"This volume takes its place, along with the correspondence between Edmund Wilson and Vladimir Nabokov, or Kingsley Amis and Philip Larkin, as consummate examples of wit, affection, and indeed—in the case of Bishop and Lowell—love."　　　　　—William H. Pritchard, *The Boston Globe*

"*Words in Air* makes an invaluable contribution to American literary scholarship, as most of the letters here have never been published before; yet it is something more. By devoting a single volume to the letters between the pair in chronological order, the editors have re-created a lifelong conversation that is intensely moving and readable . . . What finally gives *Words in Air* its emotional heft is its long continuity, which endows its pages with the immediacy of life. Joys and sorrows and puzzlements jostle; great passions blaze and fade. In the last pages, the poets bury friends and colleagues with obituaries that are frank and sometimes moving. The satisfying constant is their devotion to each other."　　　—Jamie James, *Los Angeles Times Book Review*

"*Words in Air* allows us to experience the peculiar rhythm of the Bishop-Lowell relationship, a relationship conducted almost exclusively through the mail. The letters are assiduously but unobtrusively annotated by Thomas Travisano and Saskia Hamilton, and sometimes the dullest letters are also the most weirdly revealing . . . *Words in Air* is a sad, fascinating book by two great artists."　　　　　　　—James Longenbach, *The Nation*

"The letters act as a kind of topographical map of the poets' personal and creative lives. They chart Lowell's periodic descents into psychosis, his three marriages, and his rise to become the most influential postwar poet in America. Of Bishop, living more quietly in Brazil, they offer elaborations on a sensibility that, combined with technical mastery, would cause her to win the Pulitzer Prize, the National Book Award, and the National Book Critics Circle Award. The letters also offer vivid glimpses behind the scenes of what poet James Merrill has called 'her own instinctive, modest, lifelong impersonations of an ordinary woman.'"　　　　—Dominic Luxford, *The Believer*

ELIZABETH BISHOP AND ROBERT LOWELL

WORDS IN AIR

EDITED BY THOMAS TRAVISANO WITH SASKIA HAMILTON

Elizabeth Bishop (1911–79) and Robert Lowell (1917–77) were among the greatest and most honored poets of the last century. Their poetry, prose, and letters are published by FSG.

BY ELIZABETH BISHOP

North & South (1946)

A Cold Spring (1955)

The Diary of "Helena Morley" (translation) (1957)

Brazil (with the editors of *Life*) (prose) (1962)

Questions of Travel (1965)

The Ballad of the Burglar of Babylon (1968)

The Complete Poems (1969)

An Anthology of Twentieth-Century Brazilian Poetry (edited with Emanuel Brasil) (1972)

Geography III (1976)

The Complete Poems: 1927–1979 (1983)

The Collected Prose (1984)

One Art: Letters (1994)

Exchanging Hats: Paintings (1996)

Edgar Allan Poe & The Juke Box: Uncollected Poems, Drafts, and Fragments (2006)

Elizabeth Bishop: Poems, Prose, and Letters (2008)

BY ROBERT LOWELL

Land of Unlikeness (1944)

Lord Weary's Castle (1946)

The Mills of the Kavanaughs (1951)

Life Studies (1959)

Phaedra (translation) (1961)

Imitations (1961)

For the Union Dead (1964)

The Old Glory (plays) (1965)

Near the Ocean (1967)

The Voyage & other versions of poems by Baudelaire (1969)

Prometheus Bound (translation) (1969)

Notebook 1967–68 (revised and expanded edition, *Notebook*, 1970)

History (1973)

For Lizzie and Harriet (1973)

The Dolphin (1973)

Selected Poems (1976) (revised edition, 1977)

Day by Day (1977)

The Oresteia of Aeschylus (translation) (1978)

Collected Prose (1987)

Collected Poems (2003)

The Letters of Robert Lowell (2005)

Selected Poems (expanded edition, 2007)

WORDS IN AIR

WORDS IN AIR

THE COMPLETE CORRESPONDENCE BETWEEN

ELIZABETH BISHOP

AND **ROBERT LOWELL**

EDITED BY THOMAS TRAVISANO

WITH SASKIA HAMILTON

FARRAR, STRAUS AND GIROUX / NEW YORK

Farrar, Straus and Giroux
18 West 18th Street, New York 10011

Excerpts from this book originally appeared in *The Believer,*
The Georgia Review, Poetry, and *Poetry Northwest.*

Grateful acknowledgment is made for permission to reprint the following:

Excerpts from letters written by Elizabeth Hardwick to Elizabeth Bishop, January 20, 1958, and January 17, 1964. Copyright © 2008 by Harriet Lowell and Sheridan Lowell. Printed by permission of Farrar, Straus and Giroux, LLC, on behalf of the Robert Lowell Estate.

"Typescript by Pound on Letter" by Ezra Pound, from *Previously Unpublished Material*. Copyright © 2008 by Mary de Rachewiltz and Omar S. Pound. Reprinted by permission of New Directions Publishing Corp.

"Mr Lowell of Boston" by Ezra Pound, from *Previously Unpublished Material*. Copyright © 2005 by Mary de Rachewiltz and Omar S. Pound. Reprinted by permission of New Directions Publishing Corp.

Owing to limitations of space, illustration credits can be found on page 879.

The Library of Congress has cataloged the hardcover edition as follows:
Bishop, Elizabeth, 1911–1979.
    Words in air : the complete correspondence between Elizabeth Bishop and Robert Lowell /
    edited by Thomas Travisano, with Saskia Hamilton.— 1st ed.
    p.   cm.
    Includes index.
    ISBN: 978-0-374-18543-5 (hardcover: alk. paper)
    1. Bishop, Elizabeth, 1911–1979—Correspondence.   2. Lowell, Robert, 1917–1977—
Correspondence.   3. Poets, American—20th century—Correspondence.   I. Lowell, Robert,
1917–1977.   II. Travisano, Thomas J., 1951–   III. Hamilton, Saskia, 1967–   IV. Title.

PS3503.I785Z49 2008
811'.54—dc22

                                                                                2008008919

Paperback ISBN: 978-0-374-53189-8

Designed by Jonathan D. Lippincott

www.fsgbooks.com

5   7   9   10   8   6

CONTENTS

FOR ELIZABETH BISHOP 4

by Robert Lowell, from *History*

The new painting must live on iron rations,
rushed brushstrokes, indestructible paint-mix,
fluorescent lofts instead of French *plein air*.
Albert Ryder let his crackled amber moonscapes
ripen in sunlight. His painting was repainting,
his tiniest work weighs heavy in the hand.
Who is killed if the horsemen never cry halt?
Have you seen an inchworm crawl on a leaf,
cling to the very end, revolve in air,
feeling for something to reach to something? Do
you still hang your words in air, ten years
unfinished, glued to your notice board, with gaps
or empties for the unimaginable phrase—
unerring Muse who makes the casual perfect?

INTRODUCTION:
"WHAT A BLOCK OF LIFE"

In July 1965 the great mid-century American poet Robert Lowell (1917–1977), who had recently weathered a controversy that brought him into widely publicized opposition to the nation's president, wrote affectionately to his poetic peer and close friend Elizabeth Bishop (1911–1979) from his summer retreat in Castine, Maine, "How wonderful you are Dear, and how wonderful that you write me letters . . . In this mid-summer moment I feel at peace, and that we both have more or less lived up to our so different natures and destinies. What a block of life has passed since we first met in New York and Washington!" Two years earlier, when their correspondence was briefly interrupted, Lowell acknowledged that "I think of you daily and feel anxious lest we lose our old backward and forward flow that always seems to open me up and bring color and peace." Lowell told Bishop in 1970 that "you [have] always been my favorite poet and favorite friend," and the feeling was surely mutual. For her part Bishop, with her characteristic blend of directness and wry humor, urged Lowell, "Please never stop writing me letters—they always manage to make me feel like my higher self (I've been re-reading Emerson) for several days . . ."

Through wars, revolutions, breakdowns, brief quarrels, failed marriages and love affairs, and intense poetry-writing jags, the letters kept coming. For these were not merely intimate friends, ready to share each other's lives with all their piquant and painful and funny moments, but eager readers—eager for the next letter, eager for the next poem. For each, personally as well as artistically, these letters became a part of their abidance: a part of that huge block of life they had lived together and apart over thirty years of witty and intimately confiding correspondence.

Bishop and Lowell began their lifelong exchange of letters after meeting at a New York dinner party hosted by Randall Jarrell in January 1947. When Jarrell, a gifted poet and the most discerning poetry critic of his age, introduced his old friend Robert Lowell to his new friend Elizabeth Bishop, he was bringing together the two American poets of his generation whom he most admired. The painfully shy Bishop, so often anxious and tongue-tied when among the literati, immediately felt at home with this most imposing of literary lions. Once the letters started coming, any hint of initial stiffness quickly gave way to that easy "backward and forward flow." The exchange continued for the next three decades, ending only with Lowell's death in 1977. Bishop's own death followed two years later, but not before she had written "North Haven," the most touching and incisive elegy Lowell ever received: "Fun," Bishop wrote of her "sad friend," "it always seemed to leave you at a loss . . ." Yet although both Lowell and Bishop lived lives of some disorder colored by early sorrow, each was clearly having fun with letters as frequently amusing—and often downright hilarious—as these. Indeed, the droll give-and-take of their affectionate serve and volley is perhaps the letters' most surprising and engaging feature. This complete collection of the letters between them extends by more than three hundred letters the published canon of their mutual exchange to be found separately in their selected correspondence: Bishop's *One Art: Letters* (1994), edited by Robert Giroux, and *The Letters of Robert Lowell* (2005), edited by Saskia Hamilton. The back-and-forth interchange recorded in the present volume provides a window of discovery into the human and artistic development of two brilliant poets over their last and most productive three decades.

Although Bishop confessed to Lowell in a 1975 letter that she had "been almost too scared to go" to that fateful 1947 meeting, in Lowell she discovered an artistic counterpart whose individuality, verbal flair, and dedication to craft mirrored her own. And the letters themselves are unique. For the artistic distinction of the correspondents, for the unfolding intimacy of the interchange, for its sustained colloquial brilliance of style (with neither poet ever on stilts), for its keen observation of both the ordinary and the extraordinary spiced with a wealth of literary and social history and a smorgasbord of literary gossip, it is hard to think of a parallel.

As the correspondence began in 1947, Bishop was thirty-six and Lowell had recently turned thirty. David Kalstone, in his groundbreaking *Becoming a Poet: Elizabeth Bishop with Marianne Moore and Robert Lowell* (1989), rightly observes that "they could not have met at a better moment." As poets, each had lately published a prizewinning first volume and was achieving substantial recognition for the first time. Bishop's *North & South* (1946) had won the Houghton Mifflin Poetry Prize Fellowship, which included publication and a cash prize, for a book manuscript that triumphed over more than eight hundred rival submissions. Lowell's *Lord Weary's Castle* (1946), which included new poems as well as extensive revisions from his 1944 small press *Land of Unlikeness*, had won—still more impressively—the Pulitzer Prize, making him one of the youngest poets ever to receive that award. Indeed, while both poets would receive many public honors, including a Pulitzer for Bishop in 1956, Lowell would, throughout their lifetimes, continue to enjoy a public reputation that exceeded his friend's. One prominent critic, Irvin Ehrenpreis, an admirer of both poets, dubbed their era "The Age of Lowell." Lowell appeared on a 1967 *Time* magazine cover and was regularly featured in other mainstream media not only for his poetry but for his left-of-center political interventions and for a life marked by widely publicized mental breakdowns. Bishop, by contrast, shunned publicity, was retiring by temperament, and lived for long periods in Key West or Brazil, remote from the major American cultural centers, and her work was intensely prized by a narrower circle. Bishop tended to be thought of while living as, in John Ashbery's now-famous phrase, a "writer's writer's writer." In the years since her death, however, Bishop's reputation has risen dramatically, fully catching up with Lowell's, and in the eyes of some, surpassing it. These admiring friends are now linked in many readers' minds—as they were in Jarrell's six decades before—as perhaps the two outstanding American poets of their talented mid-century generation.

On a more personal level, as Kalstone observes, their 1947 meeting came at "an unsettled time for both of them," with Lowell finalizing a divorce from Jean Stafford and Bishop facing the end of a longstanding relationship with Key West resident Marjorie Stevens. In their friendship's first two years, Bishop and Lowell would pass through a shifting and somewhat ambiguous phase of mutual attraction. Several friends thought they might soon become engaged. Bishop remained wary, however—her long-term relationships had always been with women, and she feared instability on both sides. Lowell, who had carried the thought within him that he might one day propose, later acknowledged that he could never find the right moment: "like a loon that needs sixty feet, I believe, to take off from the water, I wanted time and space, and went on assuming." Beginning in February 1949, while staying at Yaddo, the famous writers colony, Lowell suffered one of the most severe and prolonged bipolar episodes in a lifetime of severe bipolar episodes. During the long recovery process he became engaged to Elizabeth Hardwick, who had been present at Yaddo and who had supported him through this traumatic experience. They married in July of that year, and in 1950, with Lowell now recovered, he and Hardwick departed for Europe, where they would spend the next two years.

Bishop herself was suffering from bouts of depression at that time and was looking for a fresh personal direction. In 1951, on a visit to Brazil which Bishop intended to be the first leg of a freighter trip around South America, she suffered an acute allergic reaction to the fruit of the cashew. While recovering in Rio, she fell in love with Lota de Macedo Soares, a remarkable woman with whom she would spend the next sixteen years, mostly in Brazil. The lives of these two poets had taken decisively different directions since their first meeting, yet in 1957 Lowell confessed that "asking you is *the* might have been for me, the one towering change, the other life that might have been had." In 1954, lamenting the distance that separated them now that Bishop was established in and outside of Rio while he had settled down as a poet and teacher in his native Boston, Lowell observed, "We seem attached to each other by some stiff piece of wire, so that each time one moves, the other moves in another direction. We should call a halt to that." But they never did, and as Kalstone notes of Bishop, "After 1950, her friendship with Lowell was one of frequent letters and infrequent visits."

Yet their letters served as a powerful and self-renewing form of attachment, and as their correspondence moved forward year by year, Lowell sent along his poems in fresh batches or in book-length typescripts or proofs to Bishop for her appreciation and critique. According to their mutual friend Frank Bidart, Lowell used frequently to cite W. H. Auden's remark that "The best reader is someone who is crazy about your work but doesn't like all of it." Lowell found that kind of reader in Bidart, who would one day co-edit his *Collected Poems* (2003), and he found it some years earlier in Bishop. She, too, was crazy about his work but didn't like all of it, and her unfolding reactions to the evolution of Lowell's work in both form and content—her outspoken praise when she was moved and impressed and her evident disquiet and genuine concern for Lowell and his reputation when she was less persuaded—are part of what make this particular record of artistic development so revealing. The critique of this "unerring Muse" helped Lowell, as he would one day phrase it, to make "the casual perfect" by honing small details to their sharpest edge. But if Bishop's fascination with Lowell's career was unflagging, her opinions of his individual books varied. While she praised "Falling Asleep over the Aeneid" and other individual poems in his third book *The Mills of the Kavanaughs* (1951), she remained politely lukewarm about the title sequence. Moreover, Bishop famously took exception to important aspects of two Lowell volumes. Although she praised many of Lowell's free translations in *Imitations* (1961), she objected with considerable specificity to what she considered the excessive latitude of his versions of certain poems by Baudelaire and Rimbaud. Twelve years later, she objected to Lowell's extensive use in *The Dolphin* (1973) of letters from Hardwick, his recently estranged wife. Yet when Bishop liked a poem or group, her response could be glowing. Of her first reading in 1957 of the title sequence from *Life Studies* (1959), she writes:

> . . . they make a wonderful and impressive drama, and I think in them you've found the new rhythm you wanted, without any hitches . . . They all also have that sure feeling, as if you'd been in a stretch (I've felt that way for very short stretches once in a long while) when everything and anything suddenly seemed material for poetry—or not material, seemed to *be* poetry, and all the past was illuminated in long shafts here and there, like a long-waited-for sunrise.

Bishop's blurb for *Life Studies*, which Lowell confessed he was "overwhelmed by," remains one of the most perceptive appreciations that the book has ever received. In 1965 she would write appreciatively of one of Lowell's finest and most prescient poems that

> "Waking Early Sunday Morning" has many wonderful things in it— and not the least, I think, is the way it goes on in a leisurely way, like a Sunday morning—even if the meter is not leisurely, there seems to be *time*,—to think—not like week-day thoughts. "In small war on the heels of small / war"—is marvelous—and now far truer than when you wrote it, I gather by the papers I see here.

Bishop's books came more slowly than Lowell's, about one per decade, and her work appeared in Lowell's mailbox not volume by volume but poem by poem. Each effort, though proffered with her characteristic diffidence— "Here's a bit of description, for what it's worth" she writes of her masterly late "The End of March" (1975)—would be hailed in its turn by Lowell as a perfectly realized work of art. For Lowell, Bishop's "End of March" provokes an absorbed rumination on its own leisurely and intriguing metric, whose sources and effects he finds difficult to place: "What is interesting is that your rhythm slows and forces one to read it as prose—prose perhaps like M. Moore's poems, tho your rhythm has a much slower wandering quality . . ." His meditation segues into memories the poem provokes even as he continues to muse on its prosody: "now rereading I remember all sorts of talks with you: that room I got near (?) you in Brazil, filled with proletarian callgirls—the meter I see is steadily iambic . . . any number of terrific seemingly tho quiet details." Significantly, "The End of March" is one of the few poems about which Lowell offers a significant critique, observing that "I am troubled by one thing, a sort of whimsical iambic Frost tone to the last five lines or so, tho I think they are needed. New lines might make a fine poem into one of your finest." In a later letter Lowell worries that his suggestion "must have been troublesome," but Bishop took his advice to heart and, after considerable further effort, produced an ending that is among her most dazzling.

Some poems or groups, including the linked pair "The Armadillo" (dedicated by Bishop to Lowell) and "Skunk Hour" (dedicated by Lowell to Bishop), as well as the balance of Lowell's "Life Studies" sequence and Bishop's story "In the Village," became the subject of extended discussion, even long after the work had been finished and published. The correspondence thus records a series of parallel and often intertwining artistic explorations—a record of what Bidart, in an interview on his edition of Lowell's *Collected Poems*, coedited with David Gewanter, terms "the immense pleasures and satisfactions as well as the turmoil and fears about making."

Yet these letters are as much about living as they are about making, and their pages reveal a sharing of life as well as a sharing of art. Each poet's eager and surprised and excited response to the other's work emerges out of a flurry of vividly recorded everyday experience. In his insightful 1994 review of Elizabeth Bishop's *One Art: Letters* in *The Times Literary Supplement*, the poet Tom Paulin observed, "each letter occurs as a historic moment whose taut nowness can be immensely exciting." Yet there is so much of the quotidian in these letters that one sometimes feels surprised when one stumbles upon not only historic events at the moment of their happening but famous poems and sometimes whole books receiving their first readings in the context of letters brimming with impromptu bits of comic observation drawn from casual, odd, domestic moments. Such moments would continue to punctuate the letters from both sides for the next three decades, and their drily witty and unexpected—yet consistently supportive and sympathetic—playing off of each other's anecdotes and observations is one of the joys of the correspondence. Postscripts, which abound in these letters, are full of amusing throwaways, suggesting an ongoing conversation that each is reluctant to break off. One Bishop letter, written during a torrid Brazilian summer, closes apologetically: "I'm sorry—I seem to have got some of a very old & liquefied jelly-bean on this," while another Bishop postscript, written from New York and indicating a darker stain, closes, with a hint of comic challenge: "Brazilian coffee—you'd hate it; you like WEAK coffee . . ." It is hard to imagine Wordsworth ending a letter to Coleridge with either line.

When reading a fresh letter, each was in part enjoying the other's spontaneous and arresting verbal performance. Planning a seminar "on 'Letters!' " at Harvard, Bishop told friends that it would be about "just letters—as an art form or something." Paulin's investigations of this "art form or something" led him to ask, "And is there a poetics of the familiar letter?" Apparently finding none, he begins to supply the outlines of such a poetics, suggesting that letters, to qualify as literature, must paradoxically "construct themselves on an anti-aesthetic, a refusal of the literary." Speaking of a sentence in one of Bishop's early letters to Lowell, Paulin notes that "it leaps out as if she is an actor or a dancer, inspired by the intelligence and attention of her audience of one. For there is—it scarcely needs emphasizing—a keenly performative element in the epistolary art." Yet this performative element, if the letter is to be of lasting interest, must aim—again paradoxically—"to flower once and once only in the recipient's reading and then disappear immediately. The merest suspicion that the writing is aiming beyond the addressee at posterity freezes a letter's immediacy and destroys its spirit." It is the apparent absence of this interest in posterity on the part of two poets famous for their obsession with craft that gives this correspondence much of its interest and appeal.

Bishop's gusto for reading other people's letters suggests that even such an intensely private poet as she would have had scant objection to posterity's peering over her shoulder to read a fresh letter from Lowell or to scan the response she wrote at leisure or, perchance, dashed off hurriedly to catch the next day's mail. When Lowell sold his papers to Harvard's Houghton Library in 1973, he told Bishop that "Your letters are the most valuable and large single group," and he generously insisted that she accept a substantial portion of the profit he derived from the sale. This transaction might suggest a tacit understanding by both parties that such a large and valuable group of letters would be examined soon enough by scholars and might one day find a wider circle of readers. Indeed, Lowell himself declared, "When Elizabeth Bishop's letters are published (as they will be) she will be recognized as not only one of the best, but one of the most prolific writers of our century."

The focus of these poets on the performative moment emerges even in Lowell's first letter to Bishop, dated May 23, 1947, and written from his New

York apartment, in response to one of Bishop's regretting a missed meeting due to illness. Opening "Dear Miss Bishop," it begins in a friendly but comparatively formal way. Then the letter suddenly launches, without transition, into a paragraph of impromptu comic performance. From Lowell's first letter onward, neither correspondent felt the need for transitions between paragraphs—either could expect the other to follow each successive leap of thought. While much in the correspondence is in some sense historic, impromptu bits of detailed comic or lyric observation would punctuate the letters from both sides for the next three decades, as ordinary folk and distinguished personages (ranging from the modernist sculptor Alexander Calder to the quaintly learned founder of Hires Root Beer) are vividly figured forth in all their eccentric particularity. Among many pen portraits of famous writers, their lively ongoing commentary on the doings and sayings of Randall Jarrell, Marianne Moore, Robert Frost, Ezra Pound, William Carlos Williams, Allen Tate, Dylan Thomas, and Mary McCarthy feature as highlights. In these pages, too, the austere creator of *The Waste Land* makes a surprising appearance as "Elbows Eliot," so named in a Lowell postscript because he "danced so dashingly" with his new wife at a "Charles River boatclub brawl." Since Bishop and Lowell were at once historic personages, ordinary people, and extraordinarily fresh and funny observers, it should not surprise us that everywhere in the letters one finds a conjunction of hilariously descriptive performance on the one hand and literary history in the making on the other. Often these elements are inextricably intertwined.

Yet their descriptions of obscure individuals observed in passing are perhaps even more compelling. Thus, in a letter from the summer of 1948 in which Bishop has just spoken of several lonely and depressing days enclosed in the fog of Wiscasset, Maine, she writes:

> I think almost the last straw here though is the hairdresser, a nice big hearty Maine girl who asks me questions I don't even know the answers to. She told me: 1, that my hair "don't feel like hair at all." 2, I was turning gray practically "under her eyes." And when I'd said yes, I was an orphan, she said "Kind of awful, ain't it, ploughing through life alone." So now I can't walk downstairs in the morning or upstairs at night without feeling I'm ploughing. There's no place like New England.

Lowell responds perfectly with a single line in a postscript to his next letter: "There's something haunting and nihilistic about your hair-dresser."

The strong affinity as writers of these two New Englanders grew in significant part out of their eye for the telling detail, their ear for the characteristic phrase, and their shared distaste for cant and fakery. And each poet, from the start, saw the other as already a classic. Lowell told Bishop, "I think I read you with more interest than anyone now writing," and Bishop frequently yearned for new Lowell poems, because, as she said, "They really make almost everything I see look pretty dreary, or labored, or absolute silliness. . . . your poetry is as different from the rest of our contemporaries as, say, ice from slush." Yet their mutual interest grew not only out of a recognition of their many affinities but also from a recognition of their intriguing differences. Each found in the other a profound devotion to craft and a pragmatic readiness to experiment with distinct poetic manners—now free verse, now sprung rhythm, now meter and rhyme. They shared a resistance to abstract or codified theory, that keen, unpredictable, exploratory eye, and a fascination with both public and private history.

Yet along with these shared tendencies, each also found in the other qualities they wished to develop in their own work. Lowell's eye was surely keen by any reasonable standard, but he saw, behind Bishop's images, an eye yet keener and more certain. Lowell admired, too, Bishop's capacity for understatement, her gift for artistic balance and proportion, her patient waiting for each poem to come, and her willingness, as he phrased it in a public tribute, to renounce the poem "forever if it doesn't come." Lowell worried about his own capacity to compel poems into being by sheer doggedness and force of will, and he acknowledged to Bishop that, stylistically, he sometimes "beat the big drum too much." He observed with humorous self-deprecation in 1952, "You always make me feel that I have a rather obvious breezy, impersonal liking for the great and obvious—in contrast with your adult personal feeling for the odd and genuine," and in 1947, praising the naturalness of Bishop's "At the Fishhouses," he observed ruefully that "I'm a fisherman myself, but all my fish became symbols, alas!"

Bishop, for her part, admired and yearned to assimilate into her own work many of the qualities she found in Lowell: his capacity for hard and persistent poetic labor, his steady productivity, and perhaps most important, his gift for tackling seemingly any subject head-on, without apology and with compelling emotional effect. She wrote in 1947 of a recent Lowell poem, "The Fat Man in the Mirror," "I admire its sense of horror and panic extremely." Six years later she wrote of another poem, "Epitaph of a Fallen Poet" (later "Words for Hart Crane"), that she "admired its undiminished un-pulled punch." Each praised and frankly envied the differing capacities they recognized in the other. It is a measure not only of the strength of their friendship but of their strength as artists that they were able turn their life-long study of these attractive opposites to such good advantage.

Each in fact learned enormously from the other's poetic example. Lowell found means to assimilate much of Bishop's art of nuanced observation and indirection into his style without losing that "un-pulled punch" that was his characteristic feature. Lowell's *Life Studies* and *For the Union Dead* (1964), his most enduringly popular books, were written under Bishop's direct influence, as the letters make clear, and despite their power to shock they show traces everywhere of her humor, gentleness, understatement, and eye for "the odd and genuine."

Bishop, who feared Lowell's dominance—she once acknowledged that "I find your poetry so strongly influential that if I start reading it when I'm working on something of my own I'm lost"—took on Lowellian elements more slowly, perhaps, but just as surely, finding means to assimilate something of Lowell's force and directness into her understated art without relinquishing its depths of quiet suggestion. Particularly in *Geography III* (1976), perhaps her finest book, and in the handful of subsequent poems—"Pink Dog," "North Haven," "Sonnet," and "Santarém"—that she completed just before her death in 1979, Bishop produced a compelling series of self-exploratory poems that provide readers with a window into the latent yet powerful personal element that informs all of her writing. At the same time, encouraged in part by Lowell's example, this poet who worried, as she once told Lowell, that she might turn out to be merely a "minor female Wordsworth," was extending her reach into previously unexplored political and cultural borderlands.

Yet it wasn't just their poetry that was mutually influential. It is hard to avoid the conclusion that the conversationally performative quality of the letters gradually began to find its way into in a similarly casual performative quality in their poems. When Lowell felt free of the burden of his "bid for immortality," as he did when writing these letters, he was able to reveal aspects of himself that appear only fleetingly in his early poems. Bishop, no doubt, helped to draw those qualities out of Lowell in the letters, where one persistently sees Lowell's gentler, funnier, and more vulnerable side— qualities that were always there in the person. Fiction writer Peter Taylor, Lowell's close friend from their days together at Kenyon College, noted more than once in interviews that Ian Hamilton's 1982 biography failed to capture two important aspects of Lowell: his capacity for friendship and his sense of humor. According to Taylor, "He was a wonderful friend; he could make you feel good about anything. One of the problems with Hamilton's biography, although I thought it was good in many ways, was that it didn't give any impression of the other side of him. He had the most marvelous sense of humor; he was the gentlest person and the most loyal of friends." Thus, Taylor felt, "with all the book's careful delineation of his madness, there is the danger of his being seen as an unrelieved grotesque. None of his friends saw him as that—not one of them." Lowell's correspondence with Bishop may have helped him to realize in verse aspects of his character that the aggressive style of his early work could not make room for.

For as the heavily accented, radically enjambed, and harshly rhymed iambic couplets of Lowell's *Lord Weary's Castle* and *The Mills of the Kavanaughs* gave way to the conversational directness of *Life Studies*, one senses that not only Bishop's verse and autobiographical prose but the familiar style of the correspondence itself helped Lowell to master a shift toward that more casual and conversational poetic voice. In an interview shortly after the publication of *Life Studies* he admires what he calls the "drifting description" of Bishop's "Armadillo," yet much drifting description of a high order can be found already in even their earliest letters. No doubt each correspondent helped the other to articulate latent yet powerful characteristics that otherwise might have been denied full expression, and the effect of this extends beyond the letters to the poems.

Moreover, as they wrote and as they read, Bishop and Lowell seem constantly to be weighing, sampling, and trying out fragments of potential poetic material. Bishop observed in 1958 that whole paragraphs of Lowell's most recent letter appeared "almost on the point of precipitation into poetry," to which Lowell replied in a postscript, "You are the one whose letters are poetry, such a full sail, such witty stories!" Both Bishop and Lowell seem to recognize poetic possibilities in Bishop's Wiscasset hairdresser, though this "nice big hearty Maine girl" never found her way into a poem by either. However, Bishop used images and phrases from another 1947 letter to Lowell in her poem "The Bight," and many images and phrases from a 1947 letter from Bishop to Lowell found their way, fifteen years later, into Lowell's poem "Water," an imaginary colloquy with Bishop—who remains unnamed but powerfully present in the poem. Thus, along with frequent discussions of published poems or poems in draft, hints of potential poems in the makin' peek recurrently out of these letters.

The sources in the letters for "Water" and "The Bight" have rec much previous commentary, but less often noted is the use Bishop would later make of material in a letter to Lowell that she wrote from Briton Cove, Cape Breton, in August 1947.

> I like the people particularly, they are all Scotch and still speak Gaelic, or English with a strange rather cross-sounding accent. Off shore are two "bird islands" with high red cliffs. We are going out with a fisherman to see them tomorrow—they are sanctuaries where there are auks and the only puffins left on the continent, or so they tell us. There are real ravens on the beach, too, something I never saw before—enormous, with sort of rough black beards under their beaks.

Traces of this letter's description appear throughout Bishop's poem "Cape Breton," published two years later, but the clearest echo is heard in the poem's opening:

> Out on the high "bird islands," Ciboux and Hertford,
> the razorbill auks and the silly-looking puffins all stand
> with their backs to the mainland
> in solemn, uneven lines along the cliff's brown grass-frayed edge,
> while the few sheep pastured there go "Baaa, baaa."

Bishop's distinctively crafted yet conversational-sounding poem differs from her more spontaneous letter in intriguing ways, as she drops out some details (including her alluring ravens) while emphasizing or particularizing others to create the poem's uniquely balanced tone and shape. Lowell—a poetic magpie if ever there was one—for his part mined Bishop's letters for materials he would use in poems about her, not only in "Water" but in the four numbered unrhymed sonnets "For Elizabeth Bishop"—the first a fourteen-line compression of "Water"—that appear in his 1973 *History*. The last and best of these, "For Elizabeth Bishop 4," contains his most eloquent verse tribute to Bishop as a poet.

Sometimes a letter's content might reappear in a poem decades later and in a surprising shape. For example, Lowell begins a letter to Bishop in 1949 with rueful self-bemusement that on becoming aware of "a dull burning smell" in his Yaddo room one morning, he searched for some time before finding in his pocket "a lighted cigarette in holder consuming a damp piece of Kleenex. The pocket was also stuffed with kitchen matches. Oh my!" Bishop's next letter opens with the statement that "I am mailing you a SAFE if not particularly esthetic ashtray," and it goes on to detail the many practical advantages of such an unaesthetic ashtray for a working writer. In these letters Bishop and Lowell demonstrate scant interest in aesthetic theory on an abstract level. What concerned them most, whether in art or in ashtrays, were the practical problems of making poems and of living one's life, questions they approached with humility and humor, as well as with gentleness and common sense.

Yet even such casual exchanges might prove fruitful, as Bishop showed in "12 O'Clock News," an uncanny prose poem over which she had long labored and which she published at last in 1973, more than twenty years after her pragmatic riposte to Lowell's episode of near self-immolation. Here a writer's "ashtray" appears as the climactic figure in a series that includes a "gooseneck lamp," a "typewriter," a "pile of mss.," and other necessities of the writer's trade. Each item is viewed with unconscious surrealism by a condescending observer—perhaps a war correspondent—who sees in these prosaic objects evidence of battle damage suffered by "this inscrutable people, our opponents." The ashtray's crushed cigarettes metamorphose before this observer's eyes into soldiers lying in heaps:

wearing the camouflage "battle dress" intended for "winter warfare." They are in hideously contorted positions, all dead. We can make out at least eight bodies.

For Bishop as for Lowell, these letters might precipitate into poetry at surprising times and in unforeseeable ways.

As Bishop acknowledged to her fellow New Englander in the letter about her Maine hairdresser, she had in fact been virtually orphaned in early youth, and since then she had been plowing through life very nearly alone. Bishop noted the importance of support from her fellow writers, citing in a 1963 letter from Brazil a remark by Virgil Thomson, who had said: "one of the strange things about poets is the way they keep warm by writing to one another all over the world." Bishop was born half a world away from Brazil in Worcester, Massachusetts, in 1911. Her father was William Thomas Bishop, a prosperous building contractor, who died of the still-incurable Bright's disease when she was eight months old. Her mother, Gertrude Bulmer Bishop, never got over the shock of her husband's death. In 1915, when Bishop was four, her mother returned with her to the Bulmer family home in Great Village, Nova Scotia. Within a year, Bishop's mother suffered a severe mental breakdown from which she did not recover, and she was placed in a mental institution in Dartmouth, Nova Scotia, where she died in 1934. Bishop never saw her again, and she vividly portrays this decisive experience of loss in her poignant "In the Village" (1953), a story which evokes the lingering presence of "the scream"—a scream Bishop associates with her mother's final breakdown:

> The scream hangs there like that, unheard, in memory—in the past, in the present, and those years between. It was not even loud to begin with, perhaps. It just came there to live, forever—not loud, just alive forever. Its pitch would be the pitch of my village.

Lowell praised this story as "wonderful" when it first appeared in *The New Yorker*, and in 1962 he composed a poem in quatrains "derived from Elizabeth Bishop's story" entitled "The Scream." Lowell frequently mentioned "In the Village" in subsequent letters, and the story antedates his own memoir "91 Revere Street" by three years and the composition of his "Life Studies" sequence by four.

In 1917, the year after her mother's breakdown, Bishop was claimed by her wealthy paternal grandparents and transported from her beloved Great Village back to Worcester. Bishop observed of this move, in her posthumously published memoir "The Country Mouse": "I had been brought back unconsulted and against my wishes to the house my father had been born in, to be saved from a life of poverty and provincialism, bare feet, suet puddings, unsanitary school slates, perhaps even from the inverted *r*'s of my mother's family. With this surprising set of grandparents, until a few weeks ago no more than names, a new life was about to begin." In her own mind, "I felt as if I were being kidnapped, even if I wasn't." In the months that followed her unwilling return to Worcester, Bishop suffered simultaneous and nearly fatal onsets of asthma and eczema. She would struggle with severe episodes of both disorders for the rest of her life. When her paternal grandparents realized they could not care for her adequately, Bishop was passed among various maternal and paternal relatives. She lived chiefly, until she reached high school age, with her maternal aunt Maud Bulmer Shepherdson in an ethnically diverse lower-middle-class neighborhood in Revere, Massachusetts.

Thus, with these early and involuntary travels and movements up and down the social ladder, Bishop developed a fascination with geography. This may also explain the rapid juxtaposition, in her letters and in her poems, of sharply different peoples, cultures, and perspectives. After years spent quietly observing her passing world or, when the asthma struck, lying in bed "wheezing and reading," Bishop sufficiently recovered her health to attend boarding school and later Vassar College on funds provided by a trust established by her father. After graduating from Vassar in 1934, a year or two older than most of her classmates because of the time lost to illness, she embarked on an adventurous life of travel that would lead to extended sojourns in Europe, Key West, Mexico, and Brazil and briefer visits to Newfoundland and North Africa, topped near the end of her life by a journey to the Galápagos. As her letters to Lowell show, Bishop's insecurities seemed to melt away when she was on the move, and it is a widely held tenet of Bishop studies that her famous travels may have been prompted by a search for a sustaining place to be. Although, as *One Art: Letters* makes clear, she maintained a remarkably extensive circle of friends and correspondents, to many of whom she wrote nearly as voluminously as she did to Lowell, she once told him: "When you write my epitaph, you must say I was the loneliest person who ever lived." Lowell, quoting this remark back to Bishop nearly a decade later, was recalling the "long swimming and sunning Stonington [Maine] day" in 1948 when Bishop disclosed to Lowell key aspects of her early history. It was at this moment, as Lowell would recall in that 1957 letter, that he came nearest to proposing marriage to her.

Like Bishop's, Lowell's early life was deeply troubled by childhood experiences of emotional uncertainty and loss, and his work, like hers, is haunted by painful recollections of his youth. The enthusiasm they display in their letters for each other's self-exploratory writing about childhood shows that this shared experience was one source of their lasting affinity. Lowell's memoir "91 Revere Street" (1956)—inspired, as he acknowledged, by Bishop's earlier "In the Village"—focuses on the year 1927, when Lowell was ten years old and his father, Robert Traill Spence Lowell III, was making up his mind under strong pressure from his wife, born Charlotte Winslow, to resign from a promising career in the navy to take up her preferred mode of living, as an upper-crust Bostonian. This memoir, in combination with the family sequence from *Life Studies*, makes it clear that Lowell's parents were ill-matched and played out their difficulties in front of their only son. As Lowell recalled in "91 Revere Street," "I felt drenched in my parents' passions."

These passions took the form of ongoing, nightly verbal warfare overheard by the young poet-in-the-making during "the two years my mother spent in trying to argue my father into resigning from the Navy." Lowell's memoir revisits the "arthritic spiritual pains" of this period, during which "Mother had violently set her heart on the resignation. She was hysterical in her calm." The wrenching effect of this not-altogether-civil domestic combat went deep into Lowell's psyche, and his father's ultimate defenselessness, which led him to mumble, "Yes, yes, yes," in nighttime conversations overheard by their eavesdropping son, made it clear that his father would not be able to defend his son from a mother whose threatening presence was a daily reality for Lowell: "I grew less willing to open my mouth. I bored my parents, they bored me."

It was Lowell's mother who held the reins of power within his family. Lowell's father was a descendant of one of Boston's most famous families, but his was a secondary branch that had cut its ties with Boston two generations before. Lowell's great-grandfather, the first Robert Traill Spence Lowell, was an Anglican minister and the elder brother of the poet James Russell Lowell. This Lowell ancestor was a sometime missionary to Newfoundland, the pastor of a working class parish in Newark, New Jersey, a poet and novelist of minor reputation, and for three years the headmaster of St. Mark's School near Boston, the boarding school which Lowell would one day attend. Despite these accomplishments "The clan as a whole was inclined to look at him just a little askance as déraciné," or so observes Ferris Greenslet in his elegant family history *The Lowells and Their Seven Worlds*. Perhaps the principal reason for these sidelong looks of disapproval by the family's principal worthies was because this forebear ultimately relocated from Boston to "live with his wife's people in Duanesburg [New York]." The maternal Traill Spence line seems also, according to Greenslet, to have been the hereditary source of the bipolar disorder that infiltrated this branch of the family tree. Bishop may well have been aware of these bits of Lowelliana, since Greenslet was the editor of her first book at Houghton Mifflin and in October 1946, a few months before she met Lowell, Bishop congratulated Greenslet on the book's recent publication and declared her eagerness to read it, "tonight, I hope." Lowell was exaggerating, but not by much, when he said that he didn't know he was "a Lowell" until Allen Tate made clear to him the significance—and usefulness for himself as a poet—of his family position.

Lowell's mother, a descendant of the famous Winslow line, was the family's acknowledged aristocrat and its dyed-in-the-wool Bostonian, whereas when his father served as third in command of the local navy yard, he was by comparison a mere transplant and also comparatively impecunious. Without the added support of Arthur Winslow, Charlotte's wealthy father—who had made a fortune as a mining engineer before settling back into the embrace of his native city—the family would have been dependent on Commander Lowell's modest navy pay. Just as Bishop had been passed along among various grandparents, uncles, and aunts, Lowell was raised more by nurses and schoolmistresses and -masters than by his own mother or father, and he felt himself a victim both of his parents' neglect and of his mother's narcissistic overcontrol. For despite the fact that—setting James Russell and Amy Lowell aside—even the judges and captains of industry and Harvard presidents in the main Lowell line had dabbled in verse, and that his Lowell great-grandfather had been a poet of a certain note, it was Lowell's mother who declared poetry to be an impossible occupation for any son of hers. Lowell wrote to Bishop of his recently widowed mother in 1951, "Well, under the best conditions, of course, I can't begin to make sense out of her or to her. Each year since I was eighteen, it's gotten worse." Three years later, the death of Charlotte Lowell and her son's journey to Italy to recover his mother's body would trigger yet another overwhelming bipolar episode.

Certainly, these poets enjoyed real social and cultural advantages. Given their painful early histories, however, and their often turbulent personal vicissitudes, it is not surprising that they frequently found themselves viewing the world, as Adrienne Rich noted of Bishop, through "the eye of the outsider." Partly for that reason, friendship for them was a matter of the greatest possible importance. Lowell shared with Bishop a real talent for friendship. Each maintained many intense lifelong friendships, and, as Peter Taylor noted of Lowell, loyalty to friends was a crucial personal value. Lowell wrote to Bishop in 1959,

Oh we won't ever fall out, God help us! Aren't people difficult. I think, perhaps I have almost more warm intellectual friends than anyone, and have lost none except Delmore Schwartz. But it's like walking on eggs. All of them have to be humored, flattered, drawn out, allowed to say very petulant things to you. I'm sure they have to bear the same things from me—however, I don't feel the need to be diplomatic with you and Peter Taylor.

Although they did, on a few occasions, disagree—most strenuously over Lowell's use of Hardwick's letters in *The Dolphin*—and although theirs, like all friendships, contained certain areas of ambivalence, the longevity of their friendship, and its intensity, was never really in doubt.

Lowell, facing a void when it came to parental confirmation, often sought as friends elders who could also serve as mentors. Two of his earliest mentors were the poets and critics Allen Tate and John Crowe Ransom. Tate, living in his native Tennessee, provided shelter at his home, Monteagle, when Lowell, after a violent quarrel in 1938, left his family and his undergraduate career at Harvard behind. Lowell notes of his arrival at the Tates' that "Like a torn cat, I was taken in when I needed help," famously living in a tent because the house shared by Tate and his wife, Caroline Gordon, already bulged with writers. Lowell would remain under that sheet of Sears, Roebuck canvas in the yard for most of the summer. The following year, Ransom invited Lowell to room in his faculty house at Kenyon College, where the elder poet was taking up an endowed chair and the editorship of the fledgling *Kenyon Review*. There, Lowell shared the house's upper story with Jarrell, three years his senior, who had long been a disciple of Tate and Ransom and who was already serving as an English instructor and tennis coach at Kenyon. Jarrell's readings of and comments on his early poems helped Lowell to distill the style for that Pulitzer Prize–winning second book, *Lord Weary's Castle*. Bishop, six years Lowell's senior, was, like Jarrell, old enough to be a mentor but young enough to be a peer. In the years that followed their initial meeting, Bishop gradually took over Jarrell's role as the most important peer-mentor in the Lowell pantheon.

Yet if Bishop served a vital psychological and professional function for Lowell, he served a function for Bishop that may have been still more vital. While Bishop displayed a lively readiness for tackling certain practical details and was accustomed to roughing it when need be, she could seem helpless when facing major life decisions. Given her ongoing sense of diffidence about her abilities—performing at poetry readings, for example, made her deeply anxious—her approach to her career as a poet, despite her profound ambitions, sometimes threatened to be overwhelmed by passivity or shyness. Not surprisingly, she often chose as friends or as lovers people who had the skills and the interest to help her negotiate an overpowering world. Lowell, for his part, had quickly developed remarkable skills when it came to career management and, along with his brilliant reputation, maintained an extensive network of talented and influential friends. Thus, he was in a position to be of great help to Bishop with regard to her poetic career, and he put those skills entirely at Bishop's service. While Bishop lived remote from urban centers in Key West or, for two decades, in Brazil, Lowell took it upon himself to be her advocate for awards and fellowships. Thus, when Bishop hinted in 1960 that inflation in Brazil was eating into her remaining income and that a grant would come in very handy, Lowell immediately brought this to the attention of the Chapelbrook Foundation, who promptly indicated their readiness to support Bishop's writing plans. Bishop wrote back, "Heavens Cal! That was SERVICE. I feel as if I had just held out my hand to the skies." When she was about to take her first teaching job, at the University of

Washington in Seattle (a job not arranged by Lowell), he wrote with helpful pointers on how to enter upon a teaching career late in life, as Lowell himself had done in his mid-thirties. Twice, when she was chosen for major literary awards and was reluctant to travel from Brazil to America to receive them, Bishop tabbed Lowell to do the honors of formally collecting the prize. When in 1970, following the tragic death of Lota three years earlier, Bishop's Brazilian life had changed, and she was feeling trapped there, with little cash and tied to a partially renovated house that she could not sell, Lowell arranged for Bishop to succeed him in his teaching job at Harvard as he sought a new life, with a new wife, Caroline Blackwood, in England. Lowell's arrangement, three years later, to compensate Bishop for her letters as part of the sale of his papers was part of his effort to support and sustain Bishop in her endeavor to make a new life at Harvard.

The meeting of Bishop and Lowell in 1947 was fateful, both on a personal and on an artistic level. Bishop and Lowell were poets preoccupied with loss and with the curious, indistinct borderline between public and private, fiction and fact. In studying each other's lives and art while following their own "so different natures and destinies," each learned to expand his or her artistic reach across their common ground. Their poetry would very likely have been different, and their lives would certainly have been different, if they had not met. Moreover, their meeting led to the creation of an extraordinary body of correspondence whose claims to canonical status as literature must certainly be considered. What Paulin stresses in his impromptu "poetics of the familiar letter" is the quality of performative immediacy, and that is surely vital to these letters. Yet, as the letters accumulated over three decades, they took on further qualities that would have been difficult to foresee—in particular the characteristics of continuity, coherence, and development. Read from beginning to end, or even in sustained, yearlong stretches, the letters establish not just an ongoing dialogical interchange between peers and equals but a compelling narrative line. They tell a story that is immersed in the quotidian, yet one that constantly intersects with public and private history. And it emerges as a story with a surprising degree of integrity as art.

Any individual poet's "Selected Letters," however brilliant, must be of necessity partial and miscellaneous. A multivolume "Complete Letters," however inclusive, must be of necessity both one-sided and diffuse. On the other hand, these letters between Bishop and Lowell, by combining spontaneous performance focused on the moment with narrative coherence and development, may be seen, perhaps, to take on characteristics that one commonly associates with more traditional canonical genres. While the literary scene may seem an arena of constant change, preconceptions about literary genres change very slowly. Yet Bishop and Lowell themselves shared a perception that letters could be literature—and letters like these might begin to challenge preconceptions of correspondence as a secondary literary genre. Moreover, these letters link the separate published canons of these two artists in remarkable ways as we watch their parallel development as poets, as people, and as epistolary stylists. Throughout their lives both Bishop and Lowell were constantly exploring and questioning traditional artistic boundaries, so it seems fitting that we find them pushing those boundaries, once again and posthumously, in these letters.

THOMAS TRAVISANO

A NOTE ON THE TEXT AND ANNOTATION

The purpose of this edition is to reproduce the correspondence between Elizabeth Bishop and Robert Lowell in a text at once complete, faithful, and highly readable. Therefore, spelling has been silently corrected and punctuation lightly regularized. Only the most significant (and legible) canceled words and phrases have been retained.

The text was annotated to place before the reader personal or historical information that the poets do not themselves explain in the narrative, or that cannot be found in the chronology. All persons are identified in the glossary (except in rare cases where biographical information was unavailable). Because the correspondence between Bishop and Lowell records not only their friendship but their lives as readers, the editors have identified books and articles the poets were reading, as well as literary allusions. The poets also discuss in sometimes close detail their own work. We identify the poems and prose that can be found in their collected works, and quote from any surviving drafts that may vary from the final published versions.

T.T. and S.H.

LEGEND FOR BISHOP AND LOWELL WORKS CITED IN FOOTNOTES

EB: Elizabeth Bishop
EB-*Brazil*: Elizabeth Bishop with the Editors of *LIFE, Brazil* (1962)
EB-*CP*: Elizabeth Bishop, *The Complete Poems, 1927–1976* (1983)
EB-*CPR*: Elizabeth Bishop, *The Collected Prose* (1984)
EB-*EAP*: Elizabeth Bishop, *Edgar Allan Poe & The Juke-Box* (2006)
EB-*OA*: Elizabeth Bishop, *One Art: Letters* (1993)

RL: Robert Lowell

RL-*CP*: Robert Lowell, *Collected Poems* (2003)

RL-*CPR*: Robert Lowell, *Collected Prose* (1987)

RL-*Letters*: Robert Lowell, *The Letters of Robert Lowell* (2005)

RL-*OG*: Robert Lowell, *The Old Glory* (1965)

CHRONOLOGY

1911 Elizabeth Bishop born on February 8, the only child of William Thomas Bishop and Gertrude May Bulmer Bishop, in Worcester, Massachusetts. William dies of Bright's disease on October 13.

1915 Gertrude and EB move from Boston to Great Village, Nova Scotia.

1916 Gertrude Bishop is committed to the Nova Scotia Hospital in Dartmouth. EB stays with her Bulmer grandparents in Great Village.

1917 EB is moved to Worcester, Massachusetts, to be cared for by her Bishop grandparents. Begins to develop asthma.

Robert Traill Spence Lowell Jr. born on March 1, the only child of Robert Traill Spence Lowell III and Charlotte Winslow Lowell in Boston, Massachusetts.

1918 EB moves in with her Bulmer aunt Maud Shepherdson and her husband in Revere, Massachusetts.

1919 RL's family moves to Philadelphia, where RL's father works in the Philadelphia Navy Yard.

1921 RL's family moves back to Boston, where father works in the Charlestown Naval Shipyard. Begins to spend summers at his Winslow grandfather's house in Mattapoisett, Massachusetts.

1923–24 RL's uncle Devereux Winslow dies. RL's family moves to Washington, D.C.

1924–25 RL's family returns to Boston and moves into 91 Revere Street when father is named second in command of the Charlestown Naval Shipyard.

1927   EB attends the Walnut Hill School in Natick, Massachusetts.

RL's father retires from the navy. Family moves to 170 Marlborough Street in Boston.

1930   EB attends Vassar College. Intends to major in music but switches to English.

RL attends St. Mark's School in Southborough, Massachusetts. Acquires "Cal" as nickname.

1934   EB meets Marianne Moore. Gertrude Bishop dies on May 29 in the sanitarium. EB graduates from Vassar and moves to New York City.

1935   EB begins yearlong travels to Belgium, France, Morocco, England, and Spain, joined by Louise Crane.

RL attends Harvard College.

1936   EB travels to Florida with Crane. Robert Seaver, who had wanted to marry EB, commits suicide.

RL becomes engaged to Anne Dick.

1937   EB travels to Ireland and England with Crane. They meet Margaret Miller in London, then travel to Paris. On July 17, while they are driving in Burgundy, Crane's car is forced from the road. Miller loses an arm in the accident. Return to Paris. EB and Crane then travel to Rome, Florence, and Marseilles.

RL meets John Crowe Ransom and Allen Tate in Tennessee. Meets Ford Madox Ford and Jean Stafford. In the fall, attends Kenyon College in Gambier, Ohio, where he befriends Randall Jarrell and Peter Taylor. Breaks off engagement to Anne Dick. Majors in Classics.

1938   EB buys 624 White Street in Key West, Florida, with Crane.

RL's grandfather Arthur Winslow dies in the spring. During the Christmas vacation, crashes car in Boston, injuring Stafford's face.

1939   EB travels by canoe with Crane and friends to Florida's Ten Thousand Islands.

Trial over RL's accident, which Stafford wins. RL and Stafford become engaged.

1940 EB spends spring and summer in Key West. Spends part of fall in Brevard, North Carolina, then New York City.

RL marries Stafford. Graduates from Kenyon College. Begins graduate work at Louisiana State University, studying with Robert Penn Warren and Cleanth Brooks.

1941 EB returns to Key West. Moves in with Marjorie Stevens on Margaret Street.

RL received into the Catholic Church. Moves to New York, works for publishers Sheed & Ward.

1942 EB travels to Mexico with Marjorie Stevens. Meets Pablo Neruda. Returns to New York for two months, then Key West.

RL volunteers several times for army and navy but not inducted due to poor eyesight.

1943 EB works for five days grinding binocular lenses in a U.S. Navy optical shop in Key West.

RL spends winter with Stafford and the Tates. Abandons thesis on Jonathan Edwards. Allies declare a policy of unconditional surrender and firebomb Hamburg. Is called up for military service. Refuses induction as a conscientious objector and is sentenced to a year and a day. Serves five-month term, first at the West Street Jail in New York, then at the federal prison in Danbury, Connecticut.

1944 EB suffers repeatedly from asthma. Decides to leave Key West for New York.

RL's cousin Warren Winslow killed. RL released on parole and moves with Stafford to Black Rock, Connecticut. Mops corridors at the army cadet nurses' dormitory in Bridgeport, Connecticut, for the duration of his jail sentence. Publishes *Land of Unlikeness*.

1945 EB returns to Key West. In May, wins the Houghton Mifflin Poetry Prize Fellowship. In December, leaves for New York.

RL moves to Damariscotta, Maine.

1946 EB undergoes psychoanalysis with Dr. Ruth Foster. Publishes *North & South*. Travels to Nova Scotia, then returns to New York.

RL and Stafford spend part of winter with Delmore Schwartz in Cambridge, Massachusetts, then return to Damariscotta. RL separates from Stafford. Moves to New York and begins relationship with Gertrude Buckman. Publishes *Lord Weary's Castle*.

1947 EB spends winter and spring in New York. Begins to be treated by Dr. Anny Baumann for depression, asthma, and alcoholism. Wins fellowship from the Guggenheim Foundation. Summers in Cape Breton, Nova Scotia, with Stevens. Travels to Washington, D.C., to record her poems for the Library of Congress. RL introduces her to William Carlos Williams and takes her to St. Elizabeths Hospital to meet Ezra Pound. Returns to Key West, staying at the house of Pauline Pfeiffer Hemingway.

RL spends winter and spring in New York. Wins fellowships from the Guggenheim Foundation and the American Academy of Arts and Letters. Wins the Pulitzer Prize. Attends the Yaddo artists' colony in Saratoga Springs, New York, in summer. Moves to Washington, D.C., in the fall to work as poetry consultant to the Library of Congress. Meets William Carlos Williams. Begins to visit Ezra Pound at St. Elizabeths Hospital.

1948 EB travels again to Washington in spring. Summers in Maine, meeting RL at Stonington. Spends fall in New York. Attends the Bard College poetry festival in Annandale-on-Hudson. Travels to Washington, D.C., for lecture by T. S. Eliot. Suffers collapse. Returns to Key West.

RL breaks off relationship with Buckman. Begins to date Carley Dawson. Is granted divorce from Stafford. Meets EB in Maine. Breaks off relationship with Dawson. In the fall, moves to Yaddo. Attends the Bard College poetry festival in Annandale-on-Hudson. Serves on the committee that awards the Bollingen Prize to Pound for *The Pisan Cantos*. Meets T. S. Eliot.

1949 In February, EB travels to Haiti with Virginia Pfeiffer. Returns to New York in late spring. Checks into Blythewood Hospital and rest home in Greenwich, Connecticut. Attends Yaddo. Moves to Washington, D.C., to serve as poetry consultant to the Library of Congress. Begins regular visits to Ezra Pound.

RL's first major manic episode. Controversies at Yaddo and the Cultural and Scientific Conference for World Peace in New York. Hospi-

talized at Baldpate Hospital in Massachusetts. Marries Elizabeth Hardwick on July 28 in Boston. Moves to Red Hook, New York. First major depression; hospitalized at the Payne Whitney Clinic in New York City.

1950   EB lives in Washington until October, then moves to Yaddo. Befriends Kit and Ilse Barker.

RL teaches at the Iowa Writers' Workshop in the spring. Attends poetry conferences at Kenyon and Harvard. Father dies. Travels with Hardwick to Europe, settling in Florence for the winter.

1951   EB receives fellowships from Bryn Mawr College and the American Academy of Arts and Letters. Spends time at Jane Dewey's farm in Maryland, and in New York. Travels to Sable Island, Nova Scotia, where her grandfather had been lost at sea. In November, boards the SS *Bowplate* for a planned trip around the world, stopping at Santos, Brazil. Travels by train to Rio to meet Pearl Kazin and her friends Mary Stearns Morse and Lota de Macedo Soares.

RL publishes *The Mills of the Kavanaughs*. Travels in Italy, Turkey, Greece, France, and England. Moves to Amsterdam for the winter.

1952   EB eats the fruit of a cashew tree and has violent allergic reaction. Moves from Rio to Samambaia, Petrópolis, where Lota de Macedo Soares is building a country house, and is nursed by her. Travels to New York with Lota to settle her affairs and returns to Brazil in June. Tries cortisone treatment for asthma. Wins the Shelley Memorial Award.

RL leaves Amsterdam for Munich and Salzburg; teaches at the Salzburg seminars. Second major manic episode; hospitalized in Munich and at the Binswanger Sanitarium in Switzerland. Moves to Rome.

1953   EB lives mostly in Samambaia.

RL returns to America. Teaches at the Iowa Writers' Workshop. Buys house in Duxbury, Massachusetts.

1954   EB begins alcohol-aversion therapy with Antabuse, after a spell in the Hospital Estrangeiros in Rio.

RL teaches in Cincinnati. Mother has a stroke in Rapallo, Italy. Flies to Italy but arrives just after mother's death; takes a freighter home.

Third major manic episode; hospitalized in Cincinnati and at Payne Whitney. Moves to Boston.

1955 EB publishes *North & South—A Cold Spring*. House in Petrópolis full of children of Lota's adopted son and the cook, including one named for EB. Translates *Modern Brazilian Architecture* with Henrique Mindlin.

RL begins to write autobiographical prose. Spends part of summer in Castine, Maine, for the first time with his cousin Harriet Winslow. Moves to 239 Marlborough Street in Boston. Teaches at Boston University. Hardwick publishes *The Simple Truth*.

1956 EB wins the *Partisan Review* fellowship and the Pulitzer Prize for *North & South—A Cold Spring*.

1957 EB wins the Amy Lowell Poetry Travelling Scholarship. Travels to U.S. with Lota, arriving in New York on March 31. August visit to the Lowells' in Maine. Returns to Rio in November. Publishes her translation of *The Diary of "Helena Morley."* Spends Christmas at Cabo Frio.

Harriet Winslow Lowell born on January 4. RL tours West Coast in March and April, sees Theodore Roethke in Seattle and meets Allen Ginsberg and other Beat writers in San Francisco. Averts a manic episode in the spring, and again in the summer when EB visits in Castine. Spends fall in Boston.

1958 EB suffers asthma relapse in the spring.

RL's fourth major manic episode. Hospitalized at McLean. Spends summer between Castine and Boston (for psychotherapy). In the fall, teaches at Boston University, where Anne Sexton is a student.

1959 EB travels to Brasília and western Brazil with Aldous Huxley and his wife, Laura Archera.

RL teaches at Boston University in the spring, where Sylvia Plath is a student. Publication of *Life Studies*. Manic episode; hospitalized at McLean. Summer in Castine and fall in Boston.

1960 EB travels down the Amazon River with Rosalina Leão and her son, visiting Manaus, Santarém, Vigia, and Belém. Carlos Lacerda elected governor of Guanabara in April. Receives the Chapelbrook Foundation fellowship. Travels with Lota to Ouro Prêto for the first time, staying with Lilli Correia de Araújo. Travel together to Paratí and Cabo Frio. Christmas in Rio.

RL wins National Book Award for *Life Studies*. Receives Ford Foundation grant to study opera and spends fall and winter in New York City.

1961 Lota begins work on Aterro de Flamengo. Mary Stearns Morse, living with EB and Lota at Samambaia, adopts a daughter. EB invited by *Time* to write a book about Brazil. Travels with Lota to New York in the fall.

RL publishes *Imitations* and *Phaedra*. Manic episode; hospitalized at Columbia Presbyterian in New York. Buys apartment at 15 West 67th Street in New York City.

1962 EB publishes *Brazil*. EB and Lota spend more time in Rio, due to Lota's work. The Lowells visit in the summer.

Imitations receives Bollingen Prize for translation. RL teaches at the New School for Social Research. Visits Brazil. Manic episode in Brazil and Argentina; hospitalized in Argentina and then at Institute of Living in Hartford, Connecticut. Hardwick publishes *A View of My Own*.

1963 In April, EB sees police pursue a thief in Rio. Lota is hospitalized for intestinal surgery, then catches typhoid fever. EB checks into Hospital Silvestre for a rest. Fall in Rio, Christmas in Samambaia.

RL begins to teach at Harvard. Founding of *The New York Review of Books*. Visits England and France. Manic episode in winter; hospitalized at the Institute of Living.

1964 On April 1, the Brazilian military stage a coup to overthrow President Goulart. EB and Lota travel to Italy; when Lota returns to Rio, EB travels to England. Returns to Rio in July. Anny Baumann visits.

RL publishes *For the Union Dead* and *The Old Glory*. Begins to translate Aeschylus. "My Kinsman, Major Molineux" and "Benito Cereno," directed by Jonathan Miller, premieres at the American Place Theatre. Death of Harriet Winslow. Manic episode at the end of November; hospitalized at the Institute of Living until January 1965.

1965 EB travels with Ashley Brown to Ouro Prêto. Given an award by the Academy of American Poets. Returns to Ouro Prêto several times and buys a house there. Publishes *Questions of Travel.*

The Old Glory receives five Obie Awards. RL refuses Lyndon Johnson's invitation to the White House to protest American foreign policy. Visits Egypt. *Phaedra* premieres at Wesleyan University. Death of Randall Jarrell. Manic episode; hospitalized at McLean.

1966 EB teaches at the University of Washington in Seattle during the spring. Begins relationship with Suzanne Bowen. Lota suffers from professional difficulties, ill health, and depression. In the late fall, travels with Lota to the Netherlands and England. Lota hospitalized in Rio upon return.

RL begins work on *Prometheus Bound*. Befriends Frank Bidart. Manic episode in winter; hospitalized at McLean.

1967 Lota's doctor recommends a temporary separation. In January, EB enters the Casa de Reposuo for rest. Travels to Ouro Prêto. Spends two weeks in the Clinica Botofoga for asthma and drinking. Reunites with Lota in the spring. Travels down the Rio São Francisco in May. In June, doctor again recommends a separation. EB flies to New York on July 3. Lota arrives in New York on September 19, overdoses on tranquilizers, and dies on September 25. EB breaks arm. Flies to Rio on November 15. Travels to Ouro Prêto. Flies to San Francisco on Christmas Eve.

RL publishes *Near the Ocean*. Prescribed lithium. *Prometheus Bound* premieres at Yale. Participates in March on the Pentagon and other antiwar demonstrations. After Christmas, spends ten days at Center for Intercultural Documentation in Cuernavaca, Mexico.

1968 EB moves to 1559 Pacific Avenue in San Francisco with Suzanne Bowen. Breaks wrist. Awarded grant for Brazilian poetry anthology from Academy of American Poets. Travels with Bowen partway across Canada. Visits New York. Awarded grant from Ingram Merrill Foundation.

RL continues involvement in antiwar movement. Supports Eugene McCarthy's campaign for the presidency. *Endecott and the Red Cross* premieres at the American Place Theatre. Attends Democratic National Convention in Chicago.

1969 Publication of EB's *The Complete Poems*. In May, EB returns to Ouro Prêto with Bowen. Moves into Casa Marianna in Ouro Prêto at end of summer. Trouble with builders.

RL publishes *Notebook 1967–68*. Visits Israel and Spain.

1970 EB wins National Book Award for *The Complete Poems*. Bowen returns to Seattle. James Merrill visits during the summer. Teaches RL's Harvard classes in the fall, living in Harvard's Kirkland House. Meets Alice Methfessel.

RL visits Italy and the Netherlands. Fellow at All Souls College, Oxford. Affair with Caroline Blackwood. Manic episode; hospitalized at Greenways Nursing Home, London. Hardwick visits, then returns to New York. Settles alone in London at 33 Pont Street. Teaches at Essex University. Publication of *Notebook*. Visits New York at Christmas.

1971 EB travels to New York, then Ouro Prêto. Brazilian government awards her the Order of Rio Branco. Visits New York and Cambridge, returns to Ouro Prêto. Travels with Methfessel from Quito, Ecuador, to the Galápagos Islands, Machu Picchu, Lima, and Ouro Prêto. Teaches at Harvard in the fall, living at 60 Brattle Street in Cambridge. Hospitalized for asthma in November and December.

RL returns to London; moves in with Blackwood at 80 Redcliffe Square. Behavior in late spring hypomanic but manages to avert an episode. Moves with Blackwood and her daughters to Milgate Park, Maidstone, Bearsted, Kent. Robert Sheridan Lowell born on September 27. Teaches at Essex.

1972 Death of Marianne Moore. EB reads "The Moose" at Harvard's Phi Beta Kappa ceremony. Spends part of summer in Ouro Prêto. In August, travels to Scandinavia and the Soviet Union with Methfessel (Frank Bidart joins them in Norway). Teaches at Harvard in the fall.

RL teaches at Essex. Works closely with Bidart on *History, For Lizzie and Harriet*, and *The Dolphin*. Travels to New York and Santo Domingo in the fall to divorce Hardwick and marry Blackwood.

1973 EB teaches at the University of Washington in the spring. Harvard contract confirmed. Travels with Methfessel to Nova Scotia in the fall. Buys Lewis Wharf apartment. Spends Christmas alone.

RL teaches at Essex in spring. Publishes *History, For Lizzie and Harriet*, and *The Dolphin*. Moves with Blackwood to Brookline, Massachusetts, in the fall to teach at Harvard. Blackwood publishes *For All That I Found There*. Returns to Milgate at the end of term.

1974 EB breaks shoulder. Teaches at Harvard in the spring. Spends a month in Duxbury, Massachusetts. Spends summer on Sabine Farm, North Haven, Maine. Moves into Lewis Wharf apartment. Teaches at Harvard in the fall.

RL wins Pulitzer Prize for *The Dolphin*. Goes on a reading tour of the South in the spring. Returns to Milgate. Begins to write poems in *Day by Day*.

1975 EB teaches at Harvard in the spring. Spends May in Duxbury. Travels to Mexico City to participate in a film for Mexican television. Spends summer in North Haven. Teaches at Harvard in the fall. Writes "One Art." Spends Christmas and New Year's in Fort Myers, Florida, as a guest of Louise Crane.

RL spends spring term at Harvard. Fear of an impending manic episode causes him to take too much lithium; checks into Mount Sinai Hospital in New York City for observation and to reduce toxicity. Summer at Milgate. Prepares *Selected Poems* for publication and begins to work on a collection of prose. Manic episode in November, hospitalized at the Priory in Roehampton; discharges himself, hospitalized at Greenways in December.

1976 EB on medical leave from Harvard. Wins Neustadt International Prize for Literature. Reconciles with Methfessel. Travels to England, stays with Kit and Ilse Barker and the Lowells. Attends International Poetry Conference in Rotterdam. Meets Methfessel in Lisbon. Suffers acute asthma attack. Hospitalized at Cambridge Hospital on return. Spends summer at North Haven. Teaches at Harvard in the fall. Publishes *Geography III* in December.

RL committed to St. Andrew's in Northampton for two weeks in January. Returns to Milgate, writes more poems for *Day by Day*. Publishes *Selected Poems*. Travels to New York for American bicentennial production of *The Old Glory*. Summer at Milgate. Manic episode in September; hospitalized at Greenways. Blackwood leaves for Cambridge. RL follows at the end of October, staying at Blackwood's rented house and Bidart's apartment. Blackwood departs; RL returns to England. Christmas in Scotland.

1977　EB teaches at Harvard in the spring. Spends summer in North Haven. Teaches at New York University in the fall.

RL moves back to Cambridge in January. Congestive heart failure; hospitalized at McLean (medical, not psychiatric). Teaches at Harvard. Publishes *Day by Day* and *Selected Poems* (revised edition). Blackwood publishes *Great Granny Webster*. Blackwood moves to Castletown House, Ireland, where he visits her. At the end of Harvard term, Lowell moves back to 15 West 67th Street in New York. Receives Gold Medal for Literature from the American Academy of Arts and Letters. Blackwood visits RL in New York and attends ceremony. RL spends summer with Hardwick in Castine. Travels to Russia. Travels to Ireland to visit Blackwood and Sheridan. Dies of heart attack in taxi from Kennedy Airport on his return to New York on September 12.

1978　EB writes "Santarém." Receives Guggenheim Fellowship. Begins to work on projected book of poems entitled "Grandmother's Glass Eye" and a book-length "Elegy." Travels with Methfessel to the Outer Banks, North Carolina. Gives various readings. Travels to Quebec. Spends summer at North Haven. Writes "North Haven" and "Primer Class." Spends fall weekends in Duxbury. Completes "Pink Dog" and "Sonnet."

1979　EB travels to Nova Scotia, then to Greece with Methfessel, on Swan's Hellenic Cruise. On her return, buys the *Oxford English Dictionary*. Spends summer in North Haven. Spends five days on Lake Memphremagog with Methfessel and Roma Blackburn. Begins teaching verse-writing at Massachusetts Institute of Technology. Hospitalized on September 21 for anemia (a recurring problem). On October 6, writes letter to John Frederick Nims and plans to have dinner with Methfessel, Bidart, and Helen Vendler. Dies in the early evening of a cerebral aneurysm.

ONE

1947-1951

1.

46 King Street
New York
May 12th, 1947

Dear Mr. Lowell,

I don't know how to get in touch with you now that Randall is away but I should think this would reach you through Harcourt Brace. I just wanted to say that I think it is wonderful you have received the awards—I guess I'll just call them 1, 2, & 3—anyway, they are all very gratifying.[1]

I was supposed to read, too, up at the YMHA Saturday evening but couldn't make it and I hope my absence was a help rather than a hindrance. I was sorry too that that time I wanted you and the Jarrells to come here I got sick. Maybe if you're still in town you would come to see me sometime, I should like to see you very much. My telephone number is WA 5-1706, or just write me a note if you'd rather.

With best wishes and more congratulations,
Elizabeth Bishop

2.

202 E. 15th St.
New York, New York
[May 23, 1947]

Dear Miss Bishop:

Sorry to have missed dining with you yesterday, and the time before, and reading with you. I'm afraid that you have had a miserable winter.

---

1 Fellowships from the John Simon Guggenheim Memorial Foundation and the American Academy of Arts and Letters, as well as the 1947 Pulitzer Prize for *Lord Weary's Castle*.

You are a marvelous writer, and your note was about the only one that meant anything to me.

Last night at three we had a fire. The man who started it fell asleep drunk and smoking. He ran back and forth from his room to the bathroom carrying a waste-basket with a thimble-full of water shouting at the top of his lungs: "Shush, shush no fire. Stop shouting you'll wake everyone up." Then the engines came out on the street. He kept saying: "An accident. Nobody injured," until a policeman shouted: "Nobody injured? Look at all the people you've gotten up." After it was over he went on talking: "I'm an American. I fought the fire. If it hadn't been for me you'd all be dead." Today my room smells like burnt tar-paper.

I'm going to Boston on the 2nd and then to Yaddo[1] on the 9th. I hope that I will see more of you some day. The Jarrells and I had hoped to get you to go on a picnic with us tomorrow.

Good luck on your illness.

Robert Lowell

3.

Briton Cove, Cape Breton
August 14th, 1947

Dear Robert,

(I've never been able to catch that name they call you but Mr. Lowell doesn't sound right, either.) I had meant to write to you quite a while ago, to answer the note you sent me in New York, and I certainly meant to do it before your review of my book appeared in the *Sewanee Review*[2]—but someone sent me the magazine so it is too late now. However, I loaned it to some other boarders here and they made off with it so I shall have to rely on my memory which saves me some self-consciousness about it, anyway. I agreed with your review of Dylan Thomas completely—his poems are almost always spoiled for me by two or three lines that sound like padding or remain completely unintelligible. I think that last stanza of "Fern Hill" is wonderful—although I don't know what he means by "the shadow of his hand"[3]—I haven't got the poem or the review to go by. I haven't read *Paterson*[4] but your review is the

---

1 Artists' colony in Saratoga Springs, New York.
2 "Thomas, Bishop, and Williams," *Sewanee Review* (Summer 1947). See "Dylan Thomas" (RL-*CPR*).
3 "Time would take me / Up to the swallow thronged loft by the shadow of my hand"; Dylan Thomas, "Fern Hill," from lines 46–47, *Selected Writings* (1946). (RL quotes the entire last stanza of "Fern Hill" in his review.)
4 William Carlos Williams, *Paterson* (1946).

first one that has made me feel I must. The part about me I was quite over-whelmed by.[1] It is the first review I've had that attempted to find any general drift or consistency in the individual poems and I was beginning to feel there probably wasn't any at all. It is the only review that goes at things in what *I* think is the right way ... I also liked what you said about Miss Moore.[2] I wish I had it here now to tell you the many other things I liked in it, too. I suppose for pride's sake I should take some sort of stand about the adverse criticisms, but I agreed with some of them only too well—I suppose no critic is ever re-ally as harsh as oneself. It seems to me you spoke out my worst fears[3] as well as some of my ambitions.

The clipping bureau sent me the first page from the July 20th *Chicago Sun* *"Book Week"*—the one with that silly piece by

Heavens—it is an hour later—I was called out to see a calf being born in the pasture beside the house. In five minutes after several falls on its nose it was standing up shaking its head & tail & trying to nurse. They took it away from its mother almost immediately & carried it struggling in a wheelbarrow to the barn—we've just been watching it trying to lie down. Once up it didn't know how to get down again & finally fell in a heap. Now it seems to be trying *not* to go to sleep. It is dark brown and white with a sort of cap of white curly hair quite long.— The boarders & the children of the household are all pleading with Mr. MacLeod, the landlord, to keep it—such excite-ment.

Well as I was saying—by George Dillon.[4] On the back of it I saw your poem "The Fat Man in the Mirror." I am not sure but what my interpretation of it may be too literal but, whether I have it all wrong or not, I admire its sense of horror and panic extremely.

When I was in Boston, shortly after you were there, I guess, I met Jack Sweeney who asked me to make some records. In the course of making them he played me yours and I liked "The Quaker Graveyard"[5] even more than I

---

1 "The splendor and minuteness of her descriptions soon seem wonderful. Later one realizes that her large, con-trolled, and elaborate common sense is always or almost always absorbed in its subjects, and that she is one of the best craftsmen alive"; see "Elizabeth Bishop" (RL-*CPR*).

2 "It is obvious that her most important model is Marianne Moore. Her dependence should not be defined as imita-tion, but as one of development and transformation ... Compared with Moore, she is softer, dreamier, more hu-man, and more personal; she is less idiosyncratic, and less magnificent"; see "Elizabeth Bishop" (RL-*CPR*).

3 "Bishop's faults leave her best poems uninjured, and I do not need to examine them at length. A few of the shorter poems seem to me quite trivial. On rereading them, one is struck by something a little pert, banal, and over-pointed—it is as though they had been simplified for a child. Occasionally the action seems blurred and foggy, es-pecially when she is being most subjective, as in 'Anaphora' "; see "Elizabeth Bishop" (RL-*CPR*).

4 George Dillon, "The Outlaw Kingdom of Modern Poetry," *Chicago Sun Book Week* (July 20, 1947).

5 "The Fat Man in the Mirror" and "The Quaker Graveyard in Nantucket" (RL-*CP*).

had before—didn't you think it came off very well? V & VII I admired particularly. I thought making the recordings was rather fun—like a fish being angled for with that microphone—but my results were dreadful.

This is a very nice place—just a few houses and fish houses scattered about in the fields, beautiful mountainous scenery and the ocean. I like the people particularly, they are all Scotch and still speak Gaelic, or English with a strange rather cross-sounding accent. Off shore are two "bird islands" with high red cliffs. We are going out with a fisherman to see them tomorrow—they are sanctuaries where there are auks and the only puffins left on the continent, or so they tell us.[1] There are real ravens on the beach, too, something I never saw before—enormous, with sort of rough black beards under their beaks.

I think I heard before I left New York that you had received the Library of Congress post[2] for next year, although I don't believe it is mentioned in the notes in the *Sewanee Review*—if it is true congratulations and I hope it is an interesting job. Thank you again for your review and I hope I shall see you in New York sometime in the fall, or perhaps even in Washington. I am in the New York telephone book & I do hope you will get in touch with me. Maybe, if you are in correspondence with the Jarrells you could tell them the same thing—I don't know where they are.

The calf's mother has started to moo, and the cow in the next pasture is mooing even louder, possibly in sympathy. It seems that if they take the calf away immediately then they don't have the trouble of weaning it—it will drink out of a dish, says Mr. MacLeod & he has promised to call me when they try it the first time.

I hope you're liking Yaddo and I should like to hear about it sometime—I almost went there once but changed my mind.

Sincerely yours,
Elizabeth Bishop

---

1 Cf. "Cape Breton," lines 1–4 (EB-*CP*).

2 RL was to be a consultant in poetry to the Library of Congress. During the war, Archibald MacLeish established a post for poets to advise and administer projects that would improve the library's poetry collections. American consultants were elected to serve for one year by the Fellows of American Literature, who in 1947 included Allen Tate, T. S. Eliot, Louise Bogan, Robert Penn Warren, Katherine Anne Porter, W. H. Auden, Karl Shapiro, and Theodore Spencer. (Consultants in German, Spanish, and French literature included Thomas Mann, Juan Ramón Jiménez, and Saint-John Perse.)

4.

Yaddo, Saratoga Springs
[August 21, 1947]

Dear Elizabeth:

(You must be called that; I'm called Cal, but I won't explain why. None of the prototypes are flattering: Calvin, Caligula, Caliban, Calvin Coolidge, Calligraphy[1]—with merciless irony.)

I'm glad you wrote me, because it gives me an excuse to tell you how much I liked your *New Yorker* fish poem. Perhaps, it's your best. Anyway I felt very envious in reading it—I'm a fisherman myself, but all my fish became symbols, alas! The description has great splendor, and the human part, tone, etc., is just right. I question a little the word *breast* in the last four or five lines—a little too much in its context perhaps; but I'm probably wrong.[2]

Practically everything in the *Sun* was lousy; but it's exciting for us to be grouped with Nims, Ciardi and Brinnin and Howard Moss and Nerber as promising "youngsters" as W. T. Scott puts it.[3]

I was in Nova Scotia a long time ago with my Grandfather trout-fishing. All I remember of the coast is Yarmouth harbor at low-tide from a steamer called the *Yarmouth*, and some dismal low-tide gulls and a horrible after seasick feeling—something like death which as a boy I assumed I was immune to.

Glad the review was all right. I suppose what you said that night at the Jarrells started me off on a theme for your poems. I think Randall deserves the credit for reviewing you properly[4]—mine was only later and longer.

Puffins are in my book of New England birds, but I've never seen one.

I expect to be in New York sometime between Sept. 1 & 14 on my way to Washington, and if you're there then we'll try to have the dinner we missed last spring.

The Jarrells are at the Woman's College in North Carolina.

Sincerely yours,

Robert Lowell

P.S. Thanks for all the pleasant undeserved things you said in your letter.

---

1 EB's handwriting being difficult to decipher.

2 "At the Fishhouses," line 82, *The New Yorker* (Aug. 9, 1947); see EB-*CP*.

3 "A Report on Verse," *Chicago Sun Book Week* (July 20, 1947); photographs of EB and RL appeared on the cover and RL's "Fat Man in the Mirror" on page 2. Winfield Townley Scott's article, "Looking at Poetry East and West," includes RL in a group of "one-book youngsters worth keeping an eye on"; EB is not mentioned in the Scott article.

4 Randall Jarrell, "The Poet and His Public," *Partisan Review* (Sept.–Oct. 1946).

5.

[Library of Congress, Washington, D.C.]
September 19, [1947]

Dear Elizabeth:

I'd like to have you record when you come here. If you come fairly soon I think I can get you into the album that is coming out this winter, but maybe not. Anyway you'll be in the next one. We would record you at much greater length than at Harvard & then make a selection. You'll be amused when you see the list of poets that the "fellows" have provided me for the first album.

So much for that. We had a marvelous talk, and I hope you'll really come here this fall & we can go to the galleries & see the otters. I'm going to Iowa for [a] week that will include the date October 10, so if you could make it sometime after the 18th it would be swell.

This is a dull letter, but I've just been on a tour to the Library annex, had my teeth x-rayed, and when [I] look up I see the dome of our capitol.

Yours,

Cal

P.S. Of course you don't have to be recorded, but I'd like to oust some of the monstrosities on my list, if you want to let me know a few days before your arrival, so I can . . . can get the red tape rolling.

6.

[Postcard: "View of Halifax and Harbor"]

[New York, N.Y.]
September 22nd, 1947

Dear Cal,

Is the "Cosmos Club" the one you spoke of that requires one to have published a book?[1]— It was nice to hear from you. I don't remember whether I told you or not, but I'm going down to Key West as soon as possible to stay probably till sometime in January. At present I think my reservation is for the 10th or 11th, I won't know for sure until later. I'd like to stay in Washington probably the 8th &/or 9th, maybe with a friend in Georgetown, maybe at a hotel (can you recommend a moderately priced one?) Would you be there on those days or would you be gone to Iowa? Or maybe it wouldn't

---

1 RL lived at the Cosmos, a men's club for writers, artists, and scientists, located in 1947 on Lafayette Square in Washington, D.C.

be possible to make recordings then anyway? I think I'd rather see the otters than make recordings, and I'm sorry my dates are vague but I am quite sure I'll be stopping over for a day or two then and if you are there I'd like to see you, recordings or no. I am very curious about your job . . . Maybe you will send me a card about this so I'll know whether to practice my vowels and consonants or just keep on mumbling contentedly until next year.

Sincerely yours,

Elizabeth

7.

September 23, [1947]

These big envelopes are not my idea but the Library's.

Dear Elizabeth:

It looks as though I'll be gone from Oct. 6–12, just wrong. I could easily make arrangement for you to be recorded while I'm away. But then you'd miss the otters, and me, and my New Brunswick nun poem,[1] and all kinds of talk. Couldn't you push your reservations ahead four days and come here on the 13th?

I'm pretty sure I can find you a cheapish hotel, $3.00, or you could stay with my friends the Starrs,[2] who would love to have you and wouldn't impose on your time.

When poets come here, I can take off as much time as I want, and nothing said. So try and come. I'll be grieved, you know, if you don't.

Yours,

Cal

P.S. Your post-card baffled me for a minute or two. It seemed an anonymous threat. Then memory stirred, and I read the instructions for opening it. Last year, when I was at one of my disreputable rooming houses, I was told that a tall stoutish dark man with a brief case had called and refused to leave his name. I thought it was the Law. It was Allen Tate with his violin.

1 "Mother Marie Therese" (RL-*CP*).
2 Goldie and Milton Starr.

8.

[Postcard: Sanctuary of Ocotlan, Tlaxcala, Mexico, mid-eighteenth century, from the Museum of Modern Art's exhibition 20 Centuries of Mexican Art]

[October 1, 1947]

Dear Cal

You make it all sound so worthwhile that I am planning now on coming about Oct. 14th, & will stay 2 or 3 days, to see you & a friend in Georgetown whose chief interest in Washington is also these otters. It is very kind of your friends—but I guess I'd better go to a hotel. I'll write again when I have the exact date of my tickets. E.B.

9.

[Blank postcard]

[October 1, 1947]

Dear Elizabeth,

Lots of correspondence! If you come thru here before the 13th call the Poetry Consultant's secretary[1] (if you feel like reading). Shapiro[2] will be here, very nice, and anxious to meet you, but I hope you will come after the 13th. No otters, but horrible pygmy hippopotami (species discovered in 1840).

Cal

10.

[October 2 or 9, 1947]
Thursday evening—

Dear Cal:

Maybe even if you got my card you couldn't read it so I'll make another rudely rushed attempt. I think I'll be visiting a friend near Baltimore over the weekend of the 12th, and I'll probably come to Washington the evening of the 13th or the morning of the 14th. It was awfully nice of you & of the friends to suggest my staying there but I guess it would probably be better if I went to a hotel. For one thing I'll have a canary with me[3] . . . for another although I like them very much I am allergic to dogs and almost everyone I know seems to have one. If you could write me one more card please, with the name of a hotel or two, then I'll try not to bother you any more. I could

1 Phyllis Armstrong.
2 Karl Shapiro.
3 Willy.

stay with a friend in Georgetown but she has a poodle. She says one *must* hear the male gibbon scream at the zoo. (She had a gibbon once, also used to raise hamsters in the bathtub.) I am receiving all kinds of advice about the National Gallery—mostly to hire a wheel chair and take at least three days.

Thank you for all the trouble you've gone to and it will be nice seeing you—

Elizabeth

I have been thinking about a New Brunswick nun quite a lot but have come to no conclusions as to what one would possibly be like.

11.

[Postcard: Large Sea Turtle]

[Key West
October 30, 1947]

Dear Cal:

I want to write to you to thank you for *making* my trip to Washington, also to talk about the wonderful Cavanaughs.[1]—a friend of mine here is quite sick & I've been kept rather busy, so maybe this will do for a day or two longer. Anyway, I did enjoy being with you so much & hope everything is going well. Affectionately,

Elizabeth B.

12.

November 3, [1947]

Dear Elizabeth:

I've at last heard the records and some of them couldn't be better— "Faustina's" the best I think, but "Sea-Scape," "Large B. Picture," "Fish," and "Fish-Houses" are wonderful too. "Roosters" is swell in places and not so hot in others.[2] Anyway you'll get them in a few days and can judge.

But there's a catch. The N.B.C. technical part is lousy. (No worse than much we've got, but that's saying nothing.) So perhaps they won't do for publication. *I'm sorry.* I'm going to raise hell and refuse to have any

1 EB had seen an early draft of RL's "The Mills of the Kavanaughs," a six-stanza poem entitled "The Kavanaughs of Stewart Mills" (Vassar College Libraries).
2 "Faustina, or Rock Roses," "Seascape," "Large Bad Picture," "The Fish," "At the Fish-Houses," and "Roosters" (EB-*CP*).

more recordings done unless I have some guarantee—but that doesn't put Humpty-Dumpty together again. I apologize to you.

I went to the Phillips Gallery, which turned out to be on the corner opposite your hotel. It's a little place with a little of every thing—mostly good. You feel as though you'd gotten into a private house by mistake. What I remember are some very good Daumiers and Cézannes.

Since your visit Washington's been drizzly and dreary, and I've spent most of my time reading Henry Adams' scathing history of the Jefferson and Madison administrations. It's full of sentences like this: "The acts of political parties seldom show rationality, but those of the Federalists in 1809 passed the limits of understanding."[1]

Several weird people have shown up here. Dr. Swigget with a terza-rima (the only literal one in English) translation of Dante and some sonnets (privately printed) which all previous Consultants have admired. "You won't like the content, but I'm sure you'll admire the technique."

Major Dyer, who takes Pound ice-cream, was a colleague of Patton's and teaches Margaret Truman fencing. He wants to do something in letters equal to Patton's achievements. Very sympathetic about Pound and talks a blue-streak.

And Mrs. Lowell Conger, a mystic and a relative who—but the language fails me, and anyway she's gone back to California.

I hope your sick friend isn't the large bad sea turtle on your post-card. But I hope he or she is better.

Let me know how things are going with you.

Affectionately,

Cal

13.

907 Whitehead Street[2]
Key West, Florida
November 18th, 1947

Dear Cal,

Almost the first thing I noticed in my room here was the large book of pictures from The National Gallery—you've probably seen the picture by now—but the Sassetta we were looking for is a wonderful "Meeting of Saint

---

1 Henry Adams, *History of the United States During the Administrations of Jefferson & Madison* (1901 edition), 112; slightly misquoted.

2 EB was staying at Pauline Pfeiffer Hemingway's house.

Anthony and Saint Paul" with a cave, and forests, and a nice centaur in it. The book is awful—it quotes people like Aldous Huxley, Maugham, Symonds, etc. about the pictures, and the plates are poor.

I'm sorry not to have written you before and thanked you for everything in Washington—I really had an awfully nice time, thanks to you. I am very curious about the recordings—they haven't come yet—and rather relieved that the "technical part" is lousy as you say—maybe sometime I'll have a chance to do some over again, better. I almost think I could do better now. You were very patient.

I have just had a long early-morning visit from Faustina[1] who is still carrying on selling her "ticketys" (lottery tickets) bravely and walking miles every day with them, at the age of eighty-two. First she has to have a small drink of cognac, then she advises me about what number to buy this week—it's 2—then she tells me lots of gossip, except that I can't understand much of it; she speaks a sort of elementary gibberish of her own, part Spanish, part English. She is carrying all her tickets and money these days in a cardboard suit-case, brown wood-grained, with a red cross on one side, and "The Little Doctor" in large print. She also was carrying a large mirror, very tarnished, in a silver frame, that someone had given her. She is going to take out the mirror and use the frame for a photograph of, first—she said—her daughter, second thought, an improvement, the "Virgin Maria . . ."

When I first got here my friend[2] who went to Nova Scotia with me this summer, who lives here, had just got out of the hospital and was still pretty sick. Then two days later another friend from New York decided to come down to recuperate from flu and stayed here at the Hemingway house with me for almost two weeks. It was very pleasant but I really couldn't get to work at all of course and am just beginning. The swimming pool is wonderful—it is very large and the water, from away under the reef, is fairly salt. Also it lights up at night—I find that each underwater bulb is five times the voltage of the *one* bulb in the light house across the street, so the pool must be visible to Mars—it is wonderful to swim around in a sort of green fire, one's friends look like luminous frogs.

I have read both the poems now a great many times and although it isn't necessary to be comparative, I guess, "The Cavanaughs" has grown on me more than "Mother Marie Therese." I admire them both very much—I think, about "Mother M.T." that though it is all as real as real, I am not quite

1 Faustina Valdez.
2 Marjorie Stevens.

sure what the whole is about. Maybe I am wrong to look for any particular thesis. I showed it to a friend here, who has read very little of your poetry I think, and doesn't know much about poetry anyway, and I was quite delighted how she *got* almost all of it without any help from me at all. The same was true, although not quite so much, for the Cavanaughs. I wish I could be half as convincing about some of the real people I know here—Faustina, for instance—as you are about these imaginary one[s]. I'm going to try, and shall probably soon be accused of imitation. I like the saw like a "whale's jaw"[1]—I think I like stanza IV best—but in the first line of that is it supposed to be "*brocken*? pick"—maybe broken?[2] Those first lines are marvelous.— also in VI admire the lines about the poplars[3]—I've thought exactly that many times and don't know why I never said it.

I have a question to ask you, something very simple I guess. Houghton Mifflin is going to bring out a (very small) second edition of my book, also just possibly an English one. I have about six additional poems that have been published and would "fit in" all right—would you recommend adding them, or not? I guess probably not—if there were more than that I could leave out some of the first edition—or maybe I could do that anyway and substitute these to good advantage, I don't know.

I have been fishing twice with hand lines off the dock—but caught nothing. I started to go out deep-sea fishing once while the guest was here, with an old, old captain[4] I'd gone out with for years. He has "failed" a great deal and almost before we were out to sea the boat started smoking, the engine got red hot, we were in danger of blowing up, etc.—in the midst of it all, Capt. Bra lit up a cigarette and looked very remote. We finally got in safely but it was quite exciting. Someone said, "Oh Bra would like to do nothing better these days than take on a large good-paying party and head out to the gulf and never come back"—but I don't want to be in on his Viking funeral. Ernest Hemingway got a lot of stories from him—he is someone you could write about—better than Ernest, certainly better than me—

1 "Whose old, two-handed eighteenth-century saw / Hung like a whale's jaw lashed with bits of string"; "The Kavanaughs of Stuart Mills," stanza II, lines 15–16 (typescript, Vassar); cf. "The Mills of the Kavanaughs," stanza 13, lines 15–16 (RL-*CP*).

2 "The heron warps its neck, a brocken pick / To study its reflection on the scales / Or knife-bright shards of water lilies, quick / In the dead August water with their snails / And water lices"; "The Kavanaughs of Stuart Mills," stanza IV, lines 1–5 (typescript, Vassar); cf. "The Mills of the Kavanaughs," stanza 34, lines 1–5, and "In the Forties 2" (RL-*CP*).

3 "Planted poplars scatter penny leaves, / White underneath, like mussels in the dark / Chop of the shallows"; "The Kavanaughs of Stuart Mills," stanza V, from lines 6–8 (typescript, Vassar); cf. "The Mills of the Kavanaughs," stanza 35, lines 6–8 (RL-*CP*).

4 Eddie "Bra" Saunders, charter-boat captain and one of Hemingway's Key West friends.

Here are some more pictures.[1] I still think it would be nice if you could visit here sometime, maybe Christmas—if turtle soup cannot attract you maybe the Star of the Sea will . . .

Affectionately yours,
Elizabeth

14.

Dear Elizabeth:

I went through the same business about a second edition. I think you should hold back the poems. A) People who have your book won't want to buy it again for six poems, but will be annoyed at not having had them originally. B) It weakens your next book. Anyone who builds on rock as you do can take her time—let the world come to you.

Glad you like [the] poems—Randall likes them the other way around. I've made a number of little changes, but haven't good copies to send you. *Brocken* is *Broken*. The parts you pick are the ones I would. I've started a new poem to be in four 25 line stanzas and have two done, one passable.

I tried swimming—was nearly drowned and murdered by children with foot-flippers and helmets and a ferocious mother doing the crawl. Then came down with a cold.

I've seen Pound some more and won his heart by telling him that I was a collateral descendent of Aaron Burr, whose only mistake was not having shot Hamilton twenty years earlier. He remembers your work before the war as having more "address" than Mary Barnard and some New Directions' woman whose name he can't recall.[2]

Had a fine week-end with the Williams' very much like the lunch. He took me to see his old Spanish mother—91, and was like a Dickens character patting her hands and laughing and making her laugh and saying: "Mama, would you rather look at us or 20 beautiful blonds?"[3] He called your friend at NBC "that wooden-faced ass behind the glass, the typical indifferent American artisan; to hell with the company!" I read the galleys of *Paterson*:

---

1 EB enclosed two postcards, "Home of Ernest Hemingway, Key West, Florida" ("X marks my quarters"), and "St. Mary's Star of the Sea Catholic Church, Key West, Florida," with the note, "The niche is lit up at night, & all the doors are usually open & it's really quite pretty."

2 Mary Barnard's work was first published in *Five Young American Poets*, vol. I (New Directions, 1940), alongside Randall Jarrell's; the other "New Directions' woman" may have been Jeanne McGahey, in vol. II (1941), or Eve Merriam or Jean Garrigue, both in vol. III (1944).

3 Cf. "William Carlos Williams," lines 7–11 (RL-*CP*).

Book II—much better than Book One even—the best poetry by an American, I'd say, after four readings.

Not much happens to me here. I heard Anaïs Nin read—pretty thin stuff, though not unattractive personally. Finished Adams history, his life of John Randolph (a Caroline Tate sort of man), James's *Awkward Age*[1] and have grand plans for reading Sophocles with an English trot.

The Jarrells are coming on next week.

Key West tempts me—but I don't know. I'm pretty much pledged to the Taylors.[2] If you go to Nova Scotia next fall, you won't be able to shake me. We might go on a real fishing trip with guides, as I did with Grandpa—worlds ago.

Your Faustina and Captain Bra are wonderful. I wish I had an eye and the wit to use what eye I have.

Did I write you about my visit from Mrs. Lowell Conger who hears the voice of her dead son dictating her poems. "You won't mind my saying something personal. Mr. Lowell, you're a mystic. I can always tell." Or Major Dyer who takes Pound ice-cream, teaches Miss Truman fencing and was a colleague of Gen. Patton, whom in a literary way he wants to emulate—I mean he wants his poems to equal Patton's generalship.

Affectionately yours,
    Cal

P.S. Your post-cards will have me a Catholic. Wish I could come. I enclose the third poem, somehow mislaid during your stay.[3]

15.

December 3rd, 1947

Dear Cal,

I am terribly impressed with the dream poem & I gather from it that when you dream you dream in colors all right—(a psychiatrist friend of mine is writing an article on color in dreams[4] and I've heard quite a lot about it.) It is a really *stirring* poem; I don't think I've enjoyed a poem in that particular way since reading Macaulay when I was little—no, I guess some plays by Dryden affected me a little like that. There are a few spots that I am

---

1 Henry Adams, *Life of John Randolph* (1882); Henry James, *The Awkward Age* (1899).
2 Eleanor Ross and Peter Taylor.
3 Draft of "Falling Asleep over the Aeneid" (RL-*CP*).
4 Ruth Foster; see "Dear Dr.——" (EB-*EAP*).

not sure I'm getting right—I guess I'll ask you about them. I hope you don't mind—I'm not being "critical" you know, just curious or dumb . . . At first I thought I'd like the 1st three lines better in prose, but now I don't know . . .[1] But the combination of forgetting *mass* in *Concord* while reading *Vergil*—I do find it a little gratuitous, Why Concord—the "colored volunteers" marching through Concord are nice[2]—but I wonder if they aren't too much of a piece with the "Abnaki partisans"?—or is it a deliberate motif that I'm not getting very clearly. The first word that bothers me is "filings"—which so immediately suggests something else.[3] Maybe "file" is a good word for dream imagery particularly—then I see you use it again about the Italians "who must file"[4]—but "filings" does bother me. "It asks, a boy's face, through its arrow-eye . . ." puzzles me. *It* must be the "sword"—is the sword Pallas, or what?[5] (Maybe if I learn the story I'd be better off) I think the part "the design has not yet left it" etc. is very beautiful.[6] I'm not sure why the feet "turn"—they must be the feet of the men marching by rather than those of the corpse, but "turn" doesn't seem to fit either, exactly.[7] I guess I can't see "stately tears" "lathering"—although the 1st time I read it I liked it.[8] I think the sentence beginning "At the end of time," is—well, ravishing—even if I don't know what a "term" of horse is[9]— The transition of "Farewell / Forever. Mass is over . . ." is just *right*, I think (I had wondered every line how you would ever manage it)—

1 "An old man in Concord forgets to go to Mass. He falls / Asleep, while reading Virgil, and dreams that he is / Aeneas at the funeral of Pallas, an Italian prince"; "Falling Asleep over the Aeneid," lines in epigraph (typescript, Vassar); cf. "Falling Asleep over the Aeneid," prose epigraph (RL-*CP*).

2 "My aunt, / Hearing his colored volunteers parade / Through Concord, laughs"; "Falling Asleep over the Aeneid," from lines 78–80 (typescript, Vassar).

3 "Their files / Clank by the body of my comrades—miles / of filings!"; "Falling Asleep over the Aeneid," from lines 7–9 (typescript, Vassar).

4 "More pyres are rising: armored horses, bronze, / And gagged Italians, who must file by ones / Across the bitter river"; "Falling Asleep over the Aeneid," from lines 43–45 (typescript, Vassar).

5 "I hold / The sword that Dido used. It tries to speak, / A bird with Dido's sworded breast. Its beak / Clangs and ejaculates the Punic word. / I hear the bird-priest chirping like a bird. / I groan a little. 'Who am I, and why?' / It asks, a boy's face, though its arrow-eye / Is wearing from its socket"; "Falling Asleep over the Aeneid," from lines 14–21 (typescript, Vassar).

6 "A wild bee-pillaged honey-suckle brought / To the returning bridegroom—the design / Has not yet left it, and the petals shine; / The earth, its mother, has, at last, no help: / It is itself"; "Falling Asleep over the Aeneid," from lines 28–32 (typescript, Vassar).

7 "Left foot, right foot—as they turn, / More pyres are rising"; "Falling Asleep over the Aeneid," from lines 42–43 (typescript, Vassar).

8 "My marshals fetch / His squire, Acestes, white with age, to hitch / Aethon, the hero's charger, and its ears / Prick, and it steps and steps, and stately tears / Lather its teeth"; "Falling Asleep over the Aeneid," from lines 53–57 (typescript, Vassar).

9 "At the end of time, / He sets his spear, as my descendents climb / The knees of Father Time, his beard of scalps, / His scythe, the arc of steel that crowns the Alps. / The elephants of Carthage hold those snows, / Terms of Numidian horse unslip their bows"; "Falling Asleep over the Aeneid," from lines 61–66 (typescript, Vassar).

"Johnny Comes Marching Home Again" strikes me too suddenly after it I think—the three lines before it seem perfectly acceptable to a half-awake state, & so does "Virgil must keep the Sabbath"—I'm not sure what "Shadows by" etc. means—just casts a shadow by?[1] Why does the great-great aunt laugh, I wonder. The last is plain marvelous—particularly the dust business—and of course the last line— Maybe I'm wrong, maybe he isn't half awake at the end, but the "it all comes back" would indicate it, I should think—his eyes are deliberately shut at the end, surely . . .[2] I don't know why I have to reveal my naivetés like this except that I find it such a fine poem that I don't want to miss any detail.

Everything goes very well here. I have been working some on another poem called "Faustina" but it is hard to choose among the various versions she gives of her life.[3] I am also doing a couple of Cape Breton ones[4] started this summer and am beginning to worry lest I have only two poetic spigots, marked *H* & *C*. We had a small tornado last week—I was upstairs in my room here where I have quite a good view on all sides over the low roofs— palm branches and coconuts went hurtling through the air, and I watched the ground heaving up and down around several trees in the yard & thought they were going down—nothing of any consequence did, though. An enormous blue & white plastic ball blew out of the swimming pool and up into a tree where it stuck. The sun came out in an hour or so & a friend drove me around to see the damage and the ships still crashing around in the bights. The streets of colored town were full of people all out walking around as if it were a holiday and everything had a chilly bleached look—but a dreadful mess at the same time. The big excitements have been the tornado and Truman[5]—I just came in from watching him drive by the corner. A slight clapping from the people, but not much, as he sat up on the back of a car & waved his hat—I wonder why his hats, besides being so awful, always look brand new.

I hope you're over the cold, and give my kindest regards to the Jarrells if they are still there. Thank you again for the poem—it has so much richness

1 " 'Pallas,['] I raise my arm / And shout, 'Brother, eternal health. Farewell / Forever.' Mass is over, and its bell / Frightens the yellow hammers, as the Grand / Army of the Republic, with its band / Murdering *Johnny Comes Marching Home Again*, / Hobbles across the mill dam bridge and then / Mother's great aunt, who died when I was eight, / Shadows by our parlor saber. 'Boy, it's late. / Vergil must keep the Sabbath.' Eighty years! / It all comes back"; "Falling Asleep over the Aeneid," from lines 68–78 (typescript, Vassar).

2 "It is I, who hold / His sword to keep from falling, for the dust / On the stuffed birds is breathless"; "Falling Asleep over the Aeneid," from lines 84–86 (typescript, Vassar).

3 "Faustina II" (Key West Notebook I, Vassar).

4 "A Summer's Dream" and "Cape Breton" (EB-*CP*).

5 Harry S. Truman was vacationing in a house at the Key West Naval Air Station.

and almost gaiety in spite of the subject—I should think you'd be pretty pleased. I hope to see the other one sometime—

Affectionately,
Elizabeth

16.

Dear Elizabeth:

Some of your questions accord remarkably with the revisions I'd made in my *Kenyon Review* galleys.[1] 1) *Mass* is now service & *church*[2] 2) the *Johnny comes marching* is out for something else. 3) *Shadows* is *stands by*.[3]

Apologia: 1) The first 3 lines *are* prose. 2) *Filings*: one of my few puns— files of soldiers, steel filings—something uniform, filing cabinets, metal, shining, unbearably monotonous. 3) *It asks*: the corpse. *Arrow eye*: the eye used for sighting arrows. 4) The *sword* is the one Aeneas left behind him at Carthage and Dido killed herself with it. 5) It is the feet of the *men* wheeling past the bier. 5) Teeth lather works for me; it's a grotesque surrealistic image not meant to be like anything else in the poem. 6) The aunt laughs because she's a proud mad old lady, one side of her despises the Negroes and thinks the war and the parading a lot of stuff.

Of course, your objections may hold good, and I'll ponder them. It's flattering to get such a thorough going reading.

I'll mail you my new 25 line stanza poem in a few days—I just got it in decent shape. I like your two spigots and hope you'll have luck with them and send them to me before long. You know, when the next atom bombs fall there won't be any more inhabitable Atlantic coast in our life-time—so you'd better hurry. Randall has written a wonderful poem on the death of a colored child, which I think you'll like.[4]

Sat in back of the Trumans at the Symphony. They never stirred. Next to them Admiral Nimitz and his daughters smiling, craning around, saying *this is it* (when the Tchaikovsky came on) then—having ignored each other thru the music and a long intermission—the Trumans and Nimitzes suddenly recognized and shook hands with unnecessary heartiness.

1 "Falling Asleep over the Aeneid," *The Kenyon Review* (Winter 1948).
2 See "Falling Asleep over the Aeneid," epigraph and line 70 (RL-*CP*).
3 See "Falling Asleep over the Aeneid," lines 70–74 (RL-*CP*).
4 Randall Jarrell, "Lady Bates," *The Nation* (Feb. 28, 1948).

Randall's something with people he doesn't like: A pompous man of some political importance here, and a professor of political economy at Harvard, who claimed to have started Ransom (whom he called Johnnie) writing poetry (this is all one man). We were reading the galleys of *Paterson* and some manuscript of Randall's.

Pompous Man: "Can I see some of that?"

Randall, leaping up with unbelievable speed: "Oh yes." Hands Pompous Man the galleys he's already read of Paterson.

Pompous Man: "No. I want to see yours."

Endless pause

Randall: "Uh . . . uh . . . uh oh yes, I guess, but I think someone's reading them."

Pompous Man finally buries himself in Randall-manuscript. Lavish praise, "You're not obscure like the Fugitives etc. etc." Pompous Man questions the meaning of a phrase. Randall, pause, looks at Pompous Man with quiet contemptuous compassion: "You wouldn't understand it, but I think most people would. Why even my students etc. . . . . etc." This went on for about five hours on Thanksgiving till Mackie[1] & I were almost dead. I've promised to write Randall a poem like Donne's *Will* (The coals to Newcastle legacies) in which I leave him my candor.[2]

Your records[3] are on the way to Key West—see what you think?

Allen's here now—I'm going to leave him my tact in the presence of humbugs.

Affectionately,
Cal

17.

Dear Elizabeth:

Just a note to let you know I haven't forgotten you and to thank you for the lion's paws. At first they reminded me of the hands of the Cosmos Club members, but they've begun to grow on me and I keep them in my desk and look at them every now and then as a *memento mori*.

I told the Jarrells that you would probably be returning toward spring, and

1 Mackie Langham Jarrell.
2 John Donne, "The Will," lines 1–6 (1633).
3 Test pressings of EB reading her poems. Recordings of "Faustina, or Rock Roses," "Jerónimo's House," and "At the Fishhouses" were issued on *Twentieth-Century Poetry in English* (Washington, D.C.: Library of Congress, 1951).

they hope to persuade you to stop off. Here are my plans for the next six months—so we won't miss each other when you come. March 10–14, Greensboro, last week in April, Boston; June 21–July 2, Kansas. All; and enough!

In the middle of this letter my one real Library thorn has begun to prick me: the buying from Harvard at some expense and absolutely endless and incomprehensible technicalities, letters, copyright forms, discussions with the interminable Dr. Spivack of the Music Division, correspondence with Professor Packard and the president of Harvard[1]: of—John Brinnin, Paul Engle, Eberhart, Ted Spencer, JG Fletcher (something not even a poem but polyphonic prose), Jeffers (almost impossible to follow) and Miss Moore (which you've heard) Judas-Jesus!!!

But I'm doing swell otherwise—finished a new poem,[2] which I'll send in a little while; and have been writing and writing on my Kavanaugh poem— 12 hours a day—it's now 24 sections almost 400 lines, and I think it may go to about 50 sections. Wish me a lot of luck and no *Age of Anxiety*.[3]

Affectionately,
Cal

18.

630 Dey Street
Key West, Florida
January 1st, 1948

Dear Cal,

Happy New Year.

Thank you so much for sending me *The Compleat Angler*.[4] I had a copy and read it once but lost it long ago and I am delighted to have it again. It is wonderfully soothing reading & wonderfully "precious" reading here in the land of big game fish and Hemingway. I sent you something that I thought reminded me of your Bathsheba poems a little,[5] or maybe even of just your "poems" though I could only say why in the vaguest way—something masculine, emphatic and regular but sort of toughly so, and slightly somber, etc.—

1 James Bryant Conant.
2 "Thanksgiving's Over" (RL-*CP*).
3 W. H. Auden, *The Age of Anxiety: A Baroque Eclogue* (1947).
4 Modern Library edition of Izaak Walton and Charles Cotton's *The Compleat Angler* (with the inscription, "A fish for Christmas, Cal" on the half-title page).
5 Presumably the lion's paws; see letter 17. "David to Bathsheba in the Public Garden" and "Bathsheba's Lament in the Garden" (RL-*CP*).

Well, your letter just came and I'm sorry not to have written before, the new year has gone like a dream so far. I was very pleased to find how close I'd come to your changes in the wonderful Virgil poem. In the copy you sent me the first three lines of explanation all began with capitals so of course I managed to make them scan. It reminds me of the story about the Harvard professor whose pupil brought him a paper in blank verse, and the professor said he must remind him that in writing prose it wasn't customary to begin each line with a capital . . . I really understood everything except the "arrow eye" which I mistook for something like "eagle eye" or "gimlet eye." I am trying to make "lather" incorporate itself, but it still sticks out, to me, like an elbow— When is the poem to appear in the *Kenyon Review?* And are the earlier two appearing any place soon? Or Jarrell's poem about the colored child? I am beginning to get that feeling of missing things here. I received an ad for the *Hudson Review*, and I think your name was on it but I can't find it—what is it? I also just received the first 2 numbers of *The Tiger's Eye*— like a couple of simply-mad-my-dear little gas balloons, I'd say—& they must cost fortunes to get out. I wanted to see the bits of Miss Moore's notebooks in the 1st[1]—but somehow the editors have managed to ruin them too as much as possible. I don't think she should have let them use them like that. I cannot *abide* this adulation of "work in progress" stuff, and that photograph of the "little worn old books" etc. seems to me a real tear-jerker that should not have been allowed until after Marianne's death . . .

Pauline Hemingway came back at New Year's, and I moved to the above address. Some dear old friends of mine—the wife[2] is a daughter of John Dewey—come here for 2 or 3 months every winter and usually they keep the upstairs apartment for guests, but this time they kindly offered it to me— it seems to be my lucky-in-real-estate year. It isn't as deluxe as my other quarters were but better to work in in a way—the kind of meager hideousness you can look at once and forget completely—and it has a beautiful view over the harbor the fish market, etc. (When somebody says "beautiful" about Key West you should really take it with a grain of salt until you've seen it for yourself—in general it is really *awful* & the "beauty" is just the light or something equally perverse)

I like it very much but I am in a quandary. I take your remarks about writing a lot *now* very much to heart & I'd like to look forward to a long stretch

---

1 Marianne Moore, "Selections from a Poet's Reading Diary," *Tiger's Eye* (Oct. 1947).
2 Jane M. Dewey.

of nothing but work. I've been sick most of the last month—asthma—it doesn't completely incapacitate one but is a nuisance. Well—I was asked to speak at Wellesley, too, on March 22nd, and at the time I accepted. Now I am wondering if it is really worth it to go all the way back north at that time of year when: 1. I don't think I have much to say. 2. The English teacher who wrote me is an old boarding school teacher of mine, a Miss Prentiss.[1] She was very nice to me in those days but she is a very sentimental creature who doesn't really like anything she considers "modern." And I gather the audience would be mostly like her. 3. This is in confidence—I'm sort of scared. But I remember the little you told me about your speaking experiences in Washington cheered me up tremendously and I suppose I should or must begin sometime . . .

Selden Rodman has written and wants me to come to Haiti. I could board, it seems, with Margaret Sanger! He has a jeep and knows all the little villages where the painters and poets live and I know it would be beautiful, but—you can imagine why I hesitate. I suppose it is too good an opportunity to pass up, and maybe, if I can get a friend here to go with me, I may go. I seem to be talking to you like Dorothy Dix but that is because you apparently are able to do the right thing for yourself and your work and don't seem to be tempted by the distractions of traveling—that rarely offers much at all in respect to work. I guess I have liked to travel as much as I have because I have always felt isolated & have known so few of my "contemporaries" and nothing of "intellectual" life in New York or anywhere. Actually it may be all to the good.

I didn't think much of Jarrell's poem in the last *Partisan Review*, did you[2]—I re-read a little Browning & if that is the kind of poem he wants to do I think he should, too. How do you feel about Browning and why don't the critics ever mention him in connection with you?—although give me you, any time— I just finished *Trial of a Poet*[3]—& I didn't think much of that— the tone seems to me so often false. The "Recapitulations," cheap as they are, sound sincere and spontaneous anyway.

The water looks like blue gas—the harbor is always a mess, here, junky little boats all piled up, some hung with sponges and always a few half sunk or splintered up from the most recent hurricane. It reminds me a little of my desk.[4]

1 Eleanor Prentiss, EB's teacher at Walnut Hill School.
2 Randall Jarrell, "Money," *Partisan Review* (Jan. 1948).
3 Karl Shapiro, *Trial of a Poet* (1947).
4 Cf. "The Bight," lines 4–6 and 28–32 (EB-*CP*).

I don't believe I have written to you since the recordings came, have I? I played them on a friend's machine, which may have been a little slow. We couldn't adjust it and they all sounded much too slow to me. And of course so sad and dreary. I think the "Colored Singer"[1] ones came off the best, and "Faustina" next best and the others were good in spots once in a long while. The "Fishhouses" was sheer torture to listen to. But I am very glad I made them except for all the wasted time it cost you, because now I think I know what to work for to improve them. Is there anything to pay for them?

The worst thing I've read in a long time is a prose poem sent around by Alfred Kazin as a New Year's present, about Brooklyn—did you see that?

There's a doctor's wife here—a sort of provincial Jane Austenish family with four daughters—who was Caroline Gordon's roommate at college.

As soon as I can make up my mind—I hope maybe with a kind word or two of help from you—about the 2 possibilities in the 2 first paragraphs above—well, I'll know what I'm going to be doing and I hope I can manage to stay in Washington again on my way back north and see many more pictures this time. I am working on the fishing trip too and have one wonderful idea I think. I shall let you know.

The local bookshop is run by an Englishman and his wife who is about 20 years older than he, very cute, really, with dyed bright pink hair. They play chess in the corner and very much dislike being interrupted by a customer. The other day a man I knew went in to buy a book and asked for it timidly. Hugh, the Englishman, said "Good heavens, man! Can't you see I'm about to make a move?" When I first went in this year the wife asked me in her jolliest way what I was doing now? writing or what? I said writing, and she replied "Ha-ha—always *something*!"

But Good Heavens I am impressed with the long poem—was that the one in fifty-line sections. I should like very much to see it and I wonder when on earth you work, what with the problems presented by Harvard. Hope you're not freezing as well, and I shall try to profit by your stern example.

Always affectionately,

Elizabeth

---

1 "Songs for a Colored Singer" (EB-*CP*).

19.

Dear Elizabeth:

Your letters always fill me with shame for the meager illegible chaff that I send you back. So sorry to hear about your asthma—how I thank God that my imaginary asthma was cured by a chiropractor (?) and an open-air school.

Randall doesn't like people and doesn't know much of anything about them—consequently his poem . . . He's very naive about it—he wants it printed somewhere, where "thousands" of people could enjoy it, and went around imitating his old man. But it's an over-clever *tour-de-force*.

Browning had all the right ideas about material—new ones at that. But what does he do? Invents a language, ties himself up in metrical knots—often ingenious; but which have nothing to do with what he's saying. Then all his cheap simplifications! He should have been the great poet of the 19th century, but he constantly amazes and never seems to get anything really right. I suppose his best are "Caliban," "The Housekeeper," "Mr. Mudge," "Bishop Bloughram," "The Bishop Orders" and *The Ring*[1]—this probably above all, if I could ever get through it.

Yes, *Trial of a Poet* is abominable. He has a poem in this week's *Nation* that strikes me as better than anything in his book.[2] A bit flimsy, but rather delicate and metaphysical.

My *long* poem is *The Kavanaughs* of which you have six stanzas—I've now 33. I think it has my best lines, but I've a world of hard plotting to work out—I know what it will be, but that's not the same as having it written—in spite of Racine.

I'm getting to quite like Washington and my dusty club life, and think I may stay on next year, if I can afford it on my Guggenheim.

I'd go to Haiti. Rodman's a goof; but you'll probably be able to manage him—or can one? "Want to write, and do whatever you want to." We must live. The Wellesley might be fun, if it doesn't upset you too much beforehand. These things are never so bad when you're doing them. I think I've learned something from reading—that side should always be there in a poem, though, of course, we're not writing for recitals.

Friday, the Fellows meet, and I imagine that I would (probably will yet)

---

1 Robert Browning, "Caliban Upon Setebos or, Natural Theology in the Island" (1864), "The Householder" (1872), "Mr. Sludge the Medium" (1864), "Bishop Bloughram's Apology" (1855), "The Bishop Orders His Tomb at Saint Praxed's Church, Rome, 15—" (1854), and *The Ring and the Book* (1868–69).
2 Karl Shapiro, "The Minute," *The Nation* (Jan. 17, 1948).

be scared to death, if I weren't thinking about my poem. Spender was here last week-end, and to my surprise turned out to be very pleasant—no poet, though.

I've just had a rubber pad put under my chair to keep me from splintering up the floor. I feel like a baby with a wet-blanket.

Affectionately,

Cal

20.

Dear Cal,

Here is something for you to wear on your lapel . . .

I finally came up here in despair to see if I could find a decent doctor, which I have, I am glad to say—a very pleasant young man just out of the army, who has asthma himself & uses a lot of fascinating new drugs. I am going back to Key West tomorrow & as soon as I can on to Haiti for a while. I am feeling much better, maybe the drugs, maybe two new hats, or maybe just getting away from my friends who are so full of solicitude & whom I treat very ungraciously, I'm afraid.

I hope you are going to send me the new poem—book, rather. I have two new ones I'll send you when I get back, but not very serious ones I'm afraid. However I have just about finished a long & complicated one about Key West[1]—& then I hope I won't have to write about the place anymore. I am writing some more about Faustina, too, who calls on me more & more regularly—now that the prices are so high she is adding to her lottery "tickets" business by selling chances on 3 yards of dress-goods, etc., etc. She will be 82 tomorrow & I must get her a present. Another regular caller is Ben Belitt who gave me a whole new book of poems to read[2]—so egotistical one just doesn't know what to say to him—

I am reading *Poets at Work* which just arrived[3]—Auden says some rather good things, I think, having nothing whatever to do with the rest of the book—the introduction is sad & inadvertently terribly funny—but the general idea seems to be that poets often revise & usually improve their poems . . .

1 "The Bight" (EB-*CP*).

2 Probably including poems that were published in Ben Belitt's *Wilderness Stair* (1955).

3 W. H. Auden, "Squares and Oblongs," *Poets at Work: Essays Based on the Modern Poetry Collection at the Lockwood Memorial Library, University of Buffalo* (1948).

I have decided against Wellesley—I can use health as an excuse fortunately but really I'm scared—it is idiotic—

I liked Washington, too, particularly what I saw of Georgetown—but please come live in Paris, that's what I am considering doing now. I don't know whether you've been there or not but I did live there twice & was very happy there—

Miami, now—I guess it must lack a spiritual nature or something—but the people really look very well, all clean & smelling of toilet-waters— but the air smells of fried potatoes & orange-peel.

Affectionately yours,

Elizabeth

I hope you *don't* see a very poor story I had in *Harpers Bazaar*[1]—I wrote it years ago & only sold it because it was originally to appear with drawings by Loren MacIver that made it much better—the pictures would have been good.

21.

February 25 [1948]

Dear Elizabeth:

Here's my poem,[2] in time I hope to cheer you on your voyage to Haiti. Reading the *Poète Contumace*[3] after my nun poem, I felt with a shock all the things he could say that I couldn't. So this came—not much like Corbière, but starting there. I suppose it and the "Nun" complement each other.

Sorry to hear you were ailing and glad you found a good doctor. I've been thinking of Paris too, as one does come spring; but, alas, I'm a felon and can't leave the United States, except to go to "greater America."[4] Patriot though I am, I find the newness of Washington rasping at times.

Did I write you about my Santayana letters? Some one gave him my book, and he wrote me, asking me a lot of questions, and saying that my poetry was the first since Trumbull Stickney's that seemed to inhabit the same mental and moral world that he did. So I answered his questions and sent him my "Nun" and "Aeneas." He managed to get about everything I'd intended.

---

1 "The Farmer's Children," *Harper's Bazaar* (Feb. 1948); see EB-*CPR*.

2 "Thanksgiving Is Finished"; see "Thanksgiving's Over" (RL-*CP*).

3 Tristan Corbière, "Poète contumace," *Les Amours jaunes* (1873).

4 When RL was jailed as a conscientious objector in 1943, he was sentenced to a year and a day; the extra day made him a felon, restricting his civil rights.

The comments paralleled yours, even down to the Browning. It all was rather indescribably moving to me.

I have been reading masses of Pope and Faulkner—a wonderful pair to have together.

Randall's colored child will be in the next *Partisan*. I hope you'll like it as much as I do.

Isn't Ted Spencer an odious nerveless thing! What's on the inside of this page is something Ezra wants sent to 12 writers, me, Randall, Allen, Williams, Cummings, Wyndham Lewis, Auden, Spender—I forget the rest—"action within 24 hours" whatever that means. When Spencer saw him, he offered to be our academical advisor, and Pound said: "No, you're to be one of the advised." See if you can guess to whom he's sending his Confucius translation "The Unwobbling Pivot"![1] It's the most unlikely person in the world.

Affectionately,

Cal

P.S. Excited about your poems.

[on verso]

to Jarrel / Tate / Spender / ?

discuss: Brooks Adams.Frobenius, Gesell,   essential Loeb /
            Ford, W. L.[2] to Tate.

Barry Domville "Admiral to Cabin Boy"[3]

Has Tate anything of Devlin's / or has L.?
      what any one else know of him.

Tate's question re / Marianne /

O.K. but see what others think / IN ANY CASE NEVER more than ONE wumman at a time.

Tate's re /   some prof /
            ?? usual time lag or not?

---

1 *Confucius: The Unwobbling Pivot & The Great Digest*, trans. Ezra Pound (1947).

2 Wyndham Lewis.

3 Barry Domvile, *From Admiral to Cabin Boy* (1947).

22.

Dear Cal,

Thank you so much for sending me the Corbière[2]—it came at a very good moment, too. I guess it *is* a bad translation but it would be impossible to do, anyway, & it is often nice to just be able to look, when in doubt, & then to feel slightly superior to what you find. I wondered about "default" but I guess actually it's pretty good.[3] That is such a marvelous poem—some of the others I find almost unbearable—too much reality, as Eliot would say—but they're good I guess because I can see in them the kind of thing one should/could try to do but somehow half-consciously shies away from—

I came back from Miami much, much improved—bursting with health by comparison, & I think I'll be going to Haiti in about ten days, for 2 or 3 weeks—

I saw quite a nice poem by Jarrell in the *Quarterly Review*[4]—& I wish I could see his about the colored child sometime. I called this morning on my two favorite Negro babies—one is just learning to talk & her first word was *"Bad."* She looks like a golliwog.

Somebody loaned me Proust's letters when I was in the hospital & they are very good—but queer—things like "tes gens les plus gentiles ont quelquefois des périodes odieuses—"[5] & "mais l'art est un perpétuel sacrifice du sentiment à la verité—"[6] But of course what really gets me are the parts about asthma—he goes on & on about his symptoms to complete strangers—I really don't think I've capitalized enough on it. He *suggests* a little adrenaline to friends, to exhilarate them, if they're suffering from *"tension"*— So go out & buy yourself an ampoule if you are—but I hope everything is exhilarated enough without—

Affectionately yours,
Elizabeth

Sunday P.M.

---

1 In RL's hand, "Late January."
2 Tristan Corbière, *Poems*, trans. Walter McElroy (1947); RL inscribed on the flyleaf, "Dear Elizabeth, You'll probably feel insulted by any translation, especially this bad one; but I got two for Christmas.—Cal."
3 Walter McElroy's translation of Corbière's "Le Poète contumace" is "Poet by Default."
4 Randall Jarrell, "Jonah," *Virginia Quarterly Review* (Spring 1948).
5 "Even the nicest people are sometimes vile."
6 "But art is always a sacrifice of feeling to truth."

23.

Dear Cal,

I *didn't* go to Haiti, for various reasons, mostly because I wanted to stay right here and work. From what I have heard from the friends I was going with I am quite relieved that I didn't go, this particular trip, anyway. Selden, or somebody, has sent me a Haitian painting, but I haven't seen it yet. When you say you "can't leave the United States," does that mean *forever*? How awful—& does "greater America" mean Mexico & Canada?

I liked your last letter very much & have had in my mind to answer it for a long time now. Also I've read "Thanksgiving Is Finished" almost every day. But two friends, one of them partly paralyzed, had to move in with me temporarily, & I haven't had time to do anything much uninterrupted. I like the poem more than I can say—it has the most unbearable, grayest New York atmosphere for me. In fact I can shed tears over it very easily & I hardly ever do that except over trash, frequently, & over something at the other extreme, very rarely. I think one weeps over two kinds of embarrass-ment—& this is so embarrassing in the right way one wants to read it without really looking at it directly. That damned celluloid bird—& the "blue-bird in her tumbler."[1]

The rhetoric is wonderful, swaying back & forth— What I don't see is how you manage to get that effect with that metre that is so heavy the words seem to be jostling each other's shoulders. I made the mistake of reading it when I was working on a poem & it took me an hour or so to get back into my own metre. My copy[2] has two page 3's—the 1st begins "My foul was soup-bones"; the 2nd, "To the asylum"[3]—I wonder if there's a page left out? It seems to make sense all right—"hooks' chord of broken rocks"[4]—the cur-tain rods,[5]—but as I said I almost want to look the other way, & I think that's what I said about Corbière to you before—or maybe possibly rather about the experience one wants to write about—which would make my congratula-tions all the more heart-felt— There are 3 or 4 spots I don't understand—maybe when I see you again I'll ask you about them—only about 3 words I'd take objection to, at my most carping—

---

1 See "Thanksgiving's Over," lines 28–37 (RL-*CP*).
2 The typescript does not survive among EB's papers.
3 See "Thanksgiving's Over," lines 2 and 47 (RL-*CP*).
4 Cf. "Thanksgiving's Over," line 67 (RL-*CP*).
5 See "Thanksgiving's Over," line 111 (RL-*CP*).

Isn't that nice about Santayana—I can see how he would like your work very much—But I'm pretty mystified by most of Pound's message to the world—what was "Tate's question re/Marianne/" I wonder—oh, I guess maybe I have an inkling of what he's getting at there.

I'm going back to New York about the 10th or 15th of April & hope to stop off in Washington to see a couple of friends—& including to see you—will you be there then? I think I'll be staying about a week.

Have you read *Memoirs of a Secret Agent of Free France*, by Rémy[1]—an ardent de Gaullist. It is the most exciting book I've read in years, & wonderfully simple & French at the same time— I kept thinking I'm sure Cal could turn this chapter into poetry in no time—

Affectionately yours,
    Elizabeth

24.

[Washington, D.C.
March 22, 1948]
Monday

Dear Elizabeth:

Spring, but it's really mid-August—has struck and settled on Washington. Yesterday the temperature was 85, and it felt like 95.

The 15th would be much better for me. From the 12–15 there's going to be a symposium in Baltimore on Aristotle and the sublime and such matters with Ransom, Tate & Blackmur speaking. Perhaps, you'd like to go. It would be a good chance to see them, if you're interested.

When you're here why don't you stay with my friend Mrs. Dawson? She has a house with plenty of rooms. She'd like to have you, and I'd like for you to meet. You could be independent and much happier and roomier than in a hotel.

I'm delighted you liked my poem. I was afraid you'd find it violent and dry.

Frost has just finished his stay here—all very exhausting and wonderful. He wants me to send him a copy of your *North & South*.

I won't mail you any more poems, if they take you from writing your own. But there won't be any more for a long time.

---

1 Rémy, *Memoirs of a Secret Agent of Free France*, trans. Lancelot C. Sheppard (1948).

My long thing's going slowly—very! As it should.

I think I could explain what Pound means—no, I'm not so sure. I don't think I'll try. He will when you come.

So looking forward to your visit,

Affectionately,

Cal

25.

April 8th, 1948

Dear Cal:

Mrs. Dawson wrote me such a nice letter that I guess it would be very ungracious of me to go to a hotel—I have written to tell her I'd be delighted to stay there unless she has a dog (they give me asthma). I wanted to get there to see the paintings before they are returned to Berlin,[1] and now as far as I know it will be the 16th, which Mrs. Dawson said would be all right, even if she was still in Baltimore. I think I forgot to say that I'd be staying about five days—I hope that won't be too long for her. It was awfully nice of both of you to suggest it.

Everything is so beautiful here now. If it weren't for the chance of seeing those paintings, I'd be tempted to stay on a while longer. But I guess it is time to move north. Here is a poem[2]—I don't know whether it really conveys much or not, but I do know I am very sick of sounding so quiet . . . I've been reading Jarrell's *Losses*[3] and feel I keep seeing a lot of my own faults in it—except of course he has all the material in this world—also Pound's collected poems, 1926. I just noticed they are dedicated to Miss Moore's mother.[4] It's really hard to see how important a lot of them were, now—

It will be nice to see you. I'm afraid those cherry-blossoms are over—they've been in all the Supplements.

Affectionately yours,

Elizabeth

1 Paintings from the Berlin Museums, March 17–April 25, 1948, a show of paintings from the Kaiser Friedrich Museum and the Nationalgalerie that were taken to the United States by the army and stored at the National Gallery, against the wishes of museum staff.

2 "Over 2,000 Illustrations and a Complete Concordance" (EB-*CP*).

3 Published in 1948.

4 EB assumed incorrectly that "Mary Moore of Trenton," to whom Ezra Pound dedicated *Personae* (1926), was Marianne Moore's mother.

26.

April 10, [1948]

Dear Elizabeth:

There are no bears, or cats or dogs among the roses at Mrs. Dawson's, only a negress named Florence.[1] If you arrive on the 16th, we can go to the Budapest recital at the Library—a good Haydn, Mozart, Beethoven program.[2]

Will you read again for us on Monday, the 19th, I think? I have some Jack Daniels and can start you off properly slugged this time.

The German pictures are grand, but with crowds like the World Fair.

"2,000 Illustrations" is very brilliant, but I want to read it many more times before saying anything.

Affectionately,
Cal

27.

[April 22, 1948]
Thursday—

Dear Cal,

One should never change one's plans, I guess, it makes one such a nuisance to oneself and everybody else . . . I've written to Mrs. Dawson and if she can still bear the idea after the trouble I've put her to I am coming the 1st of May—and of course I can easily go to a hotel— Now I just hope you're going to be in town. There are lots of things I'd like to talk to you about. The recordings were so poor that I don't like the idea of making any more, not having done anything this winter making for improvement, but . . . I do hope to see you.

Affectionately yrs,
Elizabeth

1 Cf. Wallace Stevens, "The Virgin Carrying a Lantern," lines 1–3 (1923) (courtesy of Eleanor Cook).
2 The Budapest String Quartet, in residence at the Library of Congress.

28.

Dear Cal,

I don't know quite why I haven't written *you* a thank-you letter before now, except I guess I thought it so often & loudly to myself that I already thought I had—anyway, you were awfully kind & nice & I really had a wonderful time, & feel quite picked up again to the proper table-land of poetry for the summer, off which I guess one does gradually slip unless there are a few people like you to talk to—except I guess there aren't more than two or three. Carley couldn't have been more thoughtful & I like her very much. I found her some Marianne Moore at the Gotham Book Mart the other day—now I wish she'd write me exactly how she feels. I thought her reactions to the reindeer poem[1] so understandable & justified. I only regret that I didn't get to read your poem all the way through—or hear any more recordings.

New York is awful I think. After racking my brains I just this minute decided it is like a battered-up old alarm clock that insists on gaining five or six hours a day & has to be kept lying on its side, but maybe I can do better than that. I'm leaving just as soon as I can, but I'll be here for the lecture—readings, rather—the 25th & have already bought a ticket. I'm writing a note to Miss Moore. I'll hope to see you sometime there if you aren't too busy, but I'll understand it if you are perfectly well, so don't worry about it—

Bought a Modern Library Chaucer, the only one I could get—only the *Tales*. I have almost finished a poem about the Prodigal Son.[2] First, I think it's too much like a Lowell, then I think it isn't at all, then it seems to be again, etc.

And thank you for taking me to see Pound. I am really endlessly grateful for that experience.

Affectionately yours,
Elizabeth

---

1 Marianne Moore, "Rigorists," *What Are Years* (1941).
2 "The Prodigal" (EB-*CP*).

29.

Dear Elizabeth:

Why don't we and Miss Moore (and maybe the Tates, she and they are friendly) have dinner beforehand. There's nothing official arranged.

The Modern Library Chaucer is a convenient size with a glossary in the back. He's the author who has all the slow, open, common-sense, loving, secure, wise-in-people etc. virtues that we were talking about and that the modern world has little of. I've been reading *Middlemarch*[1]—she too, very mature, powerful, wise, if one forgets her stretches of blank Victorian prose. Not easy-going like Chaucer and Dryden—more like Milton and Wordsworth a kind of sustained tense Protestant adultness—Herbert is in between the two groups, though those categories are too vague to be worth much.

I read Carley "The Grave," "The Sweet Dead Whale," "Silence" and a few others and with the momentum of your stories, more or less converted her.[2] My admirer Flint,[3] who writes me so many letters, wrote me about how Blackmur was all wrong about her[4]—her poems being as personal as they could be. I can't write essays as letters but this fits my theory on re-reading. All the animals and places are analogies (roughly) of Miss Moore and her art—so I take the Canadian mountain which you got me to really read for the first time.[5] What a massive overwhelming poem it is. Now you must sell Carley on James. We had quite an agitated argument: "You must feel uncertain or you wouldn't be so aroused." I: "But damn it, you haven't *read* him." Then I named her a list of 50 world authors, important as James, James's peers. She: "I can't think of one except Carlyle that I wouldn't rather read than James." But I'd never dreamed of naming Carlyle in any list.

How much I enjoyed your visit—and yet it will be September before I get my poem rolling again—it worries me not writing, and yet it seems right and sensible to wait. But will the inspiration come when I call it? No peace in this world for the poet! Poor poets!

I just met someone who knew Randall since the fourth grade when he had the most beautiful Indian suit in the world. It's a fascinating subject to pursue—and the day he discovered tennis.

Be seeing you, Affectionately,

Cal

1 George Eliot, *Middlemarch* (1871–72).
2 Marianne Moore, "A Grave," "The Steeple Jack," and "Silence," *Selected Poems* (1935).
3 R. W. Flint.
4 R. P. Blackmur "The Method of Marianne Moore," *The Double Agent: Essays in Craft and Elucidation* (1935).
5 Marianne Moore, "The Octopus," *Selected Poems* (1935).

30.

Dear Cal:

To my great surprise, Marianne has accepted the invitation to have dinner before your readings. When I talked to her the other day she said that she believed on such occasions one should stay severely alone for several hours ahead of time, in order to "freeze the force" properly. Of course I irreverently suggested a shot of Novocain, but anyway, she likes Mr. Tate very much, and she began by refusing & then by imperceptible stages worked herself around into an enthusiastic acceptance. I think it will be very nice.

She suggested some place near the New School—to go on right afterwards—it seems to me that Rochimbaud place on 6th Avenue, about 11th Street, would be good—but if you have any better ideas why just let me know. I said I'd call her Tuesday morning & make the final plans. She is much concerned about whether the auditorium will be heated or not & I have just had a very funny conversation with two Scandinavians I think, "engineers," whose final statement was: "If gets real cold, we gives heat." But they "spelled" each other with me on the phone, each hardly waiting to be next to speak to this lunatic. Will you ask Mr. Tate? (Mrs.[1]—too).

I like *Middlemarch* very much but read it long ago. Last winter I read the first book, *Clerical Sketches* & parts of it are marvelous—the V. Woolf piece on G. Eliot isn't so bad.[2]

I saw the Rahvs who asked after you.[3]

I'm looking forward to Tuesday.

Yours,

Elizabeth

---

1 Caroline Gordon.
2 George Eliot, *Scenes of Clerical Life* (1857); Virginia Woolf, "George Eliot," *The Common Reader* (1925).
3 Nathalie Swan and Philip Rahv.

31.

Dear Cal,

I had a very nice time last Tuesday—hope you enjoyed it, too, in spite of the fire-alarm, etc. I think Marianne felt quite set up.— I went over to Brooklyn to dinner with her Friday night, & I don't know whether because of my conversations with you on the subject, or what, things seem to be going much better. There is another very nice story connected with the readings, but I shall save it until the next time I see you. She showed me some of the La Fontaine translations—you know that Macmillan just turned them down, after never even writing her for months, etc. I wasn't prepared to judge them as translations in such a way, but they certainly seem to sound very characteristic of Marianne, amazingly so, and even as only that, worth publishing.[1]

I hope to get away by Thursday morning. My address is just Wiscasset, & maybe you can let me know there when in August you'd like to come to visit so I can plan ahead, polish off Chaucer, etc.

Oh—Marianne has a very nice, old-fashioned steel-engraving of Burns in the front hall. I admired it; said I hoped sometime to write something about him, & didn't he look nice. She replied, "But he couldn't have looked that nice, really, of course."

Affectionately yours,
Elizabeth

32.

June 9, [1948]

Dear Elizabeth:

I want to hear your "story" about the reading. The best moment was Miss Moore changing into her heavy stockings in the crowded reception room. Fascinating woman, I liked her very much and was properly impressed.

Worked out—or nearly worked out two more stanzas to my long poem. I'm beginning to contemplate Yaddo for the winter. Only in boring solitude will I do the work! There's so much, before I even have a first draft!

You're so warm and friendly to me; It's such a joy seeing you. I called up to say goodbye, but you weren't in and then I was lost in the Tates' packing.

---

1 Marianne Moore's translation of Jean de la Fontaine's *Fables* was eventually published by Viking in 1954.

How would August 14 be for a visit? Do you think you might have room for Carley? Her little boy is here now, an angelic child, I think, and I'm not soft on children.

Did my Williams review for the *Nation*, writing all day long, and two days later the galleys came back to me. It's rather messy and enthusiastic.[1]

You must put Wiscasset "harbor" in a poem; the mud, the deadness, the quiet, the old half-turned over ship, the houses, the little drug-store where the one literary magazine is *Tomorrow*.

Affectionately,
  Cal

33.

Wiscasset, Maine

June 30th—[1948]

Dear Cal,

I talked to Carley on the phone the day before I left—you were attending a wedding or something, I think. I read the Williams review on the train with great interest but not absolute agreement—having just worked over the book again a day or two before. At least, I agree all right with what you do say and think you've done an awfully good job in the first part, of presenting the poem. But really when I re-read it all (the poem) I still felt he shouldn't have used the letters from that woman—to me it seems mean, & they're much too overpowering emotionally for the rest of it so that the whole poem suffers.[2] I noticed in Eberhart's review in *The Times* he said the prose parts were made-up, but I don't think they are, are they?[3] However—it has wonderful sections, and I think Williams has always had a streak of insensitivity. I wish I'd brought it along, now.

And then maybe I've felt a little too much the way the woman did at certain more hysterical moments. People who haven't experienced absolute loneliness for long stretches of time can never sympathize with it at all. You say something about working in "boring solitude" at Yaddo—and I had just been thinking that probably I should have tried to go to Yaddo instead of

---

1 "*Paterson* Book Two," *The Nation* (June 19, 1948), 693–94; see "William Carlos Williams" (RL-*CPR*).

2 Williams's interior monologue "is interrupted by chunks of prose: paragraphs from old newspapers, textbooks, and the letters of a lacerated and lacerating poetess. This material is merely selected by the author. That the poetry is able to digest it in the raw is a measure of power and daring—the daring of simplicity; for only a taut style with worlds of experience behind it could so resign, and give way to the anthologist"; "*Paterson* Book Two," *The Nation* (June 19, 1948). See "William Carlos Williams" (RL-*CPR*).

3 Richard Eberhart, "Energy, Movement and Reality," *The New York Times Book Review* (June 20, 1948).

this, because at least it wouldn't be quite such completely boring solitude. That is if they would take me. Could you tell me how one applies? I don't want to sound as if I were tagging along—but I had already thought I might try to go there in October, or possibly earlier if this proves to be too lonely. The house is very nice, and of course Wiscasset is amazing—so beautiful and dead as a door-nail. I think its heart beats twice a day when the train goes through. I like a moderate amount of solitude and dullness to work in but this is almost drugging. Well, I certainly shouldn't complain to you and things will undoubtedly improve.

I went to dinner with Marianne one night before I left, and then we had a confused day or two when we thought we might travel to Maine together. It is probably just as well that didn't work out. She showed me quite a lot of the La Fontaine. I just don't know what to think. It all has a sort of awkwardness & quaintness that's quite nice—& sounds very much like her, of course; I'm not sure how much like La Fontaine. And Macmillan's has treated her very badly about the whole thing and after three years work has turned her down. But I think Viking is now interested. She asked me to say grace and I had a minute's dreadful black-out, then some thing out of the remote Baptist past mercifully came to me in perfect condition—the only trouble was that M liked it very much and made me repeat it until she knew it, too. She is up near Ellsworth now—I had a letter yesterday. Apparently she is having difficulties with her hostesses because they refuse to let her mow the lawn. My best friend in N.Y. thought my poem about her[1] was "mean," which I found rather upsetting because it wasn't meant to be & it is too late to do anything about it now, I'm afraid. Well, of the readings I liked yours & hers best—I think Tate does it a little too well.

The 14th would be fine, of August, and how long can you stay—two weeks? I asked Carley to consider a visit when I talked to her, and it would be awfully nice, I think. During August I may have an old friend of mine from Key West here—very nice—or maybe not although I think she will be. I have beds for three. However, if my house is full there are several nice places I could get a room at, I think, so it would all work out all right. The only thing I'm nervous about now is that any guest of mine, unless he or she is absorbed in writing a novel, or sleeps twenty-two hours a day, is just going to die of boredom—I can't seem to discover a single thing to do except possibly go swimming. Of course if Carley had her elegant new car that would improve everything a lot—or my Key West friend might possibly have one.

---

1 "For M.M.," *Quarterly Review of Literature* (Spring 1948); see "Invitation to Miss Marianne Moore" (EB-*CP*).

I have an idea for a new book—only being half way through a [second] one yet—all about Tobias and the Angel—don't you like that story? There are wonderful birds here—3 nests in my 2 apple trees.

Is it hot in Washington? Tell me if and when & where you are having any reviews or poems printed, won't you. We might be able to take a trip to call on Marianne even though she feels that we are continents apart. Well I guess I must wander down to that dream-town and pick up the mail.

Affectionately—

Elizabeth

P.S. I really feel you should *struggle* against your feeling about children, but I suppose it's better than drooling over them like Swinburne. But I've always loved the stories about Shelley going around Oxford peering into baby-carriages, and how he once said to a woman carrying a baby, "Madame, can your baby tell us anything of pre-existence?"

34.

July 2, [1948]

Dear Elizabeth:

All the prose parts of *Paterson* are lifted, not made up. I don't know whether your point is right or not—the first two books cry out for the next two, and perhaps the proportions will come out right in the end. As it is the letters are literally left hanging. I think of their effectiveness in two ways: 1) so terrifyingly and typically real, and yet I don't think I'd want to read many of them straight—too monotonous, pathological. Yet in the poem they are placed and not pathological, the agony is absorbed. 2) Aren't they really hardest on Williams himself (Paterson), a damning of his insensitivity. She's mad, but he, like Aeneas can't handle her and shows up badly. I think that's their purpose in the poem. *Paterson* has been like water to me, and my judgment may be subjective. But doesn't true criticism come that way—the only way to penetrate an author—then after a while the intuitions become objective.

Read a good essay on Burns in an anthology of essays gotten together by F. R. Leavis.[1] I guess he's really quite a first-rate ~~poet~~, and I've followed fashion in ignoring him. It's funny, because his rhymes and stanzas are technical fire-works just on the surface. Then so much experience or observation.

1 John Speirs, "Burns," *Determinations: Critical Essays*, ed. F. R. Leavis (1931).

I don't know which, for I've never soaked in him and have trouble with Scots—more verbs I have to look up than a French poet.

My feeling about babies is mostly a joke—an imitation of Frank Parker. Still a howling one for long periods—not so hot! Then Randall thinks nothing adult is human, and how can a poor single man talk the way parents do—one's affable indifference against the afflicted mother's affectionate fury. This is meant to be non-sense.

I dropped a hint to Giroux[1] (Harcourt Brace) about trying to get the Fontaine. You should like him, in French, at least—so solid, shrewd, tender, unromantic, worldly wise, full of people—hard and soft where he should be—a perfect craftsman. He might be much larger than the other extreme, Rimbaud.

Enough talk about verse! Would you like me to write Mrs. Ames[2] about inviting you to Yaddo? Get Miss Moore to write too. You can't invite yourself, though, of course, almost all the invitations are planned. It would be marvelous to have you there. I know the solitude that gets too much. It doesn't *drug* me, but I get fantastic and uncivilized.

At last my divorce is over.[3] Looking back, it seems strange that we could survive it, and now the conclusion is allaying and satisfying. While I was in New York, I saw Jean—all very affectionate and natural, thank God.

It's funny at my age to have one's life so much in and on one hands. All the rawness of learning, what I used to think should be done with by twenty-five. Sometimes nothing is so solid to me as writing. I suppose that's what vocation means—at times a torment, a bad conscience, but all in all, purpose and direction, so I'm thankful, and call it good as Eliot would say.

Rodman was here, but I couldn't rise to the occasion: praise his anthology, care much about my ignorance of Haitian painting, pretend I hadn't read *Annus Mirabilis* and wanted to.[4] He suggested that he be included in the record albums, and that one of his friends had found me indifferent and abstracted. What do you do with such people!

Now that Carley is away, I feel that I have been trying to force something that wouldn't work. I suppose this has happened to people again and again, sad, foolish, confusing—but that's enough for a letter, enough to give substance to what must have struck you as odd generalizations in my letters.

1 Robert Giroux.
2 Elizabeth Ames, director of Yaddo.
3 RL married Jean Stafford in 1940; they separated in 1946 and divorced in 1948.
4 Selden Rodman, *The Amazing Year, May 1, 1945–April 30, 1946* (1947); cf. John Dryden, *Annus Mirabilis* (1667).

I may drive to Maine on the 1st with some cousins. In that case, how would the 6th or 7th do instead of the 14th?

Affectionately,

Cal

35.

Dear Cal:

It's very hot today, for here, and I guess I must hike down to that so-called beach and get into that icy water for a while—although I guess there's going to be a thunderstorm after a while. The robins are shrieking with that particular note they use for storms. Having just digested all the *New York Times* and some pretty awful clam-chowder I made for myself, I don't feel the slightest bit literary, just stupid. Or maybe it's just too much solitude.

Thank you for your nice long letter which did me a great deal of good. The 6th or 7th would be fine—but would you let me know as soon as you can? I'm having trouble getting the right people at the right time, with so far no one except a few rather odd New Englandish callers who mostly tell me about the state of their "nerves." I had a letter from Carley in which she said she thought she'd like to come in July, or later, in September, so I have just asked her, tentatively for the 26th.

I have no car, you know, and I am afraid any guest will be bored to death—better bring your knitting. I am working my way gradually through all the Hardy novels in the local library and find they are just the thing— Edwin Arlington Robinson is also dutifully recommended to me as a local character, but I really can't get very excited about him although I try. On the 9th I insulted several people I guess by not wanting to go to hear Mr. R. P. T. Coffin at Bowdoin. Someone asked my landlord here if he didn't have an "author" living in his house, and he replied "No, not an author, a writer."

Well, things must improve I'm sure, and the place is beautiful there's no getting round that. I am working on Tobias and "The Prodigal Son" and I just started a story called "Homesickness"[1]—all very cheerful. I think almost the last straw here though is the hairdresser, a nice big hearty Maine girl who asks me questions I don't even know the answers to. She told me: 1, that my

---

1 See "Homesickness" (EB-*EAP*).

hair "don't feel like hair at all." 2, I was turning gray practically "under her eyes." And when I'd said yes, I was an orphan, she said "Kind of awful, ain't it, ploughing through life alone." So now I can't walk downstairs in the morning or upstairs at night without feeling I'm ploughing. There's no place like New England.

I don't envy you entertaining Selden, and I think Haitian painting has deteriorated very rapidly—I got an awful one when my friends went to Haiti last winter.

I've just read a marvelous life of Juan Gris—the best book I've read in a long time, I think. Now to return to the *Trumpet Major*.[1]

Affectionately yours,
Elizabeth

36.

[July 14, 1948]
Wed.

Dear Elizabeth:

Let's make it the 6th (night) or 7th (morning), and I'll stay through about half of the next week.

Washington is not at its best—hot, empty, rainy etc. Instead of Hardy, I read through old magazines for my critical biography of modern English poets—there's luxury in putting off an assignment. I've even descended to movies and crossword puzzles—reminds me of how Jean and I used to fight for the Sunday crossword during jags of boredom—anything to kill time, the way Allen Tate must usually feel.

Cosmos Club life—saw a bat on second floor, startled an ancient man wrapped in a sheet making for the shower, dinner with an ancient man who had delivered a woman in a union suit, etc.

In the midst of this sultry club life a letter from Santayana suggesting that I visit Rome. It seemed fantastic at first, but after two days toying with it, no more so than Yaddo. I don't suppose I could interest you. The imagination roars with possibilities and inducements; but wonder if felons can travel?

Tell me how to get to your house. Are you sure one more visitor won't be too many? In Maine your friends pour in like lava—hot from their cities. I'll

---

1 Douglas Cooper, *Juan Gris: His Life and Work* (1947); Thomas Hardy, *Trumpet Major* (1880).

understand if you want a rest. No knitting; but I might bring the works of 12 minor modern British poets—say Abercrombie, Bottomly, Church and Doughty—no, an alphabet of them!

Affectionately,

Cal

P.S. There's something haunting and nihilistic about your hair-dresser.

37.

Dear Cal:

I hope I didn't sound just too grumpy and churlish in my last letter—so that you've abandoned the idea of coming to Wiscasset. Things have improved quite a bit and I don't feel quite so ungrateful about the place. I can see why this part of Maine would have a fascination for you. One of the Sortwells was telling me a long tale about the Cavanaughs of Damariscotta the other day, but I didn't really prick up my ears & connect it with your poem at all until it was too late to ask any more questions. And last night I was shown through one of the biggest houses from cellar to attic, even to the dolls in bed in the attic, paintings of all the family's ships, etc. And today, my dear, I've just returned from a church service at Head Tide. I guess you probably know all about it & its church, etc.—but I did leave before the sermon. I guess maybe what I don't like about this place is that its local atmosphere is so thick as to be distracting, like a fog. And of course, after the rather high meat of Key West, the society is like breast of chicken.

I found a place yesterday where you can rent a small sail-boat, very cheap—that might be fun when you come—at least I think you sail, don't you? I haven't for ten years and have probably forgotten how.

I hope you aren't suffering very much from the heat in Washington. It's been pretty hot here a few days, but I go & submerge myself in that ice-water once in a while, and then in the evenings it suddenly gets cool, as it's just done, and the fire-flies appear.

I found *Curtain of Green* in the local library and I liked it very much—I'd read "Why I Live at the P.O." & "Clytie" in anthologies, but the others were all new to me, and I think that last one, I think it's called "The Worn Path," about the old colored woman, is really marvelous. It's too bad her novel was so awful[1]—I should think she could write a long, long, really good Negro novel if anyone could, if she wanted to. She can do all that wonderful personification the colored people go in for so well—and then when I think how

[July 24, 1948]
Next Saturday morning—
I don't know whatever happened to this letter—I guess I thought I'd finished & mailed it. I've had a guest the past few days—asleep upstairs at the moment, so I can't type—& have let everything slide.

Can you go abroad? I've been considering a long trip of some sort this fall, & I have a wonderful catalogue of trips one can take by freighter. I'll show it to you. But the world is in such a state I don't know whether it's a good idea to go to Europe or not. But I've always promised myself I'm going to spend my declining years just taking walks in Rome. Nothing could be more profitable, I think, for the last 20 years of one's life.

Just as you come into Wiscasset, Route 27 branches off to the left of Route 1. I'm about the 4th house along it on the left, known as "Mr. Groves' Cottage"—you can't miss it; it is the only small house around, with a lot of tattered rose-bushes & 2 apple trees in front. It is DULL but pleasant, particularly when the sun shines. Yesterday we were reduced to walking in the graveyard. Carley is coming Tuesday, to stay just a week, I think. I think you should incorporate the whole Sortwell family in an epic—wait till I give you details—

Yours,
Elizabeth

38.

[Postcard: Stonington Harbor, Me.]

[Stonington, Maine
July 26, 1948]
Dear Cal—Came up here yesterday just for a day & night & I like it so much better than Wiscasset I'm hoping I'll be able to break my lease there & move up here—so please hold everything & I'll let you know— Could & would you get up this far if I do? I'm afraid this is much more my style & I am beginning to find Wiscasset *deadly*. Poor Carley—I hate to inflict it on her— Yours—
E.

1 Eudora Welty, *A Curtain of Green* (1941) and *Delta Wedding* (1946).

39.

[Washington, D.C.
July 29, 1948]

Dear Elizabeth:

Stonington!! Once I had a wild notion of fishing for a living and wound up there and sold myself on a house and sold Jean on it—till she saw it! An odd little yellow thing that she called Fatso. It was tiny and beset with neighbors. Jail, Westport, Wiscasset,* Stonington; who wouldn't have been sold.

I'll be at Spring St., Bar Harbor c/o Thorndyke after the first. Write as soon as you know what's up.¹ My best to Carley, if she's with you. Tell her I *have* written and written again.

    Cal

*An obscurity: our neighbors in Westport said that Wiscasset was a fishing center.

40.

[Postcard: Looking to North Haven from Stonington, Me.]

[Stonington, Maine
July 30, 1948]

C & I arrived an hour or so ago & it is at least 20° cooler than at Wiscasset & very nice.² Why consider Yaddo when you can come here? Tonight we are going to see *The Mating of Milly*.³

    Yours,

    E.

41.

Essex, Massachusetts
[July 31, 1948]
Saturday

Dear Elizabeth:

At the post-office with a post-office pen and Woolworth paper, while

---

1 Note for telegram in EB's hand: "Your original plan or even earlier better since I have to return to Wiscasset soon to close house. Carley returning to Cummington. Wonderful here. Possible sailing trip in offing. Please wire plans." She records the costs of "wire .73" plus "call .30."

2 Carley Dawson arrived in Wiscasset on July 26 and moved to Stonington with EB on July 30.

3 *The Mating of Milly*, dir. Henry Levin (1948).

waiting for Lesley Parker to finish her morning shopping, so that I can get back on the green cushions in the back of the Parker truck and return.

Bar Harbor turned out to have obstacles: space, children, visitors and relatives, so I'm staying here, between my parents and the Parkers—seeing people I knew 12 years ago.

I thought I'd leave here Monday, a week from the day after tomorrow, if that's convenient.

How's Stonington? Have you and Carley been fishing or sailing? Have you seen a small provincially roofed house (like an early post-office) about a block below the Gross's? Fatso, that I nearly bought.

Hope you're both having fun,

Affectionately,

Cal

42.

[Postcard: Stonington, Me. EB marks her landlady's white-clapboard house "Mrs. G.'s"
(Mrs. Gross).]

[August 2, 1948]

Dear Cal:—Either it's very dry here, or the fog gets into our bones—we wonder if when you come you'd bring something to quench the thirst or keep out the fog— Yours,

E.B.

43.

[Ipswich, Massachusetts]
August 16, 1948

Dear Elizabeth:

If you'd come to Ipswich—you'd have found waiting for you: Anne Dick, Elliott and Mrs. Chandler, the woman who almost converted Mrs. Sortwell, and my first project for you:[1] age: 41, weight: 155, hair: full black graying. He has lived for 20 years in a spic and span little white house with two aged servants tending lambs and reading Thoreau and writing a book which no one has seen. Think I can guarantee that you won't.

---

1 EB wrote to Carley Dawson that she had "commissioned [Cal] to find a rich husband in Washington. I think a nice comfy Oriental would do—one with lots of diamonds and absolutely no interest in the arts" (EB-*OA*, 165).

I interview him tomorrow. Outs: He has gone mad once or twice (very stable at present), rides, but can leave it alone, and lives with his coffin and tombstone; means small but adequate. I think we'll use him as a decoy.

I'm having a form printed. Age, weight, income, interests, apathies, aversions, past, and a composite physical examination stamped by a notary. (Do you want this before you meet them? Question of strategy.)

Here is my starting list: Joe Alsop, Ted Roethke (only makes $6000 which doesn't cover his eating and drinking, but he has a genius for sponging)—airfare: captivated by your Chicago picture. (Goodbye ball point pen!)[1] My cousins Carlisle and Pearson Winslow, and my Uncle Cot.[2]

Really the best of all: 3 houses, a yacht, $100,000 income, works from 9 to 5, absolutely no interest in the arts. He's married at the moment to Aunt Sarah, but he's already divorced an actress and knows all the ropes. This would be a personal triumph for me: I've never gotten anything from him except occasional Old Fashions, some turtle soup and a carton of paper matches marked Bobby. He's a bit old, but wonderfully preserved, ram-rod straight, and brown-haired. Mother says he was a tremendous "catch."

This is all I've been able to scare up for the first day, but things are in the saddle. You'll make your headquarters here. With each candidate you'll go on a moonlit paddle (costs a dollar which I'll pay out of my traveling expenses.) We'll see which one you would least know was in the house before five and is most entertaining after five.

Ah me, back to life. I'll write you a serious letter when I get to Washington. You were an angel to put up with all my imbecility and bad behavior.[3] I'm almost a new man thanks to you—or is one ever?

Affectionately,

Cal

P.S. Be a good girl and give Yaddo another thought.

Addenda: The man I described first has two indoor and two outdoor servants. When I telephone they ask my name and then tell me he can't be disturbed. I'm lying on my bed in the Parker library, on a prickly blue velvet counter pane, under a window shade with a picture of the St. Marks' cloisters, trying

1 RL switches to pencil.
2 Charles Edward Cotting, who was married to RL's aunt Sarah Winslow.
3 RL finally broke with Carley Dawson during his visit; she was escorted away by Tom Wanning. See letter 137.

to read the not-really-readable-in-bulk Miss Herschberger[1]—Heureux qui, comme Ulysse . . . Vivre entre ses parents le reste de son age.[2]

44.

Stonington
[August 22, 1948]
Sunday afternoon—

Dear Cal:

I think you've done an enormous amount of ground-work already & I can see I picked the right person to solve my problems about my future for me . . . I must say I like the sound of the uncle best so far, but don't like the idea of any unnecessary publicity—don't forget the Oriental angle—in fact I'd settle for some form of dignified concubinage as long as it was guaranteed . . .

Carley's room is occupied by a very cheerful lady-water-colorist who transports a Yogurt-making machine around with her, and also the works of Mary Baker Eddy. I suppose I'm going to find out how she reconciles them, although I don't want to. Another water-colorist called on her & remembered having traveled on the boat from Halifax with me last summer. They talked & giggled until midnight, & I suppose made Yogurt. A little old stone-cutter is in the little room, & I'm afraid he has silicosis, if not tuberculosis, by the coughing. The town is bursting at the seams because it is the weekend of the Granite Engineers Convention. I used to call on the Miss Moore who paints, here, & her father, & now I wish we'd done it while you were here.[3] They are both very nice, & he is a retired Latin professor, 83, from Columbia, who has been working away peacefully all through the war at a translation of Livy for the Loeb Classical Library.[4] His manuscripts went back & forth from & to England all that time without any trouble at all. He still writes Latin poetry just for amusement, or for his friends' birthdays, etc.—is very stylish & gallant & seemed like something from an earlier age & I think you would have enjoyed him. He uses Latin puns in his conversation—most of which I'm afraid I couldn't understand.

I had a wonderful letter here from *Poetry* magazine when I finally got

---

1 Ruth Herschberger, *Way of Happening* (poems, 1948); and *Adam's Rib* (essays, 1948).
2 Cf. Joachim du Bellay, "Sonnet XXXI," lines 1 and 4, *Les Regrets* (1558).
3 Janet Moore and Frank Gardner Moore.
4 Frank Moore translated books XXIII–XXX of Livy for Loeb.

back Thursday night. It requests a contribution & congratulates me on my poetry's having "perceptivity" & "sureness," etc., that "seem often to be lacking in the output of the *run-down sensibility of the forties*." I think we should make a modest fortune by working out a prescription for run-down sensibilities.

Your friend in the drug-store (whom I can't like, try as I will) keeps asking me if "Bob" is coming back, because he knows a young lady in Deer Isle, a sophomore at Holyoke, I think it is, who is writing a paper about you & would give anything to meet you. She will be very disappointed, he said.

Now I do wish we'd got to see Marianne, too. I think Tom[1] & I are going to drive on Tuesday or Wednesday & it would have been so much better with you along, too.

I do hope you had a good time in spite of all your troubles, because I did. I just hope I didn't get too teasing and opinionated which I guess I'm apt to do with any encouragement at all. Last night while the Orgy-orgy progressed next door I lay awake composing sentences of a review of your next book—I really hope I'll be up to it when the book appears. It has been beautiful here with a full moon & very light fogs at night. Mrs. Gross is blossoming like a rose—asked if I'd mind a few personal questions this morning, & sat down on a stool to inquire as to inspiration, imagination, etc., while I ate breakfast.

I am alternately thinking of Yaddo & studying my freighter-trip booklets.

Affectionately yours,
   Elizabeth

45.

[Cosmos Club, Washington, D.C.
August 23, 1948]
Monday

Dear Elizabeth:

A sticky Boston day, a lunging walk with Frank Parker half way across Boston ending with a call on Hyman Bloom—against my better judgment. We talked about printing, compared the arts, oriental mysticism, suffering, why you were always on some littoral move, why he never moved; and had five or six beers. I have misgivings but I think it went off—he's going to

---

1 Thomas Edwards Wanning.

Ipswich if Frank will fetch and return him—probably Stonington if you could get the Summers[1] to do the same. Seemed very real and witty in a somber way.

A sticky New York day, went to the end of the 3rd Avenue El alone, lunch with my publisher, said your manuscript had been refused over his head, lot of shop talk, long milk and lemonade session with Jean at the Grand Central Station and we listed about 100 useless and sordid preventatives for restlessness and solitude—but you'll laugh us to scorn.

A gummy Sunday in Washington, slept, went to the office and read my mail, the papers, went to *Henry VIII*, which I'd wanted to see for years because someone said I should or shouldn't, and a ghastly Douglas Fairbanks Jr. movie called *Catherine the Great*, did the *Times* crossword, read *Apes of God*,[2] sleep.

Now I'm back in my loose harness. I'm unhappy about the Carley business when I think of it, but it's too near and I forget as much as I can. Have you ever read Constant's *Adolphe*—it's all there, a bit worked up and romanticized, but not much.[3]

Legend: Through Betty Sortwell through Emily Dick, through Anne Dick—sordid bohemian parties in Stonington with odd Bohemians drinking absinthe.[4] I restored our vodka.

A shocking surprise—a library official with incredible diligence has written critical biographies of all the recorded poets. My pencil drops from paralyzed fingers when I try to set about cutting.

I have acquired a phony, spruce disillusioned tone—but it's only Washington.

Affectionately,
Cal

46.

[Postcard: Cartoon characters inside bubble letters spelling "Bob"]

[August 26, 1948]

Thurs.—Hyman said he had a "fine visit" with you, & was glad I'd sent you. It's too hot even here today to write a letter, but I am rather disturbed by the

1 U. T. and Joseph Summers.
2 Wyndham Lewis, *Apes of God* (1932).
3 Benjamin Constant, *Adolphe* (1816), a fictional account of his affair with Madame de Staël, several years his senior (Dawson was nine years older than RL).
4 Cf. EB to Carley Dawson, August 30, 1948 (EB-OA, 167).

round-about-news—I'd already gathered something was very wrong, & left W under a considerable cloud, I'm afraid—oh lord! & innocent, too. Hope your vocation is standing by you somewhat.

Yours,
Elizabeth

47.

Library of Congress
August 27, [1948]

Dear Elizabeth:

I started to write you a letter—after a page the heat reduced me to inertia—about my morning of being photographed for the Associated Press's rotogravure section—from all angles, sometimes as Consultant, sometimes as an expert on recording, holding a metal "mother" disc, sometimes as a typical poet reading, and all I had to read was Randall, "It was not dying. Everybody died,"[1] and "When my mother died it made me nervous,"[2] over and over again.

I too had a letter from *Poetry*, Hayden Carruth, "We admired your poem in the *Kenyon*, etc."[3] Unlike with you their comments stopped with admiration; I'm esteemed but not loved by them. Do you think their letters are the result of run-down sensibilities?

I spent a blissful two days reading *Les Liaisons Dangereuses*, one of the great books; I wish there were more. I don't know what it's like, *Troilus and Criseyde* combined with Clarissa Harlowe, with the villains made as horrible as they could without becoming lurid.[4]

I guess I've emphasized all the charms of Yaddo: large house, trees, autumn, space and economy and irresponsibility, and you can't be disturbed before 5 or 6. Perhaps, you should combine your alternatives—try Yaddo, and if it becomes oppressive, fly away on a freighter. If I can stand it, and they'll let me, I'm going to stay through the winter.

Today I record myself—the hangman with no one left to hang but himself.

From the enclosed you'll see that the poem on me has already been writ-

---

1 Randall Jarrell, "Losses," line 1.

2 Misquotation of Jarrell's "The State," line 1: "When they killed my mother it made me nervous."

3 Possibly "Falling Asleep over the Aeneid" or "Mother Marie Therese," *The Kenyon Review* (1948). Hayden Carruth was an editor at *Poetry* from 1949 to 1950.

4 Pierre Choderlos de Laclos, *Les Liaisons dangereuses* (1784); Geoffrey Chaucer, *Troilus and Criseyde* (ca. 1483); Samuel Richardson, *Clarissa* (1748).

ten. You probably would rather read his "Viable Woman," it begins "Maia was one, all gold, fire and sapphire . . . she was of Roman vocables the disburser."[1] Parody-proof; I'll mail it when I finish reading it. Thinking it over, your 1 line "My feet were cut by barnacles," doesn't sound as though you were risking much.

Ever since I've left Jean, my tongue gets blacker and blacker. I *did* enjoy Stonington.

Affectionately,
Cal

P.S. I put in Flint's letter out of vanity—the analysis seems right to me. All I know about Canada is Maine and Francis Parkman. Flint is the man who wrote Randall so many letters, and started out objecting to my Catholicism. The shoe is on the other foot.

Wish my "Kavanaughs" were done—then I'd be free, and you'd have your review to write—so far off it seems!

Dick's letter isn't quite accurate; this must be the poem he sent Randall as a review—still the kites, cold Manhattans and drive were fun.

48.

[August 30, 1948]

Dear Elizabeth:

The round-about news is nothing to *worry* over; Anne likes to make things look lurid, that's her style of gossip—the little tainting drop of poetry in everyone. There can't be any cloud—except that of leaving Wiscasset, which is of course unforgivable.

The Ipswich lamb man wrote me (note delivered by his chauffeur) "I am tired, could you see me in about two weeks." So he's off the Bishop list. So I've begun on Alsop, a very promising conversation on a book he's discovered (Joe has read all the books no one has ever heard of, and is a bit spotty on what one has) by a friend of H. James, on a man who never would or could get married.

Apologies for this flood of letters; I'm fighting the heat—the last four days were 97, 99, 99, 97—the hottest stretch in the last five years, the hottest ever for these days in August etc. And the necessity of finishing my British poets—I've written on all the ones I care about.

1 Richard Eberhart, "Speech from a Play"; "The Legend of Viable Women," *Poetry-Ireland* (Oct. 1949) and *The Kenyon Review* (Winter 1949).

Spent the week-end at Glen Echo, a tiny Revere Beach, with no beach except a lot, called "The Sand Beach" and no sea, except a sky-blue pool, with a sky-blue fountain and two thousand bathers in half an acre of water. And next day reading *Treasure Island* and *Kidnapped*,[1] with a fan, half a foot away raking me. Somehow I feel myself again, as I haven't for months, except for bits of Stonington.

During the heat, I've been living on one solid meal, and a detestable thing in blunderbuss glasses, called "orange drink."

Affectionately,
Cal

P.S. Oh, you of all people must read Jean's "Newport" in the current *New Yorker*,[2] then send it to Miss Moore.

49.[3]

Stonington, Maine
August 30th, 1948

Dearest Cal:

You sounded very tired & hot & cranky . . . It has even been frightful here for four days, so I hope you haven't died of it in Washington. But today is beautiful, cold & clear—I'm quite looking forward to September—unless it gets too lonesome. Hyman sounded very pleased that you had called—& I should think he & Frank would be good for each other. I had a letter from Marianne, & thank goodness I guess my thoughts on her came all right. She starts off, "Words fail me, Elizabeth." Her postscript is: "I hope R.L. is able to go on with things he wants to do & is not too trammeled by government and academic plans." Tom, & maybe Andy,[4] & I are going to see her Wednesday & it already promises to be quite an expedition.

Did you get a copy of Eberhart's endless *ubi sunt* poem, too? I thought it started off pretty well, for him—but really, he uses up words so fast it's a wonder he has any left by this time. Or that they'll come when he calls—like the Red-or-White Queen's remarks on Time in *Through the Looking Glass*.[5]

---

1 Robert Louis Stevenson, *Kidnapped* (1886) and *Treasure Island* (1883).
2 Jean Stafford, "Profiles: American Town," *The New Yorker* (Aug. 28, 1948).
3 Crossed with letter 48.
4 Andrews Wanning.
5 Lewis Carroll, *Through the Looking Glass* (1871).

It's probably a sign of a generous disposition even if it doesn't make very good poetry—& I imagine he is very generous.

The ex–Latin professor read me a long ode to one of his daughters on her birthday in Medieval Latin, & is going to give me some Mnemonics, too—he is very cute.

I am reading the "Nonnes Preestes Tale," which I'd never read before, & of course I was much taken with:

> "His coomb was redder than the fyn coral,
>   and batailled, as it were a castel wal.
>   His bile was black, & as the jeet it shoon;
>   like asure were his legges, & his toon:
>   His nayles whitter than the lili flour
>   and like the burned gold was his colour."

& "his sustres & his paramours," & "For Goddes love, as take some laxatyf—"[1]

I've just found the word for Mr. Tate, only for Goddes love don't tell him: hypoidalichocephaly. or -ic.

I'll read *Adolphe* sometime with the greatest interest. Please don't worry any more about *that*.

Affectionately yours,
Elizabeth

50.

Tuesday [August 31, 1948]

Dear Cal:

I guess I'd better return these letters. Really, Eberhart (after what I said to you the other day about his use of words, I keep calling him Expendable Eberhart, to myself) is extraordinary. "Thought bullet"—what *does* he mean? & "locking tremblers"—I suspect he means *temblors*, don't you? But I guess he is really fond of you & it is mean to read it as meaning anything much else than that. I'd also like to know, though, what he had in mind by the word "truth."

I like the first part of Mr. Flint's letter very much & am so glad you let me

---

1 Geoffrey Chaucer, "The Nonnes Preestes Tale," lines 93–98, 101, and 177, *The Canterbury Tales.*

see it—the part about the two notions of thought, etc. But doesn't it annoy you a little when people hand you back, like an obligation, flat statements of what you "meant"? It seems to be a sort of convention when writing to an author. I've been to Quebec, although I didn't see much of it, but when I visited my aunt in Montreal I remember—it's a long time ago—I was very much surprised to look out her window & watch the nuns & priests playing tennis. Also, have you ever been, you probably have, to the church of the Perpetual Adoration in N.Y., on 28th St.? You see those beautiful habits there. I think the "insistent rhyming" at the end is wonderful, too[1]—but I don't think "coda" is correct as applied to it, is it?

(Since you have told me the story behind the remark "Nothing is dead as a dead sister"[2] I keep wishing that more of it were stated somehow in the poem. At least, I had missed the significance of it, & was rather baffled, & so had Tom, my only literary acquaintance at the moment, been.)

You don't say anything about the rest of the letter, so I won't either. Except that you know his not being ready yet to "sort out" the Merton poems & ["]grade them" is pretty funny— Maybe he's extremely young—or what do you know about him? It's such a mixture of good interpretation & conceit.

Oh, dear Mr. E. "The spiritual is the fascinating." Let's publish an anthology of haunting lines, with a supplement on how to exorcise them.

I don't seem to remember the line about the barnacles so the blackness of your tongue was wasted on me, I'm afraid. And one more amplification or correction: I don't think Harcourt Brace ever turned me down. They were going to publish me when I had a few more poems, etc., but were very slow about it, & the Houghton Mifflin thing seemed like a good thing to try for, so I wrote to HB & got what MSS I had back from them, with their blessings, naturally, but anyway, that's the way it was.

I must see you in the rotogravure in sepia—is it for a Washington paper, or where?

Have you ever read Erich Fromm's books? I find him rather disappointing now, but still I think his summary of the Reformation in *Escape from Freedom* might interest you.[3] At least I'd like to see how it strikes you. And if you can place what I'm talking about, could you tell me once more the name of the American reporter-historian you have recommended to me several times?

---

1 See "Mother Marie Therese," lines 123–30 (RL-*CP*).
2 "He squeaked and stuttered: 'N-n-nothing is so d-dead / As a dead s-s-sister' "; "Mother Marie Therese: Drowned in 1812," from lines 75–76 (typescript, Vassar); cf. "Mother Marie Therese" (RL-*CP*).
3 Erich Fromm, *Escape from Freedom* (1941).

It is COLD here to-day—we have the DUO-THERM going—so I hope you are at least just a natural 98.8 in Washington.

Affectionately yours,
　　Elizabeth

[September 2, 1948]
Thursday—

Started to mail this yesterday & got yours of the day before, then Tom & I went to see Marianne & I decided not to mail this until after that. It was a very successful outing & Tom stood up well, considering he had to have an elaborate tea with four Blue Stockings—at least I suppose I rate as one. We were shown everything—the attic, the doll-carriage, the bathroom, the woodshed where the skunk *used* to live, the new electric iron with the special tip for ruffles, etc. M was so eager to remain in the background & show off her hostesses. She had them each reciting pieces for us before we left.

I think the Newport piece is interesting but you know how I dislike that style. We had dinner at Andy Wanning's last night with a fellow Harvard-teacher just back from a visit to Faulkner & his home town—very nice stories.

An elderly male water-colorist now has your room. He had a gray goatee & a *bass viol*—

　　E

51.

September 7, [1948]

Dear Elizabeth:

A delicate matter—the pot calling the kettle black—it's been said to me by all my friends repeatedly, and I know I'm myself beyond self-help; and at least you can spell; but! I sometimes have to use the lines you copied out from Chaucer and Eberhart as key to illegible words—at times in vain.

Since my last letter it has become autumnal (nice but muggy) and I've read *Black Arrow, Weir of Hermiston, The Master of Ballantrae,* and Graves' abridgement of *David Copperfield.* Saw *Black Arrow* as a movie too—it's a cumbersome pot-boiler at best, but redone with the plot of a western thriller it is, is—words fail me.[1] Had a drunken discussion with two Englishmen in

---

1 Robert Louis Stevenson, *Black Arrow: A Tale of the Two Roses* (1888), adapted for the screen by Gordon Douglas (1948); *Weir of Hermiston: An Unfinished Romance* (1896); and *The Master of Ballantrae* (1889). Robert Graves, *The Real David Copperfield* (1933).

which I tried to use the Socratic method, but only discovered that none of us could define "right" or "good." And finished off 23 more poets; God, how I dislike them!

More Eberhart. I wrote him a peevish letter, suggesting that a little revision wouldn't be ruinous; then had pangs and wrote him that I liked his "At Lake Geneva" in Williams.[1] Then came the enclosed—so pathetic: verse is really too hard a profession, as Randall says.

I send along the last Santayana—an example of clear hand-writing—for the comments on you. Of course, he's all wrong about your sense of reality—I guess he'd like your new poems best. But anyway, you and I and Stickney are the only modern poets he likes at all.[2]

"My feet were cut by barnacles" is an Eberhart line, the only one you found to praise.

History books: Adams (Jefferson & Madison), Parkman, W. E. Woodward, History of the U.S. His biographies of Washington, Paine and Grant are amusing.[3] What one should read are letters, diaries, etc., but I've done little myself.

Had a good afternoon with Pound, "It does me good to get unstopped." The only trouble is that it is always much the same bottle. New this time: that he went to Italy to be somewhere the French couldn't look down on; and stories about the seven male poets of England (who were they?) going to call on Wilfrid S. Blunt, and his 20 year old mistress.[4] "When I went with Dorothy the mistress was gone, but I told her all about it." "I wish I'd read Confucius when I was young, but Dorothy says I would have been the most unbearable old bore that ever lived." He's translated the Confucian odes in St. Eliz and wants them printed with a Chinese, phonetic and English texts. His family think them his best work, and I wouldn't be surprised.

I'm feeling fine except:

---

1 Richard Eberthart, "At Lake Geneva," *A Little Treasury of American Poetry*, ed. Oscar Williams (1948).

2 "I *liked* 'North & South' especially for its delicacy. If it were not for the Darky Woman who is looking for a husband that shall be monogamous ['Songs for a Colored Singer'], I should have thought that Elizabeth Bishop had little sense of reality: but I see that she sees the reality of psychic atmosphere or sentiment in their overtones, and prefers for the most part to express that. It is very nice, but a little elusive"; George Santayana to RL, August 31, 1948 (Houghton Library).

3 Francis Parkman, *France and England in North America* (1880) and *The Jesuits in North America in the Seventeenth Century* (1867); W. E. Woodward, *A New American History* (1936), *George Washington: The Image and the Man* (1926), *Tom Paine: America's Godfather* (1945), and *Meet General Grant* (1928). Woodward was a correspondent of Ezra Pound's.

4 Ezra Pound formed a committee with Richard Aldington, F. S. Flint, Frederic Manning, John Masefield, T. Sturge Moore, Victor Plarr, and W. B. Yeats in support of Blunt. Most of them called on him for a "peacock dinner" on January 18, 1914. Blunt's companion was Dorothy Carleton.

Thirty-one
Nothing done

keeps going through my head; and I hate to think of packing.

New thoughts from E's letter: Eliz. equals Betty, you might be called: Eliz, Liz, Lizzie, Betty, Bess, Bessie, Lizbeth or Lisbeth, Ba, Bee, Bet etc. But I guess I'll stick to Elizabeth, though Lizbeth is tempting.

Now, like the voice of conscience, think what you would save at Yaddo, the joy you'd give me and whatever else favorable you can think of.

Affectionately,

Cal

Next year if our books were done and we had the cash, wouldn't you like to try Italy?

52.

September 8th, 1948

Dear Cal,

I think you said a while ago that I'd "laugh you to scorn" over some conversation you & I had had about how to protect oneself against solitude & ennui—but indeed I wouldn't. That's just the kind of "suffering" I'm most at home with & helpless about, I'm afraid, and what with 2 days of fog and alarmingly low tides I've really got it bad & think I'll write you a note before I go out & eat some mackerel. The boats bringing the men back from the quarries look like convict ships & I've just been indulging myself in a nightmare of finding a gasping mermaid under one of these exposed docks. You know, trying to tear the mussels off the piles for something to eat,—horrors.[1] Also there's a small lobster-pound with 4 posts at the corners that reminds me strangely of your sunken bedstead-grave. But I can't think of any more that would be practical for the next month, so.

Sometime I wish we could have a more sensible conversation about this suffering business, anyway. I imagine we actually agree fairly well. It is just that I guess I think it is so irresistible & unavoidable there's no use talking about it, & that in itself it has no value, anyway—as I think Jarrell says at the end of "90 North," or somewhere.[2] I've just been reading through that new

1 Cf. "Water," lines 25–28 (RL-*CP*).
2 "Pain comes from the darkness / And we call it wisdom. It is pain"; Randall Jarrell, "90 North," lines 31–32.

collection of Eliot's criticism[1] (some books arrived, thank goodness) & he is one of the few poets now, I think, who can really write about it convincingly—& then I don't even like him when he gets that oh-so-resigned tone.

What I really object to in Auden's "Musee des Beaux Arts" isn't the attitude about suffering—you're probably right about that. It's that I think it's just plain inaccurate in the last part. The ploughman & the people on the boat will rush to see the falling boy any minute, they always do, though maybe not to help. But then he's describing a painting, so I guess it's all right to use it that way.[2] Oh well—I want to see what you'll think of my "Prodigal Son."

I like this story from the *N.Y. Times*—a composition by a child in the 3rd grade: "I told my little brother that when you die you cannot breathe and he did not say a word. He just kept on playing."[3]

I have just read a strange essay by Goethe on "Granite"—it seemed so appropriate. And have you ever read *The Sorrows of Werther?*[4]—which Napoleon said he read seven times & carried around with him? It makes very cheering reading these days.

Write me a note when you have the time—

Affectionately,

Elizabeth

53.

Dear Cal:

Here is a gloomy note I got off the other day—it was only a temporary mood, though, but I'll send it along. Moods at Stonington are in some algebraic equation with the weather & the tides, I guess.

In the same mail with your letter I got this card from Rome from Loren MacIver. Yes—*if* all goes well, *if* I have any money, & *if* nothing out of the ordinary happens personally, or nothing ordinary, like a war, happens impersonally—I'd like to go to Italy very much. In fact I think I'd like to go & stay quite a while, about a year, and see southern Italy, hill towns, etc., then settle in Rome for a while.

1 T. S. Eliot, *Notes Towards the Definition of Culture* (1948).

2 W. H. Auden, "Musee des Beaux Arts," lines 14–21.

3 Hannah Trimble, "Out of the Mouths of the Third Grade: in little notes to their teacher children reveal tenderness, imagery, classic rage," *The New York Times* (June 22, 1947).

4 Goethe, "Über den Granit" (ca. 1785; first published in 1878) and *The Sorrows of Young Werther* (1774).

I sang that song you sing to myself when I was twenty-one, and thirty-one, and I suppose I'll sing it at forty-one. For the meantime I guess my refrain is:

thirty-seven
& far from heaven.

I was delighted with the Santayana letter—his cell must be absolutely swamped with Oscar Williams anthologies. He may be right, in a way, about the "reality" in my book—but then, there's probably a gap of 50 years between his reality & mine, & it seems like rather an odd thing for him to pick on, doesn't it, or maybe not, since he probably isn't familiar with much contemporary writing. "Modernism that opposes modernity"[1] makes me think of Mr. Ransom's piece on Marianne in the *Quarterly Review*, which just came.[2] Of what I've read, his—"On Being Modern with Distinction"—is the only thing that's worth anything at all. I wish mine were 1/4 as good.[3] Have you seen it? Williams' piece[4] is in very bad taste, I think—as well as not making any sense. I also can't seem to make much out of Marianne's own contributions, at least not the last one. I think she must be entering upon the prophetic stage or something—

And Eberhart!—oh dear. I have an old teacher who wrote to me a little like that, too, but not nearly so bad. Your carrying the baby seems almost to have become a sort of "King's Touch" symbol for him. I wonder what the dreadful insecurity really comes from—because it seems to me he's received a good deal of attention, etc.

This being "excluded from the anthologies" sounds like a nightmare—ye gods, the poor man. As a matter of fact, for anyone so unsophisticated & unprotected, I'd say he'd done brilliantly, wouldn't you?

The Cleanth Brooks explanation of *The Waste Land* seems to me the best single one I've read—& draws the best conclusions—but of course he had an awful lot of work done for him before he took over. Should I read *The*

---

1 "It was you who first really interested me in the modern condensed method of being dramatic and profound. Besides I had a hint, from your leaning to Catholicism, of the spirit of your discontent with the world as it is: and modernism that opposes modernity has all my sympathy"; George Santayana to RL, August 31, 1948 (Houghton Library).

2 John Crowe Ransom, "On Being Modern with Distinction," *Quarterly Review of Literature* (Spring 1948).

3 "As We Like It" (a prose tribute) and "For M.M.," *Quarterly Review of Literature* (Spring 1948). See "Efforts of Affection" (EB-*CPR*) and "Invitation to Miss Marianne Moore" (EB-*CP*).

4 William Carlos Williams, "A Portrait," *Quarterly Review of Literature* (Spring 1948).

Well Wrought Urn?[1] "The Bleeding Heart," the first part anyway, reminded me a little of Wiscasset.[2] I'm just finishing a gloomy tale of my own—very undramatic, though.

There have been some beautiful days—bright blue, wisps of fog flowing in the sunshine, along with milkweed-silk, thistle-down, etc. Tom is moving his headquarters over here, in utter boredom I'm afraid, but he's bringing some more books, some whiskey, & a cribbage board, & I said I wouldn't see him till 3 P.M. every day. And I expect one more visitor,—so guess I'll hold out till October 15th. One has to admire Pound's stoic cheerfulness. I am thinking about Yaddo, but it all depends. Also I'm *trying to improve my handwriting.*

Affectionately,
Elizabeth

54.

[Postcard: Stonington, Me.]

[September 30, 1948]

Dear Cal: how are you & how is the work progressing? This is just to say I'm leaving tomorrow or the next day for New York, 46 King Street—where I hope I'll hear from you shortly. How do you like RJ's seven poems in *Poetry?*[3]

Elizabeth

55.

Yaddo, Saratoga Springs
[October 1, 1948]
Friday

Dear Elizabeth:

The place swarms with Elizabeths—Elizabeth Ames, though one wants to call her and thinks of her as Mrs. Ames, she won't allow it,—and Elizabeth Hardwick, just left, who brought back to me those days—when it was glori-

---

1 Cleanth Brooks, *Modern Poetry and the Tradition* (1939) and *The Well-Wrought Urn: Studies in the Structure of Poetry* (1947).
2 Jean Stafford, "The Bleeding Heart," *Partisan Review* (Sept. 1948).
3 Randall Jarrell, "Terms," "The Sleeping Beauty: Variation of the Prince," "The King's Hunt," and "Afterwards" (four adaptations from Corbière's *Rondels pour après*), *Poetry* (Sept. 1948).

ous and horrible to be alive—of the Tate divorce. There was even an Elizabeth Fenwick, but she was gone.

Now there are an introverted and extroverted colored man[1]; a boy of 23 who experiments with dope[2]; a student of a former Kenyon class-mate of mine, who at the age of six was in a Pathe News Reel for having a chicken that walked backwards[3]; and Malcolm Cowley, nice but a little slow.

I'm all set up with a small back room to sleep in, and large sunny room to work in—with five windows, four tables, three chairs and one work-bed. "The Kavanaughs" seems to be moving—I figure if I can do about two stanzas a week, come spring I'll have it. For December through February (possibly March) I'll pay $50 a month, "to help with the frightful fuel bill."

Léonie Adams is a queer one, so shy she mumbles inaudibly half the time, and very funny telling New York stories or about her induction tour of the Library—all for the intense lyrical Blakean kind of poetry, and though she hasn't published for almost 20 years carries around a little child's green copybook with scribblings for poems, and occasionally loses it. She said you'd told her Auden was much better than Yeats. And she'd said you'd outgrow it; and you'd said "How old are *you*?" She's a great admirer of your poetry.

An emotional last meeting with Pound: "Cal, god go with you, if you like the company."

No use describing Yaddo—rundown rose gardens, rotting cantaloupes, fountains, a bust of Dante with a hole in the head, sets called *Gems of Ancient Literature*, *Masterpieces of the World*, cracking dried up sets of Shakespeare, Ruskin, Balzac, *Reminiscences of a Happy Life* (the title of two different books), pseudo Poussins, pseudo Titians, pseudo Reynolds, pseudo and real English wood, portraits of the patroness, her husband, her lover, her children lit with tubular lights, like a church, like a museum . . .

I'm delighted.

Why don't you come?

Affectionately,

Cal

1 J. Saunders Redding and Charles Sebree.
2 James C. Harrison.
3 Flannery O'Connor, who had studied with Robie Macauley at the Iowa Writers' Workshop.

56.

[Postcard: reclining male lion]

[New York, N.Y.
October 13, 1948]

Dear Cal: Wish I could feel like this in New York—the "Senegal with machines."[1] I'm going to Boston Saturday for about a week & I'll write you from there. Yaddo sounds just right for a temporary home.

Yours, Elizabeth

I think I'll go to Bard for that week-end—will you?[2]

57.

Hotel Boston
October 23rd, 1948

Dear Cal:

It seems to me I have a good many things to tell you, but your letter I intended to answer I left behind in N.Y. I'm going back tonight & shall write you again. The week here has been literary beyond belief—parties at Andy Wanning's, Richard Wilbur's, & Dick E's—the last & far the best—one of those evenings when everyone seems to like each other a lot. He—Dick—says you're going to Bard, too. I think it must have been your invitation to that poetry orgy I forwarded just before I left. Anyway, I certainly hope you are. Maybe we can take a walk & get away from the universal good-will for a while. I've only read Wilbur for about 15 minutes before going there. It didn't seem very good to me, very relaxed, but Richard E likes it, I gather. There is a wonderful show of Kokoschka here, & also I saw the Glass Flowers in all their frigidity.[3] My reading at Wellesley wasn't too bad, or maybe I just think that because I'm surprised to be still alive. Several elderly professors slept throughout, so I guess I couldn't have made quite enough noise. I do hope you're getting lots done. After this week it seems more imperative than before.

Yours—Elizabeth

1 Federico García Lorca, *Poet in New York*, trans. Rolfe Humphries (1940).
2 The conference, organized by Theodore Weiss and Joseph Summers, was held over the weekend of November 5; it included William Carlos Williams, Louise Bogan, Jean Garrigue, Richard Wilbur, Richard Eberhart, Elizabeth Hardwick, Kenneth Rexroth, James Merrill, Lloyd Frankenberg, and Loren MacIver.
3 The Ware Collection of Glass Models of Plants, Botanical Museum, Harvard University.

58.

Dear Elizabeth:

My Bard letter had the phrase We expect poets like Bishop, Eberhart & what's his name? The guy you met with Sally Rand.[1] Yeah, I'm going; you should come back to Yaddo with me afterwards.

I now have—let me boast—53 stanzas, over 800 lines and am working harder & more steadily than ever in my life. I've decided to string my Guggenheim through two years or try to get a renewal. The poem grows, and I want a good many months just for revision. (Now, shut up about yourself, Cal!)

I like your Moore piece: genuine, shrewd, unique, etc.—especially the first part[2]—the Poe & animal business, I think would need expansion.[3] Wasn't it delightful of John to bring in Marcus Cato, as though Plutarch had just been discovered.[4]

Wilbur is a fluent Stevens imitator, with a bit of Moore, a good, rather easy ear, and just about nothing to say, so far. Dick's recommendations! Vernon Watkins, Hergesheimer, and now Wilbur; make me feel so ungenerous.

Miss Moore's poems in the *Quarterly* and her one in the *Nation* strike me as clumsy trifles with good touches. With what envy though, one rereads her old good poems! We all (not you) seem such bunglers.

I have lots of rather tame Yaddo stories, but I'll save them till I see you. O, there's a man writing a history of Harvard;[5] no, I'll save it.

Randall is in a state of incredible euphoria about Europe and says it's the final judgment on Mary McCarthy that she was disappointed.

Write some more poems—there are so few in the world now.

Affectionately,

Cal

---

1 See EB-*OA*, 589.

2 "Miss Moore and the Delight of Imitation," *Quarterly Review of Literature* (Spring 1948); see EB-*CPR*.

3 "Miss Moore and Edgar Allan Poe" and "Miss Moore and Zoography," *Quarterly Review of Literature* (Spring 1948).

4 "Let us compare her kind of human interest with that, for example, of Marcus Cato, the countryman who had come into Rome and was proceeding to reform the society of the capital. Cato, observing how the moral fibre of Romans was softening, stood out for the old austerity of living, and spent himself dangerously both in person and in his office of Censor. If so intense an effort in so elemental a situation does not meet, as we read, with some ridiculous degree of unsuccess, we will cheerfully put Cato down as among the great. And as for Miss Moore, we feel that she accepts her own society scarcely more than Cato did"; John Crowe Ransom, "On Being Modern with Distinction," *Quarterly Review of Literature* (Spring 1948).

5 Charles A. Wagner, *Harvard: Four Centuries and Freedoms* (1950).

59.

Dear Elizabeth:

The train connections were o.k. and next morning I felt wonderful at breakfast; but I noticed that I held on to my coffee cup with both hands, and when I got back to my room with the typed first draft of a stanza ugly and awful as life before me, after half an hour I discovered I was just staring at it, so I read the 3rd book of the *Dunciad*, where the Dunces contend in unmentionable contests and end by trying to see who can stay awake the longest over each other's books.[1] Then I went to bed, then I went for a long walk, then I had a really profound sleep. Now I'm back in the groove briefly before next week.

Except for the glugg (I quickly substituted it for mulled claret in my poem[2]), the readings, and the sacerdotal canon on divorce it was a marvelous week-end.

I wrote Allen and Caroline suggesting they get in touch with you and the Frankenbergs for dinner Tuesday night. If you're free let's have lunch together Wednesday—out of all the turmoil.

The Taylors are coming to New York for Christmas if they can get an apartment. If you're still around I want you to meet. I can promise you'll like each other.

One's sins catch up with one—when I started writing, it was about like Rexroth—no, not quite, but bad enough not to make any difference.

It was a lot of fun talking to you, and the long walk and meeting the Frankenbergs and the Summers.

Hope you made your dentist and have survived the *glugg*.

Affectionately,
    Cal

60.

[Postcard: L. Nauer, "Carl Maria von Weber"]

New York
[November 11, 1948]

Dear Cal:

I just called Mr. Tate to make sure of the dates, etc. You were right about

1 Alexander Pope, *The Dunciad* (1728).
2 See "The Mills of the Kavanaughs," stanza 20, line 14 (RL-*CP*).

Tuesday but it's the *16*th. I think he said you are going to Washington Wednesday the 17th—if not I was going to ask you if you'd like to go to a Bach concert Wed. night—a pianist friend of mine who is just about the best Bach player there is.[1] If there is any chance of it let me know. I *want* to write you a letter but life has been like a subway train ever since I got back—I will, though.

    Yours, Elizabeth

61.

[December 5, 1948]
Sunday morning

Dear Cal:

    This was the day, if I had got a lot done last week, I meant to take to come to see you & Yaddo with. I am sorry it hasn't worked out better but I may be able to make it yet some day next week. I now have a reservation[2] for a week from today and if I manage to get all my dentistry, Christmas shopping, etc. done—well, I'll make that trip up the Hudson. I am so sorry about Washington, but I'll explain it all when I see you—if I can, that is.[3]

    I'm afraid I haven't much news, the week having consisted mostly of very dull chores and calls. *Did* I ever tell you anything about the Sitwell party? At any rate you may have seen the picture now with everyone of the extra-select group of poets looking distorted as well as wretched.[4] Pauline kindly pointed out to me that I looked as if my head had been removed and then screwed back on again the wrong way. Marianne looks like a little ghost. She is going to speak at Harvard next week, and I wish I had remembered to write down the title of the lecture—something about MORALS, anyway, and she's going to read some of Joe Louis's recently printed autobiography,[5] also some of those last, and to me rather uninteresting, poems. I tried to read some of the Sitwell reminiscences and found them very poorly written—except for one wonderful newspaper story on page 256 of the first volume,

<hr>

1 Rosalyn Tureck.

2 For Key West.

3 EB and RL met in Washington to attend a lecture by T. S. Eliot at the Library of Congress. EB stayed at Carley Dawson's empty house and had a severe alcoholic episode; she checked herself into a Washington convalescent home for several days and missed lunch with RL and W. H. Auden (see EB-*OA*, 176–77).

4 On November 9 Bishop attended a reception for Edith and Osbert Sitwell at New York's Gotham Book Mart, with Marianne Moore, William Carlos Williams, Tennessee Williams, W. H. Auden, Stephen Spender, Delmore Schwartz, Randall Jarrell, and others. *Life* published a photograph of the group in "The Sitwells" (Dec. 6, 1948).

5 Either Joe Louis, *My Life Story* (1947) or Joe Louis, "My Story," *Life* (Nov. 8, 1948).

"The Scarlet Tree"—in case you have those books around Yaddo.[1] It will cheer you up for a whole day, I guarantee.

Tom is considering buying an English car, a *Jaguar*—he says it's "moss green," has four forward speeds, and what particularly gets him, I think, is a very elaborate tool-chest, like a jewel box, with the tools embedded in little wells of green billiard cloth. The headlights "cost ninety dollars to re-place"—but as Pauline said, "But why replace them, Tom?" I sort of hope he doesn't get it. I know I'd be scared to death to drive in it.

I am packing a trunk of books to send off to Key West. Suddenly *all* one's interests revive at the same time, so it's almost impossible to choose. I've almost decided to try to write a poem sometime about the "Mary Celeste"—there's a rather interesting theory as to what happened to her in the same copy of *Life* as the Sitwell affair.[2] She was built in Nova Scotia—I'm hoping to discover in my mother's village, which was a ship-building place then, but probably not. Anyway, don't you think it's a story that seems to mean a great deal. Every time I read the most trivial magazine article about it I am surprised at the reactions I have.

I guess that's about all the news and I must stop and pack some more and do my laundry. If I can possibly make it, Cal, I hope to get up for a day—I want to hear all that took place in Washington after I vanished from the scene, and to make my apologies in person—I hope you're well and working like a house afire.

Affectionately yours,
Elizabeth

My Key West address is, ∧ | ∧, corner of Elizabeth & Dey Sts.

---

1 Osbert Sitwell reports that a hunter caught a beaver and took it to his New York apartment (planning to return it to the country the next morning). His wife put the beaver in a wooden box lined with straw in the living room. "When they entered the next morning, they found nothing else in the room, except the beaver and a dam. The creature had apparently knocked over a small table with a vase of flowers upon it, and the consequent finding of water on the floor had brought his dam-building instinct into play. He had carefully sawed up all the eighteenth-century chairs and tables, by which his host and hostess set such store, and had, with the portions and with the aid of cushions and books, constructed a remarkably perfect example of a dam"; Osbert Sitwell, *The Scarlet Tree* (1946), 256.
2 Dod Osbourne, "The Phantom Islands," *Life* (Dec. 6, 1948). The *Mary Celeste* was found drifting derelict off the Azores in 1872. The captain, his family, and a crew of eight had disappeared without a trace. There were no signs of violence, and its abandonment has never been convincingly explained.

62.

Yaddo
[December 7, 1948]

Dear Elizabeth:

No! My apologies for Washington. Do try to come and spend the night; there's a good morning train—then we can have a fine long evening hashing the Sitwells and Washington. I have news of a kind for you.[1]

Yes, there's something about the *Marie Celeste* that makes your heart stop—when I first read it, there was a half-carved chicken on the table. All unsolved mysteries make you think of evil walking up and down in the world, like the Devil, unsatisfied.

Saratoga Springs—courtesy cab—east house Yaddo—me; or I'll meet you.

Part of your Key West address reads like this ∧ | ∧ (?)

Affectionately,
    Cal

P.S. The 3 Yaddonians[2] liked your picture.

63.

[December 18, 1948]

Dear Elizabeth:

This is a before-breakfast letter—I'm sure this practice isn't habit-forming. I've been fingering & weighing and wondering about my present—what happens if you open presents before Christmas?

But I wish you'd come instead—not for a day, but for the winter. Or summer: I'll settle for that. There are times of dry loneliness at Yaddo. I'm a bit aghast when I think of how long I'll be on this damned poem. Is anything worth so much work and isolation? Anyhow I wish you weren't so far away.

The two people at Yaddo are pleasant (particularly the little Catholic novelist; the painter has a rather withering old-maidish torpor[)][3] but they're

1 During the meeting of Library of Congress Fellows, they awarded the first Bollingen Prize to Ezra Pound for *The Pisan Cantos* (1948). They also elected Marianne Moore as the next consultant; but if she were to decline the post it would be offered to EB.
2 Flannery O'Connor, Joan Van Kirk, and Clifford Wright.
3 Flannery O'Connor and Clifford Wright.

not celebrating types. My suggestion that we have bottle egg nog for Christmas breakfast fell rather flat.

Two excerpts from a Randall letter: "I *sure* do like Elizabeth Bishop." "Edith Sitwell—a skull fattened for the slaughter."

Here's what happened at Washington—since I can no longer use it to lure you to Yaddo. If Miss Moore declines, you will be the next consultant, unless you decline. You'd better keep this to yourself. The details of the selection are intriguing, but you've got to come here to hear them. You see what pressure I'm putting on you.

I had a long discussion with Auden one evening at the Cosmos Club and the conversation turned to the Southerners. A: "I wish they'd stay off criticism. That's not what they're good at. They're not really very bright." I'm not sure that Auden shouldn't too—his ingenuity seems often to exceed his intuitions when he writes; but the remark did my wicked New England heart good.

A final shot. *Look, please, when you are sick tell me, so I won't worry!*

Affectionately, Love & Merry Christmas,

Cal

I got a huge book from Cairns, with passages in Greek, Latin, Italian, Spanish, Portuguese, French, Provencal, German and Anglo-Saxon—all with translations and have been groping for my almost forgotten Greek.[1] Did you know that Virgil spent seven years on the Georgics—2,000 lines?

Now to breakfast, just in the nick of time and unshaven.

(Did you ever see Miss Stafford again?)

Wouldn't you like to call on your neighbors, my mother & father: see postcard. Sat.

[Enclosed: Postcard of Virginia Inn on Lake Osceola, Winter Park, Florida]

Dec. 6, 1948

Dear Bobby

We arrived safely and Daddy is W. & H. It is warm and restful. I can pick oranges and grapefruit in the gardens just outside my window. We miss you.

Love

Mother

---

1 Huntington Cairns, *The Limits of Art: Poetry and Prose Chosen by Ancient and Modern Critics* (1948).

64.

[Postcard: Spotted Jew-fish—Municipal Aquarium—Key West, Florida]

611 Francis St.
[Key West, Florida]
December 21, 1948

Dear Cal:

These are the *"Fish"*[1]—I have found an absolutely marvelous apartment—large, a screened porch up in a tree, & a view of endless waves of tin roofs & palm trees—I'm going to write you—type you—a letter as soon as I get unpacked. Do let me hear from you.

Yours—

Elizabeth

65.

[December 24, 1948]
Christmas Eve

Dear Elizabeth:

The Jew-fish sure is homely; but seeing that I mistook him for a sea-robin in your poem, I can't say the picture was a shock, still the one with his (her) mouth part open . . . !

Now: no number of ingenious postcards is the equivalent of a letter; so really I've written you more than you've me. But I will stock up on what Saratoga has & send them at brief frantic intervals—each one ending "let me hear from you."

Now something I can't tell anyone else. Yesterday Peter Taylor called up from Indiana mostly to warn me that I mustn't pay much attention to his brother-in-law (who is arriving here in ten days) because he is Peter's bro. in law.[2] I "Eliz. Hardwick is arriving on the same day." Peter: "She's dangerous for you too." I: "Maybe I can interest them in each other." Peter: "Cal, that would be the most blessed thing in the world for you." Somewhere a parenthesis, Peter: "Eleanor says her brother is nice, but absolutely mad." Ah me!

My poem's like the Grapes of Tantalus. Every time I feel I'm almost done with *Book IV* (doesn't that sound grand): new stanzas and new revisions! It's now about 600 lines with a hell of a lot of re-writing to do. I tremble to think of the other "books." I had a big messy spurt in the last few days; but, damn

---

1 See "The Fish" (EB-*CP*).
2 James Ross.

it, each spurt means that the remaining books will have to be longer, and that the one I'm writing will have to be further & further revised. God!

Spent a holy evening listening to (A) the *Gloria* from Bach's B Minor Mass, (B) the *Gloria* from a Gregorian Mass, (C) The *Gloria* from a Palestrina Mass; so I too can look at a Jew-fish and cry "Rainbow, Rainbow."[1]

Now my refrain & ending from now on:

Do come to Yaddo next summer,

I miss you,

Cal

P.S. Delighted about your apartment. Got a *dies irae* note from [R.W.] Flint which I'll enclose, if I can find it.

"A screen porch in a tree" (if I read your Jew-fish postcard right) wouldn't that do for a jazz-blue-song?[2]

Been reading scraps of the *Iliad* in my Cairns anthology. It has everything in the world—but T. Weiss[3] says it's just as good in translation!

Tell me something funny about Randall at the Sitwell party in your next letter.

I suspect this is a silly letter, but I can't re-read it. The Carroll book is wonderful,[4] especially the pictures—my only other palpable present was Allen's essays from Aunt Sarah, so it was an event.[5]

I'm reading *Pride & Prejudice* aloud to the two Yaddonians—what a lovely book and lovely woman.

66.

December 31st, 1948

Dear Cal:

I'm afraid I overdid the postcards a little . . . & I think you're getting another before you're getting this, too. Now so many remarks I'd like to make have accumulated that I'm having organization-trouble. Did I tell you I wanted to take up the study of German this year or was it just a lack you felt in me? Anyway, I am delighted to have the grammar—I've read all about what's the "natural" way to learn a language in the preface, and soon I shall

1 Cf. "The Fish," line 75 (EB-*CP*).
2 See "Songs for a Colored Singer" (EB-*CP*).
3 Theodore Weiss.
4 Possibly Lewis Carroll, *Collected Verse* (1932).
5 Allen Tate, *On the Limits of Poetry: Selected Essays, 1928–1948* (1948).

get down to the unnatural work. The only really good thing I think in the Carroll book is the Tennyson parody, although I kind of like Hiawatha's Photographing, too. I think his poem "They told me you had been to her / And mentioned me to him" is wonderful—better than so much of Cummings, for example—but I guess that's in "Alice," and the one about "Little birds are tasting gratitude and gold"— Thank you so much for the grammar—a dictionary is coming and then I'll be all equipped to go on safari through the Oxford Book of German Verse.

Christmas here was quiet but very nice. I went to dinner at Pauline Hemingway's, a sort of family dinner, outdoors. We had favors and sparklers and firecrackers. Dinner was made a little tense and slow by, one: Pauline deciding that this was the year for Patrick, her oldest boy, to carve his first turkey—and we all suffered with him so; two: the special-occasion colored boy, Nathaniel, arrived in that over-meticulous stage of drunkenness—it took him forever to lower each plate, and then he had to bow from the waist and murmur apologies. I GOT a couple of nice books—the recent big Picasso one, a book by John Evelyn on "Sallets," and a book [on] Henri Michaux.[1] I'd been wanting to read him, but so far it seems like little bits of prose-poems, not very serious. I think the word "decadent" really applies to French prose-poems, if to anything. Maybe these make me particularly mad because I used to amuse myself by writing things rather like them—& then I don't think I even saved them.

Just before I left New York Randall sent me copies of "The Olive Garden" and "The Night Before the Night Before Christmas."[2] I haven't had time to write to him about them yet. I've just written him a card, I'm afraid. Today I mean to tackle it and I really don't know what to say. When someone sends you something are you supposed to "criticize" or merely appreciate? And I hesitate to tell you exactly what I do think somehow. I guess I'm afraid you'll tell him. But it does seem *limp* & more suited for a short story. But then one always feels he's "been there." Oh, I guess I'll quote you a letter I got today from Margaret Miller, my old friend who is at the Museum of Modern Art. I've always shown her everything I write, since we were in college. I sent her your book for Christmas and she says—I'll quote it all, "I have never read a word of R.L. and had suspected that at least a portion of your enthusiasm for the poetry could be laid to professional politeness. I was

---

1 John Evelyn, *Acetaria: A Discourse of Sallets* (probably a 1937 edition); René Bertelé, *Henri Michaux: Une étude* (1946).

2 Randall Jarrell, "The Olive Garden" (a translation of Rilke's "Der Ölbaum-Garten"), *The Nation* (Dec. 18, 1948); and "The Night Before the Night Before Christmas," *The Kenyon Review* (Winter 1949).

therefore unprepared for all that blacktongued piratical vigor. I can't read more than three or four poems at a sitting—it's a little like smelling salts—but they are remarkable and wonderful, though the rhymes seem a little *too* strong or crass on occasions."

I haven't anything to say about Randall's behavior, I'm afraid. It was exemplary as far as I observed. I have some bits of news though—Sally S.[1] is here, was here for quite a while before I arrived, and lives right around the corner from me but barely speaks. I finally had a letter from Joe Summers and U.T. had the baby the 22nd, a girl, Mary Elliot, after, he said "nightmares, and a Cesarean section," so I'm afraid it was pretty bad. I went to an odd party at Pauline's—but a typical Key West one—at which the guests of honor were Witter Bynner and Sarah Palfrey, the 1941 tennis champion. Witter Bynner seemed rather pleasant although towards the end of the party he was telling me he had a "strange destiny," his fame is going to rest on his translations from the Chinese when all along he'd wanted to be an English poet. He had called on Pound not long ago I gathered. They hadn't seen each other for forty years, and Pound had almost broken his ribs embracing him. Sarah Palfrey is the tennis pro at *the* hotel—really to get a divorce here—she had messages to me from Selden Rodman who is arriving shortly with his Haitian paintings and wanted me to help arrange a lecture for him here. I think he is going to be very surprised when he sees what KW[2] is really like. I had a letter from Marianne ostensibly about her Harvard lecture. Then she doesn't mention it at all of course, and I must quote this sentence: "The Wannings, Mrs. Wanning and Andrews talked of you, and Stonington, and Key West—was captivated with them—so unfalsified and mysterious—like 'Tom Wanning.' I said I was depressed about imposing myself on him for dinner (unintentionally but undeniably) and they earnestly combated regrets, in his name which made matters no better—did it?" This refers to our having dinner with Tom, I think, after the Sitwell party—and she always puts him in quotes as if it were an assumed name.— Maybe it's some kind of coyness.

I'm overcome by what you said in your first letter—about the library job. I just don't think I've done enough, although I'm tremendously flattered—but I hope Marianne will feel up to it. She's an obvious choice of course, & if only the La Fontaine is done by then I should think she might.

This is getting too long—I'm sorry the typing isn't better but the over-

1 Possibly Sally Sortwell.
2 Key West.

head light makes all the keys look like fish-scales so I'm almost using the touch system. I am about to go out to celebrate New Year's I guess. It is pretty dull here, too, but I like it. The town looks beautiful and I am very fond of the people I do see even if we haven't much to say to each other a lot of the time. I like my apartment so much that I think now I may stay on and on—and maybe come to Yaddo this summer? How soon should I inquire about it? Pauline calls to tell me we are to go with Sully,[1] the elderly boiler-maker, to the Mascotte, the toughest place in town, later on to see the fattest man in Key West do his annual New Year's dance. I guess I wasn't enthusiastic, as she said "Don't be so squeamish." I think you are most admirable—all that work—and not even a little lyric such as Miss Bogan would approve of from me. But tomorrow I'll begin. I think the gift of a German Grammar makes me feel like the heroine of a George Eliot novel. Faustina called and said tomorrow is happynewyear and she's coming to *cook* for me—oh dear. Well, I hope you have a wonderful happynewyear, anyway.

Affectionately yours,
Elizabeth

I forgot to comment on Elizabeth Hardwick's arrival—*take care.*

67.

[January 5, 1949]

Dear Elizabeth:

This is on your letter and two "Manhattans on rocks" but I do want to write you—oh yes, a whole day of "stubborn"—the last word to apply to imaginative work—(taken from Eudora Welty's reply to Wilson on Faulkner in the Christmas *New Yorker*, which you will like[2]), which produced: "Lycaon listened to Achilles speak," which must be about the bottom.[3]

---

1 James Sullivan; see *Remembering Elizabeth Bishop: An Oral Biography*, ed. Gary Fountain and Peter Brazeau (1994), 76–77.

2 "In practicing so far from such cities as produced the Flauberts, Joyces, and Jameses, Faulkner's provinciality, stubbornly cherished and turned into an asset, inevitably tempts him to be slipshod and has apparently made it impossible for him to acquire complete expertness in an art that demands of the artist the closest attention and care"; Edmund Wilson, "William Faulkner's Reply to the Civil Rights Program," *The New Yorker* (Oct. 23, 1948), 106–13. Eudora Welty's letter to the editors took exception to Wilson's review: "It's as though we were told to modify our opinion of Cézanne's painting because Cézanne lived not in Paris but by preference in Aix and painted Aix apples—'stubbornly' (what word could ever apply less to the quality of the imagination's working?)"; "To the Editor," *The New Yorker* (Jan. 1, 1949), 50–51.

3 Cf. Homer, *The Iliad*, book 21, and "The Killing of Lykaon" (RL-*CP*).

But the essential: do come to Yaddo (I'm so lonely) this summer. Mrs. Ames would be delighted to have you, looks forward to you, etc. But wouldn't it be a good idea to write now, and get it over with; then you wouldn't have to come, if . . . but you must, or I'll faint from the whole weariness of the thing. It's my dream to maneuver you and the Taylors here.

Tomorrow, the arrivals: James Ross; Eliz Hardwick and a real Yaddo ringer who knows everything and everybody—is in on everybody—and is sort of a pain.[1] The illegible letters have a sort of rhetorical effect.

(A day later)

James is here now; full of odd intro-extraverted experiences: training dogs, working in a cigarette factory; using a benzedrine inhaler till he ran 30 miles through North Carolina shooting at someone (actually sleety trees) he thought was out with his wife. He's very nice and good company. In a few hours: Miss Hardwick.

Of course, I won't tell Randall. I've only seen the "Night Before Christmas," last spring. It has lovely moments, but I don't know about the whole. Randall's defenses of his own poems are frequently overpowering. He always fills me with envy. God! Imagine writing: "Lycaon listens to Achilles speak." No black-tongued piratical vigor at all!

To my embarrassment Santayana sent me a Christmas-present. Now I'm knocking off a day or two (with that mighty line "Lycaon listens to Achilles speak" ringing in my ears) to read *Dialogues in Limbo*.[2] He sure is hot (a Randallism) and dazzling, when one is patient enough to slow down to his calm.

Affectionately,
Cal

The Yaddo summer list is being made out; so why not write now. No, I'm not trying to force your hand.

---

1 Edward Maisel.
2 George Santayana, *Dialogues in Limbo* (1948 edition).

68.

January 11th, 1949

Dear Cal:

All right—I think I shall write to Mrs. Ames right away, as soon at least as you tell me what you think would be a good month. July? I haven't any plans at all, really, except I did want to go abroad but it certainly doesn't look as though I were going to be rich enough to do that. But one month at Yaddo and another one or two in Nova Scotia would certainly be economical.

I have started in working in earnest. I know you have your problems with Lycaon listening to Achilles (speaking), etc., but I think it would be awfully nice to have one big set task. I always seem to be trying to do six or seven different poems at the same time and just hoping I can keep them all well-nurtured enough so that one of them will suddenly get strong enough to take over all by itself until it is done. I think that's more or less what happens when one does get done, but that seems like a long time ago now. The "loneliness" is pretty bad here, too—in fact I'm sure in some ways it's much more boring than Yaddo. No one interesting has turned up here for years and my dear friends (4) and I, when we get together, just are apt to sit around and discuss the fact. But there is swimming and fishing and when I feel too awful I take a long bicycle ride. You know what? My "loneliness" comes in attacks—rather brief—sometimes 2 or 3 a day, and then I don't have any for a week. This morning I decided maybe it was no more than smoking too much while I attempted to work.

Did I tell you that Selden Rodman arrived from Haiti with some of his Haitian paintings, his book about them, etc.? I can't remember. I gave a "party." I enjoyed it very much but I don't think he did. But it is impossible ever to tell what he really thinks of anything, or if he really knows what he thinks himself. We disagreed—or I disagreed with him, that is—about every poem he mentioned. Mr. Rexroth chiefly of course. It was pleasanter to watch him play tennis with the lady-ex-champ. Pauline bought one painting, a nice one, but I'm afraid S thought Key West was a pretty dreary spot compared to Haiti, or so he said, sitting on my gallery, & just then the radio next door struck up full blast "The Star-Spangled Banner" so I said, "Yes, but you see we're still in the United States here." Not a flicker.

How did you like Eliot's poem in the "Tiger's Eye" about de la Mare?[1]

I'm taking up German; it is awfully hard—& I was amazed to find, although it's probably so obvious that no one ever thought of even comment-

---

1 T. S. Eliot, "To Walter de la Mare," *Tiger's Eye* (Dec. 15, 1948).

ing on it, that Freud means "joy" (or would if it were feminine). Don't you think it's funny—what with Jung, & Adler (meaning "eagle")?

Another trivial moral problem I want to ask you about since you always seem to know about such things and I never do at all: Houghton Mifflin has written me a long typical publisher-double-talk letter about L Frankenberg's book of Poetry criticism.[1] He has "run into a snag" as they put it, meaning of course that they have, because they don't want to pay fees for all his quotes from everybody, and would I "waive" the fee and then they would. Some already have, I gather, thinking that the book is advertising after all, and some haven't, and some publishers, they say—rather contradicting themselves, I should think—on the other hand feel they should "protect" their poets. My actual representation in Lloyd's book would probably be worth about ten cents, but I just dislike the whole letter so and feel all it actually means is that HM doesn't want to spend a hundred dollars or so extra. Yet I don't want to contribute to anything that might hold up the publishing of it, etc., since although it's not too good, maybe, it does have a lot of pleasant "appreciation" and might be quite useful.

Did you read Thurber's correspondence-story about a publisher in the Jan. 8th *New Yorker* called "File & Forget." Really some of my correspondence with HM has been just as ludicrous. I guess publishers are so morally uneasy they can't write letters, & then this determination to keep up a jolly tone of informality.

Well, I'm about to go to see "Berlin Express" with a man who is rumored to be "literary" although I'm not quite sure how.[2]

I hope you're out of the doldrums. In Cowley's piece on Hemingway,[3] in which Hemingway comes off so badly in spite of Cowley's adulation, H does say one good thing I thought that might work for poetry too—to stop writing while you still feel you have something to say, from day to day, that is, and in that way you don't get stuck. But I don't know—poetry is so different. Oh dry up & get to that movie.

Affectionately,
Elizabeth

Yes—I liked E. Welty's answer to Mr. Wilson very much. It was such a feminine, capricious sort of sticking her head in the lion's-mouth.

1 Lloyd Frankenberg, *Pleasure Dome: On Reading Modern Poetry* (1949).
2 *Berlin Express*, dir. Jacques Tourneur (1948).
3 Malcolm Cowley, "A Portrait of Mister Papa," *Life* (Jan. 10, 1949).

69.

Dear Elizabeth:

A lot to write about. From Léonie:[1] "Miss Moore has written that 'she can't in conscience digress.'" So a letter is on its way through the Library machinery to you.

I don't want to force advice on you—one's dear friends can be so obtuse that way; but I think you would enjoy it. The salary is $5700. You work five days a week and *more or less* have to be there; but what you actually have to do for the Library takes no more than 2 days. The records (at least all the heavy work) will be finished, so your year will be an exceptionally light one. The duties are simple and untechnical—nothing you couldn't do better than I, except the meeting (you couldn't be more nervous than Léonie). That's not hard, & mustn't excite you. I could come down a few days early—in fact, we will all help you conduct it. The group (with the exception of Ted Spencer) is the pleasantest and most talented I've ever known. You have all the time in the world to write—you can shut yourself up alone in the office. Did a hell of a lot of reading (you could pursue your German). I wrote less and wasted a lot of time (well wasted) but I don't know that it was the job. I'm sure you'd be just swell for what little there is to do and pretty sure you'd enjoy yourself. Well, enough.

Why don't you come here in July—the month doesn't matter much (June or August might be more convenient for you) but write right away before the lists are made out. With your new money, you may want to go abroad—but pray come! Peter has just written Mrs. Ames asking, if he, his wife, and his child can come for the whole summer—there's a long chance that this will be allowed. I'm sure you and they (maybe not the child) would be friends forever, once you met. Also the Williams: I think June 15 to July 15. There's a little Catholic girl named Flannery O'Connor here now, who will remain if she can—a real writer, I think one of the best to be when she is a little older. Very moral (in your sense) and witty—whom I'm sure you'd like. It would be a marvelous summer!!

Well the H.M. Fees: they should pay you, of course. Never, never give; or think you and your publishers are throwing a party together. But under the circumstances I think you ought to let it pass—it's a trifle after all—for Lloyd's sake. But under protest (that you're doing it for friendship not pub-

1 Léonie Adams.

licity, wouldn't think of doing it again, think you should be paid if anyone else is *and etc.* as one of Ring Lardner's characters says.)

Yaddo has brightened up with Peter's brother-in-law and Eliz. H. though the fairy grumbles and gossips in the background. James Ross has a wonderful extroverted, sort of southern Ring Lardner manner (though when we talk together *seriously* he makes really just about no sense at all). Miss Elizabeth is full of talk and high-spirits. Well, for hours last night the nice Yaddonians (Flannery, James, Eliz. and *I*) read Lardner (just sick from laughing) and drank burgundy. A great discovery—you don't get tight or have hangovers and it costs $2.00 a gallon. Frank Parker always told me but . . . I think, I'll give up hard liquor pretty much, except when I emerge.

The poem is moving again. I don't see why I shouldn't take years and, perhaps, publish parts when they've cooled a bit. I work up this episode and then that, so it's not so much unlike your lyrics. Malcolm (an embarrassing article) told about that Hemingway trick, but it doesn't seem much use in verse. I do stop usually when I have first draft of a stanza or first get it so as it looks like poetry. I no longer write at night (rarely I do) but sit around and talk. This keeps one's mind up, I write most of every day—occasionally knocking off usually to read or write letters—also walk quite a bit. I get stuck and [in] the dumps every so often; but what the hell, that's writing. (I see this is a bromide paragraph.)

The Eliot poem was charming—not very strenuous though. A couple of years ago, when he'd just finished it, he said to me that verse allowed one to be much more uncritically enthusiastic, or something of the sort. I had a swell letter from him—really, he's one of the people I like best in the world.

Well, lonely girl: good luck & love,

Cal

P.S. Enjoyed your Rodman. The Star Spangled Banner was marvelous. "People are such dopes" as Randall says. Was one of the poems he sent you the "Ball Game in Salzburg"? (short).[1] I thought it was lovely—had a Mozartian gaiety and lightness. We've been listening to Don Giovanni aided by an appalling synopsis ("The Don made another virtuoso attempt at seduction.") That isn't quite the Mozart I meant for Randall's poem.

What a picture of Pauline in life; that's what she gets for saying your head was screwed on backwards. She's mightily improved. Now that this letter's done my ink has started flowing.

1 Randall Jarrell, "A Game at Salzburg," *The Nation* (Jan. 1, 1949).

70.

Dearest Cal:

I've always felt that I've written poetry more by *not* writing it than writing it, and now this Library business makes me really feel like the "poet by default." At first I felt a little over-come and inclined to wire you a frantic "no," but after having thought about it for a day or two I've concluded that it is something I *could* do (there isn't much, heaven knows) and that even if I feel I haven't written nearly enough poetry to warrant it that maybe it will be all right . . . particularly if I work hard from now until then. Another thing, I think I was pretty cheered up by the Wellesley business which really went off quite well. But I haven't heard anything from Washington so of course I suspect that everyone has changed his mind & I am not breathing any of this to anyone and if they have changed their minds I hope you're not going to be embarrassed, etc. A letter just did come from D.C., but it proved to be an invitation to a reading by Léonie Adams. I'm kind of glad I'm so far away, I'm afraid. I suppose by the "meeting" you mean when they all get together at the start of the year? The people that I already know I like and am not afraid of, and with your kind offer of help—well, I won't say any more about it until the thing is certain one way or another, except that your letter was extremely thoughtful and nice.

Things have been rather pleasant here, if dull, and not at all comparable to your intellectual carousings with burgundy. The only intellectual life, here, I gather, is taking place below stairs at the Casa Marina (that's the $40 a day hotel—where Selden stayed, and where the tennis stars are). The little Polish tennis assistant, who seemed to be Selden's amie of the moment, came to see me, bringing me his poems, and riding on a huge boy's bicycle all headlights and horns & flags, etc.[1] She said it belonged to the head dishwasher there (who also has a *horse*) and that he is avidly reading Selden's poems and wants to get hold of mine—all the dishwashers do. (When Selden came to my party he brought along the tennis champs and the elevator boy and the newspaper concession girl—all modern poetry addicts, I gathered.) Maybe I should move out to the Casa Marina as a scullery maid. The Polish girl of course writes poetry, too—I think she said one every night. Let's see. Ben Belitt arrived again, and yesterday a young man who said he met me at Bard. Anyway he's the best of the lot so far, although a little young for me, I'm afraid. There

---

1 Maria Wojciechowska, later Mrs. Rodman; see *Remembering Elizabeth Bishop: An Oral Biography*, ed. Gary Fountain and Peter Brazeau (1994), 111–13.

is a piece in the last *Sat Eve Post*—Jan. 22nd—by a friend of mine here (B. Thielen), about Key West.[1] I didn't think it was so bad although of course the "Conchs" are all mad. My landlady just came up to tell me what *she* thought of it all. I have also just had a call from Faustina—since I'm putting her in a book I feel rather mean the way I often try to get rid of her—but as Pauline says, she's too much of a lady ever to admit anyone's being rude to her, so she just settles down to her "cognac" and her cigar. I have to keep some on hand for her. Wasn't that Cowley piece awful. Poor Pauline, really, what she's put through. Anyway—where was I—read the *Sat Eve Post* piece if you're interested. Of course I still wish you'd come here sometime, say when you get a bad cold in March & have to take a rest. The new beach is nice and the fishing is marvelous, and we could take a trip to Havana—35 minutes away. You don't have to have a passport for that so I should think you could go.

I think I'll write to Mrs. Ames right now and ask about July—I think that would work out all right—I might even stay on here until then if I manage to keep working. I'm glad to hear your poem is coming along—oh, I now have a small marbleized French notebook that Loren gave me devoted exclusively to Lowell notes, with that review in mind—so far I've only covered two pages but they're awfully profound I'm sure. A wonderful tropical downpour—I have to rush around and close all the windows so the paper curtains won't dissolve—

If I get the Washington job—I don't *have* necessarily to give a lot of "readings" do I?

I just read Meyer Schapiro in the last *PR*—about a French painter & critic I don't believe I'd ever heard of—but I do think he writes wonderfully[2]; it makes one want to get to work immediately. So

Affectionately yours,
Elizabeth

I really wish Marianne had accepted—I should think she would whenever she finishes the La Fontaine, don't you?

I'm curious to know what you consider my being "moral."

---

1 Benedict Thielen, "The Cities of America: Key West," *The Saturday Evening Post* (Jan. 22, 1949).
2 Meyer Schapiro, "Fromentin as a Critic," *Partisan Review* (Jan. 1949).

71.

Dearest Elizabeth:

I was just making my bed (if you could call it "making") when I became aware of a dull burning smell. "God, I must had left my cigarette burning." I rush into my other room; no cigarette. Absentmindedly I feel in my pocket. There, a lighted cigarette in holder consuming a damp piece of Kleenex. The pocket was also stuffed with kitchen matches. Oh my!

They can't "change their minds," poor souls! Dr. Evans has to OK our choice, but he always does. Nor can we re-consider.

I've had a reading jag—*The Tempest*, bits of *Othello* (a Ring Lardner character says: "Tho I'm no Othello, I'm not as ugly as Joe Bean."), *Tartuffe*, *Le Misanthrope*, *Les Precieuses*, all of Thucydides. Isn't Molière swell!

Also your "In the Prison," a just wonderful thing.[1] You must get together a bunch of short stories—you're one of the best people writing them—and I thought all along from the way you talked that they were about like Carley's watercolors—no I didn't, but . . .

We wondered if you'd read Kafka when you wrote it. Anyway the tone, humor, description etc. is all yours. The hero is a sort of scrooge–Miss Elizabeth. I know him well.

You & Peter Taylor always make me feel something of a fake—so I love you both dearly.

The Randall German poem I liked was a short one in the *Nation*—also a lovely translation from Rilke. I wrote him that I couldn't make up my mind about the *Night Before Christmas*, but that it struck me as an "excursion," a fine piece of style but a little idle and long.[2]

A secret: Santayana has offered me a trip to Italy. I don't see how I can accept, but it's terribly touching, and I'm thinking more and more of the pilgrimage.

Did I tell you about cousin Mary and Aléxis Léger? Cousin Mary is a tall red-headed woman in her early sixties—awfully nice, mannish, worked in the Labor Department, likes to hike, drive in difficult traffic—a pure Washington Puritan. Francis Biddle was an old beau of hers. The Biddles love Léger, and cousin Mary has always detested him. Well at the party you were

---

1 "In Prison" (EB-*CPR*).

2 Randall Jarrell, "The Olive Garden" (a translation of Rilke's "Der Ölbaum-Garten"), *The Nation* (Dec. 18, 1948); and "The Night Before the Night Before Christmas," *The Kenyon Review* (Winter 1949).

at, she heard him saying something to her in French ("Je veux vous em-brasser") "Of course I didn't listen; it's pure affectation for him not to speak American." Suddenly she found herself embrasser. She's much taller; and it came out all wrong—wooden, shuddering, towering, humorous, red-headed figure.

I told Eliot the story; but after seeing him kissed by Djuna Barnes, the devil in me made me write him the rest: cousin Mary's way of describing Léger: "This greasy little Frenchman, who dyes his hair, that Bobby says is a good poet." Then E's reply: "I'm inclined to agree with both you and cousin Mary on Aléxis Léger." So I could hug *him*. This is sheer malice and don't repeat it.

I would like to visit you. Maybe in June and we could travel back to-gether.

I guess I meant your tone and humor was moral: but Flannery O'Connor's tone and humor isn't much like yours, so I don't know what I meant.

Now back to "The Kavanaughs" (a man-hunt section) after my vacation. It's fun *not* writing one's poems, I find.

Affectionately,
   Cal

You won't have to give readings; but I think the Library one pays $500.
Read Peter's play, if you can get hold of a *Sewanee Review*.[1]

72.

Dear Cal:

I am mailing you a SAFE if not particularly esthetic ashtray—I got two of them a while ago. They're the only ones I've ever found that will really hold the cigarette while you write or scratch your head, and yet if you forget it, the cigarette automatically goes out . . . I was going to give one to Lloyd Frankenberg for Christmas, but they didn't come in time and now you're go-ing to get it instead.

I still haven't heard from Washington, but then for all I know I may not be supposed to until sometime in September. But I did hear from Mrs. Ames and am hastening to fill out the forms. She says graciously that she thinks I

---

1 Peter Taylor, "The Death of a Kinsman," *Sewanee Review* (Winter 1949).

need not send any manuscript. It doesn't say how many sponsors and I'm so sick of pestering people—I think this time I'll just ask Marianne and *you* and then you could do it orally possibly. I'm saying the "July–August" period. I have read the Booklet from cover to cover . . .

Life is a little complicated right now by the fact that I just got word that my apartment house in New York is finally to be torn down starting March 31st . . . There isn't much in my place & all in pretty good order, since I sublet it, so I'm hoping now that I'll be able to get a professional mover—there must be such things—to put everything in storage so I won't have to make the trip back then. If that can be arranged I'll then stay on here until I go to Yaddo almost, I guess. I think it would be so much fun if you came here, although June would be pretty hot of course. We could go bone fishing, which I've never done but think I'm going to do next week. The gamest fish there is, very small—10 lbs. is an enormous one—& you have to pole through the mangrove keys silently and not even speak, etc. . . . Also in June the tarpon come. That's moonlight-night fishing and ravishing, but hard to catch. Bone fishing is fairly cheap—$20 a day I think. Because of the poling they don't use much gasoline.

Oh yes, I've been being the female Hemingway again, I guess. The Polish girl and a boy from the hotel—dishwasher or elevator boy I don't know which, but an expert—are teaching me pool, and Sunday I am going to the cock-fights . . . Pool will be such a useful thing to know. There's always a pool parlor wherever one goes (think I'll use this line in a poem) if one gets bored. There was even one in Stonington but Tommy was too conservative to take me.

A dear old lady just came in to tell me of how badly my friend Sally S.[1] had treated her . . . (She is here and we speak, but that's all.) The story had a very reminiscent ring . . .

I decided I was being too much of a hermit, so I've spent the last four days just loving everybody I meet and swimming, etc., but today I am back at work. I sold the *New Yorker* a medium length bit of plain description,[2] but have three more serious things just about ready to mail. Good lord—there's a fifteen year old girl next door whose voice & general personality is just about as restful as a stuck automobile horn. I love the Léger story. Pauline is now dreading his visit of course. I'm glad you like "In Prison." I had only read *The Castle* of Kafka when I wrote it,[3] and that long before so I don't know where it came from, but the *à la Turgenev* story I wrote this summer, if I can ever revise it, is

---

1 Sally Sortwell.
2 "The Bight," *The New Yorker* (Feb. 19, 1949); see EB-*CP*.
3 Franz Kafka, *The Castle*, trans. Willa and Edwin Muir (1941).

really better I think—no posing. I'll save money in W & then let's go to Italy together, if your friend lasts that long. *You* sound lively as a cricket.

    —Yours, Elizabeth

Pauline's sister is here—who lives in Rome—chiefly interested in making movies of colored people—very nice.

73.

[Grand Hotel Oloffson, Avenue Christophe, Port-au-Prince, Haiti]
February 21st, 1949

Dear Cal,

    I was sort of hoping to hear from you before I suddenly left Key West for a *petit changement*—in fact I meant to write to you again but didn't. I was afraid that, 1. you are sick. 2. you are MAD. 3.—well, various wild fancies. After my 38th birthday[1] I fell into a slough for a few days & then decided to come with Pauline's sister, Virginia Pfeiffer, to Haiti for about 10 days, & see if I could get out of it. It was a very good idea & has worked perfectly— nothing could be more of a charge than this unlikely country & I think it is much more interesting than I'd ever dreamed any of the West Indies etc., could be. I'm having one batch of mail forwarded here. I think we're going back next Saturday, & shall hope to get a note from you in that, to quiet my uneasy imagination.

    Selden, of course, is here, & 2 nights ago gave a talk (in French) on "Primitivism in Modern Poetry." I understood every word but still don't know what he means by "Primitivism"—although I missed the first 1st 5 minutes of it & so maybe the definition. It was a grand tour in his anthology—introduction style, bringing in every name since 1900. I was in the front row (between the Lewis Gannetts[2]) but kept turning around to see what the effect of all this was on his mostly black audience. A good many slept. Mr. & Mrs. G. got the fidgets & embarrassed me considerably by tearing open envelopes rather noisily & then writing each other notes on them which they handed back & forth across my knees. They are staying here, too, & presented a slight problem at first because they wanted us to go on the long trip (3 days) to Christophe's Citadelle with them & we didn't want to, but now things seemed to have worked themselves out. We're going on it

---

1 On February 8, 1949.
2 Ruth and Lewis Gannett.

Wednesday. Today we are going spear-fishing, out to islands in the harbor where you can see coral-gardens, etc. You spear-fish wearing goggles, using an oxygen-tube, & carrying an 8 ft. spear, that works by powerful springs, under your arm, so you swim only with your legs. If Jinny[1] doesn't spear *me* I'll have to write you an account of it.

The social situation is the most interesting thing about Haiti, I guess— always thorough mixture everywhere, at everything, & yet with it all a caste system that's supposed to be worse than India's.

We have a little black man who stays outside our door to protect us from burglars—clutching a knife over 2 ft. long in one hand & a large rock in the other. Mass starts at 4 AM in the churches so that the very poor (90%), who haven't any decent clothes, can come in the dark. We went to 10 o'clock mass in the cathedral—for the "elite," & then saw a lot of elite black babies baptized. The god-parents holding them shook them up & down just like cocktail shakers & it was a rather riotous baptism.

I haven't tried to work at all but yesterday morning I woke up at 4—the poorly clad were trooping by my balcony in the dark on their way to church—& wrote a lot of stuff.

Have you any further plans about Italy? The reason I ask is—Jinny lives in Rome & has just come from there. She says this is the summer to go if possible; next year is the *Holy Year* & they expect millions of Catholics from all over the world— If she'd known I had considered going a little sooner I could even have had her apartment there—I guess that's rented now, though. *If* you can get out of the U.S. I really think it would be the time for you to go—but I guess I sound interfering.

J. just took this picture of me with the new Polaroid camera that develops instantaneously. I really don't look quite so fat, nor so much like a French postcard.— This other picture is like one of Selden's primitives, only better.— I'll be in KW by next week & do hope to hear from you that you're all right, etc.—oh I read that girl's story in *PR*[2] & thought it had brilliant spots, particularly imagery—

Affectionately,
Elizabeth

---

1 Virginia Pfeiffer.
2 Flannery O'Connor, "The Heart of the Park," *Partisan Review* (Feb. 1949).

74.

Baldpate Inc.[1]
Georgetown, Massachusetts
[April 10, 1949]
Palm Sunday

Dear Elizabeth:

I don't know whether you got my last letter or not.[2] I'm in grand shape. I have your letter about beginning to write again with me. The world is full of wonders.

Love,
Cal

Thanks for being anxious about me, but I'm O.K.

75.

Yaddo
[August 5, 1949][3]
Friday PM,

I am so glad you're better—
take it easy—
I still haven't got your present from Haiti to you but shall—

Dear Cal,

I was so glad to hear from you this morning. I had been trying & trying to write to you but didn't know where to reach you and just couldn't seem to, anyway. I wish you great happiness in your marriage and I do hope your troubles are over now for good—you have had too many lately for one person.[4] I've been having quite a few of my own but things seem to have straightened out pretty much now. I was quite a[t] loose ends for this month so finally decided to come here, with some qualms. And I must say that nothing you or anyone else ever said about the place prepared me for it in the slightest. I have that huge room with 34 windows—bloody hot—but very

---

1 RL began to suffer from his first major manic episode in February 1949. He was hospitalized at Baldpate on April 4 or 5 and stayed until July.

2 If he refers to a letter other than 71, it does not survive.

3 EB's first day at Yaddo.

4 RL was released from Baldpate Hospital on July 10 after three months of treatment. He married Elizabeth Hardwick on July 28 in his parents' house in Beverly Farms, Massachusetts.

grand. I haven't been able to "work" at all, so spend most of my time very pleasantly sitting on my balcony blowing bubbles. There is something a little sinister about the place though, don't you think? I keep getting bats in my room and even met one in the woods in broad daylight, and then all those awful scummy ponds. But I think what is really the source of the trouble is the *smell*—old lunch boxes, I guess. Your friend Jim Powers is here and is very nice—Wallace Fowlie; most of the others I never heard of. One former "proletarian" novelist got put in jail for drunkenness last night and had to be bailed out this morning.

I remember hearing what a nice house Fred Dupee[1] had, and are my friends the Summerses there? They have a very pretty baby now.

A friend of mine may come up for the end of the racing season and drive me back to N.Y.—around August 31st—maybe we could stop off to call on you? I went to an auction of yearlings the other night—very interesting. Mr. Baruch was there & other celebrities I didn't recognize. Give my kindest regards to Elizabeth—

Affectionately, Elizabeth

76.

Upper Red Hook, NY
[August 16, 1949]
Tuesday

Dear Elizabeth:

I shifted my Ciardi questionnaire off onto Randall's review—said I'd just started writing again, couldn't seem to answer relevantly etc. The questions *are* too much work. The more sincerely you try to answer, the more arbitrary etc.[2]

I wouldn't bother if I were you. Of course the pay-off is that we'll have Ciardi's own introduction—approved by the author with our objections, qualifications, etc.

I think you must have the room over the driveway that I used to have. Chief delights of Yaddo—fishing in the scummy ponds—you wade up to your knees in mud, croquet, the records, talking to a few people.

1 RL and Hardwick were renting F. W. Dupee's house in Red Hook, New York, near Bard College.

2 John Ciardi asked writers included in his *Mid-Century American Poets* (1950) to respond to a questionnaire about artistic theory and practice. See Randall Jarrell, "From the Kingdom of Necessity," *The Nation* (Jan. 18, 1947). EB's response, "It All Depends," is reprinted in *Elizabeth Bishop and Her Art*, ed. Lloyd Schwartz and Sybil P. Estess (1983).

I'm enjoying life—useless and incompetent garden work, reading *Ulysses* with Gilbert's commentary[1]—not much good but explains a lot. Writing doesn't come, as often before. Hope I have another spurt.

Affectionately,
Cal

Give my best to Jim Powers. Why don't you both drive and stay with us?

77.

[Postcard: " 'Bagdad on the Subway': New York City at Night,"
a northwest aerial view of the city from the top of the Empire State Building]

Hotel Winslow, Mad. & 55th
"Bagdad" (modern)

Dear Cal:

At last I thought maybe I was driving down with a boy from Yaddo & could stop by to see you, which I'd have very much liked to, but after driving with him a few more times I decided I was too scared (a wild Texan who is used to lots of "room," I guess.) I came down by train instead—an awful trip. I began to enjoy Yaddo more towards the end, but then suddenly the last 2 days seemed quite unbearable. One particular guest stared hurting everyone's feelings, etc.—everything had been a bed of roses until then, quite unusual, I gathered. I liked Jim Powers best of all. Went to the races again & lost $17. But going to the track at 7 A.M. was the nicest activity of all, I thought—I'm going to try to write about it. I'll be here until the end of the week I think, & then on to Washington—although the way I *don't* hear from Léonie A rather encourages me about that. L. Frankenberg wants you to make a recording for his book—I did Friday & it is very easy. I do hope you're well. I wish I could see you. My regards to Elizabeth.

Love, Elizabeth

78.

[Washington, D.C.
October/November 1949]

Dear Cal:

I was up to New York briefly last week-end and tried to get hold of you

---

1 Stuart Gilbert, *James Joyce's Ulysses: A Study* (1930).

but you were out & Payne-Whitney didn't seem to have Elizabeth's telephone number.[1] I was hoping very much to see you. I'm coming up for several days at Thanksgiving though, & hope I can then.

I do hope you're feeling better. I have a friend at Chestnut Lodge here who speaks very warmly of her stay at P-W, so I hope you're liking it, too. Everything is going all right here, I think, though sometimes I'd like very much to have someone else's opinion. Sometime we must have a dreadful gossip about mutual acquaintances here. Miss A[2] is hard at work typing all these dull letters & she wishes to be remembered to you. If you want me to do anything at any time—what, I don't know, but there might be something—just ask Elizabeth to let me know, & remember me to her.

With love,
Elizabeth

79.

Library of Congress
Washington, D.C.
Elizabeth Bishop
Chair of Poetry
November 4, 1949

Dear Cal:

In reply to my letter saying that a meeting of the Fellows of the Library of Congress in American Letters had been suggested for November 17th and 18th, several of the Fellows have written that they would be unable to attend at that time. Dr. Evans has therefore recommended that the meeting be held in January, as formerly. He wishes to speak to the Fellows and has given as dates available to him the Fridays of January 6th, 13th, or 20th.

At present it appears that the business to be discussed at the meeting would probably take no more than one day. However, any matters not discussed on Friday could probably be taken care of on Saturday morning.

I am writing to find out which Friday would be convenient for the greatest number of the Fellows. Would you please reply as soon as possible?

Sincerely yours,
Elizabeth

---

1 In September 1949, RL was admitted to New York's Payne Whitney Clinic for depression. By the end of October he was allowed out on Wednesdays and weekends.
2 Phyllis Armstrong.

80.

Dear Elizabeth:

I'm afraid I'll be in Boston from Wednesday to Sunday. Is there any chance of your staying longer? We so want to see you.

Things are much better with me. I stay in our apartment weekends and go to the public library almost every afternoon—to prepare a course in modern poetry for next summer at Kenyon! Also I'm hoping to get a job teaching in February. Psycho-therapy is rather amazing—something like stirring up the bottom of an aquarium—chunks of the past coming up at unfamiliar angles, distinct and then indistinct.

Any of the January dates for the meeting except the 6th will do for me. I'm supposed to give a reading at St. John's then.

Well, it has been long since we've seen each and there's much to say. I'm dying to hear about Washington and Yaddo.

Love,
    Cal

P.S. Our number is UN4-8602

81.

Library of Congress
December 22nd, 1949

Dear Cal:

I don't know whether you're going to Boston for Christmas or not—anyway, I am, and if you're to be there I hope to see you and Elizabeth. I just had a note from Hyman who sounds in good spirits and I'm looking forward to seeing him. I'll be at the old Vendome from Sat. A.M. until Tuesday night—maybe a day or two longer if the money holds out.

Everything has suddenly become very hectic and unpleasant here, with holly ground into the linoleum and the page boys behaving worse than usual. Also it's so DAMP. Washington winter weather is rather like Paris I find, without the compensations. I had a nice letter from Jarrell with a long long poem about Austria etc. that I am still working over without too much success.[1] I seem to be losing my grip on poetry completely. Over-trained I

---

1 Randall Jarrell, "An English Garden in Austria," *Poetry* (March 1950).

guess. I'm about to go see Pound and take him some eau de cologne. So far my presents have not met with much success but maybe this will. He's reading Mirabeau's memoirs at a great rate.[1] Mrs. P[2] now has a telephone and calls me up. I think she holds out very well.

I am dying to see you and tell you about the strange tea-party for Frost, at which Carl Sandburg suddenly turned up to everyone's horror—everyone who had any sense, that is—it was very funny.

With love and best wishes for everything appropriate right now—
    Elizabeth

82.

[Library of Congress
December 31, 1949]
Saturday P.M.

Dear Cal:

I like it in here over the week-ends, so nice and silent, even the view looks improved somehow. It's the only time I can think about my own WORK, too.

Thank you thank you for the lovely book.[3] I had wanted to buy it for myself and thought I was being extravagant—now I think I'll get the Fromentin one in the same edition. Did you read any of it? It is really delightful. I have just finished Fromentin's "Dominique," too, and recommend it highly if you haven't read that.[4] In your book I notice they attribute several pictures to London, etc., that are right here now in the National Gallery—and when I see you remind me to tell you a story about Mrs. Huntington Cairns . . .

Boston, except for the actual duration of Christmas dinner, wasn't so bad. I saw a great deal of Hyman who played me all his new oriental musical instruments and seemed simply blooming with good spirits and health. He and I went and spent two days at Frank Parker's and had an awfully nice time—I had only just met Frank that time, and I am so glad to find someone I like so much. He and Hyman are engraving at a great rate. I think it's going to be particularly good for Hyman's morbid style. He was doing lizards and efflu-

1 Comte de Mirabeau, *Mémoires biographiques* (1834).

2 Dorothy Shakespear Pound.

3 Edmond and Jules de Goncourt, *French XVIII Century Painters*, trans. Robin Ironside (1948); "For Elizabeth with love and a merry Christmas, From Cal" is inscribed on the front flyleaf.

4 Eugène Fromentin, *The Masters of Past Time*, trans. Andrew Boyle (1948), and *Dominique*, trans. Edward Marsh (1948).

via from an old lady's nose etc. . . . but as cheerfully as could be. Frank's were lighter, slighter, quiet and nice. He & I went for a wonderful walk along the shore.

I saw the Eberharts in Cambridge and the Wilburs. Oh Red Warren[1] was there and said he'd seen you. I liked him very much. In fact, I just seem to love everyone these days and must stop it at once. However I won't draw the line before the end of this letter, and also wish you and Elizabeth a Happy New Year. I wrote a note to Gregory Hemingway, who is at St. John's, to go to hear you if he's there. He's a nice boy—I wish I could get there myself but I'll hope to see you Saturday anyway. If I'm out I'll be here, or I'll leave word at my boarding house: 1312 30th St., N.W., Dupont 4118. Oh, I forgot business. Serkin and a violinist are giving two concerts at the Library the nights of the 19th and 20th, and I'm supposed to ask the fellahs if they care to go and which night so as to reserve tickets. It ought to be pretty good I think. So will you tell me if you want one, or two?

Affectionately yours,

Elizabeth

83.

[January 1950]
Sunday

Dear Cal:

Yesterday was nice—I hope you weren't too exhausted. I am mailing you a small memento I forgot to present you.

I realized later that my accusations of Lloyd were probably most unfair— I remember a later, hectic conversation I had with him on the phone from Marianne's in which I may well have given him a firm *no*.[2] So please forget what I said if you can.

Best wishes to you & Elizabeth.

Elizabeth

---

1 Nickname of Robert Penn Warren.

2 Possibly a dispute about permissions for Frankenberg's *Pleasure Dome* (1949); see letters 68 and 69.

84.

[January 1950]
Monday

Dear Elizabeth:

What a comedy of errors! I reached Baltimore and finally home without any more missteps—except, perhaps, staying up to 3:30 with Santee and two students talking about symbolism, mostly *Moby Dick*. A weird room—about 10 by 8 filled with furniture from a *Good Will* store, rows of leaves in pots, glass balls, melted bottles, bits of green glass from an atomic explosion, and at least as many pictures as in Teniers painting[1]—candy-box pretties, sunsets like the inside of a blue marble, pin-up girls on calendars, photographs of cathedrals.

My term at Iowa[2] doesn't begin until the 8th, so I'll be at the poetry meeting and leave in the evening. That is unless you hear from me. We may have to leave sooner to connect with Engle. Still no apartment has been found—just a prospect.

While we were talking, my year in Washington came back like a dream: so much that I'd forgotten or never thought of again. But I think you've already taken in more than I did in my entire year.

Our telephone number is UN4-8602, if you should get to New York this weekend. Do try to come. All you really have to do for the meeting is make a list of what must be covered, then they carry themselves.

> Affectionately,
> Cal

Just got your note. I fear the Lloyd business was my fault—anyway you said all the good things. I await the "memento" or is it "monster."

85.

[Postcard: New Illuminated Fountain on Capitol Plaza, Washington, D.C.]

[January 11, 1950]

I'm pleased you are considering coming again but don't feel you should, if it rushes you too much. Ever since our conversation I've been wondering—*how* did Empson manage the 2 qts. of whiskey a day on the $20 a month?—

---

1 David Teniers the Younger, *Archduke Leopold Wilhelm in His Picture Gallery* (ca. 1647).
2 RL was invited by Paul Engle to teach the spring term at the Iowa Writers' Workshop, beginning in February 1950.

unless he codgered the whiskey, or made his own. Not that I'm considering it as a mode of living.

Best wishes—E.

86.

[January 23, 1950]
Monday morning—

Dear Cal:

Miss A has hidden away the typewriter because all those people are coming & I guess it isn't presentable enough, but I shall do my best to write LEGIBLY. Catalogues or no catalogues, you were an ANGEL & I can't thank you enough—you can come & be an angel of mine at any time, & today I really feel that is just about where I belong. A sort of numbness has set in now that everything's over.

Marcella's[1] party got rather drunken, but was very pleasant. Allen presented the flowers & the memento & little Léonie just sat there clutching it in complete silence. I really thought we might have to pour cold water over her. I think she really liked it, but insists that she wants "Bollingen Forever!"[2] added to the inscription. Mrs. Biddle's party was extremely nice—we played *charades*—& something called "adverbs," & everyone was quite hilarious. "Huntington Cairns" proved to be a good favorite for a word to act out, & my favorite moment of the party was when Huntington, acting out "Hun," put an enormous brass wood-kettle on his head & chased Léonie with a long iron lamp-base—being Attila, I think. Unfortunately the kettle fell off & onto Léonie so it all got almost too realistic. Then they acted "avuncular," & somehow or other Miss Bogan was being Ophelia with her hair down her back. Then they acted out the adverb "intimately" for the benefit of Mrs. Biddle, & Mr. Biddle was very funny, saying "Come here, little girl, & let me whisper to you." All good clean fun, as you see, & no hard feelings, I believe. My only worry now is that it all seemed to go *too* fast, & that there are probably lots of loose ends left hanging over.

I went back to the *Vienna pictures* yesterday, along with 45,800 other peo-

---

1 Marcella Comès Winslow, distant cousin of RL's.

2 Because Léonie Adams was the poetry consultant during the controversy over Pound's Bollingen, she faced the worst of what she called the "siege." The fellows were suitably grateful to her for her forbearance.

ple. Infants in arms were being lifted up to look at the Cellini salt-cellar & all kinds of improbable people were there looking mystified.[1]

Well, I wish they'd hurry up and arrive & get this tour of inspiration over so we can relax. I do hope your moving wasn't too difficult & that your new place is satisfactory. It *was* nice of you to come under the circumstances—& I thank you again. Some parts of this job don't bother me at all but I must say I'm hopeless at the public appearance part & hope I never, never have to make one again. Miss A. sends her regards—I send mine to Elizabeth.

Affectionately yours—

Elizabeth

When you have time, do send me a note about yr new job & how you like it.

I do hope Randall accepts[2]—he'd be so good.

87.

[Postcard: Greta Garbo and Robert Taylor in Camille, *directed by George Cukor, Film Library, Museum of Modern Art]*

[March 5, 1950]

Dear Cal—I haven't had word of you for so long I'm beginning to wonder how you are. I've been to N.Y. twice—saw the "CP,"[3] etc.—& all kinds of things have been going on here. I do hope you're well & liking it out there.

Yours, Elizabeth

88.

728 Bowery St.
Iowa City, Iowa
March 10, 1950

Dear Elizabeth:

Pardon my not writing sooner. Iowa City is gray-white, monotonous, friendly, spread-out, rather empty, rather reassuring. The modern museum post-card is the right note. There is a theater here that specializes in movie

1 EB visited *Art Treasures from the Vienna Collections* at the National Gallery of Art, on its final day (January 22). See the Cellini saltcellar in "The County Mouse," written ca. 1960 (EB-*CPR*).

2 After Conrad Aiken (who seemed not to want the job), Randall Jarrell was next in line for the consultantship.

3 The original American production of T. S. Eliot's *The Cocktail Party*, starring Alec Guinness (1949).

revivals—this afternoon we are going to *Ivan the Terrible*.[1] My writing class is held in a *temporary*, modern, structure—plants and a large imitation Moore statue in the window, student-art on the walls—all kinds. We arrange ourselves in a long empty, somehow dingy loop of chairs and hold mimeographed copies of the "poems of the week." All during class, people drift in and out—looking for the sociology building, warming themselves, killing time, holding whispered conferences. No one comes to look at the art, but you never forget that it is attending you.

O, and the poems! Everything from poetry society sonnets to the impenetrably dark—defended with passion, shyness, references to Kant and Empson mysticism. About six of my students are pretty good—at least, they do various things I can't and might become almost anything or nothing.

What has happened about the consultantship? I hope Randall gets it and will take it. I haven't heard from him since I left New York, but my friends the Taylors who are also at the Women's College[2] plan to come to Washington next winter, and live in the garage of a friend named Sarah Goodget. There Peter is going to write plays.

Red Warren was here about a month ago and last week I read at Minnesota—a party afterward with fifty people in a small room, most of the evening was spent talking to A) an old girl of Delmore Schwartz's, B) a whaling authority, C) an authority on Egyptian medicine.

I've been back in my long poor poem—hours and hours, have gotten some good new lines, but it's still a muddle getting it all together.

However, life in general is going very well indeed.

Affectionately,

Cal

P.S. Elizabeth sends her best. Any news on your plans for next year? I want to teach, but don't know where.

89.

May 6th, 1950

Dear Cal:

It seems that Aiken was invited about the end of March, answered in a

---

1 *Ivan the Terrible*, dir. by Sergei Eisenstein (1944).
2 Randall Jarrell and Peter Taylor both taught at the Women's College of North Carolina at Greensboro.

week, but the letter was seen by only one girl in the reference department who filed it away safely, while everyone else just wondered what had happened to Mr. Aiken for five weeks . . . I'm getting rather used to this kind of thing now, though. Mr. Aiken has *accepted*; at least we're pretty sure he has—& I'm afraid someone had told Randall (not me) & he had started to make plans. We had even discussed switching jobs next year. It's too bad. However, I wouldn't be at all surprised if Aiken changed his mind again. When Dylan Thomas was here he was very curious as to how everyone makes a living, etc., & he asked me what I was going to do after next September: "Go back on the parish?" So I guess that's wh. I shall be going, or going back on Yaddo, possibly, for a while. My vague plans for a Fulbright fell through, as I thought they might.

As you may know, Ransom is now a Fellow, & so are Thornton Wilder & Samuel Morison. Frost is still making up his mind.

May 8th

I decided it was time to go to see "The Bicycle Thief"[1] just then. Have you seen it yet? Let's see—I haven't really much news. Spring is exceptionally nice here. I've been to N.Y. 2 or 3 week-ends—saw *The Cocktail Party* which I guess I didn't like as much as you did; in fact I thought it was a MESS. I saw *The Member of the Wedding*,[2] too, & liked it very much. I had a nice time with Randall when he was here. He's in love with his new pale green convertible. Thomas's visit was the high point of my incumbency, though, & he made absolutely beautiful records. When they'll ever be used I don't know. I've been to see the baby elephants Nehru presented to the Zoo, Shontik & Asoka, Asoka being so infantile that he sucks his trunk as if it were his thumb. The "Institute" staggers along. The latest faux pas was their announcing a reading by Juan Ramón Jiménez as by José Jiménez (an inferior Brazilian) so Mr. Jiménez called it off at the last minute. It's really about as bad as calling T. S. Eliot *George* Eliot, but they all seemed unaware of the enormity of it all. I finally went to Mt. Vernon which was very nice, even with 1,000s standing in line to get in, eating ice-cream cones.

I just had a note from Aiken inquiring about where he's to live, a problem I haven't solved satisfactorily for myself yet, so I guess he's coming.

---

1 *Ladri di biciclette*, dir. by Vittorio De Sica (1948).
2 The 1950 Broadway production of Carson McCullers's *The Member of the Wedding* (1946).

Well I must get to work. Oh, tell me how you got out of having your picture painted by Marcella? I'd like to, & actually I think she's bored with the whole project now herself & would probably like to get out of it, too.

Have you settled on a place to teach yet? If you hear of any extra ones around let me know. Karl[1] told me he'd seen a couple of your students & they were very enthusiastic about you. He also said Roethke was en route here but I haven't seen him, have you?

Dr. Williams says, in print, that Peter Viereck's poetry "rises like a lovely bird from a cow pasture."[2] You see where that leaves the rest of us.

I hope you & Elizabeth are well & enjoying yourselves. I'd love to see you.

Affectionately,
    Elizabeth

90.

[Postcard: "Elk's War Memorial, Chicago"]

[Chicago
May 10, 1950]

Dear Elizabeth—

I'm just back from Kenyon where I read your "Fish" and "Fish-Houses" and a lot of my stuff glaring into the red six-feet-away, scowling face of Robert Hillyer.[3] Write how you are. We are hoping to go to Italy in September.

Affect.,
    Cal

91.

June 27th, 1950

Dear Cal:

I think you must be at Kenyon by now, but I'm not sure. I am wondering how you are & what your plans are for next year, if you are really going abroad, etc. (That is, if anyone can, by next fall.) I'm going up to Yaddo when I get through here, for 3 or 4 months, I think—as long as I can stand it & work, that is, because I want to get a new book off to Houghton Mifflin as

1 Karl Shapiro.

2 William Carlos Williams, "Diamonds in Blue Clay," *The New York Times Book Review* (March 12, 1950).

3 Robert Hillyer led the campaign to denounce the awarding of the Bollingen Prize to Ezra Pound.

soon as possible. Then in January or February I think I'll be going abroad, too, & if you're there, seeing you there. I haven't been able to do any work here at all, I don't know how you ever did, but I have made a few starts, & if I can finish about 5 poems I guess there'll be a book. I don't know.

Randall stopped over one night on his way to the Cape. He'd been painting pictures. They have asked me to visit them on my vacation, but I'm rather dubious about taking one, since I've just got over 6 weeks of bronchitis & asthma & have been out a good deal, besides which I shd. go to Nova Scotia if I go anywhere. The evening he was here—at the Starrs—I had a new asthma-machine & he said I looked exactly like the caterpillar smoking a hookah on a toadstool in "Alice in Wonderland." I can get away week-ends quite easily to Jane Dewey's anyway—the most beautiful place. I just came back from there. We attended a large party for Dos Passos, his new wife & brand-new baby (unseen.) He seemed nice, or at least in the mob of strangers he was someone I could manage to talk to, but what surprised me about him was that you & he have a good many of the same mannerisms. I couldn't think who it was, at first.

Washington is hotter than Key West—someone said hotter than Dakar. The Scotch Tape *flows* onto the photostats. I shall be very glad to leave. Marcella did paint the picture—three awful days—& I come out looking exactly like those old cartoons of char-ladies in "Punch." Did I tell you I am now living at a hotel, sort of, called "Slaughter's"?—run entirely by colored people, for Eurasians, strange gray people, poets, etc. I like it much better than the boarding house. Mrs. Aiken[1] arrived yesterday to find a place to live, found one, she wasn't at all what I'd expected.

I spent most of the week-end reading Samuel Greenberg, have you? I got so mad at the introductions—particularly Tate's—& if you haven't read the poems I recommend them highly. He was certainly one of the finest poetic *characters* I know anything about, & phrases are magnificent, & no critic has ever apparently appreciated either at their real value.[2]

I went canoeing on the Potomac—one of the few nice things to do now.

I guess I'd better get back to work. I'd love to hear from you sometime & hear about what these conferences are like. Please give my kindest regards to Elizabeth. Have you been able to get much writing done? Pound is mad at me because I put off getting something micro-filmed for him. He thought

---

1 Mary Hoover Aiken.
2 *Poems by Samuel Greenberg*, ed. Harold Holden and Jack McManis, preface by Allen Tate (1947). Greenberg, whose work influenced Hart Crane, died of tuberculosis at the age of twenty-three.

there wasn't a moment to waste because once Luther[1] (who'll be hung, anyway) finds out what inflammable material it is, etc., etc.

With love,
    Elizabeth

92.

Dear Cal:

I've had a letter from Margarita Casetoni, or Princess di Bassiono,[2] or whatever one prefers to call her, from *Botteghe Oscure* saying how she'd like to know your address & how eager she is to have a poem of yours, etc., etc. You know, she's Mrs. Biddle's sister & has always sounded awfully nice. Probably she'd be nice to call on when you get to Rome, if you *can* get to Rome considering the way things look right now. The number is 32 *B-O-*, Rome.

Just had a visit from the Dutchman[3] who works here & writes poetry incessantly. I hope he wasn't one of your problems too. One poem this time is about his soul fermenting in a barrel of sauerkraut. He's so grateful to God for sending him such marvelous ideas, but personally I'm afraid God is playing tricks on him.

Hope you & Elizabeth are doing well in spite of all the bad news now.

Love,
    Elizabeth

93.

Kenyon College
Gambier, Ohio
[July 20, 1950]
Friday

Dear Elizabeth:

Rather good news with me. Kenyon has been very easygoing, sociable, exciting etc.[4] Teaching not at all impossible and my long poem[5] is finally done—well, I think, and without re-writing any of the old stuff.

---

1 Luther H. Evans.

2 Marguerite Caetani.

3 Unidentified.

4 RL returned to Kenyon to teach for six weeks at the Kenyon School of Letters; the faculty included William Empson, Kenneth Burke, Delmore Schwartz, John Crowe Ransom, and Allen Tate.

5 "The Mills of the Kavanaughs" (RL-*CP*).

We're going to gamble on Europe anyway; it seems sort of now or never. In fact we are counting on your joining us after Yaddo.

What have you decided about your vacation? We'll be in Cambridge and Beverly Farms (where my parents live) from the 14th of August on. Perhaps we can meet there or maybe I can get down to Washington for a day early in September. I'd like to say goodbye to the Pounds and have a good idle talk with you now that the wearisome fog of depression is gone.

Kenyon is placid, with all kinds of chess-tangles and gossip I'll have to tell you. We are now on the verge of a faculty retreat with Delmore abstaining.

Elizabeth is reading all of Dickens and taken to denouncing the New Critics with great Kentucky verve—but we all do.

If prices are what my father warns us they are, we will come to the Princess Biddle holding out our hats like beggars. However, we need addresses, for we know almost no one in Italy.

We wish you were here with us.

Love,

Cal

Just finished reading a paper on Frost at the University of Akron. It was a success at the forum here, but I poked a lot of fun at the academic Philistine,—so at Akron it didn't go at all. Awful moment when you realize you must read twenty more pages to a slowly vanishing wall of disapproving old ladies.

94.

[August 1950]
Monday morning bright & early—

Dear Cal:

I was delighted to have such a cheerful letter from you & to hear that the poem is *finished*. I saw your Faber edition[1] advertised in the *London Times Lit. Supplement*, too.— I wish I could write something, no matter what, but I am hoping the minute I leave Washington it will all begin again. Miss A is away now on her vacation—I miss having her tell me what to do from minute to minute, but in some ways it's rather a relief. She'll be back the 21st. I was supposed to go to visit Randall on *my* vacation, at Dennis—my idea was to stop over a few days in Boston to see my aunt, etc. However,

1 *Poems 1938–1949* (1950).

I've been out so much that I don't feel I should go away any more—also when Phyllis gets back there'll probably be quite a lot to do before Aiken takes over. *If* I go at all I guess it will be about August 28th, for two weeks—I might see you there then—but the chances are I won't go at all. When is it that you sail? I do want to see you before you take off—either here or Boston or New York. I guess I'll be going to Yaddo around October 1st. I'm not looking forward to it too much, but if I can work it will do for a while.

It is really deadly dull here now. I read, go to movies, & return to reading some more.

I read Mr. Engle's piece in *Flair*[1]—saw us in *Harper's Bazaar*[2]—looking very cranky. I have the most hair of any poet & you have the next to most . . .

Are you going to publish your Frost paper? I'd like to see it. The records he made here this year are really wonderful, I think—those & Dylan T's have been the high points of my sojourn.

Will you please tell me if you ever replied to a letter from a M. Wilson, Harvard, Dept. of Social Relations, Psychological Clinic Annex, who wants to go interviewing various poets for hours at a stretch, giving them "picture card" tests, all to find out how they feel about their "relation to the social order"? He lists you, Williams, Shapiro, etc., but I can't make out whether you really bothered with him or had just been asked. He offers to meet me for 2 days anywhere. I think I'll pick out a nice resort & say I must also be paid a substantial fee & plied with champagne while the "picture cards" are being shown me.

I'm reading "The Green Huntsman"[3] & it's marvelous—also just finished Samuel Greenberg & Isaac Rosenberg[4] who have many strange points in common.

Give my regards to Elizabeth & I'm so pleased to hear you sounding so chipper.

Love,

Elizabeth

1 Paul Engle, "Revolution on Campus," *Flair Annual* (1950), a defense of university teaching of creative writing.

2 Photographs were taken by Marion Morehouse, third wife of E. E. Cummings.

3 Stendhal, *The Green Huntsman*, trans. Louise Varese (1950).

4 Isaac Rosenberg, *Collected Poems*, ed. Gordon Bottomley and Denys Harding, foreword by Siegfried Sassoon (1949).

95.

[Wadsworth House, Harvard University, Cambridge, Massachusetts]
August 14, [1950]

Dear Elizabeth:

If you are in Washington, you will be confused by the telegram[1] that I sent to the Library at the last minute in hopes that it would be forwarded to your "home" address which I didn't have. The Sunday in the telegram was *last* Sunday.

I am at another poets' conference and haven't seen anyone yet, but am isolated in a house for Canadian poets. None have shown themselves yet but already anthologies of Canadian verse are appearing by their bedsides. Have you ever read one?

Sorry to have missed you in Washington. Write us at my parent's address Beverly Farms Mass. so we can make arrangements not to miss each other before we sail (about the 15th if your freighter comes through).

Love,
Cal

P.S. My printing is more illegible than usual because after choosing what I thought was the best room, I discovered it had no desk.

I see Lloyd is still putting us on the map.[2]

Wish you were here.

96.

[August 17, 1950]

Dear Cal:

This is the telegram I was just handed at 3 this afternoon, Monday. It has been through a great deal, as you see, & I can't tell when you sent it, or where from, or where all it's been . . . I think it wasn't sent till Saturday, though, & I went away for the week-end early Saturday morning & didn't get back till this morning. I'm awfully sorry to have missed you & Elizabeth. Did you see Pound? I wonder. I took your ex-pupil, John Edwards, out there Friday afternoon. We had quite a pleasant visit, I thought, & Pound is very forgiving about my not coming oftener, although he sees right through me—tells everyone how I always "have to bring someone else along," etc. I see by the *N.Y.*

---

1 The telegram does not survive.

2 Lloyd Frankenberg, "The Poets: Their Spoken Words Attract a New Audience," *Harper's Bazaar* (Aug. 1950).

Times that you're at another conference at Harvard[1]—I knew Marianne was going there but didn't know who else. A funny mixture of people, & I hope you don't come to blows with P.V. or E.C.[2]—except the latter is too genteel to fight, I imagine. I wonder if you got my letter addressed to Kenyon— you'd left, I gather,—& please give me your Boston address, (if you get this) & tell me when & how you leave. I'll be in N.Y.—Hotel New Weston, probably; for Sept. 18th till Oct. 1st. I do want to see you before you go.

　　Love, Elizabeth

97.

[15 Grove Street, Beverly Farms, Massachusetts]
August 20, [1950]

Dear Elizabeth:

Our freighter, called the "Fernhill" suddenly emerged with Aug. 30 as the sailing date, so unless you could be in New York on the 29th, I guess there's not much chance of our meeting.

The conference was a crazy jumble with Viereck talking like an incoherent manic Merrill Moore, and Randall tense and inspired, very profound, cogent, rude—full of disgusts and enthusiasms—Miss Moore was our one belle. Some anonymous person gave her an orchid, and she was very cute and full of crushing compliments for her critics such as the *Harvard Wake* that had never accepted one of her poems. After I read my "Dead Brother,"[3] she said the reading was bracing and did her good. Spender was all over the place and, I'm sorry to say, very pleasant and intelligent.

Peter Taylor and I have agreed that Randall is a terror for his friends in public—you are either corrected, ignored or expected to loudly agree. You end up feeling like a boor for supporting as much as you do and a hypocrite for not going further.

I wonder if you would do me a favor and buy some flowers for my cousin Pearson Winslow who is dying (?) of cancer. They should be sent through my cousin Harriet[4] rather than directly. I hate to involve you with more florists, but this seems like the only way for me to do anything.

---

1 "Poetry Conference at Harvard," *The New York Times* (Aug. 14, 1950).

2 Peter Viereck and Elliott Coleman. Coleman had hosted a conference on literary criticism and the sublime at Johns Hopkins, attended by John Crowe Ransom, Allen Tate, R. P. Blackmur, and RL, in 1948.

3 "Her Dead Brother" (RL-*CP*).

4 Harriet Patterson Winslow, RL's maternal cousin; see "Soft Wood" and "Near the Ocean: Fourth of July in Maine" (RL-*CP*).

I guess the best way for you to reach us is through Harcourt Brace or the American Express in Rome. We'll write you at Yaddo as soon as we are settled. You must try to join us—things are bad politically, but it looks like they will be indefinitely.

My daddy is impatient to be off to the post-office, so I'd better conclude. God bless you for the coming year.

Love from us both,

Cal

P.S. Give my love to the Pounds. I had many small brushes for his sake; though almost everyone seems to be on his side now.

98.

Dear Cal:

I sent the flowers, some rather nice white chrysanthemums with petals curled up so they look like porcupine quills. I spoke to your cousin Miss Mary W on the phone to get the address, & she said, "How nice of Bobby!"

I must write to Marianne immediately to get her version of the Harvard Conference, & to hear how she enjoyed "Pakistan's Leading Poet" (so he said, but I guess it was true), whom I sent on to her in despair. He wanted to meet "poets," while here he called on Pound but seemed to retain a very confused impression of his visit, since Pound talked about nothing but Confucius, & Mr. Jasimuddin knew no Chinese (he confessed) & not much English . . . Sometime I must tell you about our luncheon-party.

Yesterday I had lunch with John Edwards'[s] wife, & 9-month old baby—they were taking *him* to spend the afternoon with Pound & I'm sorry I couldn't see that interview. Did you see MacLeish's "Poetry & Opinion"?—his usual mellifluous & meaningless periods. I am just reading Yeats' *A Vision*, or trying to.[1] Have you? Sometimes it's very Jungian. The picture of Yeats going "Woof!-woof!" in a lower berth, in the dark, in California, in order to wake up his wife who was dreaming she was a cat, is very pleasing, I think.

From here I am going (the 15th, I hope) to visit Jane Dewey for about 10 days, then a week at the new Weston in N.Y., then to Yaddo Oct. 1st. I'm

---

[1] Archibald MacLeish, *Poetry and Opinion: The Pisan Cantos of Ezra Pound* (1950); William Butler Yeats, *A Vision* (1937 edition).

going to try to get passage—probably to France—around the end of January. (I think I've told you about Jane D.—the physicist daughter of John D? At present she is in charge of "Terminal Ballistics" at the Aberdeen proving ground, & when I stay at her farm, on week-days, the rural scene shakes slightly once in a while as Jane practices her art about 15 miles away, & then there is a faint "boom." It seems there are three kinds of ballistics: Internal, External & Terminal.)

"Fernhill" is a nice name[1] & I hope you have a nice trip. Do you go straight to Italy? Did you see Eleanor Clark's endless piece about Hadrian's villa in *Kenyon*?[2] That is a *lovely* trip, to the Villa d'Este, then to the Villa. I walked it & had a beautiful time although in complete ignorance of most of what Miss C knows. You must do it, but of course you will, & I liked the Catacombs enormously.

With love,
Elizabeth

99.

Mr. Robert T. S. Lowell[3]
Beverly Farms, Massachusetts
September 18, [1950]

Dear Elizabeth:

My father died quite suddenly on the 30th of August, and we have been rusticating and maundering with my mother. His death was painless—not really tragic, for he had little besides filling the days to look forward to. He was not a suffering or heroic man, but rather as someone said "happy-seeming": always smiling or about to smile—and deep under, half-known to him: apathetic and soured. There was at least one great might-have-been—a first-rate Naval career. The death seems almost meaningless, as is perhaps always the case when the life has long resigned itself to a terrible dim, diffused pathos.

We sail now on the 28th, a Thursday, and plan to go to New York on the Monday or Tuesday before. Now, I think there's no escaping us for you. You must name some days you can see us in N.Y. or perhaps you'd prefer to come here for the week-end. *In any case* don't slip away.

1 Cf. Dylan Thomas, "Fern Hill" (1946).
2 Eleanor Clark, "Hadrian's Villa," *The Kenyon Review* (Summer 1950).
3 His father's stationery.

I'm boiling mad at Randall—I think his reading of the Aged Goethe was fatal. He gave a tremendous Philippic at Harvard against our culture that has no time or taste for poetry, something that would have made Jonathan Edwards sound like Montaigne.[1] Then what with his tennis tournaments, swimming and new enthusiasms had no time to read my poem and never apologized. Ah me!

Love,

Cal

Thanks for your goodbye wire. How did you know the ship's address?

100.

[Postcard: Photograph of a boy, "Le Petit Mohamed (Maroc)"]

[October 10, 1950]

Dear Elizabeth,

Dolphins, a school of whales, a fairy my former wife knew in Baton Rouge (first person met in Tangiers); a fairy Elizabeth knew in Kentucky who now runs a famous Tangerine bar.

Affect.,

Cal

101.

[Postcard: Roma—Acquedotto di Claudio—horse-drawn carts along the via Appia Nuova]

2 Lugarno Amerigo Vespucci, Florence

[October 1950]

Dear Elizabeth:

Large apartment and maid in Florence all waiting for you. Seen houses of Shelley, Keats, Horace, Catullus, and Pound. Roman ruins tough sledding as you can see. Language tougher. Eliz. already says things neither of us or the Italians can understand. Real Yaddos (Villa d'Este) everywhere.

Love,

Cal

1 Randall Jarrell, "The Obscurity of the Poet," *Partisan Review* (Jan.–Feb. 1951).

102.

Dear Cal:

I have had every intention of writing to you about the "Kavanaughs" ever since I got here,[1] & I will yet, but somehow I seem to feel literarily exhausted this morning, & yet I want to write you and Elizabeth a note before any more days go by, to thank you for your beautiful cards, say how nice it all sounds, etc. I am somewhat confused by the fact that although you say you're living in Florence, all the cards seem to be from Rome . . . I forgot to tell you to be sure to see my favorite church in Rome—the most beautiful, from the outside at least, I think I've ever seen—Maria del Pace[2] (probably spelt wrong)—quite a small one. A maid!—& are you both studying Italian, and have you seen Santayana, etc.

I really like Yaddo this trip, and the duller it gets the better I like it and to my great surprise I AM[3] working. (This is my brand new Royal Quiet De Luxe typewriter, 1951—at least—model, a GIFT. I just can't believe I own anything so grand and have been typing stories right off the bat on it.) I felt rather bad at first. There had been 3 deaths of people very close to me all in a couple of weeks,[4] and finally in a general state of asthmatic collapse I went to the hospital for four or five days, but I've been fine ever since. I have a suite in East house—very nice and plain and sunny. At first I shared the house with a rather elderly Negro painter whom I liked very much, but he's left now.[5] There was a little poet, May Swenson, not bad, & a nice girl, and Alfred Kazin—both gone now, too. Then there's the new secretary, Wallace Fowlie's cousin, Pauline Hanson. I *think* I sent you her book of poems[6] a while back, c/o American Express, Rome. You may not like it at all or see in it what I do, & it all may have just hit me at the right minute, but I think there are some very fine things in it, & the only 2 other poems of hers I've seen I think show great improvement—although it never "gets anywhere," and I suppose is monotonous, lots of dead lines, but some as good as *In Memoriam*,[7] I bet. At present there is only one guest besides me[8] & he is the "problem": an archeologist, explorer, grandfather, LOVER—as he leaves you in no doubt of for 2

---

1 On October 1.

2 Santa Maria della Pace.

3 "AM," "GIFT," and "LOVER" are typed with the red typewriter ribbon.

4 One was the death of Dr. Ruth Foster (see letter 15); the others are as yet unidentified.

5 Beauford Delaney.

6 Pauline Hanson, *Forever Young* (1948).

7 Alfred Lord Tennyson, *In Memoriam A.H.H.* (1849).

8 Victor Wolfgang von Hagen.

seconds—etc., and just so awful you can't believe him. Published over 25 books—at 43—& I'm horrified to think I've actually read quite a few of them because they're all about South America, naturalists, etc. He has some idea of getting me to go & trace *old Inca roads* with him in a year or so . . . at least he did have, but I guess I haven't proved quite responsive enough, turn down all offers to go watch football games on television with him, etc. He's off now, Thank God, running, I gather, the elections in Connecticut, but will be with us again tomorrow. The only thing I *don't* like is that it seems to take an awful lot of diplomacy to keep one's head above water here—rather a strain—& I'm afraid I talk too much. The Countryside is beautiful, though.

Had a funny letter from Randall. Miss A writes me Aiken had a bad nose-bleed so I'm afraid the job is telling on him already. I have to go downtown to get my Dog & Cat shot . . . Write me, & I'll really get down to serious matters next time. I hope you're both well.

With love,
Elizabeth

My plans are vague, but will take shape in a month or so, I think.

Will you send me the address of *Botteghe Obscura*? & the lady's correct name?

103.

December 5th or 6th, [1950]

Dear Cal:

You must be thinking I'm not very polite to let all this time go by without commenting on the "Kavanaughs." Well, the answer is quite simple—as soon as I got here I started to write some poems, too, rather to my surprise, and as I think I once told you before, I find your poetry so strongly influential that if I start reading it when I'm working on something of my own I'm lost. So I haven't re-read the "Kavanaughs" since the first two times way back in October. However, my own fit seems to be letting up, and this evening I'm determined to write you something about your poem.

It is absolutely beautiful here today—I just walked to town & back for my Dog & Cat shots. The people are very nice, too: a painter named Kit Barker (younger brother of George) and his wife, a German refugee, quite a good writer[1]—and another young novelist named Calvin Kentfield—actually

---

[1] Ilse Barker, who wrote under the pseudonym Kathrine Talbot.

named for Calvin Coolidge, who was president when he was born. John Cheever was here for about a week, very pleasant. I don't know what we have in store for us now. Did you ever get over to Glens Falls when you were here to see the Hyde Collection of paintings? The Barkers met the curator someplace, and we all took a little jaunt over there last week—really marvelous things. You may even remember the famous Rembrandt Christ[1] that was in the World's Fair. There's one of everyone you can think of, and all good,— and all right there in Glens Falls. But heavens I forget I am talking to someone in Florence. Well, tomorrow night the big thrill is to be that we're all going to see *King Solomon's Mines* . . .[2] You may have heard about the Hurricane. It wasn't as bad here as in N.Y. City, but it certainly was bad enough and dozens & dozens of those great old trees came crashing down. At one point, I was sitting up in bed trying to read and forget the racket. All the stucco came off the end of East House, right behind my head, with a loud report, leaving me— still—exposed to the elements except for some lathes & a thin coating of plaster. All the chimneys came down. All the birds disappeared for several days, but then came back again mysteriously, and all the squirrels and chipmunks went completely berserk trying to get their supplies re-organized. They'd run right into you on the paths, carrying apples, cobs of corn, etc.

Well, I must make myself a dish of tea.

Later

I'm sorry I forgot to send this note to you the first time I wrote. It was sent me by Miss Armstrong, I think, anyway, without benefit of envelope, like this.[3]

Well, I've gone through the "Kavanaughs" twice more and really it is one of the most harrowing things I've ever read. All the things I remember admiring in one of the earlier versions I recognized with pleasure again, and I'm sure the total effect is magnificent, horrible, what you wanted, etc.—I find it hard to tell. There is no earthly reason why I should attempt to *criticize* certainly, and so I shan't. I think "Green the clairvoyance of her deity" beautiful as some of Mallarmé and rather like him.[4] The stanza beginning "The world hushed" etc., I also find very beautiful.[5] The stone "bedstead," al-

---

1 Rembrandt van Rijn, *Portrait of Christ* (c. 1665–67).

2 *King Solomon's Mines*, dir. Compton Bennett and Andrew Marton (1950).

3 Unknown; the note does not survive.

4 "The Mills of the Kavanaughs," stanza 5, line 7, *The Kenyon Review* (Winter 1951); cf. "The Mills of the Kavanaughs," stanza 6, line 7 (RL-*CP*).

5 "The Mills of the Kavanaughs," stanza 10, *The Kenyon Review* (Winter 1951); cf. "The Mills of the Kavanaughs," stanza 11 (RL-*CP*).

though I know exactly what you mean, still bothers me, or rather I think it might bother some readers.[1] And the stanza that begins "He is St. Patrick" bothers me.[2] Is Harry St. Patrick? I thought that drink was glugg in Sweden, but maybe in Norway it's glück, etc.[3] Nothing that really amounts to a pin, as you see. Also I'm bothered by the mussels being "white underneath."[4] There are two lines I don't like. 1) which I don't mind as much as the other—"I am just a girl"—which suddenly seems to weaken the tone.[5] But it's at the end, where she says "a girl can bear just about anything" that I feel a real recoil.[6] You may think this has all just to do with gender, but I don't honestly think so. It sounds to me as if the next line should almost go "if she has a good big diamond ring." Please forgive me.

This is the next day. The maid has arrived to sweep me out so I guess I'd better *get* out first. Are you working now? Do tell me your news. I think I'll be staying on until March, then I have hopes definitely for Europe. Had a wire from Léonie last night wanting me to read with *Cummings* at the New School—on April Fool's Day, a singularly appropriate day for me to make a public appearance with Mr. Cummings, I thought. Of course I won't, but I was kind of flattered. I've just been doing a lot of short things and some stories. Hope to get down to some real work now.

Do let me hear from you & I hope you're both well.

Love to both,

Elizabeth

1 "She sees he swings a string of yellow perch / About his head to fan off gnats that mill / And wail, as his disheartened shadow tries / The buried bedstead, where his body lies—"; "The Mills of the Kavanaughs," stanza 37, lines 4–7, *The Kenyon Review* (Winter 1951). Neither the stanza nor the lines appear in the book version.

2 "He is Saint Patrick; that is why the brush / And boulders wriggle, when the children rush / Hurrahing"; "The Mills of the Kavanaughs," stanza 6, from lines 1–3, *The Kenyon Review* (Winter 1951). Cf. "The Mills of the Kavanaughs," stanza 7 (RL-*CP*).

3 "He turned the burners up, / And stirred the stoup of glück—a quart of grain, / Two quarts of claret"; "The Mills of the Kavanaughs," stanza 20, from lines 13–15, *The Kenyon Review* (Winter 1951). Cf. "The Mills of the Kavanaughs," stanza 20, lines 13–15 (RL-*CP*).

4 "The Mills of the Kavanaughs," stanza 33, line 7, *The Kenyon Review* (Winter 1951). Cf. "The Mills of the Kavanaughs," stanza 33 (RL-*CP*).

5 ". . . I am just a girl, / Just one man's and not the fleet's"; "The Mills of the Kavanaughs," stanza 31, from lines 6–7, *The Kenyon Review* (Winter 1951). Cf. "The Mills of the Kavanaughs," stanza 32, lines 6–7 (RL-*CP*).

6 "The Mills of the Kavanaughs," stanza 37, line 12, *The Kenyon Review* (Winter 1951). Neither the stanza nor the line appear in the book version.

104.[1]

Lungarno Vespucci 2
Florence
December 6, [1950]

Dear Elizabeth:

Out the window there is a statue of the 18th century playwright Goldoni. He looks like Alexander Hamilton and had his hand blown off five years ago when the bridge was mined. The city is gray and sand-colored, Bostonish, compact, very unvegetable. You live on a little more than you would in America and about 4 times as well. A maid, wine and lovely furniture for what a moderately good apartment would cost in New York.

The language, the architecture, the art, the people, the politics, the places one might go, the history—you cannot turn your head without starting up occupations, abundance in every direction, so that it seems one's energy and interest could never tire. It's another world, and we are floating.

But nothing is cheap, except time, labor, and roots, a cultivated starkness. Politics are very up-to-date, fierce, irreconcilable, a funny mixture of Dante's factions and what I'd imagine you'd find in South America. All the old buildings and history, yet the facts, necessities, and possibilities of life rawer and more nervous than with us; and the whole culture trying to forget that it is a provincial France.

Florence has a communist mayor.[2] Every so often you see scribblings on the walls such as *Death to the Criminal MacArthur*.[3] But the people are boisterous, friendly, and fearfully orderly and except at political meetings—you'd never know anything was wrong; yet in a day you could have utter civil war or more likely a communist government.

You absolutely must leave Yaddo and your horrible archeologist lover and join us, if the world survives into another temporary calm. Nothing will happen here by itself, and life is so much more sensible and joyful that you cannot imagine losing again what you have lost all your life.

Do write me what you think of the "Kavanaughs." My proofs have come and I am hammering at the fuzzy places and trying to add a stanza or two, filled with Miltonic mythology, hard for a rhetorician to resist.

Miss Hanson's book finally came. The language and stanza made it hard to take seriously; it's as though she had no experience except such as would let

---

1 Crossed with letter 103.

2 Mario Fabiani.

3 General MacArthur was leading UN forces in a counterattack against North Korea. His aggressive tactics brought China into the war and prompted fears of a global conflict.

make little refrains of Tennyson and FitzGerald, often very clumsy; but that's original and I've come on awfully good bits. She really seems to be interested in the metrical craft of her masters. I don't know anything quite like it.

We had a good, uninformed, hurried visit to Rome, saw a good deal of the Assumption Ceremony,[1] but somehow arrived always an hour late. We missed the Vatican and Capitoline museums and except for a tremendous feeling of having now been there, probably had no new impressions. The Roman ruins are at last contemporary. I went to see Santayana daily. The talk ranged from autobiography, philosophical theories on world politics, Aristotle's theory of sensation, Spanish quotations, ideas on Boston, lots of very catty and very good gossip and above all Boston and religion. The meetings were delightful for me and perfect, except that he is deaf and couldn't hear a word—shouted or whispered—that I said.

The strangest people have turned up—a room-mate of Bowden Broadwater's; a theosophist and composer I used to know at Harvard (a very able man who used to drink lemon juice, wear yellow ties and play Bach to balance his bodily fluids).[2] He told incredible Frank Parkerish stories about Roman-American society and then said that St. Augustine was the incarnation of Judas, but that he couldn't prove it. Pearl Kazin, Dunstan Thompson and Gertrude Buckman and at the far end of a huge cocktail party at the Roman Academy someone—courage failed to look twice and make sure—who looked like Carley.

O well, this is the moment to end this rambling letter. Write us and try to come soon. We hope to stay three years now.

Love,
    Cal

105.

[Postcard: Saratoga Hospital, Saratoga Springs, N.Y.]

[December] 1950

I hate to have letters cross in the mail—particularly when yours is so much better than mine. I think I sent my remarks, such as they were, on the *K*'s to Am. Exp. instead of your street address. I'll write again soon. Season's greetings to you & E—Love,
    Elizabeth

1 See "Beyond the Alps," lines 15–24 (RL-*CP*).
2 Possibly Norman Johnson, a Harvard classmate of RL's (see RL-*Letters*, 16–17).

106.

Dear Elizabeth:

An immediate *answer*! Seeing you is believing, so I suppose I don't yet think you are really sailing. You must come right here. It's the season, they say, and already it's spring-like. The opera (cheap) begins in *May* with Macbeth. In June we are going to Ischia, looping thru Venice on the way. I think (hope) you'll go with us. It sounds like my idea of Key West (in port): sand, sailing, primitivism and a horrible, brutal sport—spearing fish under water. We could all get a smallish sand and wind-swept cottage.

The *Kenyon* "Kavanaughs"[1] is unchanged but my Harcourt Brace version is all ripped up and much better, though perhaps not essentially. We went to Monte Carlo New Year's—a slightly hollow trip—and met the Parkers. First Elizabeth quarreled with Lesley, then I did. She's always right in a tense, earnest way, but jealous as a snake and untiringly watchful of Frank. Frank's fat and ruddy. They live on a floor and a half of a big house—part farm; part chateau—, a sort of squire's bohemia—polo playing, nights of red wine, singing, Negro art students, dissolute sons of generals, deaf servants, groups in cafés—all muddled and jolly. Frank now has about 15 engravings finished that I think make quite a show. He's doing one for my book, if he can do it in time.

It's exciting to think of yours. For the title, I can only think of Bishop's Gambit for a title. Won't the title of one of the poems do? Another idea. Would you think of printing 3 or 4 of your stories and perhaps sketches with the poems? It would be flashy and a novelty and seriously I think they'd read wonderfully together—more variety in unity, etc. The book even *outwardly* would be one that no one else could attempt.

Elizabeth has at last settled down to writing daily and regularly on her novel. Now that the "K's" is off I'm doing nothing but sight-seeing, Italian grammar and reading. The people one sees are welcome. They seem, though, to be mostly fairies, people of taste and students from Chicago—so there's [a] certain blank. Eleanor Clark was the most famous American in Italy. Hardly a day went by without our hearing about her. However, we haven't met since the Yaddo row.[2]

---

1 "The Mills of the Kavanaughs," *The Kenyon Review* (Winter 1951).

2 In February 1949, as RL was suffering from an acute manic episode, *The New York Times* reported that Yaddo had been under FBI surveillance because a former guest, Agnes Smedley, was suspected of espionage. Because Smedley was a friend of Yaddo director Elizabeth Ames, RL, Elizabeth Hardwick, and other guests became suspicious of Ames's role in the scandal. They organized a campaign against her, enlisting former Yaddo guests to their

Try and fly here by early in April. We'll get you a beautiful sunny room on the river two blocks away—and worlds of things to do.

Love,

Cal

P.S. Don't take these brushed off sentences for a letter, but I wanted to get something off before my natural dawdling started. Eliz. has just said "I can't understand Elen[1] & Alexei[2] leaving Italy for Yaddo (and few sharp comments on Eleanor). We can't understand your not leaving Yaddo for Italy.

107.[3]

Yaddo, January 26th, 1951

Dear Cal:

I'm not sure who owes whom what, but I can't remember thanking you & Elizabeth for the lovely Chardin—I immediately tacked it up on the closet door—room side out, of course—over the set of Yaddo rules & regulations which was beginning to get on my nerves and it covers it perfectly. It must be a beautiful picture. I must have seen it but I don't remember it at all. I've been told he did a whole series of them, others besides this and the one in the National Gallery. The little boy looks rather wicked to me.[4]

Kenyon Review came yesterday and I think the "Kavanaughs" looks most impressive. I've just been over to West house counting stanzas—I thought you'd shortened it—same number, though, as in my typescript, but I haven't gone through it yet for other changes if any. I'm sort of glad you left off the quotations at the beginning. I wasn't altogether happy about them[5]—or at least about *all* of them. If I hadn't chosen this piece of stationery I'd send you my poem on the Prodigal Son, finished at last—but then the "Kavanaughs" came to spoil my pleasure, because what I can only keep on doing for twice

---

cause and pressing the Yaddo board to investigate her. Other writers and former Yaddo guests, including Eleanor Clark, came to Ames's defense, and she was vindicated. See RL-*Letters*, 704, and Ian Hamilton, *Robert Lowell: A Biography* (1982), 151.

1 *Sic*; probably Eleanor Clark.

2 Alexei Haieff.

3 Crossed with letter 106.

4 Jean-Baptiste-Siméon Chardin, *Boy Playing Cards* (ca. 1740), Uffizi Gallery, Florence.

5 The *Kenyon Review* version of "The Mills of the Kavanaughs" has no epigraph quotations. The epigraph to "The Kavanaughs of Stewart Mills" is "Morals are the memory of success that no longer succeeds" (William Carlos Williams, *In the American Grain* [1925], 67). In the book version, RL restored the Williams and added "Ah, love let us be true / To one another! for the world, which seems / To lie before us like a land of dreams . . ." (Matthew Arnold, "Dover Beach," lines 29–31 [1867]).

14 lines I'm sure you could have kept up for pages & pages. However, I think I've almost got a book now, about 2 more to go—and *please* send me a title. I'm going crazy trying to think of one. Probably it will end up being "23 Poems" or something inspired like that.

I can't hope to compete with Florence, of course, but I'll just have to give you the simple facts of the simple life here. The Fellows meeting is Feb 8th & 9th. I'm going down. Miss Armstrong wrote me yesterday that the Poets' Room is that no longer. Mrs. Whittall has endowed it for $100,000, & it's being completely re-done in the grandest way—now called the "Poet's Corner" I believe or maybe that was Miss A's or Conrad's little joke. They're camping out in separate offices down the hall. I'll tell you more when I've been there.

Here we have the same people as before, with the exception of the composer Alexei Haieff, and a little tiny novelist of 25, with 2 babies, not along, named Peggy Bennett. Wallace Fowlie comes tonight, and Tuesday Alexei's friend & my old college class-&-cell-mate, Eleanor Clark—both just back from Rome. Fred Dupee was coming but couldn't at the last minute and that's the only one I wanted to see at all; I've always liked him. I have been doing a lot of work, for me—the holidays were rather bad and I got very blue but everything is fine now. I am in negotiations with a travel agency to get me passage on a freighter around March 20th—or if I make any money I may even fly, the winter rates are so reduced. I'm not sure whether I'll go 1st to France or Italy. Tom Wanning is thinking of coming with me, but I'm sure that three months notice is much too short for him to prepare himself mentally for such a move. Well, let's see. We play wild card games almost every evening, with something to drink 2 or 3 times a week usually, but everyone (except pampered me) is very broke. Tonight I am providing wine and roast chestnuts. We're in the midst of a January thaw, and it's just as foggy as Maine—quite beautiful—& when a churchbell rang downtown I realized that unconsciously I was just taking for granted it was a bell-buoy.

Love to you & Elizabeth—

Elizabeth

108.

Hotel Grosvenor
New York
March 31st, 1951

Dear Cal:

I can't believe I am answering a letter of yours dated January 24th. There *must* have been some exchange in between, but I'm afraid not. It's been a very confused stretch, and even now I think I'm just beginning to see the clearing through the woods. I had a freighter reservation for the 16th of this month. Then Houghton Mifflin wrote that they really, apparently, want a book for this fall and it seems very important to me to get it all off to them, etc., before I do anything else. Also I found myself in a tax tangle so that I probably would have been arrested on the dock; *also*, I was waiting to hear from a Bryn Mawr Fellowship I'd applied for, but I didn't hear until just as I left Yaddo, and then had to find out whether I should really accept it or not. It's a literary thing, a new "resident writer" fellowship, for $2,500, but I didn't want to live there.[1] Well, I got it and I don't have to live there, just make a few visits—really very generous. Also an Academy award, maybe I told you that, but not till May 23rd.[2] The other begins with the academic year. So I am hoping to get over as soon as I can get the book off, sell a story, etc. This is just a temporary address, but will reach me. I've got to find something else, see my way to earning a little money, etc. However I think I'll make a couple of reservations just on general principles.

Joe Frank wrote me from Paris a while ago that even if I wasn't around he wondered if he could see you in Florence, so I sent him your address finally—but you may have met long before now. He's awfully nice and I think you'd like him. He wanted to go to Ischia this summer, too, I gathered. I want to go to Venice. I didn't get there on my brief Italian trip. Last night I saw a travel movie of it and feel that I must go there immediately.

Harcourt Brace sent your book a couple of days ago.[3] Thank you very much. I haven't had a chance to compare texts yet, but I've read the book through a couple of times and it seems to me you have improved "Ks" a *lot*, but this is something I'm going to study Sunday, i.e. tomorrow. I like Frank's frontispiece much better than the 1st one[4]—except for the little tree to the left which seems rather weak somehow. But it's a nice-looking book & I am ea-

---

1 The Bryn Mawr Lucy Martin Donnelly Fellowship.
2 Award from the American Academy of Arts and Letters.
3 *The Mills of the Kavanaughs* (1951).
4 See RL-*CP*, 3 and 71.

ger to see what the reviews will say—out of idle curiosity rather than concern, you understand. (I feel guilty about never sending Frank back a book
of his, but I have it safe for him.)

Roethke was here this past week to read at the YMHA and see his publishers. I went to my 1st reading there. His records are much better. But I
kind of liked him. We downed a great deal of champagne together our first
meeting. I saw him off yesterday in a terrible rainstorm. We couldn't get a
cab & he almost missed his train to Seattle. He is a very sad man, I think—
not melancholy, but he makes *me* feel sad.

"Mother Marie Therese" strikes me as even better now than it did at first.
In fact, there are lots of magnificent things I'll expatiate on when I have finished with my story and my last ordeal with the Public Accountant. Now
I've got to go. This address will reach me. I'm sorry about not writing for so
long & still hope to see you—both.

Much love,
Elizabeth

109.

April 24, [1951]

Dear Elizabeth:

We are on the brink of what looks like almost unceasing movement—till
mid September! In a little more than a week we are sailing for Constantinople stopping in Athens—early in June Venice (2 or 3 weeks), Vienna (a week
or two), Paris by the 7th of July to meet old friends (the Macauleys), a trip
through Germany for about a month beginning July 20, 20th of August Paris
again to meet my mother [for] a tour of the chateaux country with her, then
by early October Naples I think for the winter and oblivion.

I am writing this on a hangover—wobbling toward a resolution to stay
off hard liquor; one must I guess. What a lot of people (mostly Americans)
we have seen going down the drain or crashing—for all sorts of almost unbelievably spectacular reasons. I suppose people come here for odd reasons,
and then their lives are so visible and discussed. Well, we have had an enjoyable winter—day in and day out, incredibly so—but idle. Elizabeth's novel
has bogged down and I've done nothing but a draft of [a] short poem[1]; oh no,
for the last week (to forget about packing) I've spent hours and hours reading *Gerusalemme Liberata*,[2] a real technician's poem—everything reminds

---

1 Unidentified; see "Uncollected Poems 1946–1951" (Houghton, bMS Am 1905, folders 2175–81).
2 Torquato Tasso, *Gerusalemme liberata* (1574).

you of something else: Dido in Virgil, *The Knight's Tale*, Spenser's Bower of Bliss, Milton's Eden, *Phédre* and Dryden's translation of the *Aeneid*. It's wonderful, though curiously anonymous in style, full of melancholy and tormented undertones, heroines like mine, but less muddied.

We've been to Pisa, Sienna, seen 5 or 6 of the wonders of the world, and visited the Princess (*Botteghe Oscure*) Caetani—a mad, sympathetic aristocratic Mrs. Ames, not deaf and really nice and kind, at least to us—but mad, so that though a grand and tireless manager, she thinks of nothing except her magazine—like an only child, a simile I understand so well.

I seem to have made up with Randall and really one misses and one feels rusty without him. Every time I drop some vague critical bromide, I hear the jump of his voice—a figure of speech. I'm not having hallucinations.

I'm cheered in a way by your difficulties finishing your book, planning your travel etc. Not really, of course, but it makes our similar difficulties seem more dignified.

I think I've almost given up expecting you—you'll only come suddenly after swearing you'll never move, or are on your way to Alaska—but do try to come and join us either this summer or next winter or both. As an old veteran of Europe, I think I can promise you—or anyway as an old friend.

Had a note from Pound, "Think at last Monsieur Lowell is larnin' to write—going into it hindquarters first like E.P."

Write us care of the American Express Florence and your letter will be forwarded. Doesn't anything on our long route allure you? Paris, anyway.

With love,

CAL

110.

[233 East 69th Street, New York, N.Y.]
July 11th, 1951

Dearest Cal:

I can't remember when I wrote to you last, & I wonder if I really have been owing you a letter ever since the end of April? I trust not—although nothing very cataclysmic has been happening to me since then. I visited in Maryland, came back & moved here. Just got back from a prolonged 4th of July visit in Maryland again. In the meantime I've done quite a lot of work, attended that dreadful Academy ordeal—Randall was there—a few parties, seen a few people, and that's about all. This place belongs to Kappo (that name embarrasses me) Phelan & Kenyon Brooks—a sort of railroad place up four flights, but very cheap, and I have it until October. I'm looking for a permanent apartment but so far have had no luck. They are so dreadfully expensive as well as scarce. I'm going to Nova Scotia for the first two weeks or so of August, mostly to try to write an article and earn some money. I'm trying to get out to Sable Island, cheerfully known as "the graveyard of the Atlantic" (my great-grandfather & his schooner and all hands were lost there, amongst hundreds of others), and if I am not fulfilling my destiny and get wrecked, too, I think I can turn it into an article and maybe a poem or two. Then I'm going to visit Randall for a week. At least that was the plan, but I haven't heard from him for quite a while & possibly he has changed his mind. He and a Starr girl, Fred Dupee & his wife, Margaret Marshall and a couple of others & I all had dinner together after the Academy tea, then came here: Randall very excited and voluble. I hadn't seen Fred for a long time. I've always liked him very much. I've been to his house since. Just before I went to visit Jane Dewey in Maryland, I had dinner with Nathalie Swan—Philip[1] is off at the U of Indiana. She seems very well and is doing a lot of work, I gathered.

Your proposed trip has me very ugly and envious. However, if the *New Yorker* takes my article[2] (they're interested) and I earn all I hope to, there's a chance I may still get abroad in the fall, after finding a place to live here, and paying my respects to Bryn Mawr—all that's expected of me, I gather. My book is about 85% at Houghton Mifflin, but I must confess it doesn't jell at all yet. Maybe the other 15% will prove to be pure pectin. I am going to call it—so far, & I hope you'll approve—"Concordance," starting off with a poem called "Over 2,000 Illustrations & a Complete Concordance."[3] On reading over what I've got on hand I find I'm really a minor female Wordsworth. At least, I don't know anyone else who seems to be such a Nature Lover. The *New Yorker*, I'm delighted to say, is quibbling with me over an indelicacy in a poem . . .[4]

My views from this tenement are very Neapolitan. I was very depressed by Naples on my short visit there, but you may like it—and of course you'll go to Paestum, which is one of the most beautiful things I've ever seen, though coming after Greece it might not be, I don't know. Margaret Miller went to Paris for 6 weeks 2 weeks ago—maybe you'll run into her. Or Joseph Frank, or a Mary Meigs—I gave her your address, I think—a painter.

What is Elizabeth's novel about? Give her my regards. Send me your

1 Philip Rahv, Nathalie Swan's husband.
2 A proposed article about her journey, never written.
3 *Partisan Review* (June 1948); see EB-*CP*.
4 Possibly "A Cold Spring."

"short poem." I really need something to give my standards a jerk, I think—but it is nice to feel awfully well (which I do) and like working. And please, if you ever have the time, write me a travel-letter. I should so much like to see you.

Love,
Elizabeth

111.

Dearest Cal:

Yes, I believe I had better put the year in, since I've let a ¼th of one go by without writing you, I think. At the moment I am in one of those curious dead-end Sunday predicaments that I'm sure you never get into—no one else I know ever does—& because I can think of nothing more alleviating than having you & Elizabeth here to talk to me about your travels I think I'll finally write to you and tell you about mine, which are the vaguest kind of sketch of "travel" really. I'm on my way to Stonington for about a week. I got off the train from Nova Scotia at 4 this morning & a taxi-driver brought me to this old but rather pleasant dump. I thought I'd get to Stonington this afternoon, but of course the bus doesn't run on Sunday. I don't like to call the two people I know there—who would probably come & get me if I did. So here I sit for 36 hours although I suppose I should go out & see the sights of Bangor.

The itinerary you wrote me—in April or May—sounded wonderful, & I've heard rumors in N.Y. of your trip—I can't remember from whom now. I wonder where you are now—Paris perhaps. You may even have run into Margaret Miller who went over for six weeks, I think she's just back. I envy you very much. I think you went to Greece, too, didn't you? I can't quite believe you'll settle in Naples for a winter though, but maybe you will—the 3 or 4 days I spent there I found very depressing, as a lot of people do. (I've noticed it's only my near-sighted or half-blind friends who profess to like it.) But the time of year & the weather have a lot to do with it—and certainly the gallery there is worth a long stay.

I've just been in Nova Scotia for two weeks. I went down—well, I'll tell you from the beginning. One day when I was visiting Jane Dewey I was sitting out doors with her Audubon bird book trying to identify some sort of sparrow, & I ran into a reference to the "Ipswich Sparrow" which does not live in Ipswich at all but only on Sable Island, which is a sandbar known as "the Graveyard of the Atlantic" about 180 miles off the coast of N.S.—where one of my great-grandfathers & his ship & all hands were supposed to have been lost, and where there are wild ponies, besides the sparrows—& my aunt had, has—she's (Pansy, the pony) about 40 now—one of them. So I've always felt a personal interest in the place. So I thought I'd go and try to write a piece about it, which I have just done—gone, I mean. The piece is just getting under way. It was quite an interesting outing; I had to get permission from Ottawa to get taken out on a lighthouse tender, etc. The actual place is nothing much except sand-dunes like Cape Cod, but its history is spectacular, just the kind of thing I feel you might like, but maybe you know something about it already.

Anyway I'm hoping to sell a travel piece about it and make some money. If I do I may take a trip of some sort, probably a long freighter one. I enjoyed the short one out there so much that I don't want to settle down in N.Y. at all. I sublet for the summer Kappo Phelan Brooks' apt. She was writing, poetry, I think, in the back room, and Jean[1] was writing a novel in the front room, when I took over. It is a very funny place. Maybe you've even seen it. It's Kenyon Brooks' really, I think, but they want to come back Oct. 1st. I have done some work but am way behind schedule on the book of poems. HM[2] wants it all in by Sept. 1st, but I'm afraid I'll never make it. It's now called "Concordance"—I hope you like that. From the title of one poem. I had my doubts but yesterday morning, just as I was leaving the hotel in Halifax, I picked up the Gideon Bible and thought I'd make one of those test-samplings, you know. My finger came right down on the concordance column, so I felt immensely cheered.

I'll be in Stonington about a week, then I'm going to visit Randall at Dennis for about a week. I haven't seen him since I did quite unexpectedly & with great relief at the Academy Award Affair. He's been in Colorado on one of those conferences, I think. I spent an evening with Nathalie shortly before I left—Philip was at Kenyon. Marianne has a selected poems coming out in the fall, and I'm attempting to review it for the *Times*. I don't know why I said I would. I'm hoping to be able to turn it into a sort of poem.

Have you been able to finish any work? I'd love to see a poem. How is Elizabeth's novel progressing? I guess it is really too nice a day to sit here in this running-water, large-saggy-bed room & I'd better go out. It would be nice if you were both coming along for one of my famous little Stonington absinthe parties. (Did I ever tell you that Sally married a Key West eccen-

---

1 Jean Stafford.
2 Houghton Mifflin.

tric?—a Dane, who has lived there for some time on a crazy old boat without any engine in it. She wrote Tom they were buying an engine, & I do so hope they have not managed to get as far as S[1] with it.)

One news item from today's *Boston Advertiser*: "Storm Sweeps on Mexico Gulf." After describing the 125-mile winds, the damage done in Jamaica, the ships lost etc., it says: "Linda Darnell of the movies was on the island, but a mountain range protected her from the worst of the blow." Would that we all had such useful Hollywood connections.

With love to you & Elizabeth & I do hope to see you in foreign parts yet.

Elizabeth

My address is c/o Brooks, 233 East 69th St. Please forgive me for not writing for so long and let me hear from you.

112.

17 Nicholaas Witsenkade
Amsterdam, Holland
November 6, [1951]

Dear Elizabeth:

It's so long since I've written you that I don't even have your address, so I'll send this to Houghton and Mifflin, hoping that they will hand it to you at the moment when you are giving them your finished manuscript. At this point you must be saying "why Holland?" Everyone has. I suppose it's the carless automobileless man, who has no command of foreign languages or scoutsmanship's substitute for burying himself in Ischia or Sardinia. It is quiet and still; as far as the outer world goes, I guess it has been still since the seventeenth century, when it was at the full tide, a baroque, worldly, Presbyterian, canal-and-brick, glorious Boston. I've been reading Motley and Fromentin,[2] and rather luxuriate in it; but it is prosy and empty, and Elizabeth doesn't like it at all. However, we have no money to unsettle again until May. By the way, the returns from my book have been rather a shock: the royalties just about cancel off the cost for revisions.

The summer was a tremendous whirl, like going through college and graduate school in one year on pills that prevent your sleeping at night. We went everywhere I wrote you we would, except Venice and Vienna. I can't

1 Stonington.
2 John Lathrop Motley, *The Rise of the Dutch Republic* (1855); Eugène Fromentin, *Les Maîtres d'autrefois* (*The Masters of Past Time*) (1876).

resist putting down the names: Naples, Barri, Lecci, Brindisi, Athens, Istanbul, Bursa, Smyrna, Athens, Delphi, Corinth, Sunnium, Naples, Genoa, Paris, Versailles, Chartres, Mont Saint Michel, The Loire Country, Fontainbleau, the Basque country, Lourdes, Pau, Brussels, Antwerp, The Hague, Haarlem, Amsterdam . . . O and London, and Eton. Also I've read gobs of Italian, German, French and Latin poetry, Greek, French and Turkish history, and art books, till my head rocks, as though it held the lantern-slides of the world. I'm convinced none of us can possibly survive on into our forties, except as hermits, unless we become bores; and that takes some doing. You can't be a happy bore without talking, without having a line that will bore anyone of any age and in any circumstances, one that is stereotyped, demands no spontaneous thought, and yet is universal enough to find openings everywhere, and blanket conversation. Since this summer I'm well on the road.

We are just finished with Mother's visit. She is a very competent, stubborn, uncurious, unBohemian woman with a genius for squeezing luxury out of rocks. That is, she has a long memory for pre-war and pre-first-world war service, and thinks nothing of calling the American ambassador if there's no toilet-paper on the train; etc. Well, under the best conditions, of course, I can't begin to make sense out of her or to her. Each year since I was eighteen, it's gotten worse. I don't suppose you can imagine three months with the three of us, all behaving very badly, then being very self-sacrificing, and fuming inside like the burning stuffings of an overstuffed Dutch chair. Now it's over; we have emerged triumphantly—so we thought, but there's a relapse and weakness, such as one gets from sulfa drugs.

At first I thought *Concordance* was too snug; but I see it's right and impregnable, as my more flashy, high-sounding titles are not. I still wish you'd put your short stories in, first because I'd like to see them, all together, but secondly because I think your poems and stories explain and light each other up, and that anyone will or should be dazzled by the combination.

Elizabeth has just finished a story[1] that I think is much her best and sent it off to *PR*. I'm deep in the thin first drafts of a long monologue about a sort of 16th century Mrs. Dawson.[2] Write me some American gossip, and heavens' sake hurry over here.

Love,
Cal

How's your poetry residence going? I've applied for Salzburg next summer.

1 Probably "Two Recent Travellers," *The Kenyon Review* (Summer 1953).
2 "The Banker's Daughter" (RL-*CP*).

TWO

1951-1958

113.

Dear Cal:

I sent you a postcard just as I was leaving N.Y., but I had to put so many stamps on it I probably completely covered up my message. It seems to me I've written to you a couple of times—Florence, Naples, or someplace—but c/o American Express so maybe sometime or other you'll get them. It wasn't until I had decided on this crazy trip and went down to see the Rahvs one evening before sailing (as I then thought, I was held up a couple of weeks by the dock strikes) that I knew where you were. Philip said you intended spending the winter in Amsterdam which somehow surprised me, but maybe no more than my decision to go through the Straits of Magellan will surprise you . . . At least I think that's where I'm bound for. At present we're approaching Santos, a couple of days late because of storms, and first I'm going to visit in Rio for a while. In case you get this before Christmas—c/o Soares, Rua Antonio Vieira 5, Leme, Rio de Janeiro, Brazil—will reach me, if you write, as I hope you will. After that, I guess, c/o the Vassar Club, N.Y. They're kind of hopeless about messages but maybe they'll be better about forwarding. Oh dear, there is so much to talk about. I wish you & Elizabeth could join me in this dining-room-saloon-etc., for a scotch & soda right now before lunch. (This is a very small freighter—smaller than yours I think. It sailed from the dock next [to] the Fern line. It's Norwegian, and hired by the Duponts to take an enormous cargo of jeeps, combines, etc. There are 9 passengers; that includes a sad young missionary—"Assemblies of God"—and wife and three little boys. The rest of us are an Uruguayan consul from N.Y., a refined but sea-sick lady, and another lady whom fortunately I like very much, otherwise these 17 days wd have been a little too much—a 6 ft. ex–

police woman who has retired after being head of the Women's Jail in Detroit for 26 ys. She's about 70; very gentle and polite—tells how she accidentally solved such and such a murder, in an apologetic way, & confessed she was written up in "True Detective Stories." She also has day-dreams of going down through the Straits & up the West coast—has also invited me to inspect a few jails with her en route.)[1]

It is funny, but I almost went to Amsterdam too—before I knew you were there—but I couldn't seem to get a cheap passage. How is it? And how is it in the winter? Lots & lots of paintings?—& what about the language?

With me on the boat I brought yr review of Randall[2] and Randall's review of you[3] . . . & I've been brooding over them both. I wrote an I hope, withering one of a book called "The Riddle of Emily Dickinson" for *The New Republic* the other day[4]—now I'm working on Miss Moore for the *Times* but find it very difficult since I left my original bright ideas behind in N.Y. I don't remember whether I wrote you, or if I did you probably didn't get it, about visiting Randall and Mackie in September. It was all rather distressing because I like them both.[5] I can understand what you mean about missing him—you wrote in the spring—his reviews infuriate me and yet that activity and that minute-to-minute *devotion* to criticism is really wonderful. I think he admires Richard Wilbur too much, though. (This is trusting you've seen the last *PR*)—I thought the Leavis piece on Pound was excellent, but probably you won't.[6]

The missionary is dictating a letter to his wife at the next table. They are so sad, and the worst aspect of the trip has been the two Sundays we've spent at sea on which he held a "small interdenominational service." There are so few of us we all had to attend and sing "Nearer my God to Thee" (after he told the story of how the people on the Titanic sang it as they went down). The 3 tiny boys sang "Jesus loves me this I know" in Spanish, and a song, with gestures, about how the house built on the sand went *splash*. I'd always wondered how it did go, but I had never thought of it as splash somehow.

I've been completely without news since getting aboard. There is a Nor-

---

1 Cf. "Arrival at Santos," lines 29–32 (EB-*CP*).

2 "With Wild Dogmatism: *The Seven-League Crutches* by Randall Jarrell," *The New York Times Book Review* (Oct. 7, 1951); see RL-*CPR*.

3 Randall Jarrell, "A View of Three Poets," *Partisan Review* (Nov.–Dec. 1951); Richard Wilbur is reviewed in same article.

4 EB, "Love from Emily," *The New Republic* (Aug. 27, 1951).

5 Mackie and Randall Jarrell were separating; they divorced in October 1952.

6 F. R. Leavis, "Ezra Pound: The Promise and the Disaster," *Partisan Review* (Nov.–Dec. 1951).

wegian news report over the wireless but the officers although very nice are the silent Viking type—you probably ran into that, too,—and don't translate. Please write to me. Send me a poem (that seems unbelievable at the moment but I can think of no Christmas present I'd like better.) I hope to get around to the west coast, maybe write an article about Punta Arenas or something on the way, and stay in Peru and Ecuador until April or May, then come back in time to put in an appearance at Bryn Mawr. Pearl Kazin went down to Rio not long ago and got married to Victor Kraft. I expect to see her. I saw Alfred just before leaving & he raved, absolutely, about "Mother Marie."[1] I must stop—obviously having no literary information that could be of the slightest interest to you,—and fill out my baggage declaration. *Please* write me about Amsterdam, how you both are, what you are each writing, etc.

> With love,
> Elizabeth

114.

February 26, [1952]

Dear Elizabeth:

I find that every day I less like writing letters and more like getting them; it's the same with poems. I.e. I am waiting for them to come in dreams: a first draft one night, uncanny revisions the next two. No, I think I'm still up to filing them.

We've spent the winter a few feet away from each other in a plump, fuzzy red plush room, reading. We both enjoy reading aloud to each other and detest listening. I'm becoming a free-trade nineteenth century liberal (bourgeois) and Elizabeth is becoming a bourgeois conservative. It's very confusing because I still use a reactionary rhetoric and she uses a radical covenanter's rhetoric.

Holland is a crowded flat country with a grey flat climate. Everyone speaks and reads *fluently* French, English and German—more of each than the average native intellectual. Their literature is, I think, something of a commentary. We like the people we have met better than literary people anywhere. However, one year is enough.

In May we are going through Germany to Vienna, then I will be teaching at Salzburg from the sixth of July until the twentieth of August. We'll spend

1 Alfred Kazin; "Mother Marie Therese" (RL-*CP*).

the winter in Florence or Rome. I've almost persuaded the Taylors to join us. But they are almost as hard to pin down as you.

Can't you be persuaded? Think of the "values." You can live like a princess on your trust fund. Endless short, infinitely varied coastal excursions to keep you from getting restless. Wine with every meal. Short run-ins with every slight acquaintance of every slight acquaintance you've ever met etc., etc. But best of all, lots of talk with me. Somehow I haven't made this too attractive. But really, you must know all the thousand sensible reasons for coming.

Joe Frank was here the other day. I was hoping for news of you, but he's even more out of touch than I am. He has a friend who came to Paris on a Fulbright[1] and is now living on his wife (not white-slaving) and ruminating an essay on James, the Racine of English novelists. That's what happens. Joe seems to be flourishing, though, and is full of travel, foreign languages, and abstruse essays that he publishes once a quarter.

I've had a weighty winter trying to avoid writing and household chores: the Nuremburg trials, Hannah Arendt, Lord Macaulay's *History*, etc.[2] There's a lot more, and I now know something of French and Italian—nothing yet of Dutch or German, to which I thought it would be a stepping-stone. Saw an *Othello* (thinking it would be *Otello*, we've become opera addicts) in which Othello was the villain. Iago was a lovable Breughelesque extrovert. Twenty grand days in London, just missed the funeral.[3] We heard every minute of it, though, for ten days on the radio. Elizabeth's iconoclastic Calvinism has obsessed her royalty; it's like a square circle. All day one subtile ramified theory follows another. I see her brooding on her red plush sofa; suddenly her face lights up: "it's because they're more ordinary than other people."

Sometimes, I suspect we see too much of one another. Accordingly, I have borrowed a houseboat for four days. I've had a glorious time, rummaged through all the books, broken the filament of the oil reading lamp, unprimed the toilet-pump, let the furnace go out, had meals of cold oatmeal soaked in cold milk, and accomplished none of my fine resolutions, except writing you, Randall and my Cousin Harriet. Don't see how you could think Wilbur flattered by Randall's review; what makes it hurt is R's leaning over backwards to be friendly—caressed by a tiger.

---

1 Probably William Burford.

2 International Military Tribunal, *The Trial of Major German War Criminals: Proceedings* (1946); Hannah Arendt, *The Origins of Totalitarianism* (1951); Thomas Babbington Macaulay, *History of England* (1849–61).

3 George VI was buried on February 15, 1952.

Write soon and tell us about Brazil. Why Brazil? That's what everyone asks us.

Love,
   Cal

P.S. You know we are a unique class, the only three American writers of our generation who don't have to work. Usury has made us; and I can hear Karl Marx muttering out a review to prove that our biases are identical.

115.

c/o de Macedo Soares
Rua Antonio Vieira 5, Leme
Rio de Janeiro, Brazil[1]
March 21st, 1952

Dear Cal:

Heavens, I started this yesterday & got interrupted & left the typewriter uncovered over night & have just had to brush off a large thick cobweb. I have a letter written Nov. 6th. I think I wrote to you just about the same time—I wrote a couple of times but I'm not sure you got either—but I just got the Nov. 6th one a week or so ago, and then right after it the Feb. 26th one. The first was apparently in that batch of mail the Vassar club pigeonholed for over three months. Well, I'm sorry. I've been wanting to hear from you so much, not knowing whether American Express in Amsterdam would reach you or not, etc. (That's where I sent one letter, I think.) I started out intending to go all over the continent but I seem to have become a Brazilian home-body, and I get just as excited now over a jeep trip to buy kerosene in the next village as I did in November at the thought of my trip around the Horn. I wasn't even particularly interested in Brazil to start with, but it was my freighter's first stop. In fact, I wanted to go around the world ending up about now visiting *you*, only they had made some mistake about my reservations on *that* freighter, so I haphazardly settled on South America. I have some Brazilian friends in Rio I used to know in N.Y.—so I went to visit for two weeks and have stayed four months. I haven't been in Rio much of the time, though—just go for a haircut or to see about a visa once in a while. Lota de M-S—my hostess, has an apartment there on that famous carte postale beach but lives mostly in the country,

---

1 The Rio apartment of Maria Carlota (Lota) Costellat de Macedo Soares; EB was writing from Samambaia, however.

though that gentle expression scarcely seems to fit, in Petrópolis, a mountain resort about 40 miles off—magnificent and wild. She is building an ultra-modern house up on the side of a black granite mountain, with a waterfall at one end, clouds coming into the living room in the middle of the conversation, etc. The house is unfinished and we are using oil-lamps, no floors—just cement covered with dogs' footprints. The "family" has consisted of another American girl, also a N.Y. friend of mine,[1] 2 Polish counts[2] for a while, the architect[3] over week-ends etc., all a strange tri- or quadri-lingual hodgepodge that I like very much. After a couple of weeks of rain (which, by some racial illusion, I think, is called the "summer") the cook left, and for about a month I did the cooking. I like to cook, etc., but I'm not used to being confronted with the raw materials, all un-shelled, unblanched, un-skinned, or un-dead. Well, I can cook goat now—with wine sauce. And we have a new cook, from the "north" (the "north" is regarded a little the way we regard the "south") who came armed with a gigantic chromium crucifix. She "loves nature," so we hope she'll stay. She loves it so much though that when you want her she's usually out gathering flowers up on the mountain. The kitchen would do Max Schling credit, orchids and all. This morning I decided I wanted an egg. I said 5 minutes, and it arrived very watery, and she said there were 2 clocks in the kitchen, and they are not running exactly together so she had no way of timing the egg, naturally.

I find it hard to stop when I get to describing, as you see, but I have had a really nice time, and I am coming back, because I still want to see some more of S.A. and do some more writing about it. I have to put in an appearance at Bryn Mawr in May. I'm leaving in a month, but shall probably return in July. Then, I think by next winter I'll have had enough for a while and will have saved enough money to go to Europe, from here, probably, or Buenos Aires. I don't know whether you'd like it or not, and I've seen so little of the country, actually, and it is so tremendous. Probably it is all too formless for you, and not nearly enough people. Lota knows "everybody"; I've met, or looked at, many of the literary lights, but as she says, she's "retired" and very fed up with Brazil, as all the Brazilians I've met are. They yearn for 1. Paris, 2. New York. (N.Y. is a recent taste, just 10 years old—it was considered rather vulgar to go there before and Lota was much criticized for spending over 2 years there). There is a great Catholic revival on, I gather, and large families are

1 Mary Stearns Morse.
2 Unidentified; however, in a letter to Ilse and Kit Barker, EB writes that on her birthday, "a neighbor [called Tomska] whom I scarcely know—because we have no known language in common, for one thing—came bringing me my lifelong dream—a TOUCAN . . . The woman who gave him & her husband are Polish refugees and ran the zoo in Warsaw, I think it was"; EB-*OA*, 234.
3 Sérgio Bernardes.

the style: 10 or 12, all the boys named "Jose" something or other and all the girls named "Maria" something or other. These are always shortened into absurd nicknames that stick for life. I met a very elegant "Magoo," for Maria Augusta—or "Dona Baby," for an elderly lady. I am now "Dona Eliza-bethchy"—and you are a Mynheer I suppose. (Almost every idea I have on the subject of Holland comes from "Hans Brinker or the Silver Skates," which I still know almost by heart.[1]) Well, I don't mind the large families if they'd only confine them to the upper class (and how it simplifies things to have almost no middle class). I have started writing again at last—finished two longish poems. I don't know anything about my book and HM has abandoned me, I guess. I haven't done much reading, although we have a wonderful library—now reading some Portuguese poetry. I can read it because of knowing Spanish, but I can't talk it at all—everyone I meet usually speaking excellent English or French.

I just wrote to Randall the day your second letter came. Strange masses of mail from the Library of C. I *saw* that Whittall poetry nook, or did I tell you—and *ye gods*. I suppose everyone will soon have to resign. At least that seems like the only dignified thing to do. Yes, we do worship the dollar, that's all there is to say. However, they worship the cruzeiro here, and I suppose the guilder or something where you are. I saw a recent Miss Bogan—about Randall, and *admiring* Eberhart.[2] I didn't think she was *that* easily taken in! I see the *New Yorker*—a month late—airmail *N.Y. Times*, air mail *Time* (full of lies even more than in the U.S., I think). This afternoon a neighbor is coming up the mountain with *Theater Arts* and the last *PR*—I wonder how many subscribers it has in Brazil. This is a young and very fashionable girl—very odd.

For heaven sakes—please keep me informed about your addresses so I can write to you, and I hope you'll write to me. I'm probably going to need it much more than you are. This will reach me until April 19th, then I'm going to Key West for a week, then Hotel Grosvenor, 5th Ave. and 10th St., for six weeks. I want to see some poems. Antonio Vieira, Lota tells me, was a minor Portuguese Saint who "suffered from bi-localization" (much funnier in French.) I am now studying the poems of the most popular modern Portuguese poet, Fernando Pessoa—ever heard of him?—who had a four-split personality; wrote four different kinds of poetry under four different names—volumes of each—and committed suicide sometime in the 30's, though if alive he'd be just Miss Moore's age. As I've already written to

1 Mary Mapes Dodge, *Hans Brinker, or the Silver Skates* (1865).
2 Louise Bogan, "Books," *The New Yorker* (Feb. 16, 1952).

Randall—maybe personality splits are particularly Portuguese—I've run into a few real-life ones, too.

Oh, my title is now (has been for months) *A Cold Spring*—a poem titled that, too. And now I suppose it will appear in November.

Give my love to Elizabeth. What is she writing? Please write again, sooner. I have a TOUCAN—named Uncle Sam in a chauvinistic outburst. He's wonderful, gulps down jewelry or pretends to, can play catch with grapes, and has brilliant blue eyes like neon lights.

With love,
    Elizabeth

116.

April 24, [1952]

Dear Elizabeth:

Our apartment is right now full of half-filled half open suit-cases, leaves are beginning to hide the canal, the sun is shining, the radio is playing a sort of Indian Summer Mozart minuet, and each of us knows that if he can only stall long enough the other will do the packing. Our long green coffin-like trunk that we counted on to hold almost everything is brimful of books.

I've gone music-mad, have just heard Bach's two *Passions* each twice, and now we are going to Brussels to hear five Mozart operas in six nights. I know all about the sonata form (a misnomer according to Tovey[1]), canons, and modulations, but have difficulty in distinguishing them when heard, and have so far failed to convince the cynical and skeptical Eliz. H. Lowell that I am not tone-deaf. I always reply by asking her "just what is a quaver?" or "When is Haydn going to modulate back into C minor?" Her replies are more airy than clear.

We have quite a group of Dutch friends. They are all very loving, urbane and hard-headed about each other. The way one would like to picture, alas, the *PR* people. One in particular likes to talk intellectual shop even more than I do.[2] We spend days that go from 11 in the morning till one the next morning reading Dutch poetry. He is able to quote Goethe's maxims, Stendahl, La Bruyère, Auden, Yeats, Valéry, Valery-Nicolas Larbaud and Randall by the hour. He can now do the same with you. He's rather like Mann's Leverkühn[3]: dry, enthusiastic, exact, and with a terrifying knowledge of German

1 Sir Donald Francis Tovey, *Essays in Musical Analysis*, 6 vols. (1935–39), which RL had read at Yaddo in 1948.
2 W. F. van Leeuwen.
3 Protagonist of Thomas Mann's *Doctor Faustus* (1947).

philosophy. The other day Bill Burford was here. He was full of himself because he is writing a long autobiographical poem, and as you know his conversation is a pure centerless flux. The three of us spent a long night. Burford managed to drink an entire quart of Dutch gin, so one had the contrast of unimaginable coherence and unimaginable incoherence. The next day my Dutch friend said, "You always felt he was about to make a point."

Elizabeth is rather down on our abode, and I think your Brazil is the one trip taken by some one else that she can bear to contemplate without envy. However, it sounds delightful. You always make me feel that I have a rather obvious breezy, impersonal liking for the great and obvious—in contrast with your adult personal feeling for the odd and genuine; but I'm not sure that Holland doesn't beat Brazil—it's not picturesque, healthy, spectacularly on the up or down, just like or just unlike home, had a post-war literary revival, not very much of anything except flat, canal-checkered and Dutch. It's probably odd and genuine; but then what isn't? Well, it *was* odd and genuine to have come here.

Elizabeth has just said the only advantage of marriage is that you can be as gross, slovenly, mean and brutally verbose as you want. This was re my asking her if she had ever told Mary McCarthy off. Can you imagine anyone telling off either Mary or Randall? At Harvard I once heard Mary say to Randall: "I think your poetry is much more obscure than Cal's." This was an obscure but hurting blow at both of us. Somehow I got caught between them. Randall laid down the law, but it wasn't a pleasure for anyone. How did you like your fresh girlish appearance in R's polemic on the critics "The Age of Criticism"?[1] I think this was one subject in which he might well have called names.

Wonderful comic strip scene: man large and smiling stretched out on a sofa with a glass of milk; nervous, puzzle-faced wife standing by a chair piled with books. Husband: "I'd get a step-ladder if you are going to fix that roller-spring. It's dangerous to stand on books. You might fall and hurt yourself. Remember how George Fink warned his wife about dragging that trunk upstairs." We're very light-hearted about leaving.

Write us care of the American Express in Vienna. We'll be there and at Salzburg most of the summer. My usual refrain: When are you sailing so I can meet you at the dock with champagne?

Love,

Cal

---

1 Randall Jarrell, "The Age of Criticism," *Partisan Review* (March–April 1952).

117.

[Postcard: Statue of "Germanina," Niederwald monument, Weinstadt Rudesheim am Rhein]

[June 1952]

Dear Elizabeth:

Apologies for my joint Paris-postcard;[1] we had a terrific, too gay 3 weeks there with Allen and others. Now I hear from a fellow named Canfield[2] that you are moving to Brazil forever. Impossible choice even for the author of *North & South*. Hear you're in wonderful tanned, talkative shape with a finished book. I'm talkative but untanned.

Love,
Cal

118.

Burlington Apts.
Burlington St.
Iowa City, Iowa.
June 14, 1953

Dear Elizabeth:

Medias res:—We've just bought a seventeen year old Packard that an old professor looked after like a baby, or rather far better. I've just gotten my driver's license, and discover unexpectedly that I am slow and reliable. We go for pleasure drives along the unscenic Iowa river, and are almost senile with joy and fatuousness.

I'm tied up with teaching from now until next June: Indiana till the first of August, back here in September, Cincinnati from February till June. After that we hope to get a house and write as worldly people with a stake in the world, or President Eisenhower—wasn't the election a misfortune!

I gather from Nathalie Rahv and other people that Brazil is incredibly the perfect place for you, and that you have good friends there. But you must keep covering the entire Atlantic seaboard with long stops in New York and Massachusetts, so that I can see you. I don't like your removal at all.

Last night I had a dream. I was in France. Paris was again falling to the Germans, but it had become such a habit that one had to look closely to see that anyone really cared. I arrived in Paris (from the front, I think, but there wasn't much of one); went to a party, where I was surrounded by acquain-

---

1 The postcard does not survive.
2 Unidentified.

tances. They became distant and shadowy when I approached them. Suddenly I saw you and gave you a tremendous hug. You moved to another table. I said: "I know where there are a couple of good French restaurants." You said: "They're all French here."

You see. You must come back.

What are you writing? Elizabeth has just finished two good essays and a story,[1] and I've three or four poems that are coming out in *Kenyon* and *PR*.[2] Also a pile of unfinished stuff.

Write and tell us how you are, and I'll answer with a good letter. Elizabeth sends her love.

Love,
  Cal

I had your address from Nathalie, but [it] vanished in a cleaning of my billfold. I'm sending this through Houghton & Mifflin. If you stay in Brazil ten years we might drive. Are there bridges over the Panama Canal?

119.

[Blank postcard]

[July 7, 1953]

Dear Elizabeth:

On the tail of my other note, but sent care of *PR* this time. I liked your dirty child story[3] very much, and seem to remember you're talking about it at Stonington. You must get out a book. Stories as well as poems. You must come back sometime soon. I'm teaching all year—never again, but for the moment I am a pillar of strength and geniality. Our old car beats anything. I never walk and even beg to be allowed to get the groceries, and lie awake thinking up useless errands.

Love,
  Cal

---

1 Elizabeth Hardwick, "The Subjugation of Women" (review of Simone de Beauvoir), *Partisan Review* (May–June 1953), "Memoirs, Conversations and Letters," *Partisan Review* (Nov.–Dec. 1953); and "Two Recent Travelers," *The Kenyon Review* (Summer 1953).
2 "Beyond the Alps," *The Kenyon Review* (Summer 1953), and "Inauguration Day: January 1953" and "A Mad Negro Soldier Confined at Munich," *Partisan Review* (Nov.–Dec. 1953); see RL-*CP*.
3 "Gwendolyn," *The New Yorker* (June 27, 1953); see EB-*CPR*.

120.

Samambaia[1]—place where I live, near Petrópolis. Rio is the address. But you gave 2! Airmail here is 10 cents. Your letter came by boat.

July 28th, 1953

Dearest Cal:

How *wonderful* to hear from you! I have been wanting to for so long, and I don't know whether you'll believe me or not, but I have right here two envelopes addressed and stamped, for you, about six months apart—one c/o the University of Iowa—only I never could find out where it is, so that's as far as that address gets, and the other c/o Harcourt Brace that gets as far as "Dear Cal." But now I have an address and you have an address, and I guess I'll just plunge in. There are so many things and they intercommunicate as *House and Garden* (that I've just been reading) says, so it will probably be a mess.

I read the interview in *Poetry*, my eyes glued to the page, of course, and it sounded most exhausting, and I was delighted to be mentioned with favor, of course.[2]

I read Elizabeth's review of Simone de Beauvoir's book, also pretty glued to the page. I had read it in French, my dear, a couple of years ago and got rather annoyed, although fundamentally of course I agree with her—and I thought Elizabeth did a fine job and she was the only reviewer I've seen who made fun of the ridiculous biological section as well, about spiders and oysters, etc., that I'm sure SB just "lifted" out of something. But then I think all the existialist writers in their urge for output at all costs do an awful lot of lifting.

I read your sonnet in *PR* and admired its undiminished un-pulled punch, but wanted very much to know who it was about.[3]

I read an ad for *Perspectives* mentioning your poem about Santayana,[4] and immediately sent for it. But they can't mail it out of the country. I thought that was the whole idea of the thing, or else it's supposed to be stunning the Brazilians here with American culture, in Portuguese, but it isn't. But I have asked Pearl Kazin to mail me a copy.

I read you in Italian in the last *Botteghe Oscure* that I just received this week—sounds grand, as far as I can judge.[5]

---

1 *Giant fern*; see "Song for the Rainy Season," line 15 (EB-*CP*).
2 "What about American poets? I asked. With the exception of Elizabeth Bishop and Randall Jarrell, he confined his remarks carefully to the older poets"; John McCormick, "Falling Asleep Over Grillparzer: An Interview with Robert Lowell," *Poetry* (Jan. 1953).
3 "Epitaph of a Fallen Poet," *Partisan Review* (Jan.–Feb. 1953); cf. "Words for Hart Crane" (RL-*CP*).
4 "Santayana's Farewell to His Nurses," *Perspectives USA* (1953); cf. "For George Santayana" (RL-*CP*).
5 "Il cimitero dei Quaccheri a Nantucket," trans. Rolando Anzilotti, *Botteghe Oscure* (1953); see "The Quaker Graveyard in Nantucket" (RL-*CP*).

So you see I've been keeping tabs. But you can't have been reading me because there hasn't been anything, to speak of. It was nice of you to like that little story because I really don't think it amounts to two pins. However, I feel a debt of gratitude to it because it's the first thing I ever wrote right off on the typewriter, in one day, just the way it is, and it started me off on several more that have been going much more easily than they used to. I think when you see them you will see they are much better. I am even doing one about 75–100 pages, my first Brazilian story, a length I never dreamed of before.[1]

My poems, *A Cold Spring* must come out late next winter or bust.

I'd like to follow it in the fall with a book of stories, but I am afraid the total effect is pretty "precious," "lovely, sensitive prose," etc. I am also translating, with Lota, the friend I'm living with here, a famous Brazilian book, a young girl's diary,[2] that I'm positive will be a success if we can sell it to a U.S. publisher, & I am in the middle of a poem called "Tierra del Fuego Unvisited,"[3] although I still have hopes of getting there.

Oh, and of course I read "Poets Among Us" in *Vogue* (that title sounds like "Beware of Pickpockets," doesn't it.) It was wonderful the way they managed to make it sound as if you and I had sort of robbed Jean Garrigue, etc., of her rightful due.[4] My friend Tom Wanning—remember him—wrote me a letter starting, "You Old Chiseller, you!" (The blurb said my poetry was written like *chiseling in quartz*—quite a feat.[5]) But "women poets" either have to be COLD or HOT, obviously.

And Oh dear! Randall on the subject of women![6] Why didn't he think it over a little more! He can't really think all those clichés or Mackie would have left years ago, I should think . . .

—a lot of thinks here—

Margaret Marshall, I think it was, wrote me he had married again, a woman with some children, but I haven't written or heard from him.[7] What do you hear?

1 EB wrote "Gwendolyn" and "In the Village" during this period (EB-*CPR*), as well as unfinished pieces about Brazil; she also wrote "The Shampoo," "The Mountain," and "Arrival at Santos" (EB-*CP*), and drafted "Crossing the Equator" (see EB-*EAP*).

2 *The Diary of "Helena Morley,"* trans. EB (1957).

3 EB never completed this poem and no draft survives.

4 *Vogue*'s profiles of RL and EB list their prizes and prize monies. Jean Garrigue is "elusive, almost unknown, appears as one of the most rewarding and least rewarded poets in the United States . . . Although she also contributes to almost every literary periodical, the single plum her work has brought her was a Fellowship in Creative Writing at Bard College"; "Poets Among Us," *Vogue* (April 15, 1953).

5 EB is "a woman of extreme heights and depths of mood, writes a cool, pared verse as if she were chiselling some remarkable quartz"; "Poets Among Us," *Vogue* (April 15, 1953).

6 Randall Jarrell, "Woman," *Botteghe Oscure* (1952).

7 Randall Jarrell married Mary von Schrader in 1952.

I am having some poems in English-Portuguese in a literary supplement, here—there are no magazines, so the newspapers cover literature in varying degrees of seriousness. *The* Brazilian poet, a man of about 65, Manuel Bandeira, is doing them and doing them extremely well, I think. I have been trying to return the compliment, I've read quite a lot of Brazilian poetry by now, and it is all graceful, and slight, I think, although Bandeira is sometimes extremely witty, like a gentler Cummings. But how hopeless to write Portuguese. But I can read Camões, etc., pretty well now, and he—his sonnets—are superb—as good as any in English, certainly.

(I'll send you a translation of one, maybe.)

Mr. Zabel is here now to give some lectures. I'm not in Rio, so probably won't hear any, but he is coming up for a day here with a journalist lady, a friend of his and Lota's. I don't know him—met him once at the Rahvs' (rather to my surprise) on my flying trip to New York about a year ago, and I thought he was rather chilly, but Lota knew him when he was here before so maybe we'll have a pleasantly literary day.

And that covers the world of letters, I think, for the time being. I am delighted to hear about Elizabeth's work and where is it going to appear? I get *PR, Hudson, & Kenyon, Botteghe Oscure, Poetry*—well, quite a lot of things, down to the *Farmer's Digest*, and Lota gets the plastic arts, and down to *Ellery Queen's Monthly*—but I do miss "little" magazines sometimes, probably.

I think it was extremely sweet of you to give me a witticism *in a dream*—it shows real, subconscious generosity.

Where is the poem about the Dutch Carley-type? You know I sometimes dream of *her?* I wonder why. And now that it's all remote you should sometime have Tom Wanning do his imitation of her: a conversation about Beethoven's *Quartets*. She also once exclaimed to Tom, referring to you, "I do wish I knew what makes that boy *tick*."

Well, I hope you are ticking away like the finest old-fashioned alarm-clock. And I hope you drive the Packard the same way its previous owner did. I want to learn to drive, but there is never a stretch of road appropriate, all up and down, or round and round, or full of Brazilian drivers, who never bother to learn at all. Or else there aren't any roads. That's the real problem here; *every*thing hinges on that.

Well, Brazil is a much more unlikely place than Amsterdam, certainly, and I'd never have picked it. But it is a combination of circumstances that make it wonderful for me now, and it really looks as though I'd stay. By next spring I think I'll be able to go away—probably to Europe, for about six months. The next trip will be to New York, for a winter, I imagine. But I don't feel "out of touch" or "expatriated" or anything like that, or suffer from lack of intellectual life, etc. I was always too shy to have much "inter-communication" in New York, anyway, and I was miserably lonely there most of the time. Here I am extremely happy, for the first time in my life. I live in a spectacularly beautiful place; we have between us about 3,000 books now; I know, through Lota, most of the Brazilian "intellectuals" already, and I find the people frank, startlingly so, until you get used to Portuguese vocab-ularies, extremely affectionate, an atmosphere that I just lap up—no I guess I mean loll in—after that dismal year in Washington and that dismaler win-ter at Yaddo when I thought my days were numbered and there was nothing to be done about it. I arrived to visit Lota just at the point where she really wanted someone to stay with her in the new house she was building. We'd known each other well in New York but I hadn't seen her for five or six years. She wanted me to stay; she offered to build me a studio, picture en-closed. I certainly didn't really want to wander around the world in a drunken daze for the rest of my life. So it's all fine & dandy.

But Brazil is really a horror; but sometime I must tell you more. You would be really fascinated by the family histories. Rio society is beyond be-lief. Proust in the tropics with a samba instead of Vinteuil's little phrase[1]— no, that's cheap,—but sort of.

Where are you going to get your house? What are you teaching at all these places? (Sometimes I think I should come back and start taking courses from all my friends. I have an uneasy feeling they know so much I don't.) How is your health? Your spirits sound very good.

I'm sending some pictures. Please write soon again. Now you are in Indi-ana, I guess, on your way to Iowa. Heavens, I've never been to Chicago, even. Well, a few more stories to the *New Yorker* and I can rocket to the moon if I care to, it seems to me. Do write and tell me gossip. How is Nathalie? I've been thinking she might come here on an architectural jaunt sometime.

Give my love to Elizabeth. With lots for yourself, as always,

Elizabeth

Here I am "Dona Elizabetchy."—always first names. You'd be "Seu Roberto." No, I guess having a degree, you'd be "Doutor Roberto."

"Caligula" would surprise no one,—I know a Tacito, an Aristides, a Theo-philis, a Praxiteles,—& the nicknames are marvelous—Magu is the cutest—a friend named Maria Augusta. Lota is really Maria Carlota + 3 more names.

1 The phrase from a sonata that haunted Proust's character Swann in *À la recherche du temps perdu.*

P.S. I have opened this up to add something I forgot to ask you completely, so maybe I am rather out of touch, after all. Whatever has happened about the Library of Congress? Have there been any meetings or anything? The last word I had was a letter from Phyllis months and months ago now, and I think Dr. Williams was there,[1] or partly there, or about to be there, or something. Never a word about a meeting last spring or winter or anything. I began to think I should resign, of course,—although for all I know I've been blackballed by now, and I wrote a letter to Mrs. Biddle from whom I'd had a note at Christmas, to ask her. I like her very much and think she has a very sensible attitude about the Fellows, etc. But she hasn't answered. Maybe she didn't get it. If it no longer exists I think someone should have let me know, or if *I* no longer exist. Will you tell me? I was pretty disgusted when I went there the last time with that ROOM, etc., and Aiken wrote me once in a while about goings on. I meant to get to Washington a year ago, but I didn't have time. My idea was to hold onto being a Fellow until I'd been able to attend one meeting, and then to resign, but now I don't know.

It just occurred to me that I think Randall and Simone de Beauvoir should exchange a few ideas—or hormones, and then try again. But really, the supreme condescension of Randall's poem! It makes me feel that women should have the Vote.

I am getting old & sentimental, but now that I have a studio I think I'd like to have some photographs to put in it. I have only one, of Marianne. Could you give me one of you?—or one of you & Elizabeth if you have that.

And—one more request—I have here a book that belongs to Frank Parker that I swore I would send back to him. Can you tell me where he is and if it is feasible now? And which *is* your address: Burlington St. or Summit Street?

    Mine is: Rua Antonio Vieira 5, Leme
             Rio de Janeiro

That's Lota's Rio apartment. Antonio Vieira was a magnificent writer and a queer saint, too—

---

1 William Carlos Williams was appointed poetry consultant to the Library of Congress in 1952 but did not serve.

121.

Dear Elizabeth:

I think about you continually—you and your studio and your Brazilian world. I'm sure you are as happy as you sound. But I don't approve at all. Like a rheumatic old aunt, I would gladly spoil all your fun just to have you back. I think I'll try and have payments on your trust fund stopped.

We've just "bought" a house in Duxbury, Mass.: 1740, red cedar shingled, 1950 oil furnace, eight rooms, kitchen, garage, three acres, stream, flagpole, ten miles from Plymouth, forty from Boston, ten thousand dollars mortgage owing—it's ours! We'll be moving in early in May, when I finally get through the last of my teaching. You must come then and we'll build a replica of your Brazilian house, and you can swing through the years back and forth from one to the other like a pendulum.

This letter may have a peculiar rhythm—that's because I've just read in *Time* that I'll have cancer of the throat in six years if I go on smoking fifty cigarettes a day (Elizabeth's figure for me). I don't think I'm scared enough to stop, but I'm starting my second day. It's surprisingly easy (anyone can do it) and unpleasant. Writing this letter is difficult; it's as though I were drunk or asleep. (You wish you were both as soon as you start to do anything that requires any thought or concentration at all.) Elizabeth started stopping a month ago, and was very Spartan and undemonstrative about it; I don't think she suffered. Now after listening to me for a few hours groaning and boasting, she's ready to quit.

I guess you've heard about Dylan Thomas's death.[1] He died four days after a brain stroke which seems to have immediately finished his mind. The details are rather gorgeously grim. He was two days incommunicado with some girl on Brinnin's staff in some New York hotel. Then his wife came, first cabling "eternal hate," and tried quite literally to kill and sleep with everyone in sight. Or so the rumors go in Chicago and Iowa City. It's a story that Thomas himself would have told better than anyone else; I suppose his life was short and shining as he wanted it—life, alas, is no joke.

What other news is there? Randall's writing a college novel with Mary McCarthy as the heroine.[2] *Partisan Review* has refused to print sections, they all say it is bad and not fiction etc. and wait with watering mouths for Mary to read it. Fiction or not, it's rather terrific writing. Randall and I are doing

---

1 Dylan Thomas died on November 9, 1953, at the age of thirty-nine.
2 Randall Jarrell, *Pictures from an Institution* (1954).

an anthology of modern poetry—we want things like fifty Yeats, fifty Hardy etc. that cost like hell. I fear we will be paying Harcourt Brace a hundred dollars a month for the rest of our lives. Elizabeth is finishing her novel.[1] I'm teaching Homer. My car won't start in the snow. We want to have a child as soon as we get to Duxbury. (Really!) I've been so busy finding ways to make teaching easy that I haven't done a stroke of work. Write us soon, and come and stay with us next summer.

Love,
Cal

122.

Dear Cal:

I was awfully glad to hear from you—and also because I thought perhaps that large envelope of bad pictures had got lost or stolen, and because I was sick in bed with bronchitis—& asthma. I can't ever seem to get quite rid of it. Now I've started on cortisone again. Did I ever mention that to you before? This is my third ride with it. To begin with it is absolutely marvelous. You can sit up typing all night long and feel wonderful the next day. I wrote two stories in a week. The let-down isn't bad if you do all the proper things, but once I didn't and found myself shedding tears all day long for no reason at all. This time I'm hoping it will help me get that last impossible poem off to H. Mifflin . . . Try it sometime. It seems to apply to just about anything.

Have you really bought a house in Duxbury? I haven't been there for years, but I think it is a wonderful place, and I remember a good many wonderful old houses. Seems to me I stayed in a real Pilgrim Father attic once, and ate succotash. I also visited there with my mother at the age of three. We visited a Mrs. Tewkesbury of Duxbury, and I had chicken-pox. But really it seems to me it would be a wonderful place to live, not too far from Boston, good beaches—you could have a sail-boat. I will send you a Brazilian flag— green, yellow, and a bright blue globe, *"Ordem e Progreso"*[2]—to fly under the Stars & Stripes. I used to sail a lot in Plymouth harbor—and I had a cottage, no longer existent, away out on a sandbar there when I was eighteen— named "Beulah," there were two: "Beulah" & "St. Elmo." I think it's a fine idea. The idea of a child overwhelms me a little—but then, people *do* have

1 Elizabeth Hardwick, *The Simple Truth* (1955).
2 "Order and Progress."

them. Here I'm getting rather against them, since everyone has at least eight, rich or poor, sick or healthy, kill the mother or not, with complete abandon.

(These seeds from a tall bright-green-trunk tree are all over the place now.)

Yes—I first saw about Dylan Thomas in *Time*, that awful magazine that you have to read here because it has the news first, at least. Then I got some letters. I suppose he had a cerebral hemorrhage or something, poor man. I liked him so much. Well, "like" isn't quite the word, but I felt such a sympathy for him in Washington, and immediately, after one lunch with him, you knew perfectly well he was only good for two or three years more. *Why*, I wonder . . . when people can live to be malicious old men like Frost, or maniacal old men like Pound, or—well—I gather that J. Malcolm Brinnin had the worst of it all, too? And that he's left the wife and three children without any money.

Well, I got a car, too—I guess since I wrote you. I think I'll even enclose another bad picture that looks as if I were heading into the Andes in it, when as a matter of fact I can't even get my license yet. I made enough on a story in the *New Yorker*[1] to get it—a slightly second-hand MG, almost my favorite car, black, with red leather. It *zooms* up the mountains with the cut-out open, but really I only like speedy *looking* cars that I can drive very slowly. (My dream is a butter-yellow Jaguar racing model, which I shall drive at about 30, with an umbrella in one hand, probably.) Then just after I bought it, we went to the movies one night just because we hadn't been for so long, and it was an awful picture with Ginger Rogers and Cary Grant taking some kind of youth-elixir[2]—and the first thing Cary G did after taking it was to rush out and buy a car exactly like mine to symbolize adolescence. Well, maybe my next will be a sedate coupe.

I've seen quite a bit of work by both you & Elizabeth recently, I think. I liked her little tale of Constantinople[3]—I think, partly, besides its own merits, because it reminded me of some of Trollope's queer travel stories—ever read any of them? They're very good sometimes. I also thought she made a very good point about memoirs, conversations, etc. You know when I read that remark about Flaubert when I was very young it prejudiced me against him for years.[4] Her view of the "Letters"—I haven't read Anderson's and

---

1 "In the Village," *The New Yorker* (Dec. 19, 1953); see EB-*CPR*.

2 *Monkey Business*, dir. Howard Hawks (1952).

3 Elizabeth Hardwick, "Two Recent Travelers," *The Kenyon Review* (Summer 1953).

4 "When I was young my vanity was such that if I found myself in a brothel with friends, I would choose the ugliest girl and would insist upon lying with her before them all without taking the cigar out of my mouth. It was no fun

don't want to much; that *effort* is so painful, I think—but I agreed with her about poor Edna St. Vincent Millay. Heavens she suffered. But *I* also suffered reading Hart Crane, and I don't think I could agree with E there very much.[1] They are awfully good, and amazingly solid for letters[2]—but his terrible rationalizations upset me for a long time—& then I liked your poems in the same number very much.[3] Each terrifying in its way. The review of Robert Penn Warren's poem I can't comment on.[4] I read the section of the poem in the magazine, but you know I've never been able to see him at all. He's a hell of a better poet than novelist, certainly, but—I still like his books best. But maybe I'd better order the book? I saw a section of that novel of Randall's, too—extremely witty, and I wonder how he keeps it up without sounding hysterical. I think Mrs. White at the New Yorker told me they'd turned down chapters of it several years ago, too. Poor Mary—I recognized her at once, of course.

Use a Dunhill Denicontina holder—though you probably already have for years. I like them very much and you can chew on it while typing, but mine are all used up now. And you can get nice bright red and blue ones. We buy American cigarettes here at enormous expense. I thought I could always smoke any old cigarette, and I liked Gaulois in Paris, etc., but Brazilian ones—I've tried dozens—are really too bad. (*Louis XV* is the best.) I remember my friends always got very cranky when they stopped smoking, and it must be a real vice in the USA now—even see ads for imitation cigarettes to suck. I only smoke when I'm working usually, otherwise three or four a day, and never more than 20. But here I have been able to stop drinking almost entirely, which is certainly more important for me. No one ever thinks of it here: a drink of Scotch if you're trying to be chic, or a gin & tonic. The beer is marvelous but I only like a little. The result of being served *cafezinhos* all the time—plus dysentery, off and on—is that I've lost 20 pounds and am still going. I don't believe you've ever even seen me my normal size.

But my news now is that sometime in March I'm going to Europe. Probably for nine months or a year. My Brazilian friend Lota is going with me and is going to buy a car. I expect we'll be in Italy most of the time but we don't know yet. Food prices here have gone up 300% since I've been here—most

at all for me; I did it for the gallery"; Gustav Flaubert, quoted in Elizabeth Hardwick, "Memoirs, Conversations and Diaries," *Partisan Review* (Nov.–Dec. 1953).

1 Elizabeth Hardwick, "Anderson, Millay and Crane in Their Letters," *Partisan Review* (Nov.–Dec. 1953).

2 Hart Crane, *Letters, 1916–1932*, ed. Brom Weber (1952).

3 "Inauguration Day: January 1953" and "A Mad Negro Soldier Confined at Munich," *Partisan Review* (Nov.–Dec. 1953); see RL-*CP*.

4 "Robert Penn Warren's 'Brother to Dragons,'" *The Kenyon Review* (Autumn 1953); see RL-*CPR*.

things accordingly. It isn't so bad for me because the dollar is so omnipotent, but by selling a car and a Land Rover here and renting her Rio apartment at a fabulous rent (to an elderly American who is with United Business Machines, and we think is really just starting to *live* at sixty-five—he talked about a "person"—no gender—who is coming to share it with him, and immediately took on the maid at twice what she's been getting) and by stopping feeding all the "help" here, who naturally eat their poor heads off under the circumstances, she will be rich in Europe.

Any information you can give me would be most welcome. Were you in Italy—I think you were—during the early spring? How cold is it? My one trip there was in November–December and Rome was wonderful, but it rained steadily in Florence. We may have to go to England first, but if we can shall probably fly straight to Rome—eventually come back by way of Spain and Portugal so she can buy things for the house and ship them from Lisboa. This all depends somewhat on my earning some more money before then, but I guess I can. (The story that bought the MG is in the Dec. 19th *New Yorker*. Please tell me exactly what you think. At first I thought it was my best, but after they took it naturally I had serious doubts. However, they keep assuring me it is extremely "experimental" for them.)

How are you teaching Homer? Not the way I was taught it, I hope. I suppose if I never teach I never *will* get my ideas in order, and sometimes I imagine what I would say to a class, but some one who has read Empson always stumps me with a question.

Oh, do you remember you gave me a volume of Adrian Stokes? Well, I was looking into it the other day preparing myself for Italy and I realized, I'd forgotten before, where Eleanor Clark got her style[1]—even some vocabulary. That "Shocking"—& "terrible" business. As if only she—& Adrian S.—really *fault*.

One nice thing here—I've read more than ever before: just about all Dickens which I'm now writing a small concentrated sonnet about,[2] & tackling some Portuguese. Camões is very much like what Ezra Pound says, but have you ever seen any of his holy sonnets?[3] They are *superb*, "Jacob & Rachel" etc. You could probably read them easily all right. I must try to write Randall. I somehow feel it was very noble of him to leave me in *Poetry and the Age*[4] and whether I am just being masochistic or not I don't know.

---

1 Eleanor Clark, *Rome and a Villa* (1952).
2 The sonnet does not survive.
3 See Ezra Pound, *The Spirit of Romance* (1910).
4 Randall Jarrell, *Poetry and the Age* (1955); it includes Jarrell's review of EB's *North & South*.

Good lord—Eberhart. I read a review by him of J Garrigue somewhere—"sailing through the archipelagos of female poets" on and on, like a real hallucination. I must go down to the house and get the next shot of cortisone—*this euphoria is wonderful*—also feed a few animals and see if the toucan is dry; it's the rainy season. One night I forgot to put the cover on his cage, and it started pouring, and when I rushed out he was standing stretched straight up with his beak in the air and his eyes shut, the water pouring down him—like Brancusi's "Bird in Flight." I didn't know he could make himself so long: the idea of least resistance, I suppose. I hope you and Elizabeth have pleasant holidays and that the novel is all done. What's it about? I wish I *could* come and visit next summer. Maybe summer after next, with luck.

Best wishes and love to you both.

Elizabeth

123.

January 1, [1954]

Dearest Elizabeth:

We have your photograph perched high on our little foot-and-a-half Maine Christmas tree, sent us by my Cousin Harriet. I'm sure you remember her from Washington. I'd never dare take the wheel holding a kitten, and I doubt if my car would be up to reaching to that roof of the world you seem to have attained. Nevertheless, I want to take a colored photograph of my own car—green, glorious, sedate, and empty—and engraved underneath, "merry Christmas from the Lowells." Maybe Williams would write some verses for us. I think it's thrilling about your losing twenty pounds, though I'm sure I shouldn't remark on it, and I wouldn't want you any different. Still it's a haunting idea. But alas, if I don't watch out I'll be gaining each ounce you drop. Except for football games, I've become a pure creature of books during the past three months. That's the trouble with living in a pioneer undecadent world.

We're both sick of Iowa City. Also I'm sick of explaining to Elizabeth why she shouldn't be. She has just finished her novel.[1] It "centers" about a student murder that happened in 1950, when we were first here. It's the best thing she's done, very stern with a subdued satirical edge. And everything she tactfully didn't say about the locale is tearing through her. So here we are in the beginning of the New Year. It has just occurred to me that I haven't

1 Elizabeth Hardwick, *The Simple Truth* (1955).

done a lick of preparation for my nine one-hour lectures on American poetry to be given in Cincinnati in a little over a month. How I wish I'd been reading Americana instead of Homer and Pindar! By the way, I had a long talk with a girl about one of your lectures. She said you were such a wise, sympathetic person, but it was a pity that you stuttered. She said she really couldn't get a word, but loved your books so. Well, after five minutes it turned out to be Elizabeth Bowen. You ought to have heard how I sweated to merge the two characters.

Your *New Yorker* story is wonderful. A great ruminating Dutch landscape feel of goneness. I could weep for the cow. I've been dragging up old conversations with you and wondering just how autobiographical both this and that other two little girls story[1] are. I feel they are perhaps parts of a Nova Scotia growing-up novel—though of course they are rounded short stories. The second is much more considerable, but somehow it raises the first. So I think of some Education of E.B. or E.B.s Downward path to Wisdom. What KA Porter's childhood stories aim towards, or a super Miss Jewett. But it could be less than a novel—something in three, four or five sections that would go for about a hundred pages. You see I'm back on my old *Mills of the Kavanaughs* rage for putting pieces together.

Glad you found Elizabeth's and my things had life in them. My best poem lately, I think, is a long thing on leaving Europe that came out in the summer *Kenyon*.[2] I'd send you a copy, but haven't one. And the thought of copying it out makes me groggy.

I am rather groggy from a three days head-inflaming cold, from lying in bed (it's all over now) and reading Carlyle's *French Revolution*. Overpowering, and almost as good as *Moby Dick* when you give in to it. Our century really can't match the best Victorians for nonfictional prose. But I am not going to start a lecture.

Do you stop in the States on your way to Europe? I wish with all my heart that you could somehow stretch things and see us. We seem attached to each other by some stiff piece of wire, so that each time one moves, the other moves in another direction. We should call a halt to that.

Now, to end impersonally. I saw Pound some two weeks ago at St. Elizabeths, the first time in four years. It's a shock how unchanged he was, the same list of books (when he learned I was only to be there for the day, he brushed aside human amenities, plunged in medias res, and told me how

---

1 "In the Village," *The New Yorker* (Dec. 19, 1953), and "Gwendolyn," *The New Yorker* (June 27, 1953); see EB-*CPR*.
2 "Beyond the Alps," *The Kenyon Review* (Summer 1953); see RL-*CP*.

to teach history from 1830–1860), the same rhetoric. But he's much fatter and healthier, jumps about, dances like a bear and no longer complains of memory gaps. O, I think he has lived because he has wanted to, and Thomas didn't. No I don't mean that exactly. Thomas wanted to live burning, burning out.

So we. I want to live to be old, and want you to.

Love,

Cal

124.

My Dearest Elizabeth:

So glad your letter to Lizzie came yesterday, for I have been meaning to write you ever since your wonderful photograph arrived, and somehow, somehow . . . A lot of water has gone under the mill-wheel, since we were last writing almost a year ago now, I have been sick again,[1] and somehow even with you I shrink both from mentioning and not mentioning. These things come on with a gruesome, vulgar, blasting surge of "enthusiasm," one becomes a kind of man-aping balloon in a parade—then you subside and eat bitter coffee-grounds of dullness, guilt etc. Well, your letter moved our hearts. Please don't worry any more. All the pieces have been picked up, and (but I see have already used at least five discordant metaphors) life has licked up.

I wish you could see our sunny-side of Commonwealth Ave. apartment. We are three twenty-foot flights up and look on two decaying churches and Boston's two hugest and most imperial life-insurance buildings. We have great rooms, look down on society, see at least one parade a month, and can't get the former tenant out of our heads—she had made her own world here, for twenty-six years she lived buried in ice-packs, syphons, trash, mammoth rose-wall-paper, signs of the zodiac and twenty-six birds, half of them uncaged. We are very, very tame in comparison. We've been moving into here *and* Duxbury for the past month and a half. Our nomadic heads are in a whirl, we don't know ourselves. Have you ever tried picking up your roots?

---

1 RL suffered a major manic episode following the death of his mother in Rapallo on February 13, 1954; he did not recover until late summer.

I think Elizabeth's *Simple Truth* is much the biggest and brightest thing she has ever written—it seems so simple, one forgets that it's a wonderful invention—I don't think any other murder trial has been its audience. There have been quite a lot of good letters and blurbs about it already. Yours is the best.

I don't have too much news. I've been reading Dickens, getting records—Berg, Schubert, Glück, not old New England lore—from the Public Library, getting a Mass. Driver's license (my old one was revoked after my accident with Jean in 1937 and that means I have to be investigated, gently but at a snail's pace) and trying to write prose[1]—a hell of a job. It starts naked, ends as fake velvet.

Do write and tell us about your trip to Portugal, much more about Brazil, very much about you. We send our love,

Cal

125.

Samambaia, November 30th, 1954

Dear Cal:

What a joy to hear from you! Heavens—I've felt much better ever since; I hadn't realized just how worried I had been, I guess. I had heard vaguely, perhaps from Zabel, about the death of your mother and felt I should have written about that but scarcely knew what to say and of course do not even now. But I am just so relieved to know you are safe & sound again and apparently cheerful and pugnacious, too.

I'm trying to think which way the numbers run on Commonwealth Avenue, and I think you must be down near Arlington or Bedford Streets. I sometimes have a hankering to live again in Boston myself, although I know I never shall. But there are many nice things about it. Do you see Frank Parker ever? I have a book of his I'd like very much to get back to him sometime if he is in the U.S. and you could give me his address. Or my old friend Hyman Bloom, who I think got married a while ago? We had an awfully nice visit, in August and September, from Agnes Mongan, the head of the drawings at the Fogg Museum; we liked her a lot. She seemed to be quite a friend of Jack Sweeney. And just now I am expecting a visit from a general, of all things—his wife seems to be a "poetry lover" & says, on the telephone, that she is doing a book with John Ciardi. I think they were sent to me by Frost,

---

1 See "91 Revere Street," "Antebellum Boston," and "Near the Unbalanced Aquarium" (RL-*CPR*).

who was also here a while ago. A General Erskine.[1] Frost put on quite a good show at our fearfully ugly embassy auditorium. Then I asked him to lunch at the house of a friend of mine in Rio—a beautiful old house and garden that I thought he might like to see. The friend had invited, among others, Brazil's "leading poet,"[2] who's an awfully nice man but who refuses to speak any English at all—Frost refuses to speak anything else—and they are both extremely deaf. So lunch was rather a strain, with me screaming away in any old language I could think of at one end of the table, and Frost's daughter Lesley holding forth endlessly to some poor bored Brazilians at the other end—and Miss Mongan—about her daughter's creditable marks at Radcliffe. Frost asked the hostess where she got the seeds for the beautiful flowers on the table and after screwing up her courage she said very loud and clear: "BURPEE."

I've been reading Dickens, too, volume by volume by volume, and having a wonderful time. That abundance and playfulness and slopping all over the place is so wonderful. Now I've just today finished V Woolf's diaries[3]— the book got held up at the docks here for almost a year and just reached me. It's awfully harrowing, and I really don't see how she fitted all those things into an ordinary *day* sometimes. Have you read it? And I'm in the middle of Lord Cecil's *Melbourne*,[4] which is really awfully good. But I'm mostly doing a translation of a Brazilian book.[5] I may have told you about it a long time ago, I'm not sure; I started it just to teach myself Portuguese, and then I decided it really might be quite successful in translation, so after some false beginnings I'm about half through it now and have acquired an English typist, etc. It's the diary of a little girl—unreal diary, however—sounds awful, I fear—a girl from 12–15, living in a mining town called Diamantina, in the '90's. There's a huge family of aunts and uncles and ex-slaves, ruled by a grandmother, all very poor and religious and superstitious, and the girl really wrote extremely well. She is funny and hard-headed and the anecdotes are very full of detail about the life, food, clothes, priests, etc. I sort of think you'll like it. She is now a rich old dowager in Rio, 75.[6] Her husband, about 80, was president of the bank of Brazil.[7] I haven't read much Brazilian literature but this is by far the best thing I have read, since the famous Machado de

---

1 General Graves Blanchard Erskine.
2 Manuel Bandeira.
3 Virginia Woolf, *A Writer's Diary: Being Extracts from the Diary of Virginia Woolf*, ed. Leonard Woolf (1954).
4 David Cecil, *Melbourne* (1954).
5 *The Diary of "Helena Morley"* (1957).
6 Alice Dayrell Caldeira Brant.
7 Dr. Augusto Mário Caldeira Brant.

Assis, that is, the only glory of letters here as far as I can see. (My friend Lota has a poet in her family tree who was ravishingly beautiful and won a prize at a costume ball in Carnival time, disguised as a woman, and wrote bad romantic poetry and died at the age of 22, saying "What a pity . . .")

I think *The Simple Truth* stays in one's mind. I keep thinking of the sad household arrangements in that one-room apartment, the girl's clothes, etc. When is it supposed to appear? (It really is awfully good, I feel surer all the time— Later)

My poems are supposed now to come out in the early spring, I think, but Houghton Mifflin and I don't seem to be getting along too well. I am sending them the sections from this translation, because I said I would mostly, but I haven't heard yet whether they are interested or not. I sent them all my stories to date, and they dropped them like a hot potato, so if you ever go by 2 Park Street you can throw stones at their windows for me, if you want to.

I haven't much "literary" news, certainly. I struggle every week or so to write Marianne another installment about her *Fables* and just hope she hasn't seen some of the reviews. I suppose the best was in *Poetry*,[1] but I really don't know what to think or say. I should be about to get a driver's license, too— my first—but I'm putting it off until the roads are a little better. I think I told you about my MG that I've had about a year now. I don't think I'd ever drive in Rio. It's all done by some other process there, anyway, not "driving" at all, I'm sure. (The head of the traffic system there just committed suicide and they decided he could have a Christian burial anyway, I suspect out of sympathy) but I'll get my license up here in Petrópolis, which isn't so bad.

I asked Foyle's, of London, to send you a book a while ago. Maybe you've received it by now—a book about George Herbert by Joe Summers.[2] Remember that boy at Bard College? I think in general it is pretty good— not very profound but a very sympathetic book. It will be a sort of Christmas present, although I may be able to send something else along by the *General*, who sight unseen has offered to take things, over the telephone. He's here for the big economic conference[3] going on in Petrópolis now in which they have again come to an impasse about coffee, I think.

It is starting to get dark and I am up at my *estudio* without a lamp, and I don't hear any signs of our generator's being started, so I must clamber

---

1 Marianne Moore, "The Fox and the Goat," "The Fox and the Bust," and "The Fox Shorn of His Tail," *Poetry* (Oct. 1953); "The Hen That Laid the Golden Eggs," "The Dog Who Dropped Substance for Shadow," and "The Woods and the Woodman," *Poetry* (March 1954).
2 Joseph H. Summers, *George Herbert: His Religion and His Art* (1954).
3 The Pan American Economic Conference.

down the mountain and start it myself. That is why we have no music at all here yet except my clavichord. The generator noise comes through a radio or victrola. In six months or so more there will be electricity all the way up here, I think, and then you can give me some advice about records. The light is darker than this page—or this ribbon—so I must stop.

December 10th

I'm awfully sorry. I thought this had been sent off with a batch of Christmas cards almost two weeks ago now, and here I have just found it in a special pile.

The luncheon with the general was quite incredible. I still can't believe he was real. He and his wife, Constance *Caraway* Erskine—a poet, I think—anyway she's working on an anthology with Ciardi, and knows Tate, etc. They are about sixty, I imagine, Southerners, and had been married two months and were radiantly happy and infatuated and wearing roses and brought a bottle of champagne, and he looked very much like Eisenhower only about three times as big . . . She called him "Bobby." Well, that's enough, except that my friend Lota was enchanted with them, vulgarity and all (the wife told us all about her horrendous "operation" during lunch), because she admires Americans so much for their endless youth and vitality, and here were certainly two living symbols of it . . .

There is a lot I'd like to say about the poems of yours I've seen in the past year, but a guest is going down to Rio early this morning—it's 8 AM now—and will mail this, so I'll stop now and write again later. I just got a year's numbers of *Encounter*—with your Ford Madox Ford poem[1]—& I've never mentioned the superb "Crossing the Alps,"[2] ever.

With best wishes to you and Elizabeth for 1955 and please do let me hear from you: about Duxbury, Boston, what you're writing, everything.

With much love and *saudades* as they say here, a very nice word that seems to include all the sentiments of missing friends in one.

Elizabeth

1 "Ford Madox Ford: 1873–1939," *Encounter* (April 1954); see RL-*CP*.
2 "Beyond the Alps," *The Kenyon Review* (Spring 1953); see RL-*CP*.

126.

Dear Elizabeth:

Oh dear! I see your last letter is dated Nov. 30th, then a coda dated Dec. 10th. I have many little items to write you and might compose this in the manner of my friend Merrill Moore, whose letters have more paragraphs than sentences, if that were possible. But first my thanks for the proofs of *Cold Spring*—good title and good to see both your books together.[1] I wrote Miss Ford a blurb, which I liked a lot but which may have struck her as rather glibly lavish. I like everything, particularly at the moment (and for years now) some of the longer ones, those scenes: "Fishhouses," "Cape Breton," "2000 Illustrations," and, of course, "Faustina." I wrote that your poems were not just poetry but showed a Russian novelist's eye for the world, or something of the sort; and hoped the publishers would have twinges about your stories.[2] According to Rosalind Wilson who works at Houghton Mifflin but was a bystander, what upset them was that your manuscript came on different sizes and colors of paper. Whenever I meet a publisher I give him your address.

What's new here? Lizzie's *Simple Truth* is out three months, *one*, in England, small sales, pretty fair reviews. Most of them are baffled by the book's being about the spectators at the trial instead of being about the killer, what they call *warmth* or *life*. She has now started a play, 3 stories (2 done), a review of Christina Stead,[3] and a novel, and is learning to drive. The safest place to learn driving in the neighborhood is a road between the Cambridge Cemetery and the Cambridge dump. We tried at first to practice in the Mount Auburn Cemetery, past J. R. Lowell, Rufus Choate etc. and were quickly spotted, and warned that the graveyard, despite appearances, was heavy with threat: bends, knolls, other heedless amateurs learning. We teach one another. I tell Lizzie what to do for an hour, then she tells me what to do for an hour.

Did you get an ancient Dutch doll from us? Very glad to get Joe Summers Herbert; but I find the Summers-Tuve,[4] *What Herbert really meant* line, rather bleeds the life out of him, as though his lines really were stones that

---

1 Because *A Cold Spring* was a short book, *North & South* was reprinted with it in a single volume.
2 "Miss Bishop has a good heart and a good eye. She has three virtues, each in itself enough to make a poet. (1) She knows her own tongue. Her tone can be Venetian gorgeous or Quaker simple; she never falls into cant or miserliness. (2) Her abundance of description reminds one, not of poets, poor symbolic, abstract creatures—but of the Russian novelists. (3) In all matters of form: meter, rhythm, diction, timing, shaping, etc., she is a master."
3 Elizabeth Hardwick, "The Neglected Novels of Christina Stead," *The New Republic* (1955).
4 Rosemond Tuve, *A Reading of George Herbert* (1952).

could be fitted together to build a temple without flaw or despair. I shouldn't say this I suppose—about two months ago after much irresolution I became an Episcopalian again (a high one). I used to think one had to be a Catholic or nothing. I guess I've rather rudely expected life to be a matter of harsh clear alternatives. I don't know what to say of my new faith; on the surface I feel eccentric, antiquarian, a superstitious, skeptical fussy old woman, but down under I feel something that makes sober sense and lets my eyes open.

All winter I've been playing at starting my autobiography, and now have about a hundred pages of drafts. It's quite clumsy, inaccurate and magical, but may work out passably. I like being off the high stilts of meter, and feel there's no limit to the prosiness and detail I can go into.

We heard from Frost that you are quite a public figure, and appear in the papers as the American poet. Also met Agnes Mongan, at a poetry panel. She seemed terribly attractive. We met at the end and didn't have much chance to talk, because while we were talking one of the poets (poor man, a secret drinker) fainted. Everyone, and your own letters, speak so well of your life and health and spirits!

Love from us,
    Cal

127.

Dearest Cal:

A few days ago Houghton Mifflin sent me your "blurb"—heavens, I am quite overcome. But it must mean that you never received either of my letters—I wouldn't have had them ask you for it in that *crude* way, naturally. I wrote a short letter a couple of months ago, I think, and then a long long one about six weeks ago[1]—I am rather relieved you didn't get it, because I think I sounded rather gloomy and apologetic. Since those things are still the custom with us I suppose we might as well do them as well as possible—and with yours I'll certainly be able to—but I do loathe them and wish the custom would go out—maybe a few people could start refusing. I don't think you should have said all that—it is really not worth it, I know damned well—but I am very pleased. Then just after that your letter of the 5th arrived—no, the same bunch of mail—your friend at HM must have got the

1 The letters do not survive.

story wrong! Probably the poems were on different colors & sizes of paper—or at least varying shades of faded yellow, by the time they were together—but the stories I'd had all freshly and beautifully typed at great expense and sent from New York . . . However, it's probably just as well. HM and I hit it off worse and worse, I'm afraid, with "faults on both sides." There weren't enough stories, anyway, and I'll never again undertake any kind of publication until every last comma is finally in place—

In my long letter I said I'd seen a couple of reviews of Elizabeth's book but unsatisfactory ones—the *N.Y. Times* and something in the *New Republic* that sounded like spite and had almost nothing to do with the book. Since then *PR,* and a very brief note in *Encounter.*[1] I'm sorry that one wasn't longer, because it seemed to me it was the first that got the point at all and showed something of what the book is *really* about. I am envious of such productivity. All *I* am doing is learning to drive, still! Well, I learned, more or less, but in order to we had to drive several miles to a good place to learn in, and then our mountain road got worse and worse. It's 2 miles or so down to the highway, and so I abandoned it until our road would be finished. Now it is, almost, and I'm starting in again and have also just ordered a new top for the MG: black with red piping, very chic and a *large* window behind—at present if the top is up you can't see a thing—and shall soon qualify for my license in Petrópolis, I trust. It is really a marvelous little car. That & marmalade-making and playing with the cook's baby take a lot of time . . . did I tell you about her, named "Maria Elizabeth," now 3 months old and lovely & fat, like milk chocolate. I'm to be the godmother, when she can "sit up and have her ears pierced." The godfather is a young white boy here,—such a bad worker we've fired him several times already. I suppose I shall provide the dress and the earrings, and pay the priest. It's the only time she'll ever go to church, probably. The church's hold here is almost non-existent. The poor are christened and buried—not married—and then the priest doesn't go to the cemetery. The family straggle along, under black umbrellas usually, carrying a crepe-paper covered box. However, the Eucharistic Congress is about to take place in Rio: 600,000 pilgrims expected, a dreadful water-shortage, not much food, and either typhus or typhoid, I don't know which, already going. It promises to be too, too medieval. One society woman has given all her jewels. I've forgotten how much they're worth, now, but 100's of 1,000's of $$$—two fistfuls—to make the *monstrum.*

1 John Brooks, "The Trial Watchers," *The New York Times Book Review* (Feb. 13, 1955); Dachine Rainer, "The Truth and the Vacuum," *The New Republic* (Feb. 14, 1955); William S. Porter, "Fiction Chronicle," *Partisan Review* (Spring 1955); and Anthony Quinton, "Ideas about Love," *Encounter* (April 1955).

Oh, and in my long letter I thanked you for the doll. In fact getting it out of customs was what occasioned the letter (first part of April). In case it never shows up I'll tell you all over again—I'd had a package there for two weeks or so and thought it was something else so didn't bother to get it until I went to Rio for a few days. It is rather fun to go to the *Alfandaga* (I rather like that word) always, even if it means all kinds of little stamps and signatures and counter signatures and sealing wax, etc. It was a fearfully hot day and everyone else there was waiting to extract sad little electrical gadgets at great cost, or things made of plastic, and one old man beside me a set of phylacteries & skull-caps, etc., so the doll made a great sensation, the only thing *antique* in years, I imagine. The man waiting on me had to call his "colleagues"—that's a favorite word here—to come to see it and I did my best in my faltering Portuguese to explain what it was. So finally it was put back in the box (and thank you for the fine supply of white tissue-paper, too) and sealed with lots of red wax and baroque seals and off we went in a taxi. It is extraordinary and I'd like to know more about it—her, rather—as I said in my other letter. I think I like the back of the pinafore, with the bows, best, but the little legs are very nice, too. I have her on the book-case in my room: some days front to the room, some days back, between a bird's nest and a clay dog from Bahia, and she looks extremely well in her sad way. The gardener, waxing the floor, said she looked just like a blond he knows . . . (There was no duty to pay, by the way.)

I wish I could reciprocate in some way, but if I ever get in a trip to the U.S., I have some strange Indian things for you. Mailing anything from here is next to impossible, except books.

Yes, I got the Tuve book, too, and read it carefully and then forgot it. Joe's I thought was simpler, and I did learn quite a bit from it. But they both obviously love the poetry & the poet, and that's nice. Neither book was written to show how Herbert should have done it.

I have just finished the Yeats *Letters*[1]—900 & something pages—although some I'd read before. He is so Olympian always, so calm, so really unrevealing, and yet I was fascinated. Imagine being able to say you'd always finished everything you'd started, from the age of 17. And he is much more kind, and more right about everything than I'd ever thought—right, until the age of 65, say. And it's too bad he discovered s-e-x so late, I feel. A lot of it would be more enjoyable coming from a younger man. And then why do so many famous men have to write hundreds of letters about after-

---

1 *The Letters of W. B. Yeats*, ed. Allan Wade (1954).

lunch-I-lie-down-for-an-hour, and now—I'm eating fruit-& vegetables . . . Well, he has magnificence, even so. I have a theory that all this business of psalteries and chanting, etc., was because he was completely tone-deaf and even the normal music of spoken verse wasn't too apparent to him, so he felt something was missing. This is based on an imitation Pound once gave me (I don't know whether it was the time I went to see him with you or later) of Yeats' singing, to show how tone-deaf he was. The imitation was so strange & bad, too, that I decided they were *both* tone-deaf . . . . Have you read *A Vision?*[1]

I am glad you told me about the Episcopalian Church. I have no right to speak about things I know so little about, but it seems to me the best things of the Christian tradition lie with it at present, maybe, rather than in the Catholic Church, and here, particularly, one feels more and more disgusted with the Catholic Church I'm afraid. Although a couple of my best and brightest friends are very Catholic, and of course everyone is by education. I wish I had the 39 articles on hand. I also wish I could go back to being a Baptist!—not that I ever was one—but I believe now that complete agnosticism and straddling the fence on everything is my natural posture, although I wish it weren't.

Frost was wrong, too, about my being a "public figure"—! !—but then, he tells so many fibs. I am a friend of THE poet (at least I keep him provided with marmalade, and he has written me a poem and I have written him one[2]) and he gave me a hammock. I have also attracted myself to a madman who arrives once in a while up the mountainside with a poem in his hand—in a taxi-cab—and has to be gently pushed down again. I know about ten people, two of them "literary," and I go to Rio once in three or four months . . . I know one American, that's all. I'm hoping very much to get in a quick trip to the US this fall, if I can earn some money before then—and possibly, possibly spend the winter of 1956 in N.Y.

Do please write an autobiography—or sketches for one. The two or three stories I've managed to do of that sort have been a great satisfaction, somehow—that desire to get things straight and tell the truth. It's almost impossible not to tell the truth in poetry, I think, but in prose it keeps eluding one in the funniest way. My translation is going along slowly—the 1st third in N.Y. now. Next week or so I'm going on a trip to the town where it all took place to write the introduction: Diamantina. It is completely god-

---

1 W. B. Yeats, *A Vision* (1937 edition).
2 See "To Manuel Bandeira, with Jelly and Jam" (EB-*EAP*).

forsaken, now—and solid, beautiful, late Portuguese baroque—white plaster and green soap-stone, fountains and bridges and churches: absolutely dead, although 100 yrs. ago it was filled with Europeans making fortunes and was known all over the world. I believe we're going to be entertained by the mayor! They are hard up for amusement, understandably. In my letter that got lost I complained bitterly about not being able to write a decent poem, ever again, etc., etc., and then after forcing myself—it took five months—to finish one rigid, 32 line, completely artificial thing,[1] it worked, and now I seem to be writing again. Please pray for me to an Anglican saint. I am so happy about your "blurb," and grateful, that that is probably helping a great deal, too.

I just went out and screamed LUZ![2] to the black mountains in a most un-Goethe like way (more like God) and miraculously someone down at the house heard me and turned on the generator. It is dark and cold and rainy. Sometime, sometime I do wish you & E. would visit me here. S.A.[3] is unrewarding for travel, I'm afraid, but some things you'd like a lot—& we have loads of room.

With love,
Elizabeth

May 21st

Just before waking up I dreamed I was Stephen Spender, and I was reciting:

"In the beautiful morning
a beautiful poem fell to the ground
from the beautiful lips of the poet . . ."

or I was *pretending* to be Stephen Spender—it seemed to be very funny at the time.

Kenyon Review came yesterday and I read your piece "The Muses Won't Help Twice" last night and thought it was very good.[4] I remember reading Golding[5] by the hour, when I was at college and reading everything Pound

1 Possibly "Squatter's Children" (EB-*CP*).

2 LIGHT! George Henry Lewes writes that Goethe's "last words audible were: More light!"; see Lewes, *The Life and Works of Goethe* (1855), 391.

3 South America.

4 "The Muses Won't Help Twice," *The Kenyon Review* (Spring 1955); see "The Metamorphoses of Ovid" (RL-*CPR*).

5 Arthur Golding, *Metamorphosis, translated into Englishe meter* (1565–67).

had said to read, but I don't think I could take much of it anymore.[1] I don't believe I've ever told you that—a year ago now—at last I got around to reading Propertius[2] and how more than ever I thought your poem from him was extraordinary and marvelous . . .[3]

But I marvel at how people like your Mr. Watts—and MacNeice & Fitzgerald and Fitts,[4] etc., etc., find *time* to do these long translations. I just don't see. My own little translation of a *child's prose* takes me hours of fussing. I'm beginning to think other people's days are twice as long as mine.

Do you go to Duxbury soon or are you already there? Please write when you have time and tell me some gossip! and what you are reading and writing.

Love, E.

I don't know whether I said this before or whether maybe I said it in the letter that got lost—I should like so much to have a picture of you, or of you and & E maybe. I never had such things before but somehow they seem to go in my *estudio*—age or Latin sentimentality I don't know which. So far I have only Marianne and 3 Brazilian birds, so it really isn't like the Gotham Book Mart. Rollie McKenna, that photographer, was here just before Christmas & took a lot of photographs—those of me are horrible, but those of the house & animals, etc., fine, and I think I'll try to get a copy or 2 for you. She told me that Dylan Thomas, in the little house he worked in,[5] had two photographs—Marianne and Walt Whitman!

128.

Sitio Da Alcobacinha
Samambaia, Est. Do Rio—(*Don't* use this!) Are you at Duxbury?
July 8th, 1955

Dear Cal:

I hope you are well and that you finally received one or the other of my

---

1 "Ezra Pound has written that he doesn't think anyone can know anything at all about the art of lucid narrative in English if he hasn't seen all fifteen books of Ovid's Elizabethan translator, Arthur Golding. This is a good way of putting it, and yet I imagine Golding has rarely been read cover to cover"; RL-*CPR*, 154. See Ezra Pound, *ABC of Reading* (1934), 113.

2 EB was probably reading Propertius in a Loeb edition, trans. H. E. Butler. See also Ezra Pound, "Homage to Sextus Propertius" (1919).

3 "Thanksgiving's Over" (RL-*CP*); see also RL-*Letters*, 93.

4 Louis MacNeice translated the *Agamemnon* (1936) and Goethe's *Faust* (1951); Robert Fitzgerald and Dudley Fitts co-translated the Oedipus cycle (1949).

5 Rollie McKenna photographed Dylan Thomas in 1953 in the bike shed at Laugharne, Dyfed.

letters that thanked you for the weird and wonderful doll and, the last one, for the wonderful and over-generous remarks to Houghton Mifflin . . . Do let me know how you are, really. I am extremely happy here, although I can't quite get used to being "happy," but one remnant of my old morbidity is that I keep fearing that the few people I'm fond of may be in automobile accidents, or suffer some sort of catastrophe . . . The word for even a small accident here is "desastre," so I often have false alarms.

A friend and neighbor of mine, Carlos Lacerda (if you ever read any news items about Brazil you must have heard of him in the past year—the young man who was really responsible for the fall and suicide of president Vargas[1]) is flying up to New York in a few days, and I'm giving him a small present to be mailed to you. It's an Amazonian Indian Adam, I think. Sometime I'm going to find you a really beautiful *Santo*, though. Who's your favorite saint? I favor the black ones here, Ephigenia and Benedito. The other night, Sunday, after the movies I went into a very primitive sort of funeral parlor in Petrópolis. The door was open and loud samba music was coming out of the back room. There wasn't anything much in the shop but one large coffin pasted over with purple and gilt paper, and a few white wax babies, almost life size—votive offerings. But I bought a small wood Benedito, the crudest kind of whittling and painting, that is really terrifying. He's holding out the baby, who is stuck on a small nail, exactly like an hors d'oeuvres. There's one man in Petrópolis who always reminds me of your poem, "The Fat Man."[2] He is enormously fat, softly, gleamingly fat, very soft-spoken and well-dressed, and he owns a plate glass and mirror shop. When you go in it you see him reflected all around you, and I think he enjoys it—(unlike your fat man). He speaks very mellifluously. He's been selling us some windows lately and took coffee with us, and his last name is: ABELARDO.[3]

---

1 See "Suicide of a Moderate Dictator (For Carlos Lacerda)," EB-*Brazil*, 127–31. Getúlio Dornelles Vargas ruled Brazil as a dictator from 1930 to 1945. A populist who stood for land reform, he resisted attempts by the extreme right and the extreme left to seize power during the Great Depression. His political machine relied increasingly on corrupt practices, however. He was deposed in 1945 and went into semiretirement, but a political system relying on bribery and favors remained in place. In 1950, he stood as the Brazilian Labor Party candidate and was returned to office. Lacerda soon began to accuse the Vargas family and government of corruption. On August 5, 1954, the palace guard "arranged, unbeknownst to Vargas, for a professional gunman to assassinate Lacerda . . . Lacerda was only slightly wounded, but his companion, Air Force Major Rubens Florentino Vaz, was killed. Lacerda returned fire as the assailant escaped. The political impact of the shooting could hardly have been greater . . . Since the 'honor' of the officer corps was at stake, the military had now been drawn directly into the political quarrel" (Thomas E. Skidmore, *Politics in Brazil* [1967], 138). In the scandal that followed, military leaders demanded that Vargas resign. Vargas replied, "if you come to depose me you will find my body," and, when they presented him with a final ultimatum on August 24, he killed himself.
2 "The Fat Man in the Mirror" (L-*CP*).
3 Cf. *The Letters of Abelard and Heloise*, trans. C. K. Scott Moncrieff (1926).

And while I'm on local color: yesterday I read in the paper about a poor backlands family who have seventeen or so children and who had just had their second set of triplets. Cosme and Damao are favorite saints here (the policemen who go in pairs are nicknamed for them) so they'd named the first set Cosmé, Damão, and Damaoina, making up the feminine form for the occasion. The last set they had named José, Maria, and Jesús.

I just was given *The Encyclopaedia Britannica* as a *present*. Lota's architect was here for lunch and I remarked that I was about to get one on the installment plan, not being able to live any longer without it, and he said, "Oh, I'll give you mine." I said didn't he want it for himself and he said, "Oh, no. I've read it." I've also just bought the Pleiade Proust, so I should be busy for a while.[1] I'm going down to Rio tomorrow to hear "Porgy and Bess," but I haven't heard it for a long time and it's a good company, the one that's been in Europe,[2] and the Brazilians I'm going with have never heard it. If I were rich I'd take the cook and her husband along.

I haven't read Flannery O'Connor's books, but I've read most of these recent stories,[3] and I think she's really pretty good, don't you?

Love,

Elizabeth

Now it's the 17th, and this really *will* get mailed tomorrow, I think. "Porgy & Bess" was awful, & I'm sure the Brazilians I took, although they were very polite, were completely baffled by it all.

I waited to make sure Carlos is really going to New York, but it seems as certain as anything ever does here. The doll may be a male or a female. They *are* certain, but I have a good specimen of each and can't make up my mind. The women have more charm, or charms—the male is very rare . . . This letter seems to have nomenclature for its theme, so I might as well add the latest newspaper item: a woman in a remote state went to the hospital and turned into a man. Her name was "Veronica," but after the transformation she, or he, chose the name of "Julius Caesar."

Seen any good poems lately?

I am really tackling some rather big ones now and feel very cheered up

---

1 Marcel Proust, *À la recherche du temps perdu*, ed. Pierre Clarac and André Ferré (1954).

2 Blevins Davis and Robert Breen's revival of George Gershwin's *Porgy and Bess* (1952).

3 Flannery O'Connor, *Wise Blood* (1952) and *A Good Man Is Hard to Find and Other Stories* (1955). Recently published O'Connor stories in journals EB subscribed to included "The Life You Save May Be Your Own," *The Kenyon Review* (Spring 1953); "A Circle in the Fire," *The Kenyon Review* (Spring 1954); and "The Artificial Nigger," *The Kenyon Review* (Spring 1955).

about them. It is all due, I suspect, to Cortisone, or rather, now, Metacortone which is even better. I get up in the freezing dawns here and begin with all the confidence in the world. The mountains look exactly as if floating in *vin rose* then, with a white bowl of milk down below us. I do wish it weren't quite so dull for guests and you and Elizabeth would consider a visit sometime. The Eucharistic Congress started yesterday and the papers are full of wonderful things like "Watch out for pickpockets while praying" (illustrated) and "Half a Ton of Host Required." To supplement the attractions of the Congress the *waxworks* from Paris, Musée Greve[1] (?) has arrived and is installed at a big hotel near here. I suppose Rio itself is too hot for it. A dowager of Lota's acquaintance drew the Cardinal of Ireland as a guest, and we hope she is spending her days genuflecting and wonder what she has done about her bathroom for him. It is solid mirror. I shouldn't make fun, though. The outdoor setting is really superb and the altars, etc. built for it are really lovely; I saw them in passing last week. The best of the "modern" architects did it. But everything here is that confusing mixture of good and bad taste, the absurd and the sad, and the natural and spontaneous & charming.

Abraços,
Elizabeth

129.

Duxbury, Massachusetts
July 16, [1955]

Dear Elizabeth:

No, your two earlier letters never arrived, but I've just read your last again, and feel as though it were many letters, and almost as though you were here in the house talking to us. I'm enclosing some photos of us and also one of a house here that we looked at and imagined buying. It's bigger than Longfellow's house and would have been quite beyond us to keep up, but for a week we dreamed of living in it, and persuading you to stay with us permanently.

E. is learning to drive, too—only it turns out she already knows, because once a long time ago she was out with a suitor who passed out, and then E., never having driven, drove home twenty miles and through traffic.

Random notes: The doll is 18th Century (?) Dutch and came from an antique store on Charles St. Her best angle is from the back, but she looked

---

1 Musée Grévin.

wonderfully alien and taking last January, so I bought her though she wasn't at all what I had intended. The customs in Boston were also quite confusing. Brazil seems to have a changing, and half-concealed, rate.

Saw Randall who is living further down the Cape at Dennis—brown, knotted, and with a great black beard with a white splash in the center. He blows hot and cold on one, and both moods are disturbing. Now he is chilly, and I think of him as a fencer who has defeated and scarred all his opponents so that the sport has come to be almost abandoned, and Randall stands leaning on his foil, one shoulder a little lower than the other, unchallenged, invulnerable, deadly, salt marsh and deserted tennis court stretching below him. Really though, he is as "good as ever" and is writing a long review of you for the fall *Yale Review*.[1]

I'm just back from a Harvard Summer School Symposium on drama. An Englishman wrote a three hundred page play in heroic blank verse on a king of Portugal who died fighting in Morocco.[2] Some one told MacLeish that Eliot and Robert Speaight had said that this was the best play in English since *Murder in the Cathedral*. So sight unseen the author was brought from England, his play, cut to a fifth was staged without costumes or motion, and a panel made up of myself, Wilbur, MacLeish, Lillian Hellman, and Francis Fergusson set up to talk about it. But Eliot had only said that he didn't suppose the play could be staged. The action was all but incomprehensible because the critics had no text, and cut and costumeless, it hardly made sense to the author. And the author! (In a few minutes he is about to arrive here for a day's visit.) Bald, red-faced, spectacled, long amber hair curling down his neck, stuttering, humorous, flattering, modest, and knowing his immense play by heart down to the last and least word. At one point during the symposium, he was asked to give a brief pithy synopsis of his play. He talked for three quarters of an hour, scene by scene, with each promising to accelerate—then suddenly as he was within seconds of his climax in which the hero is hanged, MacLeish, who wasn't following, stopped everything with a flowery little speech praising the usefulness of the synopsis and asking for questions.

(Two weeks later and after your letter.) I guess my not writing has no particular meaning, just my old habit of putting off *all* letters and then brooding about it. This has been a house-choosing summer—our set-up: an apartment in Boston and a house here hasn't seemed workable, but rather too

---

1 Jarrell's "Recent Poetry," *Yale Review* (Summer 1955), did not contain a notice of EB's *A Cold Spring*; for that, see "The Year in Poetry," *Harper's* (Oct. 1955).
2 Jonathan Griffin, *The Hidden King* (1955).

expensive, too cramped, too cumbersome, too impermanent, too much trouble. So we've been through every sort of alternative, a larger house in the country, England, and even Iowa. Each choice carries a whole way of life with it, and we have lived through them all. Our income is now sufficient for me to live quite comfortably without earning anything at all. But I don't feel much tempted that way. So I have been rocking this way, then that—each push gentle at first, a cat tap, but later strong, nettled, irresolute, now wanting to be with people, now wanting to be alone, and so the summer has passed. We have just—a week ago—bought a house in Boston; it is on Marlborough St., 239, and only blocks from where I grew up. It's gray stone, rather Parisian, four floors, two windows to a floor, white, neat, dainty Italian fire-places, a lovely foyer, a sort of stream-lined Victorian.

There's a strong piece on art and old age in the summer *PR* by Gottfried Benn.[1] By the time you are old you have broken with convention, broken with your models and heroes, and finally broken with yourself. Our time of life is apparently one of the breaking times. The thought of going back to Boston sometimes makes me feel like a flayed man, who stands quivering and shivering in his flesh, while holding out a hand for his old sheet of skin.[2] Excuse this image, it comes from bathing suits on the line, our washing-machine which became overloaded and stopped, looking at pictures of Pollaiuolo, and the heat—it is almost a hundred in the shade today.

In a few days we are moving to Castine for a month to stay in a little house near my Cousin Harriet, then in late September we will be moving into Boston. We'll have a huge airy guest-room and offer it to you indefinitely as lure to bring you to America this fall.

We had another much better day with Randall and Mary. He is like a knotted, brown old gladiator, and will be still more so when his Mercedes racer arrives. Elizabeth says he is much stranger than Dylan Thomas, and that when Randall turned up, Nature had never seen anything like him, and instantly broke the mould.

I think most people who are Christians find profession and practice something commonsensical, cow-like, customary. I'd like to take it that way. Doing much more seems extravagant. It doesn't seem possible to act, except for a few ritual motions, as though we really began to really believe. That God should really be Christ—that does seem strained, and so unlike our usual and

1 Benn, "Artists and Old Age," *Partisan Review* (Summer 1955).
2 Cf. "Near the Unbalanced Aquarium" (RL-*CPR*), 362.

soberest ways of seeing things as to be improper. Thus often our belief, our creed, seems like some simplified abstraction only intelligible to people who can no longer use their senses, a way of going to a country by not going, but by staying at home and buying a book of maps. Then you tell other people who also stay at home looking at maps that they are not getting anywhere because they have the wrong directions. This is getting off the deep end. I don't think anyone has much kick against what the Christian would like to want, we can't help seeing the same objects and the same colors.

    Cal

P.S. Don't take my heat-wave joke too seriously.

130.

[Postcard: Praça D. Pedro, Petrópolis]

[August 1955]

This is where we market & go to the movies. It is known as the town of Hortensias (hydrangeas to you) which are naturally blue here, none of those rusty nails you use on Cape Cod. I am trying to compose an answer to that Mr. Mumford of the Library—who do you suppose his "others" he mentions so often might be? Frances Parkinson Keyes? After all this time it has just dawned on me that the highest aims of the Fellows and those of the National Library are not exactly the same. I thought E's piece on C Stead (of whom I've never read a word) was very good and I wish I could get her books. Dick Eb wrote me a letter with lots of the latest news of people I've never heard of—and he re-iterated that old scene of you man-handling Dikkon[1]— "A Greek God." I am tired of it and think I'll start one of my own for him about "Cal, like a medieval saint." Did you ever get a copy of my book? HM apparently threw away the "advance" list.

    With much love,
      Elizabeth

---

1 Richard Eberhart's son.

131.

[Postcard: Photograph of Castine Bay and Islands]

[Castine, Maine]
August 24, 1955

Dear Elizabeth:

The world moves in circles: Stonington, the Eberharts, sea-fishing etc. Mighty proud of my doll, and think I am learning to like it—my Cousin Harriet saw it out of the corner of her eye for a split second when it arrived—her rejection of it was utter. We've been having a dim, cool, lazy, delightful time here—reading Cousin H.'s *who done its* and listening to Monteverdi records. How I wish you were with us!

Love,
Cal

132.

239 Marlboro St.
Boston
November 6, [1955]

Dear Elizabeth:

We are having a good fall I think, and wish your change of address had been to Boston, to us. You are much in my mind and everyone who comes to my study admires your picture where it stands next to a bearded William Empson playing baseball, a cousin Harriet, and a bearded J. R. Lowell not doing anything. Also the other day I taught your "Prodigal" to my class and found it easy to spend an hour on it, not saying anything very ambitious or profound but just telling the students to look at your words and think of the story—some like the pints behind the two-by-fours and some didn't.[1] I feel so envious, old portraitist and dramatic monologist that I am—you tell your moral with such grim kindly patience, are so there,—I'm glad Miss Moore says of you that at last we "have some one who is not a didacticist."[2]

We have nothing here to match your Eucharistic Congress. We do have a maid, whom Elizabeth intends to pay for by writing for the *New Yorker*, and our maid puts newspapers out on the side-walk periodically for arch-bishop Cushing's charities. Otherwise she is much in this world, has a very fancy car which she disappears in each evening, and is getting a portable, technicolor

---

1 See "The Prodigal," line 10 (EB-*CP*).
2 See Marianne Moore, "A Modest Expert," *The Nation* (Sept. 28, 1946).

TV set after Christmas—she grew up, oddly enough, in Nova Scotia and New England, an added reason for you to visit us. We're awfully mad at her at the moment. We feel that everything we have is tremendously grand. She doesn't. I don't think we own a plate or piece of linen that she doesn't want to have replaced.

Send something you have written or at least write another letter. I hate to think how long it's been since that long past day when you saw us off on the Norwegian boat for Genoa, when . . . but I don't know what I was going to add. But don't stay away for ever.

　　Love from us both,
　　Cal

133.

Dear Cal:

No sooner said than done. Here are the first and last poems of a bunch I've been doing. The last[1] I just wrote yesterday & probably shouldn't send it so soon. But if it doesn't work as a poem it may as a letter, that kind of thing being the daily life here. I just noticed the other day that I must have got my pigs' feet in "The Prodigal" from your spiders in "Mr. Edwards"[2] . . . And here, I'm afraid, "improvident as the dawn" is out of Yeats,[3] but anyway, I still like it. Where are you teaching? What is that spiritual exercise of the Jesuits—when they try to think in detail how the thing must have happened? Well, "The Prodigal" is an attempt at that.

Thank you so much for the pictures and I must say you look handsome and mature . . . I had quite an argument Sunday with a Brazilian beauty here for the week-end—passionate eyes, hooked nose, even a beauty spot— because she didn't think you were good-looking, but it finally came out that she is too dumb to appreciate anything but what she grew up with, the Latin type, and is very much taken with a Mexican movie star at the moment.

We loved the account of your maid. Well, here we have lots and lots. Against our wishes we're acquiring a real Brazilian style ménage. It seems to grow by subdivision, and now there are little sisters visiting and a baby in a crib in the kitchen and Singer hand-run sewing machines whizzing away

1 "Manuelzinho" (EB-*CP*).
2 "The Prodigal," line 21 (EB-*CP*); see "Mr. Edwards and the Spider," line 32 (RL-*CP*).
3 "Manuelzinho," line 74 (EB-*CP*); cf. W. B. Yeats, "The Dawn" (1919).

while they make wedding dresses—all very nice and gay. But your one probably does more than our three women and two men. The standard is: I was in bed with a cold for two days and sent my hot-water bottle to be refilled. Maria da Gloria made two trips to find out if she should use the same water over again. I intend to write for *The New Yorker* this coming year, too. I intend to jump at least three income tax brackets and go traveling, and that's the only way I can think of to do it.

We had a revolution last week,[1] an anti-revolution-revolution, and right now things look rather bad, although it started out gently enough, and it is the worst of the rainy season, so as Lota said, naturally no one would dream of going out to fight. The old dictator gang is back in again. (If you happen to read of it in the papers don't believe what they say. The *NY Times* had it completely the wrong way around,—another step for "democracy," etc.[2] I think our reporters are always told to agree with whoever's in power.) The reason I'm mentioning this is because one of my best friends here was the leader of the revolution that didn't come off—a newspaper editor and Representative who was responsible for getting rid of Vargas last year, almost single-handed.[3] He's a wonderful man, really—41, I think, very brave and intelligent, at his best as orator and TV man, and may end up as anything, of course, even dictator; Catholic, but liberally so. Well—he had to flee the country, first on a battleship (the old U.S. *"St. Louis."* Now the "Almaérante Tamardoré") then back to the Cuban Embassy, and now he's in New York. His wife and children are going up later. I've written various people in N.Y.—the Rahvs, for example,—and I wonder, if he gets to Boston, if you and E. would be interested in seeing him? I'm pretty sure you'd like him and get along. He speaks English and is interested in everything under the sun besides politics—just built a house near me here in the country and has discovered gardening and cooking. His last trip to N.Y. was for only two days, and he somehow found time to buy me 20 jars of spices.

He knows you by name, I know. I mentioned you when I wrote to him but I didn't have your address. I'll send it later. His is—and his name

1 The October 1955 elections were won by Juscelino Kubitschek de Oliveira (Vargas's political heir), but only narrowly; he would be a minority-elect president. Conservative military and civilian groups and individuals, including Carlos Lacerda, agitated against the outcome and advocated an "Emergency Regime" by coup. The war minister, Henrique Teixeira Lott, and Marshal Odílio Denys, who commanded the army in Rio, sided with arguments to protect the constitution and, in November, staged a "preventative coup" of their own to ensure Kubitschek could take office. He was inaugurated in January 1956. See EB-*Brazil*, 131–32.
2 "Brazil Stands Firm," *The New York Times* (Nov. 23, 1955).
3 Carlos Lacerda, editor of *Tribuna da Imprensa*.

Carlos Lacerda
C/O Hugo Gouthier, Consul
The Brazilian Consulate
10 Rockefeller Plaza, N.Y.

Oh, come to think of it, he's the one who mailed that doll to you for me. He tells good stories—about King Farouk on a picnic, etc. I'm writing Agnes Mongan, too. She met him when she was here. I don't think you'd find it a chore at all, and he's going to be making some broadcasts, etc. on "American Life" and I want to show him the "spiritual" side of it. Hide that automobile! I'm trying to do a complicated poem about Hopkins and E. Dickinson, after reading that new edition.[1] I am aiming as high as your Ford Madox Ford one, but have my doubts[2] . . . I'm also up to my neck, or higher, in the 2nd volume of that *Life of Freud.*[3] It's wonderful and fearful, although Dr. Jones is awfully laborious and dead-pan. I thought E's review of the Fiedler book was *excellent.*[4]

With love to you both,
Elizabeth

Manuelzinho = little Manuel *h* = *y*, in English

134.

December 29, 1955

Dear Elizabeth:

I shall have to write more of the champagne than of the poems for the moment, because Christmas with its maelstrom of cards, ornaments, sweets, extra cleanings, scattered wits etc. has hidden them completely, and I with my old woman's memory trust myself with nothing factual. Well, a little. I like the long one with Lota speculating on the Brazilian Indian with his varnished hat and praying for her enormously.[5] You seem to have a loose, seemingly careless style, very humorous, very "I am saying what amuses me and saying it without breaking my back"; but of course I know all [the] fierce labors you really go through. What I mean to say is that this last poem and your long wonder-

1 EB, "Notes for the Dickinson/Hopkins Poem" (typescript, Vassar). Emily Dickinson, *Poems*, ed. Thomas H. Johnson (1955).
2 "Ford Madox Ford" (RL-*CP*).
3 Ernest Jones, *The Life and Works of Sigmund Freud*, vol. 2 (1955).
4 Elizabeth Hardwick's review of Leslie Fiedler's *An End to Innocence* (1955), *Partisan Review* (Winter 1955).
5 "Manuelzinho" (EB-*CP*).

ful Nova Scotia story[1] both give themselves, as though you weren't writing at all, but just talking in a full noisy room, talking until suddenly everyone is quiet. I like your short poem[2] too very much and the two in the *New Yorker*, particularly the second[3]—more later, when I have the texts near me.

The fine, Brazilian S.S. Pierce champagne came at a good time. We gave a little Christmas party for eight unmarried people. It had to be on Christmas night when everyone was bursting at the seams and blue in the face with over-eating and new dieting resolutions. If it hadn't been for your champagne, costly, exotic, glorious with your name, and amazing everyone with the fact that anyone in Brazil could bring Boston's Pierce into action, (now for an anaphora[4]) if it hadn't been for your champagne we would never have gotten off the ground. There were bad moments. Two guests whom we had rather wickedly intended to throw on one another, defied us, and invited friends of their own, whom we had never met. At any moment one might look up and see each guest and each stranger off in a corner, musing sullenly, silently. I sound like notes for a Mary McCarthy novel. Have you read her last[5] in which Mary (divorced and remarried) is seduced by Wilson (divorced and remarried) after a Wellfleet reading of Racine's *Berenice?*[6] In the last chapter Mary driving to Boston for an abortion is run into and killed by a red-headed Millay-like Cape poet driving on the wrong side of the road.[7] Who can doubt that Mary really *lives* in her books? If she ever loses her mind, she'll never know which parts of her life she lived and which she wrote. She is somehow rather immense without her books ever being exactly good form or good imagination.

Last night I was reading Lord Acton's introduction to a series of lectures on modern history. He offered as a truism that needed no underlining or amplification: "Historians, learn by writing, rather than by reading."[8] This had never occurred to me. Don't you think we could mak e a fortu n e (my typewriter occasionally splutters and skips spaces with anger) by starting a sanitarium to cure victims of ceaseless reading. Across the alley in back of our house, there is a reducing school. No one eats anything; but pyramids of

1 "In the Village" (EB-*CPR*).
2 Probably "The Shampoo," *The New Republic* (July 11, 1955); see EB-*CP*.
3 "Manners (for a Child of 1918)," *The New Yorker* (Nov. 26, 1955), and "Filling Station," *The New Yorker* (Dec. 10, 1955); see EB-*CP*.
4 See "Anaphora" (EB-*CP*).
5 Mary McCarthy, *A Charmed Life* (1955). Mary McCarthy and Edmund Wilson were married from 1938 to 1944.
6 Racine, *Berenice* (1670).
7 Edna St. Vincent Millay and Edmund Wilson were lovers in 1920.
8 Lord Acton, *Lectures on Modern History* (1906).

garbage pile up—so high I sometimes can't force my car through them. This is the food they have left untouched, and the odor of its corruption is like incense, for each betokens a triumph of the will. So it would be with the book-cure; think of all the wonderful-really-necessary-for-one's-occupation-and-peace-of-mind-books one could *not* read each day! At a Christmas lunch we met a sweet old lady who was going out of her mind second by second as we watched. The reason was that on this one day out of the whole 365 she was missing her television. *Channel two* was on, and there she was eating turkey and flaming pudding. She had come to Boston from Milton in a taxi: after thirty minutes the taxi returned to take her home. Her soup was unfinished and she had left presents apparently intended for the next year, so that she should never again be disturbed. That's how I've been about reading during my vacation, la chair n'est pas triste.[1]

I hope my present has arrived and not caused you a world of trouble at the customs.

We stay on here. I am going [to] continue teaching at Boston University. We are very pretentious and sociable, sort of Poobahs; and are trying to memorize Lionel Trilling in defense of manners.[2]

Love from us both,

    Cal

135.

June 7th, 1956

Dearest Cal:

I don't know why I've been so slow about writing to you, since I think of you every day of my life I'm sure . . . But now I really must, because a week ago Saturday to my great astonishment and joy, your Christmas present arrived. Not even tarnished. Nothing to pay. They didn't even open it. I think you were very foolhardy to trust it to these mails, but I am delighted with it and we have used it for milk for tea every afternoon since. It's an awfully pretty little pitcher and where on earth did you get it; and yes, it is very much like here except for the elephants, and I don't think we have *hooded* cobras, but maybe we do. We certainly have enough of them, called *cobras*, too, and all sizes. The inscription makes me very proud and self-conscious—always hoping that some observant guest will ask me all about it; and if they don't, I tell them anyway . . .

---

1 The flesh is not weary; cf. "*La chair est triste, hélas! et j'ai lu tous les livres*," Mallarmé, "Brise Marin," line 1.
2 Lionel Trilling, "Manners, Morals, and the Novel," *The Liberal Imagination* (1950).

You probably know all about the Pulitzer business[1] . . . that, and just before that a trip to Diamantina and writing a piece about it, have pretty much
taken up the past two months. I was really surprised, having thought all
along that it had already been given out, and I'd not seen about it. It was very
funny here—a reporter from *O Globo* shouting at me over the telephone, and
I kept replying in a cool New Englandy way, "Thank you very much," and
he shouted again, "But Dona Elizabetchy, don't you understand? O Prémio
Pulítzer!" I honestly feel from the bottom of my heart that it should have
gone to Randall, for some of his war poems,[2] and I don't know why it didn't.
I really do seem on the frivolous side compared to him, and there's so little of
it. Well, one never knows about these things, or how one *should* feel about
them. As I'll never forget Caroline[3] saying to you, I'll try to "live it down."
     We had lots of fun here for a while with reporters and photographers and
their amazing fantasies . . . There was a snapshot of Portinari on the wall doing his last UN mural, and the reporters asked if we knew him, etc.[4] (He's an
old friend of Lota's.) *That* appeared in the papers as their asking her how we
carried on a conversation, since he speaks no English, and then " 'Oh—Art
is the universal language' replied the lively and intelligent Dona Lotinha." I
am taking the money, or part of it, to buy a high-fidelity victrola with. (The
reporters also said I lived "an austere life, without a radio.") If you happen to
see Harvey Breit in the *Times* don't believe it. It's all wrong, both times, except, of course that I *am* terribly handsome . . .[5]
     One journalist friend did a piece for the literary monthly. I quoted you
and Herbert and Hopkins, etc. to try to make it slightly sensible, but I am
afraid my quotations will be garbled. I quoted the lines "Salem fishermen /
Once hung their nimble fleets on the great Banks"[6] as an example of what a
single word—*hung*—can do, the enormous power[,] suggestion of accuracy,
etc. (Also "Les soirs illuminés par l'ardeur du *charbon*"[7])
     I just read yesterday Elizabeth's story about the man who lived in a hotel

---

1 *Poems: North & South—A Cold Spring* (1955) won the 1956 Pulitzer Prize.
2 Randall Jarrell, *Selected Poems* (1955).
3 Caroline Gordon.
4 Candido Portinari's murals *War* and *Peace* were commissioned by the Brazilian government as a gift to the
United Nations.
5 Breit mentions EB in two of his "In and Out of Books" columns for *The New York Times Book Review* (on
May 20, 1956, and May 27, 1956). In the first, he applauds her Pulitzer because "(1) she is a handsome woman, (2) a
friend of Marianne Moore, and (3) she once said she was opposed 'to making poetry monstrous or boring and proceeding to talk the very life out of it.'" In the second, he reports from a Brazilian correspondent who was sent to interview her in Samambaia.
6 "Salem," lines 10–11 (RL-*CP*).
7 Charles Baudelaire, "Le balcon," line 6.

room for fifteen years, did nothing, etc.[1] It reminded me uncomfortably of my friend Tom—remember him?—except that he is much richer and lives in a much worse hotel. The whole thing is so like him that I even wondered if E knew him. I think it's very well done, and the magazine editor scenes are awfully good. And now I hope that pays for your hypercritical maid for some time to come . . . I thought E's review of the Dylan Thomas book by Brinnin was superb, really.[2] It came the same day that MacNeice's review did, and that was so poor, and mean![3] Heavens, the English can be mean. He accuses Brinnin of being handicapped by his faulty American sense of humour so that he couldn't appreciate DT "as a clown," which strikes me as speaking rather well for the U.S. sense of humour . . . I thought the book suffers chiefly from a lack of common sense, or a helpless romanticism, about alcoholism—confusing it with philosophy or something—but actually I think he did have to write it, good or bad.

I went on a trip to Diamantina in April and had a wonderful time. Once I get going I lose my fears of airplanes and the Portuguese language, so much so that I really think I'll tackle an Amazon trip next year. I think you would like and appreciate Diamantina. It is very high, very tiny, with 16 tiny, solid churches and an ugly Cathedral from which they broadcast terce every evening at sundown, so that the whole place vibrates with Hail Marys. There is a remote, intense atmosphere, derived, I think, from the fact that the two consuming passions of the inhabitants are religion and gambling—or the equivalent of gambling, since they live from finding one diamond, or nugget of gold, until the next one, in great poverty. It is set in a great sea of waves of steely gray rocks that all turn blood red when the sun goes down, too, and the evenings are icy cold—then the fire-siren sounds, to announce the beginning of the movie: Betty Grable while I was there. I bought and picked up so many hunks of rock crystal that I had to pay $7 excess baggage on the home trip—brought them along with me in a lovely little black leather trunk with brass nail-heads that I acquired there, too. I've described it all in detail, probably too much, in the introduction to *Black Beans & Diamonds*[4] (my translating job) that is *just* done: just some more corrections, now.

You mentioned—months ago—Lord Acton (I'd been reading him too)

1 Elizabeth Hardwick, "The Oak and the Axe," *The New Yorker* (May 12, 1956).
2 Elizabeth Hardwick, "America and Dylan Thomas," review of John Malcolm Brinnin's *Dylan Thomas in America* (1955), *Partisan Review* (Spring 1956).
3 Louis MacNeice, "What Vomit Had John Keats," review of John Malcolm Brinnin's *Dylan Thomas in America* (1955), *New Statesman and Nation* (April 21, 1956).
4 Bishop considered "Black Beans and Diamonds" as a possible title for her translation of *The Diary of "Helena Morley."*

and history-writing. Did you know that Southey wrote a very good history of Brazil, without ever having seen it of course?[1] Lionel Trilling—well, I don't know quite why but I always feel a little suspicious of him, probably unfairly, but I did see an awfully good piece of his about Santayana's letters.[2] Did you see that? At least it put for me exactly how I feel about Santayana myself—although I haven't read the letters. I saw a piece about you by somebody named *Jumper* in the *Hudson Review*.[3] He starts out implying he's really going to tell us ALL, and then after telling nothing at all, and repeating the obvious, I thought, petered out and wound up by saying you should be more cheerful! I haven't read Mary's last and probably shant.[4] She somehow keeps chopping away at her own feet until there is nothing left at all. I read *The Quiet American*[5] expecting to be made mad, but it's just rather silly, or else poor Hemingway. I am pleased you said you liked my "Manuelzinho"—somehow when he appeared just now, in the *New Yorker*, he seemed more frivolous than I'd thought, but maybe that's just the slick, rich surroundings.[6] Please do forgive me for being so slow about writing; thank you for the really lovely pitcher, and I hope you and E are both well and flourishing on Marlborough St. Tell me more about it, and your summer plans. Why not come here?

    With much love,
    Elizabeth

136.

[Postcard of Dedo de Deus, Orgãos Mountains, Petrópolis]

June 8th, [1956]

This is "The Finger of God"—hope I haven't sent you one before, but postcards here are limited. I wrote you a letter yesterday, but I have lost so many, coming and going, lately, that I'm sending this along with it, too, as a sort of guide. This scenery is near us, higher up—we sometimes drive up & back on moonlight nights and it is not *earthly* at all—except for the fact that they raise excellent vegetables there because of all the mists, and we usually bring back strawberries, artichokes, etc. Farming here is very queer—it doesn't seem to come natural—for example, right here they use[d] to raise carrots,

---

1 Robert Southey, *History of Brazil* (1810).
2 Lionel Trilling, "That Smile of Parmenides Made Me Think," *A Gathering of Fugitives* (1956).
3 Will C. Jumper, "Whom Seek Ye?: A Note on Robert Lowell's Poetry," *The Hudson Review* (Spring 1956).
4 Mary McCarthy published *Sights and Spectacles* in 1956, but EB probably means *A Charmed Life* (1955).
5 Graham Greene, *The Quiet American* (1955).
6 "Manuelzinho (Brazil. A Friend of the Writer Is Speaking)," *The New Yorker* (May 26, 1956); see EB-*CP*.

up above our house—and bring them down the cliffs on ladders. Why? Please do come visit sometime—I'd take you to some wonderful colonial towns in the Volkswagon *bus* we're getting—holds 10—only car we can get. Red—with windows on the roof for sight-seeing.

With love,
Elizabeth

137.

[June 18, 1956]

Dearest Elizabeth:

We are going to have a child. It will come sometime in January, and already *we* are exhausted. We lie about on sofas all day eating cornflakes, no-calorie ginger-ale and yogurt. Elizabeth never moves except to turn the page of an English newspaper or buy a dress. I never move except to turn on my high-fi radio or to go on expeditions for second-hand books. E's doctor has decided that we had better not go to Maine, so we will probably spend the summer here . . . However E has been told not spend *all* her time shopping, so we may go to Maine after all. This isn't quite how it really is, but the last four days here have been scorchers, ninety-four on our coldest floor and we are very disorganized and cynical. But how we boast! People whom I had utterly felt cut off from: my barber, my dentist, the head of the Boston University English department, wives of friends, children . . . to all of them I can't stop talking and bragging. Elizabeth had rather a painful first month and still feels languid but is much more comfortable. We hear of women (Eleanor Clark) who ski all through pregnancy, give birth in bomb shelters without doctors, etc. But we don't approve, and are timid, delicate and antebellum.

I had no idea that the Christmas present would be so late, and had begun to fear that you were somehow offended, or had had to pay a fine at the customs. It really was mailed early in December . . . Five months arriving in Brazil! I must mail your next year's present early in July. The pitcher came from Treffery and Partridge, a little silver shop opposite the State House. The pitcher looks suspiciously like one we once inherited from my Aunt Beatrice, who for the first sixteen months of her marriage lived in India and had a staff of sixty servants. For the sixty remaining years of her marriage she lived in Boston and could never adapt.

I think the man in E's story is really *us*, but already several people we never met are having persecution break-downs because they recognize themselves. I saw Andrews Wanning at Bard last week-end, where I read a paper on art and bad characters.[1] Apparently Andrews' wife is famous for dreading Tom, a sort of portent of what her husband might become if his art for enjoying life were to develop any further. Ah me, how grateful I still am to Tom for driving Carley Dawson homeward from Stonington!

I am so delighted about the Pulitzer. I was on the Bollingen and National Book Award committees and tried to get the prizes given to you and/or Randall. Your chances were killed by Phyllis McGinley who thought you were serious or a woman or something. The National Book Award went to Auden, a wonderful poet with not so good a book, while the Bollingen went to Conrad Aiken, not such a good poet but with one of his best books.[2] Everyone said you and Randall were young and would have hundreds more chances. Phyllis McGinley dominated one meeting and Mrs. Biddle the other. Did you hear about Randall being made the consultant for the next two years? We were driving through Virginia at the time of the announcement. The early morning edition had a small front page picture of Randall very bearded and looking like a seedy French second Empire baron. Slowly the editors began to realize that they had a sensational photograph. All day it grew larger and larger till by evening it almost covered the entire page, blotting out the whole world!

We are liking Boston and have quite a few friends—in some groups we seem unspeakably strange and bohemian, in others we seem very grand and social. It's fun to puzzle people. But oh it's wonderful to be in one spot two successive autumns. And now a third is coming! How I wish you would come and pay us a very long visit, several years. Couldn't you translate Howells into Portuguese and spend a long time boning up on local Boston color to be used in your introduction. We can't be much farther away from you than the sources of the Amazon.

You should see the Rahvs' new house. It's what Philip calls good material, and must have cost a hundred thousand dollars once to build. It has a hundred acres or so of land. Meadows that have [to] be mown, woodchucks that Philip traps and hires someone to take away, a stream that could be dammed for a swimming pool, a kitchen that was once exhibited in *Home Beautiful*. Inside it is full of vast empty spaces, staggered modern book shelves designed by Nathalie, a clock that runs without winding for three years, but then has to be taken to the factory and re-charged for $25, dried

1 "Art and Evil" (RL-*CPR*).
2 W. H. Auden, *The Shield of Achilles* (1956); Conrad Aiken, *A Letter from Li Po* (1955).

pine trees in vases, a whole nursery wing for children, a quarter of a mile dirt driveway which the swimming pool stream overflowed and washed away for leagues and leagues this spring. The Rahvs' only neighbors are an old man's home, a girls finishing school, and a society of retired fowl hunters and active professional farmers. Philip boasts of knowing no one within forty miles, and one has a feeling of Tolstoy, versts, owned serf villages, and the grand old PR whiskey drinking gossips in that old immense room with its small bed in the back occupied by a sick and murderous cat.

I've got a big chunk of autobiography coming out in PR this fall[1]—fifty pages and hope you will approve, though it seems thin and arty after your glorious Nova Scotia mad mother and cow piece.[2] Liked your Brazilian man better than ever in the New Yorker—the most feminine of character sketches with you and Lota both speaking through each other. I very much liked the short tourist poem and hope I wrote you about it.[3]

You are on Mary McCarthy's good books, though few others are. She boasts on her book jackets of editing a college magazine with you, was very eager for you to get all the poetry prizes, and gave your childhood background but not you to one of the characters in her last novel. But she is very high horse with success, has said that my poems are brassy, that Elizabeth's next-to-last New Yorker story[4] sounds like Jean Stafford, and advised Arthur Schlesinger not to publish his ten years opus on F.D.R.[5] I think I have a lot more news, but feel I'm running down like the Rahvs' three year clock. So goodbye and all our love,

Cal

138.

September 5, 1956

Dear Elizabeth:

Many thanks for the child's scratch pads; but aren't you expecting him to be born a Lord Macaulay completely literate and a master of strange tongues? We are afraid that . . . but never mind our fears. They are mostly for our selves. We are so much older than other beginning parents. I half fear

---

1 "91 Revere Street," *Partisan Review* (Fall 1956); see RL-*CP*.
2 "In the Village" (EB-*CPR*).
3 Possibly "Questions of Travel," *The New Yorker* (Jan. 21, 1956); see EB-*CP*.
4 Elizabeth Hardwick, "A Season's Romance," *The New Yorker* (March 10, 1956).
5 Arthur M. Schlesinger Jr., *Age of Roosevelt*, published in three volumes: *The Crisis of the Old Order, 1919–1933* (1957), *The Coming of the New Deal* (1958), and *The Politics of Upheaval* (1960).

we will go to a parents and teachers meeting and there we will meet the children of our contemporaries—already parents! I do have one old friend who is having his first child this October. His name is Macauley and we already call the not yet first-born Babington.[1] I can already hear my little daughter whining seven years hence: "Daddy why do I ALWAYS have to play with that BabingTON!"

Ah me the years, the years! The day after your pads arrived, I saw a nice grey Brazilian air-mail envelope waiting for me. All day I'd been saying to myself, "Isn't it lovely and witty and typical somehow of dear Elizabeth to celebrate and take notice of our coming parenthood solely by sending those attractive Brazilian pads—one word of comment from her would really spoil everything." However, I was all atremble with excitement when I opened the letter and found the enclosed. Would I were in Brazil and twenty-seven and writing poems of verses about the infancy!

I was on a magazine conference held at Harvard this summer and saw Marianne Moore and felt like falling at her feet. She had to sum up the other speakers and spoke of Philip Rahv "looking volumes each time an intention of the *Partisan Review* was misconstrued." The Trillings, by the way, are said to be having long serious perplexed discussions and to be lying awake nights. Why? After all these years they have discovered that Philip Rahv just isn't *tonic.*

We're just back from New York and seeing the Taylors who have just landed from Italy. On the same day I saw my other closest friend. Oh what a gap and blank and sorrow that you are so far away. Miss Moore says that you hunger for news from America and keep up a correspondence with people that would ordinarily bore you to tears. Please put me back on your list.

Elizabeth is blooming and sends her love,
Cal

[Enclosed]
Rio de Janeiro, August, 22, 1956
Sir Robert Lowell,
Poet
170 Marlboro St.,
Boston, U.S.A.

Dear Sir:

I am writting this letter to you because I am a poetess. I am reading some verses of the american poets I and knew a poem

1 Lord Macaulay's full name was Thomas Babington Macaulay.

that you had written—"The Quaker Graveyar in Nantucket." I think it is a wonderfull poem and I wish very much to know you.

So I went to day at the American Embassy and I asked information about you at de Department of Informations of the Embassy Library.

I will be very glad if you could writte to me about your poetry and if you send to me some poems of your book of verses. I know you are a catholic man. I am a catholic girl. I am 27 years old. You are eleven years old than I. I think there are no importance this difference between our age. You don't?

I suppose you don't want to writte to me, but I thank you very much if you pay attention at my letter.

My addres is: Rua Barata Ribeiro, 531, Apt. 902, Copacabana Rio de Janeiro, Brasil.

Sincerelly yours,
Miss Zila Mamede

P.S.—

My subjects in the poetry are: love, the sea, the death, the people, the clouds, the land, the beach and the infancy.

139.

September 24th, 1956

My dear Sir Robert:

My apologies for being so slow about writing. I've been awfully busy lately finishing up that translation, done at last, thank goodness, and going back and forth to Rio to the dentist and to see the authoress of the translation, or the original, rather, now seventy-six years old.[1] I'm so afraid she may die before the thing appears. She says, "If only Aunt Madge could have lived to see me printed in English!" (Aunt Madge would be about 125 if she had.) Her husband, over eighty, is a phenomena. He just retired from being President of the Bank of Brazil for the 4th time and looks about 60. He goes over every word with a fine tooth-comb and sends me pages and pages, hundreds, of notes, corrections, "recommendations," "suggestions," *"Importante,"* etc.—in the tiniest, clearest hand-writing. Now he's even taken to cutting out pictures of trees, gold-panners, etc., and gluing them to the notes, and

---

1 Alice Dayrell Calderia Brant.

drawing very elaborate sketches (maps) of church processions, etc. He thinks he knows English and corrects mine—all wrong, of course. The last thing he read was Boswell's *Journal*, so he tries to force his wife's childhood diary into that style . . . I'm calling it *Black Beans & Diamonds*, but he is putting up a stiff fight for *As You Ware*, as he says it. Well, they're a marvelous couple.

Your fan-letter has been greatly appreciated. Shall I look her up for you? She lives near the apartment in Rio. Every word is literally from the Portuguese. That's the best I've ever seen, I think. I had a strange one from a boy who loves "all the arts"; his paintings and drawings are in Canada or he'd send them to me, so instead he appends a long list of all their titles "The Death of Marat," "The Bohemian," "The Musslemen," etc., & on the back of the envelope (the letter's in Portuguese) he wrote: U R 2 GOOD 2 B 4 GOT 10 But nothing can approach Miss Mamede.

I don't believe I've congratulated you yet about the baby, and I hope you are both keeping well and strong and cheerful. I'm very probaby these days. "Maria Elizabeth" is 18 months old now and beautiful as an Abyssinian Princess and learning to talk. We also have Lota's son's two older children—2 & 3— here for long stretches from time to time and run a regular nursery school and enjoy it very much.[1] Couldn't you arrange to have the christening coincide with Marianne's 70th birthday?[2] I'm really hoping to get back to the U.S.A for that.

She wrote me about her Boston visit: "then Harvard's little magazine Conference at which I *throve* (useless as I was professionally); cool pleasant weather and such companionable people . . . R & E Lowell. I do like them— heartfelt, generous, genial, initiate; and so prepossessing! Philip Rahv gave a stern A-One talk on values in use as over against mildewed dictatorial culture. The L's invited me to a tea that was notable—flowers in a stone dish— a Boston-in-its-glory pair of drawing rooms—large window embrasures and millions of books ascending the walls. William Alfred (?) was an ornament of the conference, so punctual, so learned, so cheerful."

(I hope you weren't late & gloomy.)

I saw a picture of Randall in *TIME* and think the beard is extremely becoming. I wonder if he got his Mercedes Benz. My dream car has now switched to a Giulietta convertible . . . the MG is really getting rather old . . . and I am writing *New Yorker* stories, too, with this in mind. A Giulietta with

---

1 Lota adopted a boy called Kylso, whom "she found in a garage where she was having her car fixed." He was crippled by polio and his family was too poor to afford his medical care. Lota paid for his treatment and his education. He later worked as a draftsman for Sérgio Bernardes, married, and had several children who spent time in Samambaia. See *Remembering Elizabeth Bishop: An Oral Biography*, ed. Gary Fountain and Peter Brazeau (1994), 131–32.
2 November 15, 1957.

"Spider Springs." Somebody wrote me, I can't remember who, that Catharine Carver said your autobiographical piece is "wonderful" and Philip wrote something stern and A-one masculinely equivalent, so I wish it would hurry up and appear. I loved Mary McC's saying you were "brassy"—well, I like trumpet music very much if that's what she meant . . .

We've had a house guest for over a month now, one of a pair of famous sisters, Rio "beauties," old school friends of Lota's. She really is beautiful, too—tall, grizzled blond, magnificent teeth and one blue eye and one brown eye. But she is an extreme hypochondriac, and it's a little like having Proust to visit . . . No, I'm sure she's much nicer. But "resting" and making up her face and taking endless baths occupies most of her day. One interesting thing about her is that she's still, at 45 or so, completely dominated by her old Scotch governess who died 15 yrs. ago, but was with them for thirty years. She has her picture in her prayer-book, looking just like a Scotch Highlander. I know of several of these Scotch governesses—their charges, no matter how "delicate" they are, all still take a "walk" every day and start off every morning with a dish of oatmeal (it's almost all the nourishment our guest will take) and speak perfect English with slight Scotch accents. Maria Cecilia (the guest) says: "My, you gave me a turn, as Miss Killough would say." Miss Killough bossed the mother around completely and every so often they had big fights, and she'd pack her steamer trunks to start back to Aberdeen. But when she died she left them all the money she'd saved, out of the salary they paid her, and just before the end she became a Catholic. (The 2nd case of that I know)—said her own church seemed "cold" to her. But I bet it was because of being snubbed by the English colony here, over the years, as a "governess." Well, Maria Cecilia is a fiend for "altering" clothes, darning and mending, and she's got my wardrobe in better shape than it's been in years . . . there's a nice Portuguese word meaning to make the most of or take advantage—*aproveitar*—and we've been *aproveitar*-ing shamelessly.

There's another nice humane verb that English needs—when you want to get out of an engagement, or dis-invite yourself—*desmarcar*. Something else I've found out about the language—Portugal was such a remote part of the Roman Empire that Portuguese changed more slowly than any other latin language—they still have some Roman *Republic* forms, dropped under the Empire,—and the open and close *e* & *o* correspond to differences of length in Classical Latin. Also the days of the week—"2nd Day" "3rd Day" are early Christian, when they couldn't use the names of the pagan Gods—after a while the other nations went back to *lundi, mardi*, and so on . . . However, I'm still hopeless at *speaking* languages and really only talk freely to the cook.

I've been reading a superb book—but you probably know it—Marchand's *Memoirs of Napoleon*?[1] If not, do read it immediately; I'm sure you'd like it, too. I wrote a kind of poem, not much, for Mr. Rizzardi's number on Pound.[2] Do you know him?—from Bologna. He writes very nice letters and I think he said he was going to see you. He's in the U.S. now as a Commonwealth Fellow.

The pitcher is really used every single day for tea. I hope Elizabeth is keeping well. Please write soon all the news.

With much love,
Elizabeth

No new poems to see?

140.

Dearest Elizabeth:

U R 2 good 2 B 4 got 10. What a grand line! I'm just back from a week in New York and Washington. In New York I was on some poetry committee to give a poetry prize for Brandeis College in memory of Judge Brandeis. When I arrived at the 5th Avenue palace Marianne Moore was sprawled like some Boucher goddess in a print dress and black cartwheel hat on the huge marble disc of the huge marble banister. Next to her Louise Bogan looking a little stiff, proud and shocked. We went into the ballroom, a room a mile wide and long with a green carpet, nothing anywhere except a green carpet, little rickety iron chairs hugging the wall, and a green baize-covered lopsided ping pong table. We ordered into the elevator, a matchbox that would only scarcely hold me and Miss Moore. Arriving, we entered on a man dictating, who waved us away and said without raising his eyes, "Oh heavens, first floor." But some one at the end of the corridor welcomed us. We entered a narrow room about as big as three matchboxes. There sat two secretaries and Mr. Warburg, "Piggy" as I later learned from Louis Kronenberger.[3] Mr. Warburg immediately began spouting in a stately drone and couldn't be forced to wait for the other three judges. It never stopped for an hour and three quarters. I don't think he really had any effect on our

1 Louis Marchand, *Memories of Napoleon* (1955).
2 "Visits to St. Elizabeths," *Nuova Corrente: rivistas di letteratura* (1956), an issue dedicated to Pound; see EB-*CP*.
3 Paul F. ("Piggy") Warburg.

voting, nor did we have much of any effect on him. At one time he talked for fifteen minutes on the climate and sloping banks of the islands off Vancouver, a "place where all poets should go." His voice was terrible in the little space and made one feel as though it were an airplane descending forever from a great altitude. Moore sayings: Some one proposed Padraic Colum. "Well lately he has split apart." She meant his poetry had.[1] Referring to you, "Poor Elizabeth, she does her best to bear up and rejoice." To W. C. Williams, "And his is sometimes ASTONISHINGLY RIGHT, sometimes!"[2] To Mr. Warburg, who seemed on the point of proposing a second meeting for a second ballot, "But these meetings are death to me." Some one said that he didn't suppose she often undertook the trip in from Brooklyn. Miss Moore: "I am just back from California." However, she was always small, gracious, mobile, and beautiful. I feel utterly in love with her. At the end of the meeting, Mr. Warburg, tanned, bald, brown-patched, Buddha-nosed, beaming, growing as big as Huntington Cairns, and having to be prodded by both his secretaries each time one of us spoke—at the end Mr. Warburg said to me, "Goodbye . . ." long pause. "Mr. . . ." pause. "I have always wondered if your name were pronounced Lou-well or Lowe-well."

Well, Randall! Like the earth he carries his atmosphere with him and is no different in Washington than he is in Greensboro. In the office he has his big Degas, Munch, Klee, and Vuillard (?) reproductions and a spectacled photograph, like a picture of one's wife and baby, in a leather frame on his desk: Chekhov. At his home in Chevy Chase he has big reproductions of Klee, Degas, Munch, etc. Photographs in the shadowy hall of Wallace Stevens and Marianne Moore and on his desk another photograph—this time without spectacles—of Chekhov. Randall is just back from the west coast and tells an unconsciously blood-curdling story about how he spent the evening with two young poets. One he took a shine to. The other . . . "Well he could see that I didn't like him near as well." I'll bet the guy did! Peter Taylor speaks of the time when Randall "dropped" his little daughter age five. Randall is in grand shape, and is enjoying the library where he will work 20 hours a week and have three months vacation. He sounds like Bernard Shaw when he is quoted in the papers. He also has a little white patch in his beard and is ageless—almost. Lonely and wonderful.

I loved your description of the blue-and-brown-eyed beauty—how like

---

1 Padraic Colum, *The Vegetable Kingdom* (1954).
2 William Carlos Williams, *The Desert Music* (1954).

my mother I seized on the vulnerable detail! I've shot my wad. Bear up, my dear, and come back to us. Elizabeth is grand, enormous, lovely and sends you her love, and I send mine.

~~Robert Lowell~~ Cal

P.S. My poor Cousin Harriet, frail and wonderful, she had a stroke last winter and her right arm and leg will remain paralyzed forever. I had a good visit with her and she talked just as someone my own age, only wittier and more natural. I think going out that way is even better than instant death, late in life and in full health. I saw Ezra, but I'll save that for another letter.

P.S. There's a review of Auden's *Faber Book of Verse* in the *New Statesman* by Walter Allen, who calls you the best woman poet since Emily Dickinson.[1] I know you like neither E.D. nor being called a "woman" poet.

141.[2]

December 2nd, 1956

Dearest Cal:

I was awfully glad to hear from you & hope Elizabeth continues to do well. Day before yesterday I mailed you both a book that I trust you haven't seen already, or that when you have seen you won't feel shows a terrible degeneration in my taste! I like best the TROU—page 256 . . .[3] Last night and this morning I've read your piece in *PR*, that just arrived. It is *very* good; I feel as if I'd sat through one of those Sunday dinners. And being thrown out of the Garden, just like Adam, is marvelous.[4] I hadn't realized before how closely connected with the Navy you were. In fact it is all fascinating, and I hope I see more soon. Is *PR* going to publish more, and when will the book of it appear, and how far along do you go? No, really, it's excellent. And what's more, you *keep it up,*—and can keep it up, I should think, your life being more all of a piece than—well, mine, for example. Or perhaps other people's lives always appear to be.

I'm glad it came along now because for several weeks I've been com-

---

1 *The Faber Book of Modern American Verse*, ed. W. H. Auden (1956); Walter Allen, "Aristocracy of One," *New Statesman and Nation* (Sept. 15, 1956), 316.

2 See Appendix I for EB's first draft of her reply to letter 140.

3 Unidentified French book.

4 ". . . I stood in the center of a sundial tulip bed and pelted a little enemy ring of third-graders with wet fertilizer. Office Lever was telephoned. Officer Lever telephoned my mother. In the presence of my mother and some thirty nurses and children, I was expelled from the Public Garden"; "91 Revere Street," RL-*CP* and *CPR*.

pletely absorbed in Coleridge's *Letters*—that new edition.[1] (Maybe I was when I wrote to you last; I can't remember how long it's been going on now.) Last week Lota had to go to Rio for three days & I was all alone: except for the servants, that is, the cat (being de-wormed) and the toucan (who has a sore foot) and the most terrific storm in my experience here raged all those days. (A family of seven was wiped out in a landslide in Petrópolis, the road was impassible, etc., although I knew none of this until later.) And I read Coleridge, and read him, & read him—just couldn't stop—until he and the waterfall *roaring* under the windows, and ten times its usual size, were indistinguishable to my ears. By the time he'd had "flying irregular gout," got himself drenched once more, was in debt, hating his wife, etc., I couldn't believe that I really existed, or not what you'd call *life*, compared to that: dry, no symptoms of any sort, fairly solvent, on good terms with all my friends (as far as I know). I want very much to write some sort of piece, mostly about C, but bringing in Fitzgerald's "The Crack-Up,"[2] Dylan T., H. Crane, etc., but don't know whether I know enough, or have enough material at hand. Well, your chapter was a decided change in tone.

Marianne is wonderful, that's all. If I don't mention my health she writes implying that she knows I'm concealing my dying throes from her. If I say I've never felt better in my life (God's truth) she writes *"Brave* Elizabeth!" (Lota says it's a form of aggression). She used to send one rather stolid, timid friend of ours on Errands of Mercy, to people he'd never met. She told him that *"poor* Peter Monro Jack"[3] was in desperate straits, sick, lonely, heaven knows what all, and the friend went to call, probably taking a bag of groceries or a bunch of flowers, and found a large gay party going on, with everyone in evening dress. Also Marsden Hartley—dying and all alone in a miserable garret—*he* was found to be in a friend's most luxurious apartment, with a Steinway grand and a cook and a maid waiting on his every wish! I have to repeat one of the few *bon mots* of my life here. I told the unfortunate friend, whose name was *Lester,* "You're for the Moores and Martyrdome."[4]

Yes, I saw that extravagant remark in the *New Statesman & Nation.* (The writer is probably aged 19 and known to be slightly feeble-minded by his intimates.) Did I really make snide remarks about E. Dickinson? I like, or at least admire, her a great deal more now, probably because of that good new

---

1 Samuel Taylor Coleridge, *Correspondence* (vol. 1, 1785–1800; vol. 2, 1801–06), ed. Earl Leslie Grigg (1956–71).
2 F. Scott Fitzgerald, *The Crack-Up*, ed. Edmund Wilson (1945).
3 Peter Monro Jack, book critic who wrote often for *The New York Times.*
4 Lester Littlefield; cf. Richard Crashaw, "A Hymn to the Name and Honour of the Admirable St. Teresa" (1646), line 64.

edition, really. I spent another stretch absorbed in that, and think, (along with Randall[1]) that she's about the best we have. However, she does set one's teeth on edge a lot of the time, don't you think? "Woman" poet—no. What I like to be called now is *poetress*. I was at a friend's house here the other day and he introduced me to a Brazilian lady. He murmured to her in Portuguese that this was the American poet, etc., and the lady, determined to show off her English, shook my hand enthusiastically and said, "You are the famous American poetress?" So I allowed I was. I think it's a nice mixture of poet and mistress. The lady actually turned out to be quite interesting: she & her husband a team of lawyers, & she's writing a book about the U.S. Supreme Court, has written one about Brandeis (speaking of Brandeis), all most unusual for a "woman" here!

I had a wonderful letter from Randall, after a long silence: full of news and excitement and snapshots. I was awfully pleased.

Summer is here, which means lots of visitors—this past week, too many. One a tall, elegant São Paulo *gran fina* arrived without any warning (telephoned from the top of the mountain) with her BOOK (600 pages) for me to translate. She had taken a bus and even started to walk—her five inch heels dipped in red mud—all completely unheard of here, and we were so taken with her that we kept her all afternoon. A diamond in each ear, and two on one finger, as big as this: honestly. The book an example of total recall, probably written to take her mind off her husband's notorious infi delities. *What* shall we do with it? This is the second time it's happened. The first was someone's trying to get me to translate a horrendous Life of Jesus by the leader of the Brazilian Fascist party . . . (1,000 pages.)

How is Marianne's new book?[2] She said she'd sent a copy but it hasn't arrived yet. I saw Wilbur's review.[3] Do you ever see him, by the way? Do you know what happened to my friend Hyman?— He was getting married the last I heard, from Agnes Mongan. And where is Frank Parker and is he still painting? I suspect that Marianne's *Ladies' Home Journal* poem was about Eisenhower . . .[4] Do you know that she did some campaign writing for Hoover once?—in 1929 or thereabouts. But sometimes I think that that dogmatism *works* in her poetry—sometimes, of course, not. I think (a simple

1 Randall Jarrell, "The Year in Poetry," *Harper's* (Oct. 1955).
2 Marianne Moore, *Like a Bulwark* (1956).
3 Richard Wilbur, "The Heart of the Thing," *The New York Times Book Review* (Nov. 11, 1956).
4 Marianne Moore, "Blessed Is the Man," *Ladies' Home Journal* (Aug. 1956).

thought) she must represent reassurance to all the audiences who hear her—a kind of family-feeling, and that if you'll be good you'll be happy—combined with intellectual *chic*! But heavens, what a wonderful old age she really is having—and deserving.

Our small neck-deep pool has just been cleaned—full of boulders & tree-trunks after that storm, and it looks so inviting I think I'll take a swim. It comes straight down the mountainside—the water—a steep cascade of a mile or so, and of course is icy cold. We built a dam across the end of a natural pool. Lota kept telling the man who was cementing the rocks to make it look as if God had made it. A lovely dark red snake about 3 feet long swam across it, with his head weaving about, a foot above the water, the other day while I was in it. Lunch was interrupted yesterday by the maid's shrieking that a snake was taking a baby bird from a João do Barro's nest in a tree right

 beside the house. The name means John of the mud or clay. They build big bee-hive shaped nests, like this. The snake was just coming down, over five feet long, the poor bird's feet waving feebly in his mouth, the parent birds shrieking and having hysterics. Lota got her rifle and got him with the first shot. *That* baby was dead, but there were more in the nest, I think, and after a while the parents went back. We did not go on with our lunch.

I am not economizing on my new paper but don't have any more of it up here in the *estudio* . . .

I was just interrupted by a small, dusky apparition wearing nothing but red boxer shorts with large white polka dots and a few white hair-bows—my namesake, who wanders up here when she can escape her mother and aunts. (That kind of Negro hair-do is here called a "coffee plantation.") She is learning to talk and is extremely pretty & smart. What she likes to do is to come and *jump* on me when I'm having coffee in bed in the mornings. (You'll love that.) She has been restored, howling, to *mamãi*. Well—this all sounds very peaceful and domestic in contrast to most of the rest of the sorry world.

We want to spend six months in N.Y. next year—IF, and IF. I think we'll make it, probably, but don't know quite when. Lota wants a new *red* Jaguar. We'll probably zoom up Marlborough street in it one of these days. (Yet she says her mother used to protest bitterly about her father's red Bugatti or whatever it is, and say that everyone would say he had typical South American taste!) Things are very bad here politically—threats of a new dictator.[1] We may really want to get away badly next year if they keep on.

With love to you and Elizabeth, and I hope all goes well with you both,
Elizabeth

Tell me how you like that Berryman poem about A. Bradstreet?[2] I couldn't make up my mind when I read it in *PR*. Also can't think anything—or react in any way at all, to René Char. Philip asked me to do a review on him for *PR*[3] but I had to refuse. *What* do you think? I SUSPECT there's nothing in it, as the hindu said after contemplating his navel for 7 years.

142.

[Postcard: Photograph of a church]

[n.d.]

Church in Diamantina, Minas Gerais, Brazil
This is one of my "illustrations" for my translation—Love to you & Elizabeth & best wishes for the book, & the new year—
Elizabeth

143.

[Postcard: Statue of La Musa Polimnia, Museo Nuovo del Palazzo dei Conservatori, Rome]

[January 1957]

My dear Elizabeth:

Our little girl, Harriet Winslow Lowell was just born last Friday, weight 6 pounds and 14 ounces, and already more with both feet on the ground than her fatuous and boasting parents.

Many thanks for your slice of life book. Just what I need to jolt my hazy literary French.

Will write soon.

Love,
Cal

1 In November 1956, Juscelino Kubitschek de Oliveira tried to silence political opposition by outlawing two particularly vociferous parties (including Carlos Lacerda's Lantern Club). It was rumored that he would declare a state of siege.

2 John Berryman, *Homage to Mistress Bradstreet* (1956; published in the *Partisan Review* in 1953).

3 René Char, *Hypnos Waking: Poems and Prose*, trans. Jackson Mathews, William Carlos Williams, et al. (1956).

144.

January 25th, 1957

Dear Cal:

Just a note of congratulation to Elizabeth & you on the arrival of Harriet Winslow Lowell. I hope everyone is doing nicely. What should I bring her from Brazil, I wonder: an aquamarine for future use?

We have *three* babies here now for a month—aged almost 4, almost 3, and just one. The one-year old is an enormous boy named Paulo, with legs like Doric pillars and a smile unfortunately just like John Foster Dulles', for the time being. I think he'll get over it when he gets some more teeth. They're all remarkably good, thank goodness. In fact their *baba*, or supposed nurse-maid, is much more of a problem to us than they are. We bedded her in a spare bedroom where I keep my Nova-Scotian style array of jellies, pickles, etc., and today I discovered that *Mowra* had been digging into them—lifting up the wax and probing around . . . Oh dear, she's enormous and a hopeless case of sugar-addiction, and such a hypocrite that she *pretends* she can read and tell time when she really can't . . .

Lota and I are really planning to get to New York around the first part of April. It isn't the best time to come but for various reasons we can't make it any other time. We also have to stay for six months, and I am in a quandary because I recently received an announcement that I can have an Amy Lowell scholarship if I stay *out* of the U.S. for a year, starting in September.[1] I never heard of these scholarships before. Perhaps you had something to do with my receiving it? If so I certainly thank you. I'm hoping they'll give me an extension of a month before I have to leave, as they put it, "the continent of North America." It should be a lesson to us not to leave wills with strings at-tached. I imagine they have a hard time finding a rich-expatriate-already poet like me to give it to! But not so rich it won't be extremely welcome.

You don't happen to have any New York friends who are going away for six months just then, do you?—who'd like to sublet us a nice three-room apartment? I'm a good housekeeper, I think. It will be awfully nice to see you. I'll be making a trip or two to Boston—IF we ever get off. It doesn't seem likely now but I suppose that just shows that we really should go. Oth-erwise we'll just settle back in L's grandfather's rocking chairs on the new terrace & look at the view and read paper-backs for the rest of our lives. Also an American visitor is coming for carnival, and after that I'm supposed to

1 Amy Lowell endowed a fellowship allowing American poets to travel abroad.

take a ten-day trip up the Amazon with her. If I survive that I guess we'll make it. Possibly Tom W is coming along, too.

I've just finished Mr. Wilson at 60—and in general I agree with him, at 45, so oh dear what will I be at 60.[1] Lota is boning up on the Dead Sea Scroll situation so that we can fight all week-end with a devout friend of hers—the Tom Wanning of Brazil—

Please give my love to Elizabeth and kiss HATTIE for me— And please write—with love,
      Elizabeth

She'll undoubtedly be blonde?

145.

February 7, 1957

Dearest Elizabeth:

Tremendous news about your coming here in April! We have a room all ready for you with a patchwork quilt rescued from a blazing Tennessee (Hardwick) mansion, a Confederate flag, a toy Robert E. Lee on horseback, an abstraction pasted together by Cousin Harriet . . . and I'll even loan you your rash little statuette so that you'll not miss Brazil. You must come, and I hope for long. I may go to the West Coast late in March—eastern poets (Jarrell, Eberhart, Wilbur, Marianne Moore, all in six months) are now being shipped west by barrel-load to give readings. I wish you would come to us in the second week of April. The mud will be beginning to crack, and here and there a little green will be stirring.

I reread Amy Lowell on the strength of your fellowship and half-affectionate and half-malicious proddings of Robert Frost, "Some one ought to unbury Amy." There [is] a childish bluntness to her: all the Chinese scenes that her brother Percival wrote about,[2] the little girls (Oh a pretty little girl!)[3] dancing behind her formidable form, all those counterparts—fragile, effete Watteau ladies. Poor lady, she broke her ankles, one twelve and the other, I think, fifteen times, really liked writers better than society, and died at fifty-two—a life briefer than Keats'![4]

Upstairs, Harriet Winslow Lowell is crying as rhythmically as breathing.

      •

1 Edmund Wilson, *A Piece of My Mind: Reflections at Sixty* (1956).
2 Percival Lowell wrote four books about his travels in Asia.
3 Cf. Amy Lowell, "A Roxbury Garden," *Men, Women, and Ghosts* (1916).
4 Amy Lowell died in 1925, the year of the publication of her two-volume biography of Keats.

Lizzie and our beaverlike professional baby nurse, Miss Elsemore, are not in theoretic or emotional agreement.[1] Miss Elsemore, red-haired, dumpy, in her late fifties, supported by forty years' practice and pre–Dr. Spock's baby book, believes in letting a baby cry before eating. Miss Elsemore doesn't really believe that Lizzie can enter a room correctly. Poor Lizzie isn't allowed to play with Harriet except for thirty minutes between six and six-thirty when she would like to be relaxing over an Old Fashioned. Morning, noon and night, our house shakes, quakes, and continues to stand while the opposites war—thesis and antithesis, lion and unicorn, and nothing resolved except that Miss Elsemore remains in the saddle but not unchallenged. The worst is that Miss Elsemore is so devoted, accomplished, and even in her expert style, gentle, that any substitute would be unthinkable and we have even committed ourselves to hiring as her eventual successor and *long*-term nurse, Ann (no Miss), an elderly very talkative and ladylike Anglo-Irish Quebec spinster, Miss Elsemore's girl-friend. Miss Elsemore is already foreseeing and planning Ann's regime, "with Ann toilet-sitting should begin in the eight month." Frank Parker says we are very lucky not to have a nurse that condemns *both* Father and Mother and eats all meals with the family and never allows the conversation to stray from baby-virtue and baby-care.

I'm really mad about my little daughter and feel as though I had been up to now lacking some prime faculty: eyesight, hearing, reason.

Hyman is a neighbor, and we see each other every so often, and he misses you. He has a young wife, a society girl, very much of a rebel. Hyman's friends whisper that she is only interested in riding at the Myopia Hunt. Her relatives accuse Hyman . . . But what don't they accuse Hyman of! Their hours are peculiar: Hyman gets up at noon and goes to bed at two maybe; Nina[2] gets up at seven and goes to bed at ten. Yet she is a fine and devoted girl, and I think the marriage is very happy. Hyman is awesomely consistent, brilliant, ascetic—more and more people say he is the best painter in America, and so he is, I guess, along with Graves[3] and Ben Shahn.

I've been stalling on my autobiography. So many relatives don't like it. But that isn't the trouble; rather it's laziness and feeling that I must store up more drive and wisdom.

Boston is becoming a center. Edmund Wilson is here: to educate his daughter; Ransom may retire here, if he can find a duplicate bridge group (he and his wife are expert and passionate players); and surprise: Philip and

1 Cf. "Home After Three Months Away," lines 1–3 (RL-*CP*).
2 Nina Bohlen.
3 Morris Graves.

Nathalie! I think Philip is going to teach at Brandeis and bring *PR* and even William Phillips, perhaps! with him. So spurn your rich expatriate's prize, return and be a resident poet amongst us.

Much love from us both,

Cal

146.

February 27th, 1957

Dear Cal:

You certainly make Boston sound very attractive these days. I'm not sure whether I can get there the second week in April or not. I don't think I'm arriving in N.Y. until April 5th or 6th. But we are planning to stay for six months, probably, and I'll be getting to Boston more than once, surely. How soon I go for the first time sort of depends on the condition of what my elderly aunt in Worcester calls her "Gaul bladder" ... hers, not mine, of course. Won't you be there the *third* week in April, perhaps? Thank you & Elizabeth for your kind invitation to visit you—but since Lota will be with me I think we'd better stay at the Vendome or someplace. (That sounds as if Brazilians had awful manners, but I merely mean it's a little too much visitors for you.) Once Lota went to Boston and chose the Hotel Puritan because she thought the name was so wonderful ...

I have acquired one Brazilian present for Harriet W.—if only it doesn't scare her out of her first year's growth. I just noticed another story by Elizabeth in a *New Yorker* we just received.[1] I haven't had a chance to read it yet, though. I am terribly envious and I'd feel a lot happier about this trip if I had a story or two there now ... Oh—and did *you* send *Venice Observed*? It arrived, from Boston, on my birthday, and I was awfully pleased to have it, and I think it must be from you. I was very curious to see it, probably wouldn't have bought it for myself, and I have read it with many confused sensations. In some ways I think it's extremely good. The pictures are fine, of course, and she does write awfully well. But why (let me be bitchy for a moment) should the call of "Gondola, gondola!" (like "Taxi, taxi!")—come to *"resemble an obscene cry ..."*????[2] and there are similar fancies. And speaking of my birthday—I received a tiny clipping from a Newark paper—"Today's Birthdays". Lana Turner and me. Surely that's Fame.

1 Elizabeth Hardwick, "The Classless Society," *The New Yorker* (Jan. 19, 1957).
2 "It is like the cry 'Gondola, gondola,' that meets me every day as I cross the Bridge of the Canonica till it comes to seem like an obscene suggestion"; Mary McCarthy, *Venice Observed* (1956), 142.

Miss Elsemore sounds terrifying. I supposed I'll only see "Anne," though. It's funny how caring for helpless babies builds character. I've been told that I had a nurse who bossed my grandfather who was a terrifying man, himself, made him stop smoking cigars, used his "billiard room" to park me in, etc.[1]

Today is my last day of peace for some time, I'm afraid. Tomorrow we go down to Rio to meet the American friend arriving for Carnaval—a rich, elderly, several-times married lady, who began her career by driving an ambulance for Anne Morgan[2] in the first war. We are rather dreading Carnaval, but I have never done it properly and this will be my big chance to. We have seats on the platform with the mayor of Rio,[3] etc., where we shall have to sit up ALL Sunday night while he judges the Negro Samba Schools. It's the best thing in the Carnaval, however. They spend all year long and all their money rehearsing, making costumes, composing really superb songs, etc. Mostly Carnaval has sadly degenerated. I saw one awful night of one, in the rain. It was shortly after the movie of *David & Bathsheba*[4] had been to Rio and there were thousands of D's and B's—and those who *weren't* all seemed to be men wearing false breasts.

I'd love to see Hyman. In fact, if I have any money at all, I'd like very much to get a painting to bring back here. And since you mentioned Frank Parker I think he must be on hand, and so I'm going to ask you to do something boring for me. I have a book here he loaned me long ago, *Les Jours de Notre Mort*,[5] and that I swore I'd return to him and then didn't. I've felt guilty about it all this time. I am going to mail it to you and perhaps sometime you can give it to him. Books usually arrive safely, and my luggage is already way over-weight.— I just read E. Wilson's thoughts at 60. Oh, I think I already told you *that* piece of news. Anyway—I agree with him about education!

One final session with the dressmaker this afternoon. We have five, honestly, working for us now, but I am still very much afraid that what seems chic in Rio is going to look like St. Louis 1948 in New York—or Boston. I'm leaving here about March 15th, and going with the American to Bahia and Recife, then probably on to Puerto Rico—if I can get her to give up her idea of the Amazon. I'll be in Key West for a week, until April 5th—c/o Mrs. M. C. Stevens, Box 668. Lota and I meet in N.Y., where we have a sub-let:

1 John W. Bishop, EB's paternal grandfather.
2 Anne Morgan's American Fund for French Wounded and American Fund for Devastated France (World War I).
3 Francisco Negrão de Lima.
4 *David and Bathsheba*, dir. Henry King (1951).
5 David Rousset, *Les Jours de notre mort* (1947).

address and telephone number unknown at present. I am torn between the joys of being waited on hand and foot, however sloppily, by all our little Negroes and scrambling some eggs *right* for myself . . . Lota is looking forward to breakfast foods. Did I tell you that when we flew back the last time we brought 4 quarts of homogenized milk with us, in the refrigerator on the plane, and gave a corn-flake party immediately upon arrival? It was a great success, too.

Well, I must brood about my will some more. Would you like to be left something? I can not read Amy Lowell—although she seems to be quite popular here!

Remember me to Elizabeth and I hope to see you soon.

With much love,
  Elizabeth

The latest news from Key West is that Tom W has arrived with a married woman and her 3-year old child—not his, as his aunt says when introducing them, & he was always so conservative! While you've been becoming a young father, I've become a rather wizened lady, with a lorgnette, you know!

I'm sorry—I seem to have got some of a very old & liquefied jelly-bean on this.

147.

Dearest Elizabeth:

I guess this will easily catch you before March 15, but I hurry to write on my new promptly answering typewriter lest I should be late. I meant any time *after* April 7 would be good for us. We will be here and dying to see you until the middle of June when we go to Castine. The Vendome is just a block and a half from us, so if you stay there we will all be within shouting, almost whispering, distance. Castine, by the way, is just below Stonington and perhaps familiar to you. We hope you and Lota will come and spend a large part of the summer with us there. You know the area.

Ah me "a young father and you a wizened lady with a lorgnette." Age grips me with her clutch too (or whatever Lord Vaux says it does).[1] I can now see a little skull through the very back of my head and a little in the very

---

1 "For age with stealing steps, / Hath clawde me with his crowch"; Thomas Vaux, "The Aged Lover Renounceth Love" (1557), lines 9–10.

front above the forelock. With a good short haircut, though, nothing much appears. The great brink is certainly there. I'm sure we can bear with one another with the old delight, surely. I can't tell you how much I long for your return and hope I shan't disillusion you.

I *did* send you the McCarthy. Oh, I feel bitchy too. Mary can't open her mouth about anything without my wanting (or one's wanting) to put my foot in it and block her. A great Norman horse trampling, trampling—and Bowden[1] following, tongue out and eyes drooping to his toes with spleen and fatigue. But then the glorious energy, mean at every point, the Irish pure disinterested joy in wrecking plus a Jewish seriousness, but really awfully glorious. I think she has bounded back from a terrible dry low bald point, from a time of few books and the last only *The Oasis*.[2]

I am going on a tour. It's the eastern poet's tour to the west coast, and I leave here on the 20th of March and get back on the 7th of April. Write me your New York address, and I hope I can get in touch with you on the way home (April 6 or 7) or failing that maybe the next week. I am going to read at Vassar on the 11th of April. The reading seems rather withering. I've done so few poems in the last five years and feel so far from the old ones. However the traveling has its drawing power. One mustn't die without seeing the Pacific. All my poems will look bluer to me than the Pacific by the time you get here.

Little Harriet is really terrific. I feel as though we had been living on the moon for the last two months. She is realer than all the sky, yet one wishes to pinch one's self every so often and see if she and us along with her haven't changed to glowing moon-struck cheese. What luck to have her.

With much love,
Cal

148.

Apt. 1E, 115 East 67th Street
New York
April 26th, 1957

Dearest Cal:

Heavens![3]—it was nice to hear you talking and sounding very much like yourself! I am sorry I have been so very slow about reciprocating in some

---

1 Bowden Broadwater was married to Mary McCarthy from 1946 to 1961.
2 Mary McCarthy, *The Oasis* (1949).
3 Typed with red ribbon; EB then switches to black.

way. We have been being very social and sociable, for us, and seeing people both for lunch and dinner, plus this new-fangled thing called the television we have here . . . and then I had to acquire a typewriter before I could really write, anyway. I wish to goodness we could get over to Boston right away but I don't see how we can—*perhaps* before that Ceremonial[1] on May 22nd, but I'm not sure. The chief drawback, now that the seeing people is dwindling away, is that I had to prepare the final corrected copy of that translation[2]—in, now—and a new version of the Introduction, to be sold as an article first. Since they're apparently getting to work on the book immediately, for Sept or Oct publication, I have to get it done before I can even go around here seeing art galleries, etc. I really didn't come to N.Y. to sit in a small bedroom and type all day, but that's what I seem to be doing at the moment. I've sent Lota out to buy theatre tickets, with full instructions on a sheet of paper—what buses to take, what theatres to go to, etc., and I do hope she doesn't get lost. She's lived here a lot before, but some quirk in Portuguese prevents her from thinking of high numbers as being UP and low ones DOWN, which does complicate things for her. Also, PULL on doors means, more or less, "JUMP" in Portuguese, and PUSH means "PULL," so you see.

I saw Randall, I think it was the night after we talked: went to his lecture at the YMHA, sat beside his wife (who made a one-woman audience and was shushed and glared at by our neighbors who thought she wasn't being reverent enough), and then they came back here for a short visit. Everything was just as if we'd left off the day before and we agreed or disagreed in just the same way and it was very nice. I find I can't get used to the beard and keep expecting him to take it off in one hand. This letter is partly to ask you to do something for him, or me, and it may be foolish of me; you may have already done it many times, for all I know, but anyway, in conversation with Marianne this morning I said I'd like to nominate Randall for the Institute and she immediately said she'd be one of the 2nds. So I sent off the form, suggesting you as the other 2nd. It may well be impossible. I can't but believe he's been nominated a good many times already, but as long as I'm here I thought I'd be "active" for once. And when Ciardi, John Cheever, etc. are in—well, not that any of it signifies much, but my idea is that it would be nice to have one's friends in so that those dinners, etc., might be fun in our old age. But

1 For the National Institute of Arts and Letters, to which RL and EB had been elected in 1954.
2 *The Diary of "Helena Morley,"* which was to be published in December 1957.

probably Randall has made many enemies! (I should hope so.) I did go to the dinner and it was something. It reminded me of a large and particularly painful family Thanksgiving dinner. And when I found myself being taken home in a cab by Mr. Kronenberger, in the front seat (he's all right, though, and delivered an *essay* after dinner, just like Charles Lamb), with Louis Untermeyer (whom I'd never met before) on one side of me, and Deems Taylor, my god, on the other, I had serious thoughts of resigning at once . . . Maybe one can skip the dinners, though. I think they're all so old their tastebuds have dried up. Mr. U kept telling me what a wonderful dinner it was, and I found it completely tasteless.

Marianne has called here once, looking adorable, just back from 3 weeks in Bermuda, wearing, she said, her "Toreador Hat and Teddy Bear Coat." She's been sick all the past week, though, and although she'll talk for hours on the phone she won't let me come over and do any cooking for her, as I wanted to. She's getting much franker about people—gets off some wonderful remarks, and her vision of the Institute is apocryphal and wonderful . . .

I spent one nice evening with Mary McC who invited me up to Hannah Arendt's. Philip Rahv was in fine form and terribly funny, and I had a very good time although afraid to open my mouth among such BRAINS.[1] Also I was questioned about the Brazilian Labor movement, and I'm afraid proved woefully ignorant. I wonder if you'll like my Pound poem in *PR*.[2]

But you both will be coming for May 22nd, won't you. Do you spend 2 or 3 days? What about coming back here afterwards that evening? I wish I could offer to put you up but I'm afraid it's too tiny, even if we do have 2 bathrooms . . . But you select whom you'd like to have dinner with (someplace around here?) and come back here? Can you? We can squeeze in about eight people in the living-room all right, or private, as you prefer, and if you're staying over a day, or coming the day before, we could entertain you both privately and in a group.

In the meantime, IF I get this introducing thing done, I might make a quick trip to Boston before then, but I'm rather dubious about it. I wanted to send on my presents for the baby by mail. I'm afraid if I don't she'll never be able to use one of them at all, if she's the usual American-Baby size . . . But I would rather give them in person.

---

1 For an account of the dinner party, see *Remembering Elizabeth Bishop: An Oral Biography*, ed. Gary Fountain and Peter Brazeau (1994), 152–53.
2 "Visits to St. Elizabeths," *Partisan Review* (Spring 1957).

I had Isabella Gardner here the other day. I'd never met her before but she'd sent me her book and written letters, etc. She seemed very nice and of course our greatest bond right away was contemporary architecture. Seems she lives in a Mies Van der Rohe (?) house, but deigned to be impressed by the one I live in . . .

Well—this is a poor substitute for conversation. I am dying to see you. If the Randall thing is hopeless and you'd rather not, just say so. I really know next to nothing about it, of course. Please give my love to Elizabeth and kisses to Harriet.

Devotedly yours,
Elizabeth

149.

April 29, 1957

Dear Elizabeth:

Too much like myself! We had been having martinis, and I was in a very foolish, exalted and exhausted state from my reading trip. Never again; I'm really very tame and will be all the time we see you in N.Y.

I live so far from seconds in Boston that I have never even made a stab at nominating Randall, but I had been hoping that we might combine and have even been keeping the *nominating* blank out on the top of our TV so that we could do something when you came to Boston. I'll fill my blank as soon as it arrives. I guess nominating people, once you've done it, is simple, like taking a plane or going to Europe. However, the Academy is so full of dopes that one is not hopeful. I met Jacques Barzun the other night; his candidate for fiction was Ann Goodwin Winslow, Marcella's mother-in-law. He also said, re: Tate arriving boiled and unprepared for his lectures . . . well, I forget what he said, but he blamed our age of poet-teachers. The poets rob the university and the university kills poetry. But he didn't quite put it as outright as that. I pointed out ragged lives in the past, and he said, "Darn it, Melville fulfilled his contracts."

We'll be in New York on the 22nd for two or three days. Perhaps we could have an evening with just you and Lota. I would like to see you sometime with Miss Moore but also want to see you without her.

I read your "Roosters" and "Prodigal Son" to Jack Sweeney's class and at the end felt I'd learned a lot about roosters and pigs. I am afraid I sounded a little like some sort of centaur fusion of both the other night.

Honor bright, I'm not a rowdy. Perhaps you both will reconsider staying with us.

Love,
Cal

P.S. Rizzardi showed me your Pound. I've read it aloud to people several times. Just as with the "Prodigal" and "Roosters," you are very womanly and wise. A lot better than Robert Fitzgerald in his rather pious and trap-doorish review that I've now seen in three magazines.[1] Harriet weighs 14 pounds and Elizabeth is already getting her to reduce.

150.

June 10, 1957

Dearest Elizabeth B.:

Coming home from dropping the Williams for their visit with their cousin, an 82 year old Episcopalian nun, I stopped on Charles Street to buy Sunday papers, then drifted to the wine-basket florist, and, while debating buying you a little bouquet of miniature roses, forget-me-nots, pinks etc. all arranged to look like flowers in china, I saw the pianists' car[2] swing round the corner, big as a battleship and you sitting, great car spaces about you, in the back seat. Being a Yankee, I raise an arm you couldn't have seen, and made sounds you couldn't have heard. I sent the flowers to Bill Merwin's wife[3]— he had caught a cold from me, and she had caught bronchitis from him. So . . . but I wish the flowers had journeyed on with you to dazzle your old cross aunt in Worcester!

The last morning with the Williams was touching. The delivery poem was read to Harriet and a coyly chuckling Miss Elsemore.[4] She is gobbling up the Williams *Autobiography* and one sees it stuck between the stair-rails on top of her *Reader's Digest* and her *Real Meaning of Jesus*. The book begins something like this: "I'm not going to tell about the women I've been to bed with. They're not the story."[5] When I left them at the nuns' house we all kissed goodbye, and Bill said, "You're my son. That's what I do to them." Age, Oh age!

1 Robert Fitzgerald, "A Note on Ezra Pound," *Nuova Corrente* (Jan.–July 1956) and *The Kenyon Review* (Autumn 1956); reprinted as "Gloom and Gold on Ezra Pound," *Encounter* (July 1956).
2 Arthur Gold and Robert Fizdale drove EB to visit her relatives in Worcester.
3 Dido Merwin.
4 William Carlos Williams, "From a Window," *New Directions* (1957).
5 See Williams Carlos Williams, *Autobiography* (1951), xi.

I've read your poems many times. I think I read you with more interest than anyone now writing. I know I do, but I think I would even if it weren't for personal reasons. "The Armadillo" is surely one of your three or four very best. I thought the title mistaken at first, a Moore name—though I suppose the armadillo is a much too popular and common garden animal for her—for an out-of-doors, personally seen and utterly un-Moore poem. However, "Armadillo" is right, for the little creature, given only five lines, runs off with the whole poem. Weak and armored, I suppose he is those people carrying balloons-illegal-to their local saint.[1]

Your crucifix and torture (?) wheels in Flanders poem has a grave girlish jump to it.[2] I've always wanted to write on this subject. Wilenski's *Dutch Painting*[3] gives a fierce description of the reality of the Spanish soldiery in the Brueghel "Crucifixion." Apparently he could get away with that. Maybe I'll do my poem, sad, resonant, ferocious, as a counterpiece to yours. Remember the "Bad Thief"[4] we saw at the Fogg?

Also reread the poems you recited. How true that treasure of white sunlight and energy one has in the morning; how often I've blown it off into reading a novel. "A Summer's Dream" seems to me a flattish (Jarrell adjective) variant of your exciting "Sunday, 4 A.M." I like best the mackerel-crying stanza.[5] "Armadillo" was surely by far the best poem read by anyone that day.

How easy it is for me to lay it on, and mean it. I remember reading as a boy in Bartlett's *Quotations* this arresting and immortal sentence: "Peace reigns in Warsaw."[6] I wonder who the author was? Today and yesterday, more peace has reigned in our house than we've seen for ages. See what you bring. It *kills* me that you are gone, and I do want to make a stay in New York toward the end of July.

Love,
Cal

P.S. I'm awfully relieved that Lota has my number and still likes me best of your poets. It's comforting too that you find most of the new poetry tame.

---

1 See "The Armadillo," lines 41–44 (EB-*CP*).
2 "Sunday, 4 A.M." (EB-*CP*).
3 Published in 1955.
4 Robert Campin, *Bad Thief* (c. 1420–1440).
5 "A Summer's Dream," lines 13–16 (EB-*CP*).
6 Alexandre Dumas, *Mes Mémoires* (1868–83).

151.

[Postcard: Charlie Chaplin reading the Police Gazette, *fully clothed, in a fully drawn bath, from* Payday, *Film Library, Museum of Modern Art]*

[June] 22nd [—1957][1]

Dearest Cal: We've been living like this, more or less, for the past few days—probably you have, too. Lota was all set to return to Brazil immediately, but today is cooler & perhaps I can persuade her to stick out our visit. If we do, do you think we could visit you & E. around the last week in August or 1st in Sept., in Maine? (I don't know how long you're staying.) It would just be for a few days—3 or 4—but I'd love to see Maine again (& you!) if I possibly can. I have so much to tell you. I enjoyed my stay in B so much—it will all have to wait until I can write a letter—Sat. or Sun.—I'm mailing you a record.

> Devotedly,
> Elizabeth—

June 21st—Card #2

[Buster Keaton peering out to sea with binoculars; a scene from The Navigator, *Museum of Modern Art Film Library[2]]*

Dearest Cal—I'm on my way to the P.O. now to mail you a record—it isn't the one I had in mind, but still pretty good. I've really seen enough people for a while but can't seem to stop—however, we have also seen lots of *Art* this week, and by the end of next hope to be leading a contemplative life again. I just read Randall's piece in *Art News*[3] when your letter came about the Blooms[4]—congratulations. I'll really write at length today, (or *Monday*). New York has had a fever, but is feeling better now—

> Lots of love to you & E & H—
> Elizabeth

---

1 Dates should be reversed, EB having marked the earlier card #2 by mistake ("22nd" on the first was added after the text was written).

2 See "Keaton" (B-*EAP*).

3 About abstract expressionism, Jarrell, "The Age of the Chimpanzee," *ARTNews* (Summer 1957).

4 Letter now missing; the Lowells had bought a Hyman Bloom painting, "a thunderbolting lion woman (black and silver" (RL to Sister Mary Corita, June 4, 1958, courtesy of the Cordita Art Center and Evgenia Citkowitz).

152.

Dearest Elizabeth:

I've been rather carelessly waiting for your long letter before answering your wonderfully chosen postcards. We do want you and Lota to come for the visit you suggest, but why not come much sooner and for much longer? While you vanish away in the heat, we are so cool that we've used furnace, heaters, flannel shirts and a fire-place stuffed with oak logs. We say to new-comers, such as the Dupees who've just arrived: "We can stand it; we're used to Maine." Why not spend the summer with us? We have lots of room in our house (now that Miss Elsemore is on her way out) and after that in August we can give you a little house to yourselves on the Castine shore that looks like Japan from one angle and Castine from another.

I meant to write you about Cummings' reading on the public garden,[1] but its colors have somewhat faded on me after a week in Maine. Most colorful was Allen Tate, who arrived at our house for the occasion dressed in a very pale, very delicately made khaki coat, a khaki hat with a plaid hat-band, loafers that shone like armor in a Rembrandt painting. He was smarting from the night before when Elizabeth, determined to raise his mode of existence from gossiping and violin-playing with girl graduate students, invited him to meet [a] terribly distinguished, awfully nice, awfully Bostonian former Miss Cabot, the wife of Ellery Sedgwick, nephew of the *Atlantic Monthly* man. She is the most brilliant talker about Bostonians in Boston, and so charming that ordinary mortals soon forget that one hand has been paralyzed from birth, one eye squints a little. Allen rose to the occasion enough to tell an anecdote about some one named Beezie Cabot, showed a surprising knowledge of Cabot genealogy. Then the air suddenly went out of him. He said, "At my age one never feels *absolutely* well you know," grew distracted when Mrs. Sedgwick suggested that he visit her at Stockbridge, and finally had to be prodded to escort her home around the block. This couldn't have been the night before the Cummings' reading because Allen seemed to go under-ground for days thereafter. Well, Cummings was introduced by MacLeish as some one who had been against Communism when it was still dangerous to take such a position. "Unlike Archie," Allen said loudly. And there we sat, a rather conspicuous and hateful row, the two Merwins, us, Allen, Moira Sweeney,[2] Bill Alfred—all ages, all degrees of innocence and cynicism—

1 A reading for the Boston Arts Festival on June 23, 1957.
2 Máire MacNeill Sweeney.

while Cummings read outrageous and sentimental poems, good and bad of both kinds. About eight thousand people listened and those who couldn't hear crowded in huge masses under awnings across the Public Garden pond to look at non-objectivist paintings. The Revolution has come, I guess, yet we're still creatures of flesh and blood.

Maine is restful for our jaded Boston nerves. Except for driving up it's been pure rest cure—one much needed. Oh the drive up! We had to have a trailer. Due to some uncharacteristic oversight in my planning, I found myself faced with fearful alternatives. There are two kinds of U-haul-it trailers, the open, and the covered, little ambulance-like wagons that blot out all back-view and are entirely dangerous. The covered may be returned to the nearest large city (Belfast, 25 miles from Castine), the cozy uncovered ones must be brought back to Boston, an additional drive of 458 miles. I hadn't understood, hadn't securely bound the agent to the terms I had imagined. I took the uncovered trailer. For two hundred of the two hundred and twenty-nine miles, we analyzed the flaws in this choice. And we had Miss Elsemore, furious at her dismissal, loaded with token forbearance from a last minute reading of her "What Jesus really thinks," blaming everything on Elizabeth, sweetening the journey by saying to the baby, "You're fickle, you'll soon forget me . . . You'll have to take what comes . . . Your *Daddy's* one person you'll never forget." At Wiscasset, still gloomy with the boredom you felt there many summers ago, I got out—I was beginning to nod at the wheel—and went swimming off the town dock. While I was in the water, a freight-train slowly came to a stop and cut me off from my car and family. Getting out, I cut my big toe on the step, a barnacled tire. Oh, when we got to Castine we found a young resident poet, off to the wedding of his favorite Wellesley student, and he drove the trailer back.

I want more than anything in the world to see as much as I can of you before your return. Lizzie has an old Kentucky friend, a Miss Turner,[1] who teaches at Vassar, coming here for the month of August. I'd like to come and see you both in New York then, and perhaps I could guide you both up here from there. Elizabeth is full of praise and affection for you both and is most eager for you to come.

Love,
Cal

P.S. At the end of the Cummings' reading, while I stood in line waiting to shake hands with Cummings, I ran into Paul Brooks, who said breezily to

1 Susan J. Turner.

me, "It seems absurd that I should have to ask you the address of our own author, Miss Bishop." All the age-old author and publisher rifts began to widen in me and I said, "But isn't she a Farrar and Straus author." Then I said something about how much I admired your stories, and we parted rather coldly.[1] I hope I haven't made things more of a mess.

153.

New York
July 10th, 1957
Dearest Cal:

We do want to come to visit you . . . in fact, we're determined to, and I am busy right now getting out of some other week-ends, etc., that we half-accepted in our first dazed period here. I'm not sure from your letter whether August is a good month for you, or a bad month. First you say something about your guest-house maybe being free then (we can only stay a week, so don't be alarmed!), and then you say something about Elizabeth's having a guest then and the possibility of your coming to N.Y. at that time. Well, the way things are with us: anytime between August 1st and 20th would be fine, and just possibly the rest of August, too. (Depending on whether a Brazilian friend[2] comes or not. If she comes it would be for the last week in August and first 2 in September. I should know in a few days and can let you know.) If August isn't possible for you, because of E's friend, well, maybe we can work out something in September? Katharine White (E.B.'s wife) is here in town now and when I told her I might be visiting you in Castine, she immediately made plans for a grand luncheon party for everyone. They are not far away. (She's going back in August.) She is very eager to meet you, but, she confided, "scared to death . . . ," although she likes E. very much. It might be fun. We might even call on Andy W.[3] if that isn't too far away. Anyway, you see I am an imminent visitor and one reason why I've been so bad about writing is that I've been trying to get everything on the calendar in order before I wrote. As you see, it still isn't, quite.

Your letter about your trip was marvelous. Surely E is going to put Miss E *in* something.[4] And thank you for your fine speeches to Paul Brooks. The

---

1 Houghton Mifflin had turned down *The Diary of "Helena Morley."* Robert Giroux, who had recently left Harcourt Brace to join Farrar, Straus and Company (taking several authors, including RL, with him), agreed to publish it if he could publish EB's other writing.
2 Rosalina Leão.
3 Andrews Wanning.
4 RL did; see "Home After Three Months Away."

more I know of them the less I understand publishers—honestly, they are a stupid set. One department apparently never speaks to another. HM sends me bills and things to this address all the time! I'm about to go see my wonderful agent[1] now and HM is one of the things I must discuss with her. But the latest is Farrar, Straus, etc. After a long telephone conversation with Bob G[2] about the jacket, how it should be bright and cheerful (we agreed), being a "funny" book, how the Brazilian national colors are green & yellow, with a touch of blue, and I thought they might be used somehow (& he said "Fine! Fine!"), the jacket arrives—BLACK, with enormous hollow-looking white type, and a wreath arrangement, like a memorial slab in a church. It looks like the history of the slave trade. Also, most of the facts stated on it are wrong. (Of course they never read anything they publish, do they?) Also, the *typography*—and in the galleys as well—well, it seems to me they'd save themselves so much time and expense if they'd just consult the author (or translator) sometime for fifteen minutes . . . Or even if the U.S. trade would just look at a few Faber & Faber books and admit they look pretty good and decide just to imitate them for a few years . . .

Another reason I didn't write was that I wasn't sure that just "Castine" would reach you, and I realized I'd sent my cards and the disc (horrors, I mean record) so that they arrived in Boston after you'd left. Did you have a chance to try the record and is it any good? We spent the long week-end of the 4th with Fizdale & Gold on Long Island. Lota got burned on a sparkler. We had a very nice time, really, steaming clams, going to "The Boy Friend,"[3] and seeing a good many "action" painters (who all congregate around Southampton now) in action, painting, dancing, and being sociable, which then they all do very actively and indistinguishably . . . I'd love to see the Bloom you bought. If we'd been richer we would have acquired one or two of this post-Pollock school, I think. (Randall's piece in *Art News* is right, but up to a point, I think—or in a very, very general way. But probably those talks all went together better and helped each other out when they were given in Texas.)

I'll find out about the State of Mainer train today, I think—or maybe we could fly.

Oh—about two weeks ago I got a letter from an Aileen Ward, from Vassar, asking me to come and read. I am sure that you are also responsible for this, and I am really grateful for all your strategic moves on my behalf . . . It says "Our budget limits us to an honorarium of $100.; but we can promise

1 Bernice Baumgarten.
2 Robert Giroux.
3 Sandy Wilson, *The Boy Friend* (1953).

you a hearty welcome, a comfortable room at the Alumnae House [oh dear!] and an eager audience." I haven't answered yet. Since they took 23 years to write I didn't think there was any special rush. But I wanted to ask you what you thought. I have no idea. Is that *enough?* (Lota keeps quoting an old Portuguese saying to me, about not selling one's fish cheap.) I have, however, recklessly accepted Jack Sweeney's invitation to read for the Morris Gray series,[1] which means we'll be in Boston on October 10th, and probably a few days before. I don't know what's got into me—except some "tranquilizers," making me as irresponsible—as they're said to. Possibly I shall go to Wellesley again at the same time.

I've already had a nightmare in which I was speaking to a small group, about 20, on a stony beach. I couldn't find my book, and as I groped around for it under some stones, I had the awful experience of seeing all the 20 drift away, one by one, until no one was left.

8,000 people!—

Tom made a wonderful Freudian slip when I saw him recently—speaking of Wiscasset he said "Wiscasket."

I must collect my wits and go to see Miss Baumgarten, the dentist, get a haircut, etc. I do hope our visit can be arranged; we'd really love to come, and I want Lota to see that part of Maine (next to Nova Scotia which I'm afraid is going unseen this trip). We saw Pearl Kazin the other night and she really raved about E's review of the Dylan Thomas book, also the George Eliot piece, which I had also admired but forgot to mention when I saw you.[2] E really has a very solid reputation as a critic. One nice thing about staying away so long is coming back and finding these *faits accomplis.*

With much love—to one and all,
    Elizabeth

154.

Castine, Maine
July 19, 1957

Dearest Elizabeth:

Excuse this lethargy in answering your last letter. I've been, to tell the truth as they say, a little wavery in my plans and have been toying with the idea of spending part of August alone in Boston. Nothing is nearer to

1 At Harvard University.
2 Elizabeth Hardwick, "America and Dylan Thomas," *Partisan Review* (Spring 1956), and "George Eliot's Husband," *Partisan Review* (Spring 1955).

my heart than having you with us. Do come here any time you can. You can stay with us, and we can perhaps even give you a little house and barn near us that also belongs to Cousin Harriet. This depends on just when Cousin Harriet's nurse comes here for her vacation (if she comes) and on the time set by a couple, friends of Cousin Harriet's who usually take the house for two weeks in September. Any time is wonderful for us. Do let me know as soon as you can.

I keep wondering about the "disc." Is it a reading by you, or just interesting modern music? You must have told me orally, but I remember nothing and your letters leave me in the dark.

Aileen Ward is [a] quite beautiful blond girl that Delmore Schwartz was once in love with and that Perry Miller once rather scandalously went with. This has nothing to do, though, with your reading at Vassar. I think they don't pay more than $100, at least that's all I got. The audience was easy to read to. At least they laughed at my jokes and sat in a room with good acoustics (nothing is more important for a reading). I'm sure the Harvard will go well. If I can do anything to ease your stand, let me.

There's worlds of things I want to tell you and ask you. I'm quite set on a visit to Brazil, if you are still willing. This has been a rather boy scoutish summer, first with Fred Dupee and his children and then with the Merwins: picnics in small outboards, sails, a cruise with Eberhart in his cabin cruiser that looks rather like the old Murray Hill, drives to Bar Harbor, Stonington, Camden, cocktails, whiskey sours. . . And now for almost a week I haven't touched a drop and probably won't for a good year. The first two days were very rough and surly-making. And now I am through the roughest water. I've been through all this twice before, once about a year and a half ago and know what I am taking up. Oh heavens, all the lives one wants or has to lead.

Write me your plans as soon as you can. I know you will like this part of Maine, as abrupt and green as pictures of Japan, and there are all kinds of quiet and unquiet excursions we can take up. I'm awfully keen on introducing Lota to it all.

Love, Cal

155.

Dearest Elizabeth:

I guess this may just reach you before you set off. We are so excited about your arrival here with Lota. Your stay will crown and top what has really already been a glorious summer after the withdrawal of poor Miss Elsemore. Castine is like a chunk of Wiscasset thrown into the setting of Stonington. We are between two rivers and face a thousand islands. Everyone who has come has wanted to buy a house or at least a barn. Your house is a few feet from the shore. It was once a barracks for six bricklayers and a few years ago was bought by Cousin Harriet and brightly and cleanly redone. A little off from it is a redone barn painted inside with aluminum paint and made to look sedately bohemian in contrast to the remodeled barn attached to the house we are living in (Cousin Harriet['s] house proper) which is made warmly unbohemian, where it rests quietly on a street called School on the village common.

If you are interested we might, on about the fifth, drive to Roque Island where Belle Gardner's brother lives with his wife.[1] We could drive up the coast and spend the night there in sight of Canada, which might be the next best thing to showing Lota your native Nova Scotia. A Canadian living in Brazil, how were you ever placed on Brinnin's panel of living New England poets?

Our number is Fairview 6-8786. You can wire or telephone us the time of your arrival in Bangor, and I'll be there waiting. Come as soon as you can. Fred is anxious to see you again, and we would like to have you stay with us if you arrive before the 31st, when the Dupees leave.

I won't write any more. I want to get this off in the night mail. And I've really grown too outdoorish to write anything but the most muscle-bound of letters, even to you.

Love,
Cal

[In EB's hand]
Arriving Friday 10.10 AM Northeast Airlines. Much love, Elizabeth

---

1 Robert and Ainslie Gardner.

156.

[Card: "The City of Baghdad in Flood," Persian miniature reproduced from an anthology produced at Shirwan, 1468, British Museum, London]

[Late July, 1957]

Dearest Cal:

The only plane we can get on will get us to Bangor at 10:12 AM Friday the 2nd. I do hope that will be all right with you. It certainly seems very quick—& very early.— Northeast Airlines. The exact date of our departure depends on when a Brazilian friend arrives in N.Y.—but I think we can stay ten days anyway,—again if that is all right with you—

We are very excited & counting our sweaters, sneakers, etc.— Do you want anything from here? Any books? I hope your respective lectures went well. I hope to read them both. Please don't *plan* anything—we'll be too happy just to loaf & read & be cool—

Abraços e bejos,

(hugs & kisses)

Elizabeth

157.

Castine, Maine

August 9, 1957

Dear Elizabeth:

Thanks for speaking to Lizzie about your misgivings.[1] I see clearly now that for the last few days I have been living in a state of increasing mania— almost off the rails at the end. It almost seems as if I couldn't be with you any length of time without acting with abysmal myopia and lack of considera- tion. My disease, alas, gives one (during its seizures) a headless heart.

I am not going to write very much now, but I do want you and Lota to know that I *am* at last in reverse. I am taking my anti-manic pills—75 mgs. of sparine, no more than what my doctor prescribed on the bottle but too much to drive a car or even see people much. The effect is something like the slow- ing and ache of a medium fever. One's thoughts are not directly changed and healed, but the terrible, overriding restlessness of one's system is halted so that the mind can again see life as it is.

I want you to know . . . Oh dear, I wanted you to know so many things . . .

---

1 During their visit, RL was hypomanic and suggested to EB that he visit her alone in New York, Boston, or Brazil. EB reported the Brazil suggestion to Elizabeth Hardwick. EB and Lota left Castine sooner than they had planned.

(Next morning) Yesterday was mostly bed, sparine and letting my beard grow. Today I feel certain that I am not going off the deep end. Gracelessly, like a standing child trying to sit down, like a cat or a coon coming down a tree, I'm getting down my ladder to the moon. I am part of my family again, I love my lovely family again.

When I said goodbye Lota said I was like an archangel! I see what an ass I have been. Lota has her head screwed on and is one of the loveliest and most amusing ladies I've ever met. Ask her to forgive me. And forgive me yourself, dear old friend, Boba. I'll make no solo descents on you either in New York or Brazil.

As I dully drove back over the Bango[r] toll bridge in my gray and blue Ford, the nut still rattling in the hub cap as though we were dragging a battered tin can at our heels, I looked up and a sign said, "When money talks it says, 'Chevrolet.' "

Love,
Cal

P.S. The George Herbert![1] I've really always wanted you to have it—ever since it turned up in storage four years ago. Perhaps you can add some stumbling block of humor to the dedication. I'll be mortally hurt if you don't keep it.

158.[2]

[New York, N.Y.
August 11, 1957]
Sunday morning, the 11th

Dearest Cal:

I, too, have de-frosted, and swept up a few cupfuls of New York soot. Lota is repairing two broken lamps with her new screwdrivers; so far the new hammer hasn't been called into play, but it is right at hand, ready. As I just wrote Elizabeth—the trip back was very easy, a brand-new 4-engine plane, all the usual chromium parts in copper, lemonade and macaroons

---

1 On her departure, RL gave EB *The Works of George Herbert in Prose and Verse*, 2 vols. (1852). The books had first been presented to the Rev. Robert T. S. Lowell in 1859 from the parishioners of Christ Church in Newark, New Jersey. They were passed on to "R.T.S.L. (3rd)" in 1892. RL reinscribed it to EB: "These two volumes given one August morning with ALL his heart by Robert T. S. Lowell (4th) to Elizabeth Bishop. 8/8/57 'Thy mouth was open, but thou couldst not sing' " (Houghton). "Thy mouth . . .": George Herbert, "Death," line 4.
2 Crossed with letter 157.

served en route—and we were home by 6:30, only depressed by an awful woman and child who had quarreled behind us—and the fact that we *were* home, of course. Rather than face that we dined dazedly at the nearest Schraffts and went to the nearest movie . . . We saw Loren & Lloyd[1] Saturday night and in the course of telling them all about our stay in Maine we realized more and more what a nice time you'd given us and how many things we actually had managed to get into such a short time. Ll[2] showed me a long verse-letter, very obscene, he'd received from Dylan T before D's last trip here—very clever, but it really can't be published for a long long time, he's decided. About people D. met in the U.S. etc.—one small sample: *A Streetcar named Desire* is referred to as "A truck called F———." (Lota is demanding bicycle tape, but I really don't think I can find any on a Sunday morning.)

We've had rather discouraging news about the car, and even worse about the translation—Giroux wants over $600 for corrections. Both these problems are to be faced tomorrow—I have to go over the entire galley with him, fighting every inch, I suppose. Miss Baumgarten says it's absolutely impossible and that she is growing gray. Holliday House is sending you *Seal Morning*[3]—let me know if you don't receive it in a week. They won't have the Larkin[4] in again for a while, I'm afraid, but will send it when they do. Tomorrow I'm going to send a couple more books if I can find them. I sort of hope you'll be seeing the Whites again—even if Andy isn't feeling too well at present I think you'd find him pleasant company and nice to go looking at Nature with . . . I'm sorry we didn't get clamming & blue-berry picking— and sailing with Philip B., of course.[5] Give him my regards. (the drama of the lamps—2 now—goes on—they are quite gutted & all over the living-room & at any moment I'm about to give in and go out to the drugstore for sticking plaster.)

Lota had a very funny letter from her sister whom she'd written saying we were visiting "Robert Lowell in Maine." The sister didn't know who you were but assumes that all Lota's friends are very famous, so mentioned you casually to a Rio friend and then was embarrassed when the friend didn't know, either. So then she made up that you were a poet, too, and *next-best*, she thought, to me (!) and that "Maine" was the name of your *southern*

---

1 Loren MacIver and Lloyd Frankenberg.
2 Lloyd Frankenberg.
3 Rowena Farre, *Seal Morning* (1957).
4 RL had recommended Philip Larkin's *The Less Deceived* (1955).
5 Philip Booth, a Castine neighbor.

estate . . . (Lowell-sur-Maine?)—pronounced as if it were French, naturally. She wanted to know the facts.

Yesterday I meant to write you and to do a little work, too, but it was cool and rainy and we decided to take a long walk down 3rd Avenue & take in some more of New York, as long as we're here. There are a few too many hardware stores along it for us to make much headway—but we did find one very rarified antique shop full of old signs, mostly, and things from ships. I was dying to send you a life-size gold figure-head, an elegant small brass telescope, a gigantic red tin glove, a pair of gilt and red spectacles, about a yard across, like this: and a lovely green and gilt fountain-like structure to keep tea and coffee in—but all these items were horribly expensive.

Half an hour out for a very nice TV program of Renaissance music—the Pro-Musica Antiqua—old instruments, views of Florence, etc. thrown in. Will we ever get there again?

I've been reading a lot in the Herbert—this is the first time I'd ever gone traveling without him so it is nice to have him again this way, too—even if I feel you really really shouldn't have given it away. I think we should have read H's translation of Cornaro's (whoever he was) "Treatise of Temperance & Sobriety"[1] out loud to each other. It begins "Having observed in my time many of my friends, of excellent wit & noble disposition, overthrown & undone by Intemperance; who, if they had lived, could have been an ornament to the world and a comfort to their friends: I thought fit to discover in a short Treatise, that Intemperance was not such an evil, but it might easily be remedied . . ." "For in the end I got the victory, to my great honor and no less profit, whereupon also I joyed exceedingly, which excess of joy neither could do me any hurt: By which it is manifest, That neither melancholy nor any other passion can hurt a temperate life." (He knows what he's talking about, I think.) "Moreover, I say, that even bruises, and squats, & falls, which often kill others, can bring little grief or hurt to those that are temperate."

I'm writing refusing all the readings today. Our plans at present are, more or less—we're going to Easthampton for a concert to be given by the "boys"[2] on the 25th—in a borrowed car, taking Rosinha, to show her a bit of the U.S., and probably the joys of a motel. On August 31st I think I'll fly to Key West for 5 or 6 days, probably, and return for the unveiling of the Portinari Murals at the U.N. on the 7th.[3] Sometime towards the end of Sept. I'll get to Boston again, with Lota, I hope. Or we might get over while Rosinha's

1 Luigi Cornaro, "Discorsi della vita sobria" (1558), trans. George Herbert.
2 Robert Fizdale and Arthur Gold.
3 Rosalina Leão assisted Candido Portinari when he painted his UN murals.

216

here for her to see some art—and she's a friend of Agnes Mongan's, too. But I don't know her plans, or how long she's staying. We've told Moore McCormack that we can go back any time after Oct. 1st, now, (I'm really getting anxious to get back to work & L is worrying a bit about the house) and we should know the sailing date soon.

Dear Cal, do please please take care of yourself and be an ornament to the world (you're already that) and a comfort to your friends . . . It seems to me in our conversations we just did the ground-work and never got onto the more constructive and hopeful parts of things. (Lota is going to try to get in touch with her old doctor here tomorrow, too, and I'll let you know if she recommends any good people in Boston.)— There *are* many hopeful things, too, you know. Sobriety & gayety & patience & toughness will do the trick. Or so I hope for myself and hope & pray for you, too. It was wonderful seeing you in Maine again. Any blue afternoon you might call on that Janet Moore—she's really awfully nice and knows a lot about painting and the "classics," of course, and I'm sure would love giving you a cup of tea. When you write me will you give me the name of the Boulanger collection and the Prévert? We want to get them both (the records, I mean). Lota sends love— so do I—and hope to see you again very soon.

Faithfully,
Elizabeth

Marion Cummings' photographs came & are awful—I look like a terrifying rich dowager of 65—she said herself she just can't take women.

159.[1]

[Castine, Maine
n.d. 1957]

Dear Elizabeth and Lota:

I've opened this as instructed but can make neither "head nor tail" of it except that the only date seems to be the unurgent September 15, so I am sending this by mail instead of calling in Merwin and telephoning. Hope I haven't made a mistake.

Love,
Cal

---

1 Typed on a scrap of paper; RL was forwarding mail that had arrived for EB and Lota in Castine.

160.

Dearest Cal:

I'd mailed my letter to you when yours of the 9th came. We really covered somewhat the same subjects, I think—but yours made me feel both awfully sad and extremely optimistic. You weren't "inconsiderate," Cal! You were a wonderful host, and we had such a nice time with you, really. Even if Lota does think all fir trees are deliberately planted, she liked Maine very much, and you were so good about driving us all over the coast-line.

As I'm sure she's told you, Elizabeth & I had only about three minutes' conversation, in which I told her that I was worried about your coming down to Brazil alone. I just spoke about Brazil, not New York nor Boston nor anything. (Except that I think I said I thought Boston alone in the summer didn't sound very promising, either.) What both Lota and I felt, feel, about Brazil is that much as we'd really love to have you visit us there, show you a few of the colonial towns, etc.—it's really *not* a place to spend any time in alone. Rio is absolutely beautiful, the most beautiful harbour in the world, and parts of the city are enchanting—but once you've seen it there is really very little to do there. Up in the country with us is also beautiful and peaceful and we have lots of books and hope to have the high-fi going—but I'm afraid you'd really feel restless after a stretch of it, and even a trip to Ouro Prêto (THE baroque town) only takes three or four days. Our idea was that it would be better if you all could come sometime—we could find you an apartment in Rio, find Elizabeth a maid and a *baba* (nanny) (such things do exist there) and then you might stay for two or three months and I think find it more interesting. If you got bored in Rio you could come up and visit us (1½ hours by excellent bus service, every half hour). If you got bored up there you could go back to Rio. And we really have plenty of room for you and family, too. Suggest this to E—I think she might really be able to work there, too—

When we started thinking about various friends you might stay with in Rio was really when this all grew on us—we just knew how strange, difficult, and *boring*, it might get for you—it really is much more "foreign" than Europe, you know, in some ways, and the language is difficult and there aren't cafés, simple restaurants, places to go sight-seeing, etc., etc.—

Please don't worry about anything connected with me, Cal—don't worry at all, if that's possible! I saw Giroux the other day about this awful proof and he talked & talked about how much he liked the autobiographical piece in *PR*.— I'm not going to give those readings so we think maybe we can go back to Brazil sometime the first week of October now. Lota's Dr.

Moulton (her old (former! young & beautiful) doctor) is out of town but she's written her, and any information about Boston Drs. I'll send on to you immediately. Maybe I shd. add to the inscription in the Herbert "E.B. 'the 1st' " (?) (but I shan't, of course.) I do hope and pray you are feeling better and please write me whenever you feel like it. I got the German anthology[1] right away and have found some wonderful things. Did you notice Morgenstern?—Klee-like and Stevens-like? Thank you for forwarding the letters— the Brazilian friend isn't coming until Sunday but we really needed the time to prepare for her. I plan to go to Key West for one week, starting Aug. 31st, back the 6th. I do hope to see you again before we leave. Lota sends her love and all best wishes and so do I, as I'm sure you know—

I'll write soon—

Elizabeth

161.

Castine, Maine
August 15, 1957

Dearest Elizabeth B.:

Your letter, besides bringing its cheerful tempering of the spirit, has brought me terrific relief. I feared that I was forever in exile, along with those other clinging, clutching, fevered souls, Muriel,[2] your worst Nova Scotian relatives, all those bramble-armed bugbears that have so boringly tried to tangle up your life. God be thanked, and let this letter begin as scherzo lest my last, though true and necessary, seem my one voice.

First I must solace you for having missed the voyage with Eberhart to Somes Sound. It was rich in undramatic mishaps. When the plans were being made, Dick managed to tell me ten times in the course of five sentences and five minutes that we must be off by ten. Ferried by Booth in Fred's outboard, I arrive at 9:35 at Goose Falls. We sat, blue-jeaned on the cable of the Falls' bridge. Time passed. We had a rather vexatious and repetitive talk about Phil's poem, a long narrative about a friend of his [who] was actually frozen to death while canoeing down an uncharted Canadian river. I had made the point that both in his letter applying for his Guggenheim and in the poem itself it would [be] disastrous to leave out the real adventure (which he by the way tells very powerfully in conversation) and substitute his reflections on

---

1 *The Penguin Book of German Verse*, ed. by Leonard Forster (1957).
2 Possibly Muriel Rukeyser, who had briefly been at Vassar when EB was a student there.

the destructive element, his aesthetic notions of how difficult such a poem is to write. Good points made for the second time began to pall, the cable ate into our behinds, Phil began to talk his to me maddening line about wanting to write like Muir and Merwin and Brewster Ghiselin. At eleven Eberhart appeared in his sky-blue beach wagon, and mumbled something about never being able to start on time when there are women. This became clearer when we reached the little red bungalow under Undercliff where Betty[1] and the second ex–Mrs. Rexroth[2] were waiting. The second ex–Mrs. Rexroth, tall fading red-haired, figury, black-sweatery said that she had heard me read in San Francisco but had had to leave before the end. I: "Which reading at San Francisco?" Second ex–Mrs. Rexroth: "The one at the museum. I heard all of Dick's readings but couldn't do that for anyone else." She had gone to six consecutive Eberhart readings (sometimes two a day)! In fact she was all too much astride the high, foamy wave of Eberhart's élan, and Betty was rather balky and unpoetic about obeying Dick, still a bungalow man and not yet the skipper of the *Reve*. First mishap, our skiff loaded with all our clothes, movie cameras, can of crepe suzettes etc. began to move gently out from under Undercliff into the great sea. At first it seemed to be coming back ashore, then like Kitten diving through Randall's legs for its beloved coal pile, the skiff shot toward Stonington. Suddenly Dick was splashing in all his girth, and underwear and sneakers over razor sharp rocks and bouncing on floating sea-kelp and the skiff was caught. We were off, and I began to study steering with the chart. Dick's chart-reading, though miles ahead of mine, was encouragingly incomplete and there were many pleasing puzzles for the beginner to grow strong on. We passed gloriously under the Deer Island Bridge and into Eggemoggin Reach and the many islands. Each spar and island that came up could be checked off on the chart (and in Dikkon's log book) but it was as though one were fitting some twenty screens in the twenty similar by each slightly different windows of [a] country house and had somehow gotten the order wrong. Still everything with straining and pushing *would* go on the chart. We looked at the compass (the one that Dick described as working well North and South but not so well East and West). We were going somehow due west instead of due east! There were Blue Hill, the Camden Hills, the mountains of Mount Desert. A great brown mountain loomed ahead of us like Atlantis in Dante's Ulysses canto[3]; we could already see white waves breaking. But there was no sign of what should have been the small-business-

---

1 Helen Elizabeth Eberhart, Richard Eberhart's wife.
2 Marie Kass Rexroth, who was married to Kenneth Rexroth from 1940 to 1955 (they separated in 1948).
3 Dante, *Inferno*, canto 26.

power blue smoke of the Bass Moccasin factory of the Bass Harbor, Mount Desert. We were entering Isle au Haut! Things then went swimmingly, only Dick was disconcertingly officious, old school-teacherish and skipperish about my steering; he stood at a different angle and it was impossible for me to make a turn without little shifts and corrections. Then without warning he vanished utterly and was deaf to all my calls for even the most needful advice. Then came the sinister Casco Strait. Philip Booth, who has a way of making the serenest outboard trip across Castine Harbor seem a clash of thews, seamanship and foundering, had made this part of our voyage seem an almost maniacal act of hubris. Dick put down his movie camera, ordered Betty and the ex–Mrs. Rexroth on the alert, assumed command. The Casco Strait, however, was wider than the broadest part of the Boston Basin. Yet there was a difficulty. Dick is color-blind and at this supreme moment with the eyes of the ex–Mrs. Rexroth on him he reverted to his old heresy that colors have no functional difference and spars are painted now red, now black, merely to vary their monotony. Now the *Reve* is a perfect craft, about forty feet long. It looks as though some Alice in Wonderland accident had befallen some much smaller boat and that it had doubled its size without somehow readjusting its design. Broad and covered with dark mahogany, it looks [like] some Gothic, Episcopal church built for a small town about 1900, something from that last gasp of Victorian design when the old massive designs still held but when the quality of the old massive materials was fast failing. It was, as Betty said, too big for those who might have liked it but couldn't have afforded it, yet too unsporting and bulky for those who could afford it. It developed one defect; not a ray of sun could pierce its massive after-cabin where everyone sat and watched the helmsman, a little stooped lest he bump his head, steer. We nearly froze, yet it was a broiling day.

Glorious entrance into Northeast Harbor, all the most beautiful forty thousand dollar Atlantic class 31 foot sloops racing in the yellowing late afternoon sun. We entered Southwest Harbor and by this time I had so much mastered my chart reading that for the first time I understood the meaning of the names Southwest and Northeast, an experience denied the land automobile tourist. All our fish in Castine and even the fish in Bucksport come from Southwest, and all summer we'd been hearing that one had never really tasted haddock unless one had had a Southwest Harbor haddock fresh off the fishing boats. I had determined to treat our group to a sea dinner and even had us all headed toward a famed place called Andy's when we became aware of a scarlet convertible that for several minutes refused to pass us and almost tread on our heels as we strolled down the dust[y] dockside road. The car stopped. Asked about Andy's, the driver offered to drive us. Red-faced as his car, laughing, he really made Dick seem gaunt, speechless, Charles Addamsish. Asked about Andy's, he put a hand over his mouth and said "Shh-h, Andy's my neighbor." He then proposed a place where he and his wife went when they wanted a real meal. He said that he was Captain Claaussens. He said, "I'm a gambling man, that is in my calling and I risk my life against sea-hazards. I'll make you a gambling proposition: if you are not a hundred and one per cent satisfied with the meal you are going to get you can telephone me and I'll pay for it." So we abandoned Andy's and obeyed. On the way, we passed Caruso's. Captain Claaussens said, "I'll be honest with you, if you like Italian food you can get [a] real meal there." We reached our destination. It was a sort of very provincial country version of the Northeast Harbor *Lighthouse*. Hard hunched quarters, apricot paint, spotless Maine souvenirs, no liquor. We had real bread, there was a little butter in the clam chowder, the haddock was fried in fat as thick as the deck of the *Reve*, for dessert we had horrible "rainbow superbs."

Glorious evening, Maine food-filled cruise down Somes Sound. Everything I had hoped you and Lota would see on our trip now materialized. All the great lawns, birch and elm groves, frail expensive wharves, new Swedish racing craft at the moorings, here and there a private plane; you felt you were seeing the great Roman villas described by Horace and Juvenal as examples of the glorious *sic transit gloria mundi* of the imperial Roman's middle age (His own middle age, not Rome's!) We landed at Somesville, went ashore, a rather ungracious little group, I in khaki socks, pants and shirt, Betty in blue shorts and sailor blouse looking like a boy of twelve, the ex–Mrs. Rexroth, figury, black sweatery, faded red haired, Dick, home-made Commander Whitehead, fringe-bearded, sunset red-faced, wearing a plum and beige lumber-jacket. Sweeping for a moment into control, I showed everyone the Somesville herring-run. Then foot-weary and languid, we all climbed a little hill to an old white hotel, *The Somes*. It wasn't for us. Elderly, wealthy, speechless lonely people sat about drinking carbonated water at candle-lit tables. In reply to Dick's "Do you serve the soft drink," and Betty's, "We mean beer," the manager answered "I could give you some ice tea but that would not do you any good." Ice-tealess then, we sat conspicuously on the front veranda and tried to decide whether a man named Saigan, married once to someone he called Isa Gardner, and twenty years ago followed by the ex–Mrs. Rexroth from San Francisco to New York was really *Belle* Gardner's first husband.[1]

---

1 Isabella Gardner's first husband was Harold van Kirk.

The clientele seemed to be entirely women, in evening dresses, they would rise from their little tables where they were playing probably Auction Bridge, stare at us then turn away in fatigue and horror. When we went back to our skiff it was moonlit dark, Dick with a bunchy, musclely leap pushed off, there was a blaze of phosphorous water like a Fourth of July sparkler, and poor Betty had fallen into the water, fortunately only three feet deep, but full of jelly-fish causing the phosphorescent blaze. On board the *Reve*, half the company began drinking a kind of boiler-maker, manhattans followed by beer. The ex–Mrs. Rexroth, really a rather gentle sympathetic soul, turned out to be a nurse, the ideal wife for Rexroth. The conversation turned to hospital stories. Betty showed an unexpected gift for really eccentric macabre recollections: the man with a bleeding amputated leg who asked her to kiss him on the lips her first day as a volunteer nurse; the man who had put a proposal of the offer of marriage in the back end of a hen so that the hen laid an egg containing the offer of marriage, which the girl opened at breakfast; a horrible man who had had "his tubes tied," so that he could enjoy sexual intercourse without the danger of procreation. Dick said, "Cal and I are haunted and harassed by a disaster which you girls are relieved of." We discussed the prostate operation in saturating detail. The *Reve* now offered from its hold a set of canvas curtains that completely enclosed the back cabin, and which for no reason could [be] fastened down completely on one side but not the other. Shut in, the hurricane lantern fuming, the cabin heavy with a thick canvas and coal oil dew, I took a last look through our canvas curtains at the Sound. Captain Claaussens, questioned about anchorage, had said, "Why a fish line will hold you." And yet an unfamiliar, tremendous ridged shadow, like the back of [a] crocodile seemed nearing. We had anchored correctly, letting out five and a half times our depth of rope, only we had forgotten the tides, and our anchor was actually floating a fathom or so from bottom.

I can't go on in this detail, and the rest of the *Reve*'s cruise was uneventful. Dick demanded orange juice and blueberries, blueberry pancakes and bacon and eggs and sausage. At noon we reached an island off Blue Hill where we joined up the Wanning ketch carrying Elizabeth and Susan,[1] Philip and Margaret Booth and two small Booth children. First manhattans and beer on the *Reve*, then martinis on the Wanning ketch. Andy Wanning is of course beautiful on his boat, lazily, gently, absolutely, softly in control. Only we seemed to be drifting nearer the *Reve*. Andy slowly said, "This is the strangest thing, we *are* drifting but the anchor rope is always slack." This

1 Susan Turner.

was no Eberhart ignorant paradox, but a puzzle supported by thirty years of the most patient and skillful seamanship. Meanwhile the drinks continued. Eberhart, red-faced, manhattan-breathing, began to focus his movie camera on the approaching boats. No one did a thing. Pat Wanning appeared from the hold, where orange-sweat shirted, khaki shorted, a pretty-grayed curl in the middle of her forehead, she had been working with unstopping efficiency. She said, "I am going to make a speech. I know my speeches are very unpopular in my family, nevertheless I am going to make a speech. I have prepared cold consommé, hot Canadian bean soup, hot dogs with relish and mustard, cucumber and tomato salad, coffee, tea and cocoa, but I haven't hands enough to serve you individually. When I pass the food out you must divide it yourselves." Behind her Andy, unlistening, filling another pitcher of martinis. She said to me re schools, "Of course I like yachting and my free summers too, but I think colleges and schools will have to run twelve months a year; I can't bear it when my husband and children get up in the morning with nothing they *must* do." The great beautiful ketch costing forty thousand dollars, according [to] the petrified Philip Booth, had drifted within a foot of the *Reve*. It really had. Then Andy started his motor and dragged our anchor away in safety. Meanwhile Elizabeth had drunk a whole water tumbler of the martinis to which she is allergic. She sprawled on the fore-cabin and just (?) out of hearing began [to] discuss sotto voce an amazingly frank and detailed reappraisal of our entire marriage. It went on for an hour and a half. She said that we were all leaving the next day with a trailer for Boston where we would both go [to] doctors. Susan already had her reservation back to Vassar. When we got home and ever since, it seems as though we were at last in better agreement than we have been since Harriet's birth. I think we will both go to doctors, but we are staying here, *and* poor Susan has gone home two weeks early, the one unplanned outward event of the whole summer. Elizabeth had suddenly turned gray in the face at the thought of a whole month of Susan, who cannot cook, is too recessive to carry on conversation, will talk about nothing but her doctor's thesis with Trilling and Versailles Kentucky and finds nothing Elizabeth and I do half as interesting as her own health. Now we are in one another's arms, and feeling a thousand years younger. Of course, Susan's departure was perfectly friendly, not another dislodging of Miss Elsemore.

Oh one last sailing scene. We are in the ketch, sailing under Blue Hill, before the wind at capacity speed, nine and a half knots an hour, carrying full canvas, mainsail, *Geneva*, jigger, and an exotic thing, the mizzen stay-sail that stretches almost vertical in the air between the main mast and the little stern mast. Philip Booth is at the wheel utterly transformed with excitement, quoting Merwin sea poems, Shakespeare, calling Andy "Sir." He looks up and shouts, "By G-god Sir, Sir if this boat is going to j-jibe unexpectedly I'm not going to be resp-ponsible." Then Andy sleepy, floating lightly and indifferently as a cloud, is back at the helm and Pat says, "Andy knows everything about boats but all his commands sound like questions."

Once I got started writing about the cruise, I found going on too pleasant to stop, but after so much buffoonery, like Pat Wanning I want to make my little speech. Your advice about going to a doctor and keeping up one's patience, sobriety, toughness and gaiety is dreadfully true, and I am sure that all is beginning to be well and that Elizabeth and I really profoundly love and are charmed by one another and we will be a safe happy place for little Harriet. All will come and one begins to see the ways.

Also I want you to know that you need never again fear my overstepping myself and stirring up confusion with you. My frenzied behavior during your visit has a history and there is one fact that I want to disengage from all its harsh frenzy. There's one bit of the past that I would like to get off my chest and then I think all will be easy with us.

Do you remember how at the end of that long swimming and sunning Stonington day after Carley's removal by Tommy, we went up to, I think, the relatively removed upper Gross house and had one of those real fried New England dinners, probably awful. And we were talking about this and that about ourselves and I was feeling the infected hollowness of the Carley business draining out of my heart, and you said rather humorously yet it was truly meant, "When you write my epitaph, you must say I was the loneliest person who ever lived." Probably you forget, and anyway all that is mercifully changed and all has come right since you found Lota. But at the time everything, I guess (I don't want to overdramatize) our relations seemed to have reached a new place. I assumed that would be just a matter of time before I proposed and I half believed that you would accept. Yet I wanted it all to have the right build-up. Well, I didn't say anything then. And of course the Eberharts in-laws wasn't the right stage-setting, and then there was that poetry conference at Bard and I remember one evening presided over by Mary McCarthy and my Elizabeth was there, and going home to the Bard poets' dormitory, I was so drunk that my hands turned cold and I felt half-dying and held your hand. And nothing was said, and like a loon that needs sixty feet, I believe, to take off from the water, I wanted time and space, and went on assuming, and when I was to have joined you at Key West I was determined to ask you. Really for so callous (I fear) a man, I was fearfully shy and scared of spoiling things and distrustful of being steady enough to be the least good. Then of course the Yaddo explosion came and all was over. Yet there were a few months. I suppose we might almost claim something like apparently Strachey and Virginia Woolf.[1] And of course there was always the other side, the fact that our friendship really wasn't a courting, was really disinterested (bad phrase) really led to no encroachments. So it is. Let me [say] this though and then leave the matter forever; I do think free will is sewn into everything we do; you can't cross a street, light a cigarette, drop saccharine in your coffee without really doing it. Yet the possible alternatives that life allows us are very few, often there must be none. I've never thought there was any choice for me about writing poetry. No doubt if I used my head better, ordered my life better, worked harder etc., the poetry would be improved, and there must be many lost poems, innumerable accidents and ill-done actions. But asking you is *the* might have been for me, the one towering change, the other life that might have been had. It was that way for these nine years or so that intervened. It was deeply buried, and this spring and summer (really before your arrival) it boiled to the surface. Now it won't happen again, though of course I always feel a great blytheness and easiness with you. It won't happen, I'm really underneath utterly *in* love and sold on my Elizabeth, and it's a great solace to me that you are with Lota, and I am sure it is the will of the heavens that all is as it is.

I wish we had three more weeks in low gear, drifting with the wind, sustained by three or four servants here, when you and I and Lota and Elizabeth could have passed the time without hurry or pressure. But that too will come and I am sure everyone loves, admires and approves of everyone else and are happier than a month ago now because a great block and question mark is gone.

We go to Boston on the fifth of September. Perhaps the fifteenth or thereabouts would be the ideal time for you and Lota to make your visit and I promise to take Lota to Raymonds and Iver Johnson and Charles Street and my father's old tacky beloved army navy stores—wherever there's hardware, there we'll go.

Love,

Cal

P.S. The last part is too heatedly written with too many *ands* and so forth. I guess it doesn't much matter though. The records are French Renaissance

---

1 Lytton Strachey and Virginia Woolf were briefly engaged on February 17, 1909.

Vocal Music (Nadia Boulanger) Decca; there an old and new French song concert also directed by Boulanger put out by Vox. The Prevert songs are Les Frères Jacques Polydor 1st series.[1] Have you seen the huge monthly record catalogues. They list everything under five or things crossing classifications and would be handy to take home. I guess you're wise about the readings, though we wish we could hear you. Certainly there are trifles, not interesting challenges. Why doesn't Miss Baumgarten tackle Straus[2] himself, surely he won't dare be so miserly as Giroux.

162.

115 East 67th Street
New York
August 28th, 1957

Dearest Cal:

Here is the letter Lota just received from her ex-analyst—"ex" may not be right. The man's name seems to be *Taves*—perhaps you've heard of him? At any rate, you might make an appointment to see him when he returns to Cambridge, and see how you like him. Lota's Dr. apparently has others up her sleeve, too. I do hope I'm not being awfully bossy about this—but everyone finds analysts through their friends, I think, so I guess not . . .

I wanted to answer your wonderful account of the *Reve* and her crew of *reveurs* right away, but we've been so busy ever since Rosinha arrived a week ago that this is the first time I've sat down to the typewriter. And I'm apt to be interrupted at any moment by my Brazilian friends returning from Bloomingdale's loaded down with place-mats, electric frying-pans, and cosmetics. You saw this place so you can imagine what it's getting like as Lota goes down her list of commissions—mens' suits and slacks, a plastic dinner-set for a family of 14, slickers, sou-wetters, and rubber boots for 3 grandchildren and my godchild, dozens of jars of spices, etc. that one can't get in Brazil, and under, over, and stuck between everything else a few hundred books . . . Oh—Orlon blankets and pillows (the most space-taking of all) for allergic friends . . . I have a sore toe from stubbing it on the dinner-set crate,

---

1 *French Renaissance Vocal Music*, Nadia Boulanger, conductor (Decca 9629, n.d.); *Concert of French Choral Music: La Polyphonie française à travers les siècles*, Nadia Boulanger, dir. (Vox PL 6380, n.d.). Les Frères Jacques made several recordings of Jacques Prévert's poems, including one released in 1957, mostly for Phillips. *En Sortant Ecole/Orgue Barbari* (composed by Jacques Prévert) was released by Polydor (n.d.). See RL, "Near the Ocean: Fourth of July in Maine," lines 77–80 (RL-*CP*).
2 Roger Straus.

in the hall last night. There are little lists everywhere and jotted calculations changing waist-measurements in centimeters into inches . . . I don't know how Lota does it, really; I hate to shop so.

We had a friend with a car here until today and over the week-end we went down to East Hampton where Fizdale & Gold were giving a concert. It poured and rained and the millions of automobiles on the endless highways *whished-whished* by, almost in silence. I can't imagine what Rosinha made of it—I don't know what to myself. There were super-highways and clover-leafs in 1951, but they have ex-foliated beyond my wildest dreams since then—they're really terrifying. I did my road-map tricks and got us from the Veterans' Memorial Highway to the Northeastern Highway to the Grand Central Thruway in such a way that I think I even eliminated 20 miles on the return trip, but I still can't believe in any of it and have felt rather subdued ever since. We stayed at a motel, ate horrible food, went to a party in a house made out of a windmill, had lunch the next day with Aaron Copland, walked on the dunes (Rosinha carrying her spike-heeled shoes in her hand, but bearing up bravely, even if the beaches there can compare with those of Rio no better than can those of Maine. I keep telling Lota they aren't "beaches" in Maine—that's a "coast"—but the "beaches of Maine" get worse every time she tells about them!) The concert itself was very nice—frivolous but good—Mozart, Poulenc—winding up with Milhaud's *Brasileira*[1] in our honor. Bobby F had been going to make a little speech mentioning all our names, concluding with "Cookiezinha,"[2] but lost his nerve—

We've also made other highway-trips—up the Hudson, where I thought the West Point boys all looked very fat and out-of-condition and the river at points is choked up with lines and lines of decaying freighters; and then down and around the Battery, etc., to the markets and St. Paul's. Have you been there?—the prettiest church in the U.S., inside, at least—where George Washington used to go? Perfect 18th century, rather ballroom-like.

But every time I've made a trip, a side-trip on this trip, I mean, I've come back depressed, I don't know why—I think it's mostly *automobiles*—and then decide it's just some lack of vitality in myself that makes me feel so hopeless about my own country. (Maine didn't produce this result—if we'd driven back instead of flying, it probably would have, though.) And then I feel just as hopeless about Brazil, so I suppose I am just a born worrier, and that when the personal worries of adolescence and the years after it have

---

1 Darius Milhaud, *Saudades do Brasil*, Op. 67 (1920–21).
2 Nickname given by Lota to EB for her cooking skills.

more or less disappeared I promptly have to start worrying about the decline of nations . . . But I really can't *bear* much of American life these days—surely no country has ever been so filthy rich and so hideously uncomfortable at the same time.

I'm sorry we missed the sail with Andy—the rest of it not so much!—I'd rather read your account of it, I think. An awful little anthology just arrived and I've read Miss Moore's poem on the small-magazine conference[1] and Eberhart's and Philip Booth's contributions, just to see if they're all the way I think they are, and they are. My friends have also arrived, laden with, this time, mens' shirts—stacks of them, very nice—neckties, yard-goods, and two beautiful Japanese parasols. Now we are supposed to go down to the Matisse Gallery where Loren is giving us a private showing of what's there, so I must get into my street clothes.— Another thing that's tiring about N.Y. life, maybe, is this constant shifting gears (and even that I seem to think of in automobilistic terms), from one occupation to another.

I do hope you're feeling much, much better, Cal, and realize now that I may not have written a very cheering letter. However, underneath I really am extremely cheerful and well and very eager to get back to work. I'm going down to Key West next Wednesday, probably for six days. Sometime towards the end of September I'll be getting to Boston for a couple of days—with Lota, I hope. Our boat, the "Mooremacstar," is supposed to sail the 8th of October. Please give my love to Elizabeth and I hope the baby is doing well—and able to do the cooking ~~herself~~ by now. Please do write and tell me how you are and I'll write a better letter over the week-end, I hope—

    With lots of love as always—
      Elizabeth

I just read Fanny Burney's *Journal*[2]—or selections from it. Have you read it? All the parts about her life at the court of George III are marvelous. Did you ever get the seal book? I'm trying to find you Marchand's *Memoirs* & hope to send them off before I go to Florida—

---

1 Marianne Moore, "Values in Use," *New Poems by American Poets* #2 (1957), ed. Rolfe Humphries.
2 Fanny Burney, *Diary and Letters* (1842–46).

163.

September 11, 1957

Dearest Elizabeth—

I've put off writing you till I could proudly report that I had nailed down Dr. Taves; however, he's out of town, so that will have to wait.

Really things have turned the corner! We're getting on very cheerfully and sensibly. We have been back in Boston, almost a week and have spent the time mostly with ourselves, calling up no one. The only trouble with this is that one must take what comes, and what comes is the editor of the *Yale Review*[1] with his white shoes, his fashionable conservativism and his young minister friend or our very icy Norwegian friend[2] (Have [you] noticed how every young man of talent is now a minister or a playwright or a baby-doctor? The *50's*.) who thinks he's Stendhal and who looks like Alger Hiss,[3] and who is always explaining what a success his last visit to his about to be abandoned Dutch wife[4] has been.

I've been furiously writing at poems and spent whole blue and golden Maine days in my bedroom with a ghastly utility bedside lamp on, my pajamas turning oily with sweat, and I have six poems started. They beat the big drum too much. There's one in a small voice that's fairly charmingly written I hope (called "Skunk Hour," not in your style yet indebted a little to your "Armadillo.") If I can get two short lines and a word, I'll mail it to you. The others, God willing, will come to something in the course of the winter. At least I feel I have armloads of lines and leads.

Back here I've gotten sidetracked into reading. Emerson on Montaigne,[5] the two terrible ~~trial~~ Senate scenes in *Sejanus*,[6] they beat anything of their kind, and though not exactly contemporary, yet are—change a little decor and the blank verse—almost unbearably what has happened in Russia under Stalin, might happen anywhere. Jonson has a bold steadiness and here hardly ever flinches away into parody and the clichés of exaggeration. Went through John Ransom's complete *Selected Poems*[7] (75 pages of big print)

---

1 J. E. Palmer.
2 Per Seyersted.
3 State Department official accused of membership in the Communist party during the McCarthy era.
4 Sister of RL's friend W. F. van Leeuwen.
5 Ralph Waldo Emerson, "Montaigne; or, the Skeptic," *Representative Men* (1849).
6 Ben Jonson, *Sejanus: His Fall* (1605).
7 The 1945 edition.

again. They are almost all queer Chaplin-like charades of himself: looking at children, young girls, the heavens and more often the knotted ravel of marriage. Then I went through Graves[1]—more force than Ransom, more poems and kinds of poems. There's not a banality, I think anywhere, though a somewhat sparring, boxerlike and too steely man. But what a wonderfully nervous and ever-exercised mind—each poem knocks me in a corner with a wet towel over my head. I liked the Morgenstern. He's not in the main and perhaps too glowing and grandiose German line. Have you read Heine's[2] "Morphine," and "Der Scheidende" (the ending very Jewish and German with its bluster, comicality, clicking sounds, confusion of pronouns is about the wittiest poem I know of)? Two long poems seem magnificent to me, Hebel's father and son dialogue in dialect,[3] as good as Frost or Wordsworth, and much more serene, humorous and peopled; then Carossa's long lament for destroyed Germany[4] . . . it reminds me of some of Randall's and some of mine (like me he even has the Cologne Cathedral,[5] though I suppose that's not such a coincidence). It's [a] good deal deeper than we are, and if it's a little steady and too massive in expression, that too seems right and felt. Then there's the long Holderlin[6] that [I] guess goes the furthest of all, and almost all the Goethe—he has an even-tempered agility that seems now too nimble and then too usual, there are no earthquakes, yet if one could take him, one might shed the poets' worst temptation, the temptation to get off the ground, roar and go blind. Goethe doesn't. My last reading has been Keats' letters, but I've just finished them, finished myself, and will keep quiet. Ah though! All of it just four years (in Trilling's selection)[7] and young enough to make Booth and Merwin seem gray—all the foolery, and gaiety and shouldering into what life gave.

I have meant (talking about shouldering) to wave a flag at your "so filthy rich and hideously uncomfortable." I agree mostly and we seem to strike everyone from away very harshly—vibrant, stiff, sickly. But I don't know, if it's the water one must swim in, where most of what one knows about life comes from, most of one has to love—it doesn't hurt so much. It is liveable.

1 Robert Graves, *Collected Poems* (1955).
2 Heinrich Heine.
3 Johann Peter Hebel, "Die Vergänglichkeit. Gerspräch auf der Straße von Basel zwischen Steinen und Brombach, in der Nacht."
4 Hans Carossa, "Abendländische Elegie" (1943).
5 See "The Exile's Return," lines 22–23 (RL-*CP*).
6 Friedrich Hölderlin, "Brot und Wein" (1800).
7 John Keats, *Selected Letters*, ed. Lionel Trilling (1951).

So Harriet finds. She can now manage a few consonants *Da Da dadada*—though the immensity that these words designate doesn't seem to have sunk in. She can't cook, she can now pull herself to her feet (first occasion on a cage of guinea pigs belonging to my cousin Alice's baby and removed from Harriet who had, in two seconds, half depilated them), and yesterday we caught her going through my Salem cigarettes and drooling a sweet trickle of brown juice. Come and stay with us, dear, with Lota.

Love,

Cal

P.S. Thanks for the Lora the seal; why can't *I* carry a tune![1]

164.

[Postcard: Sailboat Lake and the Mall, Central Park, New York City]

[September 24, 1957]

Dear Cal: I'm coming at 9:15 on Friday—"Merchants Ltd."[2]—shall debouch at Back Bay. I shd. leave either Sat. night or Sun. morning—

Love—

E.B.—

(This written in Grand Central in a joke shop, with difficulty)

165.

September 27, 1957 10:07 PM

NEXT WEEK END WILL BE SWELL HAVE THE BLOOMS FOR FRIDAY NIGHT LOVE

CAL

1 Rowena Farre's *Seal Morning* (1957), a memoir of growing up in a remote Scottish croft, features a seal named Lora who plays the xylophone and mouth organ and was known to sing.
2 Train connecting New York and Boston.

166.

Dearest Cal:

Thank you for your reassuring wire & I'm sorry I've been so fickle about my plans. I really had to stay here this week-end, though—Margaret Miller's mother had an operation on Friday & we here all worried about her. Everything's fine, though. And Saturday I had to go to a funeral. The next weekend is really much better, and I'll take the train that gets there at 5 o'clock, to give us a bit more time—it will be nice to see Hyman. On Saturday I shall have to have lunch or something with a cousin; aside from that I'm free. On Sunday I think if I get out to Worcester by three or four o'clock that will be early enough.

Thursday, the third, Lota & I've decided to give a bang-up party, to even scores all around—so if you or Elizabeth or any of our mutual friends I don't know of are to be in N.Y.—please come! We're giving it at Robert Fizdale's, 333 Central Park West, apt. 81, 6 PM—Marianne's coming, maybe Cummings, our mysterious scientist friend, Herbert Spencer Polin,[1] perhaps Eleanor C and Red W,[2] etc., etc. . . . this is to be our last fling and I wish you were to be here—

It's past midnight and very silent and I'm probably keeping the night doorman awake as well as Lota, and a mystery man across the garden who sits up all night with three bright lights on, as if giving himself a 3rd degree—only he always does seem to be awake, & alone. Tonight he did something very strange for a while—and finally we saw that he was (silently) playing a cello.

This is no answer to your letter at all—I'll answer it out loud. I am dying to see the poems and hope you're all well. Until next Friday—
Lots of love,
Elizabeth

The freighter now sails the 11th—

---

1 Herbert Spencer Polin invented cafelite, a form of plastics made from coffee beans.
2 Eleanor Clark and Robert Penn Warren.

167.

[Postcard: "John P. Grace Memorial 'Cooper River' Bridge, one of the highest and longest cantilever bridges in the world"]

[Charleston, South Carolina][1]

[October 17, 1957]

We approached quaint old Charleston this A.M. under this bridge to the right, & have been viewing its historic lovely homes in the pouring rain with a German-speaking taxi-driver—Thank you for your wire. The ship is all right but slightly squalid. I'll write details—

Lots of love,

Elizabeth

168.

[Postcard: The Eugene Jalmadge Bridge, Savannah]

[Savannah, Georgia]

[October 19, 1957]

Today's approach to the modern South—"by the greasy gray Limpopo River, all hung about with fever trees"[2]—

Recessively yours—

E.B.

—next stop Curoção—

169.

[239 Marlborough Street, Boston 16, Massachusetts]

October 25, 1957

My Darling receding Elizabeth:

I guess I can match Miss Moore in explosive openings! However, you never recede and I seem to be always with you in the doorway of your aunt's brown apartment, ringing the bell for her to open the door again. You are with me always.

Otherwise, my poems still go on. I now have a jail one,[3] a three and a half

---

1 The SS *Mormacstar* sailed for Brazil on October 15, stopping at the ports of Charleston, Savannah, and Curaçao, arriving in Rio on November 3.
2 See Rudyard Kipling, "The Elephant's Child," *Just So Stories* (1902).
3 "Memories of West Street and Lepke" (RL-*CP*).

page one about my being five years old and seeing my Uncle Devereux for the last time (at my Grandfather's country place) before he died of Hodgkin's disease,[1] another on my Father,[2] one on flying to Rapallo for Mother's dying[3]—all very personal! I'll type them out next week and mail them along with the others to you. I sent "Skunk Hour" with fear and trembling to Randall—he's never acknowledged the existence of my autobiography chapter. However, he's the most incredible reader—I have been looking over his comments on drafts of my old *Lord Weary* poems, so witty and enthusiastic: "This certainly is a just right poem; you were smart not to put in any of the unpleasant, stomach-upsetting details you love. (You and me both, for that matter.)" Re my *Exile's Return*. Well, he's delighted and wrote me back air mail saying, "I like the poem *very* much. The motion really has changed and is much clearer and easier." You know Randall has his own flippant natural language—I'll never forget John Ransom's writing an essay attacking Shakespeare's sonnets[4] (with which Randall couldn't have been more in disagreement with!) Randall and Ransom sat talking one evening and every minute Randall got more enthusiastic about Shakespeare and more & more breezy about Ransom's critical points. At the end Ransom said, "That boy just doesn't have a critical vocabulary." Well, I couldn't be more pleased, so I'll mail (with fear and trepidation) my other poems to the consultant in Washington. Poor fellow, he's been quite sick for the last *two* months with flu and some kind of respiratory infection. We talked on the phone and he sounded very croaking at first, but then he was soon the old Randall, telling me, "You know I've just read Dostoyevsky through. He was a very bad man, it seems."

I must tell you an indecent story about Frank Parker and the Bloom marriage. You know after six o'clock, Frank has only two interests: drinking red wine and talking about the sexual act. He was here the other night and had soon finished two quarts of red wine. Stuttering and sunrise-color he moved over to the needle-point foot-stool in front of Elizabeth. First he said, "Wasn't Hyman Elizabeth Bishop's *Grande passion*." My Elizabeth answered rather sourly "*One* of Elizabeth Bishop's grand passions!"—marvelous picture! You like George Sand scattering your heart up and down the Atlantic sea-board: Hyman, Hart Crane, Neruda, me . . . oh dear. Then Frank began on the Blooms saying that at first Nina threw herself on Hyman, almost

---

1 "My Last Afternoon with Uncle Devereux Winslow" (RL-*CP*).
2 "Commander Lowell" or "Terminal Days at Beverly Farms" (RL-*CP*).
3 "Sailing Home from Rapallo" (RL-*CP*).
4 John Crowe Ransom, "Shakespeare at Sonnets," *The Southern Review* (Winter 1938).

forced the marriage, after the marriage used to dress up and ask him, "Do I look pretty?" And Hyman would contract. Frank feels they are closer now, but he is watching like a falcon, ready to swoop—nothing attracts him more than his heroes' wives. In the middle of this rather nettle-like conversation, Leslie suddenly appeared and said, "How do you pronounce *zucchini?*" as though she and Elizabeth had never met! By the way I have two mean verbs for an evening with the Rahvs: one *blows* and the other *sags*. They are warm-hearted in their immense immobile way and have quite changed Charles Street, which their apartment looks out on. You feel you are back in the twenties, lights, sounds, hole-in-the-wall Bohemian bars.

I haven't much news and have been staying at home writing. I had a good evening with I. A. Richards alone, both of us reading our poems—he's so much quicker and more innocent than I am. Saw Wilson at the Schlesinger's; we all got quite drunk and I forget all the things he said. He thinks Waugh is a Calvinist. He said "You know some women are wonderful when you are sick["]—he has just built himself a gout-box (for sleeping) ["]and some loathe it." (Mary) We are going to visit them at Wellfleet about two weeks from now, and I'll try to stay sober and report to you. (I do not drink much really, and for daily use I have found a mild all year round Bock Beer, made by the Haffenreffers, old Rivers' School-mates.

Dearest Elizabeth, I always think of you. Send me your poems and a long letter. I loved your postals dropped like Persephone's pomegranate seeds.

Love from us both to you both,
    Cal

I must tell you that I've discovered a new poet, W. D. Snodgrass—really his name, as he well knows; one poem has the line: "Snodgrass is drifting through the universe."[1]—he was once one of my Iowa students, and I merely thought him about the best. Now he turns out to be better than anyone except Larkin. (Randall by the way, likes Larkin as much as I do: "I was just delighted with what you said about Larkin. I'm crazy about him. Say what one will, there's a surprising amount of objectivity in taste.") His— Snodgrass's—poems are much more personal than Larkin's, remind one a little of Vaughan and Traherne with a Laforgue-like wit and a perfect ear. I'll send you a bunch that are in an anthology gotten out by Hall and Simpson[2]; I'm really stunned. Elizabeth was as moved as I was by a group called *The*

1 W. D. Snodgrass, "These Trees Stand," lines 6, 12, and 22 (slightly misquoted).
2 *The New Poets of England and America*, ed. Donald Hall, Robert Pack, Louis Simpson (1957).

Heart's Needle written to his little daughter after his divorce—very amusing and heart-breaking all, in modern idiom and as measured as Herrick. Maybe you'll agree with me.

I'm sending a picture of me to be followed by one of the family, as soon as we can get one that does Harriet justice.

170.

Dearest Elizabeth:

This is just a little note to tell that in a day or so you'll get your Christmas present for once ahead of time. A "little check" for royalties and anthologies suddenly came out of the blue from Harcourt Brace, so I took the chance to go and blow it on something for you and Lizzie. And I do want to thank you for being such a brick about me during your return.

I'm enclosing the Snodgrass. I don't think I've gone off the deep end about him. I feel a little shivery being all alone so far in discovering him. I hope you'll like the poems. My own go on; I now have four you haven't seen, and next week after a little puttering and polishing I'll send the lot on to you. I've had a pleasant time exchanging poems with I. A. Richards, but all his suggestions involve putting [in] bits of unusable British idiom. He says that though he's been here almost twenty years, he still feels a tourist. Certainly his idiom is uncorrupted. Next letter I'll send you one or two of his.

Yesterday I had a curiously jolly day visiting our New Hampshire family graveyard with Aunt Sarah—young-looking and acting, rich, charmingly inconsecutive. Stopping at the toll-house on a superhighway, we asked the way to Goffstown and Dunbarton from a queer graying young man in a black leather jacket, black visor and black mustache. Our questions were helter-skelter; his answers were curt, accurate, detailed. By mistake my Aunt handed him a nickel. "What's that for?" The toll was 35 cents. My Aunt admired how much he knew about getting to Dunbarton. "I live there!!!" Then just as he was vanishing back into his little glass house, feeling he'd won all the repartee, my Aunt said with a gay little laugh—car in motion—"I'm going to be buried there." I can still see the poor man's smile fixed forever like one of the Harvard glass flowers.

My love to Lota, miss you terribly.

Cal

171.

November 8, 1957

Dearest Elizabeth:

Here are my poems and a picture with them if I can get some sort of cardboard to protect it. I won't try to write a letter now because we are setting off on our Wellfleet Wilson week-end in a few minutes, and I want to get my poems off now.

Did I tell you I've been deep in Laforgue (Smith's prose and the poems in French); it's [the] saddest story since time began; yet as he says contrasting himself with Corbière, "I have humor."[1] It never leaves him. How few writers are readable after one has finished his Hamlet![2] Read two good poems of yours in Humphries' anthology[3]—I like the outcast children very much. Wish I weren't such a rough writer, and could be inspired to do such a subject. I guess we all have our own fiddles—toute la lyre! This non-sense came into my head—I guess it means, all our different sounds are part of the show.

Love to you both,

Cal

172.

[November 21, 1957
Brazil]

POEMS LOVELY HAVENT FORGOTTEN YOU
ELIZABETH

173.

December 3, 1957

Darling Elizabeth:

"Come ye sons of art," arrived this morning, and I played it in the sunlight of my study, and felt that I myself, not Queen Mary, was having the birthday celebration. I've liked Ritchie for a long time. And the two counter tenors![4] I know nothing male that sounds so much like what I imagine the

---

1 *Selected Writings of Jules Laforgue*, trans. William Jay Smith (1956). See also "The Manipulation of Mirrors: Jules Laforgue," *New Republic* (Nov. 19, 1956), reprinted in *Elizabeth Bishop: Poems, Prose, and Letters*, ed. Robert Giroux and Lloyd Schwartz (2008).
2 Jules Laforgue, "Hamlet, or the Consequences of Filial Piety," trans. William Jay Smith (1956).
3 "The Wit" and "Squatter's Children," *New Poems by American Poets 2*, ed. Rolphe Humphries (1957); see EB-*CP*.
4 Henry Purcell, "Come, Ye Sons of Art: Ode on the Birthday of Queen Mary II" (1694), Margaret Ritchie, soprano, Alfred Deller and John Whitworth, countertenors (*L'Oiseau-Lyre* DL 53 004, 1954).

castrati must have been—unearthly, glorious. This won't be a long letter. You must feel inundated to death with letters, gifts, manuscript etc., from me. I was awfully proud of getting your cable from Brazil. Please write me your slow and cool critical opinion when you are in the mood.

I sent copies of my poems to Randall, Allen, and Ezra Pound. Allen wrote back boastfully that he was expecting a visit from Smith and Barbara Howes[1] and would write me after they left. (I wonder if Allen hasn't got a crush on Barbara Howes! Brandeis gives a yearly fifteen hundred dollar poetry prize for a poet under forty—or almost under forty. Katherine Hoskins got it last year.) Allen was a judge and it went unanimously to Barbara Howes. I've never heard of anyone who could read her. Randall hasn't answered at all. Pound wrote:

> "Mr Lowell of Boston
> No light Baby-Austin
> but when the garbage froze   or
> the vast accumulation of residues
> caused exacerbation,
>   a bulldozer
> was wanted for deep excavation . . .
>
> whether I can corrugate
> castigate or elevate this nonsense
> into somethink worthy the occasion
>   REEMains to be sawn
> rough, hew them as we will."

This does seem unusually clear for Ezra. But, whose nonsense? His or mine? I'm not sure if enthusiastic flattery is meant or fierce abuse. My other fan is Philip Rahv, who says, "Diss is da break-through for Cal and for poetry. The one real advance since Eliot." You guess how my head is turned. But really I've just broken through to where you've always been and gotten rid of my medieval armor's undermining. They are taking "Skunk Hour" and three others.[2] I'm dedicating "Skunk Hour" to you. A skunk isn't much of a present for a Lady Poet, but I'm a skunk in the poem.

---

1 William Jay Smith and Barbara Howes were married from 1947 until the mid-1960s.
2 "To Delmore Schwartz (Cambridge 1946)," "Skunk Hour," "Man and Wife," and "To Speak of Woe That Is in Marriage," *Partisan Review* (Winter 1958); see RL-*CP*.

We've talked over a lot of things together I've never mentioned to Elizabeth. If you ever feel like writing me privately (I don't mean anything by this) you can address the letter c/o The Dept. [of] English, Boston University. I really glory in the memory of your visit and miss you terribly. Our love to you and Lota.

Cal

I'm flying to Williamsburg tomorrow to read a Phi Beta Kappa poem ("Skunk Hour"!) and will spend four or five days in Washington seeing Randall and Cousin Harriet.

P.S. I enclose 3 more poems; you've seen them all before in cruder version[s]. Jesus! I've really exploded my powder writing and feel I have no force left. I hope for more next year.

174.

Petrópolis, Brazil
December 11th, 1957[1]

Dearest Cal:

I don't know why I haven't been able to write to you sooner, really. I don't often get these letter-writing-blocks, & particularly about my favorite correspondents. All the way down on our freighter I composed endless letters to you, full of profound new ideas, but they just evaporated into the ocean air. Then when we finally got here (not until November 4th) so many complications arose immediately that I couldn't write any letters for two or three weeks, or not real letters. We were kept going back and forth to Rio to get things out of the customs—in fact half our belongings are still there. At one point last week the Customs not only had our things but had lost all our papers, including our passports, etc. It was Kafka *Puro*. (For example: they *weighed* the victrola records. Wrote down the transformer as an "air-conditioner," etc., etc.) All the laws about customs have been changed recently, while we were at sea, I think, and they are three months behind with their work; the sheds are piled high with everything under the sun, from pathetic household "effects" to complete barber-shop equipments. Beside my crate of books there was a very old knife-sharpener's outfit—you know, those wheels they push about the streets. Some poor old Portuguese knife-

1 Actually December 13; see letter 175.

grinder is waiting to set up business in Rio, I suppose. We spent several days just sitting about on crates (I read two Conrads in the process), in a heavily alcoholic atmosphere. Somehow the officials always managed to break some poor immigrant's gallons of wine every single day . . . Well, this is still going on, but Lota now has a power of attorney from me to take out *my* belongings, while I supposedly stay at home to work and make us money . . .

I did write some necessary letters to aunts and agents—but I think I felt that writing you would somehow make my exile just too final again. Well, I must face it!

Thank you so much for so many things that have accumulated by now . . . The photograph is a very nice one; I'm having it framed in Petrópolis. Lota's "grandchildren," the two older ones, that is, are here and they asked me who that "disarrayed" man was. They also want to know what everyone has died of—all portraits apparently strike them as being of dead people! The Christmas present—well, I kept it unopened for a week, thinking I'd keep it that way until Christmas. But finally that label "*lava* cameo" was too much for me, and I opened it. Sydney Smith speaks somewhere of an Englishman dancing at court in Naples, wearing "volcanic silk with lava buttons," and I'd wondered what it meant.[1] It sounded slightly Emily-Dickinson-ish for Mr. Smith. Now I think I know. Perhaps "volcanic silk" was shot silk, or else just scarlet, but I think the buttons, like your cameo, must be straight from Vesuvius, don't you? It's really a marvelous, curious, quaint, and evocative piece of workmanship and I am crazy about it . . . It makes me think of the Brownings, *The Marble Faun, Roderick Hudson,*[2] and my own strange stay in Naples. Did you notice the high point of the carving—that one romantic curl that you can see through? I also like the other cruder curls of the gold, which remind me strongly of sucked dandelion stems; but I'm getting altogether too Marianne-ish about this, I'm afraid. You can see I am very much taken with it. It is really pure 19th-century romanticism, late. Do you know anything about where it came from and if I am right?

I am so glad you liked the Purcell. I had intended to send you, for Christmas, Purcell's "Dido & Aeneas," but I wasn't sure whether you had it or not. There's a version I bought with Flagstad singing Dido.[3] Do you have it? I also hesitated because although I bought it for myself, at the last minute, I haven't been able to hear it yet, so I don't know how good it is. My idea is to wean you away from those French songs, because I think the English ones

---

1 *The Letters of Sydney Smith*, ed. Nowell Smith (1953).
2 Nathaniel Hawthorne, *The Marble Faun* (1860); Henry James, *Roderick Hudson* (1875).
3 Henry Purcell, *Dido & Aeneas*, Kirsten Flagstad and Elisabeth Schwarzkopf et al. (EMI, 1952).

are so much better and so much more appropriate to us! (However, I got the Boulanger recording of Monteverdi's songs[1]—the same series as your French one—and it is ravishing. Do you have that one?) My high-fi is all here and the local carpenter is making a case for us. Jane Dewey's parting gift to me was a magnificent transformer for it! Now if we can just get it installed before another year goes by. Please let me know if you'd like that "Dido & Aeneas," and if not I'll think of something else . . .

Thank goodness you got that cable—one never knows. I am delighted with the reception your poems have been getting. In fact, the whole phenomena of your quick recovery and simultaneous productivity seems to me in looking back to be the real marvel of my summer. I'm not going to tackle them in this paragraph because I'm not sure I'll have time to do them justice before we go to town. I do want to get something in the mail to you today. *I'll write again tonight, I promise,* if I can't now. Our financier friend, Oscar,[2] is here. He came up on the bus in a great rush last night to tell us of a new investment; and after lunch we have to take him back to catch the bus to Rio again. We sat up till two like a group of wicked old capitalists, conniving. At one point I mentioned you, and immediately Oscar was off again, scribbling away and figuring the fantastic interest on $30,000. in 2½ years . . . I went to bed seeing us all millionaires. This morning we don't seem quite so rich; maybe "comfortable"! Perhaps you'd like to try a small amount, say $5,000. just to see? I think I'd feel worried if you wanted to invest a lot here the first thing. What I'm doing will bring about 100% in 2½ years, however—something quite conservative for here, and quite safe. This is a dreadful paragraph. How did I skid from poetry to percents?

Your hammer has been much admired and we keep it in our bathroom now instead of with other tools, just so it will be safe. You should hear Lota describing Maine. It sounds like the 18th century's ideas of the "Gothic." We are going to visit friends for a week over Christmas, to the seashore, a famous place called Cabo Frio, "Cold Cape," where I've never been and where I'm supposed to see Lota's ideal ocean landscape—also go fishing for amberjack, etc. The friend is the champion fisherman here—(strange the way one's life goes in little cycles). Since Brazilians are mad about anything chocolate (and get a special thrill from it because it's so bad for their "livers") I have been requested to bring along 4 dozen brownies (something I've introduced to Brazil) and a large chocolate cake . . . You see how innocent our lives are here—just making money and eating sweets.

---

1 Claudio Monteverdi, *Madrigali e arie profane*, Nadia Boulanger et al. (Gramophone, *La Voix de son maître*, 1948).
2 Oscar Maria Simon.

I asked Farrar Straus & Cudahy to send you the translation[1]—and please let me know if they don't. They've been even worse than Houghton Mifflin so far. I don't know whether you'll find it interesting at all or not. I think you just possibly might think "Helena" is funny. My introduction now strikes me as long-winded.

When you write again do tell me, if it isn't too far behind you, about your visit with Wilson. I wanted to see him again somehow, but really had no reason to, I suppose—but he has always been very nice to me.

I am so pleased Randall liked the poems—also Philip, but Randall's liking them really means infinitely more. I had him sent a copy of my translation, too, and I think it's the kind of thing he might like. However, our long and peculiar silence (which I really feel was my fault this time, probably) weighs on me, and I just don't know how to go about writing to him again. Lota also likes your poems very much and amazes me by the way she "gets" every detail—or else Maine really sank in much more profoundly than I realized! She likes "Skunk Hour" best and so do I, I think, and I'd be particularly charmed to have that one dedicated to me. The one poem I've done anything with since I've been back is a long one I started two years ago, to you and Marianne, called "Letter to Two Friends," or something like that.[2] It began on a rainy day and since it has done nothing but rain since we've been back, I took it up again and this time shall try to get it done. It is rather light, though. Oh heavens, when does one begin to write the *real* poems? I certainly feel as if I never had. But of course I don't feel that way about yours. They all seem real as real—and getting more so—

While I remember it—one small item that I may have mentioned before. If you ever do anything with the poem about me, would you change the remark my mother was supposed to have made?[3] She never did make it; in fact I don't remember any direct threats, except the usual maternal ones. Her danger for me was just implied in the things I overheard the grown-ups say before and after her disappearance. Poor thing, I don't want to have it any worse than it was. Just as I left N.Y. my aunt Grace sent me two family portraits from Nova Scotia, and I brought them down, unopened, in an enor-

---

1 *The Diary of "Helena Morley"* (1957).
2 See "Letter to Two Friends" (EB-*EAP*).
3 RL showed EB a draft of a poem about her that would later become "For Elizabeth Bishop 2. Castine, Maine" (although which draft is uncertain). In several of the surviving drafts at the Houghton Library, RL writes that EB's mother had threatened to kill her. Lines from one existing draft, in EB's voice, read: "Starlike the eagle on my locket watch, / Mother's sole heirloom. I hear her, 'All I want / To do is kill you!'—I, a child of four; / She, early American and militant" (typescript, Houghton); cf. RL-*CP*.

mous crate.[1] They are awfully nice; just as I'd remembered them, except that I'd had Uncle Arthur leaning on the red-plush-hung table and my mother leaning on the red-plush chair, instead of vice versa, I suppose because I like the chair so much. They are in huge gold frames, a little hard to reconcile with our modern architecture, but so charming we can't resist them. "Gertie" aged 8, wears little boots with one leg crossed over the other, and "Artie" aged 12, has *his* little boots crossed the other way. (He looks very much like me.) And how strange to see them in Brazil.

My buzzer is buzzing, meaning lunch. Now that I've got started I'll go on, and I have so much to say about the poems. Remember me to your lady as Sam. Johnson says (& I'm afraid the rest of the quotation applies, too)[2] and how's the lovely child—

Oh, Snodgrass—well, later. Lota sends her love.

Devotedly,

Elizabeth

175.

December 14th, 1957

Dearest Cal:

I dated my letter yesterday as of the 12th—then I found out it was really Friday the 13th. We had another deluge last night, so I didn't get back up to the estudio—settled for a few games of backgammon and then reading *War & Peace* in bed. I hadn't read it for many years & decided to go through it again and it certainly is *the* novel. Coming down on the boat I started reading Conrad. It wasn't a very good idea because the ship was very slip-shod and all our officers were much worse than Lord Jim, I'm sure, and as for that "silence" Conrad says is the reason men go to sea—there was very little of it. They drilled fore and aft all day long and in the afternoons we were treated to music above and below decks. Both the captain and the chief engineer had tape-recorders and had recorded loud mooing snatches of Kostelanetz[3] through the years. *Don't travel American*, as they say . . . The sailors wore large billowy shorts, black oxfords and socks, white linen sport caps, sun glasses—few of them spoke English and many were very fat. The captain

---

1 Family portraits of EB's mother ("Gertie") and Uncle Arthur ("Artie"); see "Memories of Uncle Neddy" (EB-CPR).

2 Johnson's customary subscription in letters to Boswell was a variation on "I am, Sir, your most affectionate humble servant." EB's edition was James Boswell, *The Life of Samuel Johnson L.L.D.* (New York: Modern Library, 1931).

3 André Kostelanetz, pioneer of easy listening.

kept scolding the steward for not wearing his new teeth. It was all just too democratic and Lota nearly died of boredom. (I stood up much better since I like the sea, but the Latin races haven't really liked it since the 15th century, I think.) We actually did go through the Doldrums—a day of them. The water absolutely slick and flat and the flying fish making sprays of long scratches across it, exactly like finger-nail scratches. Aruba is a little hell-like island, very strange. It rarely if ever rains there, and there's nothing but cactus hedges and prickly trees and goats and one broken-off miniature dead volcano. It's set in miles of oil slicks and oil rainbows and black gouts of oil suspended in the water, crude oil—and Onassis' tankers on all sides, flying the flags of Switzerland, Panama, and Liberia. Oh—our tug was named "La Creole Firme" and one young engineer had a nice tattoo, simply MY MOTHER. I guess that will be enough about our trip . . .

But what I started to say was, I was reading Conrad when the toothless steward observed me and said that was one of his favorite authors; he used to hear him lecture at Chautauquas and always liked that speech called "Acres of Diamonds."[1] Well, that was all right. The next day one lady passenger was reading Somerset Maugham and started telling me how he was her favorite author, and then all about his hunting in the green hills of Africa.[2] I began to grow a little uncomfortable. And the third day another passenger was reading Thomas Mann's short stories (this was a dear old lady of 78) and *she* started telling me all about what wonderful things Thomas Mann had done for the U.S. educational system[3]—and I began to wonder if it was me or them.

(I'm afraid Philip R would disapprove of this letter so far and I must stop being anecdotal and be serious.)

I find I have here surely a whole new book of poems, don't I? I think all the family group—some of them I hadn't seen in Boston—are really superb, Cal. I don't know what order they'll come in, but they make a wonderful and impressive drama, and I think in them you've found the new rhythm you wanted, without any hitches. Could they have some sort of general title? I see now that Randall may not have commented on them all yet, and I'd like to see what he thinks of this group. Pound's remarks mystify me completely, too, and so do Philip's, slightly! (Except that his are meant to be complimentary, obviously, and I'm with him there.) "Commander Lowell," "Terminal Days at Beverly Farms," "My Last Afternoon with Uncle Devereux Wins-

---

1 Russell H. Conwell, "Acres of Diamonds: our every-day opportunities and their wondrous, unsuspected riches" (1893).
2 Cf. Ernest Hemingway, *The Green Hills of Africa* (1935).
3 Confusing Thomas Mann with Horace Mann.

low" (the one I like best, I think. I think I'd like the title better without the "my" maybe—to go with "Terminal Days" better?), "Sailing from Rapallo," which is almost too awful to read, but a fine poem. They all also have that sure feeling, as if you'd been in a stretch (I've felt that way for very short stretches once in a long while) when everything and anything suddenly seemed material for poetry—or not material, seemed to *be* poetry, and all the past was illuminated in long shafts here and there, like a long-waited-for sunrise. If only one could see everything that way all the time! It seems to me it's the whole purpose of art, to the artist (not to the audience)—that rare feeling of control, illumination—life *is* all right, for the time being. Anyway, when I read such an extended display of imagination as this, I feel it *for* you . . .

I still like the skunk one enormously, although I suppose it's exercises compared to the other ones. I also like what you've done to the marriage sonnet one.[1] Some things I like especially: "sky-blue tracks . . . like a double-barreled shotgun,"[2] "less side than an old dancing pump,"[3] the last lines . . .[4] Practically all of Uncle D.—I'm a bit confused about why the maids shd. look like sunflowers or pumpkins.[5] Fat, in yellow dresses? I love the face in the water,[6] and the marvelous description of Uncle D., his cabin, his trousers, etc., etc.[7] In "Commander Lowell" I think the name is Helene Deutsch, isn't it?[8] (I'll look it up.) Yes. And have you ever read her? Unless your mother was very peculiar I don't think she could be "drugged to sleep" by Dr. Deutsch—she's fairly hair-raising. That's finicky, I know—but I do think that Deutsch stands in the popular mind (if for anything at all) as the ruthless exponent of female masochism. She's apt to arouse some opposition in the female reader.[9]

I'm sorry I can't seem to say all the right things I'd like to. I really should

---

1 "To Speak of Woe That Is in Marriage" (RL-*CP*).

2 "Terminal Days at Beverly Farms," lines 18–19 (typescript, Vassar). The lines in the published version are unchanged (see RL-*CP*).

3 "Terminal Days at Beverly Farms," line 30 (typescript, Vassar). The line in the published version is unchanged (see RL-*CP*).

4 "Terminal Days at Beverly Farms," lines 30 and 43–47 (typescript, Vassar). The lines in the published version are unchanged (see RL-*CP*).

5 "What were those sunflowers? Pumpkins floating sky high? / They were Sadie and Nellie," "My Last Afternoon with Uncle Devereux Winslow," lines 37–38 (typescript, Vassar); cf. "My Last Afternoon with Uncle Devereux Winslow," lines 37–38 (RL-*CP*).

6 "My Last Afternoon with Uncle Devereux Winslow," lines 59–60 (typescript, Vassar). The lines of the published version are unchanged (see RL-*CP*).

7 "My Last Afternoon with Uncle Devereux Winslow," lines 119–31 and 152 (typescript, Vassar). The lines in the published version are unchanged (see RL-*CP*).

8 "While Mother dragged to bed alone / drugged herself asleep on Helena Deutsch," "Commander Lowell," lines 47–48 (typescript, Vassar); cf. "Commander Lowell," lines 52–53 (RL-*CP*).

9 See Helene Deutsch, *Psychology of Women: A Psychoanalytic Interpretation* (1944).

learn to be more articulate, I know. Oh, your mother might read Harry Stack Sullivan. He's by far the most soporific, stylistically. But not so well known, maybe.

(I'm reading the last volume of Dr. Jones' *Life of Freud*[1] now. It is a really magnificent job; you should read it—beginning with vol. 1, though, in some ways the most interesting. I'm sure you'd be so fascinated by the time you got through that you'd rush straight to Dr. Taves to find out some more.)

But "broken through to where you've always been"—what on earth do you mean by that? I haven't got anywhere at all, I think. Just to those first benches to sit down and rest on, in a side-arbor at the beginning of the maze.

Reviewing your letters: Frank's ideas about Hyman and me are awfully funny. Who(m) else could I put on my list? I wonder if ever you see Hyman if you could find out if he did receive that book of poems I had sent him? I know he'll never write, but I'd like to know because Houghton Mifflin has made so many mistakes about mailing things. How are the Rahvs? I must confess that I got the notion when I was in Boston that perhaps they had said they couldn't bear to see *me* & you were both being tactful about it! But even if they did it doesn't seem to matter much from here. Looking back on my slight *PR* connections I realize I always feel I should be brilliant, profound, take the floor, etc., so usually stay silent—then when I try to remember what *they* said it's not particularly impressive, after all! But as I said before, I wish I were more articulate and I suppose I'll never be now, living off in the mountains and meeting only Brazilian intellectuals who got stuck at Valéry, and with whom I really *am* silent, necessarily . . . And here I must confess (and I imagine most of our contemporaries would confess the same thing) that I am green with envy of your kind of assurance. I feel that I could write in as much detail about my Uncle Artie,[2] say—but what would be the significance? Nothing at all. He became a drunkard, fought with his wife, and spent most of his time fishing . . . and was ignorant as sin. It is sad; slightly more interesting than having an uncle practicing law in Schenectady maybe, but that's all. Whereas all you have to do is put down the names! And the fact that it seems significant, illustrative, American, etc., gives you, I think, the confidence you display about tackling any idea or theme, *seriously*, in both writing and conversation. In some ways you are the luckiest poet I know!— in some ways not so lucky, either, of course. But it is hell to realize one has wasted half one's talent through timidity that probably could have been

---

1 Ernest Jones, *The Life and Work of Sigmund Freud*, vol. 3 (1957).
2 See "Memories of Uncle Neddy" (EB-*CPR*).

overcome if anyone in one's family had had a few grains of sense or education . . . Well, maybe it's not too late!

I'm not really complaining and of course am not really "jealous" in any deep sense at all. I've felt almost as wonderful a sense of relief since I first saw some of these poems in Boston as if I'd written them myself, and I've thought of them at odd times and places with the greatest pleasure every single day since, I swear.

I shouldn't complain about my Brazilian friends, either. Last night our week-end neighbors, an historian and his novelist wife,[1] gave me a beautiful Nonesuch edition of Blake,[2] with all the notes, etc., all inscribed in the Brazilian way. They'd just bought it for me in London.

The week-end before this one we took them to the circus—my first South American one. "Circo Garcia," "the greatest on the continent." It proved to be just what the circus should be—one ring, in a bright green tent with red and yellow poles. About a dozen performers did everything, appearing first with the wild animals (2 very fat, elderly lions), then bicycle tricks, then juggling, a motorcycle act, high wire (they were *good*, too)—the same two youthful couples, with unflagging energy, while Mr. & Mrs. Garcia supervised everything. When he wasn't performing he wore a blue silk dressing gown and she a red velvet evening dress with sequins on her eyelids—both very squat and strong, built exactly like tops. (And imagine them trudging, in old trucks, over these SA roads, deep red mud—maybe across the Andes. With their 2 lions, 2 elephants, 1 zebra.) The clowns were very good, too—jokes straight from Aristophanes that would never get by on our continent. The lady novelist's face was a study when the tiniest clown made an exit breaking wind in huge puffs of blue smoke, with reports like a cannon—again, and again, and finally just once more from behind the red velvet curtain. One nice moment (Cocteau would have *adored* it) was when a huge moth, a local moth, lit on the shoulder of one of the young Negro roustabouts—it was really about 8 inches down one wing, with its wings folded, just like a fairy wing on the Negro's shoulder. It rested there for a long time and of course the boy kept grinning, not knowing what the audience was laughing at. At another moment the loudspeaker announced that it was Mrs. Garcia's birthday, and the wretched 4 piece band burst into "Happy Birthday to you" while everyone cheered. Lota and Octavio (the historian) told each other that was "very Brazilian," and I think they were right—the

1 Octávio Tarquínio de Sousa and Lúcia Miguel Pereira.
2 *The Complete Writings of William Blake*, ed. Geoffrey Keynes (1957).

innocent feeling of *intimacy* the people in general seem to have. It is like what one reads of the Russians in the old days. They're confident we're all interested in the same things and in *them*.

I must get this off to you before Christmas. We go away Wed. I haven't been fishing for so long I'm afraid I don't have enough muscle to pull in an amberjack. (I once got a 65 pound one in Key West—that's really big.)

Tell me about your teaching, etc. Allen & Barbara Howes! Really, he has very strange tastes. William Jay came to see me in N.Y., and I thought he was improved; I haven't seen her for six years. But I'll never forget their coming to my railroad apartment in N.Y. and her urging him to recite his Phi Beta Kappa poem to Tom and me. It was midnight; Tom finally got out: "Er— uh—I think it's a little late for poetry reading." But it couldn't stop him. In the kitchen Tom kept asking me, "Say, what's the matter with her buzzies?" (that was the awful word he used). "Take a look and tell me. Is it her brassiere?" I finally ordered him to stop staring. They're a sad couple (of people!) I think.

I've typed myself into a fine nostalgia. I miss you very much.

Lots of love,

Elizabeth

P.S. "Snodgrass" next time—Merry Christmas—& *would* you like "*Dido & Aeneas*"?

176.

January 29th, I think—1958, I know

Dearest Cal:

I began to worry a bit when I didn't receive any answer to my two long letters to you before Christmas, then about two weeks ago I had a note from Belle Gardner mentioning in passing that you'd been sick, so I wrote Elizabeth.[1] I had a very nice letter from her (which I'll answer sometime)—and

---

1 "I didn't realize that you didn't know Cal had been in the hospital. He went in about the 9th of December, having sort of speeded up after he finished the batch of poems, probably with the excitement, etc. It was dreadful and now so much later there doesn't seem to be any point in going into the details; the details are always like a Russian novel because of the immense *activity* of these stages, the facts that things are happening, wildly, even from the hospital. The activity urge is greater than the confinement and is never fully confined. Perhaps Dostoevsky, particularly, was given to mania states as well as to epilepsy because it [is] always like one of his novels, but much more painful to live through. Cal is out of the hospital, is in fact moving back home today. He is far from well, alas" (Elizabeth Hardwick to EB, January 20, 1958 [Vassar]). He was readmitted to McLean Hospital at the end of January 1958.

by then you were better and coming home the day she wrote, I think. I am so dreadfully sorry, as you can imagine—I do hope and pray you are feeling yourself again. (Not that I pray very much, but I mean by that just intensity of hoping . . .) It is a damned shame; you'd been working so marvelously— but you do have that wonderful group of poems on hand now to console you, and we can all be grateful for them. I've read them over and over again, finally had to stop because I was trying to write some of my own, read them again just now, and every time I find more things I'd like to mention in detail. They are awfully well worked out, *real*, and I like the rather gentle, really, tone . . . more a muted trumpet this time, or even a cello.

I'm thinking in musical terms because last week we finally got the ee-fee, as we call it here, installed. It still has to be adjusted a bit, a little more sponge rubber here, felt there, and some more ground wires—but to me it sounds absolutely superb and now I seem to have everything I want here, except for a few friends I'd like to see more often. I bought that Webern you had before I left, and I'm listening to parts every day.[1] I think I'm so smart, because when you played me one piece I immediately thought it seemed like the musical equivalent of Klee. Now, according to the notes, Webern was actually a member of the Blue Rider group[2] . . . I still can't take very much of the songs. For one thing, those voices aren't too good, even if accurate, but I am crazy about some of the short instrumental pieces. They seem exactly like what I'd always wanted, vaguely, to hear and never had, and really "contemporary." That strange kind of modesty that I think one feels in almost everything contemporary one really likes—Kafka, say, or Marianne, or even Eliot, and Klee and Kokoschka and Schwitters . . . Modesty, care, *space*, a sort of helplessness but determination at the same time. Well, maybe I'm hearing too much. (—and admission of final ignorance!)

This past week has been pretty grim here but things are better now. Lota's sister was suddenly taken very sick & had to have an emergency operation. Lota went to Rio right away, and I've been here alone with the sister's fifteen year old son, Flávio—a very neurasthenic, gangling boy, with big horn rimmed glasses, who reads twenty hours a day and has asthma. He reminds me a little of myself at the same age except that I combined being asthmatic with also being athletic . . . Our mealtime conversations are pretty difficult, but we discuss books, and we have one thing in common—jazz. He brought most of his collection with him and he is gradually converting me to

1 Anton von Webern, *The Complete Works*, cond. Robert Craft (Columbia K4K 232).
2 German expressionist artists and composers.

Theolonious Monk and other "way out" cool jazz specialists, while I'm converting him to Webern. Poor boy, I should think he'd be bored to death up here—it rained for five days straight—but he seems quite happy, and my maternal instinct notices that his cheeks are getting *pink*. We also try out each other's asthma medicines . . . but now that his mother is out of danger we're both breathing again! I'm trying to get him to take fencing lessons!

Do you ever go to a Boston nightclub called Storyville?—I noticed it mentioned in Flávio's copies of *Downbeat*, etc., and he has some *very* cool records made there that I rather like. I think you might find it soothing and curious . . .

"Helena Morley" is doing awfully well, it seems—the reviews have been stupid, from my point of view, but wonderful from Bob Giroux's, apparently. I'm really surprised. Have you read it yet and when you do do tell me what you think. I sent a copy to Randall because I felt pretty sure it was the kind of thing he'd like—but I suppose he'll never write unless I do first.

Yesterday we were beginning to run out of food and because I still can't drive my MG I hiked down to the nearest bus line, about a mile and a half, and took a bus to Petrópolis—and a taxi back again. The bus goes once an hour, a tiny bus, very loose-jointed, full of signs and a St. George with a red light, etc.—two bicycle bells worked by strings to signal with. It said "20 passengers" and at one point we had 45, and we creaked and crept up the hills. I thought we'd never make it. I marketed and sat in the local café to read the newspaper and felt much more cheerful for seeing my fellow-men even if they all looked unusually ugly yesterday. At the PO I had a letter from Agnes Mongan enclosing some clippings—mostly about "Helena" but one from last March from the London *Times Literary Supplement* (I take that, but I'd missed this). It was a review damning Peter Viereck and a few others and concluding by saying: "But if one is acquainted with the work of E.B. and R.L. there is no great cause to despair of American poetry."[1] I feel very grateful to this reviewer, whoever he may be . . .

Oh dear—I just noticed that Louis, who cleaned this place yesterday, has dumped all my accumulation of old papers, ashes, Lucky Strike packages, etc., directly under my window . . . Well, he doesn't know any better, *coitado*.[2] When I give him something especially good to eat he says, "This is infernal!" He also said that the mountains made him feel "impotent." (I complained to our gorgeously beautiful but dumb maid, Gloria, that there was an

---

1 "Four American Poets," *The Times Literary Supplement* (March 8, 1957).
2 Poor thing.

old shoe lying beside the kitchen door, and she said with a sweet wondering smile, "Why, it's just an old shoe!")

Please, please let me hear from you when you feel like it Cal dear—and do take care of yourself and take it easy, etc. . . . I hope you did receive my letters; I was so slow about writing them. Remember me to Elizabeth; kiss the baby for me.

With much love,
Elizabeth

177.

Saturday, March 15, 1958

Dearest Elizabeth:

Oh dear, the record, the record! Almost immediately after writing you my last letter, I wanted to write another taking it back.[1] Elizabeth and I are happily back together; I spend long week-ends at home and will soon leave the hospital entirely. All the late froth and delirium have blown away. One is left strangely dumb, and talking about the past is like a cat's trying to explain climbing down a ladder. One would like to look at it all without moodiness or bravado.

I live in an interesting house now at McLean's, one in which no man had entered since perhaps 1860; suddenly it was made co-ed. It was like entering some ancient deceased sultan's seraglio. We were treated to a maze of tender fussy attentions suitable for very old ladies: chocolate scented milk at 8:30; a lounging and snoozing bedspread after meals, each announcement of an appointment gently repeated at ten minute intervals, an old crone waiting on table barking like television turned on full to pierce through deafness. On the other hand, it took three days to get a shaving glass. The man next to me is a Harvard Law professor. One day, he is all happiness, giving the plots of Trollope novels, distinguishing delicately between the philosophies of Holmes and Brandeis, reminiscing wittily about Frankfurter. But on another day, his depression blankets him. Early in the morning, I hear cooing pigeon sounds, and if I listen carefully, the words: "Oh terror, TERROR!" Our other male assembles microscopically exact models of clippers and three masted schooners. Both men, and I too, shrink before a garrulous Mrs. Churchill, sometimes related to the statesman and sometimes to the novelist.

---

1 Either a letter does not survive or RL regretted suggesting that EB write to him "privately" at Boston University (see letter 173).

Each of her sentences has a proper and usually Massachusetts name. "But of course it was really Francis Xavier Beamis Todd's son?" "How are you related to Thomas Arnold Lowell?" I assumed she meant James Russell Lowell, and was abysmally wrong and have never been [able] to explain. Pointing to the classical molding on the mantelpiece, she will say, "That's Cameron Forbes, the ambassador to Japan," or begin a dinner conversation with "Speaking of Rhode Island reds . . ." Sometimes with a big paper napkin stuck like an escaping bra on her throat, she will dance a little jig and talk about being presented to Queen Victoria. She was.

I've done another family poem,[1] a translation of Der Wilde Alexander's poem in the Penguin German anthology,[2] and several Montale pieces from the Penguin Italian,[3] and have improved my poem to you,[4] but it's still too fragmentary to mail.

I've filled this letter with trivia. Things are really very well. I seem [to] have come out of this awfully quickly and easily, I am faithfully contracted to a very keen doctor, and Elizabeth and I are very much at ease and thankful to be together. Let's not let my slip into the monstrous cloud our love. Love to Lota.

Cal

178.

[April 1, 1958]
APRIL FOOL'S DAY

Dearest Cal:

It's very cold and long swirling clouds of fog are blowing past the window and through the trees and re-coiling against the giant rocks above. It's just noon and two of Lota's "mens" have chosen to eat their lunch and heat their coffee on an alcohol lamp on the porch of my estudio. I went out once and one of them immediately sat on a small green apple he'd been munching, and I'm sure it was one of my eight Roman Beauties he'd stolen off the little tree, but I didn't like to go and count them right under his nose. Now he is singing a horrid monotonous ballad-like song, off tune, over and over, and

1 "Home After Three Months Away" (RL-*CP*).
2 "Children" (RL-*CP*).
3 *The Penguin Book of Italian Verse*, ed. George R. Kay (1957). See "Dora Markus," "Day and Night," "The Coast-guard House," "Arsenio," "The Chess Players," "News from Mount Amiata," "The Eel," and "Little Testament" (RL-*CP*).
4 "For Elizabeth Bishop; flying to Rio de Janeiro 1956" (typescript, Houghton, bMS Am 1905, folder 2238).

making up the words, I think—the other man laughs at every refrain. Should I be a cranky old maid and go out and tell him to shut up and go away, or what? They're just trying to get out of the damp and wind, poor things, but heavens what a dreary song. We have three little apple trees, and they have already given enough apples to make a large pie on Lota's birthday (she insisted on apple-pie and ice-cream, American style, instead of a cake), and I have my eye on the rest of them; they grow at the same time as the oranges do! Oh—now it's twelve and the men have left. Peace and quiet. (Lunch hour's from 11–12 here.)

PR with your poems in it and your letter came in the same mail, and I was pleased to see them both but extra-pleased, naturally, to have a letter from you again. You do sound well, Cal, and I hope and pray you are getting better every day. Maybe you're at home again now. McLean's is a good place, I think. I've been to see friends there and my mother stayed there once for a long time. I even have some snapshots of her in very chic clothes of around 1917, taking a walk by a pond there (?) However, I hope you don't have to stay very long—the people in such places are so fascinating I think one begins to find the usual world a bit dull by comparison. (I think I told you I was writing a hospital story,[1] didn't I, but my characters aren't as lively as yours, I'm afraid. However, I think you may like it.) The poems in PR look very impressive, I think. Of course, I love the skunk one. Actually I think the family group[2] is the more brilliant, don't you? Now you say you've added to it, too. Where is that going to be published? Also I'd love to see the translation. I like the "chocolate scented milk" and poor Mrs. Churchill—in fact that whole paragraph of your letter is almost on the point of precipitation into poetry as it is. You know there are several of our contemporary poets who always live in sanatoriums, feeling they're the only sensible place for a poet to live these days—& I've heard of one in Chile. And when Jiménez was in Washington he went around from one to the other, with his poor wife, Zenobia. He finally got to one run by Moravians or some such sect—strictly vegetarian, sparsely furnished in golden oak, and with Bibles and hymn-singing (or so I heard)—a strange place for a Spanish poet.

You say you wanted to take back the letter you wrote before this last one. I don't see why—it's a perfectly nice letter! They've all been.

Remember me to Elizabeth and the baby. She must be starting to talk, by

---

1 See "Mercedes Hospital" (EB-*PR*).
2 "Memories of West Street and Lepke," "Man and Wife," and "To Speak of Woe That Is in Marriage" (RL-*CP*).

now. We are up to our necks in babies at the moment—all Lota's little "grandchildren" and their little mother are staying in a little house down the road because there isn't any water in their little apartment in Rio . . . The youngest is 3½ months, Lota's namesake, called "Lotinha." Yesterday, in the rain, we took everybody, including the cook and *her* child, *my* namesake, to market. It was quite an expedition. Everyone sooner or later had to be fed and either taken to some very squalid bathroom—through cafes full of truck-drivers—or in the case of Lotinha, breast-fed and *changed*. We all ate ice cream and got it all over us. There was a magnificent rainbow across one end of town, over the hideous new pink obelisk—they cut down all the Emperor's trees along the canals and put up this obelisk instead. On the way home we were hailed by a priest who wanted a lift and anti-clerical Lota shouted "Can't you see we're full of children?" There were nine souls in the Volkswagen bus. Lota is magnificent with child-problems. I suspect it's because she's had so much practice with me.

Rio is crazier than ever. There is no water in parts of the city, and the gas has been going off; one elevator works in each building and there are endless queues, blocks long, to get on every tiny brilliantly enameled bus or every old open trolley car. These are in first class & second class sections, although no one pays any attention to it any more. These are a few enormous new buses—the truck & trailer variety, with a joint, and eight wheels. They are called *"papa-fílas,"* or "eat the queues," like dragons. Meanwhile Brazil is constructing a brand-new *capital* away off in the interior where there wasn't even a road until a year ago.[1] They say it is exactly like a frontier town in the movies at present, a line of temporary wooden buildings, bars and motels, and a street of mud. I'd like to go see it.

I haven't been able to work at all since I got back, I don't know quite why. I've read and read and read, that's all. I just finished *Wife to Mr. Milton,* another of Graves' re-constructions—have you read it? He hates Milton so I can't quite believe it all, though he probably was pretty bad. You once told me to read the *Claudius* books,[2] which I did. Have you ever read the *old* re-construction, though—*Marius, The Epicurean?*[3] I was reading lots of Roman history and finally re-read it, and I think it's really better than Graves, even

---

1 Brasília, which had been under construction since 1956. Provision for a new capital had been written into the Brazilian constitution of 1891 and Juscelino Kubitschek de Oliveira promised to carry it out. The project, designed by Lúcio Costa and Oscar Niemeyer, was meant to encourage development of Brazil's interior.
2 Robert Graves, *Wife to Mr. Milton: The Story of Marie Powell* (1944), *I Claudius* (1934) and *Claudius the God* (1935).
3 Walter Pater, *Marius the Epicurean: His Sensations and Ideas* (1885).

if I can't warm to the style the way I did at 15. I wonder if you've read "*Helena*" yet and if you liked her? I think you might enjoy it. It got wonderful reviews all over the place but I'm afraid isn't selling too well—not sexy. One Jesuit review said "This is an astonishing book. The author doesn't mention a single sexual aberration . . ."! etc. It's coming out in England now.

I was so sorry that Randall didn't get in that silly old Institute . . . Should we try over again, or what? And they elect people like Ciardi! Have you heard from Randall?

Tell me how you like your doctor. Is it the one the Gardner boy went to? We've been living so quietly I haven't a bit of news. I went down to Rio for one night of Carnival—the Negro Samba night—and everything was so late, hours behind schedule, that we didn't see the best things. They appeared at eleven the next morning. My darling toucan died; I still can't bear to think about it. It was all my fault. I used an insecticide the man in the store said was "inoffensive" to animals, and it killed him. There he lay, just like life only with his feet up in the air. I want to get another one, but Lota says we're having a little vacation from toucans now. I am trying to write Sammy an ode—incorporating a lot of poems I wrote about him from time to time—"Most comical of all in death . . ."[1] Well, the cat is flourishing and gets more spoiled and more beautiful every day.[2] His whiskers measure, from tip to tip, including his mouth and nose, of course, ten inches . . . Pure white whalebone.

Someone sent us *A Death in the Family*—it's pretty good—not as good as Alfred Kazin thinks, though![3] AK is getting just too sort of injured-sophistication for words—he sounds as if he were the only man in the USA who *appreciates* things. I must change my clothes and put on a raincoat and go to town again. Easter guests are starting already. I've been having the poor cook blow eggs for several weeks now, for a dyeing party—one of my favorite indoor sports. I hope the Easter Rabbit is very nice to you.

With much love as always, Cal—for heavens sake don't worry about anything you did or wrote as far as I'm concerned: There's nothing to worry about in the slightest, and I wish I could write such good letters. Send me some poems!

Yours,

Elizabeth

1 See "Sammy" (EB-*EAP*).
2 Tobias; see "Electrical Storm" (EB-*CP*).
3 James Agee, *A Death in the Family* (1957); Alfred Kazin, "A Universe of Feeling," *The New York Times Book Review* (Nov. 17, 1957).

179.

Dearest Elizabeth:

There's a saying that the true Bostonian has "a share in the Athenaeum, a lot in Mount Auburn and an uncle in McLean's." Well, "all roads lead to Rome," "God writes straight by crooked lines," etc. No matter what I do now, I shall end up as a true Bostonian.

You make sanatoria sound like ports for poets; however, I am now well out. On the last day I began *Helena Morley*. I was in a terrific room—cream mantelpiece, cream ten foot windows, in the next room a depressed Harvard law professor, reading, *Look Back in Anger*, and the *Unpublished Decisions of Brandeis*,[1] making sounds like a pigeon (sometimes it was pigeons) and moaning "Decades, Oh decades!" and "HorrOR, HorrOR." The *Helena* is really overwhelming; everything's a story. I found I was underlining on almost every page. She has so much that a real author—I've been reading *The Princesse de Cleves* and *Pere Goriot*[2]—never happen on in hundreds of pages. I like the "protector," the tattle-tale priest, her amused paraphrase of bad adult stories and flat charades. I couldn't have her worldly fresh ease in a million years. Your translation reads like an original.

Marianne Moore was here reading at Brandeis. There's no more "poor, brave Elizabeth." She is delighted with your life, knows Lota's whole history, down to the names of the "grandchildren," and has no end of praise for her competence and kindness and charm. Her reading, hard to hear and parse, was full of gentle and sharp things, as she complimented Rahv, Harry Levin, Cowley, put on her glasses, took them off, looked now like my grandmother, now like a clear-browed girl. She spoke of the "devious and interminable" introductions—this for John Ransom—to a Frost evening. The Fontaine read very dramatically; I must buy them. Also saw Zabel in Chicago, where I was meeting classes, etc. for a week. He gave the most old Empire picture of Brazil.[3] Each of his visits was preceded by "six months before I could even begin to make up my mind." On one he was kept up till three before flying by Allen Tate and Jean, and then shipped on to Caroline, who was driving Katherine Anne Porter out of her house. On another he had charge of Faulkner, drunk, photogenic, secretly supplied with some two hundred per

---

1 John Osborne, *Look Back in Anger* (first performed in 1956); Louis Brandeis, *The Unpublished Opinions of Mr. Justice Brandeis: The Supreme Court at Work* (1957).

2 Marie-Madeleine de La Fayette, *Princesse de Clèves* (1678); Honoré de Balzac, *Le Père Goriot* (1835).

3 Zabel, who taught at the University of Chicago, had been a visiting professor at the National University of Brazil from 1944 to 1946, and from 1953 to 1954.

cent Mexican drink, and lying in his shirt sleeves on the floor at some old Empire reception. Zabel lives twenty miles from the University and commutes by subway. When I saw him off and had to walk two blocks home unaccompanied, he was terrified lest I be mugged. Poor man, he is pouring out books, yet is still crushed by the *eight years* he tended his dying sister.

Chicago, magnificently waterfronted, filled with exiled Eastern seaboard professors, was like some one you've made a huge effort with all evening, and even quite converted yourself to, and in the end you find your enthusiasm is shared by no one, and you sigh with relief at your release. I used your "Armadillo" in class as a parallel to my "Skunks" and ended up feeling a petty plagiarist. I've tried other things in similar stanzas; nothing comes. The muse seems quite gone.

Sorry about Sammy. We are about to get one of those pigmy Chinese bulldogs. Lizzie has delusions that they are too small to need exercise or even watering. Do you remember the Gardners'? Harriet has gone on a strike against solids, but is two pounds overweight. "N-no, n-no," she grunts and wraps us round her wrist. We need the dog for a pseudo diversion.

Pound is out. Going to a Chinese restaurant and using a telephone for the first time in 13 years, he told his daughter-in-law "the ancestral voice is once more on the air." A joke, I think, not the beginning of a Jeremiad.

I'll try *Marius*; I used to be amazed at how *there* it was, but somehow never finished.

Love,

Cal

P.S. You are the one whose letters are poetry, such a full sail, such witty stories!

180.

May 8th, 1958

Dearest Cal:

Heavens, how nice it is to know you're well again! Please please, don't "overdo," will you—all this "meeting classes," etc., sounds very strenuous to me—but then, I couldn't do it at all, in the best of health, I suppose. Morton Z didn't happen to say anything about receiving the *Diary* did he? (I'm glad you like it)—I had him sent a copy, of course, but I've never heard, and he is so meticulous and polite I think he couldn't have received it, but naturally don't like to ask. I think I'll get Lota to—he seems to like her a lot! His letters here, to us or to a friend of ours whom he knows much better, are wonderful—like a dowager's calling list. He goes right through all the people he met here. Yes, that hideous story of Faulkner got around, all right. And now the latest rumour is that Pound is coming here. At least a friend called from Rio last night and said he has a letter about coming here in the current *Journal of Letters*. I haven't seen it yet but shall try to get a copy today or tomorrow. Can it be true? I thought he wanted to go straight back to Italy. There is an enormous Italian colony in São Paulo, and he might well have fascist friends there, and he *did* translate some of Camões,[1] and the exchange *is* extremely high now (but so are prices here) . . . so I suppose there are reasons why it may be true. It depresses me terribly, though, to think of him spreading more anti-Americanism here, where there is already a lot of it . . . Do you know anything about it? If he does come, of course, I'd like to go call on him in Rio, help Mrs. P if I could, even have him up here, maybe. But he'd probably be going to São Paulo; and if he ever saw that poem of mine, or Mrs. P saw it, he might not want to see me, anyway. Well, if you know anything please advise . . . If ever he came up here I'd have to get Lota to swear up and down first that she wouldn't let him get a rise out of her, or argue with him! (I'm a coward, I know,—but I've never seen the point of, or been able to endure, much argument.) I really hope it isn't true. There are too many crack-pots here already. However, if it is, and you know his address there, or here, will you give it to me so I can write a note? I *am* glad he's out. (And he had an unpleasant little note in the London *Times*,[2] about not being interested in poets, so for them please not to bother him—just in historians!)

Did you see, about two months ago now, a very nice little piece about Webern in the *New Statesman*?[3] I think you get that, too, so I won't cut it out to send. And speaking of music—how do you feel about our American, Ives? My oldest friend has been working on his MMS for several years now—because of her I got a couple of his records.[4] One uses "Tenting Tonight," "The Old Oaken Bucket," and a couple more old hymns. He was a fascinating man, I gather, but I haven't heard enough to know whether I really like the music or not . . .

He made millions in insurance, and then gave it all away, keeping just what he thought he should have to live on.

1 Ezra Pound, *The Spirit of Romance* (1910).
2 "Ezra Pound Regrets," letter to the editor, *The Times Literary Supplement* (April 4, 1958).
3 Andrew Porter, "Anton Webern," *New Statesman* (March 15, 1958).
4 Frani Blough Muser.

Horrors—a hummingbird came in. Panic & confusion. Now it's out again.

What do you mean by a "pigmy chinese bulldog," I wonder?—a Pekinese? I like them very much, maybe partly because so many other people don't—& Lota and I have been wanting one, too. However animals do give me asthma, and I suppose my enormous cat is enough. He is really funny. Lota had to go to Rio for a night last week, and I had Tobias in my room to keep me company. I get a little nervous once in a while, feeling that other *wings* of the house may be being ransacked and I can't do a thing about it. (The servants have a little house of their own, some distance off.) But Tobias is absolutely no comfort at such times. *He* gets so nervous—he jumps feet if I so much as turn a page, and keeps running to the window, standing up on his hind legs and peering out into the night in the most ominous way.[1] Our Boston friend Mary Morse (who went to school with Isabella Gardner) has just acquired a tiny, tiny kitten, extremely pretty but really too young to leave its mother. She's been force-feeding the poor thing with an eye dropper. Yesterday we went down to call on her, and I took it some finely chopped filet mignon, and it *ate*, for the first time. We all had the same sensation I suppose mothers have when their babies actually nurse! It was so weak its legs and head shook. You might try raw filet mignon on Harriet if she's still on her hunger strike.

As you see, I don't have much news. We are starting the garage; more like a bridge than a garage, and Lota is happy with 15 "mens" to direct. I seem to be writing poems again at last—they are all such old poems, though, it's like cleaning up the attic. Only one new one, and it's about Miami[2] . . . I'm also writing about snow in Nova Scotia—one would never think we are having such wonderful winter weather, clouds & sunsets, etc., right here under my nose. Our friend Alfredo[3]—the one we thought you might stay with in Rio—has taken up with an American girl and brings her here every Saturday or Sunday. She also was born in Worcester. She's the widow of a Brazilian composer; ex-communist, now Catholic, and writes novels. She is bringing me a proletarian one to read. Oh dear. We took a wonderful drive up to Terezopolis last week-end—a little mountain town much higher and colder, named for Dom Pedro's wife, the way Petrópolis was named for him. I'd like to have you see that scenery—and am enclosing a very bad postcard of it, to give you some idea, if I can find it. It's Chinese, somehow—thin

---

1 Cf. "Electrical Storm" (EB-*CP*).
2 See "Miami" (EB-*EAP*).
3 Alfredo Lage.

finger-like peaks; a red new moon, and down below a brightly lit roller-skating rink with men playing hockey, on roller skates—all in red or green satin outfits. Lota told Alfredo not to be a "backside driver . . ."

Tell me what you hear of Randall. Delmore Schwartz? I must write to Marianne again. Some of her poems appeared in the newspaper here, in Portuguese. (Pound, too.) Please remember me to Elizabeth and Harriet. How's the Irish girl with the sweet tooth? Forgive a very dull letter, but with lots of love,

> Elizabeth

I ordered the drawing from Hyman—an old man or old woman. I hope he's sent it—via a friend in N.Y. who's coming here.

181.

June 21, 1958

Dearest Elizabeth:

I should have set your mind at rest about Pound weeks ago. Mrs. Pound was here just after the liberation seeing her son, Omar. I gather it's pretty certain that Pound is returning to Italy sometime towards the middle of July. He seems rather to hibernate through his winters—a relative hibernation; for us it would seem fierce activity. But of course when he was released, exhausting energies appeared—a trip to Charlottesville, lunches with colonels, professors, fans, suggestions that he was about to study old Egyptian, tour Germany, France, and England. Mrs. Pound had a long list of addresses and high-spots to see in Boston. We cut them down to a morning at the John Adams' House—very grave and cool after Ezra and the pealing traffic-wrung environs of Boston.

Last Sunday, Marianne Moore read before thousands on the Public Garden. I went rather fearing that neither her poems nor her delivery would carry. They didn't very much, yet that seemed irrelevant. She entered with a black cloak and black jacket and a diamondy green dress. The cloak came off, then after slight hesitation the jacket, then another pause and the cloak went on again. She *had* her audience. Each obstruction fell into her hands: a whistle from the amplifier ("I see I have a rival"), trucks rumbling down Boylston Street, a mute bean-shaven young man, who kept pushing her back to the speaker, an unexquisite mass of red flowers, received with a disgruntled, admiring "gorgeous?" Each epigram was cheered. Jack Sweeney's Irish wife said in amazement, "Why, this is the only real American."

We're about off for Maine. Our house has a dock atmosphere as boxes of heavy clothing move downwards towards our new, shining, gun-metal-gray and meekly utilitarian ranch wagon. I return on the thirtieth of June to teach at the Harvard Summer School. It's disappointing to be away from my family, but doing something seemed altogether preferable to commuting weekly from Maine to my doctor.

We like Ives too. As soon as I put him on the phonograph a year and a half or so ago, Lizzie pricked her ears and felt he was firmly new and not just another advanced American copy of the big Europeans. I suppose he reminds one of Emily Dickinson, the queer mind, old-fashioned yet way ahead, and somehow superior to publication. I like hymns and feel assured getting them with so stern [a] discovering intelligence.

Awfully good to hear that you are writing poems again. I too have a lot of old lumber. Somehow it won't light. However, I have about enough for a book, and feel half-happy to let it rest in a drawer until the next awakening. I like the language of my new poems, but feel fatigued by their fierceness, my old serpent in the perfect garden. I wish I could be described as stubborn hopeful, summery, utilitarian.

Just read the Agee. He has something of Ives' earlier America. There's a heart-breaking brevity to its ungainly, wooden, doomful little action. I add Agee's death to his hero's and can't forget the epitaph.[1] Wish I enjoyed the telling as much as the overall momentum.

I am sending you one little new poem.[2] The ending grows untimely and needs an upstroke. We are all very jolly and close, and marvel at Harriet bursting into words. "Shoe" is her favorite, and she calls the mounted policeman in a forsythia-yellow oilskin[3] ambling down the Back Bay checking parking meter violations "doggie."

Love to you and Lota,

    Cal

P.S. I must write you about Eliot and his new bride next letter. They danced so dashingly at a Charles River boatclub brawl that he was called "Elbows Eliot."[4]

---

1 James Agee died of a heart attack in a taxicab in New York City, leaving *A Death in the Family* unfinished (it was published posthumously in 1957). The book's protagonist, Jay Follet, is killed in a car accident.
2 "Home After Three Months Away" (RL-*CP*).
3 Cf. "The Drinker," line 38 (RL-*CP*).
4 T. S. Eliot married Valerie Fletcher, his secretary at Faber and Faber, on January 10, 1957. (She was thirty-seven years his junior.) They traveled to the United States in April 1958.

I am getting a pleasing and unexpected honor, an honorary doctor's degree from Kenyon.

182.

[Postcard: Signpost, Castine, Maine: Moore's Hill. "Here, Sir John Moore, (18 years old) Lieut. and Paymaster, of H.M.B. 82nd Regiment fought his first battle July 28th 1779—defending this natural redoubt against the American attack until—having lost 7 of his 20 men—he was relieved by a rescue party sent by Gen. McLean. 'Will the Hamiltons leave me?[1] / Come back and behave like soldiers'—'They obeyed.' / I was the only officer who did not / leave his post too soon.' "]

[Castine, Maine]

[June 25th, 1958]

Dear Elizabeth:

We've just spent our first day of renewing Castine connections from tennis-playing Episcopal canon to Mr. Farley in the house opposite where you stayed last summer. Summer has come here all in one breath after a glacial spring—all very calm. Longed for you & Lota as we sat about our barn fireplace listening to Mozart.

Love,

Cal & Elizabeth

183.

August 28th, 1958

Dearest Cal:

I don't believe I have ever answered your last letter have I, although I have answered it, or at least written you many letters, in my imagination, since— The letter in which you sent me another of the "family life" poems, the one about the nurse feeding the birds with bags of salt pork . . .[2] Well, I like it very much; all together these poems will have a wonderful effect, I think—family, paternity, marriage, painfully acute and real—(Penn Warren's on the subject seem so *voulu*, don't you think?[3])

We have been having quite a social and busy time here for a change, and everything seemed to happen all at once, too. There was one dreadful Sunday when Dos Passos came for lunch. It would have been all right except that

---

1 The British 82nd Regiment was raised by the Duke of Hamilton.
2 "Home After Three Months Away," lines 4–7 (RL-*CP*).
3 Robert Penn Warren, *Promises* (1957).

our political friend brought him, and brought a lot of other people along, too, and the chicken gave out and the conversation bounced from Portuguese to English all day long—and the political friend went to sleep after lunch and snored, too. Then we discovered immediately that Dos Passos was here at the invitation of the State Dept. (B) to see Brasília and write a piece about it for *Reader's Digest*—that should have been warning enough—and as our opinions on Brasília were violently opposed that best subject of conversation had to be steered clear of . . .[1] Do you know that Dos Passos is a very beautiful Portuguese name?—probably was Our Lord of the Steps, to begin with, or something religious like that. The change in the times is indicated by the way he sometimes translates it as "Johnny Walker . . ."!

Then for the last three or four weeks Huxley and his wife have been here—and that indicates the Brazilian ignorance of Eng Literature, I suppose! To think that two writers as far apart as DP and Huxley would both be interested in seeing Brasília and—I suppose that's the idea—doing a little propaganda for it! Huxley's second wife happens to be someone I used to know, an Italian girl,[2] so we saw them quite a bit. I can't say he's exactly easy, though I think he'd like to be—even Lota was scared to death when they first came up here—but he is a remarkable man, don't you agree? He asked me about US poets and when I spoke of you said he'd met you and you were a "nice fellow." They were sent on a trip to Brasília and then beyond, with the Air Force, to see some Indians, and I went along, the best trip I've made here so far. I don't know how you feel about Indians. I had expected to be depressed by them, the most primitive people alive except for the pygmies, but actually we had a wonderful cheerful time. It's only depressing to think about their future. They are quite naked, just a few beads; handsome, plump, behaving just like gentle children a little spoiled. They were very curious about Huxley and one who spoke a little Portuguese said he was "homely . . . homely . . .". And then one, a widower, asked me to stay and marry him—this was a slightly dubious compliment. Nevertheless the other ladies along were all quite jealous. . . But I am finishing up a long piece about it[3] (and hope to goodness I can sell it and start building the garage) so I won't describe any more. Sometime I hope to go back there and

---

1 The building of Brasília was opposed by many inhabitants of Rio, including Lota and EB.
2 Laura Archera Huxley.
3 Posthumously published as "A New Capital, Aldous Huxley, and Some Indians." Cf. EB, *Poems, Prose, and Letters*, ed. Robert Giroux and Lloyd Schwartz (2008).

spend a few days—we flew over the River of Souls, the River of the Dead (and presumably over Col Fawcett's bones[1])—to the *Xingú*. The group that went along was very odd—five nationalities. On these endless flights we kept changing partners for conversation like a dance—and mostly whispering about Huxley. "Do you think he's interested in *literature* any more?" "Have you ever tried any of these new drugs?"—etc. I think it is one that you take that H talks of a great deal. In fact medicine, mysticism, and God are his present themes.

Here your summer has gone by almost and I think you have been spending it mostly in Boston, haven't you? Have you had a dull time or how has it been and have you kept on with your doctor and do you like him, etc., etc. . . . Please write and tell me what you are doing and if you [have] written any more poems. I think I have done one—the first in 18 months—but I'm not sure yet and I have been very miserable and petty-feeling about it all, wishing I could start writing poetry all over again on another planet.

Marianne writes marvelous letters to Lota, beginning "Lota—dear thing." Now we think we'll work on the Brazilian State Dept. for her to come here and cast a bright eye on Brasília, too. Why not? She's off to Vancouver now, I think. The Indians would be far too naked for her, I'm afraid.

How is Harriet? Elizabeth? Is Harriet writing articles by now? Whom do you see in Boston? Are you teaching? Have you heard from Randall. I'd like to write him but don't dare. Why don't you come here on a Fulbright? They aren't like the usual Fulbrights at all. They want well known people to come and give a talk, or talks, around in the larger cities, and they pay quite well, and the exchange is really *too* good now. Wouldn't you consider it sometime?

I miss you very much and Lota is dying to get back to New York, but the exchange is too much for her to dream of it. Perhaps we shall meet here or in Europe.

With much love,
   Elizabeth

184.

September 18, 1958

Dearest Elizabeth:
   For the first time in my life I seem to have mislaid a Bishop letter. (I read

---

1 Percy Fawcett disappeared on an expedition near the Upper Xingú.

it the day we returned from Castine and my last image of it is seeing it lying bluely by a jagged rise of fall books of poetry, fall book catalogues, bargain offers of *Newsweek*, baby toys and our new "child," *Cat* or "Lea-Lone Cat" as Harriet calls her, a black and white kitten, prematurely introverted by dodging under cover from baby rushes.) I have a memory of your voyaging up the Amazon with Huxley, but realize it must have been a lesser expedition. We met him with Eudora Welty at the Denver Lindley's. A flat Harcourt Brace evening just as we were changing publishers. We arrived after dinner; by then everyone was in a state of mute gloom, except Mrs. Lindley, black huge eyed, deafening, obsessed to prove for an hour and a half that Edmund Wilson—I think he too was leaving Harcourt Brace—was a bad stylist. Each point demanded documentation, which meant long trips to the bookcase to find old Wilson articles that never had the sentence she was looking for. Finally we got on a neutral yet publishers' subject, an appeal by Alfred Knopf for preservation of wild areas, and Huxley gave an amusing fantasy of the two elderly Knopfs building [a] lean-to, etc.

Wish you'd mail your new poem. I have four or five things you haven't seen, more or less fill-in-pieces, and have made out a trial full table of contents. I'll send them on to you in a few weeks if they seem finished. What a funny life doing these small consuming, to one's self desperately important things, that seem so out of what everyone else is doing except the myriads of run-of-the-mill poets.

I had to be in Boston at least two days a week to see my doctor and thought it best to be busy, so I taught at the Harvard Summer School, and talking about myriads of poets, I had twenty-five, mostly writing unintelligible poems about isolation. My best wrote rather lovely straight from life things, yet they made me realize that there is a point when even truth is prose and won't quite work. My next best wrote like Longfellow.

Things are much better with us. My *sturm and drang* seems over for good, I hope. Lizzie's much less tense. We are thinking of a three week trip to Spain this January during mid-term reading period. If this is too long or too expensive we might go to Jamaica. Could you and Lota possibly join us?

Summer scandal. The Rahvs separated for the summer, then rejoined just as we wrote them commiserating letters. Now all Philip can talk about is how shiftless and unserious Allen Tate is about such matters. I saw quite a bit of Allen this summer, always at noon. His nights were taken. One day he said, "Every so often I meet some one and say to myself, everything would have been all right if I met her in my twenties. I felt that way yesterday about Belle Gardner." Then rather triumphantly, "I hate that feeling." After that he spent each week-end on the Cape. Belle *seems* to have gotten quite enflamed, but nothing fatal *seems* to have happened.

Otherwise—we played a lot of frantic tennis, got to know the speedy Episcopalian minister set in Castine. There are seven, all with different dogmatic, ritualistic and domestic standards. Harriet's growing wonderfully and is very feminine, jolly and a ball of fire and assertion. Driving to Maine, I usually stopped for coffee opposite a mammoth hardware store and thought of Lota.

I miss you sorely,
    Cal

I see we are both on the jacket of May Swenson[1]—mine (tossed off while packing) the most inanely phrased thing I ever wrote. I think I'll draw an arrow to yours and say that's what I meant. You must read the Pasternak *Dr. Zhivago*,[2] badly translated but dwarfing all other post-war novels except Mann.[3] Everyone says it's great but too lyrical to be a novel. I feel shaken and haunted by the main character.

---

1 EB and RL wrote blurbs for May Swenson's *A Cage of Spines* (1958). EB: "Miss Swenson looks, and sees, and rejoices in what she sees. Her poems are varied, energetic, and full of a directness and optimism that are unusual in these days of formulated despair and/or careful stylishness." RL: "Miss Swenson's quick-eyed poems should be hung with permanent fresh paint signs."

2 Boris Pasternak, *Doctor Zhivago*, trans. Max Hayward and Manya Harari, with the poems of "Yurii Zhivago," trans. Bernard Guilbert Guerney (1958).

3 Thomas Mann, *Doctor Faustus* (1947).

THREE

1958-1962

185.

Dearest Elizabeth:

My book's done, I guess.[1] At least I've mailed it off to Farrar, and it's meant to come out in April, though there may be a delay because Harcourt is being edgy about releasing me from my old contract. I'm mailing you a copy and wish you'd point [out] any correctable flaws. *Correctable*—the big ones alas I'm stuck with. There's quite a bit you haven't seen. I've been puttering away rather numbly since last spring, and at last this fall quite a few came out. I hope you like the whole works as well as the bunch you have.

This has been a quiet fall. Lizzie's just gotten her Massachusetts driving license. We're both on the wagon. I work without killing myself at my two classes and have been reading and rereading a lot of old Russian fiction. Did I write you about Pasternak—really an earthquake—bigger perhaps than anything by Turgenev and something that alters both the old Russia and the new for us—alters our own world too.

Gossip. The Rahvs are now finally separated, and Philip seems to have a girl, a young Viennese woman, pretty and teaching sociology at Brandeis, who talks, and thinks Philip isn't aesthetic enough in his literary criticism. Philip is as devious as Stalin about it all, and we haven't met her. Nathalie has lost seventeen pounds and intends to lose seventeen more and is drinking rather less and is looking quite pretty. Still there's the awful sag when she stops talking on an evening. And last night we went with her to an exhibition of primitive art arranged by a friend of Bob Gardner's, and Nathalie's shoes began to crucify her after ten minutes and one room.

Everyone is talking about Belle Gardner and Allen Tate and no one knows anything for certain, though there was great fear in Wellfleet that

---

1 *Life Studies* (1959).

Belle's husband[1] would hear something. Allen's at Oxford and Belle's planning a trip to Europe in April which includes England. Coincidence? But no one knows. Belle was here last night. I do wish she were brighter and more sophisticated. One sinks into the wet sand of her good works, good will and enthusiasm for young poets, fresh and already trailing heavy gray clouds of ennui and oblivion.

Stanley Kunitz is teaching at Brandeis, a small, sharp, orderly Bohemian little gray man, looking rather like Kenneth Burke. We have grand talks about Ted Roethke escaping from a sanitarium dressed like a woman—and (believe it?) unrecognized for three days! And we talk metrics. I really like him immensely. Bill Alfred has written a ferocious wonderful play in blank verse, full of Irish violence, Irish alcoholism, Irish politics, religion and Brooklyn Irish eloquence.[2] Adrienne Rich is having a third baby—one that defied all preventative science—and is reading Simone de Beauvoir and bursting with benzedrine and emancipation. She and Lizzie had a forty-five minute argument, carried on in [the] dining-room, pantry and library about two people neither liked or really knew. We like her very much. Also Richards glistening with mountain-climbing—last week he slept in a sleeping bag with a frozen aluminum bottle of supposedly boiling water in zero weather—also glistening with his first book of poems[3] and carbon copies that he hands out and reads—just as well, because some are replies to Wittgenstein and Oppenheimer and Coleridge and the obscurer Plato and are written in Welsh rhyming schemes which are as intricate as Provençal poems that Pound quotes and where most of the words rhyme and are so complicated that Pound says nothing more intellectual than falling leaves can be versified in them.[4]

I really think we'll go to Spain in January. Wish you'd join us and help us with directions. Give our love to Lota. As always your absence is an aching gap for me.

Cal

1 Robert H. McCormick Jr.
2 William Alfred, *Hogan's Goat* (first performed in 1965).
3 I. A. Richards, *Goodbye Earth and Other Poems* (1958).
4 See Ezra Pound's translation of Arnaut Daniel's "Can chai la fueilla" ("When the leaf falls . . ."), *Literary Essays* (1954), 115–16.

186.

October 30th, 1958

Dearest Cal:

I've read through the BOOK again and really, it is very fine. The older poems are good in the old way and the new poems are good in a new way, and altogether they are (the new ones) solid, real, intensely interesting, honest—and very interesting metrically. I think you should feel very proud of the whole effort, and at the same time all the new ones have a strangely modest tone that I like, too, because they are all about yourself and yet do not sound conceited! They really make almost everything I see look pretty dreary, or labored, or absolute silliness (like poor dear Eberhart). At first I didn't like the title, but Lota says I'm wrong—and she has a way of being right. I don't know what the real differences are, I suppose only the *critics* know them, but your poetry is as different from the rest of our contemporaries as, say, ice from slush . . .

I do know that much. However, I'm getting so I can't judge the poets we know so well any more at all. I was craving something new—and I suspect that the poetry-audience is, too, and will like these new poems very much. I just got Cummings' latest, and a lot of it is very good Cummings.[1] I've been reading Dr. Williams and a lot of it is awfully good Williams—but one does need a change.[2] I have seen a couple of poems by Frank O'Connor I like pretty well. I like May Swenson in spots—and at least, I think it is all quite honest and real and she is enthusiastic. She really likes NATURE, too— almost no one seems to. I just read, for the first time, *The White Peacock* and you have no idea how refreshing and wonderful all that long-winded nature-description seemed.[3]

I've been asked to give a talk, or maybe 2 or 3, on U.S. poetry to the teachers, I think, of something called the *Instituto Brasil—Estados Unidos*. It's where everyone goes to learn English in Rio. I turned them down once before, but now I think I'll do it. It's not for months but now I've accepted I find I'm reading American poetry with new ideas. In fact, I think I'm going to talk about *Democracy* . . . How Concord had a kind, like a Greek city a little; Whitman's steamy variety; Amherst's variety—Miss Moore and John Dewey the only two *real* democrats I've ever met, etc. . . . . And your interest in character will be stressed. After all, I can't think of any English poet who

---

1 E. E. Cummings, *95 Poems* (1958).
2 William Carlos Williams, *Kora in Hell* (1957).
3 D. H. Lawrence, *The White Peacock* (1911).

writes about *people*, the way you do any more . . . Well, I may change my mind before the time comes. Frost—the Bad Gray Poet.[1] I read some remarks of his about Pound—just what the public wants to hear, I'm afraid.

Here is a picture of me among the Uialapiti—not very good and, I think, somewhat censored. I want to get copies of some of the better ones. I was sitting at a table; the Indians are really very short. See the baby's foot?

When your letter came I *was* reading *Dr. Jivago* (Zhivago, in English)—in French.[2] I stopped part way through because the book's owner wanted it back, and I think I'll finish it in English. I agree with you completely. I even liked the poems at the end, as much as one could tell about them. I also read some of Pasternak's autobiography and a long short story, "Recit," in French.[3] Lota kept telling me how bad the French was all the time and I thought even I could tell that it was, but I find him a very encouraging character, don't you. Since you wrote all the business about the Nobel Prize has happened.[4] However, I didn't find it "as good as" Turgenev—but intensely moving, and the first sign of real life, like the first leaves of spring, say. (At least, when I see Russian news reels or photographs of Red Square I always find it hard to believe the sun is really shining there.) I wish I could take up Russian, although I know I never will. I'm sure from what little I know about it that it's as good, if not better, than English . . .

We spent two weeks and two days in Rio recently, getting back Lota's apartment on the Avenida Atlantica. It is such a wonderful apartment that we'll never rent it again, no matter what heights rents soar to, I think. Top floor, 11th, a terrace around two sides, overlooking all that famous bay and beach. Ships go by all the time, like targets in a shooting gallery, people walk their dogs—same dogs same time, same old man in blue trunks every morning with 2 Pekinese at 7 AM—and at night the lovers on the mosaic sidewalks cast enormous long shadows over the soiled sand. I think you'd like it. Now that we have the apartment we can really invite you and Elizabeth to visit. You could stay in it for a month, if you wanted,—come up here for week-ends. The new Moore-McCormack boats are very good and take only six days, I think. Please consider it sometime. I could devise a wonderful lecture tour for you! There are five rooms, a special passage to the beach for

1 Cf. William Douglas O'Connor's book about Walt Whitman, *The Good Gray Poet: A Vindication* (1866).
2 Boris Pasternak, *Le Docteur Jivago* (Gallimard, 1958).
3 Boris Pastenak, *Essai d'autobiographie* (Gallimard, 1958); *Récit*, trans. Benjamin Goriély and Michel Aucouturier (1958).
4 Boris Pasternak won the Nobel Prize in 1958 but refused to accept, fearing he would be expelled from the Soviet Union.

bathers. Food is very cheap, for *us*—the dollar is away up. You can get Pasteurized milk now, very good. We could even get you a maid, probably (or a *baba* for Harriet). We both worked very hard while we were there, and I didn't get swimming much, but next week I'm going down again and acquire a tan. At night there are occasional candles burning in the sand, near the waves—*macumba*—(like voodoo) offerings to the Goddess of the Sea.

I am sorry to hear about the Rahvs.

Lota, too, has lost about seventeen pounds—and looks very elegant.

I have liked some Kunitz poems I've seen in magazines, but knew nothing about him. Adrienne Rich I've liked *fairly* well. Your life sounds very nice and well-peopled. Mine has been rather lonely and bookish, but I don't really care much. I'm hoping we can get to Europe—Italy & Greece—next year, but I'm not sure. N.Y. looks hopeless because of the exchange for Lota,—but maybe I'll somehow earn heaps of money . . . I made two friends on my Huxley-tour—one of those terrifyingly bright young Englishmen, diplomats, but really nice and intelligent. The other a Brazilian newspaper (best Rio paper) editor[1]—a real darling, if only he didn't *write*, too. Piles of books arrive, all autographed in the Brazilian way. But he's a marvelous source of information. A man I'd heard of in N.Y.—Kimon Friar—arrived out of the blue, on his way back to the U.S. by way of Chile to see his Greek relatives there, with a 333,333 line translation of an epic by Kazantzakis.[2] He took up where Homer left off. Odysseus goes to Africa and meets Hamlet—and Napoleon, I think. Anyway, dies adrift on an ice floe at the South Pole . . . All this has been paid for, hugely, in advance, by Simon and Schuster.

Yesterday and today we've had terrific thunder storms in the afternoons—the beginnings of "summer." The dogs and the cats all try to get on my lap at the same time, in terror, and it rains so hard I had two boys working away with *squeegees* yesterday, pushing back the water from under the doors as it came in, like a sinking ship. Then it stops suddenly and quite often there's a rainbow. There are wonderful birds now: one a blood-red, very quick, who perches on the very tops of the trees and screams to his *two* mates—wife and mistress I presume, again in the Brazilian manner. But oh dear—my aunt writes me long descriptions of the "fall colors" in Nova Scotia and I wonder if that's where I shouldn't be, after all. I have another marvelous Purcell, "Hail, Bright Cecilia" that I recommend highly.[3] I've ordered

1 Antônio Callado, editor of *Correio da Manhã*.
2 Nikos Kazantzakis, *The Odyssey: A Modern Sequel* (1958).
3 Henry Purcell, *Ode for St. Cecilia's Day*, Alfred Deller and the Ambrosian Singers (Bach Guild 559).

another opera, "The Fairy Queen"[1]—but now the customs have made it impossible to get in *anything*, except books. It has got so bad that it's bound to improve, if you know what I mean, but until it does it's an awful nuisance. A friend sent me two records for last Christmas. I got them this October, and had to pay about $7.00 duty.

I liked Spain best of all my travels, twenty years ago. (!) I don't think I could ever see a bull-fight again (I saw quite a few, and *liked* them, then), but the Prado is worth two weeks, at least. Granada, Ronda, Cadiz—I like them all tremendously. Toledo—the bitter landscape. Well, I suppose it's more worth while than here, but I wish you'd come here!

With lots of love as always,
Elizabeth

How are you liking your doctor?

Lota sends love—she now keeps the hammer in Rio.

I don't think I actually thanked you for sending the MMS—well, I am very pleased & grateful to have it. *Do you do your own typing?*

187.

November 19, 1958

Dearest Elizabeth:

Many thanks for your comments. I feel that I write only for you and Lizzie. I was just up at Dartmouth reading and talking. I read one of my old poems, "Salem," I think, and then your "Man-Moth," and said I felt like a mastodon competing with tanks, and determined to reform.

We've just had a visit from Snodgrass, touched with the fire of heaven I feel in a few of his daughter poems, but green and hysterical personally and rather unhinged by ten days in New York after three years of being buried and unknown at Rutgers. He wore plaid socks, woolly white underwear-like trousers, a coat made of white fibers and carbon and Ithaca, New York tailoring, spoke in a profound persuasive, hypnotic Jarrell-like whisper, then giggled. The Eberharts like him unreservedly; Lizzie disliked him unreservedly.

"The bad gray poet." Frost. Monstrous vanity—talking about controlling elations, he said he thought of how little his success did for his relatives.[2]

---

1 Henry Purcell, *The Fairy-Queen*, with Jennifer Vyvyan and Peter Pears (Oiseau Lyre 50139/41).
2 Cf. "Robert Frost" (RL-*CP*).

This cooled him down. Yet a mountainous, marvelous man. He's about the only friend I have who wants to hear the details of my crack-up, what I think of girls, etc. Quite a contrast to the aerial Richards, the gentle Ransom— talking about women Ransom said, "Early in life, I pitied them," and even the giddy, philandering Tate. I'll never forget Peter Taylor's amazement in discovering that Allen was no traditionalist, but a whole-hearted masher and anarchist. I think Tate's plotting to divorce Caroline and marry Belle Gardner, but breathe a word of this to no one.

Please send me a full uncensored version of your Brazilian National Geographic picture. You've heard the story of a Brazilian cannibal boy watching a jet plane and asking his mother if it were good to eat. She said, "It's like a lobster, hard to get into, but sweet inside." Glad you are still outside.

We go to Spain, I think in mid-May. Then, I'll have five weeks instead of two. I see my doctor three times a week and will continue to through next summer till August. He does me a lot of good, and I am learning not to throw my weight around the household every minute to prove I am not like my Father. Oh, and much else!

Just now the Academy ballot arrived. What a list! Still it's a pleasure annually *not* to vote for Harry Levin.

I'm sending you the American Pasternak for Christmas, and they promise it will arrive on time. But who knows? Wilson had a terrific review of it in the *New Yorker*.[1] By the way, have you seen Pritchett's review of your Diamond in the *New Statesman*? If not I'll mail it. I liked his crack at Nicolson.[2]

Do try, try, you and Lota, to join us in Spain!

My dearest love,

Cal

P.S. Harriet now says, "I am a pick up," and calls me Cal.

---

1 Edmund Wilson, "Doctor Life and His Guardian Angel," *The New Yorker* (Nov. 15, 1958).
2 "I was not surprised to see that Sir Harold Nicolson, who has lately been telling us how ungentlemanly or unladylike our men and women of genius are, was shocked by this young girl. His attention to manners is making him censorious of the springs of nature. 'Helena Morley' seems to me like any little girl one has ever seen or heard of: remorseless"; V. S. Pritchett, "A Brazilian Diamond," *New Statesman* (Oct. 25, 1958).

188.

[Typed on two postcards and Samambaia stationery. Postcard #1: Lake Kawaguchi, Nishi, Shojin from Mitsu Pass; Postcard #2: A Mulher de Pedra—Teresópolis, Brazil]

[December 1958]

Dear Cal:

This card went from Japan to the mts. of Brazil, to a Japanese shop—it's all the wrong mts. naturally. I feel like writing you something and it is the first thing at hand . . . The present got off by a Mrs. Ovalle the other day (actually a Worcester girl—the one who lives with the old friend of Lota's that we'd planned to have you stay with!)—I hope she just *mails* it, however. (I told her to.) I'm delighted to be able to drop *Dr. Jivago* (as the French have it) and wait for *Dr. Zhivago*. Now I wish I'd sent you a really good and strange samba record, but I didn't know I'd have a chance to send anything. Lota is acquiring a Siamese kitten, or did I tell you, and has decided to name it Suzuki— what are a few oriental countries in between . . . Can't we nominate Jarrell again, AND Flannery O'Connor (as soon as possible in her case?) I'll do any backing. It is beautiful here, but Lota and I are feeling horribly poor and great *saudades*[1] (that overworked word). Oh—please tell me soon—do you think you'll be getting to Sevilla on your trip to Spain? If so I want to write a friend of mine there, one of the few Brazilian poets I really like and a very nice chap—he speaks English, too, and has a car, and I know would be delighted to meet you and even drive you around Andalusia. (We've talked about you.) (He also has a wife whom I'm afraid E might not take to—and I don't know how many children by now.) His ancestry is practically pre-Roman, I gathered, and he tells very good family-tree stories (João Cabral de Melo Neto is the name—the last item of which merely means "grandson," so you see.)[2] We are now back in the right mts.—"The woman of stone."[3] You make Snodgrass sound rather sad—but so is his poetry. DON'T trust "the bad gray poet"—he tells *all*, you know, I'm sorry to say. His version of all, that is, and in the wrong places. I like the joke about the airplane—that is exactly what those Indians are like. One of my favorites was the boy on our trip who, when asked to pose for a photograph, politely removed *all* his clothes. (Then I went swimming with him.)[4] I don't know why I didn't write a letter and be done with it—but please don't ever use the above address—it is for local use only. (And the telephone is not working this week.) I wanted to tell you a nice

---

1 Yearnings.
2 EB now switches to postcard #2.
3 Translation of "Teresópolis."
4 EB continues the letter on "Sitio da Alcobaçinha" stationery.

Brazilian joke but I have just seen it told in TIME, too—but trusting you don't (have to) read that ghastly publication the way I do: The inflation here is really very bad—there have been two small almost-revolutions. Well, the man who fixes price-levels was sent to the Pope's funeral, and now the Brazilians are saying—"He got there, and the Pope went from XII to XXIII."

My specially-soft, "hospital" buzzer tells me it's dinner-time. The stars are huge—there's a deep yellow one. I have a star-book giving the heavens here every month of the year and I have never been able to make it correspond with much yet—I don't know whether it's a good idea to have to change all one's names for everything so late in life!

With much love,
Elizabeth

189.

December 12, 1958

Dearest Elizabeth:

Pleasant to have my book done, and this fall and winter has gone into joyful dissipation i.e. reading and seeing people. I've read "The Nose," "The Overcoat," quite a few of the *Sportsman's Sketches*,[1] about ten long short stories of Chekhov, Rahv's anthology of Tolstoy's novella,[2] several of Dostoyevsky's, and now a jag of Americana, Chase's brisk, over-sharp *American Novel*,[3] and once again *The Scarlet Letter*, *Gatsby*, James, Lawrence, and Melville on Hawthorne. Then a good two and a half days in New York staying with Kunitz, whose wife[4] belongs to the Guston, De Kooning, Kline group, saw three Balanchine Stravinsky Ballets in one night,[5] the Audens,[6] the McCarthys.

Boston's a pleasant place, but the home product is all dentrification and jelly. The woodiness of the old caution, now these 50 years no longer sprouting, the jelly of *Vogue* and *Literary Digest* literary tastes. We want awfully to get away for a year or two. We have been thinking of Brazil again. Do you think some little poetry teaching and reading program could be gotten for me that would pay our way. We would like to come and see you and then rapidly a little more of South America.

---

1 Nikolay Gogol, "The Nose" (1836) and "The Overcoat" (1842); Ivan Sergeyevich Turgenev, *A Sportsman's Sketches* (1852).

2 *The Short Novels of Tolstoy*, ed. Philip Rahv, trans. Aylmer Maude (1946).

3 Richard Chase, *The American Novel and Its Tradition* (1957).

4 Elise Asher.

5 Two of the performances were "Apollo" and "Agon"; the other was possibly "Firebird" or "Orpheus."

6 W. H. Auden and Chester Kallman.

People. Mary McCarthy beautifully plainly dressed, hair knot, long severe stringy camel's hair overcoat, collecting donations for Spanish Civil War derelicts, her Florence book[1] done, a novel on the thirties started,[2] marking off her list of friends all who don't like *Zhivago*. Their god now, after Hannah Arendt, is an art scholar critic, Pope-Hennessy, who has written on Donatello, and is now on the verge of fatally alienating Kenneth Clark through the Broadwaters' overeager partisanship. This I saw uptown at a rather splendid Italian restaurant, called the Baroque. Then downtown to the borders of Italian Manhattan to see Auden. Two messy rooms, expensive Oxford Press books heaped on plainness, Chester silently in another room. Then with Chester listening to records of the Brecht-Weill *Seven Deadly Sins* sung in German with the Auden-Kallman translation[3] as a trot. Auden and Mary don't agree at all on Italy—A is about to be crossed off their list for his departure poem.[4] However, he really knows worlds more about Italy in a personal non–Madison Avenue way. Ah, the British beefy, slow, eccentric normality, as against our own high-strung intensity.

I had lunch with Hyman a couple of days ago. He is shy of coming to our house. So I meet him at the Hotel Copley (on Exeter St.) Grille. Dreary, bare, noisy. He seems in his new half bachelor life—he's moved off to an apartment on Beacon St. just behind Philip Rahv's new bachelor apartment on Marlboro St.—rather gentle and haggard. Wanly himself and easier to talk to, and waiting for his next spring sale of paintings to start traveling.

What else? A good letter from Bill Williams. "Floss has just finished reading me your terrible wonderful poems . . ." and at the end, "The book took too much out of me which I don't have any more to give." A rather boozy night with Wilson loaded to the gills with Pasternak and Mosby's Civil War memoirs.[5] On Mary and Pasternak, "Eh, eh, it seemed strange to hear Mary so sold on something. It's her severe religious background—" that *Zhivago* appeals to.

Being Harriet's father quite changes Pearl for me, a rather realistic portrait of the Hawthornes' Una,[6] bursting like the Congo on their shy seclusion. James gives as examples of the old New England democracy Hawthorne's, "A shrewd gentlewoman who kept a tavern in the town was anxious to obtain two or three gravestones for the deceased members of her

1 *The Stones of Florence* (1959).
2 *The Group* (1963).
3 W. H. Auden and Chester Kallman, *The Rake's Progress* (music by Igor Stravinsky; first produced in Venice, 1951).
4 W. H. Auden, "Good-Bye to the Mezzogiorno" (1958).
5 John Singleton Mosby, *Mosby's War Reminiscences, and Stuart's Cavalry Campaigns* (1887).
6 Nathaniel Hawthorne's eldest child; see *The Scarlet Letter* (1850).

family, and to pay for those commodities by taking the sculptor to board." Pure John Ransom! James, "He speaks of all his friends as Mr., even the unconventional Thoreau and the emancipated brethren of Brook Farm."[1]

Old nineteenth century New England must have been fearful—in what other country would Thoreau, Melville, Whitman and Dickinson have been so overlooked! Yet it did sprout in a way there are no signs of now, and so many of the best writers were hardly literary men—Parkman, Motley, Adams, even Webster.

Well, I am trying to jolly you up for being in a new country. How wise and sad of you to be out of it!

The present from Brazil hasn't knocked on our door yet. I await it. Harriet awaits it. Maybe you shouldn't wait for my *Zhivago*; Edmund says the French translation is much the best, "though as usual the French squeeze all the juice out," i.e. let it escape. Love to Lota. I mourn your farness.

Love,
Cal

P.S. My *page* proofs have just gone back to Faber.

Randall on MacLeish's *JB*[2]—"as exaggerated and vulgar and awful as the mass media if they had unlimited freedom to express themselves."

Peter Taylor, "I am mad about painting. My favorite is Raphael. I love him as much as Chekhov." How deliciously un–*au courant*, after Randall and Mary M.! Remind me to write you [about] a disastrous evening with the Cummingses, Ransom, Richards and William James's son.

190.

December 16th, 1958
Dearest Cal:

Your photograph—the curly-headed one with the mysterious bric-a-brac off to the right (whose can they be?)—has just come from the framers. "*Simply* framed, Cal," as Marianne would say—just a little cedar or cypress, whichever it is that the termites won't eat, and I've just waxed you with my own hands and Lota placed you in a prominent spot on the bookcase.

This is just to say that I mentioned João Cabral de Melo to L, and she thought it was a very good idea and hoped I'd given you all the necessary in-

---

1 Henry James, *Hawthorne* (1897).
2 Archibald MacLeish, *J.B.: A Play in Verse* (1958).

formation. I'd like to write him as soon as I can because he travels around a lot. I last heard from him from Casablanca. Lota thinks he'd be so delighted to meet you and Elizabeth that he might even drive up to Madrid and drive you to Andalusia or wherever you wanted to go. He is in the diplomatic ser-vice (like all S.A. poets) and was having a good career when a few years ago he was accused of being a Communist—as far as I know completely untrue, but probably he was sympathetic. At least his poetry is the only Brazilian poetry I know that shows real sympathy, and is *about* the poor not just whimsically, that is. They're all fearfully whimsical here—the "retirantes," or "Okies," more or less—some very good ones. Anyway, he was cleared, but left in a difficult situation, and to solve it, and keep him in the service he was given a fantastically good job (Lota's Uncle's idea—he was Foreign Minister then) doing research at the Library in Seville, for six years, I think, at something like $1,000, or 2,000, or 3,000 a month, but free to come and go as he wants.

That library is apparently a vast, uncatalogued storehouse of colonial history. I know when I stayed in Seville, an English doctor (who had murdered his wife & her lover and left England) took me to call on a woman rather like Marianne, who lived in a little apartment with her old mother, and worked on Columbus's papers there. I've forgotten her name—maybe she's still there—but a few years ago she finally did publish some books about Columbus and his crew, etc. . . . This is all by the way.

It is João Cabral de Melo Neto, 20, Calle Lima, Seville. If you write to him you have to put in the Neto (grandson). Speaking to him, or introducing him, etc., leave off the Neto, but you *have* to use both the others—Cabral de Melo. João is impossible for foreigners to pronounce—call him John! Cabral discovered Brazil in 1500. That's one of the ancestors, others were the first governors here, etc. He is not very beautiful. In fact, he's a typical "northern" type—seedy, rickety, warty—generations of hot climate and bad food, but he's really charming and intelligent and a great admirer of yours. He was vice-consul in London for some time, so speaks English. I sent Pearl Kazin to call on him, and he was wonderful with her—took her to Cadiz, put her up, etc. She says he has a fine library, too, and knows all the small out-of-the way places one is apt to miss. I think he's about forty.

We had a note from Zabel the other day—in his lovely new handwriting!—and I gather he'll be in Spain about the same time you are. Oh how I wish we were going to be there, too. Will it be Holy Week? I spent that in Seville, the last one before the Civil War. There is a church—I've been trying to find the name but can't—a short-drive from S, all alone, as I remember it, formerly attached to a Carthusian monastery, that is the last word in baroque, that you should see—a wild flutter of white plaster and gold, and all the lower parts tortoise shell and marble and gold. I'm not as fond of baroque as I was twenty years ago, but it's really got to be seen to be believed. Also Cordova impressed me tremendously: the mosque, and a magnificent old bridge and a monument near the river—all very sad, solemn, strange and *solid*.

At the end of the week we're off to Cabo Frio for ten days or so. I hope to do some fishing. A friend has a very nice house there and a much too deluxe fishing boat, too. The swimming and the dunes and the light are magnificent. We went to a different, absolutely deserted, beach every day for a week last year. It's the kind of place that would be as ruined as Cape Cod in the U.S., and give Brazil fifty or sixty years, I suppose, and this will be, too. However, I was rather impressed by a (mostly silly) interview with Franz Kline in which he said that half the world spent their time complaining about the traffic on the Boston Post Road and the other half was the traffic, and he'd rather be the traffic . . . His final remark was: "Being right is the most terrific state, that nobody else is interested in."[1]

I am burbling like my poor dear Aunt Maud.

With love,
Elizabeth

Have you read Hauser's *The Social History of Art?*—it's as good as *Mimesis*[2]—not as particular, but even more illuminating, I think.

P.S. Mrs. João C. de M. is very Catholic—the niece of a famous archbishop here.

191.

February 2nd, 1959

Dearest Cal:

I should have written to you long before now, I know. When we got back from Cabo Frio, *Dr. Zhivago* was at the Post Office, so it probably did arrive in time for Christmas, if I'd been here, and I immediately settled down for almost twenty-four hours straight with it—1st beginning where I'd left off and finally going back and re-reading it all in English, because I must say French

1 Frank O'Hara, "Franz Kline Talking," *Evergreen Review* (Autumn 1958), 68.
2 Arnold Hauser, *The Social History of Art* (1951); Erich Auerbach, *Mimesis* (1953).

does draw a veil, somehow. I was completely absorbed, weren't you? And I think Wilson's review, although very good, left out a lot—the real old-fashioned "Russianness" of them all—that fantastic escape, when he tips Lara and the child out into snowbanks "for fun," then they get there and take baths, and do their *laundry*. THEN he sits down to drink vodka and write poetry for the rest of the night. I thought all the poetry-writing parts extremely good, too, didn't you?—and all much more allegorical, or allegory-within-unconscious-allegory—than even W. had said . . . I'm sure it's not a good novel, or it's in fragments, or unfinished—but it is a marvelous book. And it's such a pity it's being so mis-read and mis-used.

Tell Elizabeth I received her note and thank her very much, and I am delighted the dress actually fits—and she says will be used for a photograph in *Vogue*. Heavens! I never thought of that. When is the book coming out?—or maybe it is out; I seem to be much farther behind and further away than usual these days.

However, I have some news for you—that is, if you are still interested in coming to South America? If you are, you can almost surely count on being invited by the U.S. Embassy here (via the State Dept., I suppose)—I've been in touch with the "Cultural Attaché," a nice, well-meaning, but not very well-informed gentleman I've met once or twice. He thinks it is a fine idea and wants me to ask you just what subjects you'd want to speak about (Poetry, for one, I suppose—and maybe novels, or what else?). The idea would be for you to give two talks at the Embassy auditorium here (ugly, new, medium-sized—Frost read there), and then probably repeat them in São Paulo, Bahia (Salvador), maybe Belo Horizonte. I'm not sure of the itinerary. He also says that if you come this far, at the Embassy's invitation, of course, our other U.S. S.A. embassies will extend the invitation, too—which might make your trip very easy, because they'd put you up in the best hotels, drive you about, wine & dine you, etc. Of course this is not *certain*, but it seems fairly certain to me; if you are still interested, that is. Having got this far with Mr. Morris (the cultural attaché) I thought I might as well go on, so announced that Elizabeth is the leading critic of the younger generation, and wouldn't they like to hear her, too, on the subject of U.S. criticism, so much in the air these days?—even here. Mr. Morris rose like a trout to that, too. This is by phone, so far, but a week from Sunday—let's see, that's around the 15th—he is coming up here for lunch, to discuss it. Do you suppose you could let me know before then if you'd consider accepting the invitation, if it does work out, & what subjects you'd like to speak on; and anything else you can think of that would make you sound intriguing to a rather dumb bureaucrat? Of course I've already made you sound as glamorous as Byron, plus the capacities of Barnum, plus making Mr. M feel that anyone who is anyone knows your work backward . . . (I don't believe he'd read your poems, really,—but that doesn't matter!) Perhaps you could give me a list of where you've taught, & given readings or lectures, too. I know more or less, but probably not nearly all. Also the same for E., if she would be interested. I really feel, from what I know of the intellectuals here, that an up-to-date survey of "criticism" in the U.S. might attract quite an audience. That, or *Woman's Place in the U.S.*—that would certainly attract a female audience, at least.

They suggested August or September—or any time in your "summer vacation," I think. But probably other dates would do, too. I hope something comes of this. It would be such fun to have you come here. It would be cool in Rio at that time of year—about like April or May in the U.S., with a few hotter days. Quite cool up here; cold at nights, with fires needed, and blankets. I'd love to take you to Cabo Frio, but it may be the bad windy season. However, we'd certainly go on some expedition or other, probably to the towns of Minas—& coming after Spain, you will turn up your noses at them, but anyway.

Your New York trip sounded very good and made me feel rather envious for a bit. Did *you*, by any chance, send me the copy of Howells' *Indian Summer*[1] (& if so—thank you) I got from a N.Y. book-shop, uptown, without any name in it? It must have been either you or my friend Frani Muser, a great Howells reader, but she also sent me that "New Directions in Music" record of Boulez and Stockhausen.[2] The customs office has had a complete change of heart, or of policy, and now we are getting things, without waiting ten months, and without paying duty, on anything under $5.00. *Not a hint.* But we were so surprised to go and get records that had come in three weeks, and a pound of tea from Pierce's, and other presents. Do you know the Archive records?—very scholarly and Germanic, with information attached that looks like a dog's pedigree? I have just got a lovely tiny one of Mozart's canons[3]—some comical and indecent, etc. (The connection here was your saying you'd hear Auden's new libretto). I asked Lota to read the Auden poem about Italy, and she concentrated for a while and then said "But it's so ugly!" And don't you think she's right? Well, to go back to Boulez and Stockhausen—who go on from Webern—have you heard them? I'd like B better if it weren't a setting for René Char, whom I really cannot abide—or rarely.

---

1 William Dean Howells, *Indian Summer* (1886).

2 Pierre Boulez, *Marteau sans Maître* (a setting of René Char poems), the Craft Ensemble; Karlheinz Stockhausen, *Zeitmasse for 5 Woodwinds*, Op. 5, cond. Robert Craft (Columbia ML 5275).

3 Wolfgang Amadeus Mozart, *Secular Canons*, Norddeutscher Singkreis (DGG-ARC 3044).

We have the three oldest "grandchildren" here now—one reason I haven't written, I suppose, although I do stay up in the estudio quite a bit. They are angel children, really, but with the cook's two it makes five, and quite a lot of time is consumed in getting milk, giving baths, etc. I am even teaching the oldest one her letters. Since my Portuguese rather baffles her our lessons are very strange and exhausting on both sides. Lota is a wonderful grandma, I must say.

Have you ever read Augustus Hare?[1] Well, I just have and recommend him highly—particularly the first volumes. Horrible but all true.

We had a very nice two weeks away from domesticity—went out fishing and caught some huge dolphins and other fish. Cabo Frio is a wretched little town; all the fishing villages are ghastly these days. Apparently in the days of Capt. Slocum[2] they weren't quite so poverty-stricken, but the scenery and beaches, etc., are really unsurpassed, and rarely a soul in sight. Lota's "white sand" is true, but there are rocks, too, almost like Maine—only usually with gigantic cacti and other queer growths where one would expect firs. On New Year's Eve our host got out a magnificent telescope and we studied Mars and the moon, set off fireworks, and drank champagne. If you and E. (and H) come we'll really try to take you there for a week-end, at least—it is a very nice beach-house, Turgenev-like, somehow—thick round pillars strung with hammocks, a very overgrown little patio, and the pure white dunes rising higher than the town, like Moby Dicks. One of our fishing days was very entertaining (Manoel, the host, has a fishing boat that out-Hemingway's Hemingway's—although Manoel is a much, much nicer type.) The other guest, a young man, caught what we think, so far, is the biggest marlin ever caught off Brazil. They all got very *excited*, most unlike my fishing days in Maine, Nova Scotia, or Florida. When the monster was finally aboard we all hugged everyone, crew included, and then had a nice demi-tasse of *coffee*. When we landed, the boy's wife, sister-in-law, and children met us on the dock and the wife told me "He's been so out of humor because he hadn't caught anything big this season, so while you were out I've been at church burning a candle for him." The Cabo Frio photographer arrived to take photographs for the Rio sport (or maybe society . . .) pages and kept trying to break through the excitement and conversation: "Attenção! *Camera!*" he kept saying, thrusting in with his tripod.

Are you still planning on the Spanish trip and did you get all my well-meaning information about the poet in Sevilla? Do let me know about this

1 Augustus Hare, *Memorials of a Quiet Life* (1872–76).
2 See Joshua Slocum, *Sailing Alone Around the World* (1900).

and the Lecture Tour (of course I know very well you must be awfully busy about the book now). I hope you and your family are all well—I'd love to see you. You say it's "right" that I should be here, but I'm really not sure why. Is it? Perhaps doing just the opposite of what most U.S. poets are doing has advantages—but sometimes it's hard to see them. The Library of C. sent me a booklet of three lectures, and I think Delmore's is *excellent*. (Haven't read Ransom's yet)[1] But I feel profoundly *bored* with all the contemporary poetry except yours,—and mine that I haven't written yet.

  With much love,
    Elizabeth

The little boy, age three, has a horse—a length of yellow string that is getting dirtier every day. He drags it between his legs, galloping everywhere with it—and it has to be taken into our Volkswagen bus—or into his bed—with great care. His sisters actually go for rides on our donkey, Mimoso—but he prefers the piece of string.

192.

February 9, 1959

Dearest Elizabeth:

  I will write you a real letter in a few days, but this is just to ask a favor and make a suggestion. How would you feel about writing a blurb for my jacket? It would be the only one I'd use and of course should be written any way that pleased you and seemed natural. I know how well you like my stuff, or hope I do; however, these things are sometimes awkward and then I've dedicated "Skunk Hour" to you and a blurb mightn't be the right thing. Anyway, think it over.

  I've decided to throw the old *PR* prose piece[2] into my book, about fifty book pages and perhaps rather engulfing for the verse. But I can't see myself writing any more autobiography for ages, and hate to see my piece yellowing away in the old magazine. I am afraid I can count on my older relatives disliking the prose. However, they wouldn't have liked the personal poems anyway.

  We are just back from eight days in New York. Main event, seeing the abstract expressionist painters en masse. They are a very talkative, drinking, un-Hymanlike group. Not world-shaking, I think, except for de Kooning,

---

1 Delmore Schwartz, "The Present State of Poetry"; John Crowe Ransom, "New Poets and Old Muses"; *American Poetry at Mid-Century* (1958).
2 "91 Revere Street" (RL-*CP* and RL-*CPR*).

but awfully serious and feeling top of the world. Surely Randall is all wrong on them. His demand is like asking Chardin to be Tintoretto. I'll be seeing Randall, by the way, early in March when I go [to] Greensboro for their writing festival. Last year he thought "Skunk Hour" and the Ford[1] were the two best poems I'd ever written, but he has written no comment on the whole book.

Many thanks for Harriet's lovely dress. She [is] very keen on men now and knows how effective her new splendor is. Two weeks ago when Lizzie and I were having a somewhat impassioned discussion, she said, "Daddy's Poggie. I am a pick-up. Nathan's a pain in the neck." And we instantly reconciled.

Dear Elizabeth, I think of you every day and miss you. Our love to you and Lota.

Cal

P.S. Your letter has just arrived— We would like to come, if a tour could be arranged to pay for it. All sorts of possibilities. I think we'd like to bring Harriet plus a nurse and stay maybe three months, or maybe all winter counting the trips to other countries. Lizzie could work up two lectures, one on criticism and one on modern fiction; I, with Lizzie's help could work up one certainly on poetry, along with perhaps some off the cuff talks from notes and along with readings, the thing I've really had some experience with. Tell us how it would be with Harriet? The whole sounds quite thrilling.

I guess you know my record. Put in the Harvard summer school and my Doctor's degree at Kenyon. I wonder if my C.O. jail record is an obstacle? At least, I was never a fellow-traveler.

I had a good talk with Roger Straus, much more on the move than old Bob, now on a honeymoon with the T.S. Eliots in Nassau, and strongly urged your short stories as good as anyone had written. Don't you have all but a book; or couldn't you do a verse and prose as I am; or are you tied up for poetry with Houghton?

Pardon this jumble, but I am in flight to school and my fifteen poet students, now augmented by Lee Gardner,[2] a peacock among the rather Bennington decor of my regulars. By the way, did I tell you that Allen is now trying to get a Mexican divorce and marry Belle Gardner? We've seen a lot of both of them, and they are really fearfully goofy (especially Allen—"my

---

1 "Ford Madox Ford" (RL-*CP*).
2 Ainslie Anderson Gardner, Robert Gardner's wife.

Titianesque blond Jardinière etc.") However, I am all for it and think it would work, and God knows Allen has had little joy for the last decade.

193.

[February 1959]

Dear Cal:

I am sorry this has taken me so many days. I hope you can use it, or some of it—Do what you want with it, change the order around or use whatever sentences you want to, etc.* The image of the reading-glass may not say as much to you as it does to me but Lota likes it and urged me to send it along, too. Of course there is lots more to be said! If it's too late of course I'll understand—

I sent off a chaotic letter to Elizabeth two or three days ago—written with two week-end guests both taking an interest and a hand, and with the best idea occurring in the postscript—That Morris is so STUPID I don't know how he will ever approach the State Dept so I do think that the more you can do from your end the better— He needs to be impressed by a well-known name (like MacLeish, I suppose!) or (or Ike!)—

Please write again soon—much love,

Elizabeth

*or correct the punctuation—the word "autobiographical" is deliberate, for advertising purposes, of course—

[Enclosed]

As a child, I used to look at my grandfather's Bible under a powerful reading-glass. The letters assembled beneath the lens were suddenly like a Lowell poem, as big as life and as alive, and rainbow-edged. It seemed to illuminate as it magnified; it could also be used as a burning glass. This new book begins on Robert Lowell's now-familiar trumpet notes (see "Inauguration Day"), then with the auto-biographical group called "Life Studies" the tone changes. In these poems, heart-breaking, shocking, grotesque and gentle, the unhesitant attack, the imagery and construction, are as brilliant as ever, but the mood is nostalgic and the meter is refined. A poem like "My Last Afternoon with Uncle Devereux Winslow," or "Skunk Hour," can tell us as much about the state of society as a volume of Henry

James at his best. Whenever I read a poem by Robert Lowell I have a chilling sensation of here-and-now, of exact contemporaneity: more aware of those "ironies of American history," grimmer about them, and yet hopeful. If more people read poetry, if it were more exportable and translatable, surely his poems would go far towards changing, or at least unsettling, minds made up against us. Somehow or other, by fair means or foul, and in the middle of our worst century so far, we have produced a magnificent poet.

194.

March 5, 1959

Dearest Elizabeth:

I am overwhelmed by your blurb. I've sent it on to Giroux and said very emphatically that I wanted it used entire. (It's in good time for the jacket and will probably go on the inner flap. Frank has done a good picture in black and white of a relaxed, grieving or dreaming lion before a corridor of light bulbs—me, I suppose.) I like the way the burning glass, etc., softens one for the surprise of "in the middle of our worst century so far." I think your blurb really is a part of the book and adds much to it. Perhaps, now, my relatives will think twice before blowing up.

Finally heard from Randall, whom I'll see in two or three days. Very cordial really—"Some of the new poems are particularly good. I have a hunch this book will be most successful." He mailed two short letters—one three weeks old, the other one week.

I'll get on the job right away about getting something from Frost and Zabel. We really most want to come. I wonder if there would be anything at the University in Rio. I am really more suited to teaching students than lecturing to polite audiences. I could teach English poetry, modern poetry, or American literature—to small groups knowing English pretty well and having books with the texts of what I would be talking about in front of them. We do want to come and probably for four or five months bringing Harriet and maybe Eileen, our new wonder[ful] young nurse, if we can put her on semi-Brazilian wages.

What's new? I am waiting for a young man, 32 years old, New Zealander and interested in promoting New Zealand poetry[1]—sounds deadly, but someone sent him on to me and I can't get out of it. Lizzie has just finished a

1 Charles Doyle.

stern review of Bellow's new novel[1]—certainly "there is no refusal of greatness." Said ironically. She thinks he is only good in his short sober books— *The Victim, Seize the Day*, and completely boisterous and empty in his epics. Allen and Belle Gardner (Allen jetted in for one week from London) spent a night with us—one bedroom, despite Harriet's "two last names, two bedrooms." They really seem quite married, and we feel that in rather different ways the eventual marriage—Caroline[2] isn't helping and Allen's divorce won't come through until October—will be happiness, and gaiety, and rest for both of them. The venerable old Gardners are taking it all in their stride and are going to meet Allen this spring in London at the T. S. Eliots'. Roethke has gotten the Bollingen, the National Book Award, a Ford grant for $15,000, but is again sick and his wife is still recuperating from TB and all is gloomy there. I've written a "ringing trumpet note" blurb for Snodgrass, whose book[3] is coming out about the time mine is. I take a little the line you take with me, but briefer and less well expressed. I think he's inspired in some of the *Heart's Needle* sequence, not so much in his other poems. I do think he's better than any of our other new poets except Larkin. Fred Dupee, and James Baldwin (the colored writer) and I talked at Brandeis last week. We were each paid $200 and had limp little audiences of about thirty wriggling students. I like Baldwin's Negro essays very much[4]—no blarney like Wright's[5] when he isn't giving a real scene and has to generalize. I am now trying to obliterate my abolitionist pangs before seeing Randall.

Did I tell you that Rahv and Hyman, both separated from their wives, have apartments on opposite sides of the same Beacon-Marlboro St. alley? Rahv has a pretty little girl, American Jewish Viennese, 32, teaching sociology at Brandeis. No spark of new life. I believe he is the most cowed (yet imperious) and gloomy man in New England. Nathalie looks rather thinner and prettier and is almost talkative. They see each other once a week. Maybe they'll go back, but that too fills one's soul (theirs too) with dolor.

Lizzie has also finished a story for *The New Yorker*, two couples, a bad academic, Academy of Arts and Letters painter, and a bad, younger and egotistical bohemian painter.[6] The academic painter finally pays $700 for the other

1 Elizabeth Hardwick, "A Fantastic Voyage" (review of *Henderson the Rain King*, by Saul Bellow), *Partisan Review* (Spring 1959).
2 Caroline Gordon.
3 W. D. Snodgrass, *Heart's Needle* (1959).
4 James Baldwin, "The Hard Kind of Courage," *Harper's* (Oct. 1958); "Nobody Knows My Name (Letter from the South)," *Partisan Review* (Winter 1959); and "The Discovery of What It Means to Be an American," *The New York Times Book Review* (Jan. 25, 1959).
5 See Richard Wright, *White Man, Listen!* (1957).
6 Elizabeth Hardwick, "The Purchase," *The New Yorker* (May 30, 1959).

painter's bad painting and goes off for a mirthless affair with the bohemian wife. For the first time since Harriet, E. is really full of beans—she is now sketching a Boston sketch for *Encounter*.[1] Had a good time in New York with Mary, a little too tonic and undecadent, and Bill Williams, depressed and weak but still writing.

Our love to you and Lota,

Cal

P.S. Forgive my probable repetitions.

195.

[Gift card, MT Bird & Co. stationery, Boston]

[n.d. ca. late 1950s?]

Dear Elizabeth—

One pleasure, one for the future to fill in the gap before Webern, Boulez etc. now that the Brazil sound barriers are down.

Love,

Cal

196.

March 30th, 1959

Dearest Cal:

I went to Rio to have a tooth pulled & while there saw the assistant to the Cultural Attaché who reproached me with, "You didn't tell me that Mr. Lowell had taught at Salzburg!" So apparently they'd been doing a little research. Mr. Morris says that he's applying from his end but he seems a little uncertain as to his pull with the State Dept. And again said that the best and most certain way would be for you to make a direct application to the State Dept. It is called something like "Exchange of—?" persons? I'm going down to Rio this afternoon and shall ask again. Lota says we will exchange you for a ton of coffee beans. But the sooner the better, I gather. And if E got my long confused letter—I'd still like the information whenever she can get around to it, to use here for publicity—and also for the Brazilian Dept. of Foreign Affairs, where Lota still has considerable influ-

---

1 Elizabeth Hardwick, "Boston: The Lost Ideal," *Harper's* (Dec. 1959).

ence even if her uncle is *out*,—they might well want you both for other lectures, etc.

I didn't know until about two weeks ago that Marianne had had what they think was a slight stroke. Incredible to relate, it affected her speech for a few days—but she was better the last I heard. I'd like very much to get back to see her, and Lota and I talk hopefully of next September, but the hope is rather faint.

I think you liked my "blurb," and I am glad and relieved. They are fearfully hard to write, don't you think—at least when you really mean them and are determined to say *something* in a few words.

Now I have got out your letter of March 5th and shall answer it. I'll make inquiries while in Rio, too, about the University. However, I don't believe you'd have difficulty giving lectures here. One good idea I think is to have the poems you intend to quote or read mimeographed to hand out to the audience. They are amazing linguists, of course, but poetry is hard to get the first time. Just the poems—not the lecture itself. Spender made a mistake—gave them the whole lecture to read while he read it and the audience felt quite insulted. I suppose one should just speak a bit more slowly and clearly than usual. (Frost did marvelously, of course—the Brazilians got his every joke.) I know almost nothing about the University. There are two, anyway, the national one and Catholic University, considered the better for literature, I think. Of course the terms are all different. Summer vacation has just ended and the college year begun here.— But I'll find out what I can.

At the end of my letter to E, I suggested the apartment annex of the Copacabana Hotel as a better place to stay. I had just discovered that it was much cheaper than I'd thought. It would make everything much easier for you all,—maid service, nurse service if wanted, English-speaking (more or less) switchboard, etc.—and kitchens, too. We're just about two blocks away. We could meet on the beach for early swims. However, if you really should be at the university for a term, or plan to stay in Rio for longer than a month, our apartment would still be the best plan, I think. Well, please do apply to the State Dept! Clare Boothe Luce is about to come here as ambassador (heaven help us). I *heard* she was reading my translation which I can't quite believe, but if I ever do get a chance to meet the lady, I'll ask her about you directly, I think. These impossible interviews do have a way of taking place here, so I am not just talking through my hat.

I can't help but feel that Belle is making a great mistake—a fourth marriage at her age—but then, I'm afraid I've never understood Tate's appeal to my sex very well. I find him slightly creepy,—if amusing. Yes, I like Baldwin's essays too, but he certainly writes some bad stories.[1] There is one other poet I have found occasionally good—mostly bad in the surrealist way—but I think he's improving, and is very, very clever: Frank O'Hara. Why is Rahv "cowed"? I can't picture that. And is Nathalie practicing in Boston or what? I am delighted to hear that Elizabeth has been writing so much—although envious, too, I suppose. (See a grim little book by Melanie Klein, *Gratitude and Envy*[2]—superb in its horrid way.)

I have no news of any importance, but then, I don't believe I ever have. We had a large dinner party for 20 on Lota's birthday and it was quite successful, I think—dozens of Japanese lanterns and lots of plants and orchids our florist neighbor happened to give us at just the right moment. We set up five card tables in the "gallery"—all different colors, reflected in the rippled aluminum ceiling—very gay, if modest; and I produced an iced chestnut soufflé with fancy work in whipped cream, etc. It looked almost professional, by lantern light, at least.

We restored the children to their parents, after ten weeks. A bit too long for everyone concerned, but we hadn't the heart to send them back to their tiny Rio apartment in the fearful heat. And we have to have them back again for the month of May, probably, while the *fifth* is born. Lota behaves splendidly; I behave only fairly well, I'm afraid, alternating with fairly badly. The children think I have a speech-defect. I have just received a letter from the daughter of a friend in Conn., requesting a "picture of the Brazilian girl scout uniform and a copy of the pledge in Brazilian."

During the ten weeks I read & read & read—the 3 volume life of Byron,[3] Greville in 3 volumes,[4] Lucan (didn't you say you were reading that, too)[5]— etc, etc.—and now am finishing the new edition of Keats' letters[6]—all to what purpose I'm not sure, but all fascinating. At the moment I find the Keats the best of the lot, though. Except for his unpleasant insistence on the *palate* he strikes me as almost everything a poet should have been in his day. The class gulf between him and Byron is enormous. As Pascal says, if you can

1 James Baldwin, "Sonny's Blues," *Partisan Review* (Summer 1957), and "Come Out the Wilderness," *Mademoiselle* (March 1958).
2 Melanie Klein, *Gratitude and Envy: A Study of Unconscious Sources* (1957).
3 Leslie Marchand, *Byron: A Biography* (1957).
4 Probably the two-volume *Poems and Dramas of Fulke Greville, First Lord Brooke*, ed. Geoffrey Bullough (1945). If EB read a third volume, it may have been *Fulke Greville's The Life of the Renowned Sir Philip Sidney*, ed. Nowell Smith (1907), but this is unconfirmed (no Greville remains in her library).
5 Probably Lucan's *Civil War* (*Pharsalia*, I–X), trans. J. D. Duff (1957).
6 *The Letters of John Keats*, ed. Hyder Edward Rollins (1958).

manage to be well-born it saves you thirty years.[1] Now I am trying to finish a story called, so far, "Fancy, come faster."[2]

Did you see Randall and how is he? I wish he weren't cross with me but it can't be helped, I suppose. Please let us not have falling-outs! When is the book to appear?

We have just been cleaning the living-room light fixtures—deep bowl-shapes—because we had a short circuit last night and they all blew out. In each one we find about half a peck of baked assorted insects, moths, beetles, all sorts—completely dried-up and the color of old manuscripts. Oh, and I was hit by a thunderbolt, I believe, our last big storm. It felt like a large rock falling on my feet, so that I looked up at the sky, like Henny Penny, to see where it had come from. Bang!—it almost knocked me over. I was standing beside an outside base-plug. (Lota's fancy is to light up the scenery at night. I tell her it makes the house look like a concentration camp)

    With much love to you and your family, too,
        Elizabeth

197.[3]

                                    March 30, 1959
My Dearest Elizabeth:

I have been meaning for a good many days to write you a rather calm, almost Confucian letter. I think the Brazil trip had better wait another year. My therapy (three days a week) is really doing great things, and I begin to hope that by this time next year the knot inside me will be unsnarled. I do so want to live on into gray and white hairs, still growing. All the battering of the last ten years now seems to be paying off.

My trouble seems (just one angle for looking at it) to be to bring together in me the Puritanical iron hand of constraint and the gushes of pure wildness. One can't survive or write without both but they need to come to terms. Rather narrow walking—I can always go off the beam into hallucinations, or lie aching and depressed for months. This year I've held off depression by working and drinking rather too much. That's had its run. Lizzie and I are both loosening up a lot and have much joy and variety together.

1 "To be of noble birth is a great advantage. In eighteen years it places a man within the select circle, known and respected, as another have merited in fifty years. It is a gain of thirty years without trouble"; Blaise Pascal, *Pensees*, trans. W. F. Trotter, intro. T. S. Eliot (1936), 90.
2 Gerard Manley Hopkins, "The Wreck of the Deutschland," line 218 (1918).
3 Crossed with letter 196.

We've got our tickets to Europe and will fly on the 19th of May, then I'll be back teaching at the Harvard Summer School from July to mid-August. We are going to London (2 weeks?), Amsterdam (4 days?), Rome and Florence (2 weeks?), Paris (4 days), home.

The trip to Randall and Peter Taylor was good fun. I feel much less fed up with Boston. Greensboro, North Carolina and Columbus, Ohio really are worse. No one to talk to but the flat local English departments. The stay with Randall was like a Jesuit retreat. I'd be lying on my bed reading R's "St. Jerome" poem[1] and in he would come, wrinkled brow, hypnotic eye, to talk of our doom. The two great facts since the war are the decline of the west and our *probable* total nuclear extinction, he says. He's nuts on this. Still, it's all true, and the crass commercial vulgarity of our country goes beyond belief. Sometimes I think we will all die fighting some terrible Fascist reform movement. Randall gave me a grand introduction, "one of my two close friends" (I think he was telescoping you and Peter together—Peter said he should have said, one of his "*only* two friends") "I would be glad to introduce him every other week." Then after I'd read and explained some of the autobiographical poems, he made a concluding harangue, "Here is something you haven't heard before, someone on the platform talking naturally. If you ask is this what it is to be a poet, you might ask what it is to be a human being, even a Greensboro student." They are naïve people. Mary, "You and Elizabeth are the kind of people that make friends. Mary and Randall just aren't; if we couldn't in Washington, where could we?" Then she thanked me for writing warm letters to Randall the many times he had dropped me cold, and said "this time it's forever." "I never knew what you were like before. You were always either wild or so grave." It's fatal to be depressed with Randall. We were talking about Mackie, and I said tactfully that things end and that Jean and I also found staying married impossible. Randall, "Now I always thought you and Jean were more alike than any two people I'd ever met. I guess you would have been perhaps a little *too* spooky and haunted together. You know, I really think Jean is queerer than you are. She really is *very* queer."

I do treasure Randall, though. He has the pure, narrow steadiness of the prophet. He has a steadiness, and stands by his intuitions, while I flub and bull hither and thither. His life would kill me in a month; still he has refreshed me for twenty years.

I wish you and Lota could find some way of translating your usurious incomes into dollars and come here for a year. Boston is shining a little. Ed-

---

1 Randall Jarrell, "Jerome," *Analects* (Oct. 1960).

mund Wilson is going to be at Harvard next year, Eliot and his bride will be here in the fall—maybe for the winter. There are flocks of engaging youth—Allen Tate—drifting through. Now if we could add you!

I want to mail you my free translations if I can find a big envelope.[1] I've almost 30 pages and hope with a few more to have a book in next fall and out in the spring. I'll only teach one class at B.U. next fall and ought to have gallons of time.

The jacket has just come through with Frank's picture and no comment except your lovely blurb. I wish now it were printed inside as an introduction. I hope you won't have a hangover when you see how much you've said.

Love,
Cal

P.S. Yesterday Harriet made a tremendous family hit in her Brazilian waistless dress. Couldn't you mail me copies of all your new poems since *A Cold Spring*? Let's think more about how we must get together, here, Brazil or Europe, and very soon.

198.

April 7, 1959

Dearest Elizabeth:

What can be worse than crossed letters, and now I am continuing the asynchronization inextricably by answering your last which just missed my last.

Don't *altogether* abandon plans for our coming; I think we might do something, say, next May (1960), if a quick paid-for swoop could be arranged. History mustn't be deprived of the scene of your pleading with Mrs. Luce to OK me. She won't, will she? A lapsed Catholic! I feel very Montaigne-like about faith now. It's true as a possible vision such as *War and Peace* or St. Antony—no more though.

Oh we won't ever fall out, God help us! Aren't people difficult. I think, perhaps I have almost more warm intellectual friends than anyone, and have lost none except Delmore Schwartz. But it's like walking on eggs. All of them have to be humored, flattered, drawn out, allowed to say very petulant things to you. I'm sure they have to bear the same things from me—however, I don't feel the need to be diplomatic with you and Peter Taylor.

I'll read O'Hara. The other night Ginsberg, Corso and Orlovsky came to

---

1 See *Imitations* (1961).

call on me. As you know, our house, as Lizzie says, is nothing if not pretentious. Planned to stun people. When they came in, they all took off their wet shoes and tiptoed upstairs. They are phony in [a] way because they have made a lot of publicity out of very little talent. But in another way, they are pathetic and doomed. How can you make a go for long by reciting so-so verse to half-jeering swarms of college students? However, they are trying, I guess to write poetry. They are fairly easy to listen to. There was an awful lot of subdued talk about their being friends and lovers, and once Ginsberg and Orlovsky disappeared in unison to the john and reappeared on each other's shoulders. I haven't had the heart to tell this to Lizzie or anyone else. They also talked a lot about entering the lion's cave, a reference, I think, to my "David and Bathsheba." I think they'll die of TB.

Sorry to hear about Marianne's stroke. Did I write you about visiting poor old Bill Williams, very mournful, enjoying one day out of seven, waiting for the end, the nervous system cracking, but not the mind and courage. But it would be heaven if somehow something could bring you back for a visit next September. I feel so forlorn without you, though this has been a happy year. There's no one else I can quite talk to with confidence and abandon and delicacy.

You can't understand Allen's appeal to your sex? Me neither, except that he assays to assay your sex more than anyone I know. By the way, though, I think thru something misunderstood that I said to Blackmur, all Princeton for three days thought Allen was engaged to you! "Does she really love him? Isn't he too old?"

Keats—I read the letters fall a year ago. Better than anything except Laforgue's. I think his bold opinions on his friends impressed me more than anything. I wouldn't be that mature, if I lived to ninety, and memorized Montaigne and had hallucinations that I was Santayana.

I hope you have recovered and are not too inspired from having been thunderstruck. Neither thunder nor the muse has struck me for ages.

My love to you both,
 Cal

199.

April 19, 1959

Dearest Elizabeth:

I think we are each allowed one *nomination*. I am nominating Randall; if you'll nominate Flannery, I'll second. I am trying to get Blackmur to nominate

Mary. Then we can all second each other's candidates. I doubt if any of them except Flannery have a chance. Such disgusting fluff is proposed and elected most of the time that one hesitates to raise one's voice. I think we must, though.

I'm off in an hour or so to Washington for a week. Some ten American writers are to meet some ten European writers. Richman[1] has surpassed his own stupidity. The Americans are Eberhart, Monroe Spears, Fred Morgan, Marshall McLuhan, James Sweeney, Richmond Lattimore—the Europeans are better, Dinesen, Spender, Wain, Amis, and others of declining interest whom I forget. We were supposed to have a quiet, sort of Gray's elegy, far from the madding crowd, meeting with one another.[2] Instead, a delirium of meeting justices, ambassadors, congressmen. But it's lovely to go to Washington; we are taking Harriet and Eileen. *Both* of us are on the wagon, except for wine at dinner.

I've gotten rather a rave review from Alvarez[3] in England, so I guess the book won't be ignored, though it was turned down for the Poetry Book of the Month Club. It's awfully exciting that you've started another story.

Love to you both,
Cal

200.

May 5th, 1959

Dearest Cal:

I have two letters here from you to answer, one a particularly nice one. Also, I am going to write a recommendation for Flannery and send it on to you to second. But Lota is going to Petrópolis *right now,* and I thought I'd like to get this much in the mail for you at least. I'll write either tonight or tomorrow morning. I've been spending a great deal of time in Rio, with the dentist, and that's why I've been so slow.

You have Blackmur in mind for the second signer for Flannery? I'd like to see everyone you say in. I was glad to see Loren MacIver finally got there, and we can all be old fuddy-duddies together.

I'd love to hear about the Washington visit. Clare Boothe Luce is NOT coming here—but more later.

With love,
Elizabeth

1 Robert Richman, director of the Institute for Contemporary Art in Washington, D.C.
2 Thomas Gray, "Elegy in a Country Church-Yard," line 73 (1751).
3 A. Alvarez, "Something New in Verse," *The Observer* (April 12, 1959).

201.

Dearest Cal:

I hope these remarks about Flannery strike you as right—I don't care for "poetic" used that way, but saying what I mean exactly, in other words, would take too much space. Don't you sometimes feel green with envy the way she can cram a whole poem-idea into a sentence? The Randall one went back to you this afternoon. If you don't receive it let me know. (I've now started keeping a correspondence book—mail out and in—but I don't know how long I can keep it up.) I think I have it arranged that one of F's stories is to appear here in Portuguese—the best big literary supplement—they seem to be stalled on Salinger and Cummings now so I thought I'd give them a change—

There are three or four people in this world I really hate—Richman, Charles Olson, and a man named Lord Glenavy, who is probably dead of drink by now . . .[1] No, I think "hate" is too strong a word for Richman; he's too sad to hate. I have no idea who some of the Americans you were conferring with in Washington are. Please tell me about it. Houghton Mifflin sent me Betjeman and for weeks before it arrived (it took forever) pestered me with letters for blurbs, praise, etc., asking me to cable collect.[2] One saying how they really *loved* the *Diary*, of course, and it was all just a mistake, their turning it down!—almost the same excuses they made for their rather rude rejection of my stories. And I think my poor little English edition that fell like a dead and yellow leaf was all their fault, too—and still they seem to think I want to write them blurbs all the time. Isn't it an embarrassing line of work to be in, or don't they see it at all? And now I have all my resentments off my chest, I think.

I'd thought anthology poems of Betjeman's I'd seen were very good, but the whole book is a little too much to take, I think, and I find that morbidity and deliberate sentimentality ringing in a bit false, don't you? I have a stack of books here to write thanks for: Elizabeth Jennings (nice to begin with but awfully stilted), Berryman, Barbara Gibbs (?), an autobiography by May Sarton[3]—sent me by the publisher with whom I went to the Grand Guignol in Paris in 1936 and who thinks I'd feel tenderly reminiscent, maybe, about the Paris chapter . . . Plus three books of Brazilian poetry that are even harder to write thank-you notes for than American, I find, because so hard to place. Plus a letter from a nun who is writing a doctoral dissertation on Mari-

---

1 Probably Patrick Campbell, 3rd Baron Glenavy.

2 *John Betjeman's Collected Poems*, ed. the Earl of Birkenhead (1959).

3 Elizabeth Jennings, *Sense of the World* (1959); John Berryman, *Homage to Mistress Bradstreet* (1959); Barbara Gibbs, *Poems Written in Berlin* (1959); and May Sarton, *I Knew a Phoenix: Sketches for an Autobiography* (1959).

anne . . . I think I'd like a secretary about one day a week, and I could pace the floor and dictate "Dear Sister Maria Cecilia: Yours of March 12th . . ."

I have been spending the middles or meats of the past weeks in Rio having a lot of dentistry done; that's why I've been so slow about writing you, although I carried your last letter back and forth on two of the trips. I have a nice new dentist—Scotch, brought up in Brazil, who serves me *cafezinhos* in the chair. The Portuguese Athletic Club is in a building across the courtyard and at our early sessions the business men are doing setting-up exercises ("oh—there go the physical jerks," says the dentist) to the Blue Danube played on a piano. At the extraction of my impacted wisdom tooth we had a wonderful doll-like Japanese assistant dentist, just back from three years at Yale. I am very fond of this international potpourri—for example, I just sold my MG to a young Brazilian girl who works at the US Embassy (after six years of use, and two before I got it, I am selling it for just what I paid for it), and I have to wait for the cash until it arrives from her grandfather in Shanghai. My last trip, I had lunch at the Embassy with our friend Vera[1]—at the cafeteria. It was strange to eat sandwiches cafeteria style and to hear all the American voices. I felt as if I knew everyone, and didn't know a soul. The cultural attaché joined us, so afraid, I think, I might bring up books that he told me about his last operation. However, it seems that a circuit rider from the State Dept. had just been there (I've forgotten his name) and when they asked about you he had been very pleased and said, "Now that's the kind of person we want; and if only more good people *wanted* to go on these trips, etc." So I really think that if you still want to come in the spring of 1960 it will be easy. Also, it seems that there's a very good group already interested in having you, in Bahia (Salvador)—which would probably be an even more interesting place to visit, for a short time, than Rio—so let's please plan for it. I wonder if you did anything about it while in Washington?— Another item: I learned from Vera, who had been on a tour, that in Port Alegre there's quite a big club, of men who have been students in the U.S., called "The Cracked Bell." I don't know why, because when I told this to friends, they got quite hysterical—apparently it has obscene connotations in Portuguese. Or maybe that is why.

A few nights ago our politician-newspaper editor friend, Carlos Lacerda, came to dinner. I am sorry you didn't meet him when he was in exile because he is such a good example of the power-type—of which most poets are (or of which I am) so ignorant. While he was here *TIME* kept calling up to inter-

1 Vera Pacheco Jordão.

view him on Claire Boothe Luce's NOT coming to Brazil, after all. He was very cagey, but they kept trying to twist his remarks around to show that U.S. communists were in back of it all, or that it was a coup for communists here, etc. I am curious to see what, if anything, will appear. We happen to know the reporter, too—a really psychotic American, married to a Brazilian. He hates Brazil, Jews, Negroes, and the U.S. too—an ideal *TIME* choice.

IF the next elections go the way it looks as if they might, Carlos may get to be vice-president (even president, eventually) or at least Minister of Education. Maybe I can get the B. State dept. to invite you here then! He was very funny about a recent trip to Portugal to bring back Delgado, the general who dared defy Salazar in the elections last year.[1] (I don't know whether you keep track of any of these things or not, but that *was* international news.) Delgado is a rather unwelcome exile here now—and had been, for three months, in the Brazilian Embassy in Lisbon before that. It seems he nearly drove them crazy, storming about & saying he was a *man*, and couldn't stand being shut up away from "wine, women, and *fados*."[2] On the plane he started to go to bed and someone tried to find his suitcase, pajamas, etc.—but he drew himself up proudly and said "I sleep *nude*." He was welcomed by a very small group of Portuguese at the airport and blew kisses & wept, crying out "Stop! Stop! It is too beautiful!"

Oh dear, your "Beat" guests do sound awful. I have read some of the poetry and find it hopeless—and yet I sympathize with them. The trouble is mostly ignorance, don't you think—and lack of education, as well as talent. (I guess that takes care of *them*!)

How is Randall's home life this year? Is he still studying Freud?

Well—I had read Keats' letters *before*, I interject—but I just got that big new edition. Both he and Byron seem to have been killed off really by medical ignorance—ghastly deaths. A very stupid review by Louis Simpson of the life of Byron—in *Kenyon?*—seemed to show more lack of education.[3] The Pulitzers were in the Rio papers last night. I have read almost nothing of Kunitz[4]—just in anthologies—should I? Wilbur[5] seems to be getting more and more "nice," careful, dry, and "lovely"—dry isn't the word, but that kind of clever thinking-out process that leaves me cold. And now having

1 Humberto de Silva Delgado challenged António de Oliveira Salazar's candidacy in the 1958 Portuguese presidential elections. After losing, he was expelled from the Portuguese military and sought refuge in the Brazilian embassy, before going into exile.
2 Song.
3 Louis Simpson, "The Ancient Pistol of the Romantics," *The Hudson Review* (Autumn 1958).
4 Stanley Kunitz, *Selected Poems* (1958), winner of the 1959 Pulitzer Prize.
5 Richard Wilbur, *Things of This World* (1957), winner of the 1957 Pulitzer Prize.

damned everyone I feel awfully cheered up—sure that your book will show them a thing or two, one of which is that poetry does have some connection with emotions. And I even think I may be able to write a few simple but *gripping* lines myself.

I am underlining like Queen Victoria.

Have you ever read Capt. Slocum's books? They are wonderful—but please don't breathe a word to Randall because I'm sure he'd like them, too, and immediately write a poem about Slocum, and I really think I'd like to try one myself.

A friend is flying to N.Y. in about ten days, and I am going to send you a light-weight present by her for her to mail to you. I hope you are all keeping well—and how goes the psych-a? Before one gets bored with it there seems to be a very good stretch when anything seems possible. Remember me to Elizabeth, give Harriet a kiss. Lota and I both send our love. She is very busy getting the garden started and installing her son's family down below us— the fifth baby expected any minute now & we keep waiting for the telephone call, to rush the mother to the Petrópolis hospital. I want it to be a boy and name him *Tomás*.

Love again,
Elizabeth

I'll write about the translation next time— Heavens—I see you're almost *gone*—I'll write again, though.

202.

Robert Lowell
Castine, Maine
July 24, 1959

Dearest Elizabeth:

I feel rather creepy and paltry writing now to announce that I am all healed and stable again.[1] So it is. Five attacks in ten years make you feel rather a basket-case and it's excruciating having Brazil snatched out of my gloating jaws. Maybe when ten years have passed I'll be a sort of monument of the norm—Eberhart and Wilbur combined.

We're back in Maine, awfully tennis-playingish and beachy. Eberhart's

---

1 RL suffered a manic episode in late April on the eve of the American publication of *Life Studies*; he was hospitalized at McLean.

boat still lands, heavy with strangers and heartiness; Phil Booth still writes sea-poems. Lesley Parker is just finishing a week with us, stonelike, sleeping in the sun, full of intense unreal gossip that tries to be heroically ungossipy. I sit typing, surrounded by chintz and Cousin Harriet's somber 19th century oils of Alpine valleys. The sun comes in the window. We are really very happy and companionable. I still click but can't believe it.

I can't believe somehow that you and Lota aren't just around the corner and about to arrive here. Or maybe that we are about to disembark in Rio. Never has there been a time when we would have all enjoyed one another as neighbors—together at length and at leisure.

In the hospital I spent a mad month or more rewriting *everything* in my three books. I arranged my poems chronologically, starting in Greek and Roman times and finally rose to air and the present with *Life Studies*. I felt I had hit the skies, that all cohered. I[t] was mostly waste. However, I did four or five more translations, Heine and Baudelaire[1] and have almost enough now for a book. I've just finished a little prose sketch for Tate's *Sewanee Review* 60th birthday number.[2] Someone with strong off-Broadway connections has just called asking if I would translate Claudel's *Partage de Midi*.[3] We now plan a two or three weeks' trip this mid-winter to Spain or Italy.

Let me get this scrappy, whistling little letter into the afternoon mail. I want to write you something with a little thought soon, but this is just to relieve your mind, and cheer your mind towards thoughts of that long-promised return trip to North America.

All our love,
Cal

203.

[Othon Palace Hotel stationery, decorated with skyscrapers. An arrow drawn by EB points to a window on the nineteenth floor.]

[São Paulo, Brazil]
September 24th, 1959

Dearest Cal:

After our long dull months of reading, backgammon, gardening, cook-

---

1 RL had finished "Heine Dying in Paris" and several Baudelaire translations, including, possibly, "To the Reader," "My Beatrice," "Spleen," "Autumn," "The Virus" (later retitled "The Ruined Garden"), "The Flawed Bell," "Meditation," "The Injured Moon," and "The Abyss"; see RL-*CP*.
2 "Visiting the Tates," *Sewanee Review* (1959); see RL-*CPR*.
3 Paul Claudel, *Partage de midi* (1906).

ing, & READING, life has been almost too teeming recently. When I get back to my MACHINA I'll try to compose it into some kind of a letter. We came down to São Paulo for the opening of the Biende—4,485 works of ART—about 400 of which I have given my attention to. The best is Francis Bacon—real horror; the others just saying BOO, mostly.— We're going back to Rio this afternoon. Lota has innumerable aunts, uncles, & cousins here. Out of 66 grandchildren she is the only unmarried one, & keeps receiving *congratulations* about it. I recognized Meyer Schapiro in the lobby & got up my courage to speak to him—& he couldn't have been nicer. I hope we can see him again in Rio or up at the house. The Calders[1] (old friends of L's) have been in Rio for some time & we have seen a lot of them. He is very funny (I'm the only one who can understand him, though, since he grunts his witticisms). She looks a bit like her great-uncle Henry James, I think! I wonder if you're home again & how you are? *We are coming to N.Y. in January—through March.* If you know of a nice sub-let in N.Y. for that stretch—someone who wants a canary taken care of, say—please let me know. It will be wonderful to see you but I wish you were here now. The view, & my brain, are full of skyscrapers, just like this.[2]

    With love,
      Elizabeth

[Enclosed: postcard of the Parque Anhangabaú, São Paulo, a view of neon signs on tall buildings, one reading "GOOMTEX"]
This wonderful word (meaning unknown to me) is lit up at night, of course—in fact I've never seen so many electric signs in my life. A Japanese firm makes them & they are the biggest & best in the world, I believe—& weirdest—

204.

239 Marlboro St.
Boston, Mass.
October 3, 1959

Dearest Elizabeth:

What wonderful news! I think of Brazil, so far in the distance, blockaded behind its bad exchange barrier, myself still smarting from my stopped al-

---

1 Louisa James Calder and Alexander Calder.
2 The stationery is decorated along the left and bottom margins with imags of skyscraper hotels, intruding on EB's text.

most arrival . . . and I think you'll never come. Your skyscraper studded paper, the mysterious word, Japanese neon lighted on your postcard to make it seem nearer. I'll be in New York in about ten days—to introduce Eliot at the YMHA! and will enquire about possible apartments—maybe Mary will be off to cover another Italian city.

We've been back for about a month. No news really, except for Harriet. Three times a week, she sets off into the blue of Boston and Charles Street for her nursery school. Like an art student, she brings back her paintings, chalky spaghetti-like swirls on colored paper. Smudges on her dress, "I don't love Eileen, (her nurse), I love Miss Werner," on her lips. Twice she got closed eyes from the poisonous Boston mosquitoes, three times she had fevers that came for a day, then went in a rush of bold play. New words, a new intensity, four-part puzzles solved.

Our other excitement has been a piece Lizzie did for *Harper's* on book-reviewing,[1] which her statistics showed was 51 percent favorable and *47 percent non-committal*. Injured fans of the *Saturday Review*, and the *Times* and *Herald* book-sections (interruption to tinker with our heavy archaic downstairs toilet, still stolidly, immovably paralyzed) pour in letters of protest, an AP news release, sisters called in Kentucky, *Time* magazine telephone call and their free lance photographer. In December she is publishing a piece on Boston,[2] very brilliant and also controversial.

My life has been much like yours with tennis instead of backgammon. I can't seem to complete any more poems, except for a few translations.

Such good news about your coming. Love to Lota.

Love,

Cal

205.

[Postcard: Trolley climbing a mountain (the Estrada de Ferro Corcovado), Rio]

[October 1959]

Dearest Cal:

This is the little trolley up to that Christ on top of Rio that you must have seen pictures of. Note the peak called "The Crow's Nest" in the background—(from the Portuguese caravels). All is very lush and lovely here now—the closest we get to "spring." We still hope to get to N.Y. around

---

1 Elizabeth Hardwick, "The Decline of Book Reviewing," *Harper's* (Oct. 1959).
2 Elizabeth Hardwick, "Boston: The Lost Ideal," *Harper's* (Dec. 1959).

January 1st, or possibly for Christmas. It is not *positive*, but almost. Lota is full of gardening and high finance. I am half-full of poems. I'm going to send you some this week. We spent a very nice half-day with Meyer Schapiro. He seems to be very fond of you. He really is wonderful, isn't he. I'd never met him before. Someone sent me a weird little book about the Poet's Theatre in Boston—naming names, etc. Also Ned Rorem wrote me he'd seen you in Buffalo. He's quite a good song writer, I believe (& he thinks so, too). My love to you, E., and your school-girl. How I wish you could come here.

Elizabeth

N Rorem *might* be good enough for your, I think—"grand" styles—

206.

Dearest Elizabeth:

The three marvelous bottles of wine from S.S. Pierce made you seem just around the corner, while Harriet's "Anna Karenina" doll, dressed in the white boots you brought her, made you exotic and far away. And now the *New Yorker* poem makes you seem both.[1] By the way, have you read the story by the Hindu, Ved Mehta, that envelops and surrounds your poem?[2] He's [a] new friend of ours. Since three he has been blind, and puzzles people by loading his conversation and writings with visual images. His face and eyes quiver at you when he is talking or listening, and few people with sight are half as sensitive and knowing. When he was twenty he was teaching English in Arkansas, and went off with a Negro jazz group to New Orleans, which he describes (elaborately with visual images), and where he might be still if the whole group hadn't been locked up for being on dope—all except Ved, who had missed that one detail on his surroundings.

Your poem is one of your most beautiful, I think—wonderful description, the jungle turning into a picture, then into history and the jungle again, with a practical, absurd, sad, amused and frightened tone for the Christians. I have been rereading Lear (Edward) whom you like so much. I guess it would be far-fetched to find his hand here; yet I think he would have enjoyed your feeling, your disciplined gorgeousness, your drawing, you[r] sadness, your amusement.

---

1 "Brazil, January 1, 1502," *The New Yorker* (Jan. 2, 1960); see EB-*CP*.
2 Ved Mehta, "Indian Summer," *The New Yorker* (Jan. 2, 1960).

Barzun quotes you in his Mid Century Book Club preface for *Life Stud-ies*, more or less agrees but finds no hope. Maybe so. Anyway, no one would deny you that, yet there's no shearing off from the grim.[1] Here you'll notice a dramatic change and deepening of my type. It's been getting milder for several months, and edging up on the invisible. Sometime I must tell you about this time since last spring. After the manic attack comes an incredible formless time of irresolution, forgetfulness, inertia, all the Baudelairean vices plus what he must never have known, stupidity. Now that it is coming to an end I can tell you that nothing for a time seemed more desirable than putting off something. Anything done was to put off something else more distressing or burdensome. Except for a few more translations I've written nothing, only one poem, a black one though not personal, called "The Drinker,"[2] a mixture in style of Montale and Lowell. I'll mail it to you but hope my next news of you will be that you are in New York.

Enough of this personal glooming. The Mid Century Book advertise-ment has a postage-stamp size square with my face in the foreground and Marianne Moore—we are offered together as a choice—looking over my shoulder. A symbol! I do so long to see you. Our love to Lota.

Cal

207.

February 15th, 1960

Dearest Cal:

I don't know what got into me. I haven't written any letters for ages ex-cept the meagerest kind of note to my two elderly aunts every so often, and yet every day I have composed letters in my head to you, I think. Now I'm about to go on a trip to the Amazon at last, and I feel I have to send you some kind message before braving the mosquitoes and the rainy season and the tidal wave 40 feet high that backs up the river for 100's of miles, or maybe it backs up the river 40 miles and is 100's of feet high. A friend of L's and mine, named Rosinha Leão (Little Rose Lion) promised to take her 16-year old nephew in his summer vacation (now), and I decided to go along. Lota thinks she shouldn't leave now and doesn't want to go so very much anyway, I think. The Little Lion is an almost Proust-like character—hundreds of mysterious allergies. She has just telephoned me to say we should wear *cotton*

---

1 RL pauses to change his typewriter ribbon.
2 "The Drinker" (RL-*CP*).

stockings and gloves. Mosquitoes won't bite through cotton, and I have firmly refused. Then we checked over our medicine chest to see if we are quite prepared in case either of us has an attack of asthma. Meanwhile, L & I have discovered that we have a lithe, shiny black snake living in a stone wall inside the house. The servants are having a picnic trying to smoke the poor thing out of its hole by burning garlic on a tin plate. It came out once and dashed for another hole, and now can be anywhere at all in the house. It will be odd if I return unscathed from my trip and find that Lota has been bitten by a snake in her own front hall.

Of course I was awfully pleased to have Mary's Florence book[1]—I was wondering if I could afford to send for it when it arrived—I think it's better than the Venice one, don't you? Fewer wise-cracks (she's condensed and omitted and reproved mercilessly), but I do envy her her journalistic gifts. I think the photographs are marvelous, even if Wm Jay Smith says they are "chi-chi." Thank you so much. We've both enjoyed it thoroughly and then, too, it is one of those wonderful books to hand guests to look at when you don't know quite what to do with them—the superior type of guest, that is. The others we hand Steinberg to.[2] I do hope that wine I sent you was good. The red *should* have been equal to T. S. Eliot, I think. (I read a fascinating bit of gossip somewhere about his requesting still wines instead of champagne in Chicago—and he & his wife *both* not being able to eat shrimp, onions, etc.) I wonder if you had him to dinner again. Oh, all kinds of things have been going on, I read in the back of *POETRY* and in the *Times Book Review* section and *Evergreen Review*, etc. etc.

I see our friends got nominated for the Institute—but did they get in? Should I know by now? I received Flannery's new book last week.[3] That first section that was published somewhere before still seems superb to me—like a poem. In fact she's a great loss to the art, don't you think? And all through there are absolutely marvelous passages—conversations, bits of description—she's wonderful because it seems so effortless, and never a word wasted— There's an idiot child named for me, I think—read about him on page 91—that paragraph is beautiful—[4]

1 Mary McCarthy, *The Stones of Florence*, with photographs by Evelyn Hofer (1959).
2 Probably S. H. Steinberg, *Five Hundred Years of Printing* (1959).
3 Flannery O'Connor, *The Violent Bear It Away* (1960).
4 "The small white-haired boy shambled into the back of the hall and stood peering forward at the stranger. He had on the bottoms to a pair of blue pajamas drawn up as high as they would go, the string tied over his chest and then again, harness-like, around his neck to keep them on. His eyes were slightly sunken beneath his forehead and his cheekbones were lower than they should have been. He stood there, dim and ancient, like a child who had been a child for centuries . . . 'That's only Bishop' "; Flannery O'Connor, *The Violent Bear It Away* (1960), 91–92.

I am so glad you liked the New Year's poem. I think it is a bit artificial, but I finally had to do something with the cliché about the landscape looking like a tapestry, I suppose. And it does now in February, too. The Lent trees are just starting to come out all over the place a wonderful purple—and the pink and yellow trees are beginning, too. I have some more poems, too, of dubious value. Farrar Straus sent me a folder of advertising for your book— couldn't be more glowing—and I wonder if I have missed any of the annual prizes, etc. Did you get them all? Yes, I saw the montage photograph of you and Marianne—I wonder what surrealist advertising man thought that up! We sent a nice and fearfully rich coffee-grower friend of ours to call on Marianne at Christmas time, and she (the plantation owner) was so overcome by Marianne that she immediately sent her I don't know how much coffee. It is the best coffee in the world, I know, because we get sent some more once in a while and I suspect that Marianne is giving it to the janitor . . . Marianne adores jewels—and sure enough, in her letter about the friend she described the huge diamond rings she wears—

Please send me the poem called "The Drinker"—I have a sort of sonnet called "The Drunkard" but I've never been able to decide whether it's any good or not.[1] I'd like to see the Barzun preface—was it published separately anywhere? Also, should I get the Tate tribute? I see you are in it. How is the marriage, I wonder, and what is Caroline doing? (I am re-reading your letter of January 4th). We enjoyed Elizabeth's piece about Boston—but I wonder how Boston enjoyed it? Are you teaching, and what? Horrors, from this letter of yours I think that perhaps you think we are still coming to N.Y. I took it all back several times, but maybe not from you? The exchange is so awful for Lota now—there is a real inflation here—that we finally gave up that plan. I think it is up to me to earn $$$$ somehow or other or maybe try for another fellowship of some sort.[2] My friend Loren MacIver just got $10,000—from Ford.[3] I suppose painters get so much more because they have to buy paints—

The Calders are coming back for Carnival. There are three or four nights of it: balls, elegant, bohemian, the most famous pansy ball in the world—and parades—and Lota is getting apprehensive. We always try to go to the night of the Negro Samba Schools, but that is all—but the Calders like to stay up until 6 AM and dance and dance and dance and drink and drink and

---

1 See "A Drunkard" (EB-*EAP*).

2 With the rapid rise of inflation in Brazil, EB and Lota found it difficult to live on their incomes. EB hoped to make extra money writing journalism, including an account of her journey down the Amazon.

3 The Ford Foundation.

drink . . . I'll probably be away for some of carnival—in Belém (Bethlehem) at the mouth of the Amazon. We have had some strange social activities—in Rio, at very short notice, to help out a point-4 friend of ours—we went out on a rather small cruiser to see the bay with the ex-governor of Nevada,[1] his wife and four sons . . . It was very rough; we mis-directed the captain to the wrong island; the four huge boys sulked; all we know about Nevada is Reno . . . The point-4 boy had told me the governor was interested in literature. I hadn't really believed it of course, but our conversation was like this: "I hear you write poems." "Yes." "Well, Lucius Beebe[2] is a very good friend of mine." Poor dears, they were actually very nice, and on their way to Paraguay (Lota tactlessly groaned when they told her) and now there is a revolution going on there already. The man wore a very strange buttoned bow-tie, and as a youth he had carried gold, around his waist, for Wells Fargo.

We went away to Cabo Frio again for Christmas and had a lovely time. But actually we've been rather low lately, I'm afraid. One of my oldest friends, who was coming to visit us in April, died very suddenly of heart failure[3]—in Nassau, of all places to die—and our nicest neighbors, Brazil's best historian and his wife, very good friends of Lota's, were killed in a stupid airplane crash.[4] A man here, slightly odd, after two of his friends had died of heart attacks, pounded his plump knees and said indignantly, "There's no more guarantee!" A thought for the present.

With much love, Cal—forgive me for not writing sooner—Lota sends love, too—& best wishes for the family,

Elizabeth

208.

February 24, 1960

Dearest Elizabeth:

I've been wondering about your visit and dully assuming it wasn't to be. Last night, a little lecture accompanied the news coverage of Eisenhower's arrival; Brazil's exchange sacrifices were explained, the new capitol praised, and it was suggested that we might learn to defy all financial advice and follow the same course. So maybe there will be an exchange relief for you.

---

1 Charles H. Russell, governor of Nevada from 1951 to 1959, leading the International Cooperation Administration mission to Paraguay.

2 Lucius Beebe published one book of poems, *Corydon* (1924).

3 Marjorie Stevens died on October 21, 1959.

4 Octávio Tarquínio de Sousa and his wife, Lúcia Miguel Pereira, were killed on December 22, 1959.

The Academy elections were announced this morning. Flannery didn't reach the finals, but Mary and Randall were elected, also Eberhart, Harry Levin, De Kooning, the architect of Lever Brothers.[1] Things are better this year. Why don't we propose Flannery again. I had a long talk with Bob Giroux about her last week; her life is what you might guess. A small, managing indomitable mother, complaining that no one helps her, more or less detesting Flannery's work, impressed however, wishing she would marry—Flannery silent in her presence. A tall ancient Aunt living next to the old State Capitol, the unwanted peacocks, a doctor telling her two years ago that she couldn't expect to live[2]; then new drugs, her Mother forcing her to bathe at Lourdes, an improvement, announced as a miracle by the Mother, Flannery silent. Battles between the Mother and the Catholic priest about an unwished-for altar tapestry. And so on. Flannery's health seems safe.

I hadn't connected "Bishop" with you. Maybe you'll be rebaptized by missionaries on your trip up the Amazon. The book strikes me as incredibly professional, less humorous and more like other books than anything she has done. The fire is there—a terrifying ending, the grotesque beginning—a short story to which the rest was added—the fierce struggle of sympathy and loathing with the second uncle. Her true inspiration is a narrow, fizzling powder-line—the askew child, the torn criminal prophet, the Southern fact, the sapless ordinary world neither good nor evil. I see Flannery standing in the fire and splutter—brain, muscle and common-sense and will, working and working. I don't know whether this book is her best or just her most controlled; part of its thrill is to see the control, so perfect in many of the stories, pushed through a whole novel.

Have you seen the Italian-French film, *Black Orpheus*,[3] about your carnival? It's just a little too full-color, gorgeous, operatic, American; but the story's developed with amazing tenderness, one is really at the carnival and hears the music of your records.

Your Amazon trip sounds tough and alluring. I rather burn for motion, new things, then dread the interruption. Little engagements, little letters, little reading excursions so heap up here; the world spills through my fingers and I stand, a mountain of inefficiency. I have more or less been offered a Ford grant for next year to study opera. I would be in New York about half the week, then back here for week-ends. The delightful duties would be going to opera rehearsals, etc. at the Met and New York City Opera. Nothing produced is ex-

1 Gordon Bunshaft.
2 Flannery O'Connor was diagnosed with lupus in 1951.
3 *Orfeu Negro*, dir. Marcel Camus (1959).

actly required. I love opera and am totally ignorant of music, and hope to write dramatic scenes that would be rich enough to stand without music, a form that would owe everything to seeing opera first-hand and yet would stand on its own. A contradiction—however, I want tremendously to get away from the personal, my purely subjective and all too free as air way of writing.

I wonder when you began to feel that the first careless, regardless lunge was over, that you were waking up, that every step asked for prudence and deliberation. Lately, I've felt I was waking from a long dream, fearful, hopeful, thrilled, a great weight pulling me backwards, a great air-bubble floating me upward, and somewhere a kind of birth in the substantial.

I saw Allen and Belle in Chicago. Swarms of teachers, students, columnists, architects, champagne, people getting divorces, nick-names—Belle, resolute, nervous, corresponding and dressed like Edith Sitwell. They seem very happy, and Allen, though hardly stilled and hum-drum, does seem greatly eased.

Give our love to Lota, ours goes with you up the river. More news in the next letter.

Love,
Cal

209.

April 12th, 1960—Rio
Dearest Cal—Happy Easter—

This is just to say that and give you my congratulations. I see by the April 2nd New Yorker that you received the Book Award[1] & made a speech, etc.—and heaven knows what other honors have come to you by now, too. (I got that N Yer air mail because of my pre-Amazon poem in it. I found when I actually went there I'd been fairly accurate. The "dolphins" come in gray or pink with gray spots—pink ones are lucky.[2])

I have a long letter written to you in my head and when I get home tomorrow I'll really write it. So much has been happening—to you, mostly! Your little girl looks amazingly like you in that snapshot. Maybe in action she resembles Elizabeth, too?

With much love & lots of pink dolphins,
Elizabeth

---

1 Life Studies won the 1960 National Book Award.
2 "The Riverman," The New Yorker (April 2, 1960); see EB-CP.

210.

Dearest Cal:

This is TIRANDENTES DAY—"Toothpuller Day"—a national holiday on which I think I wrote to you last year, too. He was a patriot who tried to get rid of the Portuguese, and he had been an itinerant dentist, and he was finally cut into eight, I think it was, pieces and the pieces sent around the country . . .

Yes, I saw the *Orpheus* movie; it opened here a year ago. It was an opera to begin with, written by a poet Lota knows,[1] but we didn't attend that, and L refused to see the movie, too. I liked bits of it, but the effect, I thought, was more French than Brazilian (you say "American"!—but that footsie-game, etc., are pure French, surely). I liked the views of Rio at dawn, and they picked the best slum, of course, but had to build their own hovels, and Carnival isn't like that. It's much, much better. For one thing the Samba Schools are very proud and independent and they practice all year with professional teachers, and they *perform*; they'd never mix with the crowd like that. Carnival's one big glorious mess, but a more orderly and artistic mess, really. I was in Amazonas this year, but Lota went with the Calders, and it *rained*. The beautiful Louis XV costumes were all draggled, but they danced on until dawn. Calder stood up and watched for six hours. He is made of iron like one of his own creations, I think. Mrs. C wore an Indian shawl over her dress, magenta, and she and Lota returned in the gray dawn both dyed all over from it. It is something you really must see before it is quite ruined. Loudspeakers have almost ruined parts of it already. The "Orpheus" music is pretty fakey, too—only one true samba—and the words, being written by a *real* poet, are bad. They lack that surprise, the mis-used words, the big words, etc., that sambas always have. One of my favorites has a refrain: "Respect the ambient!" And one is about how Woman drags down Man—with all his "beauty and nobility . . ." But Lota can sing them all night when she gets going. Oh, another, "The Cathedral of Love." I should really make a good collection, and translations, I think—I suspect they're some of [the] last folk poetry to be made in the world.

The New Yorker sent me the April 2nd number airmail and so I learned that you had received the Book Award, made a speech, etc. *Congratulations*, and please tell me about it. I was hoping Flannery would get the novel one, but

---

1 Vinícius de Moraes, *Orfeu da Conceição* (1954).

maybe her book appeared too late—if it had any chance. I was sent the Roth book[1]—and thought it clever—over-clever, somehow, and very vulgar, but good in spots. You don't have to like the "Riverman" poem. Lota hates it, and I don't approve of it myself but once it was written I couldn't seem to get rid of it. Now I am doing an authentic, post-Amazon, one that I trust will be better,[2] & almost finished a story about the Amazon, too, but it is more or less a potboiler. Yes, the Flannery book is a bit disappointing, I'm afraid—one wishes she could get away from religious fanatics for a while. But just the writing is so damned good compared to almost anything else one reads: economical, clear, horrifying, *real*. I suspect that this repetition of the uncle-nephew, or father-son, situation, in all its awfulness, is telling something about her family life—seen sidewise, or in distorted shadows on the wall.

I wonder if you got my cards from the Amazon, and the ballad books?[3] (also some snapshots mailed in Rio last week). No, those are folk poetry all right, too. The form goes back to Camões, and they sell thousands of them, displays in all the markets, like Marlboro book-shops in N.Y., and people buying all the time. I know you can't read it properly, but sometimes they are quite good, and they are composed by people who can't read or write, and sung to guitars. Some stanzas go in for long lists of place-names, rhymed, or people's names, with very classical effect.

Well, speaking of opera, you'd like Manaus. Its most famous sight is the huge opera house built around 1905 at the height of the rubber boom. Rubber collapsed completely just after that and there the Opera house stands, huge, magnificent, art-nouveau-ish, with the town dwindled to nothing around it, and the Rio Negro rolling magnificently below. It is quite lovely inside, rose damask and mirrors (the last governor stole a lot of mirrors and girandoles) and armchairs with cane seats, for coolness; the plaster work is very delicate, all regional things, palms, coffee trees, alligators, etc., and huge paintings of *Guaraní*, sunrise on the river, etc. The ballroom is marble and tortoiseshell— but the pillars around the sides are *fake* marble, because that last shipload from Carrara was sunk. I've never heard *Guaraní* and suspect it's bad—but we had "Bifstek Carlos Gomes" on the menu every single day.[4]

I think your Ford grant to study opera is amazing. I got asked to *suggest* people for it, vaguely thought of myself, since I need money badly, but

1 Philip Roth, *Goodbye, Columbus* (1959), which won the 1960 National Book Award for Fiction.
2 Possibly an early draft of "Santarém" (EB-*CP*).
3 EB had sent RL *Literatura de la corda* pamphlets.
4 Antonio Carlos Gomes, *Il Guarany* (1870).

couldn't think how I could get to enough operas. Now I think I was rather stupid. Maybe we could have gone to Milan for a year! And I have dreamed of a libretto for years . . . Do you know Sam Barber? He wants one, I know—but then, I don't think much of his luscious music. However, I think a good libretto might be exactly your cup of tea. I think Auden's are too pastiche-ish. They don't have to be quite so simple, really. And as you say, there's no reason why they can't stand on their own without the music.

If you can think of anything *I* could apply for, please tell me . . . I sometimes think I have no right to, and then I realize other people who have small amounts of money do and I don't see why I shouldn't. Except that if I really worked . . . It's a problem, but I think that now in this Eisenhower splurge I might possibly get enough from Ford or Rockefeller to take a trip to Europe. I haven't been since before the war. I couldn't live on my money in the "states." In fact I find by statistics in *The New Republic* that there I am actually in the "underprivileged" class. Ford or Rockefeller—Rockefeller has long been interested in South America, and I have an idea for getting money to see some more of it and finish up a book of stories about Brazil. But I don't know where to write, and any information would be welcome. Three people I recommended got Guggenheims this year, and I am beginning to feel sorry for myself! What were you doing in Chicago? Lota was dumfounded at Belle G when she saw a photograph of Allen in the N.Y. *Times.* I did think that interview or tape-recorded gathering or whatever it was in *Kenyon*, with poor little Sylvia Beach, etc., took the cake for cheapness, didn't you? Why not just tape record everything, everything, and then cut it up into segments and advertise it madly, and not bother about art any more at all?[1] But proposing toasts to Belle & Allen, that seems gratuitously cruel to poor old Caroline (or has she died?)

I want to go back to the Amazon. I dream dreams every night. I don't know quite why I found it so affecting. Did I tell you that I have been taking photographic slides?— I always thought it was too bourgeois for words, but they really are lovely and I have a small Amazon lecture and a small Cabo Frio lecture, etc. Lota does the machine part and so far we have to look at everything twice, I don't know why, but I'm hoping to solve this problem. (She wanted me to take all the house.) Who is ever going to look at these, and when, I can't imagine. I have some of passengers going ashore in a pouring rain and up a steep ladder, etc.—it is like the Israelites. Did I tell you (oh

---

1 Jackson Mathews, "Conversation with Sylvia Beach & Co.," *The Kenyon Review* (Winter 1960); see RL-*CPR*.

dear I hope not) how we stopped at a place called "Liverpool" late one night—a narrow channel, nothing visible but a few white blurs of houses and candles, and one lantern. The ship waited and waited—then plop, plop—very gently, a canoe came out, a big one. Several men were in it, with two lanterns, one the old-fashioned burglar's kind of dark lantern. They were bringing out a dying man to be taken to the hospital in Belém. It was very hard to raise him up to the ship, in a sheet, I think, an old man with a night-cap on. The lantern light fell on his face, on the red, muddy water. It was quite incredible. They are very quiet people, and handsome—Portuguese and Indian mixed, "caboclos" and "mamalucos." I must find out where that name comes from.

But I worry a great deal about what to do with all this accumulation of exotic or picturesque or charming detail, and I don't want to become a poet who can only write about South America, etc. It is one of my greatest worries now, how to use everything and keep on living here, most of the time, probably, and yet be a New Englander-herring-choker-bluenoser at the same time . . .

Oh—I think your drunkenness poem is going to be superb! Yours is infinitely better. It started me off on mine again. Mine is more personal and yet a bit more abstract, I think. Please send me your finished one and I hope eventually to send you mine. Wasn't the Shapiro business idiotic?[1] And sad, of course. I suppose you have read the Fiedler book?[2] I finally read *The Tradition of the New* but I couldn't see quite all that Mary McC saw in it[3]—and I think he's crazy, about painting—sometimes. I saw your review of Richards.[4] Oh, I do manage to see quite a few things, but I do think we should get away this year if we can. Lota has had a very tough stretch. Two of our best friends here, a couple on whom she depended a lot for company over week-ends, a historian and his wife, were killed in a stupid plane crash at Christmas time. (I had just got him nominated for the Academy, an honorary member, too) and one of my oldest friends who was coming to visit me this month died just before Christmas. Then Lota's adopted son has been cutting up—so has her whacky sister. She has too many lawsuits on her

1 Karl Shapiro, "What's the Matter with Poetry?: It's a 'Diseased Art,' Argues a Poet Who Presents a Bill of Particulars," *The New York Times Book Review* (Dec. 13, 1959).
2 Leslie Fiedler, *Love and Death in the American Novel* (1960).
3 Harold Rosenberg, *The Tradition of the New* (1959); Mary McCarthy, "An Academy of Risk," *Partisan Review* (Summer 1959).
4 "I. A. Richards as Poet," *Encounter* (Feb. 1960); see RL-*CPR*.

hands and too much land and no cash, etc., and I haven't earned anything to speak of. I think the best thing for her would be a trip to N.Y. or Europe, preferably Europe, but she prefers N.Y.

Next week I am going on another short trip, 3 or 4 days, down the coast to a place that one can only get to by boat—so no one ever goes, of course. It is supposed to be perfect 18th century, tiny, and the tide comes up the streets every day and goes down again—no hotel. Lota refuses to have anything to do with anything Brazilian or "primitive," you know. She says she wants something more civilized rather than less when she goes traveling, so I am going with two neighbors. One is the father of a childhood friend of L's, he's almost 80, and the other is his boy-friend of over 40 years, who is about 65—a huge, handsome, Viking-like German, with the brain and soul of a small girl of 8. (Really, Tennessee Williams should come here, but please don't suggest it.) They are amazing, however—never a cross word in all these years, and they have ten times my energy, and are stupid as stupid—and we'll make a lovely trio.

Yes, I saw that Mary and Randall *got in*—and Levin!—and Nabokov[1] refused—and Calder's *in*, too. I think we might have some quite funny dinners in our old ages, don't you?

Yesterday morning at 6:30 AM we were awakened by a very noisy old truck full of 22 very noisy men, standing up, ten monks and the rest laity. Lota rushed out saying that this was private property and what was the idea, etc., and then in the midst of her outrage she remembered she'd promised one Franciscan he could bring the gang here for a hike sometime, so she piped down quickly. You must imagine this in the full red light of late sunrise, the mountains hung with red wisps of cloud, the birds shrieking, and Lota in a pasha-like, huge, Paisley dressing-gown, with red fringes, shrieking too, while the poor brown brothers cowered in their truck. So they started off, some of the monks carried *brief cases*, poor dears, and waded off through the long wet grass holding their skirts up. They came back about six last night, and I went out to talk to them. They had their hoods up and some actually had bottles of beer. It was like a bad painting. I hope you got the nuns I took at Cabo Frio. They were awfully nice, in wading. I wanted to take a picture of their boots and blue wool socks lying in the sand but I got shy.

But the church here keeps giving me deep Protestant shudders. I borrowed a nightgown in an emergency one night in Rio. When I went to bed something scratched my bosom, over the heart, and I felt around and found

---

1 Vladimir Nabokov.

something pinned to it. At first I thought it was a small powder puff, a new way of scenting one's bosom, perhaps, but when I fished it out I found printed on it in almost invisible letters "Agnus Dei." This belonged to a woman whom I'd always thought of as Catholic but *intelligent*—one of the good kinds.

You sound very well in your letter of February 25th, and I am so glad. I'm in fine shape except for these worries about money and whether I'm going to turn into solid cuteness in my poetry if I don't watch out—or if I do watch out. Aside from that everything is fine, and I've been writing a lot again. Have you done any more poems? You know how happy all this success for the book makes me, I'm sure. We know how (can't think of the right word) it is in some ways, and yet for once they've picked the right person and it is awfully gratifying and even makes one feel a bit better about all the world's horrors.

How I'd like to see you.

With much love,

Elizabeth

211.

Next Day—April [23], 1960

Dear Cal:

I forgot to enclose this yesterday. I also forgot to say that in Belém I met this young poet, Joaquim Francisco.[1] He had just received a fellowship for a year in the U.S., for the study of American poetry. When I met him he didn't know which university he'd be sent to, but thought he'd be leaving Brazil in June or July. I found him adorable, and I took the liberty of giving him a note to you and some other poets. He will probably never get within miles of you, but if he does happen to I think you'd like him, and I'm sure he wouldn't be any trouble—his manners are too good. He's only twenty-two, very handsome, gentle, and he knows all contemporary American poets by heart—which must have taken a great deal of hard work, in Belém, and was very touching. He is very serious about it all, and it is pleasant to find someone here who thinks American poetry is better than French, at present, and that you are best of all. They are doing something in Rio now called "concretionist." It seems like pre-1914 experiments, with a little "transition"[2] &

---

1 Joaquim-Francisco Coelho.
2 Modernist magazine *transition*, edited by Eugene Jolas.

Jolas, and a dash of Cummings. It's awfully sad. I was interviewed about it in Belém and said ferociously that perhaps it had "A certain nostalgic charm," & Joaquim was delighted. While the interview was going on (it was during Carnival) a masquer in a striped convict suit came into the café we were in and came straight to me. He was wearing a Chessman[1] mask and carrying a black book labeled LEX.[2] He opened it under my eyes, and it said "Only God can Kill." The two poets with me suffered agonies.

Tell me: what you think of Delmore S's new book?[3] All the *new* poems by him I've seen I thought were really bad, I'm sorry to say. Have you seen anything new by Randall? I have not liked Snodgrass since that *PR* piece of his on writing *Heart's Needle*.[4] So silly and solemn—next we'll be having radio(electro?)cardiograms of the poet writing a poem. How is THRONES? I refused to buy ROCKDRILL.[5] Pound criticism is wildly confused, don't you think, but I agree with D. Fitts that poetry is *not* to be drilled into you, nor is music—and that's one of P's—oh well—I'll skip it.[6]

I am getting as tedious with my second thoughts as Verlaine, but I realized that my financial complaints yesterday didn't sound very well after my glowing reports of money to be made in Brazil. That is still true, however, I have been investing my own small makings here in order to try to make some more, and in this particular case it has been held up for the past year. In two or three years I should have more, all right.

Harriet is going to be very good-looking, I think. Remember me to her Ma.

With love,
Elizabeth

Yes, let's nominate Flannery again. Maybe I should have said much more, but I imagine those blurbs count for little.

212.

April 28, 1960

Dearest Elizabeth:

Your marvelous second post-Amazon letter arrived yesterday, while Ted

---

1 Caryl Chessman, death row inmate and writer, whose case became a cause célèbre for opponents of capital punishment.
2 For lex talionis, the law of retaliation.
3 Delmore Schwartz, *Summer Knowledge: New and Selected Poems* (1959).
4 W. D. Snodgrass, "Finding a Poem," *Partisan Review* (Spring 1959).
5 Ezra Pound, *Thrones: 96–109 de los cantares* (1959) and *Section: Rock-Drill, 85–95 de los cantares* (1956).
6 See Dudley Fitts, "Music Fit for the Odes," *Hound & Horn* (Winter 1931).

Roethke was just ending a visit. Poor thing, a mammoth yet elfinlike, hairless, red-faced, beginning the day with a shot of bourbon, speechless except for shrewd grunted asides—behind him nervous breakdowns, before him—what? He is off to Europe with his frail wife on [a] Belgian freighter in June. We had *all* the Boston poets in to meet him. I. A. Richards read, then Ted read, saying, "I feel like a punk or a hog-caller following Thomas Hardy." Then Philip Booth read, saying "I feel like Ted," and Ted said, "Honey, that's work." When Ted read at Harvard, everything showed, the delicate glistening nerves, the wallow of flesh, the obscenity, the shyness. Well, it's awful to be driven on like a great baggy blue serge sail before the wind. Somehow, all this contrasted with you, the most all there of anyone I've ever known.

I wouldn't worry about the Amazon poem—it's the best fairy story in verse I know. It brings back an old dream of yours, you said you felt you were a mermaid scraping barnacles off a wharf-pile.[1] That was Maine, not Brazil. Your new book with this and the Pound and "The Armadillo" ought to be your very best and all in different styles.

Yes the Tate-Gardner tape was crude and cruel and cheap. I made an awful blunder last spring when I was getting high. I called up Caroline and told her she mustn't let Allen get a divorce, that Allen really loved her and that Belle was extremely stupid. Actually, the marriage is a good thing—Allen much more settled down after all his gadding. They are both a little unreally cordial and dramatic—however, there's effervescence and happiness, and who knows? love, I think.

What tremendous descriptions in your letter! The sick man on the Amazon, the monks and nuns and Lota, the sacred heart on your bosom. I have nothing to reply with except a prosaic trip to Swarthmore. I was visiting a minute, intelligent dry poet, Daniel Hoffman, midway in a book on vegetation and other myths in Melville, Hawthorne, James, Faulkner, etc. and the American humorists, and all the way through a dry intelligent, unreadable book of vegetation myths poems in strange ballad meters and the alliterative stanza of Sir Gawain.[2] Exquisite Shaker and European baroque and Swarthmore stone house; nervous, charming near-sighted wife, poetry-editor for the *Ladies Home Journal* (ten dollars a line) and a friend of Marianne Moore's—both industrious and armed with a Columbia graduate school culture, oppressed by the lazy, social non-book-writing and non-New Criticism

1 See letter 52; cf. also "Water," lines 25–28 (RL-*CP*).
2 Daniel Hoffman, *Form and Fable in American Fiction* (1961) and *A Little Geste* (1961).

world of Swarthmore. (After their huge cocktail party, I asked them who was interesting and they said, "We are."[)] In the morning I read to the Swarthmore "Collection." A churchlike hall, an organ playing and the entire faculty behind me; the entire student body, many reading papers, in front of me. A silence, an introduction. I made Quaker references and jokes—the little group of Catholics and atheists who met Quaker leaders once a month when I was in the Danbury jail—and gradually realized that only the building's frame was Quaker, not the students. Then my *"Three millionaires"* day. First the Barnes Museum,—the obligatory one year ahead application having been waived, Hoffman drove me to the back door of a sort of Frick Museum in the country—one felt one was entering Germany for the first time since the war—sinister, silent men trained on Barnes aesthetics driving power rollers. A knobbed oaken door opened a crack, so as not to let Hoffman slip in. A little old lady with dyed red hair, Miss de Mazia,[1] Barnes collaborator and supposed mistress, brought out the guest book—whispered instructions: in an hour and twenty minutes a bell would ring to tell us to leave the floor where a lecture was about to begin, but we were to be allowed our full two hours. The pictures were hung in uniform gilded oak frames & on a sort of de luxe burlap, about them bits of burnished iron, keys, hinges, scissors. The paintings were glorious—two hundred Renoirs, good Cézannes, Matisses, Demuths, Soutines, everything, even the trivia seeming to have been really *chosen*. A great feeling of the brevity and difficulty of the visit. Barnes had a great flair for nudes, done sometimes by unlikely people: a hideous Van Gogh, a Douanier Rousseau, Cézanne's late nudes. But over all, oppressive and awesome, as if the earth panted to be released from its clothes, the innumerable Renoirs, sometimes seeming mere air and nothing, and sometimes the fullness of the world. After a while Miss de Mazia lectured. Heavy Italian(?) accent: "Tradition is how man dominates his sufferings." Then later, the dates of Fra Angelico. As I left a tall Negro student said I had been pointed out to him as Mr. Lowell from his town. He said it took time to get Miss de Mazia's style, but then she had it.

(Jack Sweeney just called, and I suggested that you would welcome a grant. He was full of the highest admiration and optimistic and will let me know in a week. I do hope you and Lota will touch on New York, and not just briefly while we are there.)

Second millionaire. The Frankenthalers', a modest bulging Commonwealth Avenue house on Rittenhouse Square. Maid, but Hoffman's received

---

1 Violette de Mazia, Barnes Museum trustee and director of education.

with open arms, incredible Empire furniture, about ten paintings, a pittance after the Barnes, particularly as the pictures repeated on a small scale others I'd just seen: Seurat's models for the *Grande Jatte*, a fifth the size of the Barnes's, Renoir's *Three Graces*, somehow small and alone and shivering, a wonderful graceful Degas of Mary Cassatt looking like a James heroine, furs, small waist, face invisible. Mr. Frankenthaler's sister appeared, expensive print dress, most interested in pointing out photographs and semi-famous paintings of Orlando, her poodle, and saying "I wouldn't sell this one to my brother. Oh, here's Willie, at last." A heavy young man with a doe-skin waistcoat, a seducer's tough upper lip, a tilting posture. Then a table of drinks and sandwiches, and "I wonder where Willie has gone to." He was gone; later it turned out we were supposed to be a part of Willie's cocktail party. We left, hearing Mr. Frankenthaler's sister murmuring, "I've never seen the Barnes collection; I can tell you no one will regret Miss de Mazia's passing." I thought I would.

Third millionaire. (This will come to a stop.) After a reading at Haverford—this time real Quakers, and I felt all my poems were as soiled and disreputable as Baudelaire on his mistress—a reception by Mr. Hires of Hires Root Beer. A crew hair-cutted, black-and-gray-haired man with a heart condition, who had put up a hundred dollars for me to read. He told [me] that whenever someone had told [him] a book was supreme, he read it. He then named ancient poets I'd never heard of and Buckless *Intellectual History of the World*,[1] which he had read nine times, and I think Ingersoll, too. The guests, Haverford faculty, fawned. One said, or maybe two separately, that Mr. Hires loved books so that he had at first built a library and no dining room in his house; though, of course, he could afford a dining room. And so, home to Boston, taking in on the way a dinner at Hartford, everyone standing around for two hours before dinner, the men in one group telling memorized smut, the women in another talking about Dale Carnegie's speech courses, my hostess, whom I'd just met, apologizing for labeling my place card "Robert" instead of "Bob."

I don't know why I've stuffed all this in, except to plaintively suggest that even here one can see the world in a grain of sand.[2] Dearest, how I miss you. Someday, we will be in the same spot and long, long, long. Love to Lota.

All my love,
Cal

---

1 Probably Henry Thomas Buckle, *History of Civilization in England* (1857).
2 William Blake, "Auguries of Innocence," line 1.

P.S. I enclose a translation of Heine, almost an original poem from three of his.[1] How marvelous to have had a life that could be so written about even in terrible pain. I hope to have my translation book done by September. Bentley has asked me [to] try *Phédre* for his French-classics series,[2] and I've tried a few pages in crisp unscanned verse, and am astonished that everything *isn't* lost. Then I've half-contracted to [do] a modern poetry anthology for Anchor. I hope to give large gobs of the people I like, but it's harder now to be very original; Oscar Williams and others have gradually spread and lapped up most of the good things. Let me know of anything you like a lot. And please, if you have copies, send me all you've done since *A Cold Spring*. I carry "The Armadillo" in my billfold and occasionally amaze people with it. And more photographs. The Amazon ones were real but you were missing. Lizzie sends her love. Flannery's book is for next year; do you want to propose her again for the Academy. I'll second. I wrote Randall to this purpose, but have had no answer.

213.

May 6, 1960

Dearest Elizabeth:

Here we are. You should write a letter to the Chapelbrook Foundation, Mr. Harry K. Mansfield at Ropes, Gray, Best, and Coolidge, 50 Federal St. Boston 10, Mass. The grants are from three to four thousand for a year; Cummings has had one, and I think this will go through. What you should tell them is a) your financial circumstances, b) how the money would forward your work by allowing you to come here or go to Europe. This can be quite natural: your nearly completed book of poems, your prose, and your fears of becoming an exclusively Brazilian poet—more or less what you wrote me and in the same easy-going, sensible, personal style. Jack and I will get in touch with Archie and Murdock.[3] I don't think other sponsors will be necessary, but if they are, we will dig them up.

Agnes Mongan is very keen and would like to have a letter from you. You might write Jack[4] too, who has been very sweet. I hope a little at least of your trip will include New York and us. I don't think the Foundation cares

---

1 "Heine Dying in Paris" (RL-*CP*).
2 RL first attempted to translate Jean Racine's *Phèdre* (1677) at Yaddo in 1947; *Phaedra* was published in 1961.
3 Jack Sweeney, Archibald MacLeish, and Kenneth B. Murdock.
4 RL enclosed a letter from Jack Sweeney, who, having approached Agnes Mongan about a grant for EB, suggested to RL that Allen Tate and Marianne Moore send letters of support to Archibald MacLeish.

whether you go to Europe or America. Everyone seems brimming with willingness and enthusiasm.

Love,
Cal

214.

[From Archibald MacLeish to Robert Lowell]

Uphill Farm
Conway, Massachusetts
May 10, 1960

Dear Cal:

It is you who are the doer of good works. It seems to me that wherever I turn I see your hand held out to help somebody along. I am much moved by it. I think your Elizabeth Bishop idea is very good indeed. Do you know her well enough to suggest to her that she make application (which is what people have to do with the Chapelbrook Foundation) for a grant? If you do, why don't you ask her to write me as a trustee? She ought to describe a kind of project—the project you sketch in your note—indicating how a grant would help her to complete it within a year or two years or whatever. This isn't a formal requirement but the Board does like to have as specific an indication as possible of the way in which the grant will be helpful.

My affectionate regards to you both.

Faithfully yours,
Archie

[typed at the foot of the page]

Dearest Elizabeth:

I think this adds nothing to what I've already written you, but you might write MacLeish too—I see the tantalizing phrase *two* years. He's really quite unusually generous and industrious about getting people things. I gave my class your "Man-Moth," unidentified, last week, as an illustration of good description that also builds a new world like Kafka. How breathlessly real, the little creature,—itself, us, you,—is! I̶ ̶f̶e̶l̶t̶ I had been talking to you, all veils off, and was very much surprised.

Love,
Cal

215.

Heavens Cal! That was SERVICE. I feel as if I had just held out my hand to the skies. I got your letter when Lota and I were on the way to Rio for her tooth, for two days, and yesterday and today I have been back again and trying to compose an application. It is a little hard because I want to allow for contingencies; such as war, I suppose—and make it sound as though New York, Europe, or if I couldn't make either even if I did have more money, further S.A. travel—in Peru and Bolivia—would all serve equally well. However, I think it's done now: very simple, just about what I did say to you, and I'm giving them my bank, income tax man, etc., so they can check on the financial details if they want. I met Murdock twice, I think, years ago at Andy Wanning's, and he might remember me. MacLeish I've never met but he has always been very polite to me, and we have had some exchanges, by letter, and by telephone when I was at the Library. I'd rather *not* ask Marianne again, if possible. She has done a lot of that for me in the past. I'm writing Agnes this morning, and also I'll write a note to Jack. I feel guilty about this because I know perfectly well that if I could manage to turn out more prose I wouldn't have to go begging, or else I should be teaching like everyone else (God forbid), but anyway—I'll be delighted if it comes through and if it doesn't I'll just think I probably really didn't deserve it anyway. What is the Chapelbrook Foundation, I wonder. I never heard of it, nor had I heard of those Amy Lowell Fellowships. I had had the idea of trying Ford with a project for more South American travels, but I do prefer this plan. If it doesn't work please don't feel badly. I think if it works we shall try to get to Europe for a while. Now if I could manage this and *two stories* as well, we might make Europe *and* New York; Lota likes N.Y. best, of course—or thinks she does!

We read your letter avidly—the long one—full of news and entertainment. I like the Heine *very* much. When those dead translations enter the Cabinet of Dr. Cal,[1] they become almost too much alive. It should make a good book, all of them, and you are doing more for us all than did Longfellow,[2] at the same time.

This seems to be the term-paper stretch in the U.S.A. Never have I had so many of things like the enclosed—although not all are even that polite. And here is the nomination for Flannery again. I had a very nice letter from her in which she sounded a little upset by a silly review in *TIME*, of course, mostly

---

1 *The Cabinet of Dr. Caligari*, dir. Robert Wiene (1920).
2 See Henry Wadsworth Longfellow's translation of Dante's *Divine Comedy* (1867).

about her sickness.[1] I'd like to go to call on her sometime, although I do find her a bit intimidating.

It is odd. I had meant to remark that I have been seeing some poems around by an Anne Sexton[2] that reminded me quite a bit of you and also were quite good, at least some of them—and the same day your last letter came, Houghton Mifflin sent me her book, with your blurb on the jacket[3] and that sad photograph of her on the other side of it. She *is* good, in spots,—but there is all the difference in the world, I'm afraid, between her kind of simplicity and that of *Life Studies*, her kind of egocentricity that is simply that, and yours that has been—what would be the reverse of *sub*limated, I wonder—anyway, made intensely *interesting*, and painfully applicable to every reader. I feel I know too much about her, whereas, although I know much more about you, I'd like to know a great deal more, etc. Oh, well, it is all fairly obvious, isn't it. I like some of her really mad ones best; those that sound as though she'd written them all at once. I think she must really have been in what Lota called the other day the "Luna Bin." (You should really cultivate some foreign friends who can startle you like that several times every day.)

(& just now I was asked for a "blanket check")

Should one join the PEN club? They are now using you as an inducement for me—you, and if I hurry up and join I can soon go to a conference in Rio. A friend of mine here left it because he says it was taken over by the communists here, but I really don't know.

You made me feel somewhat better about "The Riverman" by calling it a "fairy tale." I think I have 13–15 poems towards a book, but of course always feel that the best are yet to come.— My drunkard one, and one about Trollope in Washington[4] which I like very much at the moment, and which is probably very much influenced by you. Also one about Hopkins *and* E. Dickinson,[5] at the same time. I feel so cheered up by this interest displayed in Boston that everything seems much nearer the surface, or the possible, than usual.

Oh—I am going to write to Mrs. White about that nasty little notice of Flannery's book.[6] It makes me really angry. They devote so much space to

1 "God-Intoxicated Hillbillies," *Time* (Feb. 29, 1960).
2 Anne Sexton, *To Bedlam and Part Way Back* (1960).
3 "Mrs. Sexton writes with the now enviable swift lyrical openness of a Romantic Poet, yet in her content she is a realist and describes her very personal experience with an almost Russian accuracy and abundance. Her poems stick in my mind. I don't see how they can fail to make the great stir they deserve to make."
4 "A Drunkard" (EB-*EAP*); "From Trollope's Journal" (EB-*CP*).
5 Drafts of this poem remain fragmentary. EB never titled it and it does not appear in EB-*EAP*.
6 "Briefly Noted" (review of Flannery O'Connor's *The Violent Bear It Away*), *The New Yorker* (March 19, 1960).

insignificant novels—and that notice wasn't even accurate, which they're so proud of being.

I liked Roethke when I saw him—huge people like that often have that lightning quickness. I went to Grand Central with him in a cab; he was almost missing his train to the west, and I suggested my doing something while he did something else. I forget what, but to help him catch the train, and his last words to me were, "You're a quick kid in a caper." Where is he going in Europe, I wonder? I've wanted to go to the Barnes collection for years, of course. My friend Margaret Miller is the only person I ever heard of who went cold (after having failed when she applied as a curator of the Museum of Modern Art) and not only got in but also saw Mrs. Barnes's famous shrubberies, a personally conducted tour. It is funny you mentioned Hoffman, too—because that Joaquim Francisco[1] had also translated him and was surprised when I said I'd never heard of him. Also funny the Quakers made you feel "soiled & disreputable," because I used to go calling with Jane Dewey on some awfully rich Quaker neighbors of hers who owned a whole 18th century mill in Maryland, plus all their Philadelphia houses, etc., and I remember saying after one dinner there that they made me feel really decadent, for the first time in my life. (Jane D couldn't see it.) I never can quite believe in such innocence, though. They raised lambs and watched birds and ground flour and made their own furniture, all in the utmost luxury. But to make a circle back to Roethke: I went to hear him read at the YMHA, and I just wished he wouldn't—it was real torture.

There is a new or re-modeled apartment house on Beacon Street now, "modern," three or four floors, 2 apts., quite small, that has appeared in the various architecture reviews Lota gets and that I like very much. I wonder if you've seen it or know the people who live in it? It is very elegant; squeezed in between two old houses; a beautiful job, I think. We've had a very nice English city-planner here recently. He and Lota agreed perfectly about everything, from Brasília to Basra (one of his jobs), and we were very much taken with him. He actually *noticed* "The Riverman" in a magazine,[2] sat down and read it, and patted me on the back—that was his first visit—so now we think the English are warm, talkative, gesticulate a lot, argue, and are excitable and probably passionate. One Max Lock.

I'll try to get some copies of things off to you the first of the week. We are going to Ouro Prêto (the most perfect colonial town, a long day's drive from here) next week for a few days. Oh, I think I once sent you some photo-

1 Joaquim-Francisco Coelho.
2 "The Riverman" (EB-*CP*).

graphs of sculpture by Aleijadinho, the last, and best Brazilian, baroque sculptor. That name means "little cripple"; it is not known what he had, but all his last work was done, like Renoir's, with tools tied to his hands. Ouro Prêto has whole churches by him—tiny, but lovely.

It is time for the big week-end market expedition, and I must take this to mail. Lota has been miserable with an infected tooth. We spent ten days in Rio, and two this week—but she is better now and being very funny from sheer relief. Tomorrow an English couple come to tea. The wife gave us the Siamese cat, and I think they are just coming to see if we're treating him well since we don't know them at all. But I have always *wanted* to know someone named "Featherstone."[1] When I went to their Rio house to get the kitten, I found a strange witch-like young woman with huge pale gray eyes, surrounded with cats, including one small Brazilian wild cat, all very shy and skittery, and a shy, gap-toothed husband who even wore a waistcoat. The house smelled very catty. (I assure you, ours doesn't.) They say the husband is apt to turn to guests and mumble hopelessly, "Wouldn't you like a cat?"

I must make my lists like Hamlet.[2]— Thank you, Cal, for your amazing first aid; I can almost hear the siren.

Give my love to your ladies—with lots for yourself,
    Elizabeth

Lota sends hers, too.

One wouldn't guess from this what is on all our minds—we get short wave radio here—if only K would have apoplexy.[3]

216.

June 29th, 1960
Dear Cal:

We're rushing off to Rio to two dentist's appointments and, this evening, a lottery of paintings—maybe we'll win something. I just wanted to tell you

1 Cf. Miss Featherstone, the stage name of Isabella Paul, British actress who made her name in 1853 playing Captain Macheath in *The Beggar's Opera*.

2 "Now, sir, young Fortinbras, / Of unimproved mettle hot and full, / Hath in the skirts of Norway here and there / Shark'd up a list of lawless resolutes, / For food and diet, to some enterprise / That hath a stomach in't"; William Shakespeare, *Hamlet*, I:i, 110.

3 The Soviets shot down an American U-2 spy plane on May 1, 1960. Nikita Khrushchev demanded an apology from the United States, which Eisenhower refused, causing the collapse of the Paris Summit on May 16. Given Hamlet just above, cf. "Sense, sure, you have, / Else could you not have motion; but sure, that sense / Is apoplex'd" (William Shakespeare, *Hamlet*, III:iv, 81).

I think I've written ALL the letters—except now the banker has written again to ask *how much* I want . . . That's naïve of him. I had a nice letter from Agnes—I think they all meet in September again. Now I don't know whether I should try for a Guggenheim, too, or what . . . As they all surely know—one can't really get very far in Europe—after one's got there from S.A.—on $3,600. However, IF I can finish up two stories, say, plus this, if it goes through—then we might be able to get away. It's all my own fault, anyway. Look at how Elizabeth can turn out a story! And if they feel I have already had my share of grants I'll be the first to agree with them . . .

Agnes said you were a tremendous success on Boston Common, with an audience of thousands and encore after encore[1]—"if that is what they're called when they are poems." That is wonderful—the Transcendentalists are turning green.

I had a letter from Robie Macauley who's coming here for the PEN thing (I've never met him), and another letter from someone whose name I can't read—also coming—(not you, by any chance?)

It's been the coldest winter in years—snow in Buenos Aires—and probably in the 30's here, and we have huddled around the stove, holding cats on our laps, for four or five days. This seemed to have a good effect on me. A batch of poems is getting finished at last, and here is the first one.[2] It's almost word for word out of *North America*,[3] and I trust doesn't sound too much like you! I'll probably make a lot more changes.

Thank you again for your good deeds; I am very grateful.

Please write soon—with much love,

Elizabeth

217.

[Castine, Maine]
July 12, 1960

Dearest Elizabeth:

Glad the grant seems in the bag. I hope the banker will up the amount, and oh me! I hope part of your tour will be New York. People come and come, and when some drop out, others fairly engaging replace them, but I find it hard to be so far away from you and Peter Taylor—above all, you!

I've had a funny summer translating *Phèdre* into English heroic cou-

1 RL read for the Boston Arts Festival on June 5, 1960.
2 "Trollope in Washington" (typescript, Houghton); see "From Trollope's Journal" (EB-*CP*).
3 Anthony Trollope, *North America* (1862).

plets—not really, the meter is more my own run-on couplet. It rolls off, a river of declamation. I have almost four acts done, and ought to have a version by the beginning of August. It's awfully pleasant to be able to work day after day, a labor of versification rather than inspiration, for really good poetry is, I think, impossible. Yet I'd like to go on churning this way, and hope to do a play of my own, or something a little less grueling than short poems. I was rather surprised at being able to do my Public Garden poem,[1] and see there's a certain relief in having an occasion and limits. I'll finish off my book of short translations after this, then the opera business. Then—what?

I like your Trollope, and I think you never do a poem without your own intuition. You are about the only poet now who calls her own tune—rather different from even Pound or Miss Moore, who built original styles then continue them—but yours, especially the last dozen or so, are all unpredictably different. I mightn't have known this was yours. Though it is. I'd suggest, maybe, that the sonnet division should be dropped. It's more a dramatic monologue. If you revise, you might put in more lines. I see nothing wrong though. I see one line I might have written while doing Racine, "just higher than Potomac's swampy brim."[2]

Did I ever say anything about your comments on Sexton? I'm rather abashed about my blurb—not too much, because, in an odd way she is much more inspired than she knows how to be, and has done what scores of young poets, some of them more knowing than she is, will never do: written a book that can be remembered. I don't really like the tone underneath, or care much about the experience, or rather the experience's impact on Anne Sexton.

By the way, meter is a puzzle to me now. Metrical verse and unmetrical verse seem almost two different species. Something quite pleasant both to write and to read is added by meter, but it's something free verse doesn't want at all, and which seems to have little to do with experience or intuition, though I know all the standard answers to this. I think it's some architectural, building up effect that makes meter impressive. You have something explicit and hard to do, and your reader can spot this, criticize the difficulties, and enjoy the obvious work. I'm fascinated by something in between like the great passages in *The Changeling*,[3] where meter is kept but its big, applied, laid-on-thick billows disappear. What a figure!

I write you so much helter-skelter shop talk! We've had an unusually

---

1 "For the Union Dead" (RL-*CP*), which RL read at the Public Garden for the Boston Arts Festival on June 5, 1960.
2 "From Trollope's Journal," line 6 (EB-*CP*).
3 Thomas Middleton, *The Changeling* (1653).

serene Maine summer with a good bit of picnicking and tennis. Harriet can do a terrifying thing—almost turn twist on the hand-grips(?), whatever those rings on chains four feet in the air are called. I've been feeling more that I may at last really be content not to boil over any more. I can always see the possibility, and now seem cold about it. I don't suppose there's too much I want that I don't really have—at least what I want isn't to be run after to the ends of the earth, but is at home, near at hand. I guess you found that ten years ago. I don't think you were ever much tempted by running off the edge. I wonder if you had another trouble—how naïve of me to [be] making tentative suppositions, when I know you so well—but I wonder if you ever found reading and writing curiously self-sufficient. There are times when one hardly needs people, most people, though they are welcome when they come. I guess my family does, for most purposes. I rather dread New York, or rather feel the pouring in of new impression and acquaintances ought to go to someone else who needs them more. However, the opera ought to be a delight.

Robie Macauley can be very good company. He talks well about books with plots and has a lot of plotted war impressions. He was in the intelligence service, and went to Germany and then Japan in 1945. He's an old Kenyon crony and one of my best friends. A literary man, I guess, more than a writer, and this has something to do with his character, a little pushed and yet subordinate to something. I wish I were the other guy who wrote you about coming to Brazil. I'm not.

Oh, it's terribly exciting that you are writing. Go on striking, while it's there. Then there'll be two or more books, both huge. Love to Lota, Lizzie sends hers.

Love,
Cal

218.

July 27th, [1960] I think—Friday, at any rate—and marketing-day,
and the day someone is bound to arrive . . .

Dearest Cal:

Please never stop writing me letters—they always manage to make me feel like my higher self (I've been re-reading Emerson) for several days . . . Lots of things have been happening here, at least lots for me, here. But first, I don't think I've ever really commented much on "The Drinker." I find it even more horrendous in *PR*—although I hate to give up that soap-dish.[1] The most awful line for me is "even corroded metal . . . ," and the cops at the end are beautiful, of course[2]—with a sense of release that only the poem, or another fifth of Bourbon,[3] could produce. As a cook I feel I should tell you that soured milk is NOT junket, but the picture is all too true.[4] (I have a poem that has a galvanized bucket in it, too—it is one I started in Key West[5]—and I think I even used the phrase "dead metal," oh dear—but it has nothing to do with my "Drunkard" one.[6]) The sense of time is terrifying—have hours gone by, or one awful moment? How long have the cars been parked?

That Anne Sexton I think still has a bit too much romanticism and what I think of as the "our beautiful old silver" school of female writing which is really boasting about how "nice" *we* were. V. Woolf, K.A.P.,[7] Bowen, R. West, etc.—they are all full of it. They have to make quite sure that the reader is not going to mis-place them socially, first—and that nervousness interferes constantly with what they think they'd like to say . . . I wrote a story at Vassar that was too much admired by Miss Rose Peebles, my teacher, who was very proud of being an old-school Southern lady, and suddenly this fact about women's writing dawned on me, and has haunted me ever since.

I have re-arranged the Trollope poem, taking your advice, and I think it is improved. The whole thing should really be in quotation marks, I suppose; the reason it doesn't sound like me is because it sounds like Trollope . . . It probably should be quite a bit longer. Have you ever read his *North America?* I just copied out some of the Washington chapter. Well, I don't know whether it is a virtue or not, never to sound the same way more than once or twice! It sounds too much like facility, and yet I don't feel a bit facile, God knows.

Robie Macauley wrote me that I had been made a member of the P.E.N. by John Farrar, willy-nilly, and then Lota and I were invited to the Embassy luncheon given for the U.S. group—only Lota refused to go. So I went, and met Robie & his wife, and John Brooks of *The New Yorker* and his wife, and Elmer Rice, and May Sarton, none of whom I'd ever met before. I wished so much you had been there—all else aside, I would have loved to have intro-

1 "The Drinker," *Partisan Review* (Spring 1960); see RL-*CP*. The "soap-dish" refers to a typescript sent to EB, now missing.
2 See "The Drinker," lines 25 and 36–38 (RL-*CP*).
3 See "The Drinker," line 2 (RL-*CP*).
4 See "The Drinker," line 32 (RL-*CP*).
5 Unknown draft; "galvanized" also appears in line 57 of the later "Santarém" (EB-*CP*).
6 See "The Drinker," lines 15–16 (RL-*CP*); see also "A Drunkard" (EB-*EAP*).
7 Katherine Anne Porter.

duced you to our Ambassador: "Mr. Cabot, Mr. Lowell."[1] (When I told Robie about your having read to 3,000 people on the Common, he said, "A Lowell speaks to Boston.") I liked Robie very much and am only sorry I didn't have more of a chance to talk to him. He was very busy of course being a delegate. The next day, however, Lota and I did see more of them. We dragged the Americans, with the exception of Elmer Rice, all the way up here, by Volkswagen and bus, for dinner, and I think everyone had rather a good time. But I still didn't have much chance to talk to Robie because I was too busy being a hostess, and he is very quiet, or was here at any rate. He seems very very bookish and also, from time to time, extremely funny, and I liked him a lot. The wife seems very nice, too. John Brooks, a *New Yorker* type, I think—and his wife a cute little Vassar girl with a convict hair-cut, terribly worried (after a few gin tonics) about who she *is*. May Sarton much addicted to the higher cliché—but as Lota says, it's still better than the lower cliché . . . I had a feeling she was getting on her companions' nerves by then, and I'm sure Anne Macauley would have had some wonderful things to say if she'd known me better. I remarked that I was afraid I'd had some sort of falling-out with Randall, and she said "Good!" All wives seem to feel strongly about Randall! "Never lifts a finger," etc. . . . Anyway, it was all very enjoyable; the weather not too good, nor the dinner. I only went to half a P.E.N. lecture, by Mario Praz, and found it sounded much better when read at home without the distractions of Graham Greene stomping out and Moravia scowling like a small Mussolini, etc. The advantages of that P.E.N. (a Brazilian finally told me what the letters stand for[2]) seems to be that members get sent to expensive-to-get-to places, like Japan and South America. But the disadvantage is that they don't seem to have time to see the places when they get there and just have to submit to being excruciatingly bored— but maybe I underestimate what goes on, because I didn't see much of it, after all. Oh, Miss Sarton told us that she had joined "out of a sense of obligation" and then, "when life opens a door . . . one shouldn't refuse,"—to go to Rio, I think. Afterwards Lota asked me, "Did *Life* Magazine send her, or what?"

Robie told me you are going to Copenhagen, and that should be more interesting than this affair. Also that you have swapped houses with Eric Bentley for the winter in N.Y. I wish we could get there in the spring, but I don't

1 John Moors Cabot was U.S. Ambassador to Brazil from 1959 to 1961. "And this is good old Boston / The home of the bean and the cod, / Where the Lowells talk to the Cabots, / And the Cabots talk only to God"; John Collins Bossidy, "Boston" (1910).
2 Poets, playwrights, essayists, editors, and novelists.

know. I went to see a friend off to Europe last week. She was going 3rd class on a new English ship and it is dirt cheap so I went to see what it is like and I think I could stand it for 13 days—to Lisbon and back for about $300 IF the Chapelbrook thing comes through, however, I don't feel at all sure about that.

You ask if I have ever found "reading and writing curiously self-sufficient." Well, both Lota and I read from 7 AM intermittently until 1 AM every day, and all sorts of things, good and bad, and once in a while I think—what if I should run out of things to read, in English, by the time I'm sixty and have to spend my old age reading French or Portuguese or even painfully taking up a new language? And then I've always had a day dream of being a light-house keeper, absolutely alone, with no one to interrupt my reading or just sitting, and although such dreams are sternly dismissed at 16 or so they always haunt one a bit, I suppose. I now see a wonderful cold rocky shore in the Falklands, or a house in Nova Scotia on the bay, *exactly* like my grandmother's—idiotic as it is, and unbearable as the reality would be. But I think everyone should go, or should have gone, through a stretch of it, like your 3rd Avenue stretch, maybe—a *The Notebook of Malte Laurids Brigge*[1] stretch—and perhaps it is a recurrent need. But let us not say, to quote Miss S again—"I've fallen in love with solitude!"

What you say about meter: well, I have loads of thoughts on the subject and I think I'll have to write again tomorrow. I have a theory now that all the arts are growing more and more "literary"; that it is a late stage, perhaps a decadent stage, and that un-metrical verse is more "literary" and necessarily self-conscious than metrical— If I were Shapiro I'd write a book about it.[2] (And have you read *Art & Illusion?* by one Gombrich?—it is fascinating.[3]) I find it is time to go to market. What kind of plan do you have for your opera or is it an opera? Now you must teach Harriet to swim—or have you—it is just the age to learn. I believe in swimming, flying, and crawling, and bur-rowing.

  With much love,
   Elizabeth

---

1 Rainer Maria Rilke, *The Notebook of Malte Laurids Brigge* (1910).
2 See Karl Shapiro, *In Defense of Ignorance* (1960).
3 E. H. Gombrich, *Art and Illusion: A Study in the Psychology of Pictorial Representation* (1960).

219.

Dearest Cal:

I find I have overlooked something, after all, in that application and I am writing to you very hastily, from Rio, to ask you for one more favor . . . I wrote at length to that Mr. Mansfield and then to Agnes M, and then to MacLeish, and I thought that that took care of everything, but apparently not. Mr. Mansfield has written to me twice more saying that they still haven't received a letter from my "sponsor." I waited the first time because I thought maybe it wasn't necessary, but now he has written again. The committee meets sometime in September and I should get a letter to him before then. Will you, please, be my "sponsor"?—or if you'd rather not can you think of anyone suitable? As I said, I'd rather not ask Marianne this time . . . I should think a very short letter saying that you could recommend me would do, or possibly that you had approved of *some* of the poems you know me to be working on for the volume I hope to finish in 1961, etc. . . . I HATE to ask you this but time seems short, suddenly, and for some reason I feel quite sure they are going to turn me down. (Not that it wouldn't be deserved, for my laziness and procrastination, etc. . . .)

Mr. Harry K. Mansfield

Ropes, Gray, Best, Coolidge and Rugg

50 Federal Street, Boston 10

Why not "Gray ropes best rug. Coolidge."

Lota and I are here to have one tooth extracted, each, and in some mysterious way we have both avoided it and now shall have to come back next week, probably . . . "Thou hast made me and shall thy works decay?"[1] Oh dear yes.— We attended a film festival in Petrópolis, of all places, and saw "Les 400 Coups" and "Hiroshima, mon Amour"—both excellent in parts, and in different ways—[2]

I hope you read that Aksakov (?) book if you never have, and tell me what you think—*Memories of Childhood*[3] I re-read it and then read a contemporary "Memories of C" called *Memoirs of a Public Baby*[4] and felt as if I had taken a fast, sickening fall through a hundred years—// But when I get back

1 John Donne, "Thou hast made me, and shall thy work decay?," line 1 (1635).
2 *Les Quatre cents coups*, dir. François Truffaut (1959); *Hiroshima mon amour*, dir. Alain Resnais (1959).
3 Sergey Aksakov, *Years of Childhood*, trans. Alec Brown (1960).
4 Philip O'Connor, *Memoirs of a Public Baby* (1958).

home and back to the better typewriter I shall write again. I do hope you are all well and flourishing. Child Care Note (after a PM s[p]ent helping entertain last week)—straight liquid shampoo makes marvelous soap-bubbles—the very biggest and toughest—

    With love to you and your family—
        Elizabeth

220.

August 9, 1960[1]

Dearest Elizabeth:

    I've been coming to Boston at intervals during the summer to keep up my therapy. This is the last, and I am gathering a clutter of things together to take to Maine in a few hours. Strange times, like a retreat, mostly alone here in the empty house translating, and usually a wonderful letter from you waiting for me.

    In "The Drinker," I've half put the soap-dish back (a little cute) with "the keys and used silver razor blades / shine in a saucer." The junket was a joke, I know milk turns to clabber. Liked your Sexton and old silver remarks. I feel I'm her half-discoverer and now can't keep up with her new admirers. One lags. I don't think anyone could admire the best Snodgrass more than I do, but a fellow named George Elliott, Jr. to whom I once made some qualifications on Snodgrass, now takes a swipe at me in the *Hudson*, and calls my book a fake *Heart's Needle*.[2] I guess I'll soon be fake Sexton in the *Hudson*. (I have your letter in front of me and am avoiding the pains of organization by now running through it commenting). You're not facile to be different in each poem, and except for the Trollope and perhaps the Pound in another way, your [poems] are always very much you. I just meant, you never let mere style and mannerism write your poems for you as everyone else does. "Randall never lifts a finger!" I feel solaced; I find it so hard to lift a finger and pine over it and feel it's a racket husbands ought to treasure, but a low, maddening furtive vice not to be confessed to, so I'm glad to share this with Randall, all of whose vices, unlike mine, are like Cato's, and extraordinary ones he is proud of. (I'm joking.) How truly and easily you see through people like May Sarton! That's dangerous. I think most people—I seem obsessed with this expression, and don't exactly feel so lofty—see faults out of pique and are just like the people they criticize—you're not. We have

---

1 Enclosed with letter 221.
2 George P. Elliott, "Three Imaginary Autobiographies," *The Hudson Review* (Summer 1960).

swapped with Bentley and will be at 194 Riverside Drive after mid-September. Do think again about skipping New York and going straight to Europe. I'm not going to Copenhagen, alas. The trip would have come just in the midst of moving, and I do occasionally "lift a finger."

More on solitude and meter—I've just been doing some Baudelaire in meter as strict as his, and have never had such a work-out. Three poems have about killed me. I think he is unlike any of the later Baudelairean French poets. In him the fire comes from the descent of his Racinian rhetoric into the material of Flaubert and Balzac, or something of the sort, so that if you remove the finish he's gone, though still rich in a flat prosy way. In Rimbaud and Laforgue, the finish goes; in Mallarmé and Valéry the material. This is a horrible simplification, but he is different. I never realized that such wonder could be done with a sentence, moving through its terrible balances and metric and so seldom turning into a mere fireworks of syntax. I've also done Rimbaud's "Poet at Seven"[1] in rhyming irregular lines and think I've lost his terrible bull-like perversity, jamming and crush, the detestable (as Louise Bogan would say) alexandrine, yet keeping it. I think he rather hated meter and syntax, though a great master of both, while Baudelaire gloried in both.

I guess I don't really like solitude. The fun is hammering bits of it out of a crowded life. For one's self, I think one should keep [the] door open for strict, disorderly and free meters. God knows the chances are so slim of breaking through the crust, writing something alive—one ought to have several possible techniques ready.

Gombrich, funny, just after your [letter] I had dinner with Spender and he brought up Gombrich. I must read him. Isn't poor Karl's a dull roar of bombast; it's the resonance I mind not the opinions, though and think the opinions aren't real at all but were chosen to let him thunder. But what a curse to thunder and say nothing!

Harriet is terrific, like living with the new forces.[2] I don't think she knows how frail we are, but being a child, she is heavy on her feet and we can almost keep up with her by cheating and using cunning and withdrawing into the shadows she can't understand.

Well goodbye, my Dear,

Love,

Cal

---

1 Arthur Rimbaud, "Les poètes de sept ans" (1871).
2 "The new American must be either the child of the new forces or a chance sport of nature"; Henry Adams, *The Education of Henry Adams* (1918), 501.

221.

Dearest Elizabeth:

I enclose an old, rather jaunty and silly letter I wrote two weeks ago and somehow never mailed. The summer here draws to an end, next Wednesday we leave for Boston, then two weeks later for New York. My *Phédre* is finished; at least I have a coherent version. There'll be tinkering, heightening and clarifying to be done, but you can't do much with 1600 lines, all marching in their metallic meter. I don't know what to think. Sometimes it seems overwhelmingly shining and dramatic, at others, mere carpentry and slipshod at that. I am uncertain, too, of its future. I think it may be ignored by poetry readers and lashed by Racine experts, or maybe it will be done on Broadway, and people will say I've translated an author no one has ever translated. The whole business of translating is fascinating, like living in some[one] else's house and being carried by their framework. I've now done three Baudelaire poems and drafts of four more and would like to make a little collection of ten or twenty. I know you like him particularly and will send you a bunch when I have a group. Doing anything of my own seems distasteful at the moment, and I feel a fluctuating fever to get this business finished—also a feeling of comfort, a supply of enchanting hard work, enough firewood to last me till I tire.

We're just back from Roque Island, again. The motor that used [to] drive the lobster boat at sixty miles an hour shook itself to pieces. Now the boat goes at a more conventional speed. Bob Gardner has imported three donkeys that move like skulls on the bare hillside, dreaming of corn and dresses to eat. Oil still burns in the houses, but the yawl has electricity and a telephone. Log bridges are caving in and one feels the absence of the father's iron patriarchal hand. One day we drove to St. Andrew's, where I bought an unauthenticated Burne Jones—a naked woman and a clothed woman like Titian but very English and Victorian, puritanical and improper, from two English sharks, Mrs. Fitz Maurice and Colonel St. John, distinguished service, military cross, next in line to the title of Earl of Bolinbroke, born in a fifteenth century Renaissance manor, taken over by the government for taxes—"We had to pay a shilling to see it." The Colonel grew up with the picture, and asked for documents, murmured, "I know no more about it than I know about myself." Mrs. Fitz Maurice, showing pictures of Bolinbroke Manor, said, "You see he's sound as a bell." Then we all connived like rogues in Dickens to get the painting without duty across the border. No questions were asked, but Lee

Gardner was pale and nauseated with guilt and Bob, so excited he drove fifty miles north instead of south.

Oh dear, next winter! We're looking forward to it, but I have been having long narrative dreams with plots and jagged discoveries. We rather appalled the Gardners, rather uneasily married, Lee wants to go to the beauty parlors, defend the aristocracy and accrete furniture, and Bob wants to be off anthropologizing at the ends of the earth—can I get back to my subject? by suggesting that marriage, though much the best and only conceivable way of living, was nevertheless an imposition of the gods and that we felt like accomplices in our complete harmony on this subject. We seem more ramshackle, torn, and happy than most people. Harriet is becoming just like us, full of storms and gaiety—only more adult. She acts out everything we do, and also seems like the winner of a Channel swim about to dive off for another victory.

Well, goodbye Dearest Elizabeth, till we reach the city. I've mailed the letter to Mansfield. I imagine all is set.

Love from us all to you and Lota,

Cal

222.

October 6th, 1960

Dearest Cal:

The good news came yesterday and what wonderful lovely $$$$$, 7,000 of them for 2 years . . .[1] It is all thanks to you, I know perfectly well. Perhaps some to Agnes, too, and I shall write to her next. I've already written, yesterday, to Mr. Harry K. Mansfield, who wrote me—it must be that I have a guilty conscience about all this because from his quite innocent and formal little letters I have drawn morbid conclusions that he doesn't *like* me, personally; disapproves highly of my poetry; and probably thinks it should have gone to Donald Hall or somebody . . . We are both delighted, naturally, and I honestly did not expect to receive it. It seems to me that I have a lucky streak every once in a while that I don't deserve—or perhaps it is awfully good friends. What we plan to do now is save it up until next spring and then take off for a trip, to Portugal (briefly), drive across northern Spain, spend two months or so in Italy, go to Greece, and then depending on lots of things, mostly how much *more* money we can acquire, go to London for a

1 From the Chapelbrook Foundation.

while and maybe Amsterdam . . . Election day was Monday here and so far Lota's candidate[1] is away ahead (no voting machines, so it takes 10 days or so for the returns to come in—if there isn't a *coup* in the meantime), and what with the Vargas gang being really out after 30-some years, and my being so awfully rich, Lota is more cheerful than I have seen her in ages. It had been a very bad stretch for us both, but for her particularly: troubles with her adopted son that just can't be solved, family troubles, lawsuits, all kinds of things, and, since her family has been in politics, etc. for so long, she has been so depressed about the state of the country ever since I've been here— (Thank God I don't have to take the U.S. elections so personally, although they are depressing enough.) Well, this paragraph is a fine jumble. As a matter of fact I tried to write to you yesterday, too, and found I couldn't concentrate enough—so you see the enchanting dither the Chapelbrooks have put me into. DO you know what it is?—and whose money it is, etc.? I'd sort of like to know a bit more about it; probably Agnes does, of course.

Somewhere, sometime in this paid-for stretch I hope we can see you. From what I hear of prices in New York, I don't feel as if I'd ever see it again, but maybe, if I can get two or three stories done, we might be able to get back by way of the USA, or perhaps you and Elizabeth will be going to Europe around then, too?

I have an awful lot to tell you, I think, and yet actually no news except the first item. I want very much to see the Baudelaire translations and wonder which ones you chose,—except it's usually more what one can do than what one likes best, in translating. You are right about its being the ideal backlog work, but I have always found it too *hard*, or impossible, perhaps because I tried to do it too strictly. My dream is to write stories when I can't do anything else, however, I have been doing a little translating, for that friend João Cabral de Melo.[2] *POETRY* has asked me for Brazilian translations ever since I've been here, and he is the only one I really like much, but he doesn't come out very well in English, either—too long-winded. Oh these luscious Latin languages and all that assonance and how tempting it seems to be for them to go on and on and on.

We liked being reminded of Roque Island—and no wonder the Gardner's marriage is "uneasy"! He should have married a sportswoman who wanted to go to visit the pygmies with him. (Someone more my type!) I didn't feel that Lee was a "beauty" exactly but she is the beauty-type, I'm afraid, and it

---

1 Jânio Quadros.
2 João Cabral de Melo Neto, "From *The Death and Life of a Severino*," *Poetry* (Oct.–Nov. 1963); see EB-*CP*.

must be awful to be married to. We had one to tea yesterday—an old friend of Lota's—just Lota's age—who was a *real* beauty, too, and I felt if I were her husband (she's only had two, being a pretty good Catholic) I would commit suicide—the sadness of constantly living with an aging beauty must be such. She talked on about all their mutual friends and the state they're now in: weight, skin, hair-color, face-lifting, etc. "Lotinha—I swear she is completely *deformée*," in the most luscious Spanish accent. And these ladies believe in "society" the way they believe in God; and I suspect that as a group they have changed very little since the times of the Greeks and Romans—or Egyptians. Physical beauty, then "chic," money, jewels, health, diseases— and sex away along at the end. I wonder if there is an equivalent in contemporary Russian society and I suppose there must be: ladies and gentlemen vying with each other in the cut of their dresses or uniforms and their black market toilet waters and champagnes . . . Poor Bob Gardner—your sex does get taken in. The unauthenticated Burne Jones sounds wonderful and where have you hung it? (Have I told you about my *carranca*: that is, a figurehead, from a river boat, I acquired a few months ago? I must send you a photograph: he, or she, whichever it is, is a devil with small horns, but a sweetly *dumb* face, tongue hanging out slightly, and long yellow hair—carved wood, about four feet high, and most of the paint gone. I admired some of them for a long time and when Schapiro was here to my surprise he commented on the same ones and said they were "Romanesque"—"almost as good as Vézelay." So I just trusted my taste after that and plunged in and bought one on installments . . .)

You sound very clever about your little girl, too (sympathetic perhaps I should say) and that is my worst regret in life, although I would have been such a nervous, over-devoted mother probably.

Well—George Elliott, Jr.—he keeps turning up all the time. He sent me poems several years ago which I just couldn't like; then I liked him pretty well when I met him in N.Y., but because I didn't have time to go to see him I think he thought I didn't, or his wife thought I didn't or something—it got embarrassing—and I'll probably get "swiped" at next time, too. These people are so touchy. I have just got a batch of AWFUL poetry from a Fulbright fellow apparently, in Rio, who writes to me as if he were Shakespeare writing, perhaps, to Fletcher—or someone young and *apache*-like. (slangy)[1]

---

1 Unfinished; see letter 224.

223.

194 Riverside Drive
New York City
October 10, 1960

Dearest Elizabeth:

Really just a note to let you know we've survived moving and like it here. New York seems so full of people after Boston, where intellectual women don't seem to exist (so far they haven't here, but with a difference), and our men friends all seem to drift on trust funds or hold Harvard University chairs.

Going to opera rehearsals is strangely passive. William Meredith and I go together. No one knows or cares who we are. The directors seem like tough Broadway people, the sopranos like highschool girls and the tenors like comic-strip thugs. A world of hurry, craftsmanship and controlled calculated tantrums. The singers usually have only a misty understanding of their librettos unless they are in English, and even then not much. And I can't read a note. On Monday nights I teach modern poetry at the New School and after five days of crawling non-entity become for my brief hour a maestro. I prefer being a non-entity.

My *Phédre* is done and by the end of the week I'll have enough good copies to mail you one. It's certainly hack-work, but maybe eloquent and maybe headed for money and production, though god knows how things work in theater. Can anyone recite fathoms of heroic couplets? Would anyone listen?

A beautiful poem of yours is in *The New Yorker*, rising wonderfully in the last stanza and perfect in the way several poems in *North & South* were perfect.[1]

Have you heard from the fellowship? What are your plans? Do write soon, and do plan on coming here. This is a wonderful city to meet in. Now particularly, with the turning leaves. My study looks out on the Hudson—more ocean than Maine—and Central Park gives a feeling of huge, rather park-like wilds.

We are all fine. Harriet is the only girl in her class that has been to nursery school before, and she lets the others know it to their chagrin.

Our love to you and Lota,

Cal

---

1 "Song for a Rainy Season," *The New Yorker* (Oct. 8, 1960); see EB-*CP*.

224.[1]

Dear Cal:

This first letter seemed so bad to me that I gave up, and the next morning we went to Cabo Frio for over a week and just got back. I took typewriter and all to Cabo Frio, but of course never even opened it. I have had you on my mind all this time and yesterday morning when I woke up I had been having a long dream about you—in which I was saying—"Tell E. I did admire her Chessman piece"[2]—and we seemed to be going to a *picnic* in a forest in Maine or Nova Scotia . . . Then your letter arrived the same morning. I am ashamed of not having let you know sooner about the grant—since I know I owe it to you. We plan and dream but cannot be very definite about dates yet.

The young man who sent me the bad poetry was due for lunch today but called up to say he couldn't come—he's a Fulbright, teaching at the University, and a whole small book of Brazilian poems arrived shortly after the original batch. I feel for the honor of the USA I have to be as nice as I can but I am dreading it. I get so depressed with every number of POETRY, *The New Yorker*, etc. (this one I am swearing off of, except for prose, forever, I hope) so much adequate poetry all sounding just alike and *so* boring—or am I growing frizzled small and stale[3] or however you put it? There seems to be too much of everything—too much painting, too much poetry, too many novels—and much too much money, I suppose. (Although I certainly welcomed mine.) And no one really feeling anything much . . .

Just before we went away we had 28 or so German architects arrive by bus—with half an hour's warning and the servants given the afternoon off—to see this house. Their bus driver mutinied at our mountain road and Lota made trip after trip—but a good many of them came up on foot, straight up, for about a mile, and arrived panting and red and bowing and heel-clicking and hand-kissing—fascinating long hair-dos—about 3 female architects among them—I lost track in the hubbub. Some were very nice. One cute little one with blue eyes and a small beard who cornered me in the kitchen and talked and talked—he wrote poetry, too, and wished his wife were along because "She is very active in the American German Women's Club of Heidelberg." Everywhere one looked there were large seats in loose trousers,

---

1 Posted with letter 222.
2 Elizabeth Hardwick, "The Life and Death of Caryl Chessman," *Partisan Review* (Summer 1960).
3 "Cured, I am frizzle, stale and small"; "Home After Three Months Away," line 40 (RL-*CP*).

bending over, taking photographs. We asked in one German neighbor, to help, and German, English, Spanish, Portuguese, French, a little Italian, were spoken. I can't make out what kind of architects they are—one asked me what Lota's best and biggest Calder *was*, and had never heard of Calder (who's had lots of shows in Germany, etc.) Next week we're expecting an American group.

Cabo Frio was marvelous as ever. The weather a bit windy and the water a bit cold, and no fishing—but we went swimming every day on those beaches I'd like so much to show you. One small one has a grotto at one side—the sand is mostly amethyst quartz, a deep lavender, streaked with white as the waves wash the other sand up into it, the sides full of quartzes and pot-holes with huge stones still whirling around in them as the waves come up—lots of sea-urchins in little niches, like ikons, and huge pure white or black or lavender-ish rocks, very smooth, arranged in the shadows till you'd think an extremely good Japanese gardener had been at work.

Your opera work sounds wonderful. I wish I knew a great deal more about fitting words to music and vice versa, and I hope sometime you hear the Pound poem sung and can tell me what it sounds like.[1] That same boy— Rorem—did three. I think you could do some fine recitative . . . Sam Barber has asked me for librettos every once in a while but I don't like his music at all. You sound very active and busy and I think happy.— & I still sound jumbled, I realize, and maybe it is too much sun and beach-combing. Quadros has definitely won the election and everyone feels better.[2] (*The NY Times* always calls him the "conservative" candidate, but such distinctions don't apply here at all. The last governments here have been pro-labor in the way that Perón was, more or less.) Also a friend of ours is now governor of the State of Guanabara—city of Rio—and has promised to build a school a week.[3] One feels very cheered up by this, and then reads a terrifying piece about universities in California, in TIME,[4] and wonders what education is coming to, or if there is any such thing, etc., and two of my old school-teachers write me despairing letters about Yes-or-No-answer College Board exams!

My part-time work at present seems to be baking bread. I took it up a while ago and now find I can make wonderful bread fairly quickly, once a week—it sounds food-faddish I'm afraid. Today a mason named Joaquim

1 Ned Rorem, "Visits to St. Elizabeths: (Bedlam)" (1964).
2 Jânio Quadros was inaugurated on January 31, 1961, and served until August 25 (see note to letter 238).
3 Carlos Lacerda.
4 "Master Planner," *Time* (Oct. 17, 1960).

(Portuguese, with floppy beret and a fantastic vocabulary) is building us an outdoor oven, beehive shaped. He has begun it by making the mold of the inside, a nice little heap of wet sand. Then it will be cemented, white-washed etc.—as elegant as the Taj Mahal, we hope.

Thank you for the kind words about the Rain poem—there are some words that *must* be changed, somehow—and it seems to me now it is in *rumba* rhythm . . .[1]

How did you like Mary on the novel? I thought it was pretty good—very good. I didn't like the "stink" part, but L tells me I'm wrong and that it's effective, there.[2] If you see her, remember me to her.

Please give my love to Elizabeth. I did admire the Chessman piece, and I was very interested because it arrived just after I had tried to have a fight with the man-who's-now-governor-of-the-State about the case—he used it for political capital in a way I found unworthy of him—but then, what can one expect of politicians, and I certainly never in my born days thought *I'd* be trying to pick a fight with a Latin American one— Send another snapshot of Harriet— Please do not OVERDO.— With much love, as always, and I am very very grateful to you for all your help,
　　　Elizabeth

P.S. Tell me who's your favorite saint—or favorites. One can still get beautiful ones here occasionally, and I hope eventually to be able to send you one. I have my eye on a St. Geronimo now—he keeps one from falling, E

225.

November 16, 1960
Dearest Elizabeth:

This letter might have been written under very odd circumstances: trying to be natural while Cartier-Bresson sat in my study taking occasional pictures. He's left now, but I still feel the strain of dutifully trying to forget he was here—I really *did* forget at times, but now realize that was more of a stunt than I realized.

---

1 Cf. "the brook sings loud / from a rib cage / of the giant fern; the vapor / climbs up the thick growth" and "kind to the eyes; / too indulgent, perhaps, / to silver fish, mouse" ("Song for a Rainy Season," lines 13–16 and 34–36, *The New Yorker* [Oct. 8, 1960]) with the final draft of "Song for the Rainy Season" (EB-*CP*).
2 Mary McCarthy, "The Fact in Fiction," *Partisan Review* (Summer 1960). McCarthy points to the corpse of the priest who dies "in the odor of sanctity" in Dostoyevsky's *The Brothers Karamazov*: "The stink of Father Zossiama is the natural generic smell of the novel."

Marvelous about your fellowship, and so much—not that you don't deserve more. We may go to Europe next summer. I'll surely do all I can to see that our lines cross. New York is expensive and rushed. Ever[y] day we talk about moving. There really is so much more happening than in Boston. Yet—still I rather think we *will* move for a few years.

A lot's been happening. My *Phaedra* now has a producer, a Mrs. Bel Geddes, widow of Norman Bel Geddes, blond, somewhere near sixty, 4th wife of four different men, very rich apparently, brought up in Belgium but of Scotch and German extraction, drinks Bloody Marys, is accompanied by an alert servile young man, about my age but more youthful. Well everything is hopping—letters have been sent to Callas, Mme. Feuillere, Melina Mercouri. There's even been a reply from Callas. She is interested but is about to open at La Scala and can't make any decisions. So, there's a chance. It [is] all very heady and I might make piles of money. Everything depends on getting someone tremendously good to do Phaedra. The translation is lively, but of course no masterpiece. Farrar and Straus are mailing you a copy and I am very anxious to get your opinion.

So, there's been all that. Also endless small wrangling with Eric Bentley over publications details. Also going to the Met daily, almost, to rehearsals. I feel a little like Randall and his tennis. That is, doing something very captivating for me, but which can't lead to anything much. However, Eliot writes me that he thinks Stravinsky is looking for a libretto. It would be fun, I guess, to be something unimportant in something wonderful.

We've had our election. First part spent with Philip Rahv at his new girl's apartment. A very strange "girl" by the way, a Mrs. Stillman, Long Island society, divorced, exquisite conventional, costly apartment, very dumb, she and Philip and she showing no trace of emotion. Left about 11:30, Eastern returns in, apparently a Kennedy landslide. Came home. Kennedy began to lose the whole west. Stayed up till 6, and went to bed uncertain and dead. For literally 12 hours, 93 percent of the Michigan, Illinois and Minnesota was in, the candidates a few thousand votes apart. I found I cared awfully that Kennedy win. Who knows? At least we'll have a president for a change.

Not much else. Lizzie, Harriet and I and even Eileen have had lingering, snuffly colds, and consume mountains of Kleenex. Lizzie went to Bergdorf Goodman's and bought herself broke and then accepted two reviews, one of one book and one of thirty, to pay for her dresses.

I have the best therapist I've ever had, a Dr. Viola Bernard who teaches at Columbia and knows all the names I bring up. I'm not doing much and must get back to my other translations. I teach one night a week at the New School and really love New York, but already feel seedy.

My best to Lota and love to you,

Cal

P.S. Would you like the Weill-Brecht-Lenya *Mahagonny?*[1] It's the best thing I've heard for ages and wonderfully sung. What about books? I can order you a carton of poets from the Gotham.

I could tell a hundred queer little stories about the Met. Everyone speaks Met German except for the ten Italian tenors, who can only act off stage. One grotesque scene. They are rehearsing Strauss's *Arabella.*[2] The text is an English translation done by a German. The singers are German and talk in German to the German stage director and conductor. Example: "ist es *leeps* or *lips?*" 15 minutes were spent on the translator's phrase *dubious people* "Dübeeous oder doóbyus?" Bing's whole interest seems to be whether glass crashes at the right moment off stage, whether the curtain comes down at the right moment. Terrible crisis when a plastic glass refused to shatter. Meanwhile the diva, Lisa della Casa, very beautiful, beautiful acting, beautiful singing, lovely pronunciation of the English libretto, is absolutely unintelligible from the second row even if you have just read every word. In front of me an old woman of about a hundred and nine (probably Bing's grandmother), stone deaf and loudly talking just when she shouldn't, looked after by a Marlene Dietrich–looking German woman of about 70, saying "Hush, yess eets schock-ing, neither Engglish nor Ger-r-rman."

226.

December 23, 1960

Dearest Elizabeth:

I hope these will reach you sometime near Christmas, and that you will like them and that you will let me dedicate them to you.[3] The book will come out next fall—I still hope to make changes and perhaps add two or three more poems. My Racine is on its way to you, not air mail, and should reach you soon. It will come out this spring.

---

1 Kurt Weill and Bertolt Brecht, *Aufstieg und Fall der Stadt Mahagonny (Rise and Fall of the City of Mahagonny)*, Wilhelm Brückner-Rüggeberg conducting, with Lotte Lenya repeating the role she created in Leipzig, 1930 (Columbia K3L 243).
2 Richard Strauss, *Arabella* (1933).
3 *Imitations* (1961).

We like it here so much, we have finally decided to sell our Boston house and are about to buy an apartment—15 west 67th, duplex, one huge room two stories high, artist's window, bedroom, kitchen, and dining room on first floor, three bedrooms, all fairly large, fireplace, exposed beams, elevator man, near new Lincoln Center, improving neighborhood, Central Park a few feet away for Harriet. I make this as dull as I can in haste, but we are thrilled with the move and figure we can live here for about what we can in Boston.

I've talked to Marianne Moore a couple times on the phone—"Robert, I am in eclipse." Meaning she, poor thing, had been suffering from dysentery. About The Mid Century [that] gives her book and mine away together and our photographs have been combined into one—"Like Pompeii and Herculaeum." We had a little contest saying how much we loved and admired you—Brooklyn accent, "Of course she venerates you."

Dear Elizabeth, let me know your plans. We will probably go to Boston for a month in May. I may go to England sometime in the late summer or fall if my *Phaedra* opens there. Where can we meet?? Love to you and Lota and Merry Christmas.

Cal

More news & gossip later.

227.

January 26, [1961]
[Rio]

BELIEVE MY LETTER LOST TRANSLATIONS ABSOLUTELY STUNNING PROUD AND PLEASED RECORDS RECEIVED LOVE
ELIZABETH

228.

February 15, 1961

Dearest Elizabeth:

Isn't this Valentine's Day or near it? Such an age since I've heard from you. Your telegram was a joy, but I was grieved to think of the lost letter. Please write it again. The translation book keeps growing—I've added "Mémoire," "Bateau Ivre" and "Les Chercheuses" of Rimbaud; Baudelaire's "Le Voyage," a Victor Hugo, and 12 pages of Villon's "Testament," probably my best translations along with the Baudelaire. Let me know things you question. I am supposed to have my manuscript in by April, but the book won't come out till September. The *Phaedra* will be out in April—a Greek movie and Greek tragedy girl, Melina Mercouri may do the part of Phaedra. I see her next week. We have just submitted the manuscript to the Edinburgh Festival. If they should take [it], I'll be in England in August and September and hope we can meet at length.

Mary McCarthy was here last night *fresh* from her Alabama divorce. Her new man in photographs looks like a combination of Lionel Trilling and Jim Farley—though a year or two younger than Mary, he looks of an older generation. He works in the foreign service in Warsaw.[1] Mary's more at ease and generous than we have ever seen her—no more nervous Broadwater run-downs of everyone under the sun. Bowden's improved too and really very touching—he's still Bowden.

We were invited along with 170 others—writers etc.—to the Kennedy inaugural. Strange scenes with Allen Tate, tails, white gloves, "my duty to the Republic, etc." and Belle, very at ease with Allen at least, huge, described by Francis Biddle as a "sponge wrapped in a quilt." The Kennedy business is very inspiring—with a lot of reservations, I feel like a patriot for the first time in my life. I wrote in the Kennedy guest-book, Robert Lowell, happy that at long last the Goths have left the Whitehouse. Bobby Kennedy read it, and said, "I guess we are the Visigoths." Incredible dinner at the Eberharts[2] with the Tates, Madam Perkins, K. A. Porter, Auden, Ted Spencer's sister and Betty Eberhart's German cousin. Allen, very tight, gave two identical very formal toasts to the memory of Ted Spencer, and Auden helpfully took out all our plates, still unfinished, to the pantry, and Katherine Anne announced that she was seventy.

I am now on my second month of contact lenses and feel a new man—I can see and be seen about twice as well. They're really miraculous—you can swim, sleep, dive, play football or anything under the sun in them.

Did I write you that we have sold (are selling) our Boston house and have bought an apartment, 15 West 67th St.? The apartment has two floors, four bedrooms, kitchen, dining-room, and one huge room, two stories high, with a two story window, fire-place, beams, etc. Miles away on the top of the house, there's an old servants' room which I'll use for my study. We are just off Central Park, where there is a playground for Harriet, and we are very near Broadway and the new Lincoln Center for us to play. Living in New York after Boston is like discovering that there is oxygen in the air—people

1 James West; he married McCarthy on April 15, 1961.
2 Richard Eberhart was living in Washington while he was poetry consultant at the Library of Congress (1959–61).

to talk to, plays, opera, and something in the air that somehow makes people very different here from what they are in Boston. Lizzie has stopped giving dinner parties and now has lunches out with friends. Somehow everything is much merrier, easier and more serious. Other American cities may honor writers, but they can't digest, or worse, they can, and expect you to live as they do. Harriet's a woman now, the most beautiful in New York, I tell [her], if she would stop talking 24 hours a day about what she's wearing.

I run into your old cronies: Pearl Kazin and Loren and am green with envy because they have letters from you. Dearest, please write me! Our love to you and Lota.

229.

March 1st—in like a lamb, if that means anything here—1961

Dearest Cal:

I can't believe I *haven't* written to you all this time because I've been doing it so much of the time in my head—then I did do justice, I thought, to the [*Phaedra*] and that one got lost. (I thought it had because one I mailed at the same time, in Rio, I knew did.) I have here my 1st version of it—dated New Years! Lota read it first, and of course she knows Racine much better than I do, and she was amazed by the way you managed the famous lines and the famous meter—speaking of *"noblesse"* to me. Yet it seems amazingly natural at the same time, but *pure*—but undated. Isn't real tragedy a relief for a change? I feel I've said all this to you before, of course. Anyway, seems a *tour de force* to me, and I hope something is done with it. The nice letter I got from you three days ago mentions a movie! Couldn't we all just be in Greece when they make it—if they make it there?

Also—the records came safe and sound without a cent of duty to pay. That was something I'd really been wanting a lot, too, and thank you very much. We had played it just once, I think—& some of the famous songs twice (it's wonderful)—when my player went on the blink. Today a man is coming, at last, from Petrópolis to repair it—it's something very simple this time—and this evening we'll go to *Mahagonny* again. I wanted so much to get something sent to you—but records, books, etc., are pretty silly since you are at the source. When I get a chance, however, I am going to send you something *by* somebody—something for the new duplex, or its study. I am pleased by your New York move—not that it brings you any nearer. I am lost in admiration for Mary's vitality. Isn't she wonderful. As for Katherine Anne—I know how *she* feels. I feel I'm almost there myself. Belle wrote me a letter at Christmas. She tells me her "writing projects" every year—from what you say she must be expecting a baby? I envy you the dinner party, I think, and the inauguration must have been fun, too. I see bits of it over and over in the news reels. But I don't like that Roman Empire grandeur—the reviewing stand, for example, looks quite triumphal—of course Mrs. K's hat looks Byzantine . . . I wish K weren't so damned RICH. It all turns my stomach, slightly. I am so glad you mentioned contact lenses because at last you have interested Lota in them. I've been trying to make her try them for years. Isn't it true that they are tiny things now—just covering the pupil? (Any advertising literature will be welcome . . .) I think you—we—must be getting vain. I have almost decided that before my next trip to N.Y., I'm going to have my face lifted and my hair dyed pink. As it will probably be my *last* trip, I want to leave a dashing memory behind me. Please send snapshots of Harriet. She is at the clothes-stage, I suppose—one of L's "grandchildren" visited us, aged 5, and worried us for a few days because she did nothing but change her dresses all day—but she got over it quickly, in a few months.

Pearl K wrote me she'd met you and took to you enormously. She is a very nice girl and a wonderful friend, but she appears to much better advantage alone, or with one or two people. Some other friends of mine you probably know, or will, are Bobby and Arthur—Bobby Fizdale & Arthur Gold, the 2-piano team. They are a little chi-chi but awfully nice and you ought to hear them play. They are the best going, for semi-serious music at least. Bobby just wrote us (he thought we were off to Italy) to look up the girl he almost married recently, an Italian. He says, "She's awfully nice, her only fault is that she's Mary Mc's best friend"!

We are NOT going abroad just now—in fact I'm not sure when at all now. Lota was invited by Carlos Lacerda to work for him and we both feel it is very important for her. He is an old friend, newspaper editor, politician, *the* head of the opposition for years—and now, with the complete, or almost complete, turn-over here, he's *in* at last, as Governor of the new State of Guanabara. That's the old Federal State—including Rio so it's important—now that the capital has been changed to Brasília. He has put Lota in charge of a huge new "fill" along the Rio bay[1]—about 2 miles of it—4-lane highways, etc., and enough land besides to build restaurants, parks, playgrounds, outdoor cafés. It is just the kind of thing that Lota has been really preparing herself for for years and of course it is about time her poor country made

1 To convert into a city park (the Aterro do Flamengo).

some use of her brains, and it shows how superior Carlos is that he insisted on her accepting. (He also goes to my darling female doctor[1] in N.Y., and took some more Brazilian *men* to her, too, which is probably a huge step forward for the cause of feminine equality in Brazil! Every time he goes to NY he takes her out to dinner now.) Lota has just about the world's best landscape gardener[2] working with her, and four of the best architects here[3]—and Rio being the way it is, of course they're all old friends and it is all fine so far. I am very pessimistic about temperamental and spoiled Brazilians ever cooperating for long on anything—or working under a woman—but Lota is even more skeptical than I am, so maybe she won't mind too much if she feels she has to resign after a few months. She is wonderful in action, though—just the right tone, firm but funny, the times I've seen her. We went "on location" last week—heat about 105, I think—and stared at over-passes and under-passes (already smelling of urine, which is one reason why L is trying to fight them!) and sewers and dumps and scows and steam-shovels—accompanied by a dozen melting engineers, mostly in white linen (the oddest had a small black fan) a custom I love, but I'm afraid it's going out. But I have gone back and forth to Rio with Lota every week for almost two months now, and that is one reason why I haven't written to anyone—not just you, Cal!

Then our Bostonian friend, Mary Morse, went and adopted a 2-month old baby—now 4-months. She has been living with us until her new house, near here, is ready, so we've had a small baby in the house all this time, too—which is very occupying, since we all (including the maid, cook, and cook's husband) behave rather foolishly about the nice little orphan bastard—who is a happy, healthy, *laughing* baby, thank God. I met Albertinho, the cook's husband, this morning, carrying booties in one hand and a diaper in the other—perfectly happy. Brazilians all do like babies—like Italians—and every *proletário* for miles around has been to call. Mary took her and registered her, paying a bribe of about $2.50, "Monica Stearns Morse—father unknown, mother spinster"—this will look fine on her US passport.

My work (ha ha) has suffered badly, of course, but now we are getting a system worked out, have a cleaning boy in Rio, at least, and won't have to stay there quite so much. I do wish I could see you. Perhaps if we can't get abroad for another year I might manage a quick trip to N.Y. I think I have a book of poems almost ready. How do you like JANUARY RIVER as a title?

1 Anny Baumann.
2 Roberto Burle Marx.
3 Sérgio Bernardes, Hélio Mamede, Jorge Machado Moreira, and Affonso Eduardo Reidy.

(there's a poem of that name, or with that in it at least[1]). I saw the London *Times* piece on you[2]—heavens—before Christmas, and the solemn exchange of letters about the misprints, too.[3] Some of the piece was good, I thought, and to see it, the *whole page*, was very gratifying. Your star couldn't be higher, and looking as big and bright as Venus does here these evenings.

Then, somewhere along the line, I got the book of translations with the dedication that of course made me shed tears. I went through it very rapidly and concentrated mostly on the Montale. I've never read him, or barely, and I'd love to. Then I cabled you, I think. This last week I've been at home and with some time at last, and I've been reading them all carefully. The only ones I can judge at all, of course, are the French ones—and I know them all pretty well. I think Baudelaire is more sympathetic to you, verbally, (and probably emotionally) than Rimbaud—at least those early Rimbauds you've chosen—and sometimes you've done *wonders* with his (B's) language, "mansards," "chain-smoking," "purring," "narcotics"[4]—(couldn't she look for *coco-palms* instead of *coconuts*, though?[5]). You say to let you know things I question. Well, here are one or two things that bother me because they *look* like mistakes, whether or no, and though you have left yourself "free" I don't want to think of your being attacked for mistakes. (Please forgive my sounding like French 2A): In THE SWAN; (one of my favorite B poems), I think the line shd. read "—who drink tears / and suck grief like a Wolf-Nurse"[6]; in LA MALINE ("The malicious girl"), "I listened to the clock, happy and calm. *The kitchen (door) opened with a blast /* And the."[7] In AT THE GREEN CABARET (I did this once myself), the last line is: "with its foam gilded by a ray of *late* sun."[8] (It seems important, for the atmosphere for fatigue and peace, etc.). Also: "tartines" are the little pieces of bread and butter given to French school-children.[9] And in LA BOHÈME[10]: he just holds his shoe *near* his heart, in the position of Apollo playing the lyre, although what's elastic

---

1 "On the Amazon" (EB-*EAP*).

2 "The Destructive Element," *The Times Literary Supplement* (Oct. 14, 1960).

3 Hugh B. Staples, letter to the editor, "Robert Lowell," *The Times Literary Supplement* (Nov. 25, 1960).

4 "The Swan," line 30; "To the Reader," line 29; "My Beatrice," line 29; and "To the Reader," line 25: see RL-*CP*.

5 "The Swan," line 44 (RL-*CP*).

6 "Like she-wolves giving grief a tit to suck"; "The Swan" (typescript, Vassar). Cf. "The Swan," line 47 (RL-*CP*).

7 "In the cigar-brown dining room, perfumed / by a smell of shellac and cabbage soup, / I held my plate and raked together some / God-awful Belgian dish. I blew my food, / and listened to the clock tick while I ate— / snug, warm. The kitchen gave on a buffet"; "The Indisposition" (typescript, Vassar). Cf. "Eighteen-Seventy: A Malicious Girl," lines 5–6 (RL-*CP*).

8 See "Eighteen-Seventy: At the Green Cabaret," line 12 (RL-*CP*).

9 "Half-cold, and a basket of raspberry tarts"; "At the Green Cabaret" (typescript, Vassar). Cf. "Eighteen-Seventy: At the Green Cabaret," lines 14 and 4 (RL-*CP*).

10 It should read "Ma Bohème."

I've never been able to figure out, exactly.[1] Couldn't be elastic *sided* boots—they must have used elastic shoe laces! If you want me to, I'd be glad to give you more benefits of my past experience in Rimbaud-translating. (But of course not if you don't want me to.) (I spent a month alone in Brittany once doing nothing much but that.) Sometimes it seems to me you sort of spoil his joke, or give his show away, by bringing up his horror too *soon*. Like, the "white eye" in "The Sleeper in the Valley," when R says nothing to show he's not asleep until the very last phrase,[2] or in "La Cloche Fêlée," too.[3] I just don't want you to lay yourself open to stupid or jealous misunderstandings. I lived in Paris one whole winter long ago, and most of another one, and that "endless wall of fog" haunts me still.[4] But isn't it strange how those Rimbaud sonnets (early poems, that is) sound so gay and *healthy* and normal beside Baudelaire? Do you have those Pléiade editions?[5] They're awfully good.

And, to continue being literary, will you please tell me what's a good Pasternak to get for some idea of the poems? I have a little French one here, and the English "Safe Conduct" with some poems, but I want to get a lot more.[6] Is any one better than the others? Now you have given me courage to try Italian, I think. I can read quite a bit, because it is so close to Portuguese and Spanish. Montale sounds very beautiful.

I have to go to market, I'm sorry. Please excuse me. I have been worrying so about not-writing you have no idea. Lota keeps saying that after all, most people never write letters at all anymore! Now I've started I find it is easy and want to keep on, but the butcher, baker and candle-stick maker call.

With love to you all—how's E?—and thank you very much for everything lately, letters not the least.

Abraços,
Elizabeth

I ordered Randall's book but it hasn't come yet—how is it?[7] Do you read to Harriet? Does she like nursery-rhymes?

1 See "Eighteen-Seventy: On the Road," lines 13–14 (RL-*CP*).
2 "The river sucks his hair. A white eye rolls. / He sleeps. In his right side are two red holes"; "On the Road," (typescript, Vassar). Cf. "Eighteen-Seventy: On the Road," lines 13–14 (RL-*CP*).
3 See "Eighteen-Seventy: The Sleeper in the Valley," lines 12–14, and "The Flawed Bell," lines 12–14 (RL-*CP*).
4 "La muraille immense du brouillard"; Charles Baudelaire, "Le Cygne," from line 44 (1857). RL renders it: "the Paris fog's thick wall" ("The Swan," line 43, RL-*CP*).
5 Charles Baudelaire, *Oeuvres*, ed. Y.-G. Le Dantec (1938); Arthur Rimbaud, *Oeuvres complètes*, ed. Rolland de Renéville and Jules Mouquet (1954).
6 Boris Pasternak, possibly *L'An 1905*, trans. Benjamin Goriely (1958), and *Safe Conduct*, trans. Alec Brown and Lydia Pasternak-Slater (1958).
7 Randall Jarrell, *The Woman at the Washington Zoo* (1960).

230.[1]

Dearest Cal:

I've at last made up my mind to attempt something very difficult. You said "Let me know things you question," and I'm going to and I pray you will please not be proud and sensitive. I am very much worried by the French translations, particularly the Rimbaud ones. Your English, your force and meter, are very over-riding and of course the meter of the Racine is a *tour de force*, I think. When I got the book of translations I read them too rapidly at first and concentrated on Montale, because I've never read him and have wanted to for a long time. At that point I cabled you from Rio. The atmosphere of the book as a whole seemed vivid and personal and *you*. But when I read the French ones more carefully I began to get worried.

You have been careful to call them "Free translations" and of course that does leave you free to change the line-order, interpolate, point up, call Zeus Jehovah, maybe, put in those "plebescites"[2]—all for good and obvious reasons. (In Baudelaire sometimes an up-to-date phrase has a wonderful effect.) But once in a while I think you have made changes that *sound* like *mistakes*, and are open to misinterpretation. Or you have made the poet say the opposite of what he said in the original (a few times). The Rimbaud and Baudelaire poems are all so well known that I don't think you should lay yourself open to charges of carelessness or ignorance or willful perversity . . .

I don't want to sound scared, over-cautious, afraid of criticism, but I do want you to keep your reputation for solid, severe, painstaking workmanship. Your star is so very high now. I saw that piece in The London *Times Lit. Sup.*, a while ago, for example, and there have been other things—and to publish things open to misunderstanding might produce a lot of foolish jealous haggling and criticism that you could easily avoid. The French will say, "Those Americans who think they know French!" The London *Times*, well you know how they love to niggle and compare and damn. What will Eliot, the old French scholar, think? No, I'm probably saying it all wrong. *I* don't want you to be attacked. But perhaps that is an idea; perhaps you could consult Eliot? I feel I am running an awful risk and I am suffering, writing this. I think you should consult someone both more scholarly and more "in the world" than I am, while you have time to do something about it.

If you will forgive my sounding like the teacher of French 2A, I'll give

---

1 See Appendix I for more notes.
2 See "Eighteen-Seventy: Napoleon after Sedan," line 10 (RL-*CP*).

you some examples: Here's a flat literal translation of LA MALINE = "The malicious girl"—or "sly girl." In the brown dining-room, scented by a smell of varnish and fruits, at my ease, I picked up a plate of I don't know what Belgian dish, and lay flat in my huge chair / Eating, I listened to the clock, happy and calm. The kitchen (door) opened with a blast (or gust). And the servant came in, her kerchief undone and her hair provocatively combed. And, while her trembling little finger wandered over her cheek, pink and white peach-down, and her childish lip pouted, She kept arranging the plates (or fussing with) near me, to disarm me (or as you have it) Then like that— of course to get a kiss—she whispered "Feel it—my cheek has caught a cold." (The point of the last line seems to be that she makes a mistake in gender.) Of course a lot of what you wrote is "correct," and the changes you have made for your own reasons—but I do think that "buffet" *looks* like a mistake . . .[1] The poem strikes me as so much more light-hearted than you've made it, and the girl, fussing with plates to make an opening for conversation, is feminine, flirtatious, untidy, by implication young and pretty, "naughty"—but not sordid or dirty. Although he likes to go in for adolescent shock, a lot of these early poems seem quite gay in spite of formal perfection. I just *can't* decide how "free" one has the right to be with the poet's intentions. Brecht and *The Beggar's Opera* is a good case, maybe, and of course it is for you to decide, anyway (thank heavens!)[2]

AT THE GREEN CABARET: "tartines" aren't tarts, they're the pieces of bread & butter given to French school-children. "I contemplated the very naïve subjects of the tapestry"—"And it was adorable when"—I feel as if you'd spiked it with alcohol![3] I suppose the "Belgian pictures" is to tie it to your number I?[4]

"Pink & white ham flavored with a clove of garlic": it would have been baked in the ham, not served raw, I'm pretty sure.[5]

The last is what bothers me the most: "and filled up an immense stein for me, with its foam gilded by a ray of late sun."[6] The *late* seems very impor-

---

1 See notes to letter 229.
2 Bertolt Brecht, *The Threepenny Opera* (1928); John Gay, *The Beggar's Opera* (1728).
3 See "Eighteen-Seventy: At the Green Cabaret," lines 4 and 6–8 (RL-*CP*).
4 The first poem in the sequence is "Eighteen-Seventy: A Poster of Our Dazzling Victory at Saarbrucken" (RL-*CP*), a version of Rimbaud's "L'éclatante victoire de Sarrabrück." In "Eighteen-Seventy: At the Green Cabaret," as the speaker is "entering Charleroi," RL renders "je contemplai les sujets très naïfs / De la tapisserie" as "and laughed / at the naïve Belgian pictures on the wall." In making the images "Belgian," RL makes a silent link to "L'éclatante victoire de Sarrabrück," which contemplates a "Gravure belge brillamment coloriée, se vend à Charleroi, 35 centimes."
5 See "Eighteen-Seventy: At the Green Cabaret," line 53–54 (RL-*CP*).
6 See "Eighteen-Seventy: At the Green Cabaret," line 12 (RL-*CP*).

tant, fixing the atmosphere of fatigue, late afternoon, peacefulness. I'm afraid *behind* looks like a mistake . . .

THE SLEEPER IN THE VALLEY: The little valley foams with sunbeams . . . he is stretched out in the grass, under the cloud, pale in his green bed, etc. His feet in the gladiolas (flags, or rushes), he *takes a nap.* Your "The river sucks his hair" is highly effective—but Cal, I don't think you should put in "A white eye rolls" *there.* Until the very last phrase nothing has been said to suggest that the soldier isn't simply asleep (and I'm against putting in the bruises, too, for the same reason[1])—and so it seems to me you are giving the show away, spoiling Rimbaud's little joke, etc.

231.

Rio de Janeiro—June 15th, 1961

Dearest Cal:

I have started many letters to you lately, and I have a whole untidy "file" of papers, clippings, and notes-for-letters to you that I've been carrying back and forth from here to Petrópolis for so long now—I am just going to begin. Since the Post Office has definitely deteriorated lately I don't know whether you've got my last two letters or not or whether perhaps you did answer. Anyway, I had a letter a while ago from Pearl Kazin in which she told me— hoping at the same time that she wasn't the first to let me know, although she was, that you had been sick again,[2]—very briefly, I gathered,—and were already recovered. This was awfully bad news; both Lota and I are very, very sorry and disturbed about it. Surely New York itself is partly to blame . . . I do hope you recovered as quickly as Pearl seemed to imply you had, and that you are all right again. I'm not even sure where you are now—at the new address or where. It is *cruel and unfair*—(isn't everything.)

One of the clippings I've been collecting is that page from TIME with Barzun in his Barca-Lounger and you in your Salvation Army (was it?) chair.[3] I much prefer your chair and your portrait & you wherever it was taken.— Perhaps the new apartment, since it looks somewhat unfurnished? It's a funny review. They seem to be afraid of discussing anything but pot— "stoking his lines with fire and flare"! I've seen a few others, all very favorable, but nothing really serious enough or appreciative enough as yet. Then

---

1 See "Eighteen-Seventy: The Sleeper in the Valley," line 9 (RL-*CP*).
2 RL had a manic episode in March 1961 and was hospitalized for the month at Columbia Presbyterian Hospital.
3 "French With/Without Tears," *Time* (April 28, 1961).

a week or so ago I had a letter from a man named Silvers from *Harper's*. He thought I might write them something about Brazil, and he enclosed a batch of proofs from *Harper's* just to show me how good they are these days. The proofs, of course, are of your Pasternak translations *and* Elizabeth's Book Reviews (also J. Baldwin on Martin Luther King, a sort of journalistic job).[1] Some of the Pasternaks I'd seen and some not. The introductory note is fine, I think—exactly the right words and tone.[2] How I wish I could read Russian (and German)! I am sure he is a great poet. (I probably just ignorantly repeat, like a babu, phrases you are sick of hearing in N.Y., and make my little discoveries months or years late.) Anyway, if you've conveyed that, you have done everything possible, and there are wonderful phrases, and ideas— the first probably all yours. I always like the *ideas* in P's poems, even in the feeblest translations, and now you also give some of the probable marvelousness of the real thing—the life, color, reality, etc. E's "Ingredients Everywhere" is a splendid kind of attack—and in everything she mentions that I *have* read—not much—I always agree with her completely.[3] I do wish she'd do a piece on Durrell. Those books, which I somehow got befuddled into reading (I suppose because I want to see how other people handle exotic places), are grand glittering shams—sophisticated, or pseudo-sophisticated, travel-writing at the best, but as novels—well, it would take E to do it right.[4] It's funny—it's really bad "feminine" writing—V Woolf with adrenaline. I don't think anyone has pointed it out.

I *also* have a clipping from *The Spectator*, a rather unkind review of Snodgrass,[5] but it's the first that showed me exactly why it is I don't really like him very much. (I've never liked him since that self-congratulatory & self-deluded piece in *PR*—surely a direct descendent of Poe's piece on how he wrote "The Raven"?) The point made is that Snodgrass is really saying, "I do all these awful things—but don't you really think I'm awfully *nice?*" This is the masculine version of that "our old silver" feminine-thing I wrote you

---

1 "Seven Poems by Boris Pasternak," *Harper's* (Sept. 1961); Elizabeth Hardwick, "The New Books: Ingredients Everywhere," *Harper's* (Jan. 1961); and James Baldwin, "The Dangerous Road Before Martin Luther King," *Harper's* (Feb. 1961).

2 "My purpose in these very free versions of Pasternak's poems has been to make good English poems, to capture something of the greatness that flashes through the various literal translations that have been published. I know no Russian and have snatched, stolen, and improvised from whatever versions I could find. Friends have rendered the Russian for me word by word and then checked my final results. I offer what I have done as a tribute to Pasternak, and hope I have caught something of the triumph and blaze of his tone"; "Seven Poems by Boris Pasternak," *Harper's* (Sept. 1961).

3 Hardwick, "The New Books."

4 Lawrence Durrell, *The Alexandria Quartet* (1957–60).

5 Donald Davie, "Australians and Others," *The Spectator* (March 24, 1961).

about, too, I think, and it is the vast vast difference between you and one of your better imitators. You *tell* things—but never wind up with your own darling gestures, the way he does (he'd be giving Lepke[1] home-made cookies or something). I went straight through *Life Studies* again and there is not a trace of it, and that is really "masculine" writing—courageous and honest. Even Marianne has some-what broken down in this way lately, but not that I'd criticize her! She is old enough to have the right to indulge her eccentricities, surely. Even after struggling with Carnegie Hall and Yul Brynner[2] I still think she is behaving better and more in the old Emersonian ga-ga-individualist tradition—in her old age than Frost and his ancient cautious stingy (not in quantity) wisdom. He really advises one to do all the meanest bourgeois things, if you think about it.

Have you seen the poems of a girl named Vassar Miller?[3] (I haven't, but they sound as if they just might be good.) You asked me long ago now for new poets or poems for some anthology, I think. I'm not the person to know—of course—but also you might look at Gwendolyn Brooks' last book.[4]—I haven't seen that either, and the one I did see was half-hopeless, but she did have something occasionally, and I liked her very much when I met her and talked to her, and Negroes should be paid extra attention, anyway.

I liked your review of Winters in POETRY—very fair.[5]

I think I must order Ransom's selected Hardy[6]—maybe keep it here in Rio and the big book up at Petrópolis. Is it good? I liked his Hardy piece[7]—however—I'd like to talk to you about it.

I think Mary's novel articles are awfully good, too, don't you? It's funny. Before I saw the first one I was telling Lota how wonderful *Anna Karenina* is—how it even tells you how to make raspberry jam, and I went and *made* raspberry jam from our wild raspberries just that way—excellent—and then Mary makes the same remark.[8]

I had just re-read Dostoyevsky's *The Idiot* when the Russian movie came

---

1 See "Memories of West Street and Lepke," lines 42–53 (RL-*CP*).

2 Marianne Moore, "Carnegie Hall: Rescued," *The New Yorker* (Aug. 13, 1960), and "Rescue with Yul Brynner," *The New Yorker* (May 20, 1961).

3 Vassar Miller, *Wage War on Silence* (1960).

4 Gwendolyn Brooks, *The Bean Eaters* (1960); EB had reviewed Brooks's *Annie Allen* (1949) in *United States Quarterly Book List* (March 1950).

5 "Yvor Winters, a Tribute," *Poetry* (April 1961), 40–43; see RL-*CPR*.

6 Thomas Hardy, *Selected Poems*, ed. John Crowe Ransom (1961).

7 John Crowe Ransom, "Thomas Hardy's Poems and the Religious Difficulties of a Naturalist," *The Kenyon Review* (1960).

8 "You can learn how to make strawberry jam from 'Anna Karenina' and how to reap a field and hunt ducks"; Mary McCarthy, "The Fact in Fiction," *Partisan Review* (Summer 1960). See also McCarthy, "Characters in Fiction," *Partisan Review* (March–April 1961).

to Rio, so I went to see it.[1] It's terrible, but interesting, and only goes up to the end of part one so they have a long long way to go. It's as if it were a bad movie made about the time D wrote the book. But something funny: a girl radio announcer here was supposed to announce the play—also being put on here. She apparently couldn't believe that a play would be called *The Idiot*, just like that, so she said it as if it were the name of a musical comedy (the article *the* is *o* in Portuguese & also it's an exclamation, of course. So (in her text) *written*—they could be the same thing)—O! IDIOTA!—You Idiot, You! One nice example of Brazilian political humor derived from the movies. I don't know whether a medium-good Italian movie called *The Bel Antonio* has reached N.Y. or not?[2] It deals with the daring subject of impotency. Well, Brazil's new second-hand and only air-craft carrier, that cost millions and millions of non-existent dollars and drifts slowly up and down the bay with one or two helicopters on the vast flight deck, is now called *The Bel Antonio*.

Lota is working hard and doing awfully well. She is being attacked, even, in the newspapers, and intrigue is rife and two or three people have resigned. I must have told you about her job as "Chief-Co-ordinatress of the Fill"— the *fill* being, it seems, 6 kilometers long. I hadn't realized the size of it until we went to look it over yesterday. She is refusing pay—too bad, but a good precaution. It is wonderful for her, and if it works out the way she wants it to, it will be a wonderful big shady park, two or three restaurants, playgrounds, outdoor cafes, etc.—and give all classes of Rio somewhere to go and walk and enjoy the view and sea-breezes—which they badly need. If you have any ideas on playgrounds (as you well might now) tell us . . . I asked Howard Moss that, and he wrote he had a good idea—huge cement statues of parents. (He went into raptures about your Baudelaire translations in *PR*, too.[3]) The landscape gardener (I know you probably don't share my interest in interior decoration, modern architecture, gardens, etc., but after all I do live in one of the best examples—of architecture that is—in SA, supposedly). Well, you might have heard of him—he's lectured at Harvard—and is called the modern Le Nôtre, and *I* think he is one of the real Brazilian geniuses—Roberto Burle Marx. He gave a big party out at his *fazenda* (his nursery, really—acres and acres of marvelous and somehow sad, flamboyant, and threatening subtropical trees and plants) for our pal the governor and everyone to do with the "fill." Burle Marx is also a fine cook. There were roast pigs and fish a

1 *Idiot*, dir. Ivan Pyryev (1958).
2 *Il Bell' Antonio*, dir. Mauro Bolognini (1960).
3 "Translations from Baudelaire," *Partisan Review* (Jan.–Feb. 1961); see "To the Reader," "Voyage to Cythera," "My Beatrice," "The Servant," "The Swan," and "The Game" (RL-*CP*).

yard long and fantastic fruit-and-flower-decorations yards high that everyone tore to shreds at the end of the day, to take home. Unfortunately someone had had the idea of bringing along a Chinese Trade Commission that had just arrived from a stay in Cuba—8 or 10 small-sized, slovenly-looking, youthful, long-haired Chinese who wouldn't touch alcohol and *pinned people down*, in French or bad English. (Mão-Mão—pronounced like Mow—means "bad-bad" in Portuguese and is a common expression. After they all refused Scotch and wine, again, looking grimmer & grimmer, Roberto said "Mao-Mao-Tse-Tsung.") I tried talking to one whose English was very limited and when he told me "Castro-strong-strong" shaking his fist, and "Batista bad-bad" (as if I wouldn't have heard of *him*, probably) for the first time, I think, a really cold shudder of fear and horror of Communism went down my spine. They were dreary, ignorant-looking little men, their eyes burning with righteous passion—and there we were all being very gay, admiring *plants* and Roberto's collection of Brazilian antiques, etc., and stuffing ourselves—and about to reap what we sowed.

Not immediately connected with this but perhaps partly, since I can't use my grant at present, until Lota is free to go with me—I've been thinking I'd like to do something for our new regime here, something like give advice! I realize I have picked up a vast amount of information in almost ten years here, without even trying, and thanks to Lota, I do know an awful lot of important people. I know them quite well and as a friend rather than as an official American. We have done, are doing, such stupid things here, absolutely incredible folly, some of it, and as far as "cultural exchanges" go we couldn't present ourselves in a worse light, usually, and I think I could really be of some use, if they'd want me. I had this idea before but I have been sternly ignored by the Embassy here and the "cultural attachés" have been so low-class there didn't seem to be much use in trying. I don't want a job—or pay. I just think I could really tell them a bit about who's who, and what kind of cultural importations the Brazilians would *really* like, and how to stop being quite so condescending—with the best intentions in the world, as always. (I told Lota I wanted to be a "poet engagée" and she said I wanted to be engagée to Kennedy's insolent chariot.) After your trip to the White House—do you know anyone well enough to say a word for me? I don't know anyone at all. I met Schlesinger years ago, that's all. I've composed a letter to him but I don't know whether it will even reach him, of course. I don't know about the new Ambassador here, Gordon,[1] an economist from Harvard. I could call on him, but it would

---

1 Lincoln Gordon.

all be much easier if I had some kind of recommendation from Washington—if I could get it. I'll write MacLeish, anyway. I should, to explain why I'm not using the grant this year—but it occurs to me he may not be too enthusiastic about all this fondness for a rival poet . . .

Well—I have this project, and another one or two that I'd better not speak of until certain, but one might mean a flying trip to N.Y. sometime this year, at least.

Dear Cal, if you only knew how many imaginary conversations I have with you all the time and how little any of this represents what I am really thinking, doing, etc. Lota and I talk about you a lot and we both hope and pray you are better, that things are going well, and that your life is matching the splendor and success of your work. Surely we don't have to choose between them quite as narrowly as Yeats says.[1] I realize I should get back to NY for a bit when I find all my jokes have to be translated. They translate worse than poetry, by far.

Time out to make *another* little coffee. I am sorry you left that good Boston doctor—at least he sounded extraordinarily good and it is hard to change. Robert Gardner (at least I think it must be the same one) has a strange contribution to a "movie" number of DAEDALUS—a sort of case history of an old African woman.[2] I don't quite get the point. I am sounding like a "Review of Reviews"—oh dear.

It is pouring and the sea is raging. Lota—who's developing a positively Wellingtonian style of official letter-writing—is writing hard in one room and I in another. She sends much love—so do I—

Elizabeth

I don't know where to mail this—new apt. or where—

In Feb. you wrote that Harriet was in the clothes stage—what's she like now? I'd like to send her something—I am also trying to find a *light weight* saint to send you, but no luck—

232.

June 25, 1961—Sunday morning

Dear darling Cal:

I don't know whether my letters are reaching you or not or where to ad-

---

1 "The intellect of man is forced to choose / Perfection of the life, or of the work"; William Butler Yeats, "The Choice," lines 1–2 (1933).
2 Robert Gardner, "A Human Document," *Daedalus* (Winter 1960).

dress you—I sent the last one to the old Riverside Drive address, hoping it would be forwarded—but half my letters seem to get lost these days, anyway, coming and going. A friend is jetting up to NY tonight—nine hours only now—and I'm going to give her this note to mail to you—perhaps c/o Farrar, Straus—or the new address—although I don't know when you intended moving. I am awfully worried about you, having had only that one bit of news from Pearl Kazin Bell quite a while ago now. I do hope you are well. I collect odd items or information. From England I heard you had some "marvelous" Villon translations in something there, *The Observer*, I think.[1] And yesterday Pearl sent me your interview in the *Paris Review*—old now, but I hadn't seen it. It is *excellent*—and of course I am overcome by the references to myself.[2] I had read some of the interview with Frost which was chiefly interesting for the way he *didn't* answer the questions but turned them into speeches about his own poems and how good they are . . .[3] But your remarks are so good, so useful, and true—well, you're the only poet who makes much sense to me when he speaks about poetry and technique, anyway. What you say about Marianne is fine: "terrible, private, and strange revolutionary poetry. There isn't the motive to do that now." But I wonder—isn't there? Isn't there even more—only it's terribly hard to find the exact and right and surprising enough, or un-surprising enough, point at which to revolt now? The Beats have just fallen back on an old corpse-strewn or monument-strewn battle-field—the real real protest I suspect is something quite different. (If only I could find it. Klee's picture called FEAR seems close to it, I think . . .)[4]

My one news item is that I have taken on a job that maybe I shouldn't have, but anyway—writing a small book about Brazil for LIFE's series in The World Library. They're mostly pictures, the ones I've seen—superb photographs, of course, and a superficial text of 35,000 words or so, a little of everything—but not *too* LIFE-y. I have plenty of material, and I think Lota and I can have quite a lot of fun using up our favorite jokes, putting in our favorite people, etc. My one idea is to do it *fast*, and just accept it as pot-boiling and a sort of penance for my years of idleness. (No one will ever read the text

1 "François Villon: The Grand Testament," *The Observer* (May 7, 1961); see RL-*CP*.
2 Frederick Seidel, "An Interview with Robert Lowell," *The Paris Review* (Winter–Spring 1961); see RL-*CPR*. Seidel asks RL if he admires the work of his contemporaries. "The two I've been closest to are Elizabeth Bishop . . . and Jarrell, and they're different. Jarrell's a great man of letters, a very informed man, and the best critic of my generation, the best professional poet . . . Elizabeth Bishop's poems, as I said, are more personal, more something she did herself, and she's not a critic but has her own tastes, which may be very idiosyncratic. I enjoy her poems more than anybody else's."
3 Richard Poirier, "An Interview with Robert Frost," *The Paris Review* (Summer–Fall 1960).
4 Paul Klee, *Mask of Fear* (1932), Museum of Modern Art.

anyway, probably!) The advantages are—it pays a lot, by my standards, and also pays for trips around here and a trip to NY with expenses, in October, for a month. [(]That will be hell—re-writing with *them*.) Maybe Lota will be able to come, too, if she can get away from re-making the Rio harbor long enough. Since I can't use my grant until next year, anyway, it seemed like a good idea to keep very busy for a while. I do hope you will be there then. (If you aren't, I think I'll try to get out of going at all!)

I tried and tried to find a good Saint Sebastian to send you by Mary Morse (the friend). He's the Saint I want to get because once we went swimming in that Maine ice-water near Stonington (the day poor dear C left with Tom) you inadvertently posed against a tree trunk, and looked just like Saint S for a moment! I found rather a nice St. Thomas Aquinas, with wings *and* spectacles—but when I put my own on—spectacles, not wings—to examine his face I didn't like it.

Instead, I bought myself an antique rocking-chair, jacaranda wood and cane—beautiful crude 19th century Brazilian style, almost whittled. There was a pair, one for a man and one for a woman. They must have been a rather large country couple, for Brazilians, since the woman's just fits me. The man's was bought ten minutes before I got there by the Spanish Ambassador. Now I have a rocking-chair, a purple wool sweater, and all three volumes of Mme. de Sévigné[1]—all set for old age. Have you ever read her? She is marvelous, and the wonder is that the letters survived, and are so much better than most things written on purpose.

The part about camping at the Tates' in your interview is so good, about Roethke is good, too. It makes me think I must get back to my memories of Marianne that I started and dropped.— And maybe I *should* have taught. I might not have wasted so much time. These teacher-poets seem to produce a great deal! Why don't I like Merwin's poetry? It never seems as if he really quite meant it. (Wilbur sometimes affects me the same way.) Merwin is so proficient—and yet it all seems "glazed," too. I was rather hard on Snodgrass, maybe—but it *is* self-congratulatory sometimes, in spite of his great talent—and that is the greatest sin, almost. If only one could get back to the stage of ignorance, where poems just seemed to happen, with their sense tagging along later.

I am pleased to be probably going to NY—and October is when it looks its best. Please be there!

I told you a joke about the Brazilian one big useless air-craft carrier. Now

---

1 Marquise de Sévigné, *Lettres*, ed. Gérard-Gailly (1953–57).

they are calling it "the floating debt." But my favorite story—and more Brazilian than anything else I can think of—is about the man who was insulted in the street—another man yelled a gross insult. The friend with him said, "Are you going to take that? Didn't you hear what he said? Are you a man, or aren't you?" He answered, "Yes, I'm a man—but I'm not [a] fanatic." That's been the Portuguese attitude since the Moors beat them in the 14th century, apparently.

I must get ready for Rio. Mary Morse is taking her adopted daughter, aged 8 months, along, and we are loading the car with what L calls her "collapsible" bed, diaper-bags, etc.— The baby laughs and pulls the Siamese cat's loose skin, hard, and he wriggles and his eyes get very blue and cross-eyed, but so far he hasn't scratched her. Tell me how big Harriet is—by October—so I can bring her something to wear. Size 5?— I do hope and pray you are well, Cal, and perhaps taking it easy for a while. You have been working so hard, obviously—I do hope I hear from you soon.

With much love,
    Elizabeth

233.

85 East End Ave., Apt 14 G
NYC
June 27, 1961

Dearest Elizabeth:

I'm O.K. and have been since April and have been meaning to write you since April, but I shy away from giving a lot of personal history—this has happened so many times one feels a little cut off from one's kind. I was in a hospital for five weeks or so, less high and in an allegorical world than usual and not so broken down afterwards. Once more there was a girl,[1] a rather foolish girl but full of a kind of life and earth force, and once more a great grayness and debris left behind me at home. Now we are back together, wobbly but reknit, almost.

We have sold our Boston house and bought an apartment here, 15 West 67th St. and will be here settled when you come in October. I hope you will stay with us some of the time at least.

My book is a lot bigger: a long selection from Villon, more Rimbaud—"Les Chercheuses,"[2] "The Drunken Boat," "Mémoire," now a total of eight

1 Sandra Hochman; see letter 242.
2 Arthur Rimbaud, "Les Chercheuses de Poux" (1871); see "The Lice-Hunters" (RL-*CP*).

sonnets (I took all your suggestions),[1] Baudelaire's "Le Voyage," more Pasternak, and some scraps of Homer and Sappho.[2] The whole is much more worth dedicating to you now, and I hope you'll be pleased.

I have a rather large plan, risky to mention at this point when not a line has been written, but I would like to try a long long poem about Hitler and the Second World War, done more or less chronologically, short scenes, prose, strict and free verse, and many styles. It would take many years to do, if it could be done at all, and almost anything could go in it. I could get away from the too personal, use history and perhaps catch a great chunk of the times we have endured.

I must say your Brazil book sounds much more achievable and good sense. I think you do catch that revolutionary under-pressure quality of the earlier poets—most poets, though, seem like crusts of hardening lava. By the way, Jason Epstein at Random House would very much like to see the manuscript of your stories, if it is clear of ties to Houghton and Mifflin. I have been reading over the long *New Yorker* childhood story.[3] Really no one is better either in an open Russian way or symbolically as in your "Prison"![4]

Harriet will be almost five when you arrive, strong long legs, a powerful climber, an actress whenever men [are] around. She has two boy friends her age and many mine, including me and is learning about life in large scoops.

I loved your letter as always and am thrilled at your visit—really come this time. Write again soon. Write again soon and I will be less hang-dog and more fun.

Best to Lota and love to you,
Cal

P.S. Lizzie tells me there's another letter from Boston, so I'll write again then. Somehow it's hard to write very fully, or interestingly or honestly about personal matters. I always feel my Mother's moralizing wrestling with my father's optimism. Almost from birth I decided they were both wrong and the truth lay elsewhere. Then from time [to time] I talk like both of them at once.

There's a long bit about Quadros in the last issue. When you wrote you

1 See "Nostalgia" (RL-*CP*).
2 "The Voyage," "September," "For Anna Akmatova," "Mephistopheles," "The Seasons," "Sparrow Hills," "Wild Vines," "In the Woods," "The Landlord," "Hamlet in Russia, A Soliloquy," "The Killing of Lykaon," and "Three Letters to Anaktoria" (RL-*CP*).
3 "In the Village" (EB-*CPR*).
4 "In Prison" (EB-*CPR*).

were accepting a job, I thought at first that you were entering the govern-ment like Lota and were perhaps rebuilding a city. I miss you greatly.

234.

[Postcard: Henri Rousseau, The Dream *(1910), Museum of Modern Art]*

[n.d. 1961]

Jungle to jungle! My erroneous picture of Brazil is much like this (doubtless also erroneous) of India.

Love,

CAL

235.[1]

[July 1961]

. . . sent a long cable back saying that Mr. B's[2] books dealt with "the war, crime, homosexuality, drunkenness, and insanity, and were not appropriate to distribute in Brazil" . . . Yet they are sending *him*—and of course here au-thors always exchange books the minute they say how-do-you-do. Well, maybe he's quite unlike his books, or maybe I'll find he's a compendium of the war, crime, etc., etc. . . . But isn't that incredible.

I've been doing some poems—the *N Yorker* took a long one[3] that I don't like at all (maybe I said this before), but now I have others I like a bit better and when we get back here again I think I'll send you a set of old and new.— We have had raging storms, one after the other, for two weeks—the whole week I spent in Rio watching the sea, I think—every tide came right up over the mosaic sidewalks and right to the base of our apartment house, and left the avenue covered with sand. Then this week has been very sad—Lota's mongrel dog died, aged about 12 or 14. We felt extra badly because we'd been away and if we'd got back sooner might have saved her, we think. That was bad enough, but the other dog, the 1st dog's lifelong friend, hasn't eaten for four days, and is suffering from melancholia and probably pneumonia as well by now. The vet has been treating her by telephone and I've been giving penicillin injections—didn't know I could till I tried. Today she does seem

---

1 Only the final page survives; the date is therefore speculative.
2 William S. Burroughs.
3 *The New Yorker* published "A Norther—Key West," "First Death in Nova Scotia," and "Sandpiper" in 1962 (see EB-*CP*). The longest is "First Death in Nova Scotia" (*The New Yorker,* March 10, 1962), but it may not be the one she speaks of with dislike.

better but we are taking her to Rio anyway, AND the cat we are keeping for our friend Mary Morse. It will shortly have to have a Caesarian . . . The Noah's ark is about to take off—save us. Neither of these animals is apartment-broken—oh well—I'll spare you the details and I don't really know what you know, or feel, about pets, come to think of it. *My* cat is in fine shape, in his beautiful winter coat now, and just scornfully stares the poor invalids out of countenance . . .

It seems to me I had lots more to say: I've been writing letters mentally every day. Maybe I'll get a chance in Rio to collect my thoughts and go on with this. I just wanted to tell you how happy we are that you're better.

With much love,
Elizabeth

236.

My Dearest Elizabeth:

The other night I had a dream about you, one of those dreams where there were many scattered people moving about like bits of wood in a current, much maneuvering and confusion. Somewhere on the edges you were, but we couldn't come together, and all was a headache of difficulties and distances. Finally you appeared in our apartment and said I am ready to take a walk, unless you intend to keep me waiting longer—it's already been hours. Well, I am expecting you this fall in New York and I won't keep you waiting.

There's something else. For the last two weeks, I haven't had a drop to drink. At first one feels removed from the living, that sociable drop gone that makes us all one species, in warmth, weakness and talkativeness. Then the air clears and steadies. I have so many holes in my soul, I imagine this is the only way for me to go through the rich jungle of New York on my own feet. So come soon, and we will gaze on the riches of the world in our odd sobriety. I can't say that you ever seemed to lose the slightest gaiety, rather the opposite!

We never seem to write what we plan. For a year or so, I've had a vague idea of making an opera libretto out of Melville's *Benito Cereno*.[1] It was mostly my fellow Ford Foundation Fellow, Bill Meredith's notion, and I kept delaying, sure in my heart that I would always put it off. Then after I got

---

1 Herman Melville, "Benito Cereno" (1856); "Benito Cereno" (RL-*OG*).

back here, I started. Now a draft is done, 47 pages of iambicky free verse, full of horror, charade and scenes. The grand "Gerontion"[1]-like Elizabethan monologues I proposed for myself never materialized: all is terse, rapid and direct. Lizzie is all for it, but it has gone so fast, I am very dim on what I've done.

I'll give you two of my days. First day: New York, in bed tight after too gay a time with an old Kenyon classmate and Léonie Adams (by the way Bill Troy died this spring after a long speechless drag with cancer of the throat. The funeral was a high mass with a little group of Columbia atheists, mostly women and Russian translators, with a man or two in a beret. No one knew when to stand or kneel except for Caroline Tate. Later Léonie kept getting letters from intellectual priests, who all assumed that Bill was in Purgatory and would need a lot of prayers.) Back to my day. With a terrible head-ache, I look at my watch: 7:15. I rush with a heavy head to the Lexington Avenue Subway, take a local by mistake. Stones along the side seem to crawl by, one by one in slow motion. On the Staten Island Ferry, the refreshments girl announces, "We have no coffee." I drink something that is neither tea nor coffee. Worrying furiously with this question, I read that Kennedy is calling up the reserves, and some sort of estimate that seventy million people may be killed on both sides at the first blow.[2] Pictures of the New York common man, all saying that they don't intend to be pushed around and that for the first time they feel we have a president. Leaving the ferry, I meet the conference leech, natty beret, pressed suit, a two pound portable Olivetti typewriter. In his wake, the two conference morons, tieless shirts and trousers held up by neckties. My two hour class; I am very distant, ascetic and philosophical. Lunch: ham mostly fat and terrible things, egglike, that look like they've been through a steam laundry. A joint conference on drama, poetry and fiction in which the conference director, a Mr. Rust Hills, makes more and more surly references to my colleague, Saul Bellow's, heroes. Mounting explosive heat. I side-step the conference nymphomaniac. Swimming. Something has gone wrong with the tide. At every six inches there are deflated contraceptives. Boys of five blowing them up like balloons. Hideous blue and bloated things floating. The water striped with reddish algae that stains. Red sand on the beach, that also stains. On the horizon, the houses of Brooklyn and the *Queen Mary* making for Manhattan. Saul Bellow goes off for a long, killing fiction-discussion meeting with the conference nymphomaniac, leav-

---

1 T. S. Eliot, "Gerontion" (1919).
2 Jack Raymond, "Speedy Build-Up of Army Studied in Berlin Crisis," *The New York Times* (July 17, 1961).

ing me with the conference leech, who invites me to dinner. Supper: at six, after two minutes for drinks—more laundered food. Discussion on Wagner College dormitory steps. First two shy literary agents, then Molly Kazan, deep practical New York voice, an answer for everything, obviously a woman who touches nothing that doesn't turn to gold. She is challenged by Willard Maas, the Wagner poet and poetry professor, quietly alcoholic, less quietly homosexual, a man who hasn't published for twenty years and never, at best, sold anything for a nickel. He questions the lastingness of Broadway at best. Stifling sleepless heat, sounds of intimacy, outrage and drinking. A young bearded poet announcing that he is the best poet of 24 in America, then rapping each dormitory door with a toilet brush. From the next room belonging to my other colleague, Edward Albee, a playwright—the low end-less Tennessee voice of the conference nymphomaniac reading aloud a play. At about four-thirty, all is quiet.

Second day (if I have the strength to tell it!) Our annual trip from Castine to Mount Desert. Lizzie, Harriet, I and Betty Dawson, our colored nurse. Betty is a first-rate housekeeper, a novelty in our family, but she is a slow, re-tiring soul. On the drive up, one of her few remarks was, "I don't make friends easily." Lizzie says, if most people have spark-plugs, eleven and a half of Betty's are clogged with chewing-gum. She fears nature, "why don't the folks living up these back roads get out of here?" She knows the woods are full of snakes, won't go to the ladies' room alone, and has a hundred and seventy-five dollar polaroid camera. Showing Betty the world turned out to be impossible. After two miles: "We almost there? They have dinky roads like this in Virginia." Harriet, mistakenly bought a two-note wooden flute, begins deafening, then prodding, then (this is the worst) questioning Betty. "Why is it wood? Why does it have two notes? That's funny, isn't it. Tell me something else you know!" On the great Ocean Drive, pointing out things was a failure. Betty glumly gaped inland, afraid that snakes might [come] out of the woods. At Thunder Hole, the polaroid pictures first came out gray outlines on blinding white, then formless gray on white and finally pure white. At the beach, we trampled about in the much too-cold-to-swim water, while Betty sat in the shade, head unraised, as she shifted the film in her cam-era. At last a real picture, of Elizabeth, but a brawny unknown man in trunks occupies two-thirds of the film-space. That night we slept ten hours. In the morning, Harriet woke me up, and I had to tell her the domestic life of Aunt Jemima. "She only reads her children cook-books."

I work from about ten to three-thirty, then we play tennis, then we eat and listen to music. It's really very quiet and beautiful. We go to New York about the 7th. I feel like someone washed up on land and given a new suit, after six months of floating. A cancerous impatience is wearing away, and I guess life is really much too lovely not to live out.

A few facts that I may have given you before. Our address will be 15 West 67th St. Harriet weighs forty pounds and comes to my belt. We all miss you and long to see you.

My best to Lota,

love,

Cal

237.

Rio—August 20th, 1961

Dearest Cal:

How omnipotent you are . . . I got a nice little note, signed "Arthur"[1] and headed, engraved, merely THE WHITE HOUSE. (So nice & democratic— but I can't *stop* making generalizations for a minute these days and only hope, when I get this piece for LIFE over with, that I'll be able to drop the habit.) I answered, but didn't want to go into details, of course, but I do have lots of ideas and if there is a slightly cultured Culture Attaché coming now— as surely there will be—I think I may be of some use. Thank you.

Your trips to Maine are always wonderful (—but wait till you read of the trip of the Portuguese court to Brazil. *Much* worse.— Maybe you already have—and I certainly don't ever want you to read it in my capsule-version). I do hope Maine is beautiful, cool, peaceful, that Betty behaves herself. The Melville idea sounds wonderful to me, really.

I didn't know about poor Bill Troy. How will Léonie ever live alone? We just got a big batch of mail from Petrópolis—along with your letter, all the *Dissent*s, *PR's*, *Evergreen*s, etc., that I subscribe to. I started in on the *Dissent* about New York and decided it was no wonder I'd given up trying to live there. Also *Evergreen*—a fascinatingly incredible review of Ginsberg. Only he—and maybe *you*—are any good at all.[2] I went to the theatre the other night, the first time since NY—the American Repertory Theatre is here— and saw *Miss Julie* and *Zoo Story*.[3] I thought the latter came off pretty well. I

1 Arthur Schlesinger.
2 "Only Robert Lowell and the recent work of John Ashbery match Ginsberg in this; they are constructing—each quite differently—new poetic forms"; Michel Butor, "Delphi," *Evergreen Review* (May–June 1961), 116.
3 August Strindberg, *Miss Julie* (1888); Edward Albee, *The Zoo Story* (1958).

am so dumb I was quite surprised when I realized the Brazilians around me were taking it for granted as a political allegory about the USA and the "poor" countries.

First Lota refused to go to N.Y. with me. The inflation here is so bad that the $ is absolutely impossible for her. Now I think I'll be staying at Loren MacIver's studio, 61 Perry Street (they're in Athens or Istanbul), and Lota has decided to come, too, thank goodness, because I am going to need her moral support badly. Sometime in October, I'm not sure when—and I'll have to make one quick trip to Canada, too.

(oh dear, sorry—)

I feel awful about the Hemingway suicide[1]; it seems to be the last thing he should have done, somehow. All the notices I have read have been so STUPID—including English ones that say he learned how to write conversation from "British understatement"! I'm sure he must have been very sick for several years—out of his head—perhaps you know?

Could you ask Elizabeth to give me Harriet's measurements across the shoulders and from shoulder to knee? I'd love to bring her a dress. They do make pretty ones here—and the sizes—and children's shapes—are so different. I think we'll have to give one party—a sober party—perhaps we could invite Meyer Schapiro? I do like him, and he lives right around the corner from Loren's.

Your Rousseau postcard came just at the right minute. I was working on a chapter about naturalists, the jungle, etc. LIFE is getting nervous about this—say they're more interested in people than animals. However, I have just learned that the way to keep a *coati*, if you have one, out of mischief is to give him a hairbrush and he'll spend hours brushing his own tail. These are darling, small, ring-tailed animals. I've seen quite a few pet ones—one I met, if you picked him up and said *"Dorme, dorme"* to him, would shut his eyes and pretend to go to sleep.

Or how about a monkey instead of a new dress? He would adore your various typewriters and might learn to pick out Beat poetry.

I've heard recently from Marianne, and she doesn't sound well at all. I'm glad I'm going to see her. Her publishers seem to be treating her badly, as usual—"outwitting" her, as she puts it. "I never protest at being diminished, Elizabeth, but had I known I was being outwitted I would have disrupted the peace in any language known to me." "Robert Lowell; starring, I am glad to

1 On July 2, 1961.

say. I don't know anyone who knows anything who does not like his Racine and Baudelaires . . . his firmness and working out of a problem—the rhythm." (She is always awfully impressed by RHYTHM.)

I have lots and lots to tell you and ask you but this is to be just a brief cheering interruption in the tedious flow of generalities spiced with "anecdotes." I do hope you are keeping well and I think your capacity for work— E's, too—is magnificent.

With much love, and see you soon,

Elizabeth

238.

Castine, Maine
August 31, 1961

Dearest Elizabeth:

I have been worrying and wondering about you all week in your turmoil. On television, we have seen Quadros leaving the country without a tie, Brazilian soldiers guarding the American embassy in Rio etc. I hope all is secure with you. Let me know if we can do anything, such as send you money.[1]

A few minutes ago, I finished my last play of the group.[2] It's about the Puritans coming to Merrymount, destroying the May-pole and cutting down their own English flag. My middle play is Hawthorne's "Major Molineux,"[3] a young man coming to Boston from the country, looking for his rich British relative, and finally finding him tarred and feathered by the American revolutionary mob. My three plays together will make an evening and a book.[4] I have over a hundred and ten pages. (You see I give you all the ambitious, measurable details.) For the last few minutes, I've been lying in my bed in the sea-side barn, seeing the white hairs on my chest, watching the rising tide bring the sea as close as a lake shore, enjoying the liquidity of a peach, sip-

---

1 Since July 1961 Carlos Lacerda had repeatedly attacked Jânio Quadros's foreign policy on the radio and in newspapers. On August 25, Quadros left office abruptly, alleging that "terrible forces" were aligned against him. The constitution provided for the vice president to succeed him; but João Goulart was of the opposition party and considered too radical by the military and by conservatives to be allowed to assume office. Goulart was abroad on an economic mission to China and, for the moment, "effective power was held by three military ministers . . . They quickly declared *de facto* marshal law in an attempt to prevent public demonstrations" (Thomas E. Skidmore, *Politics in Brazil* [1967], 206). During the crisis, banks were closed and the cruzeiro was devalued. On August 31, 1961, the Bank of Brazil imposed restrictions on foreign exchange.

2 "Endecott and the Red Cross" (RL-*OG*).

3 Nathaniel Hawthorne, "My Kinsman, Major Molineux" (1832); "My Kinsman, Major Molineux" (RL-*OG*).

4 *The Old Glory* (1965).

ping coffee and of course smoking. Harriet gave me her first lecture yesterday—on smoking. I explained that it was very good for me but would taste like nothing at all to her. I have an idea the plays may be pretty good or will be with another scrubbing. This is very new. I've never written fast, anything many people would read, anything in which the whole labor wasn't a meticulous worrying with each word.

Not drinking is beginning to be refreshing. Still, it will be lonely in New York, unless you come. I've developed a craving for Welch's grape juice and gingerale and drink a large concentrated bottle each afternoon at the cocktail hour. I do need some company though besides ex-alcoholics and the physically disabled. I won't believe you are in America till I see you. The Frankenberg apartment sounds grand for you both.

We've had the warmest (humanly) and most quiet and loving time we have ever spent lately. Tennis every afternoon at four, no quarrels, no haste, eight hours sleep.

My annual voyage with Eberhart was monotonous. He has mastered his boat, and this somehow drains it of interest. We were alone, except for his son Dikkon, or Rick, or Dick, a quiet, slow boy, wavering between being awfully nice and turning to vegetation. Andy Wanning says that Tom has a girl now, who has burned the old rubbish in his room, and is trying to move him to a [new] room. Andy watches the process with amused, skeptical detachment.

What news for you? Mary McCarthy will be in New York this fall to display her new husband. Her essays are out and have a lovely naïve, very intelligent dissenter's springiness to them.[1] Bob Gardner is returning from New Guinea where he has been photographing tribesmen and even their wars. Belle Gardner's daughter, a very perplexed and listless one, became engaged to a Mexican bull-fighter, who at the last moment turned out to be a pimp, so there was no wedding. Merwin turned down the Library of Congress job, and it went to Louis Untermeyer!

We leave here next Thursday, will stay a day or two in Boston and will arrive in New York on Sunday. Black Betty and her Polaroid camera have gone on ahead to clear the debris. I have to write a piece on Bill Williams,[2] all but dead, alas, now, and five pages analyzing a Stanley Kunitz poem,[3] neither of which I have much inclination to do or think I can do well.

1 Mary McCarthy, *On the Contrary* (1961).
2 "Dr. Williams," *The Hudson Review* (Winter 1961–62); see RL-*CPR*.
3 "Stanley Kunitz's 'Father and Son,'" *The Poet and His Critics II*, ed. Anthony Ostroff, *New World Writing* (1962); see RL-*CPR*.

Oh dear, I pray that we will see you and Lota soon, our love to you both. Your arrival brightens my fall!

Love,

239.

Rio—September 14th, 1961

Dearest Cal:

We are very much touched by your offer to send us money . . . I received that letter when we went up to Samambaia last week-end. We had, by chance, gone to the bank and the money changers the day before they closed here, so we were all right—in fact able to lend money to our friends who ran out. Now the banks are open again. I hadn't thought of you as watching television in Castine, somehow.— It was a sad and awful stretch for everyone here, and now we don't like the way things are one bit.[1] Lota, of course, was very much involved in everything and stayed at the Governor's Palace all night long several nights, arriving home for breakfast. You know that the Governor of the State of Guanabara is an old friend of ours, Carlos Lacerda—and he is the man who set the whole thing off—more or less. It is extremely complicated, of course. I even wrote a note to the *NY Times* about ten days ago—maybe you'll see it—maybe they won't print it.[2] But really— the US papers I've seen, or what's been quoted from them here—have everything entirely wrong. My one point was that the US doesn't believe a word of what Russia says—but when it comes to S.A. anything anyone says—dictators or would-be dic. of the right or of the left (as now) they take on faith. Things look very bad. However—I won't go into it!— I think I'll give after-dinner speeches on the Brazilian Situation when I get to N.Y. I seem to know quite a lot about it. The Navy steamed up and down right in front of our apartment here and I watched through binoculars. But Rio itself was pretty quiet—thanks to Carlos—(whom the NY *Times* calls "feudal and reactionary" etc., etc.[3] The army actually is so *un*-warlike that they backed down—and really behaved very well!)

---

1 In early September, the military and "legalists" who wanted to honor the constitution reached an awkward compromise, temporarily shifting the country to a parliamentary government, ruled by a prime minister. This allowed Goulart to assume the presidency on September 7 as figurehead, pending a national plebiscite.

2 Unpublished.

3 "The reactionary, feudalistic forces in civil and military life that brought such fierce pressures on Jânio Quadros, and that are now trying to keep his legal successor, Vice President Goulart, out of the Presidency, have done their country a great disservice"; "Brazil on the Brink," *The New York Times* (Sept. 1, 1961).

Tell E I got the measurements, and I'll soon go shopping with my tape-measure that has inches on one side and centimeters on the other— Thank her.

Another non-alcoholic drink that is quite good is tonic-water (quinine-water) with lots of ice, lemon and a drop of bitters—tastes almost exactly like a gin & tonic. Maybe I'll bring you some *matte*, too.

I am very eager to see the plays. What good ideas. Now that I know what they're about I am surprised that no one saw before what good short plays they could make.

I wonder what has happened to poor Bowdoin[1]—en—in—however he spells it. (*You* spell "polaroid"[2] more like hemorrhoid . . . And I was touched to see that Hemingway misspelled *seized* in his will.)

I have so many things to tell you—but I am at least ten days behind with this little book. We did nothing but answer the telephone, buy newspapers, scribble notes, etc. all that time—and all L's friends were here—we just sat and looked at each other, mostly. No one I know will ever *see* this book if I can help it . . . And of course now lots of parts of it are obsolete and have to be reconstructed.[3] I have an interview with the governor today, then one with the most famous female journalist, one with an *economist* (my weakest link, all right). It is wonderful you are well and doing so much work.— I am so eager to see you and your family. I suppose we'll come towards the end of October now—with much love and thank you again for writing during the crises, and offering dollars (?)—a cruzeiros disguised as a book?

Elizabeth

Saturday, the 16th

I am sorry this hasn't got mailed yet. I'll take a walk up the beach to the Co-pacabana Palace this afternoon and mail it. We have been busy, in a sort of harassed and worried way that isn't much fun. I'm mostly worried about whether Lota's job will go on or not. It all depends on whether Carlos stays in power or not. So far he's staying. But every day begins with going through all the papers—another batch at 1 PM.— I do so want her to go on with it. The situation is a mess. Don't believe what you see about "legal-ity" and the precious "constitution" being saved!— All the old crooks are

1 Bowden Broadwater.
2 RL spells "polaroid" correctly in his letter (see letter 236).
3 Chapters on "The Struggle for a Stable Democracy" and "A Nation Perplexed and Uncertain" discuss the crisis prompted by the Quadros resignation. See EB-*Brazil* (1962).

jetting back into their niches as fast as they can—& the C p[1] right out in the open now.

The big Bienale is starting soon in São Paulo—we'll have to go, I suppose. Do you know a German-Swiss called *Bissier?*— I am crazy about what I've seen of his painting—not much so far. Julius Bissier— They have 72 there, I think, and I do want to see that. A big Motherwell show from the US—and lots of smaller fry. The last two or three days we've been entertaining Monroe Wheeler—do you know him, I can't remember?—here for the show, and now in Rio recuperating—much more affable than I've ever found him before, somehow.

Do you smoke cigars?— I think not—but Brazil has excellent, famous ones, you know, and I'll bring you a box if you'd like. What shape do you prefer? I'd forgotten about their supposed merits until Monroe expatiated on them. I don't know why if they can make good cigars they can't make good cigarettes . . . Oh heavens—my smallest thought is a journalistic cliché these days. I'll have to put that into Chapter VII,[2] I suppose. Also—why does all the toothpaste turn to cement these days? What about the food and drug laws? How strong is the Julião movement in the northeast?[3] Do I really have to make another trip to that nightmare Brasília?—heaven forbid.

I am somewhat in love at the moment with the last Emperor—Dom Pedro II—surely the world's noblest emperor as far as character went. He tried to *hug* Whittier, in the Brazilian fashion, when they met. Whittier backed away, of course. When they parted, Dom Pedro chased him downstairs (this was at Longfellow's, a dinner-party) and finally did succeed in hugging him. (Dom Pedro was 6 foot 4"). He translated a very bad poem of Whittier's, "The Cry of a Lost Soul"—not about slavery, as I'd thought,[4] but about an Amazon bird—and sent him a glass case of them, stuffed.— But I mustn't give away any more of my thrilling surprises . . .

Good-bye, and see you soon—Lota sends *abraços,*

Elizabeth

---

1 Communist Party.

2 See EB-*Brazil*, 75.

3 Francisco Julião was the leader of the Peasant League movement, which had fought for the rights of people working on the large estates of northeast Brazil since the 1950s. *Brazil* features a photograph of Julião with sugarcane workers and a photograph of a "pro-Castro rally organized in Recife by the Peasant League." (EB did not write the caption.)

4 John Greenleaf Whittier, "The Cry of a Lost Soul" (1862). In *Brazil*, EB wrote that "the Emperor loathed slavery, believing it to be a shameful blot on his beautiful, beloved country, and he liberated all his own inherited slaves as early as 1840. But he also thought that emancipation would have to come gradually in the country as a whole in order not to upset the economy, which during his reign was dependent almost entirely on slave labor" (EB and the Editors of *Life, Brazil* [1962], 45–46). Slavery was abolished in Brazil in 1888.

Sunday—
I'm going to give this to Monroe to mail to you—he's leaving tonight and
you'll get it sooner—sorry I've been so slow.

240.

September 25th [1961]
Dearest Cal:
Tell E I just read her review in the *Times*—August 27th[1]—and think it's
awfully good. It gives me strength, almost, to tackle the *favela* business
here— (The Rio slums—if anyone doesn't know by now.)
This is just to be going on with—and undoubtedly shows your influence,
I think. I'll probably make some more changes.[2]
We hope to leave around October 28th—if I stall any longer we'll freeze
to death—probably shall, anyway, with our tropic-thinned blood and no fur
coats, etc.
Harriet's dress is ordered. I hope she'll like it! The dressmaker much impressed with her measurements—"These American children are so *forte* . . ."
This awful book has aged me fearfully, I feel—and probably politics has
aged Lota, although she looks about the same, to me. I feel older than
KAP.[3]— Everything is a mess here, and tragic, really. God knows what will
happen next. It looks very pro-communist to me and please tell Kennedy or
Arthur S, Jr to get busy— The whole of SA could perfectly well *curdle*—to
communism—like a bowl of milk, I think—and it is half Brazil's fault and
half ours. (Cheerful thought to leave with you.) Lota is again at "the
Palace"—she loves a fight, fortunately, but this is all a bit too much. Everyone is impeaching everyone else—and Lota is being attacked in the papers,
too—mostly out of jealousy and spite. I suppose it is just like the US, really,
but on such a small and personal scale—and *I* never was involved, in the US!
Much love—and how nice it will be to see you,
Elizabeth

As you may not know, "The Maple Leaf Forever" is the un-official Canadian
anthem—sung in school constantly.[4]

1 Elizabeth Hardwick, "Some Chapters of Personal History: A Brilliant Study of a Mexican Family Probes the
Lives of the Unknown Poor" (a review of *The Children of Sanchez* by Oscar Lewis), *The New York Times Book Review* (Aug. 27, 1961).
2 EB enclosed "First Death in Nova Scotia" (EB-*CP*).
3 Katherine Anne Porter.
4 See "First Death in Nova Scotia," line 36 (EB-*CP*).

241.

15 West 67th Street
New York, New York
October 3 ? [1961]

My dear Elizabeth:

I am overjoyed to have your letter this morning and to know at last that the date is certain. I gather you are coming by plane and will be here the 29th or 30th. Our number is Sc-4-1580. The *Harvard Advocate*[1] is having a Lowell number and I'll be in Cambridge on the first of November for a few days. We'll be meeting soon, thank heaven; call as soon as you get in.

Your elegy is very lovely and pathetic, the best in the language of its kind, I think—I mean a piece on a real little child, memorialized from your own memories. The other good ones are either imaginary children, such as Ransom's, or not personally remembered, as Jonson's Salathiel Pavy.[2] I have been thinking lately—your poems usually bring something of the sort to my mind—that there's a side to writing that's like a little bird swooping in to snatch a piece of bread, only there are so many birds bustling about, and I suppose the bread is always vanishing, so that only by miracle can the bird get it. That is, if one is very lucky and talented, there's a way of writing that is actually believable, and beyond that, a way that is rich and interesting, and beyond that, a way that really gets the bread—then a bell rings and a poem is what we call immortal. That's what you've done. Your little child is caught in all its childish, fairy story pomp and simplicity, and pushing in like black prongs are the years, autumn and maturity.

You talk of age and how your book has aged you—sometime every day, it's with me personally, impersonally, though I'm hale enough in body and soul. But there's a blankness that we and everyone else is always moving on in our one way trip to the dust, and will get there, still not understanding, for all's incomplete and not to be understood. I am enough of a Puritan to believe that I will be told at least this and can rest satisfied in my chaos—the universal human chaos, perhaps.

My play's done and almost retyped by the typist, and I don't know what I've done, an American epic, or just words for actors to turn into life, if I've done that even. So many questions! What makes a play actable, more than just actable? Have I done something solid, or just reshuffled Hawthorne and Melville? All very confusing and exciting! Among the satisfactions: the speed

---

1 "Robert Lowell Special Issue," *The Harvard Advocate* (Nov. 1961).
2 John Crowe Ransom, "Bells for John Whiteside's Daughter" (1924); Ben Jonson, "On Salathiel Pavy" (1616).

in writing, the avoidance of that feeling of getting something by the wrong end so that do what I will whatever I write will be confused, phony, pretentious, and a great freedom from myself and all my much too well known to me plot and passions.

We're settled here now. A lot's over, or begun to be over, the sweat of moving in, the nervousness of facing the damage of last year and facing it down here in New York. Our place is pleasant, a big room with a twenty-foot ceiling loaded with our old fashioned Boston furniture, rather like a club room. There's a smug pleasure in watching the parade go by, and being out of it to the extent of not drinking.

Well, I am thinking of you. It must be like living in a ruined house, now in Brazil. I was talking to Morton Zabel the other night. He was worried about you and trying to find you in New York and had been writing people in Brazil if he should make a trip to help them. He remembered Lacerda, "the hero of the Vargas affair"[1] one night in his room, wounded in the foot. I'm sorry it's all so tough for you and Lota. It's not like that here—there's just a queer, half-apocalyptic, nuclear feeling in the air, as tho nations had died and were now anachronistic, yet in their anarchic death-throes would live on for ages troubling us, threatening the likelihood of life continuing.[2] I guess this is my personal, eccentric impression, but things are very queer, as if one's clothes were full of holes!

(over)

Did I write you about having a haircut at the Ritz in Boston? When I got there there were a couple of boys ahead of me, one had about a quarter of an inch of hair left from his crew haircut and yet was waiting for that to be trimmed down. The other, I felt with relief, was at least normally in need of a haircut. Then I saw this other kept twitching and grimacing, and that his mother was begging him to calm himself and finally that his eyes were rolled so that only the whites showed. I started to read in *Life*, an article on megalitonic warfare, the 96 per cents that we and Russia could destroy of each other, the planes with bombs 24 hours in the air, any one able to get jittery or answer a false warning and let go.[3] When I was in the chair, the barber was a brownish, baldish, spectacled man, looking rather like William Carlos Williams. He was talking about fishing for flounder in Boston harbor. It was always spoiled by one or two drunks. "The world's fine except for the people in it," he said.

1 See note to letter 133.
2 See "Fall 1961," lines 6–15 (RL-*CP*).
3 "K's 100-megaton Threat," *Life* (Sept. 8, 1961).

Well, Central Park's gorgeous for Harriet, and for me as I cross it three times a week to my psychiatrist. We love a lot of people.

And you, my Dear—

Love,

Cal

Harriet's alerted for her dress and awfully *forte*.

242.

Dearest Elizabeth:

You owe me and I owe you a letter. It seems an age since you left, though nothing much has happened, except that a few things on the scene then have moved a few inches forward. Harriet got my chicken pox and so we didn't go to Puerto Rico, but spent New Years with the Peter Taylors in Columbus, Ohio, going to bed at 11:30 after a sleepy rubber of bridge. Bloomgarden has taken my *Phaedra* and it may go on this spring if it's done off Broadway. Harvard has made good its offer, and my teaching will be reduced to two days a week from September through December.[1] A lot of commuting and flying, but the students will be better and my pay doubled. I've done another little poem which I'll enclose.

Tell me something personal. What did you make of Sandra Hochman?[2] I suppose you know how mixed up with her I was last year. I haven't seen her since last summer, but Kunitz told me she was visiting you here. I knew she had intended to do a thesis on you, but somehow shyly never brought it up with you, thinking perhaps nothing had happened. She's rather a bull, I don't know how to judge her work. There's certainly bounce and unexpected images, though I don't know how much order.

I think you still have my American play, at least Dr. Baumann doesn't have it. Could you mail it back sometime? I'd love to know what you think of it. I'm about to start rewriting again. Somehow I've found excuse after excuse for dawdling—so much typing, such ignorance of the medium!

We're all set for Brazil, and chicken pox won't stop us. For Christmas I gave Harriet a jig-saw puzzle of the world and an airplane that flies around a map of the world. So she's prepared. We too, we feel a drouth from having

1 Harvard offered RL a contract to teach one semester each year.
2 With whom RL had an affair during his manic episode in 1961 (see letter 233).

been home too long. I talked to a guy at the Rockefeller Foundation who advised us to stop at Trinidad and come home by way of Lima. Jack Thompson[1] thinks the Congress for Cultural Freedom might partially finance us. Do you know someone in Rio named Keith Botsford? I knew him at Iowa. He's the agent for the Congress and is being written.

The De Lassus[2] is about as solemn as anything I've ever heard, a sort of super Gregorian chant, very wonderful. So is Supervia. We'll play her many times before we leave and steep in the sound, and people will say there's something indefinably Brazilian about us.

I loved seeing you. It was quite a lot, though a fraction of what I would have liked. I felt as close and at ease as ever, though at ease is beyond what the living are allowed. Tell me how the trip went. I hear you had trouble getting off, and spent a couple of free-from-Life Inc. days. What's happened to your book? Can we have a copy both for itself and to do our homework? What's happened since your return?

Send me some more poems. I want to see the book in print. I still wish you'd put in the stories. The Taylors thought your *New Yorker* anthology one wonderful.[3] You are a prose classic to ever so many people, as well as a poet classic.

I've just written Peter Taylor about a day here with Allen Tate getting drunker and drunker and haven't the heart to go into [it] again, but at one point, well along, he called Harriet very formally to him. He was wearing her cardboard birthday derby, green, and looking like a miniature Irish barfly, and said, "You are a Kentucky Belle, because your mother is a Kentucky Belle. You are very dear to me because your mother and father are very dear to me. You will be very dear to me when you grow up." He looked at her as if he would very much prefer her grown up. She looked at him with wonder—there was really a lot more strange blarney. Then she said, "If you are still alive."[4] I had to quickly say we would all be alive for ever.

Ah, I miss you, I miss you!

Love from all of us to you and Lota.

Cal

P.S. Lota's house seems to be the most know[n] and admired house on the continent. Everyone has heard of it.

1 John Thompson was executive director of the Farfield Foundation from 1956 to 1965; it was involved in the funding of the Congress for Cultural Freedom (in part, and covertly, by the CIA).
2 EB had sent RL Orlande de Lassus, *Seven Penitential Psalms*, Instrumentalensemble Rudolph Pohl, with Helmut Krebs, Hans Joachim Rotzsch, and Hans-Olaf Hüdemann (Archive DGG ARC 3134/5).
3 "In the Village," reprinted in *Stories from The New Yorker: 1950–1960* (1960); see EB-*CPR*.
4 See "Writers: To Allen Tate II," lines 1–9 (RL-*CP*).

243.

Dearest Cal:

I started a letter to you a few days ago, but I seem to be having trouble getting to writing anything again, even letters—then last night, Sunday, a batch of mail arrived from Petrópolis. Would that my mail were always like that, I said to Lota: a letter from you, a poem from you,[1] and a check for $3,000 (the last installment from LIFE). I did finish a note of practical information to Elizabeth. We are already preparing for your visit and I wish it were almost June. Everything looks promising—as far as the visit goes, that is. Politically I just hope nothing drastic is going to happen. We are cultivating English-speaking children of the right age to play with Harriet, and the apartment should be remodeled by then. The permit to move two walls is supposed to come tomorrow. Our trunks are in the customs now. Because of Lota's present pull, we have an Army Captain getting them out for us. I met him in his full uniform, white coat, gold lanyards (?) medals, etc. and first he saluted me, then kissed my hand, then shook it and gave me an *abraço*. I felt rather nervous, remembering the rumpled laundry, piles of old bills, etc., that he may see if they open those trunks. I am worried by the thought of those beautiful cookie-jars and hope they are safe—unbroken and unstolen.

I was also worried a little by the thought of Sandra Hochman, and I am glad you mentioned her. She wrote me a note in New York, then telephoned, saying she was writing a paper on me, etc., and I, all unknowing that she was the girl you had been involved with last summer, had lunch with her and talked with her for a couple of hours. That same evening I mentioned her to someone and, of course, was speedily informed. Then I felt a bit upset—I didn't know whether to mention it to you or not and finally decided not to. I saw her once more, briefly, at the apartment, and I went over her paper and corrected all the factual errors—didn't attempt to criticize it at all. I left it for her at LIFE and hope she got it. She had some pretty good ideas, I thought—and some were pleasantly surprising to me. I thought afterwards that it is rare to talk to someone so much younger for almost two hours, about oneself, and never have her rub one the wrong way. I also thought she was very pretty. I haven't seen any of her poems. I think she said she was sending me a book. Maybe it will turn up in the trunks, and I just don't remember getting it. Virgil Thompson seemed to think he was responsible for her calling me, etc.—"my little friend" he kept calling her.

---

1 "Fall 1961" (RL-*CP*).

Anyway, I am glad it is all clear now, and I did feel considerable sympathy for her, and curiosity, although of course I refused to ask Virgil any questions . . . She never mentioned you; during the 1st interview I did recommend your works to her very highly!

Virgil was the same as ever—you should hear him on the subject of Rio—but it's only funny in his voice (which I imitate very well, Lota says). "Once you get away from that *appalling* coast, Rio's very nice, very nice— just like *Nice* . . ." and—"the oysters are quite tasteless—not as tasteless as *English* oysters that taste like diddies,—but of course if you haven't eaten a *Peruvian* oyster you've never eaten oysters" etc., etc. I don't know why he is always so nice to me, in his way—he always has been. He kept informing Lota—"I adore Brazil—simply *adore* it—but the Brazilian *attention-span* is the shortest in the world . . ."

Yes—we finally did get away after two or three postponements due to sleet. I can't even remember exactly when now, it went on so long. I gave your plays—with a hurriedly written and illegible note—to Harold Leeds across the street at 64 Perry Street, Chelsea 3-4452. He was either going to give them to Dr. Baumann—he's a patient and friend of hers, too—or straight to you. Perhaps you have met by now. I'd like to have you, and E, see his house. It's the prettiest one I know in New York. He is a very good architect—a bit chi-chi and difficult at first, but improves rapidly, and his friend Wheaton Galentine makes, also, very good movies—really. Ask to see his Singer Sewing Machine movie sometime![1]— They are hard-working and quiet and ultra-ultra-refined. I like them both. I am awfully sorry about the plays and do hope you've got them by now. I wish I had copies here to say some more about them. I wasn't myself at all in N.Y.—just half-there, I think—and I'm horrified to think how I must have seemed to be slighting your work, not even reading it, etc. You said I seemed "serene," but I think it must have been a facial expression left-over from several months earlier in Brazil. I actually don't remember a great deal of what I did in N.Y., and everything Lota produces for me in the way of clothes and purchases is a complete surprise. I didn't *see* anything. Now I know why most people seem so unobservant all the time. They are just too harassed and over-worked.

We did get to see *A Man for All Seasons* before we left—and I was very disappointed in it— It seemed awfully thin to me, although well-acted.[2] I'm sick of all this fascination of extremes—although I suppose it's understand-

---

1 *Treadle and Bobbin* (1954).
2 Robert Bolt, *A Man for All Seasons* (1954), first performed on Broadway in 1961.

able enough. Dope-addicts—saints—either one or the other—*anything* rather than be what we are—*anything* to imply we're all victims, I guess—or that as long as you see through everything you've done all you can. I hope they put on your *Phaedra*. I don't like to think of all that flying you will be doing, to Harvard. Some of our books have arrived now, and I am going to read the *Imitations* through with my mind really on them at last—all those that appeared after I took on that book, that is. I am eager to get the records out of the customs—the ALFANDAGA—isn't that a nice Arabian word?

Supervia was *Spanish*. It's like confusing Chinese & Japanese. Be careful! You might be able to impress Bob Giroux with your knowledge of her. There was never a Carmen like hers, they say, and she died in childbirth at the age of 30 or 28. I didn't put you on my mailing list for LIFE. I was hoping you'd never see that damned—really damned—book—but maybe I'll have to send them a supplementary list. They made changes in my text even after I left—"young girl" appearing as "teenager," etc., etc.—and I don't think there are more than 20 sentences of mine left unchanged. Words like "oust" mysteriously appeared, too—oh, it's not worth the money except that now I do KNOW. Well—I am writing them that LETTER they want, but I suspect all their writers did and then didn't send it. It's like mailing a snowflake to Devils Island, more or less. The article of "The Madison Avenue Villain"[1] in the last *PR* seems meant all for me.

Lota's house—or *our* house, really, since I bought some portions of it, too, although it was started when I arrived here—is in very shabby condition now, but still beautiful. We showed Belle G photographs of it, I remember—but of course she had *two* Mies houses at that point![2] I've been going over the stories and don't think they're good enough—only IN PRISON and the last 2 *New Yorker* ones[3]—and three scarcely make a book . . . Oh, dear. Today I am really going to face the problem and write to the agent, etc. I didn't do anything for two weeks but sleep and mope.

The end of February I hope to go on another river-trip—can't seem to help myself—this time down the Rio São Francisco—ten days or so. If I survive, I think it may be worth writing about. I have plans for my own small book on Brazil now, as I guess I said. I've been reading Mary McCarthy's *On the Contrary*—also Marianne's *Reader*,[4] which I promised to review for the

1 Robert Brustein, "The Madison Avenue Villain," *Partisan Review* (1961).
2 Mies van der Rohe.
3 "Gwendolyn" and "In the Village" (EB-*CPR*).
4 *A Marianne Moore Reader* (1961).

Bryn Mawr magazine. Strange contrast—Mary so sane and mean; Marianne so mad and good—which do you choose? And they both lie like rugs—at least I shouldn't say *lie*, but anything I know at first-hand of their impressions aren't mine at all. Marianne admiring the Duke of Windsor's style! Mary giving her poor dead 1st husband another beating still: "Notions of the superman and the genius flickered across his thoughts . . ."[1] But Marianne can *astound*, and there are always some of those marvelous poems. Mary seems like all the rest of us, striving, striving.

I always used to say that I wouldn't teach or work, etc. because I was lazy. Now I've decided to change my tune and say that I am "independent." This never occurred to me before the N.Y. trip—"I'm just terribly independent . . ." How I can get around not living among my peers but running off to the hinterlands of poverty-stricken societies I don't know yet, but maybe I'll think of something.

Your poem is haunting me—I find I have it almost memorized— We had a clock that had a ship that rocked back and forth, and another one that showed something moving in the window of a house on a green hill—I always thought it was someone shaking out the sheets in the bedroom. "Radiant with terror"—but best of all, I think, are the old sayings used in the ghastly new context.[2] Please write again soon—I certainly shall because this seems like just a beginning— Thank you for all your great kindness in New York.

Love from Lota and me,
Elizabeth

P.S. I saw Marlboro advertising *Os Sertões*—"Rebellion in the Backlands"[3]— the best Brazilian book, next to Machado de Assis, & wrote them to send you a copy. You'll never read it all, but skip through the 1st half to the story part—it's wonderful, really. I suspect it influenced Hemingway—in a Spanish translation—and have almost proved it—(his retreat from Caporetto).[4]

The 23rd—
Another storm is about to break—an awful one last night, and the worst a week ago followed by a slight earthquake, Rio's first, I think. I was relieved

---

1 Harold Johnsrud, an aspiring playwright, was married to Mary McCarthy from 1933 to 1936.
2 See "Fall 1961," lines 13, 16, 17, 21, and 22 (RL-*CP*).
3 Euclides da Cunha, *Os Sertões* (1902); *Rebellion in the Backlands*, trans. Samuel Putnam (1944).
4 See Ernest Hemingway, *A Farewell to Arms* (1929).

to see it *had* been an earthquake, in the morning papers—because when I felt it, at 11:30 PM, Lota had said it was my imagination. Also—I thought the apartment house might be about to fall down, as they occasionally do.

I think Ransom's piece about you in the ADVOCATE is charming, and so nice.[1] The aristocracy one doesn't quite seem to make its point, to me—or else I have known it all all along so it doesn't strike *me* as very profound, but I was glad to see he agreed with my "exuberant" estimate![2] Anne Sexton gave me a new idea of you, and I do wish I had attended one of the New School evenings, somehow or other. (Her poetry bothers me—sometimes so good, sometimes *so* imitative of you—like in the December POETRY— those in *PR* so uneven, but fine in spots[3]). Donald Hall sounds "stingy," as always.[4] I wonder how your "week" was and how the reading was and do wish I could have got there.— I think the ad for "Salem" cigarettes on the back of the *Advocate* is a wonderful irony, after your poem about Salem "air-softens every puff" and that peaceful *canoe*.[5]

The Hugo translation is particularly fine—at least it seems to me Hugo sounds much better in your English than in his French.[6] You save him from his own vulgarity. That's a word I never mean to use again—but I can't think of any other for some qualities.

Will you please give me Stanley Kunitz's address—and his wife's name—*again?*—I'm sorry—I didn't write it down, apparently. I'd like to write him a note to thank him and perhaps send him a book.

And I didn't even notice until I got back that Eliot and I had helped you with yr. French . . .[7]

You have no idea, Cal, how really grateful to you I am and how fortunate I feel myself in knowing you, having you for a friend. When I think of

1 John Crowe Ransom, "A Look Backwards and a Note of Hope," *The Harvard Advocate* (Nov. 12, 1962).

2 "Speaking of *Life Studies*, Elizabeth Bishop says, 'a poem like "My Last Afternoon with Uncle Devereux Winslow" or "Skunk Hour" can tell us as much about the state of society as a volume of Henry James at his best.' 'Skunk Hour' is dedicated to Miss Bishop, and since it is undeniably a good poem, perhaps on these grounds alone we should be prepared to forgive what sounds like incredible exuberance"; David Berman, "Robert Lowell and the Aristocratic Tradition," *The Harvard Advocate* (Nov. 12, 1962).

3 Anne Sexton, "Classroom at Boston University," *The Harvard Advocate* (Nov. 12, 1962); "The House," *Poetry* (Dec. 1961); and "A Curse Against Elegies," "The Abortion," "With Mercy for the Greedy," "For God While Sleeping," "In the Deep Museum," and "Ghosts," *Partisan Review* (1961)

4 Donald Hall, "Lord Weary in 1947," *The Harvard Advocate* (Nov. 12, 1962).

5 See "Salem" (RL-*CP*).

6 See "Russia 1812" and "At Gautier's Grave" (RL-*CP*).

7 "I have been so free with my texts that it is perhaps an impertinence for me to thank those people, more expert in languages than I, for their scattered help. Corrections . . . in my French [were made] by Jackson Matthews, T. S. Eliot and Elizabeth Bishop"; "Acknowledgments," *Imitations*, xiv. See also T. S. Eliot to RL, June 1, 1961 (Houghton) and RL-*Letters*, 383–84 and 749.

how the world and my life would look to me if you weren't in either of them at all—they'd look very empty, I think. I am awfully happy with Lota, odd as it is in some ways, and with living in such a hopeless, helpless country, too. I don't seem to need or enjoy a lot of intellectual society—but I certainly need you. This is the early morning of the 24th now—hot as can be—7:30—brilliant, a thin but blinding haze. I'm going for a swim before too many people get out on the beach. The sand is all beaten down after the rain, and damp. The boys peddling things start off very early. Did I tell you that there is one who very cleverly shouts out the time of day—he's peddling Coca Cola or Maté—and gives the exchange for the dollar? Yesterday I saw something really weird—a couple anointing themselves with Coca Cola,—honestly. They bought a bottle so I couldn't be mistaken. Imagine how sticky.

I am hoping to "get to know Harriet better" in Brazil.

Lots of love,

Elizabeth

244.

March 10, 1962

Dearest Elizabeth:

I meant to answer your lovely full letter instantly. Then I put it off meaning to send you some new poems, then more poems kept coming in a little trickle, and I kept waiting, and somehow shying away from copying them out. We have had a succession of little pricking winter illnesses: chicken pox, tonsillitis, piles, tonsillitis, coughs—all these for me, Harriet much the same plus scarlet fever, over in three days with drugs but involving hundreds, I think, of inoculations because Mary came here before the diagnosis was made, then went to several parties and households with children.

We are very keen on our Brazil and feel heaven would be a new atmosphere. I think the Congress for Cultural Freedom will arrange for ~~us both~~ me to do readings in other countries and help pay the bills. Lizzie is planning a lecture on "plot" that might be given and would have more critical substance than my offerings.

Glad you liked Sandra. The whole business is a slightly malarial memory for me. She has surprising energy and freshness, a slice of the new age, full of references, interests and rhythms that are strange to me, a bit of what one once was or might have been at that age.

Did you see what *Time* did to us? Very impertinent, vulgar and often meaningless. You are warm, interested in people and unslick[1]—all just the opposite of what they said. Still in their ugly way, they did their best by us, putting us at the top of our little decadent, post-war empyrian. It's funny being a poet, working in a medium that can't and shouldn't have much public. You find you want a little publicity as a by-product. Something to tell you you are no worse than the rest of the human race on their own terms, terms we never sought. I wrote a little squib for Bill Meredith's guest-book.

> "Are we couth or uncouth?
> Oh it's best to be both,
> both sides of the coin,
> half man and half horse,
> poor creatures of rhyme,
> who want to rejoin
> the human race
> and life and time."

A word about the poems I'm putting in. You'll find one to you, unidentified, about that time in Stonington after the Carley Dawson departure.[2] More romantic and gray than the whole truth, for all has been sunny between us. Indeed it all started from thinking about your letter, how indispensable you are to me, and how ideally we've really kept things, better than life allows really. Also I tried versing your "In the Village." The lines about the heart[3] are Harriet's on her kindergarten society, the rest is merely your prose put into three-beat lines and probably a travesty, making something small and literary out [of] something much larger, gayer and more healthy. I let the scream throw out the joyful *clang*. Anyway, I send it with misgivings. Maybe you could use it for raw material for a really great poem. My other things don't need comment. My inspiration seems to have become minute—little lines, little subjects. By the way, I thought your *New Yorker* child was awfully good.[4] Mary and I both read it aloud one weird evening with Ted Roethke.

Roethke is in a strange monstrous state of acting himself, never happy

1 Of Roethke, RL, and EB, she is "the most limited and proficient of the three—indeed, the cool, eely slickness of her poems is sometimes repellent. They have little human warmth, no specific temperature. She seldom writes about people or their feelings. She writes about things and places with a woman's eye as keen as any since Virginia Woolf's. Above all, she has a gift of imagery"; "Poetry in English, 1945–1962," *Time* (March 9, 1962), 93.
2 "Water" (RL-*CP*).
3 "The Scream," lines 34–35 (RL-*CP*).
4 "First Death in Nova Scotia," *The New Yorker* (March 10, 1962); see EB-*CP*.

unless he is thinking about himself, and asserting he is better than anyone else. Under the fat man, less fat now but looking like a blown up Churchill even with the cigar, is a thin, sensitive, very intelligent soul, all wound up and quivering.[1] Most of the evening, he was pawing Mary in front of her husband and his wife. Meanwhile Jim[2] was taking him behind the scenes in our kitchen hallway and offering him Scotch, "the house is yours," while Mary sat on the sofa hearing his wife say only people who really hate Ted give him anything to drink. At the end Jim said, "I've never seen you in better form (their first meeting). I think it's fifty-fifty you'll get home without a quarrel with your wife." A riddling picture of us all, but rather awful!

We've rented a little two room apartment above us, and now I sit there in great sunlit silent space and it seems as if we had a house again.

Dr. Baumann has become part of our lives. Brisk sunny visits, pills, shots, conferences behind closed doors, conversations with her all-German nursing staff, bargain suppositories for piles. She's wonderful, and makes illness a treat.

Kunitz' address is 157 West 12th St. His wife's name is Elise. He's my great stand-by, and every Monday after class, I stop at his house and we talk till two, both coughing.[3] I saw Mackie Jarrell the other night when I was reading at the Conn. Women's College. She sent her love and apologies for never having answered a letter. Like Randall, she somehow can't [write] to anyone. What an imprint to have been married to Randall. She is now a PhD, a full professor, and an expert on Pope, Swift and the modern Irish, but the old stamp remains. The strong prejudices without Randall's buoyant self-certain euphoria. She can't bear his fairy stories,[4] thinks something tragically limiting happened to his life and still seems to love him.

I feel we all do less than we might in every way, yet somehow discover we are real and human, as those before us have been[5]—all shuffled forward so rapidly through this life, aching, puzzled, too good to be true. I look back on my parents as people perpetually about our age.

I think we are all at last going to Puerto Rico in ten days. We all thirst for the heat and change. It's been a rather low-tide and pinching winter getting settled in our minds here. I feel on the verge of some howling platitude, such

---

1 Cf. "Imprisoned in every fat man a thin one is wildly signaling to be let out"; Cyril Connolly, *The Unquiet Grave* (1945), 58.
2 James West, Mary McCarthy's husband.
3 RL was teaching at the New School for Social Research on West 12th Street.
4 Randall Jarrell translated stories by the Brothers Grimm in *The Golden Bird* (1962) and by Ludwig Bechstein in *The Rabbit Catcher* (1962).
5 See "Those Before Us" (RL-*CP*).

as how stunning it is to find you are almost living exactly what you would like to. That's about it. All our love to you and Lota.

Cal

P.S. Lizzie is very anxious to know more about the climate, can she wear summer dresses, what fall or winter things will we need? Thank you a thousand times for what you've already done. By the way have you run into Keith Botsford, an old Iowa acquaintance of mine, and now in charge of the Freedom Congress things in Rio? He's quite attractive in slightly too sharp and shiny [a] way. Also Fred Dupee has written from Rome wanting your address for some lady coming to Brazil, attractive and a reader of yours. "Loves English poetry, especially E. Bishop."

245.[1]

Samambaia, for a change—March?? [1962]

Dearest Cal:

I wrote simultaneously to you and Elizabeth and she has answered and you haven't—I hope you got yours? Tell her that I have made reservations for you for June at the Copacabana—but they will be checked and re-checked several times before then. You can stay between $450 and about $700 for a suite for the month—depending if you want the very best or not. I'm going to go look at the next-best ones next week, and also our friend Osh-CAR, who is a friend of the manager, of course, will try to get a re-duction, etc. Lota is also going to pick up her old acquaintance with the English-speaking baby-sitter, Francesca (German). She says, L says, she is wonderful. I do hope it doesn't sound too expensive to you. It is really ex-tremely comfortable there and a magnificent view—and the pool will be ideal for Harriet (a children's pool, etc.) plus the beach, kites, sand-castles, sand artists, pop-corn sellers, balloons, and so on. You probably won't want it for the whole month, anyway. Did you get *Rebellion in the Backlands?* And did I recommend, before, *The Masters and the Slaves* by Gilberto Freyre?— also Knopf.[2] It has awful faults but is still the most informative and readable book—allowing for a lot of exaggeration and pro-slavery feeling, etc. A funny one, at the Library, I suppose, is *Dom Pedro the Magnanimous* by some Chapel Hill lady[3]—simple but fascinating; and then you'd have lots of back-

1 Crossed with letter 244.
2 Published in 1946.
3 Mary Wilhelmine Williams, *Dom Pedro the Magnanimous* (1937).

ground . . . And maybe by now my little horror is out, too—I asked them to send you one. I hope you can distinguish between what I said and what they said. They asked and asked me to write a letter telling how the books could be "improved" and about my "experience." I finally wrote that I thought they *couldn't* be improved (under present system), and that my experience had been depressing . . . Now I have had various phone calls from Rio telling me that we-all are in *TIME* this week, and I am adding the dread of seeing that to the dread of seeing BRAZIL. God knows what idiotic things they say. Apparently I had to learn the hard way. I am still having nightmares about being back in that formica-coated building.

The city official who went to Washington to collect a few million to repair Rio, and incidentally help with Lota's park, hasn't come back yet and so Lota decided she could take ten days or so up in the country. I hope he isn't blowing the loan—we hear he is gadget-mad . . .

I finally got my hi-fi repaired and yesterday listened properly to *The Damnation of Faust*[1]—whee. I also went through the *Mahagonny* again, after many months, or as much of it as I can take at a time. I finally got Lota to listen to her theme-song, "I want a little dollar"[2] and she does like *that* part of it. I wish they'd make some good records of the Carnaval songs here, with translations. I swear some of them are as good as Brecht any day, only real folk-art. This year's words—most of them are about inflation, of course—are wonderful. I suppose if I were one of those busy people I'd have done something about them by now—before they get spoiled. Thank you for *Faust* very much. I got myself the "7 Penitential Psalms," but I am rather sorry I inflicted it on you and wish I'd given you his secular music instead. I used to be mad about him—all those weird chromatics—but the psalms don't strike me as being as weird as they used to: either the effect of so much modern music in the interim, or they really aren't. There is one of his, something about the SYBIL,[3] I used to listen to at college, that I thought was an eye-opener. Do you have any Gesualdo? If you ever find a good recording of his madrigals I wish you would get it for me. But listening to *Faust* I could just *hear* the opera you are undoubtedly doing—only what composer? Please not Sam Barber. I can't think; who?

Did you get your plays safely— Heavens, I am sorry about that delay.

I wrote a little piece about Marianne for the Bryn Mawr magazine and I

---

1 Hector Berlioz, *The Damnation of Faust* (1846).
2 "O show us the way to the next little dollar. O, don't ask why. O don't ask why"; "Alabama Song," *Aufstieg und Fall der Stadt Mahagonny* (Bertolt Brecht's original text for the song was in English).
3 Orlande de Lassus, *Twelve Prophesies of the Sybil* (c. 1560).

hope they got it in time. Once I got going I had a lot of fun and I can use it, revised, for a section in the long piece about her I am planning. I say she is a good guide for the "city life" . . . I also make fun of Stanley K (not by name and he'll never see it) for being so serious,—upset by her last *New Yorker* poems[1]—didn't you think that was rather funny and touching when he complained about them? & will you send me his address?

The Kipling I've been using for going-to-sleep reading.[2] A few I had never read and all the others mostly years ago when I went right through him at the public library. (However, I re-read the *Jungle Books* and *Just-So Stories* and *Kim*, every so often. Isn't Harriet almost old enough for the *Jungle Books?*—or some of the stories?) I think I feel about him exactly the way Max Beerbohm did—such a hideous mis-use of magnificent talents. (And also he was to blame for the worst side of Hemingway.) I don't care what he'd been through (& Randall's good about that part) but anyone who goes on all his life talking about "wonderful beatings"—for boys, men, elephants, anything—just had something too wrong with him. I never really appreciated Conrad until I had lived here a while. Now I find *Nostromo* profoundly interesting—not like Brazil at all, but some of the upper-class characters are familiar.[3] He seems to have been the only man who really understood colonialism while it was going on—and the mixed feelings of "foreigners."

I saw a French movie of La Princesse de Clèves a while ago.[4] You should see it if it gets to New York, really. It sticks exactly to the text and it is very pretty—court-life exactly as seen by a romantic *woman*. I can't think of any other movie that does that.

I am now half-way through a story about Uncle Arthur. The poem started me off, also I have his portrait as a boy here.[5] I don't know what to do with it (the story). His widow is still alive. He became the best fly-fisherman in the county but also the village drunk—or one of them—and took me fishing for the last time just before I came to Brazil.

I haven't heard from you for so long. I hope you are well and writing

1 "Lately I have heard one or two poets and critics sound upset because they don't think that the poem about Yul Brynner is as good as, say, *The Pangolin*. How solemn can one get? Surely by now Miss Moore is entitled to write any old way, any new way, she wants to"; EB, "A Sentimental Tribute," *Bryn Mawr Alumnae Bulletin* (Spring 1962), 3.

2 *The Best Short Stories of Rudyard Kipling*, ed. Randall Jarrell (1961), inscribed by RL: "Christmas 1961, Dearest Elizabeth, I seem to be giving you a collection of old friends this Christmas. Love, Cal."

3 Joseph Conrad's *Nostromo* (1904) is set in "Costaguana," a fictional South American republic.

4 *La Princesse de Clèves*, dir. Jean Delannoy (1961).

5 "Memories of Uncle Neddy" (EB-*CPR*); see "First Death in Nova Scotia," lines 9–11 (EB-*CP*).

some more poems. I am working on the three extra ones. I'm writing the publishers, etc. *now*—also Chapelbrook. We think we can get away to Italy for three months, this year—Italy and maybe Greece. I hope that will be all right with them. The $7,000 is intact—or at least one installment's still to come, I think. It cheers me up every time I remember it. We are going to market this afternoon and perhaps there will be a letter from you. I haven't had mail in over a week now. If you have written pay no attention to this. I am sorry to be so dull—very cheerful, really, but full of guilt about articles I can't write, etc., etc.—why I say I'll do these things! I wish I were Mary for a day. Ex-pres. Quadros is back. God knows what will happen next—nothing, probably. Oh it will be nice to see you.— Do write all your plans, what you'd like to do, etc. Want to meet poets? (If so I'd better hurry up and renew my faded friendships with a few . . .)

    With much love,
      Elizabeth

Carlos—the governor—was delighted with Lota's signed books. She really knows how to please people here.

246.

March 18, 1962

Dearest Elizabeth:

    Our letters crossed, and I again feel abashed at having let so much time slip by. The Cultural Congress is going to back our trip. We'll get traveling expenses and a per diem $40. I think we'll fly about the sixth of June. We are now taking a Radcliffe girl (one we know and who is marvelous with Harriet) and have to wait for her exams. We want to stop at one or two places, Trinidad, maybe Haiti, Surinam and Brasília on the way, and should arrive in Rio about the 15th and plan to stay there about a month. Then on to other countries reading and lecturing. Then either back to Brazil with no lectures or home to Maine. The Cultural Congress man is Keith Botsford care of Stefam Baciu, Associaco Brasileira do Congresso Pela liberdade da Cultura, Caixa Postal 89, Agencia Copacabana, Rio. I copy it all out to advance my Portuguese and for its strange likeness and unlikeness to your address.

    Oh dear! Colds, aches, tonsillitis, bronchitis, sweaty days, low fevers at night for a month now, though Dr. Anny's last drug seems to have killed the troubles. I weigh 173, less than at any time since school and look all too much like a poet. We are going to Puerto Rico on Tuesday for ten days and hope to return reborn.

I can't seem to find your last letter anywhere, and while I seem to remember it all I've probably forgotten just the things that need an answer or comment. I carried it to my study intending an instant full answer. Now where is it? Please forgive me if I am blank on something important.

I had a strange dream two nights ago about Philip Rahv, ascending the social ladder rung by rung as I climbed down. I think at the end his two sons were safely in Groton "de only place to send them," while Harriet was graduating from the local public school. We whittle away our inheritance. I think my last words were, "Is this what *PR* was all about?" And Philip said, "Of course." Have you ever noticed how snobbish the old rebel bohemians are. No one believes in society now except Mary and Philip. I'm rather sick of being so literary, but still turn green at the thought of Fred Morgan's coming out parties for his daughter, Natasha Spender's list of dukes they see, and the Epsteins' sending their son to St. Bernard's with conferences with Bowden—they were caught by the headmaster, while Bowden was showing them the backgrounds catalogue.[1] The child doesn't want to go, because "there is no goldfish bowl." Questioned, he says he's made "a thorough investigation."

I love the idea of the coming summer. Write soon dear, so I'll have a letter waiting when we get back. Your little Arthur looks beautiful in the *New Yorker*.[2] I don't seem able to use that much remembrance any more. Hope you liked my things. I feel I'm about to discover the common man or cooking or something homely and earth-shaking.

Love to you all,

Cal

P.S. Big change! I find the blighting tone of Henry Adams,[3] my old Bible, a terrible bore, coals to Newcastle, though I wouldn't want anyone else to say it. I guess what is so good about him is that he did too, and knew it was real illness in him—one he loved to exploit. I think his tone is a state anyone from our background should go through to be honest and alive, and then drop. I suspect anyone who hasn't been that bitter. Still, staying there is like calling malaria life. I guess what I mean is that there was real malaria under

---

1 Bowden Broadwater was the registrar for St. Bernard's School in New York City.
2 "First Death in Nova Scotia" (EB-*CP*).
3 *The Education of Henry Adams* (1918).

the jokes, exaggerations and epigrams, a sort of Baudelairean gallantry. But who could *want* what Empson says somewhere *to learn a style from a despair?*[1] I'm thinking of the white sand and full of deep nonsense today.

247.

Dearest Cal:

Speaking of piles . . . (wouldn't that be a good "opening phrase" to use for a Creative Writing Course?) I must tell you a nice Brazil-American misunderstanding over that word, when you get here . . . There are lots of lovely possibilities like that. Don't use the word *cocoa* the way we say it in English—it means *merde*. And the word "affair" in English still applies to business. A Brazilian friend of ours, a man, remarked in Calder's presence, "During the war, I was having an affair with an American Navy Officer, and he . . ."—and Calder began to burble and boil over the way he does, and had to be distracted immediately.

I am so glad Dr. Baumann is in attendance, and I do hope you are better and gaining weight—PLEASE don't go into a 19th century decline! Dr. B always made me feel that everything was possible if I only did my duty, and that my duty was plain and simple, too—of course it isn't, but it's a good way to feel sometimes. I wrote Elizabeth a very boring letter about *clothes* (and incidentally got going on the awfulness of the Brazilian book). Keith Botsford is coming to see me this afternoon and I may have more to tell her then—as you say, he sounds "bright & shiny," on the telephone. Our preparations seem to be overlapping somewhat.

The BRAZIL book IS awful; some sentences just don't make sense at all. And at least the pictures could have been good . . . Maybe, if you can read it at all, you will find a trace here & there of what I originally meant to say. However, as Lota keeps pointing out—most of the million "readers" won't read it; Brazil is very glad of any well-meant publicity at this point (the Governor has ordered dozens of copies to give away); and my name will mean nothing to most of the "readers," anyway. Headlines here every day about Cabot's introduction, "spiritual" values," and so on—when I happen to have his original introduction with me. He didn't write a word of the one that appears.

I thought our letters crossed, but I wasn't sure—that's nice, because it

---

1 William Empson, "This Last Pain," line 37.

meant I got two from you. Your dream is marvelous. And your evening with Roethke and his wife & Mary and Jim sounds hideous—but I wish I'd been there all the same. Poor Roethke! And "Jim" didn't strike me as such [a] sadistic type on the occasion we met. I thought he & Mary were in Belgrade or some place by now. Yes, the TIME is incredibly arrogant—but actually not as bad as I'd expect from them after my five weeks on the inside. They love those false, let's-face-it, summing-up cracks—they have sneaked some into BRAZIL, too. "But to say they are the best . . . is not to say much," etc. And they seem to quote the secondary of everybody—or poorer than that. So I'm "cool" and "eely"—that last word of course was unintelligible to my Brazilian friends, and I found myself translating it for them with embarrassment all that week. But everyone is interested to learn that you are actually coming here. It's too bad all the poets mentioned don't have books out right now, because I suppose they might sell a few hundred more.

Next morning— Keith B arrived, we one-up-man-shipped rapidly for an hour or so, & he never removed a large black pipe from his fairly handsome face . . . It seems he has three small children and is about to have a 4th baby. He also said he'd just celebrated his 13th wedding anniversary. He must have waited years to have a family. He has a house, swimming pool, and an imported nurse, here in the city—and thinks it would be nice to have Harriet as a caller—although all the children are younger than she is—but they speak English, at least. He had plans for getting you a vacant apartment—but I think I convinced him the hotel-apartment would be much better for a month's stay. It's impossible to cope with foreign servants, etc., and no vacation at all for Elizabeth. We agreed pretty well about everything else. WHO pays for the Congress for Cultural Freedom, anyway? I really know nothing about it, except EN-COUNTER & Nicolas Nabokov.[1] He wants more informal social life than lectures (which are usually badly attended here, anyway—but I think that's also usually due to poor advertising)—and that was my idea—also, to show you some of the country. Maybe I'll go to Bahia with you. I haven't been there yet.

To return to TIME—"cubistic Browning"! "more vivid than sensi-

---

[1] *Encounter* (edited by Stephen Spender), like *Partisan Review*, received funds from the Congress for Cultural Freedom, covertly funded by the CIA (see "A Statement on the CIA," *Partisan Review* [Winter 1962]). Nicolas Nabokov was secretary general of the Congress for Cultural Freedom.

tive"![1]—a wonderful opposition. I think Logue is better than Larkin,—from what I've seen.[2] Well, as Ginsberg put it so brilliantly: "Are you going to let your emotional life be run by *Time* Magazine?"[3]—it seems to me I have been, lately.

To return to your visit (the apartment is being torn down over my head almost—we have started remodeling and the place is full of piles of sand and bricks and bags of cement. It looks as though we were crazily building an air-raid shelter on the 11th floor.)—(If I sound rather disjointed that's why—I have to keep getting out of the way of two black and one white brick-layer every other minute.)— If E would like to lecture here I think in spite of what I said about lectures being badly attended—the U.S. NOVEL is a subject of some interest, and I'll do all the advertising I can—the personal approach works best, anyway.

I feel sorry for Mackie—she ought to marry again. I gather she hasn't. It was a great loss to them both, I think, that they couldn't stay together. Did MARY read my poem out loud? I can't imagine that, somehow. I haven't seen it yet. I have three poems about done—and a story called "Uncle Artie." I'll go on to *your* poems in a minute.

(Keith B said, tell Elizabeth, no evening clothes necessary. You may receive a small package from Calder in a month or so—a pair of earrings for me.)

Back to letter II. "Caixa" is pronounced *ky*-ish-a—*x*'s are like *sh*—and it's *box*, the French *Caisse*. I like Texaco pronounced Teshaco. (Also, here Buick rhymes with quick.) I liked Haiti very much when I stayed there ten years ago. God knows what it's like now, though—it sounds pretty bad. I think a few hours in Brasília are plenty. They have messed up what I said about it pretty much, in that book, but the general idea is still there. The point about its attracting the wrong sort was that no one wants to get into politics any more except for graft pure & simple, since it means having to live there some of the time, at least, and only the crudest political types can stand it, even for the sake of graft. A representative gets, say, about $4,000 a year—and will spend $25,000 on his election campaign—so you see. However, none of that could be put in, although I originally implied it fairly

---

1 "Lowell has limbered his forms and strengthened a strong and even peculiar personal tone that sounds a little like cubistic Browning . . . His best poems read like vigorous, carefully patterned prose. They are more vivid than sensitive; Lowell looks out at the world more often than he looks in on himself"; "Poetry in English: 1945–62," *Time* (March 9, 1962), 93–94.
2 Christopher Logue is not mentioned in the *Time* article. EB was probably reading Logue's *Songs* (1960).
3 Allen Ginsberg, "America," line 39.

clearly. (All the gift copies I have to hand out here I am correcting, in green ink—a futile job, but I can't stop doing it.)

I imagine you won't mind having the Radcliffe girl with Harriet in the extra bedroom? The suite I have in mind has a terrace overlooking the hotel pool, and beyond that, the ocean; the pool lit up at night and the effect very pretty. There are two bedrooms, a sitting room, serving pantry with large refrigerator—it's really pretty de luxe and comfortable. (We could probably get you a place to work in, too, if you wanted one.)

I must re-read Henry Adams. I haven't read him for years and never really liked him very much, although I learned an enormous amount from him, as we all have. What I've been reading lately is several of those little paper backs, the American Experience series—I started on them because one of my New England ancestors was imprisoned on that Jersey prison ship anchored in NY harbor during the Revolution—there's one little book about that— then went on to the others—some good, some indifferent. Lucy Larcom, "A New England Girlhood" I found fascinating, and so would you, I think.[1] She was one of the Lowell factory literary girls (but probably you know all this already?) She spent her childhood in Beverly, etc.—some of that part is very good. Her moralizing is tedious, and it is depressing to think she was a well-known "poetess" in her day, and I'm probably just about on par with her— but the details, the influence of hymns, etc., are nice. Beverly in 1830 was very much like Great Village in 1920, I think. The Brook Farm volume has opened my eyes to the fact that you are really very much in line with the Concord people. I hadn't realized quite how purely the stream has run until I read it. Although I studied them at college, I'd forgotten—the conversions to Catholicism, then to Anglicanism; the skating parties— And now your piece in *PR*[2]—the Cold War number—makes it seem even clearer. It is exactly what a poet should say, of course, and makes some of the rest sound like mental exercises—or a whole groaning orchestra with you as the clarinet soloist.

My aunt who still lives there has sent me an amateurish Great Village Historical publication—but fascinating, and of great help to me with "Uncle Artie." The house she lives in, I find, is insulated with birch bark; the one I used to live in was an old wayside inn, of "ill repute," that my grandfather had moved to the village—about 200 yrs. old. The saddest thing is the Literary Society—(my mother and aunts belonged)—in the early 1900's. "The

---

1 William Alfred Hinds, *American Communities* (1961); Lucy Larcom, *A New England Girlhood* (1961).
2 A response to a questionnaire about politics and the cold war, *Partisan Review* (Winter 1962); see RL-*Letters*, 395.

Society met fortnightly . . . to read & discuss great literature. A winter each was spent on Keats, Ruskin, Mrs. Browning, Milton, Shakespeare, Dante, and two winters on Browning and Tennyson." I imagine no one in that village had opened a Milton or a Browning for years now, and TV aerials rise from the shingles. The dying out of local cultures seems to me one of the most tragic things in this century—and it's true everywhere, I suppose—in Brazil, at any rate. Small towns far inland on the rivers were real centers; they had teachers of music and dancing and languages—they made beautiful furniture here—and built beautiful churches— And now they're all dead as door nails, and broken-down trucks arrive bringing powdered milk and Japanese jewelry and TIME magazine . . . (The[n] way up in Stonington the first thing that arrived every morning was the doughnut truck.)

If it isn't too late—you won't be getting this until you return from Puerto Rico, I think—you might send Fred Dupee my telephone numbers to give his friend—that's the best way to get hold of me. I'll give them all to you now, and if you are very systematic you can put them in your address book to give any Brazil-travelers in the future. I go back and forth now all the time—and mails in the country, inside Brazil, are hopeless—letters take a week to get from Rio to Petrópolis—if they don't get lost.

Petrópolis—telephone *3663*—ask, loud and clear, for "Dona Eliza-betchy" (no one knows my last name)—or for Lota.
Rio—address: Rua Antônia Vieria, 5. *Leme* Apartamento 1101. (Antô-nio Vieira was on[e] of the best early Jesuit writers—a missionary)

(If you shd. have to cable—use the Rio address—other for letters.) Leme means "rudder" and is the northern end of Copacabana Beach—we're only four blocks from where you'll be staying and we can meet on the beach on warm days for swims. I go in about 7:30 or 8 these days and it is lovely—blue, pure, cool. I only hope this June isn't too wintery; but one can usually go swimming most of the year. Would you like to see Rio by helicopter?—because Lota can arrange that for you. Then you wouldn't have to bother about the other views involving cable cars and cog railways—see it all at one swoop.

*   *   *   *   *

I don't know why I bother to write "Uncle Artie" really. I shd. just send you my first notes and you can turn him into a wonderful poem. He is even more your style than the Village story was. "The Scream" really works well, doesn't it. The story is far enough behind me so I can see it as a poem now. The first few stanzas I saw only my story—then the poem took over—and the last stanza is wonderful. It builds up beautifully, and everything of importance is there. But I was very surprised.

"Water" I like very much. Stanzas 4 & 5—the color ones—are marvelous—"iris, rotting . . ." etc. Yes, I like "grain after grain" better, too.[1] I have two minor questions, but, as usual, they have to do with my George-Washington-handicap. I can't tell a lie even for art, apparently; it takes an awful effort or a sudden jolt to make me alter facts. Shouldn't it be a *lobster* town, and further on—where the *bait, fish for bait*, was trapped[2]—(this is trivial, I know, and like Marianne, sometimes I think I'm telling the truth when I'm not.) The houses struck *me* as looking like clam-shells, because of the clapboarding—but I'll use that some other way! Oyster-shells is right because of the way they stick in beds on the rocks, exactly—if not for their color.[3] I can't read the word after "old" written in pencil. I remember reciting that parody on E St. V Millay to you—"I want to be drowned in the deep sea water (?) I want my body to bump the pier / Neptune is calling his wayward daughter / 'Edna, come over here!' " I asked Dwight McD why he hadn't put it in his parody book, and he thought it was "dated," I think he said[4]—"The sea drenched the rock" is so perfectly simple but so good.[5]

Well, "David & Bathsheba" has always been one of my favorites the way it was, but I like this version, too. (I don't have *Lord Weary's Castle* here in Rio so I can't actually compare them.) I remember the leaves "thicken to a ball" but I don't seem to remember the wonderful lions *sucking their faucets* . . . and "Everything's aground." I like *that*, all right. The upside down leaves—too.[6]

(You will notice a sad David & Bathsheba tale in my *Brazil* book—if you manage to get that far!) It is a very moving poem and very autumnal.[7]

But "The Old Flame" reduces me to tears. I rather liked those imaginary

---

1 In the draft "Water," stanza six reads: "The sea drenched the rock / at our feet all day, / and kept ~~chipping~~ chewing away / ~~flake~~ grain after ~~flake~~ grain" (typescript, Vassar); RL ultimately settled on "and kept tearing away / flake after flake"; cf. "Water" (RL-*CP*).

2 "It was a real Maine fishing town—," "Water," line 1 (typescript, Vassar); "where the fish were trapped," "Water," line 12 (typescript, Vassar). Cf. "Water" (RL-*CP*).

3 See "Water," lines 4–8 (RL-*CP*).

4 Samuel Hoffenstein, "Miss Millay Says Something Too," lines 3–4 (1946); *Parodies: An Anthology from Chaucer to Beerbohm*, ed. Dwight Macdonald (1960).

5 See "Water," line 21 (RL-*CP*).

6 See "The Public Garden," lines 11, 14, and 23 (RL-*CP*).

7 The draft is entitled "Autumnal" (typescript, Vassar); see "The Public Garden" (RL-*CP*).

bears—but maybe you're right to leave them out.[1] The red ear of corn is fine—like the decorator's orange floats in the skunk poem.[2] Is it *really* an antique shop? "simmering like wasps / in our tent of books"—I like that, too.[3] And the ending is beautiful—particularly the way you have it altered. Alas, it is too real to me for me to judge it as a poem, I think. If I read it in *Encounter* under someone else's name I wonder what I'd think?

"Jonathan Edwards" came just at the right moment—after my "American Experiment" books I was just about to take him up again—(all this nostalgia and homesickness and burrowing in the past running alongside trying to write articles about the Brazilian political situation—I can't—translating some Portuguese poems, etc.—are other writers as confused & contradictory? Or do they stick to one thing at a time?) "Booth" is a fine word there, reminding me of "Bartholomew's Fair."— The italicized stanzas are lovely.[4] Pompey, and the eleven children—the stanza with the stilts and the line from Herbert is wonderful.[5] All the quoted stanzas at the end, as well.[6]

(In Lucy Larcom—there were Indians who camped every year on the river that ran the Lowell mills—very degraded Indians, women wearing top-hats, etc. They arrived in birch bark canoes—this in 1840–50—but maybe you've read it?)

I feel I *must* write a lot of poems immediately—that is my test for "real poetry." Only they would come out, if at all, sounding like you. But (perhaps I've said this before) if after I read a poem the world looks like that poem for 24 hrs. or so I'm sure it's a good one—and the same goes for paintings. I studied a huge book on Bosch, I have for several days—and the world looked like Bosch-es for a month afterwards—not that it really doesn't anyway, these days. Then recently here I saw a Jules Bissier show (do you know his paintings?—slight, maybe, but beautiful)—and the world looked all like Bissiers for a long time, here, there, and everywhere. *Your* scenery comes and goes, half-real and half-language, all the time. The eye

1 In the draft "The Old Flame," a canceled second stanza reads, "no home for our imaginary / honey-colored bears, / with patent leather behinds, / and enima bags—those lovers / of garbage, afraid of snakes!" (typescript, Vassar).
2 "The Old Flame," line 6; "Skunk Hour," lines 21–22 (RL-*CP*).
3 See "The Old Flame," lines 13 and 34–35 (RL-*CP*).
4 "Jonathan Edwards in Western Massachusetts," lines 33 and 20–28 (RL-*CP*).
5 "Jonathan Edwards in Western Massachusetts," lines 58, 66, and 68 (RL-*CP*). Cf. "All rising is by a winding stair" ("Jonathan Edwards in Western Massachusetts," line 68) with "Is all good structure in a winding stair?" (George Herbert, "Jordan (1)," line 3). RL's line is adapted from Francis Bacon's "Of Great Place": "All rising to great place is by a winding stair; and if there be factions, it is good to side a man's self, whilst he is in the rising, and to balance himself when he is placed" (*Essays*, 1625).
6 "Jonathan Edwards in Western Massachusetts," lines 90–102 (RL-*CP*).

poem in *PR*[1] gets better and better. I wipe my reading glasses, always covered with brick-dust these last days here. I'll try to send you some things before long.

With much love,
Elizabeth

P.S. The condescension of the young! I said I thought João Cabral de Melo the best poet of his generation here (I've read him for yrs, know him, and am translating him) and Keith sucked his pipe, looked at the ceiling, and allowed I was *probably* right. He's been here 3 months. He sends you his love.

248.

April 14, 1962

Dearest Elizabeth:

"The piles are gone, no 19th Century decline"—how's that for an opening—my alternate is "We've just been invited to the White House again." Somehow I can't combine the strong points of the two, but what intolerable euphoria they give together!

Puerto Rico was lovely, all sand and beaches, Harriet more fun than a rubber ball and much more trouble, particularly when she and Lizzie would retire to their joint bedroom, wrapped in metaphysical argument on some small immediate decision, usually clothes. When we got off the plane Harriet said, "I'm sweatin'." I never dreamt we would be happy that several days were overcast so that we could stay out of the sun without charring. A lovely old sort of southern Italian town, San Juan, full of America in the shops. Then the millionaire hotel world which we saw on visits to Blair Clark and Lillian Hellman; two fruitless days of big game fishing—all very soothing. My angst is gone, but the day after I got back I had diahoerea (?), an ear ache, a sore throat, then lumbago—all now gone.

We'll leave on I think the 6th of June, stop in Trinidad, Surinam, then Salvador and Recife (whatever those two cities are called) then Rio, about the 15th. I hope you'll join us in Bahia. Isn't that Salvador? The hotel sounds marvelous. No, we don't want to keep an apartment, and we planned on "Toni" sleeping with Harriet.[2] Toni plays the flute, and is much better at

---

1 "Eye and Tooth," *Partisan Review* (Winter 1962); see RL-*CP*.
2 "We are taking our five-year-old daughter and the Radcliffe daughter of Alex Kern—you probably remember them from Iowa. Miss Kern has to leave us early in August" (RL to Keith Botsford, April 1, 1962, Beinecke Library, Yale University).

everything imaginable with her hands than we are, and it's our strategy that she will be an education for Harriet, now rather sated with our armchair volubility. We're rather saturated with H's non-stop talk and motion. How lovely of you to have fixed everything.

I was rather on tiptoe that my poems had been intrusive, and read your letter with great relief. Your suggestions on "Water" might be great improvements. By the way, the mermaid wasn't your Millay parody, but something in one of your letters, inspired by Wiscasset probably.[1] Glad this and my tampering with "In the Village" didn't annoy you. When "The Scream" is published I'll explain, it's just a footnote to your marvelous story.

We're just back from visiting Belle and Allen. They are best at home, and you really feel Belle saved Allen's life from the long inspired nightmare of Caroline. She's slow, imperious, though not to Allen, and sane—no crazy agrarian axe to grind! Fortunately, Allen had a slight ulcer and could only drink three drinks a night. Also saw John Berryman: utterly spooky, teaching brilliant classes, spending week-ends in the sanitarium, drinking, seedy, a little bald, often drunk, married to a girl of twenty-one from a Catholic parochial college, white, innocent beyond belief, just pregnant. They live in two rooms—in one Kate is asleep, getting through the first child pains, in the other, a thousand books, and John going into the 7th year on a long poem that fills a suitcase and is all spoken by John['s] first son (seven) from his second marriage. The poem is spooky, a maddening work of genius, or half genius, in John's later obscure, tortured, wandering style, full of parentheses, slang no one ever spoke, jagged haunting lyrical moments, etc.[2] One shudders to think of the child's birth.

Also saw Jim Powers, and had a marvelous time, talking ironic banter with him, just as though no time had passed. Wonderful moment, John in his exaggerated way and unbelievable accent, saying, "Why this man is the best *prose* writer in *America*. He is as good as *Chekhov*. His 'Lions and Hartes'[3] is like 'The Bishop!' " Then Jim smoking, saying slowly, face unchanged, "I don't know, I always thought Chekhov wrote too much." Jim, buried in St. Cloud all these years is as confident as Randall, though all is irony. Now his novel is coming out [after] 11 years and should be a masterpiece.[4]

I'm either getting soft, or good books are suddenly pouring out. K. A.

---

1 See letter 52.
2 See John Berryman, *77 Dream Songs* (1964).
3 J. F. Powers, "Lions, Hearts, Leaping Does," *Prince of Darkness* (1948).
4 Powers, *Morte D'Urban* (1962).

Porter's huge novel, very grim and the only *long* novel since *The American Tragedy* that needs to be long, I mean long by an American.[1] Randall's essays are very dashing and satirical and sad. I guess he's better writing about poetry than about American culture—this book is almost entirely culture, a sort of *Culture and Anarchy*, but he's terribly good reading.[2] Then Wilson's Civil War book, his best I think, with Plutarchan portraits of Lincoln, Grant, Justice Holmes etc.[3] Then Alfred Kazin's great heap of essays, surprisingly tougher and less long winded than he is.[4] And a little Jewish book that Jason Epstein discovered, "I the Money"[5] almost as good as Nathanael West. I'll bring all these things to you when we come, if you don't have them. (Oh, and wonderful, Isherwood's new novel, particularly the end.[6])

I'm very shabbily prepared to talk to Brazilian audiences. Botsford seems to assume that I can pick up a fluent reading knowledge of Portuguese in a few days, but of course I never will. I quite like a few poems of Bandeira, also Jorge de Lima, and am half thru Assis' *Epitaph of a Small Winner*— awfully good.[7] I can see the Brazilians will make me feel like a barbarian, with their French and Latin cultures we never had. It's much more bruising to find the Brazilians have it, than to see it in France where you would expect it. I am beginning to believe Eliot's rather high-handed quips at us about the maturity of the Latin mind. I'll bring a lot of anthologies etc. and guess I can spout and read aloud endlessly the poetry in English of this century. I suppose they already know the big people—or are they as ignorant as we are? No one here except for the young enthusiast[8] knows even Neruda. We do want to talk to little groups and not put on a rhetorical show. Lizzie has a grand lecture on plot, which can be given when we want to put our best foot forward. I guess I can make nice readings of selected poets with a few quick explanations, facts etc.

Where am I? I'm rushing through this letter skimming things and assuming that we'll pour out gossip to each other for hours. We seem almost in

---

1 Katherine Anne Porter, *Ship of Fools* (1962); Theodore Dreiser, *An American Tragedy* (1925).

2 Randall Jarrell, *A Sad Heart at the Supermarket: Essays & Fables* (1962); Matthew Arnold, *Culture and Anarchy* (1869).

3 Edmund Wilson, *Patriotic Gore* (1962).

4 Alfred Kazin, *Contemporaries* (1962).

5 RL confuses "I the Money" (perhaps thinking of William Carlos Williams's *In the Money*) with Burt Blechman's *How Much?* (1961).

6 Christopher Isherwood, *Down There on a Visit* (1962).

7 Joaquim Maria Machado de Assis, *Memórias Póstumas de Brás Cubas* (1881; *Epitaph of a Small Winner*, trans. William Grossman, 1952).

8 Cf. "When first the College Rolls receive his Name, / The young Enthusiast quits his Ease for Fame"; Samuel Johnson, "The Vanity of Human Wishes" (1749), lines 136–37.

Brazil now. Oh the White House—we are going there to dinner sometime next month to meet Malraux[1]; Edmund and Allen are going and I suppose legions of others. Only black tie, not white. The Puerto Rico [trip] was good for my mind and soul.

It's exciting to hear about your new stuff. Your *Brazil* has lovely Bishop touches, the humor of the opening, and everywhere you seem to dampen the hollow enthusiasm of the man who comments on the pictures—two Brasílias, yours and his. Then like *Moby-Dick* and *Paradise Lost*, those long stretches of organized information, which I wonder at and envy, though I miss your tone. It's quite an achievement, though only you in patches. I'm much too undisciplined to have even made a stab at doing such a book. Everywhere you are admired, John and Allen think you are better than Marianne and maybe Emily Dickinson. Well, you are better than anyone to me, but I don't see any reason to compare you with Marianne: you so beautifully exist together equally good, alike and opposites. As I. A. Richards said to me, "the best is still in promise." How that graveled me, I who feel I've surpassed all my small talents and deserve to retire! You must feel this too. How could anything be better than your best poems. Still I know immense things are pouring out of you.

Damn the young! My students, after I gave them a laborious six weeks on Pope, Dryden, Dr. Johnson, Goldsmith etc. turned out to have read only one poet before Hopkins—Donne of course. I feel taken in the flank. I am all pointed to explain the new poetry as a continuation, change and revolution of the old. But no one reads the old, except English professors. I'm on a Wordsworth and Blake jag. I'd like to do poems that would hit all in one flash, though loaded with subtleties of art and passion underneath. Or great clumsy structures like Wordsworth's Leech Gatherer, that somehow lift the great sail and catch the wind.[2] Most of our poets are so weak on brute, energy, flash, power, driving a sentence or a stanza to its mark, though it's good to be clotted, obscure, ingenious etc. But the typical modern poem is taken over by pedants, people who bore you to death. How wearisome the swarm of accomplished youngish poets are after some one like Powers or Mary! The poet ought to be at least as interesting a person as the prose writer![3]

Dearest, we can't wait. Our love to Lota,

Cal

---

1 André Malraux was minister of cultural affairs during the de Gaulle administration.

2 Wordsworth, "Resolution and Independence" (1807).

3 See "The language of a large portion of every good poem, even of the most elevated character, must necessarily, except with reference to the metre, in no respect differ from that of good prose," William Wordsworth, *Preface to the Lyrical Ballads* (1802), and "Poetry must be *as well written as prose*," Ezra Pound, *The Letters of Ezra Pound: 1907–1941* (1950), 48.

249.

April 26th, 1928 [1962]
Forgive this meandering book—I am tired apparently—look at the date—
Give me yr. Bahian dates when you know them—I might be able to get
there—

Dearest Cal:

I'll try to make this short (!)—but your letter of the 14th is so fascinating
it will be hard to . . . I am glad about your health and the White House invitation—but you should really snub Malraux, who has gone quite mad, I
think. He said horrid things about the U.S. when he was here—praised
Brasília to the skies in the most hypocritical way, and raved about "Latin culture"—in which he included Goethe & Beethoven, etc.—and said the U.S.
would *never* have any "culture" of its own. Very irritating, & now he's going
calling on Kennedy. Honestly—the longer Lota stays in the park business!—
the more papers we read every day, the more government people I get to
know—the more loathsome politics appears. I protested so violently about a
piece about Brazil in *The New Republic*[1] that they've asked me to write a regular letter for them. I'm going to get a good Brazilian to, I think.— It seems
that the Ambassador and Walter Lippmann and I all wrote exactly the same
things!— Thank you for being so kind about the awful book. Here I am torn
between getting angry if people don't like it and getting angry if they do—
which they mostly do, poor dears—& of course if their English isn't very
good they think it was so nice of me to say "A Century of Pride & Honor"[2]
etc. etc. . . . There are rumors, rumors of revolution; things have never been
such a mess—rich friends saying "Let's go to *Nova Zelandia* . . ." The thiev-
ery is beyond belief. Then they get huge loans from the U.S. and at the same
time the Brazilian capitalists, in a panic, have sent out more than the loan, of
their own money, to invest in the U.S. Quite mad and decadent. However—
nothing much will happen until after your visit, I'm pretty sure! I am thinking of Puerto Rico as a possible future home. But it's probably too dear.

I got Elizabeth's letter, then yours a couple of days later last week-end up
in the country. No—we'll be delighted to meet Toni and put her up when-

---

1 EB, letter to the editor, *The New Republic* (April 30, 1962), responding to Louis L. Wiznitzer, "Quadros Returns
to a Country in Chaos," *The New Republic* (March 19, 1962).
2 The title of the third chapter of *Brazil* is "Century of Honor and Pride."

ever you can get up to visit us. Does she bring the flute too? Keith B is half-Italian, I found—that's probably why he is so optimistic about yr. Portuguese—and then, he knew Spanish very well, too. If you know Spanish (?) it is fairly easy to read Portuguese—but it doesn't help a bit with understanding it or speaking it. I like Drummond (pronounced Droo-Mond)[1] better than Bandeira, I think. I don't know him. Bandeira & I were fairly friendly for a while. I used to make him marmalade[2]—but it was a friendship that has dwindled, although I'll try to take it up again for your visit. He is old and *very* spoiled & deaf. His apartment reminds me of Miss Moore's—very similar. Jorge de Lima was a mad doctor—painted & composed in his office, etc.—a really Brazilian type, I think, and some of his surrealist pieces are quite good. It's funny—I suspect Keith B of handing on some things I said to him, to you. He complained about the "lacunae" in Brazilian education and knowledge of economics, literature, etc.—and I said yes, but they—the older & middle-aged generation, at least—had solid groundings in French, all knew Racine, etc.—in fact Lota went to school *in French*—and we can't compete with that. Now he seems to be telling you! I don't really know what they know of American or English poetry—it's pretty spotty. ~~Keith B is getting Bandeira to translate some of you, but I wouldn't count on it too much~~—I think he's got someone else now; Bandeira found it too tough for him. My idea was to have a big page in the best supplement—in English—with literal translations in Portuguese down below—while you're here, or just before—and I'd be glad to check the translations etc. But K. didn't seem to take to that too much. But the people who are interested will know quite a lot of English, naturally—although you are hard for them, I know from experience. K, I think, didn't take to me too much—or there was jealousy or something, at work—and I had never heard of his novels, alas![3]—but I want to do all I can. If he hasn't said this, I think it would be a good idea to have mimeographed copies of the poems you speak of, to hand out. But not of any speech. Spender gave out translations of his speech and everyone was very insulted. I may have given Bandeira one of your books long ago. I gave him quite a lot of material for an anthology he was working on—8 yrs ago. In general they know Frost and Millay and E. Dickinson—Pound, Cummings— And Eliot, *well*.— He has been a great influence on some of them, like Vinícius de Moraes, in his early books (The "Black Orpheus" poet).

1 Carlos Drummond de Andrade.
2 See "To Manuel Bandeira, with Jam and Jelly," line 34 (EB-*EAP*).
3 Keith Botsford, *Master Race* (1955) and *Benvenuto* (1961).

(D. Thomas—yes—but they don't really understand him.) Wallace Stevens vaguely, and Marianne not at all—at least not till I got here, and I certainly have done very little propagandizing. There are one or two books published by the State Dept. here & the Ministry of Education (Brazilian), anthologies—you may have them—very bad, and mostly done by people who were here and wanted to put in a lot of their own poems, as far as I can see. But the ignorance of any American poets under fifty is pretty general.— That TIME has probably helped quite a bit!— I know almost no one literary and almost no one knows of me, and I think they think if I were any good I'd be at home, anyway! It will be very different for someone coming officially, like you. Also you're a MAN. Here a lady-poet is a male poet's mistress, as a rule, and he writes her poems for her.— With one exception—Cecília Meireles, who is old-fashioned, but quite good, rather like the earlier Louise Bogan, at her best. The funny thing I discovered was that in Belém, of all places, American poetry is much better known and liked than here in Rio—partly because it's that much closer to the U.S. and partly because a poet named Robert Pack (I think) lived there, I don't know why, for 2 or 3 years. In fact I found the 3 or 4 poets I met in my week's stay there much more congenial and less resentful, or whatever it is, than those here—and less openly anti-American. The intellectuals are apt to be anti-A of course, although with me they are pretty tactful about it. They will show you something god-awful called *Neo-Concretionism*—pure 1920's Parisian—but I've already told you about that, I think. That's the trouble—it is SO provincial the young keep going off on useless tangents and re-discoveries—and the old get spoiled awfully easily.

I haven't been to Recife or Bahia—oh dear—I heard recently that the hotel in Bahia was very *bad*. Do be careful of that exotic cooking. João Cabral de Melo (Neto just means grandson, or 3rd) comes from Recife, (Bandeira, too—long ago) and one good artist I'm going to invite to meet you—Aloísio Magalhães.[1] They might be there when you're there, or here. Aloísio is one of the few really bright people I know, to whom we can talk the way we'd talk in N.Y. In general it is pretty hard going, as I'm afraid you'll find— Do you like Neruda? Yes, I like Neruda. Do you like René Char? No, I don't like René Char, etc. (I *don't*—do you?) (I just read ÉLOGES for the 1st time and decided I liked it much the best of Perse, and it gave me lots of ideas for Florida material.[2]— But Lota read it and said it was terrible—such pompous French—and I'll have to take her word for it, while retaining my own lit-

---

1 Aloísio Magalhães was a cousin of João Cabral de Melo Neto.
2 Saint-John Perse, *Éloges* (1911).

tle inspirations from it.) There's one awful pompous Claudel-ish poet—Schmidt—who is a politician and owns all the supermarkets and soap-powders, and writes about God and Angels in the newspapers. He told Huxley that unfortunately he, Schmidt, was away over the heads of his fellow-countrymen. I've lots more literary information, of course—and Lota *knows all*—but it isn't worth repeating unless you need some of it when you get here in order not to get fooled or misguided! (Their "north" is like our "south"—in literature too!)

For E's benefit—they seem to be very interested in Faulkner at the moment and some books have appeared in Portuguese. But as in the case of Dylan Thomas, I feel they really don't understand him at all—certainly, I've had no luck getting people to read the better stories. Anything that's come out in French they're apt to know—a friend asked me solemnly last night about Wm. Styron, for example, because they subscribe to a French literary review and he is all the rage in Paris right now. (I had a letter from Loren who had met Mary McCarthy at a lecture by Styron—which seems odd all around.) (What the Vassar magazine reported of E's speech there sounded *fine*, to me.[1])—*Moby-Dick* I've seen in Portuguese—but very very few of our other "classics"—(*Huckleberry Finn*) And about poetry—you could really scarcely be too elementary, it seems to me. No one's ever heard of Tate or Ransom or Randall or Roethke. Hart Crane is vaguely familiar, maybe. (Lota's eccentric young nephew, who lends me Kerouac and jazz records, struggles valiantly with H. Crane.[2]) Henry Miller—at his anti-American worst of course. Hemingway has all been translated, of course—there was even a TV quiz on him. But Cummings, strange to say, seems best known. Not so strange, maybe—that sentimental side of Cummings, in love and "social comment," is sort of the stage they are at here—Bandeira and Drummond—oh, all of them practically—(except Cabral).

- - - - -

I was just about to order KAP's novel—if you can spare it it would be wonderful. But please don't bring books—they weigh too much & you'll have to pay twice over for them, you'll be so overweight. (Unless Harriet and her duds weigh so little you have lots of pounds to spare?) I'd be delighted to have any of those books you mention—but why don't you mail them? It's cheaper, even if a nuisance. You leave one end open, just a little hole so they

1 W. K. Rose, "The Novel: An Affirmation?," *Vassar Alumnae Magazine* (Spring 1962), a panel discussion with Elizabeth Hardwick, Paul Goodman, and Saul Bellow.
2 Flávio de Macedo Soares Regis.

can see it's a book, and they come book rate—cheap—in about 3 weeks. I'd love the Wilson on Lincoln—that was news to me. And I'll love to hear how Wilson stands up to Malraux—I think he could do it. I thought the KAP chapter on Vera Cruz, years ago, was the best thing I'd ever read about Mexico, and I've saved it all this time.[1] Other chapters I haven't liked so much; but thank heavens she finished it.

No—*I was very pleased with "The Scream."* I find it very touching to think you were worried for fear I might be annoyed.— I thought it was only I who went around imagining people were cross with me when I didn't hear from them. But living here has almost cured me. I just have to give them the benefit of the doubt; think their letters got lost, or mine did. All letter-writing is dangerous, anyway—fraught with peril.

Your literary visits & gossip are wonderful—but I'd rather read your version of it than spend those evenings . . . I am glad to hear Allen is better. I've never met Berryman, that I know. One has the feeling a 100 yrs. from now that *he* may be all the rage, or a "discovery"—*hasn't one?*

I think I was optimistic about swimming all year round—maybe I shd. now make June–July sound cooler than I think I did to E.—at least today is much too cold for swimming. Bring sweaters. You don't have to get dressed up very much, you know. If you have binoculars, they're nice for Rio or boating or Cabo Frio—if we get you there—and mine are broken at the moment. We are scheming to get a *larger* car & driver, somehow, for one or two trips.

Before you go—or maybe right now—could you send that batch of poems to Carl Brandt, Brandt & Brandt 101 Park Avenue? Maybe he'd even send a messenger to pick it up . . . He writes and writes and I am away behind. I'll do my best to get three or four more poems to you or him before May is up. Here are the only other things we want, and even they *aren't important*. I have mentioned the liquor-cigarette business—but that's if you can manage it (with yr. stop-overs it may be difficult) and don't need all you can bring for yourselves. We smoke Luckies, Phillip Morrises or Chesterfields— anything *without* filters—and any Scotch or Bourbon you won't need, we'll buy from you with pleasure. Prices are terrific here for cigarettes, U.S., & liquor. (I've told you both about the airport sales plan, I think—they put them on the plane for you, tax free.)

I can take you to my money changer—right around the corner from the hotel—and introduce you, to cash checks. You might save more that way

1 The first chapter of Katherine Anne Porter's *Ship of Fools* (1962).

than buying a lot of cruzeiros ahead. The changers give a higher rate than the banks. (But maybe this is Mr. B's department.)

Don't drink water out of the tap! *Lindoya* is the non-sparkling table water—there are lots of fizzy ones. Has Dr. B given you some shots? Trinidad I've just slept at, in the old days of piston planes. It was terrifying to drive rapidly down roads there *on the left*, in the middle of the night. Surinam I imagine as awful—but nothing could be worse than Aruba, the other Dutch place I stopped at—and I liked it—wonderful tinned ginger snaps!—goats, volcanoes, tiny ones, and oil rainbows in the ocean for miles and miles.

This couldn't be more discursive. I left E's letter in Samambia—we came down yesterday just for one day—going back tomorrow. (Lota has been sick with flu and still isn't well but she had to see how things were getting along. She is fighting everyone very bravely, and I do admire her. When you get here she'll either be very popular or out on her ear, and we won't be speaking to the Governor any more . . .) But I think this answers E's as well, pretty much. I'll see when I get back.

May Swenson's publisher insists on *one* blurb,[1] and she has asked me to write it and so I must, and right this minute . . . I am worried about Marianne—her letters get shorter and more cryptic and she doesn't sound well at all. I wish you could bring her along for us to take care of, but realize it's quite out of the question.

"Discipline"—ye gods—that's what I have least of. In the *B* book the long dull stretches I did write, some of, and got a journalist friend to help me out, finally, on recent politics, etc. Then I re-wrote and brightened it up, as I thought, and LIFE re-wrote, and as Lota says, massacred it. I even thought my chapter on "Animal, Vegetable, and Mineral" was quite *amusing*. I love Zebus and fishing, etc.—until they got through with it.[2]

Yes—I feel the same way about the few "young" I know—and I can't see they're going to improve much since no one seems to read any more. (At Putney I hear they really do learn to read and like it.) But it is rather pleasant when you finally get someone (I'm thinking of Lota's nephew) to read the real thing—Rimbaud instead of Ginsberg, etc.—or listen to Debussy rather than Thelonious Monk—and they get the point. I suppose that's as close as I come to understanding why people like to teach.

With much love to you both, and we are eagerly awaiting you—I'll try not to write again. Forgive all my useless advice and information. I think

---

1 For *To Mix with Time* (1963); see *Elizabeth Bishop: Poems, Prose, and Letters*, ed. Robert Giroux and Lloyd Schwartz (2008).
2 See EB-*Brazil*, 70–71.

Elizabeth is going to dislike most of it very much and you are going to dislike about 50% of it . . . But I'm sure we'll have fun, anyway.

Elizabeth

We had a very successful hour of *Mahagonny* with some "young people" on Easter Sunday—they loved it.

250.[1]

Rio, ~~May 8th or~~ 9th, 1962

Dearest Cal:

I've had this endless stupid letter around for weeks, I think, meaning to tear it up, and then absent-mindedly thinking I'd mailed it. If you ever get through it—but if you can't it doesn't matter at all. I, too, was coming down with that *grippy*, and that was partly why I rambled on so feverishly, I think. I'll send it anyway and you may find something useful in it. I am appalled to think I haven't delivered Keith's message that all is arranged for you in Bahia and Recife. ("O Recife" the natives call it—*The* Reef). He says you should allow a week in Bahia. All I know is that there is more to see there than anywhere else, certainly, but I don't know how much you and your family care for churches, etc. You should see some *capoeira* (foot-boxing)—and some of the good private collections of folk art. I am writing a note NOW to:

Martinho Gonçalves—
Head of the Dramatics Dept.—University of Bahia

He is a rather effete and complicated man, from Rio originally, who knows "everyone," etc.—but he also knows all about where to go and what to see in Bahia, and I'm not sure that Keith did meet him. I'll tell him to look you up at *the* hotel, and IF he gets my letter, he may be able to show you some interesting things. He's slightly silly; speaks perfect English.

If you are receiving a little magazine from the "Hand-Made Gramophone Shop"—I had them send it to you—if not, let me know—I think it's a good record guide. *Mahagonny* is really wonderful.

Keith is now coming to see me about some prose translations of you. He has come around to my idea, I gather! He comes through Rio traffic wobbling on a bicycle—with his large wobbling pipe leading.

---

1 Enclosed with letter 249.

He also says you may be going to Belém—if so, see my letter *I*. There is a nice shy poverty-stricken poet there named Ruy Barata whom I liked very much. (Almost everyone is named Barata—which also means, sad to say, "cockroach.")

There was a tidal wave. Then there was Glenn's *capsula*, in a park right near us. I went at 8 AM and stood in line and got the scare of my life. I wonder how your White House dinner party was? I have just been reading TIME about the one *before* the one you went to. I also have just read a very good, if rough, piece in KENYON called "The United Snopes Information Service"[1]— It summarizes the whole Culture-Government business very well—particularly as I'd just been to an official dinner-party last night. Ye gods, what pomposity and vanity about nothing at all.

Tell Harriet her name is going to be HENRIQUETA.

With much love—and it will be so nice to see you,

Elizabeth

There is a little anthology just out called "Modern Brazilian Poetry," translations by a John Nist (who lives right around the corner, but is going back soon)—University of Indiana Press. You might look at it—or just use my copy here. It's pretty dull in English like that. Mr. Nist is not you. 12 poets are included.

KB also much taken in by Gilberto Freyre, in Recife— He does seem sane, to meet, but is a megalomaniac, really! All Americans here fooled by him—don't be!

251.

May 15, 1962

Dearest Elizabeth:

Let me write for once at once but nothing like your marvelous imaginative sprawl. We fly on June 5—3 or 4 days in Haiti, 3 or 4 days in Trinidad—Belém, 2 days, Recife, 4 days, Bahia, a week or so, then Rio. We saw John Hunt, a higher Cultural Congress man, who must now be in Rio where he is seeing Botsford and plans on meeting you. When he gets back, and well before we go, we should know our dates exactly, and will let you know. I hope you will come to Bahia. The Congress people are rather breathless; they now

---

1 John McCormick, "The United Snopes Information Service," *The Kenyon Review* (Spring 1962).

plan for us to end up in Mexico City after Argentina, Uruguay, Chile and Peru. We have bales of books we can hardly read, even in English. Each expert is very friendly and emphatic, and one has no way of telling whether they are talking with taste and discernment or not. We also are getting reams of names to look up, and many cross-currents of opinions. I guess we'll live.

The White House! 200 guests, about a third maybe I think actually known to us—Schlesinger, absolutely top of the world squiring the Kennedy sisters, MacLeish, who told me the trumpets made his heart beat, New York types like Mark Rothko, Bundy drunk, Mrs. Lindbergh, Red Warren with whom I had a frantic search for the men's room, everyone rather drunk after dinner and cocktails and 3 wines and then more champagne, having to be told to give up their champagne and cigarettes and listen to Stern and Istomin play a long Schubert trio—and next morning we read that the President had ordered our 7th fleet to Laos. It was fun and a ball, but I think we all seemed rather silly, little colored bit of frosting. Malraux said nothing objectionable though there were many florid compliments to the U.S., and at one point in a question group he seemed to suggest that Frost was a poet maudit. I have a lot more gossip that I'll tell you.

Did I write that I was overwhelmed by da Cunha, as good in its way as Melville and what a terrible story once you get beyond the flora and fauna!

Oh me, so much somehow to do—a paper on myself, term papers, exams, letters, a New School reading, a peace reading in Boston, where Hyman and most of the other painters are auctioning off pictures for peace. But all is well. I've done two rather obscure, metrical and grandiose little poems[1]—all for a while. We have the ear-rings and will soon see you. We are really very very looking forward to all that's coming.

Our love to Lota and all my love to you.

Cal

252.

Dearest Elizabeth:

Almost zero hour, six, and tonight we have dinner with Dos Passos, also going to Brazil, then tomorrow at nine we fly for Trinidad. I assume Botsford has given you our new schedule—Belém on the 18th, giving us more

1 Possibly "The Tenth Muse" and "Lady Ralegh's Lament" (RL-*CP*).

than ten days to loaf in Trinidad, with beaches and a familiar language. I do hope you'll meet us in Bahia; it seems so much longer now till we meet. We won't reach Rio I guess till after the 25th. We should stay a month. I think we'll skip Mexico. So, we can't wait to see you. Lots of news! Quite a change from meeting in one day, your friend Vera, then a little group of Columbia U. Spanish translating republicans.

> Abraçios (?)
> Cal

I'll never learn to speak any language except our own I fear, but I do read a little. We are 80 pounds overweight!

253.

[Postcard: Photograph of a girl leaning against the trunk of a palm. Inscription: "Trinidad, Wayside Scene"]

[Trinidad & Tobago]
[June 13, 1962]

Dearest Elizabeth:

Don't be surprised if Harriet calls you Aunt Elizabeth on seeing you, & demands a large Brazilian doll, Dona Lolita, her reward for learning to swim—if she does. Here we are in a world rather like Louisiana turned on its head with an inset from *Passage to India*. I've master[ed] my only new language for the summer "Trinidadian." Can't wait to see you. Love from us all,

> Cal

254.

[Postcard: Autumnal scene of a woman dressed in hunting gear, holding a rifle, accompanied by a retriever. Inscription: "Greetings from Suriname"]

[Suriname, en route to Belém, Brazil]
[June 1962]

Dear Elizabeth:

Noble sentiments never die—here's a bit of New England autumn and the New England heart in Suriname. In Trinidad, Harriet developed a loathing for Moslem religious parades.

> Love,
> Cal

255.

[Buenos Aires, Argentina
10 September 1962][1]

DEAREST ELIZABETH COME HERE AND JOIN ME ITS PARADISE! ALL MY
LOVE

CAL

256.

Caixa Postal 279, Petrópolis, Est. do Rio
September [2]1, 1962
(actually, in Rio)

Dearest Cal:

I haven't written before because I wasn't sure when you'd be going to New
York, etc.—since I really have very little news if this does not reach you it will
be no loss at all. Lota and I are both terribly terribly sorry you got sick[2] and
hope you are feeling a great deal better. We both send you a great deal of love,
and don't forget we are thinking of you constantly. I hope the Clinica is comfortable and the doctor nice, etc.— Send us a message via Keith—or print a
note!—since I don't think you have a typewriter with you, do you? I hope you
got the telegram I sent you last Thursday, the 13th of September . . .[3]

You know what my life here is like now; it has been very quiet lately.
We've been reading and reading the books you had sent and thank you very
much. SHIP OF FOOLS is certainly awfully good—I am a little baffled by
some of it, however. It is, no doubt, allegorical, although not too much so—
Did you notice, for example, that the one Good Deed (jumping overboard to
save the life of the wretched bull-dog) was done by a steerage passenger?—
the same one who seemed to stand for the Artist, perhaps—he carved little
statues out of wood. ?? PALE FIRE is great fun—much better to read it first
and Mary's review afterwards.[4] Her review is clever, but seems meant for
those who don't intend to read the book—she tells so much! Lota is now
working on PALE FIRE—so much of it depends on plays on words, etc. that
she has to get my help once in a while. The Kazin book I find infuriating but

---

1 In EB's hand: "rec'd 11 Sat—8:30 pm." For EB's account, see EB-OA, 410–13.
2 After eight weeks in Brazil, RL flew with Botsford to Buenos Aires. There he suffered a manic episode, during
which Botsford returned to Rio. On EB's insistence, following the receipt of this telegram, Botsford returned to
Buenos Aires, where he arranged for Lowell's hospitalization in the Clinica Bethlehem.
3 EB notes the text in her diary: "We are thinking of you. Get better quick. Love always. Elizabeth."
4 Vladimir Nabokov, *Pale Fire* (1962); Mary McCarthy, "A Bolt from the Blue," *The New Republic* (June 4, 1962).

good in spots—the best spot being his review of you—the one really generous review in the whole book, I think.[1] There must be thousands of "*I*"s in that book . . . and it's badly written, as well.

I've been writing lots of letters, doing a bit of translating and getting up my courage to start working again. The night before Nicolas[2] left we had dinner with him and Raymond Aron and his wife—fortunately we've read a couple of Aron's books. He's just like the books—clever, omniscient, a good talker. Of course, Lota is now arranging an interview for *him* with Carlos. It is a good idea, however. I got Nicolas a silver coin, Pedro II, like the one I gave you, and he seemed pleased—covered us with kisses.

It is getting warmer all the time and I have been swimming almost every morning—except for two marvelous stormy days. Today the sea is like pale blue satin, with a mauve haze—huge freighters and tankers coming in slowly through the haze, like ghosts—lovely.

A little man in a white linen suit (summer *has* come) just was here under false pretenses—he corresponds with Philip Booth & writes pretty little Prévert-like verses—but what he really was after was an interview for a literary magazine here—oh dear. It ended with him telling me all about this second marriage and his daughter of three—he must be over sixty, too. He showed me a translation of Booth he has done—a long poem all about a snowstorm. Since he's never seen snow "except in a photograph": it was just about what one might expect . . . Nélida[3] has been here once to talk the higher Portuguese with me and I think she will come now twice a week. Just after you left, Lota was given a *medal*—two, rather—a medal with grosgrain ribbon, etc. to wear for dress, and a miniature—a *stick-pin* for every day. I don't know quite how she can wear that; she said she had to acquire a lapel. It is for Public Service—speeches and her picture in the papers, etc. It is nice that she is being appreciated a little bit, at least. Nicolas was very much taken with her, and in his farewell speech to me, over the telephone, got his centuries mixed, in his emotional state—first he said she was like "an 18th century Russian lady," then said she was like *him*, and belonged, just like him, to the 19th century! But Russians like Nicolas, and Brazilians, do have a lot in common—

Let's see—I've been to a couple of highbrow movies and a low-brow but very moving political rally, at which Carlos made an excellent speech—outdoors, full moon, very warm—all classes and colors and ages, under

1 Alfred Kazin, "In Praise of Robert Lowell," *Contemporaries* (1962).
2 Nicolas Nabokov.
3 Nélida Piñon.

palm trees over a hundred feet high. In front of the yellow, weird Palace—the one that made you exclaim "My God, what's that?" when we turned down the street in front of it one night. The State band was there in pure 19th century costumes, red and white,—mostly negroes—playing tubas, trombones, etc.—the national anthem, and the state anthem, which is a samba.

Lota is about to get home from work and I must stop and put some dinner on the stove. I wish you were here to have dinner with us. I wish I could do something to help you from here. Let me know if there is anything that can be sent from here—most unlikely, but anyway! I'm glad you seemed to find BA so agreeable—sometime I must hear more about what you like about it so much. Do take care of yourself, Cal—be a good boy. We all love you very much and only want you to get better fast. Please let me hear from you whenever you can.

Your devoted friend, as always,

Elizabeth

257.

Rio, October 8th [1962]—pouring rain

Darling Cal:

Heaven knows when, how, or if this will reach you—but I am hoping that the bookshop will have that edition of Sydney Smith's *Letters*[1] that I have here, in stock, and can get it to you. I can't think of any more cheering reading, really, and I go through them regularly two or three times a year—even if he is so anti-poetic, and did have one or two touches of brutality—not much, considering the age and the fact that he was a clergyman.

I wonder if you ever got any of the letters I sent off hopefully to BA—probably not—but they weren't important. I just wanted you to know that Lota and I were thinking of you and that lots of Rio people had liked you a great deal and asked after you, etc. I even toyed with the idea of going down myself—more than toyed—but I didn't think I'd be of much help, somehow—and members of my sex are particularly at a disadvantage in emergencies here, as you know.

We just had a nice note from Nicolas, from Paris. Lota's nephew, Flávio, seemed to get along well with Caroline, too—I think she is returning by way of Rio, to Paris. Flávio is getting quite a cosmopolitan set of lady-friends these days. He also gave me a poem of his own—and it is quite good,—quiet,

---

1 *The Letters of Sydney Smith*, ed. Nowell Smith (1953).

pretty, and not at all the kind of thing I had expected. Both Lota and I have been sick with "grippy"—everyone has—it lasts exactly three days, with a high fever and then you feel weak and blue for a week. I am just getting over the blue stretch today, I think. If it weren't for all the kissing Brazilians do, I think we might have avoided it—but then, the kissing's pleasant. Before we both got sick we had the Raymond Arons to dinner. I hate feeding *French* people, but we had just arrived with dozens of just-cut artichokes from our own garden & even Parisians couldn't despise those. He was fascinating— went all around Brazil and talked with all sides. He thinks Carlos's greatest danger is the fact that he is so much more intelligent than anyone else in Brazil—and can't help showing it. Not only intelligent, *I* think—he also gets up and goes to work every day, and gets things done—and thereby is a reproach to all the other politicians, and makes them dislike him even more.

Yesterday, Sunday, was election day—very quiet. The returns are just starting to come in and so far they are awful—and I'm afraid will get worse. Rachel de Queiroz (that journalist friend of ours—the one I want to get to do the anthology) has just come back, and I am seeing her today. However—I won't say anything about the anthology until I hear from you. However, I am sure she would do it, and do it well. I am at last beginning to write poetry again, I think—three or four new things going and two long old ones that shd. go in the book almost done. I liked these sentences from a Brazilian "primitive," Carolina de Jesus: "He's a polyglot reporter. He knows the continents." I want to use them.

Dear Cal—please be quite recovered by the time you get this, and write me when you can. Lota and I never stop loving you for a moment, you know.— *Abraços e saudades,*
    Elizabeth

258.

Rio, October 28th, 1962

Dearest Cal:

We're staying in Rio over this week-end because the next one is a really long one—starting Wednesday, I think—that includes All Souls' Day, Day of the Dead, and related holidays . . . The prices for flowers for this last day are strictly regulated every year—the list is in the paper today—Baby's Breath, so much, Calla Lilies, so much, etc. . . .[1] This week I've seen Spender,

---

1 See "Dropping South: Brazil," line 19 (RL-*CP*).

after all these years—just a few times and briefly and with your friend KB always on hand,—but he was very agreeable. Spender, I mean. I went to a very dull—at least I knew almost no one, so it was dull—British Council reception, and then he came here a couple of times. KB says he is like you, but I don't think so. He's 6' 3" which I think is wastefully tall, like being a Packard Limousine or something—now just 6' like you is much more sensible . . . What I liked about him particularly was that he really notices pictures, knows a lot about them, etc. (Seems he paints all the time—had just thrown away a *batch* of pictures at the hotel—& we exchanged brands of pastels—I mean this [is] the "area" we got along best in.) He was off to open a show of Francis Bacon in Germany (Lota's favorite painter just now). He also kindly took some baby clothes along for me, a present for an English friend. I went to one of his lectures, on poetry, just to be polite, really—as he warned me, I "knew it all already." It seems that the other lecture, about Eng. Lit. in general, was more entertaining and he mentioned you a lot—referring to the uproar about the Alvarez book.[1] Mary McC did not show up in Argentina—I'm sorry, I was hoping she'd appear here. I'd much rather have had Spender up in the country—but the weather has been awful, four rainy week-ends in a row—and I just couldn't face cooking lunch for six or eight people—since he was surrounded by *both*, the C for CF[2] and the British Council—the B cultural attaché, etc. etc. All this attention given on *English* poets by the Eng. here made me blush once more for my country— He talked to me about how he wanted to try mescaline—and I have heard reports of his having asked about marijuana & mescaline, etc. at a luncheon . . . That didn't go over too well! I think the Brazilians don't understand that kind of romanticism at all—they're romantic, too, but consider us *childishly* romantic . . . And I think they are *corny*, silly romantic, and I'd love to try mescaline . . .

I've now got back two letters I sent you in the north[3] away back in June—one yet to come—and I wonder if you ever got any of those I wrote to BA— KB totally uncommunicative as always, about absolutely everything. He did lend me a nice book—he said he'd lent it to Elizabeth and that is the extent of my knowledge of New York—the FM Ford *Portraits from Life*—it is charming, a wonderful style.[4] Maybe he really did talk it, to a secretary—that's the way it sounds. We had a nice letter from Toni. I had *two*

1 A. Alvarez, *The New Poetry: An Anthology* (1962), an anthology of modern British poetry that caused controversy for several reasons, including its inclusion of two Americans, RL and John Berryman.
2 Congress for Cultural Freedom.
3 The letters have not survived.
4 Ford Madox Ford, *Portraits from Life* (1937).

letters from Anne Sexton—I'm glad I wrote her; she seemed really pleased. I am at work really now, doing some poems in the mornings and some translating in the PM's. I'll send you some poems after a while, I hope. Thank you again for the books. I've now sent for Randall's, too.[1] I think I'll just write him anyway . . . why not—I do admire him!

A Sunday supplement on "Aviation" has a small headline about "Dona Carlota"—and the two circles being built for model-airplane flying in the park. It says that she has always "believed in youth and the importance of model airplane flying . . ."

We have just taken a quick drive to see how things are—and the new beach is covered with, really, *thousands* of people (the sun shining, momentarily, at least) so Lota is delighted. This beach was entirely her idea, too, although someone else unfortunately took the credit.

Let's see—odd news—a week ago today the Russian Ambassador— Brazil's first—went swimming in waves about 30 feet high off one of the wildest beaches (red flags[2] all over the place, too, but maybe he thought they weren't for him, or especially for him—either)—and drowned almost immediately. Unfortunately he called to an aide, 22 years old, who rushed right in to save him and was drowned, too. No one can understand why anyone would attempt to swim in such a sea—although he was a strong swimmer and did swim in that place. All the Russian embassy swims there, although it is always dangerous. He lay in state—very impressive, they said, with black-uniformed guards and lots more red flags. But when they moved the body the hearse had silver crosses on the doors—and all the papers have been filled with pictures of the Russians prying the crosses off, and the[n] cleaning or re-painting the hearse so the cross-shaped marks wouldn't show, either . . . How silly can nations get, really. And it seems there *are* cross-less hearses available—maybe for Jews, or Japanese.

Do you remember Jorge Moreira? We went to his house one night to see TV—he's the one I think the best architect of all, a big, sickly, rickety man with a sadly thin voice? Well—more catastrophe, but he's all right. He was in an automobile accident and will be for months in a huge plaster cast— from under his arm-pits down to this toes. Lota calls him the White Elephant. The staircase up to his penthouse is too narrow for him to be carried up in his cast—so the Fire Department is going to get him home. Lota says they have so few fires here (did you notice that?—how rarely one hears a

1 Randall Jarrell, *A Sad Heart at the Supermarket* (1962).
2 See "Dropping South: Brazil," line 8 (RL-*CP*).

fire-siren, as compared to N.Y.? I suppose because so little wood is used in building) The Fire Department is delighted to have this problem to solve. Lota, of course, has been talking on the telephone with the head of the Dept. all week. First they were going to raise him on a derrick—but now they are actually going to lower him, like a mummy, from a helicopter, into the waiting arms of his wife . . . I feel I have to go and watch this—poor Jorge will be doped unconscious, I think.— I know it is morbid of me, but I want to see.

I just got Ponge's latest books of poems and wish I hadn't bothered.— I like *Parti Pris des Choses*—I recommend it to you—but these are all feeble imitations of it.[1] Really, the French get away with murder—all those endless note-books they keep, full of things like:

Sidi-Madani, 20 decembre, 1947
HIVER D'AFRIQUE DU NORD.— Ne rien faire, sommeiller . . . Je n'ai jamais connu un tel confort. / Cette chaleur si bien distribué . . . etc etc etc.[2]

28 aout (le soir)
(Variante de la page precedente): Un verre d'eau. Ainsi soit-il.[3]

Well—perhaps my letters are almost that bad, so I'd better hold my tongue! How are you Cal dear?—please do let us hear from you soon and we both send our love and best wishes.
Abraços—
Elizabeth

Poor KB gives himself away so—one of the few things he saw fit to underline in the Ford piece on Lawrence, for example (a good piece, full of wonderful things), was Ford's remark: "I cannot say that I liked Lawrence much"![4]

---

1 Francis Ponge, *Le Grand recueil* (1962) and *Le Parti pris des choses* (1942).
2 "Sidi-Madani, 20 December 1947 / North African winter.— Do nothing, doze . . . Have never known such ease. The warmth, which permeates everything . . . etc. etc."
3 "28 August (evening) / Variation on the preceding page: A glass of water. So be it."
4 Ford Madox Ford, *Portraits from Life* (1937), 85.

259.

15 West 67 St.
November 3, 1962[1]

Dearest Elizabeth:

I come home days now from the hospital, and will be entirely finished with the hospital in four days. So all has passed over, not too gruelingly, at last now, it seems. I meant to write you much sooner, but somehow till today I put off answering everything, even details on reading engagements for next month that I have through Lizzie already accepted. I just sit in my study and read and snooze, or listen to records. It sounds like old age, but it isn't. I was really quite run down from "over-exuberance" (I guess that's the word) and a lung infection, gone now without a trace, I got in Argentina.

I hope our summer wasn't too taxing on you and Lota, because we had a wonderful time—almost a mirage, the beaches seem at this distance and on this heavy fall rainy day in New York.

I don't have any real gossip, except Stanley's reports on the poets' conference in Washington, at which Delmore was put in jail for shouting while drinking by himself I think, and was rescued by John Berryman! Stanley was insulted by Oscar Williams, called Williams a worm, and nearly knocked him down. Randall apparently read a tribute to both of us, along with Frost and others, which the library will print, and I'll mail to you, if they don't.[2] Each poet I've met has a different account of what was good, odd or great at the conference. Allen and Belle were here. During their visit, it chanced that Cousin Harriet called from Washington, saying "I know what you are in for, they were here." She meant Washington, not her house, but I think she regards all visitors to Washington, such as poets and ambassadors, as planned insults to the old Washingtonian.

Loved your letter with the account of the open air meeting and Lota's medal. She must wear the big one when she comes here next.

Love,
Cal

---

1 On October 1 RL was released from Clinica Bethlehem in Buenos Aires and returned with his friend Blair Clark to New York. He was hospitalized at the Institute for the Living in Hartford for the next six weeks.
2 Randall Jarrell, "Fifty Years of American Poetry," *Prairie Schooner* (Spring 1963).

260.[1]

Dearest Cal:

Wish I'd hear something of you . . . I can't help but worry—
I asked Holliday to send you the Sydney Smith *Letters*—if they had them
in stock—some of the most entertaining reading I know. I've had two reports, *favorable*, about your poem "The Scream"—my copy of *Kenyon* hasn't
arrived yet, though.[2]

We came down early from Petrópolis yesterday morning and in the afternoon I got up my courage—following your noble example—and finally gave
a brief reading. To the "Women's Club"! They'd asked me several times, as
have other outfits here. It sounded like the easiest to begin with, but as it
turned out I think almost any college or highbrow audience would be easier—the 200 or so ladies looked awfully blank—all nationalities, but English
& American predominating. A singer followed—a buxom lady with a pink
orchid on her bust and a fierce voice—and she got a much bigger hand. Then
there was a tea-party. First the chairwoman apologized for the meagerness of
it and said that *nine* naughty ladies had not brought the cakes they had promised . . . Thank heavens. We'd have been buried in cakes otherwise. Lota &
Rosinha went with me and behaved very well. One wonderful old Brazilian—with pearl dog collar, full mourning, cane, etc. very *grande dame*—the
founder of the Brazilian Girl Scouts and some charity hospital—with the
wonderful name of Dona Jeronima Mesquita . . . I suppose I should do this
kind of thing, much as I hate it. Now I'm afraid, in my post-tea enthusiasm
and relief, I agreed to go and talk with the English classes at the big Anglo-
American school . . . what have you started me off on. Two ladies asked me
where I got my shoes; two, my necklace—"*Eskimo*! Imagine!"

Lota's gone to see Roberto[3]—he just got back—perhaps he'll know
something of you. Then we're going to call on the poor friend in the plaster
cast—Jorge Moreira—I haven't seen him yet. The Fire Department did
raise him to his penthouse—not by helicopter however—and he insisted on
being quite conscious throughout. When he got there he criticized the decor
of all the rooms he'd passed—he looked into the windows. "Imagine, painting the children's bedroom saffron yellow!" and imagine what the children
must have thought, if they saw that huge mummy-case floating up past their
windows at 8 AM.

1 Crossed with letter 259.
2 "The Scream," *The Kenyon Review* (Winter 1962); see RL-*CP*.
3 Roberto Burle Marx.

O—the best thing about the "reading" was that the church—it was in the Anglican church hall—sells second-hand books. They had hundreds for sale at either 1½ cents each or 3 cents . . . I even picked up some F. M. Ford novels, etc.—a Blue Guide to Scotland worth about $7.50—for 3¢—even if we don't get there—etc., etc.

Up at Samambaia lots of mail, magazines, etc.—that book *Poet's Choice*[1]—since I'd just finished the Ford book of reminiscence, your poem about him struck me as even better than before. He *was* kind[2]—that's one of the nicest things about that book, its genuine kind-heartedness—so rare in our literary world, *não é?* That girl Nélida came to call—with a poet friend—pretty awful—the Teasdale school, I think. They treat me as if I were 100—help me up steps, etc.! I hate lack of respect—hate respect—never pleased, I guess. We hope you are well Cal, and send lots of love,

Elizabeth

261.

Rio, December 19th, 1962

Dearest Cal:

It was wonderful to hear from you again at last and I've been waiting to answer because I was sort of hoping to hear again—and then I wrote so many letters to various parts of the globe I seemed to have run out of news—and I'm not sure if you ever got any of them, anyway . . . And I'm not sure that Holliday Bookshop got my order for you because what I ordered for myself hasn't come yet, so maybe that letter got lost. It will all have to wait now until after Christmas. I did want you to get the Sydney Smith *Letters*, though, and did you ever?— Day after tomorrow we are going to Cabo Frio for a week or ten days, then up from there to Samambaia for the second week-end, then back again here after New Year's sometime. Lota is awfully tired—she falls asleep every time she sits down, poor dear—and we are looking forward very much to those beaches and nothing to do for awhile. I'll probably be going out marlin fishing once or twice, and I am taking paints to paint pictures for a change. Remember those wonderful "boobys"?

Bobby Kennedy has just been here, talking in "secret sessions" with the Pres., & rumour is rife. And then the Army—well—I think you had entirely

---

1 *Poet's Choice*, ed. Paul Engle and Joseph Langland (1962).
2 "Ford, / you were a kind man and you died in want"; "Ford Madox Ford," lines 44–45 (RL-*CP*).

too much of Brazil's problems when you were here so I'll skip politics. One of the better news items has been about an old lady who was going around selling "lots" (the Brazilian passion, you know)—in Heaven. She sold them on long terms, very high prices—and was doing awfully well. She had a couple of assistants, one named "Iron Chest"—(breast, that is). I don't think she's ever been caught. Two "school teachers" were among the investors. I wonder what kind of teachers they can be. Now there's a campaign going on against "False Santa Clauses." The chief of police or someone had headlines today—only *genuine* Santa Clauses are allowed, the others are to be unmasked . . . A man who works with Lota (& his mother was one of L's godmothers) raises fancy canaries and offered me one. I said I'd love one if he sang *softly*—so a bright orange, very youthful canary has appeared, wearing a leg-iron to say he's imported from Amsterdam, I think. The man's name is Dr. Catta Preta—"catch a nigger," apparently—or negress. He must be descended from a slave trader. To be gracious, I thought I'd name the canary for him, his first name, and that turned out to be *Zephyrino*. Yes, while the world quakes I scrape perches and talk to a canary—Zephyrino—who looks rather like a tangerine.

I got the 50th Anniversary POETRY—I like most of all (the whole number) the first six lines of your Jonathan Edwards poem, I think.[1] It's a marvelous image. I like a lot of the rest of it, too, of course . . . The ending of the "Child's Song" is terrific, as Calder says.[2] That is masculine intuition for you—wonderful. Here's a card for Harriet—and how does she like the Dalton school, etc.? Please tell me.

I have a lot of things going, or coming, but nothing finished—one is a sort of thank-you poem for "Skunk Hour"—same sort of plan. I'm doing some translating, too. I just read a very good little book about Santos Dumont—you might even like it, I think—by an English Air-Marshal[3]—very fair and affectionate. He—Santos Dumont—was a delicate, humming-bird like character, and it is too bad planes haven't developed the way he (& Leonardo) dreamed of them—all his planes and plans make our jets seem gross and murderous—and those beefy pilots and sexy stewardesses would have appalled him. (I want to write a poem about all this sometime.)

Where are you giving readings— How are you feeling? Have you any

1 "Edward's great millstone and rock / of hope has crumbled, but the square / white houses of his flock / stand in the open air, / out inthe cold, / like sheep outside the fold"; "Jonathan Edwards in Western Massachusetts," *Poetry* (Oct. 1962), lines 1–6; see RL-*CP*.

2 "Help, saw me in two, / put me on the shelf! / Sometimes the little muddler / can't stand itself!"; "Child's Song," *Poetry* (Oct. 1962), lines 17–20; see RL-*CP*.

3 Peter Wykeham-Barnes, *Santos-Dumont: A Study in Obsession* (1962).

more plans for the anthology, or what? The first of the year I'll start my business negotiations for my new book again—but I feel horribly reluctant about it all and may postpone it still another year until I have a few more poems I like—I hope. I have invested some of my fellowship money in air conditioners for this apartment—since it looks as though we'll have to spend three more "summers" here and I think to be cool and quieter is the only way to get any work done in Rio. I must get to packing up—get to the Post Office one last time. I do hope you are well, Cal, and only remembering the best things we did and saw here— Write when you feel like it.

With love, as always,
Elizabeth

The garbage collector came to the door for his Christmas tip with a *poem*—he's my "faithful but tired" garbage man, etc.—and always at my orders.

262.

December 24, 1962

Dearest Elizabeth:

The day of Christmas Eve, pure summer with you I imagine, but with us rather grimy, the sound of the snow-chisel banging through sidewalk ice to pavement. Today is sunny, but Harriet surprised us by slipping downstairs unnoticed during our breakfast and curling up in a blanket in the big living room. No temperature, but several aches, urine to be taken to the hospital. Dismay that she may not be up to the various Christmas preparations. She has really had a swimmingly good fall, ice-skating with her new nurse, bringing artifacts home from the Dalton School. I wish you and Lota could see her.

Last night, my friend Jack Thompson brought over a Mexican poet and a young Brazilian play director whom we met at Belém. After the usual comparative literature comparisons, the Brazilian started on America, a tale of woe. He was almost tearful, and even admired Brizola.[1] We gave our defense of Carlos, but somehow one had the impression of a man determined to get away from the agony of self-criticism and scorch whoever was nearest at hand—not us but the United States. Nietzsche says that thoughts of suicide got him through many hard nights, and I guess this turning on someone else has saved thousands of souls.

---

1 Leonel de Moura Brizola, João Goulart's brother-in-law, was a leftist politician whose support for Goulart during the 1961 crisis helped secure Goulart's right to the presidency.

Here, the atmosphere is very different from South America, and very different, I think, even from last fall. We were all either exalted or scared out of our wits by Cuba, and then relieved.[1] Now suddenly there is no criticism, and I think no government in my life time has been less hated. Yet there seems to be great malaise with our culture and a kind of numbed contentment with our place and fate in the world. Last night I felt we had given up having strong feelings about ourselves and left this to the South Americans.

After I got well, I buried myself in writing. I have finished the old poem to you that I [had] begun after you left Maine, and another about dropping in a dream on the Copacabana beach. I'll send them both to you. Then other things which I won't send, including a translation of Juvenal's Tenth Satire, "The Vanity of Human Wishes," and a long unfinished dramatic monologue on my namesake Caligula.[2] To my surprise, I have mostly written in very strict meter, even sonnets, not at all my intention, and a fact that I find disturbing to my theories of how poetry should be written. I have always thought one should be able to shift from free to counted verse and mix the two, but I am surprised to find myself shifted despite my desires, seized by the muse or perhaps only the spirit of rhetoric.

I have thought of you, Dear, frequently every day. I hope our visit wasn't crushingly fatiguing to you both. I don't think any visitors were ever so sensitively and tirelessly entertained. I guess I was beginning to go off during the last two weeks in Brazil, and this must have been painful for you to watch or at least sense. When I got to Buenos Aires, my state zoomed sky-high and I am glad you didn't see it. It's hard for the controlled man to look back on the moment of chaos and claim. I shan't try, but it was all me, and I am sorry you were touched by it. Please let us be as dear to each other as always.

I am sending you some records. We had a more original present, an antique wooden shield with cranes, alligators and jungle trees, but the post-office said it was hopeless to try to get it through and that if it got to you at all, you would be months negotiating with the customs.

Giroux says that Houghton and Mifflin have released your manuscript. Let me know if I can do anything. The unfinished poems should be tremendous from your descriptions. I guess it's grating to have fragments lying about waiting and waiting for a breath to blow. I've had the worse experience, 1 of grinding out like a machine things I'll never use. Ten sonnets of

---

1 The Cuban Missile Crisis.
2 "Water," "Dropping South: Brazil," "The Vanity of Human Wishes," and "Caligula" (RL-*CP*).

Nerval, that vanish to nothing in English, words for a symphony for the dead, that Leonard Bernstein wanted me to try and have so far produced a bilge of declamation.[1]

Are you still trying to translate Lispector stories? Jack Thompson says that the Farfield Foundation, which he works for, could probably subsidize a translation though at a very low rate, five dollars a 1000 words. I wonder if anyone in Brazil could and would undertake her novel at that amount, though of course there'd no doubt be more from the publisher on acceptance, and later from sales. They also might be able to finance a trip by Nélida to New York. She might too get a Ford if you and I and Keith sponsored her. I think she would have to apply first.

Our love to you and Lota, and mine to you.

Cal

---

1 "El Desdichado (After Gerard de Nerval)," "Christ in the Olive Grove (After Gerard de Nerval)," and "Three Poems for Kaddish" (RL-*CP*).

FOUR

1963-1970

263.

Dearest Cal:

Carnival comes next. The songs are already being sung:

> "Is that trembling cry a song?
> Can it be a song of joy?
> And so great a number poor?
> 'Tis a land of poverty."

> ["]And their sun does always shine,
> And their fields are bleak and bare,
> And their ways are fill'd with thorns.
> 'Tis eternal summer there."[1]

And it is hot as hell and thank heavens for our new air conditioners. It must have been over 100 last night. I went out to buy the papers, as always— someone had thrown out a large Christmas tree, a real one, not a Maine one, exactly, but some kind of fir that was quite thick and pretty, and there it stood, dropping its needles fast but still *smelling* a little of Martin Luther and the north, among the overpowering smells of rotten fruit and tired, sweat-polluted sea. Brazil is torn between Christmas our-style and New Years their-style. Lota got most presents on New Years. They put up a huge— 4 story high—Santa Claus, 3 dimensional, at the entrance to the Copacabana tunnel—horribly jolly in paint and plywood. We hate him, so that Sunday night, coming back from Samambaia, seriously considered shooting him full of holes with Lota's revolver. Then we thought of some whimsical headlines:

---

1 Cf. William Blake, "Holy Thursday," *Songs of Experience*, lines 5–12 (1794).

"Santa Claus Shot! Taken to Strangers' Hospital (across the street). Occupying rooms 204, 205, and 206. End of Christmas Foreseen!"

Joana[1] (our maid) had a terrible hangover after New Years, poor dear. I heard her throwing up and made her a prairie oyster. I told her it was an *"ostra das pampas"*—and it did the trick. Now she says she is NOT going to participate in Carnival, but of course she will. She really lives the life, that we can scarcely imagine, of an ancient—no books, black beans, gossip, living from holiday to holiday, finery, bloodshed—only her radio is something new, in 1,000's of years.

I had a nice letter from you in Petrópolis. Also one from May S.[2] who was thrilled with her subway ride with you . . . and adored the bird-record, as I was sure she would. She said she saw your "youngest child, a daughter aged four, with beautiful gray eyes . . ."! I hope H. wasn't "coming down with" something when you wrote, and wasn't sick over all the horrible holidays.

Yes, people must be pretty desperate to try to defend poor Brizola who is really too primary to be true—or you may remember. But one recent minister—out of office this morning—was flipping over the pages of a U.S. magazine (probably one of those swollen Christmas-time *New Yorker*s) and said to someone we know—*"And this is all at the expense of Brazil"* . . . Now Goulart seems between two stools—trying to please the Brizolas and the U.S. at the same time. He just won the plebiscite[3]—to get rid of having a Prime Minister—but this means nothing at all, really—just a matter of appeasing his vanity. Carlos L called up Lota yesterday and read her most of Dos Passos's 1st chapter of a book about Brazil over the phone.[4] Dos sent him the MMS. In it he quotes Lota three times . . . (I think it must be the page of information about the *aterro*[5] I typed out for him)—and calls Carlos "dangerous"—which Carlos loves.

But let me say once again—we do NOT approve of C. in many ways—and he is dangerous, when there is no one else. Did I tell you how Raymond Aron (I don't know how you feel about him, of course) went all over Brazil when he was here and met most of the governors, ministers, etc.—told us that Carlos was the only intelligent man he'd talked to—just "intelligent," nothing more. The others are so stupid! He said that C's big weakness

---

1 Joana dos Santos da Costa.
2 May Swenson.
3 João Goulart's victory in a national plebiscite eliminated the parliamentary structure of government that had been created to limit his authority.
4 John Dos Passos, *Brazil on the Move* (1963).
5 Landfill.

(which Lota already knows only too well, having suffered from it to the point of almost throwing up her job several times) is that he can't conceal his intelligence; he is scornful of the men who work with him, and shows it—and so he may never accomplish anything, or do something "dangerous," like try to be some sort of dictator. That's enough of that—the country seems on the edge of dissolution.

The enclosed is my idea of what politics shd. be like—I send it in case you didn't see it.[*]

Cabo Frio was wonderful—we stayed ten days; went to the "Horseshoe" beach eight of them, and the "little Oven" the other times—it is rather long and narrow, and rough, that day, with lots of diving birds. Everything looked better than when you were there because it is "summer"—a "flush of Verdure" (I am reading FitzGerald's letters and that's what he's always saying[1])—and a flush of baby horses, cows, goats, pigs, and sheep, all over the roads. One hot night Lota woke me up in the middle of the night to go out and look at the stars because they had never looked so *close* before—close and warm, apparently touching our hair—and never so many— We did a lot of reading & swimming and that was all. I found Monica[2] on the floor showing "Roger"—that pointer—the pictures in "Peter Rabbit"—right under his nose. He seemed faintly interested.

I also had a letter from Flannery—I had written her at last—that begins: "I was real pleased to hear from you." Since you were here I have acquired—at a vegetable stand—a crucifix in a bottle, like a ship in a bottle—all the accoutrements, gilded, and a rooster, nails, etc.—and I offered it to her. She said she'd like it—she'd been trying to write a story for a long time about a man who had the head of Christ tattooed on his back—she saw him in the papers. I think we have a lot in common . . .

Lota was one of the "Women of the Year"—this in the column of an early bitter enemy of the *aterro* . . . (I use that word because now you know what it means.)

You've probably read FitzGerald's letters—they're good, although not as good as I thought they were going to be. Or perhaps he reminds me a

[*]Reprinted in *The New Yorker*, November 24th, 1962, under the heading THE GOOD OLD DAYS: *(From* Niles' Weekly Register, *published in Baltimore, June 15th, 1816)* WASHINGTON, June 6.—The President and his family left this city yesterday for Montpelier, where it is expected he will spend the summer months; there being no public business at this time, particularly requiring his attendance at the seat of government.

1 *The Letters of Edward FitzGerald*, ed. J. M. Cohen (1960).
2 Mary Stearns Morse's adopted child (see letter 229).

bit too much of myself—although I'd never be able to learn Persian. But he wastes his time the way I do—and also has too much "good taste" and interest in too many arts, like me . . . But some of his judgments—for someone living off in the country like that—on contemporary painters, musicians, & poets are amazing—the only other such sure taste I can think of is Baudelaire's.

I have translated five of Clarice's stories[1]—all the very short ones & one longer one. *The New Yorker* is interested—I think she needs money, so that would be good, the $ being what it is (almost twice as much already as when you were here)—then if they don't want them, *Encounter*, *PR*, etc. Alfred Knopf is also interested in seeing the whole book. But at the moment—just when I was ready to send off the batch, except for one, she has vanished on me—completely—and for about six weeks! Lota met her—she isn't cross or anything—and she seemed *delighted* with the translations, letters of interest, etc. I am mystified; L is fed up . . . It is "temperament," maybe, or more likely just the usual "massive inertia" that one runs into at every turn—and that is driving Lota mad on her job. IT makes one despair, really. Her novels are NOT good; the "essays" she does for *Senhor* are very bad—but in the stories she has awfully good things and they do sound pretty good in English, and I was quite pleased with them. Oh dear. Well—we'll see.

The person I'd like to see get a Ford Fellowship is Rachel de Queiroz, the journalist. She was away in the north all the time you were here. She is dying to go; she has a huge reputation here and everyone reads her weekly page in CRUZEIRO—and her first novel is wonderful.[2] I don't think much of her later ones. Some of her earlier journalism is good too, and I think I'll translate a few chapters of it just for fun. She is corny, sentimental, etc.—but not "arty" (like Nélida), and she is someone worth having on our side (wherever that is). She really has tremendous influence here and is usually sensible and *right*. She is one of the people that the US should have recognized long ago, really—but she was a communist when she was 19 or 20, and then fought against Vargas—well. If there is anything I can do to help her get to the US I'll do it—write a report, etc.—if it would help any.

I don't want to be mean—but I don't think Nélida would be a good person—unless there are fellowships to spare. Her novel is so bad, really.[3] She *is* nice, personally, but arty and pretentious. I could have told you this that first time I met her, out of my superior knowledge of the language and the cus-

---

1 Clarice Lispector.
2 Rachel de Queiroz, *O Quinze* (1955).
3 Nélida Piñon, *Guia-Mapa de Gabriel Arcanjo* (1961).

toms, but for some reason I was being discreet. Someone older like Rachel—who has already made a reputation—would do wonders for "international relationships." Maybe Nélida will learn. Clarice suffers from the same kind of dated-ness, provincialism, etc.—but she *really* has talent—and I have hopes—(or had, until she disappeared.) Rachel has a tough mind, under the corniness, and knows everything about economics, history, politics, etc. here—and wants to see what she calls "the interior" of the USA—"fazenda" life, etc. I'd like to translate her first novel, about the north—one of the best Brazilian books—but the language is so colloquial it is very difficult.

Several days later—
This letter goes on & on and I think this is enough for all of 1963 almost. Yes, I heard from Brandt & Brandt and have written Carl. Will you let me see the Nerval poems—I like him—and I am eager to see the Copacabana one. Would there be any operatic possibilities in THE DYNASTS, I wonder?[1] I haven't read it for years—maybe not. I am dying to get the new records—how wonderful—maybe they'll be there this week-end. It is wonderful how you work—as an old Irish woman said to me once—"It's wonderful the way you read." I have some snapshots—from TIME—I'll send when I get copies made. With much love, as always—
    Elizabeth

Apparently I am NEVER going to get to the Post Office again—so I'll add another thought or two. Clarice was finally heard from yesterday—apologies and tears, even, I think! I couldn't even sound annoyed, of course. She has been sick, I think—and is having some sort of minor operation the end of this month—well—I think we'll be able to get off the batch of stories next week. Knopf is coming back in Feb. and it would be a good chance for her, too. I suppose the combination of Russian massive inertia and Brazilian does pile up. I do like her, too—but I have been minding my loneliness here more lately, I'm afraid. HOWEVER—dear Clarice might have telephoned, in seven weeks—or had her maid telephone!
    I got the Walcott book and was awfully disappointed in it—I can't even seem to find the good poem I thought you had taken from it—perhaps it was later?[2] Dugan is wonderful in spots and phrases and verses—but rarely all

1 Thomas Hardy, *The Dynasts* (1904–08).
2 Derek Walcott, *In a Green Night* (1962).

the way through a poem, I think.[1] Is he the one you told me worked in the plastic factory?

Would you like back the Robert Staples book, which I seem to have kept?[2] If so I'll gladly send, otherwise gladly keep it. And I wonder if you carried off, by chance, my old Oxford book of 17th Century Verse?[3] I hate to be a pest about things like that but if you did—please keep it for me, or send if it ever isn't too much bother. I am so in your debt about books I feel rather mean about this. (But I've had it so many years I'm fond of it.)

Lota brought Carlos and a secretary here for lunch two days ago—with about an hour's warning. He was in a good mood and ate everything in sight and everything went off very well. He said—"I have a nice new friend I must introduce to you . . ." (being funny)—and it turns out that our dear KB wrote him a long explanatory apologetic letter, then went to see him.

I wrote Stanley K twice over the past year—and I think he may have been hurt because I couldn't send him the autographed book he asked for, or something. Well—it is out of print. But I do hope he isn't cross with me— *too*! I hear that Bandeira has *stopped* being cross with me—too bad it wasn't before you left—and today I have already received two gift books (not B's however)—one prose, one poetry. I can't keep up with this flow—they keep coming & coming. Part of the general over-volubility—

I am just so glad you sound like yourself again—please forget everything except the good parts and forget that I, too, have "spells" (very rarely, thank God). They are a lot like yours, on a modest scale, I think—in origin and results, even— But you have to do everything on the grand scale! I learned a great deal.

We are about to drive up to Petrópolis.— I hope Harriet wasn't sick and that school goes well— I have been reading McNamara's statements[4]—it is all horrible, but he does sound like a thinker, for once—an almost Trotsky-ish dialectic tone—(Aron thought most highly of *him*, in the USA). Perhaps he will get us through another year— With love and best wishes for it—
Elizabeth

1 Alan Dugan, *Poems* (1961).
2 Possibly Hugh B. Staples, *Robert Lowell: The First Twenty Years* (1962).
3 *The Oxford Book of Seventeenth Century Verse*, ed. H.J.C. Grierson and G. Bullough (1934).
4 Robert McNamara had recently described his strategic doctrine for making nuclear weapons usable instruments of national policy; this included measures to reduce to 18 million the number of casualties in an attack. See "McNamara Thinks the Unthinkable," *The Saturday Evening Post* (Dec. 1, 1962).

January 23rd—

P.S. I did get to the PO in Petrópolis—began to think I had been mean & gossipy in this letter, and didn't mail it! On reading it over it doesn't seem so bad . . . I saw Clarice—she is having a small operation this week—but I hope we can get those five stories off anyway. Maybe I'll even do one more. Alfred Knopf is coming here again in February, I think, so I'll just give him copies. He has sent me lists and lists of awful writers. I don't know whether anyone would really be interested in publishing a book of *stories*, but I'll try. What I am most interested in is getting a fellowship for Rachel—she'd do more for international relationships with 2 or 3 of her weekly columns than almost anything or anyone I can think of.

I had letters from Marianne and Dr. B—who said she'd seen you and you were well—she was in Santa Lucia.

Lota wants me to give a lunch to three of the big brass in the government—Sunday—up at Samambaia. I must go buy a ham and bake it, etc. Mary Morse has to go to [the] U.S. tomorrow night unexpectedly—her aunt died—just for eight days—and she is leaving Monica with us, of course. We'll stay up in the country as long as Lota can, because it's easier there, then bring her here. Thank God she can't climb up to the terrace railing yet! Thank God also that she is passionately fond of swimming . . . I'll be spending most of next week playing in the sand—and I am still peeling, from too much Cabo Frio.

Dr. B says you are lecturing—where, I wonder—and whom.

Things seem extra-dull after your stay—however, I am getting down to work pretty well, I think— Please send POEMS.

With love,
E.—

This was wrung from me somewhere along the line last autumn:

> A cultured acquaintance named K——
> Faces life with a pipe in his teeth.
> He behaves,—well, in brief,
> It would be a relief
> To lay a small wreath upon K——.

264.[1]

January 23, 196[3]

Dearest Elizabeth:

We've been in a great flurry lately. Lizzie is on the board of a new book review[2] about to be set floating during the lull of the newspaper strike here that has temporarily put the New York *Times* book section out of existence. Meetings, arguments, telephone calls, and now at the end of two weeks, a fairly dazzling first number has been promised and will come out in the middle of February. One of my sideline duties was to phone Randall, who said he promised himself never again to write anything he could use in a book of essays. There was nothing he wanted to review. Then he paused and said there was one book, yours. He has been following all your new poems in *The New Yorker*, and is choosing a good many for a new anthology.

I pass this on to cheer you and perhaps prod you. The wolf with its head on its paws lies looking at the desolate yellow wastes of our present civilization, ready when your book comes to howl its welcome. This makes a difference. I remember my second book seemed lost in the dust of carping and the mildest praise, when Randall wrote a long piece violently liking and disliking. In a preface to Emily Dickinson, John Brinnin asks if she isn't the greatest woman poet, brushes away the past, and then says only Marianne Moore and Elizabeth Bishop (of the English poets of this century) reach her level.[3]

I don't suppose you need praise, but I find there are sinking times when everything I do looks about like what dozens of others are doing, or worse. It's pleasant to have an art that can never make money or much sensation; then in dry times it hardly seems to exist. You have more to offer, I think, than anyone writing poetry in English. On, Dear, with those painful, very large unfinished poems!

I am at the end of something. Up till now I've felt I was all blue spots and blotches inside, more than I could bear really, if I looked at myself, and of course I wanted to do nothing else. So day after day, I wrote, sometimes too absorbed to even stop for lunch and often sitting with my family in a stupor, mulling over a phrase or a set of lines for almost hours, hypnotized, under a spell, often a bad spell. Now out of this, I have seven poems and seven translations, just about a book when added to what I had before. Now I say to myself, "Out of jail!" I look back on the last months with disgust and gratitude. Disgust because they seem so monstrous, gratitude, because I have lived

---

1 Crossed with letter 263.
2 *The New York Review of Books.*
3 *Emily Dickinson*, ed. John Malcolm Brinnin (1960).

through the unintelligible, have written against collapse and come out more or less healed. Oh dear, have you ever felt like a man in an unreal book?

I begin my Harvard teaching next week, and have been boning up on the standard old Americans, Emerson, Longfellow, Bryant, etc. They are much farther away than they were when I was in school and college. Then they were almost something one shouldn't read much of lest they lead astray. Now the times have brought them back maybe,—hardly imitated still, they are like our own kind of revolt and competence. The Beats have blown away, the professionals have returned. Sometimes they flash—Emerson is a funny case of the poet who was all flash in theory and desire and even gifts, and somehow his equipment and instincts wouldn't let him. Then a lovely moment would come.

Harriet has had a rather hard winter getting over being shy at school. There was group dancing and singing, and she somehow got off on the wrong foot and wouldn't join and even told us trying to change "made her heart bleed." But now there's [a] burst of luncheon invitations, exchange house-visits, dancing class, swimming lessons with a friend and the sorrow is gone. She is beginning to be the girl she will be for the next ten years, living in our dense world of conscious attractions, liking this person, disliking that one. It's that time of sheer survival of energy boxing with ignorance, when I suppose only exuberance and a thousand things to do get us by the impossible obstacle of growing into something definite—bold, cheerful changing little creature!

Write and tell me about yourself, and how the hot months are going and give lots of gossip. Our minds are still in last summer. Love to Lota.

Love,
Cal

265.

February 10, 1963

Dearest Elizabeth:

So much to catch up on! A big burly letter written at different dates, the two lovely Sydney Smith volumes, and now a note asking if they had arrived. They have and I have been dipping in. Their sociable, minute, witty life far from all cant and extravagance is very attractive. I was going to say a life free from enthusiasm, but of course a continual air of enthusiasm blows through them—they are free from everything so extravagant as pessimism. That August afternoon of last summer comes back when you were picking your companions for heaven up on that tea-house on the mountain. Strange now to think how I imagined I was sipping in moderation and tolerance from you all summer! I think I was, Dear, though I hardly gave a convincing demonstration.

I suppose you have read about Frost's death,[1] though we, through the absence of New York papers, had to be told by telephone. He has been much with me: I've written a short piece on him for a new review[2] (guided by us which will be a sort of intelligent New York *Times* section), talked on television, re-read quantities and talked on him to my classes at Harvard. Walking by his house in Cambridge last Thanksgiving, I thought with some shame about how wrong I was to be bothered by his notoriety and showing off. Under the great display the life was really very bounded and simple. Pound's daughter[3] was here, looking like him and strangely like Jack Sweeney's Irish wife, Máire. Somewhere there was an awakening from father—not a disillusionment but surprise: "Until six years ago I never questioned one of his thoughts . . . Of course I wasn't prepared to be impressed by T. S. Eliot . . . When he came back, we didn't know that even he couldn't do anything . . . two years of sitting hardly raising an arm and thinking all his contemporaries' careers had gone better than his . . . stopped me from translating the *Cantos*, saying they were no good . . . Do people in such a state really feel the terrible things they say? . . . at first it was *Cantos* at every meal." She saw Frost the day before he died. "I wanted him to know that some one who loved Father didn't have bad manners." Frost said that he loved Ezra and hoped to see him in Venice, where he now is in a rather better state. She and her husband live in a Tyrolean castle, cold, too large, isolated; Dorothy Pound stays with them ("It seems she and father exhausted all they had to say to each other at St. Elizabeths") and they talk about cats and flowers, and each winter some one in the small family launches off on the New York edition of Henry James[4]—"his subtle qualifications hardly seem to fit the circumstances of my life." A strange, shy, pathetic, and in no way ugly life. She hardly knows what country she belongs to and has just taken a short course in filing at Yale to take care of her father's papers. I have been thinking of the great callousness and bravado of Ezra's existence, so free one might [think] of half-thought, of most men's waverings, feelings of being a copy, of not pur-

1 Robert Frost died on January 29, 1963.
2 "Robert Frost, 1876–1963," *The New York Review of Books* (Aug. 29, 1963); see RL-*CPR*.
3 Mary de Rachewiltz, daughter of Ezra Pound and Olga Rudge.
4 Twenty-four volumes, published between 1907 and 1909, selected, revised, and introduced by Henry James.

suing the goal, etc. Then the shell breaks and the cold air tortures the exposed flesh. Then partial recovery, though the other was a recovery of humanity.

I've started commuting to Harvard, enter my classes with apprehension, then enjoy them. One student, however, said the room seemed made up of 18 frozen introverts. I guess we'll all thaw as we get used to talking to each other. I live in Quincy House, very modern, all glass, with walls of unfinished cement brick. Their designer and installer came into my room the other day to display them. Papers with titles like *India News* come for the former occupant, Mr. Sinha, who has left behind him something I've always dreamed of, a library made up of books I've never read. And never will, alas, for they are all problems in logic and recent English philosophy.

My *Phaedra* contract has at last been signed! Now it may go on next fall, either here or in London. My next book is done, I think. I have 22 original poems and about twelve translations. It has the gentle title, *An Eye for an Eye.*[1] I'll get copies typed and send you one next month. Often it seems all acid and mannerisms to me. I may have gotten into a rather mechanical appetite for publishing. Habits come hard to me, and then seem excessive and possessive. I get a curious pleasure from getting a book off my hands and out.

I enjoyed your limerick on Keith. I finally wrote him a sort of apology and bread and butter letter. Poor thing, all ticks and angles. I gave him a hard run.

In the mail the other day came two drawings: one a very accurate Dureresque head in a surrealist design with entrails (?) and a huge thumb, the other a precise flame pattern in diamonds like good wood-carving. With them a pitiful letter about break-downs and wanting a friend. "I went to your Milton class, but didn't dare speak." And, "Oh God, why can't God be good to us!" I felt I had to ask him over. A tall young man of twenty arrived, sandy mustached, talking in images only, the son of a captain for the Grace Lines, and carrying his poems wadded in a paper bag. He had spilled milk on a bird drawing he was doing for me, and then, more out of fancy than rage, had poured milk on his poems so they stuck together. They read like [a] young man of twenty's version of the most obscure Thomas; each was finished in a day and ended where his page ended. He wanted a friend.

Let's not argue politics. I feel a fraud on the subject. One has, or I at least, such a feeling of things are in the saddle here.[2] The great machine rolls on, all

1 Cf. "Eye and Tooth" (RL-*CP*).
2 Cf. "Things are in the saddle, / And ride mankind"; Ralph Waldo Emerson, "Ode, Inscribed to W. H. Channing" (1846), lines 50–51.

in all efficiently enough, but it doesn't at the moment seem as if anyone in our lifetimes will have the force to deflect it. We trust, I suppose.

Goodbye, Dear, and our love to you and Lota. Send another letter.

Love,

Cal

Hope to see your Lispector in *The New Yorker*. Do you want me to get in touch with Jack Thompson about getting your other friend.[*] I know perfectly well who she is—the young Brazilian who was here said she and Clarice were the best prose writers in Brazil—but your letter isn't at hand, and I don't trust myself with the spelling. I'll show him your sentences and ask him to write you.

* Rachel de Queiroz.

266.

Rio, March 5th, 1963

Dearest Cal:

Should I go to Peru with Roberto BM,[1] or shouldn't I?— I am trying to decide and meanwhile I'll answer your letter. He was supposed to go today but there were both a revolution AND an earthquake—so it's been briefly postponed . . . He's having a big show in Lima, has been there many times, and it might be fun. On the other hand—Lota can't go and I haven't any CLOTHES . . .

We got back yesterday from ten days in Samambaia—stayed over Carnival. Except for the heat, I do wish you had come now, at this time of year—I have never seen the damnable country look lovelier . . . All the flowering trees are in blossom, delicate patches of color all up the mountains, and nearer to they glisten with little floating webs of mist, gold spider-webs, iridescent butterflies—this is the season for the big pale blue-silver floppy ones, hopelessly impractical, frequently frayed, in vague couples. They hover over our little pool, and pink blossoms fall into it, and there are so many dragon flies—some invisible except as dots of white or ruby red or bright blue plush or velvet—then they catch the light and you see the body and wings are really there, steely blue wire-work. We sat out in the evenings and the lightning *twitched* around us and the bigger variety of fireflies came floating along

1 Roberto Burle Marx.

like people out walking with very weak flashlights, on the hill—well—you missed this dazzlingness—and the summer storms. Lots of rainbows—a double one over the sea just now with three freighters going off under it in three different directions.

Mary finally got back to claim her child—away a month—and now we miss Monica dreadfully. There was a huge batch of mail in Petrópolis by then, including your letter of Feb. 10th, and yesterday as we came back, THE NEW YORK REVIEW. Thank you so much. It is very impressive and what a lot of work it must have taken to get it together so fast—can they keep on bringing it out, I wonder? I read it through last night—so many good pieces. Elizabeth's Grub Street awfully good, I thought—she "generalizes" awfully well. That must be the poor Brazilian you mentioned—who is he, anyway?[1] And who is the poor lady who stays in bed and reads?— I feel she must be myself but no, here I am.[2] Wolfe does take in even sophisticated foreigners—I think I finally convinced Alfredo[3] (who you never *got to know*) about him. (A typical Alfredo story—yesterday his lectures on Esthetics began at Catholic University. Due to a slight misunderstanding, they were announced as "statistics" and naturally almost no one showed up . . .) The Ring Lardner good, too—straightforward, accurate, apt[4]— I think Mary has reached the point of diminishing returns as far as frank sex-language goes.[5] There was one word I'd never heard before—maybe she's had to start inventing!— Did I ever tell you about Mary's "report" on Gide for the course in the English Novel that we took together? Mary, very young and pretty, in a tweed suit, with locks of hair falling down, at the teacher's desk with her little stack of index cards. We all *knew*, of course, and were just waiting to hear what she'd dare say. She glared at us and her voice cracked a little as she came out with the word *homosexual*—a little too loud. Miss Rose Peebles, our teacher, a real "lady" from Virginia, sat on the sidelines bravely trying to look both ladylike and modern.— And Mary has kept right on trying to shock ever since. But I think she has made her point by now and is old enough to take a different line . . .

---

1 "A South American in a brushed, blue serge suit . . . with his nervous precision, his aching repression, he declared that the huge, romantic, excessive Thomas Wolfe was the American with whom he felt the closest spiritual and personal connection. He meant to write a book on Wolfe, in Portuguese"; Elizabeth Hardwick, "Grub Street: Washington," *The New York Review of Books* (Feb. 1, 1963).
2 "Old lady writers, without means, without Social Security, reading in bed all day—dear old Sibyls, almost forgotten, hardly called upon except perhaps at midnight by a drunken couple from a pad down the street"; Elizabeth Hardwick, "Grub Street: Washington," *The New York Review of Books* (Feb. 1, 1963).
3 Alfredo Lage.
4 Elizabeth Hardwick, "Ring," *The New York Review of Books* (Feb. 1, 1963).
5 Mary McCarthy, "Déjeuner sur l'Herbe" (a review of William Burroughs's *Naked Lunch*), *The New York Review of Books* (Feb. 1, 1963).

In fact—I am appalled, bored, sickened, etc. by all the late VULGAR-
ITY. (I don't like that word but can't think of any other.) I read *Tropic of
Cancer* in 1936 or whenever it came out, and *The Black Book*, and all the rest
of them (Connolly's *Rock Pool* is a good one—and probably any day now it
will be re-issued by Random House and all the critics will jump for joy, bring
out their very frankest language, and it will be sold to Hollywood . . .)[1] and I
couldn't be more morbid and I think filth and horror are right and necessary—in the *work*. The critics are just jealous and want to use all the same
words . . . The last 2 PR's have amazed me—so much junk in them. "That
Last Visit to Hemingway"![2] More juvenile than H at his worst, & mean too,
or just insensitive.— And the letter about Miller, etc.[3] And—this isn't vulgarity—but WHO wrote those idiotic movie reviews?[4] I think she must be
somebody's mistress? Well—filth—I suppose it is a defense against the great
American slickness, perhaps—but it does sound dated, just the way the Beat
poets did, and makes me feel even more like a late late member of the
post–World War I generation rather than my own.

Your piece on Frost is awfully nice, Cal. And "Buenos Aires" is certainly
The Latin City—I'll have to go there & see why you liked it so much. I like
the first stanzas best. But I DON'T like the phallic monument, Cal.[5] This has
nothing to do with the preceding paragraph—it is just that I think it is un-
original. It seems to me I've read so many "Phallic monuments" in poetry—
Spender used to use it ad nauseam, for one. Oh I know it's the Idea, and
Peron, and Power, etc.—it couldn't be more appropriate. But I feel that *you*
can surprise us better than that.— I hope you won't mind my saying this—
The first part has so many enlightening images, then I found "phallus" too
expected.

On March 13th Jennie Tourel is singing in Carnegie Hall—one song is
my poem about Pound—called BEDLAM for the song version. I've never
heard it—perhaps you will—or some friend will who will give me a report—(She must be 70 by now!)[6]

1 Henry Miller, *Tropic of Cancer* (1939); Lawrence Durrell, *The Black Book* (1938); Cyril Connolly, *The Rock Pool* (1935).

2 Leslie Fiedler, "An Almost Imaginary Interview: Hemingway in Ketchum," *Partisan Review* (Summer 1962).

3 Alfred Chester, "Thoughts of an Unserious Reader of Erotica," *Partisan Review* (Fall 1962).

4 Pauline Kael, "Movie Chronicle: Little Men," *Partisan Review* (Fall 1962).

5 "Everywhere, the bellowing of the old bull— / the muzzled underdogs still roared / for the brute beef of Peron, / the nymphets' Don Giovanni. / On the main square / a white stone obelisk / rose like a phallus / without flesh or hair"; "Buenos Aires," *The New York Review of Books*, lines 41–48 (Feb. 1, 1963): Cf. "Buenos Aires" (RL-*CP*).

6 Jennie Tourel performed Ned Rorem's musical setting of "Visits to St. Elizabeths: (Bedlam)" at Carnegie Hall on March 13, 1963.

I spent two days in Samambaia reading a long, bad, but fascinating new life of Chekhov[1]—I bet Randall has read it, too. What a wonderful man, really—almost a saint. The son of serfs yet a greater gentleman than the estate-owning novelists. And in a country really a lot like Brazil, or even worse—and sick & poor and exhausted—look what he wrote— PEASANTS, for example, or THE RAVINE. I admire Pound's extraordinary courage, many things about him—but read this, Cal, and see how petty Pound appears, how horribly "flawed," as you say—and almost completely lacking in natural human feelings.

Brazil and France are about to go to War, it seems, over the Brazilian lobster beds—battleships standing by, hourly reports—just like a musical comedy.

That Miss Kray writes me my translations of Cabral de Melo are "brilliant"—that's nice, but I wonder how she knows? I may do that whole long poem just for fun—it goes into English fairly easily.[2]—I've also done a couple of Drummond. I wonder if you'd mind if I did "The Table"[3]—that one you liked? It's the best of the early-memory ones—and I like that part of his poetry best. Of course I do it in my painful literal way, anyway—so if you wanted to do a lively Lowell version at any time I don't think mine would interfere with yours at all—they'd be so different. Also—it turns out to have lots of Rio slang in it, not in the dictionary—so you could "look things up" in my version—(If I do it—I'll only do it if they'll pay me for more).

It is wonderful about *Phaedra*—maybe we can go to the London opening— EYE FOR AN EYE is a wonderful title, too—and I like that poem still the best of the new ones.[4] I think, the story of Pound's daughter very interesting—he wanted me to go there as a paying guest, you know, and showed me lots of photographs of her, the *castle*, etc. "Of course, you'd have to buy a desk . . ." What are the names of your courses? Cambridge must be all dirty snow and bare elms now. Have you seen Nathalie and if so how is she? Give her my love,—I think she might even like an architectural trip here sometime. I hope you don't mind the going back & forth too much—I find it disturbing and distracting here, but then—you concentrate better I'm sure, and don't mind driving or flying the way I do. Thank you for offering to help about Rachel de Queiroz. At the moment I am *off of* trying to help

---

1 Ernest Joseph Simmons, *Chekhov: A Biography* (1962).
2 EB translated part of João Cabral de Melo Neto's *The Death and Life of a Severino*; see EB-*CP*.
3 See EB's translation of Carlos Drummond de Andrade's "The Table" in EB-*CP*, first published in *The New York Review of Books* (Jan. 16, 1969).
4 "Eye and Tooth" (RL-*CP*).

anybody!—maybe it's just anybody Brazilian! They are so damned unreliable . . . It's lovely to be able to be that way and we may have sacrificed a lot, what with our consciences and all—but I have the feeling that if I did get it all arranged she might say, no, she didn't feel like it just then, or not without her husband—and go off to her drought-ridden fazendas in the north and lie in a hammock and watch the cattle die of thirst . . . Oh dear—I *do* like her, but I've had enough personality troubles for a while. She has just gone back north again for six months, just as I thought we were getting somewhere, ~~with articles for the *New Republic*, and 2 "Letters" of mine she was going to use in her column~~[1]—now everything comes to a halt again. I haven't heard about Clarice's stories, either. She volunteered to mail them several weeks ago—I bet she never did! Unfortunately I didn't discover the best one until too late. She handed me one once in a while—but maybe I'll finish it, too, just to do the job right—and then that's that.[2] Oh I'll undoubtedly relent—but for a while I want to think of my own affairs.

Do you think *The Observer* is a good place to send a poem or two? Mine has started coming. If so—will you give me the name of the editor to send poetry to? (I think you sent the water-tower one there didn't you?[3]—that's my next favorite of the new ones) They had the best short piece about Brazil I have read anywhere—by an O'Donohue,[4] I think—if you saw it—fair and sympathetic and clear. All the plays make me feel quite blue. I re-played *Mahagonny* last week. It's on in London and how I'd like to see it. Oh dear—the records you mentioned have not arrived. However, by boat, things sometimes do take months—so I haven't given up hope. But I hope it wasn't too big a bundle—and it shd. be only 2 at a time, labeled *$5.oo* . . . I am dying for some new ones. Well, they'll probably show up. Before that *.4* friend goes—not till August—I'm going to ask her to let me have some records sent to her.[5] The US sends them everything, you know—airmail, no danger of loss, customs, duty—almost no postage. She is generous about it but I don't like to ask very much.

How is little Harriet? I hate to think of all that schooling the poor child has ahead of her. I just found a long pencil-line, the length of the hall, wan-

1 Canceled by EB as "uninteresting!"
2 Clarice Lispector, "The Smallest Woman in the World," "A Hen," and "Marmosets," trans. EB, *The Kenyon Review* (Summer 1964).
3 "New York 1962: Fragment," *The Observer* (July 8, 1962); see lines 2–3 (RL-*CP*).
4 Patrick O'Donovan, "Land of Promise v. Performance," *The Observer* (Jan. 6, 1963).
5 Betty Theodorides.

dering up and down about 2 feet off the ground—as Klee said—Monica "took a walk with a line."

Lota is flabbergasting me more every day. Her latest triumph is too long to go into—but she has really saved a big hunk of the city, done a crook out of a few extra millions, all in about 48 hours. And while she saves the doomed city of Rio, I shut my self up with my air conditioner and try to forget it.

Have you seen Stanley and if so will you please ask him if he got the book I sent—or what's wrong? I sound cranky—am, probably—I hope you are not and that all goes well—we both send love; don't work too hard—keep your feet and your powder dry.

Elizabeth

Brazilian children's joke: Why is a Volkswagen like a behind?
Answer: Because everybody has one—

March 14th—

This has been in my desk a week because I thought it was too cranky & boring to send—I've just re-read it and although I don't think it's very interesting, I think it is sendable . . . Brazil has won the lobster war. My canary had a heart attack (I think). I have scarcely seen Lota for a week, but Saturday is her birthday so we are having a sort of gala in Samambaia all that day . . . I was mean about Rachel de Q. She really wants to go to the US badly, I know—and if she wrote articles for here at the same time perhaps she could afford to take her husband along, too—they're very devoted. She *should* go—the place is being flooded with violent anti-American literature, poems (I was just sent 2 books of it) etc.—all so simple minded. The poets and writers sound the way they did in the early 30's in the US, and it is a pity they seem to want to go through that all over again—they went through it here then, too—(Rachel's generation). I just read *One Day in the Life of Ivan Denisovich*—the book Philip reviewed.[1] It is heartbreaking and encouraging, I suppose—

---

1 Alexander Solzhenitsyn, *One Day in the Life of Ivan Denisovich*, trans. Ralph Parker (1963); Philip Rahv, "House of the Dead?," *The New York Review of Books* (Feb. 1, 1963).

267.

Dearest Elizabeth:

I think of you daily and feel anxious lest we lose our old backward and forward flow that always seems to open me up and bring color and peace.

Things are gayer now, but we indeed live in the current. Each Monday I fly to Boston, each Wednesday or Thursday morning I fly back. This gives me two short weeks, each with its own air and pace, instead of my old all of one cloth New York weeks. The teaching is enjoyable, not too much work really, unlocking in a mild way, except that of course one sees too many people and talks too much about poetry to too many embryonic poets. Here we are in the hectic whirl of putting out the new book review. I'm very much a bystander and admirer. But Lizzie is furiously engaged and in a way making inspired use of her abilities—for God knows we need a review that at least believes in standards and can intuit excellence. The bad side is a rush around us of the excoriated and excoriating—nerves and people. We live in the fire and burnt-outness of some political or religious movement.

I want to send you a few books or two at least. Hannah's book on revolutions[1] is somewhat diffuse and theoretical but is full of things that give me pause and I think we would both feel. She approves of the American Revolution but finds it somehow abstract and inspired no serious thought after Jefferson and the founders. The French Revolution however which she thinks doomed to violence and tyranny began with pity for the miserable, set up standards of violence and unlimited desire and has inspired generations of thinkers. She is wonderful on how sentiments of compassion get changed into blood power-lust and dictatorship. This is a very garbled way of expressing her dense thought, but she brings home to me frighteningly how certain red-capped liberal feelings can go with a sinister acceptance of the terrible.

The other book is quite different, a magical little essay on Herbert by Eliot.[2]

This is a rushed letter, much more so than my state of mind. This last week-end has been full, a trip to Washington for the magazine, then when I got back Dorine, our nurse from Rio, who had immediately gotten engaged and pregnant when she arrived here, had a miscarriage. She is now in the hospital but well and seems on the whole relieved for she and her husband are not in any position to support a child.

---

1 Hannah Arendt, *On Revolution* (1963).
2 T. S. Eliot, *George Herbert* (1962).

We are terribly interested in having you write a Brazilian letter for the Book Review—in your wonderful letter style and about anything that you want.

Love to you and Lota,
Cal

268.

May 8, 1963

Dearest Elizabeth:

I've just been rereading your old March 4th letter—ah me, such a long time. I've also reread your Cabral translations that Betty Kray lent me. I get more Lorca than Valéry out of them but the imagery is much grayer.[1] Your lines read without any feel of phoniness and as one goes into the corpse poem, the sequence begins to sound like something new that doesn't exist in English. I hope you will do the Drummond. I don't know how much more translation I'll do. I don't want my kind of improvisation to become an easy mannerism. I have a suggestion. I don't think you should pour your carefully chosen and written translations into the Bollingen stream. Couldn't you do a little Brazilian book with Cabral and Drummond and Clarice and anything else that came to mind, including your Camões sonnets? Then a shortish preface, written more or less the way you write letters?[2] I think this would really give a piece of Brazil, would make something of Brazil alive in English, and would be quite different from the great nameless industry of American translations that are now coming out—not that I object—still what you do is you in the words and selection and is much too precious to be lost. You could do a beautiful look book, you almost have one I'd think by now, in your leisure.

My Harvard commuting is over till next fall. I don't think my teaching was very inspiring, and certainly I hardly knew where I was living during those split weeks, yet it was a relief to be going through the motions of action, and my students were pretty lively. I'm rather surprised really that it could be done, and certainly have a calmer and clearer head than I had last January.

I spent a week-end with the Ransoms at Kenyon. Before my reading, John and I went to an exhibition of African masks, etc. put on by a six-foot,

---

1 See EB, "A Note on the Poet," *Poetry* (Oct.–Nov. 1963).
2 EB later coedited *An Anthology of Twentieth-Century Brazilian Poetry*, with Emmanuel Brasil (1972).

thirty year old patroness, rather charmingly dizzy with such things—some of her notices would say, "I really don't know what this was for." John stared at something, all grass and grimace, and said, "They may not have been good neighbors to each other, but they never harmed the rest of the world."[1] John has been re-writing old poems; Randall thinks the results absolutely wooden.[2] I can't judge really, because I find it so touching that he should now after twenty-five years be painfully living through his old work again, questioning not only the style but the experience. He has a lecture on music (in poetry) decaying into prose, fable into whimsy and drama into horror. He has made a map of his little garden—no Burle Marx work of art, but all genuine, and all day he and his wife solve *Nation* crosswords. He is having a delightfully innocent and firm old age.

Randall was here reading at the Y. Eric Bentley introduced him, said little about him except that he liked their common generation and loathed that before them, good art produced by hideous personalities such as Pound, Eliot and Wyndham Lewis, and also loathed the sewer of the "beats." He said a lot about fake Oxford accents from St. Louis. When Randall got up he said he had listened to Mr. Bentley and even tried to understand him, that Eliot had said James had a mind too fine to be violated by ideas, and that he hoped his audience had such minds because the ideas they had heard would only confuse what they got from his (Randall's) poems. Then he said Eliot had started out superior to everyone else but had become such a *good* man that he no longer needed to write poetry. I'm not probably giving the true impression, but Randall got rather gracefully out of a coarse simplification. Randall has written an awfully good nineteen page terza rima poem on his childhood in Hollywood, and really in his way seems to have reached a gentle honest and inspired state of life.[3] I have been thinking of what you said about Pound and Chekhov, and of course it's true. Alas, we are most of us splinters, but I see more and more that it is death to cultivate one's creases and seams.

I'll mail you Randall's "50 Years of American Poetry" lecture. The paragraph on you is only a sketch of an essay he wants to do on you. He is keener on you than on any one else, and has read and liked most of the poems since your book. Why couldn't Giroux do *all* your poetry to date? I was talking to him a week or so ago, and he seemed to like the idea.

I suppose you have been reading about the fierce and awful race riots in

1 See "Munich, 1938" (RL-*CP*).
2 John Crowe Ransom, *Selected Poems* (1963).
3 Randall Jarrell, "The Lost World," *Poetry* (Oct.–Nov. 1963).

Birmingham. We've sent a telegram and signed a petition.[1] I can imagine the Southerners, but what they are doing is barbarous, and all for a nightmare of the nerves, something that exists there, but not in fact. One felt this so strongly in Trinidad and on the whole in Brazil.

I've seen several of your friends, Summers, Gold and Fizdale, Marianne Moore who is coming here next week on the annual Academy Meeting day. We all get very bubbly about you, and of course Gold and Fizdale are wild about Lota. I don't like to think of Brazilian conditions for you, so much seems stirring under the mist and reports that one gets. Our country here seems the opposite since the fall Cuba business—a strained calm, with a little hopeful half smile, as we sit on our cushion of strength and corruption. I think there is even a slight fear that the future will be a windless monotonous ocean of order and no wars. It's easy now to hope, and under the hope lies God knows what.

I see Jack Thompson tomorrow and will speak again about Rachel de Queiroz. Your letter arrived too late for me to hear Tourel sing you. My *Phaedra* may be done next fall, Siobahm (?) McKenna would like to do it at the Dublin Festival, Peter Hall and Peter Brook are considering it for their London company, Olivier is reading it, the Phoenix Theatre here is interested. Bubbles perhaps, still something will probably happen. A wonderful young Englishman, Jonathan Miller, wants to direct my American play, and now we are trying to find a producer. So—but I feel by now my plays were written by some one else. In [the] next few weeks, I should have my poems typed and will send them to you. The Stone Phallus was meant to be awfully raw and obvious, but maybe the poem ought to end earlier. I really want to write in a new way, one I can't describe, but one that is free from a kind of shadow I still often walk under but no longer believe. The best I have done seems wizened, and yet I feverishly hope that each new trifle will catch fire.

Another *New York Book Review* will be out next Monday—long pieces by Wilson and Kenneth Burke,[2] then the *Review* will lapse till next September and then we hope come out every other week. We would [be] very eager to print anything you wanted to say about any book, or a series of Brazilian letters.

1 Dorothy Norman, Marian Willard, Alfred Barr, Stanley Kunitz, Andrew E. Norman, Mark Rothko, and RL, "Letters to the *Times*: Conduct of Officials Towards Negroes Protested," *The New York Times* (May 12, 1963).
2 Edmund Wilson, "Every Man His Own Eckerman," and Kenneth Burke, "William Carlos Williams, 1883–1963," *The New York Review of Books* (June 1, 1963).

The weather is lovely now, and the time of last year's departure is with me, and hundreds of rich moments with you return.

My love to Lota—all my love to you.

Cal

I have a feeling from the gap of time since your last letter that you must have found the clothes to go to Peru. I hope all has been well. I wish we were flying back to you.

269.

Rio, Sunday morning, May 26th, 1963

Dearest Cal:

I hope you aren't thinking that I am a: dead b: annoyed. I'm neither; but I did have *flu*—*I* thought for the first time in my life, although Lota tells me I have it frequently! When I got the letter from Elizabeth about the *N.Y. Review* I really got to work immediately—not one piece, but three. The crop of Sambas this year wasn't very good—however, I did a sort of piece that I didn't like very much, then another piece, then a poem, then stopped everything including correspondence for two or three weeks. I'm sorry— In the meantime I've had a nice letter from you, and last week—we haven't been up to Samambaia for two weeks—Mary told me a set of AIDA arrived in Petrópolis. I feel this can only be from you and is probably your Christmas present! Thank you ahead of time—I think it must be Leontyne Price?— anyway, next week-end I'll find out.[1] It's nice to look forward to.

Yes—you are right about no Valéry in the Cabral de Melo that I did, certainly—I must change that note. Thanks— However—most of the time he *is* more Valéry than Lorca—and I first did one of the cemetery poems, very Valéry-influenced—then decided a longer group from the play went together better. But you know I scarcely feel they are translations at all, in the *Higher* sense. I only chose those that seemed extremely easy and the meter is exactly the same, etc.— One Drummond came out well, I think. This bunch will be in POETRY in October—so they're not wasted on Bollingen. E. Kray hasn't answered my letter yet—or it got lost—or is on the way. I was just after another $300 or so! ENCOUNTER has Clarice's stories, but I haven't heard yet if they want any. However—Knopf apparently is definitely interested in one of her novels. I've refused to do any of that kind of translat-

1 Guiseppe Verdi, *Aida*, Rome Opera Chorus and Orchestra, cond. Georg Solti, Leontyne Price, soprano (1961).

ing, however. It's too boring & time-wasting. The idea of a small book of Brazilian selections is rather nice, I think—but there is so little I can honestly say I like or admire. I had suggested a bigger book of that sort to Alfred Knopf (who has taken to writing me at least three times a week)—since there does seem to be quite a bit of US interest in Brazil now. An anthology as lively-as-possible—well—I'll see what else I turn up this year. Things for Bollingen can be sold to magazines as well—but, as I said, I had my eye on some more $300'es if possible . . .

The pieces I started for the *NY Review* have helped get me going—one is long now and I think I'll send it to *The New Yorker*, again just for the money & they may not take it. But I have stacks of material here, diaries, sketches, etc. and it's just a matter of getting the right tone, somehow, which I now *think* I've got, to be able to make a small travel-book, story-book. The problem is where to send this kind of thing—since most of it is too sketchy or impressionistic for *The New Yorker* and I don't want to do that deadly kind of background, beginning, middle & end, reporting-piece they print—well— maybe *The New Statesman*—or something English—

Tuesday morning—28th—

To get back to this—in the meantime I've finished up your long travel-story and can't decide what to do with it. I haven't really answered you[r] letter at all, just went on about my own procrastinated affairs . . . I hope you'll send me the second *NY Review?* Is it really going on and on, now? In which case I'll subscribe, of course. These awful bulletins of all those poetry outfits I get sent have their uses—for example, did you hear Evtushenko?[1] (I can't even keep track of your probable doings.) Yes, please send Randall's lecture— AND—I asked Ostroff to send it but that was long ago—the review that has the analysis of "Skunk Hour" in it—that's what I'd really love to see.[2] Ned Rorem of all people wrote me about it (I am sure he is a pest—)

I like Ransom's remarks about the African masks & countries. Sometimes when I read about the doings in your hemisphere I immediately feel reconciled to being in a country where they just can't get organized enough to do much serious damage (aside from letting people starve, which is just normal history, I suppose)—but then it's not so consoling to realize that if they could do damage they undoubtedly would . . .

1 Yevgeny Aleksandrovich Yevtushenko.
2 In margin in RL's hand: "New World Writing." Symposium on "Skunk Hour," *New World Writing* (1962), ed. Anthony Ostroff, with essays by Richard Wilbur, John Frederick Nims, and John Berryman.

How horrible that Bentley introduction must have been! And although I don't exactly agree with what *you* said *Randall* said!—I do admire his ability to think on his feet and get out of spots like that as gracefully as possible.

How blind I am—I now have re-read the next page of your letter & see the *Review* is to come out again in September—so surely I'll get one of my three possibilities in the mail before then.

Well, Bobby & Arthur[1]—you know Lota knew them really *when*—they were still at Juilliard, and she helped them buy their first tail-suits, saw them being taught how to bow, went to their first concert, etc. . . . I've known them off and on for about 15 yrs—not well, like Lota. But I think they are amazing characters, probably very much like *Chopin*—that natural ability to adapt, please, take to elegance & money like ducks to water, rarely doing a wrong thing—perfect courtier types—that probably has something to do with the Performing Artist temperament.— (Chopin also being a great composer, but if you've ever read his letters[2]—he had this side, too. "Please see that my small salon is papered in the latest style, gray satin stripe on gray, the palest possible shade. And order me some of the finest etc pantaloons, 3 pairs, and make sure the material is dull-finished and of the best possible quality," etc. . . . This is from memory—) Of course I've never said this to them—but I think the performing artist is to music very much what the nurse is to the surgeon. Very important however— As people say "It's the nursing that counts." And with all the chichi—they really WORK. We've visited them, and heard them. But it's a hopeless Siamese-twin situation.

Well—tell me where *Phaedra* will be put on—Dublin, New York, or Tokyo—and I'll try to be there opening night. Lota works hard for three or four days, then announces—usually when getting back from a meeting, around 2 AM—"Let's go straight to London next week . . ." At least I think she might take a 6-week vacation—everyone else certainly does, and usually at government expense. She is exhausted—planned on a quiet evening at home last night and the phone rang *17* times—I counted.

I am utterly sick of public Brazil, political Brazil—the other-under-side I like more & more. I was about to go off, also with Burle Marx and Rosinha, and a botanist, chauffeur, etc., to drive to Bahia—I've not been there yet. He postponed it, but I think we'll be going fairly soon. He means to botanize all along the way and it should be interesting. OH—something I think I should tell you—I don't mean it as criticism, but I think you should change it for the next appearance. I liked your poem about Copacabana—I don't have it here

1 Robert Fizdale and Arthur Gold.
2 Probably *Frédéric Chopin: His Life and Letters*, ed. Maurycy Karasowski (1906).

458

but I remember the beginning and the *bathrobe* and the ending; I have a perfectly clear picture of the situation, so it did impress me. But *macumba* is just the name in this part of Brazil for voodoo—(Its name in most of Brazil is *candomblé*). So I don't think you can address it. It's like saying "Congregationalism!"—it's the whole practice. The goddess to whom the candles by the ocean, white flowers, etc. are offered is *Yemanjá*—goddess of the sea, also somewhat confused with the Virgin Mary. She is usually pictured as white and I think she is chaste! I almost bought you a chromo of her the other day—white, tall, walking on the water in a white nightgown—but they wouldn't sell me one without the elaborate frame. Sometimes she has a fishtail. Fertility is—well, I'd have to look her up,—another goddess, however.[1] The celebration for Yemanjá has become quite a spectacle—she's a relatively new cult. New Year's Eve.— We always invite people here to watch it from the terrace. The next day the beach is strewn with cala lilies,—always white flowers,—and the wreckage of the lovely boats they make, loaded with candles, & flowers and push out to sea. It's the only attractive *candomblé* I've ever seen.— The candles every night on the beach are minor offerings to Yemanjá. Away out on the sand dunes, five or six miles from Rio, I saw a wonderful bit of *macumba* the other night—a whole table set out for four— like a picnic—plates, chicken, white wine, the candles burning, etc.—All by itself without a soul in sight.

The head of *Folclore* here sent me a stack of bulletins.[2] One number is a collection of poems to the moon, sun, stars, Milky Way, etc.—sometimes beautiful,—short songs, rather, "serenades." Here is an off-hand translation of one folk-saying: (fishermen's)

> "Each man should make one prayer
> When he sets out to sea.
> Two when he goes to war,
> And when he gets home, three."

Carlos is supposed to run for President in 1965. *Save us*. A lot can happen before then, but if he were to get elected I'm sure Lota would be Minister of Education or an Ambassador or something . . . I would draw the line at Brasília (but so would she). I think she is really the only friend he has, sometimes—the only one who dares tell him the bitter truth once in a while, and

---

1 See "Dropping South: Brazil," lines 1, 17, 20, and 21 (RL-*CP*).
2 Comissão Nacional de Folclore (National Folklore Commission), *Cadernos de Folclore*, primeira série (1961–63).

he takes it. We took him a letter at 11 PM Sunday night in which she warned him against "McCarthy-ism"—and it's worked already. A man unjustly fired has been replaced, & last night on TV—we hear—Carlos was much more reasonable about some of these extreme factions, etc. Yet—if he doesn't get elected it would be much worse. Lota is a "councilman," I suppose it is—of the City of Copacabana—comes back with astounding bits of information— such as—C is the most densely populated part of any city in the world (that includes places like Bombay, the Lower East Side of NY, etc.). No wonder it is depressing. We have light-rationing—candles from 8:30 till nine—they say it's going to get longer. Howls of those trapped in elevators can be heard.—The best of the sambas is one against the "Light"—that is, the Canadian (supposedly—but also US, concealed) Light Company that has monopolized energy here for sixty years or so. It's called ALLADIN— perhaps I'll send. Without music & dance they're nothing, though. Goulart seems to *want* upheaval, even bloodshed. It's weird— All the communists, students, Goulart-ites, nationalists, etc. shriek about "Agrarian Reform"—as if anyone in his right mind isn't all for agrarian reform in Brazil. But what *they* mean by it is some really terrifying changes in the constitution that would give Goulart dictatorial rights. Apparently there are plenty of good laws on the books—there always *are*, here—all they have to do is start putting them into action. But by just labeling it all "Agrarian Reform," when what they mean is writing a new constitution, they have all the people befuddled, as usual, and the students shrieking that Carlos is against the peasant . . . Oh lord I'm sick of it. It backfires very nicely sometimes. Brizola worked up one bunch so that they "squatted" on private lands—only unfortunately they were some of Goulart's cabinet members' lands—and they soon got put off, by soldiers, poor things. And look how absurd—there's no lack of *land* in Brazil, for God's sake! Why break into an old worn-out plantation in the state of Rio—when—(as Carlos says!)—if the Dept. of Agriculture did what they said they would—(oh to hell with it—) I can't stand any of them—but understand how Carlos is torn—and what he might become. It is really rather nasty here.

   Something I want to ask you about—I am always appealing to you, I think—is: we'd like very much to get Flávio away for a year or two, to study. (L's nephew, you may remember) I didn't realize that he was ready to go, and dying to go, until it was too late. I sent him to get the forms for applying for a scholarship in the US but of course they are for 1964 now. I'm having him apply anyway, just in case . . . He's in his first year at Catholic University and hates it, and from what I hear of it I am entirely on his side. He is taking the course for diplomatic service. He's already passed all the exams for the Diplomatic Service except one—failed his written French, I think! He is really much too advanced for what he's getting now. In the meantime he's taking another set of exams, from the Dept. of Foreign Affairs—and if he gets high marks he may be sent as some sort of attaché, to Madrid, at $1,000.00 (US) a month . . . (The folly of Brazil knows no bounds, honestly. In N.Y. consuls, attachés, etc. get more—in *sss*—than US Ambassadors to Spain or Italy . . .) Well—I don't much care; the important thing, I think, is to get him away from here for a while, away from his ma, and his even more pernicious frustrated-architect, society-communist pa—and he realizes it. What he'd really like to do, I think, is go to some University in the US and study literature—and economics—for a year, or two years. IF I can get him a scholarship for 1964—(I'm sure he'd get in easily enough)—what places have the best literature depts? I really don't know—aside from Harvard. Undergraduate scholarships are given for "destinations unknown," apparently—and I'm afraid he'd find himself surrounded with big muscular boys who don't know how to punctuate and never heard of Beckett, etc.—and would immediately have all his worst suspicions (carefully fostered by his father) confirmed . . .

I went to see the US Cultural people about it but might as well have saved my breath. I probably did more harm than good, because they obviously regard me with such suspicion. (Really,—I'm not paranoiac!) No possible chance of anything for next semester—and the more I explained the colder they got. However, Flávio is someone worth having on our side (as I was trying to point out!) He writes really very well, in Portuguese—wrote that highbrow jazz column starting when he was 17—is now writing a lot of poetry, not "beat" as we'd expected, but delicate and sometimes quite beautiful. He is overcome by Hopkins and the metaphysicals at the moment. "Why didn't you tell me about Hopkins *before!*" he said. Meanwhile, stupid people like poor dear Vera[1] get rich fellowships and go flying all over the US and get $500 worth of books free, etc. It is much more important for someone who might be a bright next-generation Brazilian to get some of all this we're giving away, I think.

Well—anything you know about undergraduate scholarships would be most welcome—and any information as to where would be the best places to try to go to, if he gets one—Kenyon? Indiana? Minnesota? I haven't any idea at all.

He works *all* the time; is very young—but much older than most Ameri-

---

1 Vera Pacheco Jordão.

can boys his age, I think—and he's a nice boy in many ways—kind, funny, etc.—(I wish he were better-looking). Lota and I are alternately delighted with him and in despair. He brings me all the student magazines—from the *other* University—the communist one—ghastly dead stuff about Sacco & Vanzetti, Esso-congresso—etc.—etc. They seem to be trying to go through the early thirties all over again. He's GOT to see more of the world—get out of this hideous corruption. I feel he's inherited Lota's brains—the last left in that old family. I'd really much rather help him—and think it is of much more importance—than Clarice, or Raquel, or anybody. They have their fame here and are pretty well satisfied to be provincials forever. Brazilian boys are very different from US ones, allright—mistresses from 14 or so on.—(As I said to L!) They know all about l'amour—but have no idea how to make the bed. Or clean their shoes—or how to make money—or what it costs to live—or what their maid's life is *really* like. In fact, they don't see the lower class as people at all, and yet think they're communists. Poor Flávio sees some of this. I think if he could get away, it would be the best thing— He'd see Brazil is not exactly the norm.

I'm sure it's all very ancient and Mediterranean—all this immediate abstraction-izing. If you *say* it, in a flowery enough way, it's done. That's what is driving L mad on her job, too, so for once she agrees with me— I bet the Greeks did it—& talked all day long, just like here.

Sorry to run on so. I've just read the 1st 2 Edel books on James[1]—the 1st had nothing I didn't know in it, but the 2nd's better— And I admire him more. For one thing, I didn't realize he had actually earned that upper-class English mode of life entirely by his pen from an early age. I thought he'd a lot of money. But how times have changed—imagine *his* travel pieces appearing in any US magazine now—or paying well. Or an audience waiting eagerly for *Roderick Hudson*. His reaction to Henry Adams is just like mine! But what a trashy trashy world we're living in. I sometimes wish I could be 22 again and absorbed in a poetic effect for a day at a time, *one little thing.*— these spreading ripples as one grows older—more & more, and less and less.

However—I thank God that you can still concentrate the way an artist has to—and shut out things. It cheers me up to think about it!

How's the family? How are you?—are you going to Maine?

With love always—

Elizabeth

---

1 Leon Edel, *Henry James: The Untried Years, 1843–1870* (1953) and *Henry James: The Conquest of London, 1870–1883* (1962).

PS's—

Did you attend the Academy doings?—anything amusing there? How does Marianne seem? She hasn't answered my last letter yet—she's usually so prompt—of course she may not have got it; I'll write again.

I had a letter from the Ford Foundation and instead of just asking for suggestions for people for the theater project fellowships they said I'd been recommended for one. I feel you are probably in back of this? I went through torture for a couple of weeks, trying to think of some way I could decently request one—but came up with nothing . . . However, I think I'll write them a sort of stalling letter, if I can—they said for 1964 or '65— Does it *have* to be US? Couldn't one go to the theatre a lot in London?— I'd really love to write a play, of course—who wouldn't—but I haven't seen any for so long! (*Man for all Seasons*[1] was the last, I think) The new English playwrights?— The folksy things? (I've had vague ideas of a play about Nova Scotia for many years—I know it sounds awful, but it might work.) I can't bear to let that money go!—but I have, so far. Lota is really dying to get away, too— but I don't want to spend a whole winter in N.Y. I have at last interested her in London, I think—and it seems to me you spoke of friends of yours who had had those Ford things and went abroad? The trouble is I have a feeling that the new English plays are probably very much over-rated—but that's just cynicism, maybe, or sour grapes. You are so fertile of bright ideas—give me one or two!— I still have most of the Chapelbrook.

How is Harriet? School must be almost over. Mary got another daughter at last—five weeks old today—Martha Shaw Morse this time (I think it's the Shaw family of your poem.[2]) Mary hands out these names without the slightest idea of strangeness, I think—to these little mixed Indian-Portuguese-touch-of-Negro bastards . . . It's a rather nice American trait. (This baby looks pretty, so far—)

Poor Baldwin—he really doesn't seem tough enough for the spot he is in, does he—but perhaps he is, I don't know.[3] Surely the Negro business will clear up fairly soon—like a cloud lifting—in spite of all those beastly people. Randall wrote his Jewish poems—has he ever written any Negro ones, I wonder?—living all that time in North Carolina. He's so good at that wrenching[4] kind of poem.

1 Robert Bolt, *A Man for All Seasons*, which EB saw when she was in New York in 1961.
2 See "For the Union Dead" (RL-*CP*).
3 James Baldwin published *The Fire Next Time* in early 1963 and was the subject of a *Time* (May 17, 1963) cover story: "At the root of the Negro problem is the necessity of the white man to live with the Negro in order to live with himself."
4 Postscript is handwritten; below this word, in RL's hand, is his attempt to decipher the letters.

270.

Dear Cal:

We're just arriving from Petrópolis, gulping down cafezinhos, and Lota's off to work . . . I want to write you just a short note!, feeling equally sociable & grateful . . . First—some more about AIDA. I don't think you met any of our country neighbors—one a family of all very old people, interrelated in odd ways by second marriages, adopted children of mistresses, homosexual loves of 45 years' standing, etc. . . . this family beats Proust all hollow. Well— Mary Morse, to whom I'd lent AIDA, had some of them for tea and "the opera" last week—and it was a huge success. Dona Laura, 86, her brother, 84, and the brother's "friend"—about 72—German. They had all been great opera-goers when Rio had the good opera companies, and when they were richer. Mary said to Dona Laura—"Wear your jewels" and when the old lady arrived she said, "See—my jewels," and showed that she had her *teeth in* for the occasion. They sat enthralled for three solid hours—the German looked at the ceiling, Seu Henrique read the Italian, and they *all* shed tears . . . Dona Laura said "I never thought I'd hear AIDA again . . ." Isn't that nice? They're the real opera-going generation, of course, and know much more about it than we do. Now they are dying to come back for the others I have— of course they yearn, particularly Otto, the German "boyfriend," for Wag- ner—he sings it all the time—but I refuse to provide Wagner.

I received the second *New York Review*—haven't had time to read much yet but it looks equally fascinating, although I don't see your or E's names this time. I did read some of Edmund Wilson—and now I feel I was right— or I feel guilty about feeling as tempted as I did—about the Ford Fellowship thing.[1] I really have no talent whatever in that line, I know. It was all right for you—since you write dramatic poems, and there's *Phaedra*, after all, and the three plays . . .

I just realized—reading a review—that the Lillian Hellman play must have been based on that weird little book you gave me . . .[2]

I'm writing a note to F. Seidel—he IS good—but I think that the title be- trays a serious lack of sensibility . . .[3] Horrors are fine—but not *that* title— surely it should only apply, forever, to an historical horror, now?

---

1 Edmund Wilson discusses Ford Foundation grants for writers to spend time with resident theater companies in "Every Man His Own Eckerman," *The New York Review of Books* (June 1, 1963).
2 Lillian Hellman, *My Mother, My Father, and Me* (1963), based on Burt Blechman, *How Much?*
3 Frederick Seidel, *Final Solutions* (1963), reviewed by Anthony Hecht in the *The New York Review of Books* (June 1, 1963).

Thank you for the *NY Review*—or thank E—and also for the Symposium on "Skunk Hour." (I do hope the Eliot on Herbert you mentioned once wasn't in the same envelope and fell out . . . it was open. If you have sent it please don't bother to again—I can order one when I order books from England, perfectly well.)

I brooded over the "symposium" last night. The best poet[1] is by so far the best, isn't he . . . Wilbur is class-room-ish.[2] Nims—well—isn't he quoting from *his* (dreadful) translation of St. John of the Cross?[3] Oh dear I do loathe explanations, explanations, etc.—and it seems to me a "symposium" should do more, or less,—something quite different, at any rate. All this explaining shd. mostly go without saying, I think—and yet that is what people ask for. Berryman is so much brighter than the other two. I don't like his telegraphic style—but at least it does give the impression that he's right there, reacting, and not having to rack his brain for everything he can say that will show off how much he *knows*. He's the only one who really seems to like the skunk! I feel undercurrents of ENVY in the other two, too. To hell with explainers— that's really why I don't want to teach. Even talking to Isa (my "pupil") or Flávio for an hour or so about poems—I find myself impressing them with all kinds of extraneous material, twisting things just a little bit here & there so they'll laugh, or like it, or recognize something familiar . . .

How yr.-3, they belabour "fox stain"[4]—I thought I knew exactly what it meant. In fact I thought there even was such an expression—perhaps there is. And perhaps I shouldn't feel superior about thinking I understand the poem so well because after all I know the place and the time and may be more familiar with the details than they are. It's still a wonderful poem, Cal. I feel happy all over again every time I read the astounding fact that it's dedicated to me. Also—it has so much more *life* to it than you'd ever guess from those essays—and so much wonderful, distant, slightly-hesitant, but nevertheless sure-as-a-hymn kind of northern music to it.

This girl, woman rather, Isa—I find depressing. She is amazingly bright, has read everything, in English & French, *gets* almost every reference—and yet fundamentally—or "basically" as Nims says—she doesn't give a damn.

---

1 John Berryman, "Despondency and Madness," *New World Writing* (1962).
2 Richard Wilbur, "On Robert Lowell's 'Skunk Hour,' " *New World Writing* (1962).
3 John Frederick Nims quotes from *The Poems of St. John of the Cross* (Grove Press, 1959) while discussing RL's line "One dark night": "How consciously the American poet echoes the *Noche oscura* of St. John of the Cross we cannot be sure; but we do know that the Muse of the Unconscious—perhaps the only Muse—caught the echo and permitted it"; *New World Writing* (1962), 142–43.
4 "A red fox stain covers Blue Hill"; "Skunk Hour," line 18 (RL-*CP*).

She has decided that since she is so clever she must conquer poetry, too, that's all. (She was a great beauty—still is very pretty—much sought-after, two marriages, etc. etc.) But I sit there and feel rather like a horrid doctor. "Don't you *feel* anything yet?" If only she'd say *Oh!* or something equally spontaneous. You must have students like that. I'm sure she'd get all A+'s— but oh for some little dope who actually fell in love with one poet, or one poem. (Flávio is more satisfactory—he arrives reciting Hopkins—all mispronounced and out of meter—but he knows it by heart.) This may sound like a romantic notion of poetry, but I can't believe it is.

The trouble is—excuse my clichés—as people grow older, non-artists, that is, they do have to steel themselves so much, forget so much and try to pretend that everything's all right so much. They are afraid, probably rightly, that poetry—any art—if they take it hard, might upset them—so they pretend they like it while at the same time they resist it absolutely.

You shouldn't, however, say that "The Armadillo" is "better" than the skunk. I am not being modest—how I wish it were! "The Armadillo" is all right—I like it still—but not *that* good, by a long shot. It's only one fathom deep and "Skunk Hour" is five fathoms.

I'm feeling much much better these days and getting some work done, I do believe. I'll send a couple of things for you to choose for the *Review*.

Who is Leary or O'Leary[1]—the head of Eng. Lit. at Columbia? He's coming here for 3 days of lectures, conferences, etc. They want me to do something or other. I'll wait till I've met him, I think. The music festival is announced, but I am still dubious—I do hope it comes off, though.

I'm glad A. Hecht gave May S such a nice review—that's the best she's ever had as far as I know.[2]

Corpus Christi was cold and rainy all day—a half-holiday! We went to see *The Longest Day*[3]—being females we have to get our invasions vicariously like that. The dialogue is ghastly, but the spectacle occasionally superb . . . What a queer QUEER world—when in 1945 we spend billions & billions doing the real thing—then 15 years later spend millions and millions making a copy of it. But I decided it was a good sign—it's been playing to packed houses here for two months—to Brazilians, to whom the whole fray

1 Lewis Gaston Leary.

2 Anthony Hecht, "Recent Poetry," *The New York Review of Books* (June 1, 1963), a review of May Swenson, *To Mix with Time* (1963). Hecht's essay begins, "One way of indicating the distinction and quality of May Swenson's poetry is to say that she deserves to be compared to Elizabeth Bishop."

3 *The Longest Day*, dir. Ken Annakin, Andrew Marton, Bernhard Wicki, and Darryl F. Zanuck (1962).

was remote. This increasing self-consciousness of the human race—its curiosity for some kind of factual knowledge of its own history—surely it will eventually help things? It is new, after all—any general awareness of reality in events.

I can't seem to express myself very well—don't be critical! Where are you going for the summer months? How is everybody? Thank you again for all your generosity—
    and much love,
        Elizabeth

This hasn't got mailed yet—Toni[1] wrote us about her engagement. Dean GLIMP wrote from Harvard—Flávio can apply for next year—but I want desperately to get him away *now*. He got 2nd place in a poetry contest—I may have told you about. L says his poem is really "beautiful"!—& I am taking her word for it—that's a lot, from an aunt.

271.[2]

June 19, 196[3]

Dearest Elizabeth:

Tell me where you would like Flávio to apply? Some of the best colleges for English would be Columbia, Harvard, Berkeley, and Minnesota. Rutgers would be good too. I can write to people in most of these, probably all, and recommend him highly. The best thing would be for him to apply and put me down as a reference, and I could fill out the blank they would send me. Your word on him is law with me, but of course I remember him well and think very highly of him.

I'll mail you more records tomorrow. I didn't send any more, but want to. Can books too be sent through Mrs. Theodorides? If so, what would you like? I still owe you an *Oxford 17th Cent. Verse*, and would like to mail more, if they would go through.

I wasn't hurt by the correction of my macumba, and now think I have it right. It's coming out again in next winter's anniversary number of the *Kenyon Review* for Ransom.[3] I tried to make something of all your wonderful Vemanja observations (much better than my poem) but could not verse them

---

1 Toni Kern; see letter 248.
2 Crossed with letter 270.
3 "Dropping South: Brazil," *The Kenyon Review* (Winter 1964); see RL-*CP*.

into any style that was poetry for me. I have a few other poems I'll mail you. Now a puzzling project. I've more or less been asked to adapt a German play *Der Stellvertretter*, The Representative, by a man named Hochhuth.[1] It's mainly about gas chamber Germans, but its real edge comes from a group of scenes of Catholic high officials, finally ending up with one with Pius XII in which the Pope refuses to say anything concrete about the German extermination of the Jews, even though they are being removed almost before his eyes in Rome. It's a seven hour play, in loose verse, no artistic masterpiece but with a crude O'Neill-like power with a little Brecht and Schiller thrown in. I'd be adapting it with Lillian Hellman, whom I couldn't like better personally, but I suppose there'd be artistic and ideological differences, though no doubt I'd learn a lot about playwriting. In Germany it has been defended by Catholics and of course attacked by many more. The hero is a Catholic priest who ends up in Auschwitz. Well, I'm not interested in an anti-Catholic diatribe, but I think the play makes a case that must be heard, and I see it as an analogue for any institution or religion—something I personally perhaps ought to do, only partially artistic, a bit like my C.O.[2] business. Well, I'd like to try the writing, if I could do it strongly and honestly.

A couple of weeks ago I went at Nabokov's invitation to a little conference at Mrs. Agnes Meyer's estate[3]—great luxury with almost monastic regularity, a sweet old lady, nearing 80 with displaced retina trouble, bluntly bright, full of good works, personal memories of Claudel, Mann, and even Rodin. Oppenheimer presided, quivering like a hummingbird with difficult elliptical quotations on every field, beautiful-looking, rather like the monk in the Giorgione or Titian piano player scene; Nicolas subdued Rabelaisian and Russian reminiscences; kind to me, but not very interested; the architect who built Radio City, conservative in his craft but full of a gentle, worried, humane wisdom[4]—what he would build would be the opposite of Brasília; Stuart Hampshire hesitant, humorous, gossipy, pure British, and a Miss Hersch, a Jaspers student and the epitome of that kind of intellectual, Hannah A without the genius and humor; George Kennan with views almost like Khrushchev's on the arts—in a really noble old-fashioned uninformed way, wishing the world would go back to 1800, wishing the bombs were buried. Nabokov said Oppenheimer was Callas, and Kennan was Robeson and the rest of us were just honest singers. Well, I felt very young, small, ignorant

1 Rolf Hochhuth, *Stellvertreter* (*The Representative: A Christian Tragedy*, 1964).
2 Conscientious objector.
3 Seven Springs Farm Conference in Mt. Kisco, New York.
4 Wallace Harrison.

and fascinated, trying to play the role of the hesitant, muddled, intuitive poet.

What marvelous letters you've written me. You must tire of my dark inwardness and shop talk. All winter I've been full of my insides, and now for a week I've stopped drinking, dead! and really mean to make it stick. Meanwhile all my twists squirm on the surface.

A little English magazine has an interesting interview of Empson—rather sad.[1] He says most nineteenth century English poets began well, had a dismal middle-age, then wrote well again. That he himself stopped when he couldn't bear what [he] was writing. That he was interested in a kind of poetry promoted by Graves that was the working out of problems that in life one had no answer for, so that one tried to be clear as one could for the art and the working out, but really wrote for no audience, "not even Laura Riding."[2] In middle age one is too busy living, working to send a son to college, etc., to live with this kind of problem, even though underneath one seethes with scorpions. He hopes to write grand poetry when he is forced to retire at 65.

I've just been to Bob Gardner's documentary on his New Guinea expedition[3]—horrifying ritualistic wars, full of clear rules, such as stopping at night, never pushing things to much killing, skirmishing like cops and robbers, with celebrations after the death of an opponent rather like our Groton–St. Mark's football games, rather like Homer, but allowing awful things like the spearing of stray children, the men doing little else, but fight, all feathers, courtesies, psycho-somatic magic, and death, death, death— maybe a score or so on each side a year, but constant, utterly without any ideology or even purpose, except to externalize and drown the pains of the soul, wars every day, though gentle compared with ours and fun like a game, even the clamor of mourning—and it all happened. I had the guilty feeling of having gone to a gladiatorial fight.

The family's fine, awfully athletically alive, Harriet with her little girl visitors, climbing, etc. Lizzie with her magazine. Dorine is about to leave to marry. She was a good sport with Harriet, but toward the end she has become almost a call girl with gruff Argentine voices calling, "Iss mith Dorine Dere?" We have a new maid and nurse, very gentile, Argentine, meals served, clothes washed and ironed, Jehovah's Witness tracts, no English, the only old-fashioned servant we've had. On the 27th we leave for Maine.

All my love, and to Lota,

Cal

---

1 "William Empson in Conversation with Christopher Ricks," *the Review* (June 1963).
2 Laura Riding Jackson was the companion of Robert Graves from 1926 to 1939.
3 *Dead Birds*, dir. Robert Gardner (1964).

Two days later—I've just sent a little group of records through Betty Theodorides' APO, a couple of Richters, the only Messiaen I could get[1] (No Henze), Sutherland selections from *Lucia*,[2] and, extra, the last two Elliott Carter quartets.[3] I'll keep her APO number and try to send some books through the summer while her APO is still possible. The German play looks dimmer and dimmer as something I might do. It has a note of nobility coming from a West German that would all too easily seem sensational, reveling in horror etc. in English and on Broadway. I seem to teem with unused energies; one should watch this I know. I have a notion now of trying a play on Eatherly.[4] You probably know his story, he was one of the Hiroshima pilots. He became conscience-stricken through what he had done, or maybe it was in his character anyway, sent checks to Hiroshima, forged checks, twice tried to kill himself, held up banks, then didn't take the money, and wound up in a Texas sanitarium, divorced, given up by his family, somewhere between sane and insane, living to tell his story and protest against nuclear war. Noble and pitiful, hard to dramatize. I would want to write a tragedy, not a piece of peace propaganda—not at all that, for I don't think it could be done in a way that would do any good. Part of the poor man's tragedy is that although he exploded as one should and as practically no one else did, yet he has little to say, and is condemned to an almost monomaniac whittling down of his life to this one subject. Well, we'll see.

Excuse these messy copies of my poems. "Caligula" is perhaps too ugly! I wrote it last December and cut it down from four hundred lines. Hope you like something. The harshness grates on me, but I suppose it's all on the road to something less clenched. Anyway the drive to write this sort of thing seems to be dying in me—down to its roots.

Do write me in Castine.

1 Olivier Messiaen, *Le Banquet Céleste*, with organist Marcel Dupré (Mercury 50231/90231).
2 Gaetano Donizetti, *Lucia Di Lamermoor*, Joan Sutherland, soprano (London, 1961).
3 Elliott Carter, *String Quartet No. 1*, Walden Quartet (Columbia ML 5104) and *String Quartet No. 2*, Juilliard Quartet (Victor LM/LSC 2481).
4 Claude Robert Eatherly, pilot of *Straight Flush*, the weather plane serving the *Enola Gay*. See Edmund Wilson, "The Case of Major Eatherly," *The Cold War and the Income Tax: A Protest* (1963), and John Wain, "A Song About Major Eatherly," *The Listener* (Aug. 6, 1959).

272.

Dearest Cal:

Just a note—this getting mail up in the country is a nuisance, but it is safer.— Last night Mary called up and said there was a big letter from you. She opened it for me and just glanced at it. I wanted to hear if you'd got mine about Flávio, etc.—and so this is just a hasty note of gratitude, information, warning, etc., etc. I was delighted to hear about the records, naturally—have a hazy idea you've sent everything I ever thought of! But DON'T send any books via the Theodorides—it isn't necessary—I've only lost a book or two in ten years. Also—it's better not to send books unless you ask me first! I am apt to get the same ones you are—since our interests overlap, at least!—and I get most of them from England—a bit cheaper, and lots of paper books I can't get from the U.S. I have two huge orders coming right now—also a huge one from Wittenborn's for Lota.

It is terribly nice of you to offer—but also,—I don't like to exploit the poor Theodorides *too* much. They're just doing me a favor they aren't supposed to do, and maybe the State Dept. will shoot him at sunrise or something. And I already have an electric sheet, 2 pairs of "Desert Boots" and a year's supply of asthma medicine, en route. And Mr. T gets all this at the embassy and has to cart it home for me . . . Also—they like music, so are sympathetic about records—but don't care about books, that I've ever noticed . . .

I wrote—about ten days ago—a long long letter to Dean Glimp, all about Flávio. I don't know what will come of it. I suspect they might offer him something for 1964–65—but I do want to get him away before then if possible. He isn't learning a thing at that Catholic University. What he does learn he picks up for himself outside. Most of the profs. there spend their time in anti-communist propaganda, or pro-pope propaganda, of course— and there are no "liberal arts" courses, so the boys hire their own lecturers— and those mostly tend to communist propaganda. The poor students are just the objects of all the politics and get nothing in the way of education, as far as L or I can see. He is really too bright to be spending his time skipping all classes, running about doing newspaper hack-work, etc. He *is* bright, I'm convinced—how he'll turn out I can't imagine. I have all his "works" here—newspaper stuff written since he was sixteen. He was 20 the other day—and I think he must have written two *books* already. It is pretty crude, naturally—but his interests and aspirations are all right. It's just that the poor child has never really seen or learned anything first-rate, or not much.

It's all just out of books. I decided—I don't know if I said this—that Harvard was the place for him—not that I know much about it. If he goes into the diplomatic service, like his relatives, that would give him a *cachet*, I suppose, more than any other place (although that wasn't what I was thinking of to begin with.)

In my letter to GLIMP I mentioned the various people I knew and know who had anything to do with H—by way of introduction—and put in your name, but didn't say any more than that. However—I now think the "Most Magnificent Rector" or whatever he is called, of Catholic U, is going to write a note for Flávio—also his old "Ginasio," and maybe Carlos. We aren't sure whether that would be a good idea or not. (—see next page—)

I've had him translate some of his literary pieces into English for me, just to see if he could—and to my surprise he brought two back the very next day (so un-Brazilian) and they are excellent. He types them right off in English. Excellent as far as grammar, etc. goes—crudities, and wrong prepositions—but he *can* write in acceptable English, I think, and rapidly— and I gather they do make allowances for foreign students (from the little pamphlet they sent him). He thinks his French isn't good, but I think, compared to most US college-French, it is excellent, too. He is tutoring in French now for another Foreign Service exam. He also has quite a lot of Spanish. I think he'd want to study lit. & languages—and I shd. hope some economics, history, and perhaps music theory—since he knows a lot about music but not much basic theory. (He did keep up that highbrow column about US jazz weekly, for over 2 years—then switched to "bossa Nova" etc.—and it's all erudite, if imitative.) He thinks he could tutor in Portuguese to earn spending money—or even give talks—or play—Bossa Nova—and I imagine he could. He really works constantly. Poor boy—he breaks my heart really—and I think it would be the saving of him, to get him away from the chaos and trash here and let him follow his natural interests—art, lit, music, etc.—where he can at last find something *first-rate*. I think the desire comes first—and that's what counts—but if you never *see* a real Picasso, you pretend Portinari's good—or if you have never in your life heard any good music—you pretend "Bossa Nova" is good, or Villa Lobos the greatest, etc. His ignorance is appalling—but the right instincts seem to be there.

(If *only* he were a bit better-looking . . . Or if only I didn't think physical charm so important, perhaps. Girls do seem to like him . . . !)

I see on page 1, I started off saying I'd mentioned you to Dr. Glimp etc. then got sidetracked (there's a lot going on here this AM). From what Mary read me, I gathered you'd be good enough to recommend the boy, too—I imagine that would be a tremendous help—the best of all. I'll write another short note to Glimp maybe. But if you want to, it is Fred L Glimp, *Dean*, H. C., Holyoke Center, Cambridge—I can't find the street number but that shd. reach him. I hadn't realized, until Flávio got it all together for me, how much he has *done*—not academically, but outside,—and I suppose that shows "initiative," "independence," all those desirable things . . . (He did get into the top 8th in a class of 150, and has passed the diplomatic exams—first set—takes another set in July—and they are stiff ones.) (He translated "Zoo Story" into Portuguese for a theatre group here—& another play as well. Things like this keep popping up—that we hadn't known of—so maybe he's even modest—) But, all this *writing*, juvenile as it is—all these poems (that he has the amazing good sense (also un-Brazilian) NOT to want to publish right off),—being sent to Uruguay as a reporter at the age of 17—organizing the one & only jazz concert here, at the Yachty-clubby— (I heard it was a great success, too)—all kinds of odds & ends. And this in spite of the most neurotic, impossible mother, who must make life miserable for him and about whom he's never said a word of complaint, to me, at least—and a kind of semi-failure of an architect father who is a communist out of sheer spite, I suspect—because he married above him, can't make money, etc.— (However—don't mention these to Glimp!). F is dying to get away—so excited he calls me up all the time, can't eat, etc.—"hates" the US in the most conventional way, but is *dying* to go to Harvard . . . Heavens, I hope if he does get there he'll have enough good experiences to offset the bad ones, and all the pre-conceptions—I really think he's prepared enough to get into the sophomore year—on his languages alone, probably. He says "Do you suppose *Lowell* might be teaching there?" and dreams of attending a class of yours. I suppose I shd. be jealous—but I'm a prophet in my own country to him by now—as unnoticeable as "family."

Mary said there were lots of clippings, poems, etc.—in yr letter. We're going up early tomorrow—nice to look forward to a letter— I've been doing a lot of work, for me—will have some results to send soon. Have a small batch of Drummond ready to send to POETRY[1]—but I'm saving "The Table" for something bigger & better. My "note" has turned out as long-winded as usual.[2] I'll answer your letter properly when I get it—I'll try another place. It's hopeless for him here now, and *someone* might as well be

---

1 Carlos Drummond de Andrade, "Seven-Sided Poem" and "Don't Kill Yourself," trans. EB, *Shenandoah* (Spring 1965); and "Travelling in the Family," trans. EB, *Poetry* (June 1965).
2 EB, footnote to Drummond translations, *Shenandoah* (Spring 1965).

saved and educated. I'm sure he'd stay for 3 or 4 yrs—if he ever got there. But heavens, aren't the young *weird*.

much love—
Elizabeth

273.

Dearest Elizabeth:

I've been awfully remiss about Flávio. I leave here on the 12th to go to England for a week to a poetry festival and then to Nice for a week to teach at a Fulbright seminar, and will be back here about the 28th of July. Now I have your Dean Glimp letter but I don't know Flávio's last name! I'll telephone my friend Bill Alfred tonight, but maybe you could write his name to me in London, care of Faber and Faber, 24 Russell Square (London W.C.I.)—I'll be there from the 14th through the 21st. Then I'll write a very strong letter to Dean Glimp. Meanwhile, through Alfred, really the best person at Harvard and one who will take unlimited pains and pull out all the stops, I'll throw everything I can behind getting him in this year. Does he need a scholarship that pays complete expenses? Also what year will he be going in? I'm sure I can help out with some of the money, but I'd rather he didn't know, and didn't feel any need to thank me, in any way.

Oh me, it's peaceful here. A great web of New York grit, and heat and confusion seemed to lift once we arrived. Harriet is pumping about on her first bicycle with trainer wheels and talks a mile a minute about it. She's undaunted by falls. Yesterday we had Fourth of July with its costume parade for children, and she was a pyramid in an Antony and Cleopatra group, a restless pyramid, well able to walk, but only two eyes and a pair of sneakers in the group photographs. She's shy in large new bunches of children, but plays all day with someone her own age.

I've started Mary's new novel.[1] It has a rather metallic nostalgic feel that reminds me of my boarding school days in the thirties. No one seems to be remotely anyone in life, though I'm sure you'll be able to place thousands of details—one of the girls plays that "who is your best friend" game you told me Mary was fond of. Lizzie thinks it's an awful fatuous superficial book, but I've only read enough to like some things and feel others are rather crisp,

---

1 Mary McCarthy, *The Group* (1963).

blinding and mechanical—many deflowerings done with an educational touch.

A month now has gone by without my drinking a drop. I feel on the side of life or something of the sort. I have a funny increased feeling of knowing, of watching each error and mis-step and wrong feeling as they happen. You are right about older people steeling themselves to so much and forgetting so much—artists, too. The worst temptations and bad habits are wanting somehow to throw your own shadow on every scene and prospect, that and wanting to ask for a kind of help that no one can give, as if there were another life that could be thrown into your own and remove all its inertia and blindness.

I've just spent an hour or so with Phil Booth, much filled out humanly, now the commodore of the Castine yacht club, wanting terribly to move out of the backwaters of Syracuse University, where he has a good job. I used to think him fearfully green, and think I was blind to the causes of why he was so tense and jumpy. Now I am quite awed by his hard improvement, his life pulled together, if not his poetry which isn't too bad.

Well dear, I want to get this off. I'll copy a new poem I've done since I got up here. Rather more tender and even peaceful, though sad, I guess on a sad subject.

All my love,
Cal

SOFT WOOD
(For Harriet Winslow)

Sometimes I have supposed seals
must live as long as the Scholar Gypsy.[1]
Even in their barred pond at the zoo they are happy,
and now sunflower turns
more delicately to the sun
without a wincing of the will.

Here too in Maine things bend to the wind forever.
After two years away, one must get used
to the painted soft wood staying bright and clean,
to the air blasting an all-white wall whiter,

1 Matthew Arnold, "The Scholar Gypsy" (1853).

as it huffles through ~~the bleached~~ curtains and screen
touched with salt and evergreen.

The green juniper berry spills crystal-clear gin,
and even the hot water in the bathtub
is more than water,
and rich with the scouring effervescence
of something healing,
the illiminable salt.

Things last, but sometimes for days
only children seem fit to handle children,
and there's no utility or inspiration
in the wind smashing without direction.
The fresh paint ~~on the captains' houses hides softer wood~~
on the captains' houses hides softer wood.

Their square-riggers used to whiten
the four corners of the globe,
but it's no consolation to know
the possessors seldom outlast the possessions,
once warped and mothered by their touch.
Shed skin will never fit another wearer.

Yet the seal pack will bark past my window
summer after summer.
This is the season
when our friends may and will die daily.
Surely the lives of the old
are briefer than the young.

Harriet Winslow, who owned this house,
was more to me than my mother.
Dear, I think of you far off in Washington,
breathing in the heat wave
and the air-conditioning, knowing
each drug that numbs alerts another nerve to pain.[1]

1 Cf. "Soft Wood" (RL-*CP*).

274.

Dearest Elizabeth:

I am flooding you with letters. I've now talked to Bill Alfred who has talked to Dean Glimp, and now armed with Flávio's full and correct name, I've written a strong letter to Dean Glimp. Bill got the name without giving an impression of my ignorance—I didn't know about the Regis at the end of Macedo Soares. There doesn't seem to be much chance for 63 and 64, and it seems that Flávio has only applied for 64 and 65, however I urged the Dean strongly to make the scholarship this fall, if a vacancy should turn up. I feel next year is probably pretty certain. Bill said our recommendations were each worth twenty ordinary ones. I think his own backing behind ours will make a very strong case. I'm sure something from Carlos would make it still stronger. Otherwise, I guess everything has been done that can be at the moment. Harvard seems fairly sure for next year. I guess we could try Kenyon or Minnesota for this year. I'll be back here by the first of August and make calls and write letters.

Do you ever write things that turn out to be mere carpentry work? For the last three or four days I've been milling out a rather somber piece of junk in terza rima, lovely meter for narrative, if you have a story.[1] It must have been on the recoil from my high-flying, grand-subject play ideas. Did I tell you the American play may go on next February, possibly with music here and there by Virgil Thompson, who should be perfect for arranging bits from the three periods, 1638, 1776, and 1810? (This sentence seems to have gotten loose from its original question mark.)

You can sun in Maine. Our swimming pool is polluted, and now being depolluted at the usual Maine country speed and efficiency (wrong pipes etc.) I think of the Copacabana beach. But Sunday we lay on the beach behind it, and got quite burned. Harriet kept rescuing periwinkles stranded by the tide and putting them back in the sea. She calls them birthmarks. Yellow flowers she throws in the water are called corn, and grass or seaweed, Haleena Rack! To our shame, our Argentinean maid, Teresa, speaking no English, very exotic and frail Spanish features, only speaking bewildering to Castine Spanish, stayed in for half an hour, bubbling out "agua no fria." I plunged in twice for about a tenth of a second, and I don't think any one else here went more than knee-deep.

---

1 "The Severed Head" (RL-*CP*).

Lizzie is reading your Rowena Farre seal book[1] with delight. Maybe we will get one, they seem like symbols of eternity, free from all Freudian stresses and woes. Yesterday was like winter. You could feel the hot coffee thaw your toes. Today, the sun is out, and I am off to my barn.

Lying on the beach, the other day, I kept thinking of you and Rio, and realize that there were never better moments. I know I have thanked you and Lota, but never enough.

All my love to you both,
Cal

275.

Dearest Cal:

Oh dear—my typewriter must have had the tail of the Y missing—the goddess's name is *Y*emanjá[2]—or usually Iemanjá. Y seems to be the English spelling, because that's the way it's pronounced. The poem now seems perfectly right to me. Do you mean to contrast "unhappy Americas" with the singular "tropique"?[3]—I suppose you do or you'd have put "tristes tropiques." In the line "macumba candles courted Yemanjá"—I see you've put in a "the." Well, I don't think the "the" works, unless you want a very bumpy rhythm, because it's macumba—accent on the 2nd syllable.

July 12th
And that's as far as I got. Even my career as a letter-writer seems to be going to pieces, I really can't say why except that I lack the gift of self-defense to an appalling degree.

Yesterday I went back to that Palace-Museum where we met the Brazilian Russian sex-symbol-expert, as you may remember. This time I took a girl who showed up from Time-Life, etc.—a slightly superior one I felt I should be polite to, at least. But it was sadly different—she *did* everything in 15 minute stretches, then a rest; and burbled constantly about economics & race-relations, and I don't think let anything soak in more than a millimetre.

1 See letter 158.
2 "Macumba candles courted the Vemanjá"; "Dropping South: Brazil," line 17 (typescript, Vassar). Cf. "Dropping South, Brazil," line 17 (RL-*CP*).
3 "Unhappy America, ah *tristes tropique!*"; "Dropping South: Brazil," line 15 (typescript, Vassar). Cf. "Dropping South: Brazil," line 15 (RL-*CP*). See also Claude Lévi-Strauss, *Tristes tropiques* (1955).

However—I'm always glad to see the shabby old palace and some of those wonderful pots. We also went to the Indian Museum, but there were no live Indians this time. Darcy Ribeiro—who was the head of the University of Brasília when you were here (& gave you his book on feather-work[1]) has gone far & fast since then—to Minister of Education, to Head of something—Cabinet—and is locked in a death-grip with Carlos now. The evening papers say that the Gov. will impeach Carlos; the morning papers say that Carlos is suing the government! A curse on both their houses . . . We have had one nice peaceful week-end, with Alfredo along, sitting outdoors and listening to *Aida* all over again—but didn't get back last, nor shall we this one, alas. The weather has been lovely and the beach lovely—clean, shallow water with a fresh new sand-bar, and I also have a new bathing-suit I like very much . . . One Lewis Leary of Columbia is arriving and they're having some kind of literary congress. They asked me to read & I refused. Do you know Leary or of him? They also consulted me as to what he shd. speak about—saying he was going to talk on Hemingway & Faulkner. I suggested omitting Hemingway, since the Brazilians do know him pretty well and he's not so *hard*, after all. And now I've just got the program and Mr. L will speak *four* times on Faulkner. So they must have believed me; and the poor Brazilian teachers will learn about Faulkner or else. Clarice has been asked to another literary congress, at the University of Texas, and is being very coy & complicated—but I think is secretly very proud—and is going, of course. I'll help her with her speech. I suppose we are getting to be "friends"—but she's the most non-literary writer I've ever known, and "never cracks a book" as we used to say. She's never read anything, that I can discover—I think she's a "self-taught" writer, like a primitive painter.

Heavens, your letter is now three weeks old. I wonder if you are doing the Hochhuth (?) play with Lillian Hellman—seven hours—ye gods. Perhaps you can cut it as you go, instead of doing it all and then having it cut! (Now I'm answering your letter—the body of it—poems, or soul of it, later). Your conference at Mrs. Meyer's sounds like a *good* conference—at least not a boring one. I have felt rather off Oppenheimer since hearing him talk here—although it was a beautiful tale, in a way—and reading a very good but hideously depressing book, *Brighter than a Thousand Suns* by Robert Jungk (translated from German).[2] Have you read it?—the whole his-

---

1 Darcy Ribeiro, *Arte plumária dos Índios Kaapor* (1957).
2 Robert Jungk, *Brighter Than a Thousand Suns: A Personal History of the Atomic Scientists*, trans. James Cleugh (1958).

tory of the atom bomb from the beginning. I read it months ago and haven't recovered yet—never shall, I suppose.

We got invitations, as you probably did, too, to Nabokov's step-daughter's wedding—poor girl, she's getting married off early. And all the parents & grand-parents seem to have been married twice—and the males be-medaled.

Going on to your next paragraph—about Empson—I've never said it or read it—but I think I admire his prose-style as a critic more than anyone else's. He manages to say the hard-to-express in colloquial language with just the right idiosyncratic twist to it—don't you think? I wish I could do it just like that. I was delighted when I read in one of his letters to the LTLS a while back that he has a very hard time doing it, takes forever, etc.—or so he said.[1] And now Bob Gardner: well—you've probably forgotten them but at that museum here there are six big costumes—masks all-over, that is—that always seem more funny than terrifying: a leopard like a big child in a spotted sleeping garment, a big-bellied one with a spiral on the belly, exactly like Père Ubu,[2] and what looks like an ink-pot with a yellow quilled pen on top of his head, etc. I read *all* the text yesterday and found I was right—they are comic—not gods or horrors. One tribe has an institution rather like Carnival, of masked balls that sometimes go on for three days. A "host" gives them; you can't come unless you're in costume; everyone gets drunk and has to *be* his costume all that time—and at the end, an odd feature—all costumes are given to the "host." This was a rather cheering item yesterday—unfortunately it reminded me of the book by Laura Huxley (Aldous's wife) she's just sent me: *You Are Not the Target. Recipes for Living and Loving!* One recipe is "BE an animal. Take some simple food along . . ." etc. And one is "DANCE ALONE NAKED!," and so on.[3] Poor Huxley has contributed a dutiful introduction to this and says he's tried them, the "recipes." I wonder what animal he is when he's alone. What DOES California do to people's brains? But have you noticed—people who talk a lot about "loving" and "warmth," etc. are always rather cold, indifferent people? (Like Huxley, who wouldn't give a kind word to his dying grandmother.) People who love their friends or relations just take it for granted,—I believe.

---

1 None of Empson's letters to the *The Times Literary Supplement* fits this description. EB may have been thinking of, "Sir, may I testify . . . that the bits of my prose which Mr. Vallins blamed in *Good English* had been written with particular care, chiefly to avoid misunderstanding in the reader, and that I thought the complaints about them wrong-headed"; William Empson to the Editor, *New Statesman and Nation* (June 25, 1955). See *Selected Letters of William Empson*, ed. John Haffenden (2006), 245.

2 See Alfred Jarry's illustration of Père Ubu in *Ubu Roi* (1896), on the cover of the 1961 New Directions edition.

3 Laura Archera Huxley, *You Are Not the Target* (1963).

Some more records *have* arrived. I met Mr. T[1] on the street yesterday—hurray—probably yours, and what quick work. I recommend one Villa Lobos I have acquired. It's some of the "Bachianas Brasileiras," with him conducting and Victoria de Los Angeles—ALP 1603—very good.[2] Nice flute & bassoon, too—No. 6. This was sent me from England—records are IMPOSSIBLE here now—but that's the least of it, of course.

There was a long poem about Eatherly in—"The Listener" about 2 years ago, by one of those English poets whose names I can't remember.[3] It was pretty good; had been broadcast in England—but not nearly up to what you'd do with it, of course. It seems to me that it's a *hell* of a subject for you—good, that is,—hellishly. Perhaps you're well along with it by now, in the peace of Castine—or is it peaceful? Yes, I've read all about Eatherly—but not that book, which seems to have exploited him badly—[4]

$$*\quad*\quad*\quad*\quad*$$

Back to "Dropping South"—yes, I like it a lot, now—but think it shd. be "tristes tropiques"—since they're always spoken of in the plural and the sound is the same, anyway—and also think you shd. omit the "the" in front of "macumba"—as I said ten days ago. The end is lovely now—[5]

NIGHT SWEAT is very beautiful, musical, spontaneous—I like it very much. In the next to the last line I'm not sure what the first word is supposed to be—"so"? no—can't be that—something in the margin I can't read.[6] But it's a wonderful, perfectly natural poem—very *sympathetic*—"bias of existing" is wonderful because it's horribly true and suggests wringing at the same time.[7] (I don't want to sound like the intellectuals who wrote about "Skunk Hour"—but I really "get" most things, I think!) You don't need me to point out what *you've* done, as if you weren't aware of it.

THOSE BEFORE US I like in almost the same way—it is so sympathetic . . . (I suppose I mean in the French or Portuguese sense, not in our "showing sympathy") and the ending is beautiful again. The only thing that I'd question a bit is in stanza 4 (as you now have it—the one that begins "Those before us! If you look behind the screen . . .") When you say the table is still leaf-green I immediately think of the usual card-table with green

---

1 Mr. Theodorides.

2 Heitor Villa-Lobos, *Bachianas Brasileiras*, Victoria de los Ángeles, soprano (Angel/EMI 35547).

3 John Wain, "A Song about Major Eatherly," *The Listener* (Aug. 6, 1959).

4 Claude Eatherly, *Burning Conscience: The Case of the Hiroshima Pilot, Told in His Letters to Günther Anders* (1961).

5 "Dropping South, Brazil," line 17 (RL-*CP*).

6 RL had typed "aboslove" and corrected it by hand to read "absolve."

7 "Night Sweat," line 10 (typescript, Vassar); the line is unchanged in the published version (RL-*CP*).

baize top—and I've never never seen a tin one—wood and ply-wood, rather. So the table bothers me—but this is very minor of course. Also "as many holes as a fish-net" bothers me a bit—seems so unlikely![1] Aside from that the imagery is clear and just right—that muskrat, the *spoor* (one of those 1,000 time better last-minute changes, I gather) of cornflakes—Central Park comes as a bit of a shock—but perhaps it's supposed to and also does take one back nicely to the arrowheads, etc.[2]

THE NEO-CLASSICAL URN has all kinds of weird connotations for me—it begins like Africa and then looks a bit like Yaddo! The first seven lines are marvelous—I thought of them yesterday, viewing masks again— Well, all the description is fine—the park, the typical poor nymph (only I *think* she'd be cast stone, cement, even[3]—not actually plaster—even the most miserable neo-classicism couldn't use plaster because it wouldn't last a week outdoors—surely?) And of course I can't take "raw gobs of hash"[4]— but perhaps I'm right and not just squeamish—"raw gobs" might be out of their legs, etc. but they are pretty well covered with shell and the flesh has to be very small bits, I'd think.—"hash" is the word that really bothers since it suggests a quantity heaped together—not random floating bits of raw flesh. "Hash," the noun, means a *dish of hash*, a stuck-together mass . . . ? Poor old turtles . . . what a dreadful boy you were! The poem suggest the horror of an exposed brain[5]—(I've been reading about the Incas & their passion for trepanning)—the various *containers*, all vulnerable, for life—& maybe that's what it's supposed to suggest?

13th—

CALIGULA—but not as dreadful as poor Caligula . . . I have no books about Romans here in Rio so I just take your word for all these grim details . . . and a lot of it's what I remember, vaguely. I like the bad rhymes—plans/dance, etc.[6] At the moment I can't tell how this poem would strike me by itself. I wish I'd read it first, but I read them in the above order—and, as you say, this

---

1 "Those Before Us (Variation on a line by Wallace Stevens)" originally had seven stanzas, but RL canceled the second stanza, making what had been stanza five stanza four. It reads: "Those before us! If you look behind the screen / (it has as many holes as fish-net now) / you will see them conspiring, slapping the cards / across the old tin table, still leaf-green" (typescript, Vassar); cf. "Those Before Us," lines 13–16 (RL-*CP*).
2 See "Those Before Us," lines 16, 11, and 2 (RL-*CP*).
3 "I left the plaster statue of a nymph," line 13 (typescript, Vassar); see "The Neo-Classical Urn," line 13 (RL-*CP*).
4 See "The Neo-Classical Urn," line 27 (RL-*CP*).
5 See "The Neo-Classical Urn," line 4 (RL-*CP*).
6 See "Caligula," lines 42 and 43 (RL-*CP*).

is more like the old dispensation, not *telling* as much first-hand. It's just a rather terrifying canvas to me at present, like some of those wonderful Roman paintings up at the Metropolitan—(only they're not on canvas, naturally). But I admire it; oh yes! It's superb description, as always—what did you do with the other 300 odd lines, I wonder?

No—I *like* these "messy copies"—much better than final ones—a correction makes it breathe, after all—or turn over, or blink.[1] Or I see your Muse, a rather large rough type, giving you a whack across the ear.

(Mine is suffering from leukemia—just can't be bothered—hasn't tuned her lute since God knows when—)

It's a Saturday and Lota, discouraged with her job but full of energy says, "Let's go out and buy a *sports car* . . ." I feel very piddling saying I have to write a *book review*. Tell Elizabeth I got the wonderful clipping about Marianne—M had written me about that dressmaker, too, and I feel awfully out of the know.[2] Your ex-work-room hotel is now squeezed in between its two big new buildings and I'm afraid it's really about to go—it's closed. I think that Moorish tower is being squeezed upwards and will float off like a fire-balloon any evening now. Mary is here in Rio for the week-end with her two infants—the new one, 11 weeks old, asleep beside me, lulled by typing, apparently. She's awfully nice, but then I like babies best up till the age of two. But I see I can't stay here—must go do things—*até logo*.[3] With much love, and I am so grateful for the poems—they've helped enormously—

Elizabeth

Rio, July 14th—

Dearest Cal—I just got mail from Petrópolis—with yours from Castine of July 5th. How very stupid of me—Flávio's names (or at least those we have decided to use for export—he has 6 or 7) are:

Flávio de Macedo Soares Regis
Avenida Copacabana 74   Apartment 902

He was just 20—seems to me he could be a sophomore—he is so excited about going anywhere, anytime—I mean to the USA—he can't see straight,

---

1 All the drafts RL sent to EB have marginal notes and corrections.
2 Article about Marianne Moore's attendance at an opening of the clothes designer Ben Zuckerman, *The New York Times* (June 12, 1963).
3 *So long.*

poor boy, and I do hope it works out. You have been awfully kind—as always.

Lota is off to work and her secretary now mails my letters for me—an enormous help. But I can't answer your letter properly—indeed I have scarcely read it.

Love—hope you're having a nice time—and I wish I could be in London at the same time.

Elizabeth

276.

July 15th[, 1963]—Rio

Dear Cal:

I wrote you a hasty postscript yesterday—and changed the address to England, on a letter full of things you probably won't care to have on your trip—if you get any of these. (I've lost a lot lately.) It was just to give you Flávio's name and address and to thank you. Lota was leaving for work just as the mail came and I wanted to get off some sort of reply. This is to thank you again and to add that when I read the letter more carefully I realized what you had offered—the extent of your offering, to help Flávio. I didn't take it in the first time. That is more than generous of you, Cal, and we're very touched. However—IF he could get a scholarship at all—I've explained to Dr. Glimp, etc., about Brazilian money—it would have to be a full one. Flávio himself insists he can earn money on the side—teaching Portuguese, perhaps—and he has certainly done it here since he was sixteen or so—but he probably doesn't realize how very much busier he'd be in the USA. He might earn enough for spending money, I should think—according to the booklet I have here. The cruzeiro is much worse than when you were here—and dying every day—it will probably hit c$1,000. to the $. (And when Alfredo went to Princeton one generation ago, it was c$1,000.=$100.—so he lived well on what would now be seven or eight dollars a month—and was then $500.)

I'm distracted—this stuff can't be of interest in London or Nice—& why Nice, I wonder? All I mean to say is thank you deeply from Lota and me—and IF any of this works out, surely it shouldn't be necessary—and I have said my contribution to F's education will be a winter overcoat! The airplane ticket—a big item—can be arranged here. The companies usually give free trips to students who get scholarships. The only money in the family now is the great-uncle who was Foreign Minister, etc.—*extremely* rich and with only an adopted daughter, also rich. By rights he should educate Flávio—but he has always been stingy and is now quite gaga; all his money is going to the Church—this has been publicized for years—and neither F nor Lota would ask him for a penny, of course. (He gave F a pearl stick-pin once—perhaps to encourage him to take up diplomacy . . .)

I saw items about the Poetry Conference in the English newspapers— and probably you are hobnobbing with Dame S this very moment—or giving a reading at that Mermaid Theatre.[1]

Lota read NIGHT SWEAT and said simply, "It's a beauty . . ." and so it is. I suspect it is going to be one of your most "popular" poems, too. She also likes DROPPING SOUTH as it is now very much, too—and she should know! She hasn't read the others yet.

It is vacation here now and F is away for a week earning some money by reporting—so I don't know whether he's heard anything further or not—

So Mary has published *The Group*? I must read it—but rather dread it of course. It's funny, though, how long she has remained involved in college life. I can't seem to work up much interest in those days now.

4th of July—what on earth were Antony & Cleopatra doing with our Independence Day, I wonder? And the poor Pyramid—a small one.

Now I've had time to read SOFT WOOD properly—but you probably have no time to read my thoughts on the subject. I'll write a literary letter to Castine.— I love it. The seals & junipers are lovely.

In case you don't get my offering of yesterday—Flávio's name is de Macedo Soares Regis (he'd be called St. Regis, no doubt)—address 74 Avenida de Copacabana—apt 902.

Boa Viagem[2]—and *safe* viagem—with much love,
Elizabeth

277.

Rio, August 5th, 1963
Dearest Cal:

Just a note—I have two or three letters of yours here I haven't answered properly yet, and also two or three poems—including the lovely one to your aunt. Then I saw again, in the *Observer*, the one about the past—"Tess of the D'urbervilles" etc. and realized how very much I like that one— They all

---

1 Dame Edith Sitwell; RL was attending the Poets Festival in London.
2 Bon voyage.

make me happy—and GREEN with envy![1] But I'll write you later—also the latest on Flávio—I'm seeing him tonight. Our two-weeks-past mail is arriving this P.M. and I want to get a batch of notes off *before* it comes.

We've been having a difficult stretch—two weeks ago Saturday Lota was operated on for an intestinal occlusion—all very sudden. She was sick for about two days, beginning with what we thought was just a stomach upset due to over work—but that rapidly began to look much worse. Everything is fine and she's been home three days now and is getting better fast—but patience isn't her strong point and the next few weeks will probably be more difficult! The hospital is excellent—so were both doctors—and, after a few horrors, we got a good night nurse, too. They let you stay with the patient here—so I was the "accompaniante" for a week—slept in the extra bed, etc.—a very humane system, I think—in fact I liked the whole place, even the nuns. I'd lied to L for 24 hours about *not* having an operation, etc.—finally Sister Marcelina appeared and said, "Daughter, do you believe in God?" "More or less, Sister," said Lota to her, in Portuguese; then to me in English—"Well, I can see I'm going to be operated on at any minute now!" I have some wonderful anecdotes when I can get them sorted out of the nightmare parts.

The worst is the visitors . . . At the hospital the doctor did forbid them and I was tough—and Mary, who came down, tougher—but at home we're defenseless. It is all exactly like a wake. Did you ever read Santayana's auto-biographies?[2]—the only works of his I like. I remember how he describes a ghastly train trip he made with his father when he was a small boy—on & on and on—no food, no sleep, black coffee, etc.—and finally he asks permission to wash his hands and the father is furious. "Tantas requiecencias!" or something like that—"so many demands." And then S says that now he thinks Spaniards have improved—they do take better care of themselves—health—diet, sleep, children, etc. But I can't say I noticed it much in Spain—I thought them all a bit mad. I thought Brazilians so at first, too—then went through phases about them—and have now come right back to where I started—they are *mad*; it's the only explanation. The day after Lota got back—one small example—the mayor of Copacabana, a very bright, clever, honest little man, whom I really like—came and stayed 2 hours—shouting politics—upsetting teacups on the bed—pushing the bed in his excitement. I

1 "The Lesson," *The Observer* (June 16, 1963), see lines 1, 3, 7, and 18; see RL-*CP*.
2 George Santayana, *Persons and Places* (1944), *The Middle Span* (1945), and *My Host the World* (1953).

finally almost had to carry him out of the room, where Lota lay looking like death, by then. Well—they're nuts; that's all.

I don't know when she'll be able to go back to work. I'm hoping for a month's rest in the country or at Cabo Frio—but no plans yet. She's been extremely brave—she's the kind that fusses about small things but is heroic about the big ones, thank God.

Have I ever thanked you for the records (that I haven't been able to play yet)? I think not—anyway, they came safely. I *had* the Elliott Carter—but can swap it at the record store, where they'll be delighted to get it—and I can probably get 2 *old* imported ones for it. I must go out—I wonder where you are—back in Castine, I think—and I hope your wonderful writing streak is still going on. In the middle of all this sometime I had to go to the US Embassy—a dull reception—and I quoted your "Copacabana" poem to the Ambassador, who said he liked it . . . Much, much love—

    Elizabeth

Dr. Nilo (the same we got for Toni) always asks about you—many people do.

278.

Castine, Maine

August 12, 1963

Dearest Elizabeth:

Your letter has been around the world. It arrived here yesterday forwarded by Faber. I feel we have had a most vicarious joint visit to London together. I feel a terrible fraud. I was sent first class by the State Department. When I got on the plane at 8 in the evening, I found six match-boxes with my name inscribed in gold, then scarlet knitted shoe-socks, then the menu. Well, I was not drinking at all, but they offered cocktails (as many as you wanted), chilled vodka to go with the chilled caviar, red and white wine, champagne and liqueurs, then an awful elongated Elvis Presley movie of jumping 14 year-old girls. When I landed at two-thirty our time, I had breakfast with some American friends and was shown by car every sight I had ever seen in London. It took me a day in my stunned, one night's sleep lost state to understand people talking British. They all do. I guess the London weather is terrible, they all say so, but it seemed glorious to me, a sort of big Boston that functioned, or a New York with at every step some little detour or hurdle to make things more human and less sheer. *Sheer* seems to be the American's most refreshing and vexing quality.

I must tell you about seeing Randall, and later Mary McCarthy, the sheerest of all American pilgrims, both rather marvelous, almost saintly in their buoyant go ahead intensity. Randall loves England, and had spent two months with guide books planning his summer, cathedrals, plays, a long string of German castles, visits to *all* the Donatellos in Italy. He avoids all English literary people, but listens avidly to the *real* English ("England is everything the visiting Englishman isn't"). He rents chairs in Regent's Park, they wave to the children, carry bread crumbs for the pigeons, and absolutely hate France. The French customs men would not look at them. I suggested language difficulties, but Randall said wistfully, "They might smile!" Randall is having suits made, quotes his tailor, is incensed that such artisans are not considered artists, has bought a Jaguar, which he won't risk in London. And so on. I laugh a little, but they gave a lovely sparkling salt water feeling of Jamesian purity. And I too felt crazy about London, even the literary people.

My whole trip was minute little readings, stage, radio, TV, little lunches, rehearsals (six hours for a minute and 15 seconds) BBC TV recital of "Man and Wife," though of course I was with a mob of other people and didn't even rehearse more than four minutes. I saw quite a lot of Empson. They live in a hideous 18 room house on the edge of Hampstead Heath. Each room is as dirty and messy as Auden's New York apartment. Strange household: Hetta Empson, six feet tall, still quite beautiful, five or six young men, all sort of failures at least financially, Hetta's lover, a horrible young man, dark, cloddish, thirty-ish, soon drunk, incoherent and offensive,[1] William, Frank Parker red-faced, drinking gallons, but somehow quite uncorrupted, always soaring off from the conversation with a chortle. And what else? A very sweet son of 18, another, Hetta's, not William's, Harriet's age.[2] Chinese dinners, Mongol dinners. The household had a weird, sordid nobility that made other Englishmen seem like a veneer.

I don't know that I have the wind to go on with Mary. Nothing could have been less like the Empsons'. A lovely apartment, William Morris wall-paper, every item clean as a ship, and mostly brought over from England, meals planned and worked on for days, elevating, industrious trips to churches and museums, everything performed and executed to the last inch, though Mary had just gotten over a bad attack of jaundice. Jim doesn't gossip, and Mary

1 Michael Avery.
2 Jacob Empson and Simon Duval-Smith.

really seems to have become a remarkably kind, generous person, and as happily married as anyone I know. All real, I think, but there is a bubble or two. One is Mary's new novel, which will bring her maybe a quarter of a million (she is already planning to set up a foundation for peace or something with it, though they really don't have much money). She has refused the cover of *Time*, but accepted the cover of *Newsweek*, and a story in *Life*.[1] We had an incredible picnic on the grass of Saint Cloud with the Spenders, Sonia Orwell, the *Life* photographer, minor expatriates, minor embassy officials, a sixteen-foot Polish table cloth, magna of champagne, Flemish dining room groups of fruit. But no one in the know likes the book, and I dread what will happen to it in the *New York Book Review*. I've now read it through, and in my usual seesawing, indecisive way, have formed two opinions: 1) bad, that it is a very labored, somehow silly Vassar affair, awfully girlish girls, a chapter on the pessary fitting, a chapter on breast feeding, a chapter on a commitment in Payne Whitney, rather commonplace known material, documented as though she were writing about Florence; 2) good, a kind of clearness and innocence, trying to be kind to the characters—one feels she often made them dull so as not [to] resemble any of her real class-mates. The plowing and smiling through a long hard, impossible task. After all there was a kind of breathless courage and perhaps folly in giving her Vassar girls' view of the thirties. I doubt if she feels it's much of a masterpiece, still the excitement of a first commercial success is intoxicating. I'll feel wretched, if the reviewers are cruel, and take the chance to go to town on her.

Forgive me for saying that I felt comforted by your saying your Muse is dead. Mine is dead as lead, and when I try to write I feel full of a hollow aimlessness, though otherwise quite happy. What I mean of course is that if you, so much better than I, can coast along, I am somehow released for a while. I have no doubts about you; you seem much richer and more interesting than anyone else, and you *never* write junk, seldom write anything that isn't a kind of landmark, so your slow pace must be the one that wins the race. Still I brood about all those rich unfinished fragments, such a fortune in the bank, but you have done so much better than I could advise you, that I won't prod. You mustn't waver in knowing how much you have.

Thanks for your comments on my poems. I meant to bring them and your letter down to my barn today, and retouch, but I forgot. The raw gobs of hash was meant to be the turtles' food and not the turtles, and probably

---

1 "Contrary Mary: Vassar '33," *Newsweek* (Sept. 2, 1963); Jordan Bonfante, "Lady with a Switchblade," *Life* (Sept. 20, 1953).

should have the word *fed* or something of the sort put back. Maybe I had a perverse desire to blur the picture for a second. I really was too slow-witted to realize the turtles were dying. I detest the "Caligula" for feeling but find it alive as a poem. I'll get the Y of the goddess right; the *the* before *macumba* was an afterthought to make the rhythm more conversational. You are no doubt right about the jumpiness. By the "as many holes as a fishnet" I meant the screen to be some kind of metaphorical veil that shelters the past, now defenseless as one looks back with a feeling of distant detachment. *Leaf-green* is what I remember, perhaps in imagination, I hoped for a pathos in the rusty tin and the growing green, the freezing of that growing time. Glad you liked *Night Sweat*. My only product this summer is finishing another sort of like it, with Maine scenery. I'd copy it out now but no copy here is close enough for me to remember the right version. I thought [of] you in Nice, a small Rio with a rich country behind it.

All my love,
Cal

P.S. Oh, I had a letter about Flávio from the Harvard Dean. No hope this year, but I am sure it can be done next. He seemed very well disposed. Let me know what I can do. Our love to you both.

279.

August 13, 1963

Dearest Elizabeth:

I rather sensed there would be more mail from you this afternoon at the post-office, or so I wished. And there I found two, one from England, one sent direct. I am so sorry to hear of Lota's operation. Her "more or less" is about as much as one can really offer God at such a moment, though I suppose she was softening things for the Sister. Well, good, she's back home. God bless her! We have eight Episcopal clergymen and two bishops—to say nothing of others that drop off of yachts and air-planes to visit—and find I've dropped into church a couple of times. Sometimes one feels like a headless rooster—thinking of friends one's own age dying or aging—and then God seems a sort of cap.

The other night we played your Supervia records. Our heads are toward Spain, as Teresa, the new Argentinean nurse, does everything for us except learn English. We are trying to finagle a week'[s] trip for you to Mexico City through the Cultural Congress, though Lizzie and Barbara Epstein may have botched the whole business by refusing to have a Mexican number of the New York Book Review, and Jack Thompson by asking for too many good dinners, etc. There's a plan for us, the Epsteins, the Podhoretzs and the Warrens to go this November. Your little pre-Columbian statue is now sitting on our ban mantle piece, where it is greatly admired and quite drains interest from our other small objects. I gather you've sent me something at Faber's that I'll guess will be forwarded back. A thousand thanks! Did I ever tell you that Lizzie's Brazilian suit that didn't seem to fit was on backwards! It fitted perfectly.

You are so sweet about my poems. My queer remarks about your not writing were meant to mean that I wished that slowing down to your pace might result in my rising a little nearer your standard. For my Turtles I've taken your "caste stone" and put *fed* before *raw gobs of hash*. The *Y* is in and the *the* out of *Dropping South*. *Those before us* is so changed that I'll type out the new version. Also I'll put in the one new poem. What you call my big run is really a laborious, stumbling year's work, though the Cousin Harriet poem came in a couple of days, I think. I so hoped you would like it.

THOSE BEFORE US

They are all outline, uniformly gray,
unregenerate arrowheads sloughed up by the path here,
or in the corners of the eye, they play
their thankless, fill-in roles. They never were.

Wormwood on the veranda! Plodding needles
still prod the coarse pink yarn into a dress.
The muskrat that took a slice of your thumb still huddles,
a mop of hair and a heart-beat on the porch—

there's the high wastebasket where it learned to wait
for us playing dead, the slats it mashed in terror,
its spoor of cornflakes, and the packing crate
it furiously slashed to matchwood to escape.

Vacations, stagnant growth. But in the silence,
some one lets out his belt to breathe, some one
loosens her stays. Bless the confidence
of their sitting unguarded there in stocking feet.[1]

---

1 In margin in RL's hand: "Put [this stanza] after next stanza."

Those before us! If you look through the blinds,
(as full of windows as fishnets now)
you will hear them conspiring, slapping hands
across the bent card table, still leaf-green.

Sands drop from the hour-glass waist. Here on the common,
swallow-tail butterflies play cops and robbers,
as we trail their floppy shadows. Pardon them for existing.
We have stopped watching them. They have stopped watching.[1]

THE FLAW

A seal swims like a poodle through the sheet
of blinding salt. A country graveyard, here
and there on a rock, and here and there a pine,
throbs on the essence of the gasoline.
Some mote, some eye-flaw, wobbles on the heat,
hair-dark, hair-thin, the fragment of a hair—

a noose, a question? All is possible;
if there's free will, it's something like this hair,
inside my eye, outside my eye, yet free,
airless as grace, if the good God . . . I see.
Our bodies quiver. In this rustling air,
all's possible, all's unpredictable.

Old wives and husbands! Look, their gravestones wait
in couples with the names and half the date—
one future and one freedom. In a flash,
I see us whiten into skeletons,
our eager, sharpened cry, a pair of stones,
cutting like shark-fins through the boundless wash.

Two walking cobwebs, almost bodiless,
crossed paths here once, kept house, and lay in beds.
Your fingertips once touched my fingertips
and set us tingling through a thousand threads.

1 Cf. "Those Before Us" (RL-*CP*).

Poor pulsing *Fete Champetre*! The summer slips
between our fingers into nothingness.

We too lean forward, as the heat waves roll
over our bodies, grown insensible,
ready to dwindle off into the soul,
two motes, or eye-flaws, the invisible
Hope of the hopeless launched and cast adrift
on the great flaw that gives the final gift.

Dear Figure curving like a questionmark,
how will you hear my answer in the dark?[1]

So, enough. I suppose you've heard of Ted Roethke's death.[2] I had a long,
touching, grumbling letter from him three weeks earlier, and thank God I
answered in time. I tried to write an elegy on him. It didn't come off but set
me to thinking about what a tight-rope he had to walk of comedy and
grandeur, a delicacy to be true to, a bigness to live up to. Poor guy, he had a
bruised life, but he didn't dry up—somehow quite quite clean and phosphorescent in his wallow.

Our love to Lota. I hope there'll be fun in resting. Some[how] I always
feel you and I are only arm's length away.

Love,
Cal

I'd like to hold both your hands at this moment.

[Enclosed]

THE OPPOSITE HOUSE
All day the opposite house,
an abandoned police station,
just an opposite house,
is square enough—six floors,
six windows to a floor,
pigeons ganging through

---

1 Cf. "The Flaw" (RL-*CP*).
2 Theodore Roethke died on August 1, 1963, at the age of fifty-five.

broken windows and cooing
like gangs of children tooting
empty bottles.

Tonight, though, I see it shine
in the Azores of my open window.
Its manly, old fashioned lines
are gorgeously rectilinear.
It's like some firework to be fired
at the end of the garden party,
some Spanish *casa*, luminous
with heraldry and murder,
marooned in New York.

A stringy policeman is crooked
in the doorway, one hand on his revolver.
He counts his bullets like beads.
Two on horseback sidle
the crowd to the curb. A red light
whirls on the roof of an armed car,
plodding slower than a turtle.
Deterrent terror!
Viva la muerte![1]

Dear Elizabeth:

I forgot to tuck this in my letter. The poem's rather in your
style, I think, though I wish [it] were more so.

Cal

280.

Monday morning bright & early—
Rio, August 26th, 1963

Dearest Cal:

I'll start a letter to you and heaven knows when I'll finish it—(Virgil T
says "one of the strange things about poets is the way they keep warm by
writing to one another all over the world"—but I suppose you've read THE

---

1 Cf. "The Opposite House" (RL-*CP*).

STATE OF MUSIC?[1] Very funny & frivolous, but I agree with him completely when I don't occasionally think he's dead wrong:—"all God's chillun got modern art"—about psychoanalysis: "As venal a branch of science as that cannot be counted a bulwark of civilization"—and poets as "prehistoric monsters." After an evening with some of the so-called critics and writers here he does cheer me up, however, with the spectacle of what an advanced society can produce—advanced, decadent, or what you will—it's better than Brazilian barbarism any old day.)

I felt very badly when I read about poor Roethke—must have been a heart attack? Please—take care of your health! Being a poet is one of the unhealthier jobs—no regular hours—so many temptations! I was enthralled and a bit horrified by your first-class State Dept. trip. And Randall! Well— after Lota had to sell hers, I decided Jaguars are too too vulgar! Is his wife with him and is he just traveling, or what? Mary's in Paris, I gather. I think your one remark about "Jim"—"he doesn't gossip" is *almost* as good as Marianne's saying that Valéry was "unsordid." He must just listen. Do please tell me when these photographs are to be in LIFE—of your picnic—because I mustn't miss them.[2] And I suppose I must order THE GROUP; I loathed that pessary-prose-poem in *PR*—and the one in *The New Yorker* I found dull, I'm afraid[3]—and as I said before, I think, I just can't get that interested in college days any more. However—she does recapture them awfully well. How does one know beforehand about "commercial successes"—naïve of me? no doubt it's a campaign from way back. Mary has worked hard and deserves a lot of money about now—but it entails that bitterness that it's not for what she deserves it for. Those "Group" pieces, however, bring those days back only too well—sleep in a single cot with Mary with her first husband in the other one—and how they worried about their *clothes*; endless discussions of new spring outfits & pathetic interior-decoration schemes.

I'll be watching all those English reviews I take—THE LISTENER, of course—for accounts of you on the BBC . . . I am glad you seem to have survived it so well; I envy you going but not the hastiness of it. I wonder WHY ENCOUNTER has never even rejected Clarice's stories. I still don't know if Spender ever got them. I've written 2 or 3 times now. They're not much good, really—but as good as most they publish, those African ones. She is off this morning to Texas for a Literary Conference—came & read me her

1 Virgil Thompson, *The State of Music* (1939).
2 Jordan Bonfante, "Lady with a Switchblade," *Life* (Sept. 20, 1963).
3 Mary McCarthy, "Dottie Makes an Honest Woman of Herself," *Partisan Review* (Jan.–Feb. 1954) and "Polly Andrews, Class of '33," *The New Yorker* (June 29, 1963).

lecture Saturday. But she's hopeless, really. I've had a couple of charming letters from Drummond and I think I'll send you the translation of THE TABLE for the *NY Review*, with a short note about him. Would you be interested in that? (It seems it's one of his own favorites & he's pleased about having it translated.) (& I can't think of anything else Brazilian worth writing about.)

I sent two letters to you in England, just a few days apart. You seem only to have ~~received the 2nd one I think? Because you asked me if I liked~~ However—no great loss. Yes—remember I told you Virgil T's remarks about the old-fashioned 19th century parts of Rio, yellow, Frenchified villas, etc.—being "very nice, just like Nice—when one gets away from that *ghastly* coastline . . ." (You say Nice was like Rio a bit.) The Music Festival is on—and thank God I have nothing to do with it. Dreadful programs, and most of the biggest attractions not coming, of course. I went to an evening of quartets of "modern" [(]fifty years old, that is[)] music—wanted to hear Berg—took Flávio, who said it was *"away out,"* and two of his sophisticated young lady friends—Communists all—and Communists, I gather, only like Beethoven and Shostakovich, really. For an encore they played part of a late Beethoven Quartet—and so badly that I began to think they probably hadn't done so well with Berg etc. either. (I do rather like Beethoven's last quartets when I am feeling sentimental—and if you don't have them, get the *Hollywood Bowl* playing them—of all things—but it is superb playing.[1] Oh, I turned in the duplicate Carter for a very nice Purcell orchestral record). Friday night was the fatal anniversary of Vargas's suicide. President Goulart staged a monster mass-meeting right in front of the opera house—*that* concert had to be canceled. Truckloads, trainloads, ferryloads, etc. of workers were poured into the city—a division of the Army, 15,000 men—tanks all over the place—a horrible atmosphere. It was spite, pure & simple. The Army took over the city and Carlos withdrew to his palace and kept the Rio police away somewhere. (Can you imagine Kennedy moving in on his political rival in Albany?—with the US Army? and staging a monster rally in front of the State House in Albany?—well—that's what happened here. ALL MAD.) However it was a great flop, to the relief of most people. Goulart's a coward—and Brazilians do have a small sense of "fair play" and a big sense of the ridiculous—7,000 soldiers surrounded [by] 9,000 imported workers were too much, even for the pro-government newspapers. We watched intermittently on TV—because rumors of revolution were rife, of course—the best mo-

---

1 Ludwig van Beethoven, *The Late Quartets*, The Hollywood String Quartet (EMI RLS 7707).

ment was when a farmer or somebody handed the President up a monster *mandioca* root—about 25 lbs.—a huge phallic symbol—and this was so Brazilian. (Giant vegetables are revered—I have a "pumpkin big as the baby" you may remember, in a poem.[1] Just another proof of primitivism.)

Oh—Dean Glimp wrote an encouraging letter, and Flávio has applied for next year. He also has passed his next-to-last set of exams for the diplomatic service—one more in October, when the present 50 will be reduced to 25. Even if he gets in, however—I think he is still dying to go to Harvard—got so excited studying the catalogue with me he said he wanted to live in the US—and wants to take *your* course, naturally—will you be there that year? (If he is in the DS, they might give him some more money, too—so it's all to the good.)

I'm just sort of reviewing your letters. Tell E if she looks at the inside of her Brazilian skirt—there'll be a small stitched mark indicating the middle of the front . . . I am writing—oh dear I should never say this ahead—a poem about *your* Muse. *I* think it's funny, so far. She looks rather like an aunt of mine by marriage—tough, red-headed, illegitimate!

The Theodorides are leaving for three months and offered me their vacant apartment to work in—a long walk down the beach. I am delighted and hope to get that book into shape. The telephone drives me crazy here—& no matter how I shut myself up there are so many interruptions. Maybe some of those many ancient, yellowed, termite-eaten fragments will revive.

Yesterday was one of the weirder events of my life—well—to begin with I suppose came the Inauguration, Thursday, of a big show about Lota's park at the Museum of Modern Art—along with a show of Burle Marx—plants, projects & paintings. Rather to our surprise, the show is a huge success—never so many people at any opening—and the wooden models, aerial photographs, model playgrounds and toy trains, etc.—were all very attractive. I think Lota was very pleased—although she still isn't up to all the work and excitement and goes around looking like a ghost. But yesterday—9 AM—was the opening of the model airplane circles (fields?)—two of them—with surrounding garden, benches, etc.—really pretty. *Aeriomodelismo* is very popular—probably in the US, too, although I never gave it a thought, naturally; I'm sure none of us had until this year. (Even Carlos, who "opened" the thing, said "I didn't know how to pronounce this word until yesterday.") Anyway—a huge success. Lota untied the ribbon, and was dragged into the limelight & given sheaves of wilted roses. I sat on the platform, too—a very

---

1 "Manuelzinho," line 20 (EB-*CP*).

tiny one—and there were 1,000's of people. There's so little for the poor public to do in Rio; anything's a godsend. It was pretty funny—all the speeches praising Dona Maria Carlota Costellat de Macedo Soares to the skies as a lover of children & a benefactor of humanity—meanwhile Lota was yelling at and kicking at, almost, little boys who were trying to climb up on the platform, cursing photographers, etc.—with her most terrifying scowls and language. I kept poking her and saying "Try to look *pleasant!* They're all looking at you!" while Lota went right on being cruel to children. But really—when Carlos was an editor and used to come for long leisurely argumentative Sunday lunches with us—who'd ever have thought he and L would sit on a shaky platform opening a show of *aeriomodelismo* . . . What next?

I went out of curiosity to the "American Exposition" here—a big show supposed to offset the Russian one last year—and it was so bad I was embarrassed. Oh god—is *that* what we're offering the world? The State Dept. is STUPID—I could think up a better exhibition in half an hour, honestly. A huge display of FOOD, for one thing—and some of our more fantastic gadgets— Every gadget I saw they already make right here in Brazil—and only by using a US electric washer for two months can you find out it's better than a Brazilian—which it probably isn't any more, anyway. Came away very depressed and elderly and wanted to destroy the whole world and begin again with just song and dance.

Tonight a couple is coming to call—friends of Joe Frank's—the man teaching at the Faculdade de Philosophia this year.[1] (He said on the telephone, "It's great fun.") Joe wrote "they are the nicest type of American academic . . ." Well—I hope they turn out to be people we can talk to a little. (I think I smoke too much because I can't talk.) We're both quite fed up with the people here and if we can't get away will soon become hermits. But these people sound a little *young* for us. Had a card from Fizdale & Gold mysteriously saying that they and the "Lowells" are meeting in Portugal—and aren't L & I going to be there, too? Miss Moore always writes a lot about the "Lowells"—and I wish she'd stop telling me how the table was set—a CARP? in the middle?—and how many books you have—and tell me what you *said*. And I know you had that amazing blind Indian to dinner . . .[2] Is he nice? Oh dear—I don't WANT to go back to Mexico! Please! Any place in the world except Mexico—no—I don't feel much drawn to India, either. I

1 David R. Weimer.
2 Ved Mehta (see letter 206).

lived in Mexico almost a year and I had a *very* good time and met a lot of queer people—which I usually don't do when I travel—but I don't want to go back, unless to Yucatán or the southern parts—*away* off the beaten path. I imagine even Oaxaca is spoiled now, and it was so beautiful. It's a much sadder country than Brazil—and all those Indians are so awful, poor things—except the little Mayas in Yucatán—they're nice,—gentler, cleaner, don't carry guns, big hooked noses, quiet and almost gay—like little parakeets. But I've had ten years of a backward, corrupt country and, like Lota, I yearn for civilization—London, Rome, Copenhagen, Madrid (I feel I've *had* Paris, too). The impact of the clumsy and pathetic and "folk" can only last so long . . .

What "literary people" did you see in England besides Empson? Why is English Bohemianism more sordid than any other kind, I wonder. (It's always seemed so to me—[)] Oh well—the English are so much dirtier than Latins!— Brazilians who send their boys to English schools are always horrified by the bathing facilities. You should hear about that school where poor Hopkins taught!¹ And here—it is true—the only dirty *workers*—whom you see on the street in after-work hours in their work clothes, etc.—are recent immigrants from Europe—northern countries. The most miserable painter or plumber we get in here always changes his clothes to work—takes a shower in the maid's bathroom and puts on his street clothes again before going out. They live in filth, perhaps, unavoidably—but they're personally fastidious. And the English just aren't. Oxford graduates smell . . .

L's secretary Fernanda is here & will take my mail—so I'll get off this installment now and proceed immediately to the second letter of yours with your poems.

Love—
  Elizabeth

                                        August 26th,—2nd installment
Yes—I didn't understand about the turtles' food—maybe something like "*my*" raw gobs of hash??—now I feel better about the turtles! "As many holes as a fishnet"—now I can't think why I objected to that . . . It was the *tin* table being green that bothered me—just because of the standard green-felt

---

1 Gerard Manley Hopkins taught at many schools, but EB may have been thinking of his description of Mount St. Mary's College, Chesterfield, in 1878: "Life here is as dank as ditch-water and has some of the other qualities of ditch-water: at least I know that I am reduced to great weakness by diarrhoea, which lasts too, as if I were poisoned"; *The Letters of Gerard Manley Hopkins to Robert Bridges*, ed. Claude Colleer Abbott (1935), 47.

card-table—your contrast is perfect, of course. (Virgil says poets "can't observe," too—I wonder what on earth he means by that?) I don't know whether "screen" meant the interior kind or a screen door—I like the new version. "Common" is much better, isn't it—but I still like the "gun-shy shadows" & from "trunk to trunk" better[1] . . . It's a lovely poem and I understand it better and find more in it each time I read it. The one word I don't like, Cal, is "stays" because it is an archaism—hasn't really been used for well over a hundred years, I suppose—except to be funny. So if you have the men wearing "belts," not braces—the women would be in the "corset age"—(the letting out of belts is a beautiful touch.) Or perhaps your elders did use the word "stays" and I'm wrong . . . very likely—

THE FLAW is quite as beautiful as NIGHT SWEAT and will be just as justly loved, I think. In fact—I think I even like it BETTER—and that is saying a great deal—but they are equally beauties, and the reason I like "The Flaw" so much is probably because the details are my kind of country, etc. They are both so spontaneous and easy sounding—the "shark-fins" superb—(that gives me the hideous sensation in the diaphragm by which I recognize ART.) The ending is like "The Exequy"[2] a bit (—richer than most of those couplets, perhaps, but in the same tone of terror + tenderness.)

27th, AM

Well, the couple (friends of J. Frank's)—named Weimer—are very young, but very nice. He teaches at Rutgers; here teaching American Lit on a Fulbright. Beginning with Mark Twain and *Huckleberry Finn*—he was surprised that his class didn't know what "Honest Injun" meant. We laughed—and later I realized I really don't know myself—at least not why it was a sort of oath. A teacher through & through, worried already about how he's going to teach their maid to read and write, immediately. I've tried this twice—no success the first time, a very slow and very slight success with our Rio maid now. But when she does read better, what is she going to read—nothing but comic strips, signboards, and the labels on packages. (Have you ever thought how beautiful neon signs would be if you *couldn't* read?) She spends every free moment watching TV, as it is—and it's about 100 times worse here than in the US—L & I did see an American newsreel last night—all about the

---

1 Cf. draft in letter 279 with "Those Before Us" (RL-*CP*); "gunshy shadows" is restored in line 22.

2 "Dear (forgive/The crime) I am content to live / Divided, with but half a heart, / Till we shall meet and never part"; Henry King, "The Exequy" (1657), from lines 117–20.

march on Washington, etc.[1]—Baldwin suddenly popping up—one Eng. review said he looked like a "fledgling"—exactly. This Weimer boy *teaches* the
Negro novel—I don't see how—or why? Said that Mary had polished off
Salinger completely in an article somewhere—?[2] Sort of in at the kill I think.
I'm up to date on the Edel James books—and James' insistence on never
using real characters, his horror at Vernon Lee for using *him*[3]—made me
wonder what on earth he'd think of Mary. We are a brutal generation—
brutalized—and yet admirable, too—but I wouldn't say "saintly," as you do!
James says wonderful things about naturalism—the more natural just means
the more art, etc.—but try to apply that to *The Naked Lunch*, say. (I am glad
your "blurb"[4] is rather careful—*não é*[5]?) I derived a Polly-Anna-ish pleasure
from that book. I'm so happy I'm not a drug addict. But it's really not good.
The notes and medical facts and omniscience remind me very much of
Poe—he's probably very much like Poe, don't you think?

This is all I have to say on this dreamy gray morning. OH—it's old to
you now—but we were glad to see your letter in the Hannah Arendt controversy.[6] Sometimes Americans are exactly as stupid as Latin Americans—at
least that display of self-interest and lack of any sense of irony, or recognition of irony, & inability to or just laziness about following an argument—
was exactly like the "intellectuals" here. I read the book sales almost stopped
for a while. I'm in the middle of *On Revolution* now—think we'll write her a
note.

  With much love to you and your family—
    Elizabeth

1 On August 28, 1963.
2 Mary McCarthy, "J. D. Salinger's Closed Circuit," *Harper's* (Dec. 1962).
3 See Vernon Lee's *Vanitas* (1892).
4 William Burroughs, *Naked Lunch* (France, 1959). RL wrote that the book was "completely powerful and serious"
and was "as good as anything in prose or poetry written by a 'beat' writer" (Grove publicity brochure for the U.S.
publication of *Naked Lunch*, 1962).
5 Isn't it?
6 On May 19, 1963, *The New York Times Book Review* published Michael A. Musmanno's "Man with an Unspoiled
Conscience," an attack on Hannah Arendt's *Eichmann in Jerusalem* (1963). RL wrote a letter to the editor: "I cannot think of a more terrifying character in either biography or fiction or of one conceived in quite this manner. That
Eichmann is no monster on a heroic scale, but only a strangely numb and nerve-wrung part of our usual world
makes him all the more appalling. Mediocre, banal, unable in the end to speak or even think the truth, he moves
through his inferno, now wriggling in his confusion, now flying on his 'gusts of elation.' His life is as close to living
in hell as I can imagine, and I am able to see it as such because Miss Arendt has refused to simplify the picture with
melodrama or blur it with clichés. I suspect Judge Musmanno's comprehension fails before so much detail, profun-
dity and intuition"; *The New York Times* (June 23, 1963).

281.

15 West 67 St., NYC
September 11, 1963

Dearest Elizabeth:

Well, we are back in town. How strange the sticky weather, and all the big architecture and lives seem. As we were driving into town along the Hudson, I half expected to [see] the buildings and even the horses of 1900, perhaps a recoil from expecting London last summer to look like New York. After going to a movie you feel in one.

I've never seen anything like Lizzie and the magazine. Instead of her somewhat murky Kentucky Scottish reserve, all is smiles, flutter and superlatives. The first regular issue comes out on the 26th of this month, and from then on it will be every two weeks. The editors have been interviewed for *Newsweek*, and Lizzie comes home from the office talking as Eve must have about work. I am collecting poetry for the magazine. There'll be one or two in each issue, about 35 or so for the year. Please send me anything you can spare from *The New Yorker*. The Drummond would be wonderful. The poem seemed marvelous to me, probably the best modern Brazilian poem (?) Could you write a few sentences explaining it and describing Drummond? I think that would help a lot. A short paragraph would do.[1]

You are so sweet about my poems. I think I must write entirely for you. I finally cut the Buenos Aires down to 8 stanzas from 14. The phallus is out, and the whole tone is now rather wistful and gentle—much better, I think, and I hope you'll approve. I enclose one more little thing, written a hundred times I guess since last fall, and still very slight.[2] I also have a nightmarish terza rima thing, that I don't know how to finish.[3]

I've put in a clipping from the N.Y. *Times* on Carlos, a harshly simplified account, though meant, I think, to be friendly.[4] It's nice to think he is gaining ground.

Well, saintly isn't quite the word for Mary, or what anyone would think reading the *Newsweek* spread on her. However, she was so kind to me and easy to talk to that I was rather stunned, and the new marriage does make for almost a transformation. "Unsordid," "no gossip," silly, but after Bowden, high praise.

---

1 EB, introduction to her translation of Carlos Drummond de Andrade's "The Table," *The New York Review of Books* (Jan. 16, 1969).
2 "The Mouth of the Hudson" (RL-*CP*).
3 "The Severed Head" (RL-*CP*).
4 "Brazil Revising Program," *The New York Times* (Sept. 8, 1963).

Hannah has been getting a flood of attacks, Lionel Abel in *PR* and Pod-horetz in *Commentary*,[1] wrong-headed but on rather a higher level than Musamanno. Lizzie suggested Abel to *PR* under the impression that he liked the book (which he did at first) and all this has had to be explained to Hannah. She seems unshaken, and says this book is [the] only one people can understand, so they strike at her.

What a mortality year for poets! Did you read about MacNeice's death?[2] I saw him in London looking very firm and in good spirits, though Bill Alfred said he would be dead soon from drinking. I liked some of his poems, more the early ones, very much. Always a smart mind and eye, and a spring to the rhythm.

I begin again at Harvard at the end of the month. My American play will definitely go on in March, and there will soon be readings etc. at the strange roomy old church where it is being done. So, a full year is coming. I am beginning to enjoy not drinking and am almost vain about it—what a change from last fall, with its mania followed by gloom.

Let me know if I can buy anything for you and Lota. All my love, and please excuse the chipper banality of this letter.

Love,
Cal

THE MOUTH OF THE HUDSON
A single man stands like a bird-watcher,
and scuffles the pepper and salt snow
from a discarded, gray
Westinghouse Electric cable drum.
He cannot discover America by counting
the chains of condemned freight-trains
from thirty states. They jolt and jar
and junk in the siding below him.
He has trouble with his balance.
His eyes drop,
and he drifts seaward with the wild ice
ticking seaward down the Hudson,
like the blank sides of a jig-saw puzzle.

1 Lionel Abel, "The Aesthetics of Evil: Hannah Arendt on Eichmann and the Jews," *Partisan Review* (Summer 1963); Norman Podhoretz, "Hannah Arendt on Eichmann: A Study in the Perversity of Brilliance," *Commentary* (Sept. 1963).
2 Louis MacNeice died on September 3, 1963. See "Louis MacNeice 1907–63" (RL-*CP*).

The ice ticks backward like a clock.
A negro toasts
wheat-seeds over the coke-fumes
in a punctured barrel.
Chemical air
sweeps in from New Jersey
and smells of coffee.

Across the river,
ledges of suburban factories tan
in the sulpher-yellow sun
of the unforgivable landscape.[1]

282.

[September 18, 1963]

Dearest Elizabeth—

Just a note. The *Review* would like [to] have as *much* as you feel like writing on Drummond, so do as much and as little as you think appropriate. I am trying to get Randall to do a piece for us on you—you and Emily Dickinson are the only people he wants to write on.

Great flurry. The first number of the *Review*, Harvard begins next week, our Trinidad poet is here,[2] everyone is returning. We seem more prepared for New York than in the former three years. I've mailed you, it will probably be months in arriving, a reproduction of that Chardin boy at the card table, which brings back our old trip to the National Gallery.[3] Please send me any spare poems or prose you have. I am playing around with translating Dante, and have done the Brunetto Canto,[4] and hope in the course of the winter and spring to do ten more.

Love,
Cal

Poor Brazil, that terrible fire![5]

1 Cf. "Those Before Us" (RL-*CP*).
2 Derek Walcott.
3 Jean-Baptiste-Siméon Chardin, *The House of Cards* (ca. 1735), National Gallery of Art, Washington, D.C.
4 "Brunetto Latini" (RL-*CP*).
5 For ten days in September 1963, forest fires spread through the state of Paraná, killing more than 145 people.

283.

Dearest Cal:

Forgive my long silence. I wrote you a long letter a week ago from Samambaia, but I've just torn it up—too stupid. We—or rather, Lota and Brazil—have had a peck of troubles lately—and Brazil still has more to come—but our personal ones do seem over for the time being. Poor L went and caught, of all things, *typhoid fever*—because she went back to work too soon, I suppose, and was weak enough to pick it up anywhere. I forget it's endemic here and we should never neglect the shots. It isn't nearly as bad as it used to be, with the new drugs for it—but the fever goes up, and UP, & UP—and it was quite frightening. When she got a bit better she went up to the country, with the maid, and *I* went to a hospital, just for a week's "rest cure" supposedly—a very funny experience—more later. Then I joined her up there and we spent two whole weeks doing nothing much, reading and loafing and listening to music. She seems almost like herself again, at last— and I wish she hadn't got so much "fighting spirit" back—there's too much going on for her to get into at present. I couldn't seem to make much sense when I tried to write letters—too much to catch up, too many things happening, etc. (I read a review of Fellini's "8½"[1] in which it said it was about someone who was "*stuck* because he was feeling too many things at the same time," and that's been my situation exactly, I see, for about two years . . .)

I have three letters from you here—or one and two kindly notes. I see you saw about the horrible fires in the south—the US Navy flew in a lot of help. All last week there was a ridiculous political situation—Goulart demanding a "state of siege."[2] Nobody knew quite why, because everything is calm enough, the calm of absolute despair, I think. He couldn't get it—then announced he hadn't wanted it, anyway! Now we have light rationing for an hour every night. Fortunately our turn to be last has come round, so our part of town is dark from 11:45 to 12:45—and we can just go to bed. But there's a threatened strike of gas and power for next week. If that occurs we'll just give up and go back to the country—being lucky enough to have a place to go to. Two nights ago, about 9, we had a mysterious telephone call from the Governor. He was at *our* house—no names could be mentioned—we had to inform various people . . . Mary[3] was very brave—saw a car race up, and col-

---

1 *8½*, dir. Federico Fellini (1963).
2 On October 3, Joâo Goulart requested permission from the National Congress to declare martial law to combat "subversion."
3 Mary Morse.

lected poor little "Manuelzinho" (in his underwear—he'd gone to bed—with his shot-gun) and went up. All lights on in our house and strange men on the terrace. Mary shouted at them, then who should appear but Carlos—all were armed. She went and had whiskey with them (& he almost never drinks so was obviously nervous.) We think—but don't know—he started off for his own house and was probably followed, or found his house surrounded, or something. There was an attempt to kidnap him last week, too. Parachutists jumped down on a hospital he was visiting!—absolutely crazy, of course . . . I really don't care to have our house used as a "hide-out" . . . puts us in an awful spot. But I suppose he had to go *somewhere*. Well—you see how bad things are getting—

Dos Passos has a book about Brazil out[1]—so shoddy I can't even read it—and so superficial. He sent it to Lota—mentions her various times, once as "a small woman in striped pants." L is furious; says she has never had a pair of striped pants in her life . . . I read THE GROUP at last—"Helena" is my oldest friend[2]—we went to school, camp, and college together—but she was a year ahead, and in "the Group"—I wasn't. She and her mother and Mary's first husband, and Eunice Clarke Jessup[3] are the only ones I really recognize—and Mary herself, split up into two or three. All the details of her first marriage and the 30's in N.Y. are remarkably real again. But I can't *attempt* to tell how good it is, really—it's like trying to remember a dream, to me.— Some parts are awfully funny—the scene in the park, etc.—wonderful. I'm sure those set-fire-works-sex-pieces will insure huge sales. I admire her for doing it, really—

(hairdressing appointment—)

*   *   *   *   *

Well—just discovered, in the elevator, that the Swiss lady who's lived all those years on the 8th floor is passionately fond of old music and gives lessons on the *recorder*—etc. When she heard I have a Dolmetsch clavichord she nearly swooned. She's been trying to get one for years & just returned from a month in England studying with the whole Dolmetsch clan, apparently—so I've just been accompanying her on her ancient piano. We went through a Handel sonata very nicely—she playing the alto flute—didn't

---

1 John Dos Passos, *Brazil on the Move* (1963).
2 Frani Blough Muser.
3 Eunice Clark Jessup and her sister Eleanor Clark studied at Vassar with EB.

know I could still play that well.[1] I really think I'll go and play with her sometimes!— At least bring the clavichord down here, since she knows someone who can get it tuned and in condition for me. Strange—we've met in the elevator and on the beach occasionally for 10 yrs. An atmosphere like *Madame Weems*, one of my old piano teachers—coffee with cream, German mottoes about, lots of *embroidery*—

*   *   *   *   *

Riots in the Senate about Carlos—one group wants to investigate the "attack on his life," most of the others don't want to, naturally—and they came to blows. What an unseemly mess. Goulart would do almost anything to get rid of him, but at the same time doesn't want to make a martyr of him, of course, because then he'd be apt to get elected President. That clipping you sent from the N.Y. *Times* was so wrong. How can they get things so wrong, I wonder. I'd like to know what Gordon really thinks. I'd like to call up Kennedy! It's almost too bad they *didn't* get martial law—that would have shown the rest of the world how bad things are, perhaps. Carlos would have been exiled to the Amazonas, probably—if he hadn't escaped first.

Well—and now TIME—I've just waded through that—is beating the drums for Goldwater. Save us. They wrote and asked me to do a small revision job on the *Brazil* book—not much work and a hunk of money, but in about ten days, of course—and it did me good to Tel-Ex back N O . . .

We did enjoy the records up in the country. Sutherland is awfully good, isn't she. I also had a marvelous blues record—Robert Johnson—I recommend it highly.[2] He was murdered in 1938 at the age of 20—one of his ladyfriends. If you like blues—it's superb, the real thing. (Eliz. wd like him, I think)

It is sad about MacNeice—I liked his early poems very much and have two books of his—those lovely descriptions of Ireland, etc. Do please stick to tea—I mean tea, not pot! (Someone wrote me you're holding a tea-cup at the St. Cloud picnic . . .) Such a sad poem by Roethke in an English review, "I know my drinking hides the wish to die"[3]—one line something like that.

Flávio was up for one night with us to get me to help him fill out all the application blanks—dozens of them.

---

1 When EB went to Vassar, she intended to major in music but switched to English.
2 Robert Johnson, *King of the Delta Blues Singers* (Columbia, 1961).
3 "From a burnt pine the sharp speech of a crow / Tells me my drinking breeds a will to die"; Theodore Roethke, "The Marrow," lines 3–4, *The New Statesman* (Aug. 9, 1963).

Later: and just at that moment Flávio arrived, to go on filling out forms. He had written two really *good* poems—I think he should publish them here, and then send them to Harvard, too. I'm not exaggerating—they're influenced by João Cabral de Melo, but are really "felt." I am hoping so much this Harvard business works out. If he could take junior & senior years . . . It seems to me his qualifications are excellent and his English is getting better all the time. His French is also excellent. He got 100 in the Foreign Affairs English exam—takes another this month. I see Harvard even has a "School of Diplomacy" and maybe he could go to that—since he's already entered in Foreign Service here. He's improving a lot, really. Even looks a *lot* better and is gradually changing his hair-do to something a bit less European-looking. (I've refrained from comment on this, of course, but am relieved.)

How is Harriet? In the 2nd grade now? And E is busy with the *NY Review*—and you are commuting to Harvard? If you ever see Nathalie please give her my love. (She doesn't seem to be in "The Group"—or just a few vague references) Heavens—is she partly "Lakey"?!—Swan = Lake?? Life was so much pleasanter up in the country—I wish we could go back & stay. I do go up to my vacant apartment to work, mornings here, and that's a help—but the city's unpleasant these days, and Lota works too hard and we both get too tired. I suppose it will take time to get back to feeling normal again.

Oh—I went to a small hospital away up near that Christ. It used to be a wonderful clean, quiet place for just that kind of exhaustion—run by 7th Day Adventists, vegetarian, hymn-singing, etc., but good. However, after I got there (& couldn't face moving) I discovered that, in order to make ends meet, in the past year they've had to go in with one of the "syndiactos," or unions—and the place has gone to pots, as L says. I give it about 2 more months. It was—as I said to L!—like a combined church picnic and trip to Yugoslavia. The little garden has been ruined.— I screamed from my balcony one day at a couple of young hoodlums calmly tearing the slats off a bench. Fat men in pajamas, and fat ladies, each with two or three shrieking children and a pocket radio, throng the place—at all hours. No visiting hours kept any more, no quiet, nothing—cockroaches moving in, and black beans and meat on the menu once a day . . . It was a glimpse into the future, I'm afraid. When I asked the doctors or nurses about it they just shrugged and said, "That's the way things are these days . . ." and when I tried preaching my own gospel of brightening—or at least cleaning up—the corner where you are, etc., I think they thought I was really mad—a mad foreigner. However, I did begin to feel better and then minded the racket less, and the food is excellent—for Brazil—and the view superb—fantastic—particularly at night. I've almost done a short poem about it.

Your "Mouth of the Hudson" is *very* nice, and I suppose because of reading *The Group*, it takes me right back to all the train trips back and forth to & from Poughkeepsie, along the Hudson, in the gray winters.

Gottlieb got first prize at the São Paulo Bienale. We can't decide whether to go down for it or not—I am SICK of abstract art all of a sudden—and Siamese abstract art and Swiss abstract art, and Chilean AA, and so on, makes me weary to think of. Also US "pop" sculpture.

What "American" play of yours? All three of them? Please tell me all about it.— I'm about to go see the French modern *Phaedre* in the movies.[1] Wilbur sent his *Tartuffo*[2]—haven't read it yet. Burle Marx is off doing the UNESCO garden in Paris. Thank you, my dear *collega*—but you can't buy me anything at all (you asked)! If the Theodorides-es come back, I'll ask to use their address again & ask for some more records—but at present there's nothing, and no safe way of sending anything. I lose about half my mail—so should really write you half a page at a time, oftener. I'm afraid this is a second stupid letter, but I'll send this one. However, I am, we are, feeling better all the time—and I hope, brighter. Please write when you can and tell me about the city's gay life.— I hope you're well—I hated that photograph of you in the *Observer*[3]—not good at all . . . Oh—I saw Mary in *Newsweek*—I didn't think the article was too bad—not compared to TIME, at least—but that, too, was such a bad picture—not a bit like Mary; she's much prettier than that.

With much love,
Elizabeth

"Vinícius"[4]—you remember him?—has contracted his 5th marriage—run off with a 20-year old girl, daughter of the Italian Ambassador or Consul—and she was engaged to someone else. The young man who was thrown over challenged V to a fight. Then when they "went outside," he looked at poor sick drunken V, and just gave up and walked away. V left a letter for the parents—saying he knew it was bad behavior for a "diplomat," but as a "poet" he couldn't help himself . . . Everyone pities the girl . . .

1 *Phaedra*, dir. Jules Dassin (1962).
2 Molière, *Tartuffe*, trans. Richard Wilbur (1963).
3 A. Alvarez, "Robert Lowell in Conversation," *The Observer* (July 21, 1963).
4 Vinícius de Moraes.

I've had some enchanting notes from Drummond—I'll try to send "The Table" in a couple of weeks—and perhaps something *original*—

About my "rest home"—for Godssake don't think I'm against the "people" having decent hospitals!— But the "sindicatos" really have a good many, you know— It just is a pity there isn't one small place left where someone like me can go! (Our maid's "best friend" has been sick for 2 years—3 operations—one like Lota's only worse—and hasn't had to pay a penny—her "sindicato" paid all.)

P.S.—October 14th—I've at last read Abel's attack on Hannah Arendt. It seems to me he's making the same mistakes as Judge M, on a somewhat higher level . . . Neither of them—nor the other attackers—seem to get "irony." Even if it's *true*, in some countries, or some cities, that the fact of the Jews being organized led to their destruction—nothing that I remember in Hannah's book implies that *therefore* they shouldn't have been organized! I thought the pieces—I read them in *The New Yorker*,[1] not the book—were an impressive example of sustained bitter irony—the irony of history, after all—man proposes, history disposes. And I completely agree with her about the "banality" of evil and think Abel quite wrong.

But his article sounds personal, don't you think?—there's some spitefulness or jealousy at work, I'm pretty sure. I hope the next number will have some good refutations.

284.

Rio, October 17, 1963

Dearest Cal:

I mailed you a big letter the first of the week—big & boring—and now I'll add a sort of postscript—and surely you'll get one of them . . .

I have found an awfully good teacher for Portuguese—she needs some help with her degree from Cambridge (did you know that Cambridge carries on a huge correspondence school and you can get degrees by mail?)—and she is helping me with LA MESA[2]—which ought to be done in a week or two. Perhaps I'll ask Drummond to write his own autobiographical sketch. I also hope to send you a small group of my own. (I haven't had a contract with *The New Yorker* for several years now.)

---

1 *Eichmann in Jerusalem* was first published in five *New Yorker* articles between February and March 1963.
2 "The Table" (EB-*CP*).

The drought is so bad that the city is almost without water, and we are going up to Samambaia at dawn tomorrow for a long weekend—and won't come back, probably, until it has rained. Alas—the sun just came out again—the longest dry spell in 70 years. Why does everything here have to be so exaggerated? I've just read the papers and at last thought of the adjective for Brazil—EXPOSED. There is light rationing for an hour a night (power depends on rainfall, too) and if it doesn't rain this week it will go to three hours, then four, etc. . . . We have some oil lamps—and kerosene always seems to be getting on the toast. Lota's friends "at the top" have told us we might as well stay up in the country for a while—*unless it rains, hard.* (There's a lovely old samba that begins *"Se não chover . . ."* "If it doesn't rain, my mullatinha, I'll come to see you," etc., etc.)

Do you really think Flávio has a good chance of getting a scholarship? The booklet they send is discouraging—only 20 transfer students a year. It is also encouraging—if he does get in, apparently they will keep him no matter what, almost—the required marks seem very low. I ask you this because the poor boy is getting so excited at the prospect I can't bear to think he might not get in; and also—he'd turn against the US all over again,—his feelings are ambivalent as it is. We have to hide the whole plan from his mother until the last minute. His father is very anti-US and says all American students do is drink. Lota says—"but even so he'll like having Flávio go there—he can say—'My son is a terrible drunk, at HARVARD . . .' " HE brought me the first batch of forms yesterday—and I am really amazed at the letters he'd composed in English. I did NOT help him with them, except to suggest that he double-space after a full stop. But I don't see how I can tell Mr. Glimp this!— The only mistake was to spell English with a small *e*. In his "autobiography" he said that meeting you was "a thrilling privilege." Poor boy—he really works so hard. It seems he has a bit of real estate and will sell it. That should give him about $1,500—to stretch over two years, I hope—for spending money. It would be so much better if he didn't have to work on the side. We can get him his plane tickets, I am pretty sure—and also the Embassy here might come across with some financial aid—according to their booklets—if he actually gets a scholarship. However—Borer, Bore-up, and Co. are undoubtedly going to be annoyed at my "going over their heads." One nice thing about Flávio—he doesn't seem to realize at all how very easily he does learn and how easily he writes.

Rachel de Queiroz *has* been offered a trip to the US—she, too, is excited—and is dickering with them to be able to take her husband along, too. Her this week's column is a letter of mine she translated—against

ruining the landscape with signboards—but pretty funny, if I do say so myself . . .

I was sent a photostat of the cover of the music of "Visits to St. E's" by
Cocteau.[1] It must be one of his very last drawings. The usual Cocteau thing,
but a weird wreath of names around it: Ned Rorem, Ezra P, E.B., and
Cocteau—(the only one I really like is E.B.)

I read somewhere that Mary was attacking Edel's H. James books—in
SHOW (?) magazine—if so, could you tear it out and send it to me? I'd like
to see—I missed her on Salinger but this I'd like to see— What a dull letter!—well,

    With bright & shiny affection,
    Elizabeth

285.

October 27, 1963

Dearest Elizabeth:

What a time you all have been through with sickness and political turmoil. I waited breathlessly while Goulart's martial law was hanging in the
air. Sometimes I've wondered, almost enviously, what it must have been like
to have lived in the Paris of revolutions, faction, barricades. But I can see it is
only deadly, waiting with fever in your joints for your temperature to rise.

We had our little New York outburst, a Hannah Arendt evening presided
over by Irving Howe.[2] Hannah wasn't there and most of the talk went
against her. One was suddenly in a pure Jewish or Arabic world, people
hardly speaking English, declaiming, confessing, orating in New Yorkese, in
Yiddish, booing and clapping. The fire of the evening fell not on Hannah,
but on Raul Hilberg, who had written a documentary book on the Jewish ex-
terminations,[3] a book hitherto uncontroversial, but which he now quoted
original documents from and ended rather unadvisably by suggesting that
the Jews were passive by religion and even now couldn't face the facts. Then
Lionel Abel, frothing, gesturing, thumping on the table, called him banal,
boring, etc. And from then on the Jews were anything but passive. Well, it
was alive, but very rash, cheap, declamatory, etc., a sort of mixture of, say,
Irish nationalists and an Alcoholics Anonymous meeting with contending
sides. A lot of mud was thrown at Hannah, and one left disheartened and

1 *Ned Rorem Songs*, Regina Sarfaty, soprano (1964), with a black-and-white cover drawing by Jean Cocteau.
2 Hosted by *Dissent* magazine.
3 Raul Hilberg, *The Destruction of the European Jews* (1961).

even a bit scared. However, the next night there was a party, where all the contending factions were represented, though only the more articulate intellectuals. And somehow, there seemed to have been a catharsis, and everyone was friendly and relieved that what had been brewing for months had somehow boiled off. There's nothing like the New York Jews. Odd that this is so, and that other American groups are so speechless and dead.

I'm not speechless, what with teaching, occasional readings, a TV show with Kunitz on Roethke. I feel always in motion and quite frivolous and rattle-brained, though pretty calm and even dull by not drinking. Life's fairly enjoyable, but every so often I look back and see only the confused flotsam of a hundred quickly done, half-done, ill-done efforts. I'll be glad when the term's over, and wish I could spend a week on [a] hospital bed, like you, resting. So, I suppose, one fills up, but can anything be well-done that isn't accompanied by dreaming, sloth, contemplation, leisure? I feel I am tied by a wire to a plane swooping back and forth between Boston and New York.

Have you read the posthumous poems by Sylvia Plath? A terrifying and stunning group has come out in the last *Encounter*.[1] You probably know the story of her suicide.[2] The poems are all about it. They seem as good to me as Emily Dickinson at the moment. Of course they are as extreme as one can bear, rather more so, but whatever wrecked her life somehow gave an edge, freedom and even control, to her poetry. There's a lot of surrealism which relieves the heat of direct memory, touches of me, and I'm pretty sure touches of your quiet and humor. She is far better certainly than Sexton or Seidel, and almost makes one feel at first reading that almost all other poetry is about nothing. Still, it's searingly extreme, a triumph by a hair, that one almost wished had never come about.

Harriet is having her tonsils out this week. She is quite a little lady now, learning to read, answering the phone, assembling collages of corks, package handles, drawings of boats, etc. Oh, oh, oh, how time whirls us on! Do you realize that we have already outlived more than half the classic English poets. I suppose they knew no more than we what it all meant. What scatterings of experience. I do feel though that I've lost a few unbelievably narrow and stubborn poses. Do you ever feel that you have almost learned enough at last to be ready to be reborn with profit?

---

1 Sylvia Plath, "Death & Co.," "The Swarm," "The Other," "Getting There," "Lady Lazarus," "Little Fugue," "Childless Woman," "The Jailor," "Thalidomide," and "Daddy," *Encounter* (Oct. 1963).
2 Plath committed suicide on February 11, 1963.

Pardon this flurry. It's just in the nerves. I wish I could spend a few weeks with you. Let us know if we can do anything to help in this troubled moment.

Love,

Cal

286.

Dearest Cal:

I haven't really anything much to say to you—the last days have been like a bad dream, of course—but I feel like writing you a note. Lota came home early from work Friday to tell me about Kennedy[1] before I heard it on the radio. Although there's been a radio and TV strike for a week or so and only the Ministry of Education radio keeps going. The papers all got out special editions that night. We were out and the sight of the crowds was awfully moving—the streets full of people, the newsstands mobbed, and many people crying openly. The grief here has been genuine, all right—they felt, rightly or wrongly, that Kennedy was a friend of Brazil's. You know Brazilians are much more formal about death than we are now. I must have had fifteen or twenty telephone calls and quite a few calls in person—of "condolence." They feel so much closer to their politicians than we do, too—all American[s] should feel as if they'd lost a relative, to their way of thinking. And they have much quicker emotional responses than Anglo-Saxons—or than I have, at any rate. Lota had lunch with Carlos today, and he said he was just beginning to feel normal again; whereas today's the day I'm really beginning to feel badly.

One TV station came back on finally, and so we've probably seen some of the same awful newsreels you have—those blown-up cars swaying like gelatin around curves, those fat Texas faces, solemn and stupid, those endless views of cops' backsides covered with holsters and cartridges . . . Oh God what a mess. Perhaps some of it will have been cleared up by the time you get this, but I'm afraid it's going to drag on and on.

Friends of ours just came back from three months in Washington and Philadelphia—Americans—and they say they are glad to get back, horrible as the situation is here. They found the atmosphere there very Sodom &

---

1 John F. Kennedy was assassinated on November 22, 1963.

Gomorrah-ish I gather—money money money and dreadful Negro troubles. Well—here we're expecting a *golpe*[1] (from the president) at any moment. Today and yesterday the hottest so far, and VERY hot—and sort of the last straw, as far as the strikes go, is a grave-diggers' strike . . . no embalming here, and not enough refrigeration!

*   *   *   *   *

We go swimming very early—7 AM—to cool off for the day. Lota is fine, amazingly well, but depressed about the country—the park is going well, thank goodness.

I wrote to Wesleyan about Flávio, too—just not to have all our eggs in one basket, although I have a feeling Harvard will take him. So maybe you'll be hearing from Wesleyan, too, if you don't mind . . .

I'm about to go and read at the "American School"—a "select" high school group. Oh dear, why do I accept these things! It's partly your fault—you were so generous when you were here, I think I have to be, too! The Americans say that the word "Group" has become popular slang already. I am just waiting to get THE TABLE *back* from Drummond to send it on to the *N.Y. Review.*— He's taking a long time.

Oh—Sunday night people here started putting candles in the windows for Kennedy—a spontaneous demonstration—all over the city. There have been many masses, indoors and out. The biggest ones will be the 7th Day masses though. I listened to Cushing—and hated to think that millions probably were, he has such a dragged-out, hypocritical-sounding delivery.

With much love as always,
Elizabeth

How is the theatre project going?

287.

Rio, January 22nd, 1964

Dearest Cal:

It's been ages since I heard from you—sometime back in early November—and I do hope you are all right. The mails have been hopeless—so perhaps things have got lost—either way. I recently got some magazines from

---

1 Coup d'état.

September, in a batch, and a large *pink* envelope addressed to "The Bishop of the Methodist Church, Brazil."

This is just to say I have written—twice, I think—once shortly after the awful Kennedy affair. About two weeks ago I wrote & sent a small poem that I'm afraid you will consider what you call "carpentry work."[1] This week I'll send the Drummond—I'm back in Rio after almost a month in Samambaia, and I've at last got things back from him and have a little changing to do. If the *N.Y. Review* can use "The Table" (this should more properly be written to Elizabeth)—could you please send him *two copies?*

Rua Conselheiro Lafayette, 60
Copacabana, Rio de Janeiro

Also—(if they can use it)—a check for half the honorarium . . .

Also sometime in early November, I think, I sent a check to the *N.Y. Review* for a year's subscription and asked please to begin with the first number—all the back numbers, that is, since it started up again in the fall. I've got the cancelled check so they did receive it but no reviews so far. Do you think someone could inquire about this? I've heard reports, etc., and naturally I have been dying to see it, from the first new issue . . . (I think a lot of books and magazines must be held up somewhere—it's discouraging.)

All goes well here personally, and Lota's work is going famously. As for politics—well, we keep our fingers crossed, that's all. Anything may happen in the next few months.

I wonder how your theatre plans worked out, and if Phaedre has already been put on?

I think I also wrote you that I am also applying for Flávio (L's nephew) to Wesleyan—just not to have all our eggs in one basket. Dick Wilbur wrote me sometime before Christmas that you and Elizabeth were to be there next year?—and Hannah Arendt—only I thought she'd already been there. If you hear from them—I'm afraid I've already asked this—I'm sure you'd be good enough to recommend him there, too? He is in a tizzy—so eager to go it breaks my heart. He's improving a lot—passed all his awful law & theology exams at the university (I didn't think he would), and has produced two or three more poems—really quite good. Now he's doing movie criticism . . . He's also grown a lot, or filled out, or something—anyway, seems pretty manly, and very hirsute—

1 The letter does not survive.

I hope you and your family are all well—heavens, I wish I'd hear from you! I think of you often—and read you often—

Love,

Elizabeth

I wonder if you got the record I sent for Christmas?—from *Liberty*—or did that order get lost, too—

288.

Dearest Elizabeth:

You have a right to be rather flurried by my silence. As you probably know from Lizzie's letter I have been in a hospital for the last six weeks.[1] It was never really bad, and now seems like a brief fevered moment in a year that now takes up where it paused. Well, six weeks of retirement, looking at TV, talking to casual acquaintances in the sanitarium, and I am sorry to say, not answering letters. These attacks still come, but on the whole they throw me less and less off balance.

Today, I have been home a week, and am spiritless and loggy from commenting on my Harvard term papers and poems. Pardon my languor, Dear, if I don't answer everything or write a very entertaining letter. The 12th Night poem is marvelous.[2] It has the form, tightness and charm of some of your early poems, such as the one about the little horse and rider,[3] but translated into nature and direct observation. I carry it around in my bill-fold, and it seems comparable to, "The Armadillo" that I have long cherished. I think you and Auden are writing the best poems now in English; only you two have the form and personality and fullness of great poetry. Could I have mislaid "The Table"? I don't seem to have ever gotten it. I am sure the *Review* will want it. In my letter I only meant to say that Drummond was the best Brazilian poet. I, too, wouldn't think he had the power of Neruda.

From the sanitarium I called up Bill Alfred about Flávio again, and he

---

1 "Cal has been sick again, but nothing very serious. He began to get a little keyed-up around Thanksgiving and we tried to treat it with drugs at home because it was so mild, but there were so many people around and so much activity that he wasn't able to calm down. The doctor sent him to a hospital in Hartford, and he got better immediately. He was at home for a few days last week—and read your poem and your letter—and will be home in three days for good. It wasn't bad. And he doesn't seem too much discouraged. He has a lot of work to do when he gets out and that is his salvation"; Elizabeth Hardwick to EB, January 17, 1964 (Vassar).

2 "Twelfth Morning; or What You Will," *The New York Review of Books* (April 2, 1964); EB-*CP*.

3 "Cirque D'Hiver" (EB-*CP*).

seemed to think his admission was certain. I'll check up again tomorrow when I return to Harvard with my papers. Your record came, in the sense that we got a notice giving a choice of any Kirkpatrick in the catalogue. Yours wasn't in it, or had another number. I'm afraid the pink package to the Methodist Bishop isn't mine, but did you get the Chardin picture? The whole series of the *Reviews* will start flooding toward you. There's tons to disagree with of course, but the whole is awfully readable and dazzling. Lizzie unfortunately is up to her neck in controversy, first Mary (for her parody and Mailer's review) and now Arthur Schlesinger for a Washington sketch.[1] She has decided, to my relief, to lay off people we know. Hornets buzz outside but we are at peace at home.

I think I now have a book done, to be called *For the Union Dead*, and adding up to 35 poems. It will be out in September and I'll send you galleys when I have them. I think there are half a dozen poems you haven't seen. I suppose the book tries to be an advance, whatever that means, or a sort of combination of *Life Studies* and the more metrical style of my earlier stuff. I hope you'll like it. It's a little like your work, each single poem an entity, un-helped by previous poems, though I am afraid I have far more monotony and haste.

I worry about each notice from Brazil, and have no way of telling how really threatening each new disturbance is. One prays that Carlos is indestructible. I had a talk with Arthur Schlesinger the other day (while in Washington reading a little piece I had written on the Gettysburg Address[2]) *about Carlos*, and found he felt much the same as we do.

Kennedy's murder was a terrible trauma for all of us. At first it seemed the work of a Southern fanatic, then of a leftist plot. I found myself weeping through the first afternoon, then three days of television uninterrupted by advertising till the grand, almost unbearable funeral. I guess it had something to do with my crack-up. The country went through a moment of terror and passionate chaos with everyone talking wildly, and deeply fearful and suspicious. Then there was the unbelievable relief of everything seeming to go well under Johnson. Now there's the let-down, a general prosiness perhaps, and the return to thousands of every day personal and national problems. Maybe it's just my nature, but one seems to see-saw from a sort of rosy blandness to a blank, bare, cracking feeling. It's like swimming across a pond littered with pieces of wood; one wonders if one has the energy to

---

1 Elizabeth Hardwick (writing under the pseudonym Xavier Prynne), "The Gang," *The New York Review of Books* (Sept. 26, 1963) and "Grub Street: Washington," *The New York Review of Books* (Jan. 24, 1964). Norman Mailer, "The Mary McCarthy Case," *The New York Review of Books* (Oct. 17, 1963).
2 "On the Gettysburg Address," Library of Congress, January 3, 1964 (see RL-*CPR*).

push through it all, then one floats gaily and the curry[1] draws one forward.

I wish every now and then and quite often, we two could have more days on the beach, talking unhurriedly and watching the surf break.

The place where I was staying was called the Hartford Institute of Living, a grand Utopian title. It's much better being out and alive. My Harvard appointment has been renewed for two years. This week will be my last until next September. Rehearsing for a reading of my play begins in two weeks. The play will go on in September. We plan to go to Castine this summer. Harriet can read and write.

My love to Lota, and all my love to you.

Cal

Thanks worlds for everything: letters, present and poem.

289.

March 10, 196[4]

Dearest Elizabeth:

It's an iron-black warm New York morning that reminds me of Europe. With the heat turned off in my study, I hear the great huffle of nature outside and almost feel I were voyaging off into the Atlantic, till I look up and see the stationary sky-line of little sky-scrapers and wooden water towers.

There was a piece in the *Times* this morning about Goulart taking over the oil refineries and a lot of land[2]—gloomy U.S. ponderings on continued unrest. I hope there's no new trouble.

I have been listening to readings of my play for a week, and feel it is something a ghost wrote and signed my name to.[3] I have a brilliant bubbling young Englishman, Jonathan Miller, directing, and some rather optimistic but heavy drama people managing the production. I feel in a very alien element, and back Miller whenever there's division of opinion. The play has power, I think, and great length, almost four hours.

Well, the daze of returning to myself seems to be clearing and cheering. I've just finished my first new poem in months, the inner stirrings of a character, half me and part Gerard Nerval.[4] I once translated a lot of his sonnets,

1 Current?
2 Tad Szulc, "Brazil Prepares to Seize Farms and Refineries," *The New York Times* (March 10, 1963).
3 *My Kinsman, Major Molineux* and *Benito Cereno*, directed by Jonathan Miller, premiered at the American Place Theatre on November 1, 1964.
4 "Going to and Fro"; in a manuscript draft of the poem, RL dedicated the poem to "Nerval or someone" (RL-*CP*; see 1,060–61).

but the French was so simple that they almost seemed to exist already in English, and somehow their Keats-like richness was rickety and stilted in my words. I've also done a long dirge by Anna Akhmatova on her son who was taken off to Siberia in the 30's.[1] Her style is a graceful, feminine pre–Marianne Moore one, but her grief has great grandeur. Strange to write from behind such a mask!

Next week a series of readings begins, Greensboro, Toronto, Delaware, Kenyon, Baltimore. The map! Last week I did my first, and answered all the old questions that I know no answers to, the roles of poet, obscurity, what do I think of John Brinnin. By the way, there's an awful, pale dull play now running on Thomas, called *Dylan*, Alec Guinness badly miscast in the lead and a tall full-haired youth, playing John Malcolm Brinnin.[2]

I haven't read much that held me lately except [a] short autobiography by Dahlberg, *Because I Was Flesh*,[3] a marvelous, realistic, loaded with Montaigne-like classical references dirge on his Mother, a lady barber, and now Larkin's new book.[4] Rather sad now about his unmarried middle-age, but always witty, quiet and his own in style. Reading him, I had a feeling that you were the crown of his whole group, humor, the authentic tone, nothing put in to make poetry. But none of them have your splendor!

Your poem will be out in the issue after the next, I think. Everyone is very excited and proud of it. We must thank you for your present, we finally got a delightful *Goldberg Variations*.[5]

I think about you both daily. Send some news and another poem or poems. The family sends its love, and I all mine,

Cal

290.

April 3, 1964

Dearest Elizabeth:

All sounds calm and at peace in Brazil for the last day and a half, but I am still reeling as I try to imagine the stir of the last few days and surely the last weeks or months.[6] I dimly followed the marine mutiny, but our last direct

---

1 "Requiem" (RL-*CP*).
2 Sidney Michaels, *Dylan*, dir. Peter Glenville, opened at the Plymouth Theatre in January 1964; see John Malcolm Brinnin, *Dylan Thomas in America: An Intimate Journal* (1955).
3 Published in 1963.
4 Philip Larkin, *The Whitsun Weddings* (1964).
5 Ralph Kirkpatrick's 1959 recording of Johann Sebastian Bach's *Goldberg Variations*.
6 In 1963 and 1964, the political situation in Brazil was increasingly dangerous, with inflation rampant (currency

Brazilian report was several months ago from Keith, who said Goulart was offering Carlos' police higher wages in the army, and that C. was in an increasingly perilous position. So, the overturn came without a whisper or warning.[1]

Our cable must sound unduly worried, but the news changed rapidly. I was in Toronto on a two days' visit and reading. The last news I read there was that the marines were attacking the barricaded governor's palace and at the same instant Carlos' police were trying to storm the little Copacabana fort. As I flew home, there was a clear sky over the Atlantic when we reached it, and I pictured the same moon, thousands of miles south, shining on the same ocean, everything strangely nearer because the sandy shore led like a road to you, and in the mind one might walk it, and be lost as I then thought in conflicting knots of thin helmeted soldiers. Thank God it's all over. I realize that since I left Brazil all was simmering and that one week told little of what would be the reality the next. I trust the change has lessoned[2] the darkness for you and Lota and the country. Do write and tell what has been going on with you, and all that your eye lit on.

What is your personal news? I gathered from Howard Moss the other night that you have written a new long poem and that you are planning very soon a trip to London. Will you come by here—not much on the way I fear. Do you want to be in Brazil for the new order or are you eager to get away from it temporarily? I hate to think of all the strain you must have had. Here one had at times a wild wish to be on the scene. Goulart seems to have disintegrated like one of those sand houses or churches on the Copacabana beach, but it must have seemed much more fearful and hazardous from moment to moment. Carlos is everywhere here: news accounts, pictures, editorials, interviews, talking English on TV. The picture is very favorable to him, but simplified and less brilliant, bold, colorful than memory remembers. Give him our warmest wishes, etc. I felt very stricken when I thought he was in danger.

Not much news with us. We both went to the Greensboro writing festival

---

having one-tenth the value of two years previous), and political rhetoric on the right and the left escalating. At a large Rio rally on March 13, President João Goulart promised to confiscate land and nationalize private companies. Goulart's opponents accused him of pro-communist leanings and feared he would overthrow the constitution and seize total power. On April 1, the military staged a coup d'etat.

1 On March 27, 1964, *The New York Times* reported that "leftist" sailors and marines had mutinied against its officers in support of João Goulart. A navy minister appointed by Goulart pardoned the mutineers, to the outrage of the Brazilian military, which used the controversy to execute its plot to overthrow Goulart. Carlos Lacerda supported the military coup.

2 Lessened?

and saw Randall, older, smaller, grayer, and still rather shaken by the jaundice he had over a year ago and aggravated by Italian cooking this fall. He is still full of intuitions, knowledge and certainties, a grizzled belief in joy and excellence, noble and a little sad. I gave him my new book with misgivings, hardly knowing what I thought of it myself, and sure that his dislike would be unbearable. But he liked it, and thought it was my best book, and said I had the same absolutely right details that you have. On Monday I go to the University of Delaware for ten days, where I'll be received by an accomplished but unintelligible poet named Huff, but my old friend Peter Taylor will also be there, so it should be fun. Then Kenyon for two days, then nothing else till Maine, except for a reading in Baltimore.

The old get older. I've seen Marianne Moore a couple of times, once introducing Auden very wittily calling him a "fantast who was also a sage," and ending with a humorous quote from Auden that all ills of the body were ills of the soul, and "I give you Mr. Auden." Then later at a small poets party for Vernon Watkins, where for all her fragility she stayed with us 7 hours talking. Her baseball is way over my head.[1] So is John Ransom's aesthetics and philosophy. He came here for the National Book Award[2] with his post box key instead of his suitcase key, no money except his ticket, and hardly knew his hotel, yet talked with fascinating merry complexity on Kant, Valéry and Stevens. Eliot too is apparently very weak and old and fearful to be far from his wife, yet sang me a humorous song called "Mr. Caruso" on the phone.

Oh dear, let me say goodbye. Things in Brazil still sound a bit confused, but I feel such relief for you both. Dear Lota must have had her hands and mind full. How we trembled for you when the first vague news began to break! Dare I say that I hope there was humor and pleasure, as well as trouble for you in the simmering days before the overturn?

All my love,
Cal

We are both so unspeakably relieved for you and Lota! Rio scenes and memories have been spinning through my head for the last three days like movie shots.

---

1 Marianne Moore, "Baseball and Writing," *The New Yorker* (Dec. 9, 1961), reprinted in *The Arctic Ox* (1964).
2 John Crowe Ransom's *Selected Poems*, rev. and enl. ed. (1963), won the National Book Award.

291.

Dear Lowellzinhos:

Mary[1] just read me a cable from you over the telephone—since we are not going up to Samambaia this week-end.[2] I don't know when you sent it (this is Saturday morning)—but thank you very much and if I can send one, I'll try to reply this afternoon . . . Although I can't think what to say. "Everything fine" isn't right, not "calm and order" . . . nor "Reforms, yes; Communism, no . . ." nor—"Catholic Mothers against Communism . . ." "Reforms yes Communism no" would be all right if I felt a bit more hopeful . . . Well, it was a nice quick revolution in the rain—all over in less than 48 hours.[3] In fact we felt a weird let-down, having steeled ourselves to live beside the radio & TV, laid in many bags of coffee; I'd *baked*, there was no bread— etc.—also roasted a leg of pork! since we thought the gas would be cut off. Now we're eating it all up . . . Modern revolutions, I've learned, are funny—everything goes but the telephone, because it's automatic—so everyone sits in the dark, unwashed, etc. and telephones their friends all day and all night.

Lota and one other woman were the only ones in Guanabara Palace (Carlos's). She had a safe-conduct from one of the generals and went in and out, through the President's troops, which surrounded the palace. All the men inside showing each other their guns, etc.— But the place couldn't have stood an assault, there were only 100 soldiers, with just small arms. April 1, Carlos broadcast an appeal for *help*, sounding really desperate. I got it in short wave—around by way of the State of Minas, since the Gov. held the radio stations here and we just got a lot of lies and the National Anthem for two days. That was the worst moment—I knew Lota was inside—she'd insisted on going back—or hoped she was, and not picked up by the Federal army. However—an hour later it was all over. *All* the army came over and turned against Goulart—and he'd already run away, but we didn't know it. Then there was a great pouring out of people into the streets—showers of paper, flags, music, etc. I drove out with a friend to see the city. Down on the

---

1 Mary Morse.

2 The cable (referred to by RL in letter 290) does not survive.

3 The coup appeared to many Brazilians a spontaneous uprising by the military to protect local administrative structures and defend the Brazilian constitution. Military leaders, under Chief of Staff General Humberto Castelo Branco, presented themselves as temporary guardians of democratic institutions, who would relinquish power once order was restored. Carlos Lacerda's support of the coup rested on the assumption that, as the country's most prominent conservative politician, he would have the generals' support in the next presidential election.

sidewalk a real Rio touch—big hairy men in bathing trunks dancing madly, waving wet towels. The whole thing took place in violent rainstorms so all paper stuck—cars, tanks, everything, plastered with wet paper.

The last two weeks have been wilder and wilder. Goulart overplaying his hand, obviously, and apparently overestimating his strength like a fool—or being forced to. The other side (we're the "rebels"!) underestimated theirs. Monday night we watched him on TV haranguing a mass-meeting of sergeants. It was awful, almost pathetic—the ring-leaders trying to read speeches written for them and not being able to read well enough etc. L & I even said to each other—"Well that's the end, really"—and sure enough it was. The army wouldn't take it. Only one army was supposed to be loyal to him—and then April 1st, it turned, too—& that was the end. But it was rather tense when we knew Rio was completely in Federal control, except for Carlos holding out in that silly little palace, and the one "enemy" army was marching in to take us, supposedly . . . Very few people killed, at least that we know of so far. (I suspect that because of no transportation and few cars out, probably a few ~~hundred~~ dozen of the usual deaths due to being run over or crashed into were avoided . . .) The Copacabana fort played an important part, but only one soldier ~~was wounded some say killed and one officer~~ was killed. Now for two days they've been putting people in prison—oh God—most of the big shots got away.

Rio de Janeiro, April 7th, 1964

Well, that was my first account, as far as I got with it. It was an exhausting week, although things began to function as well, or as badly, as usual by the 4th. This is the depressing stretch. Over 3,000 prisoners taken in Rio alone. Carlos has issued orders over and over, no police brutality to be allowed, etc.—but incidents will happen with any police. He also made one excellent impromptu speech—press conference—and it has been officially announced since, that the labor unions are to have free elections right away, no more government appointed leaders, and that they will *not* lose anything they have gained so far . . . This is fine, if he can do it. Congress, in order to show they *can* act, immediately passed one agrarian reform act that had been waiting for ages—a constitutional one, and pretty weak, but something, at least . . . Now the struggle is whether all known communists will be kicked out of the congress or what—and who'll be president next October. A General will be for now, supposedly a moderate, bright, ironical old fellow who surprised everyone by knowing more than anyone else in the country, almost, when the II Army, in Minas, started the "rebellion." Castelo Branco—[1]

De Gaulle is using Brazil now as another anti-US weapon—don't believe any news from France! *Le Monde*'s latest is that the whole thing was engineered by Standard Oil . . . The governor of the State of Minas is getting all the credit here, but supposedly the real trigger was the wife of the head of the II Army—she was watching TV (so were we) the night of the 30th when Goulart made such an ass of himself—and she made her husband come back to watch some more—and he finally got so mad he decided the time had come, & finally got the Governor to go along with him, etc.

The most encouraging thing, really, was the parade on the 2nd. It had been planned for two weeks, as an anti-Communist demonstration. By that time, the 2nd, the revolution was over and the communists on the run, so it was no longer necessary—but more than a million people turned out and marched,—again in the pouring rain. It was really impressive. I'm sending you some picture magazines—if you get them. Really spontaneous—and they couldn't *all* have been the rich reactionary right . . . April Fools' Day here is the "Day of the Lie"—so now they say "The Truth came out on the Day of the Lie." I don't believe all the papers say, naturally—but Lota is in a position to know quite a bit. They have uncovered, so far, more than 15 tons of Chinese and Russian propaganda—and arms, explosives, etc. The *quantity* is what is impressive. I think they will have a monster exhibition of it in the big stadium, the only place big enough—and I think it's a good idea because most people had no idea how close a thing it was.

The trouble is, it was over too quickly—it gives some of the really rotten old reactionaries the chance to get right back in again. Which they are doing their best to do. I don't imagine you have any idea of what the atmosphere has been like here the past few months—but it really was a wonderful feeling to wake up those first few mornings and realize there was not going to be a bloody civil war after all, and that we didn't have to leave the country in a hurry, as we'd been thinking we might—

Some rather nice Brazilian-style stories— The Naval Fusiliers (Marines) were the pro-Goulart force that held Rio. They took over all TV, radio stations and newspapers.— At one newspaper office, the night of the 31st, one marine asked if he could use the telephone. He'd been on duty 3 days & nights and wanted to tell his wife where he was. So not only did they let the

1 Humberto de Alencar Castelo Branco.

invading marines telephone but they gave them *cafézinhos*, and a couple of reporters were allowed out to take money to the wives of some of the Marines who were afraid they hadn't been able to buy food for the children.

Another division of Marines held the sort of park where Goulart's "palace" is, protecting him—but there are also big apartment houses in it where several of our friends live. They couldn't go out at all for a couple of days. There's a small playground in the middle, and at 2 AM one friend looked out and saw marines (they're the ones that wear the pretty uniforms and Scotch bonnets with streamers) swinging in the swings, "pumping away," he said, to swing as high as possible.

What they'll do with all these prisoners I can't imagine. Goulart made it to Uruguay, where he is a most unwelcome guest. Yesterday Carlos went to open another school, to be named for a famous Uruguayan poet—and apparently the Uruguayan ambassador heaved a sigh of relief when he was invited, and the school *was* named for the poet, in spite of the fact they're harboring a lot of Goulart's followers. Brizola still at large—

The night of the 2nd we went to a party, the opening of a small art gallery by the Congress of Cultural Freedom here. (I'm against this idea of an art gallery, since artists here don't need help much, but I went just to see.) Everyone was there—painters, left & right, intellectuals—not much "society"—but then *Afranio*[1] couldn't be expected to produce that. A nice little old house they have rented, with offices upstairs. In the night sometime, after the party, the house was broken into. The gallery wasn't touched, but all the correspondence, & files, were stolen and the office generally wrecked. Since everybody knows where their money comes from it was pretty silly.— I suspect some of the beatnik boys I was talking to at the party were really there, casing the joint.

I am horribly depressed about what's going to be happening here and my one thought is to get away for awhile. England is the best place, I think—I can speak the language, more or less, and I think they really don't give a damn about Brazil, so no one will ask questions. I'm still not sure whether Lota can go first to Italy with me or not—if not, I'll try to leave by boat sometime the first week in May.

She was fearfully brave—at the worst moment she said she thought that if the Marines did attack the "palace," if she weren't flattened by a tank she'd get out and find nothing left of our red Volkswagen but a smear in the street . . .

---

1 Probably Afrânio Coutinho.

The atmosphere of wild rumors, people being cagey, etc. is most unpleasant—

Dr. Baumann is coming to visit in September. I suspect she loves Carlos a lot more than I do and it may be a bit awkward—oh well—

Lota went back to work right away. The park is looking wonderful, really—

I hope you're all well and any suggestions about places or people in England will be most welcome. I want to hear more about the plays, too—

Much love,
Elizabeth

292.[1]

April 6, 1964

Dearest Elizabeth:

Let me dash off a note, since I'll be gone in a few hours to Delaware for two weeks and may not be back in time to write you before your trip. I suppose, though, everything is unimaginably changed since March 31st, the date of your last letter.[2] You were really on the brink then, as I can see you suspected.

I don't really know too many people in London, and nothing I'm afraid about traveling through the country, an old dream of ours. Spender will be here for the next two months but his wife Natasha is a charming, vigorous soul. You could get in touch with her through *Encounter*. Then there's Karl Miller, book review editor of the *New Statesman*, a dour, sardonic, bright, hard-working young man, who could assemble anyone you would like to meet—also his brother-in-law Jonathan Miller, who is doing my play, incredibly bright and bubbling. You might like to meet Empson, heroically odd but more interesting than anyone else; and John Betjeman, who is very courteous, attentive, elaborate and gentle. There's a curious writer of gruesome light verse named Stevie Smith (woman), homely in an attractive way, and with a way of saying things. Then there's my friend A. Alvarez, 74 Fellows Road, and if you should get there, Mary,[3] 141 Rue de Rennes, Paris, telephone Lit. 1092, who would welcome you with open arms. Let me know, if you are really going, and I'll write notes.

I talked to Bill Alfred this week-end about Flávio. I think all's well there. Bob Giroux at Farrar and Straus wants your book very much. I am dying

1 Crossed with letter 291.
2 The letter does not survive.
3 Mary McCarthy.

to see the ballad[1] and the other new poems. I have been haunted ever since I left Brazil by your fragments and descriptions of the unfinished poems. Hope you've done the Darwin.

I guess I found the poet business in Randall's book an asset. He has done several other children's books.[2] I find them awfully clean, charming, innocent and a nice idyllic thing to do, but a little too much in the genre. I wish he would write something much more weird, unacceptable and his own. I can't keep up with the new poets, but several good things are coming out: Berryman, Roethke, Larkin, Sylvia Plath (?). What I saw of MacNeice in magazines looked denser than he'd been for a long time, but I don't have the book yet.[3]

It's hard to tell what is happening in Brazil underneath the headlines. No one here seems to regret Goulart. The creeping (apparently galloping at the end) advance of his regime must have been a nightmare. Well, let's hope there will be peace and not too many arrests.

Love to you both,
Cal

Maybe next winter we'll make the carnival.

293.

Rio, Monday April 13th, 1964

Dearest Cal:

I got your letter of the 6th at the Petrópolis PO on the way to Rio this morning—the mails suddenly seem to have improved, and let's hope that is auspicious. One of the Big Revelations was that the huge rise in postal rates last year went straight to Brizola—as a present from his brother-in-law to pay for his campaign—really, no fooling! But first let me say how much I appreciate your writing and how much we both like hearing from you. I really don't know how you find time to do it, you have such a complicated social and professional life.— You're in Delaware, I gather.— We aren't going away until the middle of May—May 13, probably,—Lota has got a month's vacation and that means we'll go by plane, together. (If she couldn't go, I was going sooner, by boat.) She even gets some of it paid for by the government—but since it's the first vacation she's had in three years, and she

1 "The Burglar of Babylon" (EB-*CP*).
2 Randall Jarrell, *The Bat-Poet* (1964), *The Gingerbread Rabbit* (1964), and *The Animal Family* (1965).
3 Louis MacNeice, *Selected Poems*, ed. W. H. Auden (1964).

worked for more than two without any pay at all—I think she deserves it all. We're going to rent a car and take a tour through northern Italy—neither of us has ever been to Venice, or much around that part—and then middle of June she'll fly back here and I'll go on to London. Next time—in '66—we hope to stay abroad six months or so—

Thank you for the names of London people . . . I am slightly relieved to hear that SS[1] won't be there . . . (ungracious of me). I've read some of Stevie Smith—funny, when it works at all. Larkin is one of the few poets I really care about—do you think we'd take to each other at all?—or do you know him? I'd love to *see* Empson, but I'm sure he'd scare the daylights out of me. Alvarez doesn't like my poetry, so maybe I'd better not try him—alas, I do think he's a pretty good critic, too! Of course I really won't be there too long. I'll be visiting my friends the Barkers (George B's brother, Kit, the painter) in Sussex for about a week, probably—& possibly a friend in Cambridge[2]—and I'd like very much to get to Edinburgh. Yes, I'd like to meet the *New Statesman* man, I think—I am well up on that magazine! (Lota read it during her siege at the Palace, she says.) (I saw a long quote from Elizabeth somewhere—saying how she "liked to read book reviews . . . .") Anyway— if ever I know an address I'll send it to you—or *PEN* after June 12th—and thank you so much. If I can find nothing more definite, I think I can be written to c/o the Barkers, Bexley Hill, Lodsworth, Petworth, Sussex. (They have just written, offering to drive me to Stonehenge, two different cathedrals—and I think I'll ask for Brighton, since I read Creevey through the nights of the Revolution, to get my mind off things.[3])

The Revolution—well—I hope you saw Carlos on TV?—although I haven't read the papers yet today to find out what he said. Just the headlines, saying he appeared on 166? US stations. Other headlines: "Freedom of the Press Guaranteed." "Castelo Branco: May God and Man help me Govern Well." (Amen.) When we left on Saturday 500 of the 3,000 prisoners—out on a huge old ocean liner, right under out noses—had been freed, and supposedly no students and no workers, just organizers, are being arrested[4] . . . As far

1 Stephen Spender.
2 Anne Stevenson, who was writing a critical study of EB's work.
3 Thomas Creevey, *The Creevey Papers*, ed. John Gore (1963).
4 *The New York Times* reported that 7,000 people had been arrested in Brazil, 3,000 in Rio alone. It has since emerged that the military "arrested activists on the left, such as student leaders, labor union leaders, organizers of Catholic groups . . . and rural union and peasant league organizers. Hundreds were jailed in Rio, with many confined to a makeshift prison ship in the harbor. Activists in the Northeast disappeared, were tortured or executed. In Rio, Lacerda's political police (DOPS, or *Departamento de Ordem Política e Social*) went after leftist activists whom they had long been watching" (Thomas E. Skidmore, *The Politics of Military Rule in Brazil* [1988], 16–17).

as I know, this is true. The military junta probably looks much worse from outside than it does from here. As you know, the military in Brazil have never in all its history tried to seize power *or keep it*—and Castelo Branco was reluctant to be President. We now have an awful vice-president[1]—clever but a crook—but I don't believe he'll have much power. The suspension of rights, dismissing lots of Congress, etc.—*had* to be done, sinister as it may sound. Otherwise it would have been just a "deposition" and not a "revolution"— and many of Goulart's men would still be there in Congress. And all the rich communists would get away (as some have of course,) and the poor ignorant ones get left to take the blame. Flávio [is] much concerned about all his communist student-friends—but all of them, as far as I know now, have turned up safe & sound after all, so he is quieting down. Well—we *knew* things were bad, but I'd stopped trying to tell anyone outside the country—no one would believe me. Remember when I wrote you—3 years ago—about meeting the "Chinese Trade Commission" and having cold shivers, for the first time?[2] Some of those same men have turned up. They were supposed only to have 3 months' visas (Brazil has never recognized communist China)—and all along Goulart's government has been extending their visas for years, and allowing more and more in. Rather unrealistic of the Chinese—the Russians only wanted to agitate, I think. They don't *want* Brazil. No one has been killed on purpose—and very few, accidentally—those first two days. (On the other hand, the communists had a list of 40 to be executed immediately[3]—this has not been made public—I get my information from Lota.) It is a tremendous relief—but a nerve-wracking and awful kind of "victory." The Russian Ambassador fled the country (before Goulart did I think) The R. embassy and Hungarian embassy burned such stacks of papers and films in their back yards that the ignorant neighbors called up the Sanitation Dept. to complain of the stench. The whole thing's like that—a weird mixture of the clever, brutal, unbelievably simple and crude, and funny. Easter and April Fool's Day were the perfect combination of days for this particular revolution.

It will be such a relief to get away. This constant pressure of violently opposed feeling does not suit the "artistic temperament" (all I lay claim to.)

---

1 José Maria Alckmin.

2 See letter 231.

3 "The number arrested in the coup's aftermath can only be estimated, since there was no official tally; it probably totaled between 10,000 and 50,000. Many were released within days and most within weeks. Those subjected to prolonged torture (more than a day or two) were probably several hundred. Apologists for the repression argued that any excesses paled in comparison with what the left would have perpetrated had it won power. Yet the fact remained that duly authorized police and military officers had resorted to torture"; Thomas E. Skidmore, *The Politics of Military Rule in Brazil* (1988), 25.

Well—I wrote Brandt a month ago but I'll write again, I think—he couldn't have got it.[1] Also Giroux.

I'm awfully pleased about Randall's liking your book so much, as I'm sure you are. He just couldn't falsify his feelings a bit about poetry. (I'm sure he's right, too. Well—thank God for *you*, these days!)

Did you write a poem about Shakespeare? or to a quotation? My letter—theirs to me—got lost.— I heard again quite recently so I'm afraid I'll never think of anything in time. (In fact, probably return from England hating the very name for a while.[2])

I see all kinds of things about you—and honors—the Mt. Kisco thing for example . . .[3] Oh—the Congress for Cult F robbery turned out to be the police. That was Lota's theory. They returned everything the next day and apologized. Actually I think they thought someone else might have used that office as a safe hiding place for *other* papers . . . that's how things are now.

Ballads seem to be the only way of putting it all. I have another one, but really must put a stop to it. However—the first pays my plane fare. I'm writing Chapelbrook again . . . (Have over 5,000 of that still—pretty good, I think, because I am extravagant.)

Samambaia was heavenly—all purple Lent trees blooming, and two long clear dark red sunsets—huge deep red sky, Venus never huger. Lota is wonderful these days—thinks clearly, *says* what she thinks, and gets away with it. She and one man have the reputation of being the only people who aren't afraid to yell at Carlos. Before the Revolution Carlos was silent for over a week. Someone said, "Oh—probably Lota de Macedo Soares is sitting on his chest . . ."

But this *isn't* my world—or is it?— Much love,
    Elizabeth

April 14th, AM

One postscript, and then I'll say no more about things here if I can possibly avoid it. I've just read all of Carlos's U.S. TV interview and I do hope you saw it (it was in English—4 men came especially from CBS to make it) because it is *excellent*. He is a wonderful impromptu speaker. And if you did see it and got it all—he really does answer all the major questions and doubts,

1 That is, her letter.
2 The 400th anniversary of Shakespeare's birth was in 1964.
3 See letter 271; "Colloquy on Mount Kisco," *Congress News* (Congress for Cultural Freedom, Winter 1964).

and brilliantly—only perhaps a bit too high-brow for popular consumption—& of course, too briefly, necessarily.

I'm in a RAGE about what the US papers are quoted as saying, and over the remarks of the Cultural Attaché who came to dinner with us last night . . . I know what *he* says is of no importance, and he's a very aggressive type (bright on other subjects)— But what DO the Americans want, for God's sake? Imagine their reactions if things had gone the other way!— Imagine the shrieks, the blockades, the criticisms of the weak and red & naughty Brazilians . . . Now they've got what they want, supposedly, they all begin attacking *immediately.*— Even on April 1st itself, everyone began head-shaking, and being—if they only knew it—fearfully rude to, after all, innocent, Lota. Why is everyone so sure it's all wrong?— What in HELL does the NY *Post* know about it? Won't anyone believe the real facts about that idiotic Agricultural Reform Goulart proposed?— (Carlos answered this well, but of course couldn't go into all the fantastically comical and horrifying details of what Goulart's purely demagogic plan would have entailed.) At the same time our guest was shouting away about "Reforms"—(and I don't know of a single soul who *doesn't* want reforms, after all!—and no one in power has even hinted they wanted to return to any kind of status quo,—there isn't any to return to now, anyway). He was admitting that the US was pro-Carlos although of course can't come out & say so, and that things had turned out the way they wanted. Meanwhile arguing that it's wrong to take away civil rights, etc. Well—ideally speaking, of course—but what do you do in a weak, poor country, without any police at all, to speak of? The US can cope with spies and organizers & arms-running; Brazil obviously can't. If they had taken this step 30 years ago, the first time Vargas was out—taking away his civil rights—he'd never have been able to return as a dictator, and all the years of degradation and loss of morale might have been prevented . . . R. Aron was the only person who ever made sense of things here—and I'm glad to see Carlos quoted him. Ask Hannah Arendt! I bet—if she knows anything at all about Brazil—she'd agree with Carlos now. Of course it's what he *does*—what he is able to do,—and I wish I could stay away for two years and not have to go through the next stretch.

It's funny—the Americans rave about "democracy" for years—a grand big general principle—then rave again when Chinese spies are arrested, or a dozen known crooks and stooges are driven into exile . . . It's an odd sense of proportion about countries, to say the least.

Forgive me—I *won't* say anymore, but confine myself to Wordsworthian notes from now on. But please try to see it fairly, and if you get the chance, make your liberal intellectual friends see it fairly, too—& give Brazil a little time before jumping on it.

Of course one trouble is, the US has never sent any first-rate people here. Gordon has behaved well, I gather. Then he made a joke—"Now US has its White House and Brazil has its White Castle . . ." Isn't that the perfect classroom joke the students laugh at politely?—poor little professor.

294.

May 1, 1964

Dearest Elizabeth:

I hope this catches you before you set out on the 13th. I have been writing a longish book review on Berryman, and then last night there was [an] Ungaretti evening that I presided over and wrote an introduction for.[1] My desk is awash of the unanswered, letters, manuscript, printed things—not much for most people, but a deluge for me.

It will be grand for you both to get away, the scurry, the confusion, the clashes of argument. Still, the change must be a solace, and even the strife must leave a lot that is fun to arrange in your mind, disentangle and look back on. I don't think the revolution has come off badly here. The last *Time* had an account of Goulart's land embezzlement—one per cent of Brazil's land![2] He sounds crookeder than Kubitschek. He seems madly inefficient, crooked and corrupt. Only his office, I suppose, was grand, but one could write a wonderful tragedy about how he prepared his fall. The trouble with press reports is that there are so many fixed political words. They don't mean the same thing in any two countries in actuality, and even from month to month the facts change. I think everyone here feels that Brazil was rapidly dropping into chaos, more rapidly than even Brazilians knew or anticipated till lately. The General seems like a remarkably good one. This is a very confusing time. The big wars may be over, but when have so many governments toppled, so many changes, good and bad, come by violence. The radical business has brought us a little nearer to the turbulence. The issue is clear, but the working out is all uncertain, and wrung with twisted lines.

You speak of the artistic temperament, unsuited to this stuff. But you grasp strongly, and come up with full hands. I am a numbskull in these matters. I wish you could find forms, narrative, description, fiction, poems—

1 "Introduction for Giueppe Ungaretti" (Houghton). See "Returning," which "was suggested by Giuseppi Ungarettii's' 'Canzone' " (RL-*CP*).
2 "A Goulart Audit," *Time* (May 1, 1964).

to get it out. Maybe this would need time and distance. No eye in the world has seen what yours has. I have a vague image of a sequence of poems through which the Revolution moves—no obvious argument or polemic, but the thing embodied, there in all its awfulness, absurdity—good, bad, real, confused, clarified, in the end judged. I don't mean anything neutral or beyond politics, rather the opposite, everything rescued from the giddy, hard, superficial clichés that the removed give realities, that we all give even what we know well. I am thinking really that the Revolution might give a thread for you to draw together the gathering impressions of your ten years' stay.

I don't know why I am giving advice. I have a hard time finding words, remembering faces, wiping the glaze from memory. The stay at Delaware was an empty time, except for the company of Peter Taylor: a stiff English department, a drunken poet, Robert Huff, an amiable, cowed messy weak Roethke, boisterously carrying a dull weight of defeat, pen women, nice and not very nice, with their little poems and stories written for themselves, a dearth of students, many handed in work but never appeared. Delaware is a sort of Holland in size and flatness, a fading etching of Holland. At Kenyon, Ransom was very crisp, charming and unworldly. On the stage for our symposium,[1] he wanted to sit inside me for fear of falling. Stories, opinion, gossip, and speculation poured out of him, always in his own idiom. Allen gave an elegant, dark, cryptically catholic denunciation of the times, Red Warren talked about not preparing his paper, sewing a button on his fly, and drinking, Spender asked Ransom wide-eyed questions about how he started, what poems he liked, etc. I gave a rather stiff description of where I thought the arts were. Here as everywhere else more new material is flooding in than one can begin to absorb. Here and there something strikes home to me, otherwise I think about what I've known and liked. I've started to read through Shakespeare, and must get a good annotated edition.

Red and his career are a puzzle. No one in a way could be more vivacious, full of things, kindness, duty. All this and great energy are in his new novel, *The Flood.*[2] Yet you soon feel he had already written it, that others have. Just another novel! All the reviewers are slamming it as a pot-boiler. Yet, it's just his restless need to write, work that no doubt would have moved mountains, if aimed somewhere else.

Well, soon you'll be in Venice. Soon we'll be in Maine. Harriet is gob-

---

1 On "Quo Vadimus? Or the Books Still Unwritten," with RL, Ransom, Robie Macauley, Stephen Spender, Allen Tate, and Robert Penn Warren, sponsored by *The Kenyon Review*.
2 Robert Penn Warren, *Flood: A Romance of Our Time* (1964).

bling up reading, a great lump of health and freshness, though sometimes a shy lump. She seems to grow, as we watch her. Liz has had a great winter of forays, and everyone we meet is talking about her polemic on the theater.[1] Have a lovely summer!

All my love,
Cal

P.S. Has Carlos come here? We would like to give a little party for him, if he has the leisure. We could produce a little circle that would follow him with intense interest and sympathy. Lizzie heard his TV broadcast and admired it very much.

295.

[Postcard: Johannes Vermeer, "Lady Standing at the Virginal,"
National Gallery of Art, Washington, D.C.]

[May 6, 1964]

Dearest Elizabeth:

Love and bon voyage to you both. The mails do seem much more rapid and the eye blinks at you landing so shortly in Milan. Enjoy the Majo and your long-awaited vacation.

Our love,
Cal

What a scramble, this card: Holland, Italy, Brazil, the U.S.!

296.[2]

Samambaia, May 3rd, 1964

Dearest Cal:

Forgive me for boring you—and possibly Elizabeth, too—with those long letters about the "revolution." It certainly was impossible to write letters about anything *else*, during that period—or think about anything else— and it is still almost as bad. Thank heavens we are going away. I just wish we could both stay away much longer. Heaven only knows what will happen to the poor peaceful "revolution" now—thank God Carlos has gone away, be-

1 Elizabeth Hardwick, "The Disaster at Lincoln Center," *The New York Review of Books* (April 2, 1964).
2 Crossed with letters 294 and 295.

fore he starts fighting with everyone. I wonder if you saw him on CBS? His interview with the French reporters was awful but brilliant, quick-witted, aggressive, funny—we've had letters already (the revolution does seem to have improved the mails enormously) from friends in Paris (including Hilda-from-São-Paulo) saying that for half an hour they were "proud of being Brazilian." They asked him if it were true that he had been a communist and he said yes, of course, "but nothing like your Minister Malraux." He was so violent that now de Gaulle has canceled his visit to Brazil—that's nice! But oh dear—they (the winning side) have somehow to make their revolution popular—skip denouncing Cuba and Venezuela and put down the price of beans and sugar, for the love of God—and I bet they won't . . . However, if you saw last week's TIME on Goulart (right, for once—their facts) that should convince all those who think that he too, just wanted "reforms," and the nasty old right wouldn't let him . . . He has escaped with all his money-bags, and will probably join Peron in Madrid . . .

This is our last week-end up here,—getting cold, and so beautiful and peaceful. I probably gave you these already—anyway—

May 14th, American Express, Milan—until June 12th

"   "   "   London—until August 1st.

Will you be in Maine? If you do write to Brazil after getting this, by any chance—write to Rio, please—Antônio Vieira 5, Leme, apt. 1101.

I had an ambiguously phrased letter from Keith saying that "we" (and it looks as if you were one of the "we" but I can't be sure) are doing an anthology of Latin American poetry, and requesting my Drummond translations. If you are connected with this enterprise of course I'd like to contribute, but not, I think, if you're not. "Upwards of 20 poems"—well, only if you are in on it. I mistrust Keith even more, if possible, having heard very dubious things about his activities in Mexico. And probably I do not forget or forgive as easily as you do!

I have Joe Frank's book *The Widening Gyre*[1]—haven't had time to read it yet, but think I've seen most of it. Maybe he has widened his gyre, but the subjects are the same old ones we bickered over long ago in Washington. Well, he's Germanic—and I'm Anglo-Saxon—and we'll never agree. Think I'll go see the *Lake District* with all the English-teachers . . . I have two more poems I must try to send somewhere before I leave—I hope you like them.

WHAT a relief to get away from this poor country with its feudal Portuguese adventurers trying to pretend they're 20th century democrats, etc.—

---

1 Joseph Frank, *The Widening Gyre* (1964).

I send you lots of love and lots of fond but jumbled emotions, like nostalgia, etc.

Elizabeth

May 22nd[1]—
Lota was as much surprised as I was to find ALL my letters still in her basket—she'd assured me she read this one to you and approved of it—I mean, *agreed* with—and that Fernanda had mailed everything . . . Not that it matters much!

It will seem out-of-date, but it is still what I think—the "revolution" is certainly being misrepresented in the foreign press, if the quotations I see are correct. It is a decidedly "middle class" revolution so far, with a lot of working-class support, too—as far as Rio and São Paulo go, & also in the north. That awful story in TIME last week was NOT true, or not the way they told it . . . (perhaps you didn't see it, so I won't repeat it, hoping you didn't.)[2] A lot of the misunderstanding is just semantics, as always, I think. There isn't much point in my trying to explain. I won't even try. Carlos is leaving tonight for a couple of months[3]—this odd Brazilian system is a good idea in his case—if he stayed he'd undoubtedly start fighting with Castelo Branco in another day or so—since it's his nature to fight, and now he's lost his BIG Cause, what can he fight next? I mean—he's won this round, against the "communists"—so what next? There are some very good honest people in the new cabinet— The NY Times, etc.—absolutely WRONG[4]—but I'm so sick of it all, I can't bear to think of it anymore.

I read Wilson's book on his taxes[5]—well—what a strange little book— the 1st 3rd kind of ga-ga; the rest so horribly right . . . He has such a funny naïve streak, hasn't he.

We are really going away—leave May 13th. Lota has a month; then on June 13th or so she'll return and I'll go on to London—sailing back supposedly on August 1st, Blue Star Line—a really long trip but rather nice stops— 17 days—(IF I can face Brazil again . . .) I really think when L's job is up we should spend at least a year in the US again—or someplace. I am certainly

<hr />

1 Actually May 12; EB and Lota departed for Italy on May 14.
2 Possibly "The Unmissing Man," *Time* (May 15, 1964), about Brizola's flight from Brazil.
3 Carlos Lacerda departed on an official mission to reassure the United States and friendly governments in Europe about the coup.
4 Possibly "The Brazilian Revolution," *The New York Times* (May 12, 1964), which expresses anxiety about political purges and new policies serving business and banking interests at the expense of the poor.
5 Edmund Wilson, *The Cold War and the Income Tax, a Protest* (1963).

sick of Rio. I admire her courage enormously—but she is exhausted, and discouraged, and—and— How awful to be a Brazilian, is all I can think—and yet,—how awful to be anything at all, at present— (After Wilson's book—maybe only a pygmy feels guiltless!)

With much love, as always—

Elizabeth

297.

[Postcard: Piero della Francesca, "Transporto del Sacro Ponte"]

Arezzo, [Italy]

May 28, [1964]

Dear Cal:

Have you been here, I wonder? I seem to like every place we go better than the last—the reward of pessimism. Now we are going to Sansepolcro to see "the most beautiful painting in the world."[1] Lovely weather—green wheat, wild-flowers, swallows, a ruin with a big fox.— Please write me to Milan?

Love, Elizabeth

298.

June 1, 1964

Dearest Elizabeth:

In the same mail with your Arezzo Piero postcard, the enclosed came from Harvard. I don't know whether any slight fire needs to be lighted under Flávio, probably the trouble is due to the mails, but it would be a good idea for either you or Lota to send him a note and make sure he gives Harvard the information they want. I feel they are well-disposed, and his chances are very good.

Odd, the Piero card is identical with one Mary sent me last fall. She quoted from some Italian critic that the almond-like ring in the grain of the wood of the Cross was a halo. Perfect picture, nothing could be more truly classical.

We leave in three weeks for Maine. On the whole it's been a lovely green, cool spring here, like Paris or the Majo, I think, but we will be glad to get to the true country. Today I am going to Boston, to get something called the Golden Rose, given by the New England Poetry Society—not an important prize, but the only symbolically poetical one I know of. I've just had a feeler

---

1 Aldous Huxley, "The Best Picture" (Piero della Francesca's *The Resurrection*), *Along the Road* (1925).

proposal that I do a version of the *Oresteia* for the opening of the Lincoln Center in 1965. It would be directed by Kazan, and might well be quite cheap and pretentious.[1] Still it would be performed with a splash, and I've exhausted my work at hand, and am tempted. A nice long task that couldn't completely come to nothing, and might be fairly splendid. The only other things I can think of are shorter translations. I've got three coming out now: a sequence by Akhmatova in the *Atlantic*, Canto XV of the Inferno in *Encounter*, and Juvenal's 10th maybe in *Arion*. I feel a desire to pause and get my breath on original poems. I've thought a lot about doing a play on Trotsky in exile, but don't know if I could be any good at all at it. It's funny this rage to write. I don't think it's a very good idea, but love to be at work.

How lovely you and Lota are in Italy and loving it! I saw May Swenson the other day, and we both felt happy talking about you. Whenever I see people here, I miss you, and think with a secret pride that I live a little of your life.

Love,
Cal

P.S. If you are in the mood, do look up Ungaretti whom I've just seen here, and who loves Brazil. I'm not sure whether he will be in Rome or Milan, but I think you would enjoy him. Also Montale, who is in Milan, rather gloomy but friendly.

299.

Milan, June 13th, 1964
Dearest Cal:

I got your letter at the Am. Express here—and thank you for it and for sending the one about Flávio. In the same batch of mail Flávio sent me his copy of the same letter and what he'd written them, and letters to his auntie and me . . . I'm enclosing the one to me because I think it is such a nice letter—and you can see how well he expresses himself in English. (He still makes that mistake of not capitalizing countries, nationalities, etc., however.) We DID answer every questionnaire that came along,—but two I know of did get lost and "we" asked for them again. Another thing that held us up was the incredible slowness of his professors—not Flávio, who is in a fever of excitement and efficiency—one prof. we just gave up on finally. I do hope it is all right. It is almost entirely thanks to you if it is, I know—and I hope

1 See *The Oresteia of Aeschylus* (1978); the collaboration with Elia Kazan did not materialize.

you realize it will almost literally save that boy's life . . . Lota can't speak of it without her eyes filling with tears! Everything is against him in Brazil—he has no chance of amounting to anything decent there, really—and it is some kind of miracle that he has turned out as bright and as fundamentally good as he is—with the god-awful life he's had. (I lent him Agee on the movies.[1]— he's writing movie reviews for his newspaper now,—also compiled him a sort of Young Gentleman's guide to US manners—that's what he's talking about.)

Our travels: well, we are back at our star[t]ing point and day after tomorrow we leave for different points of the compass. We had a wonderful four weeks and they very obligingly seemed much longer than that. When I see the 2 in the National Gallery again, I'll have seen all the Piero della Francesca paintings in existence, except one minor one in Perugia . . . Almost the best is the "Scourging"—you must have seen reproductions of it, if not seen it? It's the best-preserved—oil, on a wooden panel, rather small—and superb. As if there were an instrument like a telescope or microscope—for time—you're looking straight through dark centuries into bright sunlight— only it's all silent. Well—those paintings—& Torcello, which you've undoubtedly seen—Vicenza with that wonderful Palladio theatre,—and a couple of villas—etc. So much. I'll be glad of that long ocean voyage back, to consolidate my gains . . . Lota drove bravely, nobly and well, the car was fine, the weather fine and cool.— One wild trip across the Apennines in a terrific storm—the only bad weather & tense moments—because we didn't see another car and Lota wasn't sure of ours at that point. It was beautiful, though—green but cold—and there were actually the remnants of snow-drifts at the sides of the road—on May 28th. The country-side lovely—but all a bit too bland and pampered for my taste. L loves it, just because it is such a contrast to poor mis-treated Brazil.

Funny, Mary sent you the same picture. I felt it wasn't an appropriate thing for a postcard, but sent it, anyway. No—the "Scourging" is the most beautiful *now*—but the "Resurrection" is surely one of the most powerful and affecting—startling—pictures ever painted. P della F was supposed to have been very lazy—did you know? It was almost impossible to get him to do anything or finish anything.

We stopped off to see Sirmione on the way here—and for one glimpse at the Lakes, at least—and the color is just like every Italian calendar you ever saw hanging in a fruit shop in Boston—completely unreal chrono blue.

1 James Agee, *Agee on Film* (1958).

Sirmione a mess of hotels, etc.—and full of Germans, like every place here—but out at the end, among the ruins and the olive trees, one can imagine a bit what it was like and why Catullus liked living there.

Life is complicated at the moment because we have just discovered Italy has no *book-rate*—and we've been blithely acquiring quite a few—and now how to get them home without paying more than they cost. Also L bought a large *picnic basket*. Our first day in Milan I looked up from my coffee and saw her struggling across the Duomo Sq through the pigeons, with a peck basket— Well, *she*'ll have to get that to Brazil.

Congratulations on the Golden Rose! (can you wear it?) I bought a tiny book of Montale's translations of Eliot[1]—which I can read—but you know I never dream of calling on anybody! I hope your play plans work out. I *met* Mrs. Trotsky—looked at her at least—she was tragic and distrait then, c. 1942.

Will you write to London? My address is PASTORIA HOTEL, St. Martin's St., London, WC2—hotels get mail faster than the Am Express, I find.

I can't seem to find the letter—I thought I brought it—in which you kindly gave me a name or two in England—Miller (?) on the *New Statesman*—darn. I thought I really might try to be sociable, after a while. I'll be grateful—again—for anything like that. The only poet I care much for is Larkin. He lives somewhere to the north I think & I thought I might see him on my way to Scotland, if I get there. Anyone that sad shouldn't be too intimidating. Well—off to the Triennalle—opened last night by "Tony" (Princess M's husband).[2] This is Lota's ostensible excuse for being here— and mercifully it was postponed so we can only go 2 or 3 times.

Have a wonderful summer in Castine—with love,
    Elizabeth

I see "Il Gruppo" for sale here—with a photograph of "Vassar Girls" (all very Latin) in their usual evening dress, on the cover.

300.

June 15, 1964

Dearest Elizabeth:

I am returning Flávio's letter because you will probably want to keep it. It

---

1 *T. S. Eliot: tre poesie*, trans. Eugenio Montale (1963).
2 Antony Armstrong-Jones, 1st Earl of Snowden; Princess Margaret.

certainly is charming and shows a kind of innocent yet wise devotion to you that seems to ring from another age—youth's, but something more. I would also like to have read your guide to US manners, also of another age I gather with its buoyant Nova Scotia gallantry. I thought he was charming too in parrying some of your suggestions—to say "I was always pretty yellow," shows he has great courage. He had a lot of lively-witted compassion—what more could one ask for? I hope and trust all will go well with him and Harvard and later life.

Everyone here very much needs your guide to U.S. manners. Civil Rights seems the clearest of black and white issues. But the road is a rough one. There's a great flow of aimless violent incidence. Very ugly attacks, mostly by little negro gangs, and with no purpose whatever. But the effort must go on to give the negro equal rights and what is harder, and almost impossible, chances. Meanwhile, one walks the streets with a perhaps silly feeling of dread. Rich and poor, black and white, liberal and conservative might be at each other's throats. Nowhere, I suppose, is such a peril less likely, and yet we are beginning to be afraid of each other.

This kind of feeling has been growing on everyone for the last few months. Television flashes it home, but of course isn't a cause. I rather exaggerate. For the last few days I've been reading Hugh Thomas on the Spanish Civil War.[1] It simmered and simmered, then overnight it became merciless on both sides. Looking back, I would choose the Republic, but without conviction. Everyone then seems on a bloodthirst[y] drunken binge, or worse, soberly, apathetically or furiously directing forces on a drunken binge. And there is no tolerance or place for the unconvinced bystander.

There's a connection between how the world is and what the imagination lights on. What it usually lights on now is some grueling murk or release at all costs. Well, why not? It has always been so. Nothing could be more terrible than *Lear* and the *Oresteia*, both of which I have been reading. And there is no more harmless way for the elemental and black to come out than in words, paint and notes, where nothing can ever be hurt. Still life is a struggle for some equally inspired calm and balance. That sounds a little smug, and cheap and inconsistent coming from me—it's a hope, not a law, or rather it's law and support that is often unavailable.

Your Piero remarks have sent me back to the little Christmas volume of his pictures that Lizzie gave me. If he was lazy, his laziness makes others' industry reckless waste. And here's the classic calm! But no, only the technique

---

1 Hugh Thomas, *The Spanish Civil War* (1961).

is calm in "The Scourging"; all the classic order squeezes like a vise on Christ. According to my text, the young man in red in the foreground is the Duke of Urbino betrayed by the other two, his evil counselors. There's a suggestion of Poussin's harsher style. I have been thinking of the curious versatility of the man who could do both the Nativity and the Scourging, opposed worlds in meaning, yet the same world in style, a breathless peace beyond the horror, and beyond the singers.

I went to sleep last night leaving the shade up over the open window at my ear because of the heat. What I looked at was the gorgeously rectilinear facade of an old-fashioned yellowish brick abandoned building. In the day, it is drab enough, and pigeons fly in and out of its broken windows, six to each of its five low stories. It seemed like South America, staid and vibrant sweep through the city. I woke with a half dream vision of the utter metaphysical impossibility of our existence. Yet we had got by, we were, I was. And behind me stretched limitless spaces of glowing, pale, empty sky. It was a kind of peace. The sky of "The Scourging."[1] I felt how silly the dark speculation in the first part of my letter written yesterday was.

I guess Spender, now back and reachable through *Encounter*, and Karl Miller at the *New Statesman* might be the best people for you to look up for a start. Larkin is the librarian at Hull, a legendary figure, seldom seen in London. I know you will find great warmth and many admirers. We just had lunch with the Biddles who sent their tenderest love to you. We saw the Tates, sailing for Naples, Allen very brisk and witty, Belle rather morosely intense, moments of a sort of boiling vagueness under what is, of course, a very happy and devoted marriage.

We are staying on here about a week longer to see the opening of Randall's *Three Sisters*, done by the Actors' Studio.[2] I hope they surpass themselves, as indeed they must.

Love,
Cal

P.S.[3] How strange the new address, though Pastoria sounds as though you had brought a little of Brazil in your suitcase.

---

1 See "The Opposite House" (RL-*CP*).
2 Anton Chekhov, *Three Sisters*, trans. Randall Jarrell, opened at the Morosco Theater on June 22, 1964.
3 RL typed a second postscript on the envelope: "Thanks for the Sirmione 'Frater.'" See Catullus ci, line 10: "Atque in perpetuum frater ave atque vale"; and Tennyson, "Frater Ave Atque Vale" (1883), which calls into play both Catullus ci and xxxi ("o venusta Sirmio"). See also Ezra Pound, cantos 1, 3, 74, 76, 78.

301.

[Postcard: Tomb of Luiz de Camões, Mosteiro dos Jeronimos, Lisbon]

[Santa Cruz de Tenerife[1]]

July 26, 1964

Dear Cal, I have skipped several *other* poets' tombs and graves I've seen on this trip . . . This one's rather nice—eye missing, & all. Lisbon a pretty city—so neat & clear & painted-up it doesn't seem quite real.— Perhaps I really liked it because I could show off my bad Portuguese.

Love.—

Elizabeth—

302.

Aboard the S.S. "Brazil Star"

Somewhere below the equator again

July 30th, 1964

Dearest Cal:

ENGLAND will be mailing this to you, by way of England again or how, I don't know, but we can continue to use these 6-penny forms until we arrive in Rio. But after I mercilessly rubbed the superior English postal system to Lota and others all the time I was there—they went and had a P.O. strike the last week, and everything got badly held up (including two bags of ours en route from Italy). Of course nothing will be lost, strayed, or stolen, I'm sure—but it did cheer up Lota I imagine . . . When I was visiting the Barkers in Sussex I couldn't get over their having a red mail-box just a step down the country lane—as if we had one at the end of our terrace in Samambaia—and deliveries and collections twice a day. And just a step beyond that a large red telephone booth, standing in a hedge. Also garbage collection (or should one say "dustmen"?)—and here and there along the road a basket with a big shovel in it and a wire-beater like a big egg-whisk, for the citizens to put out their own fires with . . . Well, it is all amazing, and I suppose means "civilization"—or does it? I'm not sure but what they haven't gone a bit too far . . . However, the mail-box was so overgrown with blackberry vines that we got scratched mailing letters. When Kit Barker mentioned this to the postman— who must get fearfully scratched, after all—he replied "well, that's the Council's business, not mine . . ." So they're human, after all.

I had a very good time; didn't get to nearly all the places I'd planned to,

---

1 The boat from Lisbon to Brazil stopped in the Canary Islands, where this was posted.

of course, but I did see lots of people, some old friends, and some of England and a great deal of London. Went to the theatre five or six times—but either old age, or a bad season, or being over-critical—the theatre never comes up to my expectations any more—London or New York. Dick Wilbur arrived while I was there and that was nice—I saw him two or three times and reaped where he'd sown, went to the parties given for him, etc. I liked Cleanth Brooks very much, the bit I saw of him—that nice old-fashioned Southern manner. I saw Spender two or three times—etc., etc.—and at Wilbur's parties met an awful lot of poets.— I missed the Brooks' last one, or would have met just about ALL living English poets under 70, I think—and of course I saw many houses and graves of those who have gone on before (I kept you *au courant* with some of them, but gave up after it started looking morbid . . .[1]) I hope I can lure Lota back there with me sometime—at least London is surely the best shopping city in the world, and she'd like that—and I'd like to drive around the north and Scotland. I gave up the Scotch part of my trip just because we had such a good time driving in Italy I was spoiled—found I wasn't really looking forward to trains and busses, etc. Oh—I made an nice expedition alone to see Darwin's house—and meant to get to Salisbury to see Herbert's last church, but got lazy visiting and didn't make it. Where the Barkers live is exactly like being in the pages of a Beatrix Potter book (& perhaps being slightly squeezed in them)—all the individual well-known animals, the rabbits playing at evening, all the old characters around. One of Aiken's daughters[2] lives in an old pub nearby—she had to sign a paper saying she wouldn't *sell* liquor to her guests. Everything so minute, and built of *flints*—looking like soiled ancient hail-stones, to me. But you probably have seen all this long ago.

This has been a wonderful boat-ride—15 days, and we're arriving two days early. I spent a day alone in Lisbon—(more later, I think). Teneriffe— beautiful from the distance, rather disappointing close to, in spite of all the volcanic rocks, cloud-caps, etc. The Capt. has lent me a wonderful book on Weather Surveys—all about Fata Morganas, the "Green Flash" (do you know that one?), the difference between Rime & Hoarfrost, and descriptions of the "great revolving wheels" of phosphorescence that occur in the Arabian Sea—that light up the clouds and that you can read by . . . I think my next voyage will be in that direction. But seven days without even another boat is a long time. This morning one bird appeared—a hundred

---

1 See letter 299; other letters or postcards have not survived.
2 Joan Aiken.

miles from shore—I felt just like Cabral. Then, all the passengers play games all the time. One of them told me I was "naughty" not to! Honestly, the poor English! After those I met in London I'd forgotten how more dead-than-alive the average ones are . . . (It was odd to have talked away with one young man at a party, liking each other a lot, and then finding out it was John Wain! But oh dear—I'm considered an authority on 1. Latin American writing. 2. "The Group," and I can't think which I feel less interested in these days.) In London *that* is—on the boat I'm just—"the American" . . . (only one).

Well, back to the Brazilian madhouse. I listened to some news from there this morning and began to wish I weren't going back, almost—not really, but I have made a great many firm resolutions about NOT thinking about this and that and sticking more to my work. I should be able to for a year or so, I think, after this holiday. But I dread catching up on the news—US and Brazilian. (I do get a newssheet every day with coffee but pretty sketchy). Oh—a huge flattish rainbow—also a tanker, second ship today. It is quite rough but bright and beautiful, rainbows along the side, over & over, etc.— And the sun "shines bright, and on the right / Goes down into the sea . . ."[1] I realize I don't know your feelings on ocean travel at all! I only know you sleep on planes. I've done a lot of work on this trip—a long story—don't know how it will look on dry land. I am dying to hear about your play in NY—and all about Castine of course. Please write soon!

Much love—Elizabeth

303.

S.S. "Brazil Star"
After tea—installment 2[2]

2.

I find I have another of these blue sheets (the office now closed down)— and I'll write some more, because I feel I really haven't been in touch with you at all the past two months and I really haven't answered your letter of June 15th yet . . . The *Hotel Pastoria* is very nice—from my modest stand-point—tiny, but right in back of the National Gallery and all the "monu-ments" I wanted to see again, almost, within walking distance. I hadn't been to London for so long and had never seen much of England at all—Chester

---

1 Cf. Samuel Taylor Coleridge, "The Rime of the Ancient Mariner," lines 27–28 (1798).
2 Typed on a second "Air Letter"; 302 and 303 were "POSTED ON THE HIGH SEAS / S.S. BRAZIL STAR."

really the only town! I did go to Cambridge for a week-end[1]—and was punted about among the ducks and swans—like going to bed with them, almost. Unfortunately I met the ghost of a 20 year old dog in my bedroom there and had a hideous attack of asthma. In fact this allergy to dogs would probably ruin my social life in England eventually.

I hate that new US Embassy—so chunky and heavy and rich in the wrong way, somehow. Or what did you think? I heard you had immense and marvelous entertainments given for you, there, and at Faber's. Dick read at the Embassy—you know how I feel about readings in general, but he was well-received, and he was certainly generous to me far beyond the call of good manners. Somebody I'd just heard of—Gene Baro—was extremely kind. In fact everyone was very nice, although I did wish I had a large impressive MMS or something along to back up my feeble social graces.— Met Donald Hall and friends of his—he was not at all what I'd expected—not that I'd expected *him* at all! Oh so many poets—all the names at the bottoms of columns in those reviews, or at the bottoms of reviews—and most of whose poetry I can't tell apart. And all I'm afraid not terribly interesting. I'm afraid you're the only poet I find very interesting, to tell the truth! There is a deadness there—what is it—hopelessness. The poet I liked best as a person was a Portuguese! He seemed so much more grown up, and tougher— although what I know of his poetry isn't at all. That kind of defiant English rottenness—too strong a word—but a sort of piggish-ness!— As if they've thrown off Victorianism, Georgeianism, Radicalism of the '30s—and now let's all give up together. Even Larkin's poetry is a bit too easily resigned to grimness don't you think? Oh, I am all for grimness and horrors of every sort—but you can't have them, either, by shortcuts—by just saying it.

The pub versus the cafe is an interesting subject for thought. But I've left one country where they have neither for another where they don't even have the dangerous bar.

You know how you finally get down to rock bottom in the ship's library—well last night I read a life of Rupert Brooke—C Hassall, quite recent.[2] It goes on for hundreds and hundreds of pages about his problems, which seemed to be mostly that he thought he was in love with two girls at the same time—and how hideously he suffered through it all, how many pounds he lost and how he couldn't sleep. It does seem like a fantasy. And just before that I had read Queen Victoria's letters to the Princess Royal

1 To stay with Anne Stevenson.
2 Christopher Hassall, *Rupert Brooke* (1964).

(that's really worth looking at)[1]—and it is a preliminary fantasy—one leading right into the other. I hope and pray our lives and problems seem a little realer than those. However—poor Brooke—he was wittier than I thought, and it was a sad death, too.

I have heard bits of broadcasts here and there in the waste of waves about Rochester, etc. and I wonder what is going on. Goldwater! *I can't bear it . . .*

There are those marvelous Piero della Francesca's in The National Gallery—& also I was surprised to see one in Lisbon, but I think it's a fake, or so re-painted it doesn't count—St. Augustine. Lisbon is the prettiest city I've ever seen, from the Tagus—but maybe you've seen it? That little castle of Belém, as you go up the river, gray and crenellated and crumbling, looks like a postage stamp. Alas, right near it they have put up a huge and ghastly monument to all the discoverers, sort of modernistic *prows*; across on the other bank a Christ-statue, like Rio's only worse, and to make sure that "Beauty" is good and dead forever, the USA is now constructing a gigantic bridge right across the city and the river and leading off into the poverty-stricken stretches to the south—why I can't imagine—looks as big as the George Washington Bridge. The town is lovely—dead and poor, no doubt—but ravishing painted buildings, green and orange and blue—clear colors—that big square, all green buildings with white stone trim, palm trees, black & white mosaics and a big green equestrian statue in the middle. But when I saw that new monument, that Christ, that BRIDGE—all totally out of scale and killing everything else—I realized I was back in the Latin world where bad taste is ACTIVE—not just a mistake, or something passive and endurable—but almost deliberately destructive in this century. Why? Then when I saw a dead dog with stiff legs beside the road, unnoticed. I knew I was on my way back to Brazil. I lunched alone in great state at a sort of miniature Versailles of a restaurant—elderly waiters with their tail-coats hanging to the floor at their heels. I told my driver to take me to Lisbon's "best" just for fun, and I think he did. Then he took me to the Flea Market—then to see where he lived—a very exquisite slum—and then where all the students are in prison. (He was a clever boy, I think—never commented at all, just stated, and smiled at me sidewise.)

What did Randall do with *The Three Sisters* I wonder? Translate it or what? What are you doing in Castine? Any boating? How's Harriet? What are you writing? How's Elizabeth? Your dream—if you can remember a

---

1 *Dearest Child: Letters Between Queen Victoria and the Princess Royal, 1858–1861*, ed. Roger Fulford (1964).

dream of June—is a wonderful one. How this ship *heaves*, & I must pack. I am dying to see Lota—

Much love always,

Elizabeth

304.

[Castine, Maine]

August 10, 1964

Dearest Elizabeth:

Marvelous letters about England, Portugal and the boat. I think of you rather buoyantly taking in all you could contain at your own pace and seeing more than all the rushing and rushed swarms straight from the US. I loved your interview in the *Observer*, and thought Lucie-Smith had a good eye for you and your idiom and knew how to use a quote to point up his descriptions of you. Your movie of a book you'd read about England made other observations superfluous, as Miss Moore might say.[1] Your whole trip seems to have been just what it should have been, though I wouldn't have predicted what your eye would have lighted on. I was crazy about the London Pieros too, and I guess I met most of the people you did. Cleanth is rather an embattled Southerner, much more than Tate, Warren, Ransom, but the kindest man to visit or teach with.

By the way, though perhaps I should say nothing yet . . . I think you will probably get a $5,000 award from the Academy of American Poets. The candidates are now you and MacLeish, with you leading. I guess nothing is certain because there are many foolish judges on the board. You should know by September. It would be a well timed homecoming gift.

This summer in Castine has been incredible, a sort of Dutch April of overcast cold days, maybe five in the last forty have been sunny. Sometimes the sun is shining at five-thirty in the morning and then again at five-thirty in

---

1 Edward Lucie-Smith, "No Jokes in Portuguese," *The Times* (July 26, 1964): "Elizabeth Bishop is a poet of real distinction . . . and she has been visiting England for the first time since before the war—soft-voiced, immaculate, unflurried: and smilingly trenchant." EB is quizzed about American and English poetry, praises RL ("we go fishing together"), "seems rather stunned by the near-canonization which has recently overtaken Lowell here," praises Larkin, Darwin, and Empson's prose (as "slightly awkward, but so characteristic. Half a sentence, and you can tell it's by Empson"), and is asked about England: " 'They scold you a great deal,' she says with a twinkle. 'And I'm suffering from caffeine withdrawal. I haven't had a cup of what I'd call coffee since I got here. All the same, it's nice not to have to tell my jokes in Portuguese. But then, I've only thought of one funny thing since I got here—that being in England is rather like going to the movies after you've read the book.' "

the afternoon, as we start our third set of tennis doubles—in between all is cold gray rock.

It hasn't mattered to me directly, because I finally decided to do the *Oresteia*, and have worked in my barn daily and now have a draft of the *Agamemnon*. It's utterly absorbing, but not writing. I have to cut out about a third of the Greek text, and make what is noble, cloudy and deep actable. That is, make a libretto that is rapid, clear and forceful. Well, it reads pretty well, and could be overwhelming on the stage if Kazan should be inspired. But I blush a little at what I've done, and find myself frequently dreaming up prefaces that will explain what I haven't tried to do. I feel like a soldier who has left the field to mold archaic lead spearmen. I've read the galleys of my poems and sliced, with Lizzie's help, ten or fifteen pages out of my American play. Both will be out in October. It will be a busy fall.

What has been new about the summer besides the weather has been having our friends the Brookses with four children next door.[1] Harriet has learned to bike without training wheels and wanders the village alone and has had to have her charge account at Randall's Drug Store stopped. In her group, she has two girls her age, two older and three little boys. She has different feelings about each and is ever in motion. We dread the return to unfree New York for her. She came here very feminine, despising trousers, and now has to be persuaded not to go to bed in her blue jean shorts. What else has happened to her? Learning to put her finger through a candle flame, yearnings to adopt a gaunt black cat that haunts us, gossip on her coevals.

The Brookses are an odd couple. Peter is a Bostonian with an income, enough to allow him to weary of the various jobs he has had from time to time, real estate, music reviewing for the Boston *Globe*, campaigning as a volunteer for Lodge against Teddy Kennedy. Very delicate, kind, zany, hesitant, inarticulate, unwild, good at most things he turns a hand to in an unassuming way. Suddenly he has started writing articles on Boston subjects for a magazine called *Boston*—comedians, schools, a Swedish Princess at Radcliffe, and all is intense activity. Esther, his wife, runs a ballet school in Cambridge, very bright, small, muscular, dramatic dress and delivery, rather on the stage in life. Well, it's all been very easy-going and sociable, a feeling of some play being assembled that turns out to be only a picnic and a tennis match, and everywhere a great wake of children.

Did you read about Flannery O'Connor's death? I know nothing except the longish notice in the *Times* that described her career mostly. I gather she

1 Esther and Peter Brooks.

must have died of the bone disease, Lupus, that plagued her all these years. A book of short stories will come out in January.[1] It seems such a short time ago that I met her at Yaddo, 23 or 24, always in a blue jean suit, working on the last chapters of *Wise Blood*, suffering from undiagnosed pains, a face formless at times, then very strong and young and right. She had already really mastered and found her themes and style, knew she wouldn't marry, would be Southern, shocking and disciplined. In a blunt, disdainful yet somehow very unpretentious and modest way, I think she knew how good she was. I suppose she knew dimly about the future, the pain, the brevity, the peacocks, the life with her mother. She was 38 when she died, and I think always had the character of a commanding, grim, witty child, who knew she was destined to live painfully and in earnest, a hero, rather like a nun or Catholic saint with a tough innocence, well able to take on her brief, hardworking, hard, steady, splendid and inconspicuous life. I think the cards seemed heavily stacked against her, and her fates must have felt that they had so thoroughly hemmed her in that they could forget, and all would [have] happened as planned, but really she did what she had decided on and was less passive and dependent than anyone I can think of.

Tell me how Brazil is, Lota and the political world. It must be good now to be home, no longer moving from place to place, but with new memories inside you.

Our love to you both,
Cal

305.

Rio de Janeiro, August 27th, 1964

Dearest Cal:

Thank you for your letter of August 10th. I started to answer it last night when Mary[2] telephoned from Petrópolis & read me Mrs. Bullock's letter announcing the $5,000[3] (an extremely nice letter, too—very thoughtful). I'm overwhelmed and surprised, and I'll write her as soon as the letter gets down here. I do not deserve it—but I'll try to, retroactively. However, since you said it was between MacLeish & me, I comfort myself with the thought that I'm sure I need it more than he does. (I've never quite recovered from his

---

1 Flannery O'Connor died on August 3, 1964, in Milledgeville, Georgia; *Everything That Rises Must Converge* (1965).
2 Mary Morse.
3 Award from the Academy of American Poets.

coming to Key West on a hired yacht.) This will ensure a trip somewhere for next year—we were figuring desperately how to take one—and it does brighten my outlook on living here, which hadn't been too good since I came back. I am sure a lot of this is due to you and I thank you with all my heart. I know nothing of Mrs. B or that Academy (is it her own money?) except that a little while ago she asked me to "select the poems" for that blue-covered mimeographed monthly. It reminded me of being asked to choose the hymns at school, I think—so I made a small anthology of hymns, and Mrs. B seemed to like the idea so much that her letters got quite chatty, and maybe that has something to do with the $5,000 too! I really feel tremendously cheered. It was almost funny—to go on about little me for a moment. Without thinking of any connection, I got out all the work of 63–64 I'd given up in despair, and now I don't think it's so bad after all. I rarely try to work at night but last night I worked away at a poem about Robinson Crusoe until after two . . .[1] Partly the effects of one vacation and partly the promise of another—but I'm sure I have six or seven possible poems and two stories I can send off soon.

I feel awful about Flannery. Why didn't I go to visit her when she asked me to. And I hadn't even met her, or answered her last letter. Mr. Silvers wrote and asked for something about her and I wrote a page[2]—(another telephoned letter)—then when I got the letter he'd asked for something about her work & it was too late anyway. But I may send what I did. I feel awe in front of that girl's courage and discipline. I have some wonderfully funny letters from her—one about Lourdes—. Lota just read me a bit from the morning paper that Flannery would have liked: there was a fist fight in the Rio Chamber of Deputies. One Deputy who is also a priest held another Deputy in a head-lock to keep him from hitting a third Deputy, and the man screamed (the usual phrase to any priest here) "Bless me, father, bless me! Let me hit him!"

Everybody is dying. One of our best friends, the architect Affonso Reidy (I don't know if you met him—thin, tall, immaculate, more Scotch than Brazilian, and one of the best architects) just died at 54 after six terrible months. Lota has been very upset (this was one reason I left London two weeks early—to get here before he died). He & his wife had a week-end house near us, and now I think we don't have *anyone* left to go to talk with or to have for Sunday supper up there—it's a wilderness. He was one of the few

1 "Crusoe in England" (EB-*CP*).
2 "On Flannery O'Connor," *The New York Review of Books* (Oct. 8, 1964); see EB-*CPR*.

sane people Lota had working with her, too. She swears all Brazilian men are slightly insane—the women are apt to be sane but, alas, morons . . .

I used the word "immaculate." I could forgive Lucie-Smith anything in that interview since he said I was, but I am afraid it's just relative—and that it is fairly easy to appear well-dressed and immaculate in England . . . I'm sure I didn't seem "stunned by the near-canonization" of you in England! That must be a Lucie-Smith "projection." But it could have been much worse—even if he did sort of spoil my one joke.

My passion for accuracy may strike you as old-maidish—but since we do float on an unknown sea I think we should examine the other floating things that come our way very carefully; who knows what might depend on it? So I'm enclosing a clipping about raccoons. But perhaps you prefer mythology. I have a whole batch of new poems on hand here by you, several I hadn't seen before. The Dante translation was much admired in London, I know—and here two Brazilians who get ENCOUNTER have spoken to me about it.[1] The "Washington" poem is certainly Washington in the summer with a vengeance. It brings back all my feelings of misery and horrid anxiety there—only I could never put it into words like that. The image of the eyelids is lovely—and the "delectable mountains"—but the first two stanzas really hit the target. Maybe it's because I feel it so strongly that I want to pick on it—(but I know you are not morbid about these things)—but couldn't it be "rings *in* a tree?"[2] The *on* gave me an unfortunate deck-quoits picture before I realized what you meant. If it were *on* it would have to be a stump—no, that would still be *in*, really. I know the two *ons* are nicer, however. But *in* suggests the un-knowingness of the line before. Oh, I'm a fussbudget. The *PR* poems I had seen; possibly you've changed them a bit. They're both—well—*first-rate*.[3] The Hudson one, as I think I said before, touches me especially. It is like Lota's book "God's Junkyard" reduced to one final image. ENCOUNTER just came ten minutes ago and I haven't had time to study the Devil and his works yet—but naturally I love the "green ribs of a new moon" . . . But please don't age yourself that way in advance, à la Eliot. It doesn't look well saying you're "fragile" and so on![4] Anyone who can do as much work as you have lately must be about twenty-two. Aren't you rather amazed and proud yourself?

---

1 "Brunetto Latini," *Encounter* (July 1964); see RL-*CP*.

2 See "July in Washington," line 14 (RL-*CP*).

3 "Caligula" and "Mouth of the Hudson," *Partisan Review* (Spring 1964); see RL-*CP*.

4 "Going to and fro," "Myopia: A Night," and "The Returning," *Encounter* (Aug. 1964); see "Myopia: A Night," lines 46 and 43 (RL-*CP*).

Dr. Baumann arrives at 8:55 tomorrow morning. I know I'll be delighted to see her but it is hard to know how to keep her entertained and use all that energy for ten days . . . I am trying to get Lota and me in the pink for her, and I must go out on the beach now and acquire some more healthy-looking tan. Then I must go look over her hotel room—brand new one, down the other way from the Copacabana Palace. She wants to swim every morning *before breakfast*, she says.

I've almost caught up with all the back numbers of reviews. I do dislike that illustrator for the *N.Y. Review*, in fact I loathe him[1]—why do they use him, I wonder? But some good reviews—Philip very funny backing-up from Fiedler.[2] Do they pay? I don't want to sound grasping, particularly right now, but I thought I'd get a little something for that poem,[3] and perhaps it got lost. When I started running out of money on my trip I sent Elizabeth a card about it, but perhaps she didn't get that because of the English postal strike. Oh how I wish *PR* would lay off the arguments about Hannah Arendt's book. It seems to me in horrible taste, heartless as well—everyone showing off how brilliant they are in argument—when you think for a moment what it is actually about. I think Dwight did say something to that effect.[4] But can't they leave it alone now? Perhaps it's part of the new coarseness—"raw concrete" building, etc., Burroughs—filthy language. Well, we are brutes and brutalized all right.

I am very impressed by *Agamemnon* and would like to know how on earth you go about it. I am also eager to hear about *The Old Glory* . . .

Brazil—you asked me—I'd rather not think about it. I felt I couldn't endure it when I first got back, and I couldn't if it weren't for Lota, of course. Now I am getting a bit used to it again. But I have to keep reminding myself that Lota does take it, somehow; that she is doing a useful job very well, and that next year we're going to Europe again (and now that seems to be really certain). There is a mild depression on, the inflation is awful although it hasn't changed much while I was away, and one feels anxiety everywhere and all the time.

Flávio didn't get into Harvard. I feel horribly guilty about not having done all that same work for three places at least . . . I know there are many possible reasons why he didn't and that they have very few places for foreign students, etc. At the same time I am still irritated by that man's foot-note in

1 David Levine.
2 Philip Rahv, "Lettuce and Tomatoes," *The New York Review of Books* (July 9, 1964).
3 "The Table" (EB-*CP*).
4 See Dwight Macdonald, "Eichmann and the Jews," *Partisan Review* (Spring 1964).

the letter to you—about "building a fire" under poor Flávio! It may be just a phrase the man uses about students all the time—but I am getting so sensitive on the subject of Brazil that I feel it is one of those condescending preconceptions that drive me mad.— I saw Flávio trying so hard to get everything done and mailed! I wrote to Mr. Glimp once or twice myself explaining that two letters did get lost—F's professors were *awful,*—uncooperative—one never would fill out a form and finally lost it, etc. Flávio never said anything at all (I was away) but grew a beard (Lota got rid of that) and has become violently anti-US and pro-communist. He tries to be tactful about the US with me, of course. His talents are really purely literary and artistic—and he has a kind heart, etc.—and it's all just going down the drain here in this political lunacy—for which he has no brains at all, and I think no *real* interest. He is going on with his second stage of the diplomatic exams, etc. Even if he passes in October he may not get in now because of politics and his own indiscretions. I think it is a *rotten* career, anyway. Oh God. I don't know whether anyone *can* "save" anyone else.

August 30th—Sunday
Well—Dr. Baumann arrived early Friday morning, looking tanned, healthy, glowing—burnt to a crisp really by a climb on a glacier 2 days before . . . She is full of information about Brazil, has been studying it and knows my "book" by heart, and has a little notebook with lists of things to be seen, inquired about, eaten, etc. She has her finger on the pulse of Brazil and is asking it to hold out its tongue, in other words. Today we lunch with Carlos Lacerda who is then going to show us the works—his works—and says he's going to drive. Save Us! Tuesday I'm going to take her to Ouro Prêto etc. for three days. I am delighted to see her really—if only I can keep up with her!

Oh—I've been asked to be a Writer in Residence at Rutgers one term of 1966—for $7,000 or $8,000. Apparently I could live in NY and be there only 2 days a week. Also Dick W[1] said something about that Wesleyan Institute (Advance Studies or something)—didn't you or E do that once? I know absolutely nothing about either of these places or jobs & any suggestions you might have would be very welcome. I really feel teaching is not my line at all, and I'd do better to dig in and write—also I'd hate to leave Lota, if she couldn't come with me—so I don't know what to say—but a chance of getting away for a few months does appeal to me.

1 Richard Wilbur.

And what about this anthology Keith keeps writing about? He is now trying to seduce me by saying he's "sure Cal would say yes, too." Poor Keith! I must prepare myself for this strenuous and awful afternoon of tunnel-seeing, etc. . . .

With much love as always—

Elizabeth

306.

Rio, October 1st, 1964

Dearest Cal:

Just a note to say I received the new book safely a few days ago, and to thank you for it and for the cheering, comforting inscription . . .[1] It looks awfully well, a nice job—I like the new title for that poem "Colonel Shaw."[2] Three poems in it are new to me, "Severed Head," "Hawthorne," and the "Epigram." I love the Hawthorne if only for the one line about re-silvering the "smudged plate . . ."[3] I am sure it will have—probably already has—a tremendous success, because I think a couple of those poems—as I said when I first read them, "Night Sweat" and "The Flaw," are just bound to be the most *popular* you have ever written—real modern love-poems, like no others I know of. I haven't had time to do very much comparing yet—it is not my line, anyway. It is [a] fine book.

2nd—

I stopped then and, shortly afterwards, this year's Fulbright man—in American Literature at the Faculdade de Filisofia—came to dinner—first time I'd met him. An Ashley Brown—I think you must have met him—ran *Shenandoah*, seems to know lots of literary people, particularly the Southern set, has just written a book about Caroline Gordon,[4] and even had messages to me, sad to say, from Flannery, whom he knew very well. He got more and more Southern as the evening went on, and we had a sort of old-fashioned evening of reminiscences, until after 2. Rather nice, tall, thin, delicate, blinking, bookish creature—who seized on your book and did start "comparing" im-

1 *For the Union Dead* (1964); in his "Note," RL writes, " 'The Scream' owes everything to Elizabeth Bishop's beautiful, calm story, *In the Village*."
2 "Colonel Shaw and the Massachusetts 54th" was an early title of "For the Union Dead" (RL-*CP*).
3 See "Hawthorne," line 9 (RL-*CP*).
4 Ashley Brown's doctoral thesis, "Caroline Gordon and the Impressionist Novel," was never published.

mediately—obviously what he lives for! Well—it is nice to have someone here to be able to talk with once in a while—although I'm not good for such concentrated "LETTERS life" for long— The kind of man who doesn't see very much unless it is written down somewhere, I think—but I may be misjudging him. I certainly wish I had visited Flannery now, he told such good stories about Milledgeville. Did you hear of her uncle who died a few years ago and left all his property—several "plantations"—*legally* to "The robins and the bobolinks"? It took years of legal disputing and looking up similar cases in England (of course) to get the will set aside.

He seemed to know all your poems by heart—in fact, yours were the only poems he did know, but they obviously sufficed for him! And he seemed to be very knowledgeable and have good taste (perhaps a slight Southern lapse for Caroline . . .).

I must say (all over again) how beautiful the lines in "Law" about the back-lash struck me—and "and each unique set stone."[1] And in "Eye and Tooth" the summer rain "fell in pinpricks"[2]—heavens, that is lovely. And in "The Old Flame" the "simmering like wasps" image[3]—and the really exquisite last stanza of that one. "It's authentic perhaps / to have been there, if now"[4] just those two lines—are your first and only that have ever reminded me of Marianne. Not the rest!

Massa Ashley told me you had a review of Berryman's *Dream Poems*[5] in the N.Y. *Times*[6]—away back last May. I missed that—it must have got lost—and I'd certainly like to see it. I know you're too busy for such things—but if you *do* have a copy around, I'd appreciate it very much sometime. I'm pretty much at sea about that book—some pages I find wonderful, some baffle me completely. I am sure he is saying *something* important—perhaps sometimes too personally?—also feel he's probably next-best to you—(Influence of last evening) Weird influence of "Wreck of the Deutschland," I sensed.[7]

Please write when you have the time—and best wishes for the play.

Much love,

Elizabeth

---

1 "Law," lines 12 and 24 (RL-*CP*).
2 "Eye and Tooth," lines 9–11 (RL-*CP*).
3 "My Old Flame," lines 34–35 (RL-*CP*).
4 "Going to and Fro," lines 1–2 (RL-*CP*).
5 John Berryman, *77 Dream Songs* (1964).
6 "The Poetry of John Berryman," *The New York Review of Books* (May 28, 1964); RL-*CPR*.
7 Gerard Manley Hopkins, "The Wreck of the Deutschland" (1918).

307.

Dearest Elizabeth:

Just a brief note to tell you I am still here and thinking about you. Everything has been happening at once, Harvard, play rehearsals, my book coming out tomorrow, Jonathan Miller in my study. I go through the day, lying sitting standing, listening reading, rather like a horse on a carousel up and down through the gay dance, vaguely feeling nothing is well done and that essentials are being forgotten. But all's well, fun and experience, I guess and soon it will be over, leaving a wake of memories.

I liked your Flannery note very much. I think people are now beginning to assume that she is one of our best writers. She seems to be on everyone's list, Saul Bellow, Peter Taylor etc. Perhaps she was lucky to have been spared her full boom. I appear to be on the verge of mine—front page glowing reviews in the *Times* and *Tribune*, one in *Newsweek*, interviews in all three.[1] I can't say I don't find it all very occupying and exciting, but what use? More invitations to be on dull committees, more books in the mails for blurbs, more tiresome doctor's degrees. Thank god, it can't go very far for a poet.

I got your comments on the Washington poem too late for changes. I guess I'd say that the raccoons were meant to be a tired myopic image. I thought of year after year winding another ring *on* the tree, like a roll of cloth, as generation on generation filled the circles of Washington.

Sorry your architect friend died. Wasn't it in his apartment we listened to Carlos' banned, delayed television speech? Dr. Baumann glows with her visit. I travel to Brazil in my mind, but I guess I like being here, a little like a stone lost in its pile of stones. I've heard too many rehearsals, read too many letters, dipped quickly into too many books and articles, but Lizzie says I am wonderfully unexcited. On the 29th, I introduce Randall, who will be reading your poems at the Guggenheim. Everyone yearns for your new book.

Love to you and Lota,

Cal

---

1 G. S. Fraser, "Amid the Horror, a Song of Praise," *The New York Times Book Review* (Oct. 4, 1964); Richard Poirier, "Our Truest Historian," *New York Herald Tribune* (October 11, 1964); and "In Bounds," *Newsweek* (Oct. 12, 1964).

308.

Dearest Elizabeth:

Things have been thundering away at such a rate that I have no time to answer your good letters—teaching, my book, the play opening[1] and Cousin Harriet's death. I've weathered all pretty well, I think, and haven't panicked into excitement. What you say about the "Union Dead" poem is subtly true, too, I think of my life with its recovery from steps into disintegration. There must be a huge hunk of health that has survived and somehow increased through all these breakdown[s], eight or nine, I think, in about fifteen years. Pray god there'll be no more. The play has been a raving success d'estime, despite patronizing reviews from the daily critics. I'll mail you some of the best. Randall, strangely malleable and boyish without his beard, thinks the second play the best thing I've ever written.[2] So, so.

I wish you could have been invisibly present at our Bishop evening.[3] Randall's reading of your poems was odd and mannered but his comments were inspired and gave a gorgeous and very deserved and accurate personal portrait of you—I mean through the poetry. Lota's long monologue read beautifully[4]; so did "The Man Moth" and "Armadillo," which he ended with. Everything read well, and we both said you were the best poet of our generation.

Dear Love, I'm off to Harvard now (via my Monday meeting with my therapist) and can't write a decent letter, but things are now much less hectic. How I miss you, Darling.

Love to you both,

Cal

---

1 On November 1, 1964, at the American Palace Theatre.

2 See Randall Jarrell, "A Masterpiece," *The New York Times* (November 29, 1964).

3 A celebration of EB's poetry for the Academy of American Poets, with RL and Randall Jarrell, Guggenheim Museum, October 29, 1964. RL remarked: "This is a very dear evening to me. Elizabeth Bishop is the contemporary poet that both I and Randall Jarrell admire the most. Her poems come slowly. You feel she never wrote a poem just to fill a page. If the poem stops coming, she'll often put it away several years—or forever if it doesn't come. I think she's hardly ever written a poem that wasn't a real poem. There's a beautiful formal completeness to all of Elizabeth's poetry. I don't think anyone alive has a better eye than she has, the eye that sees things and the mind behind the eye that remembers, and the person that remembers would be very hard to characterize, but it's a person with a good deal of tolerance and humor. Really, it defeats me to sum up the personality, but that's far more important than the description, even" (transcript of tape recording, Academy of American Poets).

4 "Manuelzhino" (EB-*CP*).

309.

November [22], 1964

Dearest Elizabeth:

Marianne Moore was here last night and said your "Burglar" ballad was your finest poem.[1] Who knows, but it's another of your peculiar triumphs like the Pound.[2] It's surely one of the great ballads in the language, and oddly enough gives more of Brazil somehow than your whole Life book. I wonder what Carlos would make of it? I left a message at his hotel for him to call me—it was impossible to get through to him—but he never answered. I wanted, though I was sure he wouldn't have the time. I [met] your friend Eulalio again—a man of quite a different slant, I gather.[3] The ballad is really lovely, not a line too many, which is almost unbelievable in ballad quatrains.

I've just read through Marianne's new Faber collection, and rather to my surprise think it's as good as anything she's ever written—a kind of wild lyrical abandon, and four or five of her most serious poems, and almost everything good.[4] Some of them made my eyes water. Oh me, she's really so much better than Berryman or Roethke,[5] our best this year.

Well, I've weathered my excitements and everyone's astonished. It's partly Miltown,[6] a drug that somehow soothes, without heaviness and depression, preliminary panic. Now I must go and read through Shelley's *Prometheus*,[7] a task for me, I'm afraid, though scattered through it are many of his lovely verses. I like his politics well enough, but that universal European romantic rhetoric, grand without observation, humor, or the heartbreaking loving-kindness of Hardy, wearies.

Dearest friend, I miss you so!!!!

All my love,

Cal

---

1 "The Burglar of Babylon," *The New Yorker* (Nov. 21, 1964); see EB-*CP*.
2 "Visits to St. Elizabeths" (EB-*CP*).
3 Alexandre Pimenta da Cunha Eulálio, editor of literary magazine *Revista do Livro*. He was visiting the United States with the State Department's Foreign Leaders Program.
4 Marianne Moore, *The Arctic Ox* (1964).
5 John Berryman, *77 Dreams Songs* (1964); Theodore Roethke, *The Far Field* (1964).
6 See "Man and Wife," line 1 (RL-*CP*).
7 Percy Bysshe Shelley, *Prometheus Unbound* (1820).

310.[1]

Dearest Cal:

It's a hot Sunday afternoon and someone has just asked if he could bring *two* American couples for tea . . . Save us. We couldn't seem to get out of it. This is just to say that an acquaintance of mine is leaving for Boston Wednesday, and I'm giving her a small gift for you and yours (mostly) to put in the mail. I wanted to send you another Arthur Deller record—Campion songs, etc.[2]—but it's too complicated—and you may have it. If not, do get it—if you like his voice, that is. But PLEASE don't try to send me anything—as I think I may have said, the customs have now gone absolutely mad—not even books can arrive without going through customs—they're still duty-less, or almost— But there have been speeches in the Senate, etc. (Things look very revolution-like at the moment.[3]) I was told (by a *suspected* Communist, naturally) (I checked with L.) that keeping books out was a good thing because now "Brazil would produce more literature"—like cars!

I read and re-read the book and honestly think it's better every time. I am appreciating all the changes now. Aside from you I seem to read only Shakespeare these days—good old Shakespeare as Mary McC used to say . . . We are having an early hot spell and everything looks wonderful. Auden's latest says that we shouldn't live in the south because we get lecherous, flabby, and forget to pay our bills[4]—but I don't believe any of it.

These views[5] are on the way up to a small town about 1,000 feet higher than we are— But I think I have sent you the Finger of God before now, so I'd better stick to letters.

With much love,
Elizabeth

311.

Dearest Cal:

Thank you for your two notes and I hope you *really* like the ballad (you sound as if you did) because it is one of those odd ones I can't make up my

---

1 Crossed with letter 309.

2 Alfred Deller, *Music of Buxtehude and Lutenist Songs (Campion/Milano/Anonymous)*, L'Oiseau-Lyre OL 50102.

3 In November 1964, federal troops deposed the governor of the state of Goiás, who was suspected of subversion.

4 "If we try / To 'go southern,' we spoil in no time, we grow / Flabby, dingily lecherous, and / Forget to pay bills"; W. H. Auden, "Good-Bye to the Mezzogiorno," *Homage to Clio* (1960), from lines 76–79.

5 The enclosed images do not survive.

mind about . . . I am so glad to hear about the play and dear Dr. Anny sent me her program for it—very pretty. Yesterday I got the following, I mean enclosed, postcard with a note from Mrs. Gordon, the wife of the US Ambassador. The card is from their daughter, studying "theatre"—she didn't know the G's had met you, so it really is a spontaneous tribute—don't bother to return. Well—I wish I could see both plays—I did see a picture somewhere of "Benito Cereno"—but I'd like to see how they did the set for "Major Molineux."

Richard Kelly, the lighting man (he did the Seagram Building, for one—and Mass. Tech, and new houses at Harvard—in fact just about everything new and good one can think of), has been here for a week planning the lighting for Lota's Flamingo Park. He has had some really lovely ideas—I particularly like one bit I copied out for him about "shadowy areas of small scintillation, intimate areas for romance"—that is the Rio spirit! Carlos was taken with him, too, and although he came just for the park job C now wants him to do the SugarLoaf . . . etc., etc. Sounds awful—but Kelly's ideas sound lovely, even for that. Anyway—I took him print-hunting and I am sending along by him a funny lithograph I hope you will like. It is taken from a book and I *think* must be from a German-Jesuit—(or some Catholic missionaries)—Father, of around 1810–20. On the Amazon—rather an imaginary Amazon, but they did make weird straw-cornucopia boats like that. What the raft-full of jars signifies I have no idea—although they still have rafts of bigger jars—of just water—on the river now. I'll find out . . . It should be smoothed out a bit—pretty hopeless to clean it—but my friend who does such work is away, and there isn't time. Any framer could do it, though.

Carlos L is in lots of trouble now. I am awfully disappointed in him, anyway—have been for a long time, but it gets worse all the time. He said he wanted to see you but just didn't have time. He saw Dr B.—about his wife's ears, etc.— Dr B. just loves him and fortunately can't see the bad side of things. It was such a *stupid* idea to go to N.Y. at the invitation of *Reader's Digest*, of all things . . . It is a tragic waste of intelligence—and it looks now as if he had cooked his goose here, politically. It is all much too involved to go into—(I sent CL the ballad—)

I wrote to Randall to thank him—I hope he gets it. I've tentatively accepted going to teach at Roethke's old job[1]—but not till Jan. 1966—try it out for one term or two. I want to see that part of the world, and I only hope I can persuade Lota to come along for part of my stay, too.

1 At the University of Washington, Seattle.

I'd love to talk to you—so much to tell, and you have much more. Marianne's saying the ballad was my "best" makes me a bit uneasy! I think she likes the message: "Crime does not pay" too well! . . . Once I wrote an ironic poem about a drunken sailor and a slot-machine[1]—*not* a success—and the sailor said he was going to throw the machine into the sea, etc., and M congratulated me on being so morally courageous and outspoken . . . (I've ordered her new book.)

Eulalio Pimenta is a mysterious young man . . . a "monarchist!" Now I've just been "interviewed" by the man that wrote for Robie[2] a few times—so dumb, poor chap, he seemed to think I'd be furious because Dr King got the Nobel Peace prize . . .

I'll write a better letter on the week-end. Remember me to E. & H. & I hope you are all well—& KEEP WELL— With lots of love, as always,

Elizabeth

P.S.—I had a letter from May Swenson yesterday enclosing clippings from the *Village Voice.* That Ruth Herschberger—she must have taken leave of her senses!—or be suffering badly from the old disease (envy?) It is too bad you have to reply to such letters and I hope there haven't been any more.[3] May of course thinks the plays all wonderful—and heard you read & discuss "Endecott & the Red Cross."

The heat has struck at last with a vengeance—I'm being air-conditioned and it is rather nice—it does shut out the other sounds, telephones, singing maids, etc. just enough. Last summer we didn't even have to turn them on. We dined last night at the Museum (which is nothing but the best restaurant in town, anyway) with that Aloysio de Paula who gave a little party for you—you might remember him—tall, enthusiastic, shaved-head doctor, nice but foolish . . . Anyway—across the table he suddenly called to me—"How's that nice boy? SO sympathetic! I have just read a BEAUTIFUL poem by him called 'The Union Dead' " . . . And he even quoted a bit— That is really amazing for here.

But I yearn to get away. Ashley Brown is pleasant—I see him about once a week—but so literary I can't keep up with him—a sort of gazetteer of US

---

1 "The Soldier and the Slot-Machine" (EB-*EAP*).
2 While Robie Macauley was editor of *The Kenyon Review.*
3 Ruth Herschberger condemned RL's *Benito Cereno* as racist (Letter to the Editor, *The Village Voice,* Nov. 12, 1964). RL replied that Herschberger had confused his own views with the character of Captain Delano, and rebuked her letter as "malicious," "slanderous," and a "deliberate falsification" (Letter to the Editor, *The Village Voice,* Nov. 19, 1964). See RL-*Letters,* 453–54.

writing, writers, and colleges. He is giving a set of lectures here & in São Paulo. One is on you, mostly, and me, some. I have promised to help him with some details. He's really much too good to be teaching here, however, and, I suspect, wonders why he is doing it.

I must write a note to Marianne for Kelly to take along, too. How does she seem to you?

Abraços,

E.

Rainy Sunday PM in the country—

It's so cold I have a huge fire going in my fireplace. I stare out into a wonderfully Chinese landscape of bamboo and rocks and lichens and the waterfall, all lined with rain. I wish we could stay up here and am considering staying on a few days alone to work.

I opened this up to say that I got two copies of the *N.Y. Review* when I got here, and a check for the Flannery piece. I was surprised—that doesn't seem right, somehow, to receive money for that little note on such an occasion. Elizabeth's remarks are awfully good, aren't they—just right about the southern religious manias—that I had tried just to hint at—so that luckily the two pieces go quite well together, I thought[1]— But surely there will be a lot more.

Yesterday I was listening to my new Archive record of Gesualdo's madrigals[2]—an excellent record I recommend. It struck me how much your poetry reminds me of Gesualdo's music—have you ever heard him? Wild and surprising harmonies, apparently a simple thought but made suddenly so strange and penetrating. If ever you do run across any more recordings of his music I'd be grateful for them—they're hard to find. And see if you don't agree with me . . .

With much love,
Elizabeth

1 EB and Elizabeth Hardwick contributed to "Flannery O'Connor, 1925–1964," *The New York Review of Books* (Oct. 8, 1964).

2 Carlo Gesualdo, *Italian Madrigals*, Singgemeinschaft Rudolph Lamy (Archive DGG ARC 3073).

312.

Dearest Cal:

Wish I'd hear from you before I go to Ouro Prêto tomorrow—for a week or ten days—Ashley Brown is going, too—he'll stay at the hotel & I'll stay with our friend Lilli[1]—a big house and I hope I can get some work done in peace in the mornings, meet A and go sight-seeing in the afternoons— Lota could forward mail—but it would probably take forever. I know how busy you are—I can gather just from the papers and from other correspondents. Howard Moss said he sat in back of you & E at "Tiny Alice"[2]—this is my latest news! You looked well, from in back . . . "Tiny Alice," according to TIME, sounds even grimmer than WHO'S AFRAID OF VIRGINIA WOOLF[3] (I saw that in London) Dr B liked "Benito Cereno" very much— better than the 1st one. I saw the marvelous review by Brustein in the *New Republic*.[4]— Ashley tells me he has an even more enthusiastic one to show me.— Oh dear, Cal—Hollywood next?

I had a nice long letter from Randall—first in years—and he wants me to change publishers and go with Michael di Capua to Pantheon—but there isn't any point in changing. Also Chatto & Windus again—again I think thanks to you. They did so miserably by me the first time—but maybe they'll do better now. (I can't seem to get very *interested* in publishing.)

I am sure you feel very badly about Eliot; and I'm very sorry, too. [I won]der why on earth he was still in London at this time of year? And [the] picture I saw of him at the time he received that medal showed him [loo]king very sick, I thought.[5] Poor Valerie.

However—a very chipper letter from Marianne!

We spent ten days or so at Samambaia—and it rained almost continuously, but we didn't mind a bit because it kept everyone away . . . What peace. We did a monster jig-saw puzzle—took four evenings!— I did a bit of work. Have you seen the show at the M of M Art—"Architecture without Architects"? Richard Kelly sent me the book and it is wonderful[6]— However, as he said, too, there should be a page or two from Brazil in it— some of the favelas are so beautiful,—and the basket-work houses on stilts

---

1 Lilli Correia de Araújo (see letter 324).
2 Edward Albee, *Tiny Alice* (1964), with John Gielgud and Irene Worth at the Billy Rose Theatre.
3 Albee, *Who's Afraid of Virginia Woolf?* (1962), with Uta Hagen at the Piccadilly Theatre, London.
4 Robert Brustein, "We Are Two Cultural Nations," *The New Republic* (Nov. 21, 1964).
5 T. S. Eliot received the 1964 Presidential Medal of Freedom. He died on January 4, 1965. (The bracketed words in the paragraph are due to the airmail paper having been burned by cigarette ash.)
6 Bernard Rudofsky, *Architecture Without Architects: A Short Introduction to Non-Pedigreed Architecture* (1965).

along the Amazon. Rudofsky (he used to live here, you know) is funny—speaks of a "superbly underdeveloped country"—(I am using this in a poem). Flávio ran away from home—it is high time, we think—spent about a week with us, went home again, left again, and now has a rented room away up in Santa Teresa with a friend of his we like very much, fortunately—a very sensible, bright young man. Flávio is *in* the Foreign Service—but has to take another set of final exams in July. I am awfully glad now he *didn't* get to Harvard—he's in no state to do anything, really—and he is going back to the analyst (thank heavens) as soon as the a. can take him—about another month to wait. He has two newspaper jobs to keep him going, and I think just getting away from home will help a lot.— I don't know how he stood it—and he almost never said a word of complaint. I wish he'd get to the Fletcher School of Diplomacy at Tufts eventually—and he was very interested in it, too (a friend went) until he developed this really rabid anti-Americanism. Maybe he'll get over it.

Well, you have much more amusing things to think of than this superbly underdeveloped country and this backward friend! I think you and Elizabeth, too, might like to see the enclosed[1]— Of course the black girl is still a *cook*—but even so, you'd never see ads. like this in the USA—

313.

[Postcard: Holy-week Procession, S. Francisco de Assisi Church, Ouro Prêto]

[n.d. 1965?]

There seems to have been a procession and fireworks, etc. almost every night since I've been here. The whole population waited in the square the other night for a Virgin who was coming to visit St. Francis—this church— When she finally arrived—on top of a station wagon, with two or three cars full of priests, business-men, etc.— We were directed to clap our hands for the Virgin—and we did, with loud "Vivas"— It was just like an operetta. Two bands played—and the procession went round and round the square—if you remember it—as fast as it could— "A big hand for Our Lady of Fatima"—the Ouro Prêto priest screamed over the loud-speaker— "Viva!"—we all screamed.— This [(]the evening's entertainment[)] alternates with movies that seem to deal mostly with prostitution—The Life of Christine Keeler, or "Women of Sin"—etc. It's all in strong chiaroscuro—perhaps like old New England, almost?

1 The enclosure does not survive.

314.

Dear Elizabeth & Cal:

This is just a note to say I hope you are both well and that it has been ages since I have heard from you and I am a bit worried . . . Although I know, of course, how extremely busy you must both be at this time of year, and what with everything I see going on—at least I see about the previous month's goings-on—in the *NY Review*s . . . That full page ad for Cal's book has just arrived in the NY *Times Book Review*—whee—and of course I read Snodgrass, etc.[1]—probably almost everything. It is all wonderful, and gives one hope.

I hope you got the old lithograph I sent up by Richard Kelly? I *thought* he wrote he had distributed everything I sent, and it is possible that a letter from you has got lost—although I haven't lost any mail since the "revolution" (it at least paid the PO workers' back pay).

On the other hand—you may be wondering why on earth you haven't heard from me. Yesterday I turned up a bundle of un-opened letters, including a notice from the Customs office.— It says something arrived for me by Panair on December 18th. The notice itself didn't come until after January 15th . . . And I didn't get it until yesterday, because I was away for two weeks in Minas and dear illiterate Joanna gave me *some* of my mail when I got back, but not this little *cache* I just found yesterday . . . The package will be picked up today. Now it may be a piece of rotting, by this time, Canadian cheddar from my aunt—but I have a feeling it may be something from you. If it isn't—don't be embarrassed! It is just that I would like to hear from you so much that I am imagining intuitions, perhaps.

I went to Ouro Prêto with Ashley Brown, the southern Ful Prof. here this year—very pleasant and an excellent traveler. We hired a car and made some rather extensive and difficult trips—awful hotels—because I want to see everything, and perhaps write a piece about that Aleijadinho, or Brazilian rococo, something like that. I have also been polishing off the Drummond— his part of the country made me go back to it—and that should be along soon. I got so bored with it—now it's revived a bit. John Mander (ex-*Encounter*) and his wife came to Ouro Prêto, too, while we were there—but I think now they said they *didn't* see you in New York . . . I think they want Lota to run the magazine here, which would be a fine idea—if she'll do it, & if ever she gets the park finished enough to stop and just serve as president of

---

1 W. D. Snodgrass, "In Praise of Robert Lowell," *The New York Review of Books* (Dec. 3, 1964).

its Preservation Foundation—the next job in sight. It is looking like a real park—but Lota isn't looking too much like the real Lota, I'm afraid. Now the big companies are trying to bribe her—"a trip to Europe, for two, Dona Lota?" etc., for contracts.— L says she was so surprised she wasn't indignant the way she should have been—even said "thank you!" but NO. All kinds of weird gifts arrive—radios, cases of wine, boxes and boxes of dreadful chocolates—black market scent—etc.

Giroux seems to be arranging my book for this year. How do you like Randall's?[1] I must write him, and my feelings are very mixed.— I haven't seen anything by Elizabeth for some time—have I missed things? I do hope and pray you are both well—that Harriet is flourishing, too—

With much love,
Elizabeth

315.

Samambaia
February 23rd, 1965

Dearest Cal:

Yes, the mysterious package at the *alfandega*[2]—it said only Caixa Postal 279, Est. do Rio on it, so how they guessed Petrópolis and let me know, is amazing—was, as I'd felt, from you, and we brought up the three nice records last weekend. Thank you very much—they're all nice. I am particularly surprised and pleased, too, with the Azzaiolo—never heard of him or his collection before, and I wonder if you listened to that side of the Gesualdo?[3] They are lovely songs, quite funny, some of them, and "popular"— couldn't be more different from the beautiful Gesualdos—or from Bossa Nova . . . I didn't have any of this last and so I am glad to—that's the best recording of it, I think—Lyra and Jobim the two best, and quite good—even if Lota says, "It's music for the *young* . . ." in a world-weary way . . . Did we ever tell you about "Ipanema"?[4]—That's the big beach after Copacabana, where most of the rich people have moved to *now*. Well—once there was an English couple; the man had worked in Brazil all his life and finally it was time for them to retire back to a little cottage in the country in England.

1 Randall Jarrell, *The Lost World* (1965).
2 Customhouse.
3 Carlo Gesualdo/*Madrigals* and Filippo Azzaiolo/ *Villote del fiore* (Vox STDL-500.900 1962).
4 "Garota de Ipanema," written by Antônio Carlos Jobim and Vinicius de Moraes; the English lyrics of "The Girl from Ipanema" were written by Norman Gimbel, featured on *Getz/Gilberto* (1964).

They had loved Rio and the beaches so much that they named their cottage "Ipanema." A few years later an old Brazilian friend came to visit them, looked rather surprised at the letters on their house, and finally told them. It means "Dirty Water" in Indian.

I did a piece of pure journalism—impure, rather—for the N.Y. *Times*[1]— you may see it next Sunday, but I'd rather you didn't. However, it did get me going on prose again and I am up here this week trying to finish a couple of other things. Plus a poem for ENCOUNTER—if it turns out to be any good at all, it is to be dedicated to you[2] and I'll send you one—but not unless I think it's really some good. The NY *Times* (Harvey Shapiro???) is almost as foolish as LIFE—cables flying every day, "What is the population of Rio?" etc.—*surely* they could find out a few facts for themselves? However, it will finish paying for our beautiful new garage! I just hope they don't change it too much—although it's all very light-weight.

Carneval is this week-end—I think we'll actually go down late Sunday night and sit in the grandstands all night long to see the sambas. I haven't done this for three years now, and this year promises to be very good and just possibly a bit more on time. We've given up at dawn a few times without having seen the good schools. It is exhausting but one of the few things here really worth seeing—and it won't be for much longer, I'm afraid.

We hope to get to Italy in April—end of April maybe. Lota is not sure of her vacation yet, however. She needs a rest & a change badly—but has never been more successful nor famous—the 1,000's of people every day in that park are very gratifying, and every time I turn on the radio or (Joanna's) TV it seems to me they're talking about her. Well—it is nice to have such famous friends! (Elizabeth, L. & you—)

Horribly lonely here, but I don't mind for a few days. I do hope you are keeping well and not trying to do too much, if you'll forgive the cliché—and I'd love to hear from you, you know! Lots of love, and thank you again for the lovely Christmas present,

Elizabeth

I am reading Wittgenstein—with great difficulty—"Philosophical Investigations."[3]

---

1 "On the Railroad Named Delight," *The New York Times Magazine* (March 7, 1965); see EB-*CPR*.
2 Possibly "Apartment in Leme" (EB-*EAP*).
3 Ludwig Wittgenstein, *Philosophical Investigations*, trans. G.E.M. Anscombe (probably the 1958 edition).

316.[1]

Dearest Elizabeth:

The wonderful lithograph[2] is hanging to the left of our fireplace in the big room. One can stand with one eye fixed on it and the other on the silver slave's fertility decoration we bought in Brazil and have set in the middle of the dining room table—amulets against the evils of New York. Further on in the kitchen hangs the modern primitive banana painting of Keith's friend from Recife. Keith, by the way, has an article in *Commentary* entitled "My Friend Fuentes," in which he makes sure that his personal adoration doesn't blind him to flaws in the thinker and novelist.[3] Back a few sentences . . . many thanks for your lovely present. I hope the bundle in customs is our Christmas present, an unworthy return, the complete Gesualdo, two records, one of which I'm sure you already have, and a joke record. I sent them air-mail, hoping that timeliness would make up for their meagerness.

I am back from a month in the sanitarium. It was a quiet stay this time. I went in almost well and so had little of the jolting re-evaluation that usually comes. These attacks seem now almost like something woven in my nervous system and one of the ingredients of my blood-stream, and I blame them less on some fatal personal psychotic flaw. Who knows? They are nothing to be blithe about, but I feel rather composed about it all. Here I am back in the bosom of my family, and back in my study, and getting ready to finish the *Oresteia*. Life and work go on.

One can talk more easily of Randall, now that he has shaved and walks the same earth we do. Gone the noble air of pained, aloof nobility. Something touching and imposing to look at is gone, but what a relief for his friends! I'm afraid I like the perverse savage new poems best: "In Montecito" and "Three Bills," and of the straight serious poems, "Next Day." Most of the opening poems except, I think, for the long "Lost World" are good, and I found I was underlining a lot of lines in poems I didn't entirely like. His worst fault is the repetition of a style and subject, as though Housman had written rather voluminously and slopped up his meter, and strung individual poems out. Endless women, done with a slightly mannered directness, repeated verbal and syntactical tricks, an often perverse and sadistic tender-

---

1 Crossed with letter 315.
2 Brought to RL by Richard Kelly.
3 Keith Botsford, "My Friend Fuentes," *Commentary* (Feb. 1965).

ness—but I am getting into clichés in describing. I like him better than any of us except you when he is good.

I think and hope and know that I have reached the end of my publicity splash. There's a rather crude, hair-blown series of pictures and remarks by me in *Life*.[1] They threw out most of the quotes I wanted, and chose clumsily and meaninglessly from the pictures they had. Rather better is an interview with me in *Encounter*.[2] I'm awfully glad and excited that Giroux will soon be bringing out your poems. We have all been waiting, its seems for years and years to get them all together, so many favorites in this last lot, probably your best book.

While I was in the sanitarium, I went into Hartford, our town, and saw a not very good but touching performance of *Uncle Vanya*. On leaving, I heard one of the audience say, "Of course, it's hardly dramatic in our sense." Her friend answered, "Yes, it's like all Russian plays." First voice, "Yes, *The Cherry Orchard* and *The Wild Duck* are like this."[3] Tomorrow we are going to see the Russian Arts Theater do the *Cherry Orchard*.

Sorry Lota is tired. Maybe you should scoop up a bribe and both come here in the spring.

All my love,
Cal

317.

Rio, March 11th, 1965

Dearest Cal:

How wonderful to hear from you again . . . It is true that I had half-suspected, of course, but kept trying to believe I was wrong. Then just before I heard from you I had a letter from Bob Giroux mentioning your return from Hartford very naturally. He also sent me the pages from LIFE. As you say, they didn't make a very good choice, probably, of either photographs or quotations,—but, then, they never do. And some of the photographs aren't so bad! I rather like the one with both hands up, as if you were being held up (by LIFE), and the one with the actors.[4] You *do* look a lot like the cousin

---

1 "Applause for a Prize Poet," *Life* (Feb. 19, 1965).
2 A. Alvarez, "A Talk with Robert Lowell," *Encounter* (Feb. 1965).
3 Anton Chekhov, *Uncle Vanya* (1900) and *The Cherry Orchard* (1904); Henrik Ibsen, *The Wild Duck* (1884).
4 RL pictured with Roscoe Lee Browne.

Charles R L,[1] now that I study it—the same shaped forehead, the same upper lip. And the hands are good in all of them—very animated! What is this about a trip to Chile?[2] Is it true, and why, and when, and will you be coming to the east coast, too? I am so glad to hear you are out and about, and you do sound well. Nevertheless, you are probably being brave and stoical about it. But I have a feeling there will soon come a time when the bloodstream you refer to will just refuse to carry the poison one more time and throw it out forever.[3] You will then look back and wonder that it ever happened at all, and that will be as miraculous in its way as Hardy writing all that poetry in his old age & better than ever,—only you'll undoubtedly be doing that, too, dear Cal . . .

THE OPPOSITE HOUSE has many beauties—"ganging" is just right, and the noise pigeons make is perfect.[4] Why didn't someone think of it before, I wonder? And the end, the armored car, etc. I must confess I'm a little puzzled, however—because is it or isn't it abandoned? Or is it really an abandoned police station, but they use it as a blind at night—or someone else is hiding out there and they're raiding it? Forgive my being so literal—I've just been re-reading all the Hopkins letters all over again to get myself through a hideous cold in the head,—and so I am full of these strict questionings he gave all his friends' poems.[5] The "fireworks"—"set-pieces" we called them—image is fine, too.[6] In fact it's all brilliantly clear and grimly beautiful, except for this one detail of circumstance that bothers me. Because of the broken windows it would seem to be really abandoned. Well— probably one or two words would make it clear to my literal mind, or perhaps I am somehow missing something—but I don't think so. Azores is a jump from or to Puerto Rico—or Puerto Ricans, which the rest of it brings to mind—but maybe you intend it. And it makes me wonder if NY is that bad, (of course it's probably worse, really). Re-reading, I think my third guess is right—it is being used as a hideout and the police are raiding it? So I may be just dumb, because of this cold.

1 Charles Russell Lowell, pictured in the *Life* article. Of his forebears, RL says, "the one I'd most like to have known is my military cousin, Charles Russell Lowell"; *Life* (Feb. 19, 1965).
2 Probably from Robert Giroux's letter, now missing.
3 See letter 316. Cf. William Empson, "Slowly the poison the whole bloodstream fills"; "Missing Dates," lines 1, 6, 12, and 18.
4 "Pigeons ganging through / broken windows and cooing / like gangs of children tooting / empty bottles"; "The Opposite House," lines 6–9 (RL-*CP*; see also letter 279).
5 *Poems and Prose of Gerard Manley Hopkins*, ed. W. H. Gardner (1964), *The Letters of Gerard Manley Hopkins to Robert Bridges*, ed. Claude Colleer Abbott (1935), and *Further Letters of Gerard Manley Hopkins*, ed. Claude Colleer Abbott (1938).
6 "The Opposite House," line 14 (RL-*CP*).

—Time out while a *tiny* boy—he says he's 13, but I'm sure is much much shorter than your Harriet was at seven—comes to the door with a suitcase of pathetic goods to sell, and sells them to me. I now have a crude potato-peeler, cruder flint gadget for lighting the gas-stove, a blue plastic barrel to keep *something* in, and a huge dead-looking cake of yellow soap, like a small monument, that I'm sure the maid will turn up her nose at . . . Poor little boy—he had to go up and down in the elevator twice, to make change, and I think cheated himself a bit at the end. But so bright and animated and *at home*—the Brazilian type I like best. He says he goes to night school and is in the 4th grade. Well—he probably made about ten cents.— He called me "Miss Girl."

Well, yes, now that you bring it up—I *did* have the ARCHIVE Gesualdo—I got it in London last summer. But that doesn't matter a bit, because a real imported Archive is worth a lot here, and I can turn it in for two or three other records—so it is all to the good. And the other one has several I hadn't heard before, as well as the beautiful other side I've already spoken about. But I did say, too, once, I think how much he reminds me of you—that sustaining of the impossible, free, strange or wild, but never disintegrating. It's a wonderful form, really. Webern was doing something a bit like it again, I think. The hardest thing in the world to do—no rules at all—just immense skill and sensibility—and willingness to say something once and *stop*, let it go. Did you know—you probably did!—that Milton admired him and took his music back to England?

Yes, I agree with what you say of Randall—exactly. I did write him with all the compliments I could truthfully pay—now I think I have some more and shall write again. I dislike the ones on "women"—more than you do, no doubt—and wonder where he *gets* these women—they seem to be like none I—or you—know. But still & all,—he's so much better than anyone else one reads, almost. He does write about a class of American life that is strange to me—perhaps it is the "west." He makes me feel scarcely American at all, and yet I am, through and through.

Giroux is being very nice about my book, I think, and I wish I felt better about its contents.[1] I decided I'd put in "In the Village," too—to go with the several Nova Scotian poems.— At first he said no, it was imitating you too much (it was)—but then when he'd read the story he changed his mind, and is now all for including it. IF Houghton Mifflin will release it, etc. He sent me a copy of the Court Circular about Eliot's funeral—and told about Pound's

---

1 *Questions of Travel* (1967).

appearing, etc. Robie was there, I see. With the Stravinsky music, etc., it must have been wonderfully impressive.[1]

We are planning to go back to Italy for a month this spring, probably—if Lota can get away. But it's still uncertain. Kelly arrives again today (the lighting man). He's bringing me a Sony TV—larger size. I dread it, although we have to have one, because of the maid—and also Lota likes to watch the politicians late at night—and come the next revolution we'll want it, I suppose. But I never thought I'd buy one. It is hideously hot and two of our Brazilian-made air-conditioners barely work—and no one will work to repair them. Wages are so high now that the workers' ideas of consumption haven't caught up with them—it is impossible to get anything done, here or up in the country—where we are trying to finish the garage (very handsome). But the men will only show up two or three times a week—or work a week and stop, saying naively that they have enough money! I suppose it is a stage the country *has* to go through—or this section of it.—But work gets sloppier than ever, if possible, and Lota has an awful time, with the hundreds she has in the park.

I did a piece (just for money) for the NY *Times*—magazine—last Sunday, I think. But if you didn't see it, please *don't*. First they wanted only 2,500 words—then more, then more, & more—and I hate to think how they stuck it all together finally. They're as bad as LIFE—spent $100's in cables—4 or 5, I think—before they got through. So silly. But I'm glad I did it because I *did* it, and rather quickly, for me—and now I feel I can try more sketches, and possibly better ones. I don't remember if I've told you or not that I've *said* I'll go to teach at Un. of Washington, Seattle—2 terms, next spring? Lota is against it (I was hoping she'd join me for part of it and we could see some of that—west I've never seen), and I am beginning to get cold feet when I hear how rude students are these days! Sometime next week I may go to Minas again for a week or ten days. I fell in love with a small place there, Tirandentes, and want very much to get a lot of photographs and write something or other about it.

Send me some more poems! That's what I love getting—I'm sorry the one for you[2] won't make this book—damn. Maybe they'll slip it in. Will you be going to Maine or what? Do take care of yourself—I am so happy you are better again.

Love, Elizabeth

---

1 The memorial service for T. S. Eliot was held at Westminster Abbey on February 4, 1965.
2 Possibly "Apartment in Leme," EB-*EAP*.

318.

[Postcard: Photograph of the Space Needle, Mt. Rainier in the distance]

[Seattle, Wash.

p.m. May 23, 1965]

Dearest Elizabeth:

I'm here for the moment for the Roethke memorial reading. Met a nice deaf old man who thinks you are the best poet in the world.[1] Everyone is looking forward to your presence here tremendously. You'll like the calm & landscape.

Love,

Cal

Did you get a Rockefeller application?

319.

June 15, 1965

Dearest Elizabeth:

Heavens, this is the longest gap, I think, in our letters! This has been a be-calmed winter. I finished up the second of the *Oresteia* plays and now must do the third. They will be put on at the Lincoln Center all a year from this fall. I doubt if my versing has much inspiration, but the barbarous archaic grandeur of the *Agamemnon* at least is still overwhelming in my lines, the second play is exciting. But the third seems tame to me, and I fear little will be there once I have lost the genuineness of the Greek. Still a task is welcome. I plan a piece on Eliot for Tate's *Sewanee Review* number, and have started a rambling impressionistic prose essay on emblematic New England figures, the Pilgrims, Mather, Melville, Colonel Shaw, etc.[2] Thus the summer is blocked out and we go to Maine next Monday.

I've had a lot of curious publicity lately. I stumbled into accepting an in-vitation to read at the White House Arts' Festival, a rather meaningless mé-lange with Phyllis McGinley as my fellow poet, then decided that I couldn't go and wrote a public letter of refusal. The papers were full of headlines such as *poet snubs President*.[3] Letters piled in and invitations to address all sorts of

---

1 Victor L. O. Chittick.

2 See "Two Controversial Questions," *Sewanee Review* (Winter 1966), and "New England and Further" (RL-*CPR*).

3 RL used the letter to express his opposition to the Johnson administration's policies in Vietnam and the Domini-can Republic (see RL-*Letters*, 459, and RL-*CPR*, 370–71).

protesting groups. But I've had my say and want to go no further. Almost everyone I know is frightened, stunned and angry about what we are doing in our foreign policy. All may cool off. Or maybe this is the beginning of a push of American force that [will] last longer than all of us will. I feel lucky that I've been able to do the one thing that I can probably do suitably, i.e. make a personal act and statement. Now the job is to get back to my own kind of writing, which is only imaginatively controversial. I mean I still feel free, if only inspiration blows, to write or not to on national matters, if they enter my experience and find a form.

I've been remiss about saying something to you about a Rockefeller Fellowship. Did you get an application? Kunitz and I are on an advisory committee and I think could promise you a grant, if you sent in your request. The awards, however, have been made for the moment. I'm not sure what we can do to determine grants in the future, or even if more will be given, but I think the odds are that anything reasonable you ask for (up to ten or twelve thousand) will be given. Please write in.

I rather hope you'll take on the Washington job. You'll like the landscape and the relative quiet for America, and I think Heilman, the head of the department, will shape the conditions [to] suit you. He did marvels with Ted Roethke and has since had such unacademic shy people as Henry Reed and Vernon Watkins. Everyone seems terribly excited and eager for your arrival. Where you are known—it's now very wide—you have about the most convinced and authentic fans of anyone writing. I know you must have a thousand hesitations. Of course, you mustn't push yourself beyond what is tolerable and enjoyable, but you quite likely would find that teaching both gives you more of the country and by giving you a routine makes everything here more digestible. In my classes, I read poems aloud, comment, ramble and ask questions, oh and also listen. The students have either anthologies or mimeographed copies of the poems so there's no question of a performance or declamation. Classes are not lectures so much as arranged conversations, and you need do nothing but take things casually and trust yourself to your humor, sense, knowledge and personal interests.

Oh dear, I never write the sort of natural letter I would like to. This is the messy last city week. Our good Spanish maid has departed for Spain for an ear operation. Harriet has passed through the second grade "arch" and is on vacation until she enters the third grade next fall. She does things we can't, cartwheels, flips from the diving board, shows a knack for mathematics. Under the muscle and fragility of her eight years, there's so much sweetness, invention and sense.

After all the fuss of my letter, I found myself getting a doctor's degree at Williams with Allen Dulles, Luce and Adlai Stevenson. Luce greeted me with, "I like your poetry better than your politics." I felt like saying I felt the same about his, but I was polite and he was polite. Stevenson said, "I've been following your new public life with interest and I must say some satisfaction." Write me in Castine. Harriet and I are off to a Cary Grant comedy called "Father Goose."[1]

All my love,
Cal

320.

Rio, July 6th, 1965

Dearest Cal:

I'm afraid I have much to answer for—and in 45 minutes I'm taking off for a week in Bahia, but at least I'm all packed, and I have saved this time to write you a note. (I think you stopped over at Bahia, didn't you? I've never been there, after all this time here.) First, I got your card from Egypt,[2] then one from Seattle, then two week-ends ago I found a letter from you in Samambaia, and the record of *Benito Cereno* . . .[3] I had a wonderful time going to the theatre on a bright Sunday morning—I played it two times over. I have a MSS of it somewhere but couldn't locate it and now I am eager to see the book to see how they had cut it—I supposed they must have. It comes off *wonderfully*—but as you know this already, it is very late for me to say so. I like the voice of BC himself best, I think—the Capt. good but I waited to see if he'd get that Bostonian A right every time! But the whole thing somehow seems to mean more and more and more when I hear it—and it is the one thing I regret having missed in NY the past season. In fact, so apropos does it seem that I've already suggested it to the most "advanced theatre" here—I hope you don't mind. Nothing whatever may come of it—you know how inert people can be here—but I have suggested it to one poet who's helping in this theatre—and he thinks, and I think, and L thinks, and Flávio thinks—it would be a fine thing to have Brazilians see right now, at this stage in the awful game . . . Perhaps on a double bill with—well, what was suggested was *Zoo Story* (Flávio did a good translation of that 2 years ago—he could do your play, too, with my help.) However—I'll tell you more when I get back

1 *Father Goose*, dir. Ralph Nelson (1964).
2 The postcard does not survive.
3 The American Place Theatre's production of *Benito Cereno*, dir. Jonathan Miller (Columbia DOL 319).

and know more—and I'd say the chances of doing *anything* are about 25% out of 100 not-doing-anything . . . The trouble is—as far as talking or writing goes—Brazilians only like black or white, no doubts or ambiguities. But when I saw *Zoo Story* here (in English, too)—the audience appreciated it even more than I did, and so I think, dramatically presented, they might really get what you are trying to say, in all its difficulty . . . (That Ruth Herschberger—I just happened to see that VOICE (wasn't it?) and your reply—what on earth ever possessed her—or is it spite or neurosis or what . . . ?)

Of course the newspapers here mentioned your party-refusal, and then TIME. (I thought Dwight rather funny, in the next TIME, or the 2nd after, saying he was "the bad fairy at the christening."[1]) And as—I gather, I didn't see it—[a] rather mildly funny piece by Art Buchenwald (?)[2] was in the English language papers—rather pro—than otherwise, I think. I read everything I can, but, of course, it is awfully hard to see clearly from here. I wonder if by any chance you have a copy of your refusal—complete—you could send me? I'd like very much to see it—all I saw was TIME's no doubt misleading quotes . . . Of course many people asked *me* about it, as a sort of authority—and so I'd like very much to see what you actually wrote. There wasn't much fuss about the Brazilian soldiers going to Dominica[3]—people thought there would be, but there wasn't—but I lie awake and pray nights that none will be killed! (3 wounded returned so far—the first fell out of a tree—as L says, he was probably stealing fruit in the traditional Brazilian way—one blew up his own hand-grenade, nothing serious, and one was really wounded by "the enemy," again not seriously.[)] It says in the papers that the US Army has set them to "directing traffic—calmly and tranquilly"! This sounds like usual army procedure—set a blacksmith to sewing, or French-speaking soldiers to Japan . . .

Yes—I did get the Rockefeller notice, and I am delighted, and I postponed answering such a long time for various reasons—now I've heard from you I'll get it off to them. (I might have guessed you had something to do with it.) IF you can—I know you're in Maine—will you tell someone or other that I DO WANT ONE (desperately, but don't say that!) It fits in so well with a scheme I've been working on lately—I haven't time to go into

---

1 At the White House Arts Festival on June 14, 1965, Dwight Macdonald circulated a petition stating, "We share Mr. Lowell's dismay at our country's recent actions in Viet Nam and the Dominican Republic." Some guests were outraged, but Macdonald replied, "I came here to make trouble politically. I'm the bad fairy come to the christening"; *Time* (June 25, 1965).

2 Art Buchwald, "Take an Artist to Lunch," Publishers Newspaper Syndicate (June 17, 1965).

3 Brazil contributed soldiers to the Inter-American Peace Force, assisting the American intervention in the Dominican Republic.

details now, but I want to put a book together—prose pieces—about Brazil—and in order to do it I shall have to make a good many rather expensive trips by air and boat. I think writing on SA—and Brazil—has declined—sadly since the days of the great naturalists—for a 100 years, that is—and the run-of-the-mill book is written, badly, by someone who has been here three months . . . I have three pieces more or less done—before I heard from the Rockefellers—my idea is to mix places, a few life-stories short-stories, more or less, a piece on Aleijadinho, probably—perhaps popular music, etc.—and the places will those where the journalists don't go, or rarely—where life is pretty much unchanged but bound to change very fast very soon. I shall try to do all this, of course, in the most beautiful prose imaginable and with photographs—for which I shall have to buy a new camera;—& films are very dear now, etc. I had thought of staying 1 year or 18 months—since [in] your letter I see I can ask up to $12,000 and take two years—which would be that much better. So far I'm calling it (all this was in the works, so to speak before I heard from the Rs at all, so it isn't made-up specially) the old title I wanted to use before: BLACK BEANS AND DIAMONDS; (tentatively). This is more or less what I shall say in my letter to them—and I'll get it off from Bahia if I can. Anyway—it looks like a godsend to me, because of inflation here, and I do hope they give me one!

Heavens—Ashley Brown will be along in ten minutes and I must collect my luggage, do my face, etc.—I'll write again, now I've made this boring start . . .

I hated to see you looking so agonized as you did in that TIME photograph, and I hope Maine is doing you a lot of good.— Eliz's review of Mailer is superb.[1] Oh I have lots more to say—but just believe I am with you, for you, etc.—and awfully grateful for all your help.

With much love,
    Elizabeth

PS—One more boring request—do you think you could write a *short* new sentence or two about me for Bob Giroux? They've got some *old* quotes—and H. Mifflin used yours so Bob can't—and you're the only person I'd like to have say something, of course . . . But short—and please don't exaggerate, Cal dear!

---

1 Elizabeth Hardwick, "Bad Boy," *Partisan Review* (Spring 1965).

321.

Castine, Maine
July 16, 1965

My dearest Elizabeth:

Here are my sentences for your book. Not good, I fear, in comparison with yours for me, in which a marvelous image jumps into the universal, into the world. I had a pleasant day in my barn composing it.

"I am sure no living poet is as curious and observant as Miss Bishop. What cuts so deep is that each poem is inspired by her own tone, a tone of large, grave tenderness and sorrowing amusement. She is too sure of herself for empty mastery and breezy plagiarism, too interested for confession and musical monotony, too powerful for mismanaged fire, and too civilized for idiosyncratic incoherence. She has a humorous, commanding genius for picking up the unnoticed, now making something sprightly and right, and now a great monument. Once her poems, each shining, were too few. Now they are many. When we read her, we enter the classical serenity of a new country."

I hope you'll like this, and that a few phrases will stick in the minds of reviewers. Your *Life Studies* blurb is still being quoted by reviewers of my last book and counteracts an unfortunate phrase by Alvarez that somehow got on my jacket that I was too good to be criticized. But what else makes a reviewer's life livable!

I feel very guilty about not having let you in on the Rockefeller business earlier. I wasn't writing letters, and may have had a probably ill-judged hunch that Washington would be good for you. But why should you go there? The Brazil book will be something permanent, and sounds just like what you should do and only you could.

I've finished nothing worth keeping for a year. But suddenly when I got up here with letters and long distance calls still swarming in about my White House business, I got going. I enclose the long poem I wrote.[1] It sounds good, I think, and is rather witty and tragic. I guess the only thing to do is to keep writing, but only publish what has a spark in it. I am old enough almost to wait.

For the last few days the Castine flags have been at half-mast for poor Stevenson.[2] I got a degree when he did at Williams, and he said, "I've been following your new public life with interest, and I must say some enjoy-

1 "Walking Early Sunday Morning" (RL-*CP*).
2 Adlai Stevenson died on July 14, 1965.

580

ment." God knows what he meant. Contradictory reports are coming out about what he really thought about his duties at the UN. Like Louis MacNeice, whom I also saw a few weeks before his death, Stevenson looked unusually healthily red and relaxed. Reading his first volume of speeches, I was disappointed and thought such a man could only make his mark by being elected. Yet I was wrong; he graced our harsh scene with a kind of kindness, nuance, everything tinged with himself, the most attractive American statesman in our lifetimes. Yet what he said no longer had great importance, and sometimes seemed merely a rather wistful rephrasing of Washington, his nuance, but not his heart. Still such modesty, an ambitious but still true modesty, offers a lesson, though one may fail to follow it.

Glad you like *Benito*. Yes, the Spanish Captain dominates; he has a voice as perfect as a good opera singer. On the stage, he looked like a tall El Greco, but moved little (both by his own nature and his part,) and the star was Babu,[1] inexhaustibly agile, able to improvise and to change from tender servility to royal barbarism. On the TV, a non-commercial filming, the American Captain is the most important.[2] Most of the scenes are from the shoulder up, show few actors, often only one. Hope they do it in Rio. There's some talk of a double bill in London, maybe with a wild negro thing by LeRoi Jones.[3]

I don't have a copy of my statement. It's not so much, but the little personal turns of phrase are everything. Murray Kempton quoted it entire in his column as an example of courteous independence. I'll mail you a copy when I get back to the city. You might find [it] in the New York *Times* that came out Thursday, a week and a half before the 14th of June. (This last was the Arts Festival Day, and that's why I have this odd way of remembering the date of the *Times* statement.) Marvelous, your details about the poor Brazilian soldiers. I can't, of course, say what ought to be done, but feel nearly certain we are embogged in tragic futility. Maybe even Johnson can do nothing, certainly he can't, I think, psychologically. A wounded bull who doesn't know he's wounded. Still every brake helps, qualification too is part of our National character.

Your Brazil book sounds terrific. I'll write Freund[4] today. You ask me not to be overcomplimentary. I fear in my sentences I've too literally followed your advice. Still, a careful reading will show that I make huge claims that anyone should accept.

1 Roscoe Lee Browne.
2 Lester Rawlins.
3 LeRoi Jones, *Dutchman* (1964).
4 Gerald Freund, a director at the Rockefeller Foundation from 1960 to 1969.

Today I am answering mail, though nothing except writing to you is of much moment. Then I hope to quietly reread old New England classics, Thoreau, Melville etc. With the idea of writing a New England essay. I thought of a good phrase for Hawthorne— . . . "poor Hawthorne, his life like Mallarmé's and many another's, too long for comfort and too brief for perfection." If I do nothing, the reading will sink into dry sand, or I hope dry fertile earth, like Maine in this summer, good for the vacationer, but a drought for farmers.

How wonderful you are Dear, and how wonderful that you write me letters. I had a rather glowing account of you and Lota from Sylvia Marlowe. In this mid-summer moment I feel at peace, and that we both have more or less lived up to our so different natures and destinies. What a block of life has passed since we first met in New York and Washington! How much I love my little, not very well treated and indomitable family!

Love,
Cal

P.S. My poem is 112 lines and I just haven't the heart to make a copy now. Can I mail one of the New York *Review* copies next week? Since I ended this letter I've answered a month's mail. Telegraphic little post-cards mostly, but enough to tire me of typing. We had an interesting night yesterday listening to Charles Ives records, enough to make me a patriot almost. If you don't have him and would like, let me mail some records next fall.

322.

Rio, August 2nd, 1965

Dearest Cal:

I should have written to you several days ago, I know—I think I have been so overcome by your paragraph about me that I couldn't concentrate on a simple letter. You should have seen me, shedding big tears. I thought, no, this is *too* good, I'll have to tone it down . . . It came to Petrópolis and Mary read it to me over the telephone; then we went up last week end, a day or so later, and I saw it with my own eyes—also Bob already had it printed up, so the whole jacket, more or less, was there. He was naturally very pleased, too, thought it "terrific." I like especially of course, being "curious" and "sprightly"—both words I hope I really live up to. I only wish the book were worth it.— I honestly do not think it is—about 4 poems please me, that's all. I don't think I told you—but I finally decided to put your name under the Armadillo poem, since you have liked it. I have a longer, grimmer one, about Copacabana beach, too, that is to be dedicated to you—but I didn't get it done in time and I did want to mention you somehow or other in this book. Well when it appears, it may be a bit better than "The Armadillo." And well—we may be a terrible pair of log-rollers, I don't know—however—I do know that I meant every word I said and I think you do too, in the kindness of your heart. I've just read straight through a huge anthology—*A Controversy of Poets*—and your familiar three poems in that are the ONLY ones I'd—well, cross the street for.[1] Possibly one or two others are good, but not even comparable, really. The whole book I find awfully depressing and it makes me feel so *demodée*, as Lota says.— I *must* write some prose using f—— and sh—— and so on, I see that . . .—and isn't it odd, out of all the nerves & troubles that something fairly "serene" does come? Well—now I don't even care if it is badly received—what you say is enough!

I've also just read Sylvia Plath's last book,[2] and Auden's—and wonder what you think of those. Sylvia P. seems like a tragic loss to me—although I can scarcely bear to read her poems through, they are so agonized. A bit formless for my taste, too—but really a talent, don't you think? And Auden seems to be enjoying a sort of premature old age a little too much . . . There are a couple of good ones, though. I like the one to MacNeice—most of it—[3]

Yes, I felt very badly about Stevenson, too—and then I'd just seen a poem in the last POETRY by Robert Duncan speaking of "the look of Stevenson lying" (in the UN) "that the nation keep face."[4] I somehow can't believe that. I do believe he was misinformed about the Cuban invasion . . . I hope to goodness so, at least. Dr. Baumann sent me a whole batch of newspaper clippings—a lot of them about you, the President's luncheon or arts festival, etc., etc.—so now I am better informed. I like very much your considered and reasonable tone—and it certainly made a sensation! (I also rather liked what Dwight McD said, if true—according to TIME—"I'm the bad fairy at the christening") But oh I wish they wouldn't use that idiotic expression "teach-in" . . . (I've been getting some reports about those things, too.) Here, I just never know what to say to people and try to avoid saying anything most of the time. Probably it was just as well Stevenson was never President—I think he was too thoughtful and subtle-minded for that job.

I'm getting my Rockefeller letter off at last today—a very simple state-

1 *A Controversy of Poets*, ed. Paris Leary and Robert Kelly (1965).
2 Sylvia Plath, *Ariel* (Faber edition, 1965).
3 W. H. Auden, "Epilogue," *About the House* (1965).
4 Robert Duncan, "The Fire," lines 81–82, *Poetry* (April 1965).

ment. It will mean flying around quite a bit, which is expensive, and also buying a camera, since I hope to have some illustrations. But thinking it all over, I really believe I could put together something rather entertaining and informative, and, with luck, a bit surprising, about this country. The old naturalists are the only good writers on the subject I've ever read—and perhaps Lévi-Strauss.[1] I look at them all, out of curiosity, and I haven't seen one decent travel-book in years. Mine should be more of a "memoir," I think—and could even include two or three (true) short-story kind of stories.

I hope they will consider me! Living is getting so expensive here that I've had to begin on the Academy Award I was trying to save up to go traveling on—etc., etc.— And that job—I just don't know—I'm a bit afraid of the climate there in January–March, etc. from what I've heard; my bronchi really aren't too good. But I must make up my mind and write them once and for all this week.

(Flávio just here—in a wet bathing suit, I'm glad to see—I think his new girlfriend is good for him! (he has an extremely pretty one, and bright, too.) He always refers to you as *Mister Lowell*, which shows the highest respect possible I gather—no one else gets that title.)

Bahia—well, I think you paused there, or went there for a couple of rather unsatisfactory days, I seem to remember—when no one managed to meet anyone else. I had a very good time, really—but it is so poor—even compared to the worst of Rio—that it is pretty depressing. Magnificent ruins of buildings, mostly—and I heard a lot of semi-african music, and ate a lot of semi-african food.[2] The prostitutes (always around the churches, the street behind the church) almost dragged Ashley from my side, and hissed and whistled out of 2nd story windows at him. Since he is the most professorial-looking, tall, thin man, with rather thick glasses and a stoop—! I think he was slightly scared. All the "intellectuals"—such as they are—very left, if not communist—like Jorge Amado—and rather coldly polite to us Americans. We stayed eight days—

It's not the big places like that I intend writing about, however, but smaller odds and end[s], and people, and possibly music and architecture. Oh—on the hotel menu was "Tart Carmen Miranda," and I also saw a Carmen Miranda Funeral Home.

I envy you Maine right now and yearn for something cold and gray and

1 Claude Lévi-Strauss, *Tristes tropiques* (1955).
2 The site of intensive sugar cultivation, Bahia was a central locus of the African slave trade and remains the Brazilian state with the strongest links to African culture.

dry-ish—(speech or manners.) I saw a very good page on you in the London *TLS*—and I was glad they liked that Stonington poem, particularly.[1] In fact, my dear boy, you are absolutely everywhere these days and I'm just delighted.

What do you hear of Randall, and do you know how he is?

Sylvia[2] had a rather poor time of it here, I think—and she wasn't very well to begin with. But she is an "old trooper" after all, and put on a good recital, with people drilling in the street at one side and others practicing high C's over her head. Oh—thank you about the Charles Ives, but I do have a good many of his recordings. Frani ("Helena" in the Group) worked on preparing some of his MMS once, and during that stretch she sent me several records. I'm of two minds about him, though—sometimes I like the music, the hymn-tunes, etc.—and sometimes it strikes me as just too amaturerish.

Do please send me the new poem when you have a copy. I'm afraid I find this Mark Strand who is the new Fulbright prof here—well what I meant to say was I find his poems that he's given me rather uninteresting and his conversation about them the same way. Ashley was more *fun*.

Lota is much too over-worked. We just went through a bad scare about her heart. Finally, without telling her, I got the doctor and the cardiologist to come Sunday morning—and everything is all right, thank goodness—whereupon we both slept for about four hours straight—out of relief, I suppose. She is fearfully important these days and of course rumor has it (it always has, here) that she is making a "fortune" out of her park, and salting it away, some say in the USA, some say in Switzerland . . . Carlos is making mistake after mistake, it seems to me—he has lost his touch, or something—I very much doubt he'll get elected now. (And I dread it if he does)—

I may go back to Minas for a week or ten days since I have the chance of driving there and really want to finish writing some bits I started about it. Also—we're having new ceilings put in here and the noise will be too much, so I must go somewhere. I hope you're having a wonderful peaceful summer, as peaceful as can be expected, and that everything looks unchanged and beautiful there. Eat some blueberries for me. Thank you again and again Cal for your paragraph—

Lots of love—to you & your family—

Elizabeth

---

1 "Eastern Personal Time," *The Times Literary Supplement* (July 1, 1965); "Water" (RL-*CP*).
2 Sylvia Marlowe.

323.

Dearest,

So happy and relieved that you liked my lines on you. They look pretty well on the cover. I find a *Controversy of Poets* hard going and feel no joy in being tossed with a lot of Ephemera. The Snodgrass still catches my heart, and I feel I have been his pupil, but there's so much competent and incompetent waste. I've been reading the opposite kind of anthology, an Oxford American Literature compiled in the late thirties, and full of names, now rather fading: Sandburg, Jeffers, Lola Ridge, MacLeish.[1] Well, they are better and are beginning to acquire the false or true nostalgia of time, records of the period. Jeffers, a sort of country cousin to Eliot in his pessimism, is almost a great poet. I wouldn't like to be that dark, though no doubt I am.

The other day Senator Teddy Kennedy arrived here with a group of young congressmen, and Phil Booth had me over to meet them. All so young and running things, looking like Bill Merwin. I felt like a white Raccoon!

I enclose the last draft with corrections of a little poem I reduced from seventy-two lines to twenty, and my long effort. I've also written a long piece in 17 eight-line stanzas on Cousin Harriet that Lizzie finds beautiful and self-indulgent.[2] Such, and a bunch of Mandelstam translations, are all I've done.[3] I can't somehow face that last of my Aeschylus trilogy.

The new Auden was somehow better read one by one, the long series on his house is a little ingenious, difficult and dry in bulk. I liked the MacNeice too. He had a still better poem, I think, a really marvelous one in the spring *Encounter*, about a flashback to an old love-affair.[4] Sylvia, I think, has a few perfect poems, but the book as a whole troubles me with its desperation, and even more perhaps by something sprawling unfinished and disorderly, though poem after poem has flashes that are incredible and make me feel weak.

So happy Lota's trouble was nothing. Tell her to take care from us. We must all continue. This part of our lives has something of the real changing quality of childhood, more enjoyable on the whole, but with—not here yet, thank God, but ahead—diminishment, disappearance of friends, our own disappearance, etc., waiting. Premature old age! I feel we are now what the

---

1 *The Oxford Anthology of American Literature*, ed. William Rose Benét and Norman Holmes Pearson (1938).
2 "Near the Ocean: Fourth of July in Maine" (RL-*CP*).
3 "Nine Poems by Osip Mandelstam," trans. RL and Olga Carlisle, *The New York Review of Books* (Dec. 23, 1965).
4 W. H. Auden, "Since," *Encounter* (May 1965).

young inevitably look on as alien, but real. That's how I used to look on people our age. But it's all illusion, we are ageless, a little wick burning in a fog.

Love and kisses,
Cal

324.

Dearest Cal:

(as I see you are called, according to TIME, August 27th)[1]

I have had this card for you for weeks now, and I did write you a letter in answer to yours of August 16th that Lota sent on—but it struck me as too dull to send. I left Rio in an awful hurry—had the chance of a ride all the way here—and have almost no books with me, and no poetry—so I was especially pleased to have some "modern poetry." The local bookshop had provided a complete Milton in paperback, and that was all, except for the Brazilian poets, & I seem to be quite sick of them. Now I find I can turn from that wonderful:

> For who loves that, must first be wise and good;
> But from that mark how far they roave we see
> For all this waste of wealth, and loss of blood.[2]

to:

> Only man thinning out his kind
> sounds through the Sabbath noon, the blind
> swipe of the pruner and his knife
> busy about the tree of life . . .[3]

and feel the language hasn't deteriorated at all, even if the state of civilization stays the same, or just gets worse and worse.

"Walking Early Sunday Morning" has many wonderful things in it—and not the least, I think, is the way it goes on in a leisurely way, like a Sunday

---

1 "Society: Edie & Andy," *Time* (Aug. 27, 1965).
2 John Milton, "Sonnett XII: I did but prompt the age to quit their clogs," lines 12–14 (1673).
3 "Waking Early Sunday Morning," lines 101–104 (RL-*CP*).

morning—even if the meter is not leisurely, there seems to be *time*,—to think—not like week-day thoughts. "In small war on the heels of small / war"[1]—is marvelous—and now far truer than when you wrote it, I gather by the papers I see here. I think you are a bit hard on yourself in stanza three.[2] And I *love* the glass of water—a beautiful simple stanza—well, not simple,—simple like Chardin, maybe. I also like stanza 9 very much—since I feel that way myself so much of the time.[3] "Wars flicker"—& "monotonous sublime" is a wonderful ending.[4] I can't express it exactly—but sounds like Tennyson a hundred years later, *with* a sense of irony.

I like *In the Park*, too[5]—also *Stalin*[6]—and I'd love to see the one on your cousin Harriet sometime.[7] I want to go into details about these two short poems, too—but I also want to get this in the mail for you right away, I have been so slow about writing—and I'll write again this week sometime. Rio began to get just too much for me again, and so I came off up here—meaning to stay only two weeks. I've been here a month now, and shall probably stay another two weeks. Then possibly Lota can take a few days off, come up, and I'll go back with her. It has been an absolutely killing stretch for her, and I feel guilty at abandoning her—but I wasn't being much help, really— moping around the apartment in the heat, and trying to work, very unsuccessfully, while she copes with politicians and crooks and journalists for 18 hours a day . . . Now I write her almost every day and I'm sure she enjoys my letters more than my company, for the time being, *coitada!*[8] It is very dull here, but I love it.— I stay with our friend Lilli Correia de Araújo—the one who owns the hotel[9] where you stayed; but I live in her house—a huge affair built on a cliff at the edge of the town, with a gold-mine in the back yard— also ruined slave-quarters, gardens away up the hill—level after level—and water running down through a marvellous set of aqueducts, tunnels, foun-

---

1 "Near the Ocean: Waking Early Sunday Morning," lines 107–108 (RL-*CP*).
2 "Time to grub up and junk the year's / output, a dead wood of dry verse: / dim confession, coy revelation, / liftings, listless self-imitation, / whole days when I could hardly speak, / came pluming home unshaven, weak / and willing to read anyone / things done before and better done"; "Waking Early Sunday Morning," lines 17–24, *The New York Review of Books* (Aug. 5, 1965). Cf. "Near the Ocean: Waking Early Sunday Morning" (RL-*CP*).
3 "Empty, irresolute, ashamed, / when the sacred texts are named, / I lie here on my bed apart, / and when I look into my heart, / I discover none of the great / subjects: death, friendship, love and hate— / only old china doorknobs, sad, / slight, useless things to calm the mad"; "Waking Early Sunday Morning," lines 65–72, *The New York Review of Books* (Aug. 5, 1965). Cf. "Near the Ocean: Waking Early Sunday Morning" (RL-*CP*).
4 See "Near the Ocean: Waking Early Sunday Morning," lines 98 and 112 (RL-*CP*).
5 "Near the Ocean: Central Park" (RL-*CP*).
6 RL's translation of Osip Mandelstam's "Stalin" (see RL-*CP*).
7 "Near the Ocean: Fourth of July in Maine" (RL-*CP*).
8 Poor thing.
9 Chico Rey; see "For the Window" (EB-*CP*) and "Let Shakespeare and Milton" (EB-*EAP*)

tains, stone tanks, etc.—now all overgrown with ferns and moss. She has a ghastly collection of handcuffs and leg-irons dug up in the grounds. She's Danish, but married a Brazilian painter long ago, as an art student in Paris.— Our languages get very mixed up. I called her *tow-headed*, and she thought I said "Two-headed." She says "Your ass," meaning "Your ace" when we play cards. I've been doing quite a lot of work, for me, but mostly suffering because I *can't*. However—a story about that Uncle Arthur who shot the loon is almost done, and I like it fairly well[1]—and a group of horrid little Brecht-like (I think) poems about Rio[2]—and one long one about the trip here[3] that MAY work—ye gods, I hope so, being pretty discouraged about my works at the moment. I also brought all the Brazil prose to work on and really think it will make a book, so I do hope the Rockefellers decide to help me! If they don't—well, eventually I'll do it, anyway, I suppose. It was a good idea to get away for a while—it is too close in Rio—all the politics, anti-Americanism, etc. Here the backward population thinks I'm "Italian" for some reason,—or occasionally Danish, like Lilli.

I suffer from lack of company—but better none at all than bores. And a few odd critics, painters, etc. from the São Paulo Bienal turn up once in a while—then the languages fly. This afternoon we had German, French, Portuguese, and English all being spoken at once. I hear Clement Greenberg is coming next week—to Brazil—hope I get to see him.

There's a big spring that runs out just below the house—an iron pipe where there used to be a fountain—and everyone stops, always, to have a drink there—dogs, donkeys, cars—besides all the pedestrians. Just now came a huge truck, painted pink and blue and decorated with rose-buds— On the bumper it says "Here I am, the one you've waited for." Now all hands are taking a drink.— I can see seven churches and a few odd chapels. People keep stopping by to try to sell Lilli things—today so far two saints— beauties,—stirrups, wooden bowls, lettuce, locks and keys, and a wire egg-basket—so you see there is never a dull moment. I think about you a lot and I have re-read your poems many times already.— I'm always delighted to get a poem! I miss the north very much occasionally—and Lilli and I had one long nostalgic conversation all about bulb plants, birch trees, hay-lofts, etc.— Apparently, *"Up in the hay!"* is an old Danish expression for having a wild good time. She also goes on about *trolls* in a way that reminds me of

---

1 "Memories of Uncle Neddy" (EB-*CPR*).
2 "House Guest" and "Going to the Bakery" (EB-*CP*).
3 "Arrival at Santos" was first published in 1951, so perhaps EB refers to "Crossing the Equator" (EB-*EAP*).

Auden.[1]— I must hike down to the Post Office or you'll never get this, and I do hope you are all well and serene and don't have to go back to N.Y. too soon—or are you already back there because of that mystical "labor day?" How's Harriet progressing?

Always devotedly, Cal,
Elizabeth

325.

[15 West 67th Street, New York, NY
n.d., October 18 or 19?, 1965]

My dearest Elizabeth,

I imagine you may have heard by now of Randall's death.[2] He was undergoing treatment of an injured wrist at Chapel Hill, and "lunged" in front of a car on a main highway near a bypass. He had a bottle of pain-killer in his pocket. I've just come from the funeral and must soon leave for Harvard. I'll write you soon in detail. It cannot be told for certain whether the death was suicide or an accident. I think suicide, but I'm not sure, and Mary's version, the official version, is accident. All heart-breaking and ghastly. Poor Dear, he wanted to take care of himself! I'm Desolate. He was starting on a review of your book, very enthusiastic, but I think got nothing written. I know he thought "Manuelzinho" a masterpiece.

My dearest one, please take care of yourself. All my love,
Cal

P.S. I should know in a couple of weeks whether the Rockefeller grants are going to be continued. If they are I feel almost certain you will get one.

326.

October 28, 1965

Dearest Elizabeth:

It was fun looking up echolalia (again), chromograph, gesso, and roadstead—they all meant pretty much what I thought. Oh and taboret, an object I've known all my life, but not the name.[3] All the poems are good and the

---

1 See W. H. Auden and Louis MacNeice, *Letters from Iceland* (1937), 150–53.
2 Randall Jarrell died on October 14, 1965.
3 See "Squatter's Children," line 22; "First Death in Nova Scotia," line 3; "Sunday, 4 A.M.," line 21; "Visits to St. Elizabeths," line 16; and "Filling Station," line 25 (EB-*CP*).

book reads with the steady excellence of some perfect short story, say my beloved "Coeur Simple."[1] "Santos" gains a lot by being the opening door to the Brazilian section.[2] My favorites are "Brazil"—how I envy the historical stretch at the end, so beautifully coming out of the vegetation—"Manuel-zinho's" a dazzling masterpiece—"Armadillo"—how proud and swell-headed I am about the dedication, one of your absolutely top poems, your greatest quatrain poem, I mean it has a wonderful formal-informal grandeur—I see the bomb in it in a delicate way[3]—"The Riverman," a sort of forsaken Merman, and a very powerful initiation poem that somehow echoes your own entrance in Santos—"Twelfth Morning" has lovely, strange touches—"The Burglar" ballad is a special poem, and gives a huge sweep of Rio, and again, though a true narrative and ballad, tells a lot about your own judgments on your society, obliquely—"Death in Nova Scotia" haunts me (It was weird this summer when I drove through New Brunswick and Nova Scotia on a short salmon fishing trip, to see everywhere the pale Maple Leaf Flag, more like (and pleasantly at last) a boy scout flag than a na-tion's—embittered anglophiles still fly the old Union Jack)—the poem is doubly provincial and remote, in time, the Prince of Wales and all, and in place, very sad and lovely—"Filling Station," just as good I think, one of your best "awful but cheerful" poems—Trollope, the more I read it the more I think he was right about Washington—at first I took the poem as a spoof at the superficial condescending Englishman. By the way your rhythm and rim-ing are extraordinary, and of course unobtrusive—then Ezra is marvelous,[4] you get bits of your old monument[5] in it, nicely, and the whole is a success against every impossibility. By the way, I am talking on the educational TV with Marianne Moore about Pound for his 80th birthday. He seems to be completely sane now. You were very right to put your story in, it's one of your finest poems, and bridges the two sections.[6] I rather wish you'd thrown *all*, or almost all, your stories in, even though it would have made jags in the book's pattern.

The Randall business is very awful. Did I tell you his wrist injury was from putting his hand through a window last spring, though no one knows this. There was also a girl (late thirties) that Hannah met at Goucher College

1 Gustav Flaubert, "Un Coeur Simple," *Trois contes* (1877).
2 "Arrival at Santos" (EB-*CP*).
3 See "The Armadillo," lines 21–24 (EB-*CP*).
4 See "Brazil, January 1, 1502"; "Twelfth Morning; or What You Will"; "The Burglar of Babylon"; "First Death in Nova Scotia," lines 1–6 and 36; "From Trollope's Journal"; and "Visits to St. Elizabeths" (EB-*CP*).
5 "The Monument" (EB-*CP*).
6 "In the Village" (EB-*CPR*).

in Baltimore. (No one else knows this). He finally wrote her that he couldn't cope with life unless he went home to Mary. He should have had a doctor who made clear to him that getting over his manic depressive attack had nothing to do with returning to his wife—my doctor has always made that point, even to the extreme of once several years ago letting me go from the hospital to an apartment where I went on with my affair, and then went back to Lizzie, knowing that I really wanted to in my soul's center. Of course the new girl would have probably have been like Randall's other wives, but she might have tided him back to health. Nothing on earth can be as bad as ending your own life—I mean medically not morally—except murder. Well, and there was a bang up quarrel with Mary just before he went to the hospital for the last time, not mental but to have ice treatments on his wrist, made much worse by an unsuccessful operation in September. There's a small chance of accident—he was planning to have dinner with his step-daughter the next day, had begun teaching, had written one or two people that he was well and writing again, and had notes on a review of your poems which he was very keen on. In his pocket a bottle of Demerol, pain-killer, that might have fuzzed his senses. I think it was suicide, and so does every one else, who knew him well. Hannah said to me, "What is so awful was that it was so fitting." Mary was in California when he died, and didn't drive him to the hospital. The Taylors didn't think she was coming back. They are very bitter. Mary's story is that he was well, and had only temporarily turned on her in his manic state—no one knows about the suicide attempt, and she insists that the death was an accident—naturally, I guess. He seems to have been begging her for a divorce, *before* he was sick last fall. I want to stay out of it all. I've just written a ten page memorial and éloge for the *Review*, which I'll have them mail you, and which I hope you'll like.[1] His worst flaw was forcing his wives into becoming false assents to himself, agreeing on everything, having the same critical opinions, etc., making them dishonest, as one of his poem[s] even says.[2] When Peter called up Mackie, she was astonished that Randall had ever been sick, then she said, "This may sound strange, but I think this means more to you than it does to me." She meant Randall's death, not his illness. Oh, but he was an absolutely gifted, and noble man, poisoned and killed, though I can't prove it, by our tasteless, superficial, brutal culture.

1 "Randall Jarrell: 1914–1965," *The New York Review of Books* (Nov. 25, 1965); see RL-*CPR*.
2 Possibly Randall Jarrell, "Hope," *The Lost World* (1965).

Dear heart, I see you've had another *golpe*[1]—unhappy Americas, unhappy world! Hope there's nothing ominous for you and Lota.
   All my love,
      Cal

What a full and glorious book, even grander than I foresaw, thinking of the poems in ones and twos. There are marvelous things in poems I haven't mentioned—I think particularly of the title poem.[2]

327.

Dearest Cal:
   I have so much to write you about and so many things to thank you for, I scarcely know where to begin. I have also put off writing to you too long. I stayed away in Ouro Prêto for over 2 months and when I came back—Lota came up and got me, finally, which touched me very much since it's a nine hour drive—there was an awful lot to attend to, and I haven't been well—bad stretch of asthma, don't know why—but I'm recovered now. When I did get back, your letter about Randall was here, and the one about my book came soon after. I've also got the book of plays and thank you very much for that, too.
   I felt awful about Randall. We had just seemed to be getting in touch again, too, after a long silence. What do you suppose went wrong with him and had he talked to you at all frankly lately or since he was sick? I feel it must have been an accident of an unconscious-suicide kind, a sudden impulse when he was really quite out of his head—because surely it was most unlike him to make some innocent motorist responsible for his death. I feel sorry for whoever it was. When I heard about it, in Ouro Prêto—and then saw it in TIME a day or so later—I tried and tried to write to Mary, but didn't. Now, after what you wrote me, I don't know whether to or not—perhaps I shall, just conventionally. Demerol is a strong drug—at least the sleeping pills are. Maybe he'd taken some and kept going, which would certainly make anyone "fuzzy," as you say.— It is too sad, really. I hope he got the two letters I

---

1 *Coup d'état.* RL had seen "President Castelo Branco, in Sweeping Decree, Dissolves Political Parties, Increases Executive Powers, and Opens Judiciary to Appointment of New Judges," *The New York Times* (Oct. 28, 1965).
2 "Questions of Travel" (EB-*CP*).

wrote him about his book and that I managed to say something he wanted said. Another thing I found when I got back was the unbound MMS from Pantheon of his children's book for me to read[1]—it came by boat, and so had taken ages to get here. I haven't had the heart to read it yet. Don't send me anything for Christmas please!— I have no way of getting anything in safely at present.

You are awfully kind about my book and your letter was a great comfort to me. I was wheezing away and full of adrenalin and feeling just too foolish, at this advanced age, to be in such a state—when it came. I love your expression, "the bomb in it in a delicate way!" That was my idea exactly, I suppose. I haven't seen that new maple leaf flag yet but hear it is ugly—too pale, and on a white ground? Well—*Trollope* was actually an anti-Eisenhower poem, I think—although it's really almost all Trollope—phrase after phrase. You are too generous to go over the same old but so short list. I think the book itself is pretty, but the contents too slight. TIME came again—same Mr. Denis. I wanted to use the old ones of you & me[2] since they are better than he usually does, but they insisted so I finally gave in, and he was kind enough to let me see proof[s]. He's a nice man, but a dreadful photographer—about 85% of them had me with my eyes shut, looking exactly like both my grandmothers put together. (He said that I blinked "unusually fast"—that's a new one). I have a horrible feeling they're preparing to tear me limb from limb because of my quarrels with them.

I see your name everywhere, everywhere—Marianne's, too—and she is moving, or has already moved by now. I have an old Nova Scotian superstition—but it's world-wide, I think—that that is a very bad sign. I saw pictures of Pound at Spoleto looking extremely old, too—and read about his silence, etc. Who *is* Barbara Guest—the only other American besides Allen? That's about the only place I'd like to go to, to a "conference" I think—Calder has talked about it to us a lot.

I haven't heard anything from the Rockefellers and you seem to imply that perhaps they aren't giving any more fellowships. However, I think I'll write a note just to see if they ever got my application—letters from Ouro Prêto seemed more subject to loss than from here, even. In the meantime I made up my mind to go to Seattle—a few days after Christmas. I don't want to one bit, but need the money and probably it will be good for me or some-

1 Randall Jarrell, *The Animal Family* (1965).
2 EB and RL on the beach in Rio de Janeiro, August 1962.

thing!— They are running a big risk, I think, since I've never taught before and all their forms and letters just confuse me more and more. I try to think seriously for a while every day, like Isherwood, on *what poetry is all about*, etc.—but my mind wanders . . . However—they do sound nice and friendly and I do want to see the BIG TREES and Mt. Rainier—so it will probably be all right. However—if you have any ideas on the subject of textbooks (!) good anthologies, etc.—or *anything at all*—I'd be extremely grateful. They keep writing me about them (textbooks) and I don't know what to say. I'm not as dumb as I sound here, I'm sure, and I certainly see enough books— too many by far—but can't think of any all-round one, or even two or three. I've re-read all of Saintsbury on Prosody,[1] just for fun—it is a marvellous book, I think—all 3 volumes—so *funny*—and good until he meets Swin- burne—or maybe we're wrong about *him*.

I'm hoping that Lota will come up for the last month and then we can do a bit of traveling and go to San Francisco, etc. She says no—she'll never be able to get away—but I hope she'll weaken. She hates having me go—very nice of her—but after a sad scene she is now resigned!—and she is so aw- fully busy she really misses me only for about an hour at dinner-time or on long week-ends. She is now President of the board to run the park—the "Foundation"—until 1968. Takes office Monday. But it has been a hideous stretch and I am utterly sick of Brazilian politics, big and little, at the mo- ment. She is a fighter, after all, and in some ways enjoys all the bloodshed, I think—but a while ago I was afraid it would really kill us both before the thing got finished. As L says—the people are *primary*—one has to spend too much time on what they should know already.

Right now I'm in a sort of quandary—I've been invited to the Embassy for lunch to meet *Mrs.* Rusk. I try to go once a year or so just so I'll get asked when someone interesting turns up—not that they ever do. I was going to refuse, being so opposed to the OEA[2] (you have the letters around in English differently, I think) in general—but then I read in the papers that she never goes anywhere with him, hates it, and just came this time because she wants to see Rio. And his *wife* may be innocent, after all—and there are to be (says the secretary) "40 ladies—no hats"— Oh dear. Last night was the opening of the big conference. There was a very small highbrow demonstration in front of the Copacabana Palace Hotel and two or three men I know were ar-

---

1 George Saintsbury, *History of English Prosody* (1906–10).
2 Organization of American States.

rested. However—I am not too sympathetic to them, either. It is NOT a "dictatorship" here—I think they all just want to be martyred, really. On the other hand—it looks as though our Latin American diplomacy had really broken down completely and they have turned it all over to the Pentagon— this is really just a military rally, I feel. Bobby Kennedy arrives next—but you didn't say anything useful about your meeting with him: (In case I do).

I have been reading all about the blackout and wonder what happened to you and your family during it—you do have fireplaces and, I hope, had candles.[1] We are so used to them here—sometimes they are even scheduled— and there are no buildings higher than 12 floors, at least. It must have been weird and rather wonderful—and maybe a good idea, in a way—to show everyone how helpless they are without *juice*. I like Ouro Prêto because everything there was made on the spot, by hand, of stone, iron, copper, wood—and they had to invent a lot—and everything has lasted perfectly well for almost three hundred years now.— I used to think this was just sentimental of me—now I'm beginning to take it more seriously. Well—I am curious to see my native land again. I must say I hate it in *The New Yorker*. I did a couple of poems lately—one will be in that magazine soon, I think.[2] Do tell me what you are doing—at Harvard again? And I am *dying to see you & talk to you*.

Love,

Elizabeth

(Please give me your ZONE number!)

328.

[November 24, 1965]

Dearest—

Why not use De la Mare's *Come Hither* or *Love?* My favorite orthodox anthology of English poetry is the Auden and Pearson five volume Viking Portable. For modern poetry, how about the Tate and Herbert Read— Scribner's or Oxford?[3]

---

1 The Northeast Blackout of November 9, 1965.
2 "Under the Window: Ouro Prêto (for Lilli Correia de Araújo)," *The New Yorker* (Dec. 24, 1966); see EB-*CP*.
3 *Come Hither*, ed. Walter de la Mare (1923); *Love*, ed. Walter de la Mare (1943); *Poets of the English Language*, ed. W. H. Auden and Norman Pearson (1950); Allen Tate coedited *Modern Verse in English, 1900–1950* (1958) with David Cecil, not Herbert Read.

I read "Armadillo" along with Auden's "Shield of Achilles," two Randalls and one Sylvia Plath at Harvard's Sanders Theatre.

You are very subtle about dictatorships, etc. On the one hand our embassy run by the Pentagon, on the other, your General "not a dictator." I know I think what you mean and more or less agree. Washington is now even more like your Trollope poem. Why isn't it yours if you rimed and metered it so beautifully? Oh, the poems I read of yours were the Pound and "Armadillo"—the Pound is overwhelming decently read aloud. I too love Saintsbury. His book on prose, prose rhythm, etc., on the same plan as the prosody but only one volume, is lovely too.[1] He's right in a way about Swinburne, and so are we. The great Victorians for me are Tennyson, Browning, Lear, Fitzgerald, Arnold and Hopkins. I just love Marianne. We did a Pound television program together, then she came to dinner with Bob Giroux and Eliot's widow. The most *powerful* poet now writing in English!

Do Dear, take the Washington. They'll be kindness and gentleness itself. Why not read aloud from Saintsbury in your class? Marvelous portrait of Stevenson by Sevareid[2] in *Look* on Adlai Stevenson. Stev. says on Rusk, "Oh, I don't know . . . I can't make him out, . . . He is so sort of wooden." Oh, see Mrs. Rusk! Oh I think Fulbright and Bobby are our best senators, but I never met him—it was Teddy I met last summer.

Ah, what's the black-out after summers in Maine with that sort of thing happening thrice a summer. Awful, though, for the people trapped in subways and elevators. How much better candles are for restaurant eating, or conversation during the evening. Hartford was like Ouro Prêto, an island of its own light, and in Cambridge, there [are] glowing DC current houses.

I'm zone 23.[3] In our society, it [is] almost a duty for people like us to teach a *little.*— You are not being sentimental, I think, about Ouro Prêto.

I have a four hundred line sequence poem which might make a book, twenty pages on a New England essay, and my obituary on Randall. Thank God, we two still breathe the air of the living.

All my love,
Cal

---

1 George Saintsbury, *A History of English Prose Rhythm* (1912).
2 Eric Sevareid, "Adlai Stevenson: His Final Troubled Hours," *Look* (Nov. 3, 1965).
3 Postal zone.

329.

Apt. 212, 4135 Brooklyn Ave., N.E.
Seattle, Washington, 98105
Washington's Birthday
[Feb. 23, 1966]

Dearest Cal:

That Carolyn Kizer . . . She called me up late one night and told me you had been elected to the Oxford post, and in my excitement I sent off a cable, telegram, I mean, that same night—and it wasn't until two days later I read the true account in the papers here.[1] I hope you didn't think I was wool-gathering . . . although come to think of it, I certainly was, the first few weeks, and as you see, I am just getting around to writing letters *now*. I am awfully sorry you didn't get the appointment, but you undoubtedly will next time, anyway—I have been sent clippings about it and you from all over the country, I think, lots from New York, of course. Bob Giroux kept me— keeps me—quite well informed. His last letter, he had just had lunch with you and said you were very well. I am awfully glad and hope all goes well with you. Are you teaching, too, I wonder, or what?

I don't know where to begin. You are much admired here and several of my "students" (I have to keep putting everything in quotes because none of it seems quite real to me, even now) are using you for their term-papers . . . you are being compared (to his discredit) frequently with Eliot, I think— Henry Reed is here—a bright spot in my life, I must say. I had dinner with him last night and he told me how he had heard a beautiful reading of SKUNK HOUR in England—and was reported in the papers as having said in a loud aside, "That's the only poem worth a damn this whole evening." He was sorry not to have met you here and would very much like to when he goes to New York.— I'm not sure when. He is extremely funny—referred to Olivier in OTHELLO as "The Nigger of the Narcissus," to give you an idea of his wit. I shall make so bold as to give him your address. He has done a few beautiful poems since "Naming of Parts" ("to which I owe my liveli-hood," he says)[2] he has shown me—but I think writes really very little. I read my class your wonderful piece on Randall one day—I had missed that copy in Brazil, of the *NY Review*—and they were very moved by it, obvi-ously. I have also read them a lot of Randall's poems—and I did send off a few sentences for that occasion at Yale I think you were reading at, not long

---

1 The telegram does not survive. RL was nominated for the Oxford Professorship of Poetry, a five-year post that would have obliged him to lecture three times a year. Edmund Blunden, an Oxonian candidate, was elected instead.
2 Henry Reed, "Lessons of the War: I. Naming of Parts," *A Map of Verona* (1946).

ago—no—the 28th, I think—?[1] I'm not sure that they would serve, though. You really said it all much better in your piece. He doesn't seem very well known here, so I am bringing in him—and Berryman—and a few others every chance I get. They are so wrapped up in Roethke, still, and he also left an anti-Pound, anti-Eliot heritage—but I go blithely on giving them things they look blasé about—even Tennyson and Keats. This eastern influence!—only here it's west. One boy gave me *100* haikus—or haikai, as I believe the plural is. (They are all too familiar with the oriental languages—and it certainly has a disastrous effect on METER.)

Well, I was never meant to be a teacher and would never like it—but I do like the "students" (children, I call them to myself)—even if they seem awfully lacking in joie de vivre and keep telling me about their experiences with LSD and "pot" etc., and (2 girls) how they are "on the PILL"—I think this was to convince me they are serious about writing! The boys are all over six feet—some girls are, too—and the girls have huge legs—& have blue eyes; one *left-handed*—what is this high percentage of left-handiness, I wonder? Henry said he'd been warned about the *bosom* in the front row—but not about the large bare knee that starts creeping up over the edge of the table . . . I have a few extremely bright students, however—thank goodness. And they all couldn't be nicer to me,—protective, almost. Some of them found this place for me and *moved* me—even provided a lot of odd furniture. I had been quite wretched in a hotel, and a motel—this is quiet and private, and I have 2 rooms.

Now that I have at last started writing you, I realize *how* much I miss you and would love to see you; and I do hope you are feeling all well again, Cal. I see I am up for the National B A—but doubt I'll get it, since I remember you once told me that Phyllis McGinley had told you she couldn't "see a thing" in my poetry! I'd like to get it for 2 reasons: 1. for Lota—these things mean a lot there. 2. It would mean a trip to New York. But I imagine Eberhart will get it, so I don't need to worry about public appearances, etc.

Everyone has been awfully kind to me. That darling old Mr. Chittick—the "deaf old man" you wrote me a postcard from here about once—wrote after you were here, welcoming me—but alas, I didn't get it. It would have helped, too.

Bob said you had some wonderful poems for your next book[2]—I wonder

---

1 Tribute to Randall Jarrell on February 28, 1966, with RL, John Berryman, Richard Eberhart, John Hollander, Mary Jarrell, Stanley Kunitz, William Meredith, Adrienne Rich, Peter Taylor, Robert Penn Warren, and Richard Wilbur.
2 *Near the Ocean* (1967).

if I have seen them all? and certainly want to. I am not taking my good reviews or any of it very seriously, really—I know quite well it is all just because you have desisted, in a gentlemanly way, from publishing a book this year . . .

And ye gods—how good your poems are when I really get to work on one—"Between the Porch & the Altar!" was the last—with that class—and they read such feeble stuff in comparison by a lot of poets I don't know. For a while I felt if I really wanted to get away all I'd have to do would be to stand up and pull my hair one day and scream I HATE ROETHKE. However, the head of the Dept., to whom I confided this, said it wouldn't work. "A great many people would agree with you." I don't really, anyway—but one hates feeling like his ghost—and I think *some* of his influence has been very bad—although at the same time I think he attracted a lot of good potential poets here—and I am still getting some of those.

Seattle—well—those billows and billows of little wooden houses, each different, and those swooshing free-ways all over the place—I found it strange and upsetting at first; now I am getting used to it, somewhat. And the biggest seagulls I ever saw—*silent* seagulls. I like the waterfront—have been there only twice, however. I really have to work awfully hard to keep a nose ahead of the classes. I am just not used to work, anyway, and realize what a lazy and pampered life I have led—but I am enjoying most of the reading I have to do—things I should have read before, probably—and some of the social life, especially the more Bohemian friends I have made—not so much the academic ones—although everyone is KIND. Westerners are really different—it took a little getting used to. We were so genteel at Vassar, really. I don't expect to think of a poem of my own, for a moment, until June.

How are Harriet and Elizabeth? I read the latter in the *N.Y. Review*[1] and shall probably soon be reading the former.—Please write me, Cal dear, if you have time—I can imagine how busy you are— I think of you with great pride and affection and try not to talk about you too much!

Love,
Elizabeth

Saw about Bill Alfred's play in TIME[2]—still don't read it here, the newspapers so poor—

1 Elizabeth Hardwick, "Theater in New York," *The New York Review of Books* (Jan. 6, 1966).
2 "The Unfabulous Invalid," *Time* (Feb. 18, 1966), about William Alfred's *Hogan's Goat*.

330.

February 25, 1966

Dearest Elizabeth:

Wonderful your letters are pouring out again. I had terrible pictures of you despondent and lost in the new toil of teaching—lonely, cold, at sea. Lizzie taught last term at Barnard for the first time in her life. Her first comment was "the students aren't very good, but I am." She gave them various non-fiction books such as Lévi-Strauss and *In the American Grain*[1] and found them agape. Then they almost all wrote *A* papers, and she got quite enthused, had another offer from Bryn Mawr and got her Barnard salary raised. Then you can now teach probably almost anywhere, more or less on your own terms, and a year here might be a pleasant change for you and Lota. New cars are cheaper.

You are too good as always about my writing. I've just been through agonies hammering out a three page introduction to Sylvia Plath.[2] I think it does now, but the first few drafts were beneath any of my graduate student papers. No, I am laborious, too much like everyone else, and a bit harsh and perverse. While you . . . Your book is another species from most everything else. I think even the reviewers now see that there's no one, except Marianne Moore, at all comparable to you. I guess I struck Roethke under a bit more favorable circumstance. I mean last year when I came to Seattle, I was to give the Roethke Memorial reading and had worked myself into the proper state of awe. I gave a Yeats reading at Columbia at about the same time, and my head rang with resonance, all of which may show in the long, metered Marvell couplet thing I wrote all last summer.[3] Ted's worst fault was a sort of tender hard-heartedness, too great a wish to be big, so that much of the poetry is a little dead under the ringing cadences. But then he really was big and it took great courage to burn out with such a big flare—nothing much left then to his body, and very like a drunken baby to meet here on visits.

Bobby Kennedy never showed up for the dinner, but Jackie did, full of wild vignettes spoken in her breathless, almost parody voice. I thought Lizzie was horrified and discovered she was charmed. Once in a blue moon—I thought this about Alice Longworth—someone from the grand world is really delightful. Sometimes, I think I would die, if it weren't for a

---

1 William Carlos Williams, *In the American Grain* (1925).
2 "Sylvia Plath's *Ariel*," *The New York Review of Books* (May 12, 1966), reprinted as a foreword to *Ariel* (1966).
3 "Waking Early Sunday Morning" (RL-*CP*).

few platonic relations with women. Adrienne Rich used to come out twice a week to see me in the Boston hospital, and a couple of hours would whirl by in what seemed like a few minutes of talk.

I have a formidable new doctor, Kurt Eissler, sounding (I mean just his name) like a Nazi in a film, and of course out of Germany with forty volume sets of Goethe, Wieland, etc. and books of his own on Goethe, Genius and Environment, Depression, etc.[1] Maybe I'll get well. This doctor is the first I've had who is really much like an artist, though it took several days for us to speak a language intelligible to the other.

I pray you get the National Book Award. Did you say the day was the Fifth? I don't leave for Florida till the 10th. You must stay with us. You wouldn't know us, we are so soften[ed] by our doctors and guinea pigs. When we drink together, we talk about how well we get on, squeaks in the background, even splintering hopping sounds from our little laconic birds, long angora (pig) hairs on the sofa, now sinking into fluff from Harriet's turns on it.

Do tell Reed to come and see us. He must have saved your heart in exile. What a difference an intelligent voice makes. Our Guadeloupe beach was restoring, but one felt stupider than the stupidest tourist—and was!

All my love,
Cal

331.

Castine, Maine
July 16, 1966

Dearest Elizabeth:

It seems months and months since I've written you, and it is, though we've talked on the phone, and you seemed during your Washington months close in a way . . . a visit, but one I almost missed. I have a guilty feeling of almost having let something die—in me, I guess. Do you have moments of relaxing,—a relaxing to let in life, that may be a letting go?

All this comes to me on a clear day, bush and grass in the sun, bush and grass in the shadow, the sea high, like a lake shore, a few feet off now from my window. For about a month, ever since coming here, I have been working steadily on an expanded prose version of the *Prometheus*.[2] Now a first full draft is done, almost seventy pages, and I wonder why I buried myself in it

1 K. R. Eissler, *Goethe: A Psychoanalytic Study, 1775–1786* (1963).
2 *Prometheus Bound* (1969).

so, five days a week, and sometimes six. Can any truth come through the old Greek plot, the few, ever-recurring grand words? Somehow though, I find myself in a rut, where it's easier to write than not to. Oh, to break away for months! (And sometimes I feel very tired, in a not quite physical way) find ways to dream—I am always dreaming inside myself—do nothing! And I do, but am made glazed, stiff and nervous by the near at hand. I have been thinking of Whitman's huge sweep, mostly in his thirties and forties, lines pouring out, a hundred poems a year, yet with long, idle afternoons of sauntering, chatting, at ease nearly with what the eye fell on.

A couple of days ago Delmore Schwartz died from a heart-attack, just outside his room in a cheap New York hotel[1]—alone, out of touch, for a year, a shadow, a rumor seen here and there, gone underground, after he vanished and hid from Syracuse University, angry that he hadn't been given tenure. Maybe the heat killed him; the death-rate has risen lately in New York, but really his end was in the cards for long, too much drinking, a paranoia that cut him off from jobs, and even friends—for a day, there was no one to claim the body. I think back on the time when Caroline Gordon said, "This is the one mature young man I've ever met." This hurt me, but I felt dismissed with a great swarm of other young men. And it seemed true in a way. *In Dreams Begin Responsibilities* had just come out,[2] and reasonable, intuitive essays, the old new criticism, but with a new touch, in all the Quarterlies. He was much more bruised and swollen, when I knew him well, an intimate grueling year, a year or so before you and I met—Jean and he and I, sedentary, indoors souls, talking about books and literary gossip over glasses of milk, strengthened with Maine vodka, the milk intended to restore what the vodka tore down—Delmore in an unpressed mustard gabardine, a little winded, husky voiced, unhealthy, but with a carton of varied vitamin bottles, the color of oil, quickening with Jewish humor, and in-the-knowness, and his own genius, every person, every book—motives for everything, Freud in his blood, great webs of causation, then suspicion, then rushes of rage. He was more reasonable than us, but obsessed, a much better mind, but one really chasing the dust—it was like living with a sluggish, sometimes angry spider—no hurry, no motion, Delmore's voice, almost inaudible, dead, intuitive, pointing somewhere, then the strings tightening, the roar of rage—too much, too much for us! Nothing haunts me more than breaking with friends. I used to think he was the only one I broke with.

1 On July 11, 1966.
2 Published in 1938.

Are you glad to be back in Rio, or are you up in the hills? I feel I had a hand in your going to Seattle, though I didn't really, and didn't suggest it. It must have been trying and empty a lot of the time, but aren't you glad—I sound like my Mother—that now you know how simple teaching is, that you can always fall back on it? Write soon and tell me about yourself, what you did then, what you are doing now. Are you and Lota going to Italy this fall? We may go to Spain next summer. Lizzie is at work on two books: one we are supposed to do together, a high school English and world literature text-book for Harcourt Brace, the other hers, a book on poverty from five or six parts of the country, helped out with a tape-recorder. She has been going shyly and sharply around with it, no, mostly shy, to our local figures, the laundress, the caretaker's widow, Phil Booth—hard to unearth the Maine poor, or rather open them up, for they are everywhere. When the debris is finally sorted, I think she will have something brilliant, but starting is hard. I am dying to hear more of and see your Brazilian book. I suppose life is at our fingertips, millions talking prose all their lives, if one could only, not gather, but arrange it![1]

I miss you so much, Dear, and feel a third of me is dead, when we stop writing.

Our love to you and dear Lota, all mine to you!

Cal

P.S. I don't know when this will arrive, all the air lines, except, oddly enough, Maine's eccentric Northeast, are on strike.

332.

15 West 67 St., NYC
September 15, 1966

Dearest Elizabeth:

What's up? It seems almost a year since I've had anything in writing from you. I spent a summer almost without event or narrative: work through the day, two hours of doubles, evenings at home or with our undrama-torn Castine friends, though no one is untorn. I can think of almost nothing. In mid-summer, following my desire and ignoring my better judgment, I went to a birthday party for Jackie Kennedy—white turrety inn building at Cotuit,

1 Cf. "Par ma foi! il y a plus de quarante ans que je dis de la prose sans que j'en susse rien"; Molière, *Le Bourgeois gentilhomme* (1670).

rooms rented for the guests by our hostess Mrs. Paul Mellon, through the afternoon glimpses of what must be fellow guests, women with hair a foot high, smiles but no introductions, information that the launch would arrive for us at eight, that we could have a free drink, or drinks, a solitary swim—water after the ice of Maine—a solitary dull drive through Cotuit, return to assembling and drinking guests, the nearest I came to knowing any were Mike Nichols, Charles Addams, and Jerome Robbins—most of them were people like Forrestal's son, Paley, the CBS president, people with names like big figures in news, business or politics, but often not related, or poor cousins. Launch with champagne in paper cups, harbor boat pacing our boat, wonderful sunset over Cotuit accredited to Mrs. Mellon's plans—then landing, swarms of new known-unknowns with lanterns, big tent, air of very expensive rustic simplicity. Hours of waiting, feeling that no one was known from our world to any of the other guests except Mike Nichols. Air of drama and waiting for Jackie, the chartered plane (chartered by my old friend Blair Clark) for Lillian Hellman and the Styrons. After a while, Jackie suddenly present and talking to Mike Nichols, Hellman group there, both Senator Kennedys, McNamara. Later, a luxuriously simple dinner, all I can remember are blood-red lamb chops, Mike Nichols next to Jackie, later, middle-aged people dancing the new dances, not very wildly, but too young for me, a slightly tawdry untimely Marie Antoinette feeling of a festival when the age for being whole-hearted about such things had passed, the flash of the jet-set, a little lurid and in bad taste in a world of poverty and blood, a certain real ease—meeting with McNamara, Jackie putting her hand over my mouth and telling me to be polite, and I saying something awkward about liking him, but not his policy, then Jackie saying, "How impossibly banal. You should say you adore his policy, but find him dull." Few minutes talk with Styron and me arguing with McNamara, no great impact on either side, except that McNamara seemed a simple brilliant administrative soul, who [has] given little thought to moral complications, and who might have even taken the usual liberal line against Viet Nam more easily than I would. The party didn't get into the news, but somehow a month later, a gossip column in Norfolk, Virginia reported that I stayed up till five with McNamara and we had gotten on famously, and the columnist hoped I'd learned something—all nonsense. A vague feeling of a heterogeneous opposition to Johnson group. The most interesting person to talk to was Bobby Kennedy, but like Carlos, there is a scary feeling of ambition and power about him, along with frankness. Well, next day, driving rather dull and stunned back to Provincetown and the Stanley Kunitzes, I was parked in traffic, looking at a road-map to find some less traveled road, something more like the backwater of Castine, when suddenly I moved forward with a jolt, found the car had stopped, a hole through the windshield, a little of my hair in the spider web of smashed glass, the car no longer able to move. The car ahead of me wasn't damaged, no blood drawn from me, though $500 injury to my car, paid by Hertz insurance. After hours of waiting, papers, police, a wrecker, I am off to Provincetown again in an *Avis* car—the Hertz and Avis booths touched each other and I was at both, making out accident papers at one, and car-rental papers at the other. Two days later I had to appear at the Barnstable Court for inattentive driving, a roomful of indicted, adolescent carelessness, I by now in fear of losing my license, taking from my pocket a birthday poem written by William Jay Smith to Francis Biddle, beginning "In Life's great court all men are judged." Relief. I plead "Nolo," and get a twenty-five dollar fine.[1] That night I lectured at Harvard on the dead, Randall, Roethke and Delmore Schwartz, and reflected that I myself might have been dead without even knowing it. Then home and back to work. In the course of the summer, I have finished *Prometheus* at last—how like him I felt as I labored on interminably—and my new book of poems heavily revised.[2]

Now Harriet's school, my teaching and everything is starting. It's exhilarating to be still alive. Hope you will do something on Randall, the deadline has been pushed forward to May. And do write!

All our love to you and Lota,

Cal

P.S. Forgive me for sending off this little gulp of incident. If I waited for a second wind to go on, it might be days.

333.

Samambaia, September 25th, 1966

Dearest Cal:

At last I am sitting down to write to you—I have hundreds, it seems, of unanswered letters weighing on my conscience, and I only answer the business ones from time to time, never write to my friends any more . . . You do know that I'm naturally rather a letter-writer, & this [is] one of the things I didn't like about my "job." In fact,—don't repeat this where it might get

1 Cf. "Flight to New York: No Messiah," line 12 (RL-*CP*).
2 *Near the Ocean* (1967).

606

back to *them*—but I felt it was much too hard work . . . or else I took it too hard; and then its being the first time made it much harder. Also I think those poor "kids" (as the other teachers all called them) are so badly prepared and so confused, most of them, in the vastness & impersonality of such a big university. I grew very fond of a lot of them, however & had some very good graduate students in the "Types of Poetry" course . . . The writing one I think is a dreadful idea—but I really knew that before I started out. The "boss" asked me what I'd like to teach if ever I went back, and I think I upset him somewhat by replying "Remedial English." At least one would feel one was getting someplace . . . I got back the first part of July—came up here—then stayed up in Ouro Prêto seeing how my old OLD house is getting along—slowly, beautifully, and sucking up money like a sponge—but my it is lovely, and I hope sometime we can sit together on my little blue balcony overlooking the whole town, and watch the fireworks in honor of some saint or other . . . I think I owe you at least three letters. What is your secret? Do you simply have a secretary? I am experimenting with a tape recorder to see if I can get off business letters that way, but so far all I can produce are very Canadian R's—and it is hard to get a typist here whose English is good enough.

Your account of Mrs. K's birthday party is fascinating but kind of awful . . . I have a feeling she is probably a Vassar type I used to know—in fact still have a few friends of my own generation of that sort. I have been reading Schlesinger's *1,000 Days* for about a month now—just finished it—I suppose you read it?[1] In some ways it is very good, and I wish a lot of young radicals who think they could change things for the better *easily* would read it, too—but I finally began to think that S. found almost everyone just a bit too brilliant, sympathetic, hard-working, witty, lovely, etc. . . . . Up here I've just read *Is Paris Burning*[2]—quite hair-raising. I have a MMS of your poems here and maybe tonight I'll re-read those. I did, of course, in Seattle, several times, but never wrote you—never wrote anyone much except Lota. I am worried to death about her. I was hoping to find her in better shape when I got back, and Brazil as well—but everything seems much much worse and she has been in bed off & on for a month—what they used to call a "nervous breakdown" I think. She does now have 45 days off, and if we possibly can we are going to Europe—just the Netherlands, where we've never been, and London, where she has never been, and to visit friends in Sussex.[3] We'd leave

---

1 Arthur Schlesinger Jr., *A Thousand Days: John F. Kennedy in the White House* (1965).
2 Larry Collins and Dominique Lapierre, *Is Paris Burning?* (1965).
3 Kit and Ilse Barker.

around October 10th—I'll let you know. Do you have any recommendations for Amsterdam, or is that all too long ago? I'm dying to look at paintings for a while.

Are you teaching at the New School, or where? I want to begin work on the Brazil book—have quite a few chapters done, more or less—and think it m[a]y even be moderately diverting and enlightening—if I can get some good photographs, too. I'll ask the Rockefellers for a month's leave of absence from work, however, if the trip abroad materializes—I feel L's health comes first of all now, and she has really had blow after blow here. Don't ever go into politics, or anything to do with city-management—in any country—I'm sure they're all equally bad, heart-breaking, crooked, lethargic, etc. . . . I believe more in the old-fashioned idea of a "change" I think, than pills and vitamins . . . we'll see. I might see Henry Reed in London. He was a wonderful comfort to me in Seattle—and I think I was to him, too. He is a sad man, though, perhaps because he hasn't been able to work for so long— I don't really know—but funny as can be at the same time. We cheered each other up through exams by midnight telephone calls telling each other the best things we'd found. He was teaching "Romeo & Juliet" to about 60 freshmen, poor dear. My favorite of his was a girl's paper that began "Lady Capulet is definitely older than her daughter but she remains a woman." One boy: "Romeo was determined to sleep in the tomb of the Catapults" . . . etc.— Henry is going back for the winter term of the job I had, again. He wants to settle in the USA, being very romantically fond of it, I think, although he's seen nothing at all except some of the west coast. I think he is a wonderful teacher—too good, really for Un. of W.—if you have any ideas of a course he could give somewhere else I wish you'd let me know . . . I think I'll write Dick Wilbur. I know nothing of these Wesleyan things, but perhaps when my grant is over and that book is done, I might apply for one. I think it would do both Lota and me a lot of good to stay in Connecticut for a few months!—seeing New York, but not IN it. I don't think I'll ever feel tough enough for New York again, somehow.

I am curious to hear about Visnesky[1] (?)—have ordered that book of poems. You know [I] didn't even know Delmore had died—how did I miss that? I was sorry to see about Frank O'Hara in TIME[2]—I liked him a lot the 2 times I saw him, even if he was drunk and a bit disorderly . . . I'd like to have heard your talk on our recent dead—but oh dear, one hears so much

---

1 Andrey Voznesensky, *Antiworlds: Poetry*, trans. W. H. Auden and others (1966).
2 Frank O'Hara died on July 25, 1966.

about Roethke where I was—too much—and I think his influence was not at all for the good. I was entirely too sane and sober for the students' tastes after him and other legendary characters they'd had lately who got arrested, gave drinks to minors, and so on . . .

I am so sorry to hear about your accident—and another trouble of L's is that she had one, too—the first in 30 some years of driving, and not her fault—a bunch of crazy boys in a Volkswagen. I wasn't with her—a friend was—they weren't hurt at all but her little open sports car, the joy of her life, was damaged—not seriously, but in this country any repair takes months, it seems. It is beautiful up here and I wish I could stay on for months working in this nice study—but she has to get back to Rio tomorrow—and I don't like it there at all, I'm afraid. However, we'll be getting ready to go away, probably, and that is cheering. Please write me to Rio—I may not get up here again—apto 1101 Rua Antônio Vieira 5, Leme, Rio de Janeiro G B / that is quicker now. Please keep well and don't think for a moment I've forgotten you! I'll be back to normal soon

    —Much much love,
    Elizabeth

Do you have an address for Philip Booth?—I'd like to thank him for the nice review—6 months old now.[1]

334.

October 2, 1966

Dearest Elizabeth:

How lovely to hear from you again in all your old leisurely fullness. Sorry though that Seattle was a grind and that Lota has had so much too much work. I have to fly up to Harvard soon for my weekly classes there, so will just dash off this letter, trying to answer and comment on your letter. The man in charge of Wesleyan is Paul Horgan, a Colorado or Arizona novelist. We know him quite well, and will get in touch with him, if you and Lota & Henry Reed are really interested. It's a queer place, about a dozen people in residence, some with wives, some without, an office, rooms or a house. Lizzie and I were offered about $20,000 to stay there a year, but so far have held off, not wanting to change Harriet's school, preferring to be in New York. It can be rather melancholy, but all depends on who is there—

1 Philip Booth, "The Poet as Voyager," *The Christian Science Monitor* (Jan. 6, 1966).

usually several people from Europe, ages older and more uniformly distinguished than Yaddo. The I. A. Richards are there now, later the Spenders are coming. Always someone. No duties, though it's suggested that you informally meet students. It might be perfect for you both. Let me know, and I'll start writing and calling people. For Holland, I have a lot of names of old dear friends, but have lost the addresses except for one—no, wait, I'll call Adrienne Rich, who knows them all more recently, and now lives a few blocks away—. . . Line's busy, so I'll go on a minute. We loved Amsterdam, a bricky baroque Boston, humanly much coarser and more solid, wonderful untouched 17th century canal center, a delicacy, a grossness, everyone we knew speaking English as well as we do, knowing English, American, German and above all French writing. You will find many who know your poetry. Randall and the Conrads[1] (Richs) loved them as much as we . . . Here are the names: W. F. van Leeuwen, psychiatrist and literary critic, my age, one of my best friends; wife Judith,[2] younger, poet and critic, Adrienne thinks she has reviewed you, and is a great admirer; Hans Gomperts, very lively critic and poet; (Oh the van Leeuwens' address is Vondel Straat 75 A, telephone 02–732893); de Groot, Prinsengracht 1019 A, I don't know him, but he is a distinguished physicist, and his wife an anthropologist and expert on Surinam; Bep du Perron (I have no more addresses) wife of a very distinguished writer[3] who died in the war and was a friend of Malraux, looks like Virginia Woolf, and is very charming. I guess this will do. You will get in touch with everyone through the Van Leeuwens. I'd think a lot of places would like to have Henry Reed. Everyone speaks well of him, and he is quite famous and admired for his one book. He's a great friend of our friend the actress Irene Worth. Philip Booth's address is Dept. of English, Syracuse, N.Y. This is no letter, but let me get it off in time. May you both get a good rest. How I miss you!

  All my love,
   Cal

(over)

Oh yes, you are more or less right about J Kennedy, yet she's quite bright and charming; Arthur sees everyone on his side that is in power with a super-

1 Adrienne Rich was married to Alfred H. Conrad.
2 Judith Herzberg.
3 Edgar du Perron.

natural glow. Politics here are in a state of groggy confusion; everyone hates Johnson nearly in our world, but fears something worse. Who knows what the Viet Nam War will lead to. Maybe it will all simmer off, but no one can be sure. An uncertain winter ahead, but personally we are untroubled and happy. Liz sends her love.

335.

[Postcard: Night view of the Glória Church, Rio]

[Rio
October 23, 1966]

Thank you for your letter and suggestions—we haven't been able to get away until today—the 23rd—but are taking off this PM to be gone as long as the money lasts—a month or six weeks—we have been seeing Nathalie Babel here. This is all for now except to thank you and say I'll try to write somewhere along the line. I hope you and the family are all well—with much love,

E

336.

[Postcard: Contemporary Portrait of Richard II, Westminster Abbey]

London, November 10th [1966]

We're cutting our visit short & going home tomorrow—because of L's health—hope to get back next year, however. Have written in Spender's BOOK, etc.—but not done very much, really. L disapproves highly of Trafalgar Sq. & the British ladies' dress—but enjoyed the Abbey as sort of "black humor," I think. I'll TYPE a long letter next week.— I do hope you are well—

Much love,
E. Bishop

337.

Friday, February 26, 1967

Dearest Elizabeth—

I gather from Dr. Baumann you've been going through a sea of troubles—asthma, a hospital, trouble with Lota, God knows what. I've been keeping informed as best I can, but really don't know too much. I dread thinking of you in trouble, exposed, and a-wash in Rio. Somehow another country, language, Spanish nuns, etc. make it all seem more grueling and uncertain. My yearly attacks, tho bruising and troubling to everyone, and even to a degree unpredictable, *do* seem to fall into a groove of repetition, making everything easier to handle. I've just gotten over another. Nothing new worth writing about, except that I have another doctor now, and there seems to be real hope that my manic seizures can be handled by a new drug, Lithium, and that all my giddy reelings come from a kind of periodic salt deficiency in some lower part of the brain. At least, this drug is now working with many.

I'll have Giroux send you my new book.[1] There are quite a few changes from the version you saw, translations added, and pictures, which you may not like, tho I do. Nolan[2] has done over a hundred, mostly in color illustrations for my *Imitations*, much more ambitious and inspired than these.

The day after tomorrow, I'll be fifty, and Lizzie is arranging a party of almost thirty, our big room lined with long tables. Doubt if I can rise to the occasion—tho I guess still being around and hale, is a triumph for our stricken generation of poets. Last fall, Berryman wrote a marvelous sequence of new dream poems, entitled, *Opus Posthumous*[3]—they really seem ex humo, from beyond the tomb. I thought he was gone, but the experience seems to have resurrected him. In four days, I fly to London for the opening of my *Benito Cereno*.[4] I wish you could see it done; it moves very slowly, and at least on the stage, surely. One reviewer said it was unconventional in that it had nothing shocking, no sex, no perversion, just the explosion of a country, 170 years in the past.

I've been writing like a beaver for the last week revising and re-typing my *Prometheus*, pages and pages of words. It will either stun, and stupefy an audience, [or] it doesn't work. It's a sort of Shelley, or generic European declamatory romantic poem—alive maybe, if anything can breathe under the formidable armor of its rhetoric and stance.

I hear rumors that you may come here. I'll welcome you with open arms, joy, and whatever stability and wisdom my hereditary granite New England morality still retains.

---

1 *Near the Ocean* (1967).
2 Sidney Nolan.
3 John Berryman, "Opus Posthumous," nos. 1–2 and 7–13, *The Times Literary Supplement* (Dec. 1, 1966), and nos. 3–6, *The New York Review of Books* (Dec. 8, 1966).
4 *Benito Cereno*, dir. Jonathan Miller, opened at the Mermaid Theatre on March 12.

All my love. Do let me hear, do let me know how I can be of help.
Love again,
Cal

P.S. I carry your "Under the Window" in my billfold,[1] and even read it aloud to Dr. Baumann late in December before I went off to the hospital. Much to say. Your style never seems mannered, just marvelous, unguessable description, now as natural as your letters, but full of design and compression. Yes, you have man's journey, his seven ages, many wonderful flashes, like the second car's syphilitic nose, all the way thru, then the great rise, just where it is needed, with the *Morpho*.[2] It's like going on the pilgrimage of your Fish, or the poem ending awful and wonderful,[3] yet the journey is as utterly new and surprising as a first discovery of what life is all about. And so it is. If I can't stop what, I've already done, I must stop. Maybe, if I carry your "Window" around long enough, I'll learn. It's a kind of patience and freshness.

338.

March 3rd, 1967

Dearest Cal:

Well, now I know when your birthday is—I had never known before—Feb. 28th, *não é?*[4] A Pisces, like Lota. Many happy returns. I minded being 35 very much, I remember, but haven't been able to give a damn since—there are too many other things that one can do a *little* something about, possibly. I have owed you a letter for so long now & I can't remember when I wrote you last, although I do think I got off some postcards on our trip to Amsterdam, London, etc. . . . but some seem not to have arrived—the ones from Amsterdam, with its wonderful P.O. arranged like a lounge, *clean* ash-trays and so on . . . And now you are probably in London and I hope the play is a great success. I'll be reading all about it in my English reviews, a month from now, no doubt . . .

I've heard several times from dear Anny—and she did tell me you had been sick again, but were rapidly getting better. I am touched by the "reading" of my poem . . . my only poem in a year or more. Well, it is nice of you

---

1 "Under the Window: Ouro Prêto (for Lilli Correia de Araújo)," *The New Yorker* (Dec. 24, 1966); EB-*CP*.
2 See "Under the Window: Ouro Prêto," lines 38–40 and 46–52 (EB-*CP*).
3 "All the untidy activity continues / awful but cheerful"; "The Bight," lines 35–36 (EB-*CP*).
4 Isn't it? (RL's birthday was actually March 1.)

to like it; it certainly couldn't be much simpler. I hung out that window by the hour (it was written a year ago last October—damn *The New Yorker*! but it is one way of making some money)—because the OLD house I've gone and bought is diagonally across the street from Lilli's own house. You didn't meet her, she was in Europe—but she actually lives in a huge ark of an old place—about 100 years later than my house, across the street—and across a water-fall, too, that runs under the windows. I have a magnificent view— including 6 or 8 churches.— Putting on a small but authentic balcony at the back, to breakfast on or have after-dinner coffee on. THE HOUSE is 1720–40—re-made many times of course—but L and I have always wanted an *old* house to play with, and she is planning a heavenly walled garden, with fountain, etc. for it. We'll probably only spend a month or two at a time there—but I hope you'll see it one of these days.

I saw very few people in London because L began to get sicker & sicker—we had thought she was improving and that a "change"—i.e., getting away from the horrible political situation here, that threatens all her last 6 years' work—would do her good. Katy Carver[1] is now at Chatto & Windus—they are bringing out a *big* book of mine next fall—and Day-Lewis was very nice, this trip. Saw Spender, of course, and Irene Worth, and went for a day to All Souls where Joe Summers is a Fellow this year. If you go there—but you probably know this better than I do—there's a really nice pub, on the Thames, in full flood then—"The Trout." He was giving a lecture at York—Edinburgh, etc. It consisted mostly of you, I think, with a few other U.S. poets, and some of me, too. He has improved a lot—nervous but less nervous. I've always loved his wife. But we had to cut our stay short by 2 or 3 weeks. Lota was getting worse, and I was dying to get her home again—and she wanted to come, too—unlike her usual traveling self. She *hated* London—I'm not sure I'll ever be able to get her back again. Too bad, because I think it was mostly her health that made her so critical—she even convinced me that Trafalgar Square is ugly and all WRONG . . . & so was almost everything! She has had this breakdown coming on for a long time, the drs. assure me—she looked dreadful when I got back in July—but can't stop blaming me for going away in the first place, even if I thought I had to, to get out of the atmosphere here for a while—& this makes me feel guilty. She was in a clinic here for two stretches—then finally I gave out, too, and went to the same clinica (run by nuns from Barcelona) but she was ten times sicker than I was and is only gradually, gradually getting better—here now,

1 Catharine Carver.

then the 8th we're going to Samambaia for a good long stay, so if you write me *PLEASE* use the Petrópolis address . . . She IS much better, but we did have a bad stretch & I am only hoping she will give up that job entirely—it—oh well, that is all too complicated to go into and I'm sure would be the same working for a government or a city-government anywhere in the world . . . One of the bigger items is that Carlos has betrayed everyone horribly—after all the years of fighting the old Vargas gang and corruption, he has suddenly, for political reasons, gone over to them (and the communists) again. I hadn't been able to endure him for several years, at least . . . He keeps writing L love-letters, really, trying to make up with her again—but since he really left her "park" defenseless, and now it may very well just go to pieces—she is still very bitter and I don't think will ever change. To hell with all politicians, anyway.

Your book is certainly a fine piece of book-making—that's aside from the poems! Bob, I believe, had sent me a copy, and then yesterday I got your copy. Now I shall either make someone a magnificent present, or—more likely—have copies in two of our three residences . . . (We are vaguely discussing selling the Rio apt.—Copacabana is getting like all cities these days—and it costs a lot to keep Joana here now—but I don't know. We do have to come here every so often, even if L isn't working—also, she has to do *something*, to keep her brains occupied—but it is a very difficult problem—*what,*—right now . . .)

I have seen very few Sidney Nolan paintings—some at the Tate, and reproductions—and I just can't make up my mind about him. Some of the Roman ones, the shields, the bestiality, seem to go awfully well—but some I honestly can't say I like too much. I'm going to keep looking at them, however, and maybe he'll dawn on me . . . (There's a painter friend I made in Seattle, named Wesley Wehr—he will soon be having a show at the Willard Gallery in NY—I hope you'll see them. They are *very* small scale and delicate (he was 1st a composer, much taken up with Webern, etc.)—and you may not be impressed, but I like them . . .)

I see you have made many small changes but I haven't had time yet to compare things. (I was in the *clinica* almost a month—everything got away behind because they wouldn't let me type—I did read Catullus and Horace again, however. Also a rather bad new Propertius someone brought me (your one infinitely better, still).[1] I had a most spectacular attack of asthma in years—this was a good idea, it got me so much attention—besides general

1 See letter 127.

exhaustion and worry about L and so on . . . I am feeling better now than for years, and have actually done a LOT, for me, of work . . .) To go back to what I was saying: I like the "4th of July" one more and more, with all its divagations (?) and wish I had had it to show my classes—who all seemed to think that "directness" was all . . . The word "stupor" is wonderful; so are the guinea pigs . . .[1] (We had some that got eaten up by a wandering and ferocious Boxer.) I am also still quite mad about that glass of water in the first poem . . .[2] "Central Park" seems to me greatly improved from the version I remember—now please don't tell me it's just the same! (I have been so purged and purified by my hospital stay that I find I am really thinking and appreciating better—in fact I could even enjoy life again, any minute now.) That is—I still haven't read what's wrong with the USA in the *PR*—[(]afraid to break this hopeful mood.) The Horace ones seem very fine to me.[3] I am never sure I understand Latin poetry—or how it struck *them*, that is—it would surely all seem highly artificial to us, now—more so than Marianne—and I know I don't get the "effects" right, even if I was a fair Latin scholar once. But the atmosphere of your poems is *surely* right. When I get up to the country where my Loeb books are, I'll re-read the Juvenal properly. It is really all too [a] like for comfort, isn't it . . . I'll mention a book I'm sure you've read, but anyway, if you haven't—DAILY LIFE IN ANCIENT ROME . . .[4] (Carcopino) And I have had something going now on Pompeii and Herculaneum for years & years . . . Well, it is a most impressive book and can only add to your reputation a lot.

I MUST try to renew my *NY Review of Books*—it seems almost hopeless here, I don't know why—I have rarely lost a review, but almost always lost that, and other people had the same trouble. No—I'm not coming to NY now. I wonder how that idea started! I want to stay and work on the Brazil book for a year and a half more, at least—have bits done, and about three and a half whole chapters. It will be a scrapbook—may even call it that: "BRAZIL—BRASIL, A Scrapbook"—and I'm getting some wonderful photographs, I think. I've even been saving some of the LIFE pieces— mostly for the pictures. Now if only a publisher will do it properly . . . well, Knopf has offered, if Bob G. fails me.

It is fearfully HOT here & we have water-rationing and light-rationing—sit with candles and a hot oil lamp from 8 to 10 each night. City

---

1 See "Near the Ocean: Fourth of July in Maine," lines 89–104 (RL-*CP*).
2 "Waking Early Sunday Morning," lines 33–36 (RL-*CP*).
3 "The Vanity of Human Wishes" (RL-*CP*).
4 Jérôme Carcopino, *Daily Life in Ancient Rome*, ed. Henry T. Rowell, trans. E. O. Lorimer (1944).

life is getting worse & worse—we really can't take it. Do *please* don't over-do in London. I am very interested in your new Dr. & medicines—I'm always sure these things have some sort of physical basis—

With regards to your family—lots of love—and thank you for the book(s)—

Elizabeth

339.

March 23, 1967

Dearest Elizabeth:

If you could look out your window and up the coast a stretch you might almost see Lizzie and Harriet on the sands of Barbados. Letter from Harriet, "Dear Robert Lowell. It is very very hot here . . . I am dying of the heat." And in between, "There is an air-conditioner in our room which is naturally pretty constantly in use." Oh lovely English language.

What a weight off my soul that things have lightened and you and Lota are both on your feet and together! And so full of shrewd, charming never-ending observation. Your old self, enriched, coming out of the tunnel. I should have known that nothing could really suppress you, but it's awfully worrying. We all seem so frail really, under the full frail morning spider webs we spread in the sun—dull methodical articles come out on me now, and list my rather sparse stock on imagery, among them spider webs. Now I must tread cautiously.

Like what you say about Latin. It's so clipped, small in words, etc., and sparing of words, that it sometimes seems like an equivalent to language rather than language as we know it. So, if it can be translated at all, it seems a kind of miracle. Nolan has a lot of on the whole much more ambitious drawing and color pictures for my *Imitations*. Faber is going to bring out a really lovely edition of the Baudelaires, about twice as big as *Near the Ocean*, and very grand.[1]

Giroux and everyone at Farrar are terrifically excited about bringing out your collected poems. Then you'll take your grand and rightful place. Don't you think you should put in a few more stories, at least "The Prison,"[2] which everyone inquires about and can't find? A little after you, a couple of years, I'm going to bring out my collected. Rather a problem: the books somehow

---

1 RL, *The Voyage: and Other Versions of Poems by Baudelaire*, illus. by Sidney Nolan (1968).
2 "In Prison" (EB-*CPR*).

seem units, hard to cut, yet full of dross. I'm afraid the time is passed when I can do anything to the point by revision. It's not chipping off this and that, but a need for a new breath, some fountain of youth they could be boiled in, to emerge young and less blemished.

London was lovely, tho the play didn't suit most of the critics. I saw Kenneth Clark's castle in Kent, Leonard Woolf in Surrey (including a christening mug given to Virginia by James Russell Lowell), then a day at Oxford with Irene Worth, then a day with Mary back from Vietnam. Now I seem to have a huge appetite for wasting time, desultory reading, fumbling day-dreams. To be in bed early with a lot of light stuff to read seems heaven. Can this be age— Ah no.

All my love to you and Lota,
Cal

(I'm sure Farrar and Straus want to do your Brazil book. Wonderful you are back in your full tide!)

340.

(Caixa Postal 279, Petrópolis, Est. do Rio de J—better now)
April 23rd, 1967

Dearest Cal:

Your last letter is up in Petrópolis, where we mostly are these days— Lota comes down every Monday for the doctor and comes back Tuesday or Wednesday—sometimes I come along. I hate this coming & going but Samambaia is just too lonely for very long—after 6 or so; I don't mind the days but the evenings. L is better, quite a bit, but still not herself & the problem is something for her to DO. She's on "leave of absence" but still very much involved with the park, the governor[1] (NOT Carlos) etc. Carlos seems to have betrayed every single principle he ever stood for and has made friends with all those he attacked and exposed as dishonest for years & years—big pictures of him shaking hands with Kubitschek, etc.—the whole thing has been very disillusioning, if anyone ever had illusions about a politician. He keeps writing L almost love-letters, asking to see her, be friends again, how much he needs her and so on, but so far she has not replied. Pretty disgusting I think . . . We stayed on this week to go to the ballet—Fontayne and Nureyev here—went last night and once more.

1 Francisco Negrão de Lima.

Fontayne has a Brazilian grandfather—she even looks Brazilian, through my opera glasses. But somehow that Opera house here and the poor corps de ballet manage to de-glamourize anything. A rainy Saturday afternoon with nothing to do we went to the local cinema to see O GRUPO[1]—my it is dreadful; one of the worst films I've ever seen. Surely Mary had nothing at all to do with it . . . Perhaps even seemed worse than it was because the day before we'd seen *La Vieille Dame Indigne*[2]—and that is a lovely picture, in case you haven't seen it—very subtle, for the movies. I seem to be giving you my cultural and social life—well, now I am going to the dentist and then, save us, to lunch with Alfred Knopf who got married here a week ago—he being 74 and the bride 64. He is a great bore, and I am not looking forward to this very much . . . I don't think he ever reads a book he publishes. Writes me *constantly* for helpful hints and then never takes any of them . . . just sends me lots of boring books about church & state in Latin America, etc.

Carlos has started (with his ex-enemies, most of whom are officially exiled or at least can't hold office for ten years) something called the "Ample Front"! I haven't seen him for over two years. It seems he took offense at an innocent little piece I wrote for the N.Y. *Times* which was abominably cut and distorted, but dared to say Rio was in pretty poor shape and *didn't* include a eulogy of him . . .

I have started working again at last but am not too pleased with the result so far. IF I can keep going I should have a book of poems ready, besides the Brazilian book, in about 18 months. I may include a few translations of Brazilian poetry—the best ones—but don't know. The Brazilian book rather bores me, I'm afraid, but fortunately I have a lot of material I wrote when I was feeling a little livelier and more interested—this boredom is probably mostly due to L's state of acute depression; I feel if she could cheer up, I'd cheer up, too. Well—she is some better, that's all I can say. The TIME man here has been hounding me about an "essay" they're doing on *poetry*. Finally I saw him. It is a great waste of time. He says "Gide" with a hard G. I am being very bitchy, but honest to God . . . (hard G) And I don't know how G got into the conversation, anyway—oh he was quoting him to impress me, I think. I said I thought Berryman was somewhat neglected—maybe that will get in. I have been struggling with those sonnets—many beautiful lines but I do find him difficult. What does it mean when people (Swift, say) resort to

1 *The Group*, dir. Sidney Lumet (1966).
2 *La Vieille dame indigne*, dir. René Allio (1965).

baby-talk, or tough-guy talk, like Pound—something very seriously wrong, no doubt. And I wish you'd tell me what *you* think about James Dickey! I see reams of him, getting more Whitman-like all the time, and I don't know what he means by those little spaces—commas, maybe.— I have re-read *Near the Ocean*—I still like the first poem best, but "Serving Under Brutus" and "The Vanity of Human Wishes" impress me more and more. (I don't like a "cardboard crown"—my only criticism!—too anachronistic for me.[1]) I told the poor, subjugated, rather elderly TIME man that the clue to poetry at present was in your NOTE,[2] and he duly noted it down. HOWEVER (this is what I notice when I try to do anything myself) I feel we must beware of the easiness of the catastrophe!—the catastrophic way out of every poem—but how can one help but be gloomy and take a gloomy outlook?

I found your letter after all and see you say somewhat the same thing. I met Irene Worth in London, then she came here with *Gielgud* to give some Shakespeare *readings*, oh dear,—I was in Minas at the time so didn't return for them although I would have liked to have seen her again—she wrote a very "poetic" letter to me which I must answer. But she's a fine actress—at least she made "The Cocktail Party" for me years ago.

Our ambassador here presented 4,000 books to the Library in Brasília—the University—and there were student demonstrations, apparently ending with the special police chasing the students and some innocent army officers in mufti, too, through the library and hitting them over the head, etc. The ambassador's speech was interrupted. The government here is silly—why not let them demonstrate—we're silly, too. The students are *so* silly that in São Paulo they had a demonstration because their classes are overcrowded (why they should be anti-US because of that I can't figure out) and here in Rio because they wouldn't let in the extra students—just the opposite, and the US apparently to blame for both . . . This new President, sinister as his "image" was when I was in the US, is actually probably a bit more liberal than the last one, but doesn't sound very promising even so.[3] Lota has had several interviews with the new governor (who beat Carlos so badly) and he is *hopeless*—told Lota that this part of town was fine (it is falling apart) and there wasn't any use *trying* to do anything about the "north zone"—where the millions of poor live. Imagine saying it, even.

1 "The Vanity of Human Wishes," line 41 (RL-*CP*).
2 "The theme that connects my translations is Rome, the greatness and horror of her Empire. My Juvenal and Dante versions are as faithful as I am able or dare or can bear to be. The Horace is freer, the Spanish sonnets freer still. How one jumps from Rome to the America of my own poems is something of a mystery to me"; RL-*CP*, 381.
3 Artur da Costa e Silva.

Also all these landslides, with hundreds dead[1]—"It isn't my fault if the land decides to move while I am governor"—and so on—quite incredible. An old Vargas man.

As usual, I hate both sides, and wish I could forget all about them but one can't really when one has no electricity and water some of the time—climbs 11 floors carrying a candle, etc. Carlos's famous water supply (that I went all over with Dr. Baumann one strenuous day) broke down at once . . . But enough of corruption and "massive lethargy" as someone called it. Who am I to talk when I feel like a piece of massive lethargy myself.

Now for a shower, if there is water, and a new gold inlay—and AL-FRED—I have never heard him make one interesting remark except that he called Mann "Tommy!"

This is a very mean letter, and I feel very mean too. Please don't say anything about L's health when you write—she sometimes asks me to read your letters to her. She thinks you are my only "lovable" friend . . . So with lots and lots of love, and do please take care of yourself—how is the new doctor and the new pill—or are you fed up with all that by now? I may send you some poems after a while if you will really give me some criticism—I can't seem to decide quickly by myself these days.

Regards to the wife and daughter if they are with you again—
    Elizabeth

Arthur Gold has just sent me a very funny (unintentionally) book called *The Sunny Side of Diplomatic Life*[2]—I enjoyed the 1st volume of this lady's memoirs so much. Diplomatic service in the 80's and 90's—in Denmark the population stops whatever they're doing to get out and bow to the Royal carriage even if it's empty. The people only appear in these books to *clap* occasionally—constant fear of assassination—and it is all so innocent it's incredible. Clothes by Worth of course—in good detail—

---

1 In the Bairro Jardim-Laranjeiras district of Rio, 110 people were killed on February 18, 1967; many more were killed in landslides in São Paulo and Caraguatatuba in March.
2 L. de Hegermann-Lindencrone, *The Sunny Side of Diplomatic Life* (1914).

341.

[Postcard: Pelourinho Hill, Bahia, Brazil]

Bahia, June 8th, 1967

Dearest Cal:

Life, no in this case I shd. say *Time*, certainly has surprises in store for us all . . . I got here late 2 nights ago after an endless trip on the boat on the other card[1]; went out to find something to read, and found apparently the one & only copy of TIME—with you on the cover[2]—in the city. Why didn't that silly TIME man in Rio TELL me the piece was to be about you? I'd have said much more about you certainly—and he—or they—didn't even repeat what I did say—because I talked about you, mostly! I am very proud of the picture on the beach (or did they just put that one in the Latin American edition?)—you & me among the kites. I hope the article pleases you and hasn't too many of the mistakes they are given to. I wish to goodness I'd been at PROMETHEUS, too. You do look a bit disconsolate at the party—but on the other hand, what an adorable little boy you were . . .

Harriet is looking very handsome.

I went down the Rio São Francisco—it seemed endless & not nearly as interesting or as beautiful as the Amazon—but in retrospect I am glad I did it, and I have already written a *chapter*, I think.

I like N's paintings better than the drawings— With much love always, and congratulations and everything—

Elizabeth

342.

[Postcard of Steamboat]

[n.d. 1967]

(This card was dirty when I bought it . . .)

In the huge garden of my OLD house there is a big laurel tree. Someday I hope you will visit me there again in Ouro Prêto—and I'll make you a *real* laurel wreath to wear[3]— E.

1 See letter 342, enclosed with 341. EB was in Bahia for a trip down the river São Francisco to research her newly projected prose book on Brazil.
2 RL was the subject of a *Time* magazine cover story (June 2, 1967)
3 RL wears a laurel wreath in the drawing on the cover of *Time* (June 2, 1967).

343.

Dearest Elizabeth:

I guess you've seen the *Time* thing. I was almost out of my mind with dread and indignation. They had collected about 1000 pages, questioning people I hardly knew, and asking impertinent personal questions. I feared the notoriety and the heavy wounding hand. Well, it was harmless and even rather delicate and tactful for them. I liked your responses,[1] but not the description of your genius (theirs, not yours) at the end.[2] It seems to me you are full of passionate feeling, as well as a serenity, a fullness, not a coolness. By the way, the optimistic James Dickey is one of the most desperate souls I know of, dreaded by the faculties where he has read.[3] Rather good poet though, particularly on horrible things like fire-bombing.[4] I really have a much less agonized German existentialist life than they indicate. More frivolous, I'm afraid, too.

Loved your sour letter. I've been seeing quite a lot of Irene, who surely made my play at Yale. She's a bit resonant and over-interested in culture. Quite gallant, one [of] the best actresses, living from hand to mouth, or at least job to job. The whole production was lovely, a wonderful Prometheus, Kenneth Haigh, and Miller's marvelous direction.[5] After two weeks, we were in consternation. Two hours of undramatic heroic Greek speeches—a very long two hours. Somehow it worked out for those of us who liked it. What a spring of plays, traveling, readings, and *Time*!

Did the late war scare you to death?[6] It did me while it was simmering. We had a great wave of New York Jewish nationalism, all the doves turning into hawks. Well, my heart is in Israel, but it was a little like a blitzkrieg against the Comanches—armed by Russia. Nasser is like a Mussolini ruling some poverty stricken part of India. I never saw a country I would less like to stay in, yet the Egyptians were mostly subtle and sad and attractive.

1 "Lowell's friend, poet Elizabeth Bishop, says that confessional poetry 'is really something new in the world. There have been diaries that were frank—and generally intended to be read after the poet's death. Now the idea is that we live in a horrible and terrifying world, and the worst moments of horrible and terrifying lives are an allegory of the world.' Speaking of some of Lowell's confessional imitators, she adds: 'The tendency is to overdo the morbidity. You just wish they'd kept some of these things to themselves' "; "The Second Chance," *Time* (June 2, 1967), 68.
2 "Elizabeth Bishop, 56, one of America's leading women poets, is the epitome of the cool, detached, low-key observer"; "The Second Chance," *Time* (June 2, 1967), 74.
3 "James Dickey, 44, is Lowell's polar opposite—facile, exuberant, bearing joy and affirmation"; "The Second Chance," *Time* (June 2, 1967), 74.
4 James Dickey, "The Fire Bombing," *Buckdancer's Choice* (1965).
5 *Prometheus Bound*, dir. Jonathan Miller, opened at the Yale Repertory Theatre on May 10.
6 The Six-Day War started on June 5, 1967, when Israel attacked Egypt, Syria, and Jordan.

Every so often, I have a vague acute feeling of missing something or someone, and it's you—long talks on some rock, or sandy knoll, or Copacabana Beach. Letters are no substitute. You [must] come back for a long visit.

No news. I'm drained of anything to write. Not a poem for a year and a half. I wish I had a suitcase of unfinished possibilities (I've just [looked] at Eliot's juvenilia.) Some the best lines in the Waste Land come from an early quite hopeless lyric on Saint some one.[1]

I've been seeing Dr. Baumann, slightly high blood-pressure, which turns out to be nothing, but I was depressed because my mother and father had this kind of trouble. But it's nothing. By the way, don't doctors love to explain how [you] have asked the wrong question. If you say, "Aren't fingernails part of the hand?" They explain that there's no such thing as the hand that anything could be part. Both Anny and my "shrink" do this. I have a probably irritating seminar teacher's habit of doing just the opposite i.e. making sense out of non-sense.

Goodbye, my dear old love, and love to Lota. Tomorrow we set out for Castine with four angora guinea pigs.

Cal

344.

[61 Perry Street, New York, N.Y.]
I'd call up but I'm not very good at telephones, you know—
July 10th, 1967
Dearest Cal:

I think but I'm not sure that I sent you a note or some cards from Bahia, when I finally reached there after an endless river trip—on the S. Francisco, on a 70 year old stern-wheeler—about 3 weeks ago. I have your letter of June 14th with me—oh, I do remember now—the night I reached Bahia I saw you on the bookstand—bought it—went out to buy another copy, and found the only other one for sale already sold. . . But I believe I commented on that—how if the TIME man had only TOLD me it was about YOU I would certainly have tried to say something BETTER. But he probably didn't know himself . . .

Well—now I'm here. Rather reluctantly, I had meant to come later—but I can stay in the MacIver-Frankenberg studio free—they're in Paris for 2

---

1 Cf. T. S. Eliot, "The Death of Saint Narcissus," lines 1–5, *Poems Written in Early Youth* (1967), with *The Waste Land*, Section I, lines 25–29.

years. It was off-season, and I do have a lot of business to attend to, suddenly, so just up and came. I don't really know for how long. The plan is that as soon as Lota is well enough she will join me for a few weeks, and we'll go back together, in September, probably—but life has been very uncertain and very difficult this past year. She is better every day, however—even hoped to start a new job last week, but I haven't had time to get a letter yet.

Almost everyone I know except two old friends across the street[1] is either in Connecticut or on Long Island (or in Maine, meaning you), so it is a good time to work, and I am used to heat. I had a long long talk with Dr. Anny Saturday. She tells me she thinks you have to come to NY—or nearby—for a few days sometime fairly soon. I hope this is true and that I can see you. I went out this afternoon and again spotted you looking very unhappy, this time on the *NY Review of Books*. So now I have *Prometheus* in supplementary form and am planning to read it in bed tonight.[2] Well—it is better to look a bit unhappy than like a laughing warrior like Mr. Dickey . . . Oh I am sorry I couldn't see the play—never really dreamed I'd be coming here so soon. I also see you've signed a petition about the Frenchman in Bolivia . . .[3] Somehow I must get hold of Mary's later Vietnam pieces—I saw only the first one.[4] (And thought it very good as far as she'd got.)

Well—the Village will rejuvenate me, no doubt. I never appear without earrings down to my bosom, skirts almost up to it, and a guitar over my shoulder. I am afraid I am going to start writing FREE VERSE next . . . Marianne is also on Long Island I think—but I'm going to leave a note for her tonight—didn't want to startle her on the telephone. (Or maybe I over-rate my ability to startle.) I am glad I am going to see her again, at least. It seems Dr. Anny talks to her almost every day—and of course has been kind-ness itself to me—called at 8 this morning just to make sure I got off to a good Monday morning's start, I think. Oh if only life seemed as simple to me as it seems to her—or she makes it seem when I'm with her, and for a few hours afterwards. But if I do exactly what she tells me to—she is usually right. Lota has a very fine "shrink"[5]—as all my students said, and you did

1 Harold Leeds and Wheaton Galentine.
2 RL, drawn by David Levine, on the cover of *The New York Review of Books* issue featuring "*Prometheus Bound* derived from Aeschylus" (July 13, 1967).
3 Régis Debray and British photographer George Andrew Roth were arrested by the Bolivian government on sus-picion of being guerrilla sympathizers; "Régis Debray," *The New York Review of Books* (July 13, 1967).
4 Mary McCarthy, "Report from Vietnam I: The Home Program," *The New York Review of Books* (April 20, 1967), "Report from Vietnam II: The Problems of Success," *The New York Review of Books* (May 4, 1967), and "Report from Vietnam III: Intellectuals," *The New York Review of Books* (May 18, 1967).
5 Dr. Decio de Sousa.

too! I haven't been being treated, exactly, but I did go to see him once a week more or less—and thank God Lota has him and our devoted maid—I wouldn't have left otherwise. (He reads you—the "shrink"—God, too, no doubt, does.)

It is nice to be on the same continent with you again and I am sure I'll see you somehow. I've written pages and pages of the prose book—one 60 page section I'm copying now.— I can't tell, and can't finish it until I go back—but I *think* it is amusing and maybe even enlightening here & there and hair-raising there and here—I'd like to ask your opinion about some bits.

How many guinea pigs do you have now? Oh well—TIME—they have me labeled as cold and chiseled or something—but at least it is a change from being an imitation Marianne—I'm sure she's relieved, too. For them, I didn't think it was too awful—and Giroux wrote me the same thing.

A bientôt—I hope—até logo—I know almost as many languages as Whitman, you see. Also *abraços*—and take care of yourself and do let me hear from you and I hope you've finished a wonderful new poem—
    Elizabeth

345.

61 Perry Street
NYC
Thurs., July 27, 1967

Dearest Cal:

Perhaps if I send one of these forms it will go as far as Bangor by plane . . .

Just as I came in now Bob G called inviting me to lunch next week to meet R Straus (whom I've met, but no one, including me, remembers the meeting at all) and the famous Miss Sontag . . . This is almost too much for one day, particularly as I have to be bright and energetic for dinner with Anny that same night. I thought in the SUMMER in N.Y. one could avoid this kind of thing, but apparently not. I do think that was marvellous— Marianne demanding a "house call" and almost unable to speak at 12 noon, yesterday, and then refusing all help and going to a baseball game. I don't think I can bear to tell on her . . . I always thought she'd die one day on the Brooklyn Express; now I think she'll die in the bleachers.

This is just to thank you for all your hospitality—heavens, if I use this

I can't enclose the check for $20.00—well, it will come under separate cover.[1] I had it with me but it seemed a bit crass to produce a check in front of the philosopher, etc. Anyway, thank you—I had had no time to go to the bank; forgot identifications, and just had to get a few things for the weekend, etc.

I didn't have time to tell you properly how much I like the saint. I studied him till all hours last night—and I've decided he was probably one of a Crucifixion group—because of the wretched expression, the upward-tilted head, etc.—even the fingers. What saints were present then?—I'm not sure—but I would bet almost anything I am right. As I said—the little piece of black wood has been nailed on very crudely (new nails right through these nice feet). I'm going to take it to a good restorer I know in Rio and have the nails taken out, and have him cemented to a larger block of jacaranda (Brazilian rosewood)—or maybe just the bottom of a glass dome—one can get them all shapes and sizes there—same kind of wood. I can clean him myself—I'm getting good at it—with a small brush—then wax him. He does have glass eyes, too—they were a bit dull, but I'll restore the glitter— He's a beauty.

Lota writes that she bought the saint she'd had her eye on—I think the one with a PIG—"the most beautiful in the world" and fearfully expensive . . . She always loses her head like that when I go away—but sounds pretty cheerful—except that she probably has to go to Brasília and speak to the Supreme Court in person, and naturally that is a fearful thought.[2]

(And here I am with my hair all done up perfectly—that I'd intended to do for lunch today until Anny B disrupted my plans . . .)

Your tales of Castine are fascinating and tempting. I'll see how much work I can get done in the next few weeks—and tell me exactly how long you'll be there. Please give my best regards to everyone I know. The next letter will be in Provençal, probably—[3]

Love and abraços,
Elizabeth

1 EB typed her letter on an aerogramme form, "no enclosures permitted."
2 Lota attempted to retain control of the Flamengo Park foundation through a legal appeal.
3 RL told EB about his French reading group in Castine, which Mary McCarthy had joined. "Once a week, we have our old French readings with our friend, who teaches French at Exeter. But we've been rather frighteningly improved by Mary, who always does her homework . . . We have arguments as to whether *grands maistres* in Villon means masters of the monastic orders, or just the great"; RL to Adrienne Rich (August 1967), RL-*Letters*, 489–90.

P.S. I keep thinking about the horses in New York—running through that poem—and the beautiful ending to the third shorter one, about the houses[1]— Felicitations.

346.

61 Perry Street
August 19th, 1967

Dearest Cal:

If my farewells to you yesterday sounded a bit hasty it was because Margaret Miller was coming up the staircase—I hadn't known she was coming; her telephone was out of order—and I hadn't see her for—heavens—maybe ten years, I'm not sure—so I rather lost my head for a minute there . . . Anyway, she stayed and talked until 1:30 AM and we had a very nice time and I hope now I can keep in touch with her during this stay. I was telling you how F, S, & G (and I gathered you didn't know about it) want to bring out THE OLD GLORY in Brazil—have a publisher called LIDADOR (I don't know this one, but it was recommended by the Embassy). I thought I told you this when I saw you, but apparently I forgot. So when I first got here they called me about it and I said yes, very nice, but WHO is doing the translating? (They 1st asked me if I'd "go over it," when done—and of course I said I would, but my Portuguese is not that good—not for idioms enough, or turns of phrase, etc.) They had no idea who was doing it. When I pointed out to them that they'd never dream of doing this in reverse—just let any stranger translate Camus, say, into English—they saw the enormity of their behaviour, and said they'd hold up the whole thing until they heard from me again. (I also gave them a few fearful examples of what does happen to American novels, etc., when they come out in Brazil . . .) I talked to one Brazilian here I know & we both thought of either the poet Paulo Mendes Campos, or—better, I think, probably—the journalist, Rachel de Queiroz. She has written plays herself and done a lot of translating—also she is a good friend of mine and I could help her and she wouldn't mind suggestions from me (as the other might). Also, again—I am planning to visit her on her fazenda in the north—maybe on my way back—and we might work on it then. (She is the cousin of the poor little ex-president—he was visiting her when he was killed in that recent plane crash.[2]) I have an awful feeling now that I may

---

1 "Near the Ocean"; section three is "The Opposite House" (RL-*CP*).
2 Humberto de Alencar Castelo Branco died on July 18, 1967.

have told you all this before—if so forgive me. I have written her one note about it—she may not have got it, or still be too upset to answer—anyway, I'll write again this week-end . . . Lota says that in spite of corny sentiments, sometimes, she does write a beautiful classical Portuguese—so I think is the best choice, probably.

Here is the $20 I owe you & I'm sorry I went off to Maryland and forgot all about it until I got back. The poem I wrote there requires an afternoon's work in the Public Library, alas—then I'll send it—I'm not at all sure about it—just can't tell at all.[1] Lota likes it, but she is apt to like almost all of them!

Oh—I showed Margaret the saint or apostle last night, and she knew exactly where he came from, if not his name. Seems that someone imported a whole *crèche* last Christmas to sell in New York (200 figures or so)—and she is sure he was one of the figures. In spite of the silk clothes—he might be a shepherd, since his sandals do seem to be of goat-skin, or imitation goat-skin. I was glad to learn this since one caller had insisted he was Judas.

Giroux has almost swamped me with Miss Sontag's works and I am trying hard—but I don't think I'll go to the party.[2] I am still having dizzy spells from that idiotic concussion[3]—particularly when I drive—and I'm afraid I wouldn't know a soul, anyway. She certainly seems to know ten times more than I've ever forgotten—but I don't think writes very gracefully—nor with Mary's wit—and of course all the philosophy is away beyond me. However—I do admire the way she will tackle anything at all, apparently— (except poetry, I see—) Beatles, films, painting, plays. But sometimes I think that she could say a lot less and it would count for more . . .

It is HOT again—it was only 68 when I came back from Maryland—and I'd love to get away but simply can't. I am AWAY behind—about a year— with this book[4] now and really have to apply myself hard for several weeks—also go to the library about that, acquire some new dictionaries, and oh—endless details that I must get organized before Lota comes. At present her doctor says December—but we hope it will turn out to be earlier after all.

Found a lovely word at Jane Dewey's—you probably know it— ALLELOMIMETIC. (Don't DARE use it!) Margaret Miller tells me she admires your prose tremendously—and this makes me realize I did miss some

1 See "In the Waiting Room," lines 13–53 (EB-*EAP*).
2 Publication party for Susan Sontag's *Death Kit* (1967).
3 EB "had fallen at the home of Lota's doctor in Rio and the 'bump on the head and nosebleed' were much more serious than she had suspected"; Brett C. Millier, *Elizabeth Bishop: Life and the Memory of It* (1993), 393.
4 The Brazil travel essays.

reviews—however, the *NY Review* seems to be coming, at last. I got Mary's nos. II & III, too. I don't know about her conclusions, etc.—but I do admire the way she caught that awful US-abroad-language and manner—I am familiar with that from occasional run-ins with it in Brazil, of course, and ye gods it is sickening and disheartening . . .[1]

All for now and I hope to see you very soon. Please send me some poems—I am really dying to read some good ones!

With much love, as always—

Elizabeth

347.

August 30th, 1967

Dearest Cal:

You are such a bright boy—perhaps you can tell me what's the matter with this poem . . . I really mean it, and say what you think—I'll scrap it, if necessary. I like the idea—but know there's something very wrong and can't seem to tell what it is . . . I have a couple of others, but I seem to be able to judge them myself; this one I just can't. Maybe it should be cut—maybe it should rhyme—maybe it's all the fault of the damned METER. (It is one of those I dream—woke up one morning at Jane's with almost the whole thing done.) It was funny—queer—I actually went to the Library & got out that no. of the *NG*—and that title, "The Valley of 10,000 Smokes"—was *right*, and has been haunting me all my life, apparently . . .[2]

Bill Alfred has been here for a stay with his father in Brooklyn and I've had two nice evenings with him. We went to see ULYSSES[3]—it has good parts, especially at first—but I didn't feel it was worth $5.50 . . . We have talked of you a lot, of course,—and I find him awfully sympathetic.

I'm seeing Walter Allen tomorrow—have never met him . . .

Mostly I just sit here and type and try to keep *clean*—then read some Portuguese in the Library—kind of awful these days—but I MUST get this

1 McCarthy writes that American political scientists "have stamped their vocabulary and their habits of thought on this loony trial of strength in the Asian arena . . . The CIA alumni and alumnae you still find in Vietnamese government nooks—nearly every Vietnamese who speaks English seems to have attended Michigan State and to be proud of it—have a certain démodé pathos . . . Professor Fishel's lasting contribution was not Nhu's MSU-trained Secret Police, now presumably disbanded, but the introduction of the word 'semantics' into official discourse about Vietnam"; Mary McCarthy, "Report from Vietnam III: Intellectuals," *The New York Review of Books* (May 18, 1967).

2 Robert F. Griggs, "The Valley of the Ten Thousand Smokes," *National Geographic* (Feb. 1918); see "In the Waiting Room" (EB-*CP*). See also E. Torday, "Curious and Characteristic Customs of Central African Tribes," *National Geographic* (Oct. 1919).

3 *Ulysses*, dir. Joseph Strick (1967).

"book" done, or all I can of it here. I hope you are having a profitable time working and reading French (?)— Please give my regards to everyone, and I wish I could get to Maine but just don't think I can . . . With lots of love, as always,

Elizabeth

P.S. I had almost decided to re-dress the saint as a shepherd—then I noticed a hole down the back of his head. Well, that only could be for a *halo* (silver)—and I believe only the Holy Family wears halos . . . Saints and such wear ESPLENDORS—the fan-like variety. Do you suppose they would sell Joseph separately? For a *splendor*, the hole is in the top of the head . . . (I'll find him a halo in Rio—lots of spares around)

348.

[15 West 67th Street, New York, N.Y.[1]
n.d. Fall 1967]
FRIDAY MORNING

DEAREST LOWELLZINHOS:

I'LL START A SORT OF THANK*YOU LETTER TO YOU NOW WHILE WAITING FOR DR. B'S "ELSIE" TO COME PICK ME UP & GO FOR X*RAYS ETC. . . . EXCUSE THE CAPITALS * IT TAKES ME SO LONG TO TYPE CORRECTLY WITH ONE HAND.[2] EVERY-THING IS FINE AND NICOLE[3] HAS FED ME SPLENDIDLY & WE GET ALONG NICELY IN OUR DIFFERENT LANGUAGES . . . I SAW HARRIET TUESDAY & SHE WAS RATHER SHY ** WEDNESDAY WE HAD QUITE A LONG CONVERSATION, UNTIL 9:45, I THINK * WE DISCUSSED MOSTLY THE USES OF MATHEMATICS, ALGE-

1 Lota arrived in New York on September 19, in spite of advice from her physicians that she wait until December to rejoin EB. That night, in EB's apartment, Lota took an overdose of tranquilizers and went into a coma. She was admitted to St. Vincent's Hospital and never regained consciousness. Lota died on September 25. Her casket was returned to Rio, where she was met by an honor guard and received a public funeral. On Anny Baumann's advice, EB did not immediately return to Brazil. She was staying in RL's studio below the Lowells' family apartment.
2 "About a month or more ago, Elizabeth B. came over here, while I was still at Harvard, had a few vodkas, and had to be taken up stairs without clothes by Lizzie and Nicole. Next morning, when I came home, she was in the kitchen with a can of beer—all else had been hidden—during the night, she had made a foraging trip downstairs over the barricade of Harriet's bicycle—(back to my sentence) chattering in Portuguese to Nicole. I put her to bed with a sleeping pill (mild). Later, going to the bathroom, she slipped and broke her shoulder, quite badly. A worse injury maybe than anyone's in the marches and demonstrations. Then what a time of ambulances, waits in the hospital[,] calls to Dr. Baumann. Well, I think it cooled her down, so that finally she was in very good shape to go back to Brazil, and handled all the very vexing duties and encounters"; RL-*Letters*, 491–92.
3 The Lowells' maid.

BRA, & GEOMETRY IN ONE'S ELDERLY YEARS & I THINK I CON-
VINCED HER THEY OCCASIONALLY COME IN USEFUL . . .
NICOLE SAID TO INVITE A FRIEND IF I WANTED, SO LAST
NIGHT I DID INVITE MARGARET MILLER & N. GAVE US A SU-
PERB SOLE. I ASKED HER IF SHE COULD MAKE A SPANISH *FLAN*
(KNOWING MM LOVES IT) AND SHE JUST OUTDID HERSELF
WITH THAT & I FEEL I SHOULD PAY YOU FOR AN EXTRA
DOZEN EGGS, PROBABLY . . . THIS PLACE HAS BEEN A GOD-
SEND * SO MUCH MORE CHEERFUL THAN PERRY ST. * AND I'VE
HAD ELSIE THREE TIMES SO HAVEN'T HAD TO CALL ON
NICOLE AT ALL . . . EXCEPT TO WASH THE PAN I BOIL MILK
FOR BREAKFAST IN * *THAT* WAS BEYOND ME . . .

I HAVE MADE A FEW LOCAL TELEPHONE CALLS WHEN UP-
STAIRS FOR DINNER, & THREE OR FOUR FROM HERE ON THE
HOUSE TELEPHONE. I MADE A LIST UPSTAIRS * BUT ACTU-
ALLY ONLY TWO LONG DISTANCE CALLS * ONE TO DARLING-
TON OR HAVRE DE GRACE, MARYLAND, THAT MAY RUN TO 2 or
3 $$$ . . . AND I TRIED SEATTLE BUT GOT THE BABY-SITTER SO
THAT SHD REALLY BE ONLY ONE $, I THINK * (AFTER 8) (But let
me know!—they can't tell you any more, because of the COMPUTERS.[1])

I HAVE ALSO USED UP *ALL* ELIZABETH'S FIVE CENT STAMPS
* I THINK ABOUT A $ WORTH . . . I'M SORRY, BUT IT WAS SO
NICE HAVING A MAIL DROP FOR A CHANGE I JUST WROTE
ALL MY LETTERS . . . I CALLED KEEFE & KEEFE & FIND I OWE
YOU $105.00 FOR MY DELIGHTFUL AMBULANCE RIDES
THROUGH THE PARK . . . I HAVE A FEELING YOU PROBABLY
PAID THE NURSE THAT NIGHT, TOO * & HAVE NO IDEA HOW
MUCH *THAT* WAS * ANYWAY, I AM MAKING OUT A CHECK FOR
$125.00 & TRUST IT WILL MORE OR LESS COVER EVERYTHING.
NOW IF NURSES ARE $50.00 A NIGHT ** BE SURE TO LET ME
KNOW! OH * ELSIE . . .

Sunday Morning

WELL, X*RAYS FINE * DR CARTER SAID IT WAS AMAZING HOW
MUCH FASTER I IMPROVED "AT HOME" THAN IN THE HOSPI-
TAL . . . I SAID HE HAD ME WOUND UP SO TIGHT HE HAS

---

1 EB switches to pen for a marginal note.

GIVEN ME A 20'S FIGURE FOREVER . . . I SHALL LEAVE HERE
MON. AM ** WITH ELSIE'S HELP * & PACK AT PERRY ST. * FLYING
TO RIO WED. EVENING . . . ANNE HATFIELD[1] KINDLY TAKING
ME TO THE AIRPORT. I'LL PROBABLY BE SEEING YOU TOMOR-
ROW SOMETIME, ANYWAY * BUT I COULDN'T LEAVE THEN
[(]SUN.[)] BECAUSE ELSIE IS BUSY * & I HOPE YOU WON'T BE
TOO TIRED TO TELL ME WHAT CONCLUSIONS YOU AND THE
LATIN AMERICANS REACHED ABOUT "CHANGE" . . . IF YOU
ARE EXHAUSTED BY YOUR TRIP DON'T BOTHER ABOUT ME AT
ALL . . . I AM GETTING ALONG PERFECTLY WELL * CAN MAKE
MY OWN MEALS, OR GO OUT, ETC * OUT LAST NIGHT, & GO-
ING OUT TONIGHT, TOO . . . BELLE G[2] COMING TO CALL SUN-
DAY * ON HER WAY TO POETS FOR PEACE * I THINK I'LL SKIP IT
* PEACEFUL OR NOT, PEOPLE TEND TO BUMP INTO ME . . .
MRS. BULLOCK SENT SOME ANEMONES SO I DID A SMALL
CRAYON PICTURE FOR YOU * NOT UP TO MY BEST WORKS, I'M
AFRAID, BUT I REMEMBER CAL WANTED ONE, IN RIO *** I'LL
DO A BETTER ONE IN WATER*COLOR SOMETIME . . . MAR-
GARET M THINKS HARRIET IS EXTREMELY GOOD*LOOKING
(SHE MADE A BRIEF APPEARANCE THURSDAY EVENING, WITH
A NOT VERY GOOD*LOOKING PLAYMATE) THIS MORNING I
MET "ANGELA" & HER MAMA . . . I DO THINK YOU ARE LUCKY
TO HAVE NICOLE & SHE HAS TOLD ME, MANY TIMES, HOW
LUCKY SHE IS TO HAVE YOU . . .
I'M AFRAID I'VE SOMEHOW GOT THE FLOOR VERY DIRTY . . .
ASHES, MOSTLY . . . IT IS A FINE PLACE TO WORK IN ** IF EVER I
DO COME BACK TO NY TO LIVE I THINK I'LL TRY TO FIND A
PLACE UP IN THIS DISTRICT * COMPARATIVELY MUCH
CHEAPER THAN THE VILLAGE, I THINK * AND OH THE JOY OF
A DOORMAN AND A MAIL*DROP . . . I READ THE POUND BOOK,
CAL, & LEARNED A LOT * ALSO ALL THE OTHER POETS ON
HAND * BUT I'M AFRAID I DON'T SEE ALL THAT YOU & REX-
ROTH DID IN F M FORD![3] * (BUT SEE WHAT YOU MEANT . . .) I
HAVE CLEANED YOUR TYPE, ELIZABETH . . . AND NOTHING,
EVEN PUTTING ALL THE BOOKS, UPSTAIRS & DOWN, IN AL-

---

1 Ann Hatfield Rothschild, a friend of Lota's who had advised her on the interior design of the Rio apartment.
2 Isabella Gardner.
3 Ford Madox Ford, *Buckshee: Last Poems*, introductions by RL and Kenneth Rexroth (1966); see RL-*CPR*. The Pound book is unidentified.

PHABETICAL ORDER, COULD BEGIN TO SHOW MY GRATI-
TUDE OR MAKE UP TO YOU FOR THE STUPIDITY OF MY BE-
HAVIOR. (DR B BAWLED ME OUT A BIT LONGER EVERY DAY,
AND IT GOT MORE AND MORE MONSTROUS WITH EVERY
VISIT . . .) I THINK IT WAS PRIMARILY DUE TO GRIEF & EX-
HAUSTION * AT LEAST THAT STARTED ME OFF * SURELY
THINGS CAN'T EVER GET ANY WORSE. ANYWAY * I DO THANK
YOU BOTH WITH ALL MY HEART . . . NO LOCAL NEWS TODAY
SO FAR * WELCOME BACK*
Love, E.

That Spanish soup is delicious—I must get the name of it from you—

349.

15 West 67 St.
N.Y.C.
October 9, 1967

Dearest Elizabeth:

I write so few letters that I see with surprise again that the number of my street is the same as the number of the year. A gray coolish day here; my Bible reading's done; and I am getting ready to set out for the University. This troubled fall!

I hope I have been of some slight help to you. I worry until the trip to Brazil is over and you can arrange your life with fixed routine—not very fixed, just a place where you know you will be, and can go on at your leisure with your poems and Brazil book. You seem so marvelously healthy that I grieve at the thought of trips, business details, disturbing meetings, etc. The woes of your heart are enough.

It's been a joy to sit chatting with you, even in this sad time—all the more perhaps because the sorrow can be shared a little. You make most people, even the most charming, seem as if seen through a glaze, as if they lived in a glaze. And your poems and prose animals[1] have the same freshness, the wood is exposed, clean and genuine.

I won't go on. I feel for Lota, though I've no right to, rather as I did after Cousin Harriet's death; a part of my life has fallen away, a part of my life in you.

1 "Rainy Season: Sub-Tropics," *The Kenyon Review* (Nov. 1967); see EB-*CP*.

No news here. Liz and I went to a good Negro movie, *Jason.*[1] Otherwise we haven't seen or *heard* from a soul.

All my love,
Cal

350.

Dearest Cal:

I'm still at the Hotel Canterbury, but packing up to move in about an hour—to meet the telephone company over at the "flat" I've taken at the above address. I talked to Elizabeth on New Years day, I think it was, or the Sunday before—I also tried to call you all on Christmas day, after I got here, but there was no reply. Perhaps you are back from Mexico by now[2]—I imagine classes begin or have begun. I do hope you'll tell me a bit about it. I can't remember now who it was you were going to visit—in fact the last 2 or 3 months are all pretty confused, and I can't remember the sequence of anything. One thing stands out—the best news I have had in several years, I think—Elizabeth and Anny, whom I called the same day, both said you were very well. I am very happy about this—it is wonderful and makes me feel there is a little hope in the world after all . . .

I'll skip all the Brazil stay; it was really too awful to speak about—not only the packing-up, dreadful as it was—but the behaviour of people I had thought were my friends for almost 16 years. I suppose it can all be explained—Anny explained it as reactions to great grief—but I felt more as if I were being used as a sort of scapegoat—without exaggeration—and think now that Lota's death left everyone feeling somewhat guilty and then I appeared and was unconsciously used in this way. Anyway—it will take me years to forget it and I am planning how I can get back to Ouro Prêto without going near Rio—it can be done. There were some exceptions, of course, thank heavens. But if anyone there ever wants to see me again they'll have to come to Ouro Prêto to visit me.

The house there is absolutely lovely—I do hope you can see it one day. Lilli is doing a beautiful job. It should be all ready by June or July, and, if I

---

1 *Portrait of Jason*, dir. Shirley Clarke (1967).
2 In late December 1967, RL went to the Centro Intercultural de Documentación for social and religious thought in Cuernavaca, Mexico, established by Ivan Illich.

can scrape up the money, I'll try to go back then for the summer, I think. I spent ten days up there—an enormous relief, most of them. Vinícius de Moraes was also staying at the little hotel, "resting," and he was good company—he is really very sweet and kind. He took me to the plane when I left Rio (I was going alone, in a taxi, from my hotel)—and even paid part of my enormous excess baggage—otherwise I'd never had made the plane. He is supposed to be visiting New York about now, I think. Anyway—he admires you so much I did take the responsibility of giving him your apartment number (not the other one), swearing him to secrecy about it—and maybe he will look you up and you could have lunch or something . . . He was a very good friend to me that sad stretch.

For about a week I didn't think I could ever make it—thought I'd just leave my bones in Brazil—but somehow I did, after all, even with some loose ends. The sister's lawsuit[1]—well, I have no idea what is going on and shall have to depend entirely on one good friend, I think—since none of the people involved will ever write, I know. The sister had already fought with & fired her first (famous) lawyer, that's all I know. But according to Brazilian law Lota didn't have to leave her anything—and hadn't in any previous wills—and Lota had also been clever enough to get doctors' certificates saying she was sane when she wrote the will. (Anny thinks she wasn't—but this will stand up in Brazil, I think.)

My young friend Suzanne came down from Seattle, and we started looking for a place to stay and found a rather funny but comfortable flat on Pacific Avenue—a steam laundry (almost silent) on one side—a body painting (CAR, that is!) place across the street, and also the Cancer Society . . . as she says "a nowhere address," but it has lots of room and will be quite comfortable, I think, when I can get some furniture. A pea-green wooden early 20th cent. building—4 bay windows—2 fireplaces—I really like it, and right near Polk Street, a rather interesting little community, lots of good shops, etc. Suzanne has gone back to Seattle to collect her belongings and her child—gone a week; she'll get here tonight or tomorrow AM. Thank God, Cal, I have such a bright, kind, and funny companion right now—I don't think I could bear to live alone just yet, or in New York, and certainly not in Brazil.

---

1 Lota "had divided her estate just as they had agreed the year before. Mary Morse would inherit Samambaia; Elizabeth would get the Rio apartment, control of the seven offices she and Lota had owned in Rio, all the furniture and books in Rio, and what was her own in Samambaia . . . But Elizabeth had not expected that Lota's sister, Marietta Nascimento, would be so angry over being excluded from her sister's will that she would challenge it, saying that Lota had been insane when she wrote it"; Brett C. Millier, *Elizabeth Bishop: Life and the Memory of It* (1993), 396–97.

Suzanne is really a nice girl—and is typing all my business letters, will type for me, etc. "Secretary" does sound decadent to me, but maybe I've been needing one for a long time!

I saw Anthony Ostroff Sunday—he came over here and we went and ate some oysters together at the St. Francis. He seems very agreeable—and he has been having a terribly difficult time—perhaps you know—his wife has been, and is, very sick—3 or 4 operations. I am going over there Friday or Sat. to dinner—he said he'd take me to call on Josephine Miles, too—also, I hadn't known before that Miss M is so lame . . . Anthony (?) built his own house—did you know—I like that. It took him over three years. He seemed a bit hopeless—thinks he may get kicked out at any moment over Vietnam. He had a little news—about Dr. Spock, etc.[1]—and now I wonder what is happening. There has been a newspaper strike here since Friday and the radio and TV in this hotel room go on and on about nothing except transplanting hearts . . .

I've been to see some of the great Barker tribe in Mills Valley—very nice and very bohemian—been taken to Chinatown and so on— I am gradually feeling a bit more like myself and even a bit sociable. In Brazil I just packed and went to bed at 8, up at 6, packed some more, and so on—a nightmare. Petrópolis was the worst, and I shall never go back there. I finally fought with a couple of people, and maybe that was good for me—at least it is bracing to know you're RIGHT, for once. Well, backward countries produce backward and irrational people, as I should have learned by now.— Lota was a great exception and how she did it I'll never know. I feel now that it got her in the end—the backwardness and self-interest and self-deception all around her—but she did put up a noble fight. Noble is the only word to describe her, really. Oh god—the awful *waste* of a country like that—ours, too, but surely not as bad . . .

I must go out and buy some blankets—nothing in the flat yet but beds and a refrigerator on Sears installment plan . . . Oh—Carolyn's "slush fund" turned out to be another loan—without interest, but still a loan. I haven't taken it yet, but I probably will have to before long—unless miraculously I receive permission to sell the Rio apt.—lots of buyers, but it's not free yet.

This is all awful, self-centered. PLEASE write and tell me what you've been doing and how you are. Well *back to the USA.*

With much love always,

Elizabeth

1 On January 15, 1968, Benjamin Spock was indicted, along with William Coffin, Mitchell Goodman, and Marcus Raskin, for counseling draft resisters.

(Love to Elizabeth—& Harriet—& many, many thanks for your kindness in N.Y. Especially after Brazil—I'll never stop being grateful—I can use my left hand now—just can't raise the arm, but shall begin therapy this week— *swimming*, I think. Did you get note from Petrópolis?[1])

351.

Ah my Dear—

I guess one could be vexed with you or anyone, but I don't see how any-one could be *cruel* to you—never, and alone there and a woman! I wish I could have been at hand to shield you. I want you never to suffer. The trou-bles of the last couple of years and above all this last, won't be again. I'm glad tho that you are keeping Ouro Prêto; something of Brazil will be kept, and I'm sure many dear friends.

Glad you are on what seems to me the very solid ground of San Fran-cisco, glad Suzanne is with you. Dr. Baumann described her to me at great length and with the completest praise—rather like Hannah on Rosa Luxem-burg.[2] I'm laying it on a little, but not much.

Marvelous stay in Cuernavaca with a radical priest friend of mine, Mon-signor Ivan Illich (!) doing I don't know what, only I hoped to combine this trip with one to Cuba. However the State Department would not authorize my passport as a journalist. Just as well; only Mexico where I could forget everything. Queer gathering; at one moment I'd be talking to heavy Chicago nuns, and the next to Brazilian refugees with forty year sentences waiting for them.[3] Lots of climbing Toltec ruins, New Year's midnight in the market.

Now back to the cold, draft-evader protests, jury duty, my last trip to Harvard. The Spock, etc., indictment may have been a bad tactical error by the government—all sorts of tepid withdrawn people like Auden and Jason Epstein are signing protests. I've signed something which pledges my sup-port to the men indicted—saying we will take their places if they go to jail. Honor demands that one does this, but how I loathe the claptrap, the pole-mical stirrers, one, alas, must agree with! I feel like a month of bass and pick-erel fishing; still, there's a thrill—sort of like being a soldier one day a month, then sunning and gossiping the rest.

Lizzie has written a review of Lillian very blasting and (ill-judged, I

---

1 The letter does not survive.
2 Hannah Arendt, "Rosa Luxemburg: 1871–1919," *Men in Dark Times* (1968).
3 Probably Francisco Julião; see letter 352.

think) which has got us into a hornets' nest of abusive letters to the *Book Review*.[1] I've never cared too much when I've been attacked, but this riles. I feel almost physically forced to cut the writers of the letters. Strange, because as I've said I don't think the piece should have been written—on personal grounds, not critical. I've learned that it is sometimes right and necessary to be angry, even when wrong.

Yes, I'm well. The pills I am taking really seem to prevent mania. Two or three years will be necessary, but already critical months have passed. Ordinarily I would certainly have been in a hospital by now. The great thing is that even my well life is much changed, as tho I'd once been in danger of falling with every step I took. All the psychiatry and therapy I've had, almost 19 years, was as irrelevant as it would have been for a broken leg. Well, some of it was interesting, tho most was jargon.

My long poem is now over a thousand lines, and will probably go on another 500, will go on till June when it began.[2] Then I'll polish through the summer. I am writing it as if it were my last work. Someone asked me if [I] expected to die when I finished it—no, but trying to write with such openness and not holding back.

Goodbye, and all my love, and Darling, forget your troubles in Brazil,
Cal

352.

January 23rd, 1968
Dearest Cal:

Forgive this makeshift writing-paper—Harold[3] has sent on all my boxes from Perry St., and they should come today, so I didn't want to lay in another supply of paper, etc. I can't imagine, no, I can—what Cuernavaca is like these days. I spent several months there a long time ago and imagine it now has thousands more awful villas, swimming-pools and so on. The only reason I stayed there so long was because my wonderful *Spanish* Spanish teacher was there—and Neruda came down often too. I do wonder about the details of your life there and what was accomplished. Did you see Julião?[4] & if so how did he strike you? And I'd like to know more about the Brazilians—well, I wish we could have lunch so I could hear all about it.

---

1 Elizabeth Hardwick, "The *Little Foxes* Revived," *The New York Review of Books* (Dec. 21, 1967).
2 *Notebook 1967–68* (1969).
3 Harold Leeds.
4 Julião was living in Cuernevaca during his exile from Brazil.

You say I seem to be "on solid ground"—well, I don't know! I haven't begun to feel real yet, but I like this place, my funny "flat," Suzanne is wonderful company, & a good many times a day I keep reminding myself that I am really free to cheer up, free to feel happy, even, if I can. But all the business in Brazil hangs over me, a very black cloud indeed. It is strange to feel so misunderstood, even hated, there—when I don't feel that way at all here—in fact I feel quite well-loved, on the whole. Well, one shouldn't get too involved with people who can't possibly understand one, that's all, but I suppose there was no help for that. I'd love to have heard Dr B.'s comments on Suzanne . . . I was at Jane's or someplace and didn't see S when she was in New York, but she went to see the famous Dr. she'd heard so much about, and I gather they had a long conversation. We like most of the same things, music, food, furniture, and so on (although I do switch the FM from the rock and roll station to the old jazz station once in a while), and she is very good for me—has already enrolled me in Blue Cross, types business letters for me, shortens my skirts above my knees. I think it will work very well, and God knows I couldn't bear living alone just yet. We've been too busy to look up many people so far—but San Francisco seems to be one of those places people "go through" quite a lot. I'm having dinner tonight with Fizdale and Gold, and other old friends are in view. Tomorrow we're going over to Berkeley to have lunch with Tony, as I suppose I now call him, and see some of the speech-making, etc. He is in up to his neck in the Viet Nam business & apparently expects to be fired any day (after calling on J. Miles, I think).

I haven't seen E's review of the Hellman play—I hope they send me that copy: shall request it. Also want to see your letter, of course. Yes, I like what you say: "it is necessary to be angry even when wrong." This applies perfectly to some of my Brazilian troubles, so I am going right on being angry about them and think I HAVE to—otherwise I'll be treated like a doormat, I find. (I am raising hell—at least it is hell for me to be raising.) I haven't seen my bits of prose in *Kenyon*—in fact, nothing has started arriving yet and I haven't got to a library—and there has been a newspaper strike for almost three weeks here now. I buy a NY *Times* whenever I can, otherwise am quite out of the world.

The Rockefeller Grant people wrote and asked me to nominate someone for a grant this year. I asked Howard Moss if he'd like one, and he said he certainly would—he has been on the *NYer* 20 years, and would love a year off to polish up his plays, etc. So I am going to nominate him and if you happen to be on the committee or whatever it is, too, and feel you could honestly recommend him, I wish you would—you carry so much more weight than anyone else, my dear. I think Howard deserves *something* by now—

Oh it is so wonderful that you are staying well—I remind myself of that several times a day, too, particularly at evening when I tend to get morbid about the immediate past—I think: well that is a bright spot in this disgusting world.

The light in San Francisco is lovely—reminds me a bit of Key West. We have had lovely weather, too—warm and sunny. I went to a playground with Suzanne and the son yesterday—just a block away—and it was fascinating—all the quaint little Chinese and Japanese children. One can always tell them apart, although I couldn't say how. Out the window we have bits of views—a piece of a bridge, a little bit of bay—the windows in Sausalito, I think it is, catch the light—the rest is signboards that light up at night— PAINT, BANK OF AMERICA, MOTEL, BASKETBALL TONIGHT, CANCER SOCIETY OF AMERICA, VOLKSWAGEN, etc.—I really like all this but shall NOT start writing like Dr. Williams about it. I am dying to get down to hard work and shall in a day or two. Give my love to Elizabeth & Nicole! & Harriet—with lots & lots for yourself,

    Elizabeth

353.

[Postcard: Alcatraz Island, San Francisco: "Having a wonderful time . . . Wish you were here"]

             [San Francisco, Calif.]

             [February 1968]

DEAREST CAL: I WONDER WHERE YOU ARE & HOW YOU ARE & IF YOU RECEIVED MY LETTER? THIS IS JUST TO TELL YOU THE DELIGHTFUL NEWS THAT ON THE 1ST I FELL AND BROKE MY RIGHT WRIST RATHER BADLY: I WANT TO SAY THAT I WAS COLD SOBER: JUST A STEEP SLICK WET SIDEWALK & HIGH HEELS: BROKE A TOOTH A DAY AGO AND WAS GREATLY RE-LIEVED TO DISCOVER IT A FALSE ONE::: THE WORST IS THAT I CAN'T WORK AT ALL I FIND: AT THIS PACE OR WITHOUT PEN IN HAND::: SEEING BOB G TOMORROW AND E KRAY DAY AF-TER THAT: EXCEPT FOR BONES ALL GOES WELL HERE: READ SOMEONE IN *PR* ON SAN FRANCISCO[1]: WELL EVEN IF IT IS LIKE THAT I DON'T CARE; ONE HAS TO LIKE *SOMEWHERE* & IT

---

1 Richard Schlatter and Thomas R. Edwards, "California Letters," *Partisan Review* (Winter 1968).

MIGHT AS WELL BE AESTHETICALLY PLEASING AS POSSIBLE; ::
DON'T KNOW WHAT I'D BE DOING NOW WITHOUT S[1]; IN A
"HOME" NO DOUBT WRITE WHEN YOU CAN. LOVE TO YOUR
FAMILY.
    MUCH LOVE TO YOU,
      ELIZABETH

354.

February 21, 1968

Dearest Elizabeth:

Just a line or two to fling you my love before I set off for a short trip to Charlottesville and the Peter Taylors—reading, etc., much chaff with friends. I have your painting on the wall, gold frame, blue matte suggested by the framer, and oddly right. Lovely and cozy; it replaces my now exiled Baskin "Nuclear Man," shut in a closet.[2] I love you so much, and have an intuitive feeling that all's much better now, a place of light and human warmth for you! I've been happily buried; my *Endecott* play rewritten for performance in April; the long poem now 100 sections, and in the formal shape it will end with after 20 or more sections.[3] Just been reading Trilling on Joyce, the heroic annihilation of most human things to doing *Finnegans Wake*, not approved or disapproved by Trilling.[4] Thank God for my small (God knows what) talent! But even I seem to get absorbed, stop writing. Do you know what hell is? Forever meeting a new English faculty, coed, all older than one is; in one hand, cup of coffee in a paper cup, in the other hand a cookie and cigarette, and always standing, and signing copies of one's least-liked book (I'm thinking of poetry readings). The other half is the pre-reading cocktail party meant to last half an hour and lasting two, so that you can hardly walk or see.

I must stop. So looking forward to introducing you when you come here.

Much love,

    Cal

---

1 Suzanne.
2 Leonard Baskin, *Hydrogen Man* (1954).
3 *Notebook 1967–68* (1969).
4 Lionel Trilling, "James Joyce in His Letters," *Commentary* (Feb. 1968).

355.

[Postcard: Winslow Homer, Marblehead, 1880 (watercolor, Art Institute of Chicago); an image of two people in conversation on a coastal rock]

[July 29, 1968]

Out of all the masterpieces in this place I chose this to send you, for obvious reasons.[1] We spent hours here—most of the time in Chicago—I suppose you've seen it, but I had never been to C before—or believed in Nevada, Utah, and so on. Utah exactly like HELL. But it was a very nice train ride on the ZEPHYR, everyone fighting for clear views for their polaroids . . . Please write.

Hope all is well, with much love,
Elizabeth

356.

Castine, Maine
July 30, 1968

Dearest Elizabeth:

Summer sliding away; as though it were the mostly-sleep from night to morning! Maybe, it's because the weather has never been like this, almost unbroken bright, dry shirt-sleeves days—this is Maine, where July a year ago couldn't have had more than three such days; even for tennis, I don't sweat in the dry air. In two weeks Harriet will be back from camp. We've seen her twice. The first time, she was shyly quite happy; the second much more gaily happy. Camp Alamoosook is forty miles from here, over fifty campers on a lake island small enough to put in someone's garden.[2] So they do a lot of boating and mainland hiking. It's all delicate, soft-handed and well-run. This is its last year, and we are already sad.

I guess the summer goes, because I write so much. I must average six days a week nine to three-thirty. The whole book retyped with various changes, and 19 new sections added. It must end, but impulse keeps pushing up something new, and I am sure the whole is better and more, still. But I know I should stop, though I don't want to, and can't easily throw the habit.

The Wests[3] are here. I find Mary a bit hard (how shall I put it?) to get at. The beautiful big house, the beautiful big meals, the beautiful big guests, the mind, as Hannah Arendt puts it, that wants to be ninety per cent right, times

1 See "Water" (RL-*CP*).
2 See "End of Camp Alamoosook" (RL-*CP*).
3 James West and Mary McCarthy.

when nothing seems addressed to me, and nothing I say is heard—maddening when you think what you said is quite good, or the subject is one you feel could be referred to you. At times I think of Randall in his off-moods, though Mary is never discourteous, and like what I imagine Mama Anna[1] must be like, compared with the dark Randall.

I never got to New York, tho I might have tried, if I'd known you were staying on into July. It would have been such joy to see you there. It is very hard to leave here; we get so comfortable and set and unset for any other life.

I had a feeling many times that all had turned out about as well for you as we can hope or want at our age. Not that our age isn't in ways our best; I feel I know more, or at least hold on to more of what I want to know. I miss the long roll of years ahead of me. I meant to say how much we liked Suzanne!

What has happened? A dead young seal with its head gnawn off floated up on my beach—the color of a pig and hard to identify. I got some children to bury it. With the Wests, we went to a Democratic rally in Portland. Rather fun, seeing the delegates in action; they seemed to care for nothing but absolute (yellow dog) democratic loyalty. Nice clambake. We all got ourselves in the local papers and television, but did nothing and were allowed to do nothing. Lizzie's trying to get signatures for a fourth party. McCarthy nearly visited us, and we had authentic plainclothesmen inspecting my house and barn.[2] Then he couldn't come. I don't know whether our tiny prestige in the village has risen or dropped. I think we've held our own.

Loneliness; I miss you so much, as ever. I wish you were sitting here now. We could be looking out on the very blue high tide and very clear sky—and talking shop and much else and doing much else. Lizzie sends her best love to you both—I too.

All my love,
Cal

P.S. Thanks for talking to Bob and Michael[3]; often I don't know what to think of my poem.

---

1 Randall Jarrell's mother.
2 RL supported Senator Eugene McCarthy's anti–Vietnam War campaign for the Democratic presidential nomination.
3 Robert Giroux and Michael di Capua.

357.

Dear Heart:

(This is a name that I use at special times for both Lizzie and Harriet.)

If I had more time (I seem to only write when I have no time), I'd tell you about another deadly day with the Eberharts. I arrived at the same time with Dick's brother-in-law and two daughters, then sat on a dwindling strip of grass overlooking ocean, filled with binoculars; Dick had small ones he handed to guests, and a big one he didn't hand to guests—talking to a Mr. and Mrs. Batty (Sounding exactly like Beaty, in Betty Eberhart) fresh from Saigon, USIS, hard to tell whether they were hawk or dove, but easy to tell they were uninteresting—above us flapping the flag of our country, but topped by the flag of the UN, gesture almost of treason by Betty, who by the way said nothing the whole long day that wasn't either demonstrably false or doggedly banal (I mean cheerfully false)—arrival of neighboring clergy-man's wife, conversation mostly about the nearest tennis court—arrival of Dan Hoffman, poet living a mile away, thin, emaciated, intelligent, rather too dry and quivering to be interesting; sharing few virtues with Dick and fewer vices, and who with his similar wife had set his heart all summer on having all of us visit them without telling the Eberharts (they'd learn a week later), their idea, a climb up a huge knot similar to the Eberharts, but in sight of no man probably since the retreat of the glacier. Somehow Lizzie has never grabbed at this day, but I suppose anyone who lived near Dick and Betty. I won't go on. Thousands came, in ones and twos, in different cos-tumes all dull, except Buckminster Fuller, the point of the visit, who, how-ever, was deaf, so the conversation was . . . his. Very Cambridge yankee, with a quaint old-fashioned brilliance and knowledge of science.

Dear, I can't write anything serious (after this) about [the] Czech hideous business,[1] or about myself. I've done nothing much this summer, and everything, 38 more sections. Things worked out much better with Mary, but her guests are almost as dull and as many as the Eberharts: I faint at the thought of what has passed through here: American common market people with French names and American fortunes; all summer, the sweet, drunken, never silent widow of George Orwell; Kevin[2] with children from two marriages . . .

---

1 The USSR and Warsaw Pact allies invaded Czechoslovakia on August 21 to suppress Czech liberalization and put an end to the "Prague Spring." See "Prague 1968" (RL-CP).
2 Mary McCarthy's brother.

Tomorrow, I'm going to Washington to go to Chicago with McCarthy.[1] We have no chance, of course. Today, I go with Harriet and her best friend to the fish hatchery; last night we had ghosts (very kind ones) at the cemetery. We leave here on the tenth. I guess I love New York, but at this moment I'd as soon stick my head in a plastic sack. This has been the most lovely summer I've ever known. But never in the world will I see enough of you.

Love to Suzanne, and all to you,

Cal

358.

If Mary is still there, remember me to her—

August 28th, 196[8]

Dearest Cal:

I have rented a TV for the duration of the conventions—& can scarcely wait to get the damned thing out of the house, to tell the truth—but the last few days I've been watching it & hoping to catch a glimpse of *you* . . . however, you are probably rarely in that mad and boring scene, but in hotel rooms or bars talking to, I hope, more interesting people. I've seen McCarthy a good many times now—listened to him, that is—and he is just too sensible to be true—one just naturally agrees with almost everything he says. Common sense and sincerity (one hates the word) are so rare—and he'll never never get elected, of course. What a pity. I watched Humphrey the other night, and heard a very cross diatribe from him last night, too—he seems bitter, mean-tempered, cross because no one loves him any more—and I hate the, I thought, calculating sidewise looks he keeps giving—oh dear—and I suppose we're stuck with him now. Ginsberg, Burroughs, Mailer—& Genet!—it is all too weird—this listing in the papers here, but not mentioning you so far—the only one who makes any sense—oh, I suppose Mailer does, a *little*. I'd love sometime to hear about your encounters with these new critics of the political scene . . .

I just read the profiles of Ginsberg in *The New Yorker*[2]—I find him rather admirable, except for his writing!—but feel a little like an old-fashioned Southerner about the Negro—all right as long as he keeps his place . . . Haight/Ashbury here—I went once to see it and once to go to a reading—is just too sad and awful now; I couldn't bear to go there again. The stories of

1 For the 1968 Democratic National Convention, August 26 to August 29.
2 Jane Kramer, "Paterfamilias—II," *The New Yorker* (Aug. 24, 1968).

the police in Chicago today are too awful, too. Well—I don't know what is happening to us at all. (I've returned to trying to finish a poem I started about Charlemagne years ago—based on the Einhard Life[1]—and it is strange the way things that struck me as unbelievably naive and pathetic in their intellectual pretensions then, (700 AD) now seem, after about 20 years, idealistic and honest.)

I've been so pleased to get two letters from you—my summer was pretty wretched, mostly because of health and then heat (the health is better now, but that infection took forever before I felt normal again)—then since we got back we have been re-painting this whole fairly big apartment—couldn't stand our Chinese landlord's color scheme and wall-to-wall carpeting any longer. Now it is looking nice & cheerful—we got it just about all done the day before Suzanne's baby came back—day before yesterday—now two visitors, and then, God willing, maybe I'll be able to get back to work. I haven't done anything, really, for well over two years, and not much before that. I just don't seem to have any talent for protecting myself or my working time the way I should. S is very good to me and does a lot or all of the business part of things, etc.—and I'm hoping eventually we will have a solid routine—not too severe, but I really have to have one of sorts to get anything done at all. I must confess I'm pretty gloomy, however—but don't repeat it—what can one do, or should one do—I don't know. I don't think I could bear NY alone. I adore Ouro Prêto, but 2 or 3 months at a time is plenty there—and I don't have many real friends in Brazil, much as I love the country . . . And this place. Well, I've met some of the poets—and the only one I still really like is Thom Gunn . . . We went to dinner with someone named Schevill—pleasant, but such awful poetry he gave me—and then Rexroth, who seemed to be in a pet about something—there had obviously been a scene just before we got there between him and his female followers. It took me all evening to sort them out—(I'll gossip, too). There was a visiting lady-poet who was very acid. I said something sociable, just to get the ball rolling, and she jerked away from my direction and said "I can't endure any form of graciousness any more . . ." leaving me feeling like an airplane hostess . . . Rexroth wasn't at table—had to be coaxed back to finish dinner—attacked me for being late, although both S and I had clearly understood him to say "anytime after 7:30" and it was barely 8 . . . Oh well. He was a bit nicer after a while and quite funny—but I lost quite a bit of the conversation because

---

1 Einhard, *Vita Karoli Magni* (ca. 830–833). "Charlemagne," in the "Key West Notebook II" (Vassar, folder 75.4b).

they are all so familiar with the *Japanese* . . . Well, what to do—I don't think this part of the world will ever suit me, somehow. It is a pretty city, if self-conscious—but I went to one of the beaches yesterday, went to a famous park, etc.—and realize that after Brazil I am quite spoiled for California scenery. I just admire away and keep my real opinions to myself. What I've seen of the coast so far is pretty much ruined—I think I'd like to go up into the Sierras sometime, however. They may have fewer hot dogs and tamales and cars.

Since I am being so gossipy—I loved your account of yr. visit to Mr Rubberheart (as Henry R calls him). Much worse than my simple evening sallies here . . . It was particularly funny since I had just had a letter from him—Mr R—I received two copies of his last book and felt I had to say something, so wrote him a very brief note managing to say *something* honest, I thought.[1] In return I got a long letter all about people I never heard of with names like Tricksy and Adam . . . Grandma and Mrs. Crosby "both 79," etc, etc. It is marvellous and his life must just go on as you describe it day after day after day. Perhaps if one can write poetry in his mystical way one can manage to live like this at the same time—the overmind at Undercliff just clashes off high beautiful mysterious insights while feeding Grandma and flirting with Tricksy . . . And that's enough un-Christian feeling for one day. Oh I can't resist: he says he "caught scent of" me in Seattle . . . and that his son is "strong, deep, and bearded . . ." Oh well—*coitado*, is all I shd. say . . . (I miss Lota more every day of my life I'm afraid, but again please don't repeat this—and what can one do? It is so hard to get to feeling again that anything at all is really worth the doing—but then I don't feel like that all the time, of course—there are better days, or hours.) I saw a lot of Marianne—and that is an awful worry, but not anything one can do much about. She cried when she kissed me goodbye and was more affectionate than she has ever been before—really wanted me to stay in New York, I think. She does have plenty of money, thank goodness—in spite of her complaints—and good friends looking out for her interests—but she won't have anyone stay with her nights. And I also have a profound mistrust of a young man named Andreas,[2] who now seems to have taken over the Gotham B M—some of her stories about him made me—and other friends—highly suspicious. That flat of hers is just too full of valuable mementos lying about—and she is very wandering in the head from time to time . . . (Do you know anything of him?)

1 Richard Eberhart, *Shifts of Being* (1968).
2 Andreas Brown.

I am so glad you had "the most lovely summer" you have ever known—
since I think my own was just about the saddest and most futile. Well—
things surely will improve. Bill A called up yesterday and I think I'll be
flying back to read at Harvard on October 16th or some following Wednesday—it was nice to hear [from] him. Susanne Langer is coming here the
2nd—a friend of a friend—philosophers, especially German ones, terrify
me, but I met her once and she was rather nice—although not interesting like
Hannah A— A Mr. Daluna (from the moon) comes today—helping some
with that dismal anthology—he is Portuguese, jailed twice, can't go back,
tried Brazil and hated that—a very nice little gentleman, young, brought me
roses—& his Portuguese and manners made me homesick—he calls me
"Dona Elizabeth, Madame"—all of them—every phrase.

I acquired a young mynah bird—too young to speak yet. I seem to be a
bit allergic to him and his, well, merde so I don't know if I can keep him or
not, but I hope to—a very entertaining and tame bird. I am going to teach
him—or did I tell you—to say *"I too dislike it"*—let's see, what would be a
good line [of] yours. They have to be a certain length & rhythm, or the bird
will fill it in with nonsense syllables of his own—isn't that queer?

Oh—speaking of speaking—an outfit called SPOKEN ARTS has been
hounding me—mostly long distance calls—for months now. They offered
$25.00—when I said that wouldn't do at all, the man said to me: "We have al-
most 100 poets—think of the book keeping"! Well, Brandt & Brandt says one
shd get a flat $500 fee or up to 18 cents a record. I may not have this quite
right, Suzanne has the details—but they sent me their list, with you on it,
too—and I gather they have just gone around more or less stealing recordings
and only one or two poets have ever questioned them about it at all . . . This
is boring, I know, but if I suffer through any of those things, it is only to make
some money from them—a fair price, at least—so I wonder if you remember
anything about it? They really are incredibly overbearing on the telephone &
in their letters, but so many people are, ah me . . . NO—S says the co. turned
down the flat fee but will pay 18 cents per record for 2 bands—so that is what
all the poets shd. be getting . . . They complained that I was the only poet who
had raised objections "except Frost & Eliot and they are dead"!

We were robbed while we were away—just a day or two after we left—
and are fairly sure we know the man who did it—someone brought here
once, whom we couldn't stand, and who kept calling me up all the time. Two
cameras including the Rolleiflex I've had for years—Suzanne's hi-fi—a
piece or two of not very valuable jewelry, and a CASSEROLE . . . The man
we suspect left for Africa shortly afterwards. We were insured but even so I

don't think I'll ever be able to afford another such camera . . . (too good for me, anyway)—I have acquired a better hi-fi, however, a KLH—very good. Suzanne has lots of good records—mostly opera, of which she's very fond—fortunately our musical tastes are pretty similar—but I left all mine in Ouro Prêto—AND about 4,000 books, etc.—and what to do with it all . . . I wanted to leave some sort of foundation in Lota's name—and we had planned something like that together for years—but after my experience in that country of charming irresponsibles and crooks I just can't figure out how to go about it . . . I'm going to see a good WILL lawyer here—but I'm sure he won't have any idea, either. Any suggestions as to what to do with my vast property and wealth for the good of the world—or preferably [for] some Brazilian students, etc.—would be welcome . . . I must get it settled very soon. I can't get any information (or money) out of Brazil—I've had one account since I've left—8 months—and L's sister is still carrying on blaming me, I gather, & telling Rio society that I stole the family jewels! Flávio does write me nice letters, poor boy—but I'm afraid there is too much of his mother in him & not quite enough of his aunt . . .

Now I have talked & talked Cal—you are just about the only person I still CAN talk to, my dear, do you realize that. I simply hate talking about myself, more & more, the older I get—I'm afraid it is not very interesting. I hope the old brains and feelings will revive after a while—once in a while I even catch myself having an idea, I think . . . It would be lovely if you just happen to be at Harvard when I make that trip—I'll let you know the date. I doubt I'll go on to NY— I hope Elizabeth & Harriet are fine and full of good spirits. Please let me know whatever you can about Chicago—but I *do* know how busy and sought after you are. With much love always—

Elizabeth

359.

September 5, 1968

Darling Elizabeth:

Let me answer the thing I can in a word or two: I'll certainly be at Harvard for your reading, and look forward to introducing you to New York, whenever it is. The guy at the Gotham seems pleasant and capable met in passing, but I really know nothing. Eberhart had a good poem, I think, in the last book: "Cape Rosier Wedding."[1]

1 Richard Eberhart, "A Wedding on Cape Rosier," *Shifts of Being* (1968).

Oh I've had a lovely summer, but when I look inside it's sad and acid: age, death of friends, aging of everything in sight, the bad immediate future of this country, most countries, talents and decency misused, etc. The stuff of life always. And now for a second, as I sat on my dry grass lifted above the harbor, and reread your letter, I was almost you—at least I could remember back last fall and Rio. The things that cannot be done twice! I think of my parents, the *I* who lived then! Ah courage!

Chicago was as it seemed. I wasn't at the Amphitheater, or in the marches.[1] I spent much of my time in McCarthy's apartment, chatting, watching him throw an orange to his brother, hearing his rather beatnik daughter say we would have to have our gas and pistols now, and maybe, tanks. The rest of the time, I spent with Lizzie, Styron, Mailer etc. In bars. Every so often I went out into the park and sidewalks by the Hilton. One night boys with bloodied heads were brought into staff headquarters, the next our staff headquarters were raided by about twenty policemen, because some probably imaginary beer cans were thrown out the window. A club was broken. One boy had twenty stitches, another six. It was horrible and looked like the old Gestapo movies. We were terrorized. The demonstrators, on the whole, behaved beautifully, about as dangerous as a church congregation. Still, I can't sympathize much with the people who sent them in to be bashed.[2] Gene did nobly, I think, the only man of importance in either party to defy the parties, nor did he overdo it. His defeat in the voting was no surprise, but the violence was.

Five more days here. I feel my book is done, and I must read Shakespeare for Harvard, so it's not untimely. But it's hard as giving up whiskey, to give up seeing and hearing live things at every turn of the head. Oh, and to see my friends again—lovely, but so turbulent. Death to politics! The jargon is migraine; and they all seem to be activist. I seem to stumble into actions—not grand enough to suit the imagination of Keith Botsford, but I have no faith. I don't suppose Harvard will erupt on Bill Alfred, Harry Levin, and me.

Imagine two very cheerful paragraphs I was intending to write. I must get this into the mail. I feel sore since Chicago, as if a man had hit Harriet.

Look forward so to your visit.

Love,

Cal

---

1 The police used tear gas and truncheons against antiwar protesters (and some journalists), and arrested more than 600 people. The violence began on August 25 but was at its worst on August 28, while peace delegates were defeated in debate in the International Amphitheater and Vice President Hubert Humphrey was nominated for the presidency.
2 See "After the Democratic Convention" (RL-*CP*).

360.

Dearest Cal:

I tried to call you, was it last Sunday or two Sundays ago, but you weren't at home . . . I don't know why I am so bad about writing letters these days; perhaps I really don't have anything much to tell anyone. Life at last has a fairly pleasant routine here and I am really working again, at last, after two years of almost doing nothing. I bought a Volkswagen about a month ago— "Lotus White." Suzanne has a license but is very inexperienced—we go over to Berkeley & back, to work in the library—but every so often we get to the top of a hill here and turn around rather than go down it . . . Tried two approaches to Thom Gunn's place the other evening, both equally terrifying, and finally telephoned him to please walk up his hill and meet us . . . The B library has excellent Brazilian material, but hard to get, until I got permission to get into the stacks. I think the student workers just didn't put books in Portuguese back on the shelves—too difficult. Also remembered that an old Brazilian friend of mine, and his wife, have been there for several years— he's Professor of Geography[1]—and this is rather nice. (He gives mimeographed copies of my "ballad" to his classes, & his cat is named *Micuçú* . . .[2])

Well, I'm going to get to Harvard sometime on the 29th—I don't know what time yet—and shall try to stay about three days, I think, in order to see you—and one or two other friends, if I can find them. I do hope this fits in with your schedule? I am looking forward to this a lot—all except the reading, of course. Who is this Laurence Scott[3] who keeps after me? I wonder how cold it will be? (Oh—Suzanne, who has taught me to read the classified ads and the yellow pages, says that's easy—one calls the Boston weather bureau . . . She is stuffed with useful information like that—things that would never occur to me in the world . . .)

We are rather lonely here, or very snobbish, or something or other . . . And the few people we do like don't seem to combine at all. But mostly it is very pleasant. I went to two "reviews"—supposed to be brilliant satire, etc.—they have rather pleasant small theatre-night-club affairs—but found them dreary—both S and I felt we were much funnier, just at home. I feel it is a period of re-learning my own pop-culture & TV—except I've had just about enough of that, now—some of the Olympics very beautiful—*Soul on*

---

1 Carolina and Hilgard O'Reilly Sternberg.
2 EB's burglar; see "The Burglar of Babylon" (EB-*CP*).
3 An artist who produced broadside illustrations for some Harvard readings.

Ice (confused),[1] Reagan, grape boycott (the mynah bird, Jacob, glares at me when I bring him only bananas and no seedless grapes), astronauts this morning, Jackie's wedding[2]—filthy books, North beach—imagine TOP-LESS STEAMED CLAM LUNCH . . . If you get back here perhaps we should try that.

Rio taxi driver, when asked what he though[t] about the Pope and the Pill: "They shouldn't have told him." That little joke did make me feel hideously homesick—there just doesn't seem to be that kind of frivolous wit in this country.

Would there be a chance of my attending one of your classes, or would you rather not? I'd sit away at the back. Shakespeare or Bible—especially the last.

Oh it will be lovely to see you. I have here the last *NYR* with Mary on "Election Illusions" but I haven't even unfolded it yet. I think I'll vote for Paulsen . . .[3] (They elected a rhinoceros at the zoo in São Paulo once.)

I must get to work. Wallace Stevens—I'm just finishing his letters[4]—says translating is a waste of time—and here I am wasting time on some rather bad poetry. Oh—I forgot to say the de luxe VOYAGE came last week, a very handsome book.[5] You know my feelings about Nolan are not exactly yours—but it is a beautiful job and I much admire the type face & the dark gray linen. (I'd like that for my own book if I can get it.) I am re-reading all your translations again, too. The Stevens letters were much better than I'd thought—he does get awfully dogmatic in his old age, however—and obviously a great many things have been left out. But from those very *demodée* (as Lota would say) romantic beginnings, up to "Blue Guitar"[6]—it is fascinating. I am trying to say something wise about Berryman—I'll show you my paragraph, I think—& as I said before it will be *lovely* to see you.

I hope Elizabeth and Harriet are both well.

Abraços,
Elizabeth

1 Eldridge Cleaver, *Soul on Ice* (1968).

2 The five-year-long grape boycott started in 1965 by César Chávez to win civil rights for migrant workers; *Apollo 7* landed in the Atlantic on October 22; Jacqueline Kennedy married Aristotle Onassis on October 20.

3 Mary McCarthy, "Notes on the Election," *The New York Review of Books* (Oct. 24, 1968); Pat Paulsen accepted an invitation to run for president during the *Smothers Brothers Comedy Hour*.

4 Wallace Stevens, *Letters*, ed. Holly Stevens (1966).

5 *The Voyage and Other Versions of Poems by Baudelaire*, illus. Sidney Nolan (1968).

6 Wallace Stevens, *The Man with the Blue Guitar* (1937).

361.

Dearest Cal:

Heaven knows where you are—still Spain, maybe, or home again . . . It is a beautiful mild Sunday afternoon here, and I wish I could go out to the park and enjoy it instead of drudging away at all the details involved in packing up to go away for four months, almost. A lot is done already, though, but there is more dentistry, more shots, visas, sub-letting, and so on still to go through.

I've had the link-bound proof copy of your sonnets[1] here now for a couple of weeks and this is the third letter I have undertaken. I really don't know what to say at all—I am overcome by their sheer volume partly, but also by the range, the infinite fascinating detail, the richness, and everything else. I shall have to read them many more times through to get it all. I think I did say something about the earlier version to you in Boston—the kind of over-all surrealism I get from them, the skipping and returning, and repeating, and the surrealism—if that is the word—being *in* the skips, or the "pattern" rather than in the separate sonnet . . .[2] That is not well put; I'll have to work on it! I think I still like some of the Mexican ones especially—also some of the Harriet ones especially. The ending is so good I could wish I hadn't read it, since it is now predominant in a group of lines of yours that haunt my days and nights—

As for me, I barely keep my head above water. Tonight K Cleaver comes for a 2nd tape-recording session—the 1st was a weird and wild experience.[3] I think she thought better of it, too, since she suddenly turned up here again one evening, alone, and wanted to re-do it. She is extremely pretty, only 23, and 5 months pregnant, *coitada*,—as we'd say in Brazil. I'm going there May 15th if all goes well. There are rumors of an earthquake this month. Forgive me, but personally I feel I would welcome a fall into the St. Andreas fault . . .

Love to your family and lots to you, Cal, as always—and I'll hope to see you, however briefly, in Washington.

Abraços,
Elizabeth

1 *Notebook 1967–68* (1969).

2 "I lean heavily on the rational, but am devoted to surrealism"; "Afterthought," *Notebook 1967–68* (1969), 159. Cf. "I lean heavily on the rational, but am devoted to unrealism," *Notebook* (1970), 262.

3 At Bowen's suggestion, EB interviewed Kathleen Cleaver, wife of Black Panther leader Eldridge Cleaver and herself a leading spokesperson for the Black Panthers. The results have never been published.

362.

Dearest Elizabeth:

I've owed you a letter forever; and you me! Dr. Baumann has just read me over the phone a sort of joint letter from you and Suzanne to her. You've had a buffeting time. But I see you are mending, indomitable. I saw Pound here last spring, very silent and gone, he and Marianne Moore weighing less than 140 pounds. He was in a stately chair at the Public Library. Whenever a woman came up, he stood up and bowed. Once he said to me, "These chairs of state were a mistake." (That's about all he said, except once when Louise Bogan came to him, and said, "I was on the Committee," and Pound seemed at sea, then he said "I always thought that was one of Cal's jokes.") What I'm getting to is, I finally said, "For God's sake sit down, Ezra," and he, "I've done nothing but sit down all afternoon." You've been doing nothing but getting to your feet. I mean this as a great tribute, but of course you've seldom been off your feet. I keep thinking of Coleridge—you know he was medically right in his treatment of himself.[1] No, you must take care, my Dear.

Here, it's Washington March week, a fever of activity.[2] Slightly unlikely people in the van. Mary McCarthy, here from Paris for dentistry, marshaling signatures for a proclamation; my old friend Blair Clark, speaking at Purdue, Chicago, and Washington. I get less leftist, if that were possible, every day, but am going to the march again with Dwight. It's a mammoth ball, fed and checked by hopes of danger. I trust it will be mostly tame. You can't tell, quite.

I go on writing: 56 more sonnets to go into the book, scattered, for the first British edition next fall—bigger, more expensive, the title now simply NOTEBOOK. I don't seem able to do much else, tho my Harvard teaching is good fun. I'm doing Shakespeare's English histories. And as far as I prepare at all, read mostly history, not criticism. My dearest regards to Suzanne, and all my love as always to you. I seem to spend my life missing you!

Love,
Cal

---

1 See "Coleridge" (RL-*CP*).
2 The National Mobilization to End the War, on November 15, 1968.

363.

December 6, 1969

Dearest Elizabeth—

I send you always these drab letters in return for your colorful postcards.[1] If there were Purgatory, I'd spend my time making pictures to mail. O, it feels now like Christmas and vacation. Two more weeks of Harvard; my book in at last. I can't quite rest, but the pace is sinking to a crawl.

I had a day with Jim Dickey, assisting in an *Encyclopaedia Britannica* (!) movie on him. Every so often (he began drinking at 9:30 AM) he would say loathsome things like "The future of American poetry is in this room." Or "my problems are worse than yours." They are; yet at times one felt his great energy to say something, so lacking in most writers. Never forget through your troubles, how strong, moral, inspired all your work has been. And do come back, every one loves and reveres you so.

Love to you both,

Cal

364.[2]

[Ouro Prêto, Brazil]

December 9th, or 10th, 1969

Dearest Cal:

I think our letters crossed; at least I hope you received mine,[3] and also that it wasn't too gloomy-sounding. I was so glad to hear from you again. As I may, probably, have said—this has been a very very bad stretch here. As they say about NY—I think now that Ouro Prêto is a wonderful place to visit but I wouldn't want to live there . . . at least, I don't think I do. Right now we are having the most beautiful evening, after a month of rain; the rocks are wonderful; this IS the prettiest house in the world, and the china closet has been painted. However—I wish I could fly the house, or Lota's house, like that church in Italy, miraculously to Connecticut or some such state.

This is first of all a semi-business letter. Yesterday I had a letter from Stanley Lewis of a David Lewis publishing company. He says they are publishing, this spring, a volume on you called *R.L.: A Portrait of the Artist in His Time*, and he asks me to write a preface to it—any length, and what would

---

1 EB may have sent postcards to RL during this period that have not survived.
2 Crossed with letter 363.
3 The letter does not survive.

my "fee" be, and so on.[1] He enclosed some sample pages—actually, very nice looking—and the table of contents, 27 people, I think, all ending up with the Interview (the Paris Review one, I imagine). From the list of contributors & titles it seems to be a very pro- and con-kind of book . . . some of the pieces I know already; quite a few of them. Some of the writers I dislike very much: some I like. Well—naturally before I answer Mr. Lewis I want to know what you think of this book, and if you are in favor of it; if you'd like to have me try my hand at a preface, and what kind of a preface it should be, etc . . . If you say yes, I'll go ahead—but I'll ask him to send me all the text, I think, so I can refer to it or avoid repeating it, or disagree with it, or whatever . . . If you are against the book, naturally I don't want to write for it. My only thoughts on the subject so far are that I could do a kind of personal happy-hours-with-RL kind of thing, with an anecdote or two and *some* "appreciation." But I do want to hear from you first, so will you let me know as soon as you can. (F, S & G forwarded the letter by boat-mail & it was written Oct. 28th, so Mr Lewis may have given up by now, anyway . . .) And if you'd like me to try of course I'll send it to you first, to see.

It was odd—this letter came just as I was re-reading a lot of E Wilson's collection *The Shock of Recognition* and re-admiring James on Hawthorne, etc.,[2] & wondering if I can ever finish a memoir of Marianne I've had in mind for so long. Are we all going to end our days writing memoirs and prefaces and footnotes, I wonder—& editing letters . . . I've had reports from Anny about Marianne and quite recently a letter from Louise Crane[3] giving even more details of it all, and I realize I must get in order and bring back all my letters from her (& you) . . . I have several stacks here tied up with red tape—heaven knows how they have survived the moves and the termites and the book-worms. Then Emanuel (my co-editor of the miserable anthology[4]), sent me 2 large photographs of her he had taken, in her wheelchair, in Washington Sq.—in one she seems to be holding a bagel. She looks a bit better than I would have thought, after all she has been through.

Did I tell you—I probably did—that I have named this house CASA MARIANA—had an oval enamel plaque made, blue letters on white—and nailed it high enough on the doorpost so that it hasn't been stolen or defaced yet—(we're on our fourth doorbell, I think). Well—from what Louise writes, she is getting the best of care and attention, and the Rosenbachs are

1 *Robert Lowell: A Portrait of the Artist in His Time*, ed. Michael London and Robert Boyers (1970).
2 Edmund Wilson, *The Shock of Recognition* (1943); Henry James, *Hawthorne* (1879).
3 EB's Vassar classmate and former lover.
4 *An Anthology of Twentieth-Century Brazilian Poetry*, ed. Emanuel Brasil and EB (1972).

doing well by her[1]—but heavens, it is all too sad. Thank you for your account to her and Ezra. You know, we should all be grateful to Louise C for having done so much for her—not financially, but time and effort and dealing with impossible people—sometime I'll tell you the fantastic story.

Next morning—
I was called on then by a lonely young Argentinean who is staying here on some sort of Museum-curator grant—this scarcely seems the country to study museum-running in . . . I told him about your & my trip to Boa Vista and the sexologist Russian guide, and how for that entire year—was it 1963?—every time I took someone to see the best stuff, the Amazonian pottery, there were no lights, and I complained. . . He replied: "And there *still* aren't any lights—I was there recently, too . . ." In fact there weren't any in the whole museum, so he had to leave when the sun went down . . . I asked him what he was going to do when he went back to Buenos Aires, and he said he had a job waiting for him, curator of the "Museum of Writers." I said— oh dear, lots of *fountain pens*, I suppose, and he said yes, hundreds, and pairs of eye-glasses, top hats, boots, and some MMS . . . All this conversation went on full tilt until midnight in my bad Portuguese and his that is good but with a rapid, rolling, Argentinean accent, very funny . . .

To go back to the "fantastic story"—it certainly is; and please don't believe any tales you may hear because I know the facts, and believe that Marianne is still alive only because of Anny and Louise's efforts. I also know there are some strange bits of gossip about—these awful people who want to be in at the death, I suppose . . .

Vinícius Moraes was here briefly last week—followed immediately by his fifth wife, to keep her eye on him, 6 months pregnant, and with three children of her own by an earlier marriage . . . He asked all about you and had somewhere seen some of your sonnets he admired highly. *Coitado*—he looks sick and awful and just can't stop marrying & drinking—plans to come to NY in May, but I wonder if he'll make it.

I read about the Peace March, in TIME's version, of course.[2] I can't even get TIME here any more, however—it was brought me from Belo—the town is getting more decadent every day and I don't know whether it is due

---

1 The Rosenbach Museum and Library in Philadelphia collected nearly all of Marianne Moore's manuscripts and papers.
2 The antiwar protest of November 15, in which RL participated; "Parades for Peace and Patriotism," *Time* (Nov. 21, 1969).

to the political situation, or what. I used to go to the movies almost every night, just for fun, and see really good things—foreign films, old ones, sometimes advance showings. Now S and I have been twice in 7 months—all they ever show are Italian Westerns, what they call *"Bangy-bangies."* Blood curdling, but popular with the natives. Well, the Peace March sounded rather peaceful—& it is too bad Nixon doesn't seem to pay any attention, does he? (I do manage to get the best Rio newspaper.) What is Mary working on now, I wonder? (I am re-reading yr. letter.)

Suzanne has a good idea for handling the Preface-problem, if it is not already too late—so she'll enclose a couple of notes, I think. She has been wonderful the past 2 or 3 months, *fighting* mostly. We spend the mornings doing business letters, some in Portuguese—and bullying the carpenter, plumbers, and so on—still much to be done here—and the afternoons going downtown and *really* fighting—to the "Forum," district attorney, police station, judge, back to the district attorney, the gas company, lawyers, bribes (which so far I have refused to pay but am about to break down and pay one, anyway). I have a[t] least three law-suits going as far as I remember and things in Rio, and about Lota's will, too awful to think of. My piece o[f] Ouro Prêto changes every day and gets bitterer & bitterer, I'm afraid. I am trying now—or have just begun—to sell this beautiful house and somehow or other get over 3,000 books and a few saints & favorite bits of furniture back to the USA—but where & how I'll live I can't think. I may rent the house for the summer/winter—it shd. be quite livable by then—but my mind is really made up to sell, although it may take some time—cut my losses, as they say, and get out.

Do you know of any slightly eccentric millionaire who is interested in the BAROQUE (this is the center of a whole constellation of good colonial towns, churches, etc.) or art historian, or South American historian, or *psychologist*, who might be interested . . . It's a fine house and a big walled garden safe for children, 1st built around 1690 they now think—4 or 5 bedrooms, best view in the whole town, 2 baths and there will be a servants' bath in the cellar soon—(?) fireplace and stove in the study—and a lot of really good furniture, all authentic, to go with it, if wanted. I can probably sell the antiques without much trouble, however, Brazilians now being eager for them. It all looks like just too much for me, but perhaps with S's help I'll survive and make it. We are now planning a trip to the falls of Iguacu and Buenos Aires, right after Christmas, to get away a bit, and also to buy *Dexamyl*! They have stopped manufacturing it in this country and I can't get along without it. S brought back a large supply, and it was stolen from her handbag as she slept, on the plane. Oh—I didn't mean to make you into my real estate agent, above—I am getting 2 or 3 of those, too—but one never knows who may turn up in friends' lives and the luckiest things seem to happen by chance. We do have a maid we like, pretty untrained but awfully nice—and that was luck. She'd go along with the house, I think.

I'd love to see the new sonnets and the English book shd. be most impressive . . . I have been able to do nothing but work on re-writing (and translating) the original rather bad introduction to this Brazilian anthology—ten sentences maybe, in 7 months—and most of the poems scarcely seem worth the effort—a few good ones, however it is awful to think I'll probably be regarded as some sort of authority on Brazil the rest of my life. The differences in the States are interesting however, I suppose—Lota & I built that house for years, and workmen & servants in that part of the country are miserably poor too, and not too good, but they were cheerful and honest—even *witty*. Maybe it's a difference in diet . . . I have been robbed of really thousands of $$$ worth of materials etc.—all very depressing. The "Mineiro"—well, there's even a good angry book on the subject I shall quote—and maybe some of the characteristics come from their having all been brought up to steal gold from the King of Portugal for so long . . .

Wallace Stevens I find rather comforting—and although he was probably a household tyrant, I yearn for that orderly, polished, clean, self-contained kind of existence. I wish I could write a "Goodbye to Brazil"—sort of combination of his to Key West and Auden's to Ischia . . . maybe in a year or two.[1] We seem to be having sunshine at last, so I must scrape the mildew off myself and prepare for this PM's fight with the District Attorney. I feel guilty for having let Suzanne in for all this trouble—she has picked up Portuguese amazingly fast and works awfully hard, but we are both pretty tired—A huge dark woman, with a gold chain and huge gold cross on the hugest bust ever seen, rang the doorbell at 6:30 this morning, wanting to do my laundry . . . I finally got rid of her, even without benefit of Dexamyl . . .

With much love and *saudades*, always—
Elizabeth

1 See Wallace Stevens, "Farewell to Florida" (1936) and W. H. Auden, "Good-Bye to the Mezzogiorno" (1958).

365.

Dearest Cal:

I got yr. note of the 8th yesterday[1] . . . The PO is so slow & they even manage to cheat us on the prices of stamps—so we go as infrequently as possible. Yesterday a stack of mail—including one from Bea Roethke who wants to visit (I DON'T feel up to visitors at all)—& wants to be recommended as a teacher . . . Well, I suppose she could teach "creative writing" as well as anyone can . . . Yr. day with Dickey . . . He wouldn't even speak to me the one time I met him; addressed all his remarks to Roger S[2] instead . . . Your saying that I am "loved and revered" cheers me quite a lot—I certainly am neither here, and do wonder what on earth I am doing here and wish to God we could get away FAST. But so much to be done first . . . If only ONE workman knew his job and would come when he says he's coming and then not fight about the originally agreed-on pay . . . I am getting completely paranoid I'm afraid—but it is true—the whole town seems put to fleece us, even 8-year-old banana-sellers, etc.— And our maid, I'm afraid, is not all we thought, either, in spite of our giving her new teeth for Christmas and a fortune in vitamins and shoes and so on for her & her little girl. I even have doubts about going away for a "rest" now—don't dare leave the house in her charge—God, it is a thieves' nest . . . Forgive me; it is really getting me.

S had a better idea—she has written 2 letters, to mail today, c/o of Mike di C,[3] one accepting writing the Preface and one refusing . . . Then she'll call you and mail whichever you say—that shd. make it easier for you.

It has been a totally wasted stretch—and had been for a long time before that, too. Oh, maybe some of it will seem comic, sometime, but if I had stayed in NY or SF, I think I might have worked on the Brazil book & even managed to say some nice things . . . now I've forgotten what they were! I suppose I had Lota for so long to intervene for me, in Petrópolis, at least—and I really was happy there for many years. Now I feel her country really killed her—and is capable of killing anyone who is honest and has high standards and wants to do something good . . . and my one desire is to get out. But how to LIVE? What ARE Dickey's problems, anyway . . . wife-problems (if that's it) seem insignificant compared to moving and changing one's whole life around, somehow . . . Well, the carpenter did show up this AM, but our steadiest worker fell in love (they say) and has vanished with his

1 Letter 363.
2 Roger Straus.
3 Michael di Capua.

last pay check and the drainage system half-done. We put our garbage out, as we're supposed to, and before it gets picked up, little boys throw it over the wall into my waterfall, where it hangs from the rocks and trees . . . Oh well, Johnson went around with garbage hanging from his hat, they say . . . Love to all my friends you know—and much to you from me
—Elizabeth

366.

Dearest Elizabeth:

I worry about you so and wish you'd come home. We've been going through old photos and Harriet at this moment is busy gluing them into three scrapbooks. They go from my grandmother as a bride to last summer. Among them, several of Harriet in the festal Indian suit and boots you gave her—a photograph suit/dress. It brings back so much, you.

I enclose a long poem to you. It's the old "Water" poem arranged as blank verse with some care, not to be improved but not to lose. Then the old Castine poem I could never finish, and finally an all new one.[1] I hope they roll up to something more passionate than any of the parts. You may not like it, or what it says, but I hope you will. I've been reading an ardent article making the point that youth is as mature as maturity. I wouldn't really quarrel with that—it's because our civilization gives the old so little means to grow wise. How fearful, if I am not something impressively more at fifty-three than twenty-three. Perhaps we know more about being imaginatively honest, or might. I have tried, and now send it to you with love, my laurel tribute—to be solemn.

We go to Italy for three weeks on March 18, then I go on alone to Oxford. Till mid-June! My address will be care of Warden John Sparrow, All Souls' College, Oxford. A Warden isn't a prison or mental officer, but a sort of house-master.

Do write me and come back.

All my love to you, and Suzanne.

Cal

---

1 "Three Poems for Elizabeth Bishop," which are "Water," "Flying from Bangor to Rio 1957," and "Calling" (typescript, Vassar). See "For Elizabeth Bishop 1. Water," "For Elizabeth Bishop 2. Castine, Maine," and "For Elizabeth Bishop 4" (RL-*CP*).

367.

Dearest Cal:

It was wonderful to get your letter of the 20th on the 25th—that is record time for here . . . I love the poems, of course, especially, I think, #2[1]—I suppose because it is the most personal. And the last 4 lines of #3.[2] And I am always dumbfounded by your capacity for re-doing things—you say "not to lose"—but surely it would never be lost. I think I'll try to turn that damned FISH into a sonnet, or something very short and quite different. (I seem to get requests for it every day for anthologies with titles like READING AS EXPERIENCE, or EXPERIENCE AS READING, each anthologizer insisting that he is doing something completely different from every other anthologizer . . . But I'm sure this is an old story to you.) The first sonnet has the most brilliant effects, I suppose, but I do like *The Youth's Companion*[3] (I used to take it), and the Georges.[4] It's weird—I'd actually been contemplating a poem on George V myself all last week, because I had just re-read Max Beerbohm's account of him to his wife. I'll even quote, because I think you'd like it if you haven't read it:

(It's the opening of Parliament, 1914) ". . . at the end of them, hand in hand, the King & Queen. And after they had passed I found myself with tears in my eyes and an indescribable sadness—sadness for the King—the little King with the great diamonded crown that covered his eyebrows, and with eyes that showed so tragically much of effort, of the will to please—the will to impress—the will to be all that he isn't and that his Papa *was* (or seems to have been)—the will to comport himself in the way which his wife (a head taller than he) would approve."[5]

I love the inchworm, too—except that it describes the way I feel at present only too well—and not just in respect to poetry.[6] Oh, thank you; thank

---

1 "Flying from Bangor to Rio 1957"; see "For Elizabeth Bishop 2: Castine, Maine" (RL-*CP*).

2 "Do / you still hang words in the air, ten years imperfect, / joke-lettered, glued to cardboard posters, with gaps / and empties for the unimagined word, / unerring Muse who scorns less casual friendships?"; "Calling," from lines 10–14 (typescript, Vassar). Cf. "For Elizabeth Bishop 4," lines 10–14 (RL-*CP*).

3 "A twelve-foot cedar hedge screens out the human, / teenage softball makes the Castine Common a *Youth's Companion* cover"; "Flying from Bangor to Rio 1957," lines 1–3 (typescript, Vassar). Cf. "For Elizabeth Bishop 2: Castine, Maine," lines 1–3 (RL-*CP*).

4 "~~Britain's four~~ Canada's Georges rules your horoscope; / long, long, may mad King George in cap and bells / sway over your Nova Scotia"; "Flying from Bangor to Rio 1957," from lines 7–9 (typescript, Vassar). Cf. "For Elizabeth Bishop 2: Castine, Maine," lines 7–9 (RL-*CP*).

5 David Cecil, *Max* (1964), 331.

6 "Have you ever seen an inchworm crawl on a leaf, / cling to the very end, revolve in air, / feeling for something to reach something?"; "Calling," from lines 8–10 (typescript, Vassar). The lines are unchanged in "For Elizabeth Bishop 4" (RL–*CP*).

you very much—you can really never know how much this has cheered me up and made me feel a bit like myself again.

Well, you are right to worry about me, only please DON'T!— I am pretty worried about myself. I have somehow got into the worst situation I have ever had to cope with and I can't see the way out. If I could *trust* anybody in this town, I'd close up the house and leave, or leave a maid or two in it—but that would just mean coming back again, sooner or later, and although it would be a tremendous relief to get away—I don't want to do that. I am trying to sell the house, as I think I wrote you—have had several nibbles, but nothing at all certain yet. I am trying just to get everything in working order, go through all books, papers, letters, and so on—(about 3,000 or more books here) so that I can leave if the chance comes. But it may take months or years; meanwhile it is too damned lonely and disagreeable and I have not been able to work. Just the last two weeks I've done a little, but very little—there are endless, endless interruptions, noise, confusion, thefts (you wouldn't believe how much has been stolen, a lot of it somehow right under my eyes . . .), trips to Belo Horizonte for building materials, hiring, firing, rehiring, re-firing . . . It's a terrible tale of woe. Another problem is that Suzanne likes it here and doesn't want me to sell the house—and this makes for difficulties, naturally. The saddest part of all is that I really love my house and would like to stay in it, if—if—if things were different—but the only solution seems to be to sell it and get out. The very thought of all the packing and expensive shipping makes me sick—and then, where to go? How to live? I am thinking of New York—and then Dr B. writes me she thinks San Francisco is better for me! But what does she know about it? I liked the flat there—now sub-let—but again, the living arrangements just didn't work, and if I go back there I'd have to find another place, or two other places, preferably . . . I want to live alone, dismal as it is. (But please don't refer to this when you write.) Well, all I can do is to try to get ready, and endure it here, and try to work a little while I endure, and pray to get away as soon as possible . . .

It is so long ago now I can't remember the details, but I finally heard just a few days ago, that it was too late for me to write an introduction to the collection of pieces about you. This is quite all right with me—the collection looked very peculiar, and the (new) publisher sounds very peculiar, too—but please believe I answered promptly and I just wanted to do whatever you wanted me to do in the matter—if you can follow this, or, indeed, know or remember anything about it!

I had a slightly hysterical—no, just "excited" letter from Bob yester-day—all about the N B A[1]—wanting me to telephone him, then he will tele-phone me, and so on . . . I don't think he realizes it is next to impossible to telephone from here—and I haven't a telephone, anyway—it would mean a day, or days, at the tel. co. He seems to think that you and I are the possibili-ties—but one never knows, and I see Rexroth is a judge and am pretty sure he dislikes me . . . I'm afraid my feelings about it are that I think *you* deserve it, but if *I* should get it I'd be delighted to have the money, but don't see how on earth I could make it to NY— All my winter clothes being in SF, for one thing . . . and then doesn't one have to make a *speech* . . .? And McCarthy is a judge, too! All these things have so very little to do with work, and so much with personalities.

I wonder where you are going in Italy. The trip that Lota and I made there in '64 was wonderful—the last time we did anything together when she was fairly well and like herself. We had the best time of all in Venice, and she wanted to go back there. I tried and tried after that to get her to give up that disastrous job and plan to go to stay in Venice for a long stretch . . . If only she had. I miss her more every day of my life. This is one of the reasons I want to leave Brazil. (forgive me.)

Also, I wonder what you are going to do at Oxford?— I visited All Souls in '66—I had some friends there then—and was shown all over the place, some wonderful little garret apartments. Also—they wear such fascinating gowns . . . I suppose you'll be wearing one. "John Sparrow" seems always to be turning up in reference to friends—sounds so 17th century.

Have you ever gone through caves?— I did once, in Mexico, and hated it, so I've never gone through the famous ones right near here. Finally, after hours of stumbling along, one sees daylight ahead—faint blue glimmer—and it never looked so wonderful before. That's what I feel as though I were waiting for now—just the faintest glimmer that I'm going to get out of this somehow, alive. Meanwhile—your letter has helped tremendously—like be-ing handed a lantern, or a spiked walking stick— Write when you have time—I do know how busy you are—

> With much love,
> Elizabeth

---

1 EB's *Complete Poems* (1969) and RL's *Notebook 1967–68* (1969) were nominated for the National Book Award; the judges were Eugene McCarthy, William Meredith, and Kenneth Rexroth.

I prepared a speech on Stevens, Marianne, and you[1]—to be given in Belo H—then it rained steadily for 3 weeks, and I began to wheeze so from mildew, etc. that I didn't give it after all—but still may sometime.

P.S. Having nothing of my own to send, I'll send a sonnet of Vinícius Moraes that I did for this bloody anthology . . . It is almost exactly like the Portuguese and rather funny, I think . . . Well—I might as well gossip a bit, too. And it is not just gossip—it seems like a prototype of what is happening here to everyone. Vinícius came here, or to the hotel, with a young girl, *not* his 5th, or is it 7th—yes 7th—wife. The 7th wife arrived the next day, driving all the way from Rio with her 2 children by an earlier marriage, and almost 9 months pregnant. Vinícius brought the wife to call—a strong-minded, strong-looking lady, not young—not mentioning the girl, although I'd heard about her, of course. He seemed very decadent and sick. In Rio he invited all his friends for an evening, didn't drink anything at all, and at midnight made a speech, with everyone present, ordering the pregnant wife from the house. The wife went on a rampage, smashed the apartment and almost finished off several of the friends—one man I know slightly had to have nine stitches in his forehead—police, ambulances, etc. Then poor Vinícius took himself off to his favorite clinic, for a "rest."

But most of the very few people I know—or who are speaking to me— seem equally far gone these days. I called on the psychoanalyst friend of L's and mine in Rio because I felt so sorry for him, mostly—and he, too, had gone completely to pieces. Suzanne went there alone to take him something from me and he tried to ravish her—chased her all around the office—and she finally just ran away. It's hard to believe. I think it has something to do with the ghastly political situation. A couple from Belo H, an architect & his wife, had lunch here with me and on their way home were kept at the *bareira*—by the police, that is, arrested, for four or five hours because they had a tape recorder in their car. The police played it over and over—nothing but rock and roll—luckily.

I expect Flávio and the girl he "married" last Saturday,[2] tonight—on his way to live in Brasília, poor thing. (She's been married before, so I don't know how they managed it.) I haven't seen him yet. He was on a plane that was taken to Cuba—returning from Montevideo—I read about it in the papers but didn't know he was aboard.[3] They had engine trouble, etc. and went

1 EB, "Three American Poets" (typescript, Vassar).
2 Regina Célia Colônia.
3 On January 2, 1970, five Brazilians hijacked Cruizero do Sol Flight 114 to Rio; the plane landed in Cuba on January 4.

all over the map and had to live on the plane for four days . . . I want to hear
about it from him—

[Enclosed]

SONNET OF INTIMACY

Farm afternoons, there's too much blue air.
I go out sometimes, follow the pasture track,
Chewing a blade of sticky grass, chest bare,
In threadbare pajamas of three summers back,

To the little rivulets in the river-bed
For a drink of water, cold and musical,
And if I spot in the brush a glow of red,
A raspberry, spit its blood at the corral.

The smell of cow manure is delicious.
The cattle look at me unenviously
And when there is a sudden stream and hiss

Accompanied by a look not unmalicious,
All of us, animals, unemotionally
Partake together of a pleasant piss.[1]

—Vicínius de Moraes

368.

March 5th, 1970

Dearest Cal:

I hope this reaches you before you take off for Italy . . . such excitement
here about the N B A . . .[2] It was rather nice. Many wires from Bob, all
weirdly mis-spelled by the time they got here, and then when I called him we
seemed to meet in mid-Atlantic—he was calling me, at the very same
minute. I really wanted to go to NY, but it would have been an awful rush—
barely 24 hours to get ready and get from here to Rio—no cold-weather

---

1 Published in *The New Yorker* (Nov. 27, 1971)
2 EB won the 1970 National Book Award. RL accepted it on her behalf.

clothes at all—and then, the expense, even if F, S, & G would have paid the airplane fare . . . But I would have loved seeing you and other friends. I have never attended one of those functions and can't imagine what they are like. I remember reading parts of a speech by Updike, however, and feared that a speech might be expected. I hope my cable (Bob's suggestion) reached you, served the purpose, and wasn't an awful nuisance to you. It seems to me you are always doing things for me that I should somehow be able to do for myself, and I am really profoundly grateful . . . I thought of several other cables; one was "About time"—not that I'd send it—it seemed like an occasion when one shd. be quite square . . . so I hope it was all right. My stock with the PO, telephone company, and I gather, the US Embassy here, has gone way up. How I would love to have heard the judges' conversation—Rexroth and McCarthy especially. Well, I am sure I owe it all to you and thank you, as well as for the helping hand at the announcement ceremonies, if you were able to be there. These things make such a big impression on the ignorant—like here—it is nice.

Just made a birthday cake for the maid who is 18 today—Eve. I've never known so many Adams and Eves, seem to be the favorite names here. This girl and her younger sister have really made life much more bearable; clean and quiet—now if only they'll stay a while. The mother—they are 2 of 13—comes to the door every day or so and they go through a little ritual: "Bless me, mother." "God bless you, my daughter" and so on. Strange little children in the street say it to me, and I feel rather foolish, "God bless thee, my child" . . . The weather has been absolutely heavenly—such clouds, rainbows, pink rainstorms with bright green hills showing through, churches coming and going through the rain or wrapped in pale green cocoons of mist. Oh dear—I am of 2 minds about selling . . . If only things were a bit different . . . We have had such a nice young man visiting, too—a former Peace Corps boy, from Chattanooga, old Episcopalian family, one brother a minister, etc.—went to Harvard where his mother thought he would become depraved. He bought a big old fazenda with a friend and worked it—a long story he didn't go into, but the friend committed suicide, and now this boy's legal problems are very much like mine only a great deal worse. Perhaps that has cheered me up more, too. I didn't think anyone's could be worse than mine. He hung pictures, cleaned the gramophone, sorted all the records, *knew* about electricity and plumbing—and he's coming back—I'm glad to say—because he is very much taken with Suzanne, I think. I just learned today that Rothko, too, had committed suicide. I don't know anything about him except that he came from some place along the Washington coast—

that's where he got a lot of those beautiful colors.[1] Oh why, I wonder—heavens, what a vale of tears it is.

I love the sonnets and read them over and over . . . By very indirect route,—too long to explain—I heard that you liked a poem by Marianne that I haven't even seen, in *The New Yorker!*[2] I must have them start sending my copies here instead of their piling up in SF. Much much love & *boa viagem*
   —Elizabeth

Dreamed of Elizabeth last night. She was huddled in the middle of a group of three ladies all wearing fur coats. I suppose this is because my coat (in storage in SF) was one reason I couldn't go to NY—

369.

[March 11, 1970]

Dearest Elizabeth—

You[r] letter cheered me up in a somewhat shadowed moment. But also you *sounded* so calmly high-spirited, amused, at ease and easily sure. Well, it's not that way, but this exuberance must be in you despite your affliction. You cheered me too by liking the poems to you which I feared you might not. I had always wanted you in the first NOTEBOOK, yet nothing came and I even wrote an inferior sonnet form of WATER which got as far as galleys and then I withdrew it.

Ah, the award! I like to make a cut at boldness occasionally, this I think I had to do. The rather curious jury, due to Rexroth, left Pound off the listings of poets to be considered (Meredith put him on). No one even noticed the omission, but there was great clamor about *Ada* and *Portnoy* not being listed.[3] I came from the wings to the bright stage (first twenty red plush rows absolutely empty) as "recipients" do and said more or less this: That I felt very shy receiving the award for you, that you had always been my favorite poet and favorite friend, I said it was hard on the stage to say anything of much critical worth. I spoke of your enormous powers of realistic observation and of something seldom found with observation, luminism (meaning radiance and compression etc.) And so on for a few sentences. Then I said I was going

---

1 Mark Rothko's family emigrated from Czarist Russia to Portland, Oregon, when he was a boy. He died on February 25, 1970.
2 Marianne Moore, "Enough," *The New Yorker* (Jan. 17, 1970) or "Magician's Retreat," *The New Yorker* (Feb. 21, 1970).
3 Vladimir Nabokov, *Ada, or Ardor: A Family Chronicle* (1969); Philip Roth, *Portnoy's Complaint* (1969).

to say something perhaps ungracious, but that I cared not, because I would consider myself dishonored if I didn't say it. Then I spoke of the complaints (named no names) and said that on the whole I agreed with the complainers but that a much more important author, Ezra Pound who had published a little book in June, one of his good books and quite possibly his last, had been mentioned by no one.[1] (Just before me a long communication from the author of the prize-winning Huey Long biography had been read[2]—not a word of criticism, it was like Humphrey speaking of Johnson five years ago— And before that Lillian Hellman[3] had made a "courageous" attack on Agnew.) I said you've just heard about two great statesmen; Pound was a very small stateman and a very great poet. When I read your "St. Elizabeths" poem (which in the beginning I'd said I would read one of your poems, because your cable hadn't arrived). I said it was a clear poem whose meaning was hard to determine, the tone was reverential mockery or mocking reverence. I went back to my seat on stage—decent applause. Behind me a voice saying, "I announce that I sever myself from this antisemitic fascist performance." Rexroth in sideburns, tho I didn't know it at the time. Well, the master of ceremonies, he was silly little man who made nonstop after dinner jokes. Just one was quite good: Some author was writing a novel about eight bicycle thugs. He was asked how he found his plot, and answered, by taking the plot of *The Group* and changing the sex. But he saved my life by instantly saying, I want to announce that I dissassociate myself from anyone who could say what you've just heard was anti-semitic or Fascist. There was faint applause for Rexroth and more for the master of ceremonies. And so things passed off.

On the way out, I got congratulations. Eric Erikson, an acquaintance from Harvard, said, "Why did the guy do that to you?" And I, "He's one of the poetry judges." (Rexroth had made the short citation of your award break into two about equal parts describing you and some protege of his named Whalen) Then I said (Rexroth wasn't there) "The bastard." And Erikson looked at me in red-faced amazement then repeated, "The bastard."

Now. Then two days later—I was away in Cambridge and later Provincetown—the telephone rang at 5:30 AM (unlisted number) and a voice, quite calm and clear, said this is the voice of the shofar (The Jewish ramshorn for war) Quite good music; Lizzie listened a minute or so, then expecting it to change to the usual anonymous obscenities, hung up. Next

---

1 Ezra Pound, *Drafts & Fragments of Cantos CX–CXII* (1968).
2 T. Harry Williams, *Huey Long* (1969).
3 Lillian Hellman won the National Book Award for *An Unfinished Woman: A Memoir* (1969).

morning, same hour, another call. Confusion of connections. Apparently long distance. Voice of operator, saying to Lizzie, "Do you want to speak to Mr. Levin?" Disconnection, or she hung up. In about an hour, another call; voice asking for me, something about "Tell him to make peace with his God." Lizzie "I never heard anything so impertinent and absurd. He is at peace with God." Voice, something about "last rites" then "tell him on this day he is going to die." Vain threat! It sounds buffoonish as I tell it, but that was not the effect, it seemed dignified and terrifying. No more now for five days. I assume it's over. But how lousy!

All my love to you,

Cal

PS Awful week for Lizzie and Harriet. Harriet was the cooler. "Tell them if they call again, Dad is off on his trip to Israel." Also, "What do they mean by *his* God, there's only one God." Lovely translation of Vinícius & story about him. I met a man, drunk, yesterday who said his only fault was a reprobative wife.

370.

April 8th, 1970

Dearest Cal:

Now when I should be writing you a long and beautiful and grateful letter, I am going to write, or type, a hurried and badly constructed, no doubt, note—for one thing, life is far from PEACEFUL here, the way I had rather hoped it might be—in fact it has been very awful lately, but perhaps no more awful than in other parts of the world. Then I have been sick—not much, but asthma and possibly a touch of pleurisy or something—anyway, a friend is driving to Belo today and I just learned about it, so am going along, to see the doctor there, and also think it a fine idea to mail a letter to you from *there*—the chances of your getting it are far greater, I believe. I don't even trust the PO in this place anymore—I mean, one never trusts the mail service too much, but here there are more, and somewhat unpleasant, complications . . . Well.

I think I did thank you, or was that the long letter I tore up (?), for your brave and noble services on my behalf at the N B A thing . . . I have almost decided to nominate R (K R)[1]—for a "chancellor,"[2] and give as my reason:

---

1 Kenneth Rexroth.
2 Of the Academy of American Poets.

"Coals of Fire." Did I tell you Bob sent me a copy of your speech, which I thought was charming, generous, and awfully nice all around, and really felt deeply grateful for . . . I had several accounts, including clippings, but of course yours was best . . . When I saw the list of judges I guessed what would—or what had, by then—happened and fairly accurately. I DID send a cable for you to read, however (and must get my money back in Belo H today!)— Something like Wish I could be there greetings—I've forgotten what exactly. The Assistant Cultural Attaché, the requisite young black man, was here last week—he had sent it for me from there, and he went into a long explanation about why it never got there . . . I am sorry—I did send it, and exactly as Bob had instructed me to. (or BOG, as his cables to me, some of them, came signed)

I have received a rather strange note—my one repercussion, I suppose—asking me if I ever actually did meet Pound or if I made it all up . . . I am frightfully sorry about your troubles—and I am glad now you are away for a while—I wish I were in Italy, too. Will you see Pound, I wonder—and I suppose so. Another friend wrote me yesterday, from São Paulo, saying "What an awful world we live in"—then catching herself up and saying "My God—my mother used to say that and I thought it was just because she was old—so I must be old now, too . . ." But I think it is much much more than that . . . Such hideous violence, and even in small things, and *here!*—well, I shall write you sometime, or tell you—I only wish we were safe in a gondola for a few pleasant hours . . .

I must pack an overnight bag and try to lock up this too unlockable house and try not [to] think of what will be missing when I get back—it gets to be a sort of game: what goes next? Or, how many things can you count that are missing in this room? How many beginning with A? With B?

Three weeks from March 18th—you must be just about at Oxford right now. I'll write very soon again. I do want to know what you are doing there, if ever you have time to tell me. I love my three sonnets—and you, too, of course . . .

Elizabeth

371.

May 13th, 1970

Dearest Cal:

A very short, rude note—but I do want to get something in the mail to you . . . Thank you so much for your letter of the 29th[1]—received here *then*, in 5 days—I don't know why, but mail from England comes quicker than mail from the US. It was nice of you to write me so soon. I have been having a very bad time of it here—I won't go into the sad details, but Suzanne had a very bad breakdown. I have been through this now with so many close friends, and recently, too—I certainly should have recognized the symptoms long before I did—but one never seems to. Especially someone like me, who is so soft-hearted, and gives way immediately when faced with tears, and was just naturally born guilty. I'd rather you didn't tell *anyone*, please—I am trying to tell everyone here, and most people except two or three close friends, that she is just "on her holidays." It dawned on me, like—well if dawn can be like a flash of lightning—about three months ago—but since her little boy had to go back to his father the first of this month, I held on, hoping she'd make it until then. But she didn't. I got her into a hospital in Belo Horizonte—fortunately I do have some good and very kind friends there, who helped me—(*none* here) and on the 11th she took off—the doctors thought she was well enough—for Seattle. One friend went with her and the little boy to transfer her onto the right plane in Rio, and a member of her family was going to meet her in San Francisco, to help her on the last flight. I am hoping and praying her mother will have cabled me when I get to the PO today. Poor, poor child—and I feel sorriest of all for the real child, of course, little Boogie, who is so beautiful and was so upset . . . It is all too much like my own early days—but I had loving grandparents and aunts, at least—and I'm afraid I don't think much of S's family, what little I've seen of them. Of course I feel as responsible as *hell*—but the psychiatrist thinks it would have happened anyway, sooner or later. I just hope she gets better quickly— Well, this is what has been happening here for the last months—it all seems like a bad dream, but during the past ten days or so I am waking up from it and actually feel more like myself than I have in four years or so, I think. Courage!—as Carlyle keeps saying to himself . . .

Could I ask you not to tell Elizabeth? I felt she never liked Suzanne at all—but then, I'm about the only person who really liked her and partly, I think, although now I'm not so sure, understood her.

---

1 The letter does not survive.

What are you *doing* at All Souls? Just being there? Joe Summers was there in 1966 and showed me all about—don't forget to study Shelley's magnificent coral teething-ring (only it isn't a ring) and rattle . . . Also they have a lovely postcard I wish you'd send me some more of sometime—a letter from George V, written when he was a child. I was informed that James Merrill and I bought just that card . . . And he writes me he may visit me in July—I really hope he does.

But I have a much better idea—why don't *you* come back by way of Brazil? That's what Dr. B did once—you can make something called the "triangular trio" and pay something like $5.00 more—to stop over in SA. That would be wonderful, I am quite alone here, but not minding it so far— I have a fairly good, for here, maid, and the house is so beautiful I simply can't sell it after all, I find—at least not until I am quite a bit more decrepit and feel I can't cope with the mean old *mineiros* any more—then I'll try to get a fortune for it and retire to a rest home de luxe . . .

I quite envy your being there—that lovely library, and that theatre— what is it called? Never lift the port—that's about all I know. And please don't come back with small purple veins in your beautiful nose . . . Thank you for telling me about the kindly-dispensed Mrs. Herzberg—I do need a bit of encouragement to get back to feeling I really do write once in a while, again. But I think with peace and silence and solitude it will come back— No one in this town speaks to me, except dourly on business—I am a pariah— but better no friends than that kind, I suppose. (Suzanne has left me with many problems here—many things I didn't know about at all.) 17 churches and one, no two, Christian souls that I know of—

I've been reading Carlyle's life—I have a poem about him I've had around for years and thought maybe I'd finish it—very slight.[1] What a man— And inadvertently so funny, *coitado* . . . I do like this:

"Today I am full of dyspepsia, but also of hope."

"The world gets even madder with its choppings and changings and never-ending innovations, *not* for the better. My collars, too, are all on a new principle."[2]

Since I have a cast-iron stomach and have had indigestion only two or three times in my life, I probably can't understand him very well . . . but suspect he just ate all wrong. Well—I'm about to write to Blackwells, right near you, and get Horace Walpole, whom I've never read, and, I think, the *Wa-*

---

1 See "Mr. and Mrs. Carlyle" (EB-*EAP*).
2 James Anthony Froude, *Thomas Carlyle: A History of the First Forty Years of His Life, 1795–1835* (1884 edition), 39 and 260.

verly Novels.[1] So you see I am quite out of it—except for the daily paper and its inevitable new horrors. Nixon apparently tried to do the right thing last Saturday[2]—didn't he?

I have a *firm* from Belo Horizonte re-doing all plumbing, wiring, etc.—something I should have done at the start—and they are so NICE, after the local workmen, I simply can't believe it. The electrician, named "Deusmar"—I think—that's the way it is said, and means God-love, I presume—rather like Ben Jonson, don't you think[3]—has just called me. My house is now worth its weight in gold—and I am rapidly going broke—but hope to earn some money soon. I'll tell you my new work in my next—

Courage! More courage! I flatter myself we are both awfully well-preserved, don't you think? But then when I see a snapshot of myself I wonder who that pleasant, foolish-looking old lady is . . .

With much love, Cal—are you working too?

Elizabeth

P.S. S's ambivalence toward me suddenly made me remember poor Keith's toward you—remember? Exactly the same—adoration & rudeness combined. What happened to him? I have a whole theory about this now—quite interesting, really.

372.

Ouro Prêto, June 15th, 1970

Dearest Cal:

I hope you received my postcard on which I said I was accepting the Harvard job[4]—your job, that I'm sure you are responsible for being offered to me, *my dear boy*—I hope I can do it well enough—I think I did all right at the Un. of Washington. (One of my pet boy-pupils told his friends I was "brilliant but superficial" . . .) I am really looking forward to it and have started to have a lot of ideas. I am probably not going to do this—can't do the necessary preparation here in time—but I think sometime a very good course could be given on poets and their letters—starting away back. There

---

1 By Sir Walter Scott.
2 On May 9, at dawn, President Richard Nixon spent an hour chatting with a group of students among the 60,000 people gathered for a protest near the White House.
3 "For God's love," an exclamation in Ben Jonson's plays.
4 The postcard does not survive. RL had accepted an offer to teach for two years at the University of Essex, replacing Donald Davie (who had gone to Stanford); he arranged for Harvard to hire EB in his absence.

are so many good ones—Pope, Byron, Keats of course, Hopkins, Crane, Stevens, Marianne. Oh dear, don't mention it or someone will make an anthology immediately—perhaps he has already—(I swear they get out a poetry anthology every day of the week, from the permission requests I get, & you probably get many more.)

Please tell me what you think of this . . .[1] I haven't sent you a poem for many years, if ever, and I am curious—I can't tell myself, at this point. (That is, if you have time.)

I am having a lovely time just being lonely—perhaps it is the way I should live, anyway. I am so damned cheerful all the time I can't believe it— I have told my 18 year-old maid that she shouldn't be frightened when I laugh to myself (at my own witticisms) and talk out loud—it is my way of "working." I play her the Beatles and Janis Joplin and Sambas all day long and we both go about this large house dancing—it is very nice—and the house is so beautiful I can't dream any more of selling it. You must see it some day—even if you are not domestic, like me. I have you—in a beautiful youthful version—and Marianne, also twenty years younger, and the Emperor, Dom Pedro II—old and resigned, a real Nadar photograph, taken after abdication, I think—on my wall. I also have a "cannon-ball" stove, I brought two—the other's a Franklin, for the *sala*,—burning away, and I just realized last night as the lights failed in the kitchen and I fried myself an egg by the light of the oil lamp, that probably what I am really up to is re-creating a sort of de luxe Nova Scotia all over again, in Brazil. And now I'm my own grandmother.[2]

Someone sent me a little book about you—one of those Telling-what-to-think books, by a Jay Martin.[3] I haven't read it all very carefully yet, but shall—strange terms however—why does he say the *Imitations* have a "*Jamesian* boldness"? And I love phrases like this "Troy, of course, merely represents . . ." Troy and mere are wonderful . . . I have been thinking however, that perhaps all poetry writing will tend more and more, will *have* to, towards things like your *Imitations*. (This is inspired partly by seeing a few of my own poems in Danish and Italian—but especially Danish. They do look guttural.) Oh—he also mentions all the people you dedicated *Imitations* to, *except* me; must be a woman-hater.

I have just learned yesterday what I should have known all along—and I'd begun to have some suspicions—that poor dear Suzanne has a long, long

1 "In the Waiting Room" (EB-*CP*).
2 See "Sestina" (EB-*CP*).
3 Jay Martin, *Robert Lowell* (1970).

history of these breakdowns . . . I don't know whether I wish I had known or not—I think it is better I didn't, because I might have given up long ago and now I haven't even given up yet. I lost my mother, and Lota, and others, too—I'd like to try to save somebody, for a change.

Those lines of yours, Cal darling—"After loving you so much"[1]—etc.— I sometimes wish you hadn't written them or I hadn't read them. They say *everything*, and they say everything I wish I could somehow say about Lota, but probably never shall. I am trying to do a small book of poems for her, or about her—but it is still too painful. Well, I didn't mean to end on this note—so I'll write two—or 200—more sentences on this page . . . Elizabeth said you were going to teach in Sussex, not Essex, I think—and maybe for three years? I'd love to get back to London sometime—maybe I'll be able to make it during that time. However, maybe not. I am going to try, I think— although I am always a week behind and don't know, & dread to know, what is happening to Suzanne in Seattle now—to have her with me part of the time in Boston. Do you know of any good doctors there? She is very hard to please. It was worst for the little boy. I am asking her to give up her child for a year and I'll promise to take care of her there—but I don't know if she'll accept, or if by now she has been hospitalized—as she should have been immediately on her return, except that her mother apparently is an utter fool. Boston still seems like home to me in a funny way, and I'd feel safer with her nearby, at least, where I can know what's going on—ironically enough, I even wish I had now kept her here, in Belo Horizonte—Brazil of all places— She would have been better off, poor crazy girl.

I must buy some miniature blue jeans for my little beggar. I have many who make their rounds, but Adão (Adam) is the saddest, and most appealing, wretched, *tiny* child. He says he's ten, but looks six. He has no mother and lives alone with a father whose profession is driving other people's donkeys. I make him come in and sit down and eat, otherwise his camp-followers, bigger boys, take everything from him. Last night he arrived—it was very cold and I had a fire in the Franklin Stove—he'd never seen anything like it of course. Asked if it was meant to give heat. I had bought a zipper wool jacket for him and got him out of a layer of filthy cotton shirts, not a single button, and into it. He kept asking me if he could keep it, and holding tightly on to the sleeves in case I changed my mind. Then I decided I couldn't stand the dirt any longer and took him into my bathroom and scrubbed his hands and

1 "After loving you so much, can I forget / you for eternity, and have no other choice?"; "Obit," lines 13–14 (RL-*CP*).

face and EARS—my lord, I have never seen such grime come off such tiny surfaces—and combed his hair. (He is too Picasso-Blue-Period for anything—bangs, and wistfulness) The comb and wash-cloth are now soaking in detergent. Then he *ordered* me to buy him some blue jeans like the ones I had on. So I told him if he came back Wednesday I'd have some new pants for him, but first he was going to have to take a bath in that tub, & I showed him how it worked. He paled— He was clean enough so you couldn't see it by then—but said he'd come back. He also says he's in the second grade but doesn't seem to know the days of the week. Then I had—well I won't go on, because I might as well write a chapter about beggars for my "book." This town is ghastly, really—no agencies at all, or just one free clinic—and so many beggars, town idiots, "characters"—like the one I sent you the card of—she is our prize product in that line.[1] Even speaks French, and was in *Life*-y, as she says. When you give them anything they make a set speech about God aiding you, and so on—I always said thank-you, but my maid tells me the correct thing to say is *Amen*—*Amem*, here. I find this difficult, but try.

Well, this is a far cry from Oxford and the Welfare State. I'd love to know what you are teaching—or are you? I know you are extremely popular in England and hope you are having a good time and it is probably a relief to get away from the USA—maybe the universities there won't even open.

With much love, and gratefulness always,
Elizabeth

P.S. I have a little oval enameled plaque I had made, high up on the front-door post, that says CASA MARIANA on it, blue letters on white. (I told you I named the house for Marianne, didn't I? As it is on the road to Mariana, the next small town, it works very well.) A painter friend came to call and asked me about it. He thought it meant that I was one of those "Daughters of Maria"—some awful Catholic Women's organization . . .

1 The image does not survive.

FIVE

1970-1977

1970-1977

373.

33 Pont St.
London [S.W. 1]
September 11, 1970

Dearest Elizabeth:

I am living in a silly Back Bay part of London, there are many, near the Cadogan Hotel where Wilde was arrested, leading a silly but not unhappy life. I expect to get back for a couple of weeks at Christmas and trust I'll have much time to see you.

I meant to answer your last radiant letter, the gladdest I think you've ever written me, but I lost my address book, with every address in the world. Have you been getting letters in Ouro Prêto from some brassy and intrusive unknown? It isn't me. I hope your good spell has held. I was almost in the same mood. Now I am not, but in a very good one. Lizzie and I have more or less separated, though as good-naturedly as such things can be. I have someone else. And [the] future looks cheerful, but who at our age can ever tell? I still feel I can reach up and touch the ceiling of one's end. Yet I have nothing more serious than a tooth to be capped. I sometimes think our age is as full of unknowns as seventeen. We really couldn't see at all clearly then.

You'll find drawbacks and deadwood at Harvard, but I think you'll find the work light and exciting, and from time to time make permanent student friends. I'm glad they are new and not all the age of Jason Epstein. I have many friends; one I'll recommend, Frank Bidart, American Basque, and who knows my poems much better than I do—a great help in corrections and proof-reading.

Love, I wish you were with me, or I with you, and assume we soon will be.

All my love,
Cal

374.

Dearest Elizabeth:

Didn't I write about your beautiful poem?[1] It's the nearest thing you've written to a short story in verse—an *I*, you or not you, telling a naturalistic narrative, more heightened than prose fiction would accept, very personal, the way a short story can sometimes be, without too much stress, because you always, till well on in waiting, seem to be just quietly talking.[2] One of your poems that most stays with me. My dentist, I feel!

I've written thirty more poems in the meter of *Notebook*, but somehow unlike *Notebook* in tone—more strained, the Romantic romance of a married man in a hospital. Mostly I'm not very very forthright. A few may be good, but I am disheartened by the whole, and keep trying to comb out the unnecessarily grand obscurities I somehow began with.

Like you I depended on Bill[3] for everything all my years at Harvard. Once I was a year behind on my health certificate. Perhaps much more, I depended on him for companionship. I could always drop in and have drinks or a dinner or meet students. Often they, not I, came to his house at four in the afternoon and left at four in the morning. Give him my love; today I am going to Essex to teach for the first time and dreading the undefined errors I am bound to make without Bill. Give him my love.

By now you will probably have fifty poet-appliers, manuscripts double at first meeting. I tried to cut them down to 12 but usually couldn't. Then I made the mistake of letting in auditors, usually wives of physics professors, who wrote better often than most of the students in worn styles that couldn't be digest[ed] by the students. Other classes were comfortably small but insultingly so. I had three for the Bible. Some were too large to talk, others too small. Yet the students mostly in the end were ideal, or at least in class they were. I don't think you'll have troubles. I almost always left a class happy.

Natasha Spender speaking of her husband teaching English students for the first time, says he is like a boy going off from home to school for the first time.

My "someone" is Caroline Citkowitz.[4] She is 39, has published stories in the London Magazine, has three very pretty daughters, eldest ten, and was once years ago married to Freud's grandson, Lucian. You might have met;

1 EB's reply to letter 373 does not survive.
2 See "In the Waiting Room" (EB-*CP*).
3 William Alfred.
4 Caroline Blackwood, married at the time to Israel Citkowitz.

Caroline lived some time in San Francisco and later in New York, but you haven't or she would remember. However she reads you with great admiration and thinks you much brighter than Mary whom she knows. What a bare list, but how can I make the introduction? She is very beautiful and saw me through the chaffs and embarrassments of my sickness with wonderful kindness. I suppose I shouldn't forget Harriet and Lizzie, anyway I can't. Guilt clouds the morning, and though things are not embattled, nothing is settled. I'll be back in New York for Christmas, then there will perhaps be more decision. I could be happy either way, if things could be settled. But nothing is. I am happy to be in presentable spirits.

This is somewhat in the mood of waiting [to] take a train to my new work later this afternoon. If only life could be as manageable as teaching. Didn't Faust say this? England, I speak from the wisdom of a six months stay, is wonderfully unstirred after New York.

All my love,
Cal

375.

Kirkland House I 27, Harvard University
Cambridge, Massachusetts 02138
Sunday, October
Now it's Tuesday, October 20th, 1970

Dearest Cal:

I do hope you are liking Essex . . . I can't quite imagine what it is like. Some say it is "swinging"; some say like Columbia . . . Anyway, fairly new, "red-brick," and big. What are you teaching there, I wonder? Do you commute from Pont Street, etc.—do you have a "furnished flat"— Well, I do, here—sort of— With Bill's help and pushing, I think, I was offered a small apartment here and since it is cheap, convenient, and I don't have time to look for anything better, and it is for such a short time, anyway, I accepted it. One bedroom has been made into a small kitchen; living-room—(with large leather Club-style sofa) small bedroom—tiny bathroom—joining my neighbor's bathroom. All doors say EXIT in big red letters. Bill came to call and said "These places don't look so bad with boys in them but they look AWFUL with a woman in them . . ." Every time I go out, the nice secretary,[1] janitors, and maid here, bring in a new article of furnishings for me—usually

1 Alice Methfessel.

making things worse—MORE battered tables, standing lamps, dish-drainers, blue and green sheets (this must be because of someone thought them Tropical . . .) I turn the heat off & on & off, open and close the windows, go to Woolworths for more hangers, and so on— However, having a beautiful place to live in in another part of the world, I don't really care much about here. The quadrangle is full of oak trees which do not get beautiful in October—they are shedding old inner-soles at a great rate. They (master & wife) asked if I'd mind "eating with the boys" once in a while and I said not at all. The boys are mixed with girls and even babies. But one eats from a large plastic disk, divided into segments—ghastly food—quite unlike All Souls—I've done it *3* times. A nice boy I think you know is down the hall, Bill Byrom. He has a rented Burne-Jones lady over his bed . . .[1] I think I'll go call on Miss Mongan and see if I can rent something for the duration. My other neighbor—our bathrooms might as well be one—is a big black boy, finishing law school and teaching a course in Freshman English. He doesn't know beans, poor boy—so I seem to be teaching him Freshman English, too. He began with LeRoi Jones and then came to consult me about "Prufrock" . . . His whole suite is taken up with stereophonic equipment and a huge collection of records. We got acquainted when I asked him to play me a few Brazilian *discos* I had with me.

I have been rather sociable, to start with, and hope I can soon stop . . . Two very trying cocktail parties—cornered by Howard Mumford Jones (?) etc. . . . The house master & his wife—the Smithies (like baby-talk) are English—they met as *students* in Michigan and have lived in the USA all this time but sound straight from Kensington, and their son even more so—and poor Mrs. S seems nothing but a disembodied English accent by now . . . *coitada*. AND the dogs, with names like "Molesworth" and "Apollo" . . . And the Bostonian old ladies who want to come to class . . . And the poor girl named Rizza, whom I *left out* (you had her *in*, twice, she told me) & she came with her dear friend Mr. Atlas (who talks steadily) and they sat on the leather club sofa while he talked for her & she looked tragic, so of course I put her *in* right away . . . (But have only *12*) & she and Mr. Atlas praise each other until I have to interrupt. And the sex-maniac girl who only admires Mrs. *Sex*ton and outdoes her—and, I think just for more "authenticity," just got married as well . . . They mostly say you're their favorite poet—but DESPISE rhyme, of course—and it turns out they have read only LIFE STUDIES, most of them . . . Oh dear. I think I chose badly. I don't know. They are

---

1 Harvard students are allowed to rent prints from the university's Fogg Museum of Art.

DULL. Their poems are competent, and so DULL. I think I'll issue dexedrine, or pot . . . No—one nice boy who delighted me by saying "I'm just so surprised to be here at all!"—the rest think it less than their due . . . Oh—Pound's grandson, de Rachewiltz—now called Walter. He was Siegfried when I met him before. He is translating an Italian poet—and very well, I think . . . He lends a worldly touch to things—
    I just hope I am doing ALL RIGHT—I can't tell . . .
    I've been re-reading Randall—& see how he *loved* to teach.— I love some students, that's all. (And you, of course)
        Elizabeth

I said I'd read for the *Advocate*. And the CHOATE Club has asked me to dinner—the guest is supposed to talk first, then talk in general—they spoke of their fine food and wines and *armchairs* . . . Diana Trilling talked to them about "Easy Rider"[1] and they "were rough"—so Pearl Kazin Bell told me (D Bell[2] is now here)—so I don't know what to do. Did you do this? Spent five hideous days in San Francisco, packing and storing—but it is over now. My next trip is to Nova Scotia to see my aunt—that is fairly easy. Maybe Baltimore this week, to see Jane Dewey, who is very old & sick and moving to Florida for good. Then I hope to get to New York, finally—also start my dentistry here . . . Well, it is a very useful stretch, if only I felt I was teaching anybody anything! Yes—I had fifty or so MMS to read . . . I just put the list of 11 on the board and RAN, and didn't see anyone for five days. But now I wish I'd taken some of the wilder ones, bad as they were . . .
    I am sorry this is so self-centered. Maybe I'll write another form full, all about you. I do hope you are happy—I am glad the lady is beautiful; that really cheers one a lot. "Brighter than Mary"—surely no one is!—(you said she thought I was.) I feel very simple-minded these days, and can't seem to understand the most elementary red-tape business here, so just sign everything, pay everything, and hope for the best. The east *is* different— The northwest—well, the students were more ignorant, and I even gave them lessons in manners once in awhile—but they were much livelier. It must be the schooling—here they act a bit subdued. I suppose I was the same at that age. (Bill said I'd now be a "drop-out," and I take this as a compliment.) One explosion so far.// A HUGE anthology just came for me—compliments of the anthologizer, of whom I've never heard: SISTERHOOD IS POWER-

1 *Easy Rider*, dir. Dennis Hopper (1969).
2 Daniel Bell.

FUL.[1] ("Women's Lib"). Oh dear. A list of "Resistances to Consciousness": *Thinking that individual solutions are possible*. I suppose that's me. It is all so right—& yet I have always felt it beneath me to complain. (Like the aristocrats beheaded because they wouldn't kick and scream.) Finding things funny is a great handicap for the Higher Life, I'm afraid. // I must read Wallace Stevens some more—I think I can talk for 2 hrs about "The Emperor of Ice Cream," alone[2]—that shd impress them.

[Indicating stains on the aérogramme]
Brazilian coffee—you'd hate it; you like WEAK coffee . . .

376.

33 Pont St., London
November 7, 1970

Dearest Elizabeth:

You're cheerfully grumpy about Harvard. You should see Essex. Queues for the only cafeterias, often no sitting space, long tan, narrow, uniform corridors, only manageable by eccentric numbers that go up to six figures—my room 603,113. It was built in the late thirties, the time of some sensational failure in architectural design, all asbestos-white without a red brick in sight. My students, minute classes, small to the point of insult, are polite and inaudible. They would make yours seem like roughs from Seattle. Still, I like it at [that], wake up to thank myself for being in England.

I know Atlas and Rizza; Miss Rizza wrote quite sensitive, low-keyed poems for me, then met Robert Bly and wrote a flaming, eloquent lead-article in the *Crimson*, rather decently denouncing me. I lacked a feeling for large spaces—like your eastern seaboard students.[3] I think your students will brighten up, at least you will find two or three people you like to talk to—maybe out of class. I found my best were elder and not even enrolled often.

I think Lizzie and I may come back together. It's impossible to give up my child and one I've loved most my life, in my life that gave me most habits and limits. Now that I am far away and detached here, they all come back, a

1 *Sisterhood Is Powerful*, ed. Robin Morgan (1970).
2 Wallace Stevens, "The Emperor of Ice Cream" (1922).
3 "In the tradition that extends from Eliot to Lowell and those between, most poets write of themselves, in a style which Bly calls the reporting of 'news of the human mind.' Involved, ego-centered, almost embarrassingly self-aware, many contemporary poets seem to live to reveal, to confess. Again the style is very, very *good*. But . . . like the Lincoln Continental, these revelations-of-mind are a polished but exhausted perfection"; "Poetry for Galway Kinnell: Confessions, a Blessing," *The Harvard Crimson* (Dec. 1, 1969). See also Robert Bly, "A Wrong Turning in American Poetry," *Choice* (1963).

creature of habit, as if my body were only spine and ribwork. Still, I can't think of America without shuddering. Have I grown allergic?

My book is just out with good reviews from Alvarez and Connolly, particularly from Alvarez.[1] Too good maybe. I'LL see you I hope when I come back in December, around the 14th through Christmas, a trial trip.

All my love,

Cal

377.

33 Pont St., London
[Dec. 1970]

Dearest Elizabeth—

I fear I may owe you an apology for versing one of your letters into my poems on you in *Notebook*.[2] When Lamb blew up at Coleridge for calling him "Frolicsome Lamb," Coleridge said it was necessary for the balance of his composition. I won't say that, but what could be as real as your own words, and then there's only a picture that does you honor. Still, too intimate maybe, and if so I humbly ask pardon.

The other night, part of a weekend alone, I was in a Knightsbridge Portuguese restaurant *Offado*, more people worked on the tables, half in the kitchen, etc. than there were guests; even the guitarist and singer helped, then sang things like "Girls from Majorca," while I ate and consumed a carafe of rosé, their table wine.[3] After a while I expected you to come in the door any moment, even began nervously looking at my watch. So much I wanted to see you.

So much I do. I'll be in New York staying with Blair Clark about the time you get this. I think Lizzie and I are going to break. I should have done it much more cleanly some time ago. But I can't. I wonder if anyone in his right mind could. I am back to see Lizzie and Harriet, things are not even now quite settled, but they must be.

I must see you. I can easily come to Cambridge, or it could be New York if you'd like—you must be ripe to leave Cambridge by now, but I'd rather like to see Harvard. Give my love to Bill. All my love to you,

Cal

1 The Faber edition of *Notebook* (1970), revised and expanded from *Notebook 1967–68*. A. Alvarez, "A Change in the Weather," *The Observer* (Nov. 8, 1970); Cyril Connolly, "The Private and the Public," *Sunday Times* (Nov. 8, 1970).
2 Cf. "For Elizabeth Bishop 3. Letter with Poems for a Letter with Poems" (RL-*CP*) and letter 367.
3 See "Winter and London: At *Offado's*" (RL-*CP*).

378.

Belo Horizonte, May 3rd, 1971

Dearest Cal:

As well as being months late, this is an awful way to write you—but I can't seem to find your address—if it is still Pont Street—anywhere in my house in Ouro Prêto—plenty of letters, mostly in the bank vault here now—but no street number . . . But we have been out of touch entirely too long and so I am going to send you some sort of message today, even if inadequate . . . After you went back to England that mail strike began and went on I don't know how long—I didn't know when it was over, in OP, until I started getting a letter or two from England. Since then of course I have had you on my mind all the time . . . I felt so distressed about you in New York; I do hope things are all right with you.

I haven't been too well—several attacks of some sort of intestinal infection—the kind of thing I thought I was immune to here years ago—so I finally came over to Belo H a few days ago to see the doctor, have some tests made, and so on. I'm seeing him again today to hear the outcome of it all—but I'm afraid I am always a bit skeptical about Brazilian tests—maybe just because I know dear Anny is. Anyway, a diet of boiled rice and soda crackers has not been very good for the morale or the physique—I feel like a rag, as they say—an OLD rag—

I'm supposed to leave for Athens on the 12th—if I can make it—to visit Jimmy Merrill for 2 weeks, and then back to Rotterdam for some sort of poetry conference the 1st week in June.[1] I wonder if you'll be at it? I'm really going to see that new museum there,[2] I think—and maybe not going at all, since I can't seem to get any information out of them—maybe the whole thing's been called off, as far as I know! It would be wonderful if you were to be there, too. Or I might take a day or two in London—I'll try to let you know, somehow.— Jim had seen Mary and Hannah A in Paris, I gather from his last note—I don't think I'll get there, however.

I have started in trying to sell the house all over again. I've been miserable in that town this time—hate it, as a matter of fact—and realize I'll never be able to work there—constant interruptions, life just too difficult, no company, no telephone in sight, etc. etc.— I love the house,—but oh dear—and WHAT to do with 3,000 books? I hope to get a LOT of money for it—it is very beautiful now—and I'd sell most of the antique furniture along with it.

How are the sonnets going? Well—I think I have written *one* . . . I have

1 Poetry International Festival.
2 Museum Boijmans Van Beuningen.

to go out and get my hair cut and see the Dr. and KLM—and so on—and all I really want to do is *lie down*—but someone wrote "cabelude" (hairy—or long-hair—or "hippy") on my house instead of the usual dirty word the other day, so a hair cut must be necessary . . . Please, please do let me hear from you—I'll *probably* be, after the 12th—c/o Jimmy M, Athinaion Efivon 44, Athens—until June 1st. I'll try to let you know my whereabouts somehow. I would give anything to see you. I have a flat or two for next fall in Cambridge—have been doing some work on my "Letters" idea[1]—but not much of anything, really. However—things must soon get better— But I realize my Brazilian world has really come to an end and I must get out of it fast. It took me a long time to react, as usual. Heavens, but I hope you are well and everything is all right with you—

Much love always,
Elizabeth

379.

São Lucas Hospital, Belo Horizonte
May 6, 1971

POSTSCRIPT.

Well—it turned out that I have typhoid fever—like an idiot. I usually get the shots every 2 years, as a foreigner is supposed to, but think I must have skipped from 1967 . . . And I always feel immune, by now, to all these things. I've been here three days—a very good hospital—and am already feeling quite a lot better. I'll probably be going back to Ouro Prêto in a few days—so—when you get this—write me there. OR—if the poetry affair in Rotterdam does take place—never a word yet, that's the first week in June, and then I might visit Jimmy after it. But it all seems a bit up in the air.

It's only the 2nd stage of typhoid—not very bad—and mostly I just feel tired, but I've been feeling that way for some time already and think it's all just psychological . . .

This place is run by an order of nuns—Germans mostly—missionaries—Order of the Holy Spirit, I think. The ones who have called on me are all very old, and adorable—Sister Nicodema—she has relatives in Minnesota—she calls it a "district" of the USA . . . Ambrosina—oh they all have lovely names.

---

1 EB taught a seminar on "Readings in Personal Correspondence, Famous and Infamous, from the 16th to 20th centuries" in the fall 1971 term at Harvard (see EB-*OA*, viii and 548).

This is just to say please don't write to me in Athens, but please do write to me, and tell me how you are getting along and what your plans are. Do you hear from Bill? I felt towards the end of my stay he was cross with me—I really don't know why—and maybe I am imagining it; I know how overworked the dear man is all the time.

This is all for now, Cal—a friend is waiting to take my letters to the Post Office. Please do let me hear from you—I don't like this long silence. Oh—my little black maid, Vitoria, looks at your picture (20 years old at least, lots of curls, very romantic) on my study wall and insists you are a movie actor she's seen . . .

With love always,
E.

380.

80 Redcliffe Square
London
June 11, 1971

Dearest Elizabeth:

I had no letter and had lost your Brazilian address and was waiting to hear from you to reply. Very sad not to be in touch. I was very much hoping you'd come here and meet Caroline, and also look about London which I think might well suit you—full of coolness, slack and little violence. I'm sure some grant or job could be found once you got here. You mightn't stay for ever, but you could rest. You have many attractive bright admirers. Then we hoped you might stay with us in Kent.

The child will be born in October. We have three little girls, the oldest ten, and this strangely makes the arrival of another (Lowell Guinness) much less disturbing. We have to fix up a new room and employ a baby-nurse, but other things will remain much the same, tho Caroline will want to stay close and feed the baby for the first few months. All's easier though; I feel less disconsolate at losing, at partly losing Harriet. And the divorce seems less willful. Things are pleasanter between Lizzie and me than they have been, and humorous touching cards come from Harriet.

My book[1] is about 120 sonnets; all about the last year, so personal, tho never malicious or slanderous, I think, that I am only bringing out a hundred

---

1 *The Dolphin* (RL-*CP*).

copies in a little press run by Ted Hughes' sister.[1] Probably next spring. When I have a clean copy, I'll mail it to you, waiting breathless for your opinion.

I'm so sorry about your triple illness, and thank God to be writing you after it's past. You sound unscarred. The Galapagos sound terrific, but I wish it were England.[2] In early July I am going on to Edinburgh and the Orkneys for five days, then later on, Caroline and I may go to Moscow to see Madame Mandelstam who has begged me to come "before it's too late—life is not imagination."

This has been a rough, confusing year for me but for some months now, the happiest. All my love.

    Cal

381.

[60 Brattle Street, Cambridge]

Sunday, September 5th, 1971

Dearest Cal: Just back from an afternoon at the beach at Rockport—temp. about 95—& the last time I went swimming was 3 Sundays ago, in the Pacific, in the Galapagos Islands . . . (On the equator, but nice & cool.) I'm sorry that I couldn't write to you before. Bill has given me yr. country address[3] & now I shall. Alice and I are about to take him to the airport—with some dinner first. I am glad he is getting away & to Ireland. I do hope you're well—he showed me your last letter & you sounded fine. My new apt. is almost painted, and as soon as some furniture arrives from San Francisco, I'll move in. It is 60 Brattle St., apt 205, Cambridge 02138 . . . very near everything—beside the Loeb Theatre—too low down, but a lucky find, anyway. I went traveling with Alice all of August—Quito, the Galapagos (marvelous), Lima, Machu Picchu—the next best—etc.—then back to Ouro Prêto for a few days, then here— Do you know of any eccentric English who would like to rent my OP house? Big & beautiful—$300 a month . . . Please write; I'll write too—

    Much much love—

    Elizabeth

1 Olwyn Hughes's Rainbow Press.

2 There is possibly a missing letter from EB to RL. EB's illness prevented her from making the trip to Athens and Rotterdam. When she arrived in New York, a specialist in tropical diseases recommended by Dr. Baumann diagnosed her not with typhoid but with multiple dysenteries. When she recovered, EB went to the Galápagos Islands, via Ecuador and Peru. (Alice Methfessel joined her in Quito for the journey.)

3 Milgate Park, near Maidstone, Kent.

382.

October 14th, 1971
(I took the new TV to Bill's Sat. night & a small group watched *Hogan's Goat*[1]— My, it is melodramatic—all that violence, coming from Bill—there wasn't a dry eye, at the end—)

Dearest Cal:

Your letter[2] just came, and I'm going to write to you IR-regardless . . . Of 50 or so waiting letters, one class waiting for its reading-list, my apartment waiting to be furnished, and my fall wardrobe waiting to be bought . . . Of course Bill called me up when he got your cable[3] and we were both very relieved that all went well and I think it is nice it is a little boy, too—the possibilities were limited, of course, but a change is interesting . . . Since Bill got back I've really only seen him with other people and we have talked very little about his visit to you—except that he described the *threshold* of the house carefully (it sounds like a beautiful house), loved the little girls, and said Caroline was "like a queen." It must be wonderful living in Kent. Almost my only experience in Kent, I think, was my Green Line Bus trip to see Darwin's house at Down—a hot summer day (for England) and they were haying all around Darwin's house and it was lovely. Can you get to Sussex from there or are you moving back to London? (No map on hand to consult . . .) Well—it is odd I got your letter today—yesterday on my way home I went shopping for a present for Robert Sheridan—you shd. get it soon— The Eng. Dept. took 3 or 4 days to forward yr letter to me, so use my new address, above.

It is Centrally Located, as you can see—between the Window Shop (where Frank Bidart likes to go to eat sweets) and the Loeb Theatre . . . Too low down but otherwise fine—quite spacious, and a Kirkland boy painted it all white to brighten it a bit—a terrible painter, but it looks better—and with my first salary check I bought a color TV—imagine—because I am determined to keep everything bright & CHEERFUL and color TV is more cheerful than the other kind, at least . . . I can walk to everything, and spend a great deal of money, within five minutes. The classes—so far so good, I think. The poetry class much more advanced than last year—almost too much so—many have *published* poems & tend to "know what they want to

---

1 *Hogan's Goat*, dir. Glenn Jordan (1971), broadcast on PBS.
2 The letter does not survive.
3 Robert Sheridan Lowell was born on September 28, 1971.

do" only too well— However, everyone very amenable so far. The other— well, my problems with a "reserve table" are beyond belief—but I suppose I'll solve this puzzle of red tape some time . . . It is nice autumn weather—the ivy turns bright colors but the trees just an unpleasant yellow. On the library steps I realized the whole place smelt exactly like a cold, opened, and slightly rotten watermelon—

Allen Tate was here to give a reading yesterday—I went, early enough, but the hall was crowded, and fearfully hot. Bill got me a chair, in the aisle (one of the charms of being so ancient and having white hair),—but even so I left when Allen took a break. He read his own poems—almost inaudibly. Then I went to the Fitzgeralds' for dinner—he stayed with them.[1] He is so old & frail—like a little hydrocephalic blond child, out of Poe—he made me feel positively motherly. He put his arms around me and kissed me—after dinner—and whispered in my ear "Sweetie, I'm so drunk . . ." (but didn't seem especially so). It was a kind of grown-up academic dinner—although Bill & Sally F are younger, I still feel I don't belong in such gatherings and haven't anything much to say . . . But I like the Fitzgeralds—Ben F is in one of my classes. Allen talks about "my little 4-year-old boy . . ."[2] and what he said—it is very touching / something wrong with this maCHINE—no the ribbon—oh dear—

Next week—no, the 28th—I go to Vassar—there's a week of Culture going on—Mary is running a "panel" on the artist as critic of society, or something—with *Muriel Rukeyser* . . . I am sorry to miss this, but can't get away for the 1st 2 days of it. I'm going to read. I haven't been there since I graduated. I'm hoping it will be fun to see Mary—

When I woke up this morning I was dreaming I was back in the Galápagos—and that's really where I'd like to be, I think—not for a very long time, but for longer than we were up there. It and the Amazon are the best things I've ever done, I think . . . Bill hates nature, I find—in fact no one much is interested in this trip—so this weekend Alice (the friend I went with) & I are going to look at our slides all over again—private showing. Did you know Bill is thinking of buying a house in Ireland? I think he'd be too lonely—but better than Ouro Prêto, I suppose. My house is un-rented and un-sold—and an awful problem. Well, I can't go on with this ribbon, obviously.

I'd like to see your new poems. What I'd like to do is stay on here after

---

1 Robert and Sally Fitzgerald.
2 John Allen Tate; Allen Tate and his third wife, Helen Heinz, had twin sons in 1967, John Allen and Michael Paul, who was drowned in an accident as an infant. See "To Allen Tate 3. Michael Tate, August 1967–July 1968" (RL-*CP*).

this semester to work for a few months—but I may choose to go back to Ouro Prêto. Brazil is very unpleasant now—growing worse—& I had some unpleasant experiences with the *Living Theatre*[1]—if you saw anything of their Ouro Prêto escapades in the newspapers? I want to WORK—probably for the 1st time in 4 years—but don't know when I'll be able to. *I'd love to see you.* Do you take snapshots of R.S.? Please do.

    With much love always,
      Elizabeth

383.

HEALTH TO YOU AND MY BEST LOVE DEAR[2]

CAL

384.

Milgate Park
December 8, 1971

Dear Elizabeth:

    Poor dear, I should have written long ago, but didn't quite know where you were. Your last letter before the asthma attack sounded ecstatically happy and healthy in a nice grumble of tartness. It's terrible we must stand on our bodies, so much more well-stored than we are, able in minutes to knock us off our feet. I gather from Bill and Bidart, you are finishing with hospital, and had very cruel treatment in the Peter Bent. There must be more irresponsibility and torture in hospitals than jails. Our local one is kind enough, nice nurses called Sisters, though entirely secular—and no doctors. When Caroline was in with labor pains and the child feet-first, the doctor didn't see her for twenty-four hours.

    I wrote Bill about our servant-trouble, and so won't bore you with it at length—our inexpendable young man (drove, cooked, cleaned, fixed, etc.) went mad, and after he was fired eloped with our old very young nurse. We had no one, (two little girls, baby at breast, remote large house, and images

1 EB allowed the cast of the Living Theatre to stay in her house during their tour of Brazil in 1971. They were arrested and jailed in Belo Horizonte. Because EB had hosted them, she was regarded with suspicion locally.
2 Telegram sent to Peter Bent Brigham Hospital in Boston, where EB was being treated for a severe asthma attack.

of a threatening revengeful figure roaming the darkness of Kent.) It's all over now. And this minute two square Canadian hippies, man and woman, twenty-seven or so, graduates of a sort, tho not poets—we chose them out of countless, but not strong, choices. Let's hope they'll be kind to the children and responsible to us. We have weird applicants; the first wave of what America has—none.

I can't find your old letter that I so enjoyed. It's lovingly put away somewhere like the wine-cupboard. I do hope you're back as you were very soon, does Asthma go, leaving no trace? Or is it slow? I hope you'll get here. Usually things with us are haphazard but calming. And there are all sorts of country and city explorations we can make together.

All my love,
Cal

385.

January 19th, 1972

Dearest Cal:

My pet pupil of last year's writing class has just been here for a prolonged breakfast with me—Jonathan Galassi; he's at Cambridge (England)[1] & back for his roommate's wedding, I think—knows Frank well and wanted your address so he could write Frank and perhaps see him when he gets back to England. We've been talking so much about you, Frank, etc., etc., London, Cambridge—that now I feel I must write you a letter right away—even if our Sara Lee Frozen Strawberry Twirl Cake dishes are still unwashed, and the yellow chrysanthemums he brought me still un-arranged . . . He is a darling boy, or young man, and makes me realize how comparatively un-darling the classes have been this year . . . I'm afraid I have actually been growing bored with most of the students. A few good ones—a few "advanced" ones, publishing poems and whole books—but somehow so correctly "advanced"—you can just foresee the next book, with a blurb by Richard Howard, etc. . . . Anyway, it is almost over again thank goodness and perhaps I can think my own thoughts now— I hope to stay on in Cambridge a while, but I don't yet know when I have to go back to Brazil—sometime, certainly.

Thank you very much for the cable when I was sick . . . I really was

---

1 Jonathan Galassi was at Cambridge University on a Marshall Fellowship.

sick—never that sick before in my life. I thought my time had come—but didn't seem to care at all. Anything would have been a nice change at that point. Then suddenly after 8 hideous days at Peter Bent Brigham, I began to recover. The Harvard infirmary was heaven after that—even 3 weeks of it—everyone so gentle and pleasant, and I had visitors—and Frank was especially angelic. He came every single day and we consumed quarts of vanilla ice-cream together, and $$$$$$ worth of coffee from the French coffee shop—at 35 cents the paper cup-full . . . & I talked his ear off; even wept, I think, on one sad evening. At present I am still on cortisone and probably a bit abnormally cheerful, for me, but I'm almost off it and shall soon be in my usual state of cheerfulness-on-top-of-what Anny sarcastically calls "your *basic* melancholy . . ." But I never want to get that sick again, and shall try to avoid it really carefully—

I was in New York for a week or 10 days at Christmas—but still too weak to do very much—had a Japanese dinner with Anny, and saw some old friends from time to time . . . Christmas very dismal. But I don't like it anyway. I was almost relieved to get back here.

I wonder how you are and how you and Frank are working . . .[1] I ran into his friend Bob the other day and *he* had had a letter . . . and it said you were well and everyone working all day long . . . Frank took a small camera (his 1st—a friend of mine here gave it to him for Christmas) with him and I hope he is snapping away furiously at everything & everybody . . .

It is dreadful about John Berryman.[2] I didn't see the TIMES that day and heard it spoken of 2 days later—an awful shock. I've talked to Fitzgerald on the telephone since—he said that John had been on the wagon (AA of all things) for 11 months—until a disastrous bout of drinking, I gathered— It is so sad & awful. "Love & Fame" made me feel badly about him—there is something so wrong about many of those poems—sick and miserable and boasting— And I never even wrote to thank him for the copy he sent, all inscribed, "with love to Elizabeth . . ."[3]

Fitzgerald was awfully nice when I was sick—he & his wife, too. I think perhaps he is unhappy here and that's why he seems so subdued and silent all the time. I went to see him in his office (I didn't know it existed before) in Lamont, and there he seemed quite different and we had quite a gay and nor-

---

1 Frank Bidart was staying with RL to help him revise and order poems for *History*, *For Lizzie and Harriet*, and *The Dolphin*.

2 John Berryman committed suicide on January 7, 1972.

3 *Love & Fame* (1970); inscribed, "To Elizabeth my dear! be happy, John / NY 14 Dec 70."

mal conversation. He returns to Italy at the end of this month & I must invite them to dinner or something—and have only a *ping-pong* table. Lynne Lawner[1] came & had tea with me this week—I'd heard about her but we hadn't met. We seemed to talk very easily—mostly complaining to each other like a couple of affected expatriates about the food in Cambridge, the general stodginess, etc. . . . (And I just can't decide if I really want to live here & become a Cambridge old lady[2]—probably already am one—or not—this is my constant worry now—*where to live*—how doesn't seem to matter nearly so much . . .) I wonder how you are liking Essex . . . Joe Summers is coming to see me tomorrow, on his way to teach in Kent (?)—// I wonder about your new poems. // I feel very out of touch with you. In fact I feel divided from my entire life somewhat by that month in hospitals—very strange. // I have taken up cross-country skiing . . . Fell down a great deal, but so did everyone—I think with better snow, fewer people, and a few degrees less cold, it would be beautiful—silent—you *whish* along in big strides. // I am NOT going to hear Evtushenko, Stanley K, Richard W and J Dickey, etc. in Madison Sq, whatever it is . . . it sounds awful.[3] What are we coming to? You can't read poems without a "combo" or at least a drum & guitar and a bit of chanting . . . // Please please keep well—and tell me about the little boy—what does he *look* like?

    With much love, as always—kiss Robert S for me—

    Elizabeth—

386.[4]

January 19th, 1972

Dearest Cal again:

    Now that I've started I keep wanting to tell you some more—number one isn't much of a letter—before I go out to the "square" to the cobbler's, the grocery store, and so on—I'll type another of these ugly forms that no one can fold properly. Why couldn't they keep the ones they had? They were much better. Why all this change? I bought a Keiler's marmalade just so I'd have a nice crockery jar to keep pencils in and find, after consuming the marmalade, that it is now made of beige-ish *glass*.— And so it goes. My favorite

---

1 Lawner lived in Rome but was in Cambridge in 1972, on a fellowship from Radcliffe's Bunting Institute.
2 Cf. E. E. Cummings, "the Cambridge ladies who live in furnished souls" (1922).
3 Yevgeny Yevtushenko was to read with Richard Wilbur, Stanley Kunitz, James Dickey, and Eugene McCarthy in two heavily publicized shows at Madison Square Garden's Felt Forum, January 28, 1972.
4 Aerogram #2.

eye shadow—for years—suddenly comes in 3 cakes in a row and one has to work much harder at it and use all one's skill to avoid *iridescence* . . .

I didn't tell you about my trip to Vassar, did I?—that was just before I got sick, and probably had something to do with my getting sick—I'd had a cold and had bad asthma there—had to rush to the infirmary to get injections of adrenaline before I could read, but got through that somehow. It was a week of culture and "famous" old graduates—Mary headed a "panel" on the Artist as Critic—I was asked to read a paper but since I was reading anyway, refused—and Mary and a woman I don't know and Muriel Rukeyser—imagine—were the stars. I couldn't get there for this attraction—it must have been amazing. The teachers said Mary's piece was very well worked-out and good, and Muriel did her vague and high-flown best, I think—the other lady, poor dear, was not "prepared" except with quite a bit of Scotch . . . Mary & I met at breakfast the night after I got there—she looked awfully well and was very friendly and amusing. She did one very Mary-ish thing, however (someday I'll tell you)—but I am rather pleased with myself, since when I discovered it I actually *spoke* to her about it, in front of the other dinner guests, and *she* actually almost apologized . . . Same old Mary—exactly the kind of thing she did in 1933 . . . Well, the trees there have grown a lot . . . The Eng. dinner party was rather dull but pleasant—Mary enlivened it some with her accounts of the Medina trial.[1]— I think they'd like me to teach there—but I'd rather not teach at all . . .

I've seen very little of Bill—since the first bad stretch of my illness when he was very kind—even cried at one point, and pressed a rosary into my hands. I have it—I can't seem to throw it away . . . But he has had a young couple staying with him the entire term—I don't know how much longer this will last—a Larry Rhu (?) and his Dutch-Indonesian wife—very pretty, black-ish, and a good cook—and that part of it is good for Bill, probably—but I don't know how long this menage will last or what effect it is having on his life, really. The girl is nicer than the boy—who writes poetry and is a bit pretentious about it, I think—getting a PhD after teaching in Rome for several years. I think he was in one of your classes . . . But he CAN'T scan (write in meter)—and this drove me crazy and must drive Bill crazy too—and when he asked me what I thought of his works, I apparently said exactly what Fitzgerald had said—and this seems to kill his inmost soul or something . . . I couldn't stand it. I sometimes wonder if Bill

---

1 Mary McCarthy was reporting on the trial of Ernest Medina, captain of the U.S. Army company responsible for the My Lai Massacre; see McCarthy, *Medina* (1972).

is really well or all right. he looks so pale, too heavy, frantic—keeps talking of buying a house in Ireland. (But he loathes the countryside—so what would he do?) Well, Frank has probably told you of this odd domestic triangle—

It is about to rain, dismally. A friend of a N.Y. friend has a show of paintings in the Loeb and I went to see them just now—oh dear—he may be sweet & gentle (I've been told so)—but the paintings are, by way of compensation, huge, violently aggressive, mostly phallic,—some female—but mostly on the male side—and one absolute horror called "Marriage." I have to meet him. Maybe it's just my dirty mind . . . ? // Octavio Paz is here— I met him once, and his glamorous (by local standards), bleached, foreign wife[1]— He's very easy to talk to—but sort of too easy—and I suppose that is like his poetry, which I don't like very much.

I spent my skiing week-end in Woodstock, Vermont—a very small town of very big, beautiful, early 19th century houses and a beautiful replica covered bridge—made in 1935—costing $65,000, instead of the $75,000 an iron one wd. have cost—but really quite nice. Very hard to understand how such huge houses—such wealth—must have existed in that little place. The hotel's "literature" said this question was often asked, and that the people, besides farming, had "home industries"—hat-making and *comb*-making . . . Now you can't tell me you could build a 3 story brick house with cupola, 2 long wings, a big stable, etc. by making combs in the cellar . . . I brought back cider, Vermont cheese, etc. etc.— An almost deserted looking town— icy & weird—one "restaurant" beside the huge Rockefeller-owned hotel— with greasy hamburgers & last year's pop tunes on the juke box . . . // Are there any good English poets? Michael Schmidt has just sent me his last book—dedicated it to me.[2] He writes nice letters—seems very young. I can't *understand* Miss Lawner's poems[3]—although I think they get better & better from book I towards the end of book II. Maybe Frank will be able to explain them—he is wonderful at that, and has cleared up some difficult Lowell passages for me amazingly. Has he heard anything from that sadistic RH[4] about his book, I wonder? Give him my love—Alice sends him hers, too—but we're both cross because he hasn't written us.

1 Marie Jo and Octavio Paz; Paz gave the 1971–72 Charles Eliot Norton lectures on "Children of the Mire: Modern Poetry from Romanticism to the Avant-Garde" at Harvard.
2 Michael Schmidt, *Desert of the Lions* (1972), inscribed, "For Miss Bishop, affectionately, and with the dedication of the book, Michael Schmidt 10/1/72."
3 Lynne Lawner, *Wedding Night of a Nun* (1964) and *Triangle Dream* (1969).
4 Richard Howard was the director of the Braziller poetry series, which published Frank Bidart's *Golden State* (1973).

I know so few people here—my own fault, mostly—and keep thinking I must cultivate some—and feel lazy about it. But teaching, such as it is, and entertaining, too, seems too much. Perhaps I'll have a party now . . . The very thought makes me want to go to bed and read all day—

Love again & again—

E.

387.

January 28th, 1972

Dearest Cal:

It was such & surprise, & wonderful, to hear your voice Monday morning. The operator didn't speak first saying it was long distance the way they usually do—I just picked up the telephone & there you were, as if you were down the street. Immediate recognition—even the sensation of surprise lagged behind a little . . . You sound so well—so did Frank. We are so eager to see him and hear all about you first-hand—although he wrote very good letters. (& I wasn't "furious" . . . !)

Marks go in today or tomorrow—then I'll feel really free, but rather sad & guilty about some of the students this year. Last year's were more sympathetic, somehow. More "talent" this year (if one can say that when it really doesn't amount to too much), but some are lazy and bluffers & hypocrites and it makes me depressed, & I feel I should have been much tougher "early on" (as you probably say by now). Anyway, tomorrow afternoon I'm going to New Hampshire with Alice for my second attempt at cross-country skiing—around Putney. There is supposed to be snow and it should be beautiful—if only my knees were stronger! We have to go to a wedding Saturday, in Keene. Strange to say this is the first wedding I've ever been to in my life, a real church one, that is—Uncle Jack was married, at home, when I was eleven, & I attended that. Since then my friends have often eloped, or I was out of town, or they didn't marry at all . . . Plenty of funerals, 2 christenings—black babies—oh—the cook got married in Brazil, but just the legal part of it, not in church—and I couldn't be godmother to the black babies, although invited to be, because I've never been christened. That's all, about me & the sacraments . . .

Here's a clipping for you.[1] This has been all over the TIMES for days, and I've seen him on TV 2 or 3 times—he is on every interview program in

---

1 An article about Yevgeny Yevtushenko's sold-out readings at Madison Square Garden.

existence. I can't see why Stanley & Dick W. lend themselves to this sort of thing, really. Last Sunday I went to have tea with Octavio Paz and his wife, and a Portuguese poet I'd met in London and liked—Alberto de Lacerda—was there, too. He's teaching at BU—just arrived. We had a nice latin-type gossip—and I realized how I have been homesick for that kind of conversation. They're funny, completely natural, and not cautious—I suppose the last is what makes them different from people in Cambridge. The wife, a cosmopolitan type, shrieks with laughter at one's slightest remark, which is very nice— Anyway, they despise Mr. Yevtushenko—a "politician," who adapts himself to whatever country he's in like this (including Portugal—where he praised Our Lady of Fatima, etc.)—as well as a bad poet. But how can I ever have the nerve to stand up and just *read* some poems to 2 or 300 . . . ?—as I'm supposed to do in Philadelphia next week.

Kathy Spivack—who seems about to fulfill her desperate ambition to publish a book—was here yesterday & gave me, or lent me, a copy of *the Review*—with your sonnets and interview in it.[1] Going backwards—I understand *well*, I think, and like, the last FISHNET,[2] and 9,[3] and 8,[4]—also 6,[5] 5,[6] 7,[7] 4[8]—but not quite as much—like 3 a lot[9]—and 2 & 1 a great deal . . .[10] That's LONDON WINTER. The 3 FALL WEEKEND ones I like a lot, too[11]—and think I understand everything, but may not. But Frank will have to explain the first FISHNET to me, I think. After "Summer, summer . . ." all seems clear, but I'm a bit baffled by the beginning.[12] These sonnets *are* clearer, though, and full of beautiful things—especially the

---

1 "Excerpt from 'The Dolphin,'" and Ian Hamilton, "A Conversation with Robert Lowell," *the Review* (Summer 1971).

2 "Fishnet" ("I hoped to gamble with unloaded dice . . ."); see "Dolphin" (RL-*CP*).

3 "London Winter 9: Juvenilia"; see "Hospital: Juvenilia" (RL-*CP*).

4 "London Winter 8: Late Movie Meal." Removed from *The Dolphin* and added to *History*; see "After the Play" (RL-*CP*).

5 "London Winter 6: They" ("True conversation is overheard in bars"). Removed from *The Dolphin* and added to *History*, retitled "English-Speaking World"; but see also "They" ("Why are women a fraction more than us?") (RL-*CP*).

6 "London Winter 5: Tabletalk." Removed from *The Dolphin* and added to *History*, entitled "Tabletalk with Names, 1970" (RL-*CP*).

7 "London Winter 7: Flounder"; see "Winter and London 3: Flounder" (RL-*CP*).

8 "London Winter 4: At *Offado's*"; see "Winter and London 2: At *Offado's*" (RL-*CP*).

9 "London Winter 3: Pont Street Dutch." Removed from *The Dolphin*.

10 "London Winter 1: Closed Sky" and "London Winter 2: Freud"; see "Winter and London 1: Closed Sky" and "Winter and London 5: Freud" (RL-*CP*).

11 See "Fall Weekend at *Milgate*" (RL-*CP*).

12 "Any clear thing that holds up the reader— / The line must terminate, the trouvailles / glitter like vikings in the icecap. / The heights are hollow, robbers pick the gold / from the fine print and volume of the colossus, / his archetypal voice—Summer, summer, / poets die adolescents, their beat embalms them"; "Fishnet," lines 1–7. Cf. "Fishnet," lines 1–7, and "Northmen," line 14 (RL-*CP*).

weather! (*Closed Sky*—lovely[1]). I love the garbage bags at the end of 8[2]—have the same "palisade" blue and green, right behind my back on the sidewalk now— (But oh god how the waste in this country makes me sick—I can't *stand* it.)

Tonight I'm having the Fitzgeralds to dinner—just them, because I'd like to have a chance to talk to them, really, not with other Eng. teachers around the way it always has been. I am rather nervous about this—can he eat roughage or can't he (We had one rather funny conversation about our dental problems in his office in Lamont—the first time I felt completely at home with him—and that poetry-lady—never remember her name—came in just as we were each pointing at our various bridges and inlays . . .)

I must scrub the kitchen floor and so on—I can't find a good maid even for half a day—and I am awfully used to being waited on— Then write to Brazil—about my plans. Haven't any, so this is very hard. I really don't know where to go, where to live, etc.—it's an awful problem. Here I went and ordered a new sofa, bought 3 beautiful rugs yesterday—and at the same time I don't think I want to live in Cambridge. Dying elms; Longfellow's house; bookshops; tasteless delicacies at outrageous prices; everyone doing the same things . . .

The interview is awfully good, I think—I think you are too kind about Bob Dylan however . . .[3] (I tried; even bought 2 records.) And all those people are responsible for rhymes like: heads / bed // or—one of Kathy S's—fill / spills / unfulfilled / and so on—that drive me wild . . . (And then she—and everyone else—says—"But I *like* it." And I feel like Dick Wilbur's grandmother.)

Perhaps I shouldn't say this—but it antedates all Female Lib-ism by 40 years—I'd rather be called "*the 16th poet*" with no reference to my sex, than one of 4 women[4]—even if the other three are pretty good . . . I think "I don't read on with many" is a superb answer[5] & I'll probably steal it . . .

1 "London Winter 1: Closed Sky"; cf. "London and Winter: Closed Sky" (RL-*CP*).
2 "Sometimes the palisades of garbage bags / sunlit beautiful playgrounds of plastic balloons"; "London Winter 8: Late Movie Meal," lines 13–14. See "After the Play" (RL-*CP*).
3 "Bob Dylan is alloy; he is true folk and fake folk, and has a Caruso voice. He has lines, but I doubt if he has written whole poems. He leans on the crutch of his guitar"; Ian Hamilton, "A Conversation with Robert Lowell," *the Review* (Summer 1971).
4 "Few women write major poetry. Can I make this generalization. Only four stand with our best men: Emily Dickinson, Marianne Moore, Elizabeth Bishop and Sylvia Plath"; Ian Hamilton, "A Conversation with Robert Lowell," *the Review* (Summer 1971).
5 On being asked how he felt about his imitators, such as Anne Sexton: "I don't read on with many. But Anne Sexton I know well. It would be delicate to say what I thought of her. She is Edna Millay after Snodgrass. She has her bite. She is a popular poet, very first person, almost first on personality. I had a mortifying revelation. I was reading

Having put it off for a long time, I'm going to meet Anne S. next week—oh dear.

I'd love to see the baby, and meet Caroline—thank you for the invitation. I like small babies best, actually—up to about 2½—and could just watch them for hours—after that I tend to get nervous & tired after an hour—unless they are too well-behaved to be normal. The moment when they discover their hands—is it 3 months?—is wonderful,— This is being written in stolen time—

(I *must* get to work. One boy (black) wrote that Mary Wortley M[1] shd. be cut up in little pieces, alive—& so on—she & Walpole & Byron were all too frivolous for him.)

Tell Frank—if he is still there when you get this—I plan a DIVINE dessert for his arrival—

With much love,
Elizabeth

388.

Feb 6 (?), 1972

Dearest Elizabeth:

You seem to have been here during Frank's visit, both by voice and reference, (if Caroline had met you, you would have been as here as we.) (Change in type cause[d] by my disastrous stopgap of putting an Olympia ribbon on a Hermes, meaning rolls stop rolling every five minutes and have to be exhaustingly switched.)

You are so here that I started to phone you about Marianne.[2] The end of her life already ended by infirmity—she was a star in my sky 35 year ago when I first read Dick Blackmur's essay.[3] Last week I was teaching her to my poor dim students, along with Cummings whom they of course liked and got much better. For you though, it's losing *the* person. What can I say? Maybe you'll write a little book of memory and thoughts. I have never heard anyone describe her so well—or anyone else. Her death has made little stir, unlike

---

an anthology and imagined I was reading another poet I often prefer to Sexton. It was marvelous, 'much X's best poem.' I thought X had become unmuddy and personal at last; but the poem was by Anne. Then the poem sank a little, I'm afraid. I knew Anne could be personal. I read with bias"; Ian Hamilton, "A Conversation with Robert Lowell, *the Review* (Summer 1971); see L-*CPR*, 287.

1 Lady Mary Wortley Montagu; EB was grading papers for her course on letters.
2 Marianne Moore died on February 5, 1972.
3 R. P. Blackmur, "The Method of Marianne Moore," *The Double Agent* (1935).

Berryman's—on whom each English week[ly] or arts page has a bad elegy. This is right, tho I thought him doomed too ever since I ate with him last year then it was drink, later he must have died from not drinking. She was much more inspired—his heroism was in leaping into himself in his last years, ~~amazingly~~ bravely.

I think Frank and I revised 405 poems in a month. That's no way to write, but it was made more sensible by Frank's amazing filing code and total memory for my lines, even for rejected versions. The three books are my magnum opus, are the best or rather they'll do. Are they much ~~though~~? Read *Dolphin* when you have leisure. I'll send the other two fairly soon. I am going to publish, and don't want advice, except for yours. Lizzie won't like the last. What else can I offer her? There's something creepy about deliberately writing something posthumous.

Love,

Cal

I have no heart or space to write about Ivana's accident.[1] We have been ~~like~~ a lost ship.

389.

February 10th, 1972

Dearest Cal:

I've re-read the *Excerpt from "The Dolphin"* a good many times now and feel I can say a lot more about it—and now feel I understand all the sonnets pretty well (this is pre-Frank, too—who'll undoubtedly make some things even clearer for me). He arrived safely on Monday and came here for a hasty supper off the end of the ping-pong table before my first "party" began. He was woefully tired & pale but full of his visit with you and so excited by it and happy about your poems, etc. I'm having dinner with him tonight so I hope to be able to hear lots more— The party was a great success, I think— at least, I enjoyed it myself very much—it was a mixed Sports & Poetry evening, beginning and ending with some of the Olympic games on the TV (the figure skating was marvelous, especially—and I am smitten with the Dutch long distance skater,[2] too), and going on to ping-pong and poetry— all very animated. The Paz-es are most agreeable (no matter how one feels

---

1 In January 1972, Ivana (Carolina Blackwood's youngest daughter, aged six) was severely burned when she overturned a kettle of boiling water. She spent nearly nine months in hospital.
2 Ard Schenk.

about his poetry)—unpretentious and talkative and gay—and James Merrill was here—well it was very nice and I got to bed about 2:30 after washing all the dishes—

Then I got up at 7 to go to New York for Marianne's funeral—what I really am writing you about. Frank didn't even know of her death, last Saturday morning. She had had several more slight strokes fairly recently and had been really unconscious for some time—the wonderful nurse (both nurses were wonderful, also Gladys, the faithful maid) telephoned Louise Crane that morning to say Marianne had just slightly evaporated . . . I am glad it is over at last. She lay in state or whatever it's called on the Monday in the Presbyterian church on the corner of 5th Ave. & 11th street, and Warner (brother—pretty far gone these days) gave a prayer he composed, thanking everyone who had cared for her these last years. I heard bits of this later and it was fine—thank goodness, he is too frail to deliver the funeral sermon he's been working on for several years . . . The funeral, or two of them, one private and one public, were at her church in Brooklyn. She'd helped compose the "program" herself and it was very nice—hymns that she'd quoted in her poems, footnotes, etc.—and she'd wanted it in a "morning-glory blue" cover—with "Beauty is everlasting / but dust is for a time" in gilt.[1] I was going to mail you one—and left them in the airport—but Eastern Airlines found the envelope and is mailing them to me, so I'll send you one later on.

Well, these affairs are always a mixture of the moving and the awful and the funny.— I went over with Louise & Dr. Anny and Margaret Miller. A great many people we know were there, of course.— During the "lunch break" or whatever it was between the two services I talked mostly with Bob Giroux— who looks much better than he did the last time I saw him, much thinner; but he is still very depressed by Berryman's death. He told me you are writing a piece on Berryman. Lincoln Kirstein seemed to be the only person in tears— throughout—he and the nurses, but *that* was only natural. The hymns were strange and Louise whispered to me "All the singing seems to be coming from the right-hand side" (in back of us)—so I looked and of course that was where most of the Negroes were sitting. Anny looked beautiful, very chic, with a black veil on her head—then I realized that the last times I've seen her I've always had dinner with her after her office hours, very late, when she is probably extremely tired. I—and others—wondered why Auden wasn't there . . .

I do hope the little girl—Yvonne?[2]—is doing well. Frank described the

---

1 Marianne Moore, "In Distrust of Merits" (1944), lines 79–80.
2 Ivana.

hospital and I see what you meant by saying it was "cruel." Sometime when I'm feeling tough I want to go back to the Intensive Care ward at Peter Bent Brigham and see if that is as hideous as I remember it—luckily I only remember bits here & there—but why they have to be so rough and so totally indifferent to people's feelings, I don't know—// He gave me two snapshots—one of you, one of the family, including—do you call him *Sheridan?*—and you do look awfully well and really happier than when I saw you last year; that's wonderful.

I'm about to go out to Octavio P's first class—lecture—on Latin Am. Poetry, I think . . . Anyway, I know he is scared to death of lecturing—& especially the C E Norton[1] ones, in English, so I thought a friendly face in the front row might cheer him up a bit . . .

The sonnets are so lovely in spots—lines and lines, I should say, and as I think I said before—I like the emphasis on the *weather*, skies, seasons, clouds, leaves, and so on. They also—this small sampling—seem much clearer, firmer even, than many in the *Notebook*.— I'm just worried about *all* of them & hope & pray you have been reticent enough—although Frank assures me that reticence or not, it's a wonderful book . . .

This week-end—or starting tomorrow—I'm going to try hard to finish my half-, or quarter-done, small piece on Marianne—of course it should have been written long ago, but I procrastinate—and then I really haven't had time to do my own work until now. I almost wish I hadn't said I'd come back next year to do the same thing[2]—but where to go if I don't? It's an awful problem that haunts me all the time. But as the world grows smaller & every place gets to be an escape for more and more Americans—maybe I'd better hold on to the *Casa Mariana* after all . . .

With much love to you—love and best wishes to you all—
    Elizabeth

390.

March 21st, 1972

Dearest Cal:

I've been trying to write you this letter for weeks now, ever since Frank & I spent an evening when he first got back, reading and discussing THE DOLPHIN. I've read it many time since then & we've discussed it some more.

---

1 The Charles Eliot Norton Lectures.
2 That is, teach.

Please believe that I think it is wonderful poetry. It seems to me far and away better than the NOTEBOOKS; every 14 lines have some marvels of image and expression, and also they are all much *clearer*. They affect me immediately and profoundly, and I'm pretty sure I understand them all perfectly. (Except for a few lines I may ask you about.) I've just decided to write this letter in 2 parts—the one big technical problem that bothers me I'll put on another sheet—it and some unimportant details have nothing to do with what I'm going to try to say here. It's hell to write this, so please first do believe I think DOLPHIN is magnificent poetry. It is also honest poetry—*almost*. You probably know already what my reactions are. I have one tremendous and awful BUT.

If you were any other poet I can think of I certainly wouldn't attempt to say anything at all; I wouldn't think it was worth it. But because it is you, and a great poem (I've never used the word "great" before, that I remember), and I love you a lot—I feel I must tell you what I really think. There are several reasons for this—some are worldly ones, and therefore secondary (& strange to say, they seem to be the ones Bill is most concerned about—we discussed it last night) but the primary reason is because I love you so much I can't bear to have you publish something that I regret and that you might live to regret, too. The worldly part of it is that it—the poem—parts of it—may well be taken up and used against you by all the wrong people—who are just waiting in the wings to attack you. One shouldn't consider them, perhaps. But it seems wrong to play right into their hands, too.

(Don't be alarmed. I'm not talking about the whole poem—just one aspect of it.)

Here is a quotation from dear little Hardy that I copied out years ago—long before DOLPHIN, or even the *Notebooks*, were thought of. It's from a letter written in 1911, referring to "an abuse which was said to have occurred—that of publishing details of a lately deceased man's life under the guise of a novel, with assurances of truth scattered in the newspapers." (Not exactly the same situation as DOLPHIN, but fairly close.)

"What should certainly be protested against, in cases where there in no authorization, is the mixing of fact and fiction in unknown proportions. Infinite mischief would lie in that. If any statements in the dress of fiction are covertly hinted to be fact, all must be fact, and nothing else but fact, for obvious reasons. The power of getting lies believed about people through that channel after they are dead, by stirring in a few truths, is a horror to contemplate."[1]

---

1 Thomas Hardy to James Douglas, November 10, 1912, published in the *Daily News* (Nov. 15, 1912).

I'm sure my point is only too plain . . . Lizzie is not dead, etc.—but there is a "mixture of fact & fiction," and you have *changed* her letters. That is "infinite mischief," I think. The first one, page 10, is so shocking—well, I don't know what to say.[1] And page 47 . . . and a few after that.[2] One can use one's life as material—one does, anyway—but these letters—aren't you violating a trust? IF you were given permission—IF you hadn't changed them . . . etc. But *art just isn't worth that much.* I keep remembering Hopkins' marvelous letter to Bridges about the idea of a "gentleman" being the highest thing ever conceived—higher than a "Christian" even, certainly than a poet.[3] It is not being "gentle" to use personal, tragic, anguished letters that way—it's cruel.

I feel fairly sure that what I'm saying (so badly) won't influence you very much; you'll feel sad that I feel this way, but go on with your work & publication just the same. I also think that the thing *could* be done, somehow—the letters used and the conflict presented as forcefully, or almost, without *changing* them, or loading the dice so against E. [(]but you're a good enough poet to write *anything*—get around anything—after all—[)] It would mean a great deal of work, of course—and perhaps you feel it is impossible, that they must stay as written. It makes me feel perfectly awful, to tell the truth— I feel sick for *you.* I don't want you to appear in that light, to anyone— E, C,—me—your public! And most of all, not to yourself.

I wish I had here *another* quotation—James wrote a marvelous letter to someone about a *roman à clef* by Vernon Lee—but I can't find it without going to the bowels of Widener, I suppose . . . His feelings on the subject were much stronger than mine, even.[4] In general, I deplore the "confessional"— however, when you wrote LIFE STUDIES perhaps it was a necessary movement, and it helped make poetry more real, fresh and immediate. But now—ye gods—anything goes, and I am so sick of poems about the students' mothers & fathers and sex-lives and so on. All that *can* be done—but

---

1 "The Farther Shore 1: From My Wife" and "The Farther Shore 2: Old Snapshot and Carpaccio" (typescript, Vassar). The lines that shocked EB read, "What a record year, even for us—/ last March, we hoped you'd manage by yourself, / you were the true you; now finally / your clowning makes us want to vomit—you bore, / bore, bore the friends who ~~want to keep~~ wished to save your image / from ~~your~~ this genteel, disgraceful hospital." See "Hospital II: Voices" (RL-*CP*).

2 "Flight to New York 1: Fox Fur" and "Flight to New York 2: The Messiah" (typescript, Vassar). Both are versions of letters from the Elizabeth Hardwick character in the poem. EB probably also objected to the voice of Hardwick in "Burden 5: Green Sore" and "Burden 6: 'I despair of letters . . .'" (typescript, Vassar). Cf. "Foxfur," "Marriage 7: Green Sore," and "Marriage 8: Letter" (RL-*CP*).

3 Gerard Manley Hopkins to Robert Bridges, Feb. 3, 1883, *The Letters of Gerard Manley Hopkins to Robert Bridges*, ed. Claude Colleer Abbott (1935).

4 Henry James to William James, Jan. 20th [1893], *The Selected Letters of Henry James*, ed. Leon Edel (1955).

at the same time one surely should have a feeling that one can trust the writer—not to distort, tell lies, etc.

The letters, as you have used them, present fearful problems: what's true, what isn't; how one can bear to witness such suffering and yet not know how much of it one *needn't* suffer with, how much has been "made up," and so on.

I don't give a damn what someone like Mailer writes about his wives & marriages / I just hate the level we seem to live and think and feel on at present—but I DO give a damn what you write! (Or Dickey or Mary . . . !) They don't count, in the long run. This counts and I can't bear to have anything you write tell—perhaps—what we're really like in 1972 . . . perhaps it's as simple as that. But are we? Well—I mustn't ramble on any more. I've thought about it all I can and can't reach any more lucid conclusions, I'm afraid.

Now the absurd. Will you do me a great favor and tell me how much you earned for a half-term, or one term I guess it is, when you left Harvard? They have asked me to come back—when I was so sick I didn't think it through very well—for the $10,000. I got last year, & last fall, and a "slight raise." (This may be $500. I learned from Mr. Bloomfield.[1]) Of course I shd. have insisted on some sort of definite contract then and there but I didn't even think of it until later. I have rented this place for a year and another year—but I must plan ahead and I am getting fearfully old and have to think of what I'm going to do in the future years, where I'm going to live, etc. At present I'm afraid even to get a cold because I have no hospital protection— thank god I did have when I was sick. The Woman's outfit—whatever it is here—has been after me, too—asking me if I am getting the same salary that you got—and I don't know. This sounds very crass—but it's true I could earn more at other places—but prefer to stay here if I can . . . but must have some sort of definite contract, obviously. Forgive my sordidness (as Marianne wd. call it).

I had a St. Patrick's Day dinner for Bill—a few days late—and Octavio Paz, etc.—very nice. We dine off the ping-pong table . . . Now I have to go to the dentist and I'll send this without thinking. Otherwise I'll never send it.

DOLPHIN is marvelous—no doubt about that—I'll write you all the things I like sometime!— I hope all goes well with you, and Caroline, and the little daughters, and the infant son—

With much love,
Elizabeth

---

1 Chair of English at Harvard.

(Later—this is all pretty silly. The only good point is on page 2.)

These will be very petty comments—but things that held me up a bit when reading or possibly one or two small mistakes—Frank & I have argued a lot about most of them!

p.6. "machismo" is accurate for the peacock, of course—but it is such an over-worked word at present . . . a fad-word, here, at least. I thought it useful when I 1st learned it, in Brazil, about 20 yrs ago; right now I can't bear it.[1]

p.10. 2. I find the *lion* (Torcello. I remember it, too) confusing, with C's poodle (that little white dog?) in the Carpaccio, in *Venice.*—and can't make out which one is in the snapshot (possibly). I don't think you can mean "tealeaf" color which would be almost black after all[2]—or is just "strongtea color" implied?[3] I'm fiddling & quibbling—but I am so fond of the images in this one I want to get them right—

p.12. 1. "count"[4]—must mean *realize?* or "are worth"?[5]—no, "realize"? or both (as F wd. say, because he loves ambiguities)

p.13. 3. "no friend to write to . . ."[6] Oh dear, Cal! The poem being remarkable for its carefulness about the emotions, and its courage, etc.—I can't quite see this—[7]

4. "thump"—I wonder if C likes this . . . but because of *carpeted* maybe the *thumps* are all right . . .[8]

p/14—"vibrance"? I think you made it up—but suppose it works all right—[9]

15. 1. I'd like a comma, after cows I think—because I tend to see the "hud-

---

1 "The machismo of the peacock"; "Redcliffe Square 3: Oxford," line 4 (typescript, Vassar). Cf. "Redcliffe Square 4: Oxford," line 4 (RL-*CP*). RL wrote in the letter's margin, above "machismo," "show-off—showing."

2 "Carpaccio's Venice was as wide as the world, / Jerome and his lion ~~scoot~~ loped to work unfeared . . . / In Torcello, the lion snapped behind you, / *venti anni fa,* ~~still poodles his~~ keeps his poodled hair— / wherever ~~you~~ I moved his snapshot, he has moved / for twenty years. The saint and animal / swim Carpaccio's tealeaf color"; "The Farther Shore 2: Old ~~Family~~ Snapshot and Carpaccio," lines 4–10 (typescript, Vassar). Cf. "Hospital II 3: Old Snapshot from Venice 1952," lines 4–10 (RL-*CP*). RL wrote in the letter's margin, "In Venice, saint[s] are beast[s]."

3 Written above line, in RL's hand: "cup of tea."

4 "But surely it cuts the toll more than men count—"; "~~Marriage?~~ Caroline 1: Flashback to Washington Square 1966," line 12 (typescript, Vassar). Cf. "Caroline 1: Flashback to Washington Square 1966," line 12 (RL-*CP*).

5 Written above line, in RL's hand: "Lost more riches than we've kept."

6 "I have no friend to write to . . . I love you"; "Caroline 3: July–August," line 13 (typescript, Vassar). Cf. "Caroline 3: July–August," line 13 (RL-*CP*).

7 Written above line, in RL's hand: "I do not [?] send postcards home."

8 "Up the carpeted stairway, your shoes thump"; "Caroline 4: Morning Blue," line 9 (typescript, Vassar). Cf. "Caroline 5: Morning Blue," line 9 (RL-*CP*).

9 "A vibrance in the news and fat of my legs"; "Summer Between Terms," line 7 (typescript, Vassar). Cf. "Summer Between Terms 2," line 7 (RL-*CP*).

dle" of cows & leaves all together—one lump—but maybe I'm supposed to?[1] Not just the cows under the autumn-leaved tree or trees?

17. the "his" in the last line[2] . . . one has to think & think & think—and then the genders don't seem to come out right . . .

23. 5. (Mermaid) I can't bear "grapple in the aspic of your[3] flesh"[4]—Frank & I have argued at length about this . . . It's supposed to be violent and jealousy is a hideous emotion, etc.—but aspic is a *cold* jelly—all right—but "grapple *in*" well, it is supposed to be horrible, too, perhaps. Frank is so totally bewitched that he even argued for an ambiguity—"aspic" suggesting also Cleopatra's colloquial word for "asp." Well, I pointed out to him that this isn't possible—an "ambiguity" has to work equally well, or at least work, both ways . . . and you can't "grapple in" a tiny black snake, but I couldn't convince him.[5] Perhaps I'm just prejudiced from the feminine point of view, having made eggs in aspic, etc. etc.—I feel sure you'll never change this, but it does make me feel sick.

31. I am pretty sure it's Ernest Thompson Seton—he used to be my favorite author. (I saw "Rolf in the Woods" at the Coop—so I'll check on it.)[6]

33. "thirty thousand"[7]—(Frank says it was originally forty.)[8] This is the sum Fitzgerald needed annually, I remember. But oh dear, it reminds me of that unfortunate remark of Mary's in an interview a few years back "Of course we're all much richer now." Well, many of us aren't and I feel such sums not only tell against the writer of the letter but wd. be held against *you*.— Of course in time they'll probably seem absurdly small, too, but they don't now— But perhaps it is *meant* just to tell against the correspondent . . . it certainly does, to me, anyway. But it gives the sonnet—so moving otherwise— a sort of Elizabeth-Taylor-whine air . . .

1 "Here a huddle of shivering cows and feverish leaves"; "Fall Weekend at *Milgate* 1," line 11 (typescript, Vassar). Cf. "Fall Weekend at *Milgate* 1," line 11 (RL-*CP*).

2 In the typescript, "I Was Playing Records," which is in Elizabeth Hardwick's voice, addresses a letter to "dearest"; line 14 reads: "love vanquished by his mysterious carelessness." The line is unchanged in the published version, "Records" (RL-*CP*).

3 Written above line, in RL's hand: "government [?], your."

4 "I've wondered who would see and date you next, / and grapple in the aspic of your flesh"; "Mermaid 5," lines 1–2 (typescript, Vassar). Cf. "Mermaid 5," lines 1–2 (RL-*CP*).

5 In the typescript and the final version, the Caroline Blackwood character is called a "rough slitherer." See "Mermaid 5," line 10 (RL-*CP*).

6 "What ~~were~~ was the lessons of the wolverine, / the Canada of Earnest Seton Thompson"; "More London Winter 1: Wolverine," lines 1–2 (typescript, Vassar). The poem was taken out of *The Dolphin* and put into *History*; see "Wolverine, 1927" (RL-*CP*). See also Ernest Thompson Seton, *Rolf in the Woods* (1911).

7 Written above line, in RL's hand: "double [illegible]."

8 " 'We can't swing New York on less than thirty thousand' "; "Transatlantic Call," line 1 (typescript, Vassar). Cf. "During a Transatlantic Call," line 1 (RL-*CP*).

39. Really *palate*[1]? I always thought that meant the small piece of flesh that hangs downaway at the back of the throat—the OED says it can be the "roof = etc. of the mouth" so maybe it's all right— Somewhere—I can't find it right now—you wrote "with my fresh wife"— and that seemed just too much, somehow—the word "fresh," again, had a sort of Hollywood or Keith Botsford feeling that I'm sure you didn't intend—you've avoided it almost completely.[2]

Well, I could go on, of course. Most of these are trivialities & some I forgot to mark as I read through the book—many times, now. You know I am quite fiendish about trivialities, however . . . But right now they don't seem worth it. I am having trouble trying to decide how to divide this letter, but I think I'll put all my technical remarks on these pages. *This is the one big criticism I'd make*:

As far as the *story* goes—of course you haven't stuck exactly to the facts, & didn't have to. But starting about page 44, I find things a little confusing. Page 44 is titled LEAVING AMERICA FOR ENGLAND—obviously, about the idea of that. Then 47, FLIGHT TO NEW YORK. (I wonder if "Flight" is the right word here? (even if you do fly.) Then New York, and Christmas. "swims the true shark, the shadow of departure."[3] That's all about that. (The NY poems in themselves are *wonderful* . . .) (Can the line about the "play about the fall of Japan" *possibly* be true . . . ?![4]) But after the "shadow of departure" comes BURDEN—and the baby is on the way. This seems to me a bit too sudden—there is no actual return to England—and the word BURDEN and then the question "Have we got a child?" sounds almost a bit Victorian—melodramatic.[5] This is the only place where the "plot" seems awkward to me, and *I* can fill it in of course—I think it might baffle most readers—

The change, decision, or whatever happens between page 51 & 52 seems

---

1 " 'My mother really learned to loathe babies, / she loved to lick the palate of her Peke' "; "Artist's Model 3," lines 1–2 (typescript, Vassar). Cf. "Artist's Model 2," lines 1–2 (RL-*CP*).

2 "In the greenest apple lurks a breath of spirits— / I sit with my fresh wife, children, house and sky"; "Burden 7: Later Week at *Milgate*," lines 11–12 (typescript, Vassar). Cf. "Marriage 10: Late Summer at *Milgate*," lines 9–12 (RL-*CP*).

3 "Flight to New York 10: Christmas 1970," line 14 (typescript, Vassar). Cf. "Flight to New York 12: Christmas," line 14 (RL-*CP*).

4 "A ~~thick~~ heavy book, sunrise-red from Lizzie, / with, 'Why don't you try to lose yourself / and write a play about the fall of Japan?' "; "Flight to New York 10: Christmas 1970," lines 5–7 (typescript, Vassar). Cf. "Flight to New York 12: Christmas," lines 5–7 (RL-*CP*).

5 "Outliving his son, place, fortune . . . their survivor / with nothing to will. Have we got a child? / Our bastard, easily fathered, hard to name?"; "Burden 1: Knowing," lines 5–7 (typescript, Vassar). Cf. "Marriage 5: Knowing," lines 5–7 (RL-*CP*).

too sudden—after the prolongation of all the first sections, the agonies of indecision, etc.—(wonderful atmosphere of life's *stalling* ways . . .)[1]

You've left your E's trip to London?—that's not needed perhaps for the plot—but it might help soften your telling of it?—but I somehow think you need to get yourself back to England *before* the baby appears like that. (Frank took violent exception to the word bastard, I don't know why—I think it's a good old word and even find it appealing & touching. He must have worse associations with it than I have.)

391.

March 28, 1972

Dearest Elizabeth—

Let me write you right away . . . thoughtlessly, casually, ~~my~~ first scattered impressions—my thanks. The smaller things. Most of your ~~questions~~ reservations seem likely to [be] right and useful. I can't tell from a quick reading and haven't checked your remarks with my lines. I think they will help; please give me more. I am talking about your brief line to line objections. 2) The transition back to London is a hard problem maybe. I'd like to do [it] in two or preferably one sonnet. The pregnancy isn't meant to come crash on New York, tho it was only a month later, i.e. when we knew or suspected. It's problem of finding inspiration for a link, I think ~~I can~~.

Now Lizzie's letters? I did not see them as slander, but as sympathetic, tho necessarily awful for her to read. She is the poignance of the book, tho that hardly makes it kinder to her. I could say the letters are cut, doctored part fiction; I thought of it (I attribute things to Lizzie I made up, or that were said by someone else. I combed out abuse, hysteria, repetition.[)] The trouble is the letters make the book, I think, at least they make Lizzie real beyond my invention. I took out the worst things written against me, so as not to give myself a case and seem self-pitying. Or maybe I didn't want to author them. I promise I'll do what I can to answer your piercing ~~objections~~ thoughts. I've been thinking of course these things for years almost. It's oddly enough a technical problem as well as a gentleman's problem. How can the story be told at all without the letters? I'll put my heart to it. I can't bear not to publish Dolphin in good form. I am in no hurry for time, and would love to spend the summer working if the muse lets me.

---

1 That is, between the end of the "Flight to New York" sequence and the "Burden" sequence. In the revised *Dolphin*, "Burden," retitled "Marriage," is placed before "Flight to New York" (RL-*CP*).

Salary is complicated. I got $9500, I think eventually at my highest. After three years, I was given rooms at Quincy House free for two or three days a week[,] the expense of commuting. I think all salaries must be higher now. Every two or three years I got a little $500 raise. I may have started at $8500. Also I wasn't around when I was teaching. I'm sure you will get more. Maybe the best thing is to have someone practical and forceful to handle it for you, but even lambs like us can kick the bucket over.

Harriet is with us now, and tho the weather is now suddenly wintry, think it is May with us.

I feel like Bridges getting one of Hopkins' letters, as disturbed as I am grateful.

Oh, I forgot. If you can get the revised *Notebook* from Frank, particularly the section *For Lizzie and Harriet*, but also the latter part of *History*, you might get a slightly different slant on the meaning of *Dolphin*. The three books are one heap, one binding, so to speak, though not one book.

All my love,
Cal

392.

Easter Tuesday,
[April 4], 1972

Dearest Elizabeth:

Harriet has come and gone, and I'm left in a mood of wonder, so well she carried off what had to be difficult, impossible I almost thought. We talked more freely than we ever have (this is age only partly) yet not too much, and no sides had to be taken except humorously. And things went well with Caroline, Harriet's brother and the other children. A moment not to come again, for there never can be such a moment again, but it is a promise of future happiness.

Let me rephrase for myself your moral objections. It's the revelation (with documents?) of a wife wanting her husband not to leave her, and who does leave her. That's the trouble, not the mixture of truth and fiction. Fiction—no one would object if I said Lizzie was wearing a purple and red dress, when it was yellow. Actually my versions of her letters are true enough, only softer and drastically cut. The original is heartbreaking, but interminable.

I thought of doing this. It's just a sketch, because I've really only had yesterday to read through *The Dolphin*, and scribble and sketch. *First*, the entire

"Burden" section should come after "Sickday," after "Burden" come "Leaving America," and "Lost Fish," then "To New York" (new title).¹ This leaves rough edges, and falsifies the actual time sequence, but gets rid of the rather callous happy ending, and softens E's role in the New York group— she seems rather serenely gracious (I overstate) about my visit after the birth. I can go this far, but won't bring any post facto business about the baby into the New York section. *Two*, I take your moral objections are confined to the letters, and not to all of them. Several can be handled and perhaps improved by using some of the lines in italics, and giving the rest, somewhat changed, to me. "From My Wife" would be called "Voice."² Other poems do not need change maybe. "Fox Fur" and "The Messiah" become gentler when the reader assumes the child is born.

This is a sketch and not exactly what I'll do. The problem of making the poem unwounding is impossible, still I think it can be made noticeably milder without losing its life. It might be much better, for who can want to savage a thing. How can I want to hurt? Hurt Lizzie and Harriet, their loving memory? Working my poem out is a must somehow, not avoidable even though I fail—as I must partially.

What are your plans? I hope to come to New York for a week at the end of May. I wish I could talk to you face to face about this and everything. The cloud of winter seems to have lifted.

Love,
Cal

393.

April 10th (Monday) ? [1972]
Dearest Cal:

I have two letters from you here now—& I was so relieved to get the first one, especially—I was awfully afraid I'd been crude, rude, etc. . . . Look—I do see how when you have written—one has written—an absolutely wonderful, or satisfactory, poem—it's hard to think of changing anything . . . However, I think you've misunderstood me a little.

I quoted Hardy exactly, & the point was that one *can't* mix fact & fic-

---

1 In *The Dolphin*, the typescript "Burden" section was retitled "Marriage"; "Sickday" was retitled "Sick"; and "New York" was retitled "Flight to New York." The revised sequence led from "Marriage" to "Leaving America for England" to "Flight to New York." "Lost Fish" became the second poem in the "Leaving America for England" sequence.
2 The typescript "From My Wife" became "Hospital II: Voices" (in which the speaker's tone is more resigned).

tion— What I have objected to in your use of the letters is that I think you've changed them—& you had no right to do that (?)

April 12th—

Well, I was interrupted there and have stayed interrupted for two days, apparently . . . It was—is—as I was saying—the mixture of truth & fiction that bothers me. Of course, I don't know anything about your possible agreements with E. about this, etc. . . . and so I may be exaggerating terribly—

To drop this painful subject and go on to the rest—I think the rearrangements you are thinking of making will improve the last part of the poem enormously—and I see what a lot of hard work they entail, too. The idea of the italics and your saying some lines—sounds fine.

I am so glad Harriet's visit apparently went off so very well. After all, she has two very bright parents and so must have inherited a good deal of intelligence!

I am getting ready to go to New York; the Brazilian anthology, or vol. I of it, is to be launched tomorrow at a huge, I gather, party, and I must be there. I don't want to be especially, but must. This is no real answer to your letters—and thank you for being so frank about the poems—

I just wanted to get some reply to you in the mail before I left. I'll be back the 17th or 18th and then I'll write again. I even have some more of my niggling line-comments, too, if you can bear them. I read your Berryman piece with sadness—also wonder that you could do it all so fast and spontaneously.[1] I have the new book here but haven't had time really to study the poems yet.[2] It is awful, but in general his religiosity doesn't quite *convince* me—perhaps it couldn't quite convince him, either . . . He says wonderful little things, in flashes—the glitter of broken glasses, smashed museum cases,—something like that.

I am still struggling to put down all my Marianne Moore recollections. I've also done a couple of poems—one a pretty long one, still being furbished a bit—the first of this batch maybe I'll enclose.[3] It is very old-fashioned and umpty-umpty I'm afraid—but I'm grateful to get anything done these days and one usually starts me off on 2 or 3 more, with luck. Frank has also asked me for a blurb and I struggle with the phrases for that in between everything else. It is terribly hard. His poem is so personal, so con-

1 "For John Berryman: 1914–1972," *The New York Review of Books* (March 30, 1972); see RL-*CPR*.
2 John Berryman, *Delusions, etc. of John Berryman* (1972).
3 Probably "Poem" (EB-*CP*).

clusive—so definitive, almost (for Frank)—I don't see where he can go after that, really. I wish he'd try something easier. He has such amazing taste and sensitivity about other people's poetry . . . I wish he were a happier young man. I do think we've become very good friends, however. The Paz-es have also been very friendly and we had—I had—an Easter breakfast party—a great success, I think, with Frank doing best at egg-dying, and Octavio madly searching my bedroom and bathroom for eggs—all brand new to him.—these Easter rites—

It's spring—first one I've seen in many years. I had one wonderful last skiing week-end in Stowe—unbroken fields & mountainsides of snow—and then back here where everything looks very bare and still brown—and the brick walks are still bleached white by all that salt they use in the winter.

I'll really write again as soon as I return. Elizabeth *Cadwalader* is arriving to vacuum my house, thank goodness—I hope you're all well and that Robert Sheridan sits up & takes notice . . .

With much love,
Elizabeth

Just rec'd an ad for a book about you called *"Everything to be Endured"* . . .[1]

394.

April 24, 1972

Dearest Elizabeth:

I seem to have left your last letter and poem (much turned to) in London, (I almost wrote New York) in a coat left there for another taken. I can't be as accurate as I'd like. The picture poem and the dentist one are in the clearest of narrative styles, of the best short stories[2] . . . if quite a long one could be written on a page. The picture is more mysterious—when the R.A. turns up I still jump[3]—your relative seemed more of a failure than that—then you see the painting is good enough, that the poem is a life, yours, his, going to age. I want to see more of these poems. I'm sure they roll up, a huge story maybe like "In the Village," gaining in what can be held on to, in graspableness by being poetry.

Kunitz has similar reservations about *Dolphin.* But don't say this; everything seems to get back to Lizzie. There must be heavy changes. But Peter

1 R. K. Meiners, *Everything to Be Endured* (1970).
2 "Poem" and "In the Waiting Room" (EB-*CP*).
3 "Poem," line 44 (EB-*CP*).

Taylor, a kind soul, has seen my *revised Dolphin* and saw nothing wrong, except that it needed to be read with the earlier poems about Lizzie and Harriet. I think I've at last turned the thing, though there's still file-work.

I'll be in New York the week beginning the 21st of May. Will you still be in North America?

From the shattering strength of your letters and your skiing, you are in huge health. Never more force! I hope to get back to tennis, but skiing—the last time I tried about eighty years ago during the war, I failed to stop on a low mound when my skis stopped and fell on my head with my thumb under a ski—broken. Do you believe in Woman Power? I do, the shadow at the end of history. However my son feels the opposite, has broken a kitchen chair, shovels everything (rugs, blankets, silver toys, the little dachshund, Caroline and my fingers) into his two tooth mouth. Our family of women braces itself.

Dear, how I hope you'll still in Cambridge!

Love,

Cal

395.

Ouro Prêto

July 12th, 1972

Dearest Cal:

I've just written Frank what little news there is from here, I think . . . He wrote me some time ago when you were away getting another degree somewhere . . . At Brown, I sat beside the shy & solemn Dr. Freund—the Law Dept. man from Harvard, a specialist in The Supreme Court[1]—I like him but find him awfully hard to talk to. He was receiving his 13th or 14th degree. When asked what he was going to do with all those hoods, he said "I'm thinking of making a quilt," then was so overcome with his own wit that he became silent again. I hand this on to you—or Caroline—as a very practical idea . . . all those different satins would be very pretty.

Frank wrote me that you are working like beavers (?) on the new books. And that he thinks your new arrangement of *Dolphin* is fine. Well, I am eager to see it—& them—and I'm sorry I never sent you all my further finicky restrictions—I'll copy them off when I get back to Cambridge—but maybe it's too late then. They aren't very important, anyway. He also wrote me about the Poetry Festival in London. I was asked to go to that, but felt that the re-

1 Paul A. Freund.

muneration was insufficient, to quote Henry James—and I have an awful feeling I didn't even answer the letters. From what Frank wrote, however, I'm glad I didn't go—except for seeing—& I think, hearing—you.

I've been working hard here, first at getting the house cleaned up and such chores as having the underbrush cleared out, the clock repaired, the rats caught (my Siamese died while I was away—the last cat, and I can't have another because my maid doesn't really like them & I don't want to entrust a kitten to her), and the woodpile replenished . . . The house wasn't in too bad shape, considering, but very damp—no one ever airs anything unless I'm here—& I spent a few bad days, wheezing, but it's much better now, with 2 fires going most of the time. I do want to sell it, though, much as I love it. I've written PREVIEWS—that fancy international agency that specializes in exotica—but it may take years, of course. And WHAT to do with all the books . . . I've already given away several hundred and must sort out hundreds more. (There were over 3,500, what with Lota's & mine.) Now if I could just get a GOOD painter . . . Now I'm down to business—lawyers & banks and taxes and return tickets, etc. . . . It hasn't been too bad, this time, and not lonely because I have people always in the house nights—but of course I miss Lota much worse in this country, and feel I've really HAD Brazil—I can barely endure reading the newspapers with all the same old idiocies they've printed for 20 years—plus the newer and much more sinister ones . . . (The town is full of police—3 cars—paddy wagons—parked permanently in the *praça*[1]—and more around town—barred, grilled, armored, etc.)

I can't seem to find the wonderful bit from Henry James' letters about using personal material that I wanted to quote to you—& I feel I've annoyed you more than enough, no doubt, as it is, on that subject, but I can't resist this from Kierkegaard: "The law of delicacy, according to which an author has a right to use what he himself has experienced, is that he is never to utter verity but is to keep verity for himself & only let it be refracted in various ways."[2]— But maybe that is exactly what you *have* done . . . ?

I think I've improved the poems Frank took with him—especially the long one. However—I don't expect you to like it!—*honestly*—

Please give my love to your family & I'd like a snapshot of the baby *and all of you* so much. (Leaving here the 29th, probably.) With much love always—

Elizabeth

---

1 Square.
2 From Kierkegaard's 1843 journal (iv A), cited in the "Translator Introduction" to *Fear and Trembling*, trans. Walter Lowrie (1941).

396.

[To Robert Lowell and Frank Bidart; postcard of Ouro Prêto]

July 2nd, 1972

Dear Cal & Frankie:

For some reason I have been dying to get news of you these past few days . . . I hope the work is going well? I do hope it will be done in time so that F can come here, too, but I also do know how important he is to the various *Notebooks*, & shall understand if he can't. // I HATE that poem, "The Moose"—or parts of it.[1] I've changed page 2 a lot, at least, and it's better now, I hope. (I'm sick of being simple.) Please send me a few stanzas of a poem—tough ones—I am also sick of the primitive, & making conversation in a foreign language is apt to reduce everything to the primitive. The Arts Festival in full swing. The *chefe* wanted me to put up the harpsichordist, a German lady from S. Paulo. I said no—then heard she had telephoned asking if there was a field where she can land her private plane. I must meet her—but must save that bed for Frank . . . An "Afro-brasileiro" mass last night—& my maid loved it—she's very with it these days, and accepted "socially" in the local "middle class" (I suppose it is) because she works for *me* . . . Somebody please send me a line. I hope all the family is well. With much love.

397.

[July 28, 1972]

Dearest Elizabeth—

I so hope you get over the asthma attack very quickly. I suppose the worst worry after the terrible breathing difficulties is how long will this last. I'm afraid the unexpected sadness of speaking to you, made me speechless. When you said "You talk, I can't," I could only think of questions. Only asked questions, then I felt guilty of tormenting you and became speechless. But we are never speechless together. I wonder if you would like for Caroline and Sheridan to join you somewhere in Scandinavia for two or three days. Most of the girls will be in camps and we can travel light.

Let me praise you. You do all kinds of strenuous athletic things, that even at Kenyon Peter Taylor and I would never have attempted. You have written some of your loveliest poems. A graver style. I've been redoing some of my old Rilkes and Rimbauds using literal prose translations, the originals and

---

1 EB was preparing "The Moose" for publication (*The New Yorker*, July 15, 1972), having read a draft of it at Harvard and Radcliffe's Phi Beta Kappa ceremony on June 13. (She had been writing the poem since 1946.)

my own translations—by losing my old jewelled glister or whatever I make better translations, I think. Something of that has happened to our original work, though comparison is difficult.

I do want you to see Caroline and meet Sheridan—I've mixed my verbs—he's really quite beautiful, a fast crawler, and his one intelligible word is *Dada*—really!

All my love,
Cal

398.

[Postcard: North Norway]

Bodø, [Norway]¹
August 23rd, 1972

Dear Cal:

Me & my Moose—a recent picture. (I realize you haven't seen me in some time.)

Lots of love,
Elizabeth

399.

September 8th, 1972

Dearest Cal:

The mail has piled up hideously while I was away & I haven't begun to finish reading it yet, much less answer it—but I'm going to write you a note first of all . . . Frank called up a day or two ago—his mother is home from the hospital, I learned, but that was about all—and now he's in San Francisco. He told me that you wanted a copy of this "Poem"²—& what a silly title, but I couldn't think of a damned thing . . . He also told me that you & Caroline AND Sheridan and nanny are coming to the USA in October and will come to Cambridge . . . (All of you?) This is wonderful news—& will you please let me know WHEN, if you can? I have told my aunt in Nova Scotia that I'll go visit her and tentatively set Columbus Day week-end—that's to take place on Monday the 9th *this* year (no respect at all)—but I can change my visit around easily if by chance that's when you might be here . . .

1 EB and Alice Methfessel traveled to London, Stockholm, Helsinki (where Frank Bidart joined them for a few days), Oslo, and Bergen.
2 "Poem" (EB-*CP*).

Frank also said you got all the books in on time, etc. and that he'd had a wonderful time with you on the last stretch . . . I bought the London *Times* or *Observer* from time to time on my travels & by chance got the one that had a picture of the jacket of the last "Review"—with the transposed heads . . .[1] Oh dear— Is it possible to get a copy?—maybe I'll find one here—F. said it's a lot of interviews . . . And that you got my postcard—but apparently hadn't received, or Sheridan hadn't received, a small present I sent him from Tromsø, I think, or was it Bodø??? I'm afraid some of those towns are already beginning to blur together— (This is the first time I've typed in over a month and I can't seem to do it very well.) We had a wonderful trip— 12 days—Alice said she was bored one afternoon, but I wasn't for a minute—but then I'm very partial to dreary grand northern (or southern) landscape and have lived in the middle of grandeur so much I find my view of the Loeb Theatre awfully stultifying . . . The "Skerries" were marvelous, I thought—and the "Troll-fjord"—and North Cape, too—and the weather was perfect except for one day— We drank a half-bottle of Mateus Rosé at North Cape to celebrate—a very odd wine-list—and (but perhaps you've been there) what struck a very surrealist note—in a special stone niche, black granite, I think—a large, snowy-white bust of Louis Philippe—curls, sideburns, medals, epaulets & all—"qui pendant quelque temps de sa vie était exilé à Masy près du Cap Nord . . ."[2] He hid up there, my other book says, because he thought he was going to be assassinated.

In Oslo we saw the Viking ships—quite a few other things but that's what I liked best. Frank said you had some lines about them in a sonnet but later took them out?[3] A very cursory look at the Munch Museum—it was too beautiful a day and I was feeling too cheerful to be bothered with all that nordic nonsense . . .

It was nice having Frank with us for two days & as it turned out—and after having seen Bergen—it was better to have him in Helsinki than there. We spent most of our time shopping—and I spent most of my money.— I think he should travel a lot more—even perhaps learn to "rough it" a little more—awful as I sound (Hopkins said that roughing it had, he thought, something to do with coarse blankets[4]). Perhaps I'll try to get him on a bicycle this fall . . . he did seem to enjoy the Honda in Bermuda!

---

1 "The State of Poetry: A Symposium," *the Review* (Summer 1972).
2 "Who was once in exile in Masi, near Nordkapp."
3 "Northmen" (RL-*CP*).
4 "ROUGHED IT; I believe it means irritating the skin on sharp-textured blankets. These old gentlemen have always had to do it when they were your age"; Gerard Manley Hopkins to Alexander Baillie, 20 July 1864, *Further Letters of Gerard Manley Hopkins*, ed. Claude Colleer Abbott (1938), 213.

You must have a wonderful sense of relief with all that work behind you . . . Are you teaching again, or going to teach? It will be marvelous to see you—and your small family. This doesn't need any answer—just send me a postcard telling me when you think you'll be in Cambridge and for how long . . .

    With lots of love,
    Elizabeth

I haven't said anything about Russia—or, I shd. say, 3 and a half days in Leningrad. One *wants* to like it so much—but it's impossible. The city—the original city—is magnificent, & I hadn't realized the Neva was so big or that Russians were so fond of gilding . . . But good God how sad and dreary everything is—and there seems to be a new freeze on—we were treated abominably, in general. It takes hours to go over the border, in or out, and the toilets are about like those in Brazil, or worse—while a few hundred yards away, the Finnish ones are the cleanest and best fitted-up in the world . . . Only the soldiers are well-dressed and have black jack-boots. The people looked at our feet first of all—and after looking at their shoes, we knew why—

    In Stockholm I was sitting waiting for Alice (I started off with bad bronchitis or something, but got cured at sea) in the outdoor Museum and discovered I was sitting beside Swedenborg's summer-house, in a replica of his flower & herb garden . . . It was closed, the summer house, but you could look in the windows & it was a very charming room, all white and gold, with a very pretty little organ, silver pipes, etc. . . .

400.

September 10, 1972

Dearest Elizabeth:

    Love to have "Poem" again; why don't you call it Small good Picture? I don't mean this.[1]

    I think we will fly on about the 16 of October, not sooner.[2] Rather a grim trip. Sad go-over what can't be again—and lousy position of being the person who wants the divorce. And then can there be two Mrs. Lowells in one city? Our best local county counsel doctor turned out to be a bigamist and

1 EB's "Large Bad Picture" and "Poem" are about the same great-uncle, George Hutchinson.
2 RL was crossing the Atlantic to divorce Elizabeth Hardwick in New York. Blackwood in turn would obtain her divorce from Israel Citkowitz; then RL and Blackwood were to be married in Santo Domingo.

had to flee back to Australia with his new wife to support his old. As far as I know Lizzie will not dispute the divorce, but the details are complicated—trusts with different terms, etc.

Many thanks for the lovely seal slippers; they fit Sheridan and he wears them. He has just learned to walk—like that, in two days. So they were timely. Would you (seriously) like to be a godmother? We would both be honored. I would like to have Peter Taylor and Bill Alfred for Godfathers. Then we can have an English set, mostly relatives.

Don't know whether you can make Frank rough it. He must have the most fixed habits I've ever met. Once we got his eggs and toast a minute different from ours, he was actually an easy guest with predictable wants. An English friend read his Herbert White, and wondered what the parents of his Wellesley students would say if they read it.[1] Years gone before it became part of him in my imagination, I took an agonizing double-take when I looked at him. He was an angel of light to me this summer, liked as one of the family by all of us.

The other night, I was reading Sylvia Plath, then you to one or two friends here—I'm afraid she seemed rather gothic and arid in comparison. All spear-head.

Today all my books go to the publisher. They are like a guest who wouldn't leave, so I'm relieved. What to do though? Soon I'll be teaching—an exercise I seem to like less and less. Also I teach at a pleasant (Hideous new architecture though) but 2nd or third choice college, and the commuting is very tedious. I had troubles twice with visas, so am not unhappy you didn't like Russia. Loved the Viking ships; I still have them, only I took out Oslo and its museum,

all my love,
Cal

401.

[First paragraph typed on postcard: "The Beast of the Apocalypse.
Door of a hanging cupboard dated 1758," Norsk Folkemuseum, Oslo.]

September 20th, 1972
Dearest Cal:

Many thanks for your letter—& I'll be expecting to hear from you shortly after the 16th of October. Frank says you'll be coming to Cam-

---

1 See Frank Bidart, "Herbert White," *Golden State* (1973).

bridge . . . I wonder if that means all of you, or just you? And if you or all of you do come here—of course I'd like to do something (has to be pretty modest because of my small apt. & lack of equipment) to celebrate and entertain you. Just have you to dinner—or—even—have a COCKTAIL party. (I had two last year—pretty good I think.) Do you like the Fitzgeralds? I like them a lot and they are two of the very few people I know (or like) here "socially." But perhaps he regards you as a lost sheep[1]—I don't know—he certainly never said so! & I do get an uncomfortable feeling once in a while that he and Sally might have *hopes* for me, even. [(]But tell me what you (& Caroline) would like![)] // I haven't seen Bill yet—I'll try calling again today. // Oh—thank you for asking me to be a godmother—I am flattered indeed. I don't know how according-to-canon-law you intend to make this, however—I was asked to be one, twice, in Brazil, but couldn't accept because I have never been baptized. (The Catholic church there wd. have accepted me if baptized even a Protestant baptism.) If it is an unconsecrated informal, Bohemian-Type godmother you are after—I'd be delighted . . . It's too late for a silver mug—& at the rate S is progressing, from your accounts, I'd better send a monogrammed, straight-edged razor set . . .

Oh dear—now I don't want to stop talking . . .

The slippers were sent from *Bodø*—Norway. (From a shop with a stuffed polar-bear on the sidewalk in front—) (You told Frank they were from Helsinki! horrors)—I think Sheridan must really be a big boy if he can use them already. It is marvelous, watching a baby learn to walk, isn't it—so *fast*, as you say— But, Saturday I bought an English bicycle and although I haven't bicycled for over 20 years—I got on and found I could ride it. That sense of balancing never deserts one, apparently—and getting up on one's feet and staying up on them must give one the same thrill . . . (I'm NOT going to bicycle through Harvard Square, however.)

Your remark about getting F's "eggs & toast a minute different" was wonderful.— When he visited Alice & me in Helsinki we were staying at a kind of student-hotel—part of the University in the winter and students run it as an hotel in the summer. It wasn't bad at all (all we could get). Breakfast was served smorgasbord (?) style—help-yourself—but very plentifully and very good (except for the coffee, which naturally never comes up to my standards, anywhere). But Frank loathed it because the boiled eggs weren't hot enough. We made him go back and have a second breakfast with us & showed him how to reach underneath for the *hotter* eggs, & where the cream

1 For having left the Catholic Church.

pitcher was, & so on . . . Yesterday we went with him, in a howling storm, to see an apartment he had discovered & wants to buy. Alice & I both felt it was much too expensive for what it is, and that the kitchen was wretched (not that he cooks, but he might someday—& he'd be tied up in this place for years) & wd. smell up the whole place, etc. etc.—no garage and no street parking "when it snows." And—it was the first and only one he'd looked at. I do hope he'll take all our motherly advice and look around a lot more. Also I wish he'd not be so extravagant when he gets a yearly large sum of money.— He needs some good business advice, but I am scarcely the one to give it to him.— I've survived just through New England and Scotch-Canadian canniness and conservativeness, I think—

I'm to write another "blurb" for his book[1]—I must right away. What I had *planned* to say was more or less exactly what you have said—alas—now I have to think up something else. (Not yr. fault . . . !) I am awfully worried about that book—I can't believe it will be well received—but one really can't tell any more—perhaps it will be. I didn't mean for F really to "rough it"—I meant he shd. be less literary, get into the world a bit more. For example: I was telling him about the weird and absurd fellow-passengers on the bus trip to Leningrad, & my conversations with them, and he asked "But didn't you *tell* them you are a poet?" See? He may even have said "*a famous poet* . . ." Imagine their embarrassment & consternation—(& mine)

Now I must think hard about those courses.— With much love—and see you soon—wonderful!

Elizabeth

402.[2]

[September 22, 1972]

Dearest Elizabeth:

I started two letters to you, each explaining the difficulties of fixing dates etc. for our trip to America—on magnifying the difficulties—when Caroline's Cousin can take two children, when Lizzie's lawyer will be ready, when I can get leave from Essex. Who'll take car[e] of our house. Now all's more or less solved. We'll fly on the 8th of October, and stay about two weeks. We'll probably come to Cambridge about the 15th, and stay a couple of days.

I've never felt any embarrassment about our situation here—we are hus-

---

1 Frank Bidart, *Golden State* (1973); for EB's blurb, see *Elizabeth Bishop: Poems, Prose, and Letters*, ed. Robert Giroux and Lloyd Schwartz (2008).
2 Crossed with letter 401.

band, wife and son, all named Lowell, answering to the name of Lowell. But in America—"I want you to meet my wife Caroline. I am here to arrange my divorce." I exaggerate; the divorce is now wanted by everyone.

Deeper than this, one has so many thoughts, Lizzie has so many thoughts, thoughts in common—a blessed change, but one that casts a funereal shadow. I feel like I am about to have some absolutely necessary surgical operation.

We'll all see you very soon—better in Cambridge maybe than Bergen.

All my love,

Cal

403.

Dearest Elizabeth:

We'll be at Bill Alfred's sometime after the 15th, though I dread the effect of Sheridan on Bill's fragile furniture. Unfortunately he has made great strides in the last month and now walks, and I think takes strength exercises. A little girl visited him and he looked in contrast like a golden gorilla.

Has Frank invited you to apartment-hunt with him again? He may decide to give you his Norwegian chair and stay where he is.[1]

The other day I read quite a good piece on you in an old *Encounter* by Douglas Dunn. He also has a good one on Randall in the current number, tho it comes close to slandering me—after once praising me to the skies.[2]

As you can imagine, we've had puzzling difficulties with Sheridan's passport—all clear now, I hope.

Eager to meet the great Alice.

O I think I'm under the Fitzgerald shadow; it had grown dim, but now it must be black as night. Caroline is a friend of Walker Evans; a friend of Robert's surely. I'd like to see them if they would. I shiver both with excitement and fear at the thought of the trip. Coming to America with Caroline is exciting. It's all so sad with Lizzie though.

---

1 When Frank Bidart bought a large chair in Helsinki, he knew that he had no room for it, which precipitated his buying the apartment that he has lived in since.
2 Douglas Dunn, "Snatching the Bays" (review of EB's *Complete Poems*), *Encounter* (March 1971); "An Affable Misery," *Encounter* (Oct. 1972).

404.

Dearest Cal:

Your note of the 8th[1] may have overlapped my last one to you—on the other hand, it may have been an answer to it? Yes, I can see how this trip is going to be very tough for you. I do hope that everything will somehow resolve itself more easily than you now feel it possibly can . . . I do want to see you—and your family, too. I met Bill on the street yesterday, no Friday, and he says you'll be in Cambridge the 16th and 17th . . .

My (unlisted) telephone number here, in case you don't have it, is 876-4993. I'll be back from Nova Scotia the night of the 9th.

There's something I want to ask you about & I feel the sooner the better. I've "heard" (the way one does here) that you are coming back to teach at Harvard—rumours before, now more definite-sounding rumours. Frank hinted at this when I first saw him, saying you wanted to return for a term, & it seems to me you wrote me you'd *like* to in 1970—or 71—but it all sounded rather vague then.

I talked with Mr. Bloomfield before I left in February, '71, and again last year and both times I asked him if you were coming back to teach and told him that if there was any possibility of my interfering with this of course I didn't want to come back. Both times Mr. Bloomfield said that you weren't coming, as far as he knew, but the second time he added that if you did, the Dept. could "find enough money for both of you" . . . something like that, half-jokingly. However, since you have—or are?—a "Chair" I don't think money would be the problem.

I think I ought to go to talk with Mr. Heimert, the new head of the Dept., soon. I really have to make plans for the future (what there is of it). I don't feel that I can keep on living on this invitation-at-the-last-minute basis any longer, and I have to decide where I am going to live, in this country, and *how*. (I'm trying to sell the Ouro Prêto house—but of course it may take years.) I don't think we will ever suffer from "conflict of interests"—but I think I ought to know your plans so I can be "looking around" etc. I don't expect the Eng. Dept. ever to tell me anything—it's unpleasant, but that's the way it is—but I know you'll be frank with me, anyway.

Lots of love,

Elizabeth

---

1 Possibly letter 400 or 403.

405.

Dearest Elizabeth—

I'm surprised everyone is vague about my coming back. I am "signed up" to come back fall term 73. This continues my tenure, but I doubt if I'll do it again. It's too expensive, transporting children, renting a Cambridge house—too disrupting of ourselves. However I want to hold on to my American tenure against the unforseeable future. Everything at the moment makes it easier and physically pleasanter for me to live in England. But I don't feel English. The color of my blood, whatever, is in America, friends, memories.

I wonder if your tenure depends on my vacating mine. They should be separate and such an arrangement is embarrassing for both of us. I don't want to resign my chair until we've spent a term and see how we like it. But I don't see any likelihood of my remaining. I might make some arrangement, or Harvard could, that I sporadically return with due notice.

I think you should definitely get the same terms I have. We cost them so little as things go! But I can't come back yearly, or anything yearly.

Cambridge—I'm not sure. I teach here on the 25th, so must fly by the 23rd. It might be easier to fly from Boston. Aren't we the nearest major airport to Europe? I think we'll come to Harvard soon as I've finished the divorce arrangements with Lizzie. I can't tell how long. It's more psychological than financial.

I think some of the confusion about my return was this—that sometime 71? before my chair had expired—only two years leave can be taken off—I got a letter assuming I no longer had my appointment. This alarmed me, and through Bill and Bloomfield, I got myself reattached. I am sure I wrote you, because there is no secret at all, and for a year I've been telling everyone I see that we would be back in 73. Maybe one avoids putting such things in letters, because they are somehow out of mind, and not very immediate. I am unbelievably sorry to put you through this anxiety.

The divorce, however painful, must improve things—for everyone.

Love,

Cal

406.

October 26th, 1972

Dearest Cal:

It's hard to think that you & yours are up in the air 30,000 ft. or so on your way back to England . . . At least I hope you are, & that all went well those last bad days.

(This is my new & extremely complicated typewriter that I haven't mastered yet, so excuse any untidiness . . .)

After saying good-bye to you, Frank came in with me and made himself a large pot of coffee . . . Then he went home, probably to stay up the rest of the night, & I went to bed. I knew you were very tired—I think Caroline was exhausted—

This is really just to say two or three small but important things. 1. I do like Caroline and I do hope you'll be happy together. Also, I'd really like very much to see some of her writing—I wasn't just being polite. Stories—and also the article she's doing about that "free" school.

2. I have an appointment to see Mr. Heimert tomorrow morning. I have a *feeling* that your return isn't going to affect my situation here—but I might be wrong. IF they want me to come back next year, I think I'll ask if I might teach in the spring term instead of the fall term. I'd really like to have time to try to finish a book of poems, and I have a fairly good start now. Or I might teach somewhere else around here . . . Anyway, we'll see. I'm going to be quite frank with him and see what happens. It's true that if I had known you definitely were coming back, I would probably have investigated these other offers in detail, etc.—but, after all, I should be able to look out for my own interests. Please, please don't let any of this academic stuff come between us to the slightest degree. I think we both need to keep our old friends—for the rest of our lives—don't you . . . ?

My photograph by Tom Victor finally arrived—it will do, but oh dear!—not his fault—mine! and yesterday when Richard Howard telephoned about it he asked about you & I said you hadn't received yours yet, either. He swore that you would very soon.

I know it's been a fearful year for you but I'm lost in admiration for the way you continue to write through it all—and with me (& Adrienne R., I gathered) and others, I'm sure, picking on you for what you were doing. I suppose it is really nobody's business but your own, after all. I am going to put my oar in once more, however—this is something I meant to ask you about and never got around to.—Frank told me you are planning to dedicate one of the new books—HISTORY, I think—to him and to Stanley Kunitz. I wanted to ask you if you couldn't manage to dedicate that, or whatever book it is, to Frank, all by himself . . . I know Stanley is an old friend, etc.—but Frank has worked so damned hard. When he came back last winter I don't think he thought of anything else for months—he used to call me up and re-cite sonnets and sonnets from memory, re-arranging lines & commas and so on—it's fantastic.— He should be going on with his thesis on you, but I think he's just too much inside your work now to do it—I don't know how long this will last. His life seems so sad and meager to me and with so few satisfactions—*coitado*, as we say in Brazil . . . I fear for his book—in spite of Richard H's telling me how "strong" it is!— Stanley doesn't need such a big boost as your dedication would give nearly as much as our Frankie does, I think. Now forgive me for being an old busybody.

Now that the psychotic black has been removed,[1] my reading class is a dream—everyone talks like mad and the English lady PhD has discovered Marianne M. and has written a wonderful short paper about her. The Chinese brings in unintelligible, but I'm sure profound, references to the Chinese, and we are really having a good time. The black lady-poet in the writing class is in the infirmary—psychological, they told me—so I went to see her and found her without her usual turban—her head divided into neat little squares and 30 or 40 short pigtails. She is very tall and elegant—a Watutsi, I think—long long black arms & legs in a short white night-shirt. She seems to be cheering up rapidly—and I really have hopes for her. I left her reading Hopkins avidly.

Mail—ye gods, *more* Amy Lowell Traveling S. poems . . .[2] One boy wants to use it to find a Sufi guru . . . I don't think Amy would have appreciated that. Or wd. she have?

I see I must spend this lovely free day at this hyper-sensitive and over-impulsive machine.

I am so glad to have seen you & to find I like Caroline a lot—also Peter Taylor. I'm sorry I didn't see more of Sheridan.

I wish you wouldn't drink. I *know* it is bad for your health, primarily.— I had a lovely time drinking vodka and aqua-vite while traveling, but when I'm working here I find it's much better just to stop completely—that's eas-ier for me than cutting down. I don't know how it works for you. But I do know I like all my friends better when they aren't drinking— And now I have said more than enough of my mind for once.

1 See Monroe Engel's account in *Remembering Elizabeth Bishop: An Oral Biography*, ed. Gary Fountain and Peter Brazeau (1994), 292.
2 EB was serving as a judge for the Amy Lowell Poetry Travelling Scholarship.

Please do let me know how things went, how you are, how the teaching is, etc. Frank also told me that maybe you'll be living in Manchester—Bob G's relative's house or something like that—I missed that on Sunday night. That ought to be nice.— I think I'd like to live with a view of the sea, around here somewhere, maybe. Meanwhile I'm going to tackle my awful little land-lady and ask her to give me first chance at any higher up apt in this same house. However—the paper says rents may go up *30%*—horrors—I may have to go back to Ouro Prêto yet.

Give my love to Caroline—always lots for you—
Elizabeth

407.

[October 31, 1972]

Dearest Elizabeth—

I'm so glad you wrote because I didn't think we parted on the right note—so much so I didn't quite know how to write. The trip has left us bone-tired, not in spirit so much as physically—I could use one of Mailer's irritating metaphors, a boxer who has been punished for ten rounds.

I am sore about my alimony, though it's quite bearable and more or less what I outlined in my mind two and a half years ago. I keep what I make: salary, manuscript sale, royalties, I lose everything inherited, all trust inter-est, NY apartment, Maine house and barn—I thought they were Lizzie's in Cousin Harriet's will, but as I had forgotten, they were half mine by Maine law—all this is OK, but it's the small things, the difficulty of getting personal or family things, my books, silver spoons etc. I have no need of furniture, but all of ours I paid for, and some pieces were in my parents' house when I was five, or seven or eight. Well, I want little, not even many books; there's a clause in the alimony agreement saying we should agree on what should be mine—and doubtless when emotions are less keen we will agree, since not more than a couple of thousand dollars at most is in question. What really bothers me though is that Harriet will receive nothing of consequence from me—the alimony provides for her tuition through graduate school and fur-ther, but to be handled by Lizzie. I feel Harriet has been stolen from me like the dozen silver spoons. Of course, there are provisions for mutually consul-tation on her life and education—unenforcible if we are in a temper, as we are now, and mustn't be later when our blood cools—for everyone's good. So it will be, God willing—today I am enjoying the luxury of steaming.

Frank's dedication—here's what happened (but no one concerned can tell the same story about something even as simple as this). I think I said to Frank last winter that I ought to dedicate *History* to him, but that this seemed odd because he was really a collaborator. Anyway I totally forgot and dedicated it to Kunitz, who had written me a powerful letter about it, had recently nearly died, to whom for ages I had wanted to dedicate a book, etc. Frank was so upset, I made a double dedication, a solution like splitting a Bollingen, that no one quite relishes, but the only possible way out for me. I haven't dared tell Kunitz and meant to if I had had a chance to see him, not just talk to. Now I will. It's hard to express how much Frank's work with me was worth, and is—without giving an immodest evaluation to my poem. There's no other book to dedicate—the *For Lizzie and Harriet* is itself a dedication, and the *Dolphin* must be to Caroline. I'm so glad you really like her—I assumed so somehow—perhaps Frank has copies of some of her things. He must have. We're so bad about parcelling and mailing, and only have one copy of most things.

Oh God, Dear one, I do feel you must have security. I don't think I've undermined you, cannot remember not being open about my return—somehow Bloomfield assumed I had resigned when I hadn't.

If I weren't still tired I'd tell you humors of our San Domingo days—I'd say with my whole heart, we (you & I) are together till life's end,

All my love,
Cal

408.

(a day later)
[November 1, 1972][1]

Dearest Elizabeth—

I must write more softly to you, or promise I will. My late trip hardly softens one's surface, or one's depths. I feel a large something infected has been removed from me—it was not really my fault or Lizzie's. Gone it is, but I cannot take it in yet, and remain at a loss, a little tired and cross trying to reassemble myself. I pretended to be angry at first about the alimony, then found I really was. Somewhere deeper than I can reach the anger has gone.

If I have spoken to you in less than my old admiring and loving voice, forgive me.

all my love,
Cal

1 Postmarked on November 3, 1972.

409.

Dear Cal:

I'm working over at Alice's apt., to get away from the telephone and the sight of all the chores I shd. be doing . . . This is the only paper around and it depresses me & the November day is even grayer than it is. We had one day of sun—in 3 weeks like this. England is sort of the same way in the fall, isn't it—I think the last time I was there was in November . . . I was very glad to hear from you, and then to hear from you *again*—but you really didn't need to write a second time. I knew when you were here, of course, what a terrible stretch you were going through . . . I even felt badly about insisting a bit, once, on my own present problems— However, they are real enough!

I think I wrote you that I did see Mr. Heimert—who was very affable. But so far I have heard nothing more. Robert Fitzgerald telephoned once, about a week ago now, to say he knew all about it and was trying to help me, etc.—very sweet. But that's all I've heard so far. I did say I'd teach next *spring* term—I'll probably be here in Cambridge the earlier part of the year, too, but think I'll try to get some of my own work done in that stretch— we'll see. Meanwhile the Un. of Virginia pursues me hotly . . . WHY? It's strange. I had a nice letter from Peter Taylor yesterday—and some from Mr. Levenson, also phone calls from him— But—I really don't want to go away to some place where I don't know a soul, to spend my declining years— However, I'll go for 2 nights to give a reading, in January, probably and see how it looks. IF I could sell my house for a fortune, and my "papers"—I'd retire immediately, & with great relief . . .

However, the classes this time are both delightful—but I always have a feeling no one is *really* learning anything.

Frank got moved—but perhaps he's written you—and we had a sort of dinner-party there a day or two later—I took a casserole, and he provided champagne . . . The apt. looks much, much better with his furniture in it. He is having the Porsche completely overhauled and re-painted—thank goodness— I couldn't bear to think of him hurtling about, without any brakes, even . . .

I heard yesterday that Fitzgerald was taken sick and was in a hospital in Hartford—some kind of dysentery he has off and on, I think. I'll try telephoning again now . . .

—Oh dear—it is worse than I realized. I got a friend staying in their house who told me that Robert was operated on in Hartford, stomach ulcers again—two days ago, I think—Sally was there with him, fortunately.

And that is all the news for now, I think— The 15th there is a memorial service for Marianne, in Philadelphia—I'm going down for it, then on to NY for a long week-end. Oh—Betty Kray called last night—she wants to put on something for Ezra Pound at the NY Public Library, I think[1]—I think she wanted "ideas"—and maybe *you*, from something she said. But I don't seem to have any ideas on that subject any more . . .

I hope things are getting better for you now— The only thing I can really say is that I've usually thought alimony an *awful* idea . . . however, in some cases perhaps it is necessary, I don't know. It all depends . . .

With much love, and regards to your family—

Elizabeth

410.

Milgate Park
[January 3, 1973]

Dearest Elizabeth:

I'll be in America before you get this letter. I am reading on the Kray Pound program on the 4th,[2] and then will stay over about four days, ending up I hope in Boston.

Many thanks for your presents, different and more interesting than other people's. The baked beans immediately disappeared in the surf of children's sweets, then miraculously reappeared this morning at breakfast unopened. We like Sheridan's Harvard sweater or underwear top. He is less naughty and boisterous maybe than once, but we have no trust. He quietly learned how to climb out his crib. We are contemplating an eight foot metal cylinder.

The book is done and in at Faber's—over 500 poems gone over for about the thousandth time, a kind of peace that it's done. What next—trout fishing? I do plan some with a friend this spring. The trouble is I am always hooking myself.

Through my three or four days English flu. There are jokes about this being the first offering England has made to the Common Market.

Dearest, will you be in Cambridge around the seventh or eighth? I'll call from New York.

Love,

Cal

1 Ezra Pound died on November 1, 1972, in Venice.
2 "A Quiet Requiem for E.P.," the Academy of American Poets, January 4, 1973.

411.

Sunday morning, January 14th, 1973

Dearest Cal:

Before I go out in the below-freezing morning to bring in 20 lbs. of Sunday papers—19 lbs. to be thrown out within half an hour—I'll write you a note . . . Here is that check-stub or whatever it is—probably unnecessary to send back, but anyway. I've just decided to write F, S & G and ask them not to write me for permissions all the time—following your good example. However, I do like to correct when possible all those idiotic things such as my chief influence was Pablo Neruda and I lived on a farm in Nova Scotia for 18 years and so on . . . There is some magnificent music on the radio—a Bach Mass. This month the Harvard station has something called a musical "Orgy"—24 hours a day—everything from African drums to Indian music to Bach—one can telephone and they'll play your requests. After this comes music from "shows." Last year I telephoned a few times and my requests were played right away, usually with the remark "Now here's a real oldie—from 1938" . . . But I must stop listening and get to work.

I haven't heard any more from the English Department and still have the feeling that Mr. Heimert was again being humourously sadistic. And Dean Dunlop has left & gone to work for Nixon in Washington . . . IF I could sell my house, and my papers—or if & when I do—I'd really like not to teach any more, but try to get along on selling poems and readings—except I feel that readings are as much of a fraud as teaching, almost. I do NOT feel right about this "teaching." Everything the students (if you can call them that) learn from me, they should be learning on their own. I don't believe in teaching anything "contemporary"—or even recent. I agree with Eliot's ideas on this subject—only the classics, some history, the sciences, *can* be taught—and certainly no "literature" unless the author has been dead 100 years, or possibly was a "foreigner."[1] I really don't feel right about it at all. Nevertheless—some of these *children tell* me they've learned a lot—but what, I wonder? I don't like this "personality" idea at all . . . so there.

Last night I read the Cole Porter book Frank gave me, until after 2.[2] He really was quite a poet—I don't think you'd agree—but sometimes in his endless frivolity and modish detail he out-does Auden—when Auden attempted night-club songs, etc. He used (like Marianne) a rhyming dictionary—and his rhymes are better than Byron's . . . Anyway, I got a lot of ideas

1 See T. S. Eliot, "On Teaching the Appreciation of Poetry," *Critic* (Apr.–May 1960), 13–14 and 78–80; and "T. S. Eliot Deplores Modern Verse Study," *The New York Times* (Dec. 30, 1960), 1.
2 Cole Porter, *Cole*, ed. Robert Kimball (1971).

to incorporate in an endless, frivolous (but not entirely, I hope) poem I've been working on, or accreting, about my poor dead toucan . . .[1]

I've also done some of the MM piece—but I don't want it to be just funny stories & I'm afraid that's all it is so far. You know the lines from *The Frigate Pelican*—

As impassioned Handel—
meant for a lawyer and a masculine domestic
career—clandestinely studied the harpsichord
and never was known to have fallen in love,
   the unconfiding frigate-bird hides
in the height and in the majestic
   display of his art.—[2]

I've always thought they are autobiographical and could somehow be used to defend Marianne against the vicious gossip that is already in the air about her . . .

Well. I'm very literary at 9 AM. A very *neat* poem by Wilbur about Sylvia Plath makes me angry. Several people including Frank have admired it and I think it is very bad—really unfeeling. I tried to decide why and think it's because it is supposed to be ironic and isn't—"It is my office to exemplify / The published poet in his happiness"[3]—it's full of words like that. Now Ransom could have written a poem like that, neat rhymes, cliché words, and all—and the irony would have been really there and somehow chilling and deep & sad—this just seems smug, I'm afraid . . .

As you see, I wish we could go on with our recent conversations. It was lovely to see you looking so much better and seeming so much more cheerful. Bill tells me you left your marriage license behind . . . ! He wants me to dine with him and *Faye*[4] this week and I think this time I'll really have to—I can't imagine why he wants *me* to meet her. This is a strange society.

If we're going to have winter, I wish there'd be snow—heavens I'm sick of looking at the Loeb theatre and Cambridge unadorned. I want a view of the sea somewhere, or at least a harbor or inlet— But rents on the harbor are $700 a month— Where to live . . . I hope you had a bearable flight and found everyone well, no more flu. I was feeling so lousy when you called but I was glad to

---

1 See "Sammy" (EB-*EAP*).
2 Marianne Moore, "The Frigate Pelican," from lines 26–32 (1934).
3 Richard Wilbur, "Cottage Street, 1953," lines 9–10, *American Poetry Review* (Nov.–Dec. 1972).
4 Faye Dunaway, who starred in William Alfred's *Hogan's Goat* (1965).

see you anyway— Both Alice and I recovered fairly quickly from the second bout. Frank is coming in this PM—to drink 18 cups of coffee . . . But he seems better now, too, and actually seems to like his Wellesley girls and perhaps is making some new friends—something he should do, *coitado*— Now no one could say *this* is a "good letter"—you are flattering about my letters but I'm afraid I've written better ones to old school friends,—and not to you!

I hope the page proofs go well & fast— Lots of love,
Elizabeth

412.

January 24, 1973
Dearest Elizabeth:

I felt almost with the address-words of your letter, that we were so airily and happily beyond the days of our clouds. And of course I felt this the times I saw you last in Cambridge. What a lovely long night of drinks, gossip, memories, everything.

The Wilbur poem annoyed me too. Which way is the irony meant? Against Dick? Against some conventional person much like Dick, yet slashed as his opposite? Or against Sylvia? All probably. I seem to have run into people lately who are his old friends, and welcome being bitter on him. He has really always been a model acquaintance, almost friend to me, though I felt a fragile shell kept his rivalry from muddying me. Still, a good man. I've always thought, I'm afraid that Ransom did his kind of poem (Wilbur's) with genius and a character.

When Eliot made his statement about teaching contemporaries, the New York Radio or some paper called me up for comment. All I could think of was that I would be out of a job. Here, by brute force I managed to teach Shakespeare for 2 months or so, and then was hurled back by the head of our department into semester . . . term on term of modern North American poets, my specialty. I think a *writing* course in poetry might be half *reading* modern poetry. But now must think up something for Heimert. How about Milton. Is Satan the hero usually starts the students talking for several meeting[s]. But maybe that's past. I think maybe English 19th century poetry.

I have read somehow about six defenses of hermeticism in the last ten days. An impassioned text (new for the Mariner) of Coleridge by Empson.[1]

---

1 William Empson, "Introduction," *Coleridge's Verse: A Selection*, ed. William Empson and David Pirie (1972). See review in *The Times Literary Supplement* (Dec. 15, 1972) and Empson's reply (Jan. 12, 1973), reprinted in *Selected Letters of William Empson*, ed. John Haffenden (2006), 544–46.

The passionate anti-Christian and the passionate Christian (Empson and Flannery) have much the same tone. Empson believes the Mariner really experienced the spirits and Coleridge really really hid them—almost in a burning sulfur air of Tory-Trinitarian persecution. Then Kathleen Raine on Yeats['s] Journals,[1] his hermeticism that has outworn Eliot's A Catholicism. Then Graves speaking the fourth and even fifth dimension at seventy-five in his love poems.[2] And finally (this is my whole point) a great outcry about John Dee and his successor Robert Fludd, scientists and the Magi of the hermetic movement under Elizabeth and James. We live in the house Fludd lived in[3] (visitors come and we can tell them nothing—but I'm ordering books) His Jacobean bust is in the village church, and Caroline has an authenticator friend who told her the Lowells and Fludds were related. A few years ago the Lowells would have spurned this connection; now it's at a premium. But do you believe you have experienced eternity, or immortality? Another article says that Hardy did with his first wife, then denied what he had actually known by experience. I think I am unreconstructable. But it would be merry to believe such things. Particularly now, when I am having strong after-book blues, feel I've written nothing and am incapable of the minimum necessary practical effort.

The Pelican must be Marianne, but aren't all her animals her? Their carefully noted anatomies given Moorish virtue? Oh thanks thanks for your lovely magnifying paperweight. Will I someday stare thru the white flower or coral, half-blind, to read letters. Caroline sends her love—I as ever all mine.

Love,[4]

413.

March 19, 1973

Dearest Elizabeth:

I am finished (such my mood) with everything—writing, teaching, divorce, alimony, strife. Phrases come into my head, and I no longer pencil them down, hoping they'll go somewhere. It's a time of de-effervescing, more busy than toil.

We're negotiating to buy the land about our house—to keep it from be-

---

1 Kathleen Raine, *Yeats, the Tarot, and the Golden Dawn* (1972).
2 Robert Graves, *Poems 1970–1972* (1972).
3 Robert Fludd was born in Milgate House, Bearsted, Kent.
4 Unsigned.

ing turned into football fields or a golf course. Now it's grazed by sheep and cattle, and gives us ease and gentle spaces. If it were changed, we would suddenly be living in the suburbs. If we bought the land, we would still have it grazed, not make much, but it would be a safe value for us and the children. Land can hardly go down much near London.

More money. My ms. sale to Harvard[1] is coming to a conclusion, though there are still details. Your letters are the most valuable and large single group. I would like to have them pay you $5000. Of course they are yours, your writing, just as Miss Moore's letters are hers, but convention gives letters to the recipient. We should keep carbons, or rather *you* should, you who really write letters. I want to reread all yours someday—it would take a summer and would be reliving a long stretch of my life. I've seen a few of my own letters (to my mother, Roethke, incongruous couple) they aren't too much, but have words and sentences written seriously and unlike what I print. Yours have the startling eye and kept-going brilliance of a work to print. I hope you do.

Harriet comes here in four days for a week. None of the drama of last year, of the divorce not agreed on and Lizzie sending her dearest lamb, mine too, into the tiger's den. In fact, I think Lizzie is looking forward to her own vacation. Somehow the alimony and the legal decision has brought peace. I hope it survives my books. They must be troubling to Lizzie, but she has seen a good deal and won't exactly be surprised, or even maybe find them an *issue*. It is somehow very different with the divorce; Lizzie doesn't want really to go to town on, or think of herself as being injured.

Ah, but I hear you have bought a condominium! How we want to be comfortable and secure (there [is] none!) I feel the same about the fields I am looking at if we know we can go on having what we have, every breath we breathe is happier. If only age could stop; and inspiration be an irregular constant.

A new author, a first book—how pleasant to watch them. Caroline has just finished her first, *For All That I Found There* (Ulster Protestant anthem) the title is much more poetic and Irish than the book, New York California characters, Woman Lib. Black schools etc. stories, autobiography, essays, reviews, Ulster where she grew up[2]— —Rave letter from Peter Taylor about you.

all my love,

Cal

1 RL sold his papers to Harvard's Houghton Library.
2 Caroline Blackwood, *For All That I Found There* (1973).

414.[1]

60 Brattle Street, Cambridge
March 20th, 1973

Dearest Cal:

It seems to me it was much easier to write you letters from Brazil than it is from Cambridge . . . This isn't just a matter of TIME—although one does seem to be constantly busy here and I *hate* being busy—but there seems to be very little to say, strange as that may be. You *know* exactly what goes on here day after day, and know all the people far better than I do, and it rarely seems worth writing about, somehow. However, I'm about to leave to teach that spring term in Seattle & feel strongly that I should write you before I go so much further away— (However, maybe it's nearer—that flight over the North Pole.)

(This address will reach me—)

I sent you a postcard from Charlottesville, I think.[2] I spent two nights there, with the Ehrenpreises (?) because Peter has that dog, *Sugar Plum*—but I had dinner with the Taylors the night I got there, and Eleanor made a lunch the next day for eight people, & they drove me out to see their land and house somewhere in the countryside . . . They are both very nice. I loved those huge old portraits—if you remember them—especially the one with the two little girls in it—Peter's great-great-aunt or some such relative—and I loved the accents. I was also taken to Monticello—and decided that Jefferson must have been a domestic tyrant—and saw the "Lawn"—the effect so beautiful, and the details so absurd— Each student there seemed to have a pile of firewood outside his door, a nice old-fashioned touch—and also a *hibachi* (?)—one of those Japanese braziers, for cooking . . . In about two weeks the gardens must be lovely. I seem to get to places at just the wrong time—before that I spent four days at the University of Oklahoma. That was really fun; I had a won-derful time—but the desolation of that scenery, at that time of year, is in-credible.— I've seen "lonely New England farmhouses"—but nothing can compare to a lonely, small-sized, ranch-house in Oklahoma. One can see for miles—all pale tan—only the pumping oil-wells *lend animation to the scene*— even the "Wild Life Reservation"—pumping away like lost lunatics—

Oh—Eleanor gave me "A Wilderness of Ladies" and I think many of the poems are *very* good. (I'd only read her second book.)[3] I am not so crazy about Randall's introduction, however—or maybe I just never did like his

---

1 Crossed with letter 413.
2 The postcard does not survive.
3 Eleanor Ross Taylor, *A Wilderness of Ladies*, intro. Randall Jarrell (1960), and *Welcome Eumenides* (1972).

understanding & sort-of-over-sympathizing with the lot of women—but this would take explaining and is NOT just Women's Lib!

Anthony Hecht and youthful wife and 11 months old son are here—I saw them and Bill, etc. Sunday night. I gathered that Bill is still trying to find you a house—also a place for the Taylors to live. My biggest piece of news in this line is that I am in the process of buying (although it won't actually be paid for until long after my death, I think) an apartment down on Lewis Wharf, in Boston. I am very excited about this—it is a marvelous old building, huge, all granite—built in 1838. I'll have a verandah (4th floor) looking at the harbor—the Mystic River side—fireplace, & as much room, or a bit more, than I have here—although the ping-pong table will have to go. After years of being spoiled by some of the world's best scenery I've really hated looking at the Loeb Theatre and being wakened by garbage trucks etc. However—I won't be able to move in until September or October—if I don't go bankrupt before then. (Do you know it is hard for women to get mortgages?—the 1st thing the lawyer told me, after he'd said to check the "construction."— Since the walls are 18" thick and the building is in perfect condition after 135 years, *that* seems sound enough.)

I had dinner with Frank last night and he gave me a beautiful book, which he shouldn't do. He'll go bankrupt before I do. He had his page-proofs with him and I thought the book looked very impressive—much better than in MMS.

I'll be coming back here for about a week, April 8th or 9th, and think I may be able to hear Empson, who is coming about then—I'd love to hear him read.[1] Of course nary a student had ever heard of him . . .

I hope you're well and that all goes well.— I have no idea as to your "terms" there—when you're working & when you're not—or when you expect to get here. Kiss Sheridan. Remember me to Caroline. *Please stay well.*— When do the books come out?

Lots of love,
Elizabeth

---

1 William Empson read at Harvard University on April 13, 1973.

415.

University Motel, 4731 12th N E
Seattle, Washington
April 29th, 1973
(Have you a house in Cambridge yet?)

Dearest Cal:

It has been over a month since I received your last note—but just too much seems to have been happening for any kind of ordinary friendly correspondence. I was about to leave for here when it came; then after one grueling week, I had to go back to Cambridge and New York—mostly the latter—for that National Book Award affair (the Translation part of it being the minorest of the minor, of course),[1] and in between the last meeting and the grand announcements (which I fled from), James Merrill and I gave a joint reading—no, a sequential reading—at the YMHA and attended a huge party given at John Hollander's—then I escaped back to Cambridge, and then flew guiltily back to here . . .

The NBA was pretty awful, I thought—although *we* all did our part honorably, as far as I could see . . . a hell of a lot of reading, or looking into, dreary books . . . But never again. I didn't go to the lunch, the dinner, OR the grand ceremonies—but I saw some of it all, and the general "outlay," the obvious expense, money wasted, etc., was sickening, I thought. All those bars set up, travel expenses (I took my share of those, of course), food, lackeys—ye gods—and then publishers begrudge a book of poems' advertising . . .

I shouldn't speak this way, perhaps—because also in N Y I went with Bob G and Mike[2]—and I invited Frank—to that Opera Club—"Rosenkavalier,"[3] which I'd never heard. We all had a lovely time, I think—Frank was frightened at the prospect, but of course being the 3rd opera buff present he had a wonderful time and the gentlemen seemed to be getting along famously.

At the party—I was feeling quite dazed by then and there was an awful crush—Elizabeth suddenly emerged and was very nice & affectionate. I was pleased about this; I'd really been feeling disturbed by not having had the courage to do anything about seeing her for so long—I just didn't know *what* to do.

Oh! No, no, a thousand times no—or five thousand times no . . . I feel guilty enough living with the possible *intention* of selling personal letters.

1 EB served on the translation prize committee for the 1973 National Book Awards.
2 Michael di Capua.
3 Richard Strauss, *Der Rosenkavalier*, cond. Ignace Strasfogel, Leonie Rysanek, soprano.

And I have just read the collection of Auden's reviews or most of it—FORWARDS & AFTERWARDS[1]—and in almost every piece he goes on & on about the wickedness of printing private letters (although one can't help noticing he's a bit ambivalent about this sometimes—he regrets—but he does love a good bit of gossip.) And now I've just finished after reading almost all night—the last vol. of the Edel *Henry James*[2]—& James was even more severe on the matter—and *burnt* almost all his papers in his garden . . . (Maybe you've read it? Such a mess in some ways—full of contradictions & repetitions & wild interpretations—but the story is so fascinating—and HJ's *death* so marvelous—I'd never known anything about that before—that one just goes on reading & reading)

I hope the visit of Harriet went off beautifully—and have you bought that land and stocked it with sheep? (I don't think one stocks sheep, but anyway—I hope you've acquired it.) It would take 3 or 4 of these forms to tell you about my "condominium"—although I never think of it as that—except when I have to call on the special Condominium Lawyer (provided by dear Mr. Oberdorfer[3]—if you remember him?). Frank must have told you about it . . . Well—it is on Lewis Wharf, a famous old tremendous warehouse called the "Granite Warehouse," built in 1838—abandoned for years, but in wonderful condition. (The granite was quarried at Quincy—where my only "old New England" ancestors all lived—) I fell in love with the building. Wrote a will, with Mr. O; looked out the window and saw Lewis Wharf; walked down there, and all in about an hour and a half I had made a will and agreed to buy a wildly extravagant apartment . . . IF I sell the Ouro Prêto house, all will be well, I think; if not—well, off to the poorhouse—but in style, as they used to say in NS. I have a verandah—looking over part of the harbor and up the Mystic River; beamed ceilings (original beams), brick walls with iron loops and hooks still in them; a flu—flue?—for a Franklin stove—well, it is wonderful, or will be. Boston Harbor is pretty dead these days, but enough ships go by to keep using binoculars—and at night it is lovely. IF all this comes true. Of course I wish it were three times bigger—but, one *shd.* cut down on books and odds and ends at 62. The verandah is big enough to dine on—over 6' x 12'. So—I can spend my declining years watching the polluted tides rise & fall, at least—

1 W. H. Auden, *Forewords and Afterwords*, ed. Edward Mendelson (1973).
2 Leon Edel, *Henry James: The Master, 1901–1916* (1972)
3 Conrad W. Oberdorfer of Choate, Hall & Stewart, which oversees the Amy Lowell Poetry Travelling Scholarship.

All for now. I feel both foolish and overworked here—but if I can survive it I won't have to work until January & might even produce one small laborious poem, who knows— Much love,
Elizabeth

[Indicating "Additional message area"]
(Don't tell *me* what to do!) (When will C's book be out—& please send, of course—)

416.[1]

April 30, 1973

Dearest Elizabeth:

I wonder if my last ever reached you? In my wooly-witted way I mailed it to Harvard. I can't find any American to talk to about Watergate, though the English are glad to, but without one's own anguish and fervor. Sickening, fascinating gobbets come out in each paper. But it's too much, unless the country can somehow be cleaned up. I think the corruption has been going on long before Nixon, yet he is a criminal silhouette on things—government almost by the mafia—the day of Goulart. It's strange though, so many worse things have been happening to our country for the last—but what *is* the precise date?—years. One feels dirtied, or rather as if one's insides were force and money.

I am reading for ten minutes for something in behalf of paralytics and repairing the old Banqueting Hall. I suppose there's an analogy. I was asked to choose some poem not by myself and one by myself to go into a booklet. I took your "Nova Scotia," and my old "Water" (I see I've again made a mistake that I made in my *Benito Cereno* play, of making someone talk of someone's water.) A good pair, I think, and clear to read.

Philip Larkin spent last weekend with us. He looked older than T. S. Eliot—six foot one, low-spoken, bald, deaf, deathbrooding, a sculptured statue of his poems. He made me feel almost an undergraduate in health, and somehow old as the hills—he is four years younger. I asked him about a poem, "Wild Oats," where he speaks of a girl he met a few times in his twenties—"a bosomy English rose," and had kept two photos of her in his billfold[2]—and there the two photos were, her breasts invisible under a heavy coat, small, the same and no more than passport pictures. He is the best poet still writing here I think, perhaps by far.

1 Crossed with letter 415.
2 See Philip Larkin, "Wild Oats," lines 22–23.

1973 | *745*

A cut up month is on me, short reading trips to Rotterdam, Pisa—Berlin, not reading. We are trying to get up courage to go blind to Paris.

How do you like Washington? Has it dimmed since we knew it? Is Ted Roethke gone yet? I'm having a wonderfully worthless life—Caroline has just finished her book too—fishing, magazines, bit of fiction by people I've just met, movies.

Frank rather disapprovingly says you are in a motel. I wish I could fly to see you. Is Frank's book causing a heartening shock. All my love,

Cal

417.

May 3, 1973

Dearest Elizabeth—

Nothing much to say but I want to write with your letter fresh in mind. We are off for a week, three days in Paris then a bit more by myself in Florence and Pisa. The last is a poetry reading seminar round, etc. The thought of a second round of Italian poets making speeches in Italian in colorful little Apennine restaurants and Tuscan restaurants was too much for Caroline—so we added Paris. A delightful prospect, but too much for me almost.

Publication day has filled me with gloom for a long time—and now it's been put forward nearly three weeks to June 20. I must be worried about the reviews, yet it isn't that. It's the twinges of morality, one's length of life that keeps swimming into eyesight. It seems unbelievable that I've statistically lived so much much the largest division of my life. Why should a man live longer than his parents etc.? I translated a proverb line of Pasternak—it seems to me it took weeks, and yet only varies slightly from what other "translators" did (someone singled it out the other day in a piece about me) "To live a life is not to cross a field."[1] This is poignant, but this is what is comforting. We cannot cross the field, only walk it . . . finishing or not finishing this or that along the way. An image of all this is watching children and stepchildren growing into their futures I cannot see, and all from forty to fifty-five years younger than I even while I live. A rich tangle of the unseen.

All this poetry, this wisdom of the traveller stepping off for a week. We are very excited about Paris, and have been reading books by Jean Rhys and Ford about Paris in the thirties.[2] The thirties, perhaps because we expect

---

1 See "Hamlet in Russia, A Soliloquy," line 35 (RL-*CP*).
2 Jean Rhys, *The Left Bank and Other Stories*, preface by Ford Madox Ford (1970); Ford Madox Ford, *It Was the Nightingale* (1934).

them to be antediluvian, seem less far than 10 years ago. When do you join your condominium? The word doesn't seem to cover Frank's high rooms and your wharf. You seem where you've always been—I hope to sit with you there this winter, listening to the "polluted tides." We still have no house. Caroline's book comes out in September. She sends her love.

All my love as always,
Cal

418.

[Seattle, Wash.]
May 29th, 1973

Dear Cal:

I'll be going back to Cambridge in 3 or 4 days and I'll write you from there—I don't like this kind of little book very much, but I finally gave in & did this one—or *they* did—& you might as well have a copy, since I believe you like the poem—[1]

I am not feeling TOO friendly at the moment, because my "class" is finding you very difficult & much too EASTERN!—&, save me, they *won't* look up words, even the easiest, in the dictionary . . . Ye gods—I wish I were a millionaire—but anyway, never again—

Much love,
Elizabeth

419.

[60 Brattle St, Boston]
June 13th, 1973

Querido Cal:

Just now, one year ago, I was reading that "Moose" to the PBK society . . .[2] Thank goodness, I don't feel I have to attend today. We've been having one of those Boston heat waves—*ghastly* heat—but now it is supposed to rain and thunder—& lightning—I have just listened to this year's version of "Fair Harvard" on the radio . . . It was very strange: a sort of Fair *Waste Land*, I think. (Last year & the year before, two of my students did this thankless job.) But always all I can think of is "Believe-me if all these endear-

1 Possibly a letter-press printing of "Poem" for the Phoenix Book Shop, New York (1973).
2 See letter 396.

ing young charms . . ."[1] Isn't that Thomas Moore? (Marianne always said they were related.)

This typewriter seems to have suffered somewhat in the trip back east—it isn't just my bad typing. I want to tell you that the three books arrived, from Bob G., the day before I left—and I sent them in a box of books I was sending myself, to save air freight, and just got them again two or three days ago . . . I have read through HISTORY—not quite—but the other two completely. I see you've made many, many changes in the DOLPHIN one, and I think it comes out much, much better—don't you? It makes, in spite of literal time, much better sense the way it is now.[2] You've changed so many things—I'll have to write you again when I have had time to look at the MMS—and at the older *Notebooks* I have here . . . The images are as brilliant as ever—sometimes more so—and some of "To H & L" is poems I have liked for a long time, it seems to me.— Oh, heavens, I don't know *what* to say. There is the same jump from thought to thought that bothers me and that I think I called* a kind of surrealism, once—individual images that I see & understand—then a leap in thought I can't understand the reason for—However, I'll try to write you something about this when I am less tired—I just wanted you to know I'd got the books, and I'd also—if this doesn't seem too mercenary, or something—like to have the English ones.— These were sent by Bob G.—

Frank told me that you had a book "about dolphins." I wonder if you'd tell me which one this is? I have a rather scientific book about the intelligence of dolphins, but I don't think it's the same one. I am quite crazy about dolphins and whales—maybe I even wrote you about NAMU, the first killer whale I knew, when I was in Seattle? (in 1966)—(You mentioned killer whales in the sonnets[3]) Two or three weeks ago I went to Victoria, British Columbia, for the day, and the best thing there was the beautiful killer whale—Haidah—(named for the local Indian Tribe) a marvelous creature, black & white, just like Tobias, my dear deceased cat . . .

Frank seems very happy with his book—the extra copies got lost in the mail, but otherwise everything is fine & the one he showed me looked very nice, thank goodness.

When are you coming here & have you found a place to live? I have to go

1 Thomas Moore, "Believe Me, If All Those Endearing Young Charms," *Moore's Irish Melodies* (1846).
2 RL rearranged the order of the poems to change the plot of the story.
3 See "Mermaid: 4," line 1 (RL-*CP*).

to Brazil sometime, but I'm putting it off as long as possible. Please let me know about—or send me?—Caroline's book? Lots of love,

Elizabeth

*Footnote: NOT "short circuit."— It's when electricity skips a gap—

420.

Dearest Elizabeth:

My dolphin book is *The Dolphin Cousin to Man*, by Robert Sténuit, no masterpiece but mostly first-hand, easy to read, charming and fascinating as all books on this subject are.[1] My Killer Whale was actually a description of a dolphin but I wished to mask it—the whales are even smarter as well as bigger. Caroline discovered a searching fact the other day: the dolphin's heating & circulatory system is so efficient that they begin to boil if long out of water.

Glad you footnoted my jumps to jumping gaps, not short-circuiting—at first I thought you meant that I had misused the word *short-circuit* and wearily went looking for it through hundreds of pages. I owe you of course the changed order in *The Dolphin* and indirectly the new poems in *Another Summer*[2]—to plug a gap.

Shall I wait and send you the English second printing of three books? The printer made a number of errors and I have made my *last* improvements, a few really worth making.

For obvious reasons—being up too far, scandal, etc. I dreaded publication. However in England at least it's alright. It's too hot here too. We've just been to Rotterdam, a poetry festival. Attractive *entirely* new city (where the bombs fell), one that might have been rolled up after the festival and shipped to Los Angeles. A barge poetry reading which I luckily missed, encounter between Ginsberg and Günter Grass, almost totally dismayed and bewildered response of Grass, "Why he doesn't even have cymbals." Ginsberg offstage rather quiet and to me soothing.

Frank seems off to an inspiriting start with his reviews. His book seems

1 Published in 1968.
2 See "Another Summer" (RL-*CP*).

the same, only more controllably (A virtue ~~to me~~) felt. We have no sign of a house anywhere. I may have to commute from here.

    Love as ever,
      Cal

421.

[Chauncy Street, Cambridge, Mass.]
July 6th, 1973

Dear Cal:

    I am at Alice's apartment where I often come on hot days to work during the day—no telephone—calls for *me*, that is—air-conditioners, and it is up among the tree-tops and much quieter than Brattle Street—pretty impossible in the summer. But I didn't bring your letter along with me—a very nice one, as I remember . . . In fact, I shouldn't be writing letters at all—but I thought you might like to see this clipping—if you haven't already, that is.[1] Just before I read it I had received a letter from someone named Axelrod enclosing an article about all the various poems written about Col. Shaw. I'd known about the other Lowell—but not William Vaughn Moody, etc.—but you probably knew of them all, & maybe Mr. A has sent his piece to you, too? He wants to come here to "discuss" you with me—except I think he missed me for some time; I wasn't here the date he suggested. So I told him I could tell him everything *I* knew in one letter, probably . . . The article is actually quite interesting . . .[2]

    I went to Maine last week-end—from Thursday until Sunday—all the way to Stonington. It rained some, and when it didn't rain it was foggy—but very beautiful. We didn't get to Castine on the return trip—we didn't have quite enough time. Frank had requested a "present" so we bought 5 lbs of lobster—cooked for us on the spot—and I have just made an overwhelmingly rich dish for him with sherry, brandy, cream, mushrooms, etc. He is coming to dinner, & I think it is just the kind of thing he enjoys. There is also a cake of BLUEBERRY soap . . . (Not in the dinner). Maine seems to consist mostly of antique shops now. Oh, we went to Bar Harbor & I kept remembering the time you so carefully drove Lota & me around in it—and she finally admitted she thought all fir trees had been *planted*—by mankind . . .

    I was asked to that affair in Holland two years ago—and then I got amoe-

1 Probably Anatole Broyard, "Naked in His Raincoat," *The New York Times* (June 18, 1973).
2 Steven Gould Axelrod, "Colonel Shaw in American Poetry," *American Quarterly* (1972).

bic dysentery, etc. and couldn't go—& haven't been asked back! I wonder what it is like. I really dislike such affairs tremendously, but at the time it would have been very helpful—they would have paid my fare from *Brazil*—and then I was going on to visit Jimmy M[1] in Greece, where I've never been . . . What about your Italian trip? I seem to remember something about that, too—

I hope you have found a house by now—I have urged the Cambridge housing place—or did—on both Bill & Frank. There *must* be professors going away for that stretch . . . I don't know much about Lewis Wharf yet—I haven't signed the final papers yet and there are so many extra traps and loopholes, etc.—what the special CONDOMINIUM lawyer describes as "sweetheart clauses." I mean—really, what can one do with a *3' x 4'* storage space? I might put my bicycle up on end in it . . . Or paying for a swimming pool extravagantly the year round—when I dislike swimming with *others* . . .

I see by TIME, too, that Mary McC is in Washington—there she is with Senator Ervin, who is very charming, I think, too[2]—but does she know he is very much opposed to the Equal Rights Amendment?— Oh—she probably does!

Cambridge is pretty awful in the summer—but I am trying to work and not think about it— I hope you're well and everyone is flourishing in nice green Kent . . . And that the books are doing so well. I'd love to have the English edition, as I think you offered—

With love,
    Elizabeth

Yesterday was scarcely a Grand or Glorious 4th here— It started to rain in the afternoon & most fireworks were canceled—besides the overhanging clouds of you-know-what . . . I watched TV steadily for 2 days, I think, then could take no more. It has changed Frank's "life style" completely—or did for a week—he gets up *early* to take in the newspapers, and then settles down to watching the Senate inquiry—[3]

---

1 James Merrill.
2 Mary McCarthy was attending the Watergate hearings, and wrote about it for *The New York Review of Books* (see "Watergate Notes," July 19, 1973, and "Watergate," April 4, 1974). She is overheard praising Senator Ervin's intelligence and calling him "a sort of folk hero" for his role in the hearings in "People," *Time* (July 9, 1973).
3 The initial phase of the Senate's Watergate inquiry was televised from May 18 to August 7, 1973.

422.

July 12, 1973

Dearest Elizabeth:

I suppose you've seen some of my American reviews, a lampooning! I think they all have a jarring effect on Lizzie, but one by a Miss Perloff in the *New Republic* has been a calamity for Lizzie—what it says about her and Harriet.[1] The distortion of the "fictional" characters becomes a slander on the people themselves. I have been talking to people who are seeing her and to Lizzie herself. Last weekend she seemed to be suicidal, and friends had to drop in and telephone to see that she didn't take too many pills. All was confused and increased by her having total insomnia. Now her mood has quieted, but I have no certainty. We dread the telephone.

In *Newsweek*, in an otherwise discreet review, an unflattering photo of Lizzie was published, and above it a family portrait photograph (taken by Victor[2] when he was here and given without our knowledge to Newsweek) Caroline, I, a wild Ivana (labeled *Harriet*) and Sheridan looking like a secret polygamous poor white family.[3] This was so grotesque that Lizzie seems to have thought it funny. Unfortunately, she reads all the reviews, though no possible one could be pleasant.

The weather for the last three days has been close and sultry. My study is a very long room with a view of cows, fields, trees—all becalmed. If I stroll up and down, I can feel Lizzie with me, and no escape but arguing, though the past all in all gives a more joyful picture . . . and the future is only dread of what will happen. My intuitions hope, but what is that?

Your old letter of warning—I never solved the problem of the letters, and there and elsewhere of fact and fiction. I worked hard to change the letters you named and much else. The new order somehow makes the whole poem less desperate. And the letters, as reviewers have written, make Lizzie brilliant and lovable more than anyone in the book. Not enough, I know. And then I didn't want to imagine reviews in magazines with big circulations that would reduce my plot to news or scandal, politicians or actors.

My immorality, as far as intent and skill could go, is nothing in my book. No one, not even I, is perversely torn and twisted, nothing's made dishonestly worse or better than it was. My sin (mistake?) was publishing. I couldn't bear to have my book (my life) wait ~~hidden~~ inside me like a dead child.

---

1 Marjorie Perloff, "The Blank Now," *The New Republic* (July 7 and 14, 1973).
2 Thomas Victor.
3 Walter Clemons, "Carving the Marble," *Newsweek* (July 16, 1973).

All the while I've been writing, I've thought of you in the heat, and been happy to think of Alice's room among the airconditioned trees. We could use airconditioning here in the middle of the day, but at night it's cool.

all my love,
Cal

We still have no house.

423.

Dear Cal:

Your letter (July 12th) is awfully distressing . . . I've felt upset and blue all week. I'd seen only the daily TIMES review, and TIME[1] & NEWSWEEK; then Frank came to dinner Friday and brought the NEW REPUBLIC. Miss Perloff—whoever she is—does some very bad far-fetched interpreting, I'd say. Now I see an advertisement for a book about you by her[2]—but that must be pre- these last three. NEWSWEEK was unforgivably careless and cruel—but cruel mostly *because* of the carelessness. That Tom Victor—he took some picture of me and I had an awful time—months—just getting him to let me see *one* of them. (Now I'm going to demand them all from him.) Photographers and undertakers are the worst characters I know, I think. The Perloff piece—surely there must have been some personal spite behind that one—there's no foundation in the book for some of her remarks. It's too bad E couldn't NOT read any of these things—but I suppose it is impossible to resist.

Bill and I talked on the telephone two days ago and he said he had talked with E and he thought she was better. (He may also have talked with you, of course, for all I know.)

We all have irreparable and awful actions on our consciences—that's really all I can say now. I do, I know. I just try to live without blaming myself for them *every* day, at least—every *day*, I should say—the nights take care of guilt sufficiently. (But for God's sake don't quote me!)

I went to dinner at Bill's last Tuesday. I hadn't seen him—nor anyone, almost—since I got back from Seattle, I've been so immured by heat and work. Philip R. was there and an unknown young lady and the boy, Don[3]—

1 "Survivor's Manual," *Time* (July 16, 1973).
2 Marjorie Perloff, *The Poetic Art of Robert Lowell* (1973).
3 William Alfred's ward.

you asked about him once but at that point I hadn't met him. Very young, 14, but looks younger; very "tough" according to Bill, but he behaved quite well—is going to school, taking remedial reading and so on. I think Bill is very brave to become a "foster father."

Frank has several new poems and brought a long one, the latest[1]—& I'm afraid I was too hard on him about it. Alice and I took him swimming in Rockport, and again to Duxbury. His precious yellow Porsche was stolen—3 weeks ago now—I'm afraid there's not much hope of finding it, now. His mother was operated on for a breast cancer (small, he says) and naturally he has been terribly wrought up about that.

Alice is away for the week-end and I am here working in her apartment with the air-conditioners going. I think I have about 2/3rds of my MM piece done—but I'm afraid it is just too simple. However—I have at last written down most of the stories you told me many times *should* be written down . . . Lewis Wharf, the building inside and my legal problems with my contract, drag on.— I may get into the apt. in October, but think probably I'll be lucky to move before Christmas. I scan the GLOBE and the CRIMSON for houses—for you-all—surely a professor with children—enough space, I mean—will be leaving for that stretch . . .

I must get back to a trip to Coney Island with Marianne. It all comes back very vividly—even 1935 and '36—what a wonderful amazing delightful creature—

I hope all goes well with the family—

Love,

Elizabeth

424.

July 31, 1973

Dearest Elizabeth:

I was about to write you a letter of almost total gloom—no Massachusetts house, a last minute discovery that Harriet and Cathie had missed their month of barging and bicycling in Ireland by six days due to some error of the hostel agency in New York. But now it seems that Frank and Alice have found us a house in Wellesley (ah but never be sure) and Harriet's trip has been righted. It's been great fun having Harriet, and I've done more walking and sightseeing (not much) than in the last six months.

Lizzie's writing (?) a long letter to the *New Republic* against Miss Perloff

1 Frank Bidart, "The Arc"(1973).

and me, and she is half-threatening to sue Giroux and Faber. However she's in Lake Como and I feel certain nothing much will happen. Harriet doesn't really know anything is happening except a trivial dispute about a real estate quit-claim. "O she doesn't care about the book." Still, there's a tenseness. I have that unreal midsummer feeling of unreality, that by autumn or winter nothing will ever be the same. It won't.

Jean Valentine sent me (what I'm really writing about) your long "Crusoe in England"[1]—maybe your very best poem, an analogue to your life, or an Ode to Dejection.[2] Nothing you've written has such a mix of humor and desperation; I find bits of the late Randall, his sour witty downgrading of his own jokes, somehow this echo, if it is, makes the poem still more original and sealed with your voice. And finally, it expresses what I have been feeling for the last two months—(before the house.) It was all so close, it seemed truth I was writing in a dream.

I guess we'll see you soon. It's unimaginable for me to think of my being, not just visiting, in America.

Love to you,
Cal

Today I sweat as I type—for us intolerable heat.

425.

December 27th, 1973

Dear Cal:

I'm so sorry I missed you—heavens, is it a whole week ago Tuesday? I kept trying to call you up, in between things—and I gathered, from Frank, you tried to call me . . . Also that you had a hard time getting there—and so did my company, Dorothee (northwest spelling).[3] First, I took her on the sight-seeing trip all Tuesday morning—bus trip— It is really very nice, except for having to look at "Old Ironsides," which is now in dry-dock and completely gutted, for the time being. I think that rather depressed us both. By the time we got back and had some lunch it was almost time to take her to the airport. Then our troubles began—the battery in Alice's car was dead— so we tried to get a taxi. This took hours, literally, and Dorothee is a very nervous traveler . . . I was sure she'd miss the only plane to Seattle and be

1 "Crusoe in England," *The New Yorker* (Nov. 6, 1971); EB-*CP*.
2 Samuel Taylor Coleridge, "Ode to Dejection" (1802).
3 Dorothee Bowie.

stuck here until after Christmas. Finally she hailed a passing *girl* taxi-driver and said she'd give her $20.00 to make the plane. Which we did with exactly half a minute to spare—her bag, meanwhile, having been left at Kirkland house . . . By this time you were on your way to *Paris*, I think . . . & I hope you made it back to Milgate all in the same day and in one piece . . .

I was supposed to get to Ouro Prêto yesterday but decided I'd better not go away off there until I find out what has been ailing me lately. I've had a set of most unpleasant tests at the infirmary & shall hear the results—if any— this afternoon.

You know when you were here that afternoon I hadn't read that fearful review in AGENDA so I had no idea how bad it was.[1] I'm sorry—but it seems to me just extracts of *bad* parts in the LTLS, omitting all the *good* ones.[2] Please don't let it sadden you too much . . . I know it's been a bad stretch for you—let's hope we both have a better time of it in 1974.

I think I'll get up my courage now and enclose a very small poem[3]—but, alas, it is pretty sad, too, I'm afraid. Give my love to your family—and lots for you—

Elizabeth

P.S. On second thought, I'm *not* enclosing the poem—it is just too sad. Please write when you have time. I think that once December is over, things will possibly look better!

426.

[Milgate Park
January 18, 1974]

Dearest Elizabeth:

Sorry to be slow in answering your sweet letter. I'm getting, I guess, into the pace of being back—happy change and place full of space, quiet and coalfires.

You bring up the bad review in *Agenda*. I didn't want to show it to you when I was fresh from reading. All in all, the reviews haven't been bad, about three to two unfavorable, many journalism, too little tested in poetry to know very much. The moral criticism, I pass by,—that is for me to take up

---

1 Peter Dale, "Fortuitous Form," *Agenda* (Spring/Summer 1973).
2 "From Genesis to Robert Lowell," *The Times Literary Supplement* (Aug. 10, 1973).
3 Probably "Five Flights Up" (EB-*CP*).

with myself—something can be learned—the mind can change, though not the acts. I think I allow a good deal of the technical criticism.

Mistakes. Only one reviewer has shown this. I took 14 poems from *Notebook* called "Long Summer" written out of, tho not about, our 1966 summer in Maine. They are dense, symbolic, almost hallucinated (this is a mixture of the style and the mood behind it). In *History* I calm them up, make them poems about boyhood in Maine. But the first version is much better—I've spent days and days, like other revisers, spoiling by polishing. I think my great fault is rhetorical melodrama, a laborious maneuvering of this.

I see in a blurb you've written you object to confession and irony.[1] I suppose confession is the use or exploitation of painful experience that gets on ~~one's~~ conscience, that must out—but must it? Irony is being amusing (or worse acid about) about what we can't understand. I guess one can't write much without possibly falling in with these both—well they don't get one to heaven.

I feel our friendship has passed out of some shadow. Cambridge is a crowded place. Too much brushing from one friend to another, too many required shifts of attitude, and we are hardly allowed to move. It's too academic. I'm sure I am ignorant of most of what I dislike, but what I've tenderly liked stays—you. Send me your sad poem. I now have nine or ten, about being 56.[2] I mean they set off from that time of life, more interesting, less promise. Is this impertinence . . . after your sad poem? I think we are much happier now, but how [to] say it unless we get together in place?

Love,
Cal

PS. Won't it all be freer visiting, journeying to you in your new home, alone, and on the ocean?

---

1 "It's like turning the light switch off, and there in the dark—reality: all kinds of likely and unlikely things, incandescent on their own, beginning to stir and breathe. All that really needs to be said about Sandra McPherson's new poems is that they are very, very good—original, surprising, and *clean*—a delight and refreshment in the tedium of irony, confession and cuteness of contemporary verse. The title of the collection, *Radiation*, is beautifully suitable"; EB, blurb on jacket copy, Sandra McPherson, *Radiation* (1973).
2 See note to letter 428.

427.

January 22nd, 1974

Dear Cal:

This will be brief & untidy— As Frank may—but may not—have told you when he called you a few mornings ago, I broke my right shoulder Jan 2nd or 3rd so I'm typing with 2 left fingers & the right thumb . . . Neither a drunken party nor ice—just haste and distraction, I think. Anyway, I had a good rest in the infirmary and I'm recovering at home now.[1]

Frank will be by shortly—he leaves at 3 for Cal[2] & his mother's funeral. Poor boy—he was in an awful state, really—& of course the next days will be rough—but he finally did eat a lot and sleep a lot & yesterday seemed pretty composed. But he will be even lonelier now, of course—& also ~~all mixed up with~~ beset by his feelings of guilt . . . It is awful; he seems so extra-vulnerable and never seems to have had *any* of the experiences one usually has had by age 34 . . .

I think you must have seen that "blurb" I wrote for Sandra McPherson's 2nd book . . . ? Never again! But she as my 1st *best* student, in 1966—& still the best—& has had such an unbelievably hard life I did want to help her. It had to be done in a hurry. I see now that I shd. have qualified both "confession" and "irony"* . . . Of course I wasn't thinking of you for a minute!— I had in mind the 3 or 4 books or more one gets every week by *her* contemporaries—written almost to a formula of *cheap* irony, would-be-shocking confessions, and, most of all, cuteness, or *archness* . . . She does avoid those things. After all—irony has always been *my* chief stock-in-trade, and how could one live without it? "Confessions"—well, you've been blamed for starting some of that, we know—but there's all the difference in the world between *Life Studies* and those who now out-sex Anne Sexton—and most of *LS* is about *other* people, anyway (as I've now pointed out to 2 classes). One does use "painful experiences"—ALL experiences—how else could one write anything at all? But—I see I shd. have put a careful adjective in front of those words.

I was really thinking about Sandra just as she differs from the other 30- or 27-yr.-old poets who seem to publish their little bits of OBVIOUS, and

---

1 "On January 2, Elizabeth fell as she was leaving the Casablanca Bar in Harvard Square and broke her right shoulder. She was taken by the Harvard police to Stillman Infirmary, where she remained for more than a week . . . her stay at Stillman probably broke a destructive cycle of drinking, freeing her and allowing her body to recover. Only [Lloyd] Schwartz knew the real story of her fall; to others she wrote almost no details"; Brett C. Millier, *Elizabeth Bishop: Life and the Memory of It* (1993), 488–89.
2 Bakersfield, California.

usually stale, irony every day of the week and go on & on & on about f——king and so on—and of whom? I am very tired . . .

(I am afraid you took my "blurb" almost personally, perhaps?—as *my* sex is supposed to do!—but it was careless of me not to make it plainer, exactly what I meant.)

I was at Lewis Wharf Sunday & it is coming along—by the end of next week I think I'll have signed the last papers, got the mortgage, and can start on my floors and bookcases. It was beautiful Sunday—THREE large freighters arriving, lots of tugs, etc. But I'm supposed to be in Brazil *now*, and have to make it sometime—to see about shipping,—some things—try to hasten selling, etc.— IF somehow I can avoid *some* of the 25% capital gains taxes . . . !

Peter[1] was here Sunday—a nice easy frank talk—I do love him. The Pazes have been wonderful to me. Well, I see so few people I suppose the "academic" side of Cambridge doesn't harass me as much as it does you. (—Dear John Peech just called up.) I gather I shd. take a "Miss Peters?" Anyone else you can think of?—they've begun applying, calling etc. And don't you think it is about time I saw some of Caroline's articles? Or the whole book? I want to very much.— I have no extra copy of the ONE poem now, but when I can type more easily I'll send you one.— I hope you're keeping healthy and just warm enough— With love always,

Elizabeth

*I certainly don't "object" to either, theoretically!

428.

February 22, 1974

Dearest Elizabeth—

Times flies on so, slides so, a whole month has passed since your last letter—a month of sitting by red coals, enjoying desultory reading (reviews of other people) and flu, chronic. Frank did tell me of your shoulder before I wrote last but I meant to wait for you to write. I think about it, and sorrow because I suppose it must be painful and now slow.

In another envelope I am sending a long piece by Ehrenpreis in the *TLS*, the whole piece because tho you only come in at the end, it all accumulates to a powerful tribute to you.[2] A thing it says which I have always known with

1 Peter Taylor, who was teaching at Harvard for the academic year.
2 Irvin Ehrenpreis, "Viewpoint," *The Times Literary Supplement* (Feb. 8, 1974).

envy and been unable to say exactly is how inventive you are. Many of your poems start obliquely, the fire balloons, the Nova Scotia Picture, the hen in New York[1]—something beside the point and unimportant (seemingly) but is not; or a story, the Amazon, the thief, a servant.[2] I've always thought using oneself was fine because I could test the feeling by memory in revision, or better still draw on and correct the details of description. But of course anything so close allows too little for the imagination, the pleasure of pure invention, the control of plot and form. Browning was never too good[—] almost when he came close to being directly himself—he had almost limitless invention, yet there seems too much Browning-voice in his people, and then, I don't know how to say it, too little of Browning. How rich he was, and long! Your personae quite avoid this in "The Man-Moth" and "Crusoe," both you in some transformation or dream they seem so well lived. I won't send you my new poems till they come out with the power of print in April.[3] I have 9 or 10. They really reveal nothing, except the most intimate of things, being 56, and are quiet. I would like to claim that I have turned the rhetoric, the flow etc. of my sonnets. This had to be, though one's style, one's self really must not change. By the way is a confessional poem one that one would usually hesitate to read before an audience? I have many (they are a perfectly good kind) but have none in my last lot, and you have none ever.

I'll be coming back to America on the 5th or 6th of April with Harriet, and then giving a few readings in the South. I might read something at the Signet on the 27, tho it stretches my stay a bit. I'd like to see you. No word from Frank. Somehow I think he'll live it out more steadily than we might have dreamed. There was a terrible harassment as well as dependence on his mother. Do I dare come back to Cambridge? Either I or Harvard, or the British mail seems to have mislaid most of my term papers? They would all, I suppose, have been As and Bs but I can't improvise. Caroline sends her love, and Sheridan who talks now, monologues.

    Love,
      Cal

---

1 "The Armadillo," "Large Bad Picture," and "Trouvée" (EB-*CP*).
2 "The Riverman," "The Burglar of Babylon," and "Manuelzhino" (EB-*CP*).
3 "To Mother," "The Airport" (revised as "Logan Airport, Boston"), "Fourth Year" (revised as "We Took Our Paradise"), "Wellesley Free," "The Afterlife," "1. What We Were" (revised as "Robert T. S. Lowell"), "2. Before We Are" (revised as "For Sheridan"), "Ulysses Circling" (revised as section 6 of "Ulysses and Circe"), "The Exile's Return" (revised from the *Lord Weary's Castle* version), and "Homecoming," *The New Review* (April 1974). See RL-*CP*.

429.

Dear Cal:

Thank you for your nice letter & for sending the clipping—the piece by Mr. Ehrenpreis. I don't think it makes too much sense—logically speaking (? right?—sounds funny) but it is nice to have someone like me that much . . . But did you notice the weird misprint?—"the little of our earthly *crust*" instead of *trust?*[1] Misprints are so much worse when they seem to make sense . . . I can type now with both hands quite well—but if I keep it up very long I ache horribly afterwards—so this will be brief. I do hope your papers have turned up! I had a rather awful tel. conversation with Mr. Heimert (he's in bad trouble now about accepting $20,000 or so for his house—is it Lowell?) He obviously would like to get rid of me—hating both women & poets as he does—and there are now too many poets on hand . . . But of course he can't, which he must have known all along anyway . . . He was very CROSS—but at the end of the conversation I realized that he was really cross with *you* & was taking it out on me as the only poet available just now. He said he wished to hell—his language—you'd get yr. marks in and did *I* know anything about them and were you coming back in Sept. Of course I said all I knew was that I thought you planned to come back in September. Awful man—I never did hear about yr. lunch with him . . . This was several weeks ago. I've again written offering to teach Ex. Writing for a term or 2 instead of another poetry seminar—but again no reply. The classes are very good this term, on the whole. I have a lot of your ex-es, one way or another—and now I am going to make them *read* you (it doesn't seem to occur to them to read more than 2 poems of anyone . . .)

I hear (by K. Spivack) that Caroline's book is here, in one bookshop— I must see it. (I could barely get across the st. to the market for over a month—but all that is much better now.)

Oh *dear*—VP Gerald Ford was here yesterday—demonstrated against— & in Boston last night, where he was presented with a replica of one of Paul Revere's lanterns. He thanked the givers saying—"As a famous Boston poet once said 'One by day and two by night . . .' "[2]

It has been suddenly lion-like and beautiful March weather—high winds, cold, and bright blue sky with wonderful clouds—but this is too bad, be-

---

1 Irvin Ehrenpreis, "Viewpoint," *The Times Literary Supplement* (Feb. 8, 1974), misquotes lines 54–63 of EB's "Poem," *The New Yorker* (Nov. 11, 1972);—"the little that we get for free, / the little of our earthly trust"; "Poem," from lines 57–58 (EB-*CP*).

2 Cf. "One, if by land, and two, if by sea"; Henry Wadsworth Longfellow, "The Landlord's Tale: Paul Revere's Ride" (1863), line 10.

cause all the trees & lilac bushes, etc. are already in bud . . . My apt. goes on slowly and extravagantly. I shall go to Brazil for the spring vacation here—the end of this month until the 10th—with great reluctance . . .

I've seen Nathalie R several times and must telephone her now about my bookcase lumber . . . I couldn't go to Philip's funeral and N telephoned me NOT to go to the memorial service later—I had been planning to.[1] But apparently it was well handled by Aileen Ward. Let's see—no more news except that I went to hear Callas sing and was completely won over, to my great surprise—she was magnificent on her Boston night. The moral seems to be—be bitchy for 20 years and then when you behave just moderately graciously everyone goes wild with delight & gratitude.

I must stop or I'll ache all night. Here's that brief poem—in case you haven't seen it—short & sad.

I hope all the family is flourishing and—what are you writing these days? I received this invite[2] today—if I can get it in this letter—but I'll be in Brazil . . .

With love,
Elizabeth

430.

[March 20, 1974]

Dearest Elizabeth—

~~Yes~~, I had a lot of trouble with the quote and knew something must be wrong—your very beautiful ending—but I didn't have my text to check it with. I wrote Ehrenpreis, I know him slightly—and got back an odd letter of flattery and severities. He is really a rather good critic, rather prim, irritating; Peter can't bear him. Oh really very good, with a toehold in/on the *TLS*, and unknown in America, and almost in England because almost nothing is signed.

I'll be in Cambridge for a reading[,] Signet Club—on the 20th. I'm trying to get this to you before Brazil, but it will be waiting for you on the 10th. Loved the poem. It's all in the last two sad lines.[3] It goes into my billfold as a vade mecum (?) for my trip to America.

Never had lunch with Heimert, unless I'm suffering from amnesia. His crimes are greater than mine. In preparation for Harriet I've paid up my

---

1 Philip Rahv died on December 22, 1973.
2 The invitation does not survive.
3 "—Yesterday brought to today so lightly! / (A yesterday I find almost impossible to lift.)"; "Five Flights Up," lines 24–25 (EB-*CP*).

American bills, had three dental appointments, discovered where all my money is, 7 different banks mostly small sums, checked on my sales, asked for my reviews, got to work on my income tax, cleaned my study. The worst though is the redtape of getting my visa indefinitely extended. I'm almost Woman's Lib; there's a huge row in the papers—foreign husbands of English women can hardly get permission to stay, while foreign wives of men have no trouble.

God bless you *to*, *in* and *from* Brazil. Lizzie is there now.[1] My love to Frank. See you in April,

Love,

Cal

431.

*[Postcard: Rio de Janeiro: Night view of Copacabana Beach with
the Sugar Loaf in the background]*

(March 29th [1974]—Santos Dumont Airport—
waiting for a plane to Belo Horizonte)

My address book is locked in my suitcase & you may never get this because something seems very wrong about that address . . . I'll have just a week to "see to things" & I am dreading what I'll find there. Is it true you are NOT teaching the Fall Term (so Mr. Bate wrote me.) Mrs. Vendler is giving a lecture on yr. last 3 books (she adores them) April 3rd—I'll miss it—but she's sending me a copy.[2] I'll be in Washington the *15th* April—maybe I'll see you? I have nice news for you, I think—[3]

Love—

Elizabeth

432.

Milgate Park
May 1, 1974

Dearest Elizabeth:

I am far in body and spirit from Mayday this cold day in Kent, but tomorrow I go to Essex for the last of my readings—a month old strike (to release

---

1 See Elizabeth Hardwick, "Sad Brazil," *The New York Review of Books* (June 27, 1974).
2 Helen Vendler, "Lowell's Last Poems," Vassar College Libraries.
3 On April 10, RL won the Copernicus Award for Lifetime Literary Achievement from the Academy of American Poets (a $10,000 prize); EB was one of three judges.

three students who were arrested months ago.) When I got home, after arriving at Kennedy to find my passport had expired, I slept 18 hours.

My ten thousand dollars is all converted into travelers' checks. I feel that even if the world were to wash away, I'd still be able to cash my checks. And a voice whispers in my ear *squander it*. On what? Thank you so much; I've never been so tangibly rich in my life. What shall I buy, now that my vices have abandoned me? A Britannica? huge books costing more than a hundred pounds apiece on Painting Through the Ages; someone to listen to me talk; grape juice that costs more than wine; a ticket to a trout club?

I've not said what I wished to—how talking with you in Cambridge was somehow like the old days in Stonington—a lonely warmth (1948). No need to stop talking, and always when the talk stops it starts up.

Tomorrow I have to give three showings at Essex, one on translation. Then I'll be free. Do look up Frank Parker.

Love,
Cal

433.

[Cambridge, Mass.]
May 30th, 1974

Dear Cal:

Since I have just corrected 8 "take-home exams" in which the students discussed, among other things, some of yr. early works and wreaked havoc with "The Drunken Fisherman" this card seems appropriate . . .[1] *Marks in!* Oh dear—they write so badly it is heart-breaking—all except two of them. I got back a few days ago from 4 days in Seattle, a rather exhausting affair but I think it went fairly well. I forgot my reading glasses at the last minute and kept everyone waiting for ten minutes; the Pres. introduced me as a "Dr. of Laws," etc. etc. . . . Yesterday I had a letter from Ashley Brown who told me you forgot some of your papers when there, and that made me feel a lot better . . . Now I only have to face finishing my floor at Lewis Wharf, getting bookcases built, and MOVING . . . Mrs. de Planck from Argentina *can't* buy my Brazilian house, & my remaining aunt is about to die & I don't know when I can get to Nova Scotia—otherwise I am free to get to work for myself a bit—oh no—I haven't heard anything from FINK Transportes—supposedly shipping all my 3,000 books, some furniture, and so on—over a month ago. It is a

1 "Noah's Ark, from a late 15th-century German woodcut."

really cold spring—or summer—flying from east to west & back again, however, I observed that the only places on the continent where the sun was NOT shining were Boston & Seattle—it rains and is freezing in both . . .

That rather awful painter whom Frank admires so and keeps buying has done a gigantic picture based on the old photograph in TIME, of you & me on the beach in Rio . . .[1] Only he has made us our present ages, or even older, if anything, and weird-looking—I have a large *bust*, sagging sadly, and black glasses for eyes, and you are enormously long and languid, with a little hair only on the back of your head . . . This is simple vanity, no doubt, for you as well as myself, but I rather resent this—& he gives the names, too.

You wrote that you found yr. passport had expired, at Kennedy airport—then went on to the next paragraph—I wonder how you got back? Frank saw—he thought—an obituary for Mr. Citkowitz in the N.Y. *Times*—I missed it.[2] If it is true that he died, you must have been having a rather sad time to go through . . . ?

John B[3] is away for a month & is letting Alice & me use the Duxbury house—I'll probably stay down all next week to work— It is very pleasant, right on the water; last Sunday there were white herons and Canada geese as well as the usual gulls and ducks. But I may have to come back to keep on fighting to get things finished at Lewis Wharf. My new address—but not till the end of June—is: 437 Lewis Wharf, Atlantic Avenue, Boston 02110.

I saw Peter Taylor briefly in New York—as nice & funny as ever. I hope everything is going well with you and you're writing a lot. I think I'll try to tackle Old Age now myself—

With lots of love—remember me to Caroline—
Elizabeth

434.

[437 Lewis Wharf, Boston, Mass.]
September 3rd, 1974

"Tidying up!"—noble, industrious Cal! The pathos of it![4]
(That is an imitation Marianne Moore beginning.)

---

1 By Ralph Hamilton, a pencil sketch of which is reproduced on the frontispiece of *Elizabeth Bishop and Her Art*, ed. Lloyd Schwartz and Sybil P. Estess (1983).
2 Israel Citkowitz died on May 4, 1974. (*The New York Times* obituary was printed on May 6, 1974.)
3 John Malcolm Brinnin.
4 From a letter now missing, or perhaps a telephone conversation.

Well, I wish I had about three noble, industrious, strong, tasteful, and rather young, young men here, to help me do just that . . . Moving is pure hell—but unless I take a great dislike to this place, pray God I'll never do it again. There is a possibility I *might* take a dislike—the architect is fine, I think—but hopelessly impractical—has gone bankrupt 3 times, I've heard—and in order to keep things going has permitted all kinds of bars and rock & roll places to surround us. My one fear is it will turn into a sort of super–Holiday Inn . . . I of course have no car—but every other tenant seems to have either a Jaguar or a Mercedes Benz . . . And the complications with the shipment from Brazil—almost 5 months ago now . . . and, and, and— (However, I see in the GLOBE the architect or management just got a *$4.5 million* loan—) (So *someone* must believe in Lewis Wharf—)

However, I won't tell you my troubles (money being one of the worst)—but I'll survive them, I suppose. Last night Frank gave one of his enormous parties . . . the occasion was mostly because of the English Institute, I think, and a very nice friend of his who was giving a paper on 18th Century *plagiarism*, I think—at least it sounded livelier than most. One Stephen Orgul or Orgel . . . 100's of people, of whom I knew six, possibly—and of course shd. have known many more but I didn't recognize them, etc. . . . . I had determined ahead not to mention any of my Lewis Wharf troubles—just smile and say I *loved* it—& to my horror I heard Frank, behind me, telling them ALL to a group of people, including Helen Vendler. (I've been groaning to him daily over the telephone.) He has been most sympathetically sighing & groaning along with me—but all my social bravery went for nothing . . . He'll probably be with you when you get this. I could even send it by hand—maybe he'll stop by on his way to the airport tomorrow—I'll ask him to, anyway. (I'm about the last stop before the airport now.) I wonder if you have ever played a fiendish game called ANAGRAMS? It became the 2nd or 3rd of Frank's obsessions at North Haven—1st, I think, came English muffins & honey; 2nd the Judiciary Committee; then Anagrams . . . However, he bore up bravely, on the whole, and went for a walk or two on the beach, and pretended to look at wild flowers when I put them under his nose . . . (Yarrow caught his fancy, because of Wordsworth, & Queen Anne's Lace because of Dr. Williams.[1]) Alice & I were mean to him, I'm afraid—but he is essentially so sweet and affectionate and needs loving so badly—I think he makes me feel *motherly*. He says a visit to you will *cheer him up* . . . so I hope *you'll* feel motherly, too.

1 See William Wordsworth, "Yarrow Unvisited" (1807), "Yarrow Visited" (1815), and "Yarrow Revisited" (1831); and William Carlos Williams, "Queen-Anne's-Lace" (1921).

I saw Caroline's review of the Simone de Beauvoir book in *The New Review* and thought it very good.[1] (I can't *stand* S de B . . .) I also saw in a back number a very nasty piece on me by a Clive James, or James Clive . . . who is he?[2] Fortunately I always forget nasty remarks almost immediately— although agreeing with them completely at the time. Oh—Jimmy Atlas cornered me 2 or 3 times at the party—he seems a bit improved, but *why* did F, S & G give him the assignment of writing about Delmore?[3] There must be several older and wiser people much better qualified—and from the selections he made of the poems in an awful review I don't think he knows what's good in D's writing. Anne Hussey was also there—she works awfully hard and has published quite a few poems—and she is so beautiful, and so nice, that everyone loves her—I wish to goodness she wrote a little bit better! (*Don't* repeat that—I have hopes for her—)

This is the last thing I shd. be doing. WHERE is that carpenter? WHERE is the man to put up the stove-pipe? It is pouring and foggy and a huge, silent freighter just went past my elbow, apparently—that's the really nice thing here—if only most of the huge, silent ships weren't tankers . . . I know all the tugs by name now. And the sight-seeing boats—comical— something called the "booze cruise" usually goes by twice a day—one trip plays classical music, the next one rock and roll. Just like Venice—

It is almost time to start reading those submitted poems again. Oh dear. I think I'll make them *read* a lot this time, and write a lot less . . .

Here's a bit of description, for what it's worth[4]—it started out as a sort of joke thank-you-note—John B was so appalled when I said I wanted that ugly little green shack for my summer home! (He doesn't share my taste for the awful, I'm afraid.) This is the only copy I can find—& I may have made more changes already—& shd. probably make a lot more. Suggestions welcome—even to tearing it up. (No—I can't—I've already spent the *N Yorker* check.) I can barely see across the Mystic or whatever it is—to the endless dead Cunard, etc. docks.— Well, North Haven was a dream—peace and quiet and so beautiful. I want to rent it all next August but the "family" has first chance. There isn't any inn at all there now.— We were lent an 80 year old sailing dinghy . . . it looked it. There are ospreys on Pulpit Rock and 2 other places.

1 Caroline Blackwood, "Taste of the Void" (review of Simone de Beauvoir's *All Said and Done*), *The New Review* (June 1974).
2 Clive James, "Elizabeth Bishop: Everything's Rainbow," *the Review* (1971).
3 James Atlas, *Delmore Schwartz: The Life of an American Poet* (1977).
4 "The End of March, Duxbury (for John Malcolm Brinnin and Bill Read)," *The New Yorker* (March 24, 1975); see EB-*CP*.

Write me and send me some poems, to help offset the "submissions," please. I wish the Paz-es wd. get here—they're the twin suns in my gloomy skies here. I hope you and all yours are well. Wish I could think of a present to send by Frank—maybe I shall—

Love always,
Elizabeth

435.

Dearest Elizabeth:

My most guilty apologies! Your letter was slow in coming, and arrived almost two weeks after Frank left. Things with us haven't been quite as untroubled as he thought. The *Depression* is just dawning on us, and brings enormous problems and irreconcilables.[1] The question is whether I should return to America where I can earn, have friends etc. I have been thinking of trying to get an arrangement like yours at Harvard and teach full time. I don't feel particularly persona grata there—still, it seems weak and demoralized not to do something for my family more than royalty payments at this time, but I can't do much here—even someone like Spender has a hard time getting a decent university job, and his pay is small. ON THE OTHER HAND—we have our house (houses) here and four children, and transplanting them might be murderous, and the cost of moving huge. Nothing will or can be done till some time after I return to Cambridge, but these are thoughts to trouble my noon's repose.

Caroline (don't repeat this) isn't too well and is having what I think of as an old-fashioned nervous breakdown. That is there is nothing wrong with her reason—she is not manic or depressed—but is full of jerks, up and downs, panics, moments of excitement, fear, grandiosity, inertia—tho most of the time she is calm and full. Like you, she takes in everything, and this adds to the strain. I think I am describing a change of life, or its prelude. There are so many children, their troubles little and big—I make things sound more intense than they are. I know everything is working out. I wish I weren't gravely impractical by nature and habit.

I assume you will assume that I love all your poems. I have been brooding on this last one since it arrived, and have ached to live in such a house too— I have all my life—cut my losses and live the life of severe deprivation, idle-

1 Rising inflation in Britain.

ness and imagination. I think I have felt this at least from Kenyon on, and in a queer luxurious way have achieved it.[1] What is interesting is that your rhythm slows and forces one to read it as prose—prose perhaps like M. Moore's poems, tho your rhythm has a much slower wandering quality—I don't think she'd choose such a shack. All this from memory; but now rereading I remember all sorts of talks with you: that room I got near (?) you in Brazil, filled with proletarian callgirls—the meter I see is steadily iambic . . . any number of terrific seemingly tho quiet details—you arrive at your castle safely. I am troubled by one thing, a sort of whimsical iambic Frost tone to the last five lines or so, tho I think they are needed.[2] New lines might make a fine poem into one of your finest. Nothing else needed.

I'm arranging my pieces and reviews—good enough to publish maybe. Not too bad. What strings them together is my scattered firsthand descriptions of many of the poets. I have a marvelous dull title—*A Moment in American Poetry*. Tell Frank what I have just written, and ask him if he can locate my Harvard collection New England piece, and my first *New York Review of Books* Berryman.[3] I have 18 poems now, all in the same free verse—18 if I count generously calling a poem in two parts two poems. Ask Frank, if you wish to show you his xerox edition of my new poems. Tell him too that it now looks as though it will be impractical and too expensive to bring my whole family to Harvard, that I wonder if Harvard can give me some sort of two room setup in one of the colleges. (houses) Today Caroline is recovered and about to see a doctor.

We both send our love,

Love,

Cal

Oh dear, Lewis Wharf rings a bell, but perhaps it is only Rolls or Rose Wharf, I never knew which, where Daddy used to go to mysterious (naval?) banquets.

---

1 See "The End of March," lines 24–26 and 29–33 (EB-*CP*).
2 See "The End of March," esp. lines 55–63 (EB-*CP*).
3 See "New England and Further" and "John Berryman" (RL-*CPR*).

436.

437 Lewis Wharf, Boston
October 18th, 1974

Dear Cal:

The mails are certainly strange—(When did yours come? What is your *zone no.?* It might help . . . [illegible][1]—I'm sure that's why mail to you is slow—& yours to me is—(IDEA!—ZONE NOS!—Try them!—)—your letter came yesterday, taking 11 days—and apparently my next-to-last one to you took as long, or longer . . . I'm answering you right away this morning because I have several things to talk about. Last night I heard, by telephone, from Alice and then from Frank: that you'd got her by mistake, that Frank is going to call you this morning, and that—or so I gathered—contrary to what you wrote me on the 6th, and what Bill told me two nights ago (how news gets around in Cambridge . . . !), you *are* planning now to come with your family and not alone . . . Well, I'll undoubtedly hear from Frank again soon about this . . . ! You see you are on People's Minds. It seems to be almost impossible to find houses for a short stay, in Cambridge. Poor Frank—he was even feeling guilty about this, as if it were somehow his fault. But if you are coming with family, that must mean, as you wrote at the end of yr. letter, that Caroline is feeling better. (I think you wrote she was "about to see a doctor"—but couldn't really read it.) I am sorry she has had a bad stretch—however, I don't think you could say it was a "change of life or its prelude"—she's much too young for that. And, to speak as intimately as the *NY Times* now does—the menopause, when it does come (around 50 or so), frequently causes *no trouble at all* . . . I wasn't even aware of it until it was over—but I may have been lucky. (Dr. Baumann said I had "very intelligent glands.") That's my first paragraph.

2nd—& I was going to write to you about this today (my free day—Friday—after the 2 seminar days) even if I hadn't heard from you yesterday. Tuesday I got a check, by way of Mr. Oberdorfer, from your NY lawyer, I think, for $5,000.00.[2] You may remember that I resisted this money very much at first—and I'd still like to. It doesn't seem right to me. HOWEVER—it came as an absolute lifesaver and I telephoned Mr. O to say I'd accept it. Moving, as you say, is "murderous." I thought I had saved up enough money to cover everything, but I hadn't and all the week before I'd been frantic—and thinking that I'd have to sublet this place and take a room or something until I could pay off my debts. My Brazilian belongings sat in

---

1 Ink is smudged.
2 The money RL wanted to give EB from the sale of his papers to Harvard's Houghton Library.

Rio for 5 or 6 months—I THINK they're on a ship now, but still am not sure—and the moving company is going to try to soak me, I know—for storage (all their fault) and something like $900 freight from N.Y. to here—no ships from Brazil come to Boston any more. I also owed the condominium lawyer (you may remember *Leon* . . .) about $1,500.—and I just didn't have any of this . . . and so on. I'd never been in debt like that before, having always been fairly thrifty—or cautious—so you can see how extremely grateful I am for that $5,000.— It means I can stay here, where I really love being, and pay off my biggest debts. So—*thank you.*— Also have had 2 *front* teeth missing over 2 months & couldn't afford the dentist!

3rd. I think I agree with you about the "March" poem, more or less—I haven't worked at it again yet. I think I like the very last line all right—but three or four just before that have been bothering me and I wanted to change them around—it may be partly a matter of placing them differently—leading up to the last line in a different way. Anyway—I'll get it out today and see it—I'm pretty sure you're right, and thanks again—

4th. I wrote you a note[1]—a week ago more or less, I think—it may have crossed with yours to me—to ask you if you'd recommend Carlos Drummond de Andrade, second him, rather, for one of those Honorary memberships in the Academy they give to foreigners . . . Margaret Mills, the new secretary, had written asking me to suggest a Brazilian poet, and saying that Glenway W.[2] wd. second anyone I recommended. That's flattering of Glenway—but I think it wd. add considerable weight—to put it very mildly—if you'd add your name, too—and, as I've already written—if you got it—I remember you did admire some of his poems in Brazil and even suggested I translate "The Table."— I've done more, and wd. even like to do a small book of him sometime, I think.

Lewis Wharf has been semi-abandoned for many years, but it may well have been where yr. father went to banquets—I think there was some sort of club (Naval?) that met here, also a few painters had studios here, and during the war it was used by the Coast Guard (also had lobster pounds in the vast cellars). ROWES Wharf is where we used to take ferries when I was little—to where?—maybe it still exists and functions, I don't know. Anyway—it's a pity Lewis isn't still a wharf & warehouse—but decadent as it may be, as a condominium for the rich (I'm the only person here without a car—a Mercedes or Jaguar—)—I love living here. The ships go by right under my nose—a huge Japanese freighter just now, the "New Jersey Maru"—!—

1 The note does not survive.
2 Glenway Wescott.

loaded so high with "containers" that I think it must be arriving with very *light* Japanese junk products.— The other day a freighter from London—or did I tell you?—named, improbably, ACT III . . . Well, you must come to call—in the daytime I think Sheridan would even enjoy the harbor and the ships very much—maybe I'll have a Children's Luncheon.

Remember me to Caroline and I hope she keeps well— Lots of love,
Elizabeth

The writing class is unusually good, so far—the other, on the dumb side—

437.

[Milgate Park]
October 26, 1974
Dearest Elizabeth:

I meant to say that I would be honored to second Drummond, poet to compare with the best in now. Don't suppose he could come to New York.

Caroline and the children are almost certainly *not* coming to America. She wanted to call Frank and I thought it a good idea, but the difficulties seem insurmountable, and ones that shouldn't be surmounted. She is much better, and as you supposed is not having the change of life, though she has had strange menstrual bleedings. There is no immediate problem really about my coming alone— ~~the~~ all things are problems. The trouble is what to do in the future—I have to be in America for long short periods to have my feet on earth and earn money. Actually Caroline almost has to be in America too for longish for her taxes. Many confusions—my oldest step-daughter, Natalya, has been going through school problems for more than a year, increased naturally by her father's death. She was on affectionate but rocky terms with him, which in a way makes things worse—an enormous quarrel three weeks before his stroke. We are as God wills.

Lately I've been in the best physical shape I've been in for seven or eight years. Blood pressure normal, little trembling of legs and hands etc. So my doctor thinks, and I feel much better. It all comes maybe from not drinking on top of lithium, ~~the~~ it took some time to work.

The end of "The End of March"—I can see the last line with some form of the line before being very brilliant—maybe not the end of the poem where it must get huge emphasis.

Please tell Bill I *do* want a couple of rooms in one of the houses.

I'm going to Oxford and Belfast in two weeks or so. My Phaedra was per-formed—I thought dazzlingly—five days in London[1] and three in some-where called Lutton, in nice tiny theaters—100 people.

I can see and even feel from here, how glad you must be to getting [rid] of the traffic, and packing of Cambridge—freedom.

O I don't like coming to America alone without Caroline. I must learn to cook dinner of a kind; the other two meals are easy. I find night dinner alone in a restaurant fascinating and a torture.

Glad the money was timely, glad about your teeth. I seem to have been going to my dentist since June for two bridges, still unfinished.

Love,
Cal

I met a nice poet named Tony Harrison, a hard Yorkshire kind of person who makes Ted Hughes seem Parisian—he admires you more than any other American. He comes from a lower world and to my delight knows Vergil and Propertius in Latin.

438.

November 1st, 1974

Dear Cal:

I got your letter 2 days ago—that's much better time and undoubtedly due to my inspiration about *zone numbers* . . . Well—you know you could just *tele-phone* your local *Post Office* and ask them for *your* zone number—see? (For a poet, I am sometimes amazingly *practical*—as John M. Brinnin remarked the other day, when, after a night's consideration, I turned down taking over the late Anne Sexton's job at B.U.— Once a week; 4 or 6 people; but I figured out how little I'd actually earn, what with more taxes, remembered how tired I get with the two classes I have; and then began wondering how I'd ever get along with the students that had been attracted to Anne, and decided I wouldn't . . .) Then I attended a memorial service for her in the BU chapel[2]—it was well-meant, but rather awful—and after hearing a few of her students reminisce, I knew I'd been absolutely right—especially as to the last reason. It is very sad—and deplorable pieces are appearing everywhere, about her.

---

1 The Young Actors Studio production of *Phaedra* at the Theatre at New End, Hampstead, October 15–20, 1974.
2 Anne Sexton committed suicide on October 4, 1974.

Now Kathy Spivack has been asked (she says) to do a piece on me, for *Ms.* Magazine—& I am going to say NO to that, too.

Oh—a big freighter is looming up—very handsome in the early morning sunlight— The "EXXON CHESTER," going out empty. It's weird—to think of all the oil from under the Saudi Arabian deserts arriving in the sad old port of Boston . . .

I've spoken to Bill about rooms in a house for you—I hope it isn't too late in the year, but probably he can find them. I am giving my 1st "party"— sort of, very modest—here, Sunday at 1. Bill—whom I haven't really seen for months now—and Frank, and Mary de Rachewiltz, and 2 or 3 more ladies & gentlemen. I brought back kippers from Nova Scotia last week-end and we'll have them—and the apartment will smell of kippers for a week. Poor Cal—"cooking dinner"!— We'll be exchanging recipes soon . . . I am afraid things have been very difficult for you lately from what you say— *"Poor of you"* as Mary Jo Paz puts it. Well, my trip to NS was pretty grim, too—Alice went with me, thank goodness, and that it made it much more bearable. My aunt has had to be put in a nursing home in Truro—where we stayed at a motel for two nights—and I felt I had to see it with my own eyes, etc. Thank god for the Canadian Health Service—like the British— And it is better to *know*, which I now do, than *imagine*—but still it's pretty awful and there doesn't seem to be a thing in the world I can do about it. At least she recognized me from time to time and actually got up and hugged me & said she was so glad I'd come . . . We think she's 87 but no one knows for sure— the family Bible is rather undecipherable.

It's *very* nice about the *Phaedra* . . . Now I must prepare myself to go to the dentist and face the worst about those two missing front teeth . . . And where is Joe O'Connor, my carpenter-painter, supposed to arrive today at 8:30 [(]in the *morning*[)]? He got drunk two weeks ago and fell through his glass back door—he told me all about it—and has his right hand in a cast— so how he's going to work for me I don't know, but he promised to come this morning— This PM John Peech is coming with a new poem—he has written one awfully good one lately—at least I think it's about his best.— Frank has been writing his "longest"[1]—and it sounds horrific; he says there's "very little sex" in it—to reassure me, I think—I can't seem to make him understand that it isn't S-E-X as such I object to in some of his poems—I was probably reading Genet long before he was born, after all!— Oh well—the generation gap or white hair or something lead to misconceptions—

1 Frank Bidart, "Ellen West" (1975).

I hope things are going better and that Caroline and Natalya are both well— When do you get here?

    With love,
      Elizabeth

I've revised the end of my poem 3 or 4 times—it's better, I think.[1] I'm reading at the Morgan Library Dec. 4th—Octavio is introducing me—awfully nice of him. After Caroline's account of last year, I refused the pre-reading dinner . . . And Marie B.[2] actually wrote me & said to "wear something becoming"!—*the nerve* . . . Maybe I'll get myself up in her style, with orchids on my shoulder, a gold handbag, and a lamé dress . . . oh, and dyed blond hair.

439.

                                    December 3rd, [1974]

Dear Cal: I hate to nag, but will you PLEASE write a short note to Margaret Mills, at the Academy—saying you'll second (or third) Carlos Drummond de Andrade? She's written me 2 or 3 times now, & apparently has to have it with yr. own signature . . . I sent her a short sketch, etc.—but in the Pub. Library they never heard of him, and the Brazilian Culture man in NY never answers his phone etc.—(his name by the way means *Big Sad One*), // Just a note or postcard! // I had a letter from Don Stanford from London, saying the production of *Phaedre* is *awfully* good. That's nice. // Tomorrow I go to NY for *my* reading at the Morgan Library—Octavio is "introducing" me.— I refused the *dinner* and I think this will be my farewell appearance . . . // A huge ESSO tanker is looming up—and by—about as big as they can get in here. I am reading SUPERSHIP[3]—can barely stop to get anything else done—it is hair-raising & very good . . . I hope all goes well with you and I'll see you soon—

    Lots of love,
      Elizabeth

---

1 EB revised several lines in the final stanza, but not the final five. Cf. "For just a minute, set in their bezels of sand, / the drab, damp, scattered stones / were multi-colored, / and all those high enough threw out long shadows, individual shadows, then pulled them in again" ("The End of March," *The New Yorker* version, lines 55–58) with "The End of March," lines 55–58 (EB-*CP*).

2 Marie Bullock.

3 Noël Mostert, *Supership* (1974).

440.

Dearest Elizabeth:

Now that Caroline is back fresh from seeing you and Cambridge and everyone, I feel almost as if I had made the trip myself, and talked to you at some length. This letter is difficult because if I don't pay attention my most pressing news will be Caroline's trip. It's a terrific thing to have house and schools settled and know we'll be together. No three or four months that could [have] been borne perhaps because they had to be.

My suggestions for the end of your poem must have been troublesome. I think I've spent more futile hours trying to perfect something satisfactory— always pressing and invisible, the unimagined perfect lines or ending, for there it usually falls. Often I've given up, and wondered why I ever found fault. There are the experiences we haven't had, working in a spool factory etc. and can't imagine, and there are others like the end of "Lycidas" where all the experience is easily ours, but we can't turn to it, or find the right sound. I've just [spent] a week or more on three lines which finally ended in changing the position of two words. (I did other things) I hope you won't bother anymore, you were probably right all along.

I think a lot about getting things right, when I haven't enough to make it matter—and often there is sprawl that cannot be arranged. We seem to be near our finish, so near that the final, the perfect etc., is forbidden us, not even in the game.

I see us still when we first met, both at Randall's and then for a couple of years later. I see you as rather tall, long brown-haired, shy but full of des.[1] and anecdote as now. I was brown haired and thirty I guess and I don't know what. I was largely invisible to myself, and nothing I knew how to look at. But the fact is we were swimming in our young age, with the water coming down on us, and we were gulping. I can't go on. It is better now only there's a steel cord stretch[ed] tense at about arms-length above us, and what we look forward to must be accompanied by our less grace and strength. Well, no more dies irae; I wonder if Christians believing in immortality saw their lives as less circular.

Just had a letter from Peter Taylor. He writes that all his letters begin by philosophizing and end with trivia. I think he meant he felt at home with trivia. We are getting ready for Christmas, 2 families in our house, each with

---

1 Description.

four children. It's like Aunt Sarah's family Thanksgivings; unlike her, none of us can make audible feast speeches.

Give my best to Alice; Caroline sends love.

Love,
Cal

441.

[Postcard: The beach at Naples, Florida]

Fort Myers Beach
Dec. 28th, 1974

Here for two weeks or a bit more—L. Crane has a "guest-house" next door to old friends of ours[1]—very nice . . . The beach is lovely & I hope to swim a lot & get to feeling less tired of it all . . . It was nice to see Caroline and I'm glad she found a house—this will be much pleasanter for all of you . . . There was a magnificent snow-storm all Christmas day in Boston.— I had a C. Eve party for Frank & the Pazes—until after 2 . . . A good time was had by all concerned as you said at St. Marks. A happy 1974 for all of us.

Love, & see you soon—
Elizabeth

442.

January 16th, 1975

Dearest Cal:

I think I sent you a postcard from Florida, but did I really? Anyway—I had a wonderful time there; went on a 3-day sailing trip with old friends; went to a marvelous wild life sanctuary; went swimming almost every day; got very *tan*—and so on . . . And came back feeling much much better than when I left bleak Boston . . . I just got my mail yesterday & it included a letter from you, dated Dec. 18th—I left Dec. 27th—it's odd I didn't get it before I left—but no, I suppose not— The Christmas Mail . . .

Now I have just talked to Frank, who says he talked to you and that you may get here before you get this . . . Well, I'll proceed with it anyway. Frank says that you have been having arthritis (?) in your back—between the shoulders. I'm sorry to hear that—I have it rather badly, too, and a touch of it in that spot, although my hands are the worst. The only thing for it is

---

1 Charlotte and Charles Russell.

ASPIRIN—in huge doses—I go occasionally to the Robert Brigham Hospital (nothing *but* arthritis there) but have almost stopped going because with Aspirin one does as well as one possibly can, apparently— Also—hot water, and exercise— But all that aspirin upsets the stomach—or gives you ulcers—so I take a coated kind, ECOTRIN, that works very, very slowly, but doesn't produce a belly-ache. There are other brands. I take from 12 to 16 every day . . . & don't have much pain, actually. (But after seeing most of the patients at Robert Brigham I usually think I don't have arthritis at all . . .)

I am now going to be very impertinent and aggressive. Please, *please* don't talk about old age so much, my dear old friend! You are giving me the creeps . . . The thing Lota admired so much about us North Americans was our determined youthfulness and energy, our "never-say-die"ness—and I think she was right! In Florida my hostess's sister had recently married again at the age of 76, for the 3rd time—her 2nd marriage had been at 67—and she and her husband also 76, went walking miles on the beach every day, hand in hand, as happy as clams, apparently, and I loved it. (A very plump, pretty, sweet lady—as naïve as a very small child.) Of course—it's different for a writer, I know—of course I know!—nevertheless, in spite of aches & pains I really don't feel much different than I did at 35—and I certainly am a great deal happier, most of the time. (This in spite of the giant oil tankers parading across my view every day . . .) I just *won't* feel ancient—I wish Auden hadn't gone on about it so his last years, and I hope you won't.

However, Cal dear, maybe your memory *is* failing!— Never, never was I "tall"—as you wrote remembering me. I was always 5 ft 4 and ¼ inches— now shrunk to 5 ft 4 inches— The only time I've ever felt tall was in Brazil. And I never had "long brown hair" either!— It started turning gray when I was 23 or 24—and probably was already somewhat grizzled when I first met you. I tried putting it up for a very brief period, because I like long hair—but it never got even to my shoulders and is always so intractable that I gave that up within a month or so. I think you must be seeing someone else!* What I remember about that meeting is your dishevelment, your lovely curly hair, and how we talked about a Picasso show then on in N.Y., and we agreed about the Antibes pictures of fishing,[1] etc.—and how much I liked you, after having been almost too scared to go—and how Randall and his wife threw sofa pillows at each other. And Kitten, of course, *Kitten* . . . You were also rather dirty, which I rather liked, too. And your stories about the cellar room you were living in and how the neighbors drank all night and when they got

---

1 Pablo Picasso, *Night Fishing at Antibes* (1939).

too rowdy one of them wd. say "Remember the boy," meaning you— Well, I think I'll have to write *my* memoirs, just to set things straight.

It will be nice to see you— Caroline and I had a "real nice visit" as they say in Florida and I'm looking forward to seeing her again. Alice is at BU Business School, poor dear—and will soon be coming for dinner after her class on "Taxes"—which she insists she *loves*. So I must stop and slice some green beans— See you later, alligator, as they also do say in Florida—

    With love,
        Elizabeth

*so *please* don't put me in a beautiful poem tall with long brown hair!

443.

[Postcard: Air View of Mexico City, D.F.]

[Mexico City]
June 25th, [1975]

Having a *?* time. Wish you were here.[1] I have had to discuss *you* in: English, French, Spanish, Russian, & Serbo-Croat— . . . Everyone very nice—but this city has multiplied (disastrously) *10* times since I was last here— Home the 28th. I do hope you're well, & please write. Love to you & to Caroline—
    Elizabeth

444.

Milgate
July 20, 1975

Dearest Elizabeth:

I feel utterly out of touch with you. And have only written two letters in the last two months; it gives ~~one~~ a feeling of almost threatened isolation.

I gather you made Mexico City and liked it. The invitation seemed so delightful and so unlikely to be ever repeated that I tentatively accepted, all the time knowing that the six thousand mile flight, the high altitude, the new germs on top of still uncured old ones, the leaving here almost before we had arrived, and when it shone day after day—unlike so often. I had a terrible time making my ambiguous points clear to whoever carried on the negotiations after Octavio.

1 EB and RL had been invited with Octavio Paz, Joseph Brodsky, Vasko Popa, and Mark Strand to Mexico City to discuss poetry for the *Encuentro* series on Mexican television.

We've both done steady work, writing day in day out, till Caroline has finished a book of long short stories, and I, if I wished, could say my book of poems is done. I have 30, more than enough. However Bob Giroux who has seen my critical pieces, admires them and even admires *all* of them nearly—speaks of them as *makings*. 200 pages of makings! I can't at the moment imagine ever undertaking another.

I remember, I often call it up with joy, our last telephone conversation. I think we are both shy from talking emotionally, then it comes out sometimes. I never can talk anything but shop and nothings at a party. We must ~~talk~~ be more alone next year.

We have no plans much. I go to a poetry festival in Ireland end of next month, and Caroline at the same time will go with the more manageable, exportable children to Provence. Please write and tell us some news.

Best to Alice and Frank.

Love,

Cal

445.

[437 Lewis Wharf]
August 1st, 1975

Dear Cal:

I got back from North Haven Island late last night; this morning I collected my mail and there was your letter of July 20th. Before I get to work finishing unpacking EVERYTHING (after a month, there's a lot), and cleaning this dirty house, I'll write you a note. I want to because, although it may not seem odd, after all,—yesterday driving down from Maine, in terrible heat, I was composing a letter to you mentally part of the way . . . I do this sometimes & then the trouble is I can't remember whether I've really written the letter or just thought about it. This is "for real"—I think! (I don't think you will have received it before.)

Maine was marvelous—North Haven approximately my idea of heaven. I rented the "Sabine Farm" for the whole month this time and almost wept when I left yesterday. Alice came up week-ends, because she is going to summer business-school, too, to get it over with sooner, and there were a good many other guests. Frank was there for 4 or 5 days and was a perfect angel—helped me a lot and was very good and talkative and his nicest self. I was alone for two weeks (except the week-ends) with a French lady-novelist friend[1]—she typed a *500* page novel downstairs, on an ancient Baby Hermes, and I typed a *short*-story[2] upstairs on a big IBM electric, with another electric alongside in case the IBM started "mal-selecting" (as they call it), which it frequently does. Those two weeks were very foggy—beautiful fog—and good working weather. Frank read almost all the 1st or 2nd draft of the story and liked it a lot—but then, I'm afraid he is a "fan." We went bicycling together and Frank one day fell off in the town dump—oh dear, I shouldn't tell you perhaps, but it was an awful moment. Frank sprawling in the gravel just ahead of me, with all the dump right ahead of him, and hundreds of startled sea-gulls flying up . . . Fortunately he only skinned his knee a bit.

Mexico—well, I loved seeing the Paz-es and that's really why I accepted the invitation. Cuernavaca, where the Paz-es have rented a villa, has grown as much, too—but that was nicer. But I hadn't been in Mexico for 32 years and everything has changed so that I would never have recognized it—to coin a phrase. Mexico City has grown from about a million then to almost eleven million now—& if this keeps on in ten yrs. it will be the biggest city in the world. It is approximately my idea of hell, I'm afraid. I realize I've put it almost out of my mind until this minute, I disliked it so. It was my 1st (& I hope last) TV—and that was funny and, I suppose, *interesting*. Me and Octavio, and Vasko Popa (whom I liked a lot, although we didn't have much language in common) and Brodsky, whom you know & with whom I could share jokes, at least. But in general I was glad you weren't there—it was awfully exhausting and rained *steadily*, in the city, at least. But the trip was all paid for and I am really glad I went.— Octavio was as sweet as ever and he has just translated a poem of mine, and I have translated one of his for Frank's *Ploughshares* number . . .[3] Oh yes—you say you had difficulties talking with the ENCUENTRO man—so did I. And his named turned out to be *John Brown*—a nice young descendent of a famous Argentinian hero[4]—but rather incomprehensible . . .

I hope you're well—both you and Caroline and all the family. You *sound* well, I think, and it is very nice about the two books. Before he came to Maine, Frank (of course) read me your letter to him about his book by telephone—he was awfully pleased. Do you know the Forster story "The Machine Stops"—something like that?[5] I am always telling Frank that the life he

1 Célia Bertin.
2 "Memories of Uncle Neddy" (EB-*CP*).
3 Octavio Paz, "Primero de Enero/January First," trans. EB, *Ploughshares* (1975).
4 William (Guillermo) Brown.
5 E. M. Forster, "The Machine Stops" (1909).

leads now is just like the future life Forster describes in that story—everyone living underground and communicating by telephone or some other gadget. The mother asks her son—underground on another continent—"Have you had any interesting thoughts lately?" (Frank doesn't mind my teasing him this way, I *think*.) You'll probably see Helen Vendler at that Irish Festival . . . I am trying to read her G. Herbert Book but that kind of "close reading" is pretty much beyond me, I'm afraid.[1]

Give my love to Caroline; I hope I'll see the stories sometime, also any new poems by you . . .

With love, as always,
Elizabeth

446.

[Postcard: Port of Boston]

August 28th, 1975

Dear Cal: I wish I'd hear from you—although I may be the one who owes a letter . . . Maine was quite heavenly—but I'm afraid the effects are wearing off. I'm finally getting my books unpacked—2 boys come to help; sit on the balcony and clean them, then I decide what to do with them all—sell, throw away, or keep.— I found this ancient review[2] I thought you might find sad & amusing . . .

I did manage to get some work done in North Haven—I *think* in another 2 months I should have both a book of prose and of poems . . . WHICH of my later poems *don't* you like? Please say!

Frank quite obsessed by his magazine[3] & I'm afraid he'll never make a *lovable* editor! I am nervous about a let-down when the thing finally appears. We had a pleasant evening yesterday—sitting out on the balcony to watch the sunset, later to watch the moon rise. I can now see Bunker Hill monument as well as Old North Church. How are you? All—

With much love,
Elizabeth

---

1 Helen Vendler, *The Poetry of George Herbert* (1975).
2 Unidentified.
3 Frank Bidart edited the Fall 1975 issue of *Ploughshares*.

447.

Dearest Elizabeth:

I haven't done well on letters to anyone; and how can I write you who jam more into a postcard than I can on this long blue scroll? It must [be] a freedom [to] have your books out and on the wall. When I moved from Boston to New York, there were no bookcases for two months, and the books stood in their boxes ten feet high, like some backward child's pyramid. I couldn't even despair.

I've read Helen Vendler's *Herbert* too—quite a lot of it really, and found new poems. But mostly I didn't agree too much with her taste, and worse, didn't [see] how her various schemata bear. He's a strange poet, and if we don't go on reading him without thinking or questioning too much and loving our old favorites (the best way to read him ~~maybe~~); then it seems a miracle that he didn't sink under so much sophistication, metrical craft, clergyman discipline and religious genius. Helen, I guess, sees that; but her language is worried.

Worried too, I feel is Frank Bidart. I hope he is not getting his contributors to re-align, repunctuate and revise. I now have a young Mr. Stewart at Farrar Straus, with Frank's care but not his depth, who takes out my comma-dashes, and gives a basketball *center* a small *c*.[1] I am in fear I'll leave a line out and neither I nor anyone else will ever know. Occasionally, I realize I have done this in typescript. The realization a gradual blundering feeling of discovery.

We've had a good and level summer. No excursions, but a brief one to Ireland. The two countries for an American look so much alike, that it turns one topsy-turvy to realize they are not alike. Two sisters, faces and dresses the same; characters opposed.

We've almost decided to try New York for the winter; then I could commute for a night or two each week as I used to. Brookline turned out to [be] almost as far away as New York for me—rare visits, rapid returns. This way I would be in Cambridge longer, and then away. I think I give you every so often compliments on how well known you are. Even in Ireland, it is impossible to find anyone who knows poetry who doesn't know you. They all seem to admire, often violently. I've finished selecting my poems (a lot, I fear) and have a new book done[2]—to come out in 1977.

Caroline sends her love.

Cal

---

1 See "The Graduate," line 6 (RL-*CP*).
2 *Selected Poems* (1976) and *Day by Day* (1977).

448.

[The Cosmopolitan Club
122 East 66th Street, New York]
February 24th, 1976

Dear Cal:

It's been so long since I've written to you that I don't know where to begin—or what to say! And since I have no typewriter here, you probably won't be able to read it, anyway . . .

I'll just begin by saying that Frank has kept me informed about you all this time & of course I've been very distressed about you.[1] He just now (11 AM) read me bits of your last letter over the telephone[2] (naturally!—although I'm seeing him here this evening) & I'm so *glad* you are home again & better. I hope & pray it "holds"—as my doctor here says—

I haven't been too well myself[3]—too long a story to go into—& I'm over here, finally, to see Dr. Baumann, etc.—I shd. have come much sooner. She is so bright & *efficient* I wd. have saved myself a lot of unnecessary trouble if I'd come sooner, probably. I'll be going back to Lewis Wharf in a day or two, however.

Elliott Carter has put some of my poems—5 or 6, I think—to music & they're to be sung tonight at Hunter[4]—just in the next block. Frank is coming over for this big event (he is so nice about things like that) & we just had a long conversation about whether he can *shave* in the men's room *here* (I don't know, but I shd. think so!), & if it's all right to wear a *sports jacket* & not a suit . . . I assured him it wd. be a very "mixed" audience—& party afterwards—so a jacket would not be remarked on . . .

I do hope you are *keeping* well & I am so glad, again, that you're home. Frank said you said you'd written a poem, too.[5] Could I see it? (Lewis Wharf) I'm enclosing the one & only villanelle of my life, written about 6 weeks ago.[6]— Give my love to Caroline—

With much love, *comme toujours*—

Elizabeth

---

1 RL had a manic episode in November 1975. He was treated in three hospitals before being released in January 1975.

2 See RL-*Letters*, 644.

3 Distressed that Alice Methfessel might leave her, EB had an alcoholic episode over the New Year's holiday.

4 Elliott Carter, "A Mirror on Which to Dwell" (1976), performed by Speculum Musicae, Susan Davenney-Wyner, soprano, February 22, 1976.

5 Possibly "The Downlook" (RL-*CP*).

6 "One Art" (EB-*CP*).

449.

Dearest Elizabeth:

Thanks for your card, finally perfectly deciphered, and for your reassuring letter to Caroline—for months she meant to answer, saying "This is a real letter."

I had a longish though not violently troubled stay in the hospital, and have been out a month—mildly depressed as the cheerful doctors insist. Mildly is bad enough. Though I can't make too much of it. I fear the frequency of these things, fear becoming something that must be categorized as a burden. Yet I put my trust in my doctor's unruffled trust in lithium. The past was quite livable.

Your poem came to the right buyer. An aching subject, as the *art* even of losing must be.[1] Your stoical humor persuades me that loss is an advantage. Or is it the form—each rhythm, rhyme and pause right? The last 4 lines are the triumph, here the poet's voice rings out. I am reminded of Wyatt or Herbert. You command your words.

I have been writing furiously in my doldrums, and always feel on the edge of being too raw . . . and more than on the edge. This book is almost entirely free verse; but the next, God willing, may be metrical. One needs to hold a shield before one's feelings and the reader. Meter might, but really it's a matter of character and imagination. Right now I'd like to borrow your villanelle armor.

I hear you are going to Holland. I trust you'll see our friend Judith Herzberg.[2] She is a good poet and thinks you the best alive. She looks like a pretty Virginia Woolf.

Spring came on my birthday and Harriet flies in tomorrow.

Love,
Cal

450.

Dearest Elizabeth:

My typewriter ribbon dimmed, as you can see from the date above, and I thought for a minute I would sending you something unique since I was

---

1 See "One Art," line 1 (EB-*CP*).
2 Judith Herzberg translated five of EB's poems for the Rotterdam Poetry International Festival in 1976.

writing my mother from school—my illegible printed capitals longhand. However the unused *red* ribbon comes out beautifully.

I called you as often as I could both before and after your message but got no answer. Our trip to New York was driven, exciting, crowded as all such trips are—the small smoked-drenched bedroom, the noisy stopping and starting trucks worst at dawn, the cross-biased friends who could only be warily mentioned to one another, the warmth of many dear meetings, the nervous publisher with many page-proof errors. Frank caught about 40. The printer's favorite slip was putting a period for a comma but without capitalizing. My play was rather splendid I like to imagine and magnificently endless—six to eleven-thirty.[1] The actor playing Captain Delano looked into the audience, perhaps with his telescope, and saw five people in a row asleep. I was in mortal fear I might be one of them, and kept crossing and recrossing my legs, moving to the edge of my seat then almost through the back . . . and never nodded, but must have seemed afflicted. Or did I wink and was seen? Anyway, a bicentennial production, fifty players and more than fifty costumes and always the problem of racing the plays beyond their rhythm or killing the audience.

I liked your interview but must disappoint you by saying I'm still in free verse, written in the blue period after sickness, when I felt I could [do] nothing else well.[2] On the balance side and on the side of formality, I am told all my lines are lines. I do scores of revisions to make them so. I use iambics often loosened into anapests. I suppose definitions of words in the dictionary can be made to do this—anything can be scanned but not be made into decisive lines. I meant to say that I agreed with everything you said, but not in practice. How different prose is; sometimes the two mediums refuse to say the same things. I found this lately doing an obituary on Hannah Arendt.[3] Without verse, without philosophy, I found it hard, I was naked without my line-ends.

New York is weird now, or so it seemed coming from the calm of Kent or even London. America and England are mirages and happy islands to each other, both an escape from prices. Caroline and I both felt that New York

1 The American Place Theatre revival of *The Old Glory*, dir. Brian Murray and Austin Pendleton. Nicolas Coster played Captain Delano.

2 "The really youngest generation now tends to write in free verse, but it seems to me that the best poets set themselves some strict limitations. Wallace Stevens almost never got away from iambic pentameter. And Robert Lowell said in the last letter I had from him that he's going back to form, that he was tired of the loose free verse he was writing"; Anna Quindlen, "Book and Author: Elizabeth Bishop" *New York Post*, April 3, 1976, reprinted in *Conversations with Elizabeth Bishop*, ed. George Monteiro (1996), 57–58.

3 RL, "On Hannah Arendt," *The New York Review of Books* (May 13, 1976).

was too anxious and running on tiptoe for us—despite of (or because of) too many friends. Typical and almost first symbol, the Straus and Giroux elevators jam and have for months, and the only stairway is permanently locked, even to Bob Giroux because of dangerous school children. One is almost congratulated for arriving in the office without much delay.

I am alone in London for a few meditative self-help days, in exile from my family because Sheridan has mumps (fast recovering) and Caroline has to join the girls in The Hebrides, where there is a mumps epidemic.

Getting to Boston and above all seeing you was a delightful gift I was promising myself, but all was too hurried. Caroline sends her love.

All my love,

Cal

451.[1]

Lewis Wharf
April 16th, 1976

Dear Cal:

I'm so sorry I missed talking with you, at least, on your visit to New York—even if telephone-conversations are not my social strong point. I called—probably you got that message—then I had 2 French ladies for tea, and they stayed a bit longer than I'd thought they would, & when I called again I think you must already have left . . . Of course Frank keeps me, or has brought me, up to date—he was here for dinner last night. At latest report, Sheridan doesn't have mumps *very* badly—& you were in London avoiding contagion . . . (I don't know whether I've ever had mumps or not—I supposedly had them at YADDO, of all places, in 1949—but the doctor there was so dumb I really never knew. It's a good idea for *you* to avoid them, however!)

Frank was also here for a drink just before he left for England his last visit—and at the very last moment I picked up that weird balsa-wood head & thrust it on him . . . I'd been thinking I wanted to send you *something*, but hadn't been able to think of anything. I have—had, that is—two of those heads, picked up by Lota years ago—they are *ex-votos*—someone cured of a head injury or violent head-aches, etc., gave one to his church or the shrine where he'd prayed for recovery. The remaining one is different wood, much heavier, and very neatly painted, with a pert little mustache, etc.—rather like

---

1 Crossed with letter 450.

a hairdresser's sign. It wasn't until Frank had taken off that I suddenly thought, "Oh dear!—I was just looking around frantically for a souvenir for Cal—I hope to goodness he doesn't think I *meant* anything by it . . . !" (Because I certainly didn't—or certainly not consciously) Then last night Frank told me you've already written a poem about it—which of course I am dying to see . . .[1]

I hope I'll be able to get to New York to see the plays—I've never seen them. Oddly, I had a paper-back of Hawthorne's stories with me on my recent trip to Oklahoma—so I re-read *yours* on the plane . . . I've read the plays, of course—as I remember them, I liked Benito Cereno the best.— I'll try to get to a night when it is put on. I can't imagine tackling a play—so you have had—have, my admiration for them . . .

Oklahoma was strange—my 2nd trip there (3 yrs. ago I gave a reading, so I'd met quite a few of the same people that time.)[2] I just went rather doggedly through it all (because I was having asthma most of the time and felt lousy) and it was all *very* friendly, exhausting, rather impressive—and in retrospect, awfully comic—although it's mean to find so many well-intentioned and really kind souls *funny* . . . Ivar Ivask—who I hope isn't pestering you—he dictates endless letters in nine, I think it is, languages—& is rather hysterical—got so worked up he made at least five *extra* speeches. His wife, who *does* speak nine languages, is more delicate—Latvian—she showed me photographs of her old home—country home—beautiful, straight out of Tolstoy—and her father, a huge general with fierce blue eyes and a huge chest covered with medals (never heard of again, of course, after the 1st days of the war). Well, I returned with a "diploma" about 2' x 3', bound in red leather, and a silver eagle's feather—a foot long, weighing 1 lb. 4 ounces, in a green velvet-lined box—*Oklahoma* walnut—that weighs 3 and a half pounds. I had to carry this trophy in a brown paper market bag . . . The night before I left I had eaten at a Chinese restaurant and my Fortune Cookie said: YOUR FINANCIAL CONDITION WILL IMPROVE CONSIDERABLY. How true.— I can't quite decide whether I shd. use the money to pay off some of my bank loan or go on a *trip*—probably the latter . . .

I wanted very much to resign from that Institute Committee—but then I have managed (*don't ever tell her, of course*) to get Eleanor Taylor an award for this year—so maybe it is worth staying on if once in a while one can do something like that.

1 "Thanks-Offering for Recovery" (RL-*CP*).
2 EB received the $10,000 Neustadt International Prize for Literature in Norman, Oklahoma. The jurors were John Ashbery, Zbigniew Herbert, Thomas Kinsella, Dennis Brutus, H. C. ten Berge, Marie-Claire Blais, Melih Cevdet Anday, Agustí Bartra, Paal Brekke, Mohammed Dib, and Günter Kunert.

It is suddenly warm and beautiful here—an enormous, sick-looking Greek tanker, called AEOLIAN SPIRIT is being guided in by 2 tugs. (I wonder what her crew calls her—terribly rusty, listing to port . . .) Frank says you seemed in very good shape and Caroline, too—but he says himself he is so unobservant that I'd prefer a 1st-hand account. (When he came back from Kent I asked him if the grass was *green* there—it was still winter here— and he allowed that he hadn't noticed. Then an hour later he said that you had lain on it one day for 3 hours—so at least it couldn't have been frozen! However, he is a darling in spite of his ways and I'm always so glad he's here.)

I must get to work; I HOPE to get 3 more poems into that book before it's too late. I'd love to see your new poems—any of them, but of course the ex-voto one—& F. tells me the "Selected" is way over 200 pages . . . Perhaps he told you about the Elliott Carter evening?—a good time was had by all, I think . . . Give my love to Caroline and I hope *she's* had mumps! F also says she has a wonderful new story (?) I'll send this to Kent, on the chance you're home again—

Love as always—

Elizabeth

452.

May 3rd, 1976

(I forgot. Do you have DOGS? Do they go in bedrooms? Oh dear—)

Dear Cal:

This is not really an answer to your last nice long letter—the boy who was just here waxing the floors seems to have mislaid it, anyway, so I can't refer to it—but it is to ask you if I may come to see you in June, on my way to the Rotterdam affair? I'll be in London a few days and then visiting the Barkers (Kit Barker—younger brother of George, & his wife—old, old friends) a few days, and they have written me they'd drive me to your residence in Kent—apparently Kent is very near Sussex . . . (They live near Petworth, where Turner painted all those pictures.) IF you are going to be home, and not in Italy or some such place, I thought I could get to Bearstead on the 12th, a Saturday, and stay until I have to leave for Rotterdam (more likely for Amsterdam) sometime on the Monday, the 14th. Since I haven't received the final schedule from Rotterdam yet, I'm not sure if I have to *begin* on the 14th or what—so I might come on Friday & leave on Sunday. Would this be all right with you?— If you're going to be away then I might get to see you first, before going to the Barkers—sometime around June 2nd—to 4th or 5th . . . I'd like so much to see you & Caroline—and "Milgate."— Bill once showed me some snapshots of it & it looked very beautiful / / / I don't want to be in Caroline's way, nor do I expect any fancy treatment!—& if you're having other people that week-end, just let me know . . .

I gave a reading at Wellesley last week & Frank introduced me in a short and much too flattering speech— However, he wanted to emphasize the *dark* side of my poems—or personality?—and I tried to find the very saddest poems . . . The trip to Oklahoma—early this month, no, last, was wonderful and strange—but maybe I've already told you about that? A silver eagle's feather?—all kinds of things. Anyway, the money was welcome & is the reason I am making this trip—instead of being practical with it. Frank & I hope to get to see your plays in N.Y. the night of the 19th—after the Academy affair—

I hope I'll hear from you about the dates—just send a postcard. With much love to you—& Caroline—and hoping to see you—really!—soon—
Elizabeth

453.

[May 12, 1976][1]

Dearest Elizabeth:

I've just discovered since Caroline wrote you, that I must be at the Aldeburgh Festival on the 15th and 16th of June, to give a reading and hear Britten's setting of words from my *Phèdre*.[2] The second of June is a little hurried too because I'll be just getting back from getting a degree and giving a reading in Dublin. I am more looking forward to your visit than anything,— couldn't you interrupt your visit with the Barkers and come to us sometime between the 3rd and the 13th?

Nothing has been happening much all winter, except low spirits. Now the sun shines on me again, and pleasant things begin to happen, especially the charming hope of your visit. I now have a whole new book to impose on you, including the health-head. Somehow I didn't want to put poems in the

---

1 On the envelope of a May 10, 1976, letter from Caroline Blackwood to EB encouraging her to visit Milgate Park on June 12, RL typed "(Caroline sealed this letter before I could add anything. Your coming is a lovely mirage long dreamt of. love, Cal)."

2 Benjamin Britten, "Phaedra," dramatic cant., trans. RL (after J. Racine), opus 93 (1975), was first performed by Janet Baker with the English Chamber Orchestra on June 16, 1976.

mail, but have more courage face to face with you, my eager eye on your scrupulous eye.

I hope you can get to *my Old Glory*, and can sit through its length. It had amazingly good reviews.— Two kept referring to the Old Jonathan Miller performance to the disadvantage of this one, heavier than it needed to be but good enough not to injure my words. I am now showered with terminal honors, a Robert Lowell Day in an Ohio high school, a plaque to be placed on 91 Revere St. A maddening pushing man is bringing out without my cooperation a book entitled James Russell Lowell and Robert Lowell, two aristocrats.[1] If the dead had eyes, these are things they would see—éloge, slander and scandal. But I am not saddened to be noticed.

Our house is haphazard like an Irish house or something in Gogol. It's very beautiful, all the more so perhaps, because trembling on the edge of extinction by the socialist state. I think you will enjoy yourself with us, space, landscape, good company and room to disappear. You see I am pressing you to come.

Love,
Cal

454.

May 13, 1976

Dearest Elizabeth:

I have a terrible feeling that my last fuller letter was sent off without the USA on the address. Could you come to us sometime between the 3rd of June and the 13th? I will be in Dublin till the second getting a degree and giving a reading; I will be at the Aldeburgh Festival on the 15th and 16th hearing a Britten setting of part of my *Phèdre* and giving a reading. I want to see you here more than anything. Besides our beautiful Gogol-sloppy house, I have poems to show you—the *health-head* and others.

It's been a dream and hope to have you visit us now for almost six years. Please don't fail. See how warmly I urge you!

Love,
Cal

---

1 C. David Heymann, *American Aristocracy: The Lives and Times of of James Russell, Amy, and Robert Lowell* (1980).

455.

May 18th, 1976

Dear Cal—(Caroline, too, although this is addressed mostly to Cal, to correct his errors . . .)

I'm fairly sure I said in my letter, about my proposed trip, that I'd be getting to London early morning the 3rd of June. Didn't I? I have some friends to see there & some *shopping* to do—etc., and I'll probably go to the Barkers on the 7th. Then my idea was to come to Kent on Friday the 11th, and leave early the 14th—that is if I can get to Heathrow to take a plane to Rotterdam by 12 noon . . . However—you do say in your letter(s) received today that you'd welcome me up until the *13th*—so maybe my leaving early the 14th (if it's possible, anyway) wd. interfere with your getting away for Aldeburgh—in which case I can leave on the Sunday, 13th, and spend that night in London.

Somehow you got it quite wrong! I'm leaving *here* on the 2nd, getting to London early the 3rd . . . I'll be at the *Stafford Hotel*, St. James St., or Place, I forget which. The Barkers wrote they'd drive me to your place—(& I think I'll pay for the *petrol*—poor dears!). They are also taking me to see a few other historic sites (as well as Milgate Park, that is! How wonderful to have a *plaque* in Boston!) that I've never seen. In fact I've seen almost nothing of England except London and Sussex—sometime perhaps I can stay longer and see more.

If I weren't engaged to appear in Rotterdam I'd like to go to Aldeburgh, I think. And how nice to be given a degree in Dublin. (I saw Seamus Heaney for the 2nd time here not very long ago.— We have never had time to talk very much, but he has been extremely friendly both times, and I like some of his "bog people" poems very much.[1])

Your letter came, even without USA on it—it didn't go to Boston, England—I feel an interest in that place after the "St. Botolph" Club . . .[2] Thank Caroline for her very nice, kind letter—and please don't "go to any trouble" as they say . . . I really mean it. My *only* request as a visitor is to be *able to read in bed* . . . (In Oklahoma there was a hideous bright central light away up over the bed—and I sat up and *wheezed* all night, and my eyes watered . . . .)

It will be lovely to see you both soon—

Lots of love,

Elizabeth

1 Seamus Heaney, *North* (1975).
2 EB received the 1975 Arts Award from Boston's St. Botolph's Club.

456.

Dearest Elizabeth:

Frank has just told me you arrived back in Boston in a wheelchair, a sad surprise because you seemed in such good health here and safe with your new English drug.[1] I am mailing this to Lewis since I gather you will be out of the hospital by now.

I still thrill to your visit. After a little, it seemed as if almost thirty years had rolled back, and we were talking, brownhaired, callow and new in New York, Washington or Maine. Voice and image seemed much more what we were than what we are—or is the essence as it was? Glad too you liked my new poems, for I feared you mightn't. Today they are going off to Bob Giroux, and though I already miss their presence pressing on me to change, polish, do more, I have an almost physical sense of lightness, as though my shoulders weighed less, and my baggage was stored in the station for a day.

I'm sure Frank told you he found us an apartment, "better than any you've had," so say nothing to deter us. The uncertainty is so much more formidable from here. I think Cambridge will really be much more convenient academically and socially than Brookline. We only have a non-driving (like us) nurse.

Everything now seems to carry me backward. One thing I was certain of was that England didn't have real summers like my Grandfather's farm or the Tates' house in Tennessee—or at most did for no more than three successive days. But it goes on—nature's still now hidden and real heat. Sometimes I almost move to set off for the lake with my trolling rod for pickerel. How Grandfather would have pulled the place and us into order. But the soil and everything on it is crumbling and wilting, sand-browns with a blush of green.

We should be moving in about the 20th of September. Hope you are now recovered and moving to North Haven. I think on clear days you can see Castine from the northern shore. I miss it all, and am now looking forward to getting back.

Caroline sends her love,
Love, Cal

---

1 EB began suffering from asthma shortly after her visit to RL. She attended the poetry conference in Rotterdam, then traveled to Lisbon with Alice Methfessel. On the flight home her condition became severe.

457.

Dear Cal:

I'm shocked to see you wrote to me on July 12th and I haven't answered you yet . . . First, I was in the hospital about two weeks, and then when I finally got out (after missing "Tall Ship Day" completely, of course—the reason why we'd returned on July 6th), I was woefully weary for quite a stretch and had to get ready to come up here somehow . . . It is perfectly beautiful here, after a preliminary stretch of thick fog—beautiful, too, in its way—and this year I'm staying until September 12th. I wish I *owned* a place here—but another house is just what I don't need, I suppose . . . Cambridge Hospital was much nicer than Peter Bent Brigham—much—but of course I wasn't quite as sick as I'd been there. It is slightly "happy," I think—very informal and friendly and the nurses and assistant nurses and interns, etc. were all unbelievably kind and nice. I was supposed to be on the "respiratory" floor—but almost everyone else seemed to be a charity/senility case—and "Charlie"—(there were 2 Charlies, one 93, the other I don't know—but he looked like that Picasso drawing of the madman, if you know that) was treated with such consideration—I could hear a great deal of the attempts to talk with him. The day the "Tall Ships" came in my invited guests spent the day, more or less, at my apartment and had *my party*, without me.— I'd telephone once in a while and get things like "Oh!—I can't talk now—the *Constitution* is coming up the harbor . . ." A good time was had by all, I gather. Frank refused— Ships, he said, are not his "thing." He also, after many preliminaries (but I knew what was coming) asked if he could please NOT come here this summer— Nature is not his "bag." Well, I suppose there are people who would rather read—and discuss—a description by Wordsworth than actually see the place . . . I showed him *yarrow* last summer—but couldn't rouse him by literary association, even . . . A hopeless case . . .

I am writing David Perkins (head of the Eng. Dept. now) today to ask him if I can give the same "intermediate prose" course—or whatever they called it—this fall term instead of in the spring—because I think one can have too many verse-writers and too much verse-writing at the same time . . . So if you change your mind—but as far as I know you are coming in September, aren't you?—will you let me know and also Mr. Perkins? I think it will be all right. That Miss Binder has written the most god-awful paper on W. Stevens—I had to report on it. I think a moratorium on writing about the Stevens shd. be declared for at least 25 yrs.

I think my book[1] is being postponed until December or something—I *must* write Bob today—only probably he's away. I didn't think it was long enough, but he did, to begin with. I think perhaps the English publishers wanted a bit more, I don't know. Well, I'd be glad to oblige if only I could get *something* finished . . . It's been a hopeless stretch. For one thing, at the very end of the trip my writing case got lost—in a Boston taxi, we think[2]— and alas it had all the better things I was working on in it. (Plus all 3 address books, Lota's photograph, my birth certificate—notebooks, oh well—you can imagine—it's like starting life all over again.)

Alice & I have rented a very small outboard motor boat here & have made some very daring trips in it—great fun, but a bit too noisy. Our French novelist friend[3] is here now, typing in another room, and Penelope Mortimer is coming next. LOBSTERS tonight—I thought they were good in Boston, but they are infinitely better when taken right out of the water the way they are here. The bi-annual mowing of the meadows that surround Sabine Farm has just taken place and it smells wonderful—hay, "sweet grass" (do you remember that—those sewing baskets, etc.?), and juniper—where they ran over the lower branches of the junipers. There are goldfinches, 3 kinds of swallows, three *ospreys* (prs. of) (out on islands, but visible), ducks, cormorants (called "shags" here)—and they stand on rocks holding their wings out by the hour—looking in silhouette like the German imperial eagle—

Have you been to Portugal—or Madeira? Well—if not I'll *tell* you some of the high points—a very strange country, really, and I'd like to go back and see the north—Minho, etc. But we did manage to see a great deal and my Portuguese was a great help—on such occasions as when we got arrested in Evora . . .

I haven't heard anything—by way of Frank I thought I might have— about how Caroline's "tests" came out and if she is feeling better—I hope she is, lots, by now . . . My new asthma drug—you only take it when you're NOT having asthma—seems to be working very well, so far. I was told yesterday—at the "Arts & Crafts" fair . . . that now I almost pass for a regular summer North Haven-er—this is a great compliment and means you go about in faded rags, mostly, with your toes coming through your sneakers. Well, this year the "Top Sider" (leather) is *in*—and I have those, too—so pass the Cabots, Saltonstalls, etc. on the street with perfect aplomb . . .

---

1 *Geography III* (1976).
2 Later found under a blanket in the taxi.
3 Célia Bertin.

I must take this down to the mail box— With much love & see you
soon—
    Elizabeth

458.

September 4, 1976
Dearest Elizabeth:
    We'll arrive on the 15th, almost as soon as this does.
    I've been writing sad letters this morning, one to Jean Stafford and one to
Allen Tate—each may be my last. Then more cheerfully to Peter Taylor
who is planning three trips for the winter, dreaming of renting or even buying as many houses, but who writes jokingly, "never in my life could I imagine being alive six months in the future . . . now less than ever."
    I fear I've confused you again about teaching. I've written Perkins that I
will again teach poetry-writing and 19th century English poetry. I am grateful to your tact in teaching prose instead of poetry, but it's [a] gesture I
should have made. Could I? Years ago, I had [an] anthology made by Malcolm Cowley that printed key chapters of novels. I usually knew the whole
novels and often the students didn't. I found fiction much easier to talk
about, and it drew so much more talk from the students. Teaching Shakespeare was much the same. The Bible, however, turned my small seminar
into mutes. But I've never tried to teach people to actually write prose.
    We've just put Milgate on the market, not expecting any acceptable offers
for some time. Unless the imaginary golf course grabs us for a casino. The
living expenses have doubled in a year, and it's more than we can safely
carry. Our sketchy plan is to buy something smaller, as expensive to buy but
less to run, somewhere near Oxford. It's all very sad and only fragmentarily
imaginable.
    Caroline is fixedly finishing a third book, two longish stories, and a third
much longer—and this is the catch—on a seemingly trivial visit to a desolat-
ing great-grandmother when she was ten.[1] Though once finished, it is now
growing and growing, in piles of longhand notebooks—absorbing more and
more daughters, grand-daughters, grandsons, mostly with tragic lives . . .
withered but often more interesting branches of the great-grandmother.
Typing it out in order is like rebuilding a house. Even the size is uncertain.
    My book is done. It's the opposite of yours, bulky, rearranged, added-to,

---

1 Caroline Blackwood, *Great Granny Webster* (1977).

deleted two months after submission—as though the unsatiated appetite were demanding a solid extra course when dinner was meant to be over. I have no more to say . . . of course. Yet after reading Wilbur I found myself musing in iambics, not meaning to. I spent days even trying rhyme—it was no marriage, rather more like parody, but fascinating. So fascinating, that after a while one would gladly ruin a poem just to complete the exercise.

We had a dreadfully pedestrian international PEN Club meeting here— "The truth of the imagination." All middle-aged people who have published two books but can't write, can't talk, but want to talk or at least hear people who can't talk talk. The intoxicating thing about rhyme and meter is that they having nothing at all to do with truth, just as ballet steps are of no use on a hike. They are puzzles, hurdles, obstacles, expertise—they cry out for invention, and of course in the end for truth, whatever that is. It's queer though, Lawrence's Figs is de gustibus as true and surprising as Herbert's Affliction.[1] But the task of composition is different. No more. I think Frank has had a hard, surprisingly lonely summer. Best to Alice,

Caroline sitting on her heels on the floor. Staring, sorting, scribbling on more than ten [piles] of script and typescript to finish before flighttime. Ivana and Sheridan and the nanny have gone off to a movie about a car without a driver, more or less engaging to three different ages.[2] The drama of the PEN Club was frequently seeing and hearing Lizzie. It couldn't have gone off more happily, . . . but the immanent sorrow.

459.

Dear Cal:

I'm writing to you & to Mary[3] this morning to say that I hope you'll understand if I say I'd rather you *don't* come to North Haven on the 10th or whenever . . . Day before yesterday, and the day before that, seven, in all, guests left & although I love them all and we'd had a very nice time—it was just a bit too much. I've been feeling so sick I really haven't been able to do anything except read and—with the seven guests—cook, all of July. Now

---

1 D. H. Lawrence, "Figs" (1923); George Herbert, "Affliction" (1633).
2 *The Love Bug*, dir. Robert Stevenson (1968).
3 Mary McCarthy, RL's Castine neighbor; they were going to travel together to see EB in North Haven. EB was still angry about *The Group*, however, and did not want McCarthy's novelist eye to fall on her domestic arrangements. See EB-*OA*, 614–15.

there's just Célia Bertin-Reich, typing away at her biography of Marie Bona-parte[1]—& I have at last got to work on two poems. Célia and I eat mostly cottage cheese, tomatoes & such.— I hope you'll understand when I say I *must* work and not break off for a while. (I haven't written anything for over a year. & probably shan't again, once NYU starts.[2])

I've been reading DAY by DAY very thoroughly. My favorite, so far, is DOMESDAY BOOK—it's just about perfect, I think—I'd only question Turner's "steam"[3]—which I associate with his train pictures!—but no, that's all right I think. And I don't know what "splash flowers" are.[4] (Forgive my being so picky—I look up flowers in my flower guide several times a day here, so I'm very aware of them.) There are many, many good—no, gor-geous, lines—I'll show you my underlinings sometime—I also admire "Sui-cide" & "Realities"—& "Last Walk"—Frank called yesterday and he said that "Last Walk" is *his* favorite. I'll report again, maybe, on carefuller read-ing of the last pages—

I *was* feeling terrible—now, I must say, I am feeling much better, mostly because Dr. B said I could stop taking iron—maybe it strengthens the red corpuscles but it really plays hell with everything else—& she also sent me a painkiller I *can* take, and some pep-up, cheer-up pills—illegal in Boston un-less one has epilepsy or sleeping sickness . . . !

Well, I'll see you in Cambridge or New York—and Elizabeth, too, in New York—and maybe in North Haven next summer if I can get back here again.

    With much love,
    Elizabeth

---

1 Célia Bertin, *Marie Bonaparte: A Life* (1982).
2 EB taught at New York University in the 1977 fall semester.
3 "The old follies, as usual, never return— / the houses still burn / in the golden lowtide steam of Turner"; "Domesday Book," lines 61–63 (RL-*CP*).
4 "Only when we start to go, / do we noticed the outrageous phallic flare / of the splash flowers that fascinated children"; "Domesday Book," lines 64–66 (RL-*CP*).

NORTH HAVEN

by Elizabeth Bishop

In memoriam: Robert Lowell[1]

I can make out the rigging of a schooner
a mile off; I can count
the new cones on the spruce. It is so still
the pale bay wears a milky skin; the sky
no clouds, except for one long, carded horse's-tail.

The islands haven't shifted since last summer,
even if I like to pretend they have
—drifting, in a dreamy sort of way,
a little north, a little south or sidewise,
and that they're free within the blue frontiers of bay.

This month, our favorite one is full of flowers:
Buttercups, Red Clover, Purple Vetch,
Hackweed still burning, Daisies pied,[2] Eyebright,
the Fragrant Bedstraw's incandescent stars,
and more, returned, to paint the meadows with delight.

---

1 On September 12, 1977, RL died in a New York taxi from the airport as he was returning to Elizabeth Hardwick.
2 Cf. "When daisies pied, and violets blue," William Shakespeare, *Love's Labor's Lost*, 5.2, line 922 (see EB to Octavio Paz, Feb. 8, 1979, Vassar).

The Goldfinches are back, or others like them,
and the White-throated Sparrow's five-note song,
pleading and pleading, brings tears to the eyes.
Nature repeats herself, or almost does:
repeat, repeat, repeat; revise, revise, revise.

Years ago, you told me it was here
(in 1932?) you first "discovered *girls*"
and learned to sail, and learned to kiss.
You had "such fun," you said, that classic summer.
("Fun"—it always seemed to leave you at a loss . . .)

You left North Haven, anchored in its rock,
afloat in mystic blue . . . And now—you've left
for good. You can't derange, or re-arrange,
your poems again. (But the Sparrows can their song.)
The words won't change again. Sad friend, you cannot change.

APPENDIX I

First drafts of letters from Elizabeth Bishop to Robert Lowell

1. Draft of 141, typed on the envelope enclosing Lowell's 140 (not sent to him):

I'm bearing up and rejoicing like anything these days. But it does no good. Marianne asks me how I am—if I don't say she thinks I'm hiding horrors; if I say I'm fine (God's truth) she tells me I'm so brave . . . I don't remember what snide remarks I may have made about ED,[1] but I seem to like, or at least admire, her much more now—a great deal, sometimes. It's probably all because of this marvelous new edition. I never trusted any of it before; thought her relatives might have made it all up, etc. . . . But I spent about a solid week on this edition and think, along with R,[2] she's about the best we have. I haven't a copy of Melville here and can't seem to get one so don't know.

2. Draft of 230, enclosed with 229 and 230:

~~LETTER NUMBER 2 (no. 4, really)~~

Next morning—[March 1961]

Dearest Cal:

I'm going to attempt something awfully difficult. You say "Let me know things you question," and I'm going to and please don't be proud & sensitive, will you . . . I am very much worried by the French translations—the ones I know well—particularly the Rimbaud ones. I know you have called them "free translations," and you can change the line-order, interpolate, call Zeus Jehovah, maybe, point up, put in those "plebescites," etc.—for obvious

---

1 Emily Dickinson.
2 Randall Jarrell.

reasons of effect— (In the Baudelaire the up-to-date language sometimes has a wonderful effect.) But I don't think you should say the opposite of what the poet says, (as you do a few times)—or make changes that *sound like* *mistakes* in translation. These poems are well known and I'd hate to see you attacked for carelessness, ignorance, etc. — and I'm sure there are lots of crit-ies, both in the U.S. and in England, who'd enjoy doing that. Your language, force, etc. are very over-riding and the metre of the Racine is superb,— When I got the batch of translations I read them through rather fast at first, and really concentrated more on the Montale because I've never read him, and wanted to. The atmosphere of the book as a whole seemed very vivid and personal and you.— But when I read the French ones more care-fully I began to get worried. I sometimes don't understand why you've done what you've done—[??] [p.3.] // Just to give you one or two examples: (Please forgive me for sounding like French 2A, but I *don't* want you to be attacked! That's *all* I'm thinking of, before it's too late to do something it.)

LA MALINE = The malicious, or sly—girl
In the brown dining-room, scented by a smell of varnish and fruits, at my ease, I picked up a plate of I don't know what Belgian dish, and took my ease in my huge chair. // Eating, I listened to the clock,—happy and calm. The kitchen (door) opened with a blast (or a gust) And the servant came in, her kerchief undone [??] and her hair provocatively uncombed. // And, while her trembling little finger wandered over her cheek, pink and white peach-down, and her childish lip pouted, She kept arranging the plates (or "fussing with") near me, for my [??] Then, like that—to get a kiss—she whispered, "Fell it—my cheek has caught a cold" (And she makes a mistake in gender.) That's literal [??]. Most of what you've done is all right —but I do think "buffet" *looks* like a mistake . . . The poem seems to me more light-hearted than you've made it. The girl is young and fussing around with the plates in a flirtatious but feminine fashion—she's untidy, pretty,—"naughty,"—but not sordid—

AT THE GREEN CABARET (one of my favorites, as I said in my other letter— in its innocent way, too) "tartines" aren't tarts—they are the pieces of bread and butter served at French schools—"I contemplated the very naïve subjects in the tapestry"—"and it was adorable when"—You're [??] can *spike* it [??]—I suppose the "Belgian pictures" is supposed to tie in with the sonnet you've put as I 1.? "Pink and white ham flavored with a clove of garlic"—it surely would have been *baked in* the ham. (Even in a simple café I don't think the French would serve a clove of raw garlic) (cooking is more my line than yours!)—and "filled up an immense stein for me, with its foam gilded by a ray of *late* sun." The *late* seems important—the atmosphere of fatigue, late afternoon, and peacefulness.—"behind" *looks* like a mistake, I'm afraid.

THE SLEEPER IN THE VALLEY—The little valley foams with sunbeams /// he is stretched out in the grass, under the cloud, pale in his green bed. / His feet in the (gladiolas, *rushes, flags,* etc.), he sleeps. Smiling the way a sick child smiles, he *takes a nap.* "The river sucks his hair" is effective, but why put in "A white eye rolls" there.— Up until the very last phrase *nothing* has been said to indicate that the soldier isn't just asleep. I am against the interpolation about the bruises, too. You're anticipating the joke . . . giving the show away, etc.—

In your no. I—the last phrase—the soldier lying on his belly pushes his behind up and inquires "Of what?" Perhaps it could mean *WHY—Vive L'Empereur?* At least it seems better to me as a direct quotation coming from the "tres naif" soldier. (Oh dear—perhaps we are using different editions of Rimbaud?—but I've got the Pleiade here—) Could we be [??]?

In your III—"Calm, under your wooden shoes you broke the *yoke* that weighs on the soul and forehead of all humanity"—well, I guess you have just made it more pointed, with the "red-capped Christs" etc.— However— Rimbaud isn't being so partisan.

MA BOHEME—line 6—it says "To Thumb"—but that's probably a misprint for Tom Thumb, isn't it?

This poem is very *dainty*—it seems to me—you've got it all right in "fairy-crowded dark" and "ghost of a coat"— But I don't like "whose stars rang like silver coins in the night" for (literally) "My stars made a sweet rustling in the sky." And it's just "drops of dew."

And I don't think the foot should be "tucked tight against my heart"—he holds his foot *near* his heart and plucks its elastic as if it were a lyre—in the position of Apollo playing the lyre—

(I never quite got those elastics, though—can't be elastic-*sided,* obviously—perhaps they used elastic laces?—that would make it possible)

But it is delicate, gay, unreal—*humming*—like in The Tempest songs. *Oh! la! la!* he says—you know how the French say that.

In your VIII—Do you think you *should* change Nature to La Patrie? I'm afraid French critics won't like that.— The King [he's rather proud of his soldiers] doesn't "curse" the soldiers—he just *rallies* them. (Again, I feel you're sort of giving the show away too soon.)

THE POET AT SEVEN—livre de devoir—is just a copy book or exercise book (but of course you know that and wanted to bring in that Bible . . .)

Later on, in the next to the last stanza, the Bible has "cabbage-green edges"—

"Buttocks" ("fesses") is actually a stronger world than "crotch"—which after all is a euphemism—but I suspect you of putting in some Revere St. here and there!—"bloomers," for example, are pre-1928. (not French,—& not *contemporary*, either)

Well, now that I've done my worst with Rimbaud. What I'm afraid of, Cal, is now that your star is so very high (I saw that piece in The London *Times Lit. Supplement* some time ago and there have been so many honors recently.) that to publish translations open to misunderstanding may produce a lot of foolish haggling and criticism you could easily avoid. The French will say "The Americans who think they know French!"—etc.—Free Translation is fine.—but when you *seem* to make mistakes, look careless, or directly contradict the sense of the poem—I think you're laying yourself wide open.—

I hold Baudelaire in such awe that I'm rather afraid to tackle those—and he seems more sympathetic to your natural style, of course—gives you much more of a chance, verbally!—

In TO THE READER the 1st line of stanza nine would be clearer if you could use comparatives, I think—something like "there's one uglier, wickeder, filthier"

In SPLEEN—I suppose his bed is painted with fleur-de lys—and food / is syrup-green Lethean ooze seems much too rich for "Lethe's green water instead of blood"— But if that's what you want! (it is next to impossible of course to draw any lines and that's why I have hesitated to write at all—feel I may be making the mistake of my life—am full of awful doubts and worries)

AUTUMN: "labeur dur et force" is the term—what do we say?—"hard labor"—of course you've got it in [??]

Two mistakes—(I think)

LA CLOCHE FELEE: It begins gently, and the bells "sing" in the fog. The clock tower bell, "in spite of its age, alert and in good health / utters its religious cry faithfully, like an," etc.—I think again as in the Rimbaud one you're throwing away the surprise ending—(Everything is *fine* until the sestet—)—The bell is *healthy* (old)—*But me*—~~I'm cracked~~—or flawed— my soul its infeebled voice / seems like the death rattle of a wounded man *forgotten*—etc.—who dies, without moving, in his fearful efforts— But they are efforts to live, after all!

In Recueillement and again in La Lune Offensee, he uses the word *suran-*

nees. I think he likes it because he was being a dandy he was clothes-conscious and liked to describe the clothes as "old-fashioned" (Also—discreetly—a misprint) or "out-of-style"— Also in La Lune Offensee style—line 3—"The stars are going to follow you in *spruce array*"—awful, but that's the meaning—the contrast [is] well-kept, traditional, it reminds me of Milton's "bright harnest angels"—(coco-palms)

In LE GOUFFRE—I think two lines have been left out after "multiform" in my copy—or maybe it was deliberate—

In THE SWAN—the next to last stanza—I think is inverted the sense—"Or whoever has lost what is never, never found! Of those who drink tears and *suck Grief like a Wolf-Nurse.*"

In the stanza before that, third from the last—this is just personal—but couldn't you say she was looking for the *coconut palms* behind the fog wall? (I spent [??] in Paris and that fog wall is [??]—still mist—much more than rain—just coconuts doesn't seem right—too much like going shopping—

In LE JEU I ~~think~~ stanzas 2 and 3 are in the wrong order—

APPENDIX II

Elizabeth Bishop on Robert Lowell[1]

I first met Robert Lowell in late 1946 or early 1947. It was the winter that Randall Jarrell was taking the place of Margaret Marshall on The Nation, and living in Margaret Marshall's apartment on Square. I had met Jarrell only once or twice before, or had barely been introduced to him, and then he invited me to dinner, to meet Lowell. I was extremely shy at that time and I had met very few poets. I was afraid of going to dinner with Jarrell and his wife, and even more afraid of meeting Lowell, who had recently published "Lord Weary's Castle" just. I had admired some of the poems extremely. I had some difficulty understanding others, and the Catholicism bothered me a bit—but I knew next to nothing about Robert Lowell except what I had learned from the poems, and that he really was a Lowell.

That evening, that I approached in fear and trembling, turned out to be one of the pleasantest I can remember. First I found myself feeling very much at home with Randall Jarrell and his wife, and their big black cat, and Jarrell talked a blue streak while putting Kitten through his tricks. Then Lowell arrived and I loved him at first sight. He was living in a basement room on Third Avenue I think at the time, and he was rather untidy. He was wearing a rumpled dark blue suit; I remember the sad state of his shoes; he needed a hair cut, and he was very handsome and handsome in a[n] almost old-fashioned poetic way. I took to him at once; I didn't feel the least bit afraid, my shyness vanished and we started talking at once. By chance we had all scene [sic] a large show of French painting at the Knoedler Gallery and I remember the way we probably surprised each other by all remembering every picture, star[t]ing at the right as one went in and going straight around the gallery. Lowell's taste & mine agreed well; Jarrell tended to argue and make fun and at one point he demonstrated painting a picture with his

---

1 "[Lowell Reminiscences]," Bishop papers, Vassar.

feet, to show us what was coming next. (And of course it did, and with bicycles, too, but we were blissfully ignorant of the future.) We talked about poetry a lot; about Marianne Moore, I remember, but I don't remember now what we said. In my taxi on the way home to Greenwich Village [to] my re[ally] genuine garrett I remember thinking that it was the first time I had ever actually talked with some one about how one writes poetry—and thinking that it was[,] that it could be[,] strangely easy "Like exchanging recipes for making a cake."

He told some very good funny-pathetic stories late at night about his 3rd Avenue room: how the poor people gathered in the next room drinking beer would start to get loud and profane, and one of them would say "Shut up! Remember the kid . . ." meaning Lowell.

We have been friends ever since. I suppose I still occasionally think that to myself when I know a poem is going bad, or re-reading it I spot lines that shouldn't be there: "Shut up—remember the kid," *he'd* never let anything that weak get by him . . .

Our lives and fortunes have

The next meeting I remember was in Washington, when he was Consultant in poetry at the Library of Congress, and I went down from NY to make a recording for him. He came to breakfast with me at the Fairfax Hotel. He was still a bit rumpled and unkept and he had a large smear of ink across his chin, like a real poet, that I finally got up my courage to mention to him.

After the recording—during which he was very kind and kept trying to soothe my nerves—we went to the National Gallery, and then we had lunch at the Cosmos Club with Dr. Williams. Dr. Williams was on his way to St. Elizabeths to see Ezra Pound for the first time in many years, and he, too, was nervous and needed soothing. He had wanted to take Pound a present and had finally chosen a large bright pink box of chocolates. I heard a lot of literary gossip all brand new to me, and then we put Williams and his box of candy into a taxi cab and went to the National Gallery—I ~~think it was on this trip~~ had brought along a pair of flat shoes to wear for gallery going in a bag and I remember Lowell politely carrying my shoes for me—

Kindness has always been the dominant note in his attitude to me, over many years, and shown in many ways, some of them highly practical. Lord Weary's Castle, with its strictures[,] condemnations, judgments, could scarcely be called a kind book—it is not until Life Studies perhaps that this side of Lowell's character shows itself in all its possibilities of ----- - ---- and delicacy.

Skunk Hour is one of the great sources of pride in my life—

He has a way in conversation, sometimes in prose writing or letters (I might quote from a letter or two to show what I mean here[)] of prefacing a name with adjective piled on adjective—I like this very much; sometimes I disagree with an adjective or two, but usually the others will be accurate, surprising, maybe, but suddenly new and absolutely right—you can take your choice—

I have visited in Castine Maine and was provided with cornflakes, maple sugar, blueberries and cream for my breakfasts— It is an almost too good to be true example of a Maine seaport full of large solidly built white houses, and elm trees, green grass and Trinitarian Church . . . I have seen the equally large, solid, but more remote, and gray pea-green house where "The Mills of the Kavanaughs" was written—and the stream where the alewives run— He compares the clapboards to oystershells and I disagree, thinking they look more like clam shells. We went fishing with my lobsterman landlord and his wife had provided us with lunch and the regulation batch of doughnuts. Lots of doughnuts— Mr. Lowell dropped a few extra over the side and said "Now I know why they are referred to ask sinkers . . ."

Swimming, or rather standing, numb to the waist in the freezing cold water, but continuing to talk. If I were to think of any Saint in his connection then it is St. Sebastian—he stood in a rocky basin of the freezing water[,] sloshing it over his handsome youthful body and I could almost see the arrows sticking out of him

His courage—kindness—increasing good manners—gentleness with his daughter—capacity for work—

APPENDIX III

Letter of July 8, 1972, from Robert Lowell to Elizabeth Bishop[1]

July 8, 1972[2]

Dearest Elizabeth:

We've been working like steam-engines; no, very hard but like human beings. Pardon me for not answering. I think of you every day, and of course Frank is a constant reminder of you.

The work is rather peculiar and sounds almost insane.[3] We've gone over almost 400 old *Notebook* poems, with an average I suppose of 4 changes a poem, tho often the whole poem torn up trying to get rid of muddy lines, dead lines etc. I dictate the changes to Frank. Often there are many alternates, and more come to me as I talk. He remembers everything, and keeps me from throwing out silver spoons. *Notebook* was such a wilderness, now I think you'll [like] it better. Kunitz thinks it's transformed. Why boast? But I do think Frank will stay here a little longer. We just can't get through by the 15th. That's why I've given you this formidable account of my methods. I do feel guilty about his not going to Brazil, but think he wants badly to finish what's so largely done.

Not much news. Caroline is off to an all-day school picnic and circus with Ivana, the little girl who was burned. I think we'll go to Ireland for two weeks or so in August. When are you coming to Europe? I gather it will be early August. We do so wish you'd stop off here with us on your way. I could time the Ireland so as to be here. You and Kunitz are the only close American friends we haven't had. I want you to meet Caroline. She has gotten as bad as I about revising and sits on her bed all day with long foolscaps in front of her. She almost finished a book of short stories this winter—along with looking after,

---

1 RL's typescript was sent from Milgate Park to EB in Ouro Prêto. EB enclosed it in a July 17, 1972, letter to Alice Methfessel, indicating "SAVE, please—." RL's letter remained among Methfessel's papers until these were acquired by Vassar College in 2011. EB's letter in Appendix IV was discovered by Harriet Lowell in her father's briefcase in 2013.

2 Postmarked July 10, 1972, Maidstone, England.

3 EB notes to Methfessel, "*Coitado!* one can see what comes first!"

with help, three children, and in vacations four. The nicest more or less new person I've met is Angus Wilson. Met when I got a degree at Norwich, as beautiful in its way as Ouro Preto, at least when we came on it from a distance, and saw it during the long English twilight.

I like all your poems—most the "Night Flight,"[1] another of your best and one I might just not have known was by you. Very directly grim. "Moose"[2] has *lovely* moments, but others maybe too close to light verse. The midnight prose poem[3] is eerie, hard to compare with the others, because it couldn't have been written in verse. Then the marvelous RA painting poem.[4] You're sailing! I can't send you anything quite finished. I'm trying to be simple sensuous and graceful.[5] My new poems, about four are additions to the long poems. I'm sure you'll find *Dolphin* less excruciating; it can't I'm afraid entirely come clear of that. The new order, due to you, helps everything.

> All my love,
> Cal

P.S. I haven't read your anthology really,[6] but have gone over the Drummond religiously and find him one of the best living poets—a quieter Montale.

1 Evidently carried to RL in manuscript among "the poems Frank took with him," which are mentioned in EB's July 12, 1972, letter to RL (letter 395). Published as "Night City (from a Plane)" in *The New Yorker* (September 16, 1972). Retitled "Night City" in *Geography III*, 1976.
2 "The Moose," *The New Yorker* (July 14, 1972). In her July 12, 1972, letter to RL (letter 395), EB states that the improvements she had made to the poems hand-carried by Bidart concern "especially the long one," i.e., "The Moose."
3 "12 O'Clock News," *The New Yorker* (March 24, 1972).
4 "Poem (About the size of an old-style dollar bill)," *The New Yorker* (November 11, 1972). Retitled "Poem" in *Geography III*.
5 "Logic therefore so much as is useful . . . To which Poetry would be made subsequent, or indeed rather precedent, as being less suttle and fine, but more simple, sensuous and passionate" (Milton, *Of Education* [1644]. Cf. RL-*Letters*, p. 25). RL typed "garceful." He notes, while hand-correcting, "Bad word for a typo."
6 *An Anthology of Twentieth-Century Brazilian Poetry*, edited with Emanuel Brasil, 1972.

APPENDIX IV

Letter of July 23, 1977, from Elizabeth Bishop to Robert Lowell

July 23rd, 1977

Dear Cal:

Here's the ferry schedule—it is almost impossible to get a car on the ferry without a reservation long in advance—and then they seem to take real delight in turning you back if you're five minutes late . . . So you can leave your car (I suppose Elizabeth will be driving?) and we'll meet you at the ferry landing here—the big event of the day . . . Celia Bertin will be here from July 31st until about the 22nd, I think (writing a book about Marie Bonaparte); Frani & Curt from the 8th to the 15th, maybe longer (and Frani may be planning to go to Castine to see Mary; I don't know); Anne Hussey is coming over for a day, perhaps 2, and later a German friend & her husband are coming for the last week . . . We have had almost *no* guests so far which is just as well; I have been feeling so poorly—but I hope to improve as time goes on. (I feel like Felix Randall, the farrier—what was it, "seven something-disorders raged there"?) I'm afraid I really *don't* want Mary to come. I prefer to read her, at a distance.

I'd ask you to stay over if it weren't that all my company seems to want to come around the same time . . . After the big storm Thursday night, it's been beautiful—& was until then, too—some days of fog, but I like them. Like Frank—I am trying to get one small poem finished at the moment.—Oh—I read *Humboldt's Gift*—left in the laundry room at L Wharf—and I *can't* see why Bellow is so highly thought of—I was bored to tears—

—As you see by this schedule—Sunday gives you more time here—Weekdays the ferry—last one—leaves at 3—on Sundays not until 4:20. It will be nice to see you—& Elizabeth, too, if she comes—Call me—

Lots of love,
Elizabeth

GLOSSARY OF NAMES

A

Abel, Lionel (1911–2001), playwright, essayist, and novelist
Abercrombie, Lascelles (1881–1938), British poet
Acton, John Emerich Edward Dalberg, 1st Baron (1834–1902), British historian
Adams, Henry (1838–1918), historian and writer
Adams, Léonie (1899–1988), poet
Addams, Charles (1912–88), cartoonist
Adler, Alfred (1870–1937), Austrian psychiatrist
Agee, James (1909–55), author
Agnew, Spiro (1919–96), U.S. vice president (1969–73)
Aiken, Conrad (1889–1973), poet
Aiken, Joan (1924–2004), novelist
Aiken, Mary Hoover: *see* Hoover, Mary
Akhmatova, Anna (1889–1966), Russian poet
Aksakov, Sergey (1791–1859), Russian novelist
Albee, Edward (b. 1928), playwright
Alckmin, José Maria (1901–74), vice president of Brazil (1964–67)
Aldington, Richard (1892–1962), British poet
Aleijadinho (1730–1814), Brazilian sculptor
Alexander, Der Wilde (ca. late 13th century), German poet
Alfred, William (1922–99), playwright and scholar
Allen, Walter (1911–95), British writer and critic
Alsop, Joseph (1910–89), journalist and columnist
Alvarez, A. (b. 1929), British poet and critic
Amado, Jorge de Faria (1912–2001), Brazilian writer
Ames, Elizabeth (1885–1977), director of Yaddo
Amis, Kingsley (1922–95), British writer
Anday, Melih Cevdet (b. 1915), Turkish poet
Anderson, Sherwood (1876–1941), writer
Angelico, Fra (ca. 1400–55), Florentine painter
Ann, Harriet Lowell's nanny
Archera, Laura: *see* Huxley, Laura Archera
Arendt, Hannah (1906–75), German political philosopher
Aristophanes (ca. 450–ca. 388 bc), Greek playwright
Aristotle (384–322 bc), Greek philosopher

Armstrong, Phyllis, secretary to Poetry Office, Library of Congress
Arnold, Matthew (1822–88), British poet and critic
Aron, Raymond (1905–83), French historian and sociologist
Ashbery, John (b. 1927), poet
Asher, Elise (1912–2004), poet and painter
Assis, Machado de: *see* Machado de Assis, Joaquim Maria
Atlas, James (b. 1949), writer and editor
Auden, W. H. (1907–73), poet
Audubon, John James (1785–1851), artist and ornithologist
Austen, Jane (1775–1817), British novelist
Axelrod, Steven Gould (b. 1944), literary scholar
Azzaiolo, Filippo (1530–69), Italian composer

B

Babel, Nathalie (1929–2006), Slavic studies scholar, daughter of Isaac Babel
Bach, Johann Sebastian (1685–1750), German composer
Bacon, Francis (1909–92), Irish painter
Balanchine, George (1904–83), Russian-born choreographer
Baldwin, James (1924–87), writer
Balzac, Honoré de (1799–1850), French novelist
Bandeira, Manuel (1886–1968), Brazilian poet
Baraka, Amiri (b. 1934), poet, author, and playwright
Barata, Ruy (1920–90), Brazilian poet
Barber, Samuel (1910–81), composer
Barker, George (1913–91), British poet
Barker, Ilse (1921–2006), German-British writer
Barker, Kit (1916–88), British painter
Barnard, Mary (1909–2001), poet
Barnes, Albert (1872–1951), art collector and museum founder
Barnes, Djuna (1892–1982), modernist writer
Barnum, Phineas Taylor (1810–91), showman
Baro, Gene (1924–82), writer and curator
Barr, Alfred H. (1902–81), director of the Museum of Modern Art (1929–67)
Bartra, Agustí (1908–82), Catalán poet
Baruch, Bernard (1870–1965), financier and presidential adviser
Barzun, Jacques (b. 1907), historian and critic
Baskin, Leonard (1922–2000), sculptor and graphic artist
Bate, Walter Jackson (1918–99), literary scholar
Batista y Zaldívar, Fulgencio (1901–73), president of Cuba (1940–44, 1952–59)
Baudelaire, Charles (1821–67), French poet
Baumann, Anny (d. 1983), physician
Baumgarten, Bernice (1902–78), literary agent
Beach, Sylvia (1887–1962), publisher, proprietor of Shakespeare & Co. (Paris)
Beauvoir, Simone de (1908–86), French author
Beckett, Samuel (1906–89), Irish writer
Beebe, Lucius (1902–66), newspaper columnist and railroad historian
Beerbohm, Max (1872–1956), British caricaturist

Beethoven, Ludwig van (1770–1827), German composer
Bel Geddes, Edith Lutyens (1907–2002), theatrical costume designer and producer
Bel Geddes, Norman (1893–1958), theatrical and industrial designer
Belitt, Ben (1911–2003), poet
Bell, Daniel (b. 1919), sociologist
Bell, Pearl Kazin, editor and writer
Bellay, Joachim du (1522–60), French poet
Bellow, Saul (1915–2005), Canadian-born writer
Benn, Gottfried (1886–1956), German poet
Bennett, Peggy (b. 1925), novelist
Bentley, Eric (b. 1916), playwright and critic
Berg, Alban (1885–1935), Austrian composer
Berge, H. C. ten (b. 1938), Dutch poet
Bernard, Viola (1907–98), psychoanalyst
Bernardes, Sérgio (1919–2002), Brazilian architect
Bernstein, Leonard (1918–90), conductor and composer
Berryman, John (1914–72), poet
Bertelé, René, French writer and publisher
Bertin, Célia (b. 1921), French novelist and writer
Betjeman, John (1906–84), British poet
Bidart, Frank (b. 1939), poet
Biddle, Francis (1886–1968), U.S. attorney general (1941–45)
Biddle, Katherine Garrison Chapin (1890–1977), poet
Bing, Rudolph (1902–77), general manager of the Metropolitan Opera (1950–72)
Bishop, John W. (1846–1923), EB's grandfather
Bishop, Gertrude Bulmer (1879–1934) EB's mother
Bishop, William Thomas (1872–1911), EB's father
Bissier, Julius (1893–1965), German painter
Blackmur, R. P. (1904–65), poet and literary critic
Blackwood, Caroline (1931–96), Irish writer
Blais, Marie-Claire (b. 1939), Canadian writer
Blake, William (1757–1827), British poet and artist
Blechman, Burt (b. 1927), novelist
Blixen, Karen: see Dinesen, Isak
Bloom, Hyman (b. 1913), painter
Bloomfield, Morton (1913–87), literary scholar
Bloomgarden, Kermit (1904–76), Broadway producer
Blunden, Edmund (1896–1974), British poet
Blunt, Wilfrid Scawen (1840–1922), British poet
Bly, Robert (b. 1926), poet
Bogan, Louise (1897–1970), poet
Bohlen, Nina, painter
Bolt, Robert (1924–95), British scriptwriter and playwright
Booth, Margaret, wife of Philip Booth
Booth, Philip (1925–2007), poet
Bosch, Hieronymus (ca. 1450–ca. 1516), Dutch painter
Boswell, James (1740–95), Scottish biographer
Botsford, Keith (b. 1928), writer and editor
Bottomley, Gordon (1874–1948), British poet
Boucher, François (1703–70), French painter

Boulanger, Nadia-Juliette (1887–1979), French music teacher and conductor
Boulez, Pierre (b. 1925), French composer and conductor
Bowen, Elizabeth (1899–1973), Irish novelist
Bowen, Suzanne (pseudonym), EB's companion (1966–70)
Bowie, Dorothee N., Seattle friend of EB's
Bradstreet, Anne (ca. 1612–72), poet
Brancusi, Constantin (1876–1957), French sculptor
Brandeis, Louis (1856–1941), U.S. Supreme Court justice (1916–39)
Brandt, Carl, Jr., literary agent, Brandt and Brandt Literary Agency
Brant, Alice Dayrell Caldeira (1880–1970), Brazilian writer
Brant, Dr. Augusto Mário Caldeira, Brazilian bank president
Brasil, Emanuel (1940–99), Brazilian poet
Brecht, Bertolt (1898–1956), German dramatist
Breit, Harvey (1909–68), reviewer for *The New York Times Book Review* (1940–65)
Brekke, Paal (1923–93), Norwegian poet
Brinnin, John Malcolm (1916–98), writer, 92nd Street Y poetry director (1949–56)
Britten, Benjamin (1913–73), British composer
Brizola, Leonel de Moura (1922–2004), Brazilian politician
Broadwater, Bowden (1920–2005), writer and educator
Brodsky, Joseph (1940–96), Russian-born poet
Brook, Peter (b. 1925), British director
Brooke, Rupert (1887–1915), British poet
Brooks, Cleanth (1906–94), literary scholar
Brooks, Esther, dancer, wife of Peter Brooks
Brooks, Gwendolyn (1917–2000), poet
Brooks, John (1920–93), business journalist at *The New Yorker*
Brooks, Oliver Kenyon, literary critic
Brooks, Paul (b. 1909), editor in chief of Houghton Mifflin
Brooks, Peter, writer
Brown, Andreas, bookseller
Brown, Ashley (b. 1923), literary scholar
Brown, John, Mexican journalist
Brown, William (Guillermo) (1777–1857), Irish founder of Argentine navy
Browne, Roscoe Lee (1925–2007), actor
Browning, Elizabeth Barrett (1806–61), British poet
Browning, Robert (1812–89), British poet
Broyard, Anatole (1920–90), literary critic
Brueghel, Pieter the Younger (1564–1638), Flemish painter
Brustein, Robert (b. 1927), theatrical producer
Brutus, Dennis (b. 1924), South African poet and activist
Bryant, William Cullen (1794–1878), poet and editor
Brynner, Yul (1915–85), actor
Buchalter, Louis (1897–1944), murder-for-hire gangster
Buchwald, Art (1925–2007), newspaper columnist
Buckle, Henry Thomas (1821–62), British historian
Buckman, Gertrude, editor
Bullock, Marie (1911–86), founder of the Academy of American Poets
Bundy, McGeorge (1919–96), national security adviser to John F. Kennedy
Bunshaft, Gordon (1909–90), architect
Burford, William (b. 1927), poet

Burke, Kenneth (1897–1993), literary critic and philosopher
Burle Marx, Roberto (1909–94), Brazilian landscape architect
Burne-Jones, Edward Coley: see Jones, Edward Coley Burne-
Burney, Fanny (1752–1840), British novelist and diarist
Burns, Robert (1759–96), Scottish poet
Burr, Aaron (1756–1836), U.S. vice president (1801–05)
Burroughs, William S. (1914–97), writer
Bynner, Witter (1881–1961), poet
Byrom, Bill
Byron, George Gordon, 6th Baron (1788–1824), British poet

C

Cabot, John Moors (1901–81), diplomat
Cabral, Pedro Álvares (1467 or 1468–1520), Portuguese navigator
Cabral de Melo Neto, João (1920–99), Brazilian poet
Cadwalader, Elizabeth, EB's maid
Caetani, Marguerite (1880–1963), editor of *Botteghe Oscure*
Cairns, Huntington (1904–85), lawyer and editor
Cairns, Florence Butler, wife of Huntington Cairns
Calder, Alexander (1898–1976), modernist sculptor
Calder, Louisa James (1905–96), wife of Alexander Calder
Callado, Antônio (1917–97), Brazilian journalist
Callas, Maria (1923–77), Greek soprano
Camões, Luís Vaz de (1524–80), Portuguese poet
Campbell, Patrick, 3rd Baron Glenavy (1913–80), Irish journalist
Campin, Robert (ca. 1379–1444), Belgian painter
Campion, Thomas (1567–1620), British poet and musician
Campos, Paulo Mendes (1922–91), Brazilian poet and journalist
Camus, Albert (1913–60), French novelist, essayist, and dramatist
Camus, Marcel (1912–82), French filmmaker
Capua, Michael di, editor and publisher of Michael di Capua Books
Carcopino, Jérôme (1881–1970), French historian and author
Carleton, Dorothy (b. ca. 1895), Wilfred Blunt's secretary and companion
Carlisle, Olga Andreyev, writer and translator
Carlyle, Thomas (1795–1881), British writer and historian
Carnegie, Dale (1888–1955), self-help writer
Carossa, Hans (1878–1956), German poet
Carroll, Lewis: *see* Dodgson, Charles Lutwidge
Carruth, Hayden (b. 1921), poet and editor
Carter, Elliott (b. 1908), composer
Cartier-Bresson, Henri (1908–2004), French photographer
Carver, Catharine (1921–97), editor
Casa, Lisa della (b. 1919), Swiss soprano
Cassatt, Mary Stevenson (1845–1926), painter
Castelo Branco, Humberto de Alencar (1897–67), president of Brazil (1964–67)
Castro, Fidel (b. 1926), Cuban leader (1959–2008)
Cato, Marcus Porcius (234–149 bc), Roman statesman

Catta Preta, Dr. Zephyrino, Brazilian architect
Catullus, Gaius Valerius (ca. 84–ca. 54 bc), Roman poet
Cecil, Lord David (1902–86), British writer
Cellini, Benvenuto (1500–71), Florentine sculptor
Cézanne, Paul (1839–1906), French painter
Char, René (1907–88), French poet
Chardin, Jean-Baptiste-Siméon (1699–1779), French painter
Charlemagne (742–814), king of the Franks (768–814)
Chase, Richard Volney (1914–62), professor of English and writer
Chaucer, Geoffrey (ca. 1343–1400), British poet
Chávez, César (1927–93), labor leader and civil rights activist
Cheever, John (1912–82), writer
Chekhov, Anton (1816–1904), Russian writer and playwright
Chessman, Caryl (1921–60), convicted criminal and writer
Chittick, Victor L. O. (1882–1972), literary scholar
Choate, Rufus (1799–1859), American jurist
Chopin, Frédéric (1810–49), Polish composer
Christophe, Henri (1767–1820), king of Haiti (1811–20)
Church, Hubert (1857–1932), British poet
Churchill, Winston (1871–1947), novelist
Churchill, Winston Leonard Spencer (1874–1965), British prime minister (1940–45)
Ciardi, John (1916–86), poet and translator
Citkowitz, Evgenia (b. 1964), RL's stepdaughter, writer
Citkowitz, Israel (1909–74), composer
Citkowitz, Ivana (b. 1966), RL's stepdaughter, writer
Citkowitz, Natalya (1960–78), RL's stepdaughter
Clark, Blair (1921–97), journalist and editor
Clark, Eleanor (1913–96), writer
Clark, Eunice: see Jessup, Eunice Clark
Clark, Kenneth (1903–83), British art historian
Claudel, Paul (1868–1955), French poet
Cleaver, Eldridge (1935–98), writer and civil rights activist
Cleaver, Kathleen Neal (b. 1945), civil rights activist
Clemens, Samuel Langhorne (1835–1910), writer
Cocteau, Jean (1889–1963), French poet, artist, and filmmaker
Coelho, Joaquim-Francisco (b. 1938), Brazilian poet and literary scholar
Coffin, R. P. T. (1892–1955), poet
Coffin, William Sloane (1924–2006), clergyman and peace activist
Coleman, Elliott (1908–80), poet
Coleridge, Samuel Taylor (1772–1834), British poet
Collins, Larry (1930–2005), writer
Colônia, Regina Célia, Brazilian writer
Colum, Padraic (1881–1972), Irish poet and playwright
Conant, James Bryant (1893–1978), president of Harvard (1933–53)
Confucius (551–479 bc), Chinese philosopher
Conger, Mrs. Lowell, RL's relative
Connolly, Cyril (1903–74), British prose writer
Conrad, Alfred H., economist
Conrad, Joseph (1857–1924), Polish novelist
Constant, Benjamin de Rebecque (1767–30), French writer and politician

Conwell, Russell H. (1843–1925), Baptist minister and orator
Coolidge, Calvin (1872–1933), U.S. president (1923–29)
Copland, Aaron (1900–90), composer
Corbière, Tristan (1845–75), French poet
Cornaro, Luigi (ca. 1467–1566), Venetian nobleman
Correia de Araújo, Lilli, Brazilian hotel owner
Corso, Gregory (1930–2001), poet
Costa, Joana dos Santos da, EB and Lota's maid
Costa, Lúcio (1902–98), Brazilian architect and urban planner
Costa e Silva, Artur da (1902–69), president of Brazil (1967–69)
Coster, Nicolas (b. 1934), actor
Cotting, Charles Edward, husband of RL's aunt Sarah Winslow
Cotting, Sarah Winslow, RL's aunt
Cotton, Charles (1630–87), British poet
Coutinho, Afrânio (1911–2000), Brazilian literary critic
Cowley, Malcolm (1898–1989), literary critic
Crane, Hart (1899–1932), poet
Crane, Louise (1917–97), philanthropist, EB's companion
Crashaw, Richard (1572–1626), British poet
Creevey, Thomas (1768–1838), British politician
Cummings, E. E. (1894–1962), poet
Cummings, Marion Morehouse (1906–69), photographer and model
Cunha, Euclides da (1866–1909), Brazilian writer
Cushing, Richard (1895–1970), archbishop of Boston (1944–70)

D

Dahlberg, Edward (1900–77), novelist and essayist
Daluna, Mr., Brazilian acquaintance of EB's
Daniel, Margaret Truman (1924–2008), author
Dante (1265–1321), Italian poet
Darnell, Linda (1923–65), actress
Darwin, Charles (1809–82), British naturalist
Daumier, Honoré (1808–79), French caricaturist and painter
Dawson, Carley (1910–77), writer
Dawson, Elizabeth, the Lowells' nurse
Day-Lewis, Cecil (1904–72), British poet
Debray, Régis (b. 1940), French intellectual
Debussy, Claude (1862–1918), French composer
Dee, John (1527–1608), British mathematician and astronomer
Degas, Edgar (1834–1917), French painter
de Kooning, Willem (1904–97), Dutch painter
Delaney, Beauford (1901–79), painter
Delgado, Humberto da Silva (1906–65), Portuguese general and politician
Deller, Alfred (1912–79), British countertenor
de los Ángeles, Victoria (1923–2005), Spanish soprano
Demuth, Charles (1883–1935), painter
Denys, Odílio (1892–1985), Brazilian army marshal

De Sica, Vittorio (1902–74), Italian film director
Deutsch, Helene (1884–1982), Austrian psychoanalyst
Devlin, Denis (1908–59), Irish poet
Dewey, Jane M. (1900–76), physicist
Dewey, John (1859–1952), philosopher
Dib, Mohammed (1920–2003), Algerian writer
Dick, Anne (b. circa 1912), RL's fiancée
Dickens, Charles (1812–70), British novelist
Dickey, James (1923–97), poet
Dickinson, Emily (1830–86), poet
Dietrich, Marlene (1901–92), German actress
Dillon, George (1906–68), poet, editor of *Poetry* (1937–49)
Dinesen, Isak (1885–1962), Danish writer
Dix, Dorothy (1861–1951), advice columnist
Dodgson, Charles Lutwidge (1832–98), British writer
Domvile, Barry (1878–1971), British naval officer and fascist
Donatello (1386?–1466), Florentine sculptor
Donne, John (1572–1631), British poet
Dos Passos, John (1896–1970), novelist
Dostoyevsky, Fyodor Mikhaylovich (1821–81), Russian novelist
Doughty, Charles Montagu (1843–1926), British man of letters
Douglas, Gordon (1907–93), filmmaker
Doyle, Charles (b. 1928), New Zealand poet and critic
Drummond de Andrade, Carlos (1902–87), Brazilian poet
Dryden, John (1631–1700), British poet
Dugan, Alan (1923–2003), poet
Dulles, Allen (1893–1969), director of the CIA (1953–61)
Dulles, John Foster (1888–1959), U.S. secretary of state (1953–59)
Dumas, Alexandre (1802–70), French writer
Dunaway, Faye (b. 1941), actress
Duncan, Robert (1919–88), poet
Dunlop, John (1914–2003), economist and U.S. secretary of labor (1975–76)
Dunn, Douglas (b. 1942), Scottish poet
Dupee, F. W. (Fred) (1904–79), literary scholar and editor of Partisan Review
Durrell, Lawrence (1912–90), British writer
Duval-Smith, Simon Peter (b. 1956), William Empson's adopted son
Dyer, Major, Washington, D.C., acquaintance of RL
Dylan, Bob (b. 1941), singer and songwriter

E

Eatherly, Claude Robert (1918–78), U.S. Air Force pilot
Eberhart, Dikkon (b. 1946), Richard Eberhart's son
Eberhart, Helen Elizabeth (1915–93), Richard Eberhart's wife
Eberhart, Richard (1904–2005), poet
Eddy, Mary Baker (1821–1910), founder of the Church of Christ, Scientist
Edel, Leon (1907–97), literary critic and biographer
Edwards, Jonathan (1703–58), theologian
Ehrenpreis, Irvin (1920–85), literary critic

Einhard (ca. 770–840), Frankish historian
Eisenhower, Dwight D. (1890–1969), U.S. president (1953–61)
Eisenstein, Sergei (1898–1948), Russian film director
Eissler, K. R. (1908–99), Viennese psychoanalyst
Eileen, Harriet Lowell's nurse
Eliot, George: see Evans, Marian
Eliot, T. S. (1888–1965), poet and critic
Eliot, Valerie Fletcher (b. 1926), second wife of T. S. Eliot
Elizabeth I (1533–1603), British queen (1558–1603)
Elliott, George P. (1918–80), writer
Ellsberg, Margaret Rizza, literary scholar
Elsemore, Miss, Harriet Lowell's nurse
Emerson, Ralph Waldo (1803–82), poet and essayist
Empson, Jacobus Arthur Calais (b. 1945), British psychologist
Empson, Hetta (1915–96), South African sculptor
Empson, William (1906–85), British poet and critic
Engle, Paul (1908–91), writer, founder of the Iowa Writers' Workshop
Epstein, Barbara (1928–2006), editor and cofounder of *The New York Review of Books*
Epstein, Jason (b. 1928), editor and cofounder of *The New York Review of Books*
Erikson, Eric (1902–94), German-American psychoanalyst
Erskine, Constance Caraway (1906–2000), poet and arts patron
Erskine, Graves Blanchard (1897–1973), U.S. Marine major general
Ervin, Samuel (1896–1985), chair of the Senate Watergate Committee
Eulálio, Alexandre Pimenta da Cunha (b. 1932), Brazilian writer and editor
Evans, Luther H. (1902–81), librarian of Congress (1945–53)
Evans, Marian (1819–80), British novelist
Evans, Walker (1903–75), photographer
Evelyn, John (1620–1706), British diarist

F

Fabiani, Mario (1912–74), mayor of Florence (1946–51)
Farley, James A. (1888–1976), politician
Farouk I (1920–65), king of Egypt (1936–52)
Farrar, John (1896–1974), publisher, cofounder of Farrar, Straus and Company
Farre, Rowena (1922–79), British writer
Faulkner, William (1897–1962), novelist
Fawcett, Percy (1867–1925), British explorer
Featherstone, Isabella: *see* Paul, Isabella
Fellini, Federico (1920–93), Italian film director
Fenwick, Elizabeth (b. 1920), novelist
Fergusson, Francis (1904–86), literary scholar
Feuillère, Edwige (1907–98), French actress
Fiedler, Leslie (1917–2003), literary scholar
Fitts, Dudley (1903–68), poet and translator
Fitzgerald, Benedict (b. 1949), screenwriter, son of Robert Fitzgerald
FitzGerald, Edward (1809–83), British poet and translator
Fitzgerald, F. Scott (1896–1940), writer
Fitzgerald, Robert (1910–85), poet and translator

Fitzgerald, Sally (1917–2000), literary scholar
Fizdale, Robert (1920–95), pianist
Flagstad, Kirsten (1895–1962), Norwegian soprano
Flaubert, Gustave (1821–80), French novelist
Fletcher, John (1579–1625), British playwright
Fletcher, John Gould (1886–1950), British poet
Flint, F. S. (1885–1960), British poet
Flint, R. W., literary critic and translator
Fludd, Robert (1574–1637), British physician and writer
Fontaine, Jean de la (1621–95), French poet
Fontayne, Margot (1919–91), British ballerina
Forbes, William Cameron (1870–1959), U.S. ambassador to Japan (1930–32)
Ford, Ford Madox (1873–1939), British writer
Ford, Gerald Rudolph (1913–2006), U.S. president (1974–77)
Forrestal, James (1892–1949), U.S. secretary of defense (1947–49)
Forrestal, Michael (1927–89), Far Eastern affairs aide to Robert F. Kennedy
Forster, E. M. (1879–1970), British novelist
Foster, Ruth (1894–1950), psychoanalyst
Fowlie, Wallace (1909–98), French scholar
Frank, Joseph (b. 1918), literary scholar
Frankenberg, Lloyd (1907–75), poet
Frankfurter, Felix (1882–1965), U.S. Supreme Court justice (1939–62)
Freud, Lucian (b. 1922), British painter
Freud, Sigmund (1856–1939), Viennese psychoanalyst
Freund, Gerald (1931–97), scholar, philanthropies administrator
Freund, Paul A. (1908–92), constitutional scholar
Freyre, Gilberto (1900–87), Brazilian writer
Friar, Kimon (1911–93), scholar and Greek translator
Frobenius, Leo (1873–1938), German explorer and ethnologist
Fromentin, Eugène (1820–76), French painter and writer
Fromm, Erich (1900–80), psychologist
Frost, Lesley (1899–1983), writer and daughter of Robert Frost
Frost, Robert (1874–1963), poet
Froude, James Anthony (1818–94), British historian and writer
Fuentes, Carlos (b. 1928), Mexican author
Fulbright, William (1905–95), Arkansas politician
Fuller, Buckminster (1895–1983), philosopher and architect

G

Galassi, Jonathan (b. 1949), poet, translator, editor, and publisher
Galentine, Wheaton (b. 1914), documentary filmmaker
Gannett, Lewis (1891–1966), book review columnist for the *New York Herald Tribune*
Gannett, Ruth (1896–1979), illustrator
García Lorca, Federico (1898–1936), Spanish poet and dramatist
Gardner, Ainslie (Lee) Anderson, wife of Robert Gardner
Gardner, Isabella (1915–81), poet
Gardner, Robert (b. 1925), documentary filmmaker
Garrigue, Jean (1914–72), poet

Gaulle, Charles de (1890–1970), French president (1959–69)
Genet, Jean (1910–86), French writer
George III (1738–1820), British king (1760–1820)
George V (1865–1936), British king (1910–36)
George VI (1895–1952), British king (1936–52)
Gesell, Silvio (1862–1930), German economist and anarchist
Gesualdo, Carlo (1561–1613), Italian composer
Ghiselin, Brewster (1928–96), poet
Gibbs, Barbara, poet
Gide, André (1869–1951), French novelist
Gielgud, John (1904–2000), British actor
Gilbert, Stuart (1883–1969), British literary scholar and translator
Gilberto, João (b. 1931), Brazilian singer and guitarist
Ginsberg, Allen (1926–97), poet
Giorgione (ca. 1477–1511), Venetian painter
Giroux, Robert (b. 1914), editor and publisher
Glenn, John (b. 1921), astronaut and politician
Glimp, Fred L., dean of Harvard College
Gluck, Christoph Willibald (1714–87), German composer
Goethe, Johann Wolfgang von (1749–1832), German poet
Gogh, Vincent van (1853–90), Dutch painter
Gogol, Nicolay (1809–52), Russian writer
Gold, Arthur (1917–90), pianist
Golding, Arthur (ca. 1536–ca. 1606), British translator
Goldoni, Carlo (1707–93), Italian playwright
Goldsmith, Oliver (1730–74), British writer
Goldwater, Barry Morris (1909–98), politician
Gombrich, E. H. (1909–2001), Austrian-born British art historian
Gomes, Antonio Carlos (1836–96), Brazilian composer
Gomperts, Hans (1915–98), Dutch literary scholar
Gonçalves, Martinho, Brazilian theater scholar
Goncourt, Edmond de (1822–96), French writer
Goncourt, Jules de (1830–70), French writer
Goodget, Sarah, friend of Peter Taylor
Goodman, Mitchell (1924–97), antiwar activist
Gordon, Caroline (1895–1981), novelist and critic
Gordon, Lincoln (b. 1913), U.S. ambassador to Brazil (1961–66)
Gottlieb, Adolph (1903–74), painter
Goulart, João (1918–76), president of Brazil (1961–64)
Grable, Betty (1916–73), actress
Grant, Cary (1904–86), actor
Grant, Ulysses S. (1822–85), U.S. president (1869–77)
Grass, Günter (b. 1927), German novelist
Graves, Morris (1910–2001), painter
Graves, Robert (1895–1985), British poet
Gray, Morris (1856–1931), Boston attorney
Gray, Thomas (1716–71), British poet
Greco, El (1541–1614), Spanish painter
Greenberg, Clement (1909–94), art critic
Greenberg, Samuel (1893–1917), poet
Greene, Graham (1904–91), British novelist

Greenslet, Ferris (1875–1959), editor and publisher
Greville, Fulke, 1st Baron Brooke of Beauchamps Court (1554–1628), courtier and writer
Griffin, Jonathan (1907–90), British poet and playwright
Griggs, Robert F. (1881–1962), botanist
Gris, Juan (1887–1927), Spanish painter
Groot, Silvia W., Dutch anthropologist
Groot, S. R. de (b. 1916), Dutch physicist
Guest, Barbara (1920–2006), poet
Guinness, Alec (1914–2000), British actor
Gunn, Thom (1929–2004), poet
Guston, Philip (1913–80), painter

H

Hadrian (ad 76–138), Roman emperor (ad 117–138)
Hagen, Victor Wolfgang von (1908–85), archaeologist and travel writer
Haieff, Alexei (1914–94), composer
Haigh, Kenneth (b. 1931), British actor
Hall, Donald (b. 1928), poet
Hall, Peter (b. 1930), founder of the Royal Shakespeare Company
Hamilton, Alexander (1755–1804), statesman
Hamilton, Ian (1938–2001), British poet
Hamilton, Ralph (1947–2006), painter
Hampshire, Stuart (1914–2004), British philosopher
Handel, George Frideric (1685–1759), German-born British composer
Hanson, Pauline, poet
Hardwick, Elizabeth (1916–2007), writer and cofounder of *The New York Review of Books*
Hardy, Thomas (1840–1928), British novelist and poet
Hare, Augustus (1834–1903), British writer
Harrison, James C. (1925–90), painter
Harrison, Tony (b. 1937), British poet
Harrison, Wallace (1895–1981), architect
Hart, Jeanne McGahey (1906–95), poet
Hartley, Marsden (1877–1943), painter
Hassall, Christopher (1912–63), British writer
Hatfield, Ann: *see* Rothschild, Ann Hatfield
Hauser, Arnold (1892–1978), Hungarian-born British art historian
Hawthorne, Nathaniel (1804–64), novelist
Hawthorne, Una (1844–77), Nathaniel Hawthorne's daughter
Haydn, Joseph (1732–1809), German composer
Heaney, Seamus (b. 1939), Irish poet
Hebel, Johann Peter (1760–1826), German poet
Hecht, Anthony (1923–2004), poet
Hegerman-Lindecrone, Lillie Greenough de (1844–1928), singer and diplomat's wife
Heilman, Robert (1906–2004), literary scholar
Heimert, Alan (1929–99), literary scholar
Heine, Heinrich (1797–1856), German poet and critic
Hellman, Lillian (1905–84), playwright
Hemingway, Ernest (1899–1961), novelist

Hemingway, Gregory (1931–2001), son of Ernest and Pauline Hemingway
Hemingway, Pauline Pfeiffer (1895–1951), Ernest Hemingway's second wife
Henze, Hans Werner (b. 1926), German composer
Herbert, George (1593–1633), British poet
Herbert, Zbigniew (1924–98), Polish poet
Hergesheimer, Joseph (1880–1954), novelist
Herrick, Robert (1591–1674), British poet
Hersch, Jeanne (1910–2000), Swiss philosopher
Herschberger, Ruth (b. 1917), poet and feminist
Herzberg, Judith (b. 1934), Dutch poet
Heyman, C. David (b. 1945), writer
Hilberg, Raul (1926–2007), historian
Hills, L. Rust (1924–2008), Esquire fiction editor (1956–63)
Hillyer, Robert (1895–1961), poet
Hires, Charles E., Jr. (1892–1980), chairman of Hires Root Beer company
Hiss, Alger (1904–96), civil servant
Hochhuth, Rolf (b. 1931), German writer
Hochman, Sandra (b. 1936), poet
Hoffman, Daniel (b. 1923), poet
Hölderlin, Friedrich (1770–1843), German poet
Hollander, John (b. 1929), poet and literary scholar
Holmes, Oliver Wendell, Jr. (1841–1935), U.S. Supreme Court justice (1902–32)
Homer (9th–8th? century bc), Greek poet
Hoover, Herbert (1874–1964), U.S. president (1929–33)
Hoover, Mary (1907–92), artist
Hopkins, Gerard Manley (1844–89), British poet
Horace (65–8 bc), Roman poet
Horgan, Paul (1903–95), novelist
Hoskins, Katherine (1909–88), poet
Housman, A. E. (1859–1936), British poet and classical scholar
Howard, Richard (b. 1929), poet and translator
Howe, Irving (1920–93), literary critic
Howells, William Dean (1837–1920), author
Howes, Barbara (1914–96), poet
Huff, Robert (b. 1924), poet
Hughes, Olwyn (b. 1928), editor
Hughes, Ted (1930–98), poet
Hugo, Victor (1802–85), French novelist
Humphrey, Hubert (1911–78), U.S. vice president (1965–69)
Humphries, Rolphe (1894–1969), poet and translator
Hunt, John (b. 1925), novelist and Congress for Cultural Freedom administrator
Hussey, Anne (b. 1934), poet
Huxley, Aldous (1894–1963), British writer
Huxley, Laura Archera (1911–2007), Italian musician and writer

I

Illich, Ivan (1926–2002), Viennese philosopher
Ingersoll, Robert (1833–99), orator and politician

Isherwood, Christopher (1904–86), British writer
Istomin, Eugene (1925–2003), pianist
Ivask, Ivar (1927–92), Estonian poet and editor
Ives, Charles (1874–1954), composer

J

Jack, Peter Monro, literary critic
Jackson, Laura Riding (1901–91), poet
James VI and I (1566–1625), king of Scotland (1567–1603) and Great Britain (1603–25)
James, Clive (b. 1939), Australian writer
James, Henry (1843–1916), novelist
James, William (1842–1910), philosopher
James, William, Jr. (1882–1961), artist
Jarrell, Mackie Langham, literary scholar, first wife of Randall Jarrell
Jarrell, Mary von Schrader (1914–2007), writer, second wife of Randall Jarrell
Jarrell, Randall (1914–65), poet and critic
Jarry, Alfred (1873–1907), French writer
Jasimuddin (1903–76), Bengali poet
Jaspers, Karl Theodor (1883–1969), German philosopher
Jeffers, Robinson (1887–1962), poet
Jefferson, Thomas (1743–1826), U.S. president (1801–09)
Jennings, Elizabeth (1926–2001), British poet
Jessup, Eunice Clark (1911–87), writer
Jesus, Carolina Maria de (1914–77), Brazilian diarist
Jewett, Sarah Orne (1849–1909), writer
Jiménez, José, Brazilian poet
Jiménez, Juan Ramón (1881–1958), Spanish poet
Jobim, Antônio Carlos (1927–94), Brazilian composer and musician
Johnson, Lyndon B. (1908–73), U.S. president (1963–69)
Johnson, Marian Willard (1904–85), art dealer
Johnson, Norman, RL's Harvard classmate
Johnson, Robert (1911–38), Delta blues singer
Johnson, Samuel (1709–84), British poet
Johnsrud, Harold (1904–39), actor
Jolas, Eugene (1894–1952), writer and editor of *transition*
Jones, Ernest (1879–1958), British psychoanalyst
Jones, Howard Mumford (1892–1980), literary scholar
Jones, LeRoi: *see* Baraka, Amiri
Jones, Edward Coley Burne-, 1st baronet (1833–98), British painter
Jonson, Ben (1572–1637), British poet
Joplin, Janis (1943–70), singer
Jordão, Vera Pacheco, Brazilian writer
Joyce, James (1882–1941), Irish writer
Julião, Francisco Arruda de Paula (1915–99), Brazilian activist
Jumper, Will C., poet and critic
Jung, Carl Gustav (1875–1961), Swiss psychoanalyst
Jungk, Robert (1913–94), Austrian writer and journalist
Juvenal (AD 55 to 60–ca. 127), Roman poet

K

Kael, Pauline (1919–2001), film critic
Kafka, Franz (1883–1924), Czech writer
Kallman, Chester (1921–75), poet and librettist
Kalstone, David (1933–86), literary scholar
Kant, Immanuel (1742–1804), German philosopher
Kazan, Elia (1909–2003), film director
Kazan, Molly (1907–63), playwright and literary agent
Kazantzakis, Nikos (1883–1957), Greek writer
Kazin, Alfred (1915–98), writer and literary critic
Kazin, Pearl: *see* Bell, Pearl Kazin
Keats, John (1795–1821), British poet
Keeler, Christine (b. 1942), British model involved in Profumo Affair
Kelly, Richard (1911–77), architectural lighting designer
Kempton, Murray (1917–97), newspaper columnist
Kennan, George (1904–2005), diplomat and historian
Kennedy, Edward (b. 1932), U.S. senator (since 1962)
Kennedy, Jacqueline: *see* Onassis, Jacqueline Kennedy
Kennedy, John F. (1917–63), U.S. president (1961–63)
Kennedy, Robert F. (1925–68), U.S. attorney general (1961–64) and senator (1965–68)
Kentfield, Calvin (1924–75), novelist and travel writer
Kern, Toni, nanny for Harriet
Kerouac, Jack (1922–69), writer
Keyes, Frances Parkinson (1885–1970), Catholic writer
Khrushchev, Nikita (1894–1971), premier of the Soviet Union (1958–64)
Kierkegaard, Søren (1813–55), Danish philosopher
King, Henry (1592–1669), British poet
Kinsella, Thomas (b. 1928), Irish poet
Kipling, Rudyard (1865–1936), British writer and poet
Kirk, Joan Van (b. 1910), novelist
Kirkpatrick, Ralph (1911–84), harpsichordist
Kirstein, Lincoln (1907–96), writer and philanthropist
Kizer, Carolyn (b. 1925), poet
Klee, Paul (1879–1940), Swiss painter
Klein, Melanie (1882–60), British psychoanalyst
Kline, Franz (1910–62), painter
Knopf, Alfred A. (1892–1984), publisher
Kokoschka, Oscar (1886–1980), British painter
Kostelanetz, André (1901–80), Russian composer
Kraft, Victor (d. 1976), photographer
Kray, Elizabeth (1916–87), director of the Academy of American Poets (1963–81)
Kronenberger, Louis (1904–80), drama critic
Kubitschek de Oliveira, Juscelino (1902–76), Brazilian president (1956–61)
Kunert, Günter (b. 1929), German writer
Kunitz, Elise Asher: see Asher, Elise
Kunitz, Stanley (1905–2006), poet

L

La Bruyère, Jean de (1645–96), French writer
Lacerda, Alberto de (1928–2007), Portuguese poet
Lacerda, Carlos (1914–77), Brazilian newspaper editor and politician
Laclos, Pierre Choderlos de (1741–1803), French writer
La Fayette, Marie-Madeleine de (1634–93), French writer
Laforgue, Jules (1860–87), French poet
Lage, Alfredo, Brazilian journalist
Lamb, Charles (1775–1834), British essayist
Langer, Susanne K. (1895–1985), philosopher
Lapierre, Dominique (b. 1931), French writer
Larbaud, Valéry-Nicolas (1881–1957), French novelist and critic
Larcom, Lucy (1824–93), poet
Lardner, Ring (1885–1933), short-story writer
Larkin, Philip (1922–85), British poet
Lassus, Orlande de (1520 or 1532–94), Flemish composer
Lattimore, Richmond (1906–84), poet and classics translator
Lawner, Lynne (b. 1935), poet and art historian
Lawrence, D. H. (1885–1930), British poet and novelist
Leão, Rosalina, Brazilian artist and landscape architect
Lear, Edward (1812–88), British poet and painter
Leary, Lewis Gaston (1906–90), literary scholar
Leavis, F. R. (1895–1978), British literary critic
Lee, Robert E. (1807–70), Confederate general
Lee, Vernon: *see* Paget, Violet
Leeds, Harold Eliot (1913–2002), architect
Leeuwen, W. F. van (b. 1917), Dutch literary critic and psychotherapist
Léger, Alexis (1887–1975), French poet
Le Nôtre, André (1613–1700), French landscape architect
Lenya, Lotte (1898–1981), Austrian singer and actress
Leonardo da Vinci (1452–1519), Italian artist
Lepke: *see* Buchalter, Louis
Levenson, J. C. (b. 1922), literary scholar
Levin, Harry (1912–93), literary scholar
Levine, David (b. 1926), caricaturist
Lévi-Strauss, Claude (b. 1908), French social anthropologist
Lewes, George Henry (1817–78), British writer, Marian Evans's companion
Lewis, Stanley (1937–58), publisher of Parnassus
Lewis, Wyndham (1882–1957), British painter and writer
Lima, Jorge de (1895–1953), Brazilian poet
Lincoln, Abraham (1809–65), U.S. president (1861–65)
Lindbergh, Anne Morrow (1906–2001), aviator and author
Lindley, Denver (1904–82), editor at Harcourt Brace
Lippmann, Walter (1889–1974), journalist
Lispector, Clarice (1920–77), Brazilian writer
Littlefield, Lester (b. 1913), literary scholar
Livy (59 BC–AD 17), Roman historian
Lock, Max (1909–88), British architect and urban designer
Lodge, Henry Cabot (1902–85), U.S. senator (1936–44)
Logue, Christopher (b. 1926), British poet

Long, Huey (1893–1935), governor of Louisiana (1928–35)
Longfellow, Henry Wadsworth (1807–82), poet and translator
Longworth, Alice Roosevelt (1884–1980), socialite and Theodore Roosevelt's daughter
Lott, Henrique Teixeira (1894–1984), Brazilian war minister
Louis, Joe (1914–81), boxer
Louis Philippe (1773–1850), king of France (1830–48)
Lowell, Amy (1874–1925), poet
Lowell, Charles Russell (1835–64), Union Army general
Lowell, Charlotte Winslow (d. 1954), RL's mother
Lowell, Harriet Winslow (b. 1957), RL's daughter
Lowell, Ivana: see Citkowitz, Ivana
Lowell, James Russell (1819–91), poet and statesman
Lowell, Percival (1855–1916), astronomer
Lowell, Robert Sheridan (b. 1971), RL's son, activist
Lowell, Robert Traill Spence (1816–91), clergyman, RL's great-grandfather
Lowell, Robert Traill Spence III (d. 1950), naval officer, RL's father
Lucan (AD 39–65), Roman poet
Luce, Clare Boothe (1903–87), writer and politician
Luce, Henry (1898–1967), publisher and founder of *Time* and *Life*
Lucie-Smith, Edward (b. 1933), British poet
Luther, Martin (1483–1546), German theologian
Luxemburg, Rosa (1870–1919), German socialist
Lyra, Carlos (b. 1939), Brazilian singer and composer

M

Maas, Willard (1911–71), poet
MacArthur, Douglas (1880–1964), U.S. general
Macaulay, Thomas Babington, Baron (1800–59), British historian
Macauley, Anne (d. 1973), wife of Robie Macauley
Macauley, Robie (1919–95), editor and writer
Macdonald, Dwight (1906–82), cultural critic
Macedo Soares, Kylso Costellat de, Brazilian draftsman, Lota's adopted son
Macedo Soares, Maria Carlota Costellat de (d. 1967), Brazilian architect
Macedo Soares Regis, Flávio de (1943–70), Brazilian civil servant, Lota's nephew
Macedo Soares Regis, Marietta Nascimento de, Lota's sister
Machado de Assis, Joaquim Maria (1839–1908), Brazilian writer
MacIver, Loren (1909–98), painter
MacLeish, Archibald (1892–1982), poet and librarian of Congress (1939–44)
MacLeod, D. B., EB's neighbor in Briton Cove
MacNeice, Louis (1907–63), Irish poet and translator
Madison, James (1751–1836), U.S. president (1809–17)
Magalhães, Aloísio (1927–82), Brazilian graphic designer
Mailer, Norman (1923–2007), writer
Maisel, Edward, writer and theater critic
Mallarmé, Stéphane (1842–98), French poet
Malraux, André (1901–76), French novelist
Mamede, Hélio, Brazilian architect
Mamede, Zila (1925–85), Brazilian poet

Mandelstam, Nadezhda (1899–1980), Russian writer
Mandelstam, Osip (1891–1938), Russian poet
Mander, John (b. 1932), British journalist and writer
Mann, Horace (1796–1859), educator and abolitionist
Mann, Thomas (1875–1955), German novelist
Manning, Frederic (1882–1935), Australian poet and novelist
Mansfield, Harry K. (1920–2000), tax attorney
Marchand, Leslie Alexis (1900–99), literary scholar and biographer
Marchand, Louis (1807–43), Napoleon's valet
Mare, Walter de la (1873–1956), British writer
Margaret Rose (1930–2002), British princess
Marlowe, Sylvia (1908–81), harpsichordist
Marshall, Margaret (1900–74), literary editor at *The Nation*
Martin, Jay, literary scholar
Marvell, Andrew (1621–78), British poet
Marx, Karl (1818–83), Prussian revolutionary and philosopher
Mary II (1662–94), British queen (1689–94)
Masefield, John (1878–1967), British poet and novelist
Mather, Cotton (1663–1728), clergyman and writer
Mathews, Jackson (1907–78), writer and translator
Matisse, Henri (1869–1954), French painter
Maugham, Somerset (1874–1965), British novelist
Mazia, Violette de (1899–1998), educator
McCarthy, Eugene (1916–2005), U.S. senator (1959–71)
McCarthy, Kevin (b. 1914), actor
McCarthy, Mary (1912–89), writer
McCormick, John (b. 1918), literary critic and writer
McCormick, Robert H., Jr., third husband of Isabella Gardner
McCullers, Carson (1917–67), writer
McElroy, Walter, writer and translator
McGahey, Jeanne: *see* Hart, Jeanne McGahey
McGinley, Phyllis (1905–78), writer of light verse
McKenna, Rollie (1918–2003), photographer
McKenna, Siobhán (1923–86), Irish actress
McLean, Francis (1717–81), British army general
McLuhan, Marshall (1911–80), Canadian literary and communications scholar
McNamara, Robert (b. 1916), U.S. secretary of defense (1961–68)
McPherson, Sandra (b. 1943), poet
Medina, Ernest (b. 1936), U.S. Army captain
Mehta, Ved (b. 1934), Indian writer
Meigs, Mary (1917–2002), painter
Meiners, Roger Keith (b. 1932), literary scholar and poet
Meireles, Cecília (1901–64), Brazilian poet
Mellon, Paul (1907–99), philanthropist and art collector
Mellon, Rachel "Bunny" (b. ca. 1912), horticulturalist and philanthropist
Melville, Herman (1819–91), novelist and poet
Mercouri, Melina (1923–94), Greek actress and politician
Meredith, William (1919–2007), poet
Merriam, Eve (1916–92), poet and playwright
Merrill, James (1926–95), poet
Merton, Thomas (1915–68), writer and Trappist monk

Merwin, Dido, W. S. Merwin's wife
Merwin, W. S. (b. 1927), poet
Messiaen, Olivier (1908–92), French composer and organist
Methfessel, Alice (b. 1944), EB's companion and literary executor
Meyer, Agnes (1887–1970), journalist and philanthropist
Michaux, Henri (1899–1984), Belgian writer and painter
Middleton, Thomas (1570?–1627), British playwright
Miles, Josephine (1911–85), poet
Milhaud, Darius (1892–1974), French composer
Millay, Edna St. Vincent (1892–1950), poet
Miller, Henry (1891–1980), novelist
Miller, Jonathan (b. 1934), British director, writer, and physician
Miller, Karl (b. 1931), Scottish writer and editor
Miller, Margaret, curator at the Museum of Modern Art
Miller, Perry (1905–63), intellectual historian
Miller, Vassar (1924–98), poet
Mills, Margaret, secretary, the Academy of American Poets
Milton, John (1608–74), British poet
Mindlin, Henrique (1911–71), Brazilian writer and architect
Mirabeau, Comte de (1749–91), French orator and revolutionary
Miranda, Carmen (1909–55), Brazilian singer and actress
Molière (1622–73), French playwright
Mongan, Agnes (1905–96), art historian
Monk, Thelonious (1917–82), jazz pianist
Montagu, Lady Mary Wortley (1689–1762), British poet
Montaigne, Michel de (1533–92), French essayist
Montale, Eugenio (1896–1981), Italian poet
Monteverdi, Claudio (1567–1643), Italian composer
Moody, William Vaughn (1869–1910), poet and playwright
Moore, Frank Gardner (1865–1955), Latin scholar
Moore, Henry (1898–1986), British sculptor
Moore, Janet, artist
Moore, John (1761–1809), British army officer
Moore, Marianne (1887–1972), poet
Moore, Merrill (1903–57), physician and poet
Moore, Thomas (1779–1852), Irish poet
Moore, Thomas Sturge (1870–1994), British poet
Moore, Warner, Marianne Moore's brother
Moraes, Vinícius de (1913–80), Brazilian poet
Moravia, Alberto (1907–90), Italian novelist
Morehouse, Marion: see Cummings, Marion Morehouse
Moreira, Jorge Machado (1904–92), Brazilian architect
Morgan, Anne Tracy (1873–1952), philanthropist
Morgan, Frederick (1922–2004), poet and editor of *Hudson Review*
Morgan, Robin (b. 1941), feminist writer and editor
Morgenstern, Christian (1871–1914), German poet
Morison, Samuel Eliot (1887–1976), historian
Morris, William (1834–96), British poet, artist, and socialist
Morse, Mary Stearns, EB and Lota's American friend in Brazil
Mortimer, Penelope (1918–99), British novelist
Mosby, John Singleton (1833–1916), Confederate cavalry officer

Moss, Howard (1922–87), poet and editor
Motherwell, Robert (1915–91), painter
Motley, John Lathrop (1814–77), historian
Moulton, Ruth (1916–99), Austrian psychoanalyst and composer
Mozart, Wolfgang Amadeus (1756–91), Austrian composer
Muir, Edwin (1887–1959), Scottish poet and translator
Mumford, L. Quincy (1903–82), librarian of Congress (1954–74)
Munch, Edvard (1863–1944), Norwegian painter
Murdock, Kenneth B. (1895–1975), literary scholar and editor
Murray, Brian (b. 1937), British director and actor
Muser, Frani Blough, musical scholar, EB's high school and college friend
Musmanno, Michael (1897–1968), jurist
Mussolini, Benito (1883–1945), Italian fascist premier (1922–43)

N

Nabokov, Nicolas (1903–78), Russian composer
Nabokov, Vladimir (1899–1977), Russian novelist
Nadar (1820–1910), French photographer
Nasser, Gamal Abdel (1918–70), president of Egypt (1956–70)
Negrão de Lima, Francisco (1901–81), mayor of Rio de Janeiro (1956–58) and governor of
   Guanabara (1965–70)
Nehru, Jawaharlal (1889–1964), prime minister of India (1947–64)
Nerber, John, poet
Neruda, Pablo (1904–73), Chilean poet
Nerval, Gérard de (1808–55), French poet
Nichols, Mike (b. 1931), film and theater director
Nicolson, Harold George (1886–1968), diplomatist and politician
Niemeyer, Oscar (b. 1907), Brazilian architect
Nietzsche, Friedrich Wilhelm (1844–1900), German philosopher
Nilo, Dr., Brazilian doctor
Nimitz, Chester (1885–1966), commander of the Pacific Fleet during World War II
Nims, John Frederick (1913–99), poet
Nin, Anaïs (1903–77), writer and diarist
Nist, John, poet and editor
Nixon, Richard Milhous (1913–94), U.S. president (1969–74)
Nolan, Sidney (1917–92), Australian artist
Norman, Andrew E. (1931–2004), editor and philanthropist
Norman, Dorothy (1909–97), writer and photographer
Nureyev, Rudolf (1938–93), Russian ballet dancer

O

Oberdorfer, Conrad W. (1908–96), lawyer
O'Connor, Flannery (1925–64), writer
O'Connor, Frank (1903–66), Irish writer

O'Connor, Philip (1916–98), British poet and writer
O'Donovan, Patrick (1918–81), Irish journalist
O'Hara, Frank (1926–66), poet
Olivier, Laurence (1907–89), British actor
Olson, Charles (1910–70), poet
Onassis, Aristotle (1906–75), Greek shipping magnate
Onassis, Jacqueline Kennedy (1929–94), U.S. first lady (1916–63) and editor
O'Neill, Eugene (1888–1953), dramatist
Oppenheimer, J. Robert (1904–67), theoretical physicist
Orgel, Stephen, literary scholar
Orlovsky, Peter (b. 1933), poet, companion of Allen Ginsberg
Orwell, George (1903–50), British writer
Orwell, Sonia Brownell (1918–80), British literary editor
Osborne, John (1929–94), British playwright
Osbourne, Dod, journalist
Ostroff, Anthony (1923–78), poet and editor

P

Pack, Robert (b. 1929), writer and critic
Packard, Frederick C., founder of Harvard Vocarium Records
Paget, Violet (1856–1935), British writer
Palestrina, Giovanni Pierluigi da (ca. 1525–94), Italian composer
Paley, William (1901–90), broadcaster and CBS board chairman (1946–73)
Palfrey, Sarah (1912–96), tennis player
Palmer, John J. E., editor of Yale Review (1954–79)
Parker, Francis S. (1917–2005), painter
Parker, Lesley Gray, Frank Parker's first wife
Parkman, Francis (1823–93), historian
Pascal, Blaise (1623–62), French mathematician and philosopher
Pasternak, Boris (1890–60), Russian poet and novelist
Pater, Walter (1839–94), British writer
Patton, George S. (1885–1945), U.S. Army general
Paul, Issabella (1833?–79), British actress
Paula, Aloysio de (1907–90), Brazilian epidemiologist
Paulsen, Pat (1927–97), comedian and satirist
Paz, Marie-Jose Tramini, Octavio Paz's wife
Paz, Octavio (1914–98), Mexican poet
Pedro II de Alcântara, Dom (1825–91), emperor of Brazil (1831–89)
Pearson, Norman H. (1909–75), literary scholar
Peebles, Rose, literary scholar
Peech, John Michael, physicist and poet
Pendleton, Austin (b. 1940), director and actor
Pereira, Lúcia Miguel (1901–59), Brazilian literary critic
Perkins, David (b. 1928), literary scholar
Perkins, Frances (Madam Perkins) (1882–1965), U.S. secretary of labor (1933–47)
Perloff, Marjorie (b. 1931), poetry critic and professor
Perón, Juan Domingo (1895–1974), president of Argentina (1946–55, 1973–74)

Perron, Edgar du (1899–40), Dutch writer and poet
Perron-de Roos, Elisabeth du (Bep), Dutch literary critic
Perse, Saint-John: *see* Léger, Alexis
Pessoa, Fernando (1888–1935), Portuguese poet
Pfeiffer, Virginia, friend of EB
Phelan, Kappo, literary critic
Phillips, William (1907–2002), coeditor of *Partisan Review*
Picasso, Pablo (1881–1973), Spanish painter and sculptor
Piero della Francesca (ca. 1420–92), Italian painter
Pindar (ca. 522–ca. 438 bc), Greek poet
Piñon, Nélida (b. 1936), Brazilian writer
Pius XII (1876–1958), pope (1939–58)
Plarr, Victor (1863–1929), British poet
Plath, Sylvia (1932–63), poet
Plato (ca. 428–348 or 347 bc), Greek philosopher
Plutarch (ca. AD 46–after 119), Greek biographer and moralist
Podhoretz, Norman (b. 1930), editor in chief of *Commentary* (1960–95)
Poe, Edgar Allan (1809–49), poet and writer
Polin, Herbert Spencer, chemist
Pollaiuolo, Antonio (1432–98), Italian painter
Pollock, Jackson (1912–56), painter
Ponge, Francis (1899–1988), French poet
Popa, Vasko (1922–91), Serbian poet
Pope, Alexander (1688–1744), British poet
Pope-Hennessy, John (1913–94), British art historian
Porter, Cole (1891–1964), songwriter
Porter, Katherine Anne (1890–1980), writer
Portinari, Candido (1903–62), Brazilian painter
Potter, Beatrix (1866–1943), British writer and illustrator
Poulenc, Francis (1899–1963), French composer
Pound, Dorothy Shakespear (1886–1973), British artist
Pound, Ezra (1885–1972), poet
Pound, Omar (b. 1925), poet and translator, son of Ezra and Dorothy Pound
Poussin, Nicolas (1594–1665), French painter
Powers, J. F. (1917–99), writer
Praz, Mario (1896–1982), Italian literary scholar
Prentiss, Eleanor, EB's teacher
Prévert, Jacques (1900–77), French poet
Price, Leontyne (b. 1927), soprano
Pritchett, V. S. (1900–97), British writer
Propertius, Sextus (ca. 50–ca. 15 bc), Roman poet
Proust, Marcel (1871–1922), French novelist
Purcell, Henry (1659–95), British composer

Q

Quadros, Jânio (1917–92), president of Brazil (1961)
Queiroz, Rachel de (b. 1910), Brazilian novelist and journalist
Quindlen, Anna (b. 1952), journalist

R

Rachewiltz, Mary de (b. 1925), poet and daughter of Ezra Pound and Olga Rudge
Rachewiltz, Siegfried Walter de (b. 1947), writer and translator
Racine, Jean (1639–99), French dramatist
Rahv, Nathalie Swan, architect, Philip Rahv's wife
Rahv, Philip (1908–73), critic and editor of *Partisan Review*
Raine, Kathleen (1908–2003), British poet and literary scholar
Rand, Sally (1904–79), dancer and actress
Randolph, John (1773–1833), statesman
Ransom, John Crowe (1888–1974), poet and literary critic
Raphael (1483–1520), Italian painter
Raskin, Marcus (b. 1934), social critic
Rawlins, Lester (1924–88), actor
Read, Herbert (1893–1968), British poet and writer
Reagan, Ronald (1911–2004), governor of California (1967–75) and U.S. president (1981–89)
Redding, J. Saunders (1906–88), literary critic
Reed, Henry (1914–86), British poet
Reidy, Affonso Eduardo (1909–64), Brazilian architect
Rembrandt (1606–69), Dutch painter
Rémy: *see* Renault, Gilbert
Renault, Gilbert (1904–84), member of the French Resistance
Renoir, Pierre-Auguste (1841–1919), French painter
Revere, Paul (1735–1818), patriot and silversmith
Reynolds, Joshua (1723–92), British painter
Rexroth, Kenneth (1905–82), poet
Rexroth, Marie Kass, Kenneth Rexroth's second wife
Rhu, Lawrence F., literary scholar
Rhys, Jean (1890–1979), Caribbean novelist
Ribeiro, Darcy (1922–97), Brazilian anthropologist and politician
Rice, Elmer (1892–1967), playwright
Rich, Adrienne (b. 1929), poet
Richards, I. A. (1893–1979), British literary critic and poet
Richardson, Samuel (1689–1761), British novelist
Richman, Robert (1915–87), arts administrator
Richter, Sviatoslav (1915–97), Russian pianist
Ridge, Lola (1873–1941), poet and feminist
Riding, Laura: *see* Jackson, Laura Riding
Rilke, Rainer Maria (1875–1926), German poet
Rimbaud, Arthur (1854–91), French poet
Ritchie, Margaret (1903–69), British soprano
Rizza, Peggy: *see* Ellsberg, Margaret Rizza
Rizzardi, Alfredo (b. 1927), Italian poet and translator
Robbins, Jerome (1918–98), choreographer
Robeson, Paul (1898–1976), bass-baritone and actor
Robinson, Edwin Arlington (1869–1935), poet
Rodin, Auguste (1840–1917), French sculptor
Rodman, Maria Wojciechowska (1927–2002), children's book writer
Rodman, Selden (1909–2002), poet and critic
Roethke, Beatrice O'Connell, Theodore Roethke's wife
Roethke, Theodore (1908–63), poet

Rogers, Ginger (1911–95), dancer and actress
Rohe, Mies van der (1886–1969), German-born architect
Roosevelt, Franklin Delano (1882–45), U.S. president (1933–45)
Rorem, Ned (b. 1923), composer
Rosenberg, Harold (1906–78), art critic
Rosenberg, Isaac (1890–1918), British poet
Ross, James (b. 1911), journalist
Roth, George Andrew, British photojournalist
Roth, Philip (b. 1933), writer
Rothko, Mark (1903–70), painter
Rothschild, Ann Hatfield (1903–89), interior designer
Rousseau, Henri (1844–1910), French painter
Rousset, David (1912–97), French writer
Rudge, Olga (1895–1996), violinist and Ezra Pound's mistress
Rudofsky, Bernard (1905–88), Austrian architect and social historian
Rukeyser, Muriel (1913–80), poet
Rusk, Dean (1909–94), U.S. secretary of state (1961–69)
Rusk, Virginia Foisie (1916–96), Dean Rusk's wife
Ruskin, John (1819–1900), British art critic and social critic
Russell, Charles Hinton (1903–89), governor of Nevada (1951–59)
Russell, Charlotte and Charles, EB's friends
Ryder, Albert (1847–1917), painter

S

Sacco, Nicola (1891–1927), Italian-born anarchist
Saintsbury, George (1845–1933), British literary scholar
Salazar, António de Oliveira (1889–1970), Portuguese dictator (1932–68)
Salinger, J. D. (b. 1919), novelist
Sand, George (1804–76), French writer
Sandburg, Carl (1878–1967), poet and folklorist
Sanger, Margaret (1879–1966), feminist and birth-control activist
Santayana, George (1863–1952), philosopher
Santee, Frederick (1906–80), doctor and classicist
Santos-Dumont, Alberto (1873–1932), French aviation pioneer
Sappho (ca. 610–ca. 580 BC), Greek poet
Sarton, May (1912–95), writer
Sassetta (1394–1450), Italian painter
Saunders, Eddie ("Bra"), charter-boat captain
Schapiro, Meyer (1904–96), art historian
Schenk, Adrianus (Ard) (b. 1944), Dutch speed skater
Schevill, James (b. 1920), poet
Schiller, Friedrich von (1759–1805), German poet and playwright
Schlesinger, Arthur M., Jr. (1917–2007), historian
Schling, Max (1874–1943), New York florist
Schmidt, Augusto Frederico (1906–65), Brazilian poet
Schmidt, Michael (b. 1947), British poet
Schubert, Franz (1797–1828), Austrian composer

Schwartz, Delmore (1913–66), poet
Schwartz, Lloyd (b. 1941), poet, literary scholar, and music critic
Schwitters, Kurt (1887–1948), German poet
Scott, Laurence, artist and printmaker
Scott, Sir Walter (1771–1832), Scottish novelist and poet
Scott, Winfield Townley (1910–68), poet
Seaver, Robert (d. 1936), EB's friend
Sebree, Charles (1914–85), painter
Sedgwick, Ellery (1872–1960), editor and publisher of *The Atlantic Monthly*
Seidel, Frederick (b. 1936), poet
Serkin, Rudolf (1903–91), pianist
Seton, Ernest Thompson (1860–1946), writer and illustrator
Seurat, Georges (1859–91), French painter
Sévigné, Marquise de (1626–96), French letter writer
Sexton, Anne (1928–74), poet
Seyersted, Per (b. 1921), Norwegian literary critic
Shahn, Ben (1898–1969), artist
Shakespeare, William (1564–1616), playwright and poet
Shapiro, Harvey (b. 1924), poet and editor of *The New York Times Magazine*
Shapiro, Karl (1913–2000), poet
Shaw, George Bernard (1856–1950), British author
Shaw, Colonel Robert Gould (1837–63), Civil War military officer
Shelley, Percy Bysshe (1792–1822), British poet
Shepherdson, Maud Bulmer (1873–1940), EB's aunt
Shostakovich, Dmitry (1906–75), Soviet composer
Silvers, Robert (b. 1929), editor and cofounder of *The New York Review of Books*
Simon, Oscar, Brazilian financier
Simpson, Louis (b. 1923), poet
Sitwell, Edith (1887–1964), British writer
Sitwell, Osbert (1892–1969), British writer
Slocum, Joshua (1844–1909), Canadian American sailor
Smedley, Agnes (1892–1950), journalist and writer
Smith, Stevie (1902–71), British poet
Smith, Sydney (1771–1845), British essayist
Smith, William Jay (b. 1918), poet
Smithies, Arthur, British economist
Snodgrass, W. D. (b. 1926), poet
Snowden, Antony Armstrong-Jones, 1st Earl of (b. 1930), British photographer
Sontag, Susan (1933–2004), cultural critic and author
Sophocles (ca. 496–406 bc), Greek playwright
Sortwell, Betty, EB's friend
Sortwell, Sally, EB's friend
Sousa, Decio de, Brazilian psychiatrist
Southey, Robert (1774–1843), British poet
Soutine, Chaim (1893–1943), French painter
Sparrow, John (1906–92), British literary scholar
Speaight, Robert (1904–76), British actor and scholar
Spears, Monroe (1916–98), poet and editor at *Sewanee Review*
Speirs, John (1907–79), Scottish literary scholar
Spencer, Theodore (1902–49), literary scholar

Spender, Natasha (b. 1919), British pianist
Spender, Stephen (1909–95), British poet
Spenser, Edmund (1552–99), British poet
Spivack, Kathleen (b. 1938), poet
Spock, Benjamin (1903–98), physician
Staël, Anne Louise Germaine de (1766–1817), French writer
Stafford, Jean (1915–79), novelist
Stalin, Joseph (1878–1953), premier of the Soviet Union (1922–53)
Stanford, Donald E. (1913–98), poet and editor
Staples, Hugh B., literary scholar
Starr, Goldie, Milton Starr's wife
Starr, Milton (1896–1976), theater owner and arts patron
Stead, Christina (1902–83), Australian novelist
Steinberg, Saul (1914–99), cartoonist
Stendhal (1783–1842), French writer
Sténuit, Robert, marine archaeologist
Stern, Isaac (1920–2001), violinist
Sternberg, Hilgard O'Reilly (b. 1917), Brazilian geographer
Stevens, Marjorie Carr (c. 1918–59), EB's friend in Key West
Stevens, Wallace (1879–1955), poet
Stevenson, Adlai (1900–65), statesman
Stevenson, Anne (b. 1933), poet and critic
Stevenson, Robert Louis (1850–94), Scottish author
Stewart, Thomas, editor
Stickney, Trumbull (1874–1904), poet
Stockhausen, Karlheinz (b. 1928), German composer and theorist
Stokes, Adrian (1902–72), British painter, critic, and poet
Strachey, Lytton (1880–1932), British biographer
Strand, Mark (b. 1934), poet
Straus, Roger W. (1917–2004), publisher and cofounder of Farrar, Straus and Giroux
Strauss, Richard (1864–1949), German composer
Stravinsky, Igor (1882–1971), Russian composer
Strindberg, August (1849–1912), Swedish dramatist and novelist
Styron, Rose (b. 1928), poet
Styron, William (1925–2006), novelist
Sullivan, Harry Stack (1892–1949), psychiatrist
Summers, Joseph H. (1920–2003), literary scholar
Summers, U. T. Miller, writer
Supervia, Conchita (1895–1936), Spanish soprano
Sutherland, Joan (b. 1926), Australian soprano
Swan, Nathalie: see Rahv, Nathalie Swan
Swedenborg, Emanuel (1688–1772), Swedish philosopher and religious writer
Sweeney, James Johnson (1900–86), director of Guggenheim Museum (1952–60)
Sweeney, John (Jack) Lincoln, curator of Harvard Poetry Room
Sweeney, Máire MacNeill, folklorist and Celtic studies scholar
Swenson, May (1913–89), poet
Swift, Jonathan (1667–1745)
Swigget, G. L., poet
Swinburne, Algernon Charles (1837–1909), British poet
Symonds, John Addington (1840–93), British scholar

T

Talbot, Kathrine: *see* Barker, Ilse
Tarquínio de Sousa, Octávio (1889–1959), Brazilian journalist and writer
Tasso, Torquato (1544–95), Italian poet
Tate, Allen (1899–1979), poet
Tate, Caroline: *see* Gordon, Caroline
Tate, John Allen (b. 1967), son of Allen Tate and Helen Heinz
Tate, Michael Paul (1967–68), Allen Tate's son
Taves, Ernest H. (1916–2003), psychoanalyst
Taylor, Deems (1885–1966), composer
Taylor, Eleanor Ross (b. 1920), poet
Taylor, Peter (1917–94), writer
Tchaikovsky, Pyotr Ilyich (1840–93), Russian composer
Teasdale, Sara (1884–1933), poet
Teniers, David the Younger (1610–90), Flemish painter
Tennyson, Alfred, 1st Baron (1809–92), British poet
Theodorides, Angelos, U.S. diplomat in Brazil
Theodorides, Elizabeth, wife of U.S. diplomat in Brazil
Thielen, Benedict (1903–65), writer
Thomas, Dylan (1914–53), Welsh poet
Thomas, Hugh (b. 1931), British historian
Thompson, Dunstan (1918–75), poet
Thompson, John (Jack) (1918–2002), poet and literary scholar
Thomson, Virgil (1896–1989), composer
Thoreau, Henry David (1817–62), essayist and poet
Thucydides (d. ca. 401 BC), Greek historian
Thurber, James (1894–1961), writer and cartoonist
Tintoretto (ca. 1518–94), Italian painter
Titian (ca. 1488–1576), Italian painter
Tolstoy, Lev Nikolaevich (1828–1910), Russian novelist
Tourel, Jennie (1900–73), soprano
Tourneur, Jacques (1904–77), French filmmaker
Tovey, Donald Francis (1875–1940), British musicologist and composer
Traherne, Thomas (1636–74), British poet
Trilling, Diana (1905–96), cultural critic
Trilling, Lionel (1905–75), literary scholar and writer
Trimble, Hannah, journalist
Trollope, Anthony (1815–82), British novelist
Trotsky, Leon (1879–1940), Russian Communist leader
Trotsky, Natalia Sedova (1882–1962), Russian revolutionary
Troy, William (1903–61), literary critic, husband of Léonie Adams
Truman, Harry S. (1884–1972), U.S. president (1945–53)
Truman, Margaret: *see* Daniel, Margaret Truman
Tureck, Rosalyn (1914–2003), pianist and harpsichordist
Turgenev, Ivan Sergeyevich (1818–83), Russian novelist
Turner, J. M. W. (1775–1851), British painter
Turner, Lana (1929–95), movie actress
Turner, Susan J., literary scholar
Tuve, Rosemond (1903–64), literary scholar
Twain, Mark: *see* Clemens, Samuel Langhorne

U

Ungaretti, Giuseppe (1888–1970), Italian poet
Untermeyer, Louis (1885–1977), poet and anthologist

V

Valdez, Faustina, EB's friend in Key West
Valentine, Jean (b. 1934), poet
Valéry, Paul (1871–1945), French poet and philosopher
van Kirk, Harold, Isabella Gardner's first husband
van Rijn, Rembrandt: *see* Rembrandt
Vanzetti, Bartolomeo (1888–1927), Italian-born anarchist
Vargas, Getúlio Dornelles (1883–1954), president of Brazil (1930–45, 1951–54)
Vaughan, Henry (1621–95), British poet
Vaux, Thomas, 2nd Baron (1510–56), British poet
Vaz, Rubens Florentino (1922–54), Brazilian Air Force officer
Vendler, Helen (b. 1933), literary scholar
Verdi, Giuseppe (1813–1901), Italian composer
Verlaine, Paul (1844–96), French poet
Victor, Thomas (1938–89), photographer
Victoria (1819–1901), British queen (1837–1901)
Vieira, Antonio (1608–97), Portuguese Jesuit and writer
Viereck, Peter (1916–2006), historian and poet
Villa-Lobos, Heitor (1887–1959), Brazilian composer
Villon, François (1431–after 1463), French poet
Virgil (70–19 bc), Roman poet
Voznesensky, Andrey Andreyevich (b. 1933), Russian poet
Vuillard, Edouard (1868–1940), French painter

W

Wagner, Charles A. (1898–1986), poet and writer
Wagner, Richard (1813–83), German composer
Wain, John (1925–94), British poet
Walcott, Derek (b. 1930), West Indian poet and playwright
Walpole, Horace (1717–97), British author
Walton, Izaak (1593–1683), British writer
Wanning, Andrews (1913–97), literary scholar
Wanning, Patricia, Andrews Wanning's wife
Wanning, Thomas Edwards (1918–2001), EB's friend
Warburg, Paul F. (1904–65), financier and philanthropist
Ward, Aileen, literary scholar
Warren, Robert Penn (1905–89), poet and critic
Watkins, Vernon (1906–67), Welsh poet
Watteau, Antoine (1684–1721), French painter
Waugh, Evelyn (1903–66), British novelist

Weber, Carl Maria von (1786–1826), German composer and conductor
Webern, Anton von (1883–1945), Austrian composer
Webster, Noah (1758–1843), lexicographer and author
Wehr, Wesley (1929–2004), artist and paleobotanist
Weill, Kurt (1900–50), German-born composer
Weimer, David R., literary scholar
Weiss, Theodore (1916–2003), poet, editor, and critic
Welty, Eudora (1909–2001), writer
Wescott, Glenway (1901–87), novelist
West, James, diplomat, Mary McCarthy's husband
West, Nathanael (1903–40), writer
West, Rebecca (1892–1983), British novelist
Whalen, Philip (1923–2002), poet
Wheeler, Monroe (1899–1988), exhibition director at the Museum of Modern Art (1935–67)
White, E. B. (1899–1985), writer
White, Katharine (1892–1977), writer and editor at *The New Yorker*
Whitehead, Edward (1908–78), British naval officer
Whitman, Walt (1819–92), poet
Whittall, Gertrude Clarke (1867–1965), philanthropist
Whittier, John Greenleaf (1807–92), poet and abolitionist
Whitworth, John (b. 1921), British countertenor
Wieland, Christoph Martin (1733–1813), German author
Wilbur, Richard (b. 1921), poet
Wilde, Oscar (1854–1900), Irish playwright
Wilder, Thornton (1897–1975), playwright
Wilenski, R. H. (1887–1975), art historian
Willard, Marian: *see* Johnson, Marian Willard
Williams, Florence (Floss) Herman (1891–1976), wife of William Carlos Williams
Williams, Mary Wilhelmine (1878–1944), historian and feminist
Williams, Oscar (1900–64), anthropologist, editor, and poet
Williams, Tennessee (1911–83), playwright
Williams, T. Harry (1909–79), historian
Williams, William Carlos (1883–1963), poet
Wilson, Edmund (1895–1972), writer and critic
Wilson, M., Harvard researcher
Wilson, Rosalind (1923–2000), editor and daughter of Edmund Wilson
Winslow, Anne Goodwin (1875–1959), novelist
Winslow, Arthur (1860–1938), engineer, RL's grandfather
Winslow, Carlile, RL's cousin
Winslow, Devereux (1892–1923), RL's uncle
Winslow, Harriet Patterson (1882–1964), RL's cousin
Winslow, Marcella Comès, RL's distant cousin, socialite, and painter
Winslow, Mary, R's cousin
Winslow, Pearson (1888?–1950), engineer, RL's cousin
Winslow, Sarah: *see* Cotting, Sarah Winslow
Winslow, Warren (d. 1944), U.S. Navy ensign, RL's cousin
Winters, Yvor (1900–68), poet and literary critic
Wittgenstein, Ludwig (1889–1951), Austrian philosopher
Wolfe, Thomas (1900–38), novelist
Woodward, W. E. (1874–1950), historian
Woolf, Leonard (1880–1969), British writer and publisher

Woolf, Virginia (1882–1941), British writer
Wordsworth, William (1770–1850), British poet
Worth, Charles Frederick (1825–95), British couturier
Worth, Irene (1916–2002), actress
Wright, Clifford (1919–99), painter
Wright, Richard (1908–60), novelist and poet
Wyatt, Thomas (1503–43), British poet
Wykeham-Barnes, Peter (1915–95), geologist

Y

Yeats, William Butler (1865–1939), Irish poet
Yevtushenko, Yevgeny Aleksandrovich (b. 1933), Russian poet

Z

Zabel, Morton Dauwen (1901–64), literary critic

ACKNOWLEDGMENTS

There are so many people to thank. I must first of all mention Frank Bidart, whose dedication to both poets is total. Without his early enthusiasm, this project might never have begun. Jonathan Galassi's instant readiness to undertake this project, and his firm guidance along the way, were also essential.

Bidart's contemporary and friend Alan Williamson introduced me to Bishop and Lowell—many years ago now—in classrooms at the Unversity of Virginia, where he helped to bring their work to life through his immersion in poetry as art and his personal knowledge of both poets. J. C. Levenson directed a doctoral dissertation on Bishop at Virginia at a time such opportunities were rare. Lloyd Schwartz, a fellow pioneer in Bishop studies, offered me early and sustained encouragement. As this book matured, he helped me to track down many elusive references, using his knowledge of the poets' Boston and Cambridge milieu.

Francesco Rognoni also worked alongside me, helping, through the wonders of the Internet, to resolve at many points the seemingly intractable illegibility of each poet's hand and to establish the interweaving chronology of many very casually dated letters. Carmen Oliveira offered generous and unflagging guidance into all the details and nuances of Bishop's Brazilian world.

A generation of students at Hartwick College—including in particular Amy Norkus, Katherine Lomasney, and Celia Cook—performed yeoman service as they laboriously transcribed almost indecipherable manuscript into lucid typescript over a period of years. Their unflagging enthusiasm for the letters was infectious. So was the enthusiasm and insight of Hartwick's students in a series of seminars I taught on these poets. The Trustees of Hartwick College have supported the project financially through a series of faculty research grants, and the Cora A. Babcock Chair in English has provided both support and release time. A sabbatical from Hartwick and a

Winifred Wandersee Scholar-in-Residence Award provided further substantial aid.

My colleagues in the Elizabeth Bishop and Robert Lowell Societies—in particular Steven Gould Axelrod, Sandra Barry, Jacqueline Vaught Brogan, Suzanne Ferguson, Richard Flynn, Gary Fountain, Carol Frost, Lorrie Goldensohn, Laura Jehn Menides, Brett Millier, Barbara Page, Camille Roman, Kathleen Spivack, and Cheryl Walker—have been consistently supportive and have often provided substantial advice and counsel. The biographies of Bishop by Millier and Fountain and the biographies of Lowell by Ian Hamilton and Paul Mariani have, of course, served as frequent and indispensable sources of information and insight.

The librarians at Harvard's Houghton Library, at Vassar College's Libraries Archives and Special Collections, and at the Harry Ransom Center at the University of Texas at Austin have extended themselves on many occasions to make my work go more smoothly. The reference librarians at Hartwick College have also provided consistent and valuable service.

Most indispensable of all, however, has been my wife, Elsa, who will know why, and my children, Michael and Emily, who love words and have always kept life interesting.

T.T.

For this edition, first and final thanks are due to Jonathan Galassi, under whose wise guidance the text was edited and annotated, and to Annie Wedekind, for her patience, wit, and tactful assistance. The book was seen through production with grace by Zachary Woolfe and Wah-Ming Chang, and was copyedited with care by Karla Eoff. For my part of the labor, I also greatly appreciate the assistance of Dean Rogers at Vassar College Library; Leslie Morris, Heather Cole, Rachel Howarth, Denison Beach, Betty Falsey, Thomas Ford, Mary Haegert, Susan Halpert, Bridget Keown, Jennie Rathbun, Emily Walhout, and Joseph Zajac at the Houghton Library, Harvard University; and Richard Workman and Jill E. Anderson at the Harry Ransom Humanities Center, University of Texas. Thanks to Evgenia Citkowitz, Joaquim-Francisco Coelho, Eleanor Cook, Theo Cuffe, James Fenton, Robert Gardner, Brad Gooch, Mary Gordon, John Haffenden, Elizabeth Hardwick, Hugh Haughton, Richard Howard, Nicholas Jenkins, Edward Mendelson, Honor Moore, Cary Plotkin, Peter Sacks, William Sessions, Timea Szell, John C. Talbot, Meg Tyler, Jean Valentine, Margaret Vandenburg, and Rosanna Warren for trouvées and answers to queries. When turned to for help with puzzles, Frank Bidart, Alice Quinn, and Lloyd Schwartz were generous with their attention and their intimate knowledge of the poets' works. Peter Fry and John Ryle lent me opticks on Bishop's years in Brazil. For their efficient and kindly advice, their rapid and precise help with annotation, and their essential discernment, I am most deeply grateful to Paul Keegan and Christopher Ricks.

The editors regret any errors; these are our responsibility alone.

S.H.

INDEX

Brown, John, 781
Brown, William, 781*n*
Browne, Roscoe Lee, 571*n*, 581*n*
Browning, Elizabeth Barrett, 401
Browning, Robert, 25, 241, 401, 597, 760
Broyard, Anatole, 750*n*
Brueghel, Peter the Younger, 204
"Brunetto Latini" (RL), 504, 553
Brustein, Robert, 386*n*, 565
Brutus, Dennis, 788*n*
Bryant, William Cullen, 443
Brynner, Yul, 360, 394*n*
Buchalter, Louis "Lepke," 234*n*, 254*n*, 360
Buchwald, Art, 578
Buckle, Henry Thomas, 323
Buckman, Gertrude, 115
"Buenos Aires" (RL), 502; EB's view, 448;
    phallic monument, 448, 455
Bullock, Marie, 551, 552, 775
Bundy, McGeorge, 416
Bunshaft, Gordon, 312*n*
"Burden" (RL): EB's view, 708, 712; RL's
    response to EB, 713, 715
Burford, William, 132*n*, 137
"Burglar of Babylon, The" (EB), 652; Mari-
    anne Moore's view, 560; RL's view, 528,
    591, 760
Burke, Kenneth, 102*n*, 272, 455
Burle Marx, Roberto, 353*n*, 361–62, 426, 446,
    458, 497, 509
Burne-Jones, Edward Coley, *see* Jones,
    Edward Coley Burne-
Burney, Fanny, 229
Burns, Robert, 37; RL's view, 40–41
Burr, Aaron, 15
Burroughs, William S., 368*n*, 501*n*, 554,
    646
Bynner, Witter, 74
Byrom, Bill, 684
Byron, Lord, 294, 302, 703, 736

C

Cabot, John Moors, 334, 397
Cabral, Pedro Álvares, 282
Cabral de Melo Neto, João, 278, 281–82, 341,
    404, 410, 411, 449, 453, 456, 508
Cadwalader, Elizabeth, 717

Caetani, Marguerite, 102, 121
Cairns, Huntington, 70, 72, 96, 187
Calder, Alexander, xvi, 305, 310, 314, 318, 345,
    397, 399, 594
Calder, Louisa James, 305, 310, 314
"Caligula" (RL), 430, 470, 490; EB's view,
    482–83, 553
Callado, Antônio, 275
Callas, Maria, 347, 762
"Calling" (RL), 662; EB's view, 663
Camões, Luís Vaz de, 142, 149, 259, 315, 453
Campbell, James, Lord Glenavy, 300
Campin, Robert, 204*n*
Campion, Thomas, 561
Campos, Paulo Mendes, 628
Camus, Albert, 628
Camus, Marcel, 312*n*
"Cape Breton" (EB), xx, 6*n*, 18; RL's view, 157
Capua, Michael di, 565, 644*n*, 661*n*, 743*n*
Carcopino, Jérôme, 616
Carleton, Dorothy, 58*n*
Carlisle, Olga, 586*n*
Carlyle, Thomas, 35, 151, 674
Carnegie, Dale, 323
"Caroline" (RL): EB's view, 710
Carossa, Hans, 231
Carroll, Lewis, 54*n*, 72*n*, 73
Carruth, Hayden, 52
Carter, Elliott, 470, 487, 784, 789
Cartier-Bresson, Henri, 346
Carver, Catharine (Katy), 185, 614
Casa, Lisa della, 348
Cassatt, Mary Stevenson, 323
Castelo Branco, Humberto de Alencar, 525,
    529, 530, 537, 593*n*, 628*n*
Castro, Fidel, 362, 378*n*
Cato, Marcus, 65
Catta Preta, Zephyrino, 428
Catullus, 541, 543*n*, 615
"Cavanaughs, The," *see* The Mills of the
    Kavanaughs (RL)
Cecil, David, 154, 596*n*
Cellini, Benvenuto, 97
"Central Park" (RL): EB's view, 588, 616
Cézanne, Paul, 12, 75*n*, 322
Chandler, Elliott, 47
Changeling, The (Middleton), 331
Chapelbrook Foundation, xxvi, 324, 325, 326,
    335, 340*n*, 395, 463, 531
Char, René, 192, 285, 410

Cunha, Euclides da, 387n, 416
Curtain of Green, A (Welty), 44
Cushing, Richard Cardinal, 515

D

Dahlberg, Edward, 520
Daluna, Mr., 649
Daniel, Margaret Truman, 12, 16
Dante, 220, 401, 539, 553
Darnell, Linda, 125
Darwin, Charles, 545, 692
Daumier, Honoré, 12
"David and Bathsheba" (RL), 298; EB's view, 402
Dawson, Carley, 31, 32, 33, 34, 35, 38, 39, 41, 42, 45, 46, 51, 67n, 83, 180, 225, 390
Dawson, Elizabeth, 371
Day by Day (RL), 783; EB's view, 798
Day-Lewis, Cecil, 614
Debray, Régis, 625n
Debussy, Claude, 413
Dee, John, 739
Degas, Edgar, 323
de Kooning, Willem, 279, 287, 312
Delaney, Beauford, 110n
Delgado, Humberto de Silva, 302
Deller, Alfred, 238n, 561
de los Ángeles, Victoria, 481
Demuth, Charles, 322
Denys, Odílio, 172n
de Planck, Mrs., 764
Der Stellvertretter, 468
De Sica, Vittorio, 99n
Deutsch, Helene, 246
Dewey, Jane M., 22, 101, 108, 122, 123, 242, 328, 629, 685
Dewey, John, 22, 108, 273
Dialogues in Limbo (Santayana), 76
Diary of "Helena Morley," The (EB): Black Beans and Diamonds as possible title, 177, 184, 579; EB and Lota's translation work, 141, 154, 200n; EB writes introduction for, 177, 201; and Farrar, Straus, 208n, 215, 243, 251; and Houghton Mifflin, 208n, 300; Pritchett's view, 277; RL's view, 257; as success, 251, 256
Dib, Mohammed, 788n

Dick, Anne, 47, 51
Dickens, Charles, 149, 153, 154
Dickey, James, 620, 623, 625, 656, 661, 697
Dickinson, Emily, 130, 173, 241, 262, 281, 327, 409, 442, 513, 702n; comparison with EB, 188, 407, 442; EB's view, 189–90
Dietrich, Marlene, 348
Dillon, George, 5
Dineson, Isak, 299
Dix, Dorothy, 23
Dodgson, Charles Lutwidge, see Carroll, Lewis
Dolphin, The (RL), xiii, xxv; EB's view, 701–702, 706–709, 710–13, 748; Frank Bidart's role, 696n, 701, 704, 706, 711; Hardwick letters as issue, 707–709, 713, 714–15; RL's changes to, 714–15, 748, 814; RL's description, 690–91, 714; views of others, 717–18
Dolphin Cousin to Man, The (Sténuit), 749
"Domesday Book" (RL): EB's view, 798
Dom Pedro the Magnanimous, 392
Domville, Barry, 28
Donatella, 280, 488
Donne, John, 336n, 407
Dos Passos, John, 101, 263–64, 416, 436, 506
Dostoyevsky, Fyodor, 360–61
Doughty, Charles Montagu, 44
Douglas, Gordon, 57n
"Downlook, The" (RL), 784
Doyle, Charles, 290n
"Drinker, The" (RL), 262n, 308; EB's view, 310, 332–33, 337
"Dropping South: Brazil" (RL), 430, 467–68, 491; EB's view, 478, 481, 485; lines from, 421n, 423n, 459n, 478n, 481n; Lota's view, 485
Drummond de Andrade, Carlos, 409, 411, 449, 453, 456, 473, 496, 502, 504, 510, 515, 516, 517, 567, 771, 772, 775, 814
"Drunkard, A" (EB), 310, 327, 333
"Drunken Boat, The" (RL), 366
"Drunken Fisherman, The" (RL), 764
Dryden, John, 16, 35, 121
Dr. Zhivago (Pasternak), 267, 274, 278, 280, 281, 283–84
Dugan, Alan, 439–40
Dulles, Allen, 577
Dulles, John Foster, 193
Dumas, Alexandre, 204n
Dunaway, Faye, 737

Lowell, Robert (*cont.*)
97–98, 102, 103, 266, 296, 321–22, 382,
391*n*, 413, 443, 453, 503, 517–18, 519, 576,
606, 638, 686, 714, 724, 729, 738, 796;
translations, 121, 324, 330–31, 339, 343, 347,
350, 355–58, 359, 382, 386, 445, 455, 458,
504, 538–39, 550, 553, 570, 575, 602–603,
606, 612, 618, 623, 625, 773, 774, 775, 790;
travel, 114, 115, 382–83, 404, 406, 635*n*,
638, 746; view of EB's work, xvii, 126,
157*n*, 324, 337, 380, 407, 453, 590–91, 601,
613, 720, 759–60; wins fellowship from
American Academy of Arts and Letters, 3*n*;
withdrawal from White House Arts Festival, 575–76, 578, 580, 581; work process,
80, 313, 430, 442–43, 617–18, 643; writes
blurb for EB's *Questions of Travel*, 580, 582;
at Yaddo, xi, 7, 41, 52, 62–63, 66, 69, 76;
at Yale tribute to Randall Jarrell, 599*n*; *see
also titles of individual works*
Lowell, Robert Sheridan (RL's son), 692, 706,
721, 722, 724, 725, 727, 735, 760, 787
Lowell, Robert Traill Spence III (RL's fa-
ther), xxiii–xxv, 70, 108, 214
Lowells and Their Seven Worlds, The
(Greenslet), xxiv
Lucan, 294
Luce, Claire Boothe, 293, 297, 299, 302
Luce, Henry, 577
Lucie-Smith, Edward, 549, 553
Luther, Martin, 435
Luxemburg, Rosa, 638*n*
Lyra, Carlos, 568

M

Maas, Willard, 371
MacArthur, Douglas, 114
Macaulay, Thomas Babington, 16, 132, 181–82
Macauley, Anne, 120, 333, 334
Macauley, Robie, 63*n*, 120, 330, 332, 333, 334,
534*n*, 574
Macdonald, Dwight, 402, 554*n*, 578, 583, 655
Macedo Soares, Kylso Costellat de, 184, 317,
341
Macedo Soares, Maria Carlota Costellat de,
133–34, 141, 142, 143, 144, 148, 155, 156,
173, 181, 184, 185, 189, 191, 193, 194, 196,
197–98, 200, 204, 205, 209, 210, 214, 215,

226, 227–28, 229, 241, 243, 258, 259, 261,
265, 273, 274, 285, 294, 305, 310, 317–18,
327, 341, 352–53, 361, 419, 437, 451, 486–87,
505, 588, 595, 608, 611, 614, 619, 621, 625–
26, 627; death and aftermath, xii, 498, 631*n*,
636*n*, 637, 648, 659, 665, 677, 719
Macedo Soares Regis, Flávio de, 471–73, 474,
483, 484, 507–508, 511, 539–40, 541–42,
554–55, 566, 577, 584, 666
Machado de Assis, Joaquim Maria, 154–55, 406*n*
MacIver, Loren, 27, 60, 64*n*, 82, 215, 229, 299,
310, 351, 373, 411, 624
MacLeish, Archibald, 6*n*, 107, 167, 206, 281,
324, 325, 326, 336, 363, 416, 549, 551, 586
MacLeod, Mr., 5, 6
MacNeice, Louis, 163, 177, 503, 507, 528, 583,
586
Madison, James, 12
"Mad Negro Soldier Confined at Munich, A"
(RL), 139; EB's view, 148
Magalhães, Aloísio, 410
Mahagonny (opera), 348, 351, 393, 414, 450
Mailer, Norman, 518, 646, 651, 732
Maisel, Edward, 76*n*
Mallarmé, Stéphane, 112, 338, 582
Malraux, André, 407, 408, 412, 416
Mamede, Hélio, 353*n*
Mamede, Zila, 183, 184
"Man and Wife" (RL), 239, 254, 488, 560*n*
Mandelstam, Osip, 586
Mander, John, 567
Man for All Seasons, A (play), 385
"Man-Moth, The" (EB): RL's view, 276, 325,
760
Mann, Horace, 245*n*
Mann, Thomas, 6*n*, 136, 245, 621
Manning, Frederic, 58*n*
"Manners (for a Child of 1918)" (EB): RL's
view, 174
Mansfield, Harry K., 324, 336, 340
"Manuelzinho" (EB), 171, 173, 178, 497*n*; Jar-
rell's view, 559, 590; RL's view, 173, 178,
181, 591, 760
Marchand, Leslie, 294*n*
Marchand, Louis, 186, 229
Mare, Walter de la, 596
Margaret Rose, 541
Marius the Epicurean (Pater), 255, 257
Marlowe, Sylvia, 582, 585
"Marriage" (RL): EB's view, 708, 712; RL's
response to EB, 713, 715

Pollaiuolo, Antonio, 168
Pollock, Jackson, 209
Ponge, Francis, 424
Popa, Vasko, 779n, 781
Pope, Alexander, 28, 66n
Pope-Hennessy, John, 280
Porgy and Bess (opera), 165
Porter, Cole, 736
Porter, Katherine Anne, 6n, 151, 257, 333, 350, 351, 379, 406, 411, 412
Portinari, Candido, 176, 216
Potter, Beatrix, 545
Poulenc, Francis, 228
Pound, Dorothy, 58, 93, 259, 261, 444
Pound, Ezra, xvi, 12, 15, 16, 28, 31, 32, 34, 58, 62, 63, 74, 93, 100n, 101–102, 103, 105, 107, 121, 130, 147, 149, 161, 162–63, 203, 239, 245, 258, 259, 261, 272, 274, 320, 321, 409, 444–45, 449, 454, 512, 543n, 573–74, 594, 633, 655, 669; Academy of American Poets memorial service, 735; daughter, 444, 449; death, 735n; and EB's poem "Visits to St. Elizabeths," 186, 201, 345, 591, 597, 670, 672; EB's view, 620; RL visits at St. Elizabeths, 151; wins first Bollingen Prize, 69n; writing style comparison, 331
Pound, Omar, 261
Poussin, Nicolas, 63, 543
Powers, J. F. (Jim), 89, 90, 405
"Prague 1968" (RL), 645n
Praz, Mario, 334
Prentiss, Eleanor, 23
Prévert, Jacques, 227
Price, Leontyne, 456
Pride and Prejudice (Austen), 72
Pritchett, V. S., 277
"Prodigal, The" (EB), 34, 42, 60, 117, 171; RL's view, 170, 202, 203
Prometheus (Shelley), 560
Prometheus Bound (RL): featured on cover of *The New York Review of Books*, 625n; presented at Yale, 623; RL in London for, 618; RL's work on, 602–603, 606, 612
Propertius, 163, 615
prosody, 595
Proust, Marcel, 29, 143n, 165, 185
"Public Garden, The" (RL): EB's view, 402
Pulitzer Prize: EB wins, xi, 176, 180; RL wins, xi, 3
Purcell, Henry, 238n, 241, 275–76, 496

Q

Quadros, Jânio, 341n, 345, 367, 374, 376n, 377n, 395
"Quaker Graveyard, The" (RL), 140n; recording, 5–6
Queiroz, Rachel de, 421, 438, 439, 441, 446, 449–50, 455, 462, 511, 628–29
"Questions of Travel" (EB): RL's view, 181, 593
Questions of Travel (EB), 573; RL's blurb for, 580, 582
Quiet American, The (Greene), 178
Quindlen, Anna, 786n

R

Rachewiltz, Mary de, 444n, 774
Rachewiltz, Siegfried Walter de, 685
Racine, Jean, 174, 324n, 338, 339, 348, 351, 356
Rahv, Nathalie Swan, 36, 122, 124, 129, 138, 180–81, 196, 236, 266, 271, 291, 294, 449, 508, 762
Rahv, Philip, 36, 122, 124, 129, 180–81, 182, 184, 192, 196, 201, 236, 239, 245, 257, 266, 271, 280, 291, 294, 347, 451, 554; death, 762; RL's dream, 396; Tolstoy anthology, 279
Raine, Kathleen, 739
"Rainy Season: Sub-Tropics" (EB), 634n
Rand, Sally, 65
"Randall Jarrell: 1914–1965" (RL), 592n, 598
Randolph, John, 16
Ransom, John Crowe, xxv, xxvi, 31, 61, 65, 99, 102n, 106n, 195, 230, 231, 235, 257, 277, 281, 287, 360, 380, 388, 411, 453–54, 467, 522, 534, 737, 738
Raphael, 201
Raskin, Marcus, 637n
Rawlins, Lester, 581n
Read, Herbert, 596n
Reagan, Ronald, 653
"Realities" (RL): EB's view, 798
"Redcliffe Square" (RL): EB's view, 710
Redding, J. Saunders, 63n
Reed, Henry, 576, 598, 602, 608, 609, 610, 648
Reidy, Affonso Eduardo, 353n, 552
Rembrandt, 112, 206
Rémy, *see* Renault, Gilbert

V

Valdez, Faustina, 13, 14, 26, 75, 82
Valentine, Jean, 755
Valéry, Paul, 136, 338, 453, 456, 495, 522
"Vanity of Human Wishes, The" (RL), 430;
  EB's view, 616, 620
Vargas, Getúlio Dornelles, 164, 172, 382, 438,
  496, 532, 615
Vassar College, xxiii, 209–10, 211, 600,
  607
Vaughan, Henry, 236
Vaux, Thomas, 198
Vaz, Rubens Florentino, 164n
Vendler, Helen, 763, 766, 782, 783
Verdi, Giuseppe, 456n
Verlaine, Paul, 320
Victor, Tom, 730, 752
Victoria, Queen, 303, 548–49
Vieira, Antonio, 135, 144, 401
Viereck, Peter, 100, 106, 251
Villa-Lobos, Heitor, 481
villanelles, 784, 785
Villon, François, 349, 364, 366
Vinci, Leonardo da, 428
Virgil, 70, 121
"Virus, The" (RL), 304
"Visiting the Tates" (RL), 304
"Visits to St. Elizabeths" (EB): EB writes
  "Pound poem," 186, 201, 345, 597, 670,
  672; Ned Rorem musical setting, 345, 448;
  RL's view, 203, 560, 590, 591, 670
von Schrader, Mary, see Jarrell, Mary von
  Schrader
"Voyage, The" (RL), 367n
Voyage and Other Versions of Poems by Baude-
  laire, The (RL), 617n, 653
"Voyage to Cynhera" (RL), 361n
Voznesensky, Andrey, 608
Vuillard, Edouard, 187

W

Wagner, Charles A., 65n
Wagner, Richard, 464
Wain, John, 299, 546
"Waking Early Sunday Morning" (RL), 580,
  601n; EB's view, xiii, 587–88, 616

Walcott, Derek, 439, 504n
Walpole, Horace, 674, 703
Walton, Izaak, 21n
Wanning, Andrews, 57, 64, 74, 180, 208, 215,
  223, 224, 225, 229, 326, 375
Wanning, Pat (Mrs. Andrews Wanning), 74,
  180, 224, 225
Wanning, Tom, 48n, 50, 54, 56, 57, 62, 68, 74,
  85, 99, 118, 125, 141, 142, 176–77, 180, 194,
  198, 210, 249, 365, 375
Warburg, Paul F. "Piggy," 186–87
Ward, Aileen, 209, 211, 762
Warren, Robert Penn, 6n, 94, 98, 148, 233,
  416, 491, 534, 599n
Waste Land, The (Eliot), xvi, 61, 624, 747
"Water" (RL), xix, xx, 59n, 321n, 430n; EB's
  view, 402, 585, 643; RL's description, 390,
  405, 662n, 745
Watergate, 745, 751
Watkins, Vernon, 65, 576
Waugh, Evelyn, 236
Weber, Carl Maria von, 66
Webern, Anton von, 250, 251, 259, 285
Webster, Noah, 281
Wehr, Wesley, 615
Weill, Kurt, 280, 348
Weimer, David R., 498n, 500, 501
Weiss, Theodore, 72
Wellesley College, 23, 25, 27, 64, 81, 210, 724,
  738, 754, 790
"Wellesley Free" (RL), 760n
Welty, Eudora, 44–45, 75, 78, 266
Wescott, Glenway, 771
West, James, 350n, 391n, 398, 488–89, 495,
  643
West, Nathaniel, 406
West, Rebecca, 333
"We Took Our Paradise" (RL), 760n
Whalen, Philip, 670
"What We Were" (RL), 760n
Wheeler, Monroe, 378
White, E. B., 208, 215
White, Katharine, 208, 327
Whitehead, Edward, 222
Whitman, Walt, 274, 281, 603
Whittall, Gertrude Clark, 118, 135
Whittier, John Greenleaf, 378
Whitworth, John, 238n
Wieland, Christoph Martin, 602
Wilbur, Richard, 64, 65, 94, 130n, 132, 167,

Frontispiece Elizabeth Bishop and Robert Lowell, Brazil (1962): Courtesy of Vassar College Library.

Page 1 Elizabeth Bishop (1943) photographed by Josef Breitenbach: Courtesy of the Josef Breitenbach Archive Center for Creative Photography, Tucson. Robert Lowell (1947): Courtesy of Robert Giroux.

Page 127 Elizabeth Bishop: Courtesy of Vassar College Library. Robert and Harriet Lowell (1957): Courtesy of Houghton Library.

Pages 190, 191, 216 Images of Elizabeth Bishop's drawings: Courtesy of Houghton Library.

Page 269 Elizabeth Bishop and Robert Lowell in Rio (1962): Courtesy of Vassar College Library.

Page 433 Elizabeth Bishop: Courtesy of Vassar College Library. Robert Lowell: Courtesy of Harry Ransom Humanities Research Center, the University of Texas at Austin.

Page 679 Elizabeth Bishop, North Haven, Maine (1978): Courtesy of Tom Barker. Robert Lowell: Courtesy of Houghton Library.